THE ILLINOIS FACT BOOK

and

HISTORICAL ALMANAC
1673–1968

compiled and written by John Clayton

Southern Illinois University Press

Carbondale and Edwardsville

To find a simple fact is often extremely difficult. What was the population of Springfield, Illinois, in 1860, when Abraham Lincoln was elected President? Who was the secretary of state of Illinois in the administration of Frank O. Lowden? How many miles of paved highways were there in Illinois in 1905? What are the exact boundaries of the state? (This one is not as simple as it seems to be.) These are only a few of thousands of questions that can be asked about Illinois alone.

The answers can be found, but often only by experts. Moreover, they are scattered in hundreds of publications, and sometimes authoritative information can be had only in unpublished sources in the Illinois State Archives or departmental files.

To assemble all useful facts about Illinois, and also those which a person moved only by curiosity might want to know, seemed to the Illinois Sesquicentennial Commission to be an undertaking of the utmost importance. The project was approved by an advisory committee of eminent historians. It was decided, moreover, that the book should deal with the past as well as the present. Thus the title: *The Illinois Fact Book and Historical Almanac*. The task of compilation—a staggering one—was entrusted to John Clayton of Chicago, a former newspaperman and advertising executive. He has been ably assisted, in many ways, by Mary Lynn McCree, Caroline Heath, Elizabeth B. Kenyon of the Southern Illinois University Press, and Paul M. Angle, Director of Historical Publications, Illinois Sesquicentennial Commission.

In a massive collection of facts such as this there are bound to be errors. But there may not be as many as some users of the book may assume. In many instances supposedly authoritative sources are at variance. In such cases every effort has been made to resolve the discrepancies, but not always with success. And there are some instances when statistics, taken from official but unpublished archival sources, do not agree with any to be found in print. We can only say that the facts and figures presented here are based upon sources which, in the judgment of the compiler and his consultants, seemed to be most reliable.

In conclusion, I would be remiss if I did not acknowledge the unwavering support of the Illinois Sesquicentennial Commission's historical program accorded by Governor Otto Kerner, Governor Samuel H. Shapiro, and the Commission members: Hon.

FOREWORD

An

Illinois

Sesquicentennial

Book

Hudson R. Sours, Hon. Thomas A. McGloon, and Hon. Paul J. Randolph, Vice Chairmen; Gene H. Graves, Secretary; William K. Alderfer, James W. Cook, Hon. Lawrence DiPrima, Patrick H. Hoy, Goffrey Hughes, Hon. Henry J. Hyde, Hon. J. David Jones, Hon. Richard R. Larson, Hon. Edward Lehman, Hon. Edward McBroom, Hon. Robert W. McCarthy, Daniel MacMaster, Virginia L. Marmaduke, Hon. Tom Merritt, Hon. Richard H. Newhouse, Hon. James Philip, Hon. Paul Powell, Walter Schwimmer, John H. Sengstacke, Glenn H. Seymour, Hon. Harold D. Stedelin, Milton D. Thompson, and Clyde C. Walton.

Ralph G. Newman, CHAIRMAN
Illinois Sesquicentennial Commission

ACKNOWLEDGMENTS

In
Appreciation

No book that is designed to present a mass of factual material can be prepared by one person in a library reading room—or a dozen persons in as many reading rooms, for that matter. The compiler of this *Fact Book* is indebted to many men and women, often anonymous, who suggested sources, dug out family records, refuted historical errors, and supplied material unavailable in published works.

First of all should be a hearty "thank you" to the Chicago Historical Society, whose enthusiastic staff provided professional assistance of the greatest value; likewise to the staff of the Illinois State Historical Library, who were indefatigable in searching out details, checking and rechecking sources; to the staff of the Illinois State Museum, who provided facts and deductions on the prehistory of the state; to the many county clerks who searched their archives for biographical detail, and to the descendants of early men of repute, who furnished information on their forebears.

A special word of recognition is due the librarians of the *Chicago Daily News* and *Chicago Tribune* for information not to be found elsewhere. To Arthur Vesey, London correspondent of the *Chicago Tribune*, goes thanks for resolving the Effingham enigma in an interview with the present earl, and for reporting Lord Thomas Effingham's abstinence from tea in protest of the tax he resented as much as did the Bostonians.

The elected officers of the state of Illinois, who are in effect the cabinet of the governor, were unstinting in preparation of materials relating to their offices, as were the many code departments, boards and commissions which conduct the business of the state and keep its official records. All these servants of the state read, checked, and commented upon the chapters that covered the activities of their offices.

The Illinois Commerce Commission was most helpful in recommending the content of the chapter on the railroads in Illinois and in preparing special tables for this book from their voluminous files.

The remarkably detailed cooperative crop reports of the United States and the Illinois Departments of Agriculture were the source of the basic tables referring to agricultural production. Special material was developed for this *Fact Book* by the Department of Mines and Minerals and the Illinois Geological Survey, by the Department of Aviation and the Department of Conservation.

The Chicago office of the Corps of Engineers, United States Army, furnished material on canals and waterways not available elsewhere. Detailed information on sports and on the revenue received by the state from licensed mutual wagering was supplied by the Illinois Racing Board, the Harness Racing Association, the Illinois State Fair, the Du Quoin State Fair, the public relations departments of the Arlington Park Jockey Club, the Chicago White Sox, Cubs, Bears, and Black Hawks, and the commissioner of the Big Ten.

To all these hundreds of persons go the thanks and appreciation of the compiler and the Illinois Sesquicentennial Commission.

John Clayton

Contents

Primitive Man

Sometime in the remote past, during one of the last two ice ages, herds of mammoth, or perhaps mastodon or prehistoric giant bison, drifted across the land bridge from Siberia to Alaska, which at times was several hundred miles wide. Hanging on the flanks of the huge beasts, traveling with them and never losing them, man came into the vast reaches of the North American continent. This man was not the explorer. He was the nomad, the homeless hunter who followed his food supply. He was the Paleo-Indian, remote ancestor of the American Indian.

No campsite of the Paleo-Indian has been found in Illinois, but projectile points unearthed in many parts of the prairies testify to his presence here. Around 10,000 B.C. the last ice sheet receded from Illinois, and the mighty river that led from Lake Michigan to the Mississippi divided into the Chicago and the Des Plaines which, on meeting the Kankakee, became the Illinois, much as it is today. But the herds of huge prehistoric animals were gone. Gone also were all but a few of the Paleo-Indians. From this remnant came the Archaic tribes from which the Indians of historic times descended.

Modoc Rock Shelter, two miles from Prairie du Rocher in Randolph County, contains evidences of Archaic Indian culture dating back as far as 8000 B.C. The appearance of hammerstones, and later of grooved stones, connotes a need for tools other than weapons. Archeologists infer that the inhabitants occupied the shelter in the winter, spent the spring in open campsites, the summer in hunting areas, and the fall in groves of beech, oak, and hickory.

Out of this foraging stage an exploitive stage developed, perhaps as early as 5000 B.C. Grinding stones, drills, bone awls, and other fabricating tools, as well as the more primitive scrapers, blades, hammerstones, and axes, have been found not only at Modoc but also in several other parts of Illinois. As the millennia passed other changes took place in the Archaic culture. Woodworking tools appeared, and the Indians ornamented themselves and their pottery. Durable structures led to the development of small communities. Flint hoes indicate an emerging agriculture.

The Archaic culture glided easily into what archeologists call the Early Woodland phase of Indian life. In a period not much longer than a thousand years the Middle Woodland or Hopewell culture rose and

1

From Stone Age to Statehood

died in the Mississippi and Ohio valleys. Artifacts and other remains tell a story of comparative peace, wide-ranging travel, accomplishments in sculpture, weaving, and pottery, of large settlements and crops of maize, beans, squash, and tobacco. In the Final Woodland period, ending about A.D. 900, the Indians reverted to primitive customs. Training in the ancient arts and beliefs was neglected. Fields went untended. Settlements dwindled in size. The Indian went back to the forest, where he chose to live as had his ancestors.

About the time the Normans won a kingdom at Hastings a new plant-raising civilization emerged in the middle Mississippi Valley. Mounds were erected as bases for rude temples as well as for burial of the dead. One of the Cahokia Mounds, north of East St. Louis, is the largest pyramid in the world in bulk and area, if not in height. Unlike the stone pyramids of Egypt and Mexico, this mound was of earth carried in baskets and tamped into place by human feet. On its flat, level top was built a house of worship which, in the last years of this culture, attracted Indians from the Ohio River to the Wisconsin and the tribute of even more distant people.

These people and a kindred folk in a large town on the Ohio River near present Metropolis dwelt in square houses with pole and matting sides and thatched hip roofs. Other communities, on the upper Illinois, around the mouth of the Rock, at the south end of Lake Michigan, and in the forests of Wisconsin, lived in oval-shaped log houses with domed roofs which accommodated several families.

About the time that Columbus discovered America the Mississippian culture reached its height. Then disaster overtook it—not from spear or bow or tomahawk or scalping knife, but by diseases introduced by civilized men. The Indian had built up no resistance to measles and smallpox. When Hernando de Soto landed near the present site of Tampa he brought death to those he encountered on his path from Florida to the Mississippi, and to thousands he would never see.

Thus ended the golden age in the middle Mississippi Valley. Men, women, and children died and lay unburied while the living fled from the accursed dwelling places on the Ohio, the Mississippi, the Kaskaskia, and the Illinois. The temples, battered by fierce prairie winds, fell apart. Seeds of the prairie grasses, borne by those same winds, found resting places on the temple mounds. The proud city of Cahokia, religious capital of middle America, reverted to wilderness.

DATES FOR REFERENCE

20,000–8000 B.C. Aboriginal man, the hunter of mammoth and mastodon, appeared on the North American continent. From his line the primitive Paleo-Indians developed.

8000–2000 B.C. The Archaic culture developed in the caves and rock shelters of Illinois. The Archaic Indians, descendants of the Paleo-Indians, were hunters, fishers, and foragers.

2500–500 B.C. In the Early Woodland culture in Illinois the Indians were pottery makers who lived chiefly by the hunt but also collected and stored nuts and roots.

500 B.C–A.D. 400 In the Middle Woodland or Hopewell culture the Indians grew maize, beans, squash, and tobacco. They excelled at sculpture and pottery and built large settlements.

A.D. 200–900 The Late Woodland phase; artistic skills deteriorated, communities dwindled, fields were untended.

A.D. 900–1500 The Mississippian culture flowed in a new golden age, marked by sun worship and the building of temple mounds. Cahokia became the religious center of a large area.

A.D. 1540–42 Hernando de Soto led an expedition from Florida to the Mississippi River, bringing measles and smallpox to the Indians along the way. The diseases spread, wiping out families, villages, even tribes.

The French in Illinois

The year was 1634, barely a third of a century after Samuel de Champlain, founder of Canada, made his first voyage up the St. Lawrence River, and only twenty-seven years after the English founded Jamestown in Virginia. But by 1634 the French were well established at Quebec and ready to push into the interior. That summer Jean Nicolet, accompanied only by seven Huron Indians, reached Green Bay and thus became the first white man to penetrate the present Middle West.

The French in Canada waited thirty-six years to exploit Nicolet's venture into the wilderness. In 1670 Jean Talon, intendant of the colony at Quebec, ordered the Sieur de St. Lusson to search the shores of Lake Superior for copper and take possession of the territory. St. Lusson could not carry out his mission until 1671. He found no copper, but in a formal, colorful ceremony at Sault Ste. Marie, on the river that connects Lakes Huron and Superior, he took possession, in the name of France, of "Sainte Marie de Sout, as also of Lakes Huron and Superior . . . and all countries, rivers, lakes, and streams contiguous and adjacent thereunto, —both those which have been discovered and those which may be discovered hereafter."

Having proclaimed their sovereignty over a vast area, it was high time for the French to find out what it contained. For this purpose the authorities chose Louis Jolliet, a Canadian-born surveyor, map maker, and frontiersman, and Father Jacques Marquette, a thirty-six-year-old Jesuit priest. In the spring of 1673 the two men, with five unnamed *voyageurs*, set out from Mackinac. They skirted the western shore of Lake Michigan to Green Bay, then paddled up the Fox River to its source, portaged to the Wisconsin, and floated with its current to the Mississippi. Priest and geographer made their way on the great river for hundreds of miles without encountering hostile Indians. At the mouth of the Arkansas they decided they had gone far enough. They now knew that the Mississippi emptied into the Gulf of Mexico instead of the Pacific, as they had hoped, and they feared that they might encounter the Spanish along the lower reaches of the river.

On their return trip they learned of the short route to Lake Michigan offered by the Illinois River. They stopped at the Great Village of the Illinois Indians between the present cities of La Salle and Ottawa, where Marquette baptized a dying child and gave his promise to return the next year. With Indians as guides, they made their way over the portage between the Des Plaines and Chicago rivers and into Lake Michigan. Other Europeans had looked on the Mississippi before them, but they were the first white men to traverse the future state of Illinois.

In the fall of 1674 Marquette set out to redeem his promise to the Illinois. Illness compelled him and his party to spend the winter near the Chicago portage, but when spring came he pushed on to the Great Village, where he preached to a huge gathering. On the return trip his frail constitution gave out. He died on May 18, 1675, and was buried at the mouth of the Marquette River near present-day Ludington, Michigan.

The development of the region which Marquette and Jolliet had explored fell to two men of a different type: Robert Cavelier, Sieur de la Salle, French-born adventurer of boundless ambition and determination, and Henri de Tonti, a professional soldier of Italian birth. La Salle's goal was the creation of a seigniory for himself and an imperial domain for France, and in all his ventures Tonti was his faithful lieutenant. La Salle and Tonti made their first journey to Illinois in the winter of 1679, and in early 1680 erected Fort Crevecoeur on the Illinois River near present-day Peoria. In their absence during the spring mutineers destroyed the fort and deserted.

La Salle had returned to Fort Frontenac, but Tonti remained on the Illinois, living with the Illiniwek at their village not far from what is now Utica. To compound his difficulties the village was attacked by a large Iroquois war party. Tonti attempted mediation and failed. Seized by the Iroquois, he was driven out of the region and made his way to Green Bay whence he joined La Salle at Mackinac.

In the late winter of 1681–82 La Salle and Tonti set out on their greatest venture: the exploration of the Mississippi to its mouth. Early in April they reached their destination, and on the ninth day of that month La Salle assembled his men and their Indian escort for the formal ceremony so dear to the

French heart: the *prise de possession* by which claim was made to the valley of the Mississippi and the valleys of all its tributaries. That done, they headed north.

To trace in detail the events of the next two decades would be to lose oneself in senseless Indian warfare, in the construction and abandonment of forts in the Illinois country, in contests for power and prestige between religious orders at Quebec, in intrigues at Versailles. One must, however, note the death of La Salle at the hands of his own men at the Brazos River in 1687; and the persistent efforts of Tonti to carry out La Salle's plans cannot be overlooked. For nine years, from 1691 to 1700, Tonti worked from a new fort and settlement he had built at Lake Peoria to bring settlers, trade goods, and missionaries from Canada, but with no more permanent result than a small village which survived until the French lost the Illinois country in 1763.

Two hundred miles from Peoria, French settlements took deeper root. In 1699 priests of the Seminary of Quebec established the Mission of the Holy Family near the left bank of the Mississippi a short distance south of the present city of East St. Louis, and adjacent to a large village of Tamaroa and Cahokia Indians. The town attracted settlers and traders from Canada and Louisiana. Four years later the Jesuits moved the Mission of the Immaculate Conception from the west bank of the Mississippi to a site on the Kaskaskia River seven miles from its mouth. With the Jesuits went the Kaskaskia, former inhabitants of the Great Village of the Illinois. Like Cahokia, Kaskaskia drew white settlers and traders.

For two-thirds of a century these outposts were the seat of French power in the Illinois country. (A mission at Chicago lasted only from 1698 to 1702.) To protect the settlers and their Indian allies, and to repel the English if they ever penetrated to the Mississippi, the French built a succession of forts, all named De Chartres, on a site bordering the Mississippi near the village of Prairie du Rocher. The last, begun in 1753, was built of stone, and so well constructed that ten years after its completion an English officer called it "the most commodious and best built fort in North America."

The Illinois villages and Fort de Chartres had no part in the war that cost France her North American empire. The French and

Indian War, begun in 1754, resulted from conflicting claims of the French and English in the upper Ohio Valley. It came to its end in fact, though not formally, when Wolfe defeated Montcalm on the Plains of Abraham in September 1759, and when Montreal surrendered a year later. By the Treaty of Paris, 1763, France ceded all Canada to Great Britain and all her claims to territory east of the Mississippi. Illinois, it was now certain, would be settled by English-speaking people.

DATES FOR REFERENCE

1634 Jean Nicolet reached Green Bay, in what is now Wisconsin, thus becoming the first white man to penetrate the present Middle West.

1671 In a ceremony at Sault Ste. Marie the Sieur de St. Lusson took possession, in the name of France, of Lakes Huron and Superior and all contiguous and adjacent countries.

1673 Father Jacques Marquette and Louis Jolliet explored the Mississippi from the Wisconsin River as far south as the mouth of the Arkansas, and returned to their point of departure by way of the Illinois River and the Chicago portage.

1675 Marquette, returning from his second trip to the Illinois country, died on the east shore of Lake Michigan.

1680 Robert Cavelier, Sieur de la Salle and his associate, Henri de Tonti, built Fort Crevecoeur on the Illinois River near the site of present-day Peoria.

1682 At the juncture of the Mississippi and the Gulf of Mexico, La Salle took possession, in the name of France, of the valley of the Mississippi and all the land watered by its tributaries.

La Salle and Tonti built Fort St. Louis on Starved Rock to replace Fort Crevecoeur, destroyed by mutineers.

1687 La Salle was murdered by some of his own men.

1691 Tonti established a new fort and settlement, Pimitoui, on the site of Peoria.

1699 Priests of the Seminary of Quebec founded the Mission of the Holy Family and the town of Cahokia.

1703 The Jesuits established the Mission of the Immaculate Conception and the town of Kaskaskia.

1719 The French built the first Fort de Chartres near Prairie du Rocher in Randolph County.

1732 A new Fort de Chartres replaced the original structure.

1753 The third Fort de Chartres, a formidable work of stone, was begun on the site of its predecessor.

1754 The French and Indian War began.

1763 By the Treaty of Paris, France ceded all Canada to Great Britain and relinquished all claim to territory east of the Mississippi River.

Illinois Under the British

Two years, marked by Indian warfare and unrest in the West, passed before the British moved to occupy the Illinois country. In the late summer of 1765 Captain Thomas Stirling, with a detachment of the Black Watch regiment, left Fort Pitt for Illinois. On October 9 he reached his destination. The next day he received the formal surrender of Fort de Chartres.

The French villagers were unhappy. Two years earlier France had banished the Jesuits from all her territories. In Illinois, the Jesuits sold their lands and buildings at Kaskaskia and departed for New Orleans. The seminary priests at Cahokia, convinced that a Catholic mission would not fare well at the hands of the heretical English, also sold their property and, like the Jesuits, left the country. Thus the villagers found themselves without the rites and consolations of their religion. For this reason, and because they were unwilling to take the oath of allegiance to the British crown, many moved to Spanish territory west of the Mississippi.

After three years a resident priest returned to Illinois, but in aspects of life other than religion the situation was not a happy one.

The powers of government resided in the hands of the British commandants, who were relieved every two or three years. Some were kindly and upright men; others were corrupt and despotic. Prevailing conditions had no attraction for French or Canadian settlers, and Americans were forbidden by the ill-advised proclamation of October 7, 1763, to settle beyond the crest of the Allegheny Mountains. Even English trading firms from the East, lured by the hope of big profits from the fur trade, met only failure. For eleven years the French villages in Illinois stagnated while the British ministry tried unsuccessfully to work out an effective system of colonial administration. To that effort the year 1775, with Lexington, Concord, and Bunker Hill, put an end.

DATES FOR REFERENCE

May 1763–Aug. 1764 Pontiac's Rebellion threw the frontier into turmoil and delayed the British occupation of the Illinois country.

Sept. 24, 1763 By order of the French government the Jesuits were expelled from Illinois.

Oct. 7, 1763 By proclamation the British ministry forbade settlement west of the crest of the Allegheny Mountains.

Aug. 24, 1765 Captain Thomas Stirling left Fort Pitt for Illinois with a detachment of the Forty-second Highlanders, better known as the Black Watch.

Oct. 10, 1765 Louis de Bellerive St. Ange, French commandant, turned over Fort de Chartres and the French villages to Captain Stirling.

May 1769 Pontiac was murdered at Cahokia by an Illinois Indian or Indians.

June 1774 The British Parliament passed the Quebec Act, enlarging the boundaries of Quebec to include Illinois and reestablishing French civil law there.

Apr. 19, 1775 The battles of Lexington and Concord marked the outbreak of the American Revolution.

From the Revolution to Statehood

One bold officer, with never more than 200 men in his command, won Illinois, and perhaps the entire Old Northwest, for the young American nation. When the Revolutionary War broke out George Rogers Clark, born in Virginia in 1752, had already earned a reputation for courage. He had explored and surveyed lands along the Ohio River and in Kentucky, and had served as a captain of militia in Lord Dunmore's War (1774). In 1777 he conceived a plan for the conquest of the Illinois country and obtained the approval of Patrick Henry, governor of Virginia.

Early in 1778 Clark was given a lieutenant colonel's commission, was authorized to recruit 350 men for his venture and to offer as a reward to each man 300 acres of land somewhere in the Northwest. He managed to sign up only half the force he wanted. Undeterred, he gathered his volunteers together at the Falls of the Ohio (Louisville). Disembarking from their boats at Fort Massac on the Illinois side of the Ohio, the men made a six-day overland march to Kaskaskia, where they arrived the night of July 4, the second anniversary of the Declaration of Independence.

The sad state of the Illinois villages is indicated by the fact that the small British garrison had been withdrawn, and the command turned over to a Frenchman, Philippe François de Rastel, Chevalier de Rocheblave. Fort de Chartres had been abandoned; Rocheblave made his headquarters in the former house of the Jesuits. When informed of the arrival of the Americans—he was asleep at the time—Rocheblave surrendered without protest. A few days later Clark's men received the willing capitulation of the inhabitants of Cahokia, Prairie du Rocher, and, in due time, Vincennes.

Although the British had paid scant attention to the Illinois villages, they could hardly have been expected to take this bold thrust into the heart of their western territory with complacency. At Detroit, Major Henry Hamilton, lieutenant governor, decided on a counterstroke. Assembling a force of French volunteers and Indians, he set out for Vincennes in early October 1778. Captain Leonard Helm, who had only one American soldier to guard the post, surrendered. When Clark learned of the fall of Vincennes he decided to retake it at once.

With 170 men, half of them French volunteers, he marched out of the Illinois villages early in February 1779. Crossing the prairies in the mire of winter and fording the swollen streams called for the utmost in courage and endurance; Clark's men had those qualities. On February 23 they surrounded the town and Clark demanded its surrender. Hamilton refused, but most of his French and Indians deserted and left him with no choice. Two days later he accepted Clark's terms.

In the next four years Clark, with the small forces he could raise, kept the British on the defensive at Detroit and shielded the Illinois villages. His plans and maneuvers need not be followed but their result was of the utmost importance: when the commissioners met in Paris in 1783 to write the treaty ending the Revolutionary War, the West, as far as the Mississippi, was in American hands. There it remained.

Meanwhile, Virginia had taken measures for the government of Illinois, its newest county. In the spring of 1779 the parent state sent John Todd of Kentucky to Kaskaskia as county lieutenant, or civil administrator. The colony seethed with discontent. The Catholic French resented the Protestant backwoodsmen who were beginning to push in from Kentucky; land speculators had grandiose and disturbing plans; soldier and settler clashed. After six months of frustration Todd resigned, to be succeeded by Richard Winston, acting county lieutenant.

The Virginia act creating the county of Illinois included a limiting clause which required the renewal of the charter every two years. This had been done in 1780, but by the fall of 1781 Virginia leaders had decided to cede the state's western lands to the federal government. Hence the legislature took no action, and with its adjournment on January 5, 1782, the county of Illinois ceased to exist. For more than two years—until March 1, 1784, when Virginia made her cession to the federal government—the Illinois villages drifted without even nominal control by any superior authority.

Three more years passed before Congress passed An Act for the Government of the United States Territory Northwest of the Ohio River—the famous Ordinance of 1787. This act prescribed the steps to statehood. In the beginning there would be a governor, a secretary, and three judges appointed by Congress. The governor and judges would have the right to adopt such laws of the original thirteen states as suited the circumstances of the territory. When the territory acquired a population of 5,000 free white male adults, the people would elect a lower house and the Congress appoint the upper house of a territorial legislature. When any of the three or five future states designated by the act should have a population of 5,000 free white male adults, it could petition for separate territorial status. When a territory reached a population of 60,000, it could ask to be admitted to the Union as a state.

In 1787 General Arthur St. Clair, a Scotch-born former British army officer who had served in the American army during the Revolution with indifferent success, was appointed governor of the Northwest Territory. St. Clair did not visit Illinois until 1790. At that time he established the first Illinois county, which he named after himself. His attention, however, was soon diverted from Illinois by his responsibilities as commander of the United States Army and administrator of Indian affairs— responsibilities which he discharged no more efficiently than those which he had borne during the Revolution. On November 4, 1791, he suffered a disastrous defeat near Fort Wayne by a confederated Indian army led by Little Turtle. As a result, he resigned from the army and devoted himself to his duties as governor of the Northwest Territory. He had little success; he was overbearing, paternalistic, and unpopular with his constituents. He tried, unsuccessfully, to thwart any movements toward statehood. His opposition to the contrary, the Northwest Territory advanced to the second stage of territorial government in 1798, and on May 7, 1800, Congress created the territory of Indiana, which included the present state of Illinois. When St. Clair opposed the admission of Ohio in 1802, Jefferson removed him from office.

To be governor of Indiana Territory, the Congress appointed William Henry Harrison of Virginia, who made Vincennes the seat of government. During his incumbency Harrison negotiated a series of Indian treaties which gave the United States title to millions of acres in what are now the states of Indiana and Illinois. He did not succeed in restoring tranquility to the Illinois villages, where speculation in land claims and friction between the long-established French and Canadians and the increasing number of American settlers contributed to a continuing turmoil.

By 1808, Illinois claimed a population of 10,000, which more than qualified it for territorial status. On February 3, 1809, by act of Congress, it became a territory. Within its boundaries the present state of Wisconsin was included. Ninian Edwards, chief justice of the Kentucky court of appeals, was appointed governor, with Nathaniel Pope, Edwards' younger cousin, secretary.

Illinois continued to grow. In 1812 it was advanced to the second stage of territorial government. Five years later the residents began to campaign for statehood. In Congress Nathaniel . Pope, the territorial delegate, introduced an enabling act which passed on April 18, 1818. With foresight, Pope succeeded in having the northern boundary of the prospective state moved from an east and west line at the southern tip of Lake Michigan to the line of 42°30', some forty-nine and a half miles north of the northern border of Indiana, and sixty-two'and a half miles north of an east–west line tangent to the southern end of Lake Michigan, as established by the Ordinance of 1787. Under the enabling act Illinois adopted a constitution on August 26, 1818. Congress admitted the new state to the Union December 3, 1818.

DATES FOR REFERENCE

July 4, 1778   George Rogers Clark, an officer of the state of Virginia, captured Kaskaskia. Soon afterward he received the capitulation of Cahokia, Prairie du Rocher, and Vincennes.

Dec. 9, 1778   Governor Patrick Henry of Virginia created the county of Illinois by executive proclamation.

Dec. 15, 1778   Major Henry Hamilton, British lieutenant governor at Detroit, recaptured Vincennes.

Feb. 25, 1779   After a bold march across Illinois, Clark surprised Hamilton at Vincennes and retook the town.

May 1779   Colonel John Todd of Kentucky, appointed county lieutenant of the county of Illinois, arrived at Kaskaskia.

Jan. 5, 1782   The Virginia legislature adjourned without renewing the charter of the county of Illinois, thus leaving the Illinois villages without a government.

Sept. 3, 1783   By the Treaty of Paris, Great Britain ceded her American territory as far west as the Mississippi to the United States.

Mar. 1, 1784   The state of Virginia ceded to the federal government all lands which she had claimed north and west of the Ohio River, reserving 150,000 acres on the Ohio River for George Rogers Clark and the soldiers of his command.

May 20, 1785   By the Land Ordinance of 1785 the Continental Congress established a rectangular method of surveying public lands, dividing those not already surveyed into townships six miles square.

July 13, 1787   Congress passed the Ordinance of 1787, establishing the Northwest Territory and providing for its government. Soon afterward, Congress designated General Arthur St. Clair territorial governor.

Mar. 5, 1790   St. Clair arrived at Kaskaskia to inaugurate civil government.

May 18, 1796   President Washington signed An Act for the Sale of Public Lands in the Territory Northwest of the Ohio River. The act reaffirmed the rectangular system of surveys and created the office of surveyor general.

May 7, 1800   Congress established the territory of Indiana, which included what are now the states of Indiana, Illinois, Michigan, and Wisconsin.

Mar. 26, 1804   Congress passed An Act for the Disposal of Lands in the Indiana Territory, which extended the powers of the surveyor general to the Mississippi River, set aside bounty lands for veterans of the Revolution, established land offices in Detroit, Vincennes, and Kaskaskia, and provided for the sale of tracts as small as quarter sections (160 acres).

Apr. 28, 1809 President Madison signed an act of Congress creating the territory of Illinois and divided it into two counties: St. Clair and Randolph.

Feb. 15, 1813 Congress passed a preemption act which permitted persons who had settled on public land prior to 1809 and improved it to purchase the land prior to public sale.

Apr. 16, 1814 The preemption act of 1813 was extended to include squatter holdings after 1809.

Apr. 18, 1818 Congress passed an act enabling Illinois to apply for admission to the Union.

Aug. 26, 1818 Illinois adopted a constitution, a prerequisite to statehood.

Dec. 3, 1818 Illinois came into the Union as the twenty-first state.

Claimants to the soil of Illinois at the end of the Revolutionary War fell roughly into six categories: 1] states of the Confederation with charters that extended and overlapped across the territory northwest of the Ohio River; 2] Indian tribes asserting residence or hunting rights; 3] individuals with grants from the original French proprietors of lands in the vicinity of Peoria, Kaskaskia, Cahokia, and Vincennes; 4] individuals with grants from the British crown through its officers and agents, or from the state of Virginia through George Rogers Clark or John Todd; 5] land companies holding tracts by treaty with Indian tribes, such treaties having been expressly repudiated by the commonwealth of Virginia, and 6] squatters who had improved the land on which they sat.

By the spring of 1786 claims of all states of the Confederation had been extinguished by cession to the general government, and Congress had passed an act that established a uniform method of surveying the wilderness and regulated the sale of public lands. This act, approved May 20, 1785, before all cessions had been completed, required that public land be laid out in ranges six miles wide bearing north and south, and divided into townships by east-west lines six miles apart. Each township was then divided into sections a mile square (640 acres). The law further required that the first seven ranges west of Pennsylvania and south of a baseline running west from the point where the border of that state first touched the Ohio River be surveyed before any land was placed on sale.

Indians living in the eastern part of what was to become the state of Ohio held that the surveys violated several treaties between the colonies or the British crown and the tribes. They resisted bitterly, and it was not until they had beaten General Arthur St. Clair in 1791 and been, in turn, decisively defeated by General Anthony Wayne in 1794 that they submitted. The Treaty of Greenville, signed in 1795, a year after the Battle of Fallen Timbers brought the war to an end, was the first to recognize the rights of white men (except for the old French grants) northwest of the Ohio. The treaty established an Indian boundary from the mouth of the Cuyahoga River south eighty miles and then west and south by various streams and portages to the Ohio opposite the mouth of the Kentucky River. It recognized the grant by the state of Virginia of 150,000 acres to George Rogers Clark and his command and ceded an area in Indiana and Illinois

2

Descent
of Title
in Illinois

containing 2,000,000 acres centering on Vincennes. It also provided small tracts where forts could be maintained to protect travelers. Three of these, at Chicago, Peoria Lake, and the mouth of the Illinois River, were in future Illinois.

Out of dissatisfaction with some of the provisions of the Land Act of 1785, and to prepare for the opening of land granted by the Greenville agreement, Congress passed, and on May 18, 1796, President Washington signed, a new land law which confirmed the grid system of surveys and created the office of surveyor general.

With the Division Act of May 7, 1800, which split the Northwest Territory into the territories of Ohio and Indiana, a resolute and energetic man began to cast a large shadow on the western scene. William Henry Harrison, who had resigned a commission in the United States Army to become secretary of the Northwest Territory, was appointed governor of Indiana Territory, which included the present states of Indiana, Michigan, Wisconsin, and Illinois. His goal, apparent from the day he took office, was the removal of all the Indian tribes to lands beyond the Mississippi or above the Wisconsin River.

Indian tribes which occupied or hunted over various parts of Illinois at that time were eleven in number. The Iliniwek, or the Illinois, six nations which once were the spiritual and military leaders of the middle Mississippi Valley, had ranged from the Ohio to the upper Illinois. By the year 1800 they had been driven out of their traditional villages and brought low by constant battles with the Iroquois, by liquor, and by disease.

Some authorities assign only fifty families to the six nations in 1800. Others believe there were about six hundred persons among the Iliniwek.

The United Tribes of the Chippewa, Ottawa, and Potawatami, calling themselves the Three Fires, were closely related and generally made war and peace as one nation. At the beginning of the nineteenth century they numbered about two thousand and were the second largest group in Illinois. The Sauk and Fox, occupying the lower reaches of the Wisconsin and Rock rivers, the land between the Illinois and the Mississippi, and a large area west of the Mississippi from the Missouri to the Jeffreon (now the Fabius) River, were the most potent of the tribes residing in Illinois —about three thousand persons.

The Kickapoo and Mascoutin, kinfolk who separated and drifted back together, were restless, quarrelsome nomads. In 1800 the Mascoutin were about to leave Illinois for homes across the Mississippi, making the Kickapoo their heirs. These people, in two groups, laid claim to many millions of Illinois acres. One group, the Kickapoo of the Prairie, occupied the valleys of the Sangamon, the Vermilion of the Illinois, the Illinois, and the Kankakee and claimed some land on Lake Michigan on which they had ceased to reside or hunt. The Kickapoo of the Vermilion were located chiefly on the Wabash and the Vermilion of the Wabash. The two groups numbered about two thousand persons.

The Piankeshaw, first identified in the Starved Rock area about 1700, later relocated on the headwaters of the Vermilion of the Wabash, were driven out in 1792 by the Kickapoo and found homes on the Little Wabash west of Vincennes. A dying tribe, they mustered only a few families in 1800, but they laid claim to nearly 3,000,000 acres in Illinois. The Winnebago, a once-powerful tribe from the headwaters of the Rock and the lower reaches of the Wisconsin, arrived in Illinois about 1800 and settled in the Rock River Valley. Traditional enemies of the Sioux, on their arrival in Illinois their numbers had been reduced to about one thousand persons.

These tribes, totaling fewer than 10,000 persons, laid claim to more than 35,000,000 acres in Illinois, coveted by tens of thousands of land-hungry settlers pushing ever westward. By 1800, 250,000 of these

people had reached Kentucky and 75,000 had settled in Ohio. Back of them were other thousands waiting until Indian titles to western lands had been extinguished.

The first treaty bearing directly on Illinois was one completed by William Henry Harrison, governor of Indiana Territory and Indian agent at Fort Wayne, June 7, 1803, whereby the boundaries of the Vincennes Tract were established and the salt springs of the Saline River Valley ceded in return for 150 bushels of salt annually. The Treaty of Vincennes, August 13, 1803, negotiated by Harrison with the Kaskaskia, contained the first major cession of land in Illinois. By it the Kaskaskia, stating their qualification to represent the remnants of all the Illinois, gave to the general government all their lands on the Mississippi from the Ohio to the Illinois and on the Kaskaskia River and its tributaries to the ridge dividing the headwaters of that stream from those of the Sangamon, a total of 8,608,167 acres.

Survey of the Vincennes Tract that summer crystalized the pattern and nomenclature now used for surveys in most parts of the United States. Jared Mansfield, surveyor general, solved the difficult problem of linking up the Vincennes Tract with lands to the east by running a baseline from the westernmost corner of the Clark Tract and intersecting it with a meridian passing through the northeast corner of the Vincennes Tract. The survey of the Clark Tract was determined by the meridian passing through the mouth of the Great Miami River which had become the eastern boundary of Indiana. Since this meridian was the first west of the Pennsylvania line, Mansfield called his north-south reference line the Second Principal Meridian. The next line he ran two years later, through the mouth of the Ohio, he designated the Third Principal Meridian. From that day future meridians of reference were given successive ordinal numbers as names.

In 1804 a new land act extended the authority of the surveyor general to the Mississippi and authorized land offices at Vincennes, Kaskaskia, and Detroit. It also empowered territorial governors to treat with the Indians. Surveys were ordered in southern Illinois referring to the Third Principal Meridian and the Indiana baseline extended to the Mississippi River.

Governor Harrison had been ordered by Congress to allocate lands authorized for a military tract of 2,500,000 acres. This he did by entering into treaty with the Sauk and

Fox for cessions north of the Illinois River as far as the Wisconsin. The Treaty of St. Louis ceded more than 11,000,000 acres in Illinois, Missouri, and Wisconsin. However, other tribes had claims to a large part of the land, and Indian titles in parts of the cession were not extinguished for more than thirty years.

In southern Illinois the story was different. Harrison's treaty of 1805 with the Piankeshaw, complementing that with the Kaskaskia, released all of Illinois south of a line from the mouth of the Illinois River to the northwest corner of the Vincennes Tract. Sale of land in Indiana and the most eastern part of Illinois was authorized in 1807, but disputes over titles, conflict with the Indian tribes, and finally the War of 1812 delayed operations at Kaskaskia. It was not until 1814 that the first sales were made there and at Shawneetown, where a land office had been authorized in 1812. At that time most claims in southern Illinois had been established or denied by a commission of three who performed ably in sifting out the frauds. Congress had confirmed squatters in their titles subject to payment of the minimum value of the land they occupied, and survey of the Military Tract had been ordered, with lines of reference the Fourth Principal Meridian passing through the mouth of the Illinois and a baseline at the fortieth parallel, this latter by a surveyor's error actually located a few miles south of the designated line. First grants in the Military Tract were not made, however, until after Governor Ninian Edwards of Illinois Territory, William Clark of Lewis and Clark fame, and Auguste Chouteau, who as a fourteen-year-old had built the first cabin in St. Louis, quieted the claims of the Ottawa, Chippewa, and Potawatami to the area in a new Treaty of St. Louis signed on August 24, 1816.

This treaty ceded to the United States all the lands claimed by the Three Fires below a line from the southern extremity of Lake Michigan to the Mississippi ceded by the Sauk and Fox in 1804. The treaty also ceded a strip of land twenty miles wide from the mouth of the Chicago River to the Fox and Kankakee rivers. Purpose: a right of way for a Lake Michigan-Illinois River canal. In return, among other considerations, the United States re-ceded the land originally ceded by the Sauk and Fox above the Lake Michigan-Mississippi line.

Title to lands in central Illinois ceded by the Kaskaskia in the Treaty of Vincennes August 13, 1803, was clouded by claims of the Peoria, who asserted that the Kaskaskia had no authority to treat for them, and by those of the Kickapoo, who claimed title by ancestral residence in the eastern part and by conquest of the Illinois Indians fifty years before in the western part. A treaty with the Peoria negotiated at Edwardsville September 25, 1818, by Ninian Edwards and Auguste Chouteau, ceded their claims in return for a gift of silver, an increase in annuities already in effect, and a section of land on the Blackwater River in Missouri. The Kickapoo, in a second Treaty of Edwardsville nearly a year later, relinquished their rights in exchange for an annuity and land on the Osage River in Missouri. More than 8,000,000 acres were opened for survey and settlement by these two treaties. Included were the future sites of Decatur and Danville, Peoria and Springfield, Bloomington, Jacksonville, and many other towns and cities.

No further treaties were attempted until 1828, when the series of negotiations began which resulted in removal of all the tribes across the Mississippi by 1835. From a few bushels of salt in 1803 the value of Indian claims, as they were extinguished, had risen to more than $1,000,000 for the final parcel. Thirty-five million acres of land had been ceded, and even the last 1,500,000 acres in the Chicago area, at $1,000,000, had gone at bargain rates.

DATES FOR REFERENCE

Aug. 3, 1795   Treaty of Greenville, negotiated by Anthony Wayne with the Delaware, Wyandott, Shawnee, Ottawa, Chippewa, Potawatami, Miami, Eel River Miami, Wea, Kickapoo, Piankeshaw, and Kaskaskia tribes, established the boundaries of Indian lands northwest of the Ohio River, beginning on Lake Erie at the mouth of the Cuyahoga River, south and southwesterly to the Ohio at the mouth of the Kentucky River. Small tracts were ceded to the general government at important river mouths, portages, and posts such as Detroit, Chicago, and Peoria. Rights of General Clark and his men to 150,000 acres of land at the Falls of the Ohio and of French and other white settlers at Vincennes, Peoria, and the American Bottom to the land they actually possessed were confirmed.

Consideration: $20,000 on signature and $9,500 annually forever, reckoned in first cost of trade goods, divided among the tribes. (12,800 acres in Illinois)

June 7, 1803 Treaty of Fort Wayne between the United States and the tribes noted in the Treaty of Greenville, negotiated by William Henry Harrison, defined the boundaries of the Vincennes Tract, which was to be a rectangle oriented 12° east of north, seventy-two miles east and west, and forty-two miles north and south. Tribes ceded salt springs on the Saline River and a right of way for the road from Clarkville to Kaskaskia by way of Vincennes. Consideration: 150 bushels of salt yearly. (336,128 acres in Illinois, including the land ceded by Treaty of Greenville)

Aug. 13, 1803 Treaty of Vincennes, negotiated by William Henry Harrison, ceded to the United States all lands held in Illinois by the Kaskaskia tribe "which is the remains of and rightfully represents all the tribes of the Illinois Indians," reserving a tract of 350 acres near the town of Kaskaskia and one other tract of 1,280 acres. The boundaries were described as the Ohio River to the ridge between Saline Creek and the Wabash, the high ground between the Little Wabash and the Kaskaskia "to the waters which fall into the Illinois" (headwaters of the Sangamon) thence by a direct course to the Mississippi at the mouth of the Illinois, thence to the beginning. Consideration: an increase in the annuity enjoyed under the Treaty of Greenville; a house for the chief; a field for the tribe; $100 annually for seven years for the support of a priest; $300 to assist the tribe in building a church; and $580 in needed articles. (8,608,167 acres in Illinois)

Nov. 3, 1804 Treaty of St. Louis, negotiated by William Henry Harrison with the Sauk and Fox tribes, conveyed to the United States all their lands north of the Illinois River as far east as the Fox River of the Illinois; north and northwest to the Wisconsin, west to the Mississippi, south to the mouth of the Missouri, and land in Missouri lying between the Missouri and the Jeffreon (now the Fabius) rivers west to the point where the Gasconade enters the Missouri. Consideration: a perpetual annuity in goods to the amount of $1,000

first cost; immediate delivery of $2,234.50 in goods; and land for relocation of the tribes west of the Mississippi. (11,146,193 acres in Illinois)

Dec. 30, 1805 Treaty of Vincennes, negotiated by William Henry Harrison with the Piankeshaw, ceded all land in Illinois between the Wabash River and the lands ceded by the Kaskaskia Indians August 13, 1803, lying south of the northwest corner of the Vincennes Tract. Consideration: $300 annually added to the perpetual annuity granted by the Treaty of Greenville; plus $1,100 at once; and the Piankeshaw to select a tract of 1,280 acres for a village. (2,616,921 acres in Illinois)

Sept. 30, 1809 Treaty of Fort Wayne, negotiated by William Henry Harrison with the Miami, Eel River Miami, Delaware, and Potawatami tribes, dealt chiefly with land in Indiana. Article IX, however, carried cessions of land west of the Wabash above the Vincennes Tract, subject to ratification by the Kickapoo tribe. Consideration (Article IX only): $400 annuity in addition to sums promised Kickapoo in the Treaty of Greenville. (282,000 acres in Illinois)

Dec. 9, 1809 Treaty of Vincennes, negotiated by Benjamin Parke, ratified Article IX of the Treaty of Fort Wayne of September 30 and further ceded other land north of the Vincennes Tract to a point on the Vermilion River twenty miles by direct measurement from its mouth. Consideration: $100 added to the annuities granted by the treaties of Greenville and Fort Wayne; plus trade goods to the value of $700 to be delivered at once. (58,880 acres in Illinois)

Aug. 24, 1816 Treaty of St. Louis, negotiated by Ninian Edwards, William Clark, and Auguste Chouteau with the United Tribes of the Chippewa, Ottawa, and Potawatami residing on the Illinois and Weewaukee rivers and Lake Michigan, ceded to the United States lands west of the Illinois River and south of a line from the southern extremity of Lake Michigan to the mouth of the Rock River previously ceded by the Sauk and Fox tribes; also ceded a strip of land twenty miles wide from the mouth of the Chicago River to the Kankakee and Fox rivers. Consideration: the United States re-ceded to the United Tribes all land ceded by the Sauk and Fox north of the Lake Michigan-Rock River line;

increased the annuity of the three tribes by $1,000 for a period of twelve years; and promised trade goods of an unspecified value to be delivered on the Illinois no farther south than Peoria. (new acres in Illinois, 767,411; re-ceded by the United States, 4,996,000 acres)

Sept. 25, 1818   Treaty of Edwardsville, negotiated by Ninian Edwards and Auguste Chouteau with the Peoria, Kaskaskia, Michigamia, Cahokia, and Tamaroa tribes, confirmed the treaty of 1803 made by the Kaskaskia tribe on behalf of the Illinois Indians, and further ceded lands claimed by the Peoria north of the original cessions by the Kaskaskia. Consideration: $2,000 in trade goods to be divided among the tribes; plus $300 yearly for twelve years to be paid to the Peoria; and 640 acres on the Blackwater River in Missouri where some of the families resided. (new acres in Illinois, 7,138,398) Note: Kickapoo of the Prairie claimed much of the additional land ceded.

Oct. 2, 1818   Treaty of St. Marys, Ohio, negotiated by Jonathan Jennings and Benjamin Parke with the Potawatami tribe, covered land between Tippecanoe Creek and the Vermilion River in the Wabash Valley. Acreage covered was included in a later treaty with the Kickapoo, who also had rights in the area. Consideration: perpetual annuity of $2,500 in silver plus small grants to individuals. (no new acreage in Illinois)

July 30, 1819   Treaty of Edwardsville, negotiated by Auguste Chouteau and Benjamin Stephenson, extinguished all claims of Kickapoo of the Prairie in Illinois, including land previously ceded by the Peoria tribe. Consideration: $2,000 annually for fifteen years to be paid in specie at the Kickapoo town on the headwaters of the Osage; and land on the Osage in the territory of Missouri. (new acres in Illinois, 969,400)

Aug. 30, 1819   Treaty of Fort Harrison, negotiated by Auguste Chouteau and Benjamin Stephenson with the Kickapoo of the Vermilion, ceded all lands this tribe could legally claim on the Wabash River or any of its tributaries. Consideration: Kickapoo relinquished annuity of $1,000 in trade goods for an annuity of $2,000 to be paid in specie. (2,317,849 acres in Illinois) The total acres ceded in Illinois before 1820: 29,258,147.

Aug. 25, 1828   Treaty of Green Bay, negotiated by Lewis Cass and Pierre Menard with the Winnebago and the United Tribes of the Chippewa, Ottawa, and Potawatami, ceded lands in the territory of Michigan and all lands in the state of Illinois situated between the Illinois River and the Fever River and lands east of the Fox from the Lake Michigan-Rock River line to the boundary of the canal strip. In this treaty the United Tribes recognized Winnebago claims to land in the middle Rock River Valley. Consideration: $20,000 in trade goods. (new acres in Illinois, 750,888)

July 29, 1829   Treaty of Prairie du Chien, negotiated by John McNiel, Pierre Menard, and Caleb Atwater with the United Tribes of Chippewa, Ottawa, and Potawatami, extinguished title to lands between the boundaries of cessions made by the Treaty of Green Bay August 25, 1828, and the Winnebago village forty miles from the mouth of the Rock River; also lands from Lake Michigan to the Rock River from the Lake Michigan-Rock River line and an east-west line from the northeast corner of the canal strip. Consideration: payment in specie of $16,000 annually forever; $12,000 in trade goods as a present; 50 barrels of salt annually forever; and individual gifts of land to heads of families electing to remain in Illinois. (3,790,000 acres in Illinois)

Aug. 1, 1829   Treaty of Prairie du Chien, negotiated by John McNiel, Pierre Menard, and Caleb Atwater, ceded all land claimed by the Winnebago tribe in northern Illinois and southern Wisconsin. Consideration: $18,000 in specie annually for thirty years; $30,000 in goods as a present; 3,000 pounds of tobacco and 50 barrels of salt annually for thirty years; the United States to provide and support three blacksmith shops on new lands, and two yoke of oxen, one cart, and one man at the portage of the Wisconsin. (no new acreage in Illinois)

Oct. 12, 1832   Treaty of Tippecanoe River, negotiated by Jonathan Jennings, J. W. Davis, and Marks Crume with the Potawatami, ceded lands north of the Kankakee River and southeast of the canal strip. Consideration: $32,000 in goods at once; $10,000 in goods in the spring of 1833; lands totaling 72 sections granted to groups and totaling 83 sections to individuals. (565,000 acres in Illinois)

Sept. 26, 1833   Treaty of Chicago, the final act of cession, negotiated by George B. Porter, Thomas J. V. Owen, and William Weatherford with the United Tribes of the Chippewa, Ottawa, and Potawatami, conveyed to the United States the remaining land of the tribes in Illinois from the Rock River to Lake Michigan. Consideration: 5,000,000 acres west of the Mississippi in what are now Iowa, Kansas, and Nebraska; $100,000 to satisfy claims of various individuals; $150,000 to pay claims against the tribes which the commissioners judge to be just; $100,000 in trade goods; $280,000 in twenty annual payments of $14,000; $150,000 for erection of mills, farmhouses, blacksmith shops, and for support of such physicians, millers, farmers, blacksmiths, and other mechanics as the President of the United States should think proper to appoint; $70,000 for education to be invested in some safe stock, interest only to be applied; small annuities to several individuals; $3,500 in cash to two bands headed by minor chiefs in payment for land withheld by them under the first Treaty of Prairie du Chien, and now ceded by them to the United States. (about 1,300,000 acres in Illinois) The total acres ceded from 1795 through 1833: 35,664,035.

Territorial

The Ordinance of July 13, 1787, by which Congress established the method of governing the territory of the United States northwest of the Ohio River, set up general rules for the creation of future states and loosely defined their borders. The first article of this ordinance provided that subject to the consent of Virginia no fewer than three nor more than five states would be admitted to the Confederation from the vast wilderness area. The ordinance further established the boundaries of the "western" state (Illinois) in this manner: "The western State, in the said territory, shall be bounded by the Mississippi, the Ohio, and the Wabash Rivers; a direct line drawn from the Wabash and Post Vincents, due north, to the territorial line between the United States and Canada; and by the said territorial line to the Lake of the Woods and the Mississippi." The ordinance also provided that in the event of the creation of five states in the Northwest Territory, the northern boundaries of the central and western states should be an east-west line passing through the southerly extreme of Lake Michigan.

The next reference to the boundaries of Illinois in legislation or other state papers occurred in the act of Congress of February 3, 1809, which divided the territory of Indiana and created the Illinois Territory. During the intervening twenty-two years Illinois had been first part of the Northwest Territory (until 1800) and later part of Indiana Territory. In the Division Act the boundaries for Illinois were those stipulated in the fifth article of the Ordinance of 1787.

The Enabling Act of December 11, 1816, which paved the way for the admission of Indiana as the nineteenth state, clarified earlier descriptions of the Indiana-Illinois line. Here, for the first time, a point of departure, however broad, was named for this border: "the Wabash to a point where a due north line from the town of Vincennes would last touch the shore of said river."

State

Had the original provisions of the fifth article of the Ordinance of 1787 prevailed, the state of Illinois would have had no frontage on Lake Michigan. To Nathaniel Pope, territorial delegate to Congress from Illinois Territory, goes the credit for moving the state line to its present position. Pope had excellent arguments for his northward push, among them the importance of keeping the jurisdiction of the projected Illinois

3

Illinois Boundaries

and Michigan Canal within one state. He also wanted to tie the new commonwealth, through a shoreline on Lake Michigan, to the states of the East so that it might at some future time become the keystone of the Union. Pope's amendment was adopted without a division, and the northern boundary of Illinois was established at parallel 42°30′, sixty-two and a half miles north of the line originally specified.

The boundaries of Illinois are described in the Enabling Act of 1818 as follows: "Said State shall consist of all the territory included within the following boundaries, to wit; Beginning at the mouth of the Wabash River, thence up the same, and with the line of Indiana, to the northwest corner of said State; thence east, with the line of the same State, to the middle of Lake Michigan; thence north, along the middle of said lake, to north latitude forty-two degrees thirty minutes; thence west to the middle of the Mississippi River; thence down, along the middle of that river, to its confluence with the Ohio River; and thence up the latter river, along its northwestern shore, to the beginning."

Only one change has ever been made in this description. Article I of the Illinois constitution of 1848 states that Illinois "shall exercise such jurisdiction upon the Ohio River as she is now entitled to, or such as may hereafter be agreed upon by this State and the State of Kentucky."

By this definition all land east of the Mississippi and west of the Wabash belongs to Illinois. But this is not necessarily the case; rivers change their courses, especially when there is little fall and many twistings and turnings. So today after many floods

15

and freshets and many an oxbow cutoff we have bits of Missouri east of the Mississippi, one tract of a few thousand acres of Illinois west of that river, an acre or two of Kentucky above the Ohio, and parts of Illinois east of the Wabash and of Indiana west of that stream. Here are the aberrations brought about by winter floods and spring freshets to the year 1967:

Illinois west of the Mississippi: Kaskaskia Island (14,000 acres), a large oxbow cutoff above the point where the Kaskaskia River formerly joined the Mississippi. Coordinates, Township 7 south, Range 8 west, Third Principal Meridian.

Missouri east of the Mississippi: a small enclave along a chute (once the main channel) on the north bank of the Mississippi in Township 9 south, Range 4 west, Third Principal Meridian; Grand Tower Island, an oxbow cutoff in Perry County, Missouri, Township 33 north, Range 20 east, Fifth Principal Meridian.

Kentucky north of the Ohio: a small enclave just northeast of and adjacent to Mound City. This enclave once was an island in the Ohio.

Indiana west of the Wabash: a small, unnamed oxbow cutoff at Township 7 south, Range 14 west, Second Principal Meridian; Ribeyre Island, a large oxbow cutoff at Township 5 north, Range 10 west, Second Principal Meridian near New Harmony, Indiana; Aurora Bend, a large oxbow cutoff at Township 10 north, Range 11 west, Second Principal Meridian.

Illinois east of the Wabash: Hutsonville Cutoff, a small oxbow cutoff in Crawford County; York Cutoff, an oxbow cutoff at York, Clark County.

The border north of the Wabash was surveyed, marked, and accepted by both states shortly after Illinois statehood. The commissioner in charge for Indiana was John Tipton and for Illinois, Samuel McClintock. The survey was run by John McDonald and platted during the summer of 1821. It was approved by joint resolution of the Indiana legislature December 14 of that year. In Illinois, however, action could not come until the regular session of the legislature which began January 2, 1823. Meanwhile doubts arose in the Illinois commission; Tipton's plat failed to show a starting point in Vincennes for the line. Perhaps Illinois had been cheated. Not so, said McClintock, and he called on Tipton to explain. Tipton

said he was fully aware of the difficulty: the line had been started at the courthouse in Vincennes; in so doing, he, the commissioner for Indiana, had given an advantage to Illinois and, fearful that it might injure his political standing if he stated the fact in the report or field book, he refused to make any other return.

After considerable debate, with the Illinois commissioner stoutly defending his Indiana colleague, the Illinois legislature finally approved the survey February 17, 1823, more than a year after Indiana had accepted it. The Illinois act provided for placing, "where the line dividing the states of Illinois and Indiana last leaves the Wabash river, a hewn stone at least five feet in length and fifteen inches in diameter, to be inscribed on west 'Illinois,' on east 'Indiana,' and on the north '159 miles and 46 chains to Lake Michigan.' " In September 1928, this old stone marker, which had sunk below the surface, was recovered and reset on a permanent foundation.

This was as near as Illinois and Indiana ever came to a border dispute. It was settled before it began by Tipton's entry in his journal, here given with the original misspellings: "We commenced the line opisit the vincennes Hotell on the Northwest bank of Wabash." The hotel was due north of the courthouse.

A boundary dispute with Wisconsin, however, did arise and endured for several years, fanned equally by Territorial Governor J. D. Doty of Wisconsin and the citizens of northwestern Illinois who felt they were overreached by the southern counties of Illinois and doubted the validity of moving the boundary above that set up in the "sacred compact" of Article V of the Ordinance of 1787.

Congress already had ruled on the question during a dispute between Ohio and the territory of Michigan which caused Governor Cass of Michigan to call up his militia in what became known as the Toledo War, a war in which no shot was fired. Congress settled the quarrel by validating Ohio's northern border above the Lake Michigan line, and compensating Michigan with land above Lake Michigan (in what was to have been upper Wisconsin), and a cash grant for development.

The conflict over the Illinois-Wisconsin line, kept alive by Governor Doty, was cheered on by citizens of Winnebago, Ogle, Stephenson, and Boone counties of Illinois, but it failed of support in most of Wisconsin. At a county meeting in Ogle County and by ballot in Stephenson, Winnebago, and Boone counties in 1842 the proposition of union with Wisconsin had hardly a dissenting vote. In Wisconsin, however, the citizens turned down a proposition for statehood that included the Lake Michigan-Mississippi line as the southern boundary by about three to one. Thus died Governor Doty's drive for a segment of Illinois. It was buried four years later when Congress passed the enabling act for Wisconsin statehood with 42°30′ as the border with Illinois. There was no comment or controversy in either state.

However, a dispute with Missouri concerning Kaskaskia Island is still in litigation.

DATES FOR REFERENCE

July 13, 1787   Congress passed the ordinance which established boundaries of future states northwest of the Ohio.

1788   The Virginia legislature modified her Cession Act of 1784 to permit limiting number of states in Northwest Territory to five.

May 7, 1800   Division Act created territories of Ohio and Indiana, confirming boundaries as set up in Article V of the Northwest Ordinance.

Feb. 3, 1809   A division act created the territory of Illinois with the boundaries of the "western state" in the Northwest Ordinance.

Dec. 11, 1816   Enabling act for Indiana statehood defined the Illinois-Indiana boundary.

Apr. 18, 1818   Enabling act for Illinois statehood defined northern boundary as 42°30′ north latitude.

Dec. 14, 1821   Indiana legislature approved the survey of the border north of the Wabash by a joint Illinois-Indiana commission.

Feb. 17, 1823   Illinois legislature approved survey and provided for a stone marker.

Aug. 31, 1847   Draft constitution of Illinois which claimed some jurisdiction over the Ohio River for Illinois was adopted by the constitutional convention, and later ratified by the people.

4

Constitutions and Capitals

Constitutions and Conventions

The Constitution of 1818

The first constitution of the state of Illinois was drafted at the territorial capital, Kaskaskia, by delegates elected in a manner stipulated by enabling legislation passed by Congress April 18, 1818. It contained a preamble and eight articles patterned principally after the constitutions of New York, Kentucky, Ohio, and the Constitution of the United States. The drafting committee, chosen from the delegates assembling at Kaskaskia on August 3, 1818, produced a provisional document sufficient to the needs of the frontier state, and the convention, after brief debate and minor changes, adopted it on August 26, 1818.

The preamble stated the purposes of the constitution and described the boundaries of the state. Article I dealt with the distribution of powers among the legislative, executive, and judicial departments and prohibited interference by any department in the affairs of another. Article II established a bicameral legislative body, prescribed methods of electing members, arranged for the election of half of the Senate every two years, and fixed qualifications of members, rules of procedure, and methods of introducing bills. It provided the members with immunity from arrest during sessions. It excluded holders of lucrative federal or state offices from seats, established twenty-one as the qualifying age for representatives and twenty-five for senators, and established a residence qualification of one year in the district for both. The article also provided that the General Assembly allow the gov-

ernor a salary of $1,000 yearly and the secretary of state $600 yearly until the year 1824.

Article III vested the executive power of the state in a governor, established the manner of election to that office, the period of tenure (four years in any consecutive eight) and age, residence, and citizenship qualifications. The article empowered the governor to grant pardons and to convene the assembly by proclamation. It designated him commander-in-chief of the state militia except when that body was called into federal service. A further provision stated that the governor's salary should not be increased or diminished during his term of office, thus limiting the change foreseen in Article II to the beginning of the third administration at the end of 1826. Article III further established the office of lieutenant governor, named him speaker of the Senate, authorized him to debate and vote as a member of the committee of the whole, and in case of ties to cast the deciding vote.

Article III also contained a provision that led to considerable discussion, debate, and delay of legislation for three decades—the provision establishing a revisionary council consisting of the governor and justices of the Supreme Court with authority to revise all bills about to be passed by the General Assembly. The article also empowered the governor to appoint a secretary of state and several other officers, and the General Assembly by joint vote to appoint the state treasurer and public printer or printers.

Article IV vested the judicial power of the state in a Supreme Court and such inferior courts as the General Assembly from time to time might establish. It located the Supreme Court at the seat of government, ordained for it a chief justice and three associate justices, and provided for their election by joint ballot of the two chambers of the General Assembly. The article also provided for appointing the judges of the inferior courts and justices of the peace.

Article V prescribed the qualifications for membership in the militia, methods of training, election of officers (except staff), and tenure.

Article VI prohibited slavery or involuntary servitude but permitted indentured servants to complete their contracts and declared that future children of those persons should be free of contractural demands on attaining their majority.

Article VII established the method of amending the constitution.

Article VIII was a bill of rights that conferred the same privileges and immunities on the citizens of Illinois as the first ten amendments to the Constitution of the United States conferred on the people of the federal union. The document was signed by Jesse B. Thomas of St. Clair County, as president, and thirty-one other delegates. It was attested by William C. Greenup, secretary of the convention.

Attempt to amend in 1822

Four years after adoption a determined effort was made to call a convention for the purpose of amending this constitution to permit slavery, which had been expressly forbidden by the Ordinance of 1787 for the government of the territory of the United States northwest of the Ohio River. In the bitter battle which followed proslavery advocates adopted the slogan, "The convention or death!" A duly elected representative who voted against the resolution to call the convention on first reading was illegally deprived of his seat and a proslavery man appointed who provided the vote necessary for a two-thirds majority. The election to decide on a convention was ordered for the first Monday of August 1824. Governor Edward Coles led the antislavery party which, in a bitter contest, defeated the proposition by 6,822 negative votes to 4,950 affirmative votes.

The Constitution of 1848

As Illinois grew in population, industry, and gross product, so did dissatisfaction with the constitution of 1818. By 1840 mismanagement, the failure of some state banks, and a severe depression had drained the resources of the treasury. Losses sustained by expansive investment in railroads and canals had further depleted state funds. Much time was consumed each legislative session in discussion of so-called private bills. A constitutional amendment to correct these evils and to limit the powers of the General Assembly was proposed and adopted by the assembly during the session of 1840–41 but defeated by the electors in a special election on August 1, 1842.

The proposal for a constitutional convention was once more moved and voted by the assembly in 1845, and the following year the voters approved it by a margin of almost three to one. After a protracted battle over population figures on which to base representation, the convention met on June 7, 1847, to debate these principal issues:

limitation of legislative powers, abolition of state banks and the unwieldy Council of Revision, prohibition of the use of state credit by individuals, associations, or corporations and of state investment in shares of private corporations. Because of the condition of the treasury it was determined to forego printing of the debates, but these were reconstructed from manuscript notes and newspaper reports by the Illinois State Historical Library long after the convention.

The constitution of 1848, agreed upon after nearly three months of debate on August 31, 1847, ratified by the electorate on March 6, 1848, and effective April 1, 1848, consists of a preamble and fifteen articles. Of these, thirteen bear the signatures of all delegates to the convention. The final two articles have the signature of the president and the attestation of the secretary and assistant secretary.

The preamble paraphrased that of the federal constitution. Article I, dealing with boundaries of the state, incorporated one sentence not found in the constitution of 1818. This sentence provided that Illinois should exercise such jurisdiction over the Ohio River as she was entitled to, or such as might be agreed upon by Illinois and Kentucky.

Article II, defining the distribution of powers, was identical with Article I of the constitution of 1818.

Article III, regulating the organization of the legislative department, fixed the lower age limit of representatives at twenty-five and added a residence requirement of three years in the state. The minimum age of senators was raised to thirty with a residence requirement of five years in the state. The article for the first time limited the size of the General Assembly and established rules for expansion after the state had attained a population of 1,000,000, but placed a top limit of 100 for the House of Representatives. For purposes of apportionment a census was ordered for 1855 and every tenth year thereafter. This census, with the census by the federal government every ten years, provided a base for reapportionment every five years. For the purpose of curbing private legislation, much of it trivial, the constitution provided that no local law should embrace more than one subject, which should be expressed in the title. Travel pay and per diem during sessions was established at ten cents a mile and $2.00 a day for the first forty-two days, $1.00 a day thereafter.

Article V provided for election of three judges of the Supreme Court by the voters, one from each of three grand divisions of the state (set up in this article). The article also established uniform organization and jurisdiction of municipal courts among the inferior courts created. The article required five years residence for judges in the state and two years in the division, circuit, or county from which elected or appointed, and fixed the minimum age for all judges of the Supreme Court at thirty-five.

Article V further provided for the election of a judge of the circuit court in each of the judicial districts and directed that two or more terms of the circuit court be held in each county annually. It further provided for one county judge in each county, chosen by the qualified electors of the county, who would have jurisdiction over probate and certain other civil cases, and in criminal cases where punishment fixed by law should not exceed a fine of $100.

Article VI again limited qualifications for suffrage to white males twenty-one years of age and older, and increased residence requirements to one year in the state. Dates of general elections were established as the first Tuesday after the first Monday in November, biennially.

The new constitution added articles concerned with the formation and administrative organization of counties, taxes and revenues, corporations, and common lands. Article XII made more elaborate provisions for constitutional amendments. Article XIII restated the bill of rights and provided a form of oath of affirmation to be required of all persons entering upon elective or appointive state offices. Article XIV prohibited free persons of color from migrating to or settling in Illinois. Article XV laid a special tax for retiring a portion of the state debt every year. An attached schedule provided for continuity of government, established the method and date of ratification, and provided for submission of articles XIV and XV separately from the main body of the constitution.

The Convention of 1862

The constitution of 1848, while indicative of progress in social organization and political maturity, left some important issues unresolved. An attempt to call a constitutional convention in 1856 to correct these inadequacies failed, but in 1860 a second attempt succeeded, and on January 7, 1862, seventy-five delegates convened in Springfield. Their work was not without merit, but representation was strictly on party lines, and in a state which had helped elect a Republican President in 1860 the Democratic majority considered its election a mandate to castigate the conduct of the war—particularly Governor Richard Yates' administration of military affairs. When the document resulting from the labors of the convention was placed before the people of the state it was repudiated by a large majority.

The Constitution of 1870

Following the Civil War the evils of private legislation, of fixed salaries for public officials (the governor's stipend had been placed at $1,500, an absurdity in postwar times), and of inadequate courts became more and more apparent. In 1867 the legislature placed before the electorate a proposal for a constitutional convention, which was promptly ratified. On December 13, 1869, eighty-five delegates met under the presidency of Charles Hitchcock to consider revision of the constitution of 1848. After five months of debate they produced the instrument which, with a few amendments in later years, still is the organic law of Illinois.

This was a more complex document than the constitution of 1848, and in many ways it improved on the previous constitution. Establishing of salary levels for state officials was made a subject of legislation, limited only by a provision that the salary of no person in office should be altered during his term. Special legislation was greatly restricted, with action prohibited on twenty-three specific subjects. The judicial system was completely reorganized. The number of justices of the Supreme Court was increased to seven, appellate courts were authorized after the year 1874, the number of circuit court and county court judges was increased to provide for an increasing work load, and election of at least one judge in each county became mandatory. Probate courts were authorized in certain counties, state's attorneys for each county were provided for, and justices of the peace and police magistrates were to be elected rather than appointed. The problems resulting from rapid growth in Cook County were recognized by establishment of additional courts.

However, lack of flexibility was a serious drawback which would be of increasing concern as population and problems of government increased. Provision for amendment by direct submission to the voters of the state was so restrictive that it made needed changes difficult to achieve.

The constitution of 1870 consists of a brief preamble unchanged, except for punctuation, from 1848; fourteen articles; and provisions covering the relationship of the state with the Illinois Central Railroad Company, minority representation through cumulative voting, municipal subscriptions to private corporations, the status of state-owned canals, and the practice of contracting for convict labor. (This last proposition, submitted separately to the voters, was defeated.) References are more easily found in this than in previous constitutions because of headings and subheadings for each article.

Article I defines the boundaries of the state as in previous constitutions. Article II embodies the bill of rights in essentially the same language as that of Article XIII of the constitution of 1848. The distribution of powers, specified in Article III, was unchanged.

Article IV deals with the legislative department. This article fixes eligibility at age twenty-five for the Senate, twenty-one for the House of Representatives, and prescribes five-year residence in the state and two years in the district from which elected. Article IV also orders apportionment of the fifty-one senatorial districts every ten years based on the federal census. The provision calling for cumulative voting for representatives, which assures minority representation, became a part of this article. For the first time the General Assembly was charged with the responsibility of protecting miners by providing for ventilation, escape shafts, and other safety devices in coal mines. The assembly was permitted to pass legislation regarding drains, ditches, and levees and required to pass liberal homestead and exemption laws.

Article V, defining the executive powers, increased the number of elective offices to seven: governor, lieutenant governor, secretary of state, auditor of public accounts, treasurer, superintendent of public instruction, and attorney general. The governor's veto power was strengthened by increasing the number required to pass an act over his veto to two-thirds of the members elected instead of a majority of the members voting.

Article VI, describing the organization and powers of the judiciary, reduced the age of eligibility from thirty-five to thirty years and maintained former citizenship and residence requirements. The three grand judicial divisions and the existing terms were continued, except that one or more sessions of the northern division each year were specified to be held in the city of Chicago. Because of the increasing burden on the courts of Cook County, that county was declared to be one judicial circuit with five judges and more if necessary. Except in the city of Chicago, where justices of the peace were to be appointed by the governor by and with the consent of the Senate, justices of the peace and constables were to be elected and their jurisdictions made uniform.

Article VII granted suffrage to males above the age of twenty-one years resident in the state one year, the county ninety days, and the election district thirty days. Article VIII broadened provisions for common schools. Aid to sectarian schools, whether by state, county, or municipality, was forbidden.

Article IX on revenue was more detailed and restrictive than the similar section of the constitution of 1848 but included no basic changes except abolition of the capitation tax (poll tax) on free white males over twenty-one years of age. Article X restricted division or subdivision of counties for the purpose of forming new counties so that no county would be smaller than 400 square miles. (No counties have been formed in Illinois since 1859.) The article authorizes township organization or organization under boards of county commissioners.

Article XI provides for the creation and administration of corporations, prohibits state-owned banks, allows access to the records of railways within the state, and gives the General Assembly authority to regulate rates. Previous constitutions had articles regulating the militia; Article XII covers this in the 1870 document. The increasing importance of agriculture is indicated by the provisions of Article XIII for regulatory legislation regarding such things as the storage of grain and the supervision of warehouse receipts.

Article XIV made provision, however restricted, for amendment or revision of the constitution either by a convention or by the General Assembly (requiring a two-thirds majority), and approval of a majority of those voting at the election. The new constitution was adopted by the convention May 13, 1870, ratified by the people of Illinois at a special election July 2, 1870, and declared in effect August 8, 1870.

Amendments

Amendments were adopted in 1878, 1880, 1884, 1886, 1890, 1904, 1908, 1950, 1952, 1954, and 1962. The amendment of 1878, elaborating Section 31 of Article IV, provided for the organization of drainage districts with broad corporate and regulatory authority. That of 1880 prohibited the reelection of sheriffs and county treasurers. The amendment of 1884 gave the governor power to veto appropriation items rather than the whole bill. That of 1886 prohibited contracts for convict labor. The amendment of 1890 authorized the city of Chicago to issue bonds for the financing of the World's Columbian Exposition. In 1904 an amendment authorized special legislation for the city of Chicago, consolidating in the government of the city the powers vested in city, board of education, township, park, and other local governments, and providing for the assumption by the city of Chicago of debts and other liabilities of these entities. This amendment made possible absorption into the city of Chicago of a number of adjacent towns and villages. In 1908 an amendment made provision for a deep waterway from Lake Michigan to the Illinois River.

No further amendments were approved by the voters until 1950, although many were submitted. In that year, the so-called gateway amendment offered in various forms in 1892, 1896, 1924, 1932, and 1946, was accepted by the electorate. This amendment to Article XIV, Section 2 provides that three amendments during one session may be approved by a two-thirds majority of both houses of the General Assembly and submitted to the voters, instead of only one amendment as provided in 1870.

In 1952 two amendments were authorized by the electorate: one which restricted the compensation of county officers to the fees actually collected and provided for the remittance to the county treasury of all fees in excess of the authorized compensation; the other, a banking amendment.

In 1954 three amendments carried. The first called for a reapportionment of the General Assembly in 1955 to provide fifty-eight senatorial districts, of which twenty-four would be in Cook County, and fifty-nine representative districts of which thirty would be in Cook County. In 1963 and every ten years thereafter reapportionment should be made in the ratio of the actual population of Chicago, Cook County outside the limits of Chicago, and the remaining 101 counties in Illinois. The second provided for a four-year term for the state treasurer. The third, preparing for the disposition of the Illinois and Michigan Canal right-of-way, gave the state authority to sell, lease, or maintain and operate state-owned canals and waterways. In 1962 a judicial amendment was approved.

Revision Attempts since 1870

A hundred years after the great conflict over the amendment of the constitution of 1818 to permit slavery, the electorate voted for a constitutional convention. Its recommended revisions of the constitution of 1870 included more flexible revenue provisions, a state income tax, abolition of cumulative voting, limited home rule for Chicago, and increased representation for Cook County in the General Assembly. The new constitution was rejected by the electorate in 1922 by a majority of more than five to one.

A proposal for calling a convention in 1935, approved by the General Assembly, was submitted to the electorate in 1934 and defeated. Of 2,935,192 voting in the election more than 56 per cent failed to mark their ballots for or against the proposition, whereas a majority of those voting was required for approval.

Capitals and Capitols

When the territorial capital of Kaskaskia was designated capital of the newborn state of Illinois in 1818, it was already apparent that the location was inappropriate and the facilities inadequate. The center of population had moved away from the American Bottom. Tens of thousands of acres of public land under control of the land offices in Edwardsville, Shawneetown, and Vincennes had been filed upon by eager settlers. Settlement in Illinois was definitely moving toward the north. Kaskaskia already was on the periphery. So it was incumbent upon the first General Assembly to establish a new capital north and east of the Bottom.

Early in 1819 the Illinois legislature petitioned the federal government for a grant of land, which was immediately approved. A committee of five legislators selected a tiny hamlet, Reeves Bluff, eighty miles northeast of Kaskaskia on the Kaskaskia River. In 1820 the rented two-story building that had served as the first capitol was deserted, and the legislature occupied a new building of the same type in the log-and-shake town that had been christened Vandalia. Like the building left behind, it housed the lower chamber on the first floor and the Senate on the second. There also was an office for the Council of Revision. The secretary of state, auditor, and treasurer found office space elsewhere in Vandalia. During its first session the General Assembly voted to retain Vandalia as the seat of government for twenty years.

On December 9, 1823, the capitol was destroyed by fire. A brick structure, built to replace it, afforded slightly more commodious quarters for the legislature. Here in the early thirties Abraham Lincoln and Stephen A. Douglas cut their legislative teeth, and here Lincoln spearheaded a drive to move the capital to Springfield, which was much nearer the center of population and the geographical center of the state. Lincoln and eight colleagues from central Illinois who, if stretched head to toe, would have aggregated more than fifty-four feet in length (hence the name "Long Nine") battled through two sessions before they succeeded in having Springfield selected during the session of 1836–37 as the third capital of the state.

In the summer of 1836, before Springfield was chosen, the citizens of Vandalia, bent on retaining the seat of government, tore down the old brick building and, in the best traditions of the Atlantic seaboard, built a handsome structure of stone complete with cupola. The building was said to have cost the town $16,000 but it availed nothing, for on July 4, 1837, the cornerstone of a new capitol (the fifth) was laid at Springfield. On July 4, 1839, all state records and movable property were transported to the new seat of government. The recently built capitol in Vandalia was acquired by Fayette County. Much later it was returned to state jurisdiction as a historical monument.

The Springfield statehouse, which cost $260,000, was not completed until 1853. By that time it was too small. The Twenty-fifth General Assembly, in 1867, authorized

the erection of a new structure at a cost of $3,000,000 and sold the old capitol to Sangamon County. The deed was executed in 1869, and the building delivered in 1876, but it was 1878 before the courts of Sangamon County could be housed in the structure for which the county had paid. By then the estimated cost of the sixth state capitol (the fifth owned by the state) had risen to $4,500,000.

The present capitol, situated on a nine-acre plot at the head of Capitol Avenue in the heart of Springfield, is in the form of a Latin cross. It was built from the prize-winning design of John C. Cochrane of Chicago. The circular foundation, 92 1/2 feet in diameter, on which rests the massive dome, is 25 1/2 feet below the surface, set in solid rock. Walls supporting the dome are seventeen feet thick through the first story, and built of granular magnesian sandstone from quarries in Hancock County. The outer walls of the superstructure are of Niagara limestone quarried at Joliet and Lemont. The building is 379 feet long from north to south and 268 feet from east to west. The height from the ground line to the top of the dome is 361 feet, and the tip of the flagstaff is 405 feet above the ground.

The state legislative, judicial, and executive departments soon outgrew even these commodious quarters. In 1908 the Supreme Court moved into its own handsome building. Other departments overflowed into the Centennial Building begun in 1918 and completed in 1923. An archives building was completed in 1938. In 1954 ground was broken for a state office building which was occupied twenty months later. On April 4, 1963, ground was broken for an addition to the Centennial Building, which was occupied December 30, 1966.

In Chicago the state rented space in several Loop buildings until 1946, when the Burnham Building at La Salle and Randolph streets was purchased, and the name changed to the State of Illinois Building. By 1965 additional space was required and found in nearby buildings.

CHRONOLOGY OF THE CAPITOLS

Dec. 1818   A rented two-story building housed First General Assembly of Illinois.

Metropolis now stands. Because of its considerable original extent, out of which thirty-two counties or parts of counties were to be formed, and its later accretions, St. Clair County has been called Mother of Counties. At the beginning it might have been called Mother of Misrule. A district organization whereby courts sat in Kaskaskia, Cahokia, and Prairie du Rocher failed to function. Rivalry of the first two villages, both of which claimed to be the county seat, further complicated problems created by vast distances, few roads, and other obstacles to harmony. Finally, on October 5, 1795, Governor St. Clair lopped off the southern third of St. Clair County to establish Randolph County. This solved one problem. Kaskaskia and Cahokia both were now county seats. Time and understanding would solve others.

On May 7, 1800, in preparation for Ohio's statehood, Congress passed the Division Act whereby the Northwest Territory was split into the territory of Ohio and the territory of Indiana, which included Illinois. In 1801 new borders for St. Clair, Randolph, and Knox counties were ordained. St. Clair received lands from Knox as far north as the mouth of the Great Calumet River, east of present-day Gary, and all of present-day Wisconsin, adding another fifty-six Illinois counties to her brood. After the Division Act that portion of Indiana Territory west of the Wabash contained only two counties; nine years later, when Illinois became a territory in its own right, the number was the same although the boundaries were somewhat altered.

During the nine remaining years before statehood thirteen counties were established. The criterion for creating a new county: when outlying areas became settled and it was a hardship for newcomers to reach a distant county seat. The principle for the formation of a new county soon became the ability of *all* residents to visit the county seat on horseback and return the same day. In conformity with this standard four new counties were established in 1819, seven in 1821, four in 1823, and three in 1824.

The procedure for the forming of a new county began with an enabling act by the state legislature and appointment of three commissioners to supervise election of county officers and select a site for a seat of justice. Since the county seat was required to be as near as possible to the geographical center of the new county, and since the enabling act generally called for donation of land for public buildings, the site frequently was in the open prairie with no habitation in view. In such cases the newly elected county officers and judges would meet in the home of a settler to transact their business, until a town had been laid out, and a rough-hewn log courthouse and tavern, or establishment of public entertainment, had been built.

When two or more settlements were near enough to the county center to be deemed by the commissioners satisfactory locations, the choice would be determined by ballot. The prestige and trade accruing to a seat of justice were considerable. When an election took place feelings frequently ran high and violence occurred. Election results sometimes were contested in the courts, particularly when there were more ballots than eligible voters. One such conflict, with all the overtones of fist fights, ballot-box stuffing, and a court contest lasting two years, erupted a few years after the Civil War, when citizens voted on a change in Knox County from Knoxville to Galesburg. Galesburg won the battle of the ballot in 1871, but the county records stayed in Knoxville until 1873, when the Supreme Court of Illinois blessed the Galesburg victory. This, however, was long after the most prolific period of county birth.

One event that accelerated the establishment of new counties north of the Illinois River was the building of the Erie Canal. Until the end of 1824 only two counties had been formed north of the Illinois River. In 1825, with the canal pushing westward, ten new counties, all of them north of the Illinois, were formed. Most of these were in the Military Tract of 3,500,000 acres set aside for bounties granted to soldiers of the Revolution, the War of 1812, and their heirs and assignees. The completion of the Erie Canal and its formal opening on October 26, 1825, provided a direct water route via the canal, the Great Lakes, and the Illinois River to the bounty lands.

Survey of the tract, authorized May 6, 1812, and delayed by the war with England, had begun November 1, 1815, with the running of the Fourth Principal Meridian, identified with the mouth of the Illinois River, and survey of a new baseline, originally designated to follow the Fortieth Parallel, but because of a surveyor's error actually placed a few miles north. Originally

a tract of 2,000,000 acres had been authorized. In 1816 another 1,500,000 acres were
added to replace allocated lands in Michigan
that were deemed unfit for cultivation. The
northern border of the tract was placed 169
miles north of the Illinois River mouth.
So the march of counties proceeded north
from the well-settled southern areas, south
and west from Lake Michigan. Cook
County was among the five established in
1831. Six were named in 1836, six in 1837,
fifteen in 1839, seven in 1841, four in 1843,
one in 1847, one in 1853, and finally two in
1859. Ford County, proclaimed on February
17, 1859, was the last, completing the roster
of the counties of Illinois. As these 102
counties were evolving from the original
two set up by St. Clair, so was the machinery of government developing to meet new
requirements in an awakening land. The
constitution of 1818 made provision for
popular election of a sheriff, a coroner, and
three county commissioners in each county
existing at the time of statehood. Officers
such as county clerks, constables, surveyors
of highways, viewers of fences, pound
officers, judges of higher courts, and justices
of the peace were appointed by the General
Assembly. Clerks and secretaries of county
courts were appointed by the judges of those
courts.

The political township, later to become a
base of local government, had been created
by territorial legislation in 1802, when
Illinois was a part of the territory of Indiana. An act approved January 18 of that
year provided that all free males over the
age of twenty-one would meet on the first
Monday of April to elect a township clerk,
three or more trustees or managers, two or
more overseers of the poor, three fence
viewers, one lister of taxable property, a
sufficient number of supervisors of roads,
and one or more constables. This first legislation was supplemented by an act of
September 17, 1807, authorizing courts of
common pleas to divide counties into
townships. When Illinois separated from
Indiana and became a territory, this legislation was reenacted but not implemented
and became dormant until 1820, when townships were made bodies politic for school
purposes and designated as coextensive with
geographical townships created by federal
legislation in 1785.

Soon these townships conveniently became election districts within the counties,
and their borders enclosed areas of jurisdiction for the various constables, supervisors
of the poor, and other officers. In the matter

of general government, however, Illinois
clung to the Virginia pattern, with most of
the power descending from above, rather
than arising out of town (or township) meetings as in New England.

Before 1818 most settlers of Illinois came
from Virginia and the Carolinas via Kentucky and Tennessee. With the admission
of Missouri as a slave state in 1820 and the
defeat of a call for a constitutional convention to legalize slavery in Illinois, Southern-
ers passed across the southern part of the
state into Missouri, where their human
property would be secure. New Englanders,
however, finding opportunity for homes in
the bounty lands northwest of the Illinois
River and the broad prairies of middle
Illinois, continued to fill the empty places
and to long for a local system of government similar to what they had left behind.
This was one of the causes of discontent
with the organic law of Illinois that led to a
constitutional convention in 1847.

Out of this convention came the constitution of 1848 which specifically authorized counties to vote on the proposition of
township government and authorized any
county where more than half of the electorate was favorable to adopt a township form
of government. Under this system each
township (generally coextensive with a
school district and a survey township)
elected a supervisor who sat with other
supervisors as a county legislative and administrative board, and other local officers,
including constables and justices of the
peace. Elections were held at township
meetings in early April, where taxes, improvement of roads within the township,
and other matters of local interest were also
decided.

When the constitution of 1848 was ratified
by the people, ninety-nine counties had
already been formed in the Virginia pattern.
(One county was chartered in 1853 and two
more were organized during 1859, completing the roster as it exists today.) In the first
year under the new constitution, twenty-
four counties ratified a township plan of
government, seventeen of these being north
of the Illinois River. By 1860 the township
plan had been accepted by thirty-six additional counties. At the time of ratification
of the constitution of 1870, a total of seventy
counties were under the township type of
county administrative organization. At the
present time, eighty-four counties are

organized on the township plan, one (Cook County) has townships for control of local matters and a board of fifteen county commissioners for county government, and seventeen counties have retained the original plan of county government.

School affairs are on both a county and city administrative plan in Cook County and other counties with large urban populations, with both county and city superintendents functioning. In most cases, county superintendents of schools are elected; city superintendents are appointed by school boards.

Referendum votes are required either by the constitution of 1870 as amended or by statute for a number of county matters, such as: forming new counties, changing county boundaries, uniting counties (none of these has been done since the organization of Ford County in 1859), issuing bonds, levying county taxes above the constitutional limit of $0.75 per $100 of valuation (an almost forgotten limitation), and a few other county matters.

County judges, formerly administrative as well as judicial officers, are now associate justices of the circuit court, and justices of the peace are magistrates of the same court. The state's attorney is primarily a public prosecutor of criminal cases, acting in this respect as a state officer. He also is legal advisor to the county board, be it of supervisors (township plan) or commissioners.

The county clerk has the greatest variety of duties and, in most counties, is the principal administrative officer of the county. He is custodian of county records, clerk for the county board, and holds considerable authority and responsibility in elections and matters of election law, assessment and collection of taxes, and issuing certain kinds of licenses. The clerk of the circuit court keeps records of proceedings, and, in those counties which do not have a county recorder, he acts as the recorder of deeds.

The office of sheriff, together with coroner the oldest in the county organization, varies in importance with county size and population. In Cook County, where enforcement responsibilities are heavy, he has a force of sheriff's police, whereas in most counties he has only one or more deputies. However, in every county he is the principal conservator of the peace and in emergencies he may appoint special deputies, organize posses, or

call on the governor for military aid. In counties not under township organization he is district and county collector of taxes. The county treasurer has custody of county funds and responsibility for the tax rolls.

In Illinois the office of coroner is still an important instrument of criminal investigation. The coroner holds inquests on all cases of violent death to determine responsibility and on cases of death from causes unknown to determine whether they resulted from criminal action.

The county superintendent of public instruction acts as agent of the state in distributing state school funds. He inspects, supervises, and advises local school officers and performs such tasks as are assigned from time to time by legislation or by direction of the state superintendent of public instruction.

County boards of review in counties under township organization (except Cook County) are composed of the chairman of the board of supervisors and two citizens appointed annually by the circuit court. In Cook County a board of review of three members is elected. In all other counties the board of county commissioners acts as a board of review. Its functions are review and equalization of assessments of property for taxation made by the local assessors.

County superintendents of highways are generally appointed by joint action of county boards and the Department of Public Works and Buildings of Illinois. Fitness for office is determined by examinations under direction of the state authorities. In counties of more than 75,000 population, county auditors are elected. County boards appoint a variety of inspectors, minor officers, and the chairman and members of local commissions.

At the township level, supervisors, magistrates of the circuit court (formerly justices of the peace), constables, and a few other local officers are elected, and town meetings are held annually to determine matters strictly of interest to the township. Supervisors, magistrates, and constables are elected for four years. Other officers serve two years. By legislation, the powers of township and town officers in townships wholly within any city of more than 50,000 population may be exercised by county officers.

Every county of the state elects a county clerk, treasurer, sheriff, state's attorney, superintendent of schools, and coroner. Cook County elects an assessor. Recorders are elected in Adams, Champaign, Cook,

Du Page, Kane, Kankakee, Knox, Lake, La Salle, McLean, Macon, Madison, Peoria, Rock Island, St. Clair, Sangamon, Tazewell, Vermilion, Will, and Winnebago counties. Auditors are elected in Champaign, Cook, Crawford, Du Page, Kane, Lake, La Salle, McLean, Macon, Madison, Peoria, Rock Island, St. Clair, Sangamon, Tazewell, Vermilion, Will, and Winnebago counties.

The counties organized with boards of county commissioners are Alexander, Calhoun, Edwards, Hardin, Johnson, Massac, Menard, Monroe, Morgan, Perry, Pope, Pulaski, Randolph, Scott, Union, Wabash, and Williamson. Cass County elects neither commissioners nor supervisors.

Names for the counties of Illinois come from a variety of sources, one or two of them incorrectly remembered. Six were named for Presidents of the United States, but none was named for President Lincoln. Four were called for early governors of Illinois, twenty-two for military heroes, three for naval commanders, twenty-one for civic leaders never residents of Illinois, nine for counties in other states, and the rest for explorers, Indian traders and fighters, Indian tribes, and physical features of Illinois and elsewhere.

Counties of Illinois (1960 population)

Adams Created January 13, 1825, from Pike County and unorganized territory attached to Pike County. Named for John Quincy Adams (1767–1848), President of the United States, 1825–29. County seat: Quincy. Area: 866 square miles. Population: 68,467.

Alexander Created March 4, 1819, from unorganized territory south of Union County. Named for William M. Alexander, early settler, state representative, 1820–24. County seats: America, 1819; Unity, 1833; Thebes, 1843; Cairo, 1860. Area: 224 square miles. Population: 16,061.

Bond Created January 4, 1817, from part of Madison County. Named for Shadrach Bond (1773–1832), first governor of Illinois, 1818–22. County seats: Perryville, 1818; Greenville, 1821. Area: 383 square miles. Population: 14,060.

Boone Created March 4, 1837, from part of Winnebago County. Named for Daniel Boone (1734–1820). County seat: Belvidere. Area: 283 square miles. Population: 20,326.

Brown Created February 1, 1839, from part of Schuyler County. Named for General Jacob Brown (1775–1848), veteran of

the War of 1812. County seat: Mount Sterling. Area: 307 square miles. Population: 6,210.

Bureau Created February 28, 1837, from part of Putnam County. Named for Pierre de Bureo, early Indian trader. County seat: Princeton. Area: 868 square miles. Population: 37,594.

Calhoun Created January 10, 1825, from part of Pike County at the southern tip of the Military Tract. Named for John C. Calhoun (1782–1850), secretary of war, 1817–25; vice president, 1825–32; senator from South Carolina, 1832–43, 1845–50. County seats: Gilead, 1825; Hardin, 1847. Area: 259 square miles. Population: 5,933.

Carroll Created February 22, 1839, from part of JoDaviess County. Named for John Carroll of Carrollton (1735–1815), signer of Declaration of Independence. County seats: Savanna, 1839; Mount Carroll, 1844. Area: 468 square miles. Population: 19,507.

Cass Created March 3, 1837, from part of Morgan County. Named for Lewis Cass (1782–1866), governor of Michigan Territory, 1813–31; secretary of war, 1831–36; senator from Michigan, 1845–57; secretary of state, 1857–60. County seat: Virginia. Area: 370 square miles. Population: 14,539.

Champaign Created February 20, 1833, from part of Vermilion County and unorganized territory west of its boundaries. Named for an Ohio county. County seat: Urbana. Area: 1,000 square miles. Population: 132,436.

Christian Created February 15, 1839, from parts of Montgomery, Sangamon, and Shelby counties. Originally named for Nathan Dane (1752–1835), author of the article in the Ordinance of 1787 excluding slavery from the Northwest Territory. Renamed Christian (1840) for a Kentucky county. County seat: Taylorville. Area: 709 square miles. Population: 37,207.

Clark Created March 22, 1819, from part of Crawford County. Named for George Rogers Clark (1752–1818) who won Indiana and Illinois for Virginia. County seats: Aurora, 1819; Darwin, 1823; Marshall, 1837. Area: 505 square miles. Population: 16,546.

Clay Created December 23, 1824, from parts of Fayette, Crawford, and Wayne counties. Named for Henry Clay (1777–1852), representative from Kentucky, 1811–21, 1823–25; secretary of state, 1825–29;

senator from Kentucky, 1806–7, 1810–11, 1831–42, 1849–52. County seats: Maysville, 1825; Louisville, 1841. Area: 464 square miles. Population: 15,815.

Clinton Created December 27, 1824, from parts of Washington, Bond, and Fayette counties. Named for De Witt Clinton (1769–1828), governor of New York, 1817–21, 1825–28; principal promoter of the Erie Canal. County seat: Carlyle. Area: 498 square miles. Population: 24,029.

Coles Created December 25, 1830, from part of Clark County and adjacent unorganized territory. Named for Edward Coles (1786–1868), abolitionist; secretary to President James Madison, 1809–15; governor of Illinois, 1822–26. County seat: Charleston. Area: 507 square miles. Population: 42,860.

Cook Created January 15, 1831, from the northeastern part of Putnam County. Named for Daniel Pope Cook (1794–1827), Illinois territorial delegate to Congress, 1816–18; adjutant general of Illinois, 1818; representative from Illinois, 1819–27. County seat: Chicago. Area: 954 square miles. Population: 5,129,725.

Crawford Created December 31, 1816, from part of Edwards County. Named for William H. Crawford (1772–1834), senator from Georgia, 1807–13; minister to France, 1813–15; secretary of war, 1815–16; secretary of the treasury, 1816–25. County seats: Palestine, 1818; Robinson, 1843. Area: 442 square miles. Population: 20,751.

Cumberland Created March 2, 1843, from part of Coles County. Named for the Cumberland Road. County seats: Greenup, 1843; Toledo (then Prairie City), 1855. Area: 347 square miles. Population: 9,936.

De Kalb Created March 4, 1837, from part of Kane County. Named for Johann Kalb, called Baron de Kalb (1721–80), German officer who served in the Revolution and was killed at Camden, South Carolina. County seat: Sycamore. Area: 636 square miles. Population: 51,714.

De Witt Created March 1, 1839, from parts of Macon, McLean, Piatt, and Logan counties. Named for De Witt Clinton (*see* Clinton County). County seat: Clinton. Area: 399 square miles. Population: 17,253.

Douglas Created February 8, 1859, from part of Coles County. Named for Stephen A. Douglas, the "Little Giant" (1813–61), Illinois legislature, 1836–37; representative from Illinois, 1843–47; sena-

tor from Illinois, 1847–61. County seat: Tuscola. Area: 420 square miles. Population: 19,243.

Du Page Created February 9, 1839, from part of Cook County. Named for the Du Page River. County seats: Naperville, 1839; Wheaton, 1867. Area: 331 square miles. Population: 313,459.

Edgar Created January 3, 1823, from part of Clark County. Named for John Edgar (d. 1832), Kaskaskia merchant and landowner. County seat: Paris. Area: 628 square miles. Population: 22,550.

Edwards Created November 28, 1814, from parts of Madison and Gallatin counties, which then comprised some seveneighths of the territory. Named for Ninian Edwards (1775–1833), governor of Illinois Territory, 1809–18; senator from Illinois, 1818–24; governor of Illinois, 1826–30. County seat: Albion. Area: 225 square miles. Population: 7,940.

Effingham Created February 15, 1831, from parts of Crawford and Fayette counties. Named for Thomas, third earl of Effingham, who stood in the House of Lords in 1774 to declare that he would never draw his sword against fellow citizens and would serve no tea in his home until the tax was repealed. In 1775, when his regiment was ordered to North America, he resigned his commission. County seats: Ewington, 1831; Effingham, 1860. Area: 483 square miles. Population: 23,107.

Fayette Created February 14, 1821, from parts of Bond, Crawford, and Clark counties. Named for the Marquis de Lafayette, the young French nobleman who served in the American Revolutionary army from 1776 to 1781, when he commanded French troops at Yorktown. County seat: Vandalia. Area: 718 square miles. Population: 21,946.

Ford Created February 17, 1859, from unorganized territory attached to Vermilion County. Named for Thomas Ford (1800–1850), governor of Illinois, 1842–46. County seat: Paxton. Area: 488 square miles. Population: 16,606.

Franklin Created January 2, 1818, from parts of St. Clair, White, Johnson, and Gallatin counties. Named for Benjamin Franklin (1706–90). County seats: None until 1826; Frankfort, 1826; Benton, 1839. Area: 434 square miles. Population: 39,281.

Fulton Created January 28, 1823, from part of Pike County. Named for Robert Fulton (1765–1815), inventor of the first practical steamboat. County seat: Lewiston. Area: 874 square miles. Population: 41,954.

Gallatin Created September 14, 1812, from part of Randolph County. Named for Swiss-born Albert Gallatin (1761–1849), representative from Pennsylvania, 1795–1801; secretary of the treasury, 1801–14. County seats: Shawneetown, 1812; Equality, 1814; Shawneetown, 1848. Area: 328 square miles. Population: 7.638.

Greene Created January 20, 1821, from part of Madison County. Named for General Nathanael Greene (1742–86), Revolutionary War hero. County seat: Carrollton. Area: 543 square miles. Population: 17,460.

Grundy Created February 17, 1841, from part of La Salle County. Named for Felix Grundy (1777–1840), representative from Tennessee, 1811–14; senator from Tennessee, 1829–37, 1839–40; attorney general, 1838–39. County seat: Morris. Area: 432 square miles. Population: 22,350.

Hamilton Created February 8, 1821, from part of White County. Named for Alexander Hamilton (1757–1804), Revolutionary War officer, secretary of the treasury, 1789–95. Killed in duel with Aaron Burr. County seat: McLeansboro. Area: 435 square miles. Population: 10,010.

Hancock Created January 13, 1825, from unorganized territory attached to Pike County. Named for John Hancock (1737–93), president of the Continental Congress, 1775–77, 1785–86; first signer of the Declaration of Independence; governor of Massachusetts, 1780–85, 1787–93. County seat: None until 1833; Carthage, 1833. Area: 797 square miles. Population: 24,574.

Hardin Created March 2, 1839, from part of Pope County. Named for a Kentucky county. County seat: Elizabethtown. Area: 183 square miles. Population: 5,879.

Henderson Created January 20, 1841, from part of Warren County. Named for a Kentucky county. County seat: Oquawka. Area: 381 square miles. Population: 8,237.

Henry Created January 13, 1825, from unorganized territory attached to Fulton County. Named for Patrick Henry (1736–99), member of the Virginia House of Burgesses, 1765–75; member of the Continental Congress, 1774–76; governor of Virginia, 1776–79, 1784–86. County seat: None until 1833; Cambridge, 1833. Area: 826 square miles. Population: 49,317.

Iroquois Created February 26, 1833, from unorganized territory north of Vermilion County. Named for the Indian tribe. County seats: None until 1837; Montgomery, 1837; Middleport, 1839; Watseka, 1865. Area: 1,122 square miles. Population: 33,562.

Jackson Created January 10, 1816, from part of Randolph County. Named for Andrew Jackson (1767–1845), hero of the War of 1812 and President of the United States, 1829–37. County seats: Brownsville, 1817; Murphysboro, 1843. Area: 603 square miles. Population: 42,151.

Jasper Created February 15, 1831, from parts of Clay and Crawford counties. Named for Sergeant William Jasper (ca. 1750–79), who replaced the flag shot away by the British at Fort Moultrie in 1776 and was later killed at Savannah. County seat: Newton. Area: 495 square miles. Population: 11,346.

Jefferson Created March 26, 1819, from parts of Edwards and White counties. Named for Thomas Jefferson (1743–1826), author of the Declaration of Independence; President of the United States, 1801–9. County seat: Mount Vernon. Area: 574 square miles. Population: 32,135.

Jersey Created February 28, 1839, from part of Greene County. Named for the state of New Jersey. County seat: Jerseyville. Area: 374 square miles. Population: 17,023.

JoDaviess Created February 17, 1827, from parts of Mercer, Henry, and Putnam counties. Named (and misspelled) for Colonel Joseph Hamilton Daveiss (1774–1811), Kentucky lawyer and soldier fatally wounded at the Battle of Tippecanoe. County seat: Galena. Area: 614 square miles. Population: 21,821.

Johnson Created September 14, 1812, from part of Randolph County. Named for Richard M. Johnson (1780–1850), said to have killed Tecumseh in the Battle of the Thames, 1813; representative from Kentucky 1807–19, 1829–37; senator from Kentucky 1819–29; vice president of the United States, 1837–41. County seat: Vienna. Area: 345 square miles. Population: 6,928.

Kane Created January 16, 1836, from unorganized territory administered by La Salle County. Named for Elias Kent Kane (1794–1835), secretary of state of Illinois, 1818–22; senator from Illinois, 1825–35. County seat: Geneva. Area: 516 square miles. Population: 208,246.

Kankakee Created February 11, 1853, from parts of Iroquois and Will counties. An Indian name. County seat: Kankakee. Area: 680 square miles. Population: 92,063.

Kendall Created February 19, 1841, from parts of La Salle and Kane counties. Named for Amos Kendall (1789–1869), postmaster general, 1835–39; member of Andrew Jackson's "Kitchen Cabinet," 1829–37. County seat: Yorkville. Area: 320 square miles. Population: 17,540.

Knox Created January 13, 1825, from part of Fulton County and unorganized territory attached to Fulton County. Named for General Henry Knox (1750–1806), Revolutionary War hero; secretary of war, 1785–94. County seats: Knoxville (originally Henderson), 1831; Galesburg, 1873. Area: 728 square miles. Population: 61,280.

Lake Created March 1, 1839, from part of McHenry County. Named for Lake Michigan. County seats: Libertyville, 1839; Little Fort, 1841 (name changed to Waukegan, 1849). Area: 457 square miles. Population: 293,656.

La Salle Created January 15, 1831, from parts of Putnam County and unorganized territory south of the Illinois River. Named for Robert Cavelier, Sieur de la Salle (1643–87), famed explorer and entrepreneur. County seat: Ottawa. Area: 1,153 square miles. Population: 110,800.

Lawrence Created January 16, 1821, from parts of Edwards and Crawford counties. Named for Captain James Lawrence (1781–1813), commander of the U.S.S. *Chesapeake*, killed in battle with the British frigate *Shannon* during the War of 1812. Lawrence is remembered for his last words: "Don't give up the ship." County seat: Lawrenceville. Area: 374 square miles. Population: 18,540.

Lee Created February 27, 1839, from part of Ogle County. Named for Richard Henry Lee (1732–94), member of the Continental Congress, 1774–80, 1784–87; signer of the Declaration of Independence; president of the Continental Congress, 1784–85; senator from Virginia, 1789–92. County seat: Dixon. Area: 729 square miles. Population: 38,749.

Livingston Created February 27, 1837, from parts of La Salle and McLean counties and unorganized territory. Named for Edward Livingston (1764–1836), representative from New York, 1795–1801; representative from Louisiana, 1823–29; senator from Louisiana, 1829–31; secretary of state, 1831–33; minister to France, 1833–35. County seat: Pontiac. Area: 1,043 square miles. Population: 40,341.

Logan Created February 15, 1839, from part of Sangamon County. Named for Dr. John Logan (1786–1853), pioneer physician, father of General John A. Logan. County seats: Postville, 1839; Mount Pulaski, 1847; Lincoln, 1853. Area: 622 square miles. Population: 33,656.

McDonough Created January 25, 1826, from unorganized territory attached to Schuyler County. Named for Commodore Thomas Macdonough (1783–1825), who defeated the British in the Battle of Plattsburg on Lake Champlain in the War of 1812. County seat: None until 1831; Macomb, 1831. Area: 582 square miles. Population: 28,928.

McHenry Created January 16, 1836, from parts of Cook County and territory attached to La Salle County. Named for William McHenry (?–1835), White County pioneer, soldier in the War of 1812 and Black Hawk War, several times member of the Illinois General Assembly. County seat: Woodstock (originally called Centerville). Area: 611 square miles. Population: 84,210.

McLean Created December 25, 1830, from Tazewell County and unorganized territory. Named for John McLean (1791–1830), representative from Illinois, 1818–19; senator from Illinois, 1824–25, 1829–30. County seat: Bloomington. Area: 1,173 square miles. Population: 83,877.

Macon Created January 19, 1829, from territory attached to Shelby County and from parts of Piatt, Moultrie, and De Witt counties. Named for Nathaniel Macon (1758–1837), Revolutionary War soldier; representative from North Carolina, 1791–1815 (speaker, 1801–7); senator from North Carolina, 1815–28. County seat: Decatur. Area: 577 square miles. Population: 118,257.

Macoupin Created January 17, 1829, from parts of Madison County and unorganized territory attached to Greene County. The name is of Indian origin. County seat: Carlinville. Area: 872 square miles. Population: 43,524.

Madison Created September 14, 1812, from parts of St. Clair and Randolph counties. Named for James Madison (1751–1836), President of the United States, 1809–17. County seat: Edwardsville. Area: 731 square miles. Population: 224,689.

Marion Created January 24, 1823, from parts of Fayette and Jefferson counties. Named for Francis Marion (1732–95), called the Swamp Fox, because of the guerrilla tactics of his South Carolina regiment in the Revolutionary War. County seat: Salem. Area: 580 square miles. Population: 39,349.

Marshall Created January 19, 1839,

from part of Putnam County. Named for
John Marshall (1755–1835), chief justice of
the United States, 1801–35. County seat:
Lacon. Area: 395 square miles. Population:
13,334.

Mason Created January 20, 1841, from
parts of Tazewell and Menard counties.
Named for a county in Kentucky. County
seat: Havana. Area: 541 square miles. Population: 15,193.

Massac Created February 8, 1843, from
parts of Johnson and Pope counties. Named
for Fort Massac. County seat: Metropolis.
Area: 246 square miles. Population: 14,341.

Menard Created February 15, 1839,
from part of Sangamon County. Named for
Pierre Menard (1766–1844), president of
Illinois Legislative Council, 1812–18; lieutenant governor of Illinois, 1818–22. County
seat: Petersburg. Area: 312 square miles.
Population: 9,248.

Mercer Created January 13, 1825, from
unorganized territory attached to Pike
County. Named for General Hugh Mercer
(1725–77), Revolutionary soldier killed at
Battle of Princeton. County seats: None
until 1835; New Boston, 1835; Millersburg,
1836; Kiethsburg, 1847; Aledo, 1857. Area:
556 square miles. Population: 17,149.

Monroe Created January 6, 1816, from
parts of St. Clair and Randolph counties.
Named for James Monroe (1758–1831),
secretary of state, 1811–17; President of the
United States, 1817–25. County seats:
Carthage, 1816; Waterloo, 1825. Area: 380
square miles. Population: 15,507.

Montgomery Created February 12, 1821,
from parts of Madison and Bond counties.
Named for General Richard Montgomery
(1738–75), Irish-born soldier who served in
the French and Indian and Revolutionary
wars and was killed at Quebec. County seat:
Hillsboro. Area: 706 square miles. Population: 31,244.

Morgan Created January 31, 1823, from
part of Sangamon County and unorganized
territory north of Greene County. Named
for General Daniel Morgan (1736–1802),
Revolutionary War hero. County seat:
Jacksonville. Area: 565 square miles. Population: 36,571.

Moultrie Created February 16, 1843,
from parts of Macon and Shelby counties.
Named for General William Moultrie (1730–
1805), Revolutionary War soldier; governor of South Carolina, 1785–87, 1792–94.
County seats: East Nelson, 1843; Sullivan,
1845. Area: 345 square miles. Population:
13,635.

Ogle Created January 16, 1836, from

part of JoDaviess County. Named for Joseph Ogle (1741–1821), early Illinois pioneer
and militia officer. County seat: Oregon.
Area: 757 square miles. Population: 38,106.

Peoria Created January 13, 1825, from
part of Fulton County and unorganized
territory attached to Fulton County. Named
for the Indian tribe. County seat: Peoria.
Area: 624 square miles. Population: 189,044.

Perry Created January 29, 1827, from
parts of Jackson and Randolph counties.
Named for Commodore Oliver Hazard
Perry (1785–1819), victor in the Battle of
Lake Erie during the War of 1812. County
seat: Pinckneyville. Area: 443 square miles.
Population: 19,184.

Piatt Created January 27, 1841, from
parts of Macon and De Witt counties.
Named for the Piatt family, residents of the
region. County seat: Monticello. Area: 437
square miles. Population: 14,960.

Pike Created January 31, 1821, from
parts of Madison, Bond, and Clark counties. Pike County originally included all
territory north and west of the Illinois and
Kankakee rivers. Named for Zebulon Montgomery Pike (1779–1813), explorer of the
upper Mississippi River and the Southwest.
County seats: Coles Grove, 1821; Atlas,
1824; Pittsfield, 1833. Area: 829 square
miles. Population: 20,552.

Pope Created January 10, 1816, from
parts of Johnson and Gallatin counties.
Named for Nathaniel Pope (1784–1850),
secretary of the Illinois Territory, 1809–16;
Illinois territorial delegate to Congress,
1816–18; U.S. district judge, 1819–50. As
territorial delegate he procured the admission of Illinois to the Union. County
seat: Golconda. Area: 381 square miles.
Population: 4,061.

Pulaski Created March 3, 1843, from
parts of Johnson and Alexander counties.
Named for Count Casimir Pulaski (1748–
79), Polish patriot and Revolutionary War
general mortally wounded at Savannah.
County seat: Mound City. Area: 204 square
miles. Population: 10,490.

Putnam Created January 13, 1825, from
unorganized territory attached to Fulton
and Edgar counties. Named for General
Israel Putnam (1718–90), veteran of the
French and Indian War and hero of the
Battle of Bunker Hill in the Revolution.
County seat: Hennepin. Area: 166 square
miles. Population: 4,570.

Randolph Created October 5, 1795, from

the southern third of St. Clair County. Named for Edmund Randolph (1753–1813), member of the Continental Congress, 1779–82; governor of Virginia, 1786–88; U.S. attorney general, 1789–94; secretary of state, 1794–95. County seats: Kaskaskia, 1795; Chester, 1847. Area: 594 square miles. Population: 29,988.

Richland Created February 24, 1841, from parts of Clay and Lawrence counties. Named for an Ohio county. County seat: Olney. Area: 364 square miles. Population: 16,299.

Rock Island Created February 9, 1831, from part of JoDaviess County. Named for Rock Island in the Mississippi, at the mouth of the Rock River. County seat: Rock Island. Area: 420 square miles. Population: 150,991.

St. Clair Created April 27, 1790, in southwestern Illinois. Named for and by General Arthur St. Clair (1734–1818), Revolutionary War veteran; member of the Continental Congress, 1785–87; governor of the Northwest Territory, 1787–1802. County seats: Kaskaskia, 1790; Cahokia, 1795; Belleville, 1814. Area: 670 square miles. Population: 262,509.

Saline Created February 25, 1847, from part of Gallatin County. Named for salt springs which abound in the area. County seats: Raleigh, 1847; Harrisburg, 1859. Area: 384 square miles. Population: 26,227.

Sangamon Created January 30, 1821, from parts of Madison and Bond counties. An Indian name. County seat: Springfield. Area: 880 square miles. Population: 146,539.

Schuyler Created January 13, 1825, from parts of Pike and Fulton counties and unorganized territory attached to Pike County. Named for General Philip J. Schuyler (1733–1804), veteran of the French and Indian War; served in the Revolutionary War, 1775–78; member of the Continental Congress, 1775–77, 1778–81; senator from New York, 1789–91, 1792–98. County seats: Beardstown, 1825; Rushville, 1826. Area: 434 square miles. Population: 8,746.

Scott Created February 16, 1839, from part of Morgan County. Named for a county in Kentucky. County seat: Winchester. Area: 251 square miles. Population: 6,377.

Shelby Created January 23, 1827, from part of Fayette County. Named for General Isaac Shelby (1750–1826), soldier in the Revolution and War of 1812; first governor

of Kentucky, 1792–96. County seat: Shelbyville. Area: 772 square miles. Population: 23,404.

Stark Created March 2, 1839, from parts of Putnam and Knox counties. Named for General John Stark (1728–1822), veteran of the French and Indian War who served with distinction in the Revolution from 1775 until 1780. County seat: Toulon. Area: 291 square miles. Population: 8,152.

Stephenson Created March 4, 1837, from parts of JoDaviess and Winnebago counties. Named for Benjamin Stephenson (?–1822), colonel of Illinois militia in War of 1812; territorial delegate to Congress, 1814–16. County seat: Freeport. Area: 568 square miles. Population: 46,207.

Tazewell Created January 31, 1827, from part of Fayette County and unorganized territory attached to Peoria County. Named for Littleton W. Tazewell (1774–1860), senator from Virginia, 1824–33; governor of Virginia, 1834–36. County seats: Mackinaw, 1827; Tremont, 1836; Pekin, 1849. Area: 653 square miles. Population: 99,789.

Union Created January 2, 1818, from part of Johnson County. Named to commemorate a union revival meeting held in 1816 or 1817 in the southeastern part of the county by a Dunkard preacher named George Wolf and a Baptist preacher whose last name was Jones—their effigies appear on the county seal. County seat: Jonesboro. Area: 414 square miles. Population: 17,645.

Vermilion Created January 18, 1826, from unorganized territory attached to Edgar County. Named for the Vermilion River. County seat: Danville. Area: 898 square miles. Population: 96,176.

Wabash Created December 27, 1824, from part of Edwards County. Named for the Wabash River. County seat: Mount Carmel. Area: 221 square miles. Population: 14,047.

Warren Created January 13, 1825, from unorganized territory attached to Pike County. Named for General Joseph Warren (1741–75), physician-turned-soldier, killed at Battle of Bunker Hill. County seat: Monmouth. Area: 542 square miles. Population: 21,587.

Washington Created January 2, 1818, from part of St. Clair County. Named for George Washington (1732–99). County seats: Covington, 1818; Nashville, 1831. Area: 565 square miles. Population: 13,569.

Wayne Created March 26, 1819, from part of Edwards County. Named for General Anthony Wayne (1745–96), Revolutionary

War hero; commander of the U.S. Army, 1792–96. County seat: Fairfield. Area: 715 square miles. Population: 19,008.

White Created December 9, 1815, from part of Gallatin County. Named for Leonard White, state senator, 1820–24. County seat: Carmi. Area: 501 square miles. Population: 19,373.

Whiteside Created January 16, 1836, from part of JoDaviess County. Named for General Samuel Whiteside, who commanded Illinois militia in the War of 1812 and the Black Hawk War; state representative, 1818–20. County seats: Lyndon, 1839; Sterling, 1841; Lyndon, 1843; Sterling, 1849; Morrison, 1858. Area: 690 square miles. Population: 59,887.

Will Created January 12, 1836, from parts of Cook and Iroquois counties. Named for Conrad Will (1779–1835), pioneer settler of Illinois; member of Illinois legislature, 1818–35. County seat: Juliet (renamed Joliet), 1845. Area: 845 square miles. Population: 191,617.

Williamson Created February 28, 1839, from part of Franklin County. Named for a county in Tennessee. County seat: Marion. Area: 441 square miles. Population: 46,117.

Winnebago Created January 16, 1836, from part of JoDaviess County and unorganized territory attached to La Salle County. Named for the Indian tribe. County seat: Rockford. Area: 520 square miles. Population: 209,765.

Woodford Created February 27, 1841, from parts of Tazewell and McLean counties. Named for a county in Kentucky. County seats: Versailles, 1841; Hanover (Metamora), 1843; Eureka, 1894. Area: 537 square miles. Population: 24,579.

Counties in the Order of Their Formation

St. Clair	1790	April 27
Randolph	1795	October 5
Gallatin	1812	September 14
Johnson	1812	September 14
Madison	1812	September 14
Edwards	1814	November 28
White	1815	December 9
Monroe	1816	January 6
Jackson	1816	January 10
Pope	1816	January 10
Crawford	1816	December 31
Bond	1817	January 4
Franklin	1818	January 2
Union	1818	January 2
Washington	1818	January 2
Alexander	1819	March 4
Clark	1819	March 22
Jefferson	1819	March 26

Wayne	1819	March 26
Lawrence	1821	January 16
Greene	1821	January 20
Sangamon	1821	January 30
Pike	1821	January 31
Hamilton	1821	February 8
Montgomery	1821	February 12
Fayette	1821	February 14
Edgar	1823	January 3
Marion	1823	January 24
Fulton	1823	January 28
Morgan	1823	January 31
Clay	1824	December 23
Clinton	1824	December 27
Wabash	1824	December 27
Calhoun	1825	January 10
Adams	1825	January 13
Hancock	1825	January 13
Henry	1825	January 13
Knox	1825	January 13
Mercer	1825	January 13
Peoria	1825	January 13
Putnam	1825	January 13
Schuyler	1825	January 13
Warren	1825	January 13
Vermilion	1826	January 18
McDonough	1826	January 25
Shelby	1827	January 23
Perry	1827	January 29
Tazewell	1827	January 31
JoDaviess	1827	February 17
Macoupin	1829	January 17
Macon	1829	January 19
Coles	1830	December 25
McLean	1830	December 25
Cook	1831	January 15
La Salle	1831	January 15
Rock Island	1831	February 9
Effingham	1831	February 15
Jasper	1831	February 15
Champaign	1833	February 20
Iroquois	1833	February 26
Will	1836	January 12
Kane	1836	January 16
McHenry	1836	January 16
Ogle	1836	January 16
Whiteside	1836	January 16
Winnebago	1836	January 16
Livingston	1837	February 27
Bureau	1837	February 28
Cass	1837	March 3
Boone	1837	March 4
De Kalb	1837	March 4
Stephenson	1837	March 4
Marshall	1839	January 19
Brown	1839	February 1
Du Page	1839	February 9

			Henderson	1841	January 20
			Mason	1841	January 20
			Piatt	1841	January 27
Christian	1839	February 15	Grundy	1841	February 17
Logan	1839	February 15	Kendall	1841	February 19
Menard	1839	February 15	Richland	1841	February 24
Scott	1839	February 16	Woodford	1841	February 27
Carroll	1839	February 22	Massac	1843	February 8
Lee	1839	February 27	Moultrie	1843	February 16
Jersey	1839	February 28	Cumberland	1843	March 2
Williamson	1839	February 28	Pulaski	1843	March 3
De Witt	1839	March 1	Saline	1847	February 25
Lake	1839	March 1	Kankakee	1853	February 11
Hardin	1839	March 2	Douglas	1859	February 8
Stark	1839	March 2	Ford	1859	February 17

Census figures referring to the Illinois country in pioneer times are sketchy. The count, when made, was by villages during French rule, and inhabitants outside settled places were not enumerated. Only in 1752 was a fairly accurate census made of all inhabitants, including Negro and Indian slaves. After the arrival of George Rogers Clark and his Virginians several population estimates were made, but in most cases only white male adults or heads of families were reported.

In 1800, when the old Northwest Territory was divided into the territories of Ohio and Indiana, an estimate of inhabitants was made which appeared to be somewhat near the actual population. The village of Vincennes, first chartered place in Indiana Territory, was not incorporated until 1805. That same year Kaskaskia was authorized to elect a board of trustees, but did not receive a charter.

The first incorporated place in Illinois Territory was Shawneetown, chartered by the territorial legislature December 8, 1814. A week later Kaskaskia was asked to select commissioners to lay out the town. The last territorial legislature, sitting in January 1818, made Kaskaskia a city and chartered the city of Cairo and a state bank at that place.

The first legislature of the state of Illinois gave charters to Belleville, Carmi, and Edwardsville in 1819, and the Second General Assembly, in 1821, incorporated Alton and the new state capital, Vandalia. Mount Carmel was granted a charter in 1825, bringing to nine the number of incorporated places in Illinois before 1830.

On February 12, 1831, the Seventh General Assembly approved an act which established general standards for incorporating villages, towns, and cities, but continued to vest authority in the state legislature. Newton in Jasper County was the first place chartered under the new law (February 15, 1831). Knoxville followed on December 22, 1832, Urbana on February 20, 1833, and Chicago (as a village) on August 12, 1833.

Every incorporation prior to July 1, 1872, was authorized by an individual act of the General Assembly. In that year, under provisions of the third constitution of Illinois, uniform procedures were established and the secretary of state was authorized to issue certificates and charters. Places which never had received documents, or had lost them, were permitted to

6

Variations in Population of Illinois

reincorporate. All but 30 of the 379 places chartered prior to July 1, 1872, took new action. Five asked new certificates only, to replace lost, damaged, or destroyed certificates. Three hundred and forty-four reincorporated. Between July 1, 1872, and July 1, 1965, 879 new places were incorporated, bringing the total to 1,258. In the

Preterritorial population variations in Illinois

Selected place	Year		
	1723	1752	1800
Bellefontaine			286
Cahokia			
Freemen	12	89	719
Slaves*		47	
Fort de Chartres			
Freemen	126	185	
Slaves*		114	
Fort Massac			90
Kaskaskia			
Freemen	196	350	420
Slaves*		331	47
L'Aigle			250
Peoria			100
Prairie du Rocher			
Freemen		53	152
Slaves*		48	60
St. Philipe			
Freemen		70	
Slaves*		56	

* Slaves were both Indian and Negro.

tables which follow population growth is reported by decades for all places which in 1960 had attained a population of 5,000, plus a few cities and towns of historic interest and smaller size.

Population of Illinois at ten-year intervals, 1810–1960, with percentage increase and urban and rural division

Year	Population	Per-centage increase	Division Urban	Rural
1810	12,282			100
1820	55,211	349.6		100
1830	157,445	185.2		100
1840	476,183	202.4	2.0	98.0
1850	851,470	78.8	7.6	92.4
1860	1,711,951	101.1	14.3	85.7
1870	2,539,891	48.4	23.5	76.5
1880	3,077,871	21.2	30.6	69.4
1890	3,826,352	24.3	44.9	55.1
1900	4,821,550	26.0	54.3	45.7
1910	5,638,591	16.9	61.7	38.3
1920	6,485,280	15.0	67.9	32.1
1930	7,630,654	17.7	73.9	26.1
1940	7,897,241	3.5	73.6	26.4
1950	8,712,176	10.3	77.6	22.4
1960	10,081,158	15.7	80.7	19.3

The United States census, for the decades 1810–40, breaks down returns in a variety of classifications, among them age, occupation, color, and condition of servitude. However, until 1840, the county was the smallest unit for reporting population in Illinois.

Incorporated places reported separately in the United States census for 1840.

Alton	2,340	Galesburg	592
Beardstown	336	Joliet	2,558*
Belvidere	698	Lockport	2,977*
Carlinville	327	Pekin	1,467
Chicago	4,853*	Peoria	2,319*
Danville	503	Quincy	2,349*
Edwardsville	616	Shawneetown	862
Freeport	491	Springfield	2,579*
Galena	1,843		

* Six of the seven most populous cities of Illinois in 1840 were incorporated after 1830.

In 1840 a few returns were made by village, town, city, or township. With every census the number of returns by incorporated places increased until finally, in 1880, figures for some unincorporated villages appeared.

The census of 1810 lists by name every head of family in Illinois and the number of free and slave in his household, but only for Kaskaskia and Shawneetown are separate population counts included, 623 and 827 persons respectively. The Kaskaskia figures include 48 slaves.

The following publications were used in preparation of the two tables showing population variations, 1850–1960.

1850: U.S. Census Office. *U.S. Census of Population: 1850.* Robert Armstrong, Public Printer, Washington, D.C., 1853.

1860: Dept. of the Interior. *U.S. Census of Population: 1860,* Vol. 1. U.S. Govt. Printing Office, Washington, D.C., 1864.

1870 and **1880:** Dept. of the Interior, U.S. Census Office. *U.S. Census of Population: 1880,* Vol. 1. U.S. Govt. Printing Office, Washington, D.C., 1883.

1890 and **1900:** Dept. of the Interior, U.S. Census Office. *U.S. Census of Population: 1900,* Part I. U.S. Govt. Printing Office, Washington, D.C., 1901.

1910: U.S. Bureau of the Census. *U.S. Census of Population: 1910.* Vol. 1, *General Report and Analysis.* U.S. Govt. Printing Office, Washington, D.C., 1913.

1920 and **1930:** U.S. Bureau of the Census. *U.S. Census of Population: 1930.* Vol. 1, *Number and Distribution of Inhabitants.* U.S. Govt. Printing Office, Washington, D.C., 1931.

1940: U.S. Bureau of the Census. *U.S. Census of Population: 1940.* Vol. 1, *Number of Inhabitants.* U.S. Govt. Printing Office, Washington, D.C., 1942.

1950 and **1960:** U.S. Bureau of the Census. *U.S. Census of Population: 1960.* Vol. 1, *Characteristics of the Population.* Part A, "Number of Inhabitants." U.S. Govt. Printing Office, Washington, D.C., 1961.

Population variations, 1850–1900, of incorporated places having 5,000 or more inhabitants in 1960, and certain historic places.

Municipality	Year of incorporation	Population 1850	1860	1870	1880	1890	1900
Addison	1884					485	591
Alton	1821	3,585	6,332	8,665	8,975	10,294	14,210
Arlington Heights	1887					1,424	1,380
Aurora	1853		6,011	11,162	11,873	19,688	24,147
Barrington	1865			1	410	848	1,162
Batavia	1891						3,871
Beardstown	1837	1,583	3,821	2,528	3,135	4,226	4,827
Belleville	1819	2,941	7,520	8,146	10,683	15,361	17,484
Belvidere	1852		1,114	3,231	2,951	3,867	6,937
Bensenville	1894						374
Benton	1841	1	380	615	984	939	1,341
Bloomington	1839	1,594	7,075	14,590	17,180	20,484	23,286
Blue Island	1843	1	1	1	1,542	3,329	6,114
Bradley	1896						1,518
Brookfield (inc. as Grossdale)	1893						1,111[2]
Cahokia	1927				211[3]		222[3]
Cairo	1818	242	2,188	6,267	9,011	10,324	12,566
Canton	1849	1,568	2,373	3,308	3,762	5,604	6,564
Carbondale	1869			1	2,213	2,382	3,318
Carlinville	1837	433	1	1	3,117	3,293	3,502
Carmi	1819	1	479	1	2,512	2,785	2,939
Carpentersville	1887					754	1,002
Centralia	1859		1	3,190	3,621	4,763	6,721
Champaign	1861			4,625	5,103	5,839	9,098
Charleston	1839	849	2,218	2,849	2,867	4,135	5,488
Chicago (inc. as village)	1833	29,963	109,260	298,977	503,185	1,099,850	1,698,575
Cicero	1867			1,545	3,294	5,433	16,310
Clinton	1855		1,362	1,800	2,709	2,598	4,452
Collinsville	1855		1	1	2,887	3,498	4,021
Danville	1839	736	1,632	4,751	7,733	11,491	16,354
Decatur	1839	1	3,839	7,161	9,547	16,841	20,754
De Kalb	1861			1	1,598	2,579	5,904
Des Plaines (inc. as Rand)	1869			1	818	986	1,666
Dixon	1857		2,213	4,055	3,658	5,161	7,917
Dolton (inc. as Dalton Station)	1892						1,229[2]
Downers Grove	1873				586	960	2,103
Du Quoin	1861		2,212	2,807	4,052	4,353	
East Alton	1894						454
East St. Louis	1865			5,644	9,185	15,169	29,655
Edwardsville	1819	677	1,965	2,193	2,887	3,561	4,157
Effingham	1861			2,383	3,065	3,260	3,774
Elgin	1854		2,797	5,441	8,787	17,823	22,433
Evanston	1857		831	3,062	4,400	9,000[4]	19,259
Evergreen Park	1893						445
Fairfield	1840	195	508	719	1,391	1,881	2,338
Flora	1867			1,339	1,494	1,695	2,311
Franklin Park	1892						483
Freeport	1855		5,376	7,889	8,516	10,189	13,258
Galena	1835	6,004	8,196	7,019	6,451	5,635	5,005
Galesburg	1841	882	4,953	10,158	11,437	15,264	18,607
Geneseo	1855		1,794	3,042	3,518	3,182	3,356
Geneva	1867			1	1,239	1,692	2,446
Glencoe	1869			1	387	569	1,020
Glen Ellyn	1892						793
Glenview	1899						450
Granite City	1896						3,122
Harrisburg	1861			590	934	1,723	2,202
Harvey	1895						5,395
Highland Park	1869			1	1,154	2,163	2,806

Municipality	Year of incorporation	1850	1860	1870	1880	1890	1900
Hinsdale	1873				819	1,584	2,578
Homewood	1893						352
Hoopeston	1877				1,272	1,911	3,823
Jacksonville	1840	2,745	5,528	9,203	10,927	12,935	15,078
Jerseyville	1855		2,610	2,576	2,894	3,207	3,517
Joliet (inc. as Juliet)	1845	2,659	7,104	7,263	11,657	23,264	29,353
Kankakee	1855		2,984	[1]	5,651	9,025	13,595
Kaskaskia	1818	513	5	[1]	326	[1]	177
Kewanee (inc. as Berrian)	1855		1,461	[1]	2,704	4,569	8,382
La Grange	1879				531	2,314	3,969
La Grange Park	1892						730
Lake Forest	1861			[1]	877	1,203	2,215
Lansing	1893						830
La Salle	1852		3,993	5,200	7,847	9,855	10,446
Lawrenceville	1835	419	474	435	514	865	1,300
Libertyville	1882					550	864
Lincoln	1857		5,700	[1]	5,639	6,725	8,962
Litchfield	1859		1,609	3,852	4,326	5,811	5,918
Lockport	1853		2,822	1,772	1,679	2,449	2,659
Lombard	1869			[1]	378	515	590
Lyons	1888					732	951
Macomb	1841	756	1,834	2,748	3,140	4,052	5,375
Madison	1891						1,979
Marion	1841	[1]	397	[1]	[1]	1,338	2,510
Mattoon	1859		1,965	[1]	5,737	6,833	9,622
Maywood	1881					[1]	4,532
Melrose Park	1893						2,592
Mendota	1859		1,934	3,546	4,142	3,542	3,736
Metropolis	1859		1,098	[1]	2,668	3,573	4,069
Moline	1855		2,028	4,166	7,800	12,000	17,248
Monmouth	1852		2,506	4,662	5,000	5,936	7,460
Morris	1853		2,105	3,138	3,486	3,653	4,273
Morton	1877				[1]	657	894
Morton Grove	1895						564
Mount Carmel	1825	935	1,393	1,640	2,047	3,376	4,311
Mount Vernon	1837	443	709	1,167	2,324	3,223	5,216
Murphysboro	1867			[1]	2,196	3,880	6,463
Naperville	1857		2,599	1,713	2,073	2,216	2,629
Niles	1899						514
Normal (inc. as North Bloomington)	1867			1,116	2,470	3,459	3,795
Olney	1841	[1]	1,499	2,680	3,512	3,831	4,260
Ottawa	1837	3,219	6,541	7,736	7,834	9,985	10,588
Palatine	1869			[1]	731	891	1,020
Pana	1857		716	2,207	3,009	5,077	5,530
Paris	1853		1,930	3,057	4,373	4,996	6,105
Pekin	1839	1,678	3,467	5,696	5,993	6,347	8,420
Peoria	1839	5,095	14,045	22,849	29,259	41,024	56,100
Peoria Heights	1898						309
Peru	1845	[1]	3,132	3,650	4,632	5,550	6,863
Pontiac	1857		733	1,657	2,242	2,784	4,266
Princeton	1849	778	2,473	3,264	3,439	3,396	4,023
Quincy	1839	6,902	13,718	24,052	27,268	31,494	36,252
Rantoul	1869			[1]	850	1,074	1,207
Riverdale	1892						558
River Forest	1880				[1]	[1]	1,539
River Grove	1888					287	333
Riverside	1875				450	[1]	1,551
Robinson	1886					1,387	1,683
Rochelle	1869			[1]	1,892	1,789	2,073
Rock Falls	1889					1,900	2,176
Rockford	1852		6,979	11,049	13,129	23,584	31,051

Municipality	Year of incorporation	Population					
		1850	1860	1870	1880	1890	1900
Rock Island	1841	1,711	5,130	7,890	11,659	13,634	19,493
St. Charles	1839	2,132	1,822	1	1,533	1,690	2,675
Salem	1837	1	1	1,182	1,327	1,493	1,642
Savanna	1874			971³	1,000	3,097	3,325
Shawneetown	1814	1,764	1,115	1,309	1,851	1	1,698
Skokie (inc. as Niles Centre)	1888					11	529
South Holland	1894						766
Springfield	1840	4,533	9,320	17,364	19,743	24,963	34,159
Spring Valley	1886					3,837	6,214
Steger	1896						712
Sterling (inc. as Chatham)	1841	1	2,428	3,998	5,087	5,824	6,309
Streator	1882					11,414	14,079
Summit	1890					1	547
Sycamore	1859		1,226	1,967	3,028	2,987	3,653
Taylorville	1882					2,829	4,248
Tinley Park	1892						300
Urbana	1833	210	1,370	2,277	2,942	3,511	5,728
Vandalia	1821	419	1,999	1,771	2,056	2,144	2,665
Venice	1897						2,450
Washington	1857		1,578	1,607	1,397	1,301	1,459
Watseka	1867			1,551	1,507	2,017	2,505
Waukegan (inc. as Little Fort)	1852		3,433	4,507	4,012	4,915	9,426
Western Springs	1886					451	662
West Frankfort	1896						1
Wheaton	1859		645	998	1,160	1,622	2,345
Wheeling	1894						331
Wilmette	1872				419	1,458	2,300
Winnetka	1869			1	584	1,079	1,833
Woodstock (inc. as Centerville)	1852		1,327	1,574	1,475	1,683	2,502

1 Not separately reported.
2 Population at incorporation.
3 Population for historic places prior to incorporation furnished by the Illinois State Archives.
4 Estimated.
5 Destroyed by flood since last census.

Population variations, 1910–60, of incorporated places having 5,000 or more inhabitants in 1960, and certain historic places.

Municipality	Year of incorporation	Population					
		1910	1920	1930	1940	1950	1960
Addison	1884	579	510	916	819	813	6,741
Alton	1821	17,528	24,682	30,151	31,255	32,550	43,047
Arlington Heights	1887	1,943	2,250	4,997	5,668	8,768	27,878
Aurora	1853	29,807	36,397	46,589	47,170	50,576	63,715
Barrington	1865	1,444	1,743	3,213	3,560	4,209	5,434
Bartonville	1903	1,536	1,588	1,886	1,879	2,437	7,253
Batavia	1891	4,436	4,395	5,045	5,101	5,838	7,496
Beardstown	1837	6,107	7,111	6,344	6,505	6,080	6,294
Belleville	1819	21,122	24,823	28,425	28,405	32,721	37,264
Bellwood	1900	943	1,881	4,991	5,220	8,746	20,729
Belvidere	1852	7,253	7,804	8,123	8,094	9,422	11,223
Bensenville	1894	443	650	1,680	1,869	3,754	9,141
Benton	1841	2,675	7,201	8,219	7,372	7,848	7,023
Berkeley	1924			779	724	1,882	5,792
Berwyn	1908	5,841	14,150	47,027	48,451	51,280	54,224
Bloomington	1839	25,768	28,725	30,930	32,868	34,163	36,271
Blue Island	1843	8,043	11,424	16,534	16,638	17,622	19,618
Bradley	1896	1,942	2,128	3,048	3,689	5,699	8,082
Bridgeview	1947					1,393	7,334
Broadview	1913		430	2,334	1,457	5,196	8,588
Brookfield	1893	2,186	3,589	10,035	10,817	15,472	20,429

Municipality	Year of incorporation	Population					
		1910	1920	1930	1940	1950	1960
Cahokia	1927	1	1	286	465	794	15,829
Cairo	1818	14,548	15,203	13,532	14,407	12,123	9,348
Calumet City (inc. as West Hammond)	1911		7,492	12,298	13,241	15,799	25,000
Calumet Park (inc. as De Young and Burr Oak)	1912		1,237	1,429	1,593	2,500	8,448
Canton	1849	10,453	10,928	11,718	11,577	11,927	13,588
Carbondale	1869	5,411	6,267	7,528	8,550	10,921	14,670
Carlinville	1837	3,616	5,212	4,144	4,965	5,116	5,440
Carmi	1819	2,833	2,667	2,932	4,098	5,574	6,152
Carpentersville	1887	1,128	1,036	1,461	1,289	1,523	17,424
Centralia	1859	9,680	12,491	12,583	16,343	13,863	13,904
Centreville	1957						12,769
Champaign	1861	12,421	15,873	20,348	23,302	39,563	49,583
Charleston	1839	5,884	6,615	8,012	8,197	9,164	10,505
Chicago	1833	2,185,283	2,701,705	3,376,438	3,396,808	3,620,962	3,550,404
Chicago Heights	1901	14,525	19,653	22,321	22,461	24,551	34,331
Chicago Ridge	1914		176	269	376	888	5,748
Cicero	1867	14,557	44,995	66,602	64,712	67,544	69,130
Clarendon Hills	1924			933	1,281	2,437	5,885
Clinton	1855	5,165	5,898	5,920	6,331	5,945	7,355
Collinsville	1855	7,478	9,753	9,235	9,767	11,862	14,217
Crest Hill	1960						5,887
Creve Coeur	1921			350	3,535	5,499	6,684
Crystal Lake	1914		2,249	3,732	3,917	4,832	8,314
Danville	1839	27,871	33,776	36,765	36,919	37,864	41,856
Decatur	1839	31,140	43,818	57,510	59,305	66,269	78,004
Deerfield	1903	476	610	1,852	2,283	3,288	11,786
De Kalb	1861	8,102	7,871	8,545	9,146	11,708	18,486
Des Plaines	1869	2,348	3,451	8,798	9,518	14,994	34,886
Dixon	1857	7,216	8,191	9,908	10,671	11,523	19,565
Dolton	1892	1,869	2,076	2,923	3,068	5,558	18,746
Downers Grove	1873	2,601	3,543	8,977	9,526	11,886	21,154
Du Quoin	1861	5,454	7,285	7,593	7,515	7,147	6,558
East Alton	1894	584	1,669	4,502	4,680	7,290	7,630
East Moline	1907	2,665	8,675	10,107	12,359	13,913	16,732
East Peoria	1919		2,214	5,027	6,806	8,698	12,310
East St. Louis	1865	58,547	66,767	74,347	75,609	82,295	81,712
Edwardsville	1819	5,014	5,336	6,235	8,008	8,776	9,996
Effingham	1861	3,898	4,024	4,978	6,180	6,892	8,172
Elgin	1854	25,976	27,454	35,929	38,333	44,223	49,447
Elk Grove Village	1956						6,608
Elmhurst	1910	2,360	4,594	14,055	15,458	21,273	36,991
Elmwood Park	1914		1,380	11,270	13,689	18,801	23,866
Evanston	1857	24,978	37,234	63,338	65,389	73,641	79,283
Evergreen Park	1893	424	705	1,594	3,313	10,531	24,178
Fairfield	1840	2,479	2,754	3,280	4,008	5,576	6,362
Flora	1867	2,704	3,558	4,393	5,474	5,255	5,331
Forest Park	1907	6,594	10,768	14,555	14,840	14,969	14,452
Franklin Park	1892	683	914	2,425	3,007	8,899	18,322
Freeport	1855	17,567	19,669	22,045	22,366	22,467	26,628
Galena	1835	4,835	4,742	3,878	4,126	4,648	4,410
Galesburg	1841	22,089	23,834	28,830	28,876	31,425	37,243
Geneseo	1855	3,199	3,375	3,406	3,824	4,325	4,169
Geneva	1867	3,006	3,327	4,607	4,101	5,139	7,646
Glencoe	1869	1,899	3,381	6,295	6,825	6,980	10,472
Glen Ellyn	1892	1,763	2,851	7,680	8,055	9,524	15,972
Glenview	1899	652	760	1,886	2,500	6,142	18,132
Granite City	1896	9,903	14,757	25,130	22,974	29,465	40,073
Harrisburg	1861	5,309	7,125	11,625	11,453	10,999	9,171
Harvey	1895	7,227	9,216	16,374	17,878	20,683	29,071
Harwood Heights	1947					655	5,688

Municipality	Year of incorporation	Population					
		1910	1920	1930	1940	1950	1960
Hazel Crest	1911		438	1,162	1,299	2,129	6,205
Herrin	1900	6,861	10,986	9,708	9,352	9,331	9,474
Highland Park	1869	4,209	6,167	12,203	14,476	16,808	25,532
Hillside	1905	328	555	1,004	1,080	2,131	7,794
Hinsdale	1873	2,451	4,042	6,923	7,336	8,676	12,859
Hoffman Estates	1951						8,296
Hometown	1953						7,479
Homewood	1893	713	1,389	3,227	4,078	5,887	13,371
Hoopeston	1877	4,698	5,451	5,613	5,381	5,992	6,606
Jacksonville	1840	15,326	15,713	17,747	19,844	20,387	21,690
Jerseyville	1855	4,113	3,839	4,309	4,809	5,792	7,420
Joliet	1845	34,670	38,442	42,993	42,365	51,601	66,780
Kankakee	1855	13,986	16,753	20,620	22,241	25,856	27,666
Kaskaskia	1818	¹	¹	107	131	¹	¹
Kewanee	1855	9,307	16,026	17,093	16,901	16,821	16,324
La Grange	1879	5,282	6,525	10,103	10,479	12,002	15,285
La Grange Park	1892	1,131	1,684	2,939	3,406	6,176	13,793
Lake Forest	1861	3,349	3,657	6,554	6,885	7,819	10,687
Lansing	1893	1,060	1,409	3,378	4,462	8,682	18,098
La Salle	1852	11,537	13,050	13,149	12,812	12,083	11,897
Lawrenceville	1835	3,235	5,080	6,303	6,213	6,328	5,492
Libertyville	1882	1,724	2,125	3,791	3,930	5,425	8,560
Lincoln	1857	10,892	11,882	12,855	12,752	14,362	16,890
Lincolnwood	1911		355	473	752	3,072	11,744
Litchfield	1859	5,971	6,215	6,612	7,048	7,208	7,330
Lockport	1853	2,555	2,684	3,383	3,475	4,955	7,560
Lombard	1869	883	1,331	6,197	7,075	9,817	22,561
Loves Park	1947					5,366	9,086
Lyons	1888	1,483	2,564	4,787	4,960	6,120	9,936
Macomb	1841	5,774	6,714	8,509	8,764	10,592	12,135
Madison	1891	5,046	4,996	7,661	7,782	7,963	6,861
Marion	1841	7,093	9,582	9,033	9,251	10,459	11,274
Markham	1925			349	1,388	2,753	11,704
Mattoon	1859	11,456	13,552	14,631	15,827	17,547	19,088
Maywood	1881	8,033	12,072	25,829	26,648	27,473	27,330
Melrose Park	1893	4,806	7,147	10,741	10,933	13,366	22,291
Mendota	1859	3,806	3,934	4,008	4,215	5,129	6,154
Metropolis	1859	4,655	5,055	5,573	6,287	6,093	7,339
Midlothian	1927			1,775	2,430	3,216	6,605
Moline	1855	24,199	30,734	32,236	34,608	37,397	42,705
Monmouth	1852	9,128	8,116	8,666	9,096	10,193	10,372
Morris	1853	4,563	4,505	5,568	6,145	6,926	7,935
Morton	1877	1,004	1,179	1,501	2,241	3,693	5,325
Morton Grove	1895	836	1,079	1,974	2,010	3,926	20,533
Mount Carmel	1825	6,934	7,456	7,132	6,987	8,732	8,594
Mount Prospect	1917		349	1,225	1,720	4,009	18,906
Mount Vernon	1837	8,007	9,815	12,375	14,724	15,600	15,566
Mundelein (inc. as Area)	1909	358	420	1,011	1,328	3,189	10,526
Murphysboro	1867	7,485	10,703	8,182	8,976	9,241	8,673
Naperville	1857	3,449	3,830	5,118	5,272	7,013	12,933
Niles	1899	569	1,258	2,135	2,168	3,587	20,393
Normal	1867	4,024	5,143	6,768	6,983	9,772	13,357
Norridge	1948					3,428	14,087
Northbrook	1925			1,193	1,265	3,348	11,635
North Chicago	1909	3,306	5,839	8,466	8,465	8,628	20,517
Northlake	1941					4,361	12,318
North Riverside	1923			969	1,036	3,230	7,989
Oak Lawn	1909	287	489	2,045	3,483	8,751	27,471
Oak Park	1902	19,444	39,858	63,982	66,015	63,529	61,093
Olney	1841	5,011	4,491	6,140	7,831	8,612	8,780
Ottawa	1837	9,535	10,816	15,094	16,005	16,957	19,408
Palatine	1869	1,144	1,210	2,118	2,222	4,079	11,504
Pana	1857	6,055	6,122	5,835	5,966	6,178	6,432
Paris	1853	7,664	7,985	8,781	9,281	9,460	9,823

Table—continued

Municipality	Year of incorporation	Population					
		1910	1920	1930	1940	1950	1960
Park Forest	1949					8,138	29,993
Park Ridge	1910	2,009	3,383	10,417	12,063	16,602	32,659
Pekin	1839	9,897	12,086	16,129	19,407	21,858	28,146
Peoria	1839	66,950	76,121	104,969	105,087	111,856	103,162
Peoria Heights	1898	582	1,111	3,279	4,376	5,425	7,064
Peru	1845	7,984	8,869	9,121	8,983	8,653	10,460
Pontiac	1857	6,090	6,664	8,272	9,585	7,562	8,435
Princeton	1849	4,131	4,126	4,762	5,224	5,765	6,250
Quincy	1839	36,587	35,978	39,241	40,469	41,450	43,793
Rantoul	1869	1,384	1,551	1,555	2,367	6,387	22,116
Riverdale	1892	917	1,166	2,504	2,865	5,840	12,008
River Forest	1880	2,456	4,358	8,829	9,487	10,823	12,695
River Grove	1888	418	484	2,741	3,301	4,839	8,464
Riverside	1875	1,702	2,532	6,770	7,935	9,153	9,750
Robbins	1917		431	753	1,349	4,766	7,511
Robinson	1886	3,863	3,375	3,668	4,311	6,407	7,226
Rochelle	1869	2,732	3,310	3,785	4,200	5,449	7,008
Rock Falls	1889	2,657	2,927	3,893	4,987	7,983	10,261
Rockford	1852	45,401	65,651	85,864	84,637	92,927	126,706
Rock Island	1841	24,335	35,177	37,953	42,775	48,710	51,863
Rolling Meadows	1955						10,879
Round Lake Beach	1937				410	1,892	5,011
St. Charles	1839	4,046	4,099	5,377	5,870	6,709	9,269
Salem	1837	2,669	3,457	4,420	7,319	6,159	6,165
Savanna	1874	3,691	5,237	5,086	4,792	5,058	4,950
Schiller Park	1914		390	709	804	1,384	5,687
Shawneetown	1814	1,863	1,368	1,440	1,963	1,917	1,280
Skokie	1888	568	763	5,007	7,172	14,832	59,364
South Holland	1894	1,065	1,247	1,873	2,272	3,247	10,412
Springfield	1840	51,678	59,183	71,864	75,503	81,628	83,271
Spring Valley	1886	7,035	6,493	5,270	5,010	4,916	5,371
Steger	1896	2,161	2,304	2,985	3,369	4,358	6,432
Sterling	1841	7,467	8,182	10,012	11,363	12,817	15,688
Stickney	1913		550	2,005	2,446	3,317	6,239
Streator	1882	14,253	14,779	14,728	14,930	16,469	16,868
Summit	1890	949	4,019	6,548	7,043	8,957	10,374
Sycamore	1859	3,926	3,602	4,021	4,702	5,912	6,961
Taylorville	1882	5,446	5,806	7,316	8,313	9,188	8,801
Tinley Park	1892	309	493	823	1,136	2,326	6,392
Urbana	1833	8,245	10,244	13,060	14,064	22,834	27,294
Vandalia	1821	2,974	3,316	4,342	5,288	5,471	5,537
Venice	1897	3,718	3,895	5,362	5,454	6,226	5,380
Villa Park (inc. as Ardmore)	1914		854	6,220	7,236	8,821	20,391
Washington	1857	1,530	1,643	1,741	2,456	4,285	5,919
Washington Park	1917		1,516	3,837	4,523	5,840	6,601
Watseka	1867	2,476	2,817	3,144	3,744	4,235	5,219
Waukegan	1852	16,069	19,226	33,499	34,241	38,946	55,719
Westchester	1925		358	621	4,308	18,092	
West Chicago	1906	2,378	2,594	3,477	3,355	3,973	6,854
Western Springs	1886	905	1,258	3,894	4,856	6,364	10,838
West Frankfort	1896	2,111	8,478	14,683	12,383	11,384	9,027
Westmont	1921			2,733	3,044	3,402	5,997
Wheaton	1859	3,423	4,137	7,258	7,389	11,638	24,312
Wheeling	1894	260	313	467	550	916	7,169
Wilmette	1872	4,943	7,814	15,233	17,226	18,162	28,268
Winnetka	1869	3,168	6,694	12,166	12,430	12,105	13,368
Wood River	1911		3,476	8,136	8,197	10,190	11,694
Woodstock	1852	4,331	5,523	5,471	6,123	7,192	8,897
Worth	1914		240	411	702	1,472	8,196
Zion	1902	4,789	5,580	5,991	6,555	8,950	11,941

[1] Not separately reported.

44

Incorporated municipalities of Illinois

Municipality	City, town, or village	Population 1960 census	County	Date incorporation laws in force Prior to July 1, 1872	Date incorporation laws in force Since July 1, 1872	Date certificate of incorporation issued by secretary of state
Abingdon	C	3,469	Knox	Feb. 13, 1857	Mar. 23, 1920	June 9, 1920
Addieville	V	231	Washington		May 18, 1896	July 16, 1896
*Addison	V	6,741	Du Page		Oct. 6, 1884	Jan. 9, 1885
Adeline	V	130	Ogle		Aug. 21, 1882	Nov. 8, 1882
Albany	V	637	Whiteside		Apr. 26, 1887	July 14, 1897
Albers	V	566	Clinton	Apr. 19, 1869	July 1, 1954	Dec. 8, 1954
Albion	C	2,025	Edwards	Apr. 16, 1869	June 9, 1908	Sept. 15, 1909
Aledo	C	3,080	Mercer		Apr. 21, 1885	June 11, 1885
Alexis	V	878	Warren		May 31, 1873	Aug. 29, 1873
*Algonquin	V	2,014	McHenry		Feb. 27, 1890	July 6, 1894
Alhambra	V	537	Madison		Apr. 5, 1884	July 17, 1884
Allendale	V	465	Wabash		Jan. 10, 1917	Mar. 5, 1917
Allenville	V	191	Moultrie		Sept. 12, 1906	Sept. 18, 1906
Allerton	V	282	Vermilion		May 7, 1902	June 26, 1902
Alma[1]	V	358	Marion	Feb. 6, 1855	Nov. 27, 1897	Dec. 3, 1897
Alorton[2]	V	3,282	St. Clair		Sept. 26, 1944	Dec. 4, 1944
Alpha	V	637	Henry		Dec. 22, 1894	June 17, 1895
Alsey	V	248	Scott		Jan. 21, 1927	Apr. 1, 1927
*Alsip	V	3,770	Cook		Mar. 10, 1901	May 2, 1927
Altamont	C	1,656	Effingham		Apr. 16, 1901	July 12, 1901
Alton	C	43,047	Madison	Jan. 30, 1821	Sept. 11, 1877	Oct. 10, 1877
Altona[3]	V	505	Knox	Feb. 13, 1857	Mar. 31, 1874	Aug. 5, 1897
Alto Pass	V	323	Union		Apr. 8, 1882	July 3, 1882
Alvan	V	281	Vermilion		Mar. 17, 1892	May 22, 1893
Amboy	C	2,067	Lee	Feb. 16, 1857	May 8, 1888	July 17, 1888
Anchor	V	194	McLean		July 18, 1959	Aug. 28, 1959
*Andalusia	V	560	Rock Island		Apr. 24, 1884	July 5, 1894
Andover	V	295	Henry	Feb. 16, 1865	Apr. 30, 1895	May 8, 1895
Anna	C	4,280	Union		Oct. 22, 1872	Nov. 29, 1872
Annawan	T	701	Henry	Mar. 31, 1869		

Table—continued

Municipality	City, town, or village	Population 1960 census	County	Date incorporation laws in force — Prior to July 1, 1872	Date incorporation laws in force — Since July 1, 1872	Date certificate of incorporation issued by secretary of state
*Antioch	V	2,268	Lake	Feb. 16, 1857	Feb. 29, 1892	Mar. 18, 1892
Apple River	V	477	JoDaviess		July 18, 1876	July 31, 1876
Arcola	C	2,273	Douglas	Feb. 16, 1865	June 16, 1873	Aug. 9, 1873
Arenzville	V	417	Cass		Feb. 13, 1893	May 13, 1893
Argenta	V	860	Macon		Jan. 29, 1891	Oct. 30, 1894
Arlington	V	254	Bureau		June 8, 1874	Oct. 11, 1901
*Arlington Heights	V	27,878	Cook		Feb. 16, 1887	Sept. 17, 1901
Armington	V	327	Tazewell		Aug. 30, 1904	Nov. 21, 1904
Aroma Park[4]	V	744	Kankakee		June 10, 1876	May 12, 1893
Arrowsmith	V	319	McLean		Mar. 3, 1890	July 12, 1894
Arthur	V	2,120	Douglas-Moultrie		May 7, 1877	Sept. 10, 1877
Ashkum	V	601	Iroquois		Apr. 22, 1875	July 25, 1903
Ashland	C	1,064	Cass	Apr. 19, 1869	Dec. 28, 1872	June 1, 1897
Ashley	V	662	Washington	Feb. 16, 1857	Jan. 18, 1876	Apr. 17, 1876
Ashmore	V	447	Coles		Aug. 8, 1873	July 3, 1874
Ashton[5]	V	1,024	Lee	Mar. 5, 1867	July 23, 1872	Oct. 5, 1872
Assumption	C	1,439	Christian		Mar. 7, 1902	June 16, 1902
Astoria[6]	T	1,206	Fulton	Jan. 24, 1839		
Athens	C	1,035	Menard		Mar. 30, 1892	Apr. 11, 1892
Atkinson	T	944	Henry	Mar. 7, 1867		
Atlanta[7]	C	1,568	Logan	Mar. 4, 1869	Mar. 22, 1912	Mar. 26, 1912
Atwood	V	1,258	Douglas		Jan. 9, 1884	Mar. 7, 1884
*Auburn	C	2,209	Sangamon	Feb. 16, 1865	Apr. 18, 1905	Mar. 20, 1936
Augusta	V	915	Hancock	Feb. 24, 1859	Sept. 2, 1879	Oct. 28, 1879
Aurora	C	63,715	Kane	Feb. 8, 1853	Mar. 1, 1887	Apr. 8, 1887
Ava	C	665	Jackson		Apr. 18, 1901	June 6, 1901
Aviston	V	717	Clinton		Feb. 10, 1874	May 13, 1879
Avon	V	996	Fulton	Mar. 8, 1867	Oct. 6, 1873	Jan. 28, 1874
Baldwin	V	336	Randolph		July 12, 1876	Oct. 15, 1901

	Class	Pop.	County			
Banner	V	247	Fulton		June 6, 1934	Jan. 25, 1939
Bannockburn	V	466	Lake		Mar. 25, 1929	Aug. 3, 1929
Barclay	V		Sangamon		Nov. 10, 1904	Feb. 9, 1905
Bardolph	V	266	McDonough	Apr. 16, 1869	Feb. 5, 1876	Mar. 23, 1876
*Barrington	V	5,434	Cook and Lake	Feb. 16, 1865	Jan. 18, 1873	Feb. 17, 1873
*Barrington Hills[8]	V	1,726	Cook		Feb. 26, 1957	July 5, 1957
Barry[9]	C	1,422	Pike	Feb. 19, 1859	Sept. 16, 1872	Nov. 14, 1872
Bartelso	V	370	Clinton		Dec. 9, 1898	Sept. 24, 1901
*Bartlett	V	1,540	Cook		Mar. 2, 1891	June 21, 1892
Bartonville	V	7,253	Peoria		June 2, 1903	Dec. 9, 1903
Basco	V	191	Hancock		Feb. 17, 1876	Apr. 2, 1886
Batavia	C	7,496	Kane		Apr. 24, 1891	May 19, 1902
Batchtown	V	248	Calhoun	Feb. 14, 1857	Feb. 6, 1897	June 4, 1897
Bath	V	398	Mason		June 30, 1876	Sept. 7, 1876
Baylis	V	284	Pike	July 21, 1837	Sept. 1, 1887	Oct. 27, 1887
Beardstown	C	6,294	Cass		Feb. 17, 1896	May 17, 1897
Beaverville[10]	V	430	Iroquois		Sept. 7, 1872	Oct. 6, 1904
Beckemeyer	V	1,056	Clinton		Feb. 23, 1905	May 8, 1905
Bedford Park	V	737	Cook		Mar. 30, 1940	May 1, 1940
Beecher	V	1,367	Will		Nov. 5, 1883	Jan. 5, 1884
Beecher City	V	452	Effingham		Feb. 5, 1895	May 11, 1895
Belgium	V	494	Vermilion		May 19, 1908	July 17, 1908
Belknap	V	203	Johnson		July 13, 1880	July 23, 1901
Belleflower	T	389	McLean		Mar. 11, 1890	Oct. 1, 1890
Belle Prairie City	V	82	Hamilton	Mar. 30, 1869		
Belle Rive	V	303	Jefferson	Mar. 27, 1819		
Belleville	C	37,264	St. Clair		Jan. 1, 1875	Jan. 23, 1875
Bellevue	V	1,561	Peoria		May 11, 1876	Feb. 15, 1877
Bellmont	V	320	Wabash		Mar. 1, 1941	Dec. 2, 1941
*Bellwood	C	20,729	Cook	June 23, 1852	Dec. 20, 1883	July 17, 1894
Belvidere	C	11,223	Boone		Feb. 24, 1900	May 21, 1900
Bement	V	1,558	Piatt		Mar. 14, 1881	May 30, 1881
Benld	C	1,848	Macoupin		May 25, 1874	Aug. 25, 1904
*Bensenville	V	9,141	Du Page		July 30, 1904	Dec. 10, 1904
Benson	V	427	Woodford		May 19, 1894	July 17, 1894
Bently[11]	T	89	Hancock	Mar. 25, 1869	Oct. 3, 1878	Aug. 17, 1894

Municipality	City, town, or village	Population 1960 census	County	Date incorporation laws in force — Prior to July 1, 1872	Date incorporation laws in force — Since July 1, 1872	Date certificate of incorporation issued by secretary of state
Benton	C	7,023	Franklin	Jan. 7, 1841	July 9, 1902	Oct. 15, 1902
*Berkeley	V	5,792	Cook		Mar. 19, 1924	Aug. 24, 1925
Berlin	V	197	Sangamon		Mar. 27, 1896	July 6, 1900
Berwyn	C	54,224	Cook		Mar. 17, 1908	June 6, 1908
*Bethalto	V	3,235	Madison	Apr. 19, 1869	Apr. 23, 1873	July 2, 1873
Bethany	V	1,118	Moultrie		June 8, 1877	Oct. 6, 1877
Biggsville	V	345	Henderson		Apr. 14, 1879	July 9, 1894
Bingham	V	122	Fayette		Apr. 28, 1888	July 6, 1888
Birds	V	235	Lawrence		July 5, 1890	Apr. 28, 1896
Bishop Hill	V	164	Henry		Mar. 24, 1893	June 23, 1893
Blandinsville	V	853	McDonough	Feb. 24, 1859	Aug. 10, 1872	Sept. 27, 1872
Bloomingdale	V	1,262	Du Page		June 18, 1923	Oct. 8, 1923
*Bloomington	C	36,271	McLean	Mar. 2, 1839	Mar. 8, 1897	Apr. 29, 1897
*Blue Island[12]	C	19,618	Cook	Feb. 24, 1843	Apr. 16, 1901	July 11, 1901
Blue Mound	V	1,038	Macon		Feb. 17, 1876	May 9, 1876
Bluffs	V	779	Scott		Nov. 15, 1883	July 19, 1894
Bluford	V	388	Jefferson		Sept. 8, 1926	Jan. 17, 1927
Bolingbrook	V		Will		Oct. 6, 1965	Dec. 12, 1965
Bone Gap	V	245	Edwards		Mar. 30, 1892	June 14, 1892
Bonfield	V	178	Kankakee		May 31, 1888	Aug. 22, 1888
Bonnie	V	215	Jefferson		Feb. 14, 1914	Mar. 23, 1914
Bourbonnais	V	3,336	Kankakee		Apr. 13, 1875	July 9, 1875
Bowen[13]	V	559	Hancock		Dec. 29, 1898	Jan. 23, 1899
Braceville	V	558	Grundy		Feb. 12, 1880	June 29, 1894
Bradford	V	857	Stark	Mar. 27, 1869	Nov. 4, 1873	Jan. 24, 1874
*Bradley[14]	V	8,082	Kankakee		Mar. 2, 1896	June 2, 1896
Braidwood	C	1,944	Will		Mar. 4, 1873	July 15, 1873
Breese	C	2,461	Clinton		Apr. 20, 1905	Sept. 16, 1905
Bridgeport	C	2,260	Lawrence	Feb. 16, 1865	Sept. 21, 1908	Nov. 11, 1908
*Bridgeview	V	7,334	Cook		June 19, 1947	July 16, 1947

Name	Class	Population	County			
*Brighton	V	1,248	Macoupin	Feb. 23, 1859	Apr. 5, 1886	June 30, 1886
Brimfield[15]	V	656	Peoria	Mar. 2, 1843	Feb. 26, 1895	Mar. 16, 1895
*Broadlands	V	344	Champaign		Mar. 12, 1902	Apr. 29, 1902
Broadview	V	8,588	Cook	Mar. 13, 1869	Dec. 6, 1913	Jan. 22, 1914
Broadwell	V	173	Logan		Nov. 5, 1894	Nov. 24, 1894
Brocton	V	380	Edgar		Feb. 1, 1890	Sept. 9, 1901
Brookfield[16]	V	20,429	Cook		Nov. 7, 1893	Aug. 24, 1905
Brooklyn	C	1,922	St. Clair		Aug. 2, 1873	Sept. 28, 1901
Brookport	V	1,154	Massac		Nov. 13, 1888	May 31, 1902
Broughton	V	235	Hamilton		Oct. 5, 1897	Feb. 23, 1899
Browning	V	300	Schuyler		Nov. 16, 1882	May 18, 1899
Browns	V	251	Edwards		May 25, 1892	July 16, 1892
Brownstown	V	659	Fayette		Dec. 6, 1909	Jan. 26, 1910
Brussels	V	201	Calhoun		Apr. 28, 1888	June 27, 1888
Bryant	V	346	Fulton		Aug. 10, 1874	July 19, 1894
Buckingham	V	152	Kankakee		July 15, 1902	Aug. 14, 1902
Buckley	V	690	Iroquois		Dec. 28, 1872	Jan. 11, 1873
Buckner	V	610	Franklin		July 2, 1912	Mar. 15, 1913
Buda	V	732	Bureau		Aug. 7, 1872	Nov. 5, 1872
Buffalo	V	356	Sangamon		Mar. 29, 1879	June 7, 1879
*Buffalo Grove	V	1,492	Cook		Mar. 7, 1958	Apr. 24, 1958
Bulpitt	V	307	Christian		Apr. 27, 1914	July 10, 1914
Buncombe	V	200	Johnson		Jan. 20, 1916	July 28, 1916
Bunker Hill	C	1,524	Macoupin	Feb. 17, 1857	Nov. 25, 1872	May 14, 1873
Bureau Junction	V	401	Bureau		Aug. 10, 1874	Sept. 16, 1901
Burlington	V	360	Kane		July 16, 1906	Oct. 5, 1906
Burnham	V	2,478	Cook		Feb. 8, 1907	Mar. 29, 1907
Burnt Prairie[17]	V	118	White		Mar. 12, 1928	June 22, 1928
Burr Ridge[18]	V	299	Du Page		Oct. 30, 1956	Jan. 29, 1957
Bush	V	459	Williamson	Feb. 16, 1865	Sept. 7, 1905	Oct. 18, 1905
Bushnell	C	3,710	McDonough		July 10, 1878	Aug. 22, 1878
Butler	C	249	Montgomery		Mar. 18, 1873	Aug. 2, 1873
Byron	C	1,578	Ogle		Apr. 22, 1904	July 1, 1904
Cabery	V	293	Ford		Nov. 12, 1881	July 26, 1894
Cahokia	V	15,829	St. Clair		Mar. 28, 1927	Aug. 1, 1927

Table—continued

Municipality	City, town, or village	Population 1960 census	County	Date incorporation laws in force — Prior to July 1, 1872	Date incorporation laws in force — Since July 1, 1872	Date certificate of incorporation issued by secretary of state
Cairo	C	9,348	Alexander	Jan. 9, 1818	Jan. 7, 1873	Mar. 18, 1873
Calhoun	V	188	Richland		July 11, 1912	Sept. 20, 1912
*Calumet City[19]	C	25,000	Cook		July 22, 1911	Aug. 1, 1911
*Calumet Park[20]	V	8,448	Cook		June 24, 1912	Dec. 2, 1925
Camargo	V	276	Douglas		Apr. 13, 1904	May 23, 1904
Cambria[21]	V	568	Williamson		Jan. 5, 1905	Feb. 4, 1905
Cambridge	V	1,665	Henry	Feb. 21, 1861	Mar. 7, 1874	July 13, 1896
Camden	V	116	Schuyler		Feb. 27, 1925	Jan. 8, 1934
Campbell Hill	V	263	Jackson		Nov. 24, 1875	Nov. 13, 1899
Camp Point	V	1,092	Adams	Feb. 13, 1857	Feb. 7, 1874	May 5, 1874
Campus	V	165	Livingston		June 10, 1892	Sept. 7, 1892
Canton	C	13,588	Fulton	Feb. 8, 1849	Apr. 4, 1892	Apr. 11, 1892
Cantrall	V	115	Sangamon		Nov. 20, 1894	Feb. 18, 1895
Capron	V	656	Boone		Oct. 4, 1873	Oct. 9, 1901
Carbon Cliff	V	1,268	Rock Island		Dec. 10, 1906	Mar. 9, 1907
*Carbondale	C	14,670	Jackson	Apr. 15, 1869	July 7, 1873	Aug. 14, 1873
Carbon Hill	V	236	Grundy		Jan. 23, 1892	June 4, 1892
Carlinville	C	5,440	Macoupin	Mar. 4, 1837	Apr. 5, 1887	May 31, 1887
Carlock	V	318	McLean		Oct. 8, 1959	Jan. 6, 1960
*Carlyle	C	2,903	Clinton	Feb. 10, 1837	Apr. 17, 1884	Apr. 26, 1902
Carmi	C	6,152	White	Mar. 24, 1819	Mar. 10, 1873	July 22, 1873
*Carol Stream	V	836	Du Page		Jan. 5, 1959	Mar. 13, 1959
Carpentersville	V	17,424	Kane		June 13, 1887	June 26, 1894
Carrier Mills	V	2,006	Saline		Sept. 19, 1894	Nov. 20, 1894
Carrollton	C	2,558	Greene	Feb. 21, 1861	Apr. 17, 1883	May 15, 1883
Carterville	C	2,643	Williamson		Mar. 8, 1892	July 30, 1894
Carthage	C	3,325	Hancock	Feb. 27, 1837	Apr. 17, 1883	May 31, 1883
*Cary	V	2,530	McHenry		Feb. 3, 1893	July 17, 1894
Casey	C	2,890	Clark		Mar. 9, 1896	June 9, 1896
*Caseyville	V	2,455	St. Clair	Apr. 15, 1869	Apr. 22, 1875	May 7, 1875

Name	Class	Population	County			
*Catlin	V	1,263	Vermilion		Apr. 15, 1873	June 21, 1873
Cave in Rock	V	495	Hardin		Jan. 7, 1901	Apr. 19, 1901
Cedar Point	V	308	La Salle		Oct. 3, 1907	June 22, 1908
Cedarville[22]	V	570	Stephenson		May 31, 1884	Aug. 1, 1894
Central City	V	1,422	Marion	Feb. 12, 1849	Mar. 21, 1891	May 29, 1958
Central City	C	30	Grundy	Feb. 14, 1857	Dec. 30, 1886	Feb. 21, 1887
Centralia	C	13,904	Marion	Feb. 18, 1859	Feb. 13, 1893	May 4, 1893
Centreville	V	12,769	St. Clair		Oct. 9, 1957	Dec. 30, 1957
Cerro Gordo	V	1,067	Piatt		July 25, 1873	Nov. 7, 1901
Chadwick	V	602	Carroll		Aug. 8, 1892	Oct. 7, 1892
Champaign	C	49,583	Champaign	Feb. 21, 1861	Apr. 17, 1883	Apr. 24, 1883
Chandlerville	V	718	Cass	Feb. 21, 1861	July 21, 1874	July 23, 1875
Channahon	V		Will		Dec. 11, 1961	Aug. 17, 1962
Chapin	V	477	Morgan	Mar. 2, 1839	May 17, 1873	Mar. 7, 1899
*Charleston	C	10,505	Coles		Oct. 12, 1872	Nov. 20, 1872
*Chatham	T	1,069	Sangamon		Mar. 24, 1874	July 23, 1874
Chatsworth	V	1,330	Livingston	Mar. 8, 1867	May. 29, 1874	June 5, 1874
Chebanse	C	995	Iroquois	Mar. 13, 1869	Aug. 5, 1872	Nov. 10, 1955
Chenoa	V	1,523	McLean	Feb. 16, 1865	Oct. 28, 1905	Dec. 6, 1905
Cherry	V	501	Bureau		Mar. 17, 1896	July 29, 1897
Cherry Valley[23]	V	875	Winnebago	Jan. 31, 1857	Mar. 29, 1873	July 14, 1873
*Chester	C	4,460	Randolph	Jan. 7, 1835	Aug. 22, 1881	Jan. 2, 1882
Chesterfield	V	280	Macoupin		Apr. 23, 1875	May 12, 1875
Chicago	C	3,550,404	Cook	Feb. 11, 1835	Feb. 28, 1901	Apr. 3, 1901
Chicago Heights	C	34,331	Cook		Sept. 1, 1914	Oct. 27, 1914
*Chicago Ridge	V	5,748	Cook	Feb. 22, 1861	Feb. 11, 1873	June 23, 1873
Chillicothe	C	3,054	Peoria		Feb. 17, 1900	Mar. 9, 1900
Chrisman	C	1,221	Edgar		Jan. 15, 1910	July 20, 1910
Christopher	V	2,854	Franklin			
Cicero	T	69,130	Cook	Feb. 28, 1867	Feb. 17, 1896	Sept. 26, 1901
Cisco	V	398	Piatt		Jan. 15, 1898	Oct. 18, 1901
Cisne	V	615	Wayne		July 13, 1891	Nov. 23, 1891
Cissna Park	V	803	Iroquois			
Claremont	V	223	Richland			June 29, 1894
Clarendon Hills	V	5,885	Du Page	Mar. 7, 1866	Jan. 22, 1924	June 27, 1924
Clark City	V		Kankakee		Dec. 6, 1890	May 12, 1893

51

Table—continued

Municipality	City, town, or village	Population 1960 census	County	Date incorporation laws in force Prior to July 1, 1872	Date incorporation laws in force Since July 1, 1872	Date certificate of incorporation issued by secretary of state
Clay City	V	1,144	Clay	Mar. 27, 1869	Feb. 9, 1874	May 4, 1874
Clayton	V	774	Adams	Feb. 27, 1837	Feb. 9, 1880	July 14, 1880
Clear Lake	V	219	Sangamon		Aug. 12, 1955	Dec. 20, 1955
Cleveland	V	251	Henry	July 21, 1869	Mar. 20, 1873	Feb. 14, 1941
Clifton	V	1,018	Iroquois	Jan. 17, 1867	May 23, 1874	Oct. 28, 1901
Clinton	C	7,355	De Witt	Feb. 15, 1855	Apr. 18, 1882	May 4, 1882
Coal City	V	2,852	Grundy		Sept. 22, 1881	Nov. 11, 1881
Coalton	V	352	Montgomery		June 3, 1916	July 24, 1916
*Coal Valley	V	435	Rock Island		Mar. 11, 1876	May 9, 1876
Coatsburg	V	178	Adams	Apr. 15, 1869	June 10, 1875	Oct. 30, 1901
Cobden[24]	V	918	Union		Nov. 17, 1875	Sept. 13, 1901
Coffeen	C	502	Montgomery		Dec. 5, 1910	Feb. 6, 1911
Colchester	C	1,495	McDonough	Feb. 16, 1867	May 12, 1884	July 18, 1884
Coleta	V	197	Whiteside		Mar. 4, 1914	Mar. 19, 1914
Colfax	V	894	McLean		Dec. 15, 1881	Apr. 27, 1882
Collinsville	C	14,217	Madison	Feb. 15, 1855	Oct. 1, 1872	Nov. 30, 1872
*Colona	V	491	Henry		July 6, 1903	May 15, 1905
Colp	V	201	Williamson		Dec. 13, 1913	Apr. 16, 1914
Columbia	C	3,174	Monroe	Feb. 19, 1859	Mar. 22, 1927	Mar. 20, 1933
Columbus	V	109	Adams	Mar. 1, 1849	Jan. 24, 1885	Mar. 30, 1885
Compton	V	366	Lee		Dec. 6, 1875	Dec. 10, 1875
Concord	V	210	Morgan		Jan. 30, 1914	Feb. 18, 1914
Congerville	V		Woodford		Dec. 21, 1959	Feb. 25, 1960
Cooksville	V	221	McLean		Nov. 7, 1901	Mar. 22, 1902
Cordova	V	502	Rock Island		Mar. 12, 1877	July 6, 1894
Cornell	V	524	Livingston		June 18, 1873	Oct. 17, 1901
Cortland	T	461	De Kalb	Feb. 16, 1865		
Coulterville[25]	V	1,022	Randolph		July 15, 1874	Aug. 18, 1874
*Country Club Hills	C		Cook		July 15, 1958	Oct. 3, 1958
*Countryside	C	3,421	Cook		Apr. 26, 1960	July 27, 1960

Name	Class	Pop.	County			
Cowden	V	575	Shelby		June 4, 1875	Aug. 27, 1875
Crainville	V	421	Williamson		June 28, 1881	Oct. 19, 1901
Creal Springs	C	784	Williamson		Aug. 12, 1892	Apr. 14, 1898
Cresent City[26]	V	393	Iroquois		Oct. 13, 1884	Dec. 2, 1884
Crest Hill	C	5,887	Will		Jan. 22, 1960	Apr. 8, 1960
Creston[27]	V	454	Ogle		Dec. 7, 1872	Feb. 25, 1873
*Crestwood	V	1,213	Cook		Sept. 25, 1928	Nov. 30, 1928
*Crete	V	3,463	Will		Mar. 27, 1880	July 16, 1880
Creve Coeur	V	6,684	Tazewell		Feb. 4, 1921	July 25, 1921
Crossville	V	874	White		Sept. 30, 1895	Oct. 22, 1895
*Crystal Lake	C	8,314	McHenry		Sept. 23, 1914	Dec. 9, 1914
Cuba[28]	C	1,380	Fulton	Jan. 26, 1853	Mar. 4, 1895	June 3, 1895
Cullom	V	555	Livingston		July 27, 1882	Oct. 17, 1901
Cutler	V	445	Perry		Feb. 18, 1907	May 16, 1907
Cypress	V	264	Johnson		Jan. 9, 1905	Feb. 15, 1905
Dahlgren	V	480	Hamilton		Dec. 24, 1887	Jan. 24, 1888
Dakota	T	363	Stephenson	Mar. 11, 1869		
Dallas City	C	1,276	Hancock	Feb. 18, 1859	Apr. 14, 1905	May 9, 1905
Dalton City	V	386	Moultrie		Aug. 6, 1877	Feb. 26, 1879
Dalzell	V	496	Bureau		Nov. 24, 1903	Feb. 11, 1904
Dana	V	240	La Salle		Sept. 20, 1875	Jan. 13, 1876
Danforth	V	394	Iroquois		Nov. 30, 1878	Aug. 8, 1894
Danvers[29]	V	783	McLean		June 10, 1878	Aug. 7, 1878
Danville	C	41,856	Vermilion	Feb. 3, 1839	Mar. 17, 1874	June 9, 1874
Davis	V	434	Stephenson		May 1, 1873	June 6, 1873
Dawson	V	393	Sangamon		Sept. 22, 1883	Dec. 20, 1883
Decatur	C	78,004	Macon	Mar. 9, 1867	Apr. 21, 1881	May 3, 1881
Deer Creek	V	583	Tazewell		Dec. 26, 1899	Mar. 21, 1900
*Deerfield	V	11,786	Lake		Apr. 14, 1903	June 22, 1903
Deer Grove	V	86	Whiteside		May 27, 1937	Aug. 4, 1937
Deer Park	V	476	Lake		Nov. 14, 1957	Jan. 20, 1958
*De Kalb	C	18,486	De Kalb	Feb. 2, 1861	Feb. 27, 1873	June 20, 1873
Deland	V	422	Piatt		Sept. 19, 1899	Mar. 7, 1900
Delavan	C	1,377	Tazewell		Apr. 17, 1888	July 17, 1888
Depue[30]	V	1,920	Bureau	Feb. 18, 1867	July 2, 1888	Oct. 29, 1901

Municipality	City, town, or village	Population 1960 census	County	Date incorporation laws in force — Prior to July 1, 1872	Date incorporation laws in force — Since July 1, 1872	Date certificate of incorporation issued by secretary of state
De Soto	V	723	Jackson		May 11, 1895	May 16, 1895
*Des Plaines[31]	C	34,886	Cook	Apr. 15, 1869	Feb. 2, 1925	Apr. 16, 1925
Detroit	V	126	Pike		Mar. 14, 1903	Apr. 10, 1903
De Witt	V	245	De Witt		July 3, 1879	Oct. 1, 1894
Diamond	V	250	Grundy		June 27, 1895	Aug. 23, 1895
Dieterich	V	591	Effingham		Apr. 1, 1893	July 30, 1894
Divernon	V	997	Sangamon		Jan. 2, 1900	Sept. 20, 1909
Dix[32]	V	181	Jefferson		June 3, 1873	Aug. 7, 1894
Dixmoor[33]	V	3,076	Cook		Nov. 1, 1922	Jan. 15, 1923
Dixon	C	19,565	Lee	Feb. 14, 1857	Mar. 7, 1904	Apr. 25, 1904
*Dolton[34]	V	18,746	Cook		Dec. 28, 1892	Mar. 30, 1893
Dongola	V	757	Union		Aug. 24, 1883	Apr. 8, 1884
Donnellson	V	292	Montgomery		May 13, 1897	June 13, 1897
Donovan	V	320	Iroquois		Apr. 16, 1901	Aug. 12, 1901
Dorchester	V	161	Macoupin		Mar. 2, 1875	June 28, 1875
Dover	V	171	Bureau		May 21, 1873	Oct. 1, 1894
Dowell	V	453	Jackson		Aug. 19, 1919	Jan. 7, 1920
*Downers Grove	V	21,154	Du Page		Mar. 29, 1873	July 11, 1873
*Downs	V	497	McLean		Jan. 6, 1917	May 10, 1917
Du Bois [35]	V	229	Washington	Apr. 1, 1869	July 8, 1896	Oct. 7, 1896
Dunfermline	V	284	Fulton		May 24, 1947	Aug. 11, 1947
Dunlap	V	564	Peoria		Nov. 3, 1951	Apr. 25, 1952
Dupo	V	2,937	St. Clair		Aug. 5, 1907	July 8, 1912
Du Quoin	C	6,558	Perry	Feb. 22, 1861	May 17, 1873	July 14, 1873
Durand[36]	V	797	Winnebago		Feb. 27, 1886	July 6, 1886
Dwight	V	3,086	Livingston	Mar. 24, 1869	July 23, 1872	Jan. 29, 1874
Eagarville	V	149	Macoupin		Oct. 28, 1915	Mar. 28, 1916
Earlville	C	1,420	La Salle	Mar. 27, 1869	Feb. 6, 1877	May 19, 1902
East Alton	V	7,630	Madison		May 4, 1894	May 7, 1894

East Brooklyn	V	68	Grundy		July 1, 1903	Nov. 1, 1904
East Carondelet	V	463	St. Clair		Aug. 21, 1876	Aug. 8, 1894
*East Chicago Heights	V	3,270	Cook		Jan. 11, 1949	May 27, 1949
*East Dubuque[37]	C	2,082	JoDaviess	Feb. 16, 1865		June 5, 1879
East Dundee	V	2,221	Kane		June 13, 1887	Sept. 20, 1901
East Galesburg[38]	V	660	Knox		Dec. 6, 1893	Mar. 31, 1894
East Gillespie	V	208	Macoupin		Mar. 23, 1938	June 21, 1938
East Hazelcrest	V	1,457	Cook		Mar. 2, 1918	July 17, 1918
East Moline	C	16,732	Rock Islanc		Apr. 8, 1907	Aug. 1, 1907
*East Peoria[39]	C	12,310	Tazewell		Apr. 15, 1919	Mar. 20, 1936
East St. Louis[40]	C	81,712	St. Clair	Feb. 16, 1865	Jan. 22, 1878	Apr. 18, 1878
Easton	V	361	Mason		Mar. 19, 1896	June 16, 1896
Eddyville	V	125	Pope		Apr. 30, 1883	Aug. 1, 1894
Edgewood	V	515	Effingham		Apr. 24, 1882	June 23, 1882
Edinburg	V	1,003	Christian		May 5, 1874	June 6, 1874
Edwardsville	C	9,996	Madison	Feb. 23, 1819	Sept. 23, 1872	Dec. 16, 1872
Effingham	C	8,172	Effingham	Feb. 20, 1861	Jan. 21, 1873	Apr. 3, 1873
Eileen[41]	V	384	Grundy		Apr. 26, 1902	May 12, 1902
Elburn	V	960	Kane		Jan. 18, 1886	Jan. 21, 1886
El Dara	V	98	Pike		Apr. 23, 1881	July 15, 1881
Eldorado	C	3,573	Saline		Mar. 11, 1873	Mar. 29, 1894
Eldred	V	302	Greene		Mar. 27, 1905	June 22, 1905
Elgin	C	49,447	Kane	Apr. 24, 1854	Oct. 18, 1880	Jan. 18, 1881
Elizabeth	V	729	JoDaviess		May 3, 1887	Aug. 13, 1887
Elizabethtown	V	524	Hardin	Feb. 13, 1857	June 23, 1873	July 21, 1875
*Elk Grove Village	V	6,608	Cook	Feb. 22, 1861	July 17, 1956	Oct. 9, 1956
Elkhart City	T	418	Logan			
Elkville	V	743	Jackson		Apr. 19, 1897	May 28, 1897
Elliott	V	343	Ford		July 1, 1903	Oct. 7, 1903
Ellis Grove	V	218	Randolph		Feb. 4, 1894	May 23, 1894
Ellisville	V	140	Fulton		Nov. 18, 1872	Mar. 30, 1874
Ellsworth	V	224	McLean		Mar. 5, 1925	May 18, 1925
*Elmhurst	C	36,991	Du Page	Feb. 27, 1867	Apr. 11, 1910	July 13, 1910
Elmwood	C	1,882	Peoria		May 24, 1892	June 14, 1892
Elmwood Park	C	23,866	Cook		Mar. 24, 1914	June 24, 1914
El Paso	C	1,964	Woodford	Feb. 22, 1861	Apr. 6, 1891	May 18, 1891

Table—continued

Municipality	City, town, or village	Population 1960 census	County	Date incorporation laws in force — Prior to July 1, 1872	Date incorporation laws in force — Since July 1, 1872	Date certificate of incorporation issued by secretary of state
Elsah	V	218	Jersey		Apr. 12, 1873	Sept. 2, 1873
Elvaston	V	232	Hancock	Dec. 14, 1869		July 6, 1894
Elwood	V	746	Will	June 19, 1869	June 21, 1873	Sept. 12, 1873
Emden	V	502	Logan		Mar. 31, 1894	June 11, 1894
Emmington	V	133	Livingston		Dec. 20, 1883	Oct. 8, 1901
Energy[42]	V	507	Williamson		Aug. 8, 1907	June 22, 1914
Enfield	V	791	White	Mar. 15, 1869	July 30, 1875	Sept. 22, 1875
Equality	V	665	Gallatin	Feb. 11, 1851	Oct. 28, 1872	Dec. 11, 1872
Erie	V	1,215	Whiteside		Aug. 20, 1872	Aug. 4, 1876
Essex	V	328	Kankakee	Feb. 23, 1859	Mar. 31, 1885	June 17, 1885
Eureka	C	2,538	Woodford	Feb. 17, 1857	Apr. 16, 1895	June 28, 1895
Evanston[43]	C	79,283	Cook	Apr. 15, 1869	Mar. 29, 1892	May 26, 1892
Evansville	V	829	Randolph		Sept. 29, 1885	Aug. 8, 1903
*Evergreen Park	V	24,178	Cook		Dec. 20, 1893	Feb. 7, 1894
Ewing	V	250	Franklin		Sept. 1, 1891	June 16, 1892
Exeter	V	77	Scott		Jan. 3, 1876	Mar. 23, 1876
Fairbury	C	2,937	Livingston	Jan. 31, 1840	Mar. 12, 1895	June 13, 1895
Fairfield	C	6,362	Wayne		Feb. 20, 1884	Feb. 26, 1884
Fairmont City	V	2,688	St. Clair		Mar. 3, 1914	Sept. 27, 1923
Fairmount	V	725	Vermilion		June 18, 1894	July 11, 1894
Fairview	V	544	Fulton	Feb. 24, 1859	July 2, 1900	Apr. 28, 1902
Farina	V	692	Fayette		Mar. 29, 1875	June 29, 1875
Farmer City[44]	C	1,838	De Witt	Mar. 27, 1869	Aug. 8, 1872	Oct. 23, 1872
Farmersville	V	495	Montgomery		July 3, 1893	July 17, 1894
Farmington	C	2,831	Fulton	Feb. 18, 1857	Mar. 14, 1887	Mar. 17, 1887
Fayetteville	V	294	St. Clair	Apr. 15, 1869	Dec. 17, 1881	Apr. 4, 1960
Ferris	V	208	Hancock		Feb. 9, 1882	Feb. 10, 1886
Fidelity	V	125	Jersey		Feb. 16, 1884	May 14, 1884
Fieldon	V	239	Jersey	Feb. 7, 1857	June 12, 1883	Aug. 23, 1883

Name	Class	Population	County			
Fillmore	V	360	Montgomery		Aug. 12, 1890	June 29, 1893
Findlay	V	759	Shelby		May 16, 1892	May 8, 1894
*Fisher	V	1,155	Champaign		May 3, 1895	May 19, 1902
Fithian	V	495	Vermilion		Mar. 3, 1896	May 2, 1896
Flanagan	V	841	Livingston		Aug. 3, 1882	Oct. 16, 1901
Flat Rock	V	497	Crawford		Nov. 7, 1891	Feb. 25, 1892
Flora	C	5,331	Clay	Feb. 27, 1867	Apr. 15, 1884	July 1, 1894
Florence	V	99	Pike		Aug. 31, 1935	Jan. 30, 1939
*Flossmoor	V	4,624	Cook		June 20, 1924	Aug. 19, 1924
Foosland	V	150	Champaign		July 1, 1959	Dec. 16, 1959
Forest City	V	249	Mason		Sept. 25, 1891	May 7, 1897
Forest Park[45]	V	14,452	Cook		Aug. 12, 1907	Aug. 27, 1907
Forest View	V	1,042	Cook		Dec. 8, 1924	Jan. 12, 1925
Forrest	V	1,220	Livingston		Mar. 27, 1874	July 30, 1874
Forreston	V	1,153	Ogle	Apr. 1, 1869	Aug. 2, 1888	Sept. 5, 1888
Forsyth	V	424	Macon		Jan. 7, 1958	May 22, 1958
*Fox Lake	V	3,700	Lake		Dec. 15, 1906	Apr. 13, 1907
Fox River Grove	V	1,866	McHenry		Aug. 21, 1919	Nov. 24, 1919
*Frankfort	V	1,135	Will		Aug. 25, 1879	May 31, 1890
Franklin	V	500	Morgan	July 21, 1837	June 13, 1887	June 25, 1887
Franklin Grove	V	773	Lee	Feb. 13, 1865	July 16, 1872	Oct. 10, 1872
Franklin Park	V	18,322	Cook		Aug. 3, 1892	Nov. 26, 1892
Freeburg	V	1,908	St. Clair	Feb. 21, 1859	Mar. 8, 1875	Apr. 26, 1875
Freemanspur	V	406	Williamson		May 28, 1913	Mar. 7, 1921
Freeport	C	26,628	Stephenson	Feb. 14, 1855	Apr. 18, 1882	July 7, 1882
Fulton	C	3,387	Whiteside	Feb. 18, 1859	Mar. 30, 1899	June 14, 1899
Fults	V	90	Monroe		Apr. 12, 1937	June 29, 1937
Galatia	V	830	Saline	Feb. 21, 1861	May 31, 1875	July 14, 1958
Galena	C	4,410	JoDaviess	Jan. 7, 1835	Apr. 18, 1882	June 12, 1882
Galesburg	C	37,243	Knox	Jan. 27, 1841	July 20, 1876	Apr. 11, 1877
Galva	C	3,060	Henry	Feb. 16, 1867	Dec. 4, 1905	Mar. 24, 1906
Gardner	V	1,041	Grundy	Mar. 30, 1869	Jan. 13, 1914	Jan. 22, 1914
Garrett	V	249	Douglas		Mar. 19, 1903	Mar. 3, 1903
Gays	V	263	Moultrie		Nov. 8, 1905	June 25, 1906
Geneseo	C	4,169	Henry	Feb. 14, 1855		Jan. 25, 1906

Table—continued

Municipality	City, town, or village	Population 1960 census	County	Date incorporation laws in force — Prior to July 1, 1872	Since July 1, 1872	Date certificate of incorporation issued by secretary of state
*Geneva	C	7,646	Kane	Feb. 25, 1867	Apr. 19, 1887	May 27, 1887
*Genoa	C	2,330	De Kalb		Apr. 18, 1911	Sept. 9, 1911
Georgetown	C	3,544	Vermilion	Mar. 8, 1869	Apr. 21, 1909	July 21, 1909
Germantown	V	983	Clinton		May 30, 1874	June 27, 1879
German Valley	V	224	Stephenson		Feb. 19, 1907	Oct. 31, 1923
Gibson	C	3,453	Ford		Apr. 17, 1894	June 6, 1894
Gifford	V	609	Champaign		May 12, 1954	May 20, 1954
Gilberts	V	238	Kane		June 2, 1890	June 3, 1893
Gillespie	C	3,569	Macoupin	Mar. 30, 1869	Mar. 4, 1907	May 2, 1907
Gilman	C	1,704	Iroquois	Mar. 4, 1867	Feb. 10, 1874	July 30, 1874
Girard	C	1,734	Macoupin	Feb. 14, 1855	Sept. 14, 1880	Feb. 17, 1881
Gladstone	V	356	Henderson		Apr. 20, 1881	June 26, 1894
Glasford[46]	V	1,012	Peoria		Feb. 2, 1889	June 5, 1889
Glasgow	V	166	Scott	Aug. 23, 1867		July 17, 1894
Glen Carbon	V	1,241	Madison		June 6, 1892	July 10, 1894
Glencoe	V	10,472	Cook	Mar. 29, 1869		
*Glendale Heights[47]	V	173	Du Page		July 13, 1959	Oct. 26, 1959
*Glen Ellyn[48]	V	15,972	Du Page		May 10, 1892	June 27, 1892
*Glenview	V	18,132	Cook		June 20, 1899	Nov. 2, 1901
*Glenwood	V	882	Cook		Feb. 4, 1903	Mar. 11, 1903
Godley	V	97	Will		Mar. 14, 1888	May 3, 1888
Golconda	C	864	Pope	Mar. 1, 1845	June 4, 1923	July 20, 1923
Golden[49]	V	491	Adams		Apr. 26, 1873	Oct. 26, 1880
Golden Gate	V	156	Wayne		May 14, 1897	Oct. 18, 1901
Golf	V	409	Cook		Feb. 27, 1928	Mar. 14, 1928
Good Hope[50]	V	394	McDonough	Mar. 3, 1869	May 6, 1875	Aug. 22, 1894
Goodfield	V	286	Woodford		Mar. 9, 1957	Apr. 25, 1957
Goreville	V	625	Johnson		Apr. 17, 1900	July 5, 1900
Gorham[51]	V	378	Jackson		July 18, 1906	Feb. 13, 1913
Grafton	C	1,084	Jersey	Feb. 12, 1853	Apr. 9, 1907	May 16, 1907

Grand Ridge	V	659	La Salle		Jan. 14, 1891	June 15, 1891
Grand Tower	C	847	Jackson		Nov. 18, 1872	Feb. 13, 1873
Grandview	V	2,214	Sangamon		June 3, 1939	Sept. 1, 1939
Granite City	C	40,073	Madison		Mar. 9, 1896	June 8, 1896
Grantfork[52]	V	134	Madison		Feb. 18, 1886	Dec. 28, 1917
Grant Park	V	757	Kankakee		Apr. 16, 1883	June 4, 1883
Granville	V	1,048	Putnam	Feb. 21, 1861	Dec. 28, 1880	Feb. 24, 1881
*Grays Lake	V	3,762	Lake		Jan. 26, 1895	May 11, 1895
Grayville	C	2,280	White and Edwards	Feb. 15, 1851	Apr. 16, 1884	May 27, 1884
Greenfield	C	1,064	Greene	Feb. 26, 1867	Apr. 7, 1884	June 2, 1884
Green Oaks[53]	V	198	Lake		Jan. 25, 1960	Apr. 20, 1960
Green Rock	C	2,677	Henry		June 3, 1950	Sept. 7, 1950
Greenup	V	1,477	Cumberland	Feb. 15, 1855	Sept. 14, 1872	July 20, 1875
Green Valley	V	552	Tazewell	Mar. 30, 1869	Mar. 11, 1916	July 29, 1916
Greenview	V	796	Menard	Feb. 15, 1855	Mar. 22, 1877	June 22, 1877
Greenville	C	4,569	Bond	Apr. 1, 1869	Aug. 13, 1872	Nov. 11, 1872
Gridley	V	889	McLean		Oct. 2, 1905	Nov. 18, 1905
Griggsville	C	1,240	Pike		Oct. 4, 1878	Dec. 24, 1878
Gulfport	V	214	Henderson		May 31, 1928	Jan. 22, 1934
*Gurnee	V	1,831	Lake		Mar. 6, 1928	June 21, 1929
Hainesville	V	132	Lake		July 23, 1902	July 21, 1903
Hamburg	V	264	Calhoun	Feb. 26, 1847	Jan. 22, 1897	Jan. 16, 1902
Hamel	V	362	Madison		Feb. 24, 1955	May 6, 1955
*Hamilton	C	2,228	Hancock	Feb. 24, 1859	Sept. 18, 1872	Oct. 18, 1872
Hamletsburg	V	107	Pope		Apr. 20, 1897	July 14, 1897
Hammond	V	471	Piatt		Apr. 18, 1890	Sept. 14, 1907
Hampshire	V	1,309	Kane		Oct. 28, 1876	July 18, 1877
*Hampton	V	742	Rock Island	Feb. 10, 1849	Apr. 22, 1876	July 5, 1894
Hanaford	V	289	Franklin		July 20, 1909	May 25, 1910
Hanna City	V	1,056	Peoria		Apr. 18, 1903	Sept. 9, 1903
Hanover	V	1,396	JoDaviess	Feb. 12, 1849	Apr. 28, 1877	July 17, 1894
*Hanover Park[54]	V	451	Cook and Du Page		Aug. 14, 1958	Oct. 29, 1958
Hardin	V	356	Calhoun		May 22, 1880	July 14, 1894
Harmon	V	214	Lee		Oct. 12, 1900	Feb. 22, 1901
Harrisburg	C	9,171	Saline	Feb. 21, 1861	Apr. 16, 1889	July 11, 1889

Table—continued

Municipality	City, town, or village	Population 1960 census	County	Date incorporation laws in force — Prior to July 1, 1872	Since July 1, 1872	Date certificate of incorporation issued by secretary of state
Hartford	V	2,355	Madison		Mar. 9, 1920	June 10, 1920
Hartsburg	V	300	Logan		Dec. 20, 1886	Oct. 1, 1901
*Harvard	C	4,248	McHenry	Feb. 26, 1867	Apr. 7, 1891	Aug. 25, 1891
Harvel	V	285	Montgomery		Jan. 14, 1873	Apr. 27, 1877
*Harvey	C	29,071	Cook		Apr. 15, 1895	May 22, 1895
*Harwood Heights	V	5,688	Cook		Nov. 25, 1947	Mar. 4, 1948
Havana	C	4,363	Mason	Feb. 12, 1853	July 13, 1872	Oct. 11, 1872
Hawthorn Woods	V	239	Lake		Mar. 10, 1958	Apr. 25, 1958
*Hazel Crest	V	6,205	Cook		Oct. 19, 1911	Feb. 12, 1912
Hebron	V	701	McHenry		Sept. 23, 1895	Jan. 16, 1896
Hecker	V	313	Monroe		Nov. 12, 1895	Nov. 24, 1895
Henderson	V	212	Knox		June 10, 1876	Apr. 24, 1895
Hennepin	V	391	Putnam	Mar. 2, 1839	Aug. 7, 1872	Sept. 5, 1872
Henning	V	271	Vermilion		Sept. 5, 1904	Dec. 6, 1904
Henry	C	2,278	Marshall	Mar. 1, 1854	Mar. 31, 1879	June 9, 1879
Herrick	V	440	Shelby		Jan. 25, 1890	Apr. 29, 1890
Herrin	C	9,474	Williamson		Apr. 17, 1900	Aug. 17, 1900
Herscher	V	658	Kankakee		Apr. 27, 1882	Dec. 11, 1909
Hettick	V	253	Macoupin		May 10, 1892	Sept. 21, 1892
Heyworth	V	1,196	McLean	Mar. 31, 1869	Mar. 23, 1901	May 4, 1901
*Hickory Hills	V	2,707	Cook		Sept. 8, 1951	Nov. 14, 1951
Hidalgo	V	126	Jasper		Nov. 5, 1900	May 5, 1902
Highland	C	4,943	Madison	Feb. 14, 1863	Apr. 7, 1884	June 5, 1884
*Highland Park	C	25,532	Lake	Mar. 11, 1869	Dec. 17, 1888	Feb. 5, 1876
Highwood[55]	C	4,499	Lake		July 17, 1888	Oct. 5, 1904
*Hillcrest	V	224	Ogle		Mar. 27, 1958	June 6, 1958
Hillsboro	C	4,232	Montgomery	Feb. 14, 1855	Mar. 8, 1882	Mar. 26, 1913
Hillsdale	V	490	Rock Island		May 27, 1950	Feb. 19, 1951
*Hillside	V	7,794	Cook		Dec. 6, 1905	Mar. 15, 1906
Hillview	V	305	Greene		July 6, 1903	Jan. 20, 1904

Name	Class	Population	County	Incorporated	Organized	Other
Hinckley	V	940	De Kalb	May 22, 1877	Aug. 22, 1877	
Hindsboro	V	376	Douglas	Nov. 18, 1899	Apr. 10, 1900	
*Hinsdale	V	12,859	Du Page	Apr. 1, 1873	Sept. 23, 1901	
*Hodgkins	V	1,126	Cook	July 1, 1896	Oct. 31, 1901	
Hoffman	V	235	Clinton	May 13, 1950	July 19, 1950	
*Hoffman Estates	V	8,296	Cook	Sept. 23, 1959	Jan. 12, 1960	
Hollowayville	V	96	Bureau	June 17, 1893	Nov. 3, 1893	
Homer	C	1,276	Champaign	Aug. 10, 1872	Aug. 16, 1894	
Hometown	V	7,479	Cook	June 6, 1953	Nov. 18, 1953	
*Homewood	V	13,371	Cook	Feb. 11, 1893	Mar. 30, 1893	
Homewood Park	C		Cook	June 16, 1933	Mar. 14, 1934	
Hoopeston	C	6,606	Vermilion	Apr. 17, 1877	July 20, 1877	
Hooppole	V	227	Henry	June 30, 1917	July 18, 1917	
Hopedale	V	737	Tazewell	Sept. 9, 1872	Aug. 4, 1894	
Hoyleton	V	475	Washington	Apr. 20, 1881	Aug. 17, 1894	
*Hudson	V	493	McLean	Jan. 16, 1888	July 1, 1902	
Huey[56]	V	212	Clinton	Aug. 3, 1891	Aug. 6, 1891	
Hull	V	535	Pike	Jan. 13, 1892	Aug. 7, 1894	
Humboldt [57]	V	342	Coles	Apr. 16, 1878	Aug. 28, 1878	
Hume	V	449	Edgar	Dec. 19, 1881	Oct. 22, 1901	
Huntley	V	1,143	McHenry	Aug. 19, 1872	Oct. 4, 1872	
Hurst	V	863	Williamson	Dec. 29, 1905	Mar. 15, 1906	
Hutsonville	V	583	Crawford	Jan. 12, 1875	Mar. 30, 1875	Feb. 3, 1853
Illiopolis[58]	V	995	Sangamon	Sept. 25, 1883	July 15, 1884	Mar. 6, 1867
Ina	V	332	Jefferson	July 15, 1898	Nov. 28, 1898	
Indian Creek	V	239	Lake	July 16, 1958	Aug. 18, 1958	
*Indian Head Park	V	385	Cook	June 9, 1959	Aug. 4, 1959	Feb. 19, 1867
Indianola[59]	V	295	Vermilion	July 15, 1882	Sept. 30, 1901	
Industry	V	514	McDonough	Jan. 23, 1873	Apr. 15, 1873	
Inverness	V		Cook	May 8, 1962	May 25, 1962	
Iola	V	155	Clay	May 9, 1914	July 13, 1914	Jan. 26, 1853
Ipava[60]	V	623	Fulton	July 17, 1872	Aug. 23, 1872	
Iroquois	V	231	Iroquois	Aug. 15, 1881	Oct. 5, 1894	Mar. 29, 1869
Irving	V	570	Montgomery	May 10, 1873	Aug. 9, 1873	
Irvington	V	387	Washington	Nov. 10, 1881	Jan. 27, 1882	

Table—continued

Municipality	City, town, or village	Population 1960 Census	County	Date incorporation laws in force Prior to July 1, 1872	Date incorporation laws in force Since July 1, 1872	Date certificate of incorporation issued by secretary of state
Irwin	V	92	Kankakee		Aug. 6, 1902	Oct. 25, 1902
Island Lake	V	1,639	Lake		Feb. 11, 1950	June 25, 1952
*Itasca	V	3,564	Du Page		Jan. 31, 1890	Oct. 17, 1901
Iuka[61]	V	378	Marion		May 10, 1882	July 29, 1882
Ivesdale	V	360	Champaign		Sept. 14, 1872	Mar. 11, 1894
Jacksonville	C	21,690	Morgan	Feb. 3, 1840	Apr. 4, 1887	Apr. 11, 1887
Jeffersonville	V	330	Wayne		Mar. 27, 1907	May 20, 1907
Jerome	V	1,666	Sangamon		Mar. 18, 1939	June 17, 1939
Jerseyville	C	7,420	Jersey	Feb. 14, 1855	Apr. 17, 1883	May 31, 1883
Jewett	V	238	Cumberland		Oct. 22, 1901	Nov. 2, 1901
Johnsonville	V	96	Wayne		Nov. 27, 1897	Oct. 19, 1091
Johnston City	C	3,891	Williamson		Feb. 24, 1905	May 13, 1905
Joliet[62]	C	66,780	Will		Aug. 5, 1876	Aug. 25, 1876
Jonesboro	C	1,636	Union		Dec. 14, 1872	Apr. 9, 1873
Joppa	V	578	Massac		Oct. 28, 1901	Jan. 24, 1902
Joy	V	503	Mercer		June 15, 1901	July 25, 1901
Junction	V	238	Gallatin		Nov. 11, 1909	May 20, 1910
Junction City	V	315	Marion		May 6, 1912	July 22, 1912
*Justice	V	2,803	Cook		Oct. 17, 1911	Nov. 26, 1911
Kampsville	V	453	Calhoun		Oct. 8, 1887	Nov. 21, 1887
Kane[63]	V	469	Greene	Mar. 15, 1869	May 7, 1883	July 24, 1883
Kangley	V	267	La Salle		Feb. 21, 1888	Mar. 29, 1888
Kankakee	C	27,666	Kankakee	Feb. 15, 1855	Mar. 15, 1892	Apr. 26, 1892
Kansas[64]	V	815	Edgar	Feb. 24, 1859	Oct. 12, 1872	Aug. 23, 1873
Kappa	V	119	Woodford		July 7, 1884	Sept. 9, 1884
Karnak	V	667	Pulaski		Jan. 11, 1915	Oct. 17, 1923
Kaskaskia	V	97	Randolph	Jan. 6, 1818	May 26, 1873	Aug. 14, 1903
Keenes	V	114	Wayne		June 16, 1958	Aug. 7, 1958

Name	Class	Population	County			
Keensburg	V	263	Wabash		June 15, 1906	May 12, 1908
Keithsburg	C	963	Mercer	Feb. 16, 1857	Mar. 18, 1889	June 6, 1889
Kell	V	194	Marion		Mar. 23, 1925	Oct. 19, 1925
Kempton	V	252	Ford		Jan. 2, 1889	Sept. 20, 1901
Kenilworth	V	2,959	Cook		Feb. 4, 1896	May 6, 1896
Kenney	V	400	De Witt	Feb. 14, 1855	Nov. 20, 1875	Aug. 14, 1902
Kewanee[65]	C	16,324	Henry		Jan. 4, 1897	Jan. 18, 1897
Keysport	V	412	Clinton		Sept. 8, 1887	Feb. 20, 1888
Kilbourne	V	352	Mason		Nov. 24, 1903	Jan. 20, 1904
Kildeer	V	173	Lake		Mar. 25, 1958	Sept. 16, 1960
Kincaid	V	1,544	Christian		Jan. 5, 1915	Jan. 26, 1934
Kinderhook	V	276	Pike	Mar. 29, 1869	Jan. 25, 1896	Feb. 14, 1896
Kingston	V	406	De Kalb		Feb. 8, 1866	May 7, 1886
Kingston Mines	V	375	Peoria		Dec. 12, 1894	Nov. 9, 1901
Kinmundy	C	813	Marion	Feb. 25, 1867	Apr. 6, 1875	Apr. 23, 1875
Kinsman	V	134	Grundy		Mar. 26, 1886	June 22, 1886
Kirkland	V	928	De Kalb		Aug. 16, 1882	Oct. 28, 1882
Kirkwood[66]	V	771	Warren		May 22, 1874	May 28, 1874
Knoxville[67]	C	2,560	Knox	Dec. 22, 1832	Mar. 10, 1873	Mar. 29, 1873
Lacon[68]	C	2,175	Marshall	Dec. 10, 1839	Mar. 28, 1873	May 27, 1873
Ladd	V	1,255	Bureau		June 10, 1890	Sept. 8, 1890
La Fayette	V	269	Stark		Sept. 18, 1872	Dec. 7, 1872
*La Grange	V	15,285	Cook		June 11, 1879	Aug. 20, 1879
*La Grange Park	V	13,793	Cook		July 14, 1892	June 21, 1894
La Harpe	C	1,322	Hancock	Feb. 24, 1859		
Lake Barrington	V	172	Lake		Nov. 2, 1959	Jan. 12, 1960
*Lake Bluff	V	3,494	Lake		Oct. 26, 1895	Nov. 8, 1895
*Lake Forest	C	10,687	Lake	Feb. 21, 1861		
Lake in the Hills	V	2,046	McHenry		Nov. 29, 1952	Apr. 20, 1953
Lakemoor	V	736	McHenry		Nov. 27, 1951	July 8, 1952
Lake Villa	V	903	Lake		Feb. 26, 1901	Oct. 26, 1879
Lakewood	V	635	McHenry		July 10, 1933	June 6, 1934
*Lake Zurich	V	3,458	Lake		Sept. 29, 1896	Oct. 20, 1896
La Moille[69]	V	655	Bureau	Feb. 25, 1867	Oct. 20, 1888	Dec. 4, 1888
Lanark	C	1,473	Carroll	Feb. 28, 1867	May 2, 1876	July 7, 1876

Table—continued

Municipality	City, town, or village	Population 1960 census	County	Date incorporation laws in force — Prior to July 1, 1872	Since July 1, 1872	Date certificate of incorporation issued by secretary of state
*Lansing	V	18,098	Cook		Mar. 4, 1893	Mar. 30, 1893
La Prairie	T	115	Adams	Apr. 15, 1869		
La Rose	V	192	Marshall		May 16, 1887	June 29, 1894
La Salle	C	11,897	La Salle	June 23, 1852	May 22, 1876	Mar. 1, 1877
Latham	V	389	Logan		July 22, 1884	July 19, 1894
Lawrenceville	C	5,492	Lawrence	Feb. 12, 1835	June 2, 1894	Mar. 26, 1895
Leaf River	C	546	Ogle		Aug. 17, 1882	Nov. 10, 1882
Lebanon	C	2,863	St. Clair	Feb. 16, 1857	Apr. 13, 1874	July 28, 1874
Lee	V	228	Lee and De Kalb		June 23, 1874	Nov. 4, 1874
Leland[70]	V	642	La Salle		Oct. 30, 1872	Nov. 30, 1872
Leland Grove	C	1,731	Sangamon		Apr. 21, 1950	July 13, 1950
*Lemont	V	3,397	Cook		June 9, 1873	Feb. 19, 1874
Lena	T	1,552	Stephenson	Mar. 30, 1869		
Lenzburg	V	420	St. Clair		Jan. 5, 1884	May 2, 1884
Leonore	V	195	La Salle		Apr. 20, 1891	June 15, 1891
Lerna	V	296	Coles		Feb. 5, 1890	May 6, 1890
*Le Roy	C	2,088	McLean	Feb. 18, 1857	July 16, 1874	Oct. 5, 1874
Lewistown	C	2,603	Fulton	Feb. 16, 1857	Apr. 3, 1882	Apr. 20, 1882
Lexington	C	1,244	McLean	Feb. 25, 1867	Apr. 21, 1890	May 14, 1890
Liberty	V		Adams		Nov. 25, 1959	July 11, 1960
*Libertyville	V	8,560	Lake	Feb. 28, 1847	Mar. 28, 1882	July 6, 1894
Lima	V	160	Adams	Feb. 18, 1857	Sept. 28, 1886	Apr. 4, 1887
*Lincoln[71]	C	16,890	Logan		Mar. 8, 1886	May 21, 1886
*Lincolnshire	V	555	Lake		Aug. 5, 1957	Dec. 2, 1957
*Lincolnwood[72]	V	11,744	Cook		Sept. 29, 1911	Dec. 11, 1935
*Lindenhurst	V	1,259	Lake		Oct. 1, 1956	Jan. 16, 1957
Lisbon	V	234	Kendall		July 5, 1894	Aug. 21, 1894
*Lisle	V	4,219	Du Page		June 26, 1956	Sept. 7, 1956
Litchfield	C	7,330	Montgomery	Feb. 16, 1859	Feb. 29, 1896	May 6, 1896
Littleton	V	176	Schuyler		May 15, 1911	June 23, 1911

Name	Class	Population	County			
Little York	V	329	Warren		May 11, 1894	Sept. 8, 1894
Liverpool	V	184	Fulton		June 18, 1956	Apr. 26, 1957
Livingston	V	964	Madison		Nov. 15, 1905	Feb. 7, 1906
Loami	C	450	Sangamon		July 29, 1875	Oct. 25, 1875
*Lockport	C	7,560	Will	Feb. 12, 1853	Apr. 21, 1904	July 26, 1904
Loda	V	585	Iroquois	Mar. 13, 1869	Sept. 2, 1873	Nov. 14, 1905
Lomax	V	535	Henderson		Nov. 4, 1913	Jan. 28, 1914
*Lombard	V	22,561	Du Page	Mar. 29, 1869	Aug. 25, 1903	Oct. 13, 1903
London Mills	V	170	Fulton		Nov. 27, 1883	Sept. 10, 1894
Long Grove	V	640	Lake		Dec. 31, 1956	Mar. 27, 1957
Long Point	V	307	Livingston		July 27, 1899	Oct. 2, 1901
Long View	V	270	Champaign		July 1, 1903	Aug. 11, 1903
Loraine	V	303	Adams		June 20, 1881	Oct. 8, 1901
Lostant[73]	V	460	La Salle	Feb. 16, 1865	Sept. 4, 1873	Nov. 16, 1874
Louisville	V	906	Clay	Mar. 1, 1867	Aug. 25, 1882	May 16, 1883
*Loves Park	C	9,086	Winnebago		Apr. 30, 1947	June 7, 1947
Lovington	V	1,200	Moultrie		May 24, 1873	June 29, 1894
Ludlow	V	460	Champaign		June 1, 1876	Aug. 25, 1876
Lyndon	V	677	Whiteside		Mar. 3, 1874	July 20, 1874
Lynnville	V	97	Morgan	Feb. 27, 1837	June 6, 1895	Oct. 26, 1895
Lynwood	V	255	Cook		Dec. 23, 1959	Mar. 7, 1960
*Lyons	V	9,936	Cook		July 18, 1888	Oct. 13, 1888
Macedonia	V	96	Franklin		Mar. 3, 1894	May 18, 1894
Mackinaw	V	1,163	Tazewell		Mar. 19, 1897	June 9, 1897
*Macomb	C	12,135	McDonough	Jan. 31, 1840	Apr. 18, 1882	June 23, 1882
Macon	C	1,229	Macon	Jan. 27, 1841	Apr. 17, 1879	June 24, 1879
Madison	C	6,861	Madison	Apr. 15, 1869	Nov. 2, 1891	July 10, 1894
Magnolia	V	245	Putnam	Jan. 15, 1859		Oct. 27, 1894
Mahomet	V	1,367	Champaign		Aug. 9, 1872	Feb. 3, 1873
Makanda	V	164	Jackson		Feb. 7, 1888	May 7, 1888
Malden[74]	V	258	Bureau		Apr. 22, 1882	June 19, 1890
Malta	V	782	De Kalb	Mar. 29, 1869	May 1, 1913	May 26, 1913
Manchester	V	282	Scott	Feb. 21, 1861	Mar. 25, 1904	May 31, 1904
Manhattan	V	1,117	Will		Dec. 20, 1886	July 19, 1890
Manito	V	1,093	Mason		Apr. 20, 1876	July 19, 1877

Table—continued

Municipality	City, town, or village	Population 1960 census	County	Date incorporation laws in force — Prior to July 1, 1872	Since July 1, 1872	Date certificate of incorporation issued by secretary of state
Manlius	V	374	Bureau		June 21, 1905	July 26, 1905
*Mansfield	V	743	Piatt		Mar. 3, 1876	May 9, 1876
*Manteno	V	2,225	Kankakee		Apr. 20, 1878	July 8, 1878
Maple Park[75]	V	592	Kane		July 18, 1872	Nov. 6, 1901
Mapleton	V	309	Peoria		Apr. 2, 1959	July 1, 1959
Maquon	V	386	Knox		Apr. 19, 1873	July 30, 1894
Marengo	C	3,568	McHenry	Feb. 9, 1857	Aug. 14, 1893	Sept. 25, 1893
Marietta	V	201	Fulton		Jan. 4, 1909	Feb. 6, 1909
Marine	V	813	Madison	Mar. 8, 1867	Apr. 23, 1888	July 20, 1888
Marion	C	11,274	Williamson	Feb. 24, 1841	Apr. 10, 1874	Sept. 8, 1905
Marissa	V	1,722	St. Clair		May 26, 1882	Feb. 15, 1883
Mark	V	445	Putnam		Dec. 4, 1905	Feb. 26, 1906
*Markham	V	11,704	Cook		Oct. 23, 1925	Dec. 9, 1925
Maroa	C	1,235	Macon	Mar. 7, 1867	Apr. 8, 1889	July 13, 1889
Marquette Heights	C	2,517	Tazewell		June 27, 1956	Sept. 6, 1956
Marseilles	C	4,347	La Salle	Feb. 21, 1861	Apr. 25, 1891	July 17, 1891
Marshall	C	3,270	Clark	Feb. 10, 1853	Aug. 6, 1872	May 14, 1873
Martinsville	C	1,351	Clark		June 13, 1905	Sept. 12, 1905
Martinton	V	314	Iroquois		Sept. 7, 1875	Apr. 28, 1876
Maryville	V	675	Madison		June 4, 1902	July 21, 1902
*Mascoutah[76]	C	3,625	St. Clair	Feb. 16, 1839	Apr. 2, 1883	June 11, 1883
Mason	T	332	Effingham	Feb. 15, 1865		
Mason City	C	2,160	Mason	Mar. 4, 1869	Aug. 5, 1872	Aug. 23, 1872
Mathersville	V	612	Mercer		Mar. 27, 1911	June 9, 1911
*Matteson	V	3,225	Cook		Mar. 20, 1889	July 20, 1894
Mattoon	C	19,088	Coles	Feb. 22, 1859	Feb. 25, 1879	May 2, 1879
Maunie	V	363	White		July 22, 1901	Sept. 3, 1901
Mayestown	V	158	Monroe		Mar. 28, 1904	June 15, 1904
*Maywood	V	27,330	Cook		Oct. 31, 1881	Apr. 3, 1882
Mazon	V	683	Grundy		Apr. 30, 1895	May 28, 1895

Name	Class	No.	County			
McCook	V	441	Cook		Apr. 12, 1926	May 26, 1926
McCullom Lake	V	759	McHenry		Apr. 7, 1955	May 31, 1955
McHenry	C	3,336	McHenry	Feb. 15, 1855	June 4, 1923	May 12, 1924
McLean	C	758	McLean		Jan. 23, 1873	Feb. 22, 1873
McLeansboro	C	2,951	Hamilton	Jan. 31, 1840	Apr. 20, 1886	June 11, 1886
McNabb	V	176	Putnam		June 23, 1959	Aug. 4, 1959
Mechanicsburg	V	428	Sangamon	Mar. 26, 1869	Mar. 4, 1907	June 29, 1907
Media	V	165	Henderson		Jan. 1, 1902	Mar. 5, 1902
Medora	V	447	Macoupin		Jan. 10, 1874	Nov. 3, 1874
Melrose Park[77]	V	22,291	Cook		Mar. 13, 1893	May 21, 1894
Melvin	V	559	Ford		Mar. 12, 1889	July 10, 1894
Mendon[78]	V	784	Adams	Feb. 12, 1839	June 9, 1891	July 15, 1891
*Mendota	C	6,154	La Salle	Feb. 19, 1859	Mar. 5, 1883	May 7, 1883
Menominee	V	191	JoDaviess		May 9, 1935	May 1, 1941
Meredosia	V	1,034	Morgan	Feb. 25, 1867	Mar. 7, 1906	Mar. 15, 1906
*Merrionette Park	V	2,354	Cook		Feb. 18, 1947	May 17, 1947
Metamora[79]	V	1,808	Woodford	Feb. 21, 1845	Apr. 26, 1875	Mar. 17, 1876
Metcalf	V	278	Edgar		Feb. 16, 1885	Sept. 1, 1901
Metropolis	C	7,339	Massac	Feb. 18, 1859	Mar. 6, 1873	June 6, 1873
*Mettawa	V	126	Lake		Jan. 25, 1960	Apr. 20, 1960
Middletown	V	543	Logan		Nov. 17, 1900	Feb. 15, 1901
*Midlothian	V	6,605	Cook		Mar. 22, 1927	May 2, 1927
*Milan[80]	V	3,065	Rock Island		Mar. 13, 1893	May 13, 1893
Milford	V	1,699	Iroquois		Mar. 16, 1874	Oct. 12, 1901
Mill Creek	V	102	Union		Apr. 24, 1898	June 14, 1898
Milledgeville	V	1,208	Carroll		May 24, 1887	July 15, 1887
Millington	V	309	Kendall		May 3, 1893	Jan. 3, 1894
Mill Shoals	V	322	White		Mar. 7, 1896	May 4, 1896
Millstadt[81]	V	1,830	St. Clair	Feb. 21, 1861	Jan. 16, 1878	July 19, 1894
Milton	V	309	Pike		Oct. 28, 1874	May 17, 1877
Mineral	V	330	Bureau		Aug. 16, 1899	Oct. 5, 1901
Minier	V	847	Tazewell		July 17, 1872	Oct. 11, 1872
Minonk	C	2,001	Woodford	Mar. 7, 1867	Sept. 20, 1872	Nov. 19, 1872
Minooka	V	539	Grundy	Mar. 27, 1869		
Modesto	V	228	Macoupin		Mar. 16, 1896	June 11, 1896
*Mokena	V	1,332	Will		May 24, 1880	May 22, 1890

Table—continued

Municipality	City, town, or village	Population 1960 census	County	Date incorporation laws in force Prior to July 1, 1872	Since July 1, 1872	Date certificate of incorporation issued by secretary of state
Moline	C	42,705	Rock Island	Feb. 14, 1855	Aug. 6, 1872	Nov. 15, 1872
Momence	C	2,949	Kankakee		Apr. 30, 1874	Dec. 13, 1910
Monee	V	646	Will		Nov. 9, 1874	Mar. 5, 1875
Monmouth	C	10,372	Warren	June 21, 1852	Apr. 3, 1882	July 3, 1882
Monsanto	V	324	St. Clair		Aug. 14, 1926	Oct. 26, 1926
*Montgomery	V	2,122	Kane		Sept. 26, 1894	Dec. 20, 1894
*Monticello	C	3,219	Piatt	Jan. 27, 1841	Nov. 4, 1872	Jan. 23, 1873
Montrose	V	320	Effingham		Mar. 21, 1892	July 24, 1894
Morris	C	7,935	Grundy	Feb. 12, 1853	Dec. 18, 1877	Mar. 13, 1878
Morrison	C	4,159	Whiteside	Feb. 27, 1867	Nov. 12, 1872	Jan. 20, 1873
Morrisonville	V	1,129	Christian		Oct. 19, 1872	Sept. 6, 1901
*Morton	V	5,325	Tazewell		Aug. 18, 1877	Nov. 13, 1877
*Morton Grove	V	20,533	Cook		Sept. 24, 1895	Dec. 24, 1895
Mound City[82]	C	1,669	Pulaski	Jan. 29, 1857	May 14, 1873	Nov. 29, 1873
Mound Station	V	204	Brown		Dec. 10, 1901	Dec. 23, 1901
Mounds[83]	C	1,835	Pulaski		July 11, 1908	Aug. 18, 1908
Mount Auburn	V	502	Christian		Feb. 4, 1878	Apr. 18, 1878
Mount Carmel	C	8,594	Wabash	Jan. 10, 1825	May 7, 1877	May 21, 1877
Mount Carroll	C	2,056	Carroll	Feb. 25, 1867	June 23, 1913	Sept. 2, 1913
Mount Clare	V	320	Macoupin		Apr. 16, 1915	May 28, 1934
Mount Erie	V	134	Wayne		Mar. 26, 1895	May 10, 1895
Mount Morris	V	3,075	Ogle	Feb. 13, 1857	Mar. 27, 1875	June 16, 1875
Mount Olive	C	2,295	Macoupin		Feb. 19, 1917	May 15, 1917
*Mount Prospect	V	18,906	Cook		Feb. 3, 1917	May 4, 1917
Mount Pulaski	C	1,689	Logan		Jan. 4, 1893	Mar. 7, 1893
Mount Sterling	C	2,262	Brown	Feb. 10, 1837	Mar. 13, 1875	Apr. 22, 1875
Mount Vernon	C	15,566	Jefferson	Feb. 10, 1837	Aug. 5, 1872	Aug. 24, 1872
Mount Zion	V	925	Macon		Apr. 13, 1881	Aug. 4, 1881
Moweaqua	V	1,614	Shelby		May 26, 1877	June 15, 1877
Muddy	V	95	Saline		Dec. 14, 1955	Feb. 27, 1956

Name		Population	County			
Mulberry Grove[84]	V	745	Bond	Feb. 7, 1857	Apr. 8, 1881	May 5, 1883
Muncie	V	195	Vermilion		Oct. 3, 1898	Jan. 14, 1899
*Mundelein[85]	V	10,526	Lake		July 12, 1909	Apr. 8, 1925
*Murphysboro	C	8,673	Jackson	Mar. 5, 1867	June 28, 1875	Sept. 22, 1875
Murrayville	V	442	Morgan	Feb. 22, 1867	Mar. 17, 1914	June 8, 1914
*Naperville	C	12,933	Du Page	Feb. 7, 1857	Mar. 17, 1890	Mar. 24, 1890
Naplate	V	738	La Salle		Dec. 9, 1947	Dec. 27, 1947
*Nashville	C	2,606	Washington	Feb. 12, 1853	Aug. 7, 1872	Aug. 26, 1873
Nason	C	188	Jefferson		Dec. 12, 1924	Feb. 17, 1925
National City	V	117	St. Clair		July 19, 1907	Sept. 5, 1907
Nauvoo	C	1,039	Hancock	Feb. 1, 1841	Apr. 10, 1899	July 11, 1899
Nebo	V	441	Pike		Aug. 3, 1885	June 29, 1894
Nelson	V	283	Lee		Aug. 1, 1923	Aug. 20, 1923
Neoga	C	1,145	Cumberland		Apr. 5, 1930	Aug. 4, 1930
Neponset	V	495	Bureau	Feb. 25, 1867	Oct. 9, 1882	Jan. 16, 1883
Newark[86]	V	489	Kendall	Feb. 28, 1843	Feb. 13, 1875	May 1, 1875
New Athens[87]	V	1,923	St. Clair	Mar. 29, 1869	Apr. 25, 1881	May 21, 1881
New Baden[88]	V	1,464	Clinton	Feb. 28, 1867	May 21, 1884	May 2, 1904
New Bedford	V	166	Bureau		Nov. 7, 1950	Jan. 31, 1951
New Berlin	V	627	Sangamon		Feb. 2, 1895	Sept. 28, 1901
New Boston	C	726	Mercer	Feb. 21, 1859	July 9, 1879	Nov. 10, 1879
New Burnside	T	227	Johnson	Mar. 31, 1869		
New Canton	V	449	Pike		Dec. 16, 1874	Sept. 18, 1901
New Douglas	V	367	Madison		Nov. 10, 1890	Feb. 4, 1891
New Grand Chain	V	282	Pulaski		Mar. 27, 1873	Aug. 7, 1894
New Haven	V	642	Gallatin	Feb. 15, 1839	June 7, 1897	Aug. 2, 1897
New Holland	V	314	Logan		May 25, 1946	Oct. 4, 1946
*New Lenox	C	1,750	Will		Jan. 15, 1895	Feb. 20, 1895
Newman	C	1,097	Douglas		June 9, 1877	Sept. 11, 1894
New Minden	V	166	Washington	Feb. 15, 1831		
Newton	C	2,901	Jasper		Aug. 6, 1887	Sept. 3, 1887
Niantic	V	629	Macon		Aug. 23, 1894	Nov. 15, 1894
*Niles	V	20,393	Cook		Aug. 24, 1899	Sept. 26, 1901
Nilwood	T	274	Macoupin	Mar. 9, 1867		
Noble	V	761	Richland	Mar. 27, 1869	Sept. 20, 1873	June 29, 1909

Table—continued

Municipality	City, town, or village	Population 1960 census	County	Prior to July 1, 1872	Since July 1, 1872	Date certificate of incorporation issued by secretary of state
Nokomis	C	2,476	Montgomery	Mar. 9, 1867	Feb. 6, 1893	Apr. 28, 1893
Nora	V	229	JoDaviess	Feb. 25, 1867	May 7, 1883	Sept. 25, 1901
*Normal[89]	T	13,357	McLean			
*Norridge	V	14,087	Cook		Dec. 4, 1948	Mar. 29, 1949
Norris	V	307	Fulton		Aug. 19, 1908	Oct. 29, 1908
Norris City	V	1,243	White		Nov. 6, 1901	Dec. 4, 1901
*North Aurora	V	2,088	Kane		Mar. 13, 1905	Oct. 13, 1905
North Barrington	V	282	Lake		Nov. 2, 1959	July 15, 1960
North Chicago	C	20,517	Lake		Feb. 18, 1890	Apr. 12, 1909
North Chillicothe	V	2,259	Peoria		May 2, 1890	Sept. 10, 1890
North City	V	362	Franklin		Aug. 3, 1915	Dec. 3, 1915
North Henderson	V	210	Mercer		Apr. 22, 1957	Aug. 5, 1957
North Pekin	V	2,025	Tazewell		Apr. 5, 1947	July 19, 1949
*North Riverside	V	7,989	Cook		July 30, 1923	Dec. 1, 1923
North Utica	V	1,014	La Salle	Mar. 25, 1869	May 8, 1885	Aug. 24, 1885
*Northbrook[90]	V	11,635	Cook		Jan. 8, 1923	Jan. 15, 1923
Northfield[91]	V	4,005	Cook		Oct. 26, 1926	July 9, 1927
*Northlake	C	12,318	Cook		Apr. 23, 1949	July 19, 1949
Norwood	V	626	Peoria		Oct. 17, 1956	Dec. 27, 1956
*Oakbrook	V	324	Du Page		Feb. 21, 1958	May 12, 1958
Oakbrook Terrace[92]	C	1,121	Du Page		June 24, 1958	Nov. 24, 1958
Oakford	V	301	Menard		Mar. 22, 1892	June 1, 1892
*Oak Forest	V	3,724	Cook		May 10, 1947	Aug. 20, 1947
Oak Grove[93]	V	888	Rock Island		Dec. 8, 1955	Feb. 7, 1956
Oak Grove Park	V	237	Woodford		May 26, 1954	July 26, 1954
Oakland[94]	C	939	Coles	Feb. 9, 1855	Apr. 24, 1896	June 16, 1896
*Oak Lawn	V	27,471	Cook		Feb. 4, 1909	May 13, 1909
Oak Park	V	61,093	Cook		Nov. 13, 1901	Mar. 18, 1902
Oakwood	V	861	Vermilion		Aug. 3, 1903	Nov. 4, 1903

Municipality	Class	Population	County			
Oakwood Hills	V	1,817	McHenry		Aug. 11, 1958	Feb. 24, 1961
Oblong	V	257	Crawford	Feb. 25, 1867	Apr. 14, 1883	June 15, 1883
Oconee	V	936	Shelby	Feb. 1, 1869	Mar. 27, 1906	Apr. 9, 1906
Odell	V	1,242	Livingston	Feb. 16, 1865	Aug. 5, 1872	Sept. 25, 1872
Odin	C	4,018	Marion	Feb. 15, 1865	Mar. 18, 1874	Apr. 9, 1874
*O'Fallon	V	515	St. Clair		Mar. 16, 1905	Mar. 24, 1905
Ogden	C	4,215	Champaign		June 18, 1883	June 26, 1894
Oglesby[95]	V	489	La Salle		Dec. 23, 1902	Aug. 5, 1913
Ohio	V	215	Bureau		Dec. 28, 1876	Mar. 9, 1877
Ohlman	V	931	Montgomery		Nov. 18, 1957	Feb. 7, 1958
Okawville	V	217	Washington		Dec. 22, 1894	Jan. 17, 1895
Old Marissa	V	149	St. Clair		Mar. 27, 1893	May 18, 1893
Old Mill Creek[96]	V	150	Lake		Oct. 20, 1958	Jan. 9, 1959
Old Ripley	V	433	Bond		June 25, 1906	Sept. 4, 1906
Old Shawneetown	V	475	Gallatin	Feb. 24, 1841	July 2, 1956	Sept. 6, 1956
Olmstead	C		Pulaski		Sept. 29, 1888	Dec. 27, 1888
Olney	V	8,780	Richland		Feb. 15, 1911	Apr. 29, 1911
*Olympia Fields	V	1,503	Cook		Aug. 5, 1927	Oct. 5, 1927
Omaha	V	312	Gallatin	Mar. 9, 1867	Mar. 30, 1888	July 9, 1890
Onarga	C	1,397	Iroquois	Mar. 31, 1869	Mar. 30, 1876	Apr. 10, 1876
Oneida	V	672	Knox	Feb. 11, 1857		May 5, 1902
Oquawka	V	1,090	Henderson	Mar. 7, 1867	Aug. 3, 1880	May 29, 1873
Orangeville	V	491	Stephenson		Mar. 22, 1873	Mar. 2, 1954
Oreana	V	464	Macon		July 21, 1952	July 9, 1873
Oregon[97]	C	3,732	Ogle	Feb. 21, 1843	Mar. 29, 1873	Sept. 11, 1917
Orient	C	588	Franklin		Apr. 14, 1917	Aug. 27, 1894
Orion	V	1,269	Henry		Aug. 19, 1873	Aug. 15, 1894
*Orland Park	V	2,592	Cook		May 31, 1892	June 8, 1881
Oswego	V	1,510	Kendall	Feb. 18, 1857	Apr. 20, 1881	May 13, 1882
Ottawa	C	19,408	La Salle	July 21, 1837	Mar. 20, 1882	May 31, 1902
Otterville	T	140	Jersey	Mar. 7, 1867		Jan. 13, 1948
Owaneco	V	290	Christian		Jan. 20, 1902	Oct. 2, 1901
*Palatine	V	11,504	Cook	Apr. 25, 1869	Mar. 21, 1887	Jan. 13, 1948
Palestine	T	1,564	Crawford	Feb. 15, 1855		Mar. 21, 1887
Palmer	V	265	Christian		Feb. 25, 1873	Oct. 2, 1901

Table—continued

Municipality	City, town, or village	Population 1960 census	County	Date incorporation laws in force — Prior to July 1, 1872	Date incorporation laws in force — Since July 1, 1872	Date certificate of incorporation issued by secretary of state
Palmyra	V	811	Macoupin		July 15, 1881	Jan. 18, 1882
*Palos Heights	C	3,775	Cook		Apr. 16, 1959	July 22, 1959
Palos Hills	C	3,766	Cook		Jan. 26, 1959	Feb. 25, 1959
Palos Park	V	2,169	Cook		Oct. 31, 1914	Dec. 22, 1923
Pana	C	6,432	Christian	Feb. 16, 1857	May 21, 1877	July 19, 1877
Panama	V	487	Montgomery		Nov. 16, 1906	Dec. 29, 1906
Panola	V	43	Woodford	Feb. 28, 1867	May 15, 1875	June 18, 1902
Papineau	V	169	Iroquois		Oct. 20, 1874	Aug. 14, 1894
Paris	C	9,823	Edgar	Feb. 10, 1853	Mar. 18, 1873	Apr. 2, 1873
*Park City	C	253	Lake		Jan. 27, 1958	Mar. 24, 1958
Parkersburg	V		Richland		Feb. 8, 1927	May 3, 1927
*Park Forest	V	29,993	Cook		Feb. 1, 1949	May 24, 1949
*Park Ridge	C	32,659	Cook		Apr. 25, 1910	Aug. 3, 1910
Patoka	V	601	Marion	Apr. 15, 1869	June 15, 1885	Sept. 12, 1885
Pawnee	V	1,517	Sangamon		Dec. 12, 1891	June 26, 1894
Paw Paw	V	725	Lee	Feb. 16, 1865	June 7, 1882	Aug. 21, 1894
Paxton	C	4,370	Ford	Apr. 15, 1869	Aug. 6, 1872	Nov. 11, 1872
Payson	V	502	Adams		Apr. 11, 1903	June 29, 1903
Pearl	V	348	Pike		Sept. 1881	Oct. 6, 1894
Pearl City[98]	V	488	Stephenson	Mar. 4, 1869	June 4, 1891	Mar. 21, 1893
Pecatonica[99]	V	1,659	Winnebago	Mar. 2, 1839	May 9, 1881	Sept. 14, 1901
*Pekin	C	28,146	Tazewell	Feb. 26, 1839	Apr. 20, 1874	Aug. 10, 1874
Peoria	C	103,162	Peoria		Oct. 20, 1891	Jan. 13, 1892
Peoria Heights	V	7,064	Peoria		Nov. 21, 1898	Nov. 10, 1901
Peotone	V	1,788	Will	Mar. 25, 1869	Feb. 25, 1879	Mar. 7, 1879
Percy	V	810	Randolph		Apr. 14, 1887	Aug. 1, 1887
Perry	V	442	Pike		Dec. 12, 1899	Oct. 10, 1901
*Peru	C	10,460	La Salle	Feb. 25, 1845	Mar. 15, 1890	May 13, 1890
Pesotum	V	468	Champaign		Feb. 24, 1906	May 24, 1906
Petersburg	C	2,359	Menard	Feb. 23, 1841	Apr. 4, 1882	June 14, 1882

Phillipstown[100]	V	69	White		June 29, 1874	Aug. 8, 1874
Philo	V	740	Champaign	Jan. 29, 1840	Apr. 19, 1875	July 10, 1875
Phoenix	V	4,203	Cook		Aug. 29, 1900	Sept. 20, 1900
Pierron[101]	V	451	Bond and Madison		Mar. 24, 1893	Apr. 21, 1893
Pinckneyville	C	3,085	Perry	Feb. 21, 1861	Apr. 17, 1888	June 27, 1888
Pingree Grove	V	173	Kane		Feb. 14, 1907	Apr. 30, 1907
Piper City	V	807	Ford	Mar. 13, 1869	May 23, 1876	Mar. 21, 1877
Pittsburg	V	485	Williamson		Feb. 10, 1909	May 5, 1909
Pittsfield	C	4,089	Pike	Mar. 30, 1869	Mar. 31, 1893	Apr. 25, 1893
Plainfield	V	2,183	Will	Mar. 9, 1869	June 30, 1877	Aug. 13, 1877
Plainville	V	227	Adams		Feb. 19, 1896	May 8, 1896
*Plano	C	3,343	Kendall	Feb. 16, 1865	Dec. 3, 1883	Feb. 2, 1884
Pleasant Hill[102]	V	950	Pike	Mar. 1, 1845	July 3, 1905	July 15, 1905
Pleasant Plains	V	518	Sangamon		Apr. 8, 1876	July 24, 1876
Plymouth	V	781	Hancock	Feb. 15, 1865	June 29, 1876	July 20, 1876
Pocahontas[103]	V	718	Bond	Feb. 25, 1847	Oct. 13, 1882	July 19, 1894
Polo	C	2,551	Ogle	Feb. 16, 1857	June 25, 1877	July 13, 1877
Pontiac	C	8,435	Livingston	Feb. 10, 1857	Aug. 16, 1872	Nov. 12, 1872
Pontoon Beach	V		Madison		Dec. 12, 1962	July 17, 1963
Pontoosuc	V	210	Hancock		Dec. 17, 1901	Sept. 27, 1901
Poplar Grove	V	460	Boone		Apr. 11, 1895	Oct. 17, 1901
Port Byron	V	1,153	Rock Island		Nov. 10, 1876	Jan. 20, 1877
Posen	V	4,517	Cook		Dec. 1, 1900	Sept. 18, 1901
Potomac[104]	V	661	Vermilion		Dec. 19, 1905	Feb. 2, 1906
Prairie City	V	613	McDonough		Dec. 17, 1873	Feb. 21, 1874
Prairie du Rocher	V	679	Randolph		Apr. 7, 1873	July 19, 1894
Princeton	C	6,250	Bureau	Feb. 8, 1849	Jan. 7, 1884	Feb. 8, 1884
Princeville	V	1,281	Peoria	Apr. 15, 1869	Mar. 24, 1874	Apr. 18, 1874
Prophetstown	C	1,802	Whiteside	Feb. 22, 1859	Feb. 6, 1884	Mar. 24, 1884
Pulaski	V	415	Pulaski		Feb. 26, 1898	July 1, 1898
Quincy	C	43,793	Adams	Feb. 21, 1839	Feb. 12, 1895	Aug. 5, 1897
Radom	V	137	Washington		July 12, 1929	Sept. 30, 1929
Rainbow Gardens[105]	V	107	Boone		June 22, 1951	Jan. 4, 1952
Raleigh	V	225	Saline	Feb. 16, 1865	Nov. 23, 1876	June 12, 1935

Table—continued

Municipality	City, town, or village	Population 1960 census	County	Date incorporation laws in force — Prior to July 1, 1872	Date incorporation laws in force — Since July 1, 1872	Date certificate of incorporation issued by secretary of state
Ramsey	V	815	Fayette		Aug. 29, 1877	Jan. 24, 1880
Rankin	V	761	Vermilion		Aug. 17, 1886	July 6, 1894
Ransom	V	415	La Salle		Aug. 1, 1885	Aug. 2, 1886
*Rantoul	V	22,116	Champaign	Mar. 30, 1869	Feb. 19, 1890	Mar. 1, 1890
Rapids City	V	675	Rock Island		Aug. 12, 1875	Nov. 27, 1875
Raritan	V	182	Henderson		May 21, 1959	Aug. 24, 1959
Raymond	V	871	Montgomery		May 6, 1873	July 14, 1873
Red Bud	C	1,942	Randolph	Apr. 25, 1867	Jan. 19, 1875	Mar. 2, 1875
Reddick	V	205	Kankakee and Livingston		Apr. 8, 1902	May 6, 1902
Redmon	V	175	Edgar		Mar. 1, 1899	Sept. 14, 1901
Reynolds	V	494	Rock Island		June 8, 1894	Jan. 22, 1897
Richmond	V	855	McHenry	Feb. 16, 1865	Aug. 5, 1872	Nov. 11, 1872
Richton Park	V	933	Cook		June 8, 1926	Sept. 1, 1926
Richview[106]	V	255	Washington	Feb. 9, 1855	June 3, 1873	July 28, 1873
Ridge Farm	V	894	Vermilion		Mar. 24, 1874	July 30, 1894
Ridgway	V	1,055	Gallatin		Jan. 4, 1886	Sept. 25, 1901
Ridott	V	221	Stephenson		Apr. 18, 1874	Aug. 15, 1874
Rio	V	177	Knox		Apr. 14, 1958	July 11, 1958
Ripley[107]	V	167	Brown	July 20, 1837	Apr. 10, 1874	Apr. 16, 1902
*Riverdale	V	12,008	Cook		Dec. 28, 1892	Mar. 30, 1893
River Forest	V	12,695	Cook		Sept. 24, 1880	June 26, 1894
River Grove	V	8,464	Cook		Oct. 6, 1888	Jan. 7, 1889
Riverside	V	9,750	Cook		July 10, 1875	Oct. 8, 1875
Riverton[108]	V	1,536	Sangamon		Aug. 16, 1873	Oct. 25, 1901
*Riverwoods	V	96	Lake		Dec. 14, 1959	Apr. 20, 1960
Roanoke	V	1,821	Woodford		July 10, 1874	June 29, 1894
Robbins	V	7,511	Cook		Dec. 14, 1917	Feb. 21, 1918
Roberts	V	504	Ford		Aug. 14, 1886	Dec. 13, 1886
Robinson	C	7,226	Crawford		Apr. 20, 1886	Aug. 27, 1886

Town	Population		County			
*Rochelle[109]	7,008	C	Ogle		Sept. 27, 1872	Jan. 27, 1873
*Rochester	742	V	Sangamon		June 2, 1873	Mar. 12, 1874
Rockbridge	253	V	Greene		Jan. 25, 1881	May 12, 1881
Rock City	202	V	Stephenson		Dec. 9, 1882	Feb. 20, 1883
Rockdale	1,272	V	Will		Feb. 9, 1903	Mar. 19, 1903
Rock Falls	10,261	C	Whiteside		June 21, 1889	July 8, 1889
*Rockford	126,706	C	Winnebago	Jan. 3, 1852	June 8, 1880	July 28, 1880
Rock Island[110]	51,863	C	Rock Island	Feb. 27, 1841	Nov. 4, 1879	Dec. 8, 1879
Rockton[111]	1,833	V	Winnebago	Feb. 26, 1847	July 31, 1872	July 14, 1902
Rockwood[112]	98	V	Randolph	Feb. 16, 1865	Feb. 16, 1891	Aug. 8, 1903
*Rolling Meadows	10,879	C	Cook		May 2, 1955	June 21, 1955
*Romeoville	3,574	V	Will		Jan. 21, 1895	Oct. 2, 1901
Roodhouse	2,352	C	Greene		Mar. 1, 1881	May 17, 1881
Roscoe		V	Winnebago		Mar. 15, 1965	July 13, 1965
Rose Hill	117	V	Jasper		June 19, 1901	Apr. 8, 1902
*Roselle	3,581	V	Du Page		Oct. 7, 1922	Jan. 2, 1934
*Rosemont	978	V	Cook		Jan. 20, 1956	Apr. 11, 1957
Roseville	1,065	V	Warren		May 8, 1875	Aug. 26, 1875
Rosiclare[113]	1,700	C	Hardin		Apr. 19, 1932	Aug. 6, 1932
Rossville	1,470	V	Vermilion		Aug. 3, 1872	May 17, 1894
Round Lake	997	V	Lake		Dec. 14, 1908	July 15, 1909
Round Lake Beach	5,011	V	Lake		Feb. 5, 1937	Jan. 10, 1937
Round Lake Heights	1,099	V	Lake		Apr. 4, 1960	Feb. 12, 1960
*Round Lake Park	2,565	V	Lake		Oct. 18, 1947	May 20, 1947
Roxana	2,090	V	Madison		Apr. 7, 1921	Dec. 20, 1947
Royal	171	V	Champaign		Aug. 10, 1953	Jan. 26, 1934
Royalton	1,225	V	Franklin		June 3, 1907	Oct. 14, 1953
Ruma	138	V	Randolph		May 10, 1879	May 20, 1908
Rushville	2,819	C	Schuyler	Mar. 2, 1839	Apr. 13, 1898	Aug. 28, 1879
Russellville	197	V	Lawrence		Mar. 17, 1875	Apr. 6, 1954
Rutland[114]	509	V	La Salle		Mar. 28, 1876	Oct. 16, 1901
Sadorus	384	V	Champaign		Mar. 18, 1873	July 31, 1874
Sailor Springs	187	V	Clay		Dec. 29, 1892	Feb. 18, 1893
Salem	6,165	C	Marion	Feb. 10, 1837	Feb. 19, 1894	May 18, 1894
Sandoval	1,356	V	Marion	Feb. 18, 1859	Feb. 20, 1873	May 27, 1873

Table—continued

Municipality	City, town, or village	Population 1960 census	County	Date incorporation laws in force		Date certificate of incorporation issued by secretary of state
				Prior to July 1, 1872	Since July 1, 1872	
*Sandwich	C	3,842	De Kalb	Feb. 21, 1859	Nov. 19, 1872	Jan. 6, 1873
San Jose	V	595	Mason		June 12, 1876	July 24, 1894
*Sauk Village	V	4,687	Cook		Mar. 12, 1957	May 8, 1957
Saunemin	V	392	Livingston		June 30, 1883	Aug. 11, 1894
Savanna	C	4,950	Carroll		Apr. 20, 1874	Sept. 29, 1874
Savoy	V	339	Champaign		Apr. 10, 1956	Oct. 8, 1956
Sawyerville	V	362	Macoupin		June 12, 1907	Oct. 21, 1907
Saybrook	V	859	McLean	Mar. 7, 1867	Nov. 4, 1872	Apr. 15, 1873
Scales Mound	V	399	JoDaviess		June 9, 1877	June 27, 1877
*Schaumburg[115]	V	986	Cook		Feb. 27, 1956	Mar. 5, 1956
*Schiller Park	V	5,687	Cook		Jan. 20, 1914	Mar. 21, 1914
Schram City	V	698	Montgomery		May 13, 1907	June 24, 1907
Sciota[116]	V	120	McDonough		May 12, 1885	Sept. 17, 1885
Scottville	V	186	Macoupin	Jan. 31, 1840	May 8, 1885	June 25, 1885
Seaton	V	235	Mercer		Aug. 10, 1907	Sept. 26, 1907
Seatonville	V	363	Bureau		June 10, 1889	July 31, 1889
Secor	V	427	Woodford	Feb. 21, 1867	June 11, 1903	July 7, 1903
Seneca[117]	V	1,719	La Salle	Feb. 16, 1865	Dec. 2, 1874	Jan. 22, 1875
Sesser	C	1,764	Franklin		Oct. 8, 1906	Apr. 18, 1919
Shabbona	V	690	De Kalb		Feb. 20, 1875	June 12, 1875
Shannon	V	766	Carroll	Apr. 15, 1869	Apr. 6, 1876	July 11, 1876
*Shawneetown	C	1,280	Gallatin	Dec. 8, 1814	May 22, 1874	July 29, 1874
Sheffield	V	1,078	Bureau		May 1, 1882	June 5, 1883
Shelbyville	C	4,821	Shelby	Mar. 2, 1839	Mar. 11, 1889	May 31, 1889
Sheldon	V	1,137	Iroquois		Dec. 23, 1901	Jan. 11, 1902
Sheridan	V	704	La Salle		Apr. 28, 1903	June 13, 1903
Sherman	V	209	Sangamon		Dec. 30, 1959	Feb. 24, 1960
Sherrard	V	574	Mercer		Oct. 10, 1896	Oct. 20, 1896
Shiloh	V	701	St. Clair		July 18, 1905	Oct. 13, 1905
Shipman	T	417	Macoupin	Mar. 6, 1867		

Place		Population	County			
*Shorewood	V	358	Will		Nov. 27, 1957	Aug. 25, 1958
Shumway	V	212	Effingham		July 20, 1895	Sept. 20, 1895
Sibley	V	386	Ford		Dec. 10, 1880	Mar. 8, 1881
Sidell	V	614	Vermilion		Oct. 7, 1889	Dec. 30, 1889
Sidney	T	686	Champaign		Aug. 5, 1874	Sept. 5, 1874
Sigel	C	387	Shelby	Mar. 7, 1867		
Silvis	C	3,973	Rock Island		May 22, 1920	Aug. 3, 1920
Simpson	V	89	Johnson		Mar. 2, 1893	July 20, 1901
Sims	V	376	Wayne		Nov. 27, 1909	Mar. 21, 1910
*Skokie[118]	V	59,364	Cook		Feb. 16, 1888	May 18, 1888
*Sleepy Hollow	V	311	Kane		Apr. 29, 1958	May 5, 1958
Smithboro	V	213	Bond		Jan. 15, 1889	Aug. 7, 1894
Smithfield	V	329	Fulton		Mar. 1, 1889	July 28, 1894
Smithton	V	629	St. Clair		Jan. 23, 1878	July 6, 1894
Somonauk	V	899	De Kalb		July 18, 1872	Oct. 1, 1872
Sorento	V	681	Bond		Mar. 11, 1885	Dec. 1, 1894
South Barrington	C		Cook		Dec. 14, 1959	Mar. 1, 1960
South Beloit	V	3,781	Winnebago		June 16, 1917	Oct. 4, 1917
South Chicago Heights	V	4,043	Cook		Mar. 20, 1907	Aug. 17, 1907
*South Elgin[119]	V	2,624	Kane		Apr. 20, 1897	Aug. 3, 1897
*South Holland	V	10,412	Cook		May 12, 1894	May 16, 1894
*South Jacksonville	V	2,340	Morgan		July 7, 1911	Aug. 10, 1911
South Pekin	V	1,007	Tazewell		Apr. 12, 1917	Sept. 23, 1921
South Wilmington	V	730	Grundy		Aug. 22, 1899	Nov. 3, 1899
*Southern View	V	1,485	Sangamon		Mar. 27, 1939	July 17, 1939
Sparland	V	534	Marshall	Mar. 5, 1867	Aug. 17, 1904	Sept. 7, 1904
Sparta	C	3,452	Randolph		Mar. 18, 1873	Jan. 29, 1874
Spaulding	V	178	Sangamon		Nov. 20, 1905	Feb. 14, 1906
Spillertown[120]	V	177	Williamson		Mar. 3, 1900	May 29, 1900
Spring Bay	V	285	Woodford	Feb. 9, 1849	Jan. 18, 1938	Feb. 15, 1939
Springerton	V	232	White		Feb. 25, 1890	Aug. 30, 1894
Springfield	C	83,271	Sangamon	Feb. 3, 1840	Apr. 6, 1882	Apr. 20, 1882
Spring Grove	V	301	McHenry		Sept. 10, 1902	Feb. 9, 1903
Spring Valley	C	5,371	Bureau		Jan. 22, 1886	Mar. 15, 1886
St. Anne	V	1,378	Kankakee		Sept. 28, 1872	Jan. 9, 1873
St. Augustine	V	201	Knox		Aug. 21, 1878	Aug. 13, 1894

Table—continued

Municipality	City, town, or village	Population 1960 census	County	Date incorporation laws in force Prior to July 1, 1872	Since July 1, 1872	Date certificate of incorporation issued by secretary of state
*St. Charles[121]	V	9,269	Kane	Feb. 9, 1839	Oct. 17, 1874	Dec. 21, 1874
St. David	V	862	Fulton		July 25, 1885	Sept. 7, 1894
St. Elmo	C	1,503	Fayette		July 1, 1903	July 13, 1903
St. Francisville[122]	C	1,040	Lawrence	Mar. 3, 1843	July 16, 1907	July 27, 1907
St. Jacob	V	529	Madison		Sept. 8, 1875	July 19, 1894
St. Johns	V	206	Perry		Apr. 6, 1903	Nov. 6, 1912
St. Joseph	V	1,210	Champaign		Feb. 25, 1881	June 13, 1881
St. Libory	V	346	St. Clair		Mar. 19, 1895	Sept. 24, 1901
St. Marie	V	347	Jasper		Feb. 1, 1873	Mar. 28, 1873
St. Peter	V	397	Fayette		Sept. 22, 1909	Nov. 12, 1909
Standard	V	282	Putnam		Oct. 16, 1907	Nov. 25, 1907
Standard City	V	182	Macoupin		June 14, 1920	July 12, 1920
Stanford[123]	V	479	McLean		June 27, 1874	May 10, 1875
Staunton	C	4,228	Macoupin	Feb. 23, 1859	Apr. 22, 1891	June 3, 1891
Steeleville[124]	V	1,569	Randolph	Feb. 17, 1851	July 2, 1888	Aug. 8, 1903
Steger	V	6,432	Cook and Will		Dec. 24, 1896	Feb. 23, 1897
Sterling[125]	C	15,688	Whiteside	Feb. 17, 1841	Mar. 3, 1884	June 2, 1884
Steward	V	264	Lee		Apr. 13, 1903	Sept. 1, 1903
Stewardson	V	656	Shelby		Sept. 30, 1874	Mar. 13, 1895
Stickney	V	6,239	Cook		Nov. 10, 1913	Dec. 29, 1913
Stillman Valley	V	598	Ogle		Dec. 11, 1911	Mar. 3, 1912
Stockton	V	1,800	JoDaviess		Apr. 15, 1890	May 22, 1890
Stonefort[126]	V	349	Saline and Williamson		June 21, 1875	July 24, 1894
*Stone Park	V	3,038	Cook		Apr. 26, 1939	May 12, 1939
Stonington	V	1,076	Christian		June 13, 1885	Dec. 10, 1886
Stoy	V	185	Crawford		Nov. 29, 1907	May 29, 1909
Strasburg	V	467	Shelby		Nov. 15, 1877	Apr. 3, 1878
Strawn	V	152	Livingston		Dec. 1, 1879	Nov. 10, 1880
*Streamwood	V	4,821	Cook		Feb. 11, 1957	Feb. 25, 1957
Streator	C	16,868	La Salle		Apr. 18, 1882	Aug. 16, 1882

Municipality	Class	Population	County			
Stronghurst	V	815	Henderson		May 5, 1894	Aug. 8, 1894
Sublette	V	306	Lee		Dec. 27, 1892	Mar. 20, 1893
*Sugar Grove	C	326	Kane		Apr. 9, 1957	July 2, 1957
Sullivan	C	3,946	Moultrie	Mar. 26, 1869	Dec. 21, 1872	Jan. 10, 1873
Summerfield	V	353	St. Clair	Mar. 29, 1869	July 20, 1872	Oct. 18, 1872
Summit	V	10,374	Cook		June 20, 1890	May 4, 1891
Sumner	C	1,035	Lawrence		Apr. 19, 1887	June 10, 1887
Sunnyside	V	303	McHenry		Apr. 9, 1956	June 29, 1956
Swansea	C	3,018	St. Clair		Apr. 8, 1895	Oct. 21, 1901
Sycamore	C	6,961	De Kalb	Feb. 21, 1859	Sept. 10, 1872	Nov. 18, 1872
Symerton	V	123	Will		Sept. 27, 1904	Jan. 3, 1905
Table Grove[127]	V	500	Fulton		May 17, 1881	June 30, 1881
Tallula	V	547	Menard		May 18, 1873	May 20, 1874
Tamaroa	V	696	Perry	Feb. 5, 1867	June 7, 1875	July 20, 1875
Tamms	V	548	Alexander		July 31, 1905	Sept. 7, 1905
Tampico	V	790	Whiteside		Jan. 16, 1875	Aug. 1, 1894
Taylor Springs	V	550	Montgomery		Sept. 10, 1909	Oct. 26, 1909
*Taylorville	C	8,801	Christian		Apr. 20, 1882	June 22, 1882
Tennessee	V	206	McDonough		Nov. 23, 1872	Mar. 6, 1873
Teutopolis	V	1,140	Effingham	Feb. 27, 1845	May 30, 1874	Aug. 27, 1874
Thawville	V	246	Iroquois		Apr. 16, 1903	July 15, 1905
Thayer	V	649	Sangamon		Oct. 30, 1901	Dec. 17, 1901
Thebes	V	471	Alexander	June 23, 1852	Dec. 5, 1899	Jan. 27, 1900
Third Lake	V	458	Lake		Nov. 23, 1959	Apr. 20, 1960
Thomasboro	V	428	Champaign		Sept. 1, 1900	Nov. 27, 1900
Thompsonville	V	543	Franklin		July 17, 1880	Aug. 26, 1880
Thomson[128]	V		Carroll	Feb. 16, 1865	Mar. 10, 1873	May 26, 1873
*Thornton	V	2,895	Cook		Aug. 4, 1900	Sept. 11, 1900
Tilden	V	808	Randolph		Apr. 14, 1904	Oct. 30, 1923
Tilton	V	2,598	Vermilion		Mar. 17, 1884	Sept. 5, 1884
Time	V	45	Pike		Nov. 9, 1874	Jan. 18, 1875
*Tinley Park	V	6,392	Cook		June 28, 1892	Sept. 19, 1892
Tiskilwa[129]	V	951	Bureau	Apr. 6, 1840	Mar. 31, 1890	Apr. 2, 1890
Toledo[130]	V	998	Cumberland	Feb. 10, 1857		
*Tolono	V	1,539	Champaign		Apr. 1, 1873	July 11, 1894
Toluca	C	1,352	Marshall		Mar. 13, 1894	July 17, 1894

Table—continued

Municipality	City, town, or village	Population 1960 census	County	Date incorporation laws in force Prior to July 1, 1872	Since July 1, 1872	Date certificate of incorporation issued by secretary of state
Tonica	V	750	La Salle	Dec. 26, 1859	Aug. 16, 1873	Oct. 16, 1901
Topeka	T	77	Mason	Apr. 10, 1869	Oct. 11, 1905	Dec. 4, 1905
Torino	V		Will			
Toulon	C	1,213	Stark	Feb. 11, 1859	Apr. 22, 1909	May 12, 1909
Tovey[131]	V	646	Christian		Oct. 15, 1914	Jan. 22, 1934
Towanda	V	586	McLean		Jan. 30, 1875	May 5, 1875
Tower Hill	V	700	Shelby		July 17, 1872	Oct. 4, 1872
Tremont	V	1,558	Tazewell		Aug. 12, 1878	Oct. 5, 1894
*Trenton	C	1,866	Clinton	Feb. 16, 1865	Aug. 22, 1887	Dec. 3, 1887
Troy	C	1,778	Madison	Feb. 18, 1857	Apr. 12, 1892	July 7, 1892
Troy Grove	V	271	La Salle		Apr. 3, 1886	Aug. 2, 1886
Tuscola	C	3,875	Douglas	Feb. 22, 1861	Aug. 12, 1872	Oct. 16, 1872
Ullin	V	577	Pulaski		Feb. 19, 1900	Mar. 9, 1900
Union	V	480	McHenry		Aug. 30, 1897	Nov. 12, 1897
Union Hill	V	80	Kankakee		Dec. 23, 1903	Mar. 1, 1904
Urbain	V	54	Franklin		May 15, 1917	June 23, 1917
Urbana	C	27,294	Champaign	Feb. 20, 1833	Apr. 19, 1873	June 30, 1873
Ursa	V		Adams		Aug. 30, 1963	Feb. 1, 1964
Valier	V	649	Franklin		July 11, 1918	Oct. 15, 1918
Valley City	V	109	Pike		Dec. 8, 1956	Apr. 11, 1956
Valley View	V	1,741	Kane		Jan. 17, 1957	Jan. 29, 1957
Valmeyer	V	709	Monroe		Dec. 4, 1909	Jan. 3, 1910
Vandalia	C	5,537	Fayette	Feb. 15, 1821	Apr. 15, 1884	May 8, 1884
Varna	V	373	Marshall		Oct. 17, 1873	Oct. 9, 1901
Venedy	V	143	Washington		Feb. 22, 1881	July 30, 1894
Venice	C	5,380	Madison		Feb. 5, 1897	Mar. 16, 1897
Vergennes	V	298	Jackson		Feb. 14, 1887	May 29, 1895
Vermilion	V	317	Edgar	Apr. 15, 1869	Apr. 5, 1873	Dec. 20, 1873

Name	Class	Pop.	County			
Vermont	V	903	Fulton	Feb. 13, 1857	Sept. 23, 1879	Jan. 14, 1880
Vernon	V	235	Marion		June 26, 1908	July 27, 1911
*Vernon Hills	V	123	Lake		July 16, 1958	Sept. 22, 1958
Verona	V	192	Grundy		Sept. 9, 1903	Jan. 15, 1904
Versailles	V	427	Brown	Feb. 21, 1861	Feb. 6, 1917	May 1, 1917
Victoria	V	453	Knox		Oct. 18, 1886	Aug. 16, 1894
Vienna	C	1,094	Johnson	Feb. 27, 1837	July 25, 1893	May 25, 1901
Villa Grove	C	2,308	Douglas		Apr. 28, 1913	June 28, 1913
*Villa Park[132]	V	20,391	Du Page		Aug. 8, 1914	Oct. 15, 1917
Viola	V	812	Mercer	Mar. 12, 1870	Apr. 10, 1873	Oct. 24, 1901
Virden	C	3,309	Macoupin	Feb. 16, 1865	Sept. 10, 1872	Nov. 21, 1872
Virginia	C	1,669	Cass	Feb. 19, 1857	Aug. 12, 1872	Sept. 11, 1872
Wadsworth	V	219	Lake		May 9, 1962	Sept. 6, 1962
Waggoner	V	1,192	Montgomery		June 8, 1895	Aug. 1, 1895
Walnut	V	153	Bureau		Oct. 26, 1872	June 23, 1900
Walnut Hill	V	123	Marion		Apr. 26, 1928	June 22, 1928
Walshville	V	394	Montgomery	Oct. 31, 1863	Oct. 31, 1902	Dec. 9, 1902
Waltonville	V	1,394	Jefferson		Mar. 6, 1911	May 17, 1911
Wamac	C	526	Washington		July 25, 1916	Sept. 30, 1916
Wapella	V	1,470	De Witt		Feb. 26, 1876	Apr. 14, 1876
Warren	V	681	JoDaviess	Feb. 24, 1859	July 24, 1876	Aug. 26, 1876
Warrensburg	V	1,938	Macon		July 8, 1880	Nov. 10, 1901
Warsaw	C	1,064	Hancock	Feb. 27, 1837	Mar. 12, 1906	June 5, 1906
Washburn[133]	V	5,919	Woodford	Feb. 7, 1857	July 11, 1873	July 30, 1894
Washington	C	6,601	Tazewell	Feb. 10, 1857	Mar. 2, 1878	May 28, 1878
Washington Park	V		St. Clair		Nov. 27, 1917	Dec. 19, 1923
Wataga	V	570	Knox		Apr. 27, 1874	May 18, 1874
*Waterloo	C	3,739	Monroe	Feb. 12, 1849	Apr. 17, 1888	Mar. 15, 1889
Waterman	V	916	De Kalb		Mar. 17, 1877	Sept. 7, 1877
Watseka	C	5,219	Iroquois	Feb. 19, 1867	Nov. 16, 1872	Feb. 7, 1873
Watson	V	247	Effingham		Dec. 30, 1882	July 16, 1895
*Wauconda	V	3,227	Lake		Aug. 18, 1877	Nov. 9, 1877
Waukegan[134]	C	55,719	Lake	June 15, 1852	Feb. 12, 1890	May 3, 1890
Waverly	C	1,375	Morgan	Feb. 25, 1867	Mar. 21, 1878	June 19, 1878
Wayne	V	373	Du Page		Sept. 15, 1958	Nov. 14, 1958

Table—continued

Municipality	City, town, or village	Population 1960 census	County	Date incorporation laws in force — Prior to July 1, 1872	Date incorporation laws in force — Since July 1, 1872	Date certificate of incorporation issued by secretary of state
Wayne City	V	903	Wayne		Mar. 10, 1883	Sept. 22, 1885
Waynesville	V	510	De Witt		July 19, 1875	July 6, 1894
Weldon	V	449	De Witt		May 25, 1892	Oct. 1, 1894
Wellington	V	334	Iroquois		Jan. 21, 1902	Apr. 8, 1902
Wenona	C	1,005	Marshall	Feb. 28, 1867	Aug. 26, 1872	Mar. 17, 1875
Wenonah	V	102	Montgomery		Jan. 24, 1917	Apr. 16, 1917
West Brooklyn	V	182	Lee		Sept. 3, 1894	May 20, 1895
*West Chicago[135]	C	6,854	Du Page		Aug. 18, 1906	Sept. 4, 1906
West City	V	814	Franklin		Apr. 24, 1911	July 10, 1911
West Dundee	V	2,530	Kane		Mar. 15, 1887	June 3, 1890
West Frankfort	C	9,027	Franklin		May 16, 1901	Sept. 18, 1901
West Point	V	234	Hancock		May 2, 1893	Aug. 16, 1893
West Salem[136]	V	956	Edwards	Feb. 8, 1857	July 30, 1914	Sept. 2, 1914
Westchester	V	18,092	Cook		Oct. 13, 1925	Jan. 14, 1926
*Western Springs	V	10,838	Cook		Jan. 30, 1886	Mar. 31, 1886
Westfield	V	636	Clark		Aug. 31, 1875	Jan. 3, 1876
*Westhaven	V		Cook		June 30, 1961	Feb. 2, 1962
Westmont	V	5,997	Du Page		Nov. 10, 1921	Mar. 24, 1925
Weston	V		Du Page		May 21, 1963	Oct. 8, 1963
Westville	C	3,497	Vermilion		Aug. 17, 1896	Oct. 21, 1901
*Wheaton	C	24,312	Du Page	Feb. 24, 1859	Mar. 31, 1890	Apr. 24, 1890
Wheeler	V	173	Jasper		June 1, 1894	May 10, 1895
*Wheeling	V	7,169	Cook		July 17, 1894	Aug. 27, 1894
Whiteash	V	160	Williamson		June 16, 1905	Aug. 24, 1905
White City	V	197	Macoupin		June 21, 1907	Nov. 1, 1907
White Hall	C	3,012	Greene	Jan. 1, 1837	Feb. 18, 1884	Mar. 25, 1884
Williamsfield	V	548	Knox		Jan. 6, 1896	Apr. 3, 1896
Williamson	V	324	Madison		Mar. 14, 1907	May 13, 1907
Williamsville[137]	V	735	Sangamon		May 15, 1884	Aug. 13, 1884
Willisville	V	532	Perry		Mar. 5, 1900	Oct. 10, 1901

Place		Population	County			
Willowbrook	V	157	Du Page		Jan. 18, 1960	Feb. 23, 1960
Willow Hill[138]	V	335	Jasper		Nov. 11, 1901	Nov. 14, 1901
Willow Springs[139]	V	2,348	Cook		June 1, 1892	Aug. 23, 1892
*Wilmette	V	28,268	Cook		Aug. 15, 1872	Apr. 17, 1873
Wilmington	C	130	Greene		Dec. 25, 1875	Jan. 7, 1876
Wilmington[140]	V	4,210	Will	July 31, 1837	Jan. 12, 1902	Feb. 3, 1902
Wilsonville	V	688	Macoupin		May 28, 1919	July 25, 1921
Winchester	C	1,657	Scott	Mar. 4, 1843	Sept. 11, 1876	Nov. 16, 1876
Windsor	V	658	Mercer	Aug. 14, 1869	Apr. 22, 1878	Oct. 22, 1901
Windsor	C	1,021	Shelby	Feb. 16, 1865	June 13, 1908	Sept. 8, 1908
*Winfield	V	1,575	Du Page		Apr. 18, 1921	May 17, 1921
Winnebago[141]	V	1,059	Winnebago	Feb. 9, 1855	Dec. 22, 1877	Mar. 30, 1878
Winnetka	V	13,368	Cook	Mar. 10, 1869		
Winslow	V	366	Stephenson		May 20, 1889	June 26, 1889
Winthrop Harbor	V	3,848	Lake		July 15, 1901	Oct. 12, 1901
Witt	C	1,101	Montgomery	June 22, 1852	Apr. 27, 1911	May 6, 1911
*Wood Dale	V	3,071	Du Page		Oct. 20, 1928	Jan. 18, 1929
Woodhull	V	779	Henry		Mar. 19, 1875	Oct. 10, 1901
Woodland	V	344	Iroquois		Dec. 1, 1897	Oct. 12, 1901
Woodlawn	V	241	Jefferson		Jan. 5, 1879	May 10, 1879
*Woodridge	V	542	Du Page		Aug. 24, 1959	Oct. 26, 1959
Wood River[142]	C	11,694	Madison		June 16, 1911	July 6, 1911
Woodson	V	229	Morgan		Apr. 9, 1894	June 29, 1895
Woodstock[143]	C	8,897	McHenry	June 22, 1852	Mar. 24, 1873	May 31, 1873
Worden	V	1,060	Madison		Oct. 22, 1877	Apr. 4, 1878
*Worth	V	8,196	Cook		Aug. 29, 1914	Oct. 8, 1914
Wyanet	V	938	Bureau	Mar. 29, 1869	May 26, 1891	June 10, 1891
Wyoming	C	1,559	Stark	Feb. 16, 1865	Apr. 19, 1898	May 4, 1898
Xenia	V	491	Clay	Feb. 16, 1865	Mar. 16, 1875	Feb. 4, 1876
Yale	V	123	Jasper		Nov. 23, 1929	Dec. 28, 1929
Yates City	V	802	Knox	Mar. 4, 1869	Nov. 28, 1911	Apr. 1, 1912
Yorkville[144]	V	1,568	Kendall		July 8, 1873	Oct. 7, 1873
Zeigler	C	2,133	Franklin		Jan. 3, 1914	June 12, 1914
*Zion	C	11,941	Lake		Mar. 31, 1902	Apr. 2, 1902

* Special census.
1 Formerly Rantoul.
2 Formerly Alcoa.
3 Formerly LaPier and Walnut Grove.
4 Formerly Waldron.
5 Formerly Ogle Station.
6 Formerly Vienna.
7 Formerly Zenia.
8 Middlebury annexed to.
9 Formerly Wooster.
10 Formerly St. Marye.
11 Formerly Sutton.
12 Formerly Portland.
13 Formerly Bowensburg.
14 Formerly Bradley City.
15 Formerly Charleston.
16 Formerly Grossdale.
17 Formerly Liberty.
18 Formerly Harvester.
19 Formerly West Hammond.
20 Formerly De Young and Burr Oak.
21 Formerly Reeves.
22 Formerly Harrison.
23 Formerly Butler.
24 Formerly South Pass.
25 Formerly Grand Cote.
26 Formerly Crescent.
27 Formerly Dement.
28 Formerly Centerville.
29 Formerly Concord.
30 Formerly Sherman and Trenton.
31 Formerly Rand.
32 Formerly Rome.
33 Formerly Specialville.
34 Formerly Dalton Station.
35 Formerly Coloma.
36 Formerly Howard.
37 Formerly Dunleith.
38 Formerly Randall.
39 Formerly Hilton.
40 Formerly Illinoistown.
41 Formerly Blackberry.
42 Formerly Fordville.

43 Formerly Ridgeville
44 Formerly Mt. Pleasant.
45 Formerly Harlem.
46 Formerly Glascoe.
47 Formerly Glendale.
48 Formerly Prospect Park.
49 Formerly Keokuk Junction.
50 Formerly Sheridan.
51 Formerly Fordyce.
52 Formerly Saline.
53 Formerly Oak Grove.
54 Formerly Wapello.
55 Formerly Ft. Sheridan.
56 Formerly Clement.
57 Formerly Milton.
58 Formerly Wilson.
59 Formerly Dallas and Chillicothe.
60 Formerly Pleasantville.
61 Formerly Middleton.
62 Formerly Juliet.
63 Formerly Halidayburg.
64 Formerly Midway.
65 Formerly Berrian.
66 Formerly Young America.
67 Formerly Henderson.
68 Formerly Columbia.
69 Formerly Greenfield.
70 Formerly Whitfield.
71 Formerly Postville and Camden.
72 Formerly Tessville.
73 Formerly Ellsworth.
74 Formerly Wiona.
75 Formerly Lodi.
76 Formerly Mechanicsburg.
77 Formerly Melrose.
78 Formerly Fairfield.
79 Formerly Hanover.
80 Formerly Camden Mills.
81 Formerly Centreville.
82 Formerly Emporium City.
83 Formerly Beechwood.
84 Formerly Huston.
85 Formerly Area.

86 Formerly Georgetown.
87 Formerly Athens.
88 Formerly Baden.
89 Formerly North Bloomington.
90 Formerly Shermerville.
91 Formerly Wau-Bun.
92 Formerly Utopia.
93 Formerly Oak Grove Park.
94 Formerly Independence.
95 Formerly Portland.
96 Formerly Mill Creek.
97 Formerly Florence.
98 Formerly Yellow Creek.
99 Formerly Lysander.
100 Formerly Victoria.
101 Formerly Millersburg.
102 Formerly Fairfield.
103 Formerly Amity.
104 Formerly Marysville.
105 1950 census.
106 Formerly Richmond.
107 Formerly Centerville.
108 Formerly Howlet and Jamestown.
109 Formerly Lane.
110 Formerly Stephenson.
111 Formerly Pecatonica.
112 Formerly Liberty.
113 Formerly Rose Clare.
114 Formerly New Rutland.
115 Formerly Schaumburg Center.
116 Formerly Clarkeville.
117 Formerly Crotty.
118 Formerly Niles Centre.
119 Formerly Clintonville.
120 Formerly Tazewell.
121 Formerly Charleston.
122 Formerly Van Buren.
123 Formerly Allin.
124 Formerly Georgetown.
125 Formerly Chatham.
126 Formerly Bolton.
127 Formerly Laurel Hill.
128 Formerly York.

129 Formerly Indiantown and Windsor.
130 Formerly Prairie City.
131 Formerly Humphrey.
132 Formerly Ardmore.
133 Formerly Uniontown and Mantera.
134 Formerly Little Fort.

135 Formerly Turner.
136 Formerly New Salem.
137 Formerly Benton.
138 Formerly New Liberty.
139 Formerly Spring Forest.

140 Formerly Winchester.
141 Formerly Elyda.
142 Formerly East Wood River.
143 Formerly Centerville.
144 Bristol annexed to.

Incorporated municipalities of Illinois

Special federal census

Municipality	Population	Date of census
Addison	13,273	Oct. 22, 1963
Algonquin	2,692	Feb. 8, 1963
Alsip	6,636	Sept. 15, 1964
Andalusia	769	Apr. 28, 1964
Antioch	2,778	May 4, 1965
Arlington Heights	40,622	Jan. 19, 1965
Auburn	2,441	Sept. 13, 1965
Barrington	6,525	Aug. 11, 1965
Barrington Hills	2,301	Aug. 12, 1963
Bartlett	2,291	Mar. 25, 1964
Bellwood	22,821	June 2, 1965
Bensenville	11,057	Jan. 21, 1963
Bensenville	12,212	Dec. 3, 1965
Berkeley	6,326	Apr. 3, 1964
Bethalto	5,404	Mar. 28, 1966
Bloomington	37,791	Oct. 4, 1965
Blue Island	21,986	June 14, 1966
Bradley	9,381	Aug. 12, 1965
Bridgeview	9,273	Mar. 17, 1966
Brighton	1,502	Jan. 27, 1965
Broadview	9,638	Aug. 8, 1963
Buffalo Grove	3,429	Aug. 5, 1963
Calumet City	27,420	July 9, 1964
Calumet Park	10,037	Mar. 17, 1965
Carbondale	18,531	Nov. 19, 1964
Carbondale (annexed portion)	1,985	Jan. 24, 1966
Carlyle	3,193	Jan. 17, 1966
Carol Stream	2,514	Nov. 9, 1962
Cary	3,204	Feb. 14, 1963
Cary	3,839	May 17, 1966
Caseyville	2,856	July 6, 1965
Catlin	1,600	Jan. 31, 1966
Charleston	13,611	Mar. 7, 1966
Chatham	2,023	May 25, 1965
Chester	5,300	Jan. 19, 1965
Chicago Ridge	6,786	Sept. 20, 1963
Coal Valley	2,284	Apr. 20, 1965
Colona	906	Feb. 21, 1963
Country Club Hills	4,771	Oct. 13, 1961
Countryside	2,626	Aug. 25, 1964
Crestwood	3,918	Jan. 29, 1963
Crete	3,788	Apr. 16, 1964
Crystal Lake	10,211	Oct. 25, 1965
Deerfield	14,318	July 8, 1963
De Kalb	23,103	Oct. 28, 1963
Des Plaines	50,789	Feb. 9, 1965
Dolton	22,557	Mar. 2, 1965
Downers Grove	22,612	Oct. 8, 1964
Downs	654	Oct. 3, 1962
East Chicago Heights	4,295	July 10, 1962
East Chicago Heights	4,715	Dec. 13, 1965
East Dubuque	2,312	Sept. 21, 1964
Elk Grove Village	13,155	Apr. 28, 1964
Elmhurst	40,329	Feb. 26, 1963
Elmhurst (annexed portion)	3,268	Apr. 4, 1966
Evergreen Park	25,284	Dec. 5, 1962
Fisher	1,330	Oct. 25, 1965
Flossmoor	5,921	Oct. 27, 1965
Fox Lake	3,886	June 17, 1965
Frankfort	1,523	Mar. 23, 1965
Geneva	8,573	Feb. 28, 1966
Genoa	2,862	Apr. 27, 1965
Glendale Heights	5,244	June 12, 1964
Glendale Heights	7,419	Nov. 3, 1965
Glen Ellyn	18,620	Oct. 14, 1964
Glenview	22,364	June 4, 1963
Glenview	23,521	Apr. 1, 1966
Glenwood	3,506	Jan. 13, 1966
Grays Lake	4,347	Apr. 26, 1965
Gurnee	2,167	Aug. 25, 1965
Hamilton	2,516	Mar. 28, 1966
Hampton	992	Sept. 28, 1964
Hanover Park	3,713	May 6, 1963
Hanover Park	6,620	Oct. 11, 1965
Harvard	5,019	June 25, 1965
Harvey	33,230	Mar. 10, 1965
Harwood Heights	6,955	May 22, 1963
Harwood Heights	8,808	Aug. 20, 1965
Hazel Crest	8,907	Oct. 27, 1964
Hickory Hills	6,946	Mar. 4, 1965
Highland Park	30,054	July 12, 1965
Hillcrest	534	Nov. 26, 1963
Hillside	9,404	May 21, 1964
Hinsdale	14,738	June 22, 1965
Hodgkins	1,592	May 10, 1965
Hoffman Estates	15,896	May 5, 1965
Homewood	15,164	June 20, 1963
Hudson	623	Mar. 16, 1966
Indian Head Park	442	June 22, 1966
Itasca	3,930	Mar. 12, 1964
Justice	5,252	July 28, 1965
La Grange	16,326	Feb. 11, 1963
La Grange Park	15,430	Oct. 14, 1963
Lake Bluff	4,345	Feb. 12, 1964
Lake Forest	13,345	Nov. 4, 1965
Lake Zurich	3,851	May 10, 1966
Lansing	20,926	Dec. 4, 1964
Lemont	4,034	May 5, 1964
Le Roy	2,436	May 2, 1966
Libertyville	9,241	Jan. 5, 1965
Lincoln	17,364	Apr. 26, 1965
Lincolnshire	999	June 3, 1963
Lincolnshire	1,390	Nov. 30, 1965
Lincolnwood	13,546	Aug. 2, 1965
Lindenhurst	1,773	May 13, 1963
Lisle	5,037	Nov. 10, 1964
Lockport	8,785	Sept. 29, 1964
Lombard	25,296	July 12, 1962
Lombard	28,151	Apr. 8, 1965
Loves Park	10,880	Nov. 16, 1964
Lyons	10,891	Apr. 28, 1964
Macomb	16,094	Sept. 20, 1965
Mansfield	843	Oct. 29, 1965
Manteno	2,448	May 18, 1964
Markham	14,595	June 2, 1964
Mascoutah	4,664	Mar. 21, 1966
Matteson	3,898	May 17, 1965
Maywood	28,805	Nov. 12, 1965
Mendota	6,714	Mar. 7, 1966
Merrionette Park	2,521	July 21, 1966
Mettawa	267	June 6, 1966
Midlothian	8,749	Sept. 19, 1963

Municipality	Population	Date of census
Midlothian	11,789	July 14, 1965
Milan	3,941	Apr. 28, 1964
Mokena	1,376	Mar. 23, 1965
Montgomery	2,744	Mar. 30, 1965
Monticello	3,511	Nov. 5, 1965
Morton	6,929	Feb. 26, 1964
Morton	8,248	July 6, 1966
Morton Grove	25,154	Sept. 9, 1963
Mount Prospect	27,349	June 24, 1964
Mount Prospect	30,202	Apr. 13, 1966
Mundelein	14,368	Dec. 5, 1963
Murphysboro	9,393	Apr. 6, 1965
Naperville	16,091	Sept. 30, 1963
Nashville	2,805	June 27, 1966
New Lenox	2,367	Apr. 12, 1966
Niles	29,497	Oct. 28, 1964
Normal	17,525	Nov. 14, 1963
Normal	20,676	Nov. 23, 1965
Norridge	17,126	July 28, 1965
North Aurora	3,448	July 15, 1963
North Riverside	8,401	Nov. 26, 1962
Northbrook	15,204	Aug. 28, 1964
Northlake	14,115	May 6, 1964
Oakbrook	1,644	July 30, 1963
Oak Forest	7,952	June 16, 1964
Oak Lawn	43,676	June 3, 1964
Oak Lawn	49,084	Aug. 17, 1965
O'Fallon	4,705	Mar. 27, 1963
O'Fallon	5,796	Apr. 21, 1966
Olympia Fields	2,124	Sept. 13, 1963
Olympia Fields	2,578	Sept. 29, 1965
Orland Park	4,509	July 20, 1964
Palatine	15,189	Oct. 18, 1962
Palatine	19,146	May 5, 1965
Palos Heights	5,303	Sept. 7, 1965
Park City	2,131	Sept. 24, 1964
Park Forest	31,324	May 11, 1965
Park Ridge	39,065	Oct. 8, 1964
Pekin	29,624	July 21, 1964
Peru	11,443	May 10, 1966
Plano	4,059	Feb. 19, 1964
Rantoul	27,533	Feb. 7, 1966
Riverdale	13,761	Jan. 20, 1964
Riverwoods	1,287	July 6, 1965
Rochelle	7,554	Feb. 3, 1964
Rochester	1,265	Feb. 3, 1965
Rockford	132,109	Jan. 9, 1964
Rolling Meadows	13,177	Dec. 9, 1963
Romeoville	6,358	Apr. 22, 1963
Roselle	4,827	July 8, 1963
Rosemont	2,283	Aug. 12, 1964
Round Lake Park	2,921	July 28, 1964
Sandwich	4,500	Nov. 5, 1965
Sauk Village	5,774	Aug. 1, 1961
Schaumburg	3,296	July 2, 1962

Municipality	Population	Date of census
Schaumburg	6,454	Jan. 4, 1966
Schiller Park	8,610	Jan. 10, 1964
Shawneetown	1,399	July 18, 1961
Shorewood	994	Dec. 9, 1963
Skokie	67,865	June 16, 1964
Sleepy Hollow	778	July 22, 1963
South Elgin	3,589	Oct. 25, 1965
South Holland	14,587	Apr. 29, 1964
South Holland	17,758	July 6, 1966
South Jacksonville	2,654	Apr. 19, 1965
Southern View	1,667	Sept. 16, 1965
St. Charles	11,158	Sept. 24, 1965
Stone Park	4,242	Nov. 8, 1963
Streamwood	6,751	Apr. 5, 1962
Streamwood	10,252	Nov. 15, 1965
Sugar Grove	565	Oct. 20, 1965
Thornton	3,667	Apr. 29, 1963
Tinley Park	7,810	Aug. 21, 1963
Tinley Park	8,750	Mar. 29, 1966
Tolono	1,802	Feb. 25, 1966
Trenton	2,095	Sept. 7, 1965
Vernon Hills	681	Apr. 21, 1964
Villa Park	23,294	June 26, 1962
Villa Park	25,697	Aug. 24, 1965
Wauconda	4,775	May 8, 1963
Wauconda	5,343	June 1, 1966
West Chicago	8,174	July 22, 1966
Western Springs	12,408	July 25, 1963
Westhaven	463	Sept. 1, 1965
Wheaton	26,263	May 13, 1963
Wheeling	11,756	Sept. 15, 1964
Wilmette	31,685	Mar. 4, 1965
Winfield	2,452	June 28, 1963
Wood Dale	4,424	Mar. 20, 1963
Woodridge	2,306	Feb. 4, 1963
Woodridge	5,263	Mar. 21, 1966
Worth	10,313	July 8, 1964
Zion	14,106	Aug. 21, 1964

Special municipal census

Municipality	Population	Date of census
Countryside	2,393	June 28, 1961
East Peoria	13,011	July 10, 1963
East Peoria	13,370	June 7, 1966
Hoffman Estates	12,570	March 1963
Taylorville	9,170	Dec. 16, 1963
Waterloo	4,076	June 1966

7

Results of Presidential Elections and the Illinois Vote

In the last 150 years citizens of Illinois have participated in 38 Presidential elections. They have given the state's electoral vote to winners 34 times and to losers 4 times (1840, 1848, 1884, and 1916). In the second election in which Illinois participated two electors voted for Jackson, the loser. One voted for John Quincy Adams, the winner. In this election (1824) Adams, who was second in the popular vote among four candidates, was voted into office by the House of Representatives of the United States. On two occasions a President who was second in the popular vote was chosen by the electoral college. Grover Cleveland was a candidate in both these elections. He was 23,005 votes behind James G. Blaine in 1884 but had a majority of electoral votes 219 to 182. In 1888 Cleveland had a lead of 100,476 in the popular vote, but mustered only 168 electoral votes to 233 for Benjamin Harrison. Illinois voted against Cleveland on both occasions and for him in 1892 when he was chosen for a second term.

Three times after 1820 a candidate who received considerably less than a majority of votes cast was chosen for the Presidential office. In 1856 James Buchanan, with about 45 per cent of the popular vote, had 174 electoral votes to 122 for his two opponents. In 1860 Abraham Lincoln, with about 40 per cent of the votes in a four-candidate struggle, had 180 electoral votes to 123 for his three opponents. In 1912 a split in the Republican party swept Woodrow Wilson into office with less than 42 per cent of the total ballot. On all occasions Illinois was with the winner.

After 1820 every President elected in a year evenly divisible by twenty died in office. William Henry Harrison (1840) served only one month of his term. Abraham Lincoln (1860) was assassinated during the second month of his second term. James A. Garfield (1880) was shot July 2, 1881, and died September 19. William McKinley, elected to a second term in 1900, was shot at Buffalo, New York, September 6, 1901, and died September 14. Warren G. Harding, elected to office in 1920, died August 2, 1923. Franklin D. Roosevelt, elected to a third term in 1940, died during the second month of his fourth term April 12, 1945. John F. Kennedy (1960) was murdered November 22, 1963.

The first Prohibition candidate for President ran in 1872, but none was admitted to the ballot in Illinois until 1880 when Neal Dow received 443 votes. Illinois never gave an electoral vote to a dissident third party; never returned a majority for a Whig candidate, and from 1860 through 1928 only twice gave its electoral vote to other than a Republican (Cleveland in 1892 and Wilson in 1912).

In preparing the tabulation of votes for the Presidency, four major sources were consulted, and little agreement on national or Illinois totals found. In Illinois, we had access to the official count as recorded in the state archives. No figures, however, were available for 1824, because the electors on the ballot were not identified by party or by preference for a Presidential candidate. In two of three Illinois districts, men favoring Andrew Jackson received a plurality of the votes. In one district an elector favoring John Quincy Adams was chosen, and for the only time in Illinois history the electoral vote of the state was split, two for Jackson, one for Adams.

In the election of 1828 voters cast 14,244 valid ballots. Not all, however, were marked for three Presidential electors. In the table we report the greatest number of votes cast for a Jackson elector and for an Adams elector. Similarly, for 1832 we report the largest totals for a Jackson elector and for a Clay elector. For 1836 and 1840 we use the largest count for a Van Buren elector and a Harrison elector. In 1840, when Abraham Lincoln was a candidate for Presidential elector on behalf of William Henry Harrison, he received nearly 200 less votes than did the other four Harrison men. These went to James H. Ralston, Democrat favoring Martin Van Buren.

In preparing our tables we consulted: *The Presidency* by Stephan Lorant (New

York: Macmillan Co., 1951), *A Statistical History of the American Presidential Elections* by Sven Petersen (New York: Unger, 1963), *Presidential Ballots 1836 to 1892* by Walter Dean Burnham (Baltimore: Johns Hopkins Press, 1955), and *Historical Review: Presidential Candidates from 1788 to 1960* (Washington: Congressional Quarterly, Inc., 1961). We generally selected the totals reported in the last volume. However, in this compilation there were differences between a table entitled A Century of Presidential Elections, which gave popular vote totals from 1856 to 1960 received by Democrats and Republicans, and other tables reporting the votes for all candidates.

We finally selected those covering all candidates. They doubtless contain errors, because this is one of the cloudiest areas in American historical research. The greatest differences occur in the reports for the election of 1832, where there was a variation of about 75,000 votes among the four cited authorities, and in the election of 1864. The variations in 1864 seem to depend largely on inclusion or exclusion of the soldier vote, which was about 117,000 for Abraham Lincoln and 34,000 for George B. McClellan.

Results of Presidential elections, 1820–1968

Year	Candidates	Party	Popular vote	Electoral vote	Illinois vote	Illinois electors
1820	James Monroe-Daniel D. Tompkins	DR	na	231	938	3
	John Quincy Adams-Richard Stockton	DR	na	1	328	
1824	John Quincy Adams-John C. Calhoun[1]	NR	114,023	84	na	1
	Andrew Jackson	D	152,001	99	na	2
	Henry Clay	DR	47,217	37	na	
	William H. Crawford	DR	46,979	41	na	
1828	Andrew Jackson-John C. Calhoun	D	647,276	178	9,582	3
	John Quincy Adams-Richard Rush	NR	508,064	83	4,662	
1832	Andrew Jackson-Martin Van Buren	D	687,502	219	14,617	3
	Henry Clay-John Sergeant	DR	530,189	49	6,745	
1836	Martin Van Buren-Richard M. Johnson	D	762,978	170	18,412	5
	William Henry Harrison-Francis Granger	W	735,561	73	15,220	
1840	William Henry Harrison[2]-John Tyler	W	1,275,016	234	27,273	
	Martin Van Buren-Richard M. Johnson	D	1,129,102	60	29,231	5
1844	James K. Polk-George M. Dallas	D	1 338,464	170	58,795	9
	Henry Clay-Theodore Frelinghuysen	W	1,299,062	105	45,854	
1848	Zachary Taylor[3]-Millard Fillmore	W	1,300,097	163	52,853	
	Lewis Cass-William O. Butler	D	1,220,544	127	55,952	9
	Martin Van Buren-Charles Francis Adams	FS	291,263		15,702	
1852	Franklin Pierce-William Rufus Devane King	D	1,601,117	254	80,368	11
	Winfield Scott-William A. Graham	W	1,385,453	42	64,733	
	John P. Hale-George W. Julian	FS	155,825		9,863	
1856	James Buchanan-John C. Breckinridge	D	1,838,169	174	105,528	11
	John C. Fremont-William L. Dayton	R	1,341,264	114	96,278	
	Millard Fillmore-Andrew J. Donelson	FS	871,731	8	37,531	
1860	Abraham Lincoln-Hannibal Hamlin	R	1,866,452	180	172,161	11
	Stephen A. Douglas-Herschel V. Johnson	D	1,375,157	12	160,205	
	John Bell-Edward Everett	CU	592,906	39	4,913	
	John C. Breckinridge-Joseph Lane	SD	848,356	72	2,332	

Year	Candidates	Party	Popular vote	Electoral vote	Illinois vote	Illinois electors
1864	Abraham Lincoln[4]-Andrew Johnson	R	2,213,665[4]	212	189,519	16
	George B. McClellan-George H. Pendleton	D	1,805,237[4]	21	158,724	
1868	Ulysses S. Grant-Schuyler Colfax	R	3,012,833	214	250,293	16
	Horatio Seymour-Francis P. Blair	D	2,703,249	80	199,143	
1872	Ulysses S. Grant-Henry Wilson	R	3,597,132	286	241,237	21
	Horace Greeley-B. Gratz Brown	C	2,834,125	5	184,772	
	Charles O'Conor-John Quincy Adams, II	D	29,489		3,138	
1876	Rutherford B. Hayes-William A. Wheeler	R	6	185	278,232	21
	Samuel J. Tilden-Thomas A. Hendricks	D		184	258,601	
	Peter Cooper-Samuel F. Carey	IG	81,737		17,207	
1880	James A. Garfield[7]-Chester A. Arthur	R	4,454,416	214	318,037	21
	Winfield S. Hancock-William H. English	D	4,444,952	155	277,321	
	James B. Weaver-Benjamin J. Chambers	IG	308,578		26,358	
1884	Grover Cleveland-Thomas A. Hendricks	D	4,851,981	219	312,351	
	James G. Blaine-John A. Logan	R	4,874,986	182	337,469	22
	John P. St. John-William Daniel	Pr	150,369		12,074	
1888	Benjamin Harrison-Levi P. Morton	R	5,439,853	233	370,475	22
	Grover Cleveland-Allen G. Thurman	D	5,540,329	168	348,371	
	Clinton B. Fisk-John A. Brooks	Pr	249,506		21,703	
1892	Grover Cleveland-Adlai E. Stevenson	D	5,556,918	277	426,281	24
	Benjamin Harrison-Whitelaw Reid	R	5,176,108	145	399,288	
	James B. Weaver-James G. Field	PP	1,029,846	22	22,207	
	John Bidwell-James B. Cranfill	Pr	264,133		25,871	
1896	William McKinley-Garret A. Hobart	R	7,104,779	271	607,130	24
	William J. Bryan-Arthur Sewall	D	6,502,925	176	464,523	
	Joshua Levering-Hale Johnson	Pr	132,007		9,796	
1900	William McKinley[8]-Theodore Roosevelt	R	7,207,923	292	597,985	24
	William J. Bryan-Adlai E. Stevenson	D	6,358,133	155	503,061	
	John G. Woolley-Henry B. Metcalf	Pr	208,914		17,626	
	Eugene V. Debs-Job Harriman	SDem.	87,814		9,687	
1904	Theodore Roosevelt-Charles W. Fairbanks	R	7,623,486	336	632,645	27
	Alton B. Parker-Henry G. Davis	D	5,077,911	140	327,606	
	Eugene V. Debs-Benjamin Hanford	S	402,283		69,225	
	Silas C. Swallow-George W. Carroll	Pr	258,536		34,770	
1908	William H. Taft-James S. Sherman	R	7,678,908	321	629,932	27
	William J. Bryan-John W. Kern	D	6,409,104	162	450,810	
	Eugene V. Debs-Benjamin Hanford	S	420,793		34,711	
	Eugene W. Chafin-Aaron S. Watkins	Pr	253,840		29,364	
1912	Woodrow Wilson-Thomas R. Marshall	D	6,293,454	435	405,048	29
	Theodore Roosevelt-Hiram W. Johnson	P	4,118,571	88	386,478	
	William H. Taft-James S. Sherman	R	3,484,980	8	253,593	
	Eugene V. Debs-Emil Seidel	S	900,672		81,278	
	Eugene W. Chafin-Aaron S. Watkins	Pr	206,275		15,710	
1916	Woodrow Wilson-Thomas R. Marshall	D	9,129,606	277	950,229	

Year	Candidates	Party	Popular vote	Electoral vote	Illinois vote	Illinois electors
	Charles Evans Hughes-					
	Charles W. Fairbanks	R	8,538,221	254	1,152,549	30
	Allen L. Benson-					
	George R. Kirkpatrick	S	585,103		61,394	
	James Frank Hanly-Ira D. Landrith	Pr	220,506		26,047	
1920	Warren G. Harding[9]-					
	Calvin Coolidge	R	16,152,200[9]	404	1,420,480	29
	James M. Cox-Franklin D. Roosevelt	D	9,147,353[9]	127	534,395	
	Eugene V. Debs-Seymour Stedman	S	919,719[9]		74,747	
	Parley P. Christensen-					
	Maximilian S. Hayes	FL	265,411[9]		49,630	
	Aaron S. Watkins-David L. Colom	Pr	189,408[9]		11,216	
1924	Calvin Coolidge-Charles Gates Dawes	R	15,725,016	382	1,453,321	29
	John W. Davis-Charles W. Bryan	D	8,386,503	136	576,975	
	Robert M. La Follette-					
	Burton K. Wheeler	P	4,831,289	13	432,027	
1928	Herbert C. Hoover-Charles Curtis	R	21,391,381	444	1,770,723	29
	Alfred E. Smith-					
	Joseph Taylor Robinson	D	15,016,443	87	1,312,235	
	Norman Thomas-James H. Maurer	S	267,420		19,138	
1932	Franklin D. Roosevelt-					
	John N. Garner	D	22,821,857	472	1,882,304	29
	Herbert C. Hoover-Charles Curtis	R	15,761,841	59	1,432,756	
	Norman Thomas-James H. Maurer	S	881,951		67,252	
1936	Franklin D. Roosevelt-John N. Garner	D	27,751,597	523	2,282,999	29
	Alfred M. Landon-W. Franklin Knox	R	16,679,583	8	1,570,393	
	William Lemke-Thomas C. O'Brien	U	882,479		89,439	
	Norman Thomas-George A. Nelson	S	187,720		7,530	
1940	Franklin D. Roosevelt-					
	Henry A. Wallace	D	27,244,160	449	2,149,934	29
	Wendell L. Willkie-Charles L. McNary	R	22,305,198	82	2,047,240	
1944	Franklin D. Roosevelt[10]-					
	Harry S. Truman	D	25,602,504	432	2,079,479	28
	Thomas E. Dewey-John W. Bricker	R	22,006,285	99	1,939,314	
1948	Harry S. Truman-Alben W. Barkley	D	24,104,031	303	1,994,715	28
	Thomas E. Dewey-Earl Warren	R	21,971,004	189	1,961,103	
	Henry A. Wallace-Glenn H. Taylor	P	1,157,172		[11]	
	J. Strom Thurmond-Fielding Wright	SR	1,169,063	39	[11]	
	Norman Thomas-Tucker P. Smith	S	139,414		11,522	
1952	Dwight D. Eisenhower-					
	Richard M. Nixon	R	33,778,963	442	2,457,327	27
	Adlai E. Stevenson-John J. Sparkman	D	27,314,992	89	2,013,920	
1956	Dwight D. Eisenhower-					
	Richard M. Nixon	R	35,579,190	457	2,623,327	27
	Adlai E. Stevenson-Estes Kefauver	D	26,027,983	73	1,175,682	
1960	John F. Kennedy[12]-					
	Lyndon B. Johnson	D	34,221,463	303	2,377,846	27
	Richard M. Nixon-Henry Cabot Lodge	R	34,108,582	219	2,368,988	
1964	Lyndon B. Johnson-					
	Hubert H. Humphrey	D	43,126,506	486	2,796,833	26
	Barry M. Goldwater-William E. Miller	R	27,176,799	52	1,905,946	
1968	Richard M. Nixon-Spiro T. Agnew	R	31,770,237	301	2,174,774	26
	Hubert H. Humphrey-					
	Edward S. Muskie	D	31,270,533	191	2,039,814	
	George C. Wallace-Curtis LeMay	APP	9,897,141	46	390,958	

Table—*continued*

na—Data not available
Party designations
  APP—American Peoples Party
  C—Coalition
  CU—Constitutional Union
  D—Democrat
  DR—Democrat-Republican
  FL—Farmer Labor
  FS—Free Soil
  IG—Independent Greenback
  NR—National Republican
  P—Progressive
  PP—People's Party of America
  Pr—Prohibition
  R—Republican
  S—Socialist
  SD—Southern Democrat
SDem.—Social Democrat
  SR—States' Rights
  U—Union
  W—Whig
[1] Elected by House of Representatives
[2] Harrison died April 4, 1841.
[3] Taylor died July 9, 1850.

[4] Totals include 116,887 soldier votes for Lincoln, 33,748 for McClellan. Lincoln shot April 14, 1865; died during the early morning hours April 15.
[5] Because of Greeley's death, November 29, 1872, the electoral votes for the coalition of Democrats and Liberal Republicans were not tallied. The regular Democratic ticket received no electoral votes.
[6] Vote count disputed in four states. Each candidate received about 4,000,000 votes. Senate canvassed the ballots from Florida, Louisiana, Oregon, and South Carolina and declared Hayes elected by one vote. House of Representatives refused to recognize Hayes, but the courts decided he was the winner.
[7] Garfield shot July 2, 1881; died September 19.
[8] McKinley shot at Buffalo, New York, September 6, 1901; died September 14.
[9] Women voted for the first time. Harding died August 2, 1923.
[10] Roosevelt died April 12, 1945.
[11] Not on ballot in Illinois.
[12] Kennedy assassinated November 22, 1963.

Constitution of 1818 Governor and lieutenant governor were elected by plurality of the popular vote. Tenure, four years. Neither could succeed himself, but could be elected for a second term four years after termination of the first. The secretary of state was appointed by the governor by and with the consent of the Senate. Tenure, at pleasure of governor and Senate. Treasurer and auditor were elected by joint vote of both houses of the General Assembly. Tenure, at pleasure of the assembly. United States senators elected by joint vote of both houses of the General Assembly. Tenure, six years, except that Ninian Edwards was elected in 1818 to serve to March 3, 1819, reelected for a six-year term and served March 4, 1819, to March 4, 1824 (resigned). Terms began on March 4 following election and ended on March 3, six years later, except that Jesse B. Thomas, elected in November 1818 for term beginning March 4, 1819, sat from December 3, 1818, by courtesy of the Senate. United States representatives elected by plurality of the popular vote in the district of residence. (In 1818 only one district existed in Illinois.) Terms began on March 4 following election, terminated March 3, two years later. Chief justice and three associate justices of the Supreme Court of Illinois elected by joint vote of the General Assembly. Commissions of those first elected ran until 1826, thereafter during good behavior.

Constitution of 1848 Method of electing the governor and lieutenant governor, tenure and restrictions on succession unchanged. (Gov. Augustus C. French was permitted to run for reelection on the ground that his original term had not been completed.) Secretary of state, treasurer, and auditor elected by plurality of popular vote in general elections the same years that governor and lieutenant governor were chosen. The treasurer could not succeed himself. Term, four years. (The term of the treasurer became two years with the election of 1856.) No positive provision being made for the office of attorney general, it remained unfilled until 1867, when office and duties were defined by legislation. Term, four years; elected with governor. Office of superintendent of public instruction created by legislation in 1854. Term, four years; elected at general elections in non-Presidential years. Provisions for electing United States senators and representatives were unchanged. Three justices of the

8

State Officers, United States Senators and Congressmen, 1818–1969

Supreme Court of Illinois were elected, one from each of three judicial divisions, one for three, one for six, and one for nine years. Thereafter one justice was elected every three years. After 1854, tenure was nine years. Seniority determined the choice of chief justice.

Constitution of 1870 Restrictions on succession of governor and lieutenant governor were lifted; those on treasurer remained in force. By amendment to the constitution in 1954, term of office of the treasurer was increased to four years, beginning with the treasurer taking office in January of 1959. Restriction on succession remained. Election of United States senators by joint ballot of both houses of the General Assembly remained in force until May 31, 1913, when the Seventeenth Amendment to the Constitution of the United States made election by plurality of popular vote mandatory. There was no change in the method of electing representatives to the Congress. By federal legislation in 1934 terms of senators and representatives begin and end on January 3 of odd-numbered years. Seven judicial districts were created by the constitution of 1870, one justice being elected from each district. Chief justices served by seniority (but not if a justice had presided within six years). Term was one year from June to June, the month of judicial elections; later from September to September, coinciding with opening of the fall term of the court. By constitutional amendment in 1962, the number of judicial districts was reduced to five, with three justices of the Illinois Supreme Court elected from the first district (Cook County) and one each from the other four. Effective January 1, 1964, tenure of supreme court justices became ten years, and the court selected one of its members to serve as chief justice for a term of three years.

The *Dictionary of American Biography* and the *Biographical Directory of Congress, 1778 to 1961* were the chief sources for biographical information used in this chapter. Most early Illinois officials not found in these works were described in the *Governors' Letter Books, 1818–1834* (Illinois State Historical Society Library, 1909) and the same, *1840–1853* (Illinois State Historical Society Library, 1911). Further information was found in *Illinois Election Returns, 1818–1848* (Illinois State Historical Society Library, 1923), Bateman and Selby's *Historical Encyclopedia of Illinois* (Rock Island County edition, 1911), and a few additional Illinois county histories. We also used information from the libraries of newspapers holding material from the nineteenth century, and from records of family societies, county clerks, and city clerks. For twentieth century officials, the *Illinois Blue Book*, published biennially, was a valuable source.

All terms of office have been checked in the official records held by the Illinois State Archives, Springfield. Dates of commission, not of election, are used throughout.

Members of the U.S. Senate and the Illinois Supreme Court are listed by seniority under each administration, members of the U.S. House of Representatives by seniority for each two-year term. Numbers in brackets refer to the administration during which the person first served and indicate where his biographical sketch can be found.

Illinois has been omitted after names of places in the state in the biographies. Where terms of office are not specified they coincide with those of the administration. Where a justice of the Illinois Supreme Court held no other state office, his political affiliation is not given.

Glossary of Abbreviations

Academic Degrees

A.B.	*Bachelor of Arts*	C.J.	*Chief Justice*	MTO	*Mediterranean*
A.M.	*Master of Arts*	Cand.	*Candidate*		*Theater of*
B.E.	*Bachelor of*	Capt.	*Captain*		*Operations*
	Engineering	Cav.	*Cavalry*	N.	*Near*
B.Ed.	*Bachelor of*	Chm.	*Chairman*	Nat.	*National*
	Education	Co.	*County*	N.G.	*National Guard*
B.L.	*Bachelor of Letters*	Col.	*Colonel*	O.R.C.	*Officers' Reserve*
B.Lit.	*Bachelor of*	Coll.	*Collector*		*Corps*
	Literature	Comm.	*Commissioner*	O.R.T.C.	*Officers' Reserve*
B.S.	*Bachelor of Science*	Conf.	*Conference*		*Training Corps*
B.Sc.	*Bachelor of Science*	Cong.	*Congress*	P.M.	*Postmaster*
B.S. in	*Bachelor of Science*	Const.	*Constitutional*	Pract.	*Practice or prac-*
Ed.	*in Education*	Conv.	*Convention*		*ticed (generally,*
D.D.	*Doctor of Divinity*	Corp.	*Corporation*		*began practice)*
D.Ed.	*Doctor of Education*	Cpl.	*Corporal*	Pres.	*President or*
D.Sc.	*Doctor of Science*	D.	*Died*		*Presidential*
Ed.B.	*Bachelor of*	Del.	*Delegate*	Prin.	*Principal*
	Education	Dem.	*Democrat*	Prof.	*Professor*
Ed.D.	*Doctor of Education*	Dept.	*Department*	Prog.	*Progressive*
E.E.	*Electrical Engineer*	D.F.C.	*Distinguished*	Pros.	*Prosecuting*
J.D.	*Juris Doctor*		*Flying Cross*	PTO	*Pacific Theater of*
	(Doctor of Laws)	Dir.	*Director*		*Operations*
LL.B.	*Bachelor of Law*	Dist.	*District*	Pub.	*Public*
LL.D.	*Doctor of Law*	Div.	*Division*	Pvt.	*Private*
LL.M.	*Master of Law*	D.S.C.	*Distinguished*	Q.M.	*Quartermaster*
M.A.	*Master of Arts*		*Service Cross*	Rcvr.	*Receiver of Public*
M.D.	*Doctor of Medicine*	D.S.M.	*Distinguished*		*Moneys*
M.Ed.	*Master of*		*Service Medal*	Reg.	*Register*
	Education	Ed.	*Editor*	Regt.	*Regiment*
M.S. in	*Master of Science*	ETO	*European Theater*	Rep.	*Republican*
Ed.	*in Education*		*of Operations*	Res.	*Resident*
M.S. in	*Master of Science*	Exec.	*Executive*	R.R.	*Railroad*
Ed.	*in Educational*	F.A.	*Field Artillery*	Sec.	*Secretary*
Adm.	*Administration*	FBI	*Federal Bureau of*	Sem.	*Seminary*
Ph.B.	*Bachelor of*		*Investigation*	Sen.	*Senate*
	Philosophy	Fed.	*Federal*	Sgt.	*Sergeant*
Ph.D.	*Doctor of*	G.A.R.	*Grand Army of*	Spec.	*Special*
	Philosophy		*the Republic*	Spkr.	*Speaker*
		Gen.	*General*	Supt.	*Superintendent*

General

		Gov.	*Governor*	Tech.	*Technical*
A.A.F.	*Army Air Forces*	Grad.	*Graduate or*	Ter.	*Territory or*
Acad.	*Academy*		*graduated*		*territorial*
Adj.	*Adjutant*	H.R.	*House of*	Treas.	*Treasurer*
Adm.	*Administration*		*Representatives*	Twp.	*Township*
Adv.	*Advocate*	H.S.	*High School*	U.	*University*
A.E.F.	*American Expedi-*	Indp.	*Independent (in*	U.S.A.	*United States Army*
	tionary Force		*politics)*	U.S.A.F.	*United States Air*
A.F.	*Air Force*	Inf.	*Infantry*		*Force*
Agr.	*Agriculture*	Inst.	*Institute*	U.S.A.R.	*United States Army*
Ald.	*Alderman*	Instr.	*Instruction or*		*Reserve*
Amb.	*Ambassador*		*instructor*	U.S.M.A.	*United States Mili-*
App.	*Appointed*	Int. Rev.	*Internal Revenue*		*tary Academy,*
Art.	*Artillery*	J.P.	*Justice of the*		*West Point*
Assoc.	*Associate*		*Peace*	U.S.M.C.	*United States*
Asst.	*Assistant*	Jud.	*Judicial*		*Marine Corps*
Att.	*Attorney*	Just.	*Justice*	U.S.N.	*United States Navy*
Aud.	*Auditor*	Leg.	*Legislature or*	U.S.N.A.	*United States*
A.U.S.	*Army of the United*		*legislative*		*Naval Academy,*
	States	Lt.	*Lieutenant*		*Annapolis*
B.	*Born*	Maj.	*Major*	Vol.	*Volunteer*
Biog.	*Biographical*	M.C.	*Medical Corps*	V.P.	*Vice President*
Brig.	*Brigadier*	Med.	*Medical*	Y.M.C.A.	*Young Men's*
Bvt.	*Brevet or brevetted*	Mem.	*Member*		*Christian*
C. in C.	*Commander in*	Mfr.	*Manufacturer*		*Association*
	Chief	Min.	*Minister*		
Ca.	*About*	Mun.	*Municipal*		

1. Administration of Shadrach Bond, Oct. 6, 1818, to Dec. 5, 1822. Voting for governor: Bond, 3,427, unopposed. **Governor** Shadrach Bond, res. St. Clair Co. Dem. b. Frederickstown, Md., Nov. 24, 1773. Mem. Ind. Ter. leg., 1805–8. Pvt. War of 1812, promoted col. Del. U.S.H.R. from Ill. Ter., 1812–14. Rcvr. Kaskaskia land office, 1814–18. Reg. Kaskaskia land office, 1823 until death, April 12, 1832. **Lieutenant Governor** Pierre Menard, res. Randolph Co. Dem. b. St. Antoine, Quebec, Oct. 7, 1766. Moved to Vincennes, Ind. Ter., 1788, to Kaskaskia, 1790. Fur trader, Indian agent, treaty negotiator. Presiding officer Ill. Ter. leg. council, 1812–18. With Ninian Edwards, negotiated Treaty of St. Louis covering military tract in Ill. d. Kaskaskia, June 13, 1844. **Secretary of State** Elias Kent Kane, res. Randolph Co. Dem. b. New York, N.Y., June 7, 1794. A.B. Yale, 1813; admitted N.Y. bar. Moved to Kaskaskia, 1814. Ter. judge, 1814–18. Del. Ill. const. conv., 1818. U.S. Sen., March 4, 1825, until death, Washington, D.C., Dec. 12, 1835. **Auditor** Elijah C. Berry, res. Randolph and Fayette cos. Dem. Aud., Oct. 9, 1818 (continuing ter. assignment) to Aug. 29, 1831 (resigned). Dir. State Bank, March 23, 1819, pres., Jan. 12, 1825. Printer, co-publisher *Western Intelligencer*, Kaskaskia, and *Illinois Intelligencer*, Vandalia. Adj. gen. Ill. militia, June 11, 1821, reappointed, Dec. 19, 1828. No further biog. data. **Treasurers** John Thomas, res. St. Clair Co. Treas., Oct. 9, 1818, until death in office, July 1819. No further biog. data. Robert K. McLaughlin, res. Fayette Co. Dem. Treas., Aug. 2, 1819, to Dec. 5, 1822. b. Va., Oct. 25, 1779. Moved to Ky., 1799; admitted Ky. bar, 1800. Moved to Belleville, 1815. Engrossing clerk Ill. Ter. leg. and leg. council, 1816–18. Ill. H.R., 1826–28. Ill. Sen., 1828–32, 1836–38. Reg. Vandalia land office, 1837–45. d. Vandalia, May 29, 1862. **Attorneys General** Daniel Pope Cook, res. Madison Co. Dem. Att. gen., March 5–15, 1819 (resigned to accept election to U.S.H.R.). b. Scott Co., Ky., 1794. Admitted Ky. bar; moved to Kaskaskia, 1815, to Edwardsville, 1816. Copublisher *Western Intelligencer*. Credited with pushing statehood ahead a year or more by his writings. Aud. Ill. Ter., 1816. Ter. judge Western Circuit, 1817. U.S.H.R., March 15, 1819,

to March 3, 1827. d. Scott Co., Ky., Oct. 16, 1827. William Mears, res. St. Clair Co. Dem. Att. gen., Dec. 14, 1819, to Feb. 2, 1821. b. Ireland, 1768. Att. gen. Ill. Ter., June 23, 1813, to Feb. 17, 1818. d. Belleville, 1826. No further biog. data. Samuel D. Lockwood, res. Madison Co. Dem. Att. gen., Feb. 26, 1821, to Dec. 28, 1822 (resigned). b. Poundridge, N.Y., Aug. 2, 1789. Admitted N.Y. bar; moved to Carmi, 1818. Resigned as att. gen. to become sec. state from Dec. 28, 1822, to April 2, 1823. Resigned to become rcvr. Edwardsville land office and agent Board of Canal Comms., 1823–25. Assoc. just. Ill. Supreme Court, Jan. 19, 1825, to Nov. 3, 1848 (resigned). Trustee of Ill. Central R.R. for state of Ill., 1851–74. d. Batavia, April 23, 1874. **United States Senators** Ninian Edwards, res. Randolph and Madison cos. Dem. U.S. Sen., Dec. 3, 1818, to March 4, 1824 (resigned). b. Montgomery Co., Md., March 1775. Grad. Dickinson, 1792. Moved to Ky. as father's agent. Ky. H.R., 1796–98; admitted Ky. bar, 1798. Judge, circuit court, 1803; court of appeals, 1804–8. C.J. Ky. Supreme Court, 1808. Appointed gov. Ill. Ter., 1809; served until statehood, 1818. Resigned U.S. Sen. to become min. to Mexico. Gov. Ill., 1826–30. d. Belleville, July 20, 1833. Jesse Burgess Thomas, res. Madison Co. Whig. U.S. Sen., Dec. 3, 1818, to March 3, 1829. b. Hagerstown, Md., March 1777. Moved to Boone Co., Ky., with parents, 1779. Clerk Boone Co. Court, 1799–1803. Admitted Ky. bar and moved to Vincennes, Ind. Ter., 1803. Ind. Ter. H.R., 1805–8. Del. U.S.H.R. from Ind. Ter., Oct. 22, 1808, to March 3, 1809, vice Benjamin Parke, resigned. Author Division Act establishing ter. of Ill. Fed. judge Western Dist., 1809–18. Moved to Edwardsville, 1818. Presided const. conv., 1818. Pract. law Mount Vernon, Ohio. d. Mount Vernon, Ohio, May 4, 1853. **United States Congressmen** John McLean, res. Gallatin Co. Dem. U.S.H.R., Dec. 3, 1818, to March 3, 1819. b. Guilford Co., N.C., Feb. 4, 1791. Moved with parents to Logan Co., Ky., 1795. Moved to Gallatin Co., 1815. Admitted Ill. bar; pract. Shawneetown, 1816. U.S. Sen., Nov. 23, 1824, vice Edwards, to March 3, 1825; March 4, 1829, to Oct. 14, 1830 (d.). Ill. H.R. 1820–22, 1826–28 (spkr.). d. Shawneetown. Daniel Pope Cook (see Att. Gen. above).

Phillips, res. Randolph Co. C.J. Ill. Supreme
Court, Oct. 9, 1818, to July 4, 1822 (resigned). b. Tenn., late 1700's. Capt. War
of 1812. Sec. Ill. Ter., 1816–18. Resigned
from Court to become cand. for gov., 1822.
Defeated and returned to Tenn. No further
biog. data.

Thomas Reynolds, res. Randolph Co.
Dem. C.J. Ill. Supreme Court, Aug. 31,
1822, vice Phillips, to Jan. 19, 1825 (resigned). b. Bracken Co., Ky., March 12,
1796. Admitted Ky. bar. Pract. Kaskaskia,
1817. Clerk Ill. H.R., 1818–22. Mem. Ill.
H.R., 1826–28. Moved to Mo., 1829; gov.
Mo., 1841, d. in office, Feb. 9, 1844
(suicide).

John Reynolds, res. St. Clair Co. Dem.
Assoc. just. Ill. Supreme Court, Oct. 9,
1818, to Jan. 19, 1825. b. Montgomery Co.,
Pa., Feb. 26, 1789. Moved with parents to
Ill., 1800. Attended college Knoxville,
Tenn., 1809–10. Ranger War of 1812. Ill.
H.R., 1826–30, 1846–48, 1852–54 (spkr.).
Gov., Dec. 9, 1830, to Nov. 17, 1834 (resigned to accept election to U.S.H.R.).
U.S.H.R., Dec. 1, 1834, to March 3, 1837;
March 4, 1839, to March 3, 1843. Historian
and author. d. Belleville, May 8, 1865.

William P. Foster, elected assoc. just.,
1818, but never served. No biog. data.

William Wilson, res. White Co. Assoc.
just. Ill. Supreme Court, Aug. 17, 1819,
vice Foster, to Jan. 19, 1825. C.J., Jan. 19,
1825, to Dec. 4, 1848. b. Loudon Co., Va.,
April 27, 1794. Moved to Ky. and in 1817
to Ill.; admitted Ill. bar, 1817. Served until
Supreme Court reorganized under new
constitution, 1848. Pract. Carmi to 1856. d.
Carmi, April 29, 1857.

Thomas C. Browne, res. Gallatin Co.
Assoc. just. Oct. 9, 1818, to Dec. 4, 1848.
b. Ky., late 1700's. Admitted Ky. bar and
moved to Shawneetown to pract., 1812. Ill.
Ter. leg. council, 1816–18. Served until
Supreme Court reorganized, 1848. d. San
Francisco, Calif., ca, 1858.

2. Administration of Edward Coles, Dec.
5, 1822, to Dec. 6, 1826. Voting for
governor: Coles, 2,854. Joseph Phillips,
2,687. Thomas C. Browne, 2,443. James
B. Moore, 622.

Governor Edward Coles, res. Madison
Co. Dem. b. Albemarle Co., Va., Dec. 15,
1786. Virginia abolitionist. Pvt. sec. to Pres.
Madison, 1810–14. Spec. envoy to Russia,
1815. App. reg. Edwardsville land office,
1819, freed inherited slaves en route and
bought land for them in Ill. Successfully

led opposition to call for const. conv. to
legalize slavery. Moved to Philadelphia,
Pa., 1833, where he died, July 7, 1868.

Lieutenant Governor Adolphus Frederick Hubbard, res. Gallatin Co. Ill. H.R.,
1818–20. Lawyer and proslavery advocate
of const. conv. Tried to unseat Coles when
latter briefly absent from state. Unsuccessful
cand. gov., 1826, receiving less than 5 per
cent of vote cast. No further biog. data.

Secretaries of State Samuel D. Lockwood[1] (resigned April 2, 1823).

David Blackwell, res. St. Clair and
Fayette cos. Dem. Sec. state, April 2, 1823,
to Oct. 15, 1824 (resigned). Copublisher
Illinois Intelligencer, opposing proslavery
const. conv. call. Ill. H.R., 1820–22, 1824–
28 (spkr., 1826). No further biog. data.

Morris Birkbeck, res. Edwards Co. Dem.
Sec. state, Oct. 15, 1824, to Jan. 15, 1825
(resigned). b. Wanborough, England, probably 1763. English Quaker, author, philanthropist, migrated to Edwards Co., 1817;
founded an English settlement. Fought proslavery conv. call. App. sec. state by Gov.
Coles; resigned when assembly refused confirmation. d. (drowning) n. home, June 24,
1825.

George Forquer, res. Monroe and
Sangamon cos. Dem. Sec. state, Jan. 15,
1825, to Dec. 31, 1828. b. Uniontown, Pa.,
1794 (half-brother Thomas Ford, seventh
gov.). Moved with twice-widowed mother
to St. Louis, Mo., 1803 and to New Design,
1804. Ill. H.R., 1824–25 (resigned). Att.
gen., Jan. 23, 1829, to Dec. 3, 1832
(resigned). Ill. Sen., 1832–35 (resigned).
Jacksonian Dem. leader in Ill. d. New
Design, 1837.

Auditor Elijah C. Berry[1].

Treasurer Abner Field, res. Union and
JoDaviess cos. Dem. Treas., Jan. 14, 1823,
to Feb. 12, 1827. b. Ky. (probably Louisville), 1799. Filed on land Union Co., 1818.
Clerk, first comms. court of Union Co.,
1818, 1819. Clerk Ill. circuit court, 1821,
1822. Removed to JoDaviess Co. with
appointment as J.P., Feb. 17, 1827. Judge
probate court, recorder and clerk of comms.
court JoDaviess Co. No further biog. data.

Attorneys General Samuel D. Lockwood[1] (resigned Dec. 28, 1822).

James Turney, res. Washington and
Greene cos. Dem. Att. gen., Feb. 28, 1823,
to Jan. 23, 1829. Lawyer; came to Ill. about
1819. Sec. Ill. Sen., 1820–22. Ill. H.R., 1822–
23 (resigned Feb. 18, 1823, to become att.

gen.); 1835–36, vice Link. Ill. Sen., 1836–39 (resigned end second session). No further biog. data.

United States Senators Jesse Burgess Thomas[1]; Ninian Edwards[1] (resigned March 4, 1824); John McLean[1] (vice Edwards).

United States Congressman Daniel P. Cook[1].

Justices Illinois Supreme Court Thomas Reynolds, C.J.[1] (resigned Jan. 19, 1825); John Reynolds[1]; William Wilson[1] (assoc. just. to Jan. 19, 1825; C.J. to 1848); Thomas C. Browne[1]; Samuel D. Lockwood[1] (from Jan. 19, 1825).

Theophilus Washington Smith, res. Madison Co. Just. Ill. Supreme Court, Jan. 19, 1825, to Dec. 26, 1842 (resigned). b. New York, N.Y., Sept. 28, 1784. Read law with Aaron Burr. Admitted N.Y. bar, 1805; pract. New York City. Moved to Edwardsville, 1816. Ill. Sen., 1822–25 (resigned). Impeached 1832, and secured negative acquittal (twelve for guilty, ten against, insufficient to convict). d. Chicago, May 6, 1846.

3. Administration of Ninian Edwards, Dec. 6, 1826, to Dec. 6, 1830. Voting for governor: Edwards, 6,280. Thomas Sloo, Jr., 5,834. Adolphus Frederick Hubbard, 580.

Governor Ninian Edwards[1].

Lieutenant Governor William Kinney, res. St. Clair Co. Dem. b. Ky., 1781. Settled in St. Clair Co. before 1818. Baptist preacher and politician who favored proslavery conv. call during adm. of Coles. Ill. Sen., 1818–20, 1822–24. Twice cand. for gov. Pres. Board Pub. Works, 1838. d. Belleville, 1843.

Secretaries of State George Forquer[2] (resigned Dec. 31, 1828).

Alexander Pope Field, res. Union Co. Dem. Sec. state, Jan. 23, 1829, to Nov. 30, 1840. b. Louisville, Ky., Nov. 30, 1800 (nephew of U.S. Judge Nathaniel Pope). Filed on land near Jonesboro prior to 1818. Admitted Ill. bar about 1820. Ill. H.R., 1822–24, 1826–30. Helped unseat Nicholas Hansen, seat John Shaw to secure passage of proslavery const. conv. call. Served continuously as sec. state until removed by Gov. Carlin and the General Assembly. Sec. Wis. Ter., 1841. Pract. St. Louis for several years after 1841. Moved to New Orleans; elected to 38th Cong. from La.,

1862, but not seated. d. New Orleans, La., Aug. 19, 1876.

Auditor Elijah C. Berry[1].

Treasurers Abner Field[2] (to Feb. 12, 1827).

James Hall, res. Gallatin, Fayette, and Hamilton cos. Dem. Treas., Feb. 12, 1827, to Feb. 1, 1831. b. Philadelphia, Pa., Aug. 19, 1793. Navy War of 1812, with Decatur vs. pirates of North Africa, 1815. Moved to Shawneetown, and admitted Ill. bar, 1820. Copublisher *Illinois Monthly Magazine*, first Ill. periodical. Judge circuit court, 4th Circuit, Jan. 19, 1825, to Jan. 12, 1827. Ill. H.R., 1826–30, 1832–34. Moved to Cincinnati where he wrote western travel sketches, Indian history, and fiction. d. Cincinnati, Ohio, July 5, 1868.

Attorneys General James Turney[2] (to Jan. 23, 1829); George Forquer[2].

United States Senators Jesse Burgess Thomas[1] (to March 3, 1829); Elias Kent Kane[1]; John McLean[1] (d. Oct. 14, 1830).

David J. Baker, res. Randolph Co. Dem. Served thirty days, Nov. 12–Dec. 11, 1830, vice McLean. b. East Haddon, Conn., Sept. 7, 1792. A.B. Hamilton, 1816. Moved to Kaskaskia, admitted Ill. bar, 1819. Probate judge Kaskaskia, 1827–30. U.S. dist. att. for Ill., 1833–41. Pract. Alton until his death, Aug. 6, 1869.

United States Congressmen Daniel P. Cook[1].

Joseph Duncan, res. Jackson and Morgan cos. Dem. and (from 1842) Whig. U.S.H.R., March 4, 1827, to Sept. 21, 1834 (resigned, elected gov.). b. Paris, Ky., Feb. 22, 1794. Commanded troops War of 1812, received sword from Cong. for gallantry Ft. Stephenson. Moved to Morgan Co., 1818. Maj. gen. Ill. militia. Ill. Sen., 1824–27 (resigned to accept U.S.H.R. seat). Author first free school law in Ill. Gov., Dec. 3, 1834, to Dec. 7, 1838. Ran for second term, 1842, as Whig and lost. d. Jacksonville, Jan. 15, 1844.

Justices Illinois Supreme Court William Wilson, C.J.[1]; Thomas C. Browne[1]; Samuel D. Lockwood[1]; Theophilus W. Smith[2].

4. Administration of John Reynolds, Dec. 9, 1830, to Dec. 3, 1834. Voting for governor: Reynolds, 12,837. William Kinney, 8,938.

Governors John Reynolds[1] (resigned Nov. 17, 1834, to accept seat U.S.H.R.).

William Lee Davidson Ewing, res. Fayette Co. Dem. Gov., Nov. 17–Dec. 3, 1834. Lt. gov., March 1, 1833, to Nov. 17,

1834. b. Paris, Ky., Aug. 31, 1795. Moved to Ill., 1818. Rcvr. Vandalia land office, 1820–26. Clerk Ill. H.R., 1826–30. Mem. Ill. H.R., 1830–32 (spkr.), 1838–42. Ill. Sen., 1832 (pres. pro tem.). On Casey's resignation became acting lt. gov. and on Reynolds' resignation became gov. U.S. Sen., Dec. 30, 1835, vice Kane, to March 3, 1837. Aud. Ill., 1843 until death, Vandalia, March 25, 1846.

Lieutenant Governor Zadok Casey, res. Jefferson Co. Dem. Lt. gov., Dec. 9, 1830, to March 1, 1833 (resigned, elected to U.S.H.R.). b. Greene Co., Ga., March 7, 1796. Moved to Ill., 1817, credited with founding Mount Vernon. Ill. H.R., 1822–26, 1849–52 (spkr., 1849–50). Ill. Sen., 1826–30, 1861 until his death. Action at Kellogg's Grove Black Hawk War. U.S.H.R., 1833–43, secured land grant for Illinois and Michigan Canal. Del. const. conv., 1847. d. Caseyville, Sept. 4, 1862.

Secretary of State Alexander P. Field[3].

Auditors Elijah C. Berry[1] (resigned Aug. 29, 1831).

James T. Stapp, res. Fayette Co. Dem. Aud., Aug. 29, 1831, to Nov. 16, 1835 (resigned). b. Woodford Co., Ky., April 13, 1804. Moved with widowed mother to Kaskaskia. Clerk to Aud. Berry at Vandalia, 1824–31. Pres. State Bank Vandalia, Nov. 16, 1835. Adj. 3rd Ill. Vols. Mexican War. Rcvr. Vandalia land office, 1850–55. d. Decatur, 1876.

Treasurers James Hall[3] (resigned Feb. 1, 1831).

John Dement, res. Franklin Co. Dem. Treas., Feb. 1, 1831, to Dec. 3, 1836 (resigned). b. Sumner Co., Tenn., April 1804. Moved with parents to Franklin Co., 1817. Sheriff Franklin Co., 1826–28. Ill. H.R., 1828–32. Served with distinction Black Hawk War. Resigned treas. to return to Ill. H.R. from Fayette and Effingham cos.; resigned house seat to become rcvr. Dixon land office. d. Dixon, Jan. 16, 1883.

Attorneys General George Forquer[2] (resigned Dec. 3, 1832).

James Semple, res. Madison Co. Dem. Att. gen., Jan. 30, 1833, to Sept. 1, 1834. b. Green Co., Ky., Jan. 5, 1798. Moved to Edwardsville, 1818, to Mo., 1820. Studied law Louisville, Ky.; admitted Ky. bar; pract. Clinton Co., Ky. Returned to Edwardsville, 1827. Brig. gen. Ill. militia Black Hawk War. Ill. H.R., 1832–38 (spkr., 1834–38). Min. to Colombia, 1837. Assoc. just. Ill. Supreme Court, Jan. 16–Aug. 16, 1843, vice Breese, (resigned). U.S. Sen., Dec. 4, 1843, to

March 3, 1847, vice McRoberts. d. Elsah, Dec. 20, 1866.

Ninian Wirt Edwards, res. Sangamon Co. Whig to 1850, then Dem. Att. gen., Sept. 1, 1834, to Feb. 7, 1835 (resigned). b. Frankfort, Ky., April 15, 1809 (son of third gov.). A.B. Transylvania, 1833. App. att. gen. while residing St. Clair Co.; moved to Springfield, 1835. Ill. H.R. (one of the "Long Nine" from Sangamon Co.), 1836–40 (resigned), 1849–51 (resigned). Ill. Sen., 1844–48. Del. Ill. const. conv., 1847. First supt. of pub. instr., March 24, 1854, to Jan. 12, 1857. d. Springfield, Sept. 2, 1889.

United States Senators Elias Kent Kane[1].

John McCracken Robinson, res. White Co. Dem. U.S. Sen., Dec. 11, 1830, to March 3, 1841 (vice McLean to March 3, 1835). b. Scott Co., Ky., April 10, 1794. A.B. Transylvania, 1818. Moved to Carmi; admitted Ill. bar, 1818. Assoc. just. Ill. Supreme Court, March 6–April 27, 1843. d. Ottawa, April 27, 1843.

United States Congressmen Joseph Duncan[3] (resigned Sept. 21, 1834); Zadok Casey (see Lt. Gov. above).

Charles Slade, res. St. Clair and Washington cos. Dem. U.S.H.R., March 4, 1833, to his death, July 26, 1834. b. England, emigrated to Va. with parents. Moved to St. Clair Co., as merchant about 1818. Ill. H.R., 1820–22, 1826–28, from Washington Co. d. en route home from Washington, D.C., at Vincennes, Ind.

Justices Illinois Supreme Court William Wilson, C.J.[1]; Thomas C. Browne[1]; Samuel D. Lockwood[1]; Theophilus W. Smith[2].

5. Administration of Joseph Duncan, Dec. 3, 1834, to Dec. 7, 1838. Voting for governor: Duncan, 17,349. William Kinney, 10,229. Robert K. McLaughlin, 4,315. James Adams, 887.

Governor Joseph Duncan[3].

Lieutenant Governors Alexander M. Jenkins, res. Jackson Co. Whig. Lt. gov., Dec. 5, 1834, to Dec. 9, 1836. No birth record. Moved to Ill. about 1817; constable Brownsville. Ill. H.R., 1830–34 (spkr., 1832–34). Resigned as lt. gov. to become pres. Ill. Central R.R. Del. Ill. const. conv., 1847. Judge circuit court, 3rd Circuit, Aug. 29, 1859, to death in Jackson Co., Feb. 13, 1864.

William H. Davidson, res. White Co.

Dem. Acting lt. gov., Dec. 9, 1836, to Dec. 7, 1838. b. Antietam, Va., Sept. 8, 1805. Early orphaned; moved to Carmi, 1828. Ill. Sen., 1832–44 (pres., 1836–38). Moved to Louisville, Ky., 1851, where he died, Oct. 24, 1861.

Secretary of State Alexander Pope Field[3].

Auditors James T. Stapp[4] (resigned Nov. 16, 1835).

Levi Davis, res. Fayette Co. Dem. Aud., Nov. 16, 1835, to March 4, 1841. b. Cecil Co., Md., July 20, 1806. A.B. Jefferson, 1828. Admitted Md. bar, 1830. Moved to Vandalia, 1831, to Alton, 1846. Pract. Alton until death, March 4, 1897.

Treasurers John Dement[4] (resigned Dec. 3, 1836).

Charles Gregory, res. Greene Co. Dem. Treas., Dec. 5, 1836, to March 4, 1837. b. Conn., May 28, 1797. Ill. H.R., 1830–32, 1834–36. Col. Ill. militia Black Hawk War. No further biog. data.

John D. Whiteside, res. Monroe Co. Dem. Treas., March 4, 1837, to March 6, 1841. b. Whiteside's Station, 1794. Brig. gen. Ill. militia. Ill. H.R., 1830–36, 1844–46. Ill. Sen., 1836–37 (resigned). Carried Shields' challenge to Lincoln. Del. Ill. const. conv., 1847. d. Whiteside's Station, 1850.

Attorneys General Ninian W. Edwards[4] (resigned Feb. 7, 1835).

Jesse Burgess Thomas, Jr., res. Madison Co. Dem. Att. gen., Feb. 12, 1835, to Jan. 8, 1836 (resigned). b. Lebanon, Ohio, July 31, 1806. LL.B. Transylvania, 1828. Admitted Ill. bar; pract. Edwardsville. Sec. Ill. Sen., 1830–34. Ill. H.R., 1834 (resigned Feb. 12, 1835, to become att. gen.). Moved to Springfield. Judge circuit court, 1st Circuit, July 20, 1837, to 1839 (resigned). Assoc. just. Ill. Supreme Court, Aug. 24, 1843, vice Douglas, to Aug. 8, 1845 (resigned); Jan. 27, 1847, vice Young, to Dec. 4, 1848 (court dissolved). Pract. law Springfield, Galena, Chicago, d. Chicago, Feb. 21, 1850.

Walter B. Scates, res. Jefferson Co. Dem. Att. gen. Ill. Jan. 18–Dec. 26, 1836 (resigned). b. Halifax Co., Va., Jan. 18, 1808. Taken to Ky. by parents, 1809. Moved to Frankfort; admitted Ill. bar, 1831. Moved to Vandalia, Jan. 1836. Judge circuit court, 3rd Circuit, Dec. 26, 1836, to Feb. 1841 (resigned). Assoc. just. Ill. Supreme Court, Feb. 15, 1841, to Jan. 11, 1847 (resigned). Moved to Chicago. Del. Ill. const. conv.,

1847. Assoc. just. Ill. Supreme Court, July 13, 1853, to June 1855. C.J., June 1855 to May 1857 (resigned). Maj. on McClernand's staff, 1862, mustered out, 1866. Coll. customs Chicago, 1866–69. Pract. Chicago until death, Evanston, Oct, 26. 1886.

Usher F. Linder, res. Coles Co. Whig. and Dem. Att. gen., Feb. 4, 1837, to June 11, 1838 (resigned). b. Hardin Co., Ky., March 20, 1809. Moved to Charleston, 1835. Admitted Ill. bar; elected to Ill. H.R., 1836 (resigned to become att. gen.), 1846–52. Del. Dem. conv. Charleston, S.C., 1860. Pract. Chicago until his death, June 5, 1876.

George W. Olney, res. Madison Co. Dem. Edwardsville att. and orator. App. att. gen., June 26, 1838 (resigned Feb. 1, 1839). No further biog. data.

United States Senators Elias Kent Kane[1] (d. Dec. 12, 1835); John M. Robinson[4]; William L. D. Ewing[4] (vice Kane, to March 3, 1837).

Richard Montgomery Young, res. Union Co. Dem. U.S. Sen., 1837–43; b. Fayette Co., Ky., Feb. 20, 1798. Admitted Ky. bar, 1816. Moved to Jonesboro, 1817. Ill. H.R., 1820–22. Judge circuit court, 3rd Circuit, Jan. 19, 1825, to Jan. 12, 1827, 5th Circuit, Jan. 23, 1829, to Jan. 2, 1837. Just. Ill. Supreme Court, Feb. 24, 1843, vice Smith, to Jan. 25, 1847 (resigned). Comm. General Land Office, Washington, D.C., 1847–49. Clerk U.S.H.R., 1850–51. d. Washington, D.C., Nov. 28, 1861.

United States Congressmen Zadok Casey[4]; John Reynolds[1].

William L. May, res. Sangamon Co. Dem. U.S.H.R., Dec. 1, 1834, to March 3, 1839. b. Ky., 1793. Moved to Edwardsville. J.P. Madison Co., Dec. 10, 1817. Capt. Ill. militia, 1822. Moved to Jacksonville. J.P. Morgan Co., Aug. 6, 1827, to Aug. 29, 1829. Ill. H.R., 1828–30. Moved to Sangamon Co. Rcvr. Springfield land office, 1829–34. Built first bridge over Ill. River, Peoria. Joined gold rush, 1849. d. Sacramento, Calif., Sept. 29, 1849.

Adam Wilson Snyder, res. St. Clair Co. Dem. U.S.H.R., 1837–39. b. Connellsville, Pa., Oct. 6, 1799. Moved to Cahokia, 1817; admitted Ill. bar, 1820. Ill. Sen., 1830–36, 1840–42. Capt. militia Black Hawk War. d. Belleville, May 14, 1842.

Justices Illinois Supreme Court William Wilson[1], C.J.; Thomas C. Browne[1]; Samuel D. Lockwood[1]; Theophilus W. Smith[2].

6. Administration of Thomas Carlin, Dec. 7, 1838, to Dec. 8, 1842. Voting for

governor: Carlin, 30,668. Cyrus Edwards 29,722.

Governor Thomas Carlin, res. Greene Co. Dem. b. Fayette Co., Ky., July 18, 1789. Moved to St. Louis, 1803, where father died; moved to Ill. Served under Ninian Edwards Ill. militia. Settled in Greene Co., 1818; Carrollton, county seat laid out on his land. Carlinville, county seat Macoupin Co., named in his honor. Ill. Sen., 1824–32. Capt. of spies Black Hawk War. Reg. Quincy land office, 1834–38. Ill. H.R., 1849–50, vice Fry. d. Carrollton, Feb. 14, 1852.

Lieutenant Governor Stinson H. Anderson, res. Jefferson Co. Dem. b. Sumner Co., Tenn., 1800. Lt. Black Hawk War. Ill. H.R., 1832–36 (resigned). Capt. regular army, 1842, served in Seminole War. U.S. marshall for Ill., 1844–48. Warden Ill. penitentiary Alton during 1850's. d. Alton, 1857.

Secretaries of State Alexander P. Field[3] (removed from office Nov. 30, 1840).

Stephen Arnold Douglas, the "Little Giant," res. Adams and Cook cos. Dem. Sec. state, Nov. 30, 1840, to Feb. 27, 1841 (resigned). b. Brandon, Vt., April 23, 1813. Moved to Winchester to teach school and read law. Admitted Ill. bar, 1834; pract. Jacksonville. State's att. Morgan Co., 1835. Ill. H.R., 1836–37 (resigned). Reg. Springfield land office, 1837. Just Ill. Supreme Court, Feb. 15, 1841, to June 28, 1843 (resigned). U.S.H.R., 1843–47. Elected to U.S. Sen., 1846, served from March 4, 1847, until his death Chicago, June 3, 1861. Defeated Lincoln for U.S. Sen. in 1858 after campaign that featured the famous debates. Pres. cand., 1860.

Lyman Trumbull, res. St. Clair and Cook cos. Dem., Anti-Nebr. Dem., and Rep. Sec. state, March 1, 1841, to March 4, 1843 (removed from office). b. Colchester, Conn., Oct. 10, 1813. Taught school Ga.; admitted Ga. bar; pract. Greenville, 1837. Removed to Ill., same year; pract. Belleville. Ill. H.R., 1840–42. Just. Ill. Supreme Court, Dec. 4, 1848, to July 4, 1853 (resigned). U.S. Sen., 1855–73. d. Chicago, June 25, 1896.

Auditors Levi Davis[5] (resigned March 4, 1841).

James Shields, res. Randolph and St. Clair cos. Dem. Aud., March 4, 1841, to May 26, 1843. b. Tyrone, Ireland, May 10, 1806. Emigrated to U.S., 1823; moved to Ill. Admitted Ill. bar, 1832; pract. Kaskaskia. Ill. H.R. 1836–38. Assoc. just. Ill. Supreme Court, Aug. 16, 1843, vice

Semple, to April 2, 1845 (resigned). Comm. General Land Office, Washington, D.C., 1846–47. Brig. gen. Mexican War, promoted maj. gen. for gallantry Cerro Gordo. Gov. Oreg. Ter., 1848; elected to U.S. Sen. same year, denied seat on grounds no Ill. citizenship. Requalified as Ill. citizen, reelected, Oct. 7, 1849, served to March 3, 1855. Moved to Minn.; elected to U.S. Sen., 1858. Resigned to accept commission brig. gen. vols., 1861. Mustered out, 1863; moved to Calif.; moved to Mo. Elected U.S. Sen. from Mo., Jan. 22, 1879, only man sent to U.S. Sen. from three states. d. Ottumwa, Iowa, June 1, 1879.

Treasurers John D. Whiteside[5] (to March 6, 1841).

Milton Carpenter, res. Hamilton Co. Dem. App. treas., March 6, 1841, elected under new constitution, 1848. Ill. H.R., 1834–41 (resigned). d. in office, Springfield, Aug. 1848. No further biog. data.

Attorneys General George W. Olney[5] (resigned Feb. 1, 1839).

Wyckliffe Kitchell, res. Crawford Co. Dem. Att. gen., March 5, 1839, to Nov. 19, 1840 (resigned). b. N.J., May 21, 1789. Moved to Ohio, 1812, to Ind.; admitted Ind. bar, 1814. Moved to Palestine, 1817. Ill. H.R., 1820–22, 1840–42. Ill. Sen., 1828–32. Moved to Hillsboro, pract. law until his death, Jan. 2, 1869.

Josiah Lamborn, res. Morgan Co. Dem. Att. gen., Dec. 23, 1840, to Jan. 12, 1843. b. Pa. Moved as child to Cincinnati, Ohio, thence to Washington Co., Ky. LL.B. Transylvania, about 1830. Early lawyer in Ind. and Ill. d. White Hall, March 31, 1847.

United States Senators John M. Robinson[4] (to March 3, 1841); Richard M. Young[5].

Samuel McRoberts, res. Monroe Co. Dem. U.S. Sen., March 4, 1841, to March 22, 1843 (d.). b. Monroe Co., April 12, 1799. LL.B. Transylvania, 1821. Admitted Ill. bar, 1821. Clerk Monroe Co. Court, 1818–21. Judge circuit court, 2nd Circuit, Jan. 19, 1825, to Jan. 12, 1827. Ill. Sen., 1828–30, from Clinton Co., vice Joseph A. Beaird. U.S. dist. att., 1830–32. Solicitor for General Land Office, Washington, D.C., 1839–40. Died n. Cincinnati, Ohio, during first term in U.S. Sen.

United States Congressmen John Reynolds[1]; Zadok Casey[4]; William L. May[5]; Adam W. Snyder[5] (to March 3, 1839).

John Todd Stuart, res. Sangamon Co. Whig and Dem. U.S.H.R., 1839–43 (Whig), 1863–65 (Dem.). b. Lexington, Ky., Nov. 10, 1807. A.B. Centre, 1826. Moved to Springfield; admitted Ill. bar, 1828. Maj. Black Hawk War. Law partner Lincoln. Ill. H.R., 1832–36 (one of "Long Nine"). Ill. Sen., 1849–52. d. Springfield, Nov. 28, 1885.
Justices Illinois Supreme Court William Wilson[1] C.J.; Thomas C. Browne[1]; Samuel D. Lockwood[1]; Theophilus W. Smith[2].

Justices appointed under reorganization of the Supreme Court, Feb. 15, 1841:

Samuel Hubbel Treat, res. Sangamon Co. Just. Ill. Supreme Court, Feb. 15, 1841, to March 23, 1855. b. Plainfield, N.J., June 21, 1811. Moved to Springfield, 1834. Judge circuit court, 8th Circuit, May 27, 1839, to 1841 (resigned). Acting C.J. Ill. Supreme Court, 1848; C.J., 1848–55. Elected to Court under new constitution of 1848. Resigned 1855 to become judge U.S. Dist. Court, Southern Dist. Ill. d. in office, March 27, 1887, after forty-eight years of continuous jud. service.

Thomas Ford, res. Monroe and Ogle cos. Dem. Just. Ill. Supreme Court, Feb. 15, 1841, to Aug. 1, 1842 (resigned to run for gov.). b. Uniontown, Pa., Dec. 5, 1800. Removed with twice-widowed mother to St. Louis, Mo., 1803, then to New Design, 1804. Attended Transylvania with aid of half-brother, George Forquer. Read law in office with Forquer, Edwardsville; admitted Ill. bar, 1824. Judge circuit court, Jan. 19, 1835, to 1837 (resigned), Feb. 25, 1839, to Feb. 15, 1841 (resigned). Gov., 1842–46; recommended const. revision, resulting in conv. call, 1847. d. Peoria, Nov. 3, 1850. His *History of Illinois, 1818 to 1848* published posthumously.

Sidney Breese, res. Clinton Co. Dem. Just. Ill. Supreme Court, Feb. 15, 1841, to Jan. 1, 1843 (resigned), Nov. 23, 1857, to June 28, 1878. b. Whitesboro, N.Y., July 15, 1800. A.B. Union, Schenectady, 1818. Moved to Kaskaskia; admitted Ill. bar, 1820. U.S. dist. att. Ill., 1827–29. Lt. col. militia Black Hawk War. Judge circuit court, 2nd Dist., Aug. 1835 to Feb. 1841. U.S. Sen., 1843–49. Ill. H.R., 1851–52 (spkr.). Judge circuit court, 2nd Dist., June 25, 1855, to Feb. 1857 (resigned). Ill. Supreme Court, Nov. 23, 1857, to 1878. C.J., June 1867 to June 6, 1870, 1873–74. d. Pinckneyville, June 28, 1878.

Walter B. Scates[5]; Stephen A Douglas (see Sec. State above).
John Dean Caton, res. Cook Co. Just. Ill. Supreme Court, Aug. 9, 1842, vice Ford, to Jan. 7, 1864 (resigned). C.J., March–June 1855, Oct. 1857 to Jan. 7, 1864. b. Monroe Co., N.Y., March 19, 1812. Moved to Cook Co.; admitted Ill. bar, 1833. J.P. Chicago, 1834; ald., 1837–38. Became wealthy with early telegraph lines. Retired, 1864; traveled and wrote. d. Chicago, July 30, 1895.

7. Administration of Thomas Ford, Dec. 8, 1842, to Dec. 9, 1846. Voting for governor: Ford, 46,452. Joseph Duncan, 39,429.
Governor Thomas Ford[6].
Lieutenant Governor John Moore, res. McLean Co. Dem. b. Lincolnshire, England, Sept. 8, 1793. Emigrated to Ill., 1830. Ill. H.R., 1836–40. Ill. Sen., 1840–42. Lt. col. 4th Ill. Vols. Mexican War. 1848. Treas., Aug. 14, 1848, to Jan. 12, 1857. d. Sept. 23, 1863.
Secretaries of State Lyman Trumbull[6] (removed from office March 4, 1843).

Thompson Campbell, res. JoDaviess Co. Dem. Sec. state, Mar. 6, 1843, to Dec. 23, 1846. b. Ireland, 1811. Emigrated with parents to Chester Co., Pa. LL.B. Jefferson; admitted Penn. bar. Moved to Galena and acquired mining interests. Resigned sec. state to become del. Ill. const. conv., 1847. U.S.H.R., 1851–53. Moved to Calif. as U.S. comm. of Mexican land grants, 1853. Returned to Ill., 1855. Del. Dem. nat. conv. Charleston, S.C., 1860. Returned to Calif., 1861; supported Union. Del. Rep. nat. conv. Baltimore, 1864. d. San Francisco, Calif., Dec. 6, 1868.
Auditors James Shields[6] (resigned May 26, 1843); William L. D. Ewing[4] (d. March 25, 1846).

Thomas H. Campbell, res. Randolph Co. Dem. Aud., March 26, 1846, to Jan. 12, 1857. Appointed by Gov. Ford, elected under constitution of 1848; only elective office. b. Pa., May 21, 1815. Chief clerk, office of aud., 1842–46. d. Springfield, Nov. 22, 1862.
Treasurer Milton Carpenter[6].
Attorneys General Josiah Lamborn[6] (to Jan. 12, 1843).

James A. McDougall, res. Morgan Co. Dem. App. att. gen., Jan. 12, 1843, to Dec. 21, 1846 (resigned). b. Bethlehem, N.Y., Nov. 19, 1817. Moved to Pike Co. Admitted Ill. bar, 1837; pract. Jonesboro. Explored Colorado River, 1849. Moved to San Francisco, Calif. Att. gen. Calif., 1850. U.S.H.R. from Calif., 1850–52. U.S. Sen.

from Calif., 1861–67. d. Albany, N.Y., Sept. 3, 1867.

United States Senators Richard M. Young[5] (to March 3, 1843); Samuel McRoberts[6] (d. March 22, 1843); Sidney Breese[6]; James Semple[4] (vice McRoberts).

United States Congressmen Zadok Casey[4] (to March 3, 1843); John Reynolds[1] (to March 3, 1843); John T. Stuart[6] (to March 3, 1843); Stephen A. Douglas[6].

Robert Smith, res. Madison Co. Dem. U.S.H.R., 1843–49, 1857–59. b. Peterborough, N.H., June 12, 1802. Teacher, merchant, mill hand; admitted N.H. bar, about 1825. Moved to Alton, 1832, where he became merchant and landowner. Ill. H.R., 1836–40. Paymaster U.S.A., 1861–65. d. Alton, Dec. 21, 1867.

John Alexander McClernand, res. Gallatin Co. Dem. U.S.H.R., 1843–51, Dec. 5, 1859, vice Harris, to Oct. 28, 1861 (resigned). b. Breckenridge Co., Ky., May 30, 1812. Moved to Shawneetown as infant; admitted Ill. bar, 1832. Served Black Hawk War. Ill. H.R., 1836–38 (resigned), 1840–44. Recruited troops for Union army; commanded troops in Ark. and Miss. as maj. gen.; resigned, Nov. 30, 1864. Judge circuit court, 30th Circuit, July 12, 1870, to June 1, 1873. Mem. Utah Commission, 1890. d. Springfield, Sept. 20, 1900.

Orlando Bell Ficklin, res. Coles Co. Dem. U.S.H.R., 1843–49, 1851–53. b. Scott Co., Ky., Dec. 16, 1808. LL.B. Transylvania, 1830. Moved to Mount Carmel, admitted Ill. bar, 1830. Q.M. Black Hawk War. State's att. Wabash Circuit, 1835. Moved to Charleston, 1837. Ill. H.R., 1838–40, 1842–43 (resigned). Del. Ill. const. conv., 1869. d. Charleston, May 5, 1886.

John Wentworth, res. Cook Co. Dem. (Rep. 1856). U.S.H.R., 1843–51, 1853–55, 1865–67. b. Sandwich, N.H., March 5, 1815. A.B. Dartmouth, 1836. Moved to Chicago, Ed. weekly *Chicago Democrat*, 1837. Bought *Democrat*, began publication as daily, 1840. Aide to Gov. Carlin 1838–42. Studied law Harvard, admitted Ill. bar, 1841. Mayor Chicago, 1857–63. d. Chicago, Oct. 16, 1888.

Joseph Pendleton Hoge, res. JoDaviess Co. Dem. U.S.H.R., 1843–47. b. Steubenville, Ohio, Dec. 15, 1810. A.B. Jefferson, 1832. Admitted Ohio bar, moved to Galena, 1836. Moved to Calif., 1853. Judge San Francisco Superior Court, 1889 until death in San Francisco, Calif., Aug. 14, 1891.

John J. Hardin, res. Morgan Co. Whig.

U.S.H.R., 1843–45. b. Frankfort, Ky., Jan 6, 1810. A.B. Transylvania, 1830. Admitted Ky. bar, moved to Jacksonville, 1831. Served in Black Hawk War. Maj. gen. Ill. militia during Mormon troubles. Pros. att. Morgan Co., 1832–36. Ill. H.R., 1836–42. Col. 1st Ill. Vols. Mexican War, killed at Buena Vista, Feb. 3, 1847.

Edward Dickinson Baker, res. Sangamon Co. Whig and Rep. U.S.H.R., March 4, 1845, to Dec. 30, 1846 (resigned), 1849–51. b. London, England, Feb. 24, 1811. Emigrated with parents to Philadelphia, Pa., 1815. Moved to Carrollton, 1825; admitted Ill. bar, 1830. Ill. H.R., 1837–38, vice Stone; 1838–40. Ill. Sen., 1840–44. Col. 4th Ill. Vols. Mexican War, promoted brig. gen. Cerro Gordo. Moved to Galena, 1847, to San Francisco, Calif., 1851. U.S. Sen. from Oreg., 1860–61. Col. 71st Penn. Inf., promoted maj. gen., Sept. 21, 1861; killed, Ball's Bluff, Oct. 21, 1861.

Justices Illinois Supreme Court William Wilson[1] C.J.; Thomas C. Browne[1]; Samuel D. Lockwood[1]; Theophilus W. Smith[2] (resigned Dec. 26, 1842); Samuel H. Treat[6]; Sidney Breese[6] (resigned Jan. 1, 1843, to enter U.S. Sen.); Walter B. Scates[5]; Stephen A. Douglas[6] (resigned June 28, 1843); Richard M. Young[5] (from Feb. 24, 1843, vice Smith); John D. Caton[6] (resigned March 6, 1843; from April 27, 1843, succeeding Robinson); John M. Robinson[4] (March 6, vice Caton, to death, April 27, 1843); Jesse B. Thomas, Jr.[5] (vice Douglas, resigned Aug. 8, 1845); James Semple[4] (Jan. 16–Aug. 16, 1843, vice Breese); James Shields[6] (vice Semple, resigned April 2, 1845).

Gustave Philipp Koerner, res. St. Clair Co. Dem. (became Rep. 1856). Assoc. just. Ill. Supreme Court, April 2, 1845, vice Shields, to Dec. 4, 1848 (court reorganized). b. Frankfurt-am-Main, Germany, Nov. 20, 1809. LL.D. Heidelberg, 1832. Wounded, fled Germany in Bursenschaft rising, Frankfurt, 1833. Admitted Ill. bar; settled in St. Clair Co. Ill. H.R., 1842–44 (resigned to become assoc. just. Ill. Supreme Court); 1870–72. Lt. gov., Jan. 10, 1853, to Jan. 12, 1857. Stumped state for Lincoln, 1858 and 1860. Min. to Spain, 1862–64. Author legal commentaries, history, and delightful memoirs. d. Belleville, April 9, 1896.

Norman Higgins Purple, res. Peoria Co. Assoc. just. Ill. Supreme Court, Aug. 8, 1845, vice Thomas, to Dec. 4, 1848 (Court reorganized). b. Otsego Co., N.Y., March 29, 1803. Moved to Pa., studied law, admitted Pa. bar, 1836. Moved to Peoria. State's att. 9th Jud. Dist., 1837. Compiled Ill. statutes in volume called *The Purple Statutes*, covering period from 1818 to 1857. d. Chicago, Aug. 9, 1863, while compiling statutes from 1857 to 1863.

8. First administration of Augustus C. French, Dec. 9, 1846, to Jan. 8, 1849. Voting for governor: French, 58,657. Thomas M. Killpatrick, 37,003. Richard Ells, 5,154.

Governor Augustus C. French, res. Crawford Co. Dem. b. Merrimack Co., N.H., Aug. 2, 1808. Attended Dartmouth; admitted N.H. bar, 1831. Moved to Albion, 1831, and Paris, 1832. Ill. H.R., 1836–37 (resigned), 1838–39 (resigned). Gov., 1846–53 (first to serve two terms). During his administration Ill. const. conv. and people approved a new constitution. d. Lebanon, Sept. 4, 1864.

Lieutenant Governor Joseph B. Wells, res. Rock Island Co. Dem. b. N.H., date unknown. App. state's att. 7th Jud. Circuit, Dec. 1843. After term as lt. gov. app. state trustee for Illinois and Michigan Canal for two-year term, succeeding Charles Oakley. Col. 6th Ill. Vols. Mexican War. State trustee Illinois and Michigan Canal, 1851–53 (second term). Pract. law Chicago. d. on visit to New York, N.Y., Dec. 26, 1855.

Secretaries of State Thompson Campbell[7] (to Dec. 23, 1846).

Horace S. Cooley, res. Adams Co. Dem. Sec. state, Dec. 23, 1846, to April 2, 1850 (d.). Appointed by Gov. French, elected under constitution of 1848. b. Hartford, Conn., 1806. Admitted Maine bar. Removed to Rushville, then Quincy, 1840. Q.M. gen. Ill. militia, 1841. d. Springfield.

Auditor Thomas H. Campbell[7].

Treasurers Milton Carpenter[6] (d. Aug. 1848); John Moore[7] (Aug. 14, 1848, to Jan. 12, 1857).

Attorney General David B. Campbell, res. Sangamon Co. Dem. Att. gen., Dec. 26, 1846, to Dec. 4, 1848. State's att. 8th Judicial Circuit, Feb. 25, 1839 (no terminal date of appointment), and from Nov. 10, 1848, to end of 1854. No further biog. data.

Under the constitution of 1818 the attorney general was appointed by the General Assembly. The office was neglected in the constitution of 1848, and was not filled from 1848 until Feb. 27, 1867, when an act specifically creating the office was approved.

United States Senators Sidney Breese[6]; James Semple[4] (to March 3, 1847); Stephen A. Douglas[6].

United States Congressmen Stephen A. Douglas[6] (to March 3, 1847); Joseph P. Hoge[7] (to March 3, 1847); Orlando B. Ficklin[7]; Robert Smith[7]; John A. McClernand[7]; John Wentworth[7].

John Henry, res. Morgan and Sangamon cos. Whig. U.S.H.R., Feb. 5–March 3, 1847, vice Baker. b. Stanford, Ky., Nov. 1, 1800. Moved to Springfield in 1820's. Pvt. Black Hawk War. Ill. H.R., 1834–36, 1838–40 from Morgan Co. Ill. Sen., 1840–48. Supt. State Insane Asylum, 1850–55. Q.M. Dept. Union army, 1861–65. d. St. Louis, Mo., April 28, 1882.

Abraham Lincoln, res. Sangamon Co. Whig. U.S.H.R., 1847–49. b. Hardin Co., Ky., Feb. 12, 1809. Moved to Ind. with parents, 1816, to Macon Co., then to Sangamon Co., 1830. Capt. Sangamon Rifles Black Hawk War. Clerk, surveyor, postmaster New Salem. Ill. H.R., 1834–42 (leader of the "Long Nine"). Declined gov. Oreg. Ter. Beaten by Douglas for U.S. Sen., 1858. Pres. U.S., 1861–65. Assassinated, Washington, D.C., April 15, 1865.

Thomas Johnston Turner, res. Stephenson Co. Dem. and Anti-Nebr. Dem. U.S.H.R., 1847–49. b. Trumbull Co., Ohio, April 5, 1815. Moved with parents to Pa., 1825; to Lake Co., Ind., 1837; to Freeport, 1838. Admitted Ill. bar, 1840. Probate judge Stephenson Co.; state's att., 1845. Established weekly *Prairie Democrat*, 1846. Ill. H.R., 1855–56 (spkr.). Col. 15th Ill. Vols., 1861 and 1862. Pract. law Chicago, 1871–74. d. Hot Springs, Ark., April 4, 1874.

William Alexander Richardson, res. Shelby, Schuyler, and Adams cos., Dem. U.S.H.R., Dec. 6, 1847, vice Douglas, to Aug. 25, 1856 (resigned); Jan. 21, 1861, to Jan. 29, 1863 (resigned, elected to U.S. Sen.). b. Lexington, Ky., Jan. 16, 1811. Attended Walnut Hill College, Centre, and Transylvania. Admitted Ky. and Ill. bars, 1831; pract. Shelbyville. State's att. Shelby Co., 1834 and 1835. Ill. H.R., 1836–38, 1844–46 (spkr.). Served Mexican War as capt. and maj. Moved to Quincy, 1849. U.S. Sen., 1863–65, succeeding Browning. d. Quincy, Dec. 27, 1875. .

Justices Illinois Supreme Court William Wilson[1] C.J. (to Dec. 4, 1848, Court dissolved); Thomas C. Browne[1] (to Dec. 4, 1848); Samuel D. Lockwood[1] (resigned

Nov. 3, 1848); Samuel Treat[6]; Walter B. Scates[5] (resigned Jan. 11, 1847); Richard M. Young[5] (resigned Jan. 25, 1847); John D. Caton[6]; Gustave P. Koerner[7] (to Dec. 4, 1848); Norman H. Purple[7] (to Dec. 4, 1848); Jesse B. Thomas, Jr.[5] (vice Young, to Dec. 4, 1848); Lyman Trumbull[6] (from Dec. 4, 1848).

William A. Denning, res. Alexander and Franklin cos. Assoc. just. Ill. Supreme Court, Jan. 18, 1847, vice Scates, to Dec. 4, 1848. Capt., 1836, col., 1837, Ill. militia. Ill. H.R., 1844–46 from Alexander Co., reelected but resigned to become Supreme Court just. Judge circuit court, 3rd Circuit, Dec. 4, 1848, to Jan. 14, 1854. No further biog. data.

David Meade Woodson, res. Greene Co. Just. Ill. Supreme Court, Nov. 3, vice Lockwood, to Dec. 4, 1848. b. Jasmine Co., Ky., May 18, 1806. Grad. Transylvania; read law with father. Moved to Greene Co. in early 1830's. Ill. H.R., 1840–42, 1869–70. Judge circuit courts, 1848–67. Mem. const. convs., 1847 and 1869–70. d. Carrollton, 1877.

On December 5, 1848, the Court, under the new constitution, consisted of Samuel Treat, C.J., John D. Caton, and Lyman Trumbull.

9. Second administration of Augustus C. French, Jan. 8, 1849, to Jan. 10, 1853. Voting for governor: French, 67,828. Charles V. Dyer, 4,962. William D. Morrison, 5,659.

Governor Augustus C. French[8].

Lieutenant Governor William McMurtry, res. Knox Co. Dem. b. Mercer Co., Ky., Feb. 20, 1801. Admitted Ky. bar. Moved to Knox Co., 1829. Ill. H.R., 1836–38. Ill. Sen., 1842–46. After term as lt. gov. retired to private practice. d. Knox Co., April 10, 1875.

Secretaries of State Horace S. Cooley[7] (d. April 2, 1850).

David L. Gregg, res. Will and Du Page cos. Dem. b. Albany, N.Y., ca. 1810. Moved to Joliet (then Juliet), 1839; pract. law; edited *Juliet Courier*. Del. Ill. const. conv., 1847. Ill. H.R., 1842–46. Sec. state April 2, 1850, to Jan. 10, 1853. Head, mission to Hawaii, 1853; adviser to King Kamehameha IV, 1853–63. Rcvr. Carson City, Nev., land office, 1863–58. d. Carson City, Nev., Dec. 23, 1868.

Auditor Thomas H. Campbell[7].

Treasurer John Moore[7].

United States Senators Stephen A. Douglas[6]; James Shields[6].

United States Congressmen Orlando B. Ficklin[7] (to March 3, 1849, and 1851–53); Robert Smith[7] (to March 3, 1849); John A. McClernand[7] (to March 3, 1851); John Wentworth[7] (to March 3, 1851); Thompson Campbell[7] (from March 4, 1851); William A. Richardson[8].

William Harrison Bissell, res. St. Clair and Monroe cos. Dem., Anti-Nebr. Dem., and Rep. U.S.H.R., 1849–55. b. Hartwick, N.Y., April 25, 1811. M.D. Jefferson Med. Moved to Monroe Co., 1835. Ill. H.R., 1840–42. During term studied law, admitted Ill. bar, moved to Belleville and began practice, 1842. Pros. att. St. Clair Co., 1844–46. Col. 2nd Ill. Inf. Mexican War. Challenged to duel by Jefferson Davis in quarrel over quality of Northern troops; meeting prevented by Pres. Tyler. Nominated for gov. by a coalition of Anti-Nebr. Dems. and Whigs. First Rep. gov. Ill., Jan. 12, 1857. d. in office, March 18, 1860.

Timothy Roberts Young, res. Clark Co. Dem. U.S.H.R., 1849–51. b. Dover, N.H., Nov. 19, 1811. A.B. Bowdoin, 1835; admitted N.H. bar, 1836. Moved to Marshall, 1838; pract. Marshall. Moved to Mattoon, 1851; mfr. plug tobacco; farmer. d. Oilfield, May 12, 1898.

Thomas Langrell Harris, res. Menard Co. Dem. U.S.H.R., 1849–51, 1855 to Nov. 24, 1858 (d). b. Norwich, Conn., Oct. 29, 1816. A.B. Washington (now Trinity), Hartford, Conn. Admitted Conn. bar; moved to Petersburg, 1842. Capt. and maj. 4th Ill. Vols. Mexican War. Sword from Ill. for gallantry Cerro Gordo. Died during third term U.S.H.R.

Willis Allen, res. Williamson Co. Dem. U.S.H.R., 1851–55. b. n. Roanoke, Va., Dec. 15, 1806. Moved to Ill., 1830; admitted Ill. bar Franklin Co. (now Williamson Co.); pract. Marion. Sheriff Franklin Co., 1834–38. Ill. H.R., 1838–40. Ill. Sen., 1844–48. Del. const. conv., 1847. Judge circuit court, 26th Circuit, March 2, 1859. Died while holding court Harrisburg, April 15, 1859.

Richard S. Moloney, res. Boone Co. Dem. U.S.H.R., 1851–53. b. Northfield, N.H., June 28, 1811. M.D. Dartmouth, 1838. Moved to Belvidere to pract. Del. Dem. conv. Baltimore, 1852. Farmer in Humboldt, Nebr., 1866–91. d. Humboldt, Nebr., Dec. 14, 1891.

Richard Yates, res. Morgan Co., Whig and Rep. U.S.H.R., 1851–55. b. Warsaw,

Ky., Jan. 18, 1818. Moved to Springfield, 1831, then to Berlin (now New Berlin). A.B. Illinois College, Jacksonville, 1835; attended Transylvania. Admitted Ill. bar, 1837, pract. Jacksonville. Ill. H.R., 1842–46, 1849–50. Gov., Jan. 14, 1861, to Jan. 16, 1865. U.S. Sen., 1865–71. d. St. Louis, Mo., Nov. 27, 1873.

Justices Illinois Supreme Court Samuel H. Treat[6], C.J.; John D. Caton[6]; Lyman Trumbull[6].

10. Administration of Joel Aldrich Matteson, Jan. 10, 1853, to Jan. 12, 1857.

Voting for governor: Matteson, 80,789. E. B. Webb, 64,408. D. A. Knowlton, 9,024.

Governor Joel Aldrich Matteson, res. Will Co. Dem. b. Watertown, N.Y., Feb. 8, 1808. Clerk, schoolteacher, railway construction foreman, moved to Joliet (then Juliet), 1834. Contractor Illinois and Michigan Canal. Ill. Sen., 1842–52. Pres. Chicago & Alton R.R., 1857. d. Chicago, Jan. 31, 1873.

Lieutenant Governor Gustave P. Koerner[7].

Secretary of State Alexander Starne, res. Pike and Sangamon cos. Dem. b. Philadelphia, Pa., Nov. 21, 1813. Moved to Ill., 1836. Comm. Pike Co., 1839–42. Ill. H.R., 1842–46. Clerk circuit court Pittsfield, 1846–52. Pres. Hannibal & Naples R.R., 1857. Treas. Ill., Jan. 12, 1863, to Jan. 9, 1865. Ill. Sen., 1871–74. Owned coal mines. d. Springfield, March 31, 1886.

Auditor Thomas H. Campbell[7].

Treasurer John Moore[7].

Superintendent of Public Instruction (new office, created by an act of the Illinois General Assembly, March 24, 1854) Ninian W. Edwards[4].

United States Senators Stephen A. Douglas[6]; James Shields[6] (to March 3, 1855); Lyman Trumbull[6].

United States Congressmen William H. Bissell[9] (to March 3, 1855); Orlando B. Ficklin[7] (to March 3, 1853); Willis Allen[9] (to March 3, 1855); William A. Richardson[8] (resigned Aug. 25, 1856); Thompson Campbell[7] (to March 3, 1853); Richard S. Moloney[9] (to March 3, 1853); John Wentworth[7] (to March 3, 1855); Richard Yates[9] (to March 3, 1855).

James Cameron Allen, res. Crawford Co. Dem. U.S.H.R., 1853–57, 1863–65. b. Shelby Co., Ky., Jan. 29, 1822. Moved with

parents to Ind., 1830; admitted Ind. bar, 1843. Moved to Palestine, 1848. Ill. H.R., 1851–52. Clerk U.S.H.R., 1857–59. Judge circuit court, 25th Circuit, July 1861 to Dec. 31, 1862; June 16, 1873, to Aug. 20, 1877. Pract. Olney, 1876–1907. d. Olney, Jan. 30, 1912.

James Knox, res. Knox Co. Whig. U.S.H.R., 1853–57. b. Canajoharie, N.Y., July 4, 1807. A.B. Yale, 1830; admitted N.Y. bar, 1833. Moved to Knoxville, 1836. Except for two terms in Cong., pract. Knoxville. d. Oct. 8, 1876.

Jesse Olds Norton, res. Will Co. Rep. U.S.H.R., 1853–57, 1863–65. b. Bennington, Vt., Dec. 25, 1812. A.B. Williams, 1835. Moved to Ill.; admitted Ill. bar, 1840. Del. Ill. const. conv., 1847. Ill. H.R., 1851–52. Judge circuit court, 11th Circuit, March 14, 1857, to July 1, 1861. Pract. Chicago after 1862. d. Chicago, Aug. 3, 1875.

Elihu Benjamin Washburne, res. Jo-Daviess Co. Whig. U.S.H.R., 1853 to March 6, 1869 (resigned). b. Livermore, Maine, Sept. 23, 1816. Journalist; studied law Harvard; admitted Maine bar, 1840. Moved to Galena, 1840. Del. nat. Whig convs., 1844, 1852. Sec. state Grant's cabinet, resigned to become min. France. Protected foreign embassies and legations in Paris during Franco-Prussian War and the Commune. Returned to Ill., 1877. Pres. Chicago Historical Society, 1884–87. d. Chicago, Oct. 22, 1887.

Samuel Scott Marshall, res. Hamilton Co. Dem. U.S.H.R., 1855–59, 1865–75. b. Shawneetown, March 12, 1821. Attended Cumberland College, Ky. Admitted Ill. bar, 1845; pract. McLeansboro. Ill. H.R., 1846–48. State's att. 3rd Jud. Circuit, 1847–48, judge, 1851–54, 1861–64. d. McLeansboro, July 26, 1890.

James Hutchinson Woodworth, res. Cook Co. Rep. U.S.H.R., 1855–57. b. Greenwich, N.Y., Dec. 4, 1804. Moved to Fabius, Onondaga Co., N.Y.; taught school and engaged in mercantile pursuits. Moved to Erie, Pa., 1827; J.P., 1829–32. Moved to Chicago, 1833; engaged in dry goods business. Ill. Sen., 1838–40. Ill. H.R., 1842–44. Ald., 1845–48; mayor Chicago, 1848–50. Pres. Merchants & Mechanics Bank of Chicago and Treasury Bank of Chicago. One of founders of first U. of Chicago. d. Highland Park, March 26, 1869.

Jacob Cunningham Davis, res. Hancock Co., Dem. U.S.H.R., Nov. 4, 1856, vice Richardson, to March 3, 1857. b. Augusta Co., Va., Sept. 16, 1820. Attended William and Mary. Moved to Warsaw, 1838;

studied law; admitted Ill. bar, pract. Warsaw. Clerk circuit court, 1841. Ill. Sen., 1842–48, 1851 to Nov. 4, 1856 (resigned to accept seat U.S.H.R.). No further pub. office. Moved to Mo., 1857. d. Alexandria, Mo., Dec. 25, 1883.

James Lowery Donaldson Morrison, res. St. Clair Co. Dem. U.S.H.R., Nov. 4, 1856, to March 3, 1857, vice Trumbull (resigned, elected to U.S. Sen.). b. Kaskaskia, April 12, 1816. App. midshipman U.S.N., 1832, served until 1839. Studied law, admitted Ill. bar; pract. Belleville, 1840. Ill. H.R., 1844–46. Lt. col. Bissell's regiment Mexican War, presented with sword by Ill. leg. for gallantry Buena Vista. After 1857 pract. law Belleville. No further pub. office. d. St. Louis, Mo., Aug. 14, 1888.

Justices Illinois Supreme Court Samuel Treat[6], C.J. (resigned March 23, 1855); John D. Caton[6], C.J., March–June 1855; Lyman Trumbull[6] (resigned July 4, 1853); Walter B. Scates[5] (vice Trumbull), C.J. from June 1855.

Onias C. Skinner, res. Adams Co. Assoc. just. Ill. Supreme Court, June 23, 1855, vice Treat, to April 19, 1858. b. Oneida Co., N.Y. Moved to Peoria, 1836. Studied law Ohio, admitted Ohio bar, returned to Carthage, 1840. Ill. H.R., 1849–50. Judge 15th Circuit, May 22, 1851, to June 1855. Pract. Quincy until his death in accident, Feb. 4, 1877.

11. Administration of William H. Bissell, Jan. 12, 1857, to Jan. 14, 1861. Voting for governor: Bissell, 111,466. William A. Richardson, 106,769. Buckner S. Morris, 19,088.

Governors William H. Bissell[9] (d. March 18, 1860).

John Wood, res. Adams Co. Whig and Rep. Lt. gov., Jan. 12, 1857, to March 20, 1860. Gov., March 21, 1860, to Jan. 14, 1861. b. Moravia, N.Y., Dec. 20, 1798. Moved to Adams Co., 1820, built first log cabin on site of Quincy. Ill. Sen., 1851–54 (resigned). App. by Lincoln Q.M. for Ill., 1861. Col. 137th Ill. Vols., 1864. d. Quincy, June 11, 1880.

Acting Lieutenant Governor Thomas A. Marshall, res. Coles Co. Whig and Rep. No record of birth. Succeeded to office, Jan. 7, 1861, on convening of Sen., served seven days. Ill. Sen., 1859–62. d. Charleston, Nov. 11, 1873.

Secretary of State Ozias M. Hatch, res. Pike Co. Rep. b. Hillsborough Centre, N.H., April 11, 1814. Moved to Griggsville, 1836; kept store to 1841. Clerk circuit court, 1841–

48. Ill. H.R., 1851–52. Ill. sec. state, 1857–65; declined third term; retired. d. Springfield, March 12, 1893.

Auditor Jesse K. Dubois, res. Lawrence Co. Whig and Rep. Aud., Jan. 12, 1857, to Dec. 12, 1864. b. of old French stock, Lawrence Co., Jan. 14, 1811. Ill. H.R., 1834–40, 1842–44. Reg. Palestine land office, 1841; rcvr. Palestine land office, 1849–53. Del. first Rep. conv., 1854. d. Sangamon Co., Nov. 22, 1876.

Treasurers James Miller, res. McLean Co. Rep. Treas., Jan. 12, 1857, to Aug. 27, 1859 (resigned). b. Rockingham Co., Va., May 23, 1795. Came to Bloomington, 1835. Merchant, landowner. Treas. only pub. office. d. Bloomington, Sept. 23, 1872.

William Butler, res. Sangamon Co. Rep. b. Adair Co., Ky., Dec. 15, 1797. Moved to Sangamon Co., 1828. Clerk circuit court, 1836. App. treas., Sept. 3, 1859. Elected, 1860, to serve from Jan. 14, 1861, to Jan. 12, 1863. d. Springfield, Jan. 11, 1876.

Superintendents of Public Instruction William H. Powell, res. Peoria Co. Rep. Supt. pub. instr., Jan. 12, 1857, to Aug. 1, 1859 (resigned). No biog. record.

Newton Bateman, res. Morgan Co. Rep. Supt. pub. instr., Aug. 1, 1859, to Jan. 12, 1863, and Jan. 10, 1865, to Jan. 11, 1875. b. Fairfield, N.J., July 27, 1822. A.B. Illinois College, Jacksonville, 1843; A.M., 1844; honorary LL.D. Taught at college level, h.s. prin. Ill. and Mo. Supt. schools Morgan Co. Pres. Knox, 1875–93. Compiled biog. encyclopedia and history of Ill. with Paul Selby. d. Galesburg, Oct. 21, 1897.

John P. Brooks, res. Sangamon Co. Dem. Supt. pub. instr., Jan. 12, 1863, to Jan. 10, 1865. No biog. record.

United States Senators Stephen A. Douglas[6]; Lyman Trumbull[6].

United States Congressmen James C. Allen[10] (to March 3, 1857); James Knox[10] (to March 3, 1857); Jesse O. Norton[10] (to March 3, 1857); Jacob C. Davis[10] (to March 3, 1857); James L. D. Morrison[10] (to March 3, 1857); James H. Woodworth[10] (to March 3, 1857); Thomas L. Harris[9] (d. Nov. 24, 1858); Samuel S. Marshall[10] (to March 3, 1859); Robert Smith[7] (March 4, 1857, to March 3, 1859); Elihu B. Washburne[10]; John A. McClernand[7] (Dec. 5, 1859, to Oct. 28, 1861, resigned).

John Franklin Farnsworth, res. Cook Co. Rep. U.S.H.R., 1857–61, 1863–73. b. Eaton,

Ontario, March 27, 1820. Moved to Ann Arbor, Mich., about 1837; admitted Mich. bar. Moved to St. Charles, then to Chicago, 1841. Pract. Chicago, 1841–57. Col. 8th Ill. Vol. Cav., 1861, brig. gen., 1862. Resigned March 4, 1863, to return to Congress. Pract. Chicago, 1873–80, Washington, D.C., 1880–97. d. Washington, D.C., July 14, 1897.

Charles Drury Hodges, res. Greene Co. Dem. U.S.H.R., Jan. 14–March 3, 1859, vice Harris. b. Queen Anne, Md., Feb. 4, 1810. A.B. Trinity, Hartford, Conn., 1829. Admitted Md. bar, 1831; moved to Carrollton, 1833. Ill. H.R., 1851–54. Judge county court, 1854–58. Judge circuit court, 1st Circuit June 27, 1867, to June 1, 1873. Ill. Sen., 1875–78. d. Carrollton, April 1, 1884.

William Kellogg, res. Fulton and Peoria cos. Rep. U.S.H.R., 1857–63. b. Kelloggsville, Ohio, July 8, 1814. Moved to Canton; admitted Ill. bar about 1836. Ill. H.R., 1849–50. Judge circuit court, 1st Circuit, Feb. 12, 1850, to Nov. 1852. C.J. Nebr. Ter., 1865–67. Coll. int. rev. Peoria, 1867–69. d. Dec. 20, 1872.

Owen Lovejoy, res. Bureau Co. Rep. U.S.H.R., 1857 to March 25, 1864 (d). b. Albion, Maine, Jan. 6, 1811. A.B. Bowdoin, 1832. Moved to Alton, 1836. Ordained min. Congregational Church Princeton, 1839, serving to 1856. Ill. H.R., 1855–56. d. Brooklyn, N.Y., during third term U.S.H.R.

Isaac Newton Morris, res. Adams Co. Rep. U.S.H.R., 1857–61. b. Bethel, Ohio, Jan. 22, 1812. Attended Miami; moved to Warsaw. Admitted Ill. bar, 1836; moved to Quincy, 1838. Pres. Illinois and Michigan Canal Board, 1841. Ill. H.R., 1846–48. App. by Pres. Grant comm. Union Pacific R.R., 1869. d. Quincy, Oct. 29, 1879.

Aaron Shaw, res. Lawrence and Crawford cos. Dem. U.S.H.R., 1857–59, 1883–85. b. n. Goshen, N.Y., Dec. 19, 1811. Moved to Lawrenceville; admitted Ill. bar, 1833; pract. Lawrenceville. Ill. H.R., 1851–52 from Lawrence Co., 1860–62 from Crawford Co. Judge circuit court, 25th Circuit, March 2, 1863, to June 1869. d. Olney, Jan. 7, 1887.

James Carroll Robinson, res. Clark Co. Dem. U.S.H.R., 1859–65, 1871–75. b. n. Paris, Aug. 19, 1823. Corp. Mexican War. Admitted Ill. bar, 1850; pract. Marshall. Moved to Springfield, 1869 and pract. d. Springfield, Nov. 3, 1886.

Philip Bond Fouke, res. St. Clair Co. Dem. U.S.H.R., 1859–63. b. Kaskaskia, Jan. 23, 1818. Civil engineer and publisher

Belleville Advocate, 1841. Admitted Ill. bar, 1845. Ill. H.R., 1851–1852, vice Harbert Patterson. Col. 30th Ill. Vol. Inf., 1861, wounded at Belmont. Pract. law Washington, D.C., 1865 until death in Washington, D.C., Oct. 3, 1876.

John Alexander Logan, res. Jackson and Cook cos. Dem. in 1859, Rep. after Civil War. U.S.H.R., 1859–1861 (resigned effective April 2, 1862), 1867–71. b. Murphysboro, Feb. 9, 1826. Second lt. Mexican War. LL.B. Louisville, 1851; admitted Ill. bar, 1852. Ill. H.R., 1853–54, 1857–58. U.S. pros. att. 3rd Dist. Illinois, 1853–57. Col. 31st Ill. Vol. Inf., Sept. 18, 1861. Promoted brig. gen. Ft. Donelson, March 21, 1862; maj. gen., Nov. 29, 1862. Commanding gen. 15th Corps Vicksburg; commanding gen. Army of the Tennessee, 1864. Declined commission regular army. U.S. Sen., 1871–77, 1879–86. d. first year third term, Dec. 26, 1886.

Justices Illinois Supreme Court John D. Caton[6], C.J. from Oct. 1857; Onias S. Skinner[10] (to April 19, 1858); Walter B. Scates[5], C.J. (resigned May 1857); Sidney Breese[6] (vice Scates, from Nov. 23, 1857).

Pinckney H. Walker, res. Schuyler and McDonough cos. Just. Ill. Supreme Court, April 19, 1858, vice Skinner, to Feb. 16, 1885 (d.). C.J., Jan. 1864 to June 1867, 1874, 1879. b. Adair Co., Ky., June 8, 1815. Moved to Rushville, 1834, to Macomb, 1838. Admitted Ill. bar, 1839; pract. Macomb until 1848, Rushville, 1848–53. Judge circuit court, 5th Circuit, March 17, 1853, to April 19, 1858.

12. Administration of Richard Yates, Jan. 14, 1861, to Jan. 16, 1865. Voting for governor: Yates, 172,196. James C. Allen, 159,253. T. M. Hope, 2,049. John Todd Stuart, 1,626. J. W. Chickering, 1,148.

Governor Richard Yates[9].

Lieutenant Governor Francis A. Hoffman, res. Cook Co. Whig and Rep. b. Herford, Prussia, 1822. Emigrated to Chicago, 1839; bootblack, schoolteacher. Ald., 1852–60. Elected lt. gov. on Lincoln ticket. Rep. elector, 1864. Ed. farm paper in southern Wis. d. Chicago, Jan. 23, 1903.

Secretary of State Ozias M. Hatch[11].

Auditors Jesse K. Dubois[11] (to Dec. 24, 1864).

Orin H. Miner, res. Sangamon Co. Rep. Aud., Dec. 24, 1864, to Jan. 11, 1869. b. Vt., May 13, 1825. Watchmaker, came to Chicago from Ohio, 1851. Explored canal route in Nicaragua with Gen. Walker, 1855. Moved to Springfield, Chief clerk aud. office, 1857–64. d. Springfield, 1879.

Treasurers William Butler[11] (to Jan. 12, 1863); Alexander Starne[10] (Jan. 12, 1863, to Jan. 9, 1865).

Superintendent of Public Instruction Newton Bateman[11].

United States Senators Stephen A. Douglas[6] (d. June 3, 1861); Lyman Trumbull[6]; William A. Richardson[8] (1863–65).

Orville Hickman Browning, res. Adams Co. Whig and Rep. b. Cynthiana, Ky., Feb. 10, 1806. Admitted Ky. bar, 1831. Moved to and pract. in Quincy. Ill. Sen., 1836–40. Ill. H.R., 1842–44. Del. Rep. conv. Bloomington, 1856, Chicago, 1860. App. U.S. Sen., June 1861, vice Douglas, to 1863. Sec. interior, 1866–69. Pract. Quincy, 1869–71. d. Quincy, Aug. 10, 1881.

United States Congressmen John F. Farnsworth[11] (to March 3, 1861, 1863–65); Isaac N. Morris[11] (to March 3, 1861); John A. McClernand[7] (resigned Oct. 28, 1861); John A. Logan[11] (resigned effective April 2, 1862, but was in Union army Sept. 1861); William Kellogg[11] (to March 3, 1863); Philip B. Fouke[11] (to March 3, 1863); Owen Lovejoy[11] (d. March 25, 1864); Elihu B. Washburne[10]; William A. Richardson[8] (resigned Jan. 29, 1863); James C. Allen[10] (1863–65); John F. Farnsworth[11] (from March 4, 1863); Jesse Olds Norton[10] (1863–65); John Todd Stuart[6] (1863–65); James C. Robinson[11].

William Joshua Allen, res. Williamson Co. Dem. U.S.H.R., June 2, 1862, to 1865. b. Wilson Co., Tenn., June 9, 1829. Moved with father to Franklin Co., 1830, to Marion, 1839. Admitted Ill. bar, 1849, pract. Metropolis. Enrolling and engrossing clerk second session Ill. H.R., 1849–50, 1851–52. Mem. Ill. H.R., 1855–56. Returned to Marion, 1853. Judge circuit court, 26th Circuit, June 24, 1859 to June 1861. Returned to prac. Marion, 1865. Judge U.S. Dist. Court, 1887–1901. d. on visit to Hot Springs, Ark., Jan. 26, 1901.

Isaac Newton Arnold, res. Cook Co. Rep. U.S.H.R., 1861–65. b. Hartwick, N.Y., Nov. 30, 1815. Admitted N.Y. bar, 1835. Moved to Chicago, 1836. Ill. H.R., 1842–46, 1857–58. Aud. U.S. Treasury, 1865–66. Pract. law Chicago and wrote until his death, April 24, 1884.

John Rice Eden, res. Moultrie Co. Dem. U.S.H.R., 1863–65, 1873–79, 1885–87. b. Bath Co., Ky., Feb. 1, 1826. Moved to Ind. as child. Moved to Sullivan; admitted Ill.

bar, 1853. State's att. 17th Dist. Ill., Nov. 17, 1856, to Dec. 1, 1860. Pract. law Sullivan until death, June 9, 1909.

Charles Murray Harris, res. Henderson Co. Dem. U.S.H.R., 1863–65. b. Munfordville, Ky., April 10, 1821. Admitted Ky. bar, moved to Oquawka about 1843. One term in Cong. only pub. office. d. Chicago, Sept. 20, 1896.

Ebon Clark Ingersoll, res. Peoria and Gallatin cos. Rep. U.S.H.R., May 20, 1864, vice Lovejoy, to 1871. b. Dresden, N.Y., Dec. 12, 1831. Moved to Wis., then to Ill., 1843. Admitted Ill. bar, 1854; pract. Peoria. Ill. H.R., 1857–58 from Gallatin Co. Pract. Washington, D.C., 1871 until death, May 31, 1879.

Anthony Lausett Knapp, res. Jersey Co. Dem. U.S.H.R., Dec. 12, 1861, to 1865. b. Middleton, N.Y., June 14, 1828. Moved with parents to Jerseyville, 1839. Admitted Ill. bar about 1850. Ill. Sen., 1859–62. Pract. Chicago, 1865–67, Springfield, 1867 until death, May 24, 1881.

William Ralls Morrison, res. Monroe Co. Dem. U.S.H.R., 1863–65, 1873–87. b. Waterloo, Sept. 14, 1825. Pvt. Mexican War. Attended McKendree. Joined gold rush, 1849; returned Ill., 1851. Admitted Ill. bar, 1855. Clerk Monroe Co. Court, 1852–54. Ill. H.R., 1855–60 (spkr., 1859–60). Col. 49th Ill. Inf., 1861–63; wounded at Ft. Donelson. Ill. H.R., 1871–72. Interstate Commerce Commission, 1887–97 (chairman 1892–97). Pract. Waterloo, 1897 until death, Sept. 29, 1909.

Lewis Winans Ross, res. Fulton Co. Dem. U.S.H.R., 1863–69. b. n. Seneca Falls, N.Y., Dec. 8, 1812. Moved to Ill; attended Illinois College, Jacksonville, 1837. Admitted Ill. bar; pract. Lewistown, 1839. Ill. H.R., 1840–42, 1844–46. Pract. Lewistown, 1869 until death, Oct. 20, 1895.

Justices Illinois Supreme Court John D. Caton[6], C.J. (resigned Jan. 7, 1864); Sidney Breese[6]; Pinckney H. Walker[11], C.J. from Jan. 1864.

Croydon Beckwith, res. Cook Co. b. Vt., 1823. Admitted Vt. bar. Moved to Chicago, 1853. App. Ill. Supreme Court to complete Caton's term, served to June 6, 1864. d. Chicago, Aug. 18, 1890.

Charles B Lawrence, res. Adams Co. Just. Ill. Supreme Court, July 22, 1864, vice Beckwith, to June 1873. C.J., 1870–73. b. Vergennes, Vt., Dec. 17, 1820. Admitted Mo. bar St. Louis, 1844; moved to Quincy.

Judge circuit court, 10th Circuit, July 1, 1861, to July 4, 1864 (resigned). Moved to Chicago, 1873; defeated by David Davis for U.S. Sen., 1877. d. Decatur, Ala., April 9, 1883.

13. First administration of Richard James Oglesby, Jan. 16, 1865, to Jan. 11, 1869.
Voting for governor: Oglesby, 190,376. James C. Robinson, 158,701.

Governor Richard James Oglesby, res. Macon Co. Whig and Rep. b. Oldham Co., Ky., July 25, 1824. Orphaned at eight, accompanied uncle to Decatur, 1836. Worked at carpentry, farming, rope-making while studying law. Admitted Ill. bar, 1845; pract. Sullivan. Lt. 4th Ill. Vols. Mexican War, served with distinction at Vera Cruz, Cerro Gordo. Joined Calif. gold rush; returned to Ill. and completed legal education Louisville Law School, Ky. Ill. Sen., 1861 (resigned). Col. 8th Ill. Vols., cited for gallantry Fts. Henry and Donelson, and at Corinth, where wounded. Promoted maj. gen., 1862. Retired (disability), 1864. Again elected gov., 1872, commissioned Jan. 13, 1873, but resigned Jan. 23, 1873, to become U.S. senator, 1873–79. Elected gov. third time, 1884; served full term. d. Elkhart, April 24, 1899.

Lieutenant Governor William Bross, res. Cook Co. Whig and Rep. b. Montague, N.J., Nov. 4, 1813. A.B. Williams, 1838. Journalist *Chicago Press*, 1852–58, *Chicago Tribune*, 1858–90. Signed ratification Thirteenth Amendment in absence of Oglesby. d. Chicago, Jan. 27, 1890.

Secretary of State Sharon Tyndale, res. St. Clair Co., Rep. b. Philadelphia, Pa., Jan. 19, 1816. Moved to Belleville, 1833; surveyor, merchant. B.E. Cambridge (now Massachusetts) Inst. of Technology, 1851. County surveyor St. Clair Co., 1857. P.M. Belleville, 1861–65. Slain by robbers, April 29, 1871.

Auditor Orin H. Miner[12].

Treasurers James H. Beveridge, res. De Kalb Co. Rep. Treas., Jan. 9, 1865, to Jan. 10, 1867. b. Washington Co., N.Y., 1828 (brother, Gov. John L. Beveridge). Dairy farmer n. Sandwich. Clerk circuit court and recorder De Kalb Co., 1852–60. Sec. Ill. State House Commission, 1867–77. Died on his farm, Jan. 1896.

George Washington Smith, res. Cook Co. Rep. Treas., Jan. 10, 1867, to Jan. 11, 1869. b. Brooklyn, N.Y., Jan. 8, 1837. Taught school Ark. LL.B. Albany; moved to Chicago, 1858. Capt. 88th Ill. Inf., 1862; wounded and captured, Stone River; escaped. Cited for bravery Gordon's Mills; wounded Missionary Ridge. Battlefield promotion bravery Kenesaw Mt. to lt. col., and to col. for bravery Franklin, Ga. Promoted brig. gen., 1865. Treas. only pub. office. Trustee Chicago Historical Society and V.P. board. d. Chicago, Sept. 16, 1898.

Superintendent of Public Instruction Newton Bateman[11].

Attorney General (office restored Feb. 28, 1867) Robert G. Ingersoll, res. Peoria Co. Rep. from 1864. Att. gen., Feb. 28, 1867, to Jan. 11, 1869. b. Dresden, N.Y., Aug. 11, 1833. Admitted Ill. bar; pract. Shawneetown with brother. Moved to Peoria, 1857. Col. 11th Ill. Cav., 1862. Famous as orator, author, and agnostic. d. Dobbs Ferry, N.Y., July 21, 1899.

United States Senators Lyman Trumbull[6]; Richard Yates[9]; William A. Richardson[8] (to March 3, 1865).

United States Congressmen William J. Allen[12] (to March 3, 1865); Isaac N. Arnold[12] (to March 3, 1865); John R. Eden[12] (to March 3, 1865); Charles M. Harris[12] (to March 3, 1865); Anthony L. Knapp[12] (to March 3, 1865); William R. Morrison[12] (to March 3, 1865); John F. Farnsworth[11]; Elihu B. Washburne[10]; John Wentworth[7]; Ebon C. Ingersoll[12]; Lewis W. Ross[12]; Samuel S. Marshall[10]; John A. Logan[11].

Jehu Baker, res. St. Clair Co. Rep. U.S.H.R., 1865–69, 1887–89, 1897–99. b. Lexington, Ky., Nov. 4, 1822. Moved to Lebanon with father, 1829. Attended McKendree. Admitted Ill. bar, 1846; pract. Belleville. Master in chancery St. Clair Co., 1861–65. U.S. min. to Venezuela, 1878–85. d. Belleville, March 1, 1903.

Henry Pelham Holmes Bromwell, res. Coles Co. Rep. U.S.H.R., 1865–69. b. Baltimore, Md., Aug. 26, 1823. Moved with parents to Cincinnati, Ohio, 1824, to Cumberland, 1836. Admitted Ill. bar, pract. Vandalia, 1853. Judge Fayette County Court, 1853–57. Moved to Charleston, 1857. After two terms in Cong. moved to Denver, Colo. Compiled *General Statutes of Colorado*. d. Denver, Colo., Jan. 7, 1903.

Albert George Burr, res. Scott and Greene cos. Dem. U.S.H.R., 1867–71. b. Batavia, N.Y., Nov. 8, 1829. Brought to Ill. by mother, 1830. Taught school. Admitted Ill. bar, 1856; pract. Winchester. Ill. H.R., 1861–64. Moved to Greene Co., 1868. Del. Ill. const. conv., 1869. Judge circuit court,

7th Circuit, Aug. 20, 1877, to June 1879. d. Carrollton, June 10, 1882.

Burton Chauncey Cooke, res. La Salle Co. Rep. U.S.H.R., 1865 to Aug. 26, 1871 (resigned). b. Pittsford, N.Y., May 11, 1819. Moved to Ottawa, 1835. Admitted Ill. bar, 1840. State's att. 9th Ill. Dist., 1846–52. Ill. Sen., 1853–60. Seconder for Lincoln, 1860, nominated him, 1864. Resigned during third term U.S.H.R., pract. Evanston from 1871. d. Evanston, Aug. 18, 1894.

Shelby Moore Cullom, res. Sangamon Co. Rep. U.S.H.R., 1865–71. b. Wayne Co., Ky., Nov. 22, 1829. Moved with parents to Tazewell Co., 1830. Attended Rock River Sem., Rockford. Admitted Ill. bar, 1855. City att. Springfield, 1855. Ill. H.R., 1857–58, 1861–62, 1873–76 (spkr., 1873–74). Twice elected gov., served from Jan. 8, 1877, to his resignation, Feb. 6, 1883, to accept seat U.S. Sen. Served continuously in Sen. to March 3, 1913. d. Washington, D.C., Jan. 8, 1914.

Abner Clark Harding, res. Warren Co., Rep. U.S.H.R., 1865–69. b. East Hampton, Conn., Feb. 10, 1807. Admitted N.Y. bar, 1827. Moved to Monmouth, 1838. Del. const. conv., 1847. Ill. H.R., 1849–50. Enlisted 83rd Ill. Vol. Inf., 1861. Promoted through several grades to col., for gallantry to brig. gen., 1864. Banker, railroad builder, 1869–74. d. Monmouth, July 19, 1874.

Norman Buel Judd, res. Cook Co. Rep. U.S.H.R., 1867–71. b. Rome, N.Y., Jan. 10, 1815. Admitted N.Y. bar; moved to Chicago, 1836. City att. Chicago, 1837–39. Ill. Sen., 1844–60. Del. Rep. conv., 1860, nominated Lincoln. Min. to Prussia, 1861–65. Coll. Port of Chicago, Dec. 5, 1872, until death, Chicago, Nov. 10, 1878.

Andrew Jackson Kuykendall, res. Johnson Co. Rep. U.S.H.R., 1865–67. b. Gallatin Co., March 3, 1815. Admitted Ill. bar, 1840; pract. Vienna. Ill. H.R., 1842–46. Ill. Sen., 1851–62, 1879–82. Maj. 31st Ill. Vol. Inf., 1861–62. Pract. Vienna, 1867–73. Probate judge Johnson Co., 1873–81. d. Vienna, May 11, 1891.

Samuel Wheeler Moulton, res. Shelby Co. Dem. and (from 1896) Rep. U.S.H.R., 1865–67, 1881–85. b. Wenham, Mass., Jan. 20, 1821. Taught school Ky. and Miss. Moved to Coles Co., 1845. Admitted Ill. bar; pract. Sullivan. Moved to Shelbyville, 1849. Ill. H.R., 1853–58. Pres. Ill. State Board of Education, 1859–76. d. Shelbyville, June 3, 1905.

Anthony Thornton, res. Shelby Co. Dem. U.S.H.R., 1865–67. b. Bourbon Co., Ky., Nov. 9, 1814. Attended Centre; A.B. Miami, 1834. Studied law, admitted Ky. bar; pract. Paris, Ky. Moved to Shelbyville, 1836. Maj. Ill. militia Mexican War. Del. Ill. const. conv., 1847. Ill. H.R., 1851–52. Just. Ill. Supreme Court, July 2, 1870, to May 31, 1873 (resigned). Chm. Ill. Board of Arbitration, 1895–97. d. Shelbyville, Sept. 10, 1904.

Green Berry Raum, res. Saline Co. Rep. U.S.H.R., 1867–69. b. Golconda, Dec. 3, 1829. Admitted Ill. bar, 1853; pract. Golconda. Moved to Kansas, 1856, to Harrisburg, 1858. Maj. 56th Ill. Vol. Inf., 1861, rose to brig. gen., 1864. Railroad builder, lawyer after 1869. U.S. comm. int. rev., 1876–83. U.S. comm. pensions, 1889–93. Pract. Chicago, 1893 to death, Dec. 18, 1909.

Justices Illinois Supreme Court Sidney Breese[6], C.J. from June 1867; Charles B. Lawrence[12]; Pinckney H. Walker[11].

14. Administration of John McAuley Palmer, Jan. 11, 1869, to Jan. 13, 1873. Voting for governor: Palmer, 249,912. John R. Eden, 199,813.

Governor John McAuley Palmer, res. Macoupin and Sangamon cos. Dem. and Rep. b. Eagle Creek, Ky., Sept. 13, 1817. Moved with parents to Ill., 1831. LL.B. Shurtleff, 1839. Admitted Ill. bar, Dec. 1839; pract. Carlinville. Probate judge Macoupin Co., 1843, reelected, 1847. Ill. Sen., 1851–52, vice Witt, 1853–56 (resigned). Chaired first Rep. conv. Bloomington, 1856. Col. commanding 14th Ill. Vol. Inf., 1861, promoted brig. gen., Dec. 20, 1861, maj. gen., Nov. 29, 1862. Commanding gen. 14th Army Corps. During his term as gov. the present Ill. const. was framed in convention, 1869, and accepted by the people of Ill., 1870. U.S. Sen., 1891–97. Pres. cand. (Sound Money Dem.), 1896. d. Springfield, Sept. 25, 1900.

Lieutenant Governor John Dougherty, res. Union Co. Rep. b. Dutch Creek, Ohio, May 6, 1806. After father's death moved with mother to Ill., 1808. Taught school, mined; read law in office of Alexander Pope Field, Jonesboro. Admitted Ill. bar, 1831; pract. Jonesboro. Ill. H.R., 1832–35 (resigned), 1836–38, 1840–42, 1857–58. Ill. Sen., 1842–48. Rep. elector, 1864. Judge circuit court, 1st Circuit, Aug. 20, 1877, to 1879. d. Jonesboro, Sept. 7, 1879.

Secretary of State Edward Rummell, res. Peoria Co. Rep. b. Baden, Germany,

Nov. 1838. Emigrated to Chicago at age thirteen. Ed. *Chicago Republican*, 1854–58. Moved to Peoria, published *Deutsche Zeitung*, Rep. party organ in German. Defeated for reelection, 1872. d. Chicago, Sept. 7, 1894.

Auditor Charles Elliott Lippincott, res. Cass Co. Rep. Aud., 1869–77. b. Edwardsville, Jan. 26, 1825. M.D. St. Louis Medical, 1849; pract. Chandlerville. In Calif., 1852–56; Calif. Sen., 1853–55. Returned Cass Co., 1861, recruited company of inf. attached 33rd Ill. Vol. Inf. Promoted col., Sept. 17, 1862, brig. gen., Feb. 17, 1865. Sec Ill. Sen., 1867 (resigned). First supt. Ill. Soldiers' and Sailors' Home, Quincy. d. in accident, Sept. 13, 1887.

Treasurer Erastus Newton Bates, res. Marion Co. Rep. Treas., 1869–71; Reelected under new const., 1870, and served to Jan. 13, 1873. b. Plainfield, Mass., Feb. 29, 1828. A.B. Williams, 1853. Moved to Minn. prior to 1856, to Centralia, 1859. Admitted Ill. bar. Maj. 80th Ill. Vol. Inf., Aug. 25, 1862, promoted to lt. col., Jan. 25, 1865, col., and bvt. brig. gen. Prisoner war Libby Prison and Charleston, 1864 to end of Civil War. Ill. H.R., 1867–68. d. Minneapolis, Minn., May 29, 1898.

Superintendent of Public Instruction Newton Bateman[11].

Attorney General Washington Bushnell, res. La Salle Co., Dem. b. Madison Co., N.Y., Sept. 30, 1825. Moved to Kendall Co. with parents, 1837. Taught school; admitted to Ill. bar Ottawa. Ill. Sen., 1861–68. d. Ottawa, June 30, 1885.

United States Senators Lyman Trumbull[6]; Richard Yates[9] (to March 3, 1871); John A. Logan[11].

United States Congressmen Elihu B. Washburne[10] (resigned March 6, 1869, to enter Pres. Grant's cabinet); Lewis W. Ross[12] (to March 3, 1869); Jehu Baker[13] (to March 3, 1869); Henry P. H. Bromwell[13] (to March 3, 1869); Green B. Raum[13] (to March 3, 1869); John A. Logan[11] (to March 3, 1871, elected to U.S. Sen.); Ebon C. Ingersoll[12] (to March 3, 1871); Albert G. Burr[13] (to March 3, 1871); Shelby M. Cullom[13] (to March 3, 1871); Norman B. Judd[13] (to March 3, 1871); Burton C. Cooke[13] (resigned Aug. 26, 1871); James C. Robinson[11] (from March 4, 1871); John F. Farnsworth[11]; Samuel S. Marshall[10].

John Lourie Beveridge, res. Cook Co.

Rep. U.S.H.R., Dec. 4, 1871, to Jan. 4, 1873 (resigned). b. Greenwich, N.Y., July 6, 1824. Moved to De Kalb Co., 1842. Attended Rock River Sem., Rockford. Studied and taught school Knoxville, Tenn.; admitted Tenn. bar. Returned to Sycamore, 1851; moved to Chicago, 1854. Maj. 8th Ill. Vol. Cav., Sept. 18, 1861; col. 17th Ill. Vol. Cav., Jan. 28, 1864; bvt. brig. gen., March 7, 1865. Sheriff Cook Co., 1866. Ill. Sen., 1871–72 (resigned). Lt. gov., Jan. 13–Jan. 23, 1873, became gov. on resignation of Richard J. Oglesby. d. Los Angeles, Calif., May 3, 1910.

Horatio Chapin Burchard, res. Stephenson Co. Rep. U.S.H.R., Dec. 6, 1869, to March 3, 1879. b. Marshall, N.Y., Sept. 22, 1825. B.A. Hamilton, 1850. Admitted Ill. bar; pract. Freeport, 1854. Ill. H.R., 1863–66. Dir. U.S. Mint, 1879–85. Pract. Freeport until death, May 14, 1908.

John Montgomery Crebs, res. White Co. Dem. U.S.H.R., 1869–73. b. Middleburg, Va., April 9, 1830. Moved with parents to White Co., 1837. Admitted Ill. bar, 1852; pract. Carmi. Lt. col. 87th Ill. Vol. Inf., 1862; col., 1864, commanded brigade. U.S.H.R. only pub. office. d. Carmi, June 26, 1890.

Charles Benjamin Farwell, res. Cook Co. Rep. U.S.H.R., 1871 to May 6, 1876, 1881–83. b. Painted Post, N.Y., July 1, 1823. Moved to Ill., 1838. Real estate broker and banker. Clerk Cook Co., 1853–61. Wholesale merchant Chicago. Chm. Cook Co. Board of Supervisors, 1868–75. Election to U.S.H.R. in 1875 contested, he was unseated, May 6, 1876. Reelected to Cong. in 1881. U.S. Sen., Jan. 19, 1887, vice Logan, to 1891. d. Lake Forest, Sept. 23, 1903.

John Baldwin Hawley, res. Rock Island Co. Rep. U.S.H.R., 1869–75. b. Hawleyville, Conn., Feb. 9, 1831. Moved with parents to Carthage; attended Illinois College, Jacksonville. Admitted Ill. bar, 1854; pract. Rock Island. State's att., 1856–60. Capt. 45th Ill. Vol. Inf., 1861–62 (resigned, injuries). Asst. sec. treas. 1877–80 (resigned). Returned to pract. Chicago to 1886, and later Omaha, Nebr. Gen. att. North Western R.R. western lines. d. Hot Springs, S. Dak., on visit, May 24, 1895.

John Breese Hay, res. St. Clair Co. Rep. U.S.H.R., 1869–73. b. Belleville, Jan. 8, 1834. Admitted Ill. bar, 1851. Pros. att. 24th Jud. Circuit, 1860–68. Served with 130th Vol. Inf. P.M. Belleville, 1881–85. Judge St. Clair Co. Court, 1886–1900, 1905–14. d. Belleville, June 16, 1916.

Thompson Ware McNeely, res. Menard

Co. Dem. U.S.H.R., 1869–73. b. Jackson-ville, Oct. 5, 1835. A.B. Lombard, Gales-burg, 1856; LL.B. Louisville. Admitted Ill. bar; pract. Petersburg, 1857. After two terms U.S.H.R. returned to pract. Petersburg. Master in chancery Menard Co., 1910 to death, Petersburg, July 23, 1921.

Jesse Hale Moore, res. Macon Co. Rep. U.S.H.R., 1869–73. b. Lebanon, April 22, 1817. A.B. McKendree, 1842. Taught school 1842–48. Ordained Methodist min., 1849. Col. 115th Ill. Vol. Inf., Sept. 13, 1862; bvt. brig. gen., May 15, 1865, for meritorious service. Presiding elder, Decatur Dist. Ill. Methodist Conf., 1868. U.S. pension agent Springfield, 1873–77. Consul Callao, Peru, 1881–83. d. Callao, Peru, July 11, 1883.

Edward Young Rice, res. Montgomery Co. Dem. U.S.H.R., 1871–73. b. Logan Co., Ky., Feb. 8, 1820. Admitted Ky. bar, 1844. Moved to Hillsboro, 1847. Ill. H.R., 1849–50. Judge Montgomery Co. Court, 1851–52. Master in chancery, 1853–57. Judge circuit court, 18th Circuit, April 13, 1857, to Aug. 20, 1870 (resigned). Pract. Hillsboro and Springfield. d. Hillsboro, April 16, 1883.

Henry Snapp, res. Will Co. Rep. U.S.H.R., Dec. 4, 1871, vice Cook, to March 3, 1873. b. Livonia, N.Y., June 30, 1822. Moved with parents to Homer, Will. Co., 1833. Admitted Ill. bar; pract. Joliet, 1843. Ill. Sen., 1869–71 (resigned). No other pub. offices. d. Joliet, Nov. 26, 1895.

Bradford Newcomb Stevens, res. Bureau Co. Dem. U.S.H.R., 1871–73. b. Boscawen, N.H., Jan. 3, 1813. A.B. Dartmouth, 1835. Moved to Tiskilwa, 1846. Merchant, farmer, mayor Tiskilwa. One term U.S.H.R. only state office. d. Tiskilwa, Nov. 10, 1885.

Justices Illinois Supreme Court (Per constitution of 1870, court enlarged to seven justices, with senior serving as C.J. Tenure nine years. For this reason almost all justices served one or more terms as chief. Terms ran from June to June, unless otherwise stated.) Sidney Breese[6]; Charles B. Lawrence[12]; Pinckney H. Walker[11]; Anthony Thornton[13].

William K. McAllister, res. Cook Co. Just. Ill. Supreme Court, Aug. 8, 1870, to Nov. 26, 1875 (resigned). b. Washington Co. N.Y., 1818. Admitted N.Y. bar. Moved to Chicago, 1854. Judge Recorder's Court Chicago, 1868–70. Judge Circuit Court Cook Co., Nov. 26, 1875; assigned to appellate court, 1879. Served in both courts until his death in office, Oct. 29, 1888.

John M. Scott, res. McLean Co. Just. Ill. Supreme Court, Aug. 8, 1870, to 1888. C.J., 1875, 1882, 1886. Refused third term. b.

St. Clair Co., Aug. 1, 1824. Admitted Ill. bar Belleville, 1848; moved to McLean Co. Co. judge, 1852–62. Judge circuit court, 8th Circuit, Dec. 2, 1862, to Aug. 7, 1870 (resigned). Author *History of the Illinois Supreme Court*. d. Bloomington, Jan. 21, 1898.

Benjamin R. Sheldon, res. JoDaviess and Winnebago cos. Just. Ill. Supreme Court, Aug. 8, 1870, to 1888. C.J., 1876, 1883, 1887. b. Mass., 1813. A.B. Williams, 1831. LL.B. Yale, admitted Conn. bar, 1836. Moved to Hennepin, then to Galena. Judge circuit court, 6th Circuit, Dec. 4, 1848, to May 1851; 14th Circuit, June 18, 1851, to Aug. 7, 1870. Retired to pract. Rockford, 1888. d. Rockford, April 13, 1897.

15. Second administration of Richard J. Oglesby, Jan. 13–23, 1873, and John L. Beveridge, Jan. 23, 1873, to Jan. 8, 1877. (Oglesby elected to two posts, served ten days as governor, then went to U.S. Sen.) Voting for governor: Oglesby, 237,774. Gustave P. Koerner, 197,084. B. G. Wright, 2,185.

Governors Richard J. Oglesby[13]; John L. Beveridge[14].

Lieutenant Governors John Early, res. Winnebago Co. Rep. Acting lt. gov., Jan. 23, 1873, to Jan. 8, 1875. b. Essex West Co., Ontario, March 17, 1828. Moved to Boone Co., 1846, to Rockford, 1852. Pioneer insurance agent. Ill. Sen., 1871 to Sept. 2, 1877 (d.). d. Highland Park.

Archibald A. Glenn, res. Brown Co. Rep. Acting lt. gov., Jan. 8, 1875, to Jan. 8, 1877. b. Nicholas Co., Ky., Jan. 30, 1819. Moved to Vermilion Co., 1828, to Schuyler Co., 1831, where father died and boy helped support family. Printer's apprentice, printer, reporter, 1838–44. Publisher Whig news-papers, 1844. Ill. Sen., 1873–76. Removed to Kans. about 1878. d. Wichita, Kans., May 21, 1901.

Secretary of State George H. Harlow, res. Tazewell Co. Rep. Sec. state, Jan. 13, 1873, to Jan. 17, 1881. b. Sackett's Harbor, N.Y., 1830. Moved to Pekin, 1854. Com-mission merchant, mayor Pekin, one of eight founders of the Union League of America to oppose proslavery Sons of Liberty during Civil War. Pvt. sec. Gov. Oglesby, 1865–69. Asst. sec. state, 1872. d. Chicago, Sept. 22, 1909.

Auditor Charles E. Lippincott[14].

Treasurers Edward Rutz, res. St. Clair

Co. Rep. Treas., Jan. 13, 1873, to Jan. 11, 1875. b. Baden, Germany, May 5, 1829. Emigrated to Ill., 1848. Farmer in St. Clair Co. Moved to Calif., 1857. Enlisted 3rd U.S. Art., 1861; served to 1865. Returned to St. Clair Co.; served as co. treas. Three times Ill. treas., Jan. 13, 1873, to Jan. 11, 1875; Jan. 8, 1877, to Jan. 13, 1879; Jan. 10, 1881, to Jan. 5, 1883. d. Calif., 1905.

Thomas S. Ridgeway, res. Gallatin Co. Rep. Treas., Jan. 11, 1875, to Jan. 8, 1877. b. Carmi, Aug. 30, 1826. Early orphaned. Merchant in Shawneetown, 1845–65. Banker, railroad builder; Rep. del. all state and nat. convs., 1868–96. Dir. McCormick Theological Sem.; trustee Southern Illinois Normal. d. Shawneetown, Nov. 17, 1897.

Superintendents of Public Instruction Newton Bateman[11] (to Jan. 11, 1875).

Samuel M. Etter, res. McLean Co. Rep. Supt. pub. instr., Jan. 11, 1875, to Jan. 13, 1879. b. Newville, Pa., May 16, 1830. Grad. Kalamazoo; taught Perrysburg, Ohio, Lacon and Galva. Supt. schools Henry Co., 1861; supt schools Bloomington, 1868. Continued as educator until death, Joliet, Jan. 27, 1889.

Attorney General James K. Edsall, res. Lee Co. Rep. Att. gen., Jan. 13, 1873, to Jan. 10, 1881. b. Windham, N.Y., May 10, 1831. Admitted N.Y. bar Albany, 1852. Moved to Wis., 1852, Kans. Ter., 1854. Mem. Free Soil ter. leg., 1855, which was broken up by U.S. troops. Moved to Dixon, 1856; mayor Dixon, 1863. Ill. Sen., 1871–72. d. Chicago, June 10, 1892.

United States Senators John A. Logan[11]; Richard J. Oglesby[13].

United States Congressmen John M. Crebs[14] (to March 3, 1873); John F. Farnsworth[11] (to March 3, 1873); John B. Hay[14] (to March 3, 1873); Thompson W. McNeely[14] (to March 3, 1873); Jesse H. Moore[14] (to March 3, 1873); Edward Y. Rice[14] (to March 3, 1873); Henry Snapp[14] (to March 3, 1873); Bradford N. Stevens[14] (to March 3, 1873); Samuel S. Marshall[10] (to March 3, 1875); James C. Robinson[11] (to March 3, 1875); James B. Hawley[14] (to March 3, 1875); Charles B. Farwell[14] (unseated May 6, 1876); Horatio C. Burchard[14]; John R. Eden[12]; William R. Morrison[12].

Granville Barrere, res. Fulton Co. Rep. U.S.H.R., 1873–75. b. Highland Co., Ohio, July 11, 1829. Admitted Ohio bar, 1853. Moved to Marion, Ark., 1850, to Blooming-

ton, then to Canton, 1855. One term in Cong. only pub. office. d. Canton, Jan. 13, 1889.

Joseph Gurney Cannon, "Uncle Joe," res. Douglas Co. Rep. U.S.H.R., 1873–91, 1893–1913, 1915–23. b. Guilford, N.C., May 7 1836. Moved with parents to Bloomington, Ind., 1840. Attended Cincinnati Law School. Admitted Ind. bar, began practice Terre Haute, 1858. Moved to Tuscola, 1859. State's att., 27th Jud. Dist., March 1861 to Dec. 1868. Moved to Danville, 1878. Speaker of U.S.H.R., 1903–11. Retired, March 3, 1923. d. Danville, Nov. 12, 1926.

Bernard Gregory Caulfield, res. Cook Co. Dem. U.S.H.R., Feb. 1, 1875, vice John B. Rice, to 1877. b. Alexandria, Va., Oct. 18, 1828. A.B. Georgetown, 1848; LL.B. Pennsylvania, 1850. Admitted Ky. bar; pract. Lexington, Ky., 1850. Pract. Chicago, 1853–78. Moved to Dak. Ter. d. Deadwood, Dec. 18, 1887.

Isaac Clements, res. Jackson Co. Rep. U.S.H.R., 1873–75. b. Franklin Co., Ind., March 31, 1837. Grad. Asbury (now DePauw), 1859. Taught school Ill., 1859–61. Second lt. 9th Ill. Vol. Inf., 1861; served until 1864 and was twice promoted. Reg. in bankruptcy, 1867. Mem. U.S. Penitentiary Commission, 1877. U.S. pension agent Chicago, 1890–93. Supt. Soldiers' Orphans Home Normal, 1899. Gov. National Home for Disabled Volunteer Soldiers Danville. d. Danville, May 31, 1909.

Franklin Corwin, res. La Salle Co. Rep. U.S.H.R., 1873–75. b. Lebanon, Ohio, Jan. 12, 1818. Admitted Ohio bar, 1839. Ohio H.R., 1846–47; Ohio Sen., 1847–49. Moved to Peru, 1857. Ill. H.R., 1865–70 (spkr. from 1867). d. Peru, June 15, 1879.

Greenbury Lafayette Fort, res. Marshall Co. Rep. U.S.H.R., 1873–81. b. French Grant, Ohio, Oct. 17, 1825. Moved with parents to Marshall Co., 1834. Admitted Ill. bar, 1847; pract. Lacon. Sheriff Marshall Co., 1850–52; Co. clerk, 1852–57. Judge Marshall Co. Court, 1857–61. Second lt. 11th Ill. Vol. Inf., 1861, rose through ranks to bvt. lt. col., March 13, 1865. Mustered out, March 20, 1866. Ill. Sen., 1867–70. d. Lacon, Jan. 13, 1883.

Stephen Augustus Hurlbut, res. Boone Co. Whig and Rep. U.S.H.R., 1873–77. b. Charleston, S.C., Nov. 29, 1815. Admitted S.C. bar, 1837. Moved to Belvidere, 1848. Ill. H.R., 1859–62, 1867–68. Brig. gen. Ill. Vol. Inf., May 17, 1861; maj. gen., Sept. 17, 1862, to 1865. A founder of the G.A.R., first c. in c., 1866–68. Min. to Colombia, 1869–72, to Peru, 1881–82. d. Lima, Peru, March 27, 1882.

Robert McCarty Knapp, res. Jersey Co. Dem. U.S.H.R., 1873–75, 1877–79. b. New York, N.Y., April 21, 1831. Moved with parents to Jerseyville, 1840. Admitted Ill. bar, 1855; pract. Jerseyville. Ill. H.R., 1867–68. Mayor Jerseyville, 1871–76. d. Jerseyville, June 24, 1889.

James Stewart Martin, res. Marion Co. Rep. U.S.H.R., 1873–75. b. Scott Co., Va., Aug. 19, 1826. Moved to Salem, 1846. Served in Mexican War. Admitted Ill. bar, 1861. Col. 111th Ill. Vol. Inf., Sept. 18, 1862; bvt. brig. gen., Feb. 26, 1865. Judge Marion Co. Court, 1865–69. U.S. pension agent, 1869–73. Pract. Salem, where he died, Nov. 20, 1907.

John McNulta, res. McLean Co. Rep. U.S.H.R., 1873–75. b. New York, N.Y., Nov. 9, 1837. Moved to Attica, Ind., 1853, to Bloomington, 1859. Capt. 1st Ill. Vol. Cav., July 3, 1861, to July 14, 1862. Lt. col. 94th Ill. Vol. Inf., Aug. 20, 1862; col. March 21, 1863; bvt. brig. gen. for gallantry, March 13, 1865. Admitted Ill. bar, Oct. 1865. Ill. Sen., 1869–72. Pract. until his death, Washington, D.C., Feb. 22, 1900.

William Henry Ray, res. Schuyler Co. Rep. U.S.H.R., 1873–75. b. Amenia, N.Y., Dec. 14, 1812. Moved to Rushville, 1834; banker. Mem. first board of equalization, 1867–69. d. Rushville, Jan. 25, 1881.

John Blake Rice, res. Cook Co. Rep. U.S.H.R., 1873 to Dec. 27, 1874 (d.). b. Easton, Md., May 28, 1809. Actor; theater manager. Moved to Chicago, 1847. Mayor Chicago, 1865–69. d. during first term U.S.H.R. in Norfok, Va.

Joseph Delos Ward, res. Cook Co. Rep. U.S.H.R., 1873–75. b. Java, N.Y., Feb. 1, 1829. Moved to Chicago in childhood. Admitted Ill. bar, 1852; pract. Chicago. Ald., 1855–56, 1859–60. Enlisted Western Engineers, 1861, mustered out, 1862. Ill. Sen., 1863–70. U.S. att. Northern Dist. Ill., 1875–77. Moved to Leadville, Colo., 1877. Dist. judge Colo., 1881; pract. Denver. d. Denver, Colo., Aug. 6, 1902.

William Black Anderson, res. Jefferson Co. Dem. U.S.H.R., 1875–77. b. Mount Vernon, April 2, 1830. A.B. McKendree, 1850. Admitted Ill. bar, never practiced. Farmer Elk Prairie. Ill. H.R., 1857–60. Pvt. 60th Ill. Vol. Inf., 1861; lt. col., Feb. 17, 1862; col., April 4, 1863; bvt. brig. gen. for gallantry, March 13, 1865. Del. Ill. const. conv., 1869. Ill. Sen., 1871–72. Coll. int. rev. Southern Dist. Ill., 1885–89. U.S. pension

agent Chicago, 1893–97. d. Chicago, Aug. 28, 1901.

John Courts Bagby, res. Schuyler Co. Dem. U.S.H.R., 1875–77. b. Glasgow, Ky., Jan. 24, 1819. Grad. Bacon, Harrodsburg, Ky., 1840. Admitted Ky. bar, 1845. Moved to Rushville, pract., 1846. Judge Schuyler Co. Court, 1882–85. Judge circuit court, 6th Circuit, June 1, 1885, to June 1, 1891. d. Rushville, April 4, 1896.

Alexander Campbell, res. La Salle Co. Indp. U.S.H.R., 1875–77. b. Concord, Pa., Oct. 4, 1814. Managed iron works in Pa., Ky., and Mo. until 1850, coal mines in La Salle Co. Mayor La Salle, 1852 and 1853. Ill. H.R., 1859–60. Retired at end of term, March 3, 1877. d. La Salle, Aug. 8, 1898.

Carter Henry Harrison, res. Cook Co. Dem. U.S.H.R., 1875–79. b. Lexington, Ky., Feb. 15, 1825. A.B. Yale, 1845; LL.B. Transylvania; admitted Ky. bar, 1855. Moved to Chicago. Mem. Board of Cook Co. Comms., Dec. 4, 1871, to Dec. 3, 1874. Mayor Chicago, 1879–87. Cand. for gov., 1884. Owner *Chicago Times*, 1891–93. Again elected mayor, assassinated early in term, Oct. 28, 1893.

William Hartzell, res. Randolph Co. Dem. U.S.H.R., 1875–79. b. Canton, Ohio, Feb. 20, 1837. Moved with parents to Danville, 1840, and to Mexico, 1844. Returned to Ill., 1853. A.B. McKendree, 1859. Admitted Ill. bar, 1864; pract. Chester. Judge circuit court, 3rd Circuit, June 18, 1897, to June 17, 1903. d. Chester, Aug. 14, 1903.

Thomas Jefferson Henderson, res. Stark Co. Rep. U.S.H.R., 1875–95. b. Brownsville, Tenn., Nov. 29, 1824. Moved with parents to Ill., 1835. Clerk Stark Co. Board of Supervisors, 1847–49. Clerk Stark Co. Court, 1849–53. Admitted Ill. bar, 1852; pract. Toulon. Ill. H.R., 1855–56. Ill. Sen., 1857–60. Col. 112th Ill. Vol. Inf., Sept. 22, 1862, to 1863; bvt. brig. gen., Nov. 30, 1864. Opened law office Princeton. Coll. int. rev. 5th Dist., 1871–75. Mem. board of managers National Home for Disabled Volunteer Soldiers. Civilian mem. Board of Fortifications, Washington, D.C., until his death, Feb. 6, 1911.

John Valcoulon Le Moyne, res. Cook Co. Dem. U.S.H.R., May 6, 1876, to 1877. b. Washington Co., Pa., Nov. 17, 1828. A.B. Washington and Jefferson, 1847. Admitted Pa. bar; moved to Chicago, 1852.

Successfully contested election Charles B. Farwell, 1875; seated May 6, 1876. Defeated in other attempts for pub. office. Retired to Baltimore, 1887. d. Baltimore, Md., July 27 1918.

William Andrew Jackson Sparks, res. Clinton Co. Dem. U.S.H.R., 1875–83. b. New Albany, Ind., Nov. 19, 1828. Moved with parents to Ill., 1836. A.B. McKendree, 1850. Admitted Ill. bar; pract. Carlyle, 1851. Rcvr. Edwardsville land office, 1853–56. Ill. H.R., 1857–58; Ill. Sen., 1863–64. Comm. U.S. General Land Office, 1885–88. Pract. Carlyle and Springfield, 1889 until death, St. Louis, Mo., May 7, 1904.

William McKendree Springer, res. Sangamon Co. Dem. U.S.H.R., 1875–95. b. New Lebanon, Ind., May 30, 1836. Moved with parents to Jacksonville, 1848. Attended Illinois College, Jacksonville; A.B. Indiana, 1858. Admitted Ill. bar, 1859; pract. Lincoln and Springfield. Ill. H.R., 1871–72. Fed. just. Ind. Ter.; C.J. U.S. Court of Appeals Ind. Ter., 1895–1900. Opened law office Washington, D.C., where he died, Dec. 4, 1903.

Adlai Ewing Stevenson, res. McLean Co. Dem. U.S.H.R., 1875–77, 1879–81. b. Christian Co., Ky., Oct. 23, 1835. Moved with parents to Bloomington, 1852. Attended Illinois Wesleyan and Centre. Admitted Ill. bar, 1858; pract. Metamora. Master in chancery Woodford Co., 1860–64. Dist. att. Woodford Co., 1865–68. First asst. postmaster gen., 1885–89. V.P. U.S., 1893–97. d. Chicago, June 14, 1914.

Richard Henry Whiting, res. Peoria Co. Rep. U.S.H.R., 1875–77. b. West Hartford, Conn., Jan. 17, 1826. Moved to Altona, 1850, to Galesburg, 1860, where he built a gas works. Paymaster of vols., 1862–66. Assessor int. rev. 5th Dist. Ill., 1870–73; coll. same district, 1873–75. d. New York, N.Y., May 24, 1888.

Scott Wike, res. Pike Co. Dem. U.S.H.R., 1875–77, 1889–93. b. Meadville, Pa., April 6, 1834. Moved with parents to Quincy, 1838, to Pike Co., 1844. B.A. Lombard, Galesburg, 1857; LL.B. Harvard, 1859. Admitted Ill. bar; pract. Pittsfield, 1859. Ill. H.R., 1863–66. Asst. sec. treas., 1893–97. d. Barry, Jan. 15, 1901.

Justices Illinois Supreme Court Sidney Breese[6]; Charles B. Lawrence[12] (to June 1873); Pinckney H. Walker [11]; John M. Scott[14]; Benjamin R. Sheldon[14]; William K. McAllister[14] (resigned Nov. 26, 1875);

Anthony Thornton [13] (resigned May 31, 1873).

John Scholfield, res. Clark Co. Just. Ill. Supreme Court, June 16, 1873, vice Thornton, to Feb. 13, 1893 (d.). C.J., 1877, 1884, 1890. b. Clark Co., 1834. LL.B. Louisville, admitted Ill. bar, 1856.; pract. Marshall. State's att. Clark Co., 1856. Ill. H.R., 1861–62.

Alfred M. Craig, res. Knox Co. Just. Ill. Supreme Court, 1873–1900. C.J., 1878, 1881, 1888, 1895. b. Edgar Co., Jan. 15, 1831. A.B. Knox, 1853. Admitted Ill. bar, 1854. State's att. and co. judge Knox Co. Del. const. conv., 1869. Retired after twenty-seven years service Supreme Court. d. Knoxville, Sept. 11, 1911.

Theophilus Lyle Dickey, res. La Salle and Cook cos. Just. Ill. Supreme Court, Dec. 28, 1875, vice McAllister, to July 22, 1885 (d.). C.J., 1880. b. Paris, Ky., Oct. 2, 1811. A.B. Miami, 1834. Admitted Ill. bar Macomb, 1835. Moved to Rushville, then Ottawa, 1839. Capt. Ill. Vols. Mexican War. Judge circuit court, 9th Circuit, Dec. 4, 1848, to May 1853. Col. 4th Ill. Cav., 1861–65. Resumed practice Ottawa. U.S. dist. att., 1868–70. d. Atlantic City, N.J., during holiday.

16. First administration of Shelby M. Cullom, Jan. 8, 1877, to Jan. 10, 1881. Voting for governor: Cullom, 279,263. Lewis Steward, 272,465.

Governor Shelby M. Cullom[13].

Lieutenant Governor Andrew Shuman, res. Cook Co. Rep. b. Manor, Pa., Nov. 8, 1830. Attended Hamilton. Journalist, came to Chicago, 1856, to edit *Evening Journal*. One term as lt. gov. only state office. Journalist in Chicago until death, May 5, 1890.

Secretary of State George H. Harlow[15].

Auditor Thomas B. Needles, res. Washington Co. Rep. b. Monroe Co., April 26, 1835. After several moves, family settled in Richview; merchant with father until 1861. Co. clerk Washington Co., 1861–77. Ill. Sen., 1881–84. U.S. marshal Ind. Ter., 1887. Ill. H.R., 1895–98. Member Dawes Commission to settle claims of civilized Indians, 1899–1907. Pres. First Nat. Bank Nashville, 1903 to death, St. Louis, Mo., June 4, 1914.

Treasurers Edward Rutz[15] (to Jan. 13, 1879).

John C. Smith, res. JoDaviess and Cook cos. Rep. Treas., Jan. 13, 1879, to Jan 10, 1881. Carpenter Chicago, 1854; miner Galena, 1856. Pvt. 74th Ill. Vol. Inf., 1861.

Capt. 96th Ill. Inf., 1862. Distinction at Ft. Donelson, promoted maj., Sept. 6, 1862; lt. col., Nov. 1, 1863. Action at Missionary Ridge; wounded Kenesaw Mountain, promoted col., 1864; bvt. brig. gen., June 20, 1865. Served two times as treas., 1879–81 and Jan. 5, 1883, to Jan. 30, 1885. Lt. gov. third Oglesby adm., 1885–89. d. Chicago, Dec. 31, 1910.

Superintendents of Public Instruction Samuel M. Etter[15] (to Jan 13, 1879).

James P. Slade, res. St. Clair Co. Supt. pub. instr., Jan. 13, 1879, to Jan. 5, 1883. b. Westerlo, N.Y., Feb. 9, 1837. Moved to Belleville, 1856. Prin. Belleville H.S. Supt. schools St. Clair Co.; Supt. schools East St. Louis, 1872–78, 1883–1908. d. April 18, 1908.

Attorney General James K. Edsall[15].

United States Senators John A. Logan [11] (to 1877, 1879–86); Richard Oglesby[13] (to 1879).

David Davis, res. McLean Co. Indp. U.S. Sen., 1877–83. b. Cecilton, Md., March 8, 1815. A.B. Kenyon, 1832; LL.D. Yale, admitted Ill. bar, 1835; pract. Pekin; moved to Bloomington, 1836. Ill. H.R., 1844–46. Del. Ill. const. conv., 1847. Judge circuit court, 8th Circuit, Dec. 4, 1848, to Oct. 1862 (resigned). Just. U.S. Supreme Court, Oct. 4, 1862 to March 4, 1877 (resigned to accept seat U.S. Sen.). Pres. pro tem. U.S. Sen., Oct. 13, 1881, to March 3, 1883. d. Bloomington, June 26, 1886.

United States Congressmen William B. Anderson[15] (to March 3, 1877); John C. Bagby[15] (to March 3, 1877); Alexander Campbell[15] (to March 3, 1877); Bernard G. Caulfield[15] (to March 3, 1877); Stephen A. Hurlbut[15] (to March 3, 1877); John V. Le Moyne[15] (to March 3, 1877); Adlai E. Stevenson[15] (to March 3, 1877); Richard H. Whiting[15] (to March 3, 1877); Scott Wike[15] (to March 3, 1877); Horatio C. Burchard[14] (to March 3, 1879); John R. Eden[12] (to March 3, 1879); Carter H. Harrison[15] (to March 3, 1879); William Hartzell[15] (to March 3, 1879); Robert M. Knapp[15] (to March 3, 1879); William R. Morrison[12]; Joseph G. Cannon[15]; Greenbury L. Fort[15]; Thomas J. Henderson[15]; William A. J. Sparks[15]; William M. Springer[15].

William Aldrich, res. Cook Co. Rep. U.S.H.R., 1877–83. b. Greenfield Center, N.Y., Jan. 19, 1820. Teacher, merchant at Jackson, Mich., 1846–51, Two Rivers, Wis., 1851–56. Supt. schools Two Rivers, Wis., 1855–56. Chr. board of supervisors, 1857–58. Wis. H.R., 1859. Moved to Chicago,

1861; wholesaler. Presiding ald. Chicago City Council, 1876. d. on visit Fond du Lac, Wis., Dec. 3, 1885.

Thomas Alexander Boyd, res. Fulton Co. Rep. U.S.H.R., 1877–81. b. Bedford, Pa., June 25, 1830. B.A. Marshall, Mercersburg, Pa., 1848; admitted Pa. bar; pract. Bedford, Pa. Moved to Lewistown, 1856. Capt. 17th Ill. Vol. Inf. Civil War. Ill. Sen., 1867–72. Pract. Lewistown after leaving U.S.H.R. d. May 28, 1897.

Lorenzo Brentano, res. Cook Co. Rep. U.S.H.R., 1877–79. b. Mannheim, Baden, Germany, Nov. 4, 1813. Attended Heidelberg; J.D. Freiburg. Practiced before Supreme Court of Baden; mem. Chamber Deputies; elected to Frankfurt Parliament, 1848. Pres. Provisional Republic, 1849; sentenced to life imprisonment, fled to U.S. Farmed in Kalamazoo Co., Mich., 1849–59. Admitted Ill. bar, 1859; pract. Chicago. Ill. H.R., 1863–64. Pres. Chicago Board Education, 1862–68. U.S. Consul Dresden, 1872 to April 1876. Author and lawyer. d. Chicago, Sept. 18, 1891.

William Lathrop, res. Winnebago Co. Rep. U.S.H.R., 1877–79. b. Genesee Co., N.Y., April 17, 1825. Moved to Knoxville, 1850. Admitted Ill. bar, moved to Rockford, 1851. City clerk and city att., 1852. Ill. H.R., 1857–58. Pract. Rockford except for one term U.S.H.R. d. Rockford, Nov. 19, 1907.

Phillip Cornelius Hayes, res. Grundy Co. Rep. U.S.H.R., 1877–81. b. Granby, Conn., Feb. 3, 1833. Moved as infant with parents to La Salle Co. A.B. Oberlin, 1860; D.D. Oberlin Sem., 1863. Capt. 103rd Ohio Vol. Inf., July 16, 1862; lt. col., Nov. 18, 1864; bvt. col. and brig. gen. for gallantry, March 13, 1865. Supt. schools Mount Vernon, Ohio, 1866. Moved to Morris, 1874. Journalist Morris to 1892, Joliet, 1892–1916. d. July 13, 1916.

Benjamin Franklin Marsh, res. Hancock Co. Rep. U.S.H.R., 1877–83, 1893–1901, 1903 to June 2, 1905 (d.). b. Wythe Twp., Hancock Co., 1839. Attended Jubilee, Peoria. Admitted Ill. bar, 1860; pract. Warsaw. Enlisted 16th Ill. Vol. Inf., 1861. Recruited troop of cav., commissioned capt., assigned 2nd Ill. Vol. Cav., 1862, served until June 1866. Pract. Warsaw, 1866–77. Farmer, stockman. Ill. R.R. and Warehouse Commission, 1889–93. d. Warsaw, during recess ninth term U.S.H.R.

Thomas Foster Tipton, res. McLean Co. Rep. U.S.H.R., 1877–79. b. Franklin Co.,

Ohio, Aug. 29, 1833. Moved with parents to McLean Co., 1843. Admitted Ill. bar, 1854; pract. Bloomington. State's att. 8th Jud. Circuit, 1867–68. Judge circuit court, 8th Circuit, Aug. 18, 1870, vice John M. Scott, to 1873; 14th Circuit, June 2, 1873, to 1877 (resigned); 11th Circuit, June 1, 1891, to June 1, 1897. d. Bloomington, Feb. 7, 1904.

Richard Wellington Townshend, res. Gallatin Co. Dem. U.S.H.R., 1877 to March 9, 1889 (d). b. Prince Georges Co., Md., April 30, 1840. Moved to Washington, D.C., with parents, 1846. Page U.S.H.R., 1857. Moved to Cairo, 1858. Admitted Ill. bar, 1862; pract. McLeansboro. Clerk circuit court Hamilton Co., 1863–68. Pros. att. 12th Jud. Dist., 1868–73. Moved to Shawneetown, 1873. d. Washington, D.C., fifth day of seventh term U.S.H.R.

Hiram Barber, Jr., res. Cook Co. Rep. U.S.H.R., 1879–81. b. Queensburg, N.Y., March 24, 1835. Moved to Wis., 1846. Admitted Wis. bar, 1856; pract. Juneau, Wis. Pros. att. Jefferson Co. Wis., 1861–62; asst. att. gen. Wis., 1865–66. Moved to Chicago, 1866. Rcvr. Mitchell, S. Dak., land office, 1881–88. Returned to Chicago; master in chancery Cook Co. Superior Court, 1891–1914. d. Lake Geneva, Wis., Aug. 5, 1924.

George Royal Davis, res. Cook Co. Rep. U.S.H.R., 1879–85. b. Palmer, Mass., Jan. 3, 1840. A.B. Williston Sem., Easthampton, Mass., 1860. Capt. 8th Mass. Vol. Inf., 1862; maj. 3rd R.I. Cav., 1863. Moved to Chicago, 1866. Mfr., financial agent. Senior col. 1st Reg. Ill. N.G. Treas. Cook Co., 1886–90; dir. gen. World's Columbian Exposition, 1893. d. Chicago, Nov. 25, 1899.

Albert Palaska Forsythe, res. Edgar Co. Rep. U.S.H.R., 1879–81. b. New Richmond, Ohio, May 24, 1830. Attended Asbury, (now DePauw). Itinerant Methodist min., 1853–61. Lt. Ind. Vol. Inf., 1861–64. Moved to Edgar Co., 1865; master state Grange. Moved to Liberty, Kans., 1882. Regent Kansas State, 1886–92. d. Independence, Kans., Sept. 2, 1906.

Robert Moffett Allison Hawk, res. Carroll Co. Rep. U.S.H.R., 1879 to June 29, 1882 (d). b. Hancock Co. Ind., April 23, 1839. Moved with parents to Freedom Twp., Carroll Co., 1844; attended Eureka. First lt. Ill. vols., Sept. 4, 1862, capt., Feb. 1863, bvt. maj., April 10, 1865. Moved to Mount Carroll. Clerk Carroll Co. Court, Dec. 13,

1865, to Feb. 27, 1879. d. Washington, D.C., during second term U.S.H.R.

John Crocker Sherwin, res. Kane Co. Rep. U.S.H.R., 1879–83. b. Gouverneur, N.Y., Feb. 8, 1838. Moved to Ill; attended Lombard, Galesburg. Admitted Ill. bar, 1859. City att. Aurora, 1859–61. Enlisted 89th Ill. Vol. Inf., served to end of war. d. Benton Harbor, Mich., Jan. 1, 1904.

James Washington Singleton, res. Brown and Adams cos. Dem. U.S.H.R., 1879–83. b. Winchester, Va., Nov. 23, 1811. Moved to Mount Sterling, 1834; studied and pract. medicine. Admitted Ill. bar, 1838; pract. Mount Sterling. Brig. gen. Ill. militia, 1844. Del. Ill. const. conv., 1847. Ill. H.R., 1851–52, vice John C. Moses; 1853–54. Moved to Quincy. Ill. H.R., 1861–62. Mem. U.S. commission concerning year-round navigation Great Lakes. Railroad builder and pres.; raised fine stock n. Quincy, 1883–91. Moved to Baltimore, Md., where he died, April 4, 1892.

John Robert Thomas, res. Massac Co. Rep. U.S.H.R., 1879–89. b. Mount Vernon, Oct. 11, 1846. Attended Hunter Collegiate Inst., Princeton, Ind. Enlisted pvt., rose through ranks to capt. 120th Ind. Vol. Inf., 1861–65. Admitted Ill. bar, 1869; pract. Metropolis. City att., 1869–70; state's att. Massac Co., 1871–74. After five terms U.S.H.R. pract. Muskogee, Okla.; mem. Okla. Code Commission, 1908–10. d. McAlester, Okla., Jan. 19, 1914.

Justices Illinois Supreme Court Benjamin R. Sheldon[14] (to June 1877); Pinckney H. Walker[11]; Sidney Breese[6] (d. June 28, 1878); John M. Scott[14]; John Scholfield[15]; Alfred M. Craig[15]; T. Lyle Dickey[15].

David J. Baker, res. Alexander Co. Just. Ill. Supreme Court, July 9, 1878, vice Breese, to 1879; June 16, 1888, to June 18, 1897. C.J., 1893. b. Kaskaskia, Nov. 20, 1834. A.B. Shurtleff, 1854. Mayor Cairo, 1864–65. Judge circuit court, 19th Circuit, March 22, 1869, to June 1, 1873; 26th Circuit (became 1st Circuit in 1877), June 2, 1873, to Aug. 13, 1878 (resigned); June 16, 1879, to June 1, 1885 (resigned). d. Chicago, March 13, 1899.

John H. Mulkey, res. Alexander and Massac cos. Just. Ill. Supreme Court, 1879–88. C.J., 1885. b. Monroe Co., Ky., May 24, 1824. Attended Bacon, Harrodsburg, Ky. Moved to Benton, 1845. Second lt. 2nd Ill. Vol. Inf. Mexican War. Read law Marion. Admitted Ill. bar, 1853; pract. Marion and Cairo. Judge of common pleas, 1861–67, assigned to circuit court, 3rd

Circuit, April 22, 1864, vice Alexander M. Jenkins, to Dec. 1865. After one term Ill. Supreme Court retired to Metropolis where he practiced law, farmed, and wrote. d. Metropolis, July 9, 1905.

17. Second administration of Shelby M. Cullom, Jan. 10, 1881, to Feb. 6, 1883 (completed by John Marshall Hamilton, Feb. 6, 1883, to Jan. 30, 1885). Voting for governor: Cullom, 314,565. Lyman Trumbull, 277,532. A. G. Streeten, 28,898.

Governors Shelby M. Cullom[13]. John Marshall Hamilton, res. McLean Co. Rep. b. Union Co., Ohio, May 28, 1847. Brought by father to McLean Co., 1854. Enlisted 141st Ill. Vol. Inf., 1864; mustered out in ninety days. Attended Illinois Wesleyan. Admitted Ill. bar, 1868; pract. Bloomington. Ill. Sen., 1877–80. Elected lt. gov., Nov. 1880; served as gov. from resignation of Cullom, Feb. 6, 1883, to Jan. 30, 1885. Pract. Chicago. d. Chicago, Sept. 23, 1905.

Lieutenant Governors John M. Hamilton (see above).

William J. Campbell, res. Cook Co. Rep. Acting lt. gov., Feb. 6, 1883, to Jan. 30, 1885. b. Philadelphia, Pa., Dec. 12, 1850. Moved to Cook Co. with parents, 1852. LL.B. Pennsylvania. Admitted Ill. bar, 1875; pract. Chicago. Ill. Sen., 1877–86. Prin. att. Armour & Company; active Armour Mission; pres. board Armour Inst. Technology. d. Riverside, March 4, 1896.

Secretary of State Henry D. Dement, res. Lee Co. Rep. Sec. state, Jan. 17, 1881, to Jan. 14, 1889. b. Galena, 1840. Enlisted 13th Ill. Vol. Inf., 1861; promoted 1st lt., made honorary capt. by Gov. Yates for gallantry. Mfr. Dixon, 1866. Ill. H.R., 1873–76. Ill. Sen., 1877–80. Warden Joliet penitentiary, 1891–93. d. Memphis, Tenn., 1928.

Auditor Charles P. Swigert, res. Kankakee Co. Rep. Aud., Jan. 10, 1881, to Jan. 14, 1889. b. Baden, Germany, Nov. 27, 1843. Emigrated to Chicago about 1848, then to 500-acre farm in Kankakee Co. Enlisted pvt. 42nd Ill. Vol. Inf.; lost right arm at Corinth. Treas. Kankakee Co., 1869–80. d. Chicago, June 30, 1903.

Treasurers Edward Rutz[15] (to Jan. 5, 1883); John C. Smith[16] (Jan. 5, 1883, to Jan. 30, 1885).

Superintendents of Public Instruction James P. Slade[16] (to Jan. 5, 1883).

Henry Raab, res. St. Clair Co. Dem. Supt. pub. instr., Jan. 5, 1883, to Jan. 6,

1887; Jan. 12, 1891, to Jan. 14, 1895. b. Wetzler, Rhenish Prussia, June 20, 1837. Emigrated with parents to Ill. Taught Belleville; supt. schools Belleville from 1870's until death, Belleville, March 31, 1901, except while holding state office.

Attorney General James McCartney, res. Wayne and Cook cos. Rep. b. Northern Ireland, Feb. 14, 1835. Brought by parents to Pa., 1837, to Ohio, 1845. Moved to Monmouth, 1857. Admitted Ill. bar, 1858; pract. Monmouth. Judge adv. and asst. adj. Army of the Ohio, 1861–65. As att. gen. initiated lakefront suits behalf Chicago, 1884. d. Sherman, Tex., May 13, 1911.

United States Senators John A. Logan[11]; David Davis[16] (to March 3, 1883); Shelby M. Cullom[13] (from March 4, 1883).

United States Congressmen Thomas A. Boyd[16] (to March 3, 1881); Hiram Barber, Jr.[16] (to March 3, 1881); Albert P. Forsythe[16] (to March 3, 1881); Phillip C. Hayes[16] (to March 3, 1881); Robert M. A. Hawk[16] (d. June 29, 1882); Charles B. Farwell[14] (1881–83); William A. J. Sparks[15] (to March 3, 1883); William Aldrich[16] (to March 3, 1883); Benjamin F. Marsh[16] (1881–83); John C. Sherwin [16] (to March 3, 1883); James W. Singleton[16] (to March 3, 1883); Aaron Shaw[11] (1883–85); William R. Morrison[12]; Samuel W. Moulton[13]; Joseph G. Cannon [15]; Thomas J. Henderson[15]; William M. Springer[15]; George R. Davis[16]; John R. Thomas[16]; Richard E. Townshend[16].

William Cullen, res. La Salle Co. Rep. U.S.H.R., 1881–85. b. Co. Donegal, Ireland, March 4, 1826. Emigrated to Pittsburgh, Pa., with parents, 1832, to Adams Twp., La Salle Co., 1846. Sheriff La Salle Co., 1864–65. Moved to Ottawa. Political ed. *Ottawa Republican*, 1871–87. d. Ottawa, Jan. 17, 1914.

Robert Roberts Hitt, res. Ogle Co. Rep. U.S.H.R., Dec. 4, 1882, to Sept. 19, 1906. b. Urbana, Ohio, Jan. 16, 1834. Moved with parents to Ogle Co., 1837. Attended Asbury (now DePauw). Reported Lincoln-Douglas debates, 1858. First sec. and chargé d'affaires Paris, Dec. 1874 to March 1881. Asst. U.S. sec. state, 1881–82. Comm. Hawaiian Islands, 1898. d. Narragansett Pier, R.I., Sept. 19, 1906.

John Henry Lewis, res. Knox Co. Rep. U.S.H.R., 1881–83. b. Tompkins Co., N.Y., July 21, 1830. Moved with parents to Fulton

Co., 1836, to Knox Co., 1847. Admitted Ill. bar, 1860; pract. Knoxville. Clerk circuit court, 1860–64. Ill. H.R., 1875–76. d. Knoxville, Jan. 26, 1929.

Lewis Edwin Payson, res. Livingston Co. Rep. U.S.H.R., 1881–91. b. Providence, R.I., Sept. 17, 1840. Moved with parents to Ill., 1852; attended Lombard, Galesburg. Admitted Ill. bar, 1862; pract. Ottawa. Moved to Pontiac, 1865. Judge Livingston Co. Court, 1869–73. Pract. Washington, D.C., from 1891 to death, Oct. 4, 1909.

Dieterich Conrad Smith, res. Tazewell Co. Rep. U.S.H.R., 1881–83. b. Ost Friesland, Germany, April 4, 1840. Emigrated with parents to Tazewell Co., 1850. Lt. 8th Ill. Vol. Inf., 1861; capt. 139th Ill. Vol. Inf., 1864. Active lay Methodist. Ill. H.R., 1877–78. Banker, railroad builder. d. Pekin, April 18, 1914.

George Everett Adams, res. Cook Co. Rep. U.S.H.R., 1883–91. b. Keene, N.H., June 18, 1840. Moved with parents to Chicago, 1853. A.B. Harvard, 1860. First lt. Ill. Vol. Art., 1861. Attended Harvard Law School. Admitted Ill. bar, 1865; pract. Chicago. Ill. Sen., 1881 84. Pract. Chicago until his death at summer home, Peterborough, N.H., Oct. 5, 1917.

Ransom Williams Dunham, res. Cook Co. Rep. U.S.H.R., 1883–89. b. Savoy, Mass., March 21, 1838. Moved to Chicago, 1857. Grain and provision commission merchant. Pres. Chicago Board of Trade, 1882. d. Springfield, Mass., on visit, Aug. 19, 1896.

Reuben Ellwood, res. De Kalb Co. Rep. U.S.H.R., 1883–85. b. Minden, N.Y., Feb. 21, 1821. Mfr. agricultural implements. N.Y. State Assembly, 1851. Moved to Sycamore, 1854; mfr. and merchant. Reelected 1884; d. Sycamore, July 1, 1885, before Cong. assembled.

John Frederick Finerty, res. Cook Co. Dem. U.S.H.R., 1883–85. b. Galway, Ireland, Sept. 10, 1846. Emigrated to N.Y. Enlisted 99th N.Y. Militia for last year of war, 1864. Moved to Chicago, 1865, correspondent *Chicago Times* in Mont. with Gen. Crook, 1876, with Gen. Miles and Gen. Merritt, 1879 (Sioux and Ute wars), with Gen. Carr, 1881 (Apache campaign). *Chicago Times* Washington correspondent, 1879–81. In 1882 founded *Chicago Weekly Citizen*, which he edited until death, June 10, 1908.

William Henry Neece, res. McDonough Co. Dem. U.S.H.R., 1883–87. b. Sangamon Co., Feb. 26, 1831. Admitted Ill. bar, 1858; pract. Macomb. Ill. H.R., 1865–66, 1871–72. Del. Ill. const. conv., 1869. Ill. Sen., 1879–81. Raised cattle and pract. law Macomb until death, Jan. 3, 1909.

James Milton Riggs, res. Scott Co. Dem. U.S.H.R., 1883–87. b. Scott Co., April 17, 1839. Attended Eureka. Sheriff Scott Co., 1864–66. Admitted Ill. bar, 1867; pract. Winchester. Ill. H.R., 1871–72. State's att. Scott Co., 1872–76. Mayor Winchester, 1876–77. Pres. Ill. Bar Association, 1891. Judge Scott Co. Court, 1922–30. d. Winchester, Nov. 18, 1933.

Jonathan Harvey Rowell, res. McLean Co. Rep. U.S.H.R., 1883–91. b. Haverhill, N.H., Feb. 10, 1833. A.B. Eureka. Served with 17th Ill. Vol. Inf., 1861. LL.B. Chicago, admitted Ill. bar, 1866; pract. Bloomington. State's att. 8th Jud. Circuit, 1868–72. d. Bloomington, May 15, 1908.

Nicholas Ellsworth Worthington, res. Peoria Co. Dem. U.S.H.R., 1883–87. b. Brooke Co., Va. (now W. Va.), March 30, 1836. A.B. Allegheny. Moved to Ill., 1860; admitted Ill. bar; pract. Peoria. Supt. schools Peoria Co., 1865–72. Mem. Ill. State Board of Education, 1869–72. Judge circuit court, 10th Circuit, 1891–1915. d. Peoria, March 4, 1916.

Justices Illinois Supreme Court Pinckney H. Walker[11]; John M. Scott[14]; John Scholfield[15]; Benjamin R. Sheldon[14]; Alfred M. Craig[15]; T. Lyle Dickey[15]; John H. Mulkey[16].

18. Third administration of Richard J. Oglesby, Jan. 30, 1885, to Jan. 14, 1889. Voting for governor: Oglesby, 344,234. Carter Henry Harrison, 319,635. James B. Hobbs, 10,905. Jesse Harper, 8,605.

Governor Richard J. Oglesby[13].

Lieutenant Governor John C. Smith[16].

Secretary of State Henry D. Dement [17].

Auditor Charles P. Swigert[17].

Treasurers Jacob Gross, res. Cook Co. Rep. Treas., Jan. 30, 1885, to Jan. 6, 1887. b. Germany, Feb. 11, 1840. Moved to Chicago, 1855. 82nd Ill. Vols., Aug. 1862 to Feb. 1865; lost right leg at Dallas, Ga. Mun. posts Chicago, 1866–72. Clerk circuit court Cook Co., 1872–84. Pres. Commercial Bank Chicago. d. Chicago, Dec. 28, 1918.

John R. Tanner, res. Clay Co. Rep. Treas., Jan. 6, 1887, to Jan. 14, 1889. b. Warwick Co., Ind., April 4, 1844. Brought to Ill. by parents as infant. Grew up on farm n. Carbondale. Enlisted 98th Ill. Vols.,

1863; lost father, two brothers in war. Miller, merchant. Sheriff Clay Co., 1870–72. Clerk circuit court, 1872–76. Ill. Sen., 1881–84. U.S. marshal, 1883–85. Asst. U.S. treas. Chicago, 1892–93. Gov., Jan. 11, 1897, to Jan. 14, 1901. d. Springfield, May 23, 1901.

Superintendents of Public Instruction Henry Raab[17] (to Jan. 6, 1887).

Richard Edwards, res. Bureau Co. Rep. Supt. pub. instr., Jan. 6, 1887, to Jan. 12, 1891. b. Cardiganshire, Wales, Dec. 23, 1822. Emigrated to Portage Co., Ohio, A.B. Massachusetts State Normal; B.S. and C.E. Polytechnic Institute of Troy (now Rensselaer). Established State Normal at St. Louis, Mo. Pres. Illinois State Normal, 1862–76. Pastor First Congregational Church Princeton, 1876–85. Pres. Blackburn, 1891–92. Retired to Bloomington. d. March 8, 1908.

Attorney General George Hunt, res. Edgar Co. Rep. b. Knox Co., Ohio, 1841. Orphaned, joined uncle in Edgar Co., 1855. Enlisted 12th Ill. Inf., July 1861, served to 1865; rose through the ranks to capt. Admitted Ill. bar Paris, 1867. Ill. Sen., 1875–84 (resigned). While att. gen. defeated appeals in 1887 and 1890–92 of accused anarchists convicted in Haymarket riots Chicago, 1887. Served to Jan. 10, 1893. Resumed pract. law Paris. d. March 17, 1901.

United States Senators Shelby M. Cullom[13]; John A. Logan[11] (d. Dec. 26, 1886); Charles B. Farwell[14] (from Jan. 19, 1887, vice Logan).

United States Congressmen Aaron Shaw[11] (to March 3, 1885); George R. Davis[16] (to March 3, 1885); William Cullen[17] (to March 3, 1885); John F. Finerty[17] (to March 3, 1885); Reuben Ellwood[17] (d. July 1, 1885); John R. Eden[12] (to March 3, 1887); William R. Morrison[12] (to March 3, 1887); William H. Neece[17] (to March 3, 1887); James M. Riggs[17] (to March 3, 1887); Nicholas E. Worthington[17] (to March 3, 1887); Jehu Baker[13] (1887–89); Joseph G. Cannon[15]; Thomas J. Henderson[15]; William M. Springer[15]; John R. Thomas[16]; Richard W. Townshend[16]; George E. Adams[17]; Ransom W. Dunham[17]; Robert R. Hitt[17]; Lewis E. Payson[17]; Jonathan H. Rowell[17].

Albert Jarvis Hopkins, res. Kane Co. Rep. U.S.H.R., Dec. 7, 1885, vice Ellwood, to March 3, 1903. b. Cortland, Aug. 15, 1846. A.B. Hillsdale, 1870. Admitted Ill. bar, 1871; pract. Aurora. Pros. att. Kane

Co., 1872–76. U.S. Sen., 1903–9. Pract. Aurora and Chicago. d. Aurora, Aug. 23, 1922.

Silas Zephaniah Landes, res. Ogle Co. Dem. U.S.H.R., 1885–89. b. Augusta Co., Va., May 15, 1842. Moved to Ill. Admitted Ill. bar by Supreme Court, 1863; pract. Mount Carmel. Pros. att. Wabash Co., 1872–84. Judge circuit court, 2nd Circuit, 1891–97. d. Mount Carmel, May 23, 1910.

Frank Lawler, res. Cook Co. Dem. U.S.H.R., 1885–91. b. Rochester, N.Y., June 25, 1842. Moved with parents to Chicago, 1854. Railroad news agent, brakeman; union organizer. Ald. Chicago, 1876–85; elected ald. for 1896. d. Chicago, Jan. 17, 1896.

Ralph Plumb, res. La Salle Co. Rep. U.S.H.R., 1885–89. b. Busti, N.Y., March 29, 1816. Merchant, moved to Ohio in 1850's. Ohio H.R., 1855. Admitted Ohio bar, 1857; pract. Oberlin, Ohio. Capt. and Q.M. Ohio Vols., 1861–65, bvt. lt. col. Moved to Streator, 1866. Railroad builder, coal miner, banker. Mayor Streator, 1882–85. d. Streator, April 8, 1903.

James Hugh Ward, res. Cook Co. Dem. U.S.H.R., 1885–87. b. Chicago, Nov. 30, 1853. A.B. Notre Dame, 1873; LL.B. Union College of Law (now Northwestern), admitted Ill. bar, 1876. Pract. and mun. office to 1885. Returned to pract. Chicago until death, Aug. 15, 1916.

George Alburtus Anderson, res. Adams Co. Dem. U.S.H.R., 1887–89. b. Botetourt Co., Va., March 11, 1853. Moved with parents to Hancock Co., 1855. A.B. Carthage, 1876; admitted Ill. bar, 1878; pract. Quincy, 1880. City att., 1884 and 1885. Except for one term U.S.H.R. pract. Quincy. d. Jan. 31, 1896.

William Harrison Gest, res. Rock Island Co. Rep. U.S.H.R., 1887–91. b. Jacksonville, Jan. 7, 1838. Moved with parents to Rock Island, 1842. A.B. Williams, 1860. Admitted Ill. bar, 1862; pract. Rock Island. Judge circuit court, 14th Circuit, 1897 until death, Aug. 9, 1912.

Edward Lane, res. Montgomery Co. Dem. U.S.H.R., 1887–95. b. Cleveland, Ohio, March 27, 1842. Moved with parents to Hillsboro, 1858. Taught school. Admitted Ill. bar, 1865; pract. Hillsboro. City att. Hillsboro, 1866–69. Judge Montgomery Co. Court, Nov. 1869 to 1873. Resumed pract. Hillsboro where he died, Oct. 30, 1912.

William Ernest Mason, res. Cook Co. Rep. U.S.H.R., 1887–91, 1917 to June 16, 1921 (d.). b. Franklinville, N.Y., July 7, 1850. Moved with parents to Iowa, 1858. Taught school Des Moines while studying law. Moved to Chicago. Admitted Ill. bar, 1872; pract. Chicago. Ill. H.R., 1879–80. Ill. Sen., 1883–86. U.S. Sen., 1897–1903. d. Washington, D.C.

Philip Sidney Post, res. Knox Co. Rep. U.S.H.R., 1887 to Jan. 6, 1895 (d.). b. Florida, N.Y., March 19, 1833. A.B. Union, 1855. Moved to Ill.; admitted Ill. bar, 1856; pract. Galesburg. Served with 59th Ill. Vol. Inf.; lt., July 21, 1861; maj., Jan. 17, 1862; col., March 20, 1862. Bvt. brig. gen. for gallantry, Dec. 16, 1864. Congressional Medal of Honor, March 3, 1893, for heroism Dec. 15 and 16, 1864. Consul Vienna, 1866. Consul gen. to Austria-Hungary, 1874–79 (resigned). Commander Dept. Ill. G.A.R., 1886. d. Washington, D.C., Jan. 6, 1895.

Justices Illinois Supreme Court Pinckney H. Walker[11] (d. Feb. 16, 1885); John M. Scott[14] (to June 1888); Benjamin R. Sheldon[14] (to June 1888); T. Lyle Dickey[15] (d. July 22, 1885); John Scholfield[15]; Alfred M. Craig[15]; John H. Mulkey[16] (to June 1888); David J. Baker[16] (from June 16, 1888).

Damon C. Tunnicliff, res. McDonough Co. Just. Ill. Supreme Court, Feb. 16– June 16, 1885, vice Walker. b. Herkimer Co., N.Y., Aug. 20, 1829. Moved to McDonough Co., 1849. Admitted Ill. bar, pract. Macomb, 1853. Pres. elector, 1868. No other pub. office. d. Macomb, Dec. 20, 1901.

Simeon P. Shope, res. Cook Co. Just. Ill. Supreme Court, 1885–94. C.J., 1889. b. Ohio, Dec. 3, 1834. Admitted Ill. bar, 1858. Judge circuit court, 6th Circuit, Aug. 20, 1877, to 1885. d. (auto accident) Chicago, Jan. 23, 1920.

Joseph M. Bailey, res. Stephenson Co. Just. Ill. Supreme Court, 1888 to Oct. 16, 1895 (d.). C.J., 1892. b. Middlebury, N.Y., June 22, 1833. A.B. Rochester, 1854. Moved to Ill., admitted Ill. bar, 1855. Moved to Freeport, 1856. Ill. H.R., 1866–70. Pres. elector, 1876. Judge circuit court, 13th Circuit, Aug. 20, 1877, to 1888 (resigned). d. Freeport.

B. D. Magruder, res. Cook Co. Just. Ill. Supreme Court, Nov. 16, 1885–88, vice Dickey; 1888–1906. C.J., 1891, 1896, 1902.

b. Natchez, Miss., Sept. 27, 1838. A.B. Yale, 1856; LL.B. Louisiana, admitted Tenn. bar, 1859. Moved to Chicago, June 1861. Supporter of the federal union. Master in chancery Cook Co., 1868. d. Chicago, April 21, 1910.

Jacob W. Wilkin, res. Vermilion Co. Just. Ill. Supreme Court, 1888–1906. C.J., 1894, 1901. b. Licking Co., Ohio, June 7, 1837. Moved to Ill. with parents, 1849; A.B. McKendree. Served three years 130th Ill. Vol. Inf., promoted maj. Admitted Ill. bar, 1866. Pres. elector, 1872. Judge circuit court, 4th Circuit, 1879–88 (resigned). d. Danville, April 4, 1907.

19. Administration of Joseph W. Fifer, Jan. 14, 1889, to Jan. 10, 1893. Voting for governor: Fifer, 367,860. John M. Palmer, 355,313. David H. Harts, 18,874.

Governor Joseph W. Fifer, res. McLean Co. Rep. b. Staunton, Va., Oct. 28, 1840. Moved to McLean Co. with father, 1857. Bricklayer and brickmaker. Pvt. 33rd Ill. Inf., wounded Jackson, Miss., 1863; recovered and rejoined regiment. A.B. Illinois Wesleyan, 1868. Admitted Ill. bar, 1870. Corp. counsel Bloomington, 1871. State's att. McLean Co., 1872. Ill. Scn., 1881–84. d. Bloomington, Aug. 6, 1938.

Lieutenant Governor Lyman B. Ray, res. Grundy Co. Rep. b. Crittenden Co., Vt., Aug. 7, 1831. Moved to Grundy Co., 1852. Ill. H.R., 1873–74. Ill. Sen., 1883–86. Merchant Morris, 1894–1912. d. Joliet, Aug. 22, 1916.

Secretary of State Isaac N. Pearson, res. McDonough Co. Rep. b. Centerville, Pa., July 27, 1842. Moved to Macomb, 1858. Clerk circuit court, 1872–80. Ill. H.R., 1883–84. Ill. Sen., 1887–88 (resigned). d. Macomb, Feb. 27, 1908.

Auditor Charles W. Pavey, res. Jefferson Co. Rep. b. Highland Co., Ohio, Nov. 8, 1835. Moved to Mount Vernon, 1859. First lt. 80th Ill. Vol. Inf.; wounded and captured Sand Mt.; exchanged, 1864. Brig. gen. Ill. N.G.; active in G.A.R. Coll. int. rev. d. Mount Vernon, May 11, 1910.

Treasurers Charles Becker, res. St. Clair Co. Rep. Treas., Jan. 14, 1889, to Jan. 12, 1891. b. Germany, 1840. Emigrated to St. Clair Co. with parents, 1851. Enlisted 12th Mo. Inf.; 1861; lost leg at Pea Ridge, Ark. Sheriff St. Clair Co., 1866–70. Clerk county court, 1872–80. d. Belleville, Jan. 2, 1908.

Edward S. Wilson, res. Richland Co., Dem. Treas., Jan. 12, 1891, to Jan. 10, 1893. b. Palestine, June 25, 1839. Read law;

admitted Ill. bar, pract. Olney, 1861. State treas. only pub. office. With two sons, operated ice and cold storage plant Olney. d. Olney, June 1924.

Superintendents of Public Instruction Richard Edwards[18] (to Jan. 12, 1891); Henry Raab[17].

Attorney General George Hunt[18].

United States Senators Shelby M. Cullom[13]; Charles B. Farwell[14] (to 1891); John M. Palmer[14] (from 1891).

United States Congressmen Jehu Baker[13] (to March 3, 1889); John R. Thomas[16] (to March 3, 1889); Ransom W. Dunham[17] (to March 3, 1889); George A. Anderson[18] (to March 3, 1889); Silas Z. Landes[18] (to March 3, 1889); Ralph Plumb[18] (to March 3, 1889); Richard W. Townshend[16] (d. March 9, 1889); Joseph G. Cannon[15] (to March 3, 1891); George E. Adams[17] (to March 3, 1891); Lewis E. Payson[17] (to March 3, 1891); Jonathan H. Rowell[17] (to March 3, 1891); William H. Gest[18] (to March 3, 1891); Frank Lawler[18] (to March 3, 1891); William E. Mason[18] (to March 3, 1891); Thomas J. Henderson[15]; William M. Springer[15]; Scott Wike[15]; Robert R. Hitt[17]; Albert J. Hopkins[18]; Edward Lane[18]; Philip S. Post[18].

George Washington Fithian, res. Jasper Co. Dem. U.S.H.R., 1889–95. b. Willow Hill, July 4, 1854. Printer at Mount Carmel. Admitted Ill. bar, 1875; pract. Newton. Pros. att. Jasper Co., 1876–84. Ill. R.R. and Warehouse Commission, 1895–97. Operated farms at Newton and at Falcon, Miss., 1897 to death, Memphis, Tenn., Jan. 21, 1921.

William St. John Forman, res. Washington Co. Dem. U.S.H.R., 1889–95. b. Natchez, Miss., Jan. 20, 1847. Moved with father to Nashville, 1851. Attended Washington Sem., Nashville. Admitted Ill. bar, 1870; pract. Nashville. Mayor Nashville, 1878–84. Ill. Sen., 1885–88. Moved to East St. Louis, 1895. Comm. int. rev., 1895–99. d. Champaign, on journey, June 10, 1908.

Charles Augustus Hill, res. Will Co. Rep. U.S.H.R., 1889–91. b. Truxton, N.Y., Aug. 23, 1833. Moved to Will Co., 1854. Taught school, studied in Ind. Admitted Ind. bar; returned to Will Co., 1860; pract. Joliet. Enlisted 8th Ill. Vols., Aug. 1862, lt. and capt. with Negro troops, 1862–65. Pros. att. Will and Grundy cos., 1868–72. Asst. att. gen. Ill., 1897–1900. d. Joliet, May 29, 1902.

George Washington Smith, res. Jackson Co. Rep. U.S.H.R., 1889 to Nov. 30, 1907

(d.). b. Putnam Co., Ohio, Aug. 18, 1846. Moved with father to Wayne Co., 1850. B.Lit. McKendree, 1868; LL.B. Indiana, admitted Ill. bar, 1870; pract. Murphysboro. Master in chancery Jackson Co. Court, 1880–88. d. Murphysboro during tenth term in Cong.

Abner Taylor, res. Cook Co. Rep. U.S.H.R., 1889–93. b. Bangor, Maine, 1829. Moved to Ohio, 1832, to Iowa, and finally to Chicago, 1860. Contractor. Ill. H.R., 1885–86. Resumed construction work, 1893, in Washington, D.C., where he died, April 13, 1903.

James Robert Williams, res. White Co. Dem. U.S.H.R., Dec. 2, 1889, vice Townshend, to 1895, 1899–1905. b. Carmi, Dec. 27, 1850. A.B. Indiana, 1875; LL.B. Union College of Law (now Northwestern), admitted Ill. bar, 1876; pract. Carmi. Master in chancery White Co. Court, 1880–82. Judge White Co. Court, 1882–86. d. Loma Linda, Calif., Nov. 8, 1923.

Samuel Thompson Busey, res. Champaign Co. Dem. U.S.H.R., 1891–93. b. Greencastle, Ind., Nov. 16, 1835. Moved with parents to Urbana. Advanced from 1st sgt. to col. Ill. vol. regiments, 1861–63; served to 1865. Bvt. brig. gen. for gallantry Fort Blakely, Ala., April 9, 1865. Mayor Urbana, 1880–89; banker. d. Urbana, Aug. 12, 1909.

Benjamin Taylor Cable, res. Rock Island Co. Dem. U.S.H.R., 1891–93. b. Georgetown, Ky., Aug. 11, 1853. Moved with parents to Rock Island, 1856. Grad. Michigan, 1876. Active in Dem. party, mfr., farmer, stockman in Ill. and Tex. d. Rock Island, Dec. 13, 1923.

Allan Cathcart Durborow, Jr., res. Cook Co. Dem. U.S.H.R., 1891–95. b. Philadelphia, Pa., Nov. 10, 1857. Moved with parents to Ind., 1862. Grad. Indiana, 1877. Moved to Chicago, 1880. Insurance agent. d. Chicago, March 10, 1908.

Lawrence Edward McGann, res. Cook Co. Dem. U.S.H.R., 1891 to Dec. 2, 1895 (resigned). b. Galway, Ireland, Feb. 2, 1852. Emigrated to Mass. with mother, 1855, and to Chicago, 1865. Supt. streets Chicago, 1885–May 1891 (resigned). Reelection to U.S.H.R. in 1894 contested by Hugh Belknap, who succeeded him, Dec. 27, 1895. Pres. Chicago General R.Rs., 1896–97. Comm. public works Chicago, 1898–1901, 1911–15. Controller Chicago, 1901–7. d. Oak Park, July 22, 1928.

Walter Cass Newberry, res. Cook Co. Dem. U.S.H.R., 1891–93. b. Sangerfield, N.Y., Dec. 23, 1835. Pvt. 81st N.Y. Vol. Inf., promoted lt., 1861, capt., 1862. Maj. 24th Regt. N.Y. Cav., 1863, lt. col. and col., 1864. Bvt. brig. gen. for bravery Dinwiddie Court House, March 31, 1865. Mayor Petersburg, Va., 1869–70 (resigned). Supt. pub. property Va., 1870–74. Moved to Chicago, 1876. P.M., 1888–89. Retired after one term U.S.H.R. d. Chicago, July 20, 1912.

Owen Scott, res. McLean Co. Dem. U.S.H.R., 1891–93. b. Effingham Co., July 6, 1848. Attended Illinois State Normal. Supt. schools Fffingham Co., 1873–81. Admitted Ill., bar, 1873. Published *Effingham Democrat*, 1882. Mayor Effingham, 1882. Moved to Bloomington, 1884, bought *Daily* and *Weekly Bulletins*. Moved to Decatur, manager *Herald*, 1893–1904. Insurance agent, 1904–21. d. Decatur, Dec. 21, 1928.

Herman Wilbur Snow, res. Iroquois Co. Dem. U.S.H.R., 1891–93. b. Michigan City, Ind., July 3, 1836. Moved as child to Ky., then to Ill. Admitted Ill. bar; pract. Sheldon. Advanced from pvt. to capt. in 139th Ill. Vol. Inf., to lt. col. in 151st, 1861–64. Taught Chicago h.s., 1865–68. Resided briefly in Tazewell Co., elected to Ill. H.R., 1873–74. Returned to Sheldon, engaged in banking. Sgt. at arms U.S.H.R., 1893–95. Moved to Kankakee; banker. d. Aug. 25, 1914.

Lewis Steward, res. Kendall Co. Dem. U.S.H.R., 1891–93. b. Wayne Co., Pa., Nov. 21, 1824. Moved with parents to Kendall Co., 1838. Admitted Ill. bar, 1860, but did not pract. Farmer with large holdings, mfr. agricultural implements, Plano and West Pullman. One term U.S.H.R. only pub. office. d. Plano, Aug. 27, 1896.

Justices Illinois Supreme Court John Scholfield[15]; Alfred M. Craig[15]; David J. Baker[16]; Simeon P. Shope[18]; Joseph M. Bailey[18]; B. D. Magruder[18]; Jacob W. Wilkin[18].

20. Administration of John Peter Altgeld, Jan. 10, 1893, to Jan. 11, 1897. Voting for governor: Altgeld, 425,558. Joseph W. Fifer, 402,676. Robert Link, 24,808. Nathan M. Barnett, 20,103.

Governor John Peter Altgeld, res. Cook Co. Dem. b. Nieder Selters, Nassau, Germany, Dec. 30, 1847. Brought by parents to Ohio, 1848. Enlisted 164th Ohio Inf., 1863; mustered out, 1865. Studied in St. Louis, Mo.; admitted Mo. bar, 1869. Pros. att. Andrew Co., Mo., 1874–75. Resigned and moved to Chicago, Oct. 1875. Defeated for Cong., 1884. Judge Cook Co. Superior Court, Dec. 6, 1886. Resigned to run for gov., 1892. When elected he became first Dem. gov. since 1856. Defeated for gov., 1896. d. Joliet, March 12, 1902.

Lieutenant Governor Joseph B. Gill, res. Jackson Co. Dem. b. Williamson Co., Feb. 17, 1862. A.B. Southern Illinois Normal, 1884; LL.B. Michigan, 1886. Ed. *Murphysboro Independent*. Ill. H.R., 1889–92. Moved to San Bernardino, Calif., 1897. Lumber merchant, banker, mem. Calif. const. conv., 1930–31. Mem. state highway advisory committee. d. San Bernardino, Calif., Sept. 22, 1942.

Secretary of State William Henry Hinrichsen, res. Morgan Co. Dem. b. Franklin, May 27, 1850. A.B. Illinois Industrial (now Illinois), 1868. Sheriff Morgan Co., 1880–82. Ed. *Illinois Courier* Jacksonville, 1880–86, 1890–1907. Ed. *Quincy Herald*, 1886–90. Clerk Ill. H.R., 1891–92. U.S.H.R., 1897–99. d. Jacksonville, Dec. 18, 1907.

Auditor David Gore, res. Macoupin Co. Dem. b. Trigg Co., Ky., April 5, 1827. Moved with parents to Madison Co., 1834. Served in Mexican War. Farmer. Ill. Sen., 1885–88. Mem. state board agr. d. Carlinville, date unknown.

Treasurers Rufus N. Ramsay, res. Clinton Co. Dem. Treas., Jan. 10, 1893, to Nov. 11, 1894 (d.). b. Clinton Co., May 20, 1838. Attended Illinois College, Jacksonville, McKendree, and grad. Indiana, 1864. Admitted Ill. bar, 1865. Banker Lebanon and Carlyle. County clerk Clinton Co., 1865–69. Ill. H.R., 1889–92. d. Carlyle.

Elijah P. Ramsay, res. Clinton Co., Dem. Treas., Nov. 14, 1894, to Jan. 14, 1895. b. Carlyle, March 11, 1872. Grad. Wentworth Military Acad., 1890. Employed by Marshall Field. Returned to Carlyle to assist in father's bank during father's term as treas. On father's death app. by Gov. Altgeld to complete term. Only pub. office. No record of death.

Henry Wulff, res. Cook Co. Rep. Treas., Jan. 14, 1895, to Jan. 11, 1897. b. Meldorf, Germany, Aug. 24, 1854. Brought to Chicago by parents, 1863. Co. clerk, 1890–94. d. Chicago, Dec. 27, 1907.

Superintendents of Public Instruction Henry Raab[17] (to Jan. 14, 1895). Samuel Inglis, res. Jackson Co. Rep. Supt. pub. instr., Jan. 14, 1895, to June 23,

1898 (d.). b. Marietta, Pa., Aug. 15, 1838. Moved to Ill., 1856. A.B. Mendota, La Salle Co., 1861. Served briefly with 104th Ill. Inf. Supt. schools Bond Co., 1868–83. Prof. mathematics and literature Southern Illinois Normal.

Attorney General Maurice T. Moloney, res. La Salle Co. Dem. b. Listowel, Kerry Co., Ireland, July 26, 1849. Grad. classical schools before age fourteen. In 1867 came to U.S., studied theology, taught school. LL.B. Virginia, admitted Ill. bar, 1871; pract. Ottawa. City att., 1879–83. State's att. Ottawa Co., 1884–88. Legal adviser to La Salle Co. Board of Supervisors. After one term as att. gen., removed to Chicago to pract. law, but returned to Ottawa, 1899. Mayor of Ottawa. d. Ottawa, March 9, 1917.

United States Senators Shelby M. Cullom[13]; John M. Palmer[14].

United States Congressmen Scott Wike[15] (to March 3, 1893); Abner Taylor[19] (to March 3, 1893); Samuel T. Busey[19] (to March 3, 1893); Benjamin T. Cable[19] (to March 3, 1893); Walter C. Newberry]19] (to March 3, 1893); Owen Scott[19] (to March 3, 1893); Herman W. Snow[19] (to March 3, 1893); Lewis Steward[19] (to March 3, 1893); Philip S. Post[18] (d. Jan. 6, 1895); Thomas J. Henderson[15] (to March 3, 1895); William M. Springer[15] (to March 3, 1895); Edward Lane[18] (to March 3, 1895); George W. Fithian[19] (to March 3, 1895); Allen C. Durborow, Jr.[19] (to March 3, 1895); William St. John Forman[19] (to March 3, 1895); James R. Williams[19] (to March 3, 1895); Lawrence E. McGann[19] (contested, unseated Dec. 2, 1895); Joseph G. Cannon[15]; Benjamin F. Marsh[16]; Robert R. Hitt[17]; Albert J. Hopkins[18]; George W. Smith[19].

James Franklin Aldrich, res. Cook Co. Rep. U.S.H.R., 1893–97. b. Two Rivers, Wis., April 6, 1853. Moved with parents to Chicago, 1861. Attended Chicago, grad. Rensselaer Polytechnic Inst., 1877. Mfr. Mem. Board Cook Co. Comms., 1886–88 (pres., 1887). Comm. public works, May 1, 1891, to Jan. 1, 1893. Rcvr. nat. banks and r.r. appraiser state of Ill., 1898–1923. d. Chicago, March 8, 1933.

John Charles Black, res. Cook Co. Dem. U.S.H.R., 1893 to Jan. 12, 1895 (resigned). b. Lexington, Miss., Jan. 27, 1839. Moved with parents to Danville, 1847. Union army, 1861–65; rose through ranks pvt. to col. Bvt. brig. gen. for gallantry Ft. Blakely, Ala., April 9, 1865. Congressional Medal of Honor, Oct. 31, 1893. Grad. Wabash, 1866. Admitted Ill. bar Chicago, 1867; pract. Danville. U.S. comm. pensions Chicago, March 17, 1885, to March 27, 1889. C. in C. G.A.R., 1903–4. U.S. civil service comm. Chicago, 1904–13. d. Chicago, Aug. 17, 1915.

Robert A. Childs, res. Du Page Co. Rep. U.S.H.R., 1893–95. b. Malone, N.Y., March 22, 1845. Moved with parents to farm n. Belvidere, 1852. Served with 15th Ill. Vol. Inf., 1861–65. Grad. Illinois State Normal, 1870. Admitted Ill bar, 1872; pract. Belvidere. Moved to Hinsdale, 1873, pract. Chicago. d. Hinsdale, Dec. 19, 1915.

Benjamin Franklin Funk, res. McLean Co. Rep. U.S.H.R., 1893–95. b. Funks Grove Twp., McLean Co., Oct. 17, 1838. Interrupted studies to enlist 68th Ill. Vol. Inf.; served five months during 1862. Grad. Illinois Wesleyan, 1865. Moved to Bloomington, 1869; mayor Bloomington 1871–76, 1884–86. Pres. board trustees Illinois Wesleyan. d. Bloomington, Feb. 14, 1909.

Julius Goldzier, res. Cook Co. Dem. U.S.H.R., 1893–95. b. Vienna, Austria, Jan. 20, 1854. Emigrated with parents to New York, N.Y., 1866; admitted N.Y. bar, 1872. Moved to Chicago. Ald. Chicago, 1890–92 and 1899. d. Chicago, Jan. 20, 1925.

Andrew Jackson Hunter, res. Edgar Co. Dem. U.S.H.R., 1893–95, 1897–99. b. Greencastle, Ind., Dec. 17, 1831. Moved to Paris with parents as infant. Civil engineer, 1852–56. Admitted Ill. bar, 1856; pract. Paris. Ill. Sen., 1865–68. Defeated four times for U.S.H.R. Judge Edgar Co. Court, 1886–92. d. Paris, Jan. 12, 1913.

John James McDannold, res. Brown Co. Dem. U.S.H.R., 1893–95. b. Mount Sterling, Aug. 29, 1851. LL.B. Iowa, admitted Ill. bar, 1874; pract. Mount Sterling. Master in chancery Brown Co., 1885, Judge co. court, 1886–92. Moved to Chicago, 1895; pract. until his death, Feb. 3, 1904.

Hamilton Kinkaid Wheeler, res. Kankakee Co. Rep. U.S.H.R., 1893–95. b. Saratoga Co., N.Y., Aug. 5, 1848. Moved to Kankakee Co. with parents, 1852. Admitted Ill. bar, 1871; pract. Kankakee. Ill. Sen., 1885–88. d. Kankakee, July 19, 1918.

Hugh Reid Belknap, res. Cook Co. Rep. U.S.H.R., Dec. 27, 1895, to 1899. b. Keokuk, Iowa, Sept. 1, 1860. Worked for B & O R.R., 1878–90 (resigned). Supt.

South Side Rapid Transit R.R. of Chicago, 1890. Contested election of McGann, 1894, seated Dec. 27, 1895. Paymaster U.S.A. in Philippines, Feb. 2, 1901, until death in Calamba, Laguna, P.I., Nov. 12, 1901.

Orlando Burrell, res. White Co. Rep. U.S.H.R., 1895–97. b. Newton, Pa., July 26, 1826. Moved with parents to White Co., 1834. Farmer. Raised company of cav., 1861; commissioned capt., attached 1st Ill. Vol. Cav. Judge White Co. Court, 1873–81. Sheriff White Co., 1892–94. d. Carmi, June 7, 1922.

James Austin Connolly, res. Sangamon Co. Rep. U.S.H.R., 1895–99. b. Newark, N.J., March 8, 1843. Moved with parents to Ohio, 1850; admitted Ohio bar, 1859. Moved to Charleston, 1861. Served with 123rd Ill. Vol. Inf. rising from pvt. to maj. and bvt. lt. col. Moved to Springfield, 1865. Ill. H.R., 1873–76. U.S. att. Southern Dist. Ill., 1876–85, 1889–93. d. Springfield, Dec. 15, 1914.

Edward Dean Cooke, res. Cook Co. Rep. U.S.H.R., 1895 to June 24, 1897 (d.). b. Cascade, Iowa, Oct. 17, 1849. LL.B. Columbian (now George Washington), admitted Ill. bar, 1873; pract. Chicago. Ill. H.R., 1883–84. d. Washington, D.C., during second term U.S.H.R.

Finis Ewing Downing, res. Cass Co. Dem. U.S.H.R., 1895 to June 5, 1896 (unseated). b. Virginia, Aug. 24, 1846. Merchant in Ill. and Mo. Mayor Virginia, 1878–80. Clerk circuit court Cass Co., 1880–92. Admitted Ill. bar, 1887. Journalist. Seat in U.S.H.R. contested by John I. Rinaker, who was seated June 5, 1896. Pract. Virginia until death, March 8, 1936.

George Edmond Foss, res. Cook Co. Rep. U.S.H.R., 1895–1913, 1915–19. b. West Berkshire, Vt., July 2, 1863. A.B. Harvard, 1885; LL.B. Union College of Law (now Northwestern), admitted Ill. bar, 1889; pract. Chicago. d. Chicago, March 15, 1936.

Joseph Verdi Graff, res. Tazewell Co. Rep. U.S.H.R., 1895–1911. b. Terre Haute, Ind., July 1, 1854. Attended Wabash. Moved to Delavan, 1873. Admitted Ill. bar, 1879; pract. Delavan. Moved to Pekin, inspector of schools, 1891. Moved to Peoria, 1899, pract. until his death, Nov. 10, 1921.

William Flavius Lester Hadley, res. Madison Co. Rep. U.S.H.R., Dec. 2, 1895, to 1897, vice Remann. b. Madison Co.,

June 15, 1847. A.B. McKendree, 1867; LL.B. Michigan, admitted Ill. bar, 1871; pract. Edwardsville. Ill. Sen., 1887–90. Banker. d. Riverside, Calif., on journey, April 25, 1901.

William Lorimer, res. Cook Co. Rep. U.S.H.R., 1895–1901, 1903 to June 17, 1909 (resigned). b. Manchester, England, April 27, 1861. Emigrated to Mich. with parents, 1866. Worked from age ten. Moved to Chicago, 1870. Served U.S. Sen., June 18, 1909, to July 13, 1912 (resigned at request of Sen.). Bank pres., lumber interests. d. Chicago, Sept. 13, 1934.

Everett Jerome Murphy, res. Randolph Co. Rep. U.S.H.R., 1895–97. b. Nashville, July 24, 1852. Moved to Sparta with parents. City clerk Sparta, 1877–78 (resigned). Moved to Chester. Deputy clerk circuit court; sheriff Randolph Co. Ill. H.R., 1887–88. Warden Menard penitentiary, 1889. Moved to East St. Louis, 1892. Mem. state Board of Pardons, 1897–99. Warden Joliet penitentiary, 1899–1913, 1917 to death, Joliet, April 10, 1922.

George Washington Prince, res. Knox Co. Rep. U.S.H.R., Dec. 2, 1895, vice Post, to 1913. b. Tazewell Co., March 4, 1854. Grad. Knox, 1878. Admitted Ill. bar, 1880; pract. Galesburg. City att. Galesburg, 1881–83. Ill. H.R., 1889–92. Moved to Los Angeles, Calif., 1913. d. Sept. 26, 1939.

Walter Reeves, res. La Salle Co. Rep. U.S.H.R., 1895–1903. b. Brownsville, Pa., Sept. 25, 1848. Moved with parents to La Salle Co, 1856. Admitted Ill. bar Mount Vernon, 1875; pract. Streator. d. Streator, April 9, 1909.

Frederick Remann, res. Fayette Co. Rep. U.S.H.R., March 4–July 14, 1895 (d.). b. Vandalia, May 10, 1847. Corp. 143rd Ill. Vol. Inf. Attended Mifflin, Pa., Acad. before and after service. Grad. Iron City Business College, Pittsburgh, Pa., 1865; grad. Illinois College, Jacksonville, 1868. Ill. H.R., 1877–78. d. Vandalia, July 14, 1895, before Cong. convened.

John Irving Rinaker, res. Macoupin Co. Rep. U.S.H.R., June 5, 1896, to 1897 (won election contest with Downing). b. Baltimore, Md., Nov. 1, 1830. Moved with parents to Springfield, Dec. 1836. Grad. McKendree, 1851. Admitted Ill. bar, 1854; pract. Carlinville. Raised 122nd Ill. Vol. Inf., 1862; commissioned col., Sept. 4, 1862. Commanded brigade in 16th Corps Army of the Tennessee; bvt. brig. gen., Feb. 13, 1865, for gallantry. Chm. board Ill. R.R. and Warehouse Commission, 1885–89. d. Eustis, Fla., Jan. 15, 1915.

Vespasian Warner, res. De Witt Co. Rep. U.S.H.R., 1895–1905. b. Mount Pleasant (now Farmer City), April 23, 1842. Moved with parents to Clinton, 1843. Attended Lombard, Galesburg. Pvt. and sgt., 1861; 2nd lt., Feb. 4, 1862; capt., Feb. 10, 1865, 20th Ill. Vol. Inf. Bvt. maj., March 13, 1865, for merit. LL.B. Harvard, admitted Ill. bar, 1868; pract. Clinton. Comm. pensions, March 4, 1905, to Nov. 25, 1909. Banker. real estate owner and manager Clinton. d. March 31, 1925.

George Elon White, res. Cook Co. Rep. U.S.H.R., 1895–99. b. Millbury, Mass., March 7, 1848. Enlisted pvt. 57th Mass. Vet. Vol. Inf., 1864; in combat Wilderness to Appomatox. Moved to Chicago, 1867. Lumber merchant, pres. White Lumber Company. Ill. Sen., 1879–86. d. Chicago, May 17, 1935.

Benson Wood, res. Effingham Co. Rep. U.S.H.R., 1895–97. b. Bridgewater, Pa., March 31, 1839. Attended Wyoming, Pa., Sem. Moved to Lee Co. and taught school, 1859–61. First lt., capt. 34th Ill. Vol. Inf., 1861–63. LL.B. Chicago, admitted Ill. bar, 1864; pract. Effingham. Ill. H.R., 1873–74. Mayor Effingham, 1881–83. Pres. Ill. Bar Association, 1899–1900. Pres. Effingham State Bank, 1903–12; chm. board, 1912–15. d. Effingham, Aug. 27, 1915.

Charles Walhart Woodman, res. Cook Co. Rep. U.S.H.R., 1895–97. b. Aalborg, Denmark, March 11, 1844. Emigrated to Philadelphia, Pa., 1863; enlisted Gulf Squadron U.S.N. Moved to Chicago, 1865. LL.B. Chicago, admitted Ill. bar, 1871; pract. Chicago. Pros. att. lower courts, 1877–81. J.P., 1881–84. d. Elgin, March 18, 1898.

Justices Illinois Supreme Court John Scholfield[15] (d. Feb. 13, 1893); Alfred M. Craig[15]; David J. Baker[16]; Simeon P. Shope[18] (to June 1894); Joseph M. Bailey[18] (d. Oct. 16, 1895); B. D. Magruder[18]; Jacob W. Wilkin[18].

Jesse J. Phillips, res. Montgomery Co. Just. Ill. Supreme Court, June 5, 1893, vice Scholfield, to Feb. 16, 1901 (d.). C.J., 1897. b. Montgomery Co., May 22, 1837. Admitted Ill. bar, 1860. Capt 9th Ill. Inf.; thrice wounded at Shiloh; cited for gallantry; bvt. brig. gen., 1865. Judge circuit court, 5th Circuit, Hillsboro, June 16, 1879, to July 31, 1893.

James H. Cartwright, res. Ogle Co. Just. Ill. Supreme Court, Dec. 17, 1895, vice Bailey, to May 18, 1924 (d.). C.J., 1899, 1905, 1908, 1914, 1920. b. Maquoketa, Iowa, Dec. 1, 1842. Pvt. 140th Ill. Vol. Inf.,

1862, promoted capt. A.B. Michigan, 1867. Admitted Ill. bar, 1870; pract. Oregon. Master in chancery, 1876. Judge superior court, 1888–95.

Joseph N. Carter, res. Adams Co. Just. Ill. Supreme Court, 1894–1903. C.J., 1898. b. Hardin Co., Ky., March 12, 1843. Taught school Tuscola. A.B. Illinois College, Jacksonville, 1866; LL.B. Michigan, 1868. Admitted Ill. bar, 1869; pract. Quincy. Ill. H.R., 1879–82. d. Quincy, Feb. 6, 1913.

21. Administration of John R. Tanner, Jan. 11, 1897, to Jan. 14, 1901. Voting for governor: Tanner, 587,637. John P. Altgeld, 474,256. George W. Gere, 14,559.

Govenor John R. Tanner[18].

Lieutenant Governor William A. Northcott, res. Bond Co. Rep. Lt. gov., 1897–1905. b. Murfreesboro, Tenn., Jan. 28, 1854. Attended U.S.N.A. (resigned). Admitted to W. Va. bar, 1877. Moved to Greenville, 1879. State's att. Bond Co., 1882–90. U.S. dist. att. Southern Dist. Ill., 1905–14. d. Excelsior Springs, Mo., June 25, 1917.

Secretary of State James A. Rose, res. Pope Co. Rep. Sec. state, Jan. 11, 1897, to May 23, 1912 (d.). b. Golconda, Oct. 13, 1850. Grad. Illinois Normal. Teacher; co. supt. schools, 1873. Admitted Ill. bar, elected state's att. Pope Co., 1881.

Auditor James S. McCullough, res. Champaign Co. Rep. Aud., Jan. 11, 1897, to Feb. 3, 1913. b. Franklin Co., Pa., May 4, 1843. Moved to Urbana with father, 1854. Enlisted 76th Ill. Vol. Inf.; fought at Vicksburg, Jackson, other campaigns; lost left arm in assault on Ft. Blakely. County clerk McLean Co., 1873–96. d. Urbana, June 22, 1914.

Treasurers Henry L. Hertz, res. Cook Co. Rep. Treas., Jan. 11, 1897, to Jan. 11, 1899. b. Copenhagen, Denmark, 1847. A.B. Copenhagen, 1866. Emigrated to Chicago, 1869. Salesman, farmer, city employee. Coroner Cook Co., 1884–92. d. Chicago, July 3, 1926.

Floyd K. Whittemore, res. Sangamon Co. Rep. Treas., Jan. 11, 1899, to Jan. 14, 1901. b. N.Y. Treasury officer in Chicago; banker in Springfield. Treas. only state office. d. Springfield, March 4, 1907.

Superintendents of Public Instruction Samuel Inglis[20] (d. June 23, 1898). Joseph H. Freeman, res. Ogle and Kane cos., Rep. Supt. pub. instr., June 23, 1898, to Jan. 11, 1899. b. Poland, Maine, May 13, 1841. Attended Episcopal Sem. (now Bates). Second lt. 23rd Maine Vol. Inf., 1862; returned to school, 1863; served as capt. 14th Maine Vol. Inf., 1864; mustered out, 1865. M.A. Bates, 1866. Moved to Ill.; prin. Leland schools, 1870; supt. schools Polo, 1874. Mayor Polo, 1876. Asst. supt. pub. instr., 1895. Prin. East Aurora H.S., 1899. d. Aurora, June 12, 1931.

Alfred Bayliss, res. La Salle Co. Rep. Supt. pub. instr., Jan. 11, 1899, to Dec. 1, 1906 (resigned). b. Mich., 1846. 1st Mich. Cav., 1863–65. A.B. Hillsdale, 1870. Supt. schools LaGrange, Ind., 1871–74. Supt. schools Sterling, 1874–98. Prin. Western Illinois State Normal, 1906–11. d. Macomb, 1911.

Attorney General Edward C. Akin, res. Will Co. Rep. b. Will Co., July 10, 1852. Attended Michigan. Banker Joliet. Admitted Ill. bar, 1878. City att. Joliet, 1888. State's att., Will Co. 1888–95. Mayor Joliet, 1896. Pract. Springfield, 1901 until death, Joliet, June 20, 1936.

United States Senators Shelby M. Cullom[13];William E. Mason[18].

United States Congressmen James F. Aldrich[20] (to March 3, 1897); Orlando Burrell[20] (to March 3, 1897); William F. L. Hadley[20] (to March 3, 1897); Everett J. Murphy[20] (to March 3, 1897); John I. Rinaker[20] (to March 3 1897); Benson Wood[20] (to March 3, 1897); Charles W. Woodman[20] (to March 3, 1897); Edward Dean Cooke[20] (d. June 24, 1897); Jehu Baker[13] (1897–99); Hugh R. Belknap[20] (to March 3, 1899); James A. Connolly[20] (to March 3, 1899); William H. Hinrichsen[20] (1897–99); Andrew Jackson Hunter[20] (to March 3, 1899); George E. White[20] (to March 3, 1899); Joseph G. Cannon[15]; Benjamin F. Marsh[16]; Robert R. Hitt[17]; Albert J. Hopkins[18]; George W. Smith[19]; George E. Foss[20]; Joseph V. Graff[20]; William Lorimer[20]; George W. Prince[20]; Walter Reeves[20]; Vespasian Warner[20]; James R. Williams [19] (from March 4, 1899).

Henry Sherman Boutell, res. Cook Co. Rep. U.S.H.R., Nov. 23, 1897, vice Cooke, to March 3, 1911. b. Boston, Mass., March 14, 1856. A.B. Northwestern, 1874, Harvard, 1876. A.M. Harvard, 1876; LL.B. Northwestern, 1879; LL.D. Northwestern, 1904. Admitted Ill. bar, 1879; pract. Chicago. Ill. H.R., 1885–86. Trustee Northwestern,

1899–1911. Min. to Portugal, 1911, to Switzerland, 1912–13. Prof. const. law Georgetown, 1914–23. d. San Remo, Italy, March 11, 1926, on journey.

James Romulus Campbell, res. Hamilton Co. Dem. U.S.H.R., 1897–99. b. Hamilton Co., May 4, 1853. Attended Notre Dame. Admitted Ill. bar, 1877; pract. McLeansboro. Ed. *McLeansboro Times* 1870–98. Ill. H.R., 1885–88. Ill. Sen., 1889–96. Col. 9th Ill. Vols. Spanish-American War; lt. col. 13th Regt. regulars, 1899; brig. gen. vols., 1901. Miller and banker McLeansboro, 1901 until death, Aug. 12, 1924.

Thomas Marion Jett, res. Montgomery Co. Dem. U.S.H.R., 1897–1903. b. Bond Co., May 1, 1862. Attended Valparaiso. Admitted Ill. bar, 1887; pract. Nokomis. Moved to Hillsboro, 1889. Pros. att. Montgomery Co., 1889–96. Judge circuit court 4th Circuit, 1919–39, appellate court, 1922–36. d. Litchfield, Jan. 10, 1939.

James Robert Mann, res. Cook Co. Rep. U.S.H.R., 1897 to Nov. 30, 1922 (d.). b. Bloomington, Oct. 20, 1856. Grad. Illinois, 1876; LL.B. Union College of Law (now Northwestern), 1881; LL.M. Illinois, 1892; LL.D. Illinois, 1903. Admitted Ill. bar, 1881; pract. Chicago. Master in chancery Superior Court of Cook Co. Ald. Chicago, 1892–96. Chm. Ill. Rep. conv., 1894. Minority floor leader U.S.H.R., 1911–19. d. Washington, D.C., during fourteenth term U.S.H.R.

Daniel Webster Mills, res. Cook Co. Rep. U.S.H.R., 1897–99. b. Warren Co., Ohio, Feb. 25, 1838. Capt. 180th Ohio Vols., 1861–65. Moved to Chicago, 1865. Lake shipping, 1866–69. Real estate broker Chicago, 1869–1904. Ald., 1889–93. d. Chicago, Dec. 16, 1904.

Benjamin Franklin Caldwell, res. Sangamon Co. Dem. U.S.H.R., 1899–1905, 1907–9. b. Greene Co., Aug. 2, 1848. Moved to Chatham with parents, 1853. Board of Supervisors Sangamon Co., 1877–78. Ill. H.R., 1883–86. Ill. Sen., 1891–94. Pres. Farmers National Bank Springfield, 1885–98. Pres. Caldwell State Bank Chatham, 1909 until his death, Springfield, Dec. 29, 1924.

Joseph Burns Crowley, res. Crawford Co. Dem. U.S.H.R., 1899–1905. b. Coshocton, Ohio, July 19, 1858. Moved with parents to Jasper Co., 1860, to Robinson, 1872. Admitted Ill. bar, 1883; pract. Robinson. Master in chancery Crawford Co., 1886–90. Judge Crawford Co. Court, 1886–93. Treasury agent (seal fisheries) Alaska, 1893–98. State's att. Crawford Co., 1912–16.

Pract. Robinson until death, June 25, 1931. Thomas Cusac, res. Cook Co. Dem. U.S.H.R., 1899–1901. b. Kilrush, Ireland, Oct. 5, 1858. Emigrated with parents to New York, N.Y., 1861. Orphaned, moved to relatives in Chicago, 1863. Owned Outdoor Advertising Company, 1875–1926. Board Education, 1891–98. Col. Ill. militia on Gov. Altgeld's staff 1893–97. d. Chicago, Nov. 19, 1926.

George Peter Foster, res. Cook Co. Dem. U.S.H.R., 1899–1905. b. Dover, N.J., April 3, 1858. Moved to Chicago with parents, 1867. Attended Chicago; LL.B. Union College of Law (now Northwestern), admitted Ill. bar, 1882; pract. Chicago. J.P. South Chicago, 1891–99. Asst. corp. counsel Chicago, 1912–22. Retired to Wheaton, 1928. d. Nov. 11, 1928.

Edward Thomas Noonan, res. Cook Co. Dem. U.S.H.R., 1899–1901. b. Macomb, Oct. 23, 1861. Admitted Ill. bar, 1882; LL.B. Michigan, 1883; pract. Chicago. Ill. Sen., 1891–94. Col. Ill. militia on Gov. Altgeld's staff, 1893–97. Pract. Chicago, 1901 until death, Dec. 19, 1923.

William August Rodenberg, res. St. Clair Co. Rep. U.S.H.R., 1899–1901, 1903–13, 1915–23. b. Chester, Oct. 30, 1865. A.B. Central Wesleyan, Warrenton, Mo., 1884; A.M., 1887. Admitted Ill. bar, 1893; pract. East St. Louis. U.S. civil service comm., 1901–2. Pract. Washington, D.C., 1923 to death, Alpena, Mich., on visit, Sept. 10, 1937.

William Ezra Williams, res. Pike Co. Dem. U.S.H.R., 1899–1901. 1913–17. b. Pike Co., May 5, 1857. Attended Illinois College, Jacksonville. Admitted Ill. bar, 1880; pract. Detroit and Pittsfield; State's att. Pike Co., 1886–92. Trial lawyer City R.R. Company Chicago, 1903–13. Pract. Pittsfield until death, Sept. 13, 1921.

Justices Illinois Supreme Court David J. Baker[16] (to June 1897); Alfred M. Craig[15] (to June 4, 1900); B. D. Magruder[18]; Jacob W. Wilkin [18]; Jesse J. Phillips[20]; James H. Cartwright[20]; Joseph N. Carter[20].

Carroll Curtis Boggs, res. Wayne Co. Just. Ill. Supreme Court, 1897–1906. C.J., 1900. b. Fairfield, Oct. 19, 1844. A.B. McKendree, admitted Ill. bar, 1867; pract. Wayne Co. State's att. Wayne Co. 1873. Judge Wayne Co. Court, 1877–85. Judge circuit court, 1885–91, appellate court, 1891–97. Pract. Fairfield until death, Dec. 16, 1923.

John P. Hand, res. Henry Co. Just. Ill. Supreme Court, 1900 to July 16, 1913

(resigned). C.J., 1903 and 1907. b. Henry Co., Nov. 10, 1850. A.B. Iowa State, 1872. Asst. U.S. att. Northern Dist. Ill. d. Cambridge, May 22, 1923.

22. Administration of Richard Yates, Jan. 14, 1901, to Jan. 9, 1905. Voting for governor: Yates, 580,199. Samuel Alschuler, 518,966. Visschler V. Barnes, 15,643.

Governor Richard Yates, res. Morgan Co. Rep. b. Jacksonville, Dec. 12, 1860 (son of Civil War gov.). A.B. Illinois College, Jacksonville, 1880; J.D. Michigan, 1884. Admitted Ill. and Mich. bars and licensed to pract. U.S. Circuit and Supreme Courts. City att. Jacksonville, 1885–89. Fed. dist. judge, 1894–97. Coll int. rev. Springfield, 1897–1900. U.S.H.R., 1919–33. d. Springfield, April 11, 1936.

Lieutenant Governor William A. Northcott[21].

Secretary of State James A. Rose[21].

Auditor James S. McCullough[21].

Treasurers Moses O. Williamson, res. Knox Co. Rep. Treas., Jan. 14, 1901, to Jan. 12, 1903. b. at sea, July 14, 1850. Self-educated. Banker. Pres. Peoples Trust & Savings Bank Galesburg to 1930. d. Galesburg, Feb. 24, 1935.

Fred A. Busse, res. Cook Co. Rep. Treas., Jan. 12, 1903, to Jan. 9, 1905. b. Chicago, March 3, 1866. Merchant. Ill. H.R., 1895–98. Ill. Sen., 1899–1902. P.M. Chicago, Jan. 8, 1906, to April 11, 1907 (resigned). Mayor Chicago, 1907–11. d. Chicago, July 9, 1914.

Superintendent of Public Instruction Alfred Bayliss[21].

Attorney General Howland J. Hamlin, res. Shelby Co. Rep. b. St. Lawrence Co., N.Y., July 13, 1850. Ed. B. N.Y. State Normal, Potsdam. Moved to Ill., 1870. Supt. schools Windsor. Admitted Ill. bar, 1875. d. Windsor, Dec. 12, 1909.

United States Senators Shelby M. Cullom[13]; William E. Mason[18] (to March 3, 1903); Albert J. Hopkins[18] (from 1903).

United States Congressmen Thomas Cusac[21] (to March 3, 1901); Edward T. Noonan[21] (to March 3, 1901); William E. Williams[21] (to March 3, 1901); William Lorimer[20] (to March 3, 1901, and from 1903); Benjamin F. Marsh[16] (to March 3, 1901, and from 1903); William A. Rodenberg[21] (to March 3, 1901, and from

1903); Albert J. Hopkins[18] (to March 3, 1903); Walter Reeves[20] (to March 3, 1903); Thomas Marion Jett[21] (to March 3, 1903); Joseph G. Cannon[15]; Robert R. Hitt[17]; George W. Smith[19]; George E. Foss[20]; Joseph V. Graff[20]; George W. Prince[20]; Vespasian Warner[20]; Henry S. Boutell[21]; Benjamin F. Caldwell[21]; Joseph B. Crowley[21]; George P. Foster[21]; James R. Mann[21]; James R. Williams[19].

John Joseph Feely, res. Cook Co. Dem. U.S.H.R., 1901–3. b. Will Co., Aug. 1, 1875. Grad. Niagara, 1895; LL.B. Yale, 1897. Admitted Conn. bar, 1897. Moved to Chicago, 1898. d. Chicago, Feb. 15, 1905.

Frederick John Kern, res. St. Clair Co. Dem. U.S.H.R., 1901–3. b. St. Clair Co., Sept. 2, 1864. Attended Illinois State Normal. Miner, teacher, journalist. Ed. *East St. Louis Gazette*. Bought *Belleville News-Democrat*, 1891 and published it forty years. Pres. State Board Adm., 1913–19. d. Belleville, Nov. 9, 1931.

William Frank Mahoney, res. Cook Co. Dem. U.S.H.R., 1901 to Dec. 27, 1904 (d.). b. Chicago, Feb. 22, 1856. Merchant. Ald. Chicago 1884–87, 1890–96.

James McAndrews, res. Cook Co. Dem. U.S.H.R., 1901–5, 1913–21, 1935–41. b. Woonsocket, R.I., Oct. 22, 1862. Moved to Chicago as youth. Building comm. Chicago. d. Aug. 31, 1942.

J. Ross Mickey, res. McDonough Co. Dem. U.S.H.R., 1901–3. b. McDonough Co., Jan. 5, 1856. Admitted Ill. bar, 1889; pract. Macomb. Judge McDonough Co. Court, 1898–1901 (resigned). Pres. Mystic Workers of the World, 1908–18; dir., 1918–28. d. Excelsior Springs, Mo., on visit, March 20, 1928.

Thomas Jefferson Selby, res. Calhoun Co. Dem. U.S.H.R., 1901–3. b. Delaware Co., Ohio, Dec. 4, 1840. Moved to Ill. about 1860. Sheriff Jersey Co., 1864–66. Published *Jersey County Democrat*, 1866–70. Admitted Ill. bar, 1869; pract. Jerseyville, 1875. County clerk Jersey Co., 1869–77. Mayor, Jerseyville, 1877–81. Moved to Hardin; state's att. Calhoun Co., 1888–1900. d. Hardin, March 10, 1917.

Martin Emerich, res. Cook Co. Dem. U.S.H.R., 1903–5. b. Baltimore, Md., April 27, 1846. Importer. Md. House of Delegates, 1881–83. Aide-de-camp to Gov. W. T. Hamilton, 1880–84, and to Gov. E. E. Jackson, 1884–87. Moved to Chicago. Merchant, brickmaker. Board Cook Co.

Comms., 1892–94. Retired, 1907. d. New York, N.Y., on visit, Sept. 27, 1922.

Charles Eugene Fuller, res. Boone Co. Rep. U.S.H.R., 1903–13, 1915–June 25, 1926. b. Boone Co., March 31, 1849. Attended Wheaton. Admitted Ill. bar, 1870; pract. Belvidere. City att. Belvidere, 1875–76. Pros. att. Boone Co., 1876–78. Ill. Sen., 1879–82, 1889–92. Ill. H.R., 1883–88. Col. 13th Ill. Inf. Spanish-American War. Judge circuit court, 17th Circuit, 1897–1903. d. Rochester, Minn., during eleventh term U.S.H.R.

Phillip Knopf, res. Cook Co. Rep. U.S.H.R., 1903–9. b. Lake Co., Nov. 18, 1847. Served with 147th Ill. Vol. Inf. in Civil War. Moved to Chicago, 1866; owned trucking company. Ill. Sen., 1887–94. Clerk Cook Co., 1894–1902. d. Chicago, Aug. 14, 1920.

Henry Thomas Rainey, res. Greene Co. Dem. U.S.H.R., 1903–21, 1923 to Aug. 19, 1934 (d.). b. Carrollton, Aug. 20, 1860. Attended Knox; A.B. Amherst, 1883; A.M. Amherst, 1886; LL.B. Union College of Law (now Northwestern), admitted Ill. bar, 1885; pract. Carrollton. Master in chancery Greene Co. Court, 1887–95. Died during his fifteenth term U.S.H.R. in a St. Louis, Mo., hospital.

Howard Malcolm Snapp, res. Will Co. Rep. U.S.H.R., 1903–11. b. Joliet, Sept. 27, 1855. Attended Forest U., Chicago. Admitted Ill. bar, 1878; pract. Globe, Ariz. Returned to Joliet, 1880. Master in chancery Will Co. Court, 1884–1903. Pract. Joliet, 1911 to his death, Aug. 14, 1938.

John Allen Sterling, res. McLean Co. Rep. U.S.H.R., 1903–13, 1915 to Oct. 17, 1918 (d.). b. McLean Co., Feb. 1, 1857. A.B. Illinois Wesleyan, 1881, A.M. 1887. Supt. schools Lexington, 1881–83. Admitted Ill. bar, 1884; pract. Bloomington. State's att. McLean Co., 1892–96. d. in auto accident near Pontiac, during seventh term U.S.H.R.

William Warfield Wilson, res. Cook Co. Rep. U.S.H.R., 1903–13, 1915–21. b. Ohio, Bureau Co., March 2, 1868. Attended Michigan; LL.B. Chicago-Kent, admitted Ill. bar, 1893; pract. Chicago. Gen. counsel Alien Property Custodian, 1922–27. Pract. Chicago 1921 until death, July 22, 1942.

Justices Illinois Supreme Court Jesse J. Phillips[20] (d. Feb. 16, 1901); Joseph N. Carter[20] (to June 1903); B. D. Magruder[18]; Jacob W. Wilkin[18]; James H. Cartwright[20]; Carroll C. Boggs[21]; John P. Hand[21].

James B. Ricks, res. Christian Co. Just.

Ill. Supreme Court, May 25, 1901, vice Phillips, to June 4, 1906. C.J., 1904. b. Taylorville, Dec. 23, 1852. Grad. Illinois Wesleyan. Admitted Ill. bar, 1874. Master in chancery Christian Co., mayor of Taylorville. d. Taylorville, July 23, 1906.

Guy C. Scott, res. Mercer Co. Just. Ill. Supreme Court, June 16, 1903, to May 1909 (d.). C.J., 1906. b. Henderson Co., Aug. 14, 1863. Grad. Knox, admitted Ill. bar, 1886. County and city offices, including mayor of Aledo, 1886–1903.

23. First administration of Charles S. Deneen, Jan. 9, 1905, to Jan. 18, 1909. Voting for governor: Deneen, 634,029. Lawrence B. Stringer, 334,880. Robert H. Patton, 35,390. John Collins, 59,062.

Governor Charles S. Deneen, res. Cook Co. Rep. b. Edwardsville, May 4, 1863. A.B. McKendree, 1882. Taught school Jasper and Madison cos. LL.D. Union College of Law (now Northwestern); admitted Ill. bar, 1885. Ill. H.R., 1893–94. Pros. att. Cook Co., 1896–1904. Fostered direct primary law, municipal courts for Chicago, a state highway commission, and a deep waterway Lake Michigan to Illinois River. U.S. Sen., 1925–31. d. Chicago, Feb. 5, 1940.

Lieutenant Governor Lawrence Y. Sherman, res. McDonough Co. Rep. b. Miami, Ohio, Nov. 8, 1858. A.B. McKendree, 1882. Admitted Ill. bar; elected city att. Macomb, 1882. Judge McDonough Co. Court, 1886–90. Ill. H.R., 1897–1904 (spkr., 1899–1902). U.S. Sen., 1913–15, vice Lorimer; 1915–21. Pract. Springfield, 1921–24, Daytona Beach, Fla., 1924–33. d. Daytona Beach, Fla., Sept. 15, 1939.

Secretary of State James A. Rose[21].

Auditor James S. McCullough[21].

Treasurers Len Small, res. Kankakee Co. Rep. Treas. Jan. 9, 1905, to Jan. 10, 1907, Jan. 8, 1917, to Jan. 8, 1919. b. Kankakee, June 16, 1862. Grad. Illinois State Normal. Supervisor Kankakee Co., 1895. Clerk circuit court, 1896. Pres. board trustees Kankakee State Hospital. Gov., Jan. 10, 1921, to Jan. 14, 1929. Built 4,800 miles hard roads authorized during Lowden adm. and obtained bond issue for more roads. Banker, pres. First Trust and Savings Bank, Kankakee. d. Kankakee, May 17, 1936.

John F. Smulski, res. Cook Co. Treas. Jan. 10, 1907, to Jan. 18, 1909. Rep. b. Poland, Feb. 4, 1867. Brought by father to Ill., 1869, to Chicago, 1875. Admitted Ill. bar, 1889. Ald. three terms. City att., 1903–

6. Banker. Active for Polish independence Paris, 1919. Organized American flying unit for Polish army, 1920. d. Chicago, March 18, 1928.

Superintendents Public Instruction Alfred Bayliss[21] (to Dec. 1, 1906).

Francis Grant Blair, res. Coles Co. Rep. Supt., pub. instr., Dec. 1, 1906, vice Bayliss, to Jan. 14, 1935. b. Nashville, Oct. 30, 1864. Grad. Illinois State Normal, 1892. M.A. Swarthmore, 1893. Returned to Ill. as supervisor of training, Eastern Illinois Normal, 1899. Pres. Nat. Education Association, 1926–27. Wrote pageants and anthologies. d. Springfield, Jan. 26, 1942.

Attorney General William H. Stead, res. La Salle Co. Rep. Att. gen., Jan. 9, 1905, to Feb. 3, 1913. b. La Salle Co., June 12, 1858. Grad. DePauw, admitted Ill. bar, 1883. City att. Ottawa, 1887–89. State's att. La Salle Co., 1896–1900. d. Chicago, April 15, 1919.

United States Senators Shelby M. Cullom[13]; Albert J. Hopkins[18].

United States Congressmen James R. Williams[19] (to March 3, 1905); Vespasian Warner[20] (to March 3, 1905); Joseph B. Crowley[21] (to March 3, 1905); George P. Foster[21] (to March 3, 1905); Benjamin F. Caldwell[21] (to March 3, 1905; from March 4, 1907); Benjamin F. Marsh[16] (d. June 2, 1905); James McAndrews[22] (to March 3, 1905); Martin Emerich[21] (to March 3, 1905); Robert R. Hitt[17] (d. Sept. 19, 1906); George W. Smith[19] (d. Nov. 30, 1907); Joseph G. Cannon[15]; George E. Foss[20]; Joseph V. Graff[20]; William Lorimer[20]; George W. Prince[20]; Henry S. Boutell[21]; James R. Mann[21]; William A. Rodenberg[21]; Charles E. Fuller[22]; Phillip Knopf[22]; Henry T. Rainey[22]; Howard M. Snapp[22]; John A. Sterling[22]; William W. Wilson[22].

Pleasant Thomas Chapman, res. Johnson Co. Rep. U.S.H.R., 1905–11. b. Johnson Co., Oct. 8, 1854. A.B. McKendree, 1876. Supt. schools Johnson Co., 1877–82. Admitted Ill. bar, 1878; pract. Vienna. Banker, farmer. Judge Johnson Co. Court, 1882–90. Ill. Sen., 1891–1902. Law and banking from 1911 until his death, Jan. 31, 1931.

Frank Stoddard Dickson, res. Fayette Co. Rep. U.S.H.R., 1905–7. b. Hillsboro, Oct. 6, 1876. Taught school. Pvt. 4th Ill. Vol. Inf. Spanish-American war. Asst. adj. gen. Ill., 1908–10; adj. gen., 1910–22. Sec. to Sen.

Medill McCormick, 1924–25. Gen. counsel Nat. Board Fire Underwriters. d. Washington, D.C., Feb. 24, 1953.

Frank Orren Lowden, res. Ogle Co. Rep. U.S.H.R., Nov. 6, 1906, to 1911. b. Sunrise City, Minn., Jan. 26, 1861. Moved with parents to Point Pleasant, Iowa, 1868; taught school at age fifteen. A.B. Iowa State, 1885 (valedictorian); LL.D. Union College of Law (now Northwestern), admitted Ill. bar, 1887; pract. Chicago. Lt. col. 1st Ill. Inf. Spanish-American War. Gov., Jan. 8, 1917, to Jan. 10, 1921. Author Lowden Code for reorganization of state boards and depts. Proposed and promoted $60,000,000 bond issue for hard roads. Pract. Chicago after 1921. d. Tucson, Ariz., on sojourn, March 20, 1943.

Martin Barnaby Madden, res. Cook Co. Rep. U.S.H.R., 1905, to April 27, 1928 (d.). b. Darlington, England, March 20, 1855. Emigrated to Chicago with parents, 1860. Business education. Ald. 1889–97 (presiding, 1891–93). Pres. Ill. Mfrs. Association, 1901–2. Died in the Capitol during twelfth term U.S.H.R.

Charles McGavin, res. Cook Co. Rep. U.S.H.R., 1905–9. b. Riverton, Jan. 10, 1874. Admitted Ill. bar, 1897; pract. Springfield. Moved to Chicago, 1899. City att., 1903–4. Pract. Chicago and Los Angeles, Calif. d. Chicago, Dec. 17, 1940.

William Brown McKinley, res. Champaign Co. Rep. U.S.H.R., 1905–13, 1915–21. b. Petersburg, Sept. 5, 1856. Banker, utility operator in Champaign. U.S. Sen., 1921 until his death in office, Dec. 7, 1926.

James McKinney, res. Mercer Co. Rep. U.S.H.R., Nov. 7, 1905, vice Marsh, to 1913. b. Oquawka, April 14, 1852. A.B. Monmouth, 1874. Pres. Aledo Bank, 1892–1907. Pres. Ill. Bankers Association, 1908–9. Real estate loan business, 1913–34. d. Aledo, Sept. 29, 1934.

Anthony Michalek, res. Cook Co. Rep. U.S.H.R., 1905–7 (seat contested on basis citizenship). b. Radvanov, Czechoslovakia, Jan. 16, 1878. Brought to Chicago as infant by parents. Pub. school teacher. First man of Bohemian blood elected to U.S.H.R. Pres. and manager of a music conservatory. d. Chicago, Dec. 21, 1916.

Zeno John Rives, res. Montgomery Co. Rep. U.S.H.R., 1905–7. b. Greenfield, Ind., Feb. 22, 1874. Moved with parents to Litchfield, 1880. Admitted Ill. bar, 1901; pract. Litchfield. City clerk, 1903. P.M.

Litchfield, 1912–16. Moved to Decatur, 1919; pract. law, real estate broker. d. Decatur, Sept. 2, 1939.

Charles Stuart Wharton, res. Cook Co. Rep. U.S.H.R., 1905–7. b. Aledo, April 22, 1875. Moved with parents to Chicago, 1878. LL.B. Michigan, admitted Ill. bar, 1896; pract. Chicago. Asst. city att., 1903. Asst. corp. counsel, 1919. Asst. state's att., 1920–23. Operated restaurant and wrote several books. d. Chicago, Sept. 4, 1939.

Martin David Foster, res. Richland Co. Dem. U.S.H.R., 1907–19. b. Edwards Co., Sept. 3, 1861. Grad. Eclectic Med. Inst., Cincinnati, Ohio, 1882, and Hahnemann Med. College, Chicago, 1884. Practiced medicine Olney. Mem. board U.S. Examining Surgeons, 1885–89, 1893–97. d. Olney, Oct. 20, 1919.

James Thomas McDermott, res. Cook Co. Dem. U.S.H.R., 1907 to July 21, 1914 (resigned) and 1915–17. b. Grand Rapids, Mich., 1872. Moved with parents to Detroit, 1884. Telegrapher. Moved to Chicago, 1889. Tobacco retailer, Dem. political leader. d. Chicago, Feb. 7, 1938.

Adolph Joachim Sabath, res. Cook Co. Dem. U.S.H.R., 1907 to Nov. 6, 1952 (d.). b. Zabori, Czechoslovakia, April 4, 1866. Emigrated to Chicago, 1881. LL.B. Chicago (now Chicago-Kent) College of Law, 1891. Admitted Ill. bar, 1892. Dem. ward committeeman, district leader, 1892–1944. J.P. Chicago, 1895. Police magistrate, 1897–1906. Died at Bethesda Naval Hospital, Md., during twenty-fourth term in Cong.

Napoleon Bonaparte Thistlewood, res. Alexander Co. Rep. U.S.H.R., Feb. 15, 1908, vice Smith, to 1913. b. Harrington, Del., March 30, 1837. Moved to Mason, 1858. Merchant. Pvt., 1862, capt., 1864, 98th Ill. Vols.; wounded Selma, Ala., April 2, 1865. Commission merchant at Mason and Cairo. Mayor Cairo, 1879–83, 1897–1901. Commander Ill. G.A.R., 1901. Retired, 1913. d. Cairo, Sept. 15, 1915.

Justices Illinois Supreme Court B. D. Magruder[18] (to June 4, 1906); Jacob W. Wilkin[18] (d. April 4, 1907); James H. Cartwright[20]; Carroll C. Boggs[21] (to June 4, 1906); John P. Hand[21]; James B. Ricks[22] (to June 4, 1906); Guy C. Scott[22].

William M. Farmer, res. Fayette Co. Dem. Just. Ill. Supreme Court, June 18, 1906, to July 1, 1931 (resigned). C.J., 1909, 1915, 1923, 1929. b. Fayette Co., June 5, 1853. LL.B. Union College of Law (now Northwestern), admitted Ill. bar, 1876; pract. Vandalia. State's att. Fayette Co., 1880–84. Ill. H.R., 1889–90. Ill. Sen.,

1891–94. Judge circuit court, 4th Circuit, June 18, 1897, to June 1906 (resigned). d. Vandalia, Aug. 28, 1931.

Alonzo Knox Vickers, res. Johnson Co. Rep. Just. Ill. Supreme Court, June 18, 1906, to Jan. 21, 1915 (d.). C.J., 1910. b. Massac Co., Sept. 25, 1853. Admitted Ill. bar Metropolis, 1877; pract. to 1886. Ill. H.R., 1887–88. Judge circuit court, 1st Circuit, June 1, 1891, to June 1903; appellate court, 1903–6.

Orrin N. Carter, res. Cook Co. Just. Ill. Supreme Court, June 18, 1906, to June 2, 1924. C.J., 1911, 1917, 1924. b. Jefferson Co., N.Y., Jan. 22, 1854. Moved with parents to Du Page Co., 1864. A.B. Wheaton, admitted Ill. bar, 1877. State's att. Grundy Co., 1882–88. Moved to Chicago. Gen. counsel for Sanitary District, 1892–94. Co. judge, 1894–1906. Served bar association and many civic enterprises. d. Glendale, Calif., Aug. 15, 1928.

Frank Dunn, res. Coles Co. Just. Ill. Supreme Court, June 13, 1907, vice Wilken, to 1933. C.J., 1912, 1919, 1925, 1930. b. Mount Gilead, Ohio, Nov. 13, 1854. A.B. Kenyon, 1873; LL.B. Harvard, 1875. Moved to Ill., admitted Ill. bar, 1875; pract. Charleston to 1897. Judge circuit court, 5th Circuit, 1897–1903. Pract. Charleston until death, Aug. 7, 1940.

24. Second administration of Charles S. Deneen, Jan. 18, 1909, to Feb. 3, 1913. Voting for governor: Deneen, 550,076. Adlai E. Stevenson, 526,912. Daniel R. Sheen, 33,922. James H. Brower, 31,293. George W. McCaskrin, 10,883.

Governor Charles S. Deneen[23].

Lieutenant Governor John G. Oglesby, res. Logan Co. Rep. Lt. gov., 1909–13, 1917–21. b. Decatur, March 19, 1878 (son of Gov. Richard J. Oglesby). Capt. 1st Ill. Cav. Spanish-American War (reserve list, 1905, as col.). Pvt. sec. Gov. Yates., 1901–4. Ill. H.R., 1905–8. Author direct primary law. Farmer near Elkhart. d. Elkhart, May 27, 1938.

Secretaries of State James A. Rose[21] (d. May 23, 1912).

Cornelius J. Doyle, res. Greene Co. Rep. Sec. state, June 1, 1912, to Feb. 3, 1913. b. Carlinville, Dec. 6, 1871. Attended Lincoln Memorial; admitted Ill. bar, 1906. City att. Greenfield, 1906–8. Mayor Greenfield, 1908–12. First Ill. fire marshal, 1911–12. App. sec. state by Gov. Deneen to complete Rose's fourth term. Pract. Springfield. d. April 19, 1938.

Auditor James S. McCullough[21].

Treasurers Andrew Russel, res. Morgan Co. Rep. Treas., Jan. 8, 1909, to Jan. 11, 1911; Feb. 20, 1915, to Jan. 8, 1917. b. Jacksonville, June 17, 1856. Grad. Illinois College, Jacksonville. Banker in Jacksonville. Chm. Board of Pardons, 1901–6. Aud. Ill., 1917–25. Board of Pardons and Paroles, 1929–33. Convicted of violating nat. banking act, July 1934, sentenced to eighteen months imprisonment fed. detention farm Milan, Mich. where he died Nov. 22, 1934.

Edward E. Mitchell, res. Jackson Co. Rep. Treas., Jan. 11, 1911, to Feb. 3, 1913. b. Corinth, Nov. 11, 1858. Prior to 1893 sec. Ill. Rep. central committee. Moved to Carbondale, 1893. Established First Nat. Bank of Carbondale, pres.; retired, 1913. Organizer Chicago & Carterville Coal Company about 1900. Mayor Carbondale, 1903–4. d. Carbondale, Sept. 19, 1938.

Superintendent of Public Instruction Francis G. Blair[23].

Attorney General William H. Stead[23].

United States Senators Shelby M. Cullom[13]; William Lorimer[20].

United States Congressmen Phillip Knopf[22] (to March 3, 1909); Charles McGavin[23] (to March 3, 1909); William Lorimer[20] (resigned June 17, 1909); Joseph V. Graff[20] (to March 3, 1911); Henry S. Boutell[21] (to March 3, 1911); Howard M. Snapp[22] (to March 3, 1911); Pleasant T. Chapman[23] (to March 3, 1911); Frank O. Lowden[23] (to March 3, 1911); Joseph G. Cannon[15]; George E. Foss[20]; George W. Prince[20]; James R. Mann[21]; William A. Rodenberg[21]; Charles E. Fuller[22]; Henry T. Rainey[22]; John A. Sterling[22]; William W. Wilson[22]; William B. McKinley[23]; James McKinney[23]; Martin B. Madden[23]; Martin D. Foster[22]; James T. McDermott[23]; Adolph J. Sabath[23]; Napoleon B Thistlewood[23].

Thomas Gallagher, res. Cook Co. Dem. U.S.H.R., 1909–21. b. Concord, N.H., July 6, 1850. Moved to Chicago, 1866. Iron molder, merchant, banker. Ald. Chicago, 1893–97. Dem. co. and state committeeman. Retired after six terms U.S.H.R. d. on visit, San Antonio, Tex., Feb. 24, 1930.

James McMahon Graham, res. Sangamon Co. Dem. U.S.H.R., 1909–15. b. Castleblayney, Ireland, April 14, 1852. Emigrated with family to Sangamon Co., 1868. Attended Illinois and Valparaiso. Teacher, 1878–85. Admitted Ill. bar, 1885; pract.

Springfield, Pros. att. Sangamon Co., 1892–96. Pract. Springfield, 1915 until death, Oct. 23, 1945.

Frederick Lundin, res. Cook Co. Rep. U.S.H.R., 1909–11. b. Vestra Tollstad, Sweden, May 18, 1868. Emigrated with parents to Chicago, 1880. Mfr. of chemicals and medicines. Ill. Sen., 1895–98. Retired, 1916. d. Beverly Hills, Calif., Aug. 20, 1947.

William James Moxley, res. Cook Co. Rep. U.S.H.R., Nov. 23, 1909, vice Lorimer, to 1911. b. County Cork, Ireland, May 22, 1851. Brought by parents to Chicago as infant. Mfr. and banker. Active in Rep. politics, served only one term public office. d. Delavan, Wis., Aug. 4, 1938.

Frank Buchanan, res. Cook Co. Dem. U.S.H.R., 1911–17. b. Jefferson Co., Ind., June 14, 1862. Bridge builder, structural iron worker, Chicago. Business agent Chicago local International Structural Iron Workers. International pres., 1901. d. Chicago, April 18, 1930.

Ira Clifton Copley, res. Kane Co. Prog. Rep. U.S.H.R., 1911–23. b. Knox Co., Oct. 25, 1864. Moved with parents to Aurora, 1867. A.B. Yale, 1887; LL.B. Union College of Law (now Northwestern), 1889. Utilities owner. Owner and publisher *Aurora Beacon-News* from 1905, *Elgin Courier-News* from 1908, and *Joliet Herald-News* from 1913. Operated newspaper chain in Ill. and Calif. d. Aurora, Nov. 1, 1947.

Lynden Evans, res. Cook Co. Dem. U.S.H.R., 1911–13. b. La Salle Co., June 28, 1858. Grad. Knox, 1882. Taught in La Salle and Evanston. Admitted Ill. bar, 1885; pract. Chicago. Author legal texts. Lecturer corp. law John Marshall Law School, 1907 and 1908. d. Chicago, May 6, 1926.

Hiram Robert Fowler, res. Hardin Co. Dem. U.S.H.R., 1911–15. b. Pope Co., Feb. 7, 1851. Grad. Illinois Normal, 1880; LL.B. Michigan, admitted Ill. bar, 1884; pract. Elizabethtown. State's att. Hardin Co., 1888–92. Ill. H.R., 1893–94. Ill. Sen., 1901–1904. d. Elizabethtown, Jan. 5, 1926. ˙

John Charles McKenzie, res. JoDaviess Co. Rep. U.S.H.R., 1911–25. b. Woodbine Twp., JoDaviess Co., Feb. 18, 1860. Attended Valparaiso. Taught school. Admitted Ill. bar, 1890; pract. Elizabeth. Mem. Ill. Claims Commission, 1896–1900. Ill. Sen., 1901–1911 (resigned). Member Nitrate Utilization Commission, Muscle Shoals, Ala., 1925. d. Elizabeth, Sept. 17, 1941.

Edmond John Stack, res. Cook Co.,

Dem. U.S.H.R., 1911–13. b. Chicago, Jan. 31, 1874. LL.B. Lake Forest, admitted Ill. bar, 1895; pract. Chicago. Asst. corp. counsel and chief trial att. Chicago. After one term U.S.H.R. resumed law practice, Chicago, where he died, April 12, 1957.

Claudius Ulysses Stone, res. Peoria Co. Dem. U.S.H.R., 1911–17. b. Menard Co, May 11, 1879. Attended Western Illinois Normal. Schoolman. Corp. 4th Ill. Vol. Inf. Cuba, 1898–99. Attended Michigan and George Washington. Supt. schools Peoria Co., 1902–10. Admitted Ill. bar, 1909; pract. Peoria. P.M. Peoria, 1917–20. Master in chancery circuit court, 1928–48. Published *Peoria Star*, 1938–49. d. Peoria, Nov. 13. 1957.

Justices Illinois Supreme Court James H. Cartwright[20]; John P. Hand[21]; Guy C. Scott[22] (d. May 1909); William M. Farmer[23]; Alonzo K. Vickers[23]; Orrin N. Carter[23]; Frank Dunn[23].

George Anderson Cooke, res. Mercer Co. Just. Ill. Supreme Court, Oct. 1, 1909, vice Scott, to Jan. 9, 1919 (resigned). C.J., 1913. b. New Athens, Ohio, July 3, 1869. Orphaned. Moved to Ill., 1880. A.B. Knox, admitted Ill. bar, 1892; partner Guy C. Scott at Aledo, 1896–1900. Ill. H.R., as Dem., 1903–6. Pract. Chicago, 1919–38. d. Chicago, Dec. 6, 1938.

25. Administration of Edward Fitzgerald Dunne, Feb. 3, 1913, to Jan. 8, 1917. Voting for governor: Dunne, 443,120. Charles S. Deneen, 318,469. Frank H. Funk, Prog. Rep., 303,401. John C. Kennedy, 78,679. Edwin R. Worrell, 15,231.

Governor Edward Fitzgerald Dunne, res. Cook Co. Dem. b. Waterville, Conn., Oct. 12, 1853. Moved to Peoria with parents, 1854. A.B. Trinity, Dublin, Ireland. Admitted Ill. bar, 1878. Circuit judge Cook Co., Dec. 1, 1892, vice George Driggs, to 1905 (resigned). Mayor Chicago, 1905–7. Elected gov. when Theodore Roosevelt split the Rep. party. Lake Michigan–Illinois River deep waterway bill and Women's Suffrage bill became laws during his administration. Published five-volume *History of Illinois*, 1933. d. Chicago, May 24, 1937.

Lieutenant Governor Barrett O'Hara, res. Cook Co. Dem. b. St. Joseph, Mich., April 28, 1882. With survey party in Nicaragua, 1897; youngest soldier at Santiago in Spanish-American War, 1898. Sports ed., journalist; at thirty he was youngest lt. gov. Ill. history. A.B. Northwestern, 1910; J.D. Chicago–Kent College of Law, admitted Ill. bar, 1912. Served World War I, 1917–19, maj. and judge adv. 15th Div. U.S.H.R., 1949–51, 1953 to Jan. 3, 1969.

Secretaries of State Harry Woods, res. Cook Co. Dem. Sec. state, Feb. 3, 1913, to Oct. 11, 1914 (d.). b. Canada, 1863. Moved to Chicago with parents, 1877. Messenger, broker grain trader.

Lewis G. Stevenson, res. McLean Co. Dem. Sec. state, Oct. 11, 1914, to Jan. 8, 1917. b. Chicago, Aug. 15, 1868 (son of U.S. V.P. Adlai; father of Ill. Gov. Adlai E. Stevenson). Private sec. to his father; farmer; journalist. Ill. Board Pardons and Paroles, 1912–14. App. sec. state by Gov. Dunne vice Woods. Spec. investigator Navy Dept. 1917–19. d. Bloomington, April 5, 1929.

Auditor James J. Brady, res. Cook Co. Dem. b. Chicago, June 10, 1878. Active in Dem. politics during long period of Rep. domination. Aud., 1913–17, only state office. d. Chicago, Feb. 11, 1941.

Treasurers William D. Ryan, Jr., res. Vermilion Co. Dem. Treas., Feb. 3, 1913, to Feb. 20, 1915. b. Danville, 1872. Grad. St. Viator's, Bourbonnais, 1892. Lt. Ill. vols. Spanish-American War. Carriage maker in Danville to 1912. d. Danville, Aug. 20, 1942.

Andrew Russel[24] (Feb. 20, 1915, to Jan 8, 1917).

Superintendent of Public Instruction Francis G. Blair[23].

Attorney General Patrick J. Lucey, res. La Salle Co. Dem. b. Ottawa, May 2, 1872. Admitted Ill. bar, 1896; pract. Streator. City att.; three times mayor. Mem. Pub. Utilities Commission, 1917–21. Moved to Chicago. Co-receiver Corporation Securities Company, 1932. Asst. corp. counsel Chicago, 1939 until death, Nov. 17, 1947.

United States Senators Lawrence Y. Sherman[23].

James Hamilton Lewis, res. Cook Co. Dem. U.S. Sen., 1913–19, 1931–39. b. Danville, Va., May 18, 1863. Moved with parents to Ga., 1866, and later to Tex. Attended Ohio Northern and Baylor. Admitted Tex. bar, 1883. Moved to Wash. Ter., served in ter. sen. U.S.H.R. from Wash., 1897–99. Inspector gen. Spanish-American War. Moved to Chicago, 1903. War work France, 1917–19; knighted by kings of Belgium and Greece. d. Washington, D.C., April 9, 1939.

United States Congressmen George E. Foss[20] (to March 3, 1913, and from 1915); George W. Prince[20] (to March 3, 1913);

Napoleon B. Thistlewood[23] (to March 3, 1915); Lynden Evans[24] (to March 3, 1913); Joseph G. Cannon[15] (to March 3, 1913, and from 1915); William A. Rodenberg[21] (to March 3, 1913, and from 1915); Charles E. Fuller[22] (to March 3, 1913, and from 1915); John A. Sterling[22] (to March 3, 1913, and from 1915); William W. Wilson[22] (to March 3, 1913, and from 1915); William B. McKinley[23] (to March 3, 1913, and from 1915); James R. Mann [21]; William E. Williams[21]; James McAndrews[22]; Henry T. Rainey[22]; Martin D. Foster[23]; Martin B. Madden [23]; James T. McDermott[23] (to July 21, 1914, resigned, and from 1915); Adolph J. Sabath[23]; Hiram R. Fowler[24] (to March 3, 1915); James M. Graham[24] (to March 3, 1915); Frank Buchanan[24]; Ira C. Copley[24]; Thomas Gallagher[24]; John C. McKenzie[24]; Claudius U. Stone[24].

William Nicholas Baltz, res. St. Clair Co. Dem. U.S.H.R., 1913–15. b. Millstadt, Feb. 5, 1860. Farmer, miller, banker. St. Clair Co. Board of Supervisors, 1897–1913. d. Millstadt, Aug. 22, 1943.

Charles Martin Borchers, res. Macon Co. Dem. U.S.H.R., 1913–15. b. Lockville. Ohio, Nov. 18, 1869. Moved to Macon Co. with parents, 1875. Teacher. Admitted Ill, bar, 1897; pract. Decatur. Mayor Decatur. 1909–11, 1919–23. d. Decatur, Dec. 2, 1946.

Frederick Albert Britten, res. Cook Co. Rep. U.S.H.R., 1913–35. b. Chicago, Nov. 18, 1871. Attended Heald's Business College, San Francisco, Calif. Construction work Chicago from 1893. Ald. Chicago, 1908–12. Mem. exec. committee Interparliamentary Union, 1923–31. Exec. in Chicago and New York. Retired, lived in Washington, D.C. d. Washington, D.C., May 4, 1946.

Louis FitzHenry, res. McLean Co. Dem. U.S.H.R., 1913–15. b. Bloomington, June 13, 1870. LL.B. Illinois Wesleyan, admitted Ill. bar, 1897; pract. Bloomington. City att., 1907–11. U.S. dist. judge, 1918–33. U.S. Circuit Court of Appeals until his death, Normal, Nov. 18, 1935.

George Edmund Gorman, res. Cook Co. Dem. U.S.H.R., 1913–15. b. Chicago, April 13, 1873. LL.B. Georgetown, admitted Ill. bar, 1895; pract. Chicago. Asst. pros. att. Chicago, 1897–1900. Asst. state's att. Cook Co., 1920–28. Master in chancery Circuit Court of Cook Co., 1930 until his death, Chicago, Jan. 13, 1935.

Robert Potter Hill, res. Williamson Co. Dem. U.S.H.R., 1913–15. b. Franklin Co., April 18, 1874. Grad. Ewing College, Ewing, 1896. Moved to Marion; J.P., 1899. Admitted Ill. bar, 1902. City att. Marion, 1908–10. Ill. H.R., 1911–12. After one term U.S.H.R. moved to Okla. Dist. judge, 1931–36. U.S.H.R. from Okla., 1937. d. Oklahoma City, Okla., Oct. 29, 1937.

William Henry Hinebaugh, res. La Salle Co. Rep. and Prog. Rep. U.S.H.R., 1913–15. b. Calhoun Co., Mich., Dec. 16, 1867. Attended Michigan Normal and Michigan. Moved to Ottawa, 1891. Admitted Ill. bar, 1893; pract. Ottawa. Asst. pros. att. La Salle Co., 1900–1902. Judge La Salle Co. Court 1902–12. Asst. att. gen. Ill., 1916–22. Pres. Central Life of Chicago, 1922–33. Pract. Albion, Mich., 1933 until death, Sept. 22, 1943.

Stephen Arnold Hoxworth, res. Knox Co. Dem. U.S.H.R., 1913–15. b. Maquon Twp., Knox Co., May 1, 1860. One term U.S.H.R. only pub. office. Farmed in Nebr. and Ill. d. Rapatee, Jan. 25, 1930.

Frank Trimble O'Hair, res. Edgar Co. Dem. U.S.H.R., 1913–15. b. Edgar Co., March 12, 1870. LL.B. DePauw, admitted Ill. bar, 1893; pract. Paris. One term U.S.H.R. only pub. office. d. Paris, Aug. 3, 1932.

Lawrence Beaumont Stringer, res. Logan Co. Dem. U.S.H.R., 1913–15. b. Atlantic City, N.J., Feb. 24, 1866. Moved with parents to Ill., 1876. Grad. Lincoln College, Lincoln, 1887. Ill. H.R., 1890–94. LL.B. Chicago College of Law, admitted Ill. bar, 1896; pract. Lincoln. Ill. Sen., 1901–4. Defeated for gov., 1904. C.J. Ill. Court of Claims, 1905–13. Judge Logan Co. Court from 1918 until his death, Lincoln, Dec. 5, 1942.

Clyde Howard Tavenner, res. Livingston Co. Dem. U.S.H.R., 1913–17. b. Cordova, Feb. 4, 1882. Printer, journalist. Dir. publicity Dem. Nat. Congressional Committee, 1910–12. Propagandist for Philippine independence, published *The Philippine Republic*, Washington, D.C., 1919–32. Mem. Philippine mission to Europe, 1931 and 1932. Legislative analyst to House Committee on Rules, 1939 until death, Washington, D.C., Feb. 6, 1942.

Charles Marsh Thomson, res. Cook Co. Rep. and Prog. Rep. U.S.H.R., 1913–15. b. Chicago, Feb. 13, 1877. Grad. Washington and Jefferson, 1899; LL.B. North-

western, admitted Ill. bar, 1902; pract. Chicago. Ald Chicago, 1908–13. Judge Circuit Court of Cook Co., 1915–27, court of appeals, 1917–27. Trustee C & E I R.R., 1933–39, North Western R.R., 1939 until death, Dec. 30, 1943.

Burnett Mitchell Chiperfield, res. Fulton Co. Rep. U.S.H.R., 1915–17, 1930–33. b. Dover, June 14, 1870. Attended Illinois and Hamline. Admitted Ill. bar, 1891; pract. Canton. Pros. att. Fulton Co., 1896–1900. Ill. H.R., 1903–4, 1907–12. Judge adv. 30th Div., 1917 and 1918. Judge adv. Ill. Corps Army of Occupation, 1918–19. Cited for gallantry in action. Lt. col. O.R.C., 1921. Brig. gen. on retirement, 1934. d. Canton, June 24, 1940.

Edward Everett Denison, res. Williamson Co. Rep. U.S.H.R., 1915–31. b. Marion, Aug. 28, 1873. B.A., B.L. Baylor, 1895; A.B. Yale, 1896. LL.B., LL.M. Columbian Law School (now George Washington), admitted Ill. bar, 1899; pract. Marion. d. Carbondale, June 17, 1953.

Edward John King, res. Knox Co. Rep. U.S.H.R., 1915 to Feb. 17, 1929 (d). b. Springfield, Mass., July 1, 1867. Moved to Galesburg with parents, 1880. B.S. Knox, admitted Ill. bar, 1893; pract. Galesburg. City att., 1893–94. Ill. H.R., 1907–14. Died in office during seventh term U.S.H.R.

Loren Edgar Wheeler, res. Sangamon Co. Rep. U.S.H.R., 1915–23, 1925–27. b. Havana, Oct. 7, 1862. Attended Graylock Inst., Mass. Moved to Springfield, 1880. Ice and coal business until 1910. Ald., 1895–97. Mayor Springfield, 1897–1901. P.M., 1901–13. Advertising agent Springfield, 1910–15 and 1927 until his death, Jan. 8, 1932.

Thomas Sutler Williams, res. Clay Co. Rep. U.S.H.R., 1915 to Nov. 11, 1929 (resigned). b. Louisville, Feb. 14, 1872. Attended Austin College, Effingham. Admitted Ill. bar, 1897; pract. Louisville. City att., 1897–99. Ill. H.R., 1899–1900. Mayor Louisville, 1907–9. Pros. att. Clay Co., 1908–15. Owner, publisher *Clay County Republican*. Moved to Harrisburg, 1926. Resigned U.S.H.R. to become judge U.S. Court of Claims. Served until his death in Washington, D.C., April 5, 1940.

Justices Illinois Supreme Court James H. Cartwright[20]; John P. Hand[21] (resigned July 16, 1913); Alonzo K. Vickers[23] (d. Jan. 21, 1915); Frank Dunn[23]; William M. Farmer[23]; Orrin N. Carter[23]; George A. Cooke[24].

Charles C. Craig, res. Knox Co. Dem. Just. Ill. Supreme Court, Oct. 24, 1913, vice Hand, to June 13, 1918. C.J., 1916. b. Knoxville, June 16, 1865. Attended Knox and Notre Dame. LL.B. Illinois Wesleyan, admitted Ill. bar, 1888; pract. Knoxville. Capt. horse art. Ill. N.G. Spanish-American War. Ill. H.R., 1899–1902. Pract. Galesburg, 1918–44. Pres. Bank of Galesburg, 1918–30. Trustee Knox College. d. Galesburg, Aug. 25, 1944.

Albert Watson, res. Jefferson Co. Just. Ill. Supreme Court, Feb. 17, 1915, vice Vickers, to June 4, 1915. b. Mount Vernon, April 15, 1857. B.S. McKendree, 1876. Admitted Ill. bar, 1880; pract. Mount Vernon. City att.; master in chancery Jefferson Co. Court. d. Mount Vernon, Nov. 25, 1944.

Warren W. Duncan, res. Marion Co. Just. Ill. Supreme Court, June 21, 1915, to 1933. C.J., 1918, 1924 (from June 3). b. Williamson Co., Jan. 21, 1857. A.B. Ewing College, Ewing, 1879. LL.B. St. Louis Law School, 1885. Judge circuit court, 1st Circuit, 1903–15. Also served in appellate court. d. Marion, April 11, 1938.

26. Administration of Frank O. Lowden, Jan. 8, 1917, to Jan. 10, 1921. Voting for governor: Lowden, 696,535. Edward F. Dunne, 556,654. Seymour Stedman, 52,316. John R. Golden, 15,309.

Governor Frank O. Lowden[23].

Lieutenant Governor John G. Oglesby [24].

Secretary of State Louis F. Emmerson, res. Jefferson Co. Rep. Sec. state, 1917–29. b. Albion, Dec. 27, 1863. Merchant Mount Vernon, 1887–1921. Bank pres., 1921. Gov. of Ill., 1929–33. Returned to business, 1933. d. Mount Vernon, Feb. 4, 1941.

Auditor Andrew Russel[24].

Treasurers Len Small[23] (to Jan. 8, 1919).

Fred E. Sterling, res. Winnebago Co. Rep. Treas., Jan. 8, 1919, to Jan. 10, 1921. Journalist, ed.-owner-publisher *Rockford Register-Gazette* and *Rockford Star*. Lt. gov. Ill., Jan. 10, 1921, to Jan. 9, 1933; only three-time lt. gov. Rep. state chm., 1916. d. Rockford, Feb. 10, 1934.

Superintendent of Public Instruction Francis G. Blair[23].

Attorney General Edward J. Brundage, res. Cook Co. Rep. Att. gen., 1917–25. b. Campbell, N.Y., May 13, 1869. Moved to Chicago, 1885. LL.B. Chicago (now Chicago-Kent) College of Law, 1893. Ill. H.R., 1899–1900, 1903–4. Pres. Cook Co. Board of Comms., 1904–7. Corp. counsel,

1907–11. Judge court of claims, 1915. Rcvr. Milwaukee R.R., 1925–28. d. Chicago Jan. 20, 1934.

United States Senators James Hamilton Lewis[25] (to March 3, 1919); Lawrence Y. Sherman[23]; Medill McCormick (from March 4, 1919), see U.S. Congressmen below.

United States Congressmen William E. Williams[21] (to March 3, 1917); Joseph T. McDermott[23] (to March 3, 1917); Claudius U. Stone[24] (to March 3, 1917); Burnett M. Chiperfield[25] (to March 3, 1917); Clyde H. Tavenner[25] (to March 3, 1917); John A. Sterling[22] (d. Oct. 17, 1918); Martin D. Foster[23] (to March 3, 1919); Joseph G. Cannon[15]; William E. Mason[18]; George W. Foss[20]; James R. Mann[21]; William A. Rodenberg[21]; Charles E. Fuller[22]; James McAndrews [22]; Henry T. Rainey[22]; William W. Wilson[22]; Richard Yates[22] (from March 4, 1919); Martin B. Madden[23]; William B. McKinley[23]; Adolph J. Sabath[23]; Ira C. Copley[24]; Thomas Gallagher[24]; John C. McKenzie[24]; Frederick A. Britten[25]; Edward E. Denison[25]; Edward J. King[25]; Thomas S. Williams[25]; Loren E. Wheeler[25].

Medill McCormick, res. Cook Co. Rep. U.S.H.R., 1917–19. b. Chicago, May 16, 1877. A.B. Yale, 1899; LL.B. Chicago, admitted Ill. bar, 1900. Owner with brother Robert R. and cousin Joseph Medill Patterson of controlling interest *Chicago Tribune*. Supported Prog. party, 1912–14. Ill. H.R., 1913–16. U.S. Sen., 1919 to Feb. 25, 1925, when he died, Washington, D.C., at beginning of second term.

William Johnson Graham, res. Mercer Co. Rep. U.S.H.R., 1917 to June 7, 1924 (resigned). b. Lawrence Co., Pa., Feb. 7, 1872. Moved with parents to Aledo, 1879. LL.B. Illinois, 1893. Admitted Ill. bar, 1895; pract. Aledo. Pros. att. Mercer Co., 1901–9. Ill. H.R., 1915–16. Resigned U.S.H.R. to accept appointment by Pres. Coolidge as presiding judge U.S. Court of Customs Appeals. Continued in office until death, Washington, D.C., Nov. 10, 1937.

Clifford Cady Ireland, res. Peoria Co. Rep. U.S.H.R., 1917–23. b. Washburn, Feb. 14, 1878. Attended Knox and Wisconsin, LL.B. Illinois College of Law, Chicago, 1908. Admitted Ill. bar, 1909; pract. Peoria. Pvt. Ill. N.G. Spanish-American War. Pres. Western Livestock

Insurance Company. A director of Ill. Dept. Trade and Commerce, 1923–26. d. on visit to Chicago, May 24, 1930.

Niels Juul, res. Cook Co. Rep. U.S.H.R., 1917–21. b. Randers, Denmark, April 27, 1859. Emigrated to Chicago, 1880. Publisher. LL.B. Lake Forest, 1898. Admitted Ill. bar, 1899; pract. Chicago. Ill. Sen., 1899–1914. Coll. customs Chicago, 1921–22. d. Chicago, Dec. 4, 1929.

Charles Martin, res. Cook Co. Rep. U.S.H.R., March 3, 1917, to Oct. 28, 1917 (d.). b. Ogdensburg, N.Y., May 20, 1856. Moved with parents to Chicago, 1860. Sewer contractor. Ald., 1894–1903, 1905–7, 1910–13, 1915–17. d. Chicago before Cong. convened.

John William Rainey, res. Cook Co. Dem. U.S.H.R., April 2, 1918, vice Martin, to May 4, 1923 (d.). b. Chicago, Dec. 21, 1880. LL.B. Chicago-Kent College of Law, 1909. Admitted Ill. bar, 1910; pract. Chicago. Asst. judge Probate Court Cook Co., 1910–12. Clerk circuit court, 1912–16. d. Chicago during his fourth term U.S.H.R.

Edwin Bruce Brooks, res. Jasper Co. Rep. U.S.H.R., 1919–23. b. Newton, Sept. 20, 1868. Grad. Valparaiso, 1892. Supt. schools Newman, 1894–97; Newton, 1897–1903; Greenville, 1903–5; Paris, 1905–12; Jasper Co., 1914–18. Supt. Ill. Charities, 1924–30. Asst. att. gen., 1930–32. d. Newton, Sept. 18, 1933.

Carl Richard Chindblom, res. Cook Co. Rep. U.S.H.R., 1919–33. b. Chicago, Dec. 21, 1870. A.B. Augustana, Rock Island, 1890. Teacher. LL.B. Kent (now Chicago-Kent) College of Law, 1898. Admitted Ill. bar, 1900; pract. Chicago. Mem. Cook Co. Board of Comms., 1906–10. Cook Co. att., 1912–14. Master in chancery Circuit Court of Cook Co., 1916–18. Referee in bankruptcy U.S. Dist. Court, 1934–42. d. Chicago, Sept. 12, 1956.

Frank Leslie Smith, res. Livingston Co. Rep. U.S.H.R., 1919–21. b. Dwight, Nov. 24, 1867. Teacher, banker, insurance agent, and real estate operator. Chm. Ill. Pub. Utilities Commission, 1921–26. App. U.S. Sen., Dec. 16, 1926, vice McKinley, having been elected to succeed him. Was refused appointve seat, not permitted to qualify for elective seat. Resigned Feb. 9, 1928. d. Dwight, Aug. 30, 1950.

Justices Illinois Supreme Court James H. Cartwright[20]; Orrin N. Carter[23]; Frank Dunn[23]; William M. Farmer[23];

George A. Cooke[24] (resigned Jan. 9, 1919); Charles C. Craig[25] (to June 13, 1918); Warren W. Duncan[25].

Clyde E. Stone, res. Peoria Co. Just. Ill. Supreme Court, June 14, 1918, to Jan. 14, 1948 (d.). C.J., 1921, 1926, 1931, 1935, 1942–43. b. Mason City, March 23, 1876. LL.B. Illinois, admitted Ill. bar Peoria, 1903. First asst. state's att. Peoria Co., 1906–9. Co. judge, 1910–15. Judge circuit court, 10th Circuit, 1915–18.

Floyd E. Thompson, res. Rock Island Co. Just. Ill. Supreme Court, April 9, 1919, vice Cooke, to July 25, 1928 (resigned). C.J., 1922. b. Roodhouse, Dec. 25, 1887. Self-educated in law; admitted Ill. bar, 1911; pract. Rock Island. Resigned Court to run for gov. Ill. Pract. Chicago, 1928 until death, Evanston, Oct. 17, 1960.

27. First administration of Len Small, Jan. 10, 1921, to Jan. 12, 1925. Voting for governor (women voted for first time): Small, 1,243,148. James Hamilton Lewis, 731,551. Andrew Lafin 58,998. John H. Walker, 56,480.

Governor Len Small[23].

Lieutenant Governor Fred E. Sterling [26].

Secretary of State Louis F. Emmerson [26].

Auditor Andrew Russel[24].

Treasurers Edward E. Miller, res. St. Clair Co. Rep. Treas., Jan. 10, 1921, to Jan. 4, 1923. b. East St. Louis, July 22, 1880. Businessman. U.S.H.R., 1923–25. d. East St. Louis, Aug. 1, 1940.

Oscar E. Nelson, res. Kane Co. Rep. Treas., Jan.⁑4, 1923, to Jan. 12, 1925. b. Sweden, April 22, 1874. Emigrated to Geneva, 1880. Banker. Aud. Ill. 1925–33. City clerk Geneva five terms; mayor two terms. d. Geneva, April 2, 1951.

Superintendent of Public Instruction Francis G. Blair[23].

Attorney General Edward J. Brundage [26].

United States Senators Lawrence Y. Sherman[23] (to March 3, 1921); Medill McCormick[26]; William B. McKinley[23].

United States Congressmen George E. Foss[20] (to March 3, 1919); James McAndrews[22] (to March 3, 1921); William B. McKinley[23] (to March 3, 1921, elected to U.S. Sen.); Thomas Gallagher[24] (to March 3, 1921); Edwin B. Brooks[26] (to March 3, 1923); Niels Juul[26] (to March 3, 1921); Frank L. Smith[26] (to March 3, 1921); Henry T. Rainey[22] (to March 3, 1921, and from 1923); William E.

Mason[18] (d. June 16, 1921); James R.
Mann[21] (d. Nov. 30, 1922); Joseph G.
Cannon[15] (to March 3, 1923); William
A. Rodenberg[21] (to March 3, 1923); Ira
C. Copley[24] (to March 3, 1923); Loren E.
Wheeler[25] (to March 3, 1923); Edwin B.
Brooks[26] (to March 3, 1923); Clifford C.
Ireland[26] (to March 3, 1923); John W.
Rainey[26] (d. May 4, 1923); Charles E.
Fuller[22]; Richard Yates[22]; Martin B.
Madden[23]; Adolph J. Sabath[23]; John
C. McKenzie[24]; Frederick A. Britten[25];
Edward E. Denison[25]; Edward J. King[25];
Thomas S. Williams[25]; Carl Chindblom
[26]; William J. Graham[26] (resigned June
7, 1924); Edward E. Miller (see Treas.
above).

Frank Hamilton Funk, res. McLean Co.
Rep. and Prog. Rep. U.S.H.R., 1921–27.
b. Bloomington, April 5, 1869. Ph.B.Yale,
1891. Farmer and stockman. Prog. cand.
gov. Ill., 1912. Prog. cand. U.S. Sen., 1914.
d. Bloomington, Nov. 24, 1940.

John Jerome Gorman, res. Cook Co.
Rep. U.S.H.R., 1921–23, 1925–27. b. Minneapolis, Minn., June 2, 1883. Moved with
parents to Chicago as infant. Business
college education. Letter carrier, clerk
Chicago post office. LL.B. Loyola of
Chicago; admitted Ill. bar, 1914. Two terms
U.S.H.R. only pub. office. d. Chicago, Feb.
24, 1949.

Winifred Mason Huck, res. Cook Co.
Rep. U.S.H.R., Nov. 7, 1922, to March
3, 1923. b. Chicago, Sept. 14, 1882. Completed father's (William E. Mason) term in
U.S.H.R. (only pub. office). Journalist,
lecturer. d. Chicago, Aug. 24, 1936.

Stanley Henry Kunz, res. Cook Co. Dem.
U.S.H.R., 1921–31, April 5, 1932, to March
3, 1933. b. Nanticoke, Pa., Sept. 26, 1864.
Attended St. Ignatius, Chicago. Ill. H.R.,
1889–90. Ill. Sen., 1903–6. Ald. Chicago,
1891–1921. Breeder thoroughbreds and
racing stock Palatine, 1910–33. Contested
election Peter C. Granata, 1930, seated
April 5, 1932. d. Chicago, April 23,
1946.

Magne Alfred Michaelson, res. Cook Co.
Rep. U.S.H.R., 1921–31. b. Kristiansund,
Norway, Sept. 7, 1878. Emigrated to
Chicago with parents, 1885. Grad. Chicago
Normal, 1898. Taught Chicago schools.
Mem. common council Chicago, 1915–
18. Retired 1931. d. Chicago, Oct. 26,
1949.

Allen Francis Moore, res. Piatt Co. Rep.
U.S.H.R., 1921–25. b. St. Charles, Sept.
30, 1869. Moved with parents to Monticello,
1870. Grad. Lombard, Galesburg, 1889.

Mfr. proprietary medicines. Banker. Moved
to San Antonio, Tex. to develop oil, 1939.
d. San Antonio, Tex., Aug. 18, 1945.

Guy Loren Shaw, res. Cass Co. Rep.
U.S.H.R., 1921–23. b. Pike Co., May 16,
1881. Attended Illinois. Farmer and de-
veloper of overflow lands along Ill. River.
Real estate broker Beardstown, Urbana,
and Normal. d. Normal, May 19, 1950.

Elliott Wilford Sproul, res. Cook Co.
Rep. U.S.H.R., 1921–31. b. Apohaqui,
New Brunswick, Dec. 28, 1856. Moved to
Boston, 1879, to Chicago, 1880. Ald., 1896–
99. Building contractor. Retired, 1931. d.
Chicago, June 22, 1935.

William Wright Arnold, res. Crawford
Co. Dem. U.S.H.R., 1923 to Sept. 16, 1935
(resigned). b. Oblong, Oct. 14, 1877.
Attended Austin; LL.B. Illinois, admitted
Ill. bar, 1901; pract. Robinson. U.S. Board
of Tax Appeals (now Tax Court of the U.S.),
July 29, 1935, to June 30, 1950. Banker,
farmer. d. Robinson, Nov. 23, 1957.

James Richard Buckley, res. Cook Co.
Dem. U.S.H.R., 1923–25. b. Chicago, Nov.
18, 1870. Minor city offices, 1893–1923. Ald.
Chicago, 1910–12. d. Chicago, June 22,
1945.

Thomas Aloysius Doyle, res. Cook Co.
Dem. U.S.H.R., Nov. 6, 1923, vice John
Rainey, to 1931. b. Chicago, Jan. 9, 1886.
Real estate broker, insurance agent, 1903–
26. Ald., 1914–18. Ill. H.R., 1919–23
(resigned). d. Chicago, Jan. 29, 1935.

William Perry Holaday, res. Vermilion
Co. Rep. U.S.H.R., 1923–33. b. Vermilion
Co., Dec. 14, 1882. LL.B. Illinois, admitted
Ill. bar, 1905; pract. Danville. Ill. H.R.,
1909–22. d. Georgetown, Jan. 29, 1946.

Morton Dennison Hull, res. Cook Co.
Rep. U.S.H.R., April 3, 1923, vice Mann,
to 1933. b. Chicago, Jan. 13, 1867. A.B.
Harvard, 1889; LL.B. Harvard, admitted
Ill. bar, 1892; pract. Chicago. Ill. H.R.,
1907–14. Ill. Sen., 1915–20. d. at summer
home n. Bennington, Vt., Aug. 20, 1937.

William Edgar Hull, res. Peoria Co. Rep.
U.S.H.R., 1923–33. b. Lewiston, Jan. 13,
1866. Attended Illinois College, Jackson-
ville. Pres. Manito Chemical Company.
P.M. Peoria, 1898–1906. After five terms
U.S.H.R. resumed business pursuits. d.
Toronto, Ontario, while on visit, May 30,
1942.

James E. Major, res. Montgomery Co.
Dem. U.S.H.R., 1923–25, 1927–29, 1931 to
Oct. 6, 1933 (resigned). b. Donnellson, Jan.

5, 1887. LL.B. Illinois College of Law, Chicago, 1909. Admitted Ill. bar, 1910; pract. Hillsboro. Pros. att. Montgomery Co., 1912–20. Judge U.S. Dist. Court, 1933–37. Judge U.S. Court of Appeals, 1931–56 (resigned); chief judge, 1948–54.

Henry Riggs Rathbone, res. Cook Co. Rep. U.S.H.R., 1923 to July 15, 1928 (d). b. Washington, D.C., Feb. 12, 1870. A.B. Yale, 1892; LL.B. Wisconsin, 1894. Admitted Ill. bar, 1895; pract. Chicago. d. Chicago.

Frank R. Reid, res. Kane Co. Rep. U.S.H.R., 1923–35. b. Aurora, April 18, 1879. Attended Chicago and Chicago-Kent College of Law. Admitted Ill. bar, 1901; pract. Aurora. Pros. att. Kane Co. and state's att., 1904–8. Ill. H.R., 1911–12. Pract. Aurora and Chicago. d. Aurora, Jan. 25, 1945.

Justices Illinois Supreme Court James H. Cartwright[20] (d. May 18, 1924); Orrin N. Carter[23] (to June 2, 1924); Frank Dunn[23]; William M. Farmer[23]; Warren W. Duncan[25]; Floyd E. Thompson[26]; Clyde E. Stone[26].

Oscar E. Heard, res. Stephenson Co. Just. Ill. Supreme Court, June 11, 1924, to 1933. C.J., 1927, 1932. b. Freeport, June 26, 1856. LL.B. Union College of Law (now Northwestern), admitted Ill. bar, 1879. State's att. Stephenson Co., 1884–90. Judge circuit court, 15th Circuit, 1909–24. Pract. with son Freeport, 1933–40. Honored by bar association for fifty years service Ill. bar. d. Freeport, July 15, 1940.

Frederic R. DeYoung, res. Cook Co. Rep. Just. Ill. Supreme Court, June 16, 1924, to Nov. 16, 1934 (d.). C.J., 1928. b. Chicago, Sept. 12, 1875. LL.B. Northwestern, admitted Ill. bar, 1897. Ill. H.R., 1915–18. Judge circuit court Cook Co., 1921–23. Judge superior court Cook Co., 1923–24.

28. Second administration of Len Small, Jan. 12, 1925, to Jan. 14, 1929. Voting for governor: Small, 1,366,436. Norman L. Jones, 1,021,408. Andrew Lafin, 15,191.

Governor Len Small[23].
Lieutenant Governor Fred E. Sterling [26].
Secretary of State Louis F. Emmerson [26].
Auditor Oscar E. Nelson[27].
Treasurers Omer N. Custer, res. Knox Co. Rep. Treas., Jan. 12, 1925, to Jan. 5,

1927; Jan. 14, 1929, to Jan. 12, 1931. b. Lafayette Co., Pa., Dec. 25, 1873. Moved with parents to Galesburg. With *Republican-Register* from boyhood. Treas. Knox Co., 1906. Chm. Ill. State Tax Commission, 1930–31. d. Galesburg, Oct. 17, 1942.

Garrett De F. Kinney, res. Peoria Co. Rep. Treas., Jan. 5, 1927, to Jan. 14, 1929. b. Rensselaer Co., N.Y., 1869. Moved to Peoria with parents, 1874. A.B. Cornell, 1891. Manufacturer, banker. Rep. Central Committee, Rep. State Committee. d. June 23, 1933 (suicide).

Superintendent of Public Instruction Francis G. Blair[23].

Attorney General Oscar E. Carlstrom, res. Mercer Co. Rep. Att. gen., Jan. 12, 1925, to Jan. 9, 1933. b. Aledo, July 16, 1878. 39th U.S. Vol. Inf. in Philippines, 1899–1901. Admitted Ill. bar, 1903. Capt. inf. Dec. 12, 1916, transferred to art., served in France, 1918–19. Organizing mem. American Legion. Retired to private practice Aledo. d. Aledo, March 5, 1948.

United States Senators William B. McKinley[23] (d. Dec. 7, 1926); Charles S. Deneen[23]; Frank L. Smith[26] (vice McKinley, resigned Feb. 9, 1928).

Otis F. Glenn, res. Jackson Co. Rep. U.S. Sen., Dec. 3, 1928, vice Smith, to 1933. b. Mattoon, Aug. 27, 1879. LL.B. Illinois, admitted Ill. bar, 1900. State's att. Jackson Co., 1906–8, 1916–20. Ill. Sen., 1921–24. Moved to Chicago to pract. d. Portage Point, Mich., March 11, 1959.

United States Congressmen John C. McKenzie[24] (to March 3, 1925); Allen F. Moore[27] (to March 3, 1925); Charles E. Fuller[22] (d. June 29, 1926); Loren E. Wheeler[25] (to March 3, 1927); Frank H. Funk[27] (to March 3, 1927); John J. Gorman[27] (to March 3, 1927); Martin B. Madden[23] (d. April 27, 1928); Edward J. King[25] (d. Feb. 17, 1929); Henry T. Rainey[22]; Richard Yates[22]; Adolph J. Sabath[23]; Frederick A. Britten[25]; Edward E. Denison[25]; Thomas S. Williams[25]; Carl R. Chindblom[26]; William W. Arnold[27]; Thomas A. Doyle[27]; William P. Holaday[27]; Morton D. Hull [27]; William E. Hull[27]; Stanley H. Kunz [27]; James E. Major[27] (to March 3, 1925, and 1927–29); Magne A. Michaelson[27]; Henry R. Rathbone[27]; Elliott W. Sproul [27]; Frank R. Reid[27].

Charles Adkins, res. Piatt Co. Rep. U.S.H.R., 1925–33. b. Pickaway Co., Ohio, Feb. 7, 1863. Moved to farm in Piatt Co., 1885. Pres. Piatt Co. Farmers' Inst. Mem. Piatt Co. Board of Supervisors,

1902–6. Ill. H.R., 1907–12 (spkr., 1912). Pres. Ill. Livestock Breeders Association, 1914 and 1915. Dir. of agr. Ill., 1916–20. Moved to Decatur. d. Decatur, March 31, 1941.

John Clayton Allen, res. Warren Co. Rep. U.S.H.R., 1925–33. b. Hinesburg, Vt., Feb. 4, 1860. Moved to Lincoln, Nebr., 1881, McCook, Nebr., 1886. Merchant. Sec. state Neb., 1891–95. Moved to Monmouth, 1896. Pres. John C. Allen & Company dept. store and Peoples Nat. Bank. d. Monmouth, Jan. 12, 1939.

Edward Michael Irwin, res. St. Clair Co. Rep. U.S.H.R., 1925–31. b. Crawford Co., Mo., April 14, 1869. Taught school. Attended Missouri; M.D. Missouri Med. College, St. Louis, 1892. Pract. New Athens, 1892–1903. Coroner St. Clair Co., 1904–8. Active Rep. politics. Resumed med. practice, 1931. d. Belleville, Jan. 30, 1933.

John Theodore Buckbee, res. Winnebago Co. Rep. U.S.H.R., 1927 to April 23, 1936 (d.). b. Rockford, Aug. 1, 1871. European-trained horticulturist. Died during fifth term U.S.H.R.

Homer William Hall, res. McLean Co. Rep. U.S.H.R., 1927–33. b. Shelbyville, July 22, 1870. Moved with parents to Bloomington, 1876. Attended Illinois Wesleyan. Admitted Ill. bar, 1892; pract. Bloomington. Banker, farmer. Co. judge McLean Co., 1909–14, 1934–42. Probate judge, 1909–14. Master in chancery, 1916–18. d. Bloomington, Sept. 22, 1954.

James Thomas Igoe, res. Cook Co. Dem. U.S.H.R., 1927–33. b. Chicago, Oct. 23, 1883. Attended St. Ignatius, Chicago. Printer, publisher, real estate broker.

William Richard Johnson, res. Stephenson Co. Rep. U.S.H.R., 1925–33. b. Rock Island, May 15, 1875. Moved with parents to Freeport, 1879. Attended College of Commerce, Freeport. Locomotive blacksmith Ill. Central R.R. Freeport, 1894–99. Mem. U.S. Capitol Police, served as pvt., sgt., lt., and capt., 1901–19. Clerical staff U.S.H.R., 1919–25. d. Freeport, Jan. 2, 1938.

Justices Illinois Supreme Court Frank Dunn[23]; William M. Farmer[23]; Warren W. Duncan[25]; Clyde E. Stone[26]; Floyd E. Thompson[26] (resigned July 25, 1928); Oscar E. Heard[27]; Frederic R. DeYoung [27].

Cyrus Dietz, res. Rock Island Co. Just. Ill. Supreme Court, Nov. 27, 1928, vice Thompson, to Sept. 13, 1929 (d.). b. Iroquois Co., March 17, 1876. LL.B. Northwestern, admitted Ill. bar, 1902.

Moved to Moline, 1904. Spec. asst. att. gen. Ill. in lake levels litigation.

29. Administration of Louis F. Emmerson, Jan. 14, 1929, to Jan. 9, 1933. Voting for governor: Emmerson, 1,709,818. Floyd E. Thompson, 1,284,897. George Koop, 12,974.

Governor Louis F. Emmerson[26].
Lieutenant Governor Fred E. Sterling [26].
Secretary of State William J. Stratton, res. Lake Co. Rep. b. Ingleside, Jan. 28, 1886. Farmer. Active in Rep. politics. Deputy game warden, 1916; chief game warden, 1921. First dir. Ill. Dept. of Conservation. d. Ingleside, May 28, 1938.
Auditor Oscar E. Nelson[27].
Treasurers Omer N. Custer[28] (to Jan. 12. 1931).
Edward J. Barrett, res. Cook Co. Dem. Treas., Jan. 12, 1931, to Jan. 9, 1933. b. Chicago, March 10, 1900. 131st Inf. World War I (wounded). B.S. Mayo College, Chicago. Active in American Legion; mem. Disabled American Veterans. Aud., 1933–41. Sec. state Ill., 1945–53. App. clerk Cook Co., vice Dalcy, 1955; elected 1956, 1958, 1962, 1966.
Superintendent of Public Instruction Francis G. Blair[23].
Attorney General Oscar E. Carlstrom [28].
United States Senators Otis F. Glenn [28]; Charles S. Deneen[23] (to 1931); J. Hamilton Lewis[25] (from 1931).
United States Congressmen Thomas S. Williams[25] (resigned Nov. 11, 1929); James E. Major[27] (to March 3, 1929, and from 1931); Edward J. Denison[25] (to March 3, 1931); Thomas A. Doyle[27] (to March 3, 1931); Magne A. Michaelson[27] (to March 3, 1931); Elliott W. Sproul[27] (to March 3, 1931); Edward M. Irwin[28] (to March 3, 1931); Henry T. Rainey[22]; Richard Yates[22]; Adolph J. Sabath[23]; Frederick A. Britten[25]; Carl R. Chindblom[26]; Stanley H. Kunz[27]; William P. Holaday[27]; Morton D. Hull[27]; William E. Hull[27]; Frank R. Reid[27]; John C. Allen[28]; Charles Adkins[28]; William W. Arnold[27]; William R. Johnson[28]; John T. Buckbee[28]; Homer W. Hall[28]; James T. Igoe[28]; Burnett M. Chiperfield[25] (vice King, took seat Dec. 1, 1930).

Oscar De Priest, res. Cook Co. Rep. U.S.H.R., 1929–35. b. Florence, Ala.,

March 9, 1871. Moved to Kans. with parents, 1878. Attended Kansas Normal, Salina. Moved to Chicago, 1889. Real estate broker. Mem. Cook Co. Board of Comms., 1904–8. Ald., 1915–17, 1943–47. d. Chicago, May 12, 1951.

Ruth Hanna McCormick, res. Winnebago Co. Rep. U.S.H.R., 1929–31. b. Cleveland, Ohio, March 27, 1880 (daughter of Mark Hanna, wife of Medill McCormick). Owner and operator dairy and stock farm. Pres. and publisher Rockford Consolidated Newspapers, Inc. Active women's suffrage movement. Widowed Feb. 25, 1925. Remarried Albert Gallatin Simms, U.S.H.R. from N. Mex. d. Chicago, Dec. 31, 1944.

Claude Van Cleve Parsons, res. Pope Co. Dem. U.S.H.R., Dec. 1, 1930, vice Williams, to Jan. 3, 1941. b. Pope Co., Oct. 7, 1895. Grad. Southern Illinois Normal, 1923. Supt. schools Pope Co., 1922–30. First asst. administrator U.S. Housing Authority, Feb. 14, 1941, until death, Washington, D.C., May 23, 1941.

Frank Marion Ramey, res. Montgomery Co. Rep. U.S.H.R., 1929–31. b. Hillsboro, Sept. 23, 1881. Attended Eastern Illinois Normal. Taught school Hillsboro, 1902–5. Admitted Ill. bar, 1907; pract. Hillsboro. City att., 1907–11. State's att. Montgomery Co., 1920–28. Asst. dist. att., 1931–34. Examiner Ill. Commerce Commission, 1942. d. Hillsboro, March 27, 1942.

Harry Peter Beam, res. Cook Co. Dem. U.S.H.R., 1931 to Dec. 6, 1942 (resigned). b. Peoria, Nov. 23, 1892. Moved with parents to Chicago, 1899. Grad. St. Ignatius, Chicago, 1912; LL.B. Loyola of Chicago, admitted Ill. bar, 1916; pract. Chicago. Seaman World War I. Asst. corp. counsel Chicago, 1923–27. Judge mun. court Chicago, 1942–60.

William Henry Dieterich, res. Cass Co. Dem. U.S.H.R., 1931–33 (elected U.S. Sen.). b. Brown Co., March 31, 1876. Grad. Kennedy Normal, Rushville; LL.B. Valparaiso, admitted Ill. bar, 1901; pract. Rushville. City att., 1903–7. Judge Schuyler Co. Court, 1906–10. Moved to Chicago, 1911, to Beardstown, 1912. Spec. inheritance tax att. for Ill., 1913–17. Ill. H.R., 1917–20. U.S. Sen., 1933–39. d. Springfield (on visit), Oct. 12, 1940.

Peter C. Granata, res. Cook Co. Rep. U.S.H.R., March 3, 1931, to April 5, 1932 (seat successfully contested by Stanley H. Kunz). b. Chicago, Oct. 28, 1898. Grad.

Bryant & Stratton, 1912. Coal and oil dealer. Ill. H.R., 1935–42, 1945–64, from 1967. Asst. dir. finance Ill., 1941–43.

Charles Adam Karch, res. St. Clair Co. Dem. U.S.H.R., 1931 to Nov. 6, 1932 (d.). b. St. Clair Co., March 17, 1875. Grad. Northern Illinois Normal, 1894. Taught school, 1895–1900. LL.B. Illinois Wesleyan, admitted Ill bar, 1898; pract. Belleville. Ill. H.R., 1905–6, 1911–14. U.S. att. Eastern Jud. Dist. Ill., 1914–18. d. St. Louis, Mo., Nov. 6, 1932.

Kent Ellsworth Keller, res. Jackson Co. Dem. U.S.H.R., 1931–41. b. Jackson Co., June 4, 1867. Grad. Southern Illinois Normal, 1890. Journalist, schoolteacher. Studied Heidelberg, Germany, 1891 and 1892. LL.B. St. Louis, 1896. Pract. Ava. Moved to Mexico for health, 1899; returned to Ava, 1912. Ill. Sen., 1913–16. Spec. advisor to U.S. amb. Mexico, 1945 and 1946. d. Ava, Sept. 3, 1954.

Edward Austin Kelly, res. Cook Co. Dem. U.S.H.R., 1931–43, 1945–47. b. Chicago, April 3, 1892. Grad. Orris Business College, 1911. Played professional baseball, 1912–16. Sgt. 332nd F.A. World War I, 1917–19. Real estate broker. Asst. to C.J. municipal court Chicago, 1943–45. Mem. Chicago Planning Commission, 1944–46.

Leonard William Schuetz, res. Cook Co. Dem. U.S.H.R., 1931 to Feb. 13, 1944 (d.). b. Posen, Germany (later Poland), Nov. 16, 1887. Emigrated to Chicago with father, 1888. Worked from age ten. Grad. Bryant & Stratton Business College. Exec. Swift & Company, 1906–23. Pres. Schuetz Construction Company, 1923. d. Chicago during seventh term U.S.H.R.

Justices Illinois Supreme Court Frank Dunn[23]; William M. Farmer[23] (resigned July 1, 1931); Warren W. Duncan[25]; Clyde E. Stone[26]; Oscar E. Heard[27]; Frederic R. DeYoung[27]; Cyrus Dietz[28] (d. Sept. 13, 1929).

Paul Samuell, res. Morgan Co. Just. Ill. Supreme Court, Oct. 18, 1929, vice Dietz, to June 2, 1930. b. Mason Co., Oct. 2, 1886. LL.B. Illinois Wesleyan, 1910. Admitted Mont. and Ill. bars. Pract. Mont., 1910–13. Moved to Jacksonville. Co. judge Morgan Co., 1916–24. Private pract. Jacksonville, 1930–38. Mem. Ill. Commerce Commission, 1932–33. d. Jacksonville, March 22, 1938.

Warren H. Orr, res. Hancock Co. Just Ill. Supreme Court, 1930–39. C.J., 1933. b. Hannibal, Mo., Nov. 5, 1886. A.B. Missouri, 1909, LL.B., 1911. Admitted Ill. and Mo. bars. Moved to Hamilton. City att., 1913–18. Co. judge Hancock Co., 1918–30. Moved to Chicago, 1939. Pract. until retirement, 1958. d. Evanston, Jan. 12, 1962.

Norman L. Jones, res. Greene Co. Just. Ill. Supreme Court, Aug. 31, 1931 vice Farmer, to Nov. 15, 1940 (d.). C.J., 1934, 1940. b. Patterson, Sept. 19, 1870. Ill. H.R., 1893–96. Admitted Ill. bar, 1896. Partner Congressman Henry T. Rainey, 1896–1914. Judge circuit court, 7th Circuit, 1914–21; appellate court, 1921–31.

30. First administration of Henry Horner, Jan. 9, 1933, to Jan. 4, 1937. Voting for governor: Horner, 1,930,330. Len Small, 1,364,043. Roy E. Burt, 39,389. Leon Dies McDonald, 12,466.

Governor Henry Horner, res. Cook Co. Dem. b. Chicago, Nov. 30, 1879. LL.B. Kent, 1899; admitted Ill. bar, LL.D. Knox; honorary LL.D. Lincoln Memorial. Collector Lincolniana. Mem. Chicago charter conv. Probate judge Cook Co., 1914–32. Introduced Horner Plan for handling veterans' estates without legal costs, expenses, or att. fees. Died in office during second term gov., Oct. 6, 1940.

Lieutenant Governor Thomas Fanning Donovan, res. Will Co. Dem. b. Livingston Co., Dec. 17, 1871. B.S. Valparaiso, 1893, LL.B., 1894. Admitted Ill. bar; pract. Kankakee, 1894. City att. Kankakee, 1897–1901. Pract. Joliet and Chicago, 1905. After term as lt. gov. returned to pract. Joliet and Chicago. d. Chicago, Nov. 17, 1946.

Secretary of State Edward J. Hughes, res. Cook Co. Dem. Sec. state, Jan. 9, 1933, to June 28, 1944 (d.). b. Chicago, July 26, 1888. Bridge builder. Ill. Sen., 1915–30. Cook Co. Board of Review, 1930.

Auditor Edward J. Barrett[29].

Treasurers John C. Martin, res. Marion Co. Dem. Treas., Jan. 9, 1933, to Jan. 14, 1935. b. Salem, April 29, 1880. Grad. Illinois College, Jacksonville. Chm. Ill. Tax Commission, 1935–36. Chm. Ill. Emergency Relief Commission, 1935–38. U.S.H.R., 1939–41. Banker, dir. Fed. Reserve Bank St. Louis, 1922–33. d. Long Beach, Calif., Jan. 27, 1952.

John Stelle, res. Hamilton Co. Dem. Treas., Jan. 14, 1935, to Jan. 4, 1937. b. McLeansboro, Aug. 10, 1891. Grad. Washington, St. Louis. Pvt., lt., capt. 30th Div. World War I (wounded and gassed). Asst. treas., 1931. Asst. aud., 1933. Lt. gov., Jan. 4, 1937, to Oct. 6, 1940. Became gov. on death Henry Horner. Pres. Askatex

Ceramic Corp., 1937–62. d. Brazil, Ind., July 5, 1962.

Superintendents of Public Instruction Francis G. Blair[23] (to Jan. 14, 1935).

John Adam Wieland, res. Cook Co. Dem. Supt. pub. instr., Jan. 14, 1935, to Jan. 11, 1943. b. Clark Co., March 19, 1892. Grad. Eastern Illinois, 1912. Served in World War I. Taught rural schools seven years, h.s. three years. Supt. schools Bradley, 1925–28. Calumet City, 1928–35.

Attorney General Otto Kerner, res. Cook Co. Dem. Att. gen., Jan. 9, 1933, to Nov. 23, 1938 (resigned to become just. U.S. Court of Appeals, 17th Dist., Chicago). b. Chicago, Feb. 22, 1884. LL.B. Chicago-Kent College of Law, admitted Ill. bar, 1905. City prosecutor, 1911; ald., 1913–19. Master in chancery Circuit Court of Cook Co., 1915–27. Judge Circuit Court of Cook Co., 1927–31, appellate court, 1931–32 (resigned, cand. att. gen.). Served as just. 17th Dist., 1938 until his death in Chicago, Dec. 13, 1952.

United States Senators J. Hamilton Lewis[25]; William H. Dieterich[29].

United States Congressmen Richard Yates[22] (to March 3, 1933); Carl R. Chindblom[26] (to March 3, 1933); Stanley H. Kunz[27] (to March 3, 1933); William P. Holaday[27] (to March 3, 1933); William E. Hull[27] (to March 3, 1933); Morton D. Hull[27] (to March 3, 1933); John C. Allen[28] (to March 3, 1933); Charles Adkins[28] (to March 3, 1933); Homer W. Hall[28] (to March 3, 1933); James T. Igoe[28] (to March 3, 1933); William R. Johnson[28] (to March 3, 1933); William H. Dieterich[29] (to 1933, elected to U.S. Sen.); James E. Major[27] (resigned Oct. 6, 1933); Henry T. Rainey[22] (d. Aug. 19, 1934); Frederick A. Britten[25] (to Jan. 3, 1935); Frank R. Reid[27] (to Jan. 3, 1935); Oscar De Priest[29] (to Jan. 3, 1935); Wiliam W. Arnold[27] (resigned Sept. 16, 1935); John T. Buckbee[28] (d. April 23, 1936); Adolph J. Sabath[23]; Harry P. Beam[29]; Kent E. Keller[29]; Edward A. Kelly[29]; Claude V. Parsons[29]; Leonard W. Schuetz[29]; James McAndrews[22] (from Jan. 3, 1935).

Jackson LeRoy Adair, res. Adams Co. Dem. U.S.H.R., 1933–37. b. Clayton, Feb. 23, 1887. Attended Illinois College, Jacksonville; LL.B. Michigan, admitted Okla. bar, 1911; pract. Muskogee, Okla. Moved to Quincy, 1913. City att., 1914–16. Pros. att. Adams Co., 1916–20, 1924–28. Ill. Sen.,

1929–32. U.S. Dist. judge Southern Dist. Ill., 1937 until his death, Quincy, Jan. 19, 1956.

Leo Ellwood Allen, res. JoDaviess Co. Rep. U.S.H.R., 1933–61. b. Elizabeth, Oct. 5, 1898. Sgt. 123rd F.A. World War I, 1917–19. Grad. Michigan, 1923. Taught school Galena, 1922–23. Clerk circuit court JoDaviess Co., 1924–32. Admitted Ill. bar, 1930; pract. and resides in Galena.

Martin Adlai Brennan, res. McLean Co. Dem. U.S.H.R., 1933–37. b. Bloomington, Sept. 21, 1879. LL.B. Illinois Wesleyan, admitted Ill. bar, 1902; pract. Bloomington. Presiding judge Ill. Court of Claims, 1913–17. Census supervisor McLean Co., 1920. Ill. H.R., 1921–24. d. Bloomington, July 4, 1941.

Everett McKinley Dirksen, res. Tazewell Co. Rep. U.S.H.R., 1933–49. b. Pekin, Jan. 4, 1896. Attended Minnesota. Pvt. and 1st lt. f.a. World War I. Comm. finance Tazewell Co., 1927–31. Studied law, admitted Ill. bar, 1936. Elected to U.S. Sen., 1950; reelected, 1956, 1962, 1968. Minority leader from 1961.

Donald Claude Dobbins, res. Champaign Co. Dem. U.S.H.R., 1933–37. b. Champaign Co., March 20, 1878. Attended Illinois and George Washington. Teacher, 1896–99. Stenographer and correspondent, 1900–1906. U.S. post office inspector, 1906–9. Admitted Ill. bar, 1909; pract. Champaign. d. Champaign, Feb. 14, 1943.

Frank Gillespie, res. McLean Co. Dem. U.S.H.R., 1933–35. b. White Sulphur Springs, W. Va., April 18, 1869. Attended Concord Normal and Central College, Danville, Ind. Admitted W. Va. bar, 1892; pract. Charleston, W. Va. Moved to Bloomington, 1894. Ill. H.R., 1913–14. Pract. until his death, Bloomington, Nov. 26, 1954.

Leo Paul Kocialkowski, res. Cook Co. Dem. U.S.H.R., 1933–43. b. Chicago, Aug. 16, 1882. Orphaned, worked from boyhood. Tax appraisal and supervision delinquent taxes Cook Co., 1916–32. Member Civil Service Commission of Cook Co., 1945–49. d. Chicago, Sept. 27, 1958.

James Andrew Meeks, res. Vermilion Co. Dem. U.S.H.R., 1933–39. b. New Matamoras, Ohio, March 7, 1864. Moved with parents to farm Vermilion Co., 1865. Attended Illinois College, Jacksonville. Admitted Ill. bar, 1890; pract. Danville. Master in chancery circuit court, 1903–15.

Corp. counsel Danville, 1925–31. d. Danville, Nov. 10, 1946.

Patrick Henry Moynihan, res. Cook Co. Rep. U.S.H.R., 1933–35. b. Chicago, Sept. 25, 1869. Printer, publisher, coal merchant. Ald., 1921–29 (chm. 1928 and 1929). d. Chicago, May 20, 1946.

Walter Nesbit, res. St. Clair Co. Dem. U.S.H.R., 1933–35. b. Belleville, May 1, 1878. Coal miner, 1892–1912. Officer United Mine Workers until 1933. Night club operator Belleville, 1935–38. d. Belleville, Dec. 6, 1938.

Thomas Joseph O'Brien, res. Cook Co. Dem. U.S.H.R., 1933–39, 1943 to April 14, 1964 (d.). b. Chicago, Apr. 30. 1878. Took courses in business law and accounting. Ill. H.R., 1909–10, 1929–32. State bank examiner, 1913–24. Pub. accountant, 1918. Sheriff Cook Co., 1939–42. d. Bethesda Naval Hospital, Md., during fourteenth term U.S.H.R.

Edward Martin Schaefer, res. St. Clair Co. Dem. U.S.H.R., 1933–43. b. Belleville, May 14, 1887. B.E. Washington, St. Louis, 1910. Chemical engineer, gen. supervisor, gen. supt. Morris & Company (packers), 1913–28. Treas. St. Clair Co., 1930–32. Mem. board Griesedieck-Western Brewing Company, 1943 to his death, St. Louis, Mo., Nov. 8, 1950.

James Simpson, Jr., res. Cook Co. Rep. U.S.H.R., 1933–35. b. Chicago, Jan. 7, 1905. Attended Harvard. Admitted Ill. bar, 1939. Owner, operator farms in Lake Co. and in Culpeper, Va. U.S.M.C., 1943–46, two years PTO, discharged capt. Civilian aide to Sec. of the Army Stevens, 1953–54. Dir. Marshall Field & Company, 1931–60. d. Wadsworth, Feb. 29, 1960.

Chester Charles Thompson, res. Rock Island Co. Dem. U.S.H.R., 1933–39. b. Rock Island, Sept. 19, 1893. Plastering contractor, 1910–32. World War I coast art. Treas. Rock Island Co., 1922–26. Mayor Rock Island, 1927–33. Pres. and chm. board government-owned Inland Waterways Corp. under direction of sec. of commerce, 1939–44. Retired 1957.

Leslie Cornelius Arends, res. Ford Co., Rep. U.S.H.R. from 1935. b. Melvin, Sept. 27, 1895. U.S.N. World War I, 1918–19. Attended Oberlin. Farmer, banker, mem. Ford Co. Farm Bureau. Rep. whip since 1943.

Ralph E. Church, res. Cook Co., Rep. U.S.H.R., 1935–41, 1943 to March 21, 1950 (d.). b. Vermilion Co., May 5, 1883. A.B. Michigan, 1907; A.M. and LL.B. Northwestern, 1909. Admitted Ill. bar;

pract. Chicago. Ill. H.R., 1917–32. Lt. com. U.S.N.R., 1938–41. Del. interparliamentary conf. Oslo, Norway, 1939. d. while appearing before committee on expenditures of exec. dept.

Michael Lambert Igoe, res. Cook Co. Dem. U.S.H.R., Jan. 3, 1935, to June 2, 1935 (resigned to become U.S. att. Northern Dist. Ill., 1935–38). b. St. Paul, Minn., April 16, 1885. Removed to Chicago with parents as child. Attended De La Salle Inst., Chicago; LL.B. Georgetown, admitted Ill. bar, 1908; pract. Chicago. Ill. H.R., 1913–20, 1923–24, 1927–32. Chief asst. U.S. att. Northern Dist. Ill., 1915–17. Comm. South Park Board, 1924–34. Dem. nat. committeeman, 1932–34. Cand. for U.S. Sen., 1938. Judge U.S. Dist. Court, Northern Dist. Ill., March 4. 1939, to 1965 (resigned). d. Chicago, Aug. 21, 1967.

Scott Wike Lucas, res. Mason Co. Dem. U.S.H.R., 1935–39. b. n. Chandlerville, Feb. 19, 1892. LL.B. Illinois Wesleyan, 1914. Admitted Ill. bar, 1915; pract. Havana. World War I pvt., 1917, promoted lt., 1918. State's att. Mason Co., 1920–25. U.S. Sen., 1939–51. Pract. law Springfield and Washington, D.C. d. Rocky Mount, N.C., en route to Fla., Feb. 22, 1968.

Harry Howland Mason, res. Sangamon Co. Dem. U.S.H.R., 1935–37. b. De Witt Co., Dec. 16, 1873. Moved with parents to Tazewell Co. Newspaper publisher Pawnee. Sec. to Congressman James Earl Major, 1930–33. Treas. Sangamon Co., 1933–34. d. Springfield, March 10, 1946.

Raymond Stephen McKeough, res. Cook Co. Dem. U.S.H.R., 1935–43. b. Chicago, April 29, 1888. Grad. De La Salle Inst., Chicago, 1905. Commission business, 1905–9. Railroad clerk, 1909–25. Investment securities broker, 1925–35. Regional administrator Office of Price Administration, 1943 and 1944; Maritime Commission, 1945–50; International Claims Commission, 1951–53. Administrative asst. to state's att. (criminal div.) Chicago, 1956–60. General insurance from 1960.

Arthur Wergs Mitchell, res. Cook Co. Dem. U.S.H.R., 1935–43. b. Chambers Co., Ala., Dec. 22, 1883. Attended Tuskegee, Columbia, and Harvard. Teacher. Founder Armstrong Agricultural School, West Butler, Ala. LL.B. Wilberforce, admitted D.C. bar, 1927; pract. Washington, D.C. Moved to Chicago, 1929. Was first Negro to address a nat. conv. From 1943, lawyer, farmer, active interracial affairs Petersburg, Va.

Chauncey William Reed, res. Du Page Co. Rep. U.S.H.R., 1935 to Feb. 9, 1956 (d.). b. West Chicago, June 2, 1890. Attended Northwestern; LL.B. Webster College of Law, Chicago, admitted Ill. bar, 1915; pract. Naperville. Sgt. 86th Div. World War I. State's att. Du Page Co., 1920–35. Died during eleventh term U.S.H.R. at Bethesda Naval Hospital, Md.

Justices Illinois Supreme Court Frank Dunn[23] (to June 5, 1933); Warren W. Duncan[25] (to June 5, 1933); Clyde E. Stone[26]; Oscar E. Heard[27] (to June 5, 1933); Frederic R. DeYoung[27] (d. Nov. 16, 1934); Norman L. Jones[29]; Warren H. Orr[29].

Paul Farthing, res. St. Clair Co. Just. Ill. Supreme Court, 1933–42. C.J., 1937. b. Odin, April 12, 1887. Sight destroyed in boyhood. J.D. McKendree, admitted Ill. bar, 1909. Co. judge St. Clair Co., 1930–33. Dir. Equity Savings Association of East St. Louis from 1942.

Lott R. Herrick, res. De Witt Co. Just. Ill. Supreme Court, June 5, 1933, to Sept. 18, 1937 (d.). C.J., 1936. b. Farmer City, Dec. 8, 1871. A.B. Illinois, 1892; LL.B. Michigan, admitted Ill. bar, 1894. Co. att. De Witt Co., 1902–4. Pract. with father and brother.

Elwyn R. Shaw, res. Stephenson Co. Just. Ill. Supreme Court, 1933–42. C.J., 1938. b. Lyndon, Oct. 19, 1888. LL.B. Michigan, admitted Ill. bar, 1910; pract. Freeport. Fed. dist. judge, 1944–50. d. Cedarville, July 18, 1950.

Francis S. Wilson, res. Cook Co. Just. Ill. Supreme Court, July 1, 1935, vice DeYoung, to March 14, 1951 (d.). C.J., 1939. b. Youngstown, Ohio, Feb. 7, 1872. LL.B. Western Reserve, admitted Ohio bar, 1895. Moved to Chicago, 1897. Partner with Clarence Darrow, Edgar Lee Masters. Cook Co. att., 1911–12. Commissioned capt. World War I, promoted maj., served 1917 and 1918. Judge Cook Co. Court, 1921–27, appellate court, 1927–33. Nominated by both parties to fill DeYoung's place; renominated by both parties, 1942.

31. Second administration of Henry Horner, Jan. 4, 1937, to Oct. 6, 1940 (d), (succeeded by John Stelle, Oct. 6, 1940, to Jan. 13, 1941).

Voting for governor: Horner, 2,067,861. C. Wayland Brooks, 1,682,685. William Hale Thompson, 128,962.

Governor Henry Horner[30].

Lieutenant Governor John Stelle[30].
Secretary of State Edward J. Hughes [30].
Auditor Edward J. Barrett[29].
Treasurers John C. Martin[30] (to Jan. 4, 1939).
Louie E. Lewis, res. Franklin Co. Dem. Treas., Jan. 4, 1939, to Jan. 13, 1941. b. Franklin Co., July 20, 1893. Taught school, farmed and published newspaper. Ill. H.R., 1933-38. Cand. lt. gov., 1940.
Superintendent of Public Instruction John A. Wieland[30].
Attorneys General Otto Kerner[30] (resigned Nov. 23, 1938).
John E. Cassidy, res. Peoria Co. Dem. Att. gen., Nov. 23, 1938, to Jan. 13, 1941. b. Ottawa, Jan. 31, 1896. LL.B. Notre Dame, admitted Ill. bar, 1917. World War I 26th Div., fought in every major drive; wounded second Battle of Argonne, Purple Heart. Legal dept. Aetna Life Chicago and Peoria, 1920-21. Private pract., 1921-34. Dir. Nat. Emergency Council for Ill., 1934. App. att. gen. by Gov. Horner vice Kerner. Dir. Ill. Chamber of Commerce; pres. Peoria Chamber of Commerce. Mem. board of govs. Ill. Bar Association Pract. Peoria.

United States Senators J. Hamilton Lewis[25] (d. April 9, 1939); William H. Dieterich[29] (to March 4, 1939); Scott W. Lucas[30] (from 1939).

James M. Slattery, res. Cook Co. Dem. U.S. Sen., April 24, 1939, vice Lewis, to Nov. 21, 1940. b. Chicago, July 29, 1878. LL.B. Illinois College of Law, Chicago, admitted Ill. bar, 1908. Taught Illinois College of Law, 1909-12. Counsel Lincoln Park Comms., 1934; Park Dist., 1934-36. App. U.S. Sen. by Gov. Horner. d. Lake Geneva, Wis., Aug. 28, 1948.

Charles Wayland Brooks, res. Cook Co. Rep. U.S. Sen., Nov. 22, 1940, to 1949. b. West Bureau, March 8, 1897. World War I lt. 6th U.S.M.C. 2nd Div.; wounded seven times; D.S.C., Navy Cross, Purple Heart, Croix de Guerre. Attended Illinois; LL.B. Northwestern, admitted Ill. bar, 1926. Asst. state's att. Chicago, 1926-32. Defeated for gov., 1936. Elected U.S. Sen. to complete Lewis' term, 1940; reelected, 1942. Pract. Chicago, 1949 until death, Jan. 14, 1957.

United States Congressmen Scott W. Lucas[30] (to Jan. 3, 1939, elected to U.S. Sen.); James A. Meeks[30] (to Jan. 3, 1939); Chester C. Thompson[30] (to Jan. 3, 1939); James McAndrews[22]; Adolph J. Sa-

bath[23]; Harry P. Beam[29]; Kent E. Keller[29]; Edward A. Kelly[29]; Claude V. Parsons[29]; Leonard W. Schuetz[29]; Leslie C. Arends[30]; Leo E. Allen[30]; Ralph E. Church[30]; Everett M. Dirksen[30]; Leo P. Kocialkowski[30]; Raymond S. McKeough[30]; Arthur W. Mitchell[30]; Thomas J. O'Brien[30]; Chauncey W. Reed[30]; Edward M. Schaefer[30]; John C. Martin[30] (from 1939).

Laurence Fletcher Arnold, res. Jasper Co. Dem. U.S.H.R., 1937-43. b. Newton, June 8, 1891. Attended Chicago. Wholesaler of hay and grain. Ill. H.R., 1923-26, 1933-36. Pres. Peoples Bank, Newton.

Lewis Leonard Boyer, res. Adams Co. Dem. U.S.H.R., 1937-39. b. Adams Co., May 19, 1886. Taught school and studied engineering, 1904-15. Supt. highways Adams Co., 1915-36. Retired after one term U.S.H.R. and defeat for Ill. Sen. in 1940 and 1942. d. Quincy, March 12, 1944.

Edwin Van Meter Champion, res. Peoria Co. Dem. U.S.H.R., 1937-39. b. Mansfield, Sept. 18. 1890. LL.B. Illinois, admitted Ill. bar, 1912; pract. Peoria. World War I 86th Div. 2nd lt., 1917, to capt., 1919. Asst. state's att. Peoria Co., 1919 and 1920. State's att., 1932-36. After one term U.S.H.R. resumed pract. Peoria.

Robert Bruce Chiperfield, res. Fulton Co. Rep. U.S.H.R., 1939-63. b. Canton, Nov. 20, 1899. Pvt. World War I. A.B. Harvard, 1922; LL.B. Boston U., admitted Ill. bar, 1925; pract. Canton. City att. Canton. Pract. with father, Burnett M. Chiperfield.

Frank William Fries, res. Macoupin Co. Dem. U.S.H.R., 1937-41. b. Hornsby, May 1, 1893. Moved with parents to Gillespie, 1904. Coal miner. Sgt. 53rd Depot Brigade World War I. Mine operator, insurance agent. Moved to Carlinville, 1930. Sheriff Macoupin Co., 1930-34. Ill. H.R., 1935-36. Since 1941 an arbiter in coal mine disputes.

Lewis Marshall Long, res. De Kalb Co. Dem. U.S.H.R., 1937-39. b. Gardner, June 22, 1883. Attended Illinois. Telegrapher and station agent, 1904-30. LL.B. John Marshall Law School, 1929. Admitted Ill. bar, 1930; pract. Sandwich. Mayor, 1935-36. Chief examiner Ill. Div. Motor Carriers, 1939-41. Nat. War Labor Board, 1943-47. d. Sandwich, Sept. 9, 1957.

Noah Morgan Mason, res. La Salle Co. Rep. U.S.H.R., 1937-63. b. Glamorganshire, Wales, July 19, 1882. Emigrated with parents to La Salle. Grad. Illinois State Normal, 1902. Teacher Oglesby, 1902-5. Supt. schools Oglesby, 1908-36. City comm., 1918–26. B.Ed. Illinois State Normal, 1925. Ill. Sen., 1931–36.

Hugh McPheeters Rigney, res. Moultrie Co. Dem. U.S.H.R., 1937–39. b. Arthur, July 31, 1873. Printer, owner, and publisher *Arthur Graphic Clarion*, 1900–25. Ill. H.R., 1935–36. Worked in office Ill. sec. state, 1943–50. d. Springfield, Oct. 12, 1950.

James Marten Barnes, res. Morgan Co. Dem. U.S.H.R., 1939–43. b. Jacksonville, Jan. 9. 1899. World War I U.S.M.C. overseas. A.B. Illinois College, Jacksonville, 1921; LL.B. Harvard, admitted Ill. bar, 1924; pract. Jacksonville. Judge Morgan Co. Court, 1926–34. Administrative asst. to Pres. Roosevelt, 1943–45. Pract. Washington, D.C., until his death, June 8, 1958.

Anton Joseph Johnson, res. McDonough Co. Rep. U.S.H.R., 1939–49. b. Peoria, Oct. 20, 1878. Attended Missouri. First sgt. 5th Inf. Ill. N.G., 1898–1901. Farmer n. Peoria, 1913–21. Moved to Macomb, 1926. Pres. Ill. Milk Dealers Association, 1931–36; Ill. Milk Products Association, 1937. Mayor Macomb, 1949–51 (resigned). d. Macomb, April 16, 1958.

Anton Frank Maciezewski, res. Cook Co. Dem. U.S.H.R., 1939 to Dec. 8, 1942 (resigned). b. Anderson, Tex., Jan. 3, 1893. Attended Lewis Inst., Chicago. Resided Cicero. Coal merchant. Active Dem. politics. Cook Co. Board of Supervisors, 1942 until death, Cicero, Sept. 25, 1949.

Thomas Vernor Smith, res. Cook Co. Dem. U.S.H.R., 1939–41. b. Blanket, Tex., April 26, 1890. A.B. U. of Texas, 1915. Pvt. World War I, 1917–19. Ph.D. Chicago, 1922. Faculty of Texas Christian, 1916–17, U. of Texas, 1919–21, Chicago, 1948. Ed. *International Journal of Ethics*, 1931–48. Ill. Sen., 1935–38. Chm. Ill. Leg. Council, 1937–38. World War II lt. col. and col., A.U.S., 1943–46. Dir. of education Allied Control Commission, Italy. Writer and faculty member Syracuse from 1946. Resides Syracuse, N.Y.

Jesse Sumner, res. Iroquois Co. Rep. U.S.H.R., 1939–47. b. Milford, July 17, 1898. A.B. Smith, 1920. Studied law Chicago, Columbia, and Oxford. Admitted Ill. bar, 1923; pract. Chicago. Legal staff Chase Nat. Bank, 1928–37. Returned to Milford. Judge Iroquois Co. Court, 1937. After four terms U.S.H.R. resumed active charge family business of farming, banking in Milford.

William Howard Wheat, res. Champaign Co. Rep. U.S.H.R., 1939 to Jan. 16, 1944 (d.). b. Kahoka, Mo., Feb. 9, 1879. Attended Chaddock College and Gem City

Business College, Quincy. Bookkeeper and bank cashier Thomasboro, 1900. Bank pres. Rantoul. d. Washington, D.C., during third term U.S.H.R.

Justices Illinois Supreme Court Clyde E. Stone[26]; Warren H. Orr[29] (to June 5, 1939); Norman L. Jones[29] (d. Nov. 15, 1940); Paul Farthing[30]; Lott R. Herrick[30] (d. Sept. 18, 1937); Elwin R. Shaw[30]; Francis S. Wilson[30].

Walter T. Gunn, res. Vermilion Co. Just. Ill. Supreme Court, June 27, 1938, vice Herrick, to 1951. C.J.; Nov. 1940 to Sept. 1941; Sept. 1946 to Sept. 1947. b. La Salle Co., June 4, 1879. LL.B. Illinois Wesleyan, admitted Ill. bar, 1902. Pract. Danville until elected to Supreme Court and after 1951. d. Danville, Oct. 13, 1956.

Loren E. Murphy, res. Warren Co. Just. Ill. Supreme Court, 1939–48. C.J.; Sept. 1941 to Sept. 1942, Sept. 8, 1947, to June 1948. b. Cuba, July 23, 1882. LL.B. Michigan, admitted Ill. bar, 1906; pract. Monmouth. Co. judge Warren Co., 1910–18. Pract. Monmouth to Nov. 1932. Judge circuit court, 9th Circuit, 1932–33; appellate court, 1933–39. Pract. Monmouth, 1948 until death, June 2, 1963.

32. First administration of Dwight H. Green, Jan. 13, 1941, to Jan. 8, 1945. Voting for governor: Green, 2,197,778. Harry B. Hershey, 1,940,833.

Governor Dwight H. Green, res. Cook Co. Rep. b. Ligonier, Ind., Jan. 9, 1897. World War I A.A.F., 1917–18. Ph.B. Chicago, 1920; J.D. Chicago, admitted to Ill. bar; licensed to pract. fed. courts, 1922. Served Int. Rev. Dept. Chicago, Washington, and elsewhere, 1922–32. Prosecuted many notorious gangsters. Dist. att. Cook Co., 1932–35. Active in American Legion, Masonry. d. Chicago, Feb. 28, 1958.

Lieutenant Governor Hugh W. Cross, res. Jersey Co. Rep. b. Jerseyville, Aug. 24, 1896. LL.B. Illinois, admitted Ill. bar, 1921; pract. Jerseyville. Ill. H.R., 1933–40 (spkr., 1939–40). Served two terms as lt. gov.

Secretaries of State Edward J. Hughes [30] (d. June 28, 1944).

Richard Yates Rowe, res. Morgan Co. Rep. Sec. state, June 30, 1944, to Jan. 8, 1945. b. Jacksonville, 1889 (nephew of Richard Yates, Civil War gov.). World War I U.S.N. seaman 3rd class to ensign. An organizer of the American Legion. Trustee MacMurray. App. sec. state by Gov. Green.

Treas., Jan. 8, 1947, to Jan. 10, 1949. Sec. Ill. Budgetary Commission.

Auditor Arthur C. Lueder, res. Cook Co. Rep. Aud., Jan. 13, 1941, to Jan. 10, 1949. b. Elmhurst, March 12, 1876. A.B. Elmhurst, 1900; LL.B. Chicago, 1902. Real estate broker. P.M. Chicago, 1921–33. Pres. Ill. Association and Nat. Association of Postmasters. Mem. civic and charitable boards. d. Lombard, May 7, 1957.

Treasurers Warren E. Wright, res. Sangamon Co. Rep. Treas., Jan. 13, 1941, to Jan. 11, 1943; Jan. 10, 1955, to Jan. 14, 1957. b. Murrayville, March 26, 1893. World War I army. Active in Morgan Co. Rep. party. Steward Ill. Racing Board, 1962. d. March 29, 1962.

William G. Stratton, res. Grundy Co. Rep. Treas., Jan. 11, 1943, to Jan. 8, 1945; Jan. 8, 1951, to Jan. 12, 1953. b. Lake Co., Feb. 26, 1914 (son of William J. Stratton, Ill. sec. state, 1922–33). B.S. Arizona, 1934. World War II lt. U.S.N. PTO, 1945–46. U.S.H.R., 1941–43, 1947–49. Gov., Jan. 12, 1953, to Jan. 9, 1961. Chm. Governors' Conf., 1957. Pres. Council State Governments, 1958.

Superintendents of Public Instruction John A. Wieland[30] (to Jan. 11, 1943).

Vernon L. Nickell, res. Champaign Co. Rep. Supt. pub. instr., Jan. 11, 1943, to Jan. 12, 1959. b. Bellflower, March 2, 1891. B.Ed. Illinois State Normal, 1929; M.A. Illinois 1932. Taught rural schools eight years. Supt. schools Champaign, 1930–42. Ill. del. to Nat. Educational Association. Honorary Ed.D. Illinois Wesleyan, 1944. Chm. of board State Life Insurance Company of Ill. from 1959.

Attorney General George F. Barrett, res. Cook Co. Rep. Att. gen., 1941–49. b. Chicago, Nov. 17, 1907. B.A. Illinois, 1929; J.D. Northwestern, admitted Ill. bar, 1932; pract. Chicago. Master in chancery Superior Court of Cook Co., 1936–38.

United States Senators Scott W. Lucas[30]; C. Wayland Brooks[31].

United States Congressmen Harry P. Beam[29] (resigned Dec. 6, 1942); Anton J. Maciezewski[31] (resigned Dec. 8, 1942); Edward A. Kelly[29] (to Jan. 3, 1943); Leo P. Kocialkowski[30] (to Jan. 3, 1943); Raymond S. McKeough[30] (to Jan. 3, 1943); Arthur W. Mitchell[30] (to Jan. 3, 1943); Edward M. Schaefer[30] (to Jan. 3, 1943); Laurence F. Arnold[31] (to Jan. 3, 1943); James M. Barnes[31] (to Jan. 3,

1943); William H. Wheat[31] (d. Jan. 16, 1944); Leonard W. Schuetz[29] (d. Feb. 13, 1944); Adolph J. Sabath[23]; Leo E. Allen[30]; Leslie C. Arends[30]; Everett M. Dirksen[30]; Thomas J. O'Brien[30]; Chauncey W. Reed[30]; Robert B. Chiperfield[31]; Anton J. Johnson[31]; Noah M. Mason[31]; Jessie Sumner[31]; Ralph E. Church[30] (from Jan. 3, 1943); William G. Stratton (see Treas. above).

Cecil William Bishop, res. Williamson Co. Rep. U.S.H.R., 1941–55. b. Johnson Co., June 29, 1890. Attended Union Acad., Anna. Telephone lineman, miner, played and managed professional baseball and football. City clerk Carterville, 1915–18. P.M., 1923–33. Congressional liaison asst. Post Office Dept., 1955–57. Supt. Div. Industrial Planning and Development Ill., 1957–58. Dept. Labor conciliator for Ill., 1958–60. Retired, 1960.

Stephen Albion Day, res. Cook Co. Rep. U.S.H.R., 1941–45. b. Canton, Ohio, July 13, 1882. A.B. Michigan, 1905. Sec. to C. J. Melville W. Fuller, U.S. Supreme Court, 1905–7. Post grad. Michigan, admitted Ohio bar, 1907; pract. Cleveland, Ohio. Moved to Evanston, 1908. Spec. counsel Comptroller of Currency Washington, D.C., 1926–28. Author. d. Evanston, Jan. 5, 1950.

Charles Schuvelt Dewey, res. Cook Co. Rep. U.S.H.R., 1941–45. b. Cadiz, Ohio, Nov. 10, 1882. Moved with parents as infant to Chicago. Ph.B. Yale, 1904. World War I U.S.N.R., 1917–19; lt. on discharge. Banker, trust officer. Financial adviser Poland, 1927–30. Much decorated, including French Legion of Honor. Agent Joint Committee (U.S. Cong.) on Foreign Cooperation, 1948–52. Resides Washington, D.C.

James Vandaveer Heidinger, res. Wayne Co. Rep. U.S.H.R., 1941 to March 22, 1945 (d.). b. Wayne Co., July 17, 1882. Attended Northern Illinois and Valparaiso; LL.B. Northern Illinois College of Law, Dixon, admitted Ill. bar, 1908; pract. Fairfield. Judge Wayne Co. Court, 1914–26. Asst. att. gen. Ill., 1927–33. d. during sojourn Phoenix, Ariz., during third term U.S.H.R.

Evan George Howell, res. Sangamon Co. Rep. U.S.H.R., 1941 to Oct. 5, 1947 (resigned). b. Marion, Sept. 21, 1905. B.S. Illinois, 1927. Taught h.s. and u., 1927–30. LL.B. Illinois; admitted Ill. bar, 1930. O.R.C. from 1933. Referee in bankruptcy U.S. Dist. Court, Southern Dist. Ill., 1937–41. Resigned U.S.H.R. to accept appointment judge U.S. Court of Claims (resigned

Sept. 30, 1953). Chm. Ill. Toll Highway
Commission, 1953–55. Pract. Springfield
from 1953.

George Arthur Paddock, res. Cook Co.
Rep. U.S.H.R., 1941–43. b. Winnetka,
March 24, 1885. B.L. Virginia, 1906; LL.B.
Virginia, admitted Ill. bar, 1907; pract.
Chicago. O.R.T.C. Plattsburg, N.Y., 1916.
Fort Sheridan, 1917. Capt. and maj. 86th
Div. World War I, 1917–19. Investment
banker from 1921. Founders' medal American Legion. d. Winnetka, Dec. 29, 1964.

Fred Ernst Busbey, res. Cook Co. Rep.
U.S.H.R., 1943–45. 1947–49, 1951–55. b.
Tuscola, Feb. 8, 1895. Attended Armour
Inst. Technology (now Illinois Inst. of Technology), Northwestern. World War I sgt.
U.S.A. 33rd Div., 1917–18; sgt. maj., 1919.
Investment broker; retired, 1958. Resides
Cocoa Beach, Fla.

William Levi Dawson, res. Cook Co. Dem.
U.S.H.R. from 1943. b. Albany, Ga., April
26, 1886. Grad. Albany Normal, 1905; A.B.
(magna cum laude) Fisk, 1909; LL.B.
Northwestern. Admitted Ill. bar, 1920;
pract. Chicago. World War I 1st lt. 365th
Inf., 1917–19; wounded; Purple Heart.
Ald. Chicago, 1933–39. Dem. ward committeeman. Member American Legion.

Thomas Sylvy Gordon, res. Cook Co.
Dem. U.S.H.R., 1943–59. b. Chicago, Dec.
17, 1893. Grad. St. Stanislaus College,
Chicago, 1912. Clerk to office manager
Polish Daily Zgoda, 1921–42. Banker.
Comm. Chicago West Parks, 1933–36. d.
Chicago, Jan. 22, 1959.

Martin Gorski, res. Cook Co. Dem.
U.S.H.R., 1943 to Dec. 4, 1949 (d.). b.
Poland, Oct. 30, 1886. Emigrated with
parents to Chicago, 1889. LL.B. Chicago-
Kent College of Law, admitted Ill. bar,
1917; pract. Chicago. Asst. state's att.,
1918–20. Master in chancery Superior Court
of Cook Co., 1929–42. d. Chicago during
fourth term U.S.H.R.

Calvin Dean Johnson, res. St. Clair Co.
Rep. U.S.H.R., 1943–45. b. Fordsville, Ky.,
Nov. 22, 1898. Moved with parents to St.
Clair Co., 1904. Gen. contractor, 1922–44.
Mem. St. Clair Co. Board of Supervisors,
1930–34. Ill. H.R., 1935–40. Exec. asst. to
pres. Remington Rand Corp. Washington,
D.C., from 1952.

Rolla Coral McMillen, res. Macon Co.
Rep. U.S.H.R., June 13, 1944, to 1951 (vice
Wheat). b. Piatt Co., Oct. 5, 1880. Attended
Illinois at Chicago; LL.B. Michigan, admitted Ill. bar, 1906; pract. Decatur. Ill.
Housing Board, 1940–44. d. Evanston, May
6, 1961.

William A. Rowan, res. Cook Co. Dem.
U.S.H.R., 1943–47. b. Chicago, Nov. 24,
1882. Grad. Chicago. Journalist, 1907–27.
Ald., 1927–42. U.S. comptroller customs
Chicago, 1947–53. d. Chicago, May 31,
1961.

Sidney Elmer Simpson, res. Greene Co.
Rep. U.S.H.R., 1943 to Oct. 26, 1958 (d.).
b. Carrollton, Sept. 20, 1894. World War I
U.S.A. overseas. Owner Simpson Auto and
Simpson Bus companies. d. Pittsfield during
eighth term U.S.H.R.

Charles Wesley Vursell, res. Marion Co.
Rep. U.S.H.R., 1943–59. b. Salem, Feb. 8,
1881. Hardware merchant, 1904. Sheriff
Marion Co., 1910–14. Ill. H.R., 1915–16.
Owner and publisher *Salem Republican*,
1916–48. Resides in Salem.

Justices Illinois Supreme Court Clyde E.
Stone[26]; Paul Farthing[30] (to June 8,
1942); Elwin R. Shaw[30] (to June 8, 1942);
Francis S. Wilson[30]; Walter T. Gunn[31];
Loren E. Murphy[31].

Charles H. Thompson, res. Saline Co.
Rep. Just. Ill. Supreme Court, 1942–51.
C.J., Sept. 10, 1945, to Sept. 1946; Sept. 12,
1949, to Sept. 1950. b. Mount Vernon, Ind.,
Dec. 11, 1886. Moved to Ill., 1914. LL.B.
Chicago-Kent College of Law, 1918; admitted Ill. bar, 1919. State's att. Saline Co.,
1920–24. Ill. Sen., 1927–34, 1939–42.

June C. Smith, res. Marion Co. Just. Ill.
Supreme Court, Feb. 25, 1941, vice Jones,
to Feb. 7, 1947 (d.). C.J., Sept. 13, 1943, to
Sept. 1944. b. Irvington, March 24, 1876.
Admitted Ill. bar, 1904; pract. Centralia.
State's att. Marion Co. 1904–8. Asst. att.
gen., 1909–13. Served World War I maj. inf.
Mem. Jud. Advisory Council for Ill., 1929–
33.

William J. Fulton, res. De Kalb Co.
Just. Ill. Supreme Court, 1942 to Nov. 1,
1954 (resigned). C.J., Sept. 1944 to Sept.
1945, June 21, 1948, to Sept. 1949. b. Lynedoch, Ontario, Jan. 14, 1875. Moved with
parents to Waterman, 1880. A.B. Illinois,
1898; LL.B. Illinois, 1900; admitted Ill. bar,
1901. City att. Sycamore, 1903–9. Master in
chancery De Kalb Co., 1913–23. Judge
circuit court, 16th Circuit, 1923–30, appellate court, 1930–42. d. Sycamore, March 24,
1961.

33. Second administration of Dwight H.
Green, Jan. 8, 1945, to Jan. 10, 1949.
Voting for governor: Green, 2,013,270.
Thomas J. Courtney, 1,940,999.

Governor Dwight H. Green[32].
Lieutenant Governor Hugh Cross[32].
Secretary of State Edward J. Barrett[29].
Auditor Arthur C. Leuder[32].
Treasurers Conrad F. Becker, res. Randolph Co. Rep. Treas., Jan. 8, 1945, to Jan. 8, 1947. b. Red Bud, Nov. 12, 1905. Ballplayer. Miller. Mayor Red Bud, 1927–29. Warden Menard penitentiary, 1941–44. d. Red Bud, Aug. 16, 1965.

Richard Yates Rowe[32], treas., Jan. 8, 1947, to Jan. 10, 1949.
Superintendent of Public Instruction Vernon L. Nickell[32].
Attorney General George F. Barrett[32].
United States Senators Scott W. Lucas[30]; C. Wayland Brooks[31].
United States Congressmen James V. Heidinger[32] (d. March 22, 1945); Edward A. Kelly[29] (to Jan. 3, 1947); Jessie Sumner[31] (to Jan. 3, 1947); Evan G. Howell[32] (resigned Oct. 5, 1947); Adolph J. Sabath [23]; Leo E. Allen[30]; Leslie C. Arends[30]; Ralph E. Church[30]; Everett M. Dirksen[30] (elected to U.S. Sen., 1950); Thomas J. O'Brien[30]; Chauncey W. Reed[30]; Robert B. Chiperfield[31]; Anton J. Johnson[31]; Noah M. Mason[31]; Cecil W. Bishop[32]; Fred E. Busbey[32]; William L. Dawson[32]; Thomas S. Gordon[32]; Martin Gorski[32]; Rolla C. McMillen[32]; Sidney E. Simpson[32]; William G. Stratton[32]; Charles W. Vursell[32]; William A. Rowan[32] (from Jan. 3, 1943).

Roy Clippinger, res. White Co. Rep. U.S.H.R., Nov. 6, 1945, vice Heidinger, to 1949. b. Fairfield, Jan. 13, 1886. Printer, newspaper publisher in Carmi from 1909. d. Carmi, Dec. 24, 1962.

Emily Taft Douglas, res. Cook Co. Dem. Wife of Sen. Paul H. Douglas. U.S.H.R., 1945–47. b. Chicago, April 19, 1899. A.B. Chicago, 1920. Actress, organizer Ill. League of Women Voters. Sec. International Relations Center Chicago. Resides Chicago and Washington, D.C.

William Walter Link, res. Cook Co. Dem. U.S.H.R., 1945–47. b. Swiec, Poland, Feb. 12, 1884. Emigrated to Chicago with parents, 1897. Studied engineering at Lewis Inst., Chicago. Gen. sec. Polish American Dem. Organization of Ill., 1932–50. Banker, businessman. V.P. Board of Local Improvements Chicago, 1912–32. Chief clerk Superior Court of Chicago, 1942–43. V.P. Board Civil Service Comms. of Cook Co., 1943–44. d. Chicago, Sept. 23, 1950.

Charles Melvin Price, res. St. Clair Co. Dem. U.S.H.R. from 1945. b. East St. Louis, Jan. 1, 1905. Attended St. Louis U. Journalist, 1925–33. Mem. St. Clair Co. Board of Supervisors. Sec. to Congressman Edward M. Schaefer, 1933–43. A.U.S. Camp Lee, Va., until elected to U.S.H.R. in 1944.

Alexander John Resa, res. Cook Co. Dem. U.S.H.R., 1945–47. b. Chicago, Aug. 4, 1887. LL.B. John Marshall Law School, admitted Ill. bar, 1911; pract. Chicago. Mem. faculty John Marshall, 1918–42. Asst. corp. counsel Chicago, 1937–44. Retired Dec. 31, 1959. d. Evanston, July 4, 1964.

Edward Halsey Jenison, res. Edgar Co. Rep. U.S.H.R., 1947–53. b. Fond du Lac, Wis., July 27, 1907. Attended Wisconsin. Journalist, 1925–37. Publisher Paris, 1938. Lt. com. U.S.N.R. (air) World War II. Dir. Dept. Finance, 1960–61. Resides Paris.

Thomas Leonard Owens, res. Cook Co. Rep. U.S.H.R., 1947 to June 7, 1948 (d.). b. Chicago, Dec. 21, 1897. Attended Northwestern and De Paul; LL.B. Loyola of Chicago, 1926. Admitted Ill. bar, 1927; pract. Chicago. U.S.H.R., only pub. office. d. Bethesda Naval Hospital, Md.

Robert Joseph Twyman, res. Cook Co. Rep. U.S.H.R., 1947–49. b. Indianapolis, Ind., June 18, 1897. Attended Georgetown U. Mfr. construction equipment. Ensign U.S.N.R. World War I, 1917–19. U.S.N.R. World War II, Feb. 1941 to Sept. 1945. One term U.S.H.R. only pub. office. Retired; resides Stuart, Fla.

Richard Bernard Vail, res. Cook Co. Rep. U.S.H.R., 1947–49, 1951–53. b. Chicago, Aug. 31, 1895. Attended Chicago Teachers and John Marshall Law School. Lt. inf. A.U.S. World War I. Mfr. steel products; chm. board, Vail Mfg. Company. d. Chicago, July 29, 1955.

Justices Illinois Supreme Court Clyde E. Stone[26] (d. Jan. 14, 1948); Francis S. Wilson[30]; Walter T. Gunn[31]; Loren E. Murphy[31] (to June 1948); William J. Fulton[32]; June C. Smith[32] (d. Feb. 7, 1947); Charles H. Thompson[32].

Jesse L. Simpson, res. Madison Co. Just. Ill. Supreme Court, Aug. 14, 1947, vice Smith, to June 18, 1951. C.J., Sept. 11, 1950, to June 18, 1951. b. Troy, Jan. 13, 1884. LL.B. Illinois Wesleyan, admitted Ill. bar, 1909. City att. Edwardsville. Co. judge Madison Co., 1946.

Joseph E. Daily, res. Peoria Co. Just. Ill. Supreme Court, June 21, 1948, vice Stone, to July 1, 1965 (d.). C.J., June 18, 1951, to

Sept. 1952; Sept. 8, 1958, to Sept. 14, 1959. b. Manito, Jan. 22, 1888. LL.B. Yale, admitted Ill. bar, 1909. City att. Peoria, 1911–15. Judge circuit court, 10th Circuit, 1926 to June 5, 1948. Albert M. Crampton, res. Rock Island Co. Just. Ill. Supreme Court, June 21, 1948, to March 13, 1953 (d.). C.J., Sept. 8, 1952, to March 13, 1953. b. Moline, Jan. 7, 1900. LL.B. Cornell, 1922; admitted Ill. bar, 1923. Judge city court, 1931–43. Served frequently in Cook Co. Circuit and Superior courts. Past commander American Legion. Board govs. Ill. Bar Association.

34. Administration of Adlai Ewing Stevenson, Jan. 10, 1949, to Jan. 12, 1953. Voting for governor: Stevenson, 2,250,074. Dwight H. Green, 1,678,007. **Governor** Adlai Ewing Stevenson, res. Lake Co. Dem. b. Los Angeles, Calif., Feb. 5, 1900. U.S.N. World War I, 1917–18. Ph.B. Princeton, 1922; J.D. Northwestern, admitted Ill. bar, 1926. Spec. counsel Agricultural Adjustment Administration, 1933–34. Spec. asst. Sec. Navy Frank Knox, 1941–43. Mission to ETO; asst. sec. state, 1944. Senior adviser to U.S. delegation London meeting to formulate plans for United Nations, 1945. Delegate to General Assembly United Nations San Francisco, Calif., 1946. Dem. cand. Pres., 1952 and 1956. Amb. United Nations, 1961–65. d. London, England, July 14, 1965.

Lieutenant Governor Sherwood Dixon, res. Lee Co. Dem. b. Dixon, June 19, 1896. Sgt. World War I. LL.B. Notre Dame; admitted Ill. bar, 1920. Col. World War II.

Secretary of State Edward J. Barrett[29].

Auditor Benjamin O. Cooper, res. St. Clair Co. Dem. b. East St. Louis, Dec. 7, 1903. Engineer East St. Louis Park Dist. Pres. board trustees East St. Louis Sanitary Dist., 1940–44. Chief clerk office of Ill. sec. state, 1945–49.

Treasurers Ora Smith, res. Henderson Co. Dem. Treas., Jan. 10, 1949, to Jan. 8, 1951. b. New Market, Iowa, Dec. 3, 1884. Merchant and farmer. Ill. H.R., 1937–48. William G. Stratton[32] (Jan. 8, 1951, to Jan. 12, 1953).

Superintendent of Public Instruction Vernon L. Nickell[32].

Attorney General Ivan A. Elliot, res. White Co. Dem. b. Phillips Twp., White Co., Nov. 18, 1889. Attended Illinois; LL.B. Illinois Wesleyan, 1916. Admitted Ill. bar, 1917; pract. Carmi. World War I A.E.F. lt., capt. art. Asst. state's att. White Co., 1936–42. Brig. gen. Ill. Military Reserve, 1940–42.

World War II lt. col. A.U.S., 1942–44. U.S.A.R., 1944–49; retired U.S.A.R. from 1949. Pract. Carmi from 1953.

United States Senators Scott W. Lucas [30] (to March 4, 1951); Everett M. Dirksen[30] (from 1951).

Paul Howard Douglas, res. Cook Co. Dem. U.S. Sen., 1948–66. b. Salem, Mass., March 26, 1892. A.B. Bowdoin, 1913; Ph.D. Columbia U., 1915. Instructor economics Illinois, 1916–17; Reed, 1917–18. Assoc. prof. economics U. of Washington, 1919–20. Asst. prof. industrial relations Chicago, 1920–23, assoc. prof. 1925–49. Ald. Chicago, 1939–42. Enlisted U.S.M.C. May 1942; rose through ranks to col.; twice wounded, Bronze Star, Purple Heart. Resides Washington, D.C., and Chicago.

United States Congressmen Martin Gorski[32] (d. Dec. 4, 1949); Rolla C. McMillen[32] (to Jan. 3, 1951); Ralph E. Church [30] (d. March 21, 1950); Barrett O'Hara[25] (1949–51); Adolph J. Sabath[23] (d. Nov. 6, 1952); Leo E. Allen[30]; Leslie C. Arends[30]; Robert B. Chiperfield[31]; Noah M. Mason[31]; Chauncey W. Reed [30]; Thomas J. O'Brien[30]; Cecil W. Bishop [32]; William L. Dawson[32]; Fred E. Busbey[32] (from 1951); Thomas S. Gordon[32]; Sidney E. Simpson[32]; Charles W. Vursell[32]; Edward H. Jenison[33]; Charles M. Price[33]; Richard B. Vail[33] (from 1951).

James Vincent Buckley, res. Cook Co. Dem. U.S.H.R., 1949–51. b. Saginaw, Mich., May 15, 1894. Auto worker, real estate broker, builder. Pres. United Auto Workers Local 714. d. Hammond, Ind., July 30, 1954.

Chester Anton Chesney, res. Cook Co. Dem. U.S.H.R., 1949–51. b. Chicago, March 9, 1916. B.S. De Paul, 1939. Professional football Chicago Bears, 1939 and 1940. World War II U.S.A.F. pvt. to maj., 1941–46; served PTO, ETO. Asst. chief spec. services Hines Veterans Adm. Hospital, 1946 and 1947. Postgrad. Northwestern. Exec. Montgomery, Ward & Company. One term U.S.H.R. only pub. office. Dir. Avondale Savings and Loan Association. Resides Chicago.

Richard William Hoffman, res. Cook Co. Rep. U.S.H.R., 1949–57. b. Chicago, Dec. 23, 1893. Veteran World War I. Printer, publisher, owner two radio stations. Resides Riverside.

Edgar Allen Jonas, res. Cook Co. Rep.

U.S.H.R., 1949–55. b. Mishicot, Wis., Oct. 14, 1885. B.Ed. Manitowoc County Normal, Wis., 1903. LL.B. Chicago-Kent College of Law, 1908; admitted Ill. bar, 1909; pract. Chicago. J.D. Chicago-Kent College of Law, 1910. Asst. corp. counsel, 1919–21. Judge Municipal Court of Chicago, 1923–37. Judge Superior Court of Cook Co., 1941–42. Mem. Ill. Board Pardons and Paroles, 1945–47. Resides Chicago.

Niel Joseph Linehan, res. Cook Co. Dem. U.S.H.R., 1949–51. b. Chicago, Sept. 23, 1895. Electrical engineer. World War I overseas with 85th Div. Pres. Linehan Electric Company, 1942–55. Dir. price stabilization Chicago dist., 1959. Resides Chicago.

Peter Francis Mack, Jr., res. Macoupin Co. Dem. U.S.H.R., 1949–63. b. Carlinville, Nov. 1, 1916. Attended Blackburn and St. Louis U. Took spec. aviation courses Springfield Junior College and St. Louis U. Served World War II U.S.N.R. (air) pilot, jet-rated. Awarded citations and other honors for around world single-engine flight in *Friendship Flame*, 1951 and 1952. Resides Carlinville.

Harold Himmel Velde, res. Edgar Co. Rep. U.S.H.R., 1949–57. b. Tazewell Co., April 1, 1910. Attended Bradley; B.S. Northwestern, 1931. Coach and h.s. teacher, 1931–35. LL.B. Illinois, admitted Ill. bar, 1937; pract. Pekin. World War II A.U.S. (Signal Corps), 1942–43. Spec. agent FBI sabotage and counter-intelligence unit, 1943–46. Judge Tazewell Co. Court, 1946–49. Pract. law Urbana.

Sidney Richard Yates, res. Cook Co. Dem. U.S.H.R., 1949–63 and from 1965. b. Chicago, Aug. 27, 1909. A.B. Chicago, 1931; LL.B. Chicago, admitted Ill. bar, 1933; pract. Chicago. Asst. att. for Ill. bank receiver, 1935–37. Lt. U.S.N.R., 1944–46. Cand. U.S. Sen., 1964. Resides Chicago.

Marguerite Stitt Church, res. Cook Co. Rep. Widow of Congressman Ralph E. Church. U.S.H.R., 1951–63. b. New York, N.Y., Sept. 13, 1892. A.B. Wellesley, 1914; A.M. Columbia U., 1917. Consulting psychologist State Charities Aid Association New York, N.Y., World War I. Lecturer, writer. Resides Evanston.

John Carl Kluczynski, res. Cook Co. Dem. U.S.H.R. from 1951. b. Chicago, Feb. 15, 1896. Cpl. 8th F.A. World War I overseas, 1918 and 1919. Caterer since 1920.

Ill. H.R., 1933–48. Ill. Sen., 1949–50. Resides Chicago.

William Estes McVey, res. Cook Co. Rep. U.S.H.R., 1951 to Aug. 10, 1958 (d.). b. Clinton Co., Ohio, Dec. 13, 1885. B.S. Ohio, 1916; A.M. Chicago, 1919; Ph.D. Chicago, 1942. Schoolman, author. Divisional Supt. Bureau of Education Philippine Islands, 1908–14. Dir. Extension Services Ohio U., 1916–19. Supt. Thornton Twp. H.S. and Junior College, Harvey, 1919–47. Pres. North Central Association Colleges and Secondary Schools. Died during fourth term U.S.H.R.

Timothy Patrick Sheehan, res. Cook Co. Rep. U.S.H.R., 1951–59. b. Chicago, Feb. 21, 1909. B.S. Northwestern, 1931. Food importer, wholesaler. Pres. Silver Brook Beverage and Swedish Produce companies since 1945. Resides Chicago.

William Lee Springer, res. Champaign Co. Rep. U.S.H.R. from 1951. b. Sullivan, Ind., April 12, 1909. B.A. DePauw, 1931; LL.B. Illinois. Admitted Ill. bar, 1935; pract. Champaign, 1936. U.S.N.R., 1942–45, overseas nineteen months World War II. Judge Champaign Co. Court, 1946–50. Resides Champaign.

Justices Illinois Supreme Court Francis S. Wilson[30] (d. March 14, 1951); Walter T. Gunn[31] (to June 18, 1951); William J. Fulton[32]; Charles H. Thompson[32] (to June 18, 1951); Albert M. Crampton[33]; Joseph E. Daily[33]; Jesse L. Simpson[33] (to June 18, 1951).

George W. Bristow, res. Edgar Co. Just. Ill. Supreme Court, June 18, 1951, to Nov. 12, 1961 (d.). C.J., Sept. 13, 1954, to Sept.12, 1955; Sept. 11, 1961, to Nov. 12, 1961. b. Grand Chain, Sept. 23. 1894. A.B. Illinois, 1916; studied law Harvard. World War I enlisted July 1917, served until June 1919. Admitted Ill. bar, 1920. State's att. Edgar Co., 1920–24. Master in chancery, 1924–27. Judge circuit court, 5th Circuit, 1927–42. Judge appellate court, 1942–51. d. in office at beginning of second term as C.J.

Harry B. Hershey, res. Christian Co. Just. Ill. Supreme Court, June 18, 1951, to Nov. 7, 1966 (resigned). C.J., Sept. 12, 1955, to Sept. 10, 1956; Nov. 12, 1961, vice Bristow, to Sept. 10, 1962. b. Richland Co., Ohio, March 8, 1885. A.B. Illinois, 1909; J.D. Chicago, admitted Ill. bar, 1911; pract. Taylorville. City att. Taylorville, 1912. State's att. Christian Co., 1912–20. Dem. cand. gov., 1940. Dir. of Insurance Ill., 1949–50.

Ralph L. Maxwell, res. Washington Co. Just. Ill. Supreme Court, June 18, 1951, to

Aug. 29, 1956 (d.). b. Nashville, April 9, 1905. A.B. Illinois, 1931; LL.B. Illinois, admitted Ill. bar, 1932; pract. Nashville. State's att. Washington Co., 1936–45. Judge circuit court, 3rd Circuit, 1945–51. Walter V. Schaefer, res. Cook Co. Just. Ill. Supreme Court from March 1951, vice Wilson. C.J., March 23, 1953, vice Crampton, to Sept. 13, 1954; Sept. 12, 1960, to Sept. 11, 1961. b. Grand Rapids, Mich., Dec. 10, 1904. LL.B. Chicago, admitted Ill. bar, 1928. Asst. corp. counsel Chicago, 1937–40. Prof. law Northwestern, 1940–51.

35. First administration of William G. Stratton, Jan. 12, 1953, to Jan. 14, 1957. Voting for governor: Stratton, 2,291,812 Sherwood Dixon, 2,043,021.

Governor William G. Stratton[32].

Lieutenant Governor John W. Chapman, res. Sangamon Co. Rep. Lt. gov., 1953–61. b. Crete, Nebr., Sept. 8, 1894. B.A. Chicago, 1915; J.D. Chicago, 1917; admitted Ill. bar, 1919. Ald. Chicago, 1927–29. Exec. sec. to Gov. Green, 1941–49. Pract. Chicago to 1953 and in Springfield after 1961. Resides Fla.

Secretary of State Charles F. Carpentier, res. Rock Island Co. Rep. Sec. state, Jan. 12, 1953, to April 3, 1964 (d.). b. Moline, Sept. 19, 1896. Attended St. Ambrose College, Moline. East Moline City Council, 1924–28; mayor, 1929–38. Ill. Sen., 1939–40, 1943–52. Died during third term sec. state.

Auditors Orville E. Hodge, res. Madison Co. Rep. Aud., Jan. 12, 1953, to July 18, 1956 (resigned at request of gov.). b. Anderson, Ind., Oct. 1, 1904. Real estate broker. Ill. H.R., 1947–52.

Lloyd Morey, res. Champaign Co. Rep. App. aud., vice Hodge, by Gov. Stratton; served to Jan. 14, 1957. b. Ladonia, Mo., Jan. 15, 1886. A.B. Illinois, 1911. Honorary LL.D. Lawrence College, 1935, Southern Illinois, 1954, Michigan State, 1955. Aud. U. of Illinois, 1912–16; comptroller, 1916–53; pres., 1953–55; named pres. emeritus, 1955. Composer of music, author of texts on accounting. d. Champaign, Sept. 29, 1965.

Treasurers Elmer J. Hoffman, res. Du Page Co. Rep. Treas., Jan. 12, 1953, to Jan. 10, 1955; Jan. 14, 1957, to Jan. 12, 1959. b. farm n. Wheaton, July 7, 1899. Farmer, trucker. Sheriff Du Page Co., 1938–42, 1946–50. U.S.H.R. 1959–65.

Warren Wright[32] (Jan. 10, 1955, to Jan. 14, 1957).

Superintendent of Public Instruction Vernon L. Nickell[32].

Attorney General Latham Castle, res.

De Kalb Co. Rep. Att. gen., Jan. 12, 1953, to May 9, 1959 (resigned). b. Sandwich, Feb. 27, 1900. A.B. Northwestern, 1922; LL.B. Northwestern, admitted Ill. bar, 1924. State's att. De Kalb Co., 1928–40. Asst. att. gen., 1940–42. Judge De Kalb Co. Court, 1942–53. Judge U.S. Court of Appeals Chicago from 1959. Chief judge from May 1, 1968.

United States Senators Paul H. Douglas[34]; Everett M. Dirksen[30].

United States Congressmen Barrett O'Hara[25]; Leo E. Allen[30]; Leslie C. Arends[30]; Robert B. Chiperfield[31]; Thomas J. O'Brien[30]; Chauncey W. Reed[30]; Noah M. Mason[31]; Cecil W. Bishop[32]; Fred E. Busbey[32]; William L. Dawson[32]; Thomas S. Gordon[32]; Sidney E. Simpson[32]; Charles W. Vursell[32]; Charles M. Price[33]; Marguerite Stitt Church[34]; Richard W. Hoffman[34]; Edgar A. Jonas[34]; John C. Kluczynski[34]; Peter F. Mack, Jr.[34]; William E. McVey [34]; Timothy P. Sheehan[34]; William L. Springer[34]; Harold H. Velde[34]; Sidney R. Yates[34].

James Bernard Bowler, res. Cook Co. Dem. U.S.H.R., July 7, 1953, vice Sabath, to July 18, 1957 (d.). b. Chicago, Feb. 5, 1875. Professional cyclist and racer. Ald. Chicago, 1906–23, 1928–53 (pres. pro tem. eight years). License comm. Chicago, 1934. d. Chicago during third term U.S.H.R.

Charles Augustus Boyle, res. Cook Co. Dem. U.S.H.R., 1955 to Nov. 4, 1959 (d.). b. Spring Lake, Mich., Aug. 13, 1907. Moved alone to Chicago as youth. Ph.B. Loyola of Chicago, 1930; J.D. Loyola, 1933, admitted Ill. bar, 1934; pract. Chicago. Zone att. Fed. Housing Bureau, 1937–38. d. auto accident Chicago during third term U.S.H.R.

Kenneth James Gray, res. Franklin Co. Dem. U.S.H.R. from 1955. b. West Frankfort, Nov. 14, 1924. World War II crew chief 12th A.F. North Africa, 1943, wounded. Combat engineer Italy, 1944. Returned to 12th A.F.; discharged 1st sgt., 1945. Owner Gray Motors, 1942–54. Licensed pilot, operated own air service, 1948–52. A founder of the Walking Dog Society for the blind.

James Cunningham Murray, res. Cook Co. Dem. U.S.H.R., 1955–57. b. Chicago, May 16, 1917. Attended De Paul; LL.B. De Paul, admitted Ill. bar, 1940. Ill. Bell contracts div. 1940–42. A.A.F. World War II, discharged sgt., Oct. 1945. Regional enforcement dir. Office Price Stabilization, 1951–53. Asst. state's att. Cook Co., 1953–55. Ald. from 1959.

Justices Illinois Supreme Court William J. Fulton[32] (resigned Nov. 1, 1954); Joseph E. Daily[33]; Albert M. Crampton[33] (d. March 13, 1953); George W. Bristow[34]; Harry B. Hershey[34]; Ralph L. Maxwell[34]; Walter V. Schaefer[34].

Charles H. Davis, res. Winnebago Co. Just. Ill. Supreme Court, March 7, 1955, to 1960. C.J. Sept. 9, 1957, to Sept. 8, 1958. b. Fairfield, Jan. 7, 1906. A.B. Illinois, 1928. J.D. Chicago, admitted Ill. bar, 1931; pract. Rockford until elected to Ill. Supreme Court, vice Fulton. Pract. Rockford from 1960.

Ray I. Klingbiel, res. Rock Island Co. Just. Ill. Supreme Court from July 24, 1953, vice Crampton. C.J., Sept. 10, 1956, to Sept. 9, 1957; Jan. 2, 1964, to Dec. 31, 1966. b. Moline, March 2, 1901. LL.B. Illinois, admitted Ill. bar, 1924. City att. East Moline, 1927–39; mayor, 1939–45. Judge circuit court, 14th Circuit, 1945–53. First C.J. chosen for three-year term after reorganization of Court in 1962.

36. Second administration of William G. Stratton, Jan. 14, 1957, to Jan. 9, 1961.

Voting for governor: Stratton, 2,171,786. Richard B. Austin, 2,134,909.

Governor William G. Stratton[32].

Lieutenant Governor John W. Chapman[35].

Secretary of State Charles F. Carpentier[35].

Auditor Elbert S. Smith, res. Macon Co. Rep. b. farm in Sangamon Co., Oct. 27, 1911. A.B. Millikin, 1934; LL.B. Alabama, admitted Ill. bar, 1936; pract. Decatur. World War II U.S.N.R. lt. (j.g.); Silver Star, two Bronze Stars. Ill. Sen., 1949–56. Pract. Decatur from 1961.

Treasurers Elmer J. Hoffman[35] (to Jan. 12, 1959).

Joseph D. Lohman, res. Cook Co. Dem. Treas., Jan. 12, 1959, to Sept. 1, 1961 (resigned). b. New York, N.Y., Jan. 31, 1910. B.A. Denver, 1930; M.A. Wisconsin, 1931. Assoc. prof. econ. Wisconsin and Chicago. Visiting prof. Washington of St. Louis, Michigan, Louisville, Denver, and American U. Chm. Ill. Parole Board, Civilian adviser Korea, 1952. Sheriff Cook

Co., 1954–58. Prof. criminology California from Sept. 1, 1961.

Superintendents of Public Instruction Vernon L. Nickell[32] (to Jan. 12, 1959).

George T. Wilkins, res. Madison Co. Dem. Supt. pub. instr., Jan. 12, 1959, to Jan. 14, 1963. b. Anna, Jan. 16, 1905. B.Ed. Southern Illinois Normal, 1937; M.Ed. Illinois, 1940. Taught rural schools, 1923–29. Prin. and coach Wolf Lake H.S., 1929–37. Supt. schools Wolf Lake, 1937–39; Thebes, 1939–43; Madison, 1943–47; Madison Co., 1947–59. Honorary LL.D. McKendree. Assoc. prof. Southern Illinois from 1963.

Attorneys General Latham Castle[35] (resigned May 9, 1959).

Granville Beardsley, res. Cook Co. Rep. App. att. gen., vice Castle, by Gov. Stratton; served to June 17, 1960 (d.). b. Salem, Iowa, Jan. 12, 1898. Service World War I. LL.B. John Marshall Law School, admitted Ill. bar, 1923, pract. Chicago. Asst. state's att. Cook Co., 1929–33. Served World War II. 1942–45; lt. col. at separation. Asst. att. gen. Chicago office, 1953. d. Springfield.

William L. Guild, res. Du Page Co. Rep. Att. gen., June 17, 1960, to Jan. 9, 1961. b. Elgin, 1910. Grad. Wheaton, 1931, Northwestern Law School, admitted to Ill. bar, 1934; pract. Wheaton. Capt. judge adv. gen. office World War II. State's att. Du Page Co., 1952–58. Co. judge, 1958 to June 1960. Assoc. just. circuit court, 18th Circuit, in Wheaton from 1960.

United States Senators Paul H. Douglas[34]; Everett M. Dirksen[30].

United States Congressmen James B. Bowler[35] (d. July 18, 1957); William E. McVey[34] (d. Aug. 10, 1958); Sidney E. Simpson[32] (d. Oct. 26, 1958); Charles W. Vursell[32] (to Jan. 3, 1959); Timothy P. Sheehan[34] (to Jan. 3, 1959); Thomas S. Gordon[32] (d. Jan. 22, 1959); Charles A. Boyle[35] (d. Nov. 4, 1959); Barrett O'Hara[25]; Leo E. Allen[30]; Leslie C. Arends[30]; Thomas J. O'Brien[30]; Robert B. Chiperfield[31]; Noah M. Mason[31]; William L. Dawson[32]; Charles M. Price [33]; Marguerite Stitt Church[34]; John C. Kluczynski[34]; Peter F. Mack, Jr.[34]; William L. Springer[34]; Sidney R. Yates [34]; Elmer J. Hoffman[35]; Kenneth J. Gray[35].

Emmet Francis Byrne, res. Cook Co. Rep. U.S.H.R., 1957–59. b. Chicago, Dec. 6, 1896. Attended Loyola of Chicago. Served in World War I. Admitted Ill. bar, 1919; pract. Chicago. LL.B. De Paul, 1920. Asst. corp. counsel Chicago, 1921–23. Asst.

state's att. Cook Co., 1923–28. Admitted to pract. U.S. Supreme Court, 1925. Hearing officer for Ill. Commerce Commission, 1947–48, 1955 and 1956. Pract. Chicago from 1959.

Harold Reginald Collier, res. Cook Co. Rep. U.S.H.R. from 1957. b. Lansing, Mich., Dec. 12, 1915. Attended Lake Forest, 1934–37. Ed. *Berwyn Beacon*, 1937–41. Advertising and pub. relations. Ald. Berwyn, 1951, twp. supervisor, 1953–56.

Russell Watson Keeney, res. Du Page Co. Rep. U.S.H.R., 1957 to Jan. 11, 1958 (d.). b. Pittsfield, Dec. 29, 1897. Moved to Naperville as child. LL.B. De Paul, admitted Ill. bar, 1919; pract. Naperville. LL.M. De Paul, 1921. J.P. and asst. state's att. Du Page Co., 1924–35. State's att., 1936–39. Judge Du Page Co. Court, 1940–52. d. Bethesda Naval Hospital, Md., during first term U.S.H.R.

Roland Victor Libonati, res. Cook Co. Dem. U.S.H.R., Dec. 31, 1957, vice Bowler, to 1965. b. Chicago, Dec. 29, 1900. Served World War I. Grad. Lewis Inst., Chicago, 1918; Michigan, 1921; LL.B. Northwestern, admitted Ill. bar, 1924; pract. Chicago. Ill. H.R., 1933–34, 1941–42. Ill. Sen., 1943–56 (Dem. whip, 1945–56).

Robert Henry Michel, res. Peoria Co. Rep. U.S.H.R. from 1957. b. Peoria, March 2, 1923. World War II combat inf. ETO, 1943–46; wounded; Bronze Star, Purple Heart, four battle stars. B.S. Bradley, 1948. Administrative asst. to Congressman Harold H. Velde, 1949–56, succeeded him in 1957.

Edward Joseph Derwinski, res. Cook Co. Rep. U.S.H.R. from 1959. b. Chicago, Sept. 15, 1926. World War II inf. and occupation forces Japan, 1944–46. B.S. Loyola of Chicago, 1951. Insurance broker, pres. West Pullman Savings & Loan Association. Ill. H.R., 1957–58. Active American Legion and Catholic War Veterans.

William Thomas Murphy, res. Cook Co. Dem. U.S.H.R. from 1959. b. Chicago, Aug. 7, 1899. Served World War I U.S.A. LL.B. Loyola of Chicago, 1926. Admitted Ill. bar, 1927; pract. Chicago. Ald. Chicago, 1935–59. Mem. Chicago Planning Commission, 1947–49. Licensed engineer and registered surveyor.

Roman Conrad Pucinski, res. Cook Co. Dem. U.S.H.R. from 1959. b. Buffalo, N.Y., March 13, 1919. Moved to Chicago as child. Attended Northwestern, 1938–41. World War II pvt. 106th Cav., transferred to U.S.A.F. Pilot 20th A.F., led his group on first B29 raid over Tokyo, forty-eight

missions; D.F.C. and Air Medal with clusters. Chief investigator for Congressional committee investigating mass murder 15,000 Polish officers by Communists.

Daniel David Rostenkowski, res. Cook Co. Dem. U.S.H.R. from 1959. b. Chicago, Jan. 2, 1928. Cpl. 7th Inf. Korea, 1946–48. Grad. Loyola of Chicago, 1951. Ill. H.R., 1953–54. Ill. Sen., 1955–58. Active in youth work. Mem. Veterans of Foreign Wars. Northtown chm. Joint Appeal, 1958, polio drive, 1961.

George E. Shipley, res. Richland Co. Dem. U.S.H.R. from 1959. b. Olney, April 21, 1927. Pvt. U.S.M.C., Dec. 1944 to May 1947; served PTO. Chief deputy sheriff Richland Co., 1950–54; sheriff 1954–58.

Edna Oakes Simpson, res. Greene Co. Rep. Widow of Congressman Sidney E. Simpson. U.S.H.R., 1959–61. b. Carrollton, Oct. 26, 1891. Housewife; resides Carrollton.

Justices Illinois Supreme Court Joseph E. Daily[33]; George W. Bristow[34]; Harry B. Hershey[34]; Ralph L. Maxwell[34] (d. Aug. 29, 1956); Walter V. Schaefer[34]; Ray I. Klingbiel[35]; Charles H. Davis[35] (to 1960).

Byron O. House, res. Washington Co. Just. Ill. Supreme Court from March 11, 1957, vice Maxwell. C. J., Sept. 14, 1959, to Sept. 1960. b. St. Louis, Mo., Sept. 27, 1902. LL.B. Illinois, admitted Ill. bar, 1926; pract. until 1956 at Nashville. State's att. Washington Co., 1945–46. Judge circuit court, 3rd Circuit, 1956–57.

Roy J. Solfisberg, res. Kane Co. Just. Ill. Supreme Court from June 14, 1960. C.J., Sept. 10, 1962, to Sept. 9, 1963, from Jan. 2, 1967. b. Aurora, Sept. 9, 1926. LL.B. Illinois, admitted Ill. bar, 1940. Corp. counsel Aurora, 1949–53. Comm. court of claims, 1953–54. Master in chancery Kane Co., 1954–56. Judge circuit court, 16th Circuit, 1956–57, appellate court, 1957–60 (presiding, 1959–60).

37. First administration of Otto Kerner, Jan. 9, 1961, to Jan. 11, 1965. Voting for governor: Kerner, 2,594,731. William G. Stratton, 2,070,479.

Governor Otto Kerner, res. Cook Co. Dem. Gov., Jan. 9, 1961, to May 19, 1968 (resigned to become just. U.S. Court of Appeals, 17th Dist., Chicago). b. Chicago, Aug. 15, 1908. A.B. Brown, 1930; postgrad. Cambridge, England. J.D. Northwestern, admitted Ill. bar, 1934. (Honorary degrees: LL.D. Brown, Quincy, McKendree, Southern Illinois, and Bradley; L.H.D. Lincoln College.) Black Horse Troop pvt., 1934, to capt., 1941. Served World War II MTO and PTO; released from active duty March 1946 as lt. col. Reorganized 33rd Div. Ill. N.G., promoted brig. gen., 1951, retired as maj. gen., 1954. U.S. att. 17th Dist., 1947–54. Judge Cook Co. Court, 1954–60. Mem. board Chicago Area Council, Boy Scouts of America since 1948.

Lieutenant Governor Samuel H. Shapiro, res. Kankakee Co. Dem. Lt. gov., Jan. 9, 1961, to May 19, 1968; gov., May 19, 1968, to Jan. 13, 1969. b. Estonia, April 27, 1907. Brought by parents to Kankakee in infancy. LL.B. Illinois, admitted Ill. bar, 1929. State's att. Kankakee Co., 1936–40. World War II U.S.N. antisubmarine warfare. Ill. H.R., 1947–60. Succeeded to governorship on resignation of Otto Kerner, May 19, 1968; took oath May 20.

Secretaries of State Charles F. Carpentier[35] (d. April 3, 1964).

William H. Chamberlain, res. Sangamon Co. Dem. Sec. state, April 3, 1964, to Jan. 11, 1965. b. Springfield, Jan. 22, 1931. B.S. Illinois, 1953. LL.B. Illinois, admitted Ill. bar, 1955. Exec. asst. to Gov. Kerner, April 1961 to April 3, 1964. Judge circuit court, 7th Circuit, from 1965.

Auditor Michael J. Howlett, res. Cook Co. Dem. b. Chicago, Aug. 30, 1914. Attended De Paul. All-American water polo. Ill. bank examiner, 1934–37. Insurance agent, 1937–42. Dir. for Chicago area, Nat. Youth Adm., 1940–42. Served World War II U.S.N., Aug. 1942 to June 1945. Exec. dir. office organization and adm. Chicago Park Dist., 1945–51. Regional dir. Office Price Stabilization, 1951–52. V.P. Sun Steel Company, 1952–60.

Treasurers Joseph D. Lohman[36] (resigned Sept. 1, 1961).

Francis S. Lorenz, res. Cook Co. Dem. App. treas., vice Lohman, by Gov. Kerner; served to Jan. 14, 1963. b. Chicago, Sept. 4, 1914. LL.D. De Paul, admitted Ill. bar, 1938; pract. Chicago. Asst. corp. counsel specializing in eminent domain. Clerk Superior Court of Cook Co., 1956–58. Treas. Cook Co., 1958–61. Dir. Dept. Pub. Works and Buildings from 1963.

William J. Scott, res. Cook Co. Rep. Treas., Jan. 14, 1963, to Jan. 9, 1967. b.

Chicago, Nov. 11, 1926. World War II U.S.N.R., 1945 and 1946. Attended Pennsylvania. LL.B. Chicago-Kent College of Law, admitted Ill. bar, 1950. Advertising dir. American Nat. Bank, 1953–58. V.P. Nat. Boulevard Bank, 1959–62. Spec. asst. U.S. att. Chicago, 1959. Att. gen. from Jan. 8, 1969.

Superintendents of Public Instruction George T. Wilkins[36] (to Jan. 14, 1963).

Ray Page, res. Sangamon Co. Rep. Supt. pub. instr. from Jan. 14, 1963. b. Sangamon Co., Dec. 8, 1921 (both parents teachers). Served U.S.A.F. World War II. B.S. Western Illinois, 1943; M.S. Illinois, 1951; D.Ed. Merrimack, 1967. Prin. and coach Williamsville H.S., 1952–54. Teacher and coach Springfield H.S., 1954–62.

Attorney General William Clark, res. Cook Co. Dem. b. Chicago, July 16, 1924. LL.B. De Paul, 1946; admitted Ill. bar, 1947. Licensed to pract. before U.S. Supreme Court. Ill. H.R., 1953–54, 1957–60. Ill. Sen., 1955–58 (resigned). Reelected 1964.

United States Senators Everett M. Dirksen[30]; Paul H. Douglas[34].

United States Congressmen Robert B. Chiperfield[31] (to Jan. 3, 1963); Noah M. Mason[31] (to Jan. 3, 1963); Marguerite Stitt Church[34] (to Jan. 3, 1963); Peter F. Mack, Jr.[34] (to Jan. 3, 1963); Sidney R. Yates[34] (to Jan. 3, 1963); Thomas J. O'Brien[30] (d. April 14, 1964); Barrett O'Hara[25]; Leslie C. Arends[30]; William L. Dawson[32]; Charles M. Price[33]; John C. Kluczynski[34]; William L. Springer[34]; Elmer J. Hoffman[35]; Kenneth J. Gray[35]; Ronald V. Libonati[36]; Robert H. Michel [36]; Harold R. Collier[36]; Edward J. Derwinski[36]; William T. Murphy[36]; Roman C. Pucinski[36]; Daniel D. Rostenkowski[36]; George E. Shipley[36].

Edward Rowan Finnegan, res. Cook Co. Dem. U.S.H.R., 1961–65. b. Chicago, June 5, 1905. LL.B. De Paul, admitted Ill. bar, 1930; pract. Chicago. Asst. state's att. Cook Co., 1945–57. Asst. corp. counsel, 1956–57. Resides Chicago.

John Bayard Anderson, res. Winnebago Co. Rep. U.S.H.R. from 1961. b. Rockford, Feb. 15, 1922. World War II f.a. A.U.S. ten months ETO. A.B. Illinois,1942; J.D. Illinois, admitted Ill. bar, 1946. LL.M. Harvard, 1949. Pract. Rockford. State Dept. foreign service, 1952–55. State's att. Winnebago Co., 1956–60.

Paul Findley, res. Pike Co. Rep. U.S.H.R. from 1961. b. Jacksonville, June 23, 1921. A.B. Illinois College, Jacksonville, 1943.

World War II lt. (j.g.) U.S.N.R., served with Seabees Guam invasion, occupation forces Japan. Pres. and publisher *Pike County Press* since 1947. Active American Legion, Veterans of Foreign Wars, Navy League.

Robert McClory, res. Cook Co. Rep. U.S.H.R. from 1963. b. Riverside, Jan. 31, 1908. Attended Dartmouth; LL.B. Chicago-Kent College of Law, admitted Ill. bar, 1932; pract. Waukegan. Ill. H.R., 1951–52. Ill. Sen., 1953–62 (resigned).

Robert T. McLoskey, res. Warren Co. Rep. U.S.H.R., 1963–65. b. Monmouth, June 26, 1907. Grad. Monmouth, 1928. Stockman, dir. Prime Beef Association. Ill. H.R., 1953–62.

Charlotte Thompson Reid, res. Kankakee Co. Rep. U.S.H.R. from 1963. b. Kankakee, Sept. 27, 1913. Attended Illinois College, Jacksonville, 1930–32. Studied voice Chicago, 1932–36. Featured vocalist (as Annette King) Don McNiell's Breakfast Club, 1936–39.

Donald Rumsfeld, res. Cook Co. Rep. U.S.H.R. from 1963. b. Evanston, July 9, 1932. A.B. Princeton, 1954. U.S.N.R. (active duty), 1954–57. Asst. to Congressman David S. Dennison of Ohio, 1958. Mem. of staff and campaign manager for Congressman Robert P. Griffing of Mich., 1959–60.

Justices Illinois Supreme Court (Under a const. amendment of Nov. 1962, effective Jan. 1, 1964, the tenure of justices was increased to ten years. Tenure of C.J. [elected by the Court] was increased from one to three years.) Joseph E. Daily[33]; George W. Bristow[34] (d. Nov. 12, 1961); Harry B. Hershey[34]; Walter V. Schaefer[34]; Ray I. Klingbiel[35]; Byron O. House[36]; Roy J. Solfisberg[36].

Robert C. Underwood, res. McLean Co. Just. Ill. Supreme Court from May 2, 1962, vice Bristow. b. Bloomington, Oct. 27, 1915. A.B. Illinois Wesleyan, 1937; LL.B. Illinois, admitted Ill. bar, 1939; pract. Normal. City att. Normal; state's att. McLean Co. Judge McLean Co. Court, 1946–62.

38. Second administration of Otto Kerner, Jan. 11, 1965, to May 19, 1968 (Samuel H. Shapiro, May 19, 1968, to Jan. 13, 1969). Voting for governor: Kerner, 2,318,394. Charles H. Percy, 2,239,095.
Governor Otto Kerner[37].
Lieutenant Governor Samuel H. Shapiro[37].
Secretary of State Paul Powell, res.

Johnson Co. Dem. b. Vienna, Jan. 21, 1902, Merchant. Ill. H.R., 1935–64 (spkr., 1949, 1959, 1961; minority leader, 1947, 1951. 1953, 1963; minority whip, 1945). Dir. Ill. Associaton County Fairs.
Auditor Michael J. Howlett[37].
Treasurers William J. Scott[37] (to Jan. 9, 1967).

Adlai E. Stevenson III, res. Cook Co. Dem. Treas. from Jan. 9, 1967. b. Chicago, Oct. 10, 1930. A.B. Harvard, 1952; LL.B. Harvard, 1957. Marine tank officer Korea, 1952–54. Mem. Chicago Crime Commission. Treas. Commission on Ill. Government. Trustee Hull House; dir. Jane Addams Center. Ill. H.R., 1965–66.
Superintendent of Public Instruction Ray Page[37].
Attorney General William Clark[37].
United States Senators Everett M. Dirksen[30].

Charles H. Percy, res. Cook Co. Rep. U.S. Sen. from Jan. 3, 1967. b. Pensacola, Fla., Sept. 26, 1919. Moved with parents to Chicago as child. B.S. Chicago, 1941; university marshal. Mem. board Bell & Howell Company, 1942. U.S.N. 1943–45, seaman to lt. (j.g.). Sec. Bell & Howell, 1945, pres., 1949, chm. board and chief exec. officer, 1961 and 1962, chm., 1961–66. Chm. Rep. Committee on Program and Progress, 1959; Rep. Platform Committee, 1960. Cand. gov., 1964. Trustee Chicago and California Inst. of Technology. Dir. Chicago Boys Clubs.

United States Congressmen Barrett O'Hara[25]; Leslie C. Arends[30]; William L. Dawson[32]; Charles M. Price[33]; John C. Kluczynski[34]; William L. Springer[34]; Sidney R. Yates[34]; Kenneth J. Gray[35]; Harold R. Collier[36]; Edward J. Derwinski[36]; Robert H. Michel[36]; William T. Murphy[36]; Roman C. Pucinski[36]; Daniel Rostenkowski[36]; George E. Shipley[36]; John B. Anderson[37]; Paul Findley[37]; Robert McClory[37]; Charlotte T. Reid[37]; Donald Rumsfeld[37].

Frank Annunzio, res. Cook Co. Dem. U.S.H.R. from 1965. b. Chicago, Jan. 12, 1915. B.S. and M.A. De Paul. Taught h.s. Chicago ten years. Legislative and educational representative United Steel Workers, 1943–48. Dir. Labor Ill., 1949–52. Business, 1954–64.

John M. Erlenborn, res. Du Page Co. Rep. U.S.H.R. from 1965. b. Chicago, Feb. 8, 1927. U.S.N., 1942–46. LL.B. Loyola of

Chicago, admitted Ill. bar, 1949; pract. Elmhurst.

Daniel J. Ronan, res. Cook Co. Dem. U.S.H.R. from 1965. b. Chicago, July 3, 1914. Grad. Loyola of Chicago, 1938. Cryptographer CBI theater, 1942–45. Ill. H.R., 1949–52. Ald. Chicago, 1951–64.

Gale Schisler, res. Fulton Co. Dem. U.S.H.R., Jan. 3, 1965, to Jan. 3, 1967. b. Knox Co., March 2, 1933. U.S.A.F., 1952– 55. A.B. Western Illinois, 1959. Prin. London Mills Jr. H.S., 1959–64.

Thomas F. Railsback, res. Rock Island Co. Rep. U.S.H.R. from Jan. 3, 1967. b. Moline, Jan. 22, 1932. Attended Grinnell; J.D. Northwestern, admitted Ill. bar, 1955. U.S.A. Ft. Riley, 1955–56. Pract. Moline from 1965. Ill. H.R., 1963–66.

Justices Illinois Supreme Court Ray I. Klingbiel[35], C.J. to Dec. 31, 1966; Joseph E. Daily[33] (d. July 1, 1965); Harry B. Hershey[34] (resigned Nov. 7, 1966); Walter V. Schaefer[34]; Byron O. House[36]; Roy J. Solfisberg[36], C.J. from Jan. 2, 1967; Robert C. Underwood[37].

Thomas E. Kluczynski, res. Cook Co. Just. Ill. Supreme Court from Dec. 13, 1966. b. Chicago, Sept. 29, 1903. Attended Chicago; J.D. Chicago, admitted Ill. bar, 1927; pract. Chicago. Circuit court judge Cook Co., 1950–63. Just. appellate court, 1st District, 1963–66. Elected Nov. 8, 1966, to complete term of Hershey which expires June 1970.

Daniel P. Ward, res. Cook Co. Just. Ill. Supreme Court from Dec. 5, 1966. b. Chicago, Aug. 30, 1918. A.B. St. Viator, Bourbonnais, 1937; LL.B. De Paul, admitted Ill. bar, 1941. Asst. prof. law Southeastern U., 1941–42. Sgt. combat engineers ETO, 1942–45, five battle stars. Pract. Chicago, 1945–48. Asst. U.S. dist. att. prosecuting criminal cases, 1948–54. Dean De Paul Law School, 1955–60. State's att. Cook Co., 1960–66. Elected Nov. 8, 1966, to complete term of Daily which expires June 1974.

39. Administration of Richard B. Ogilvie, from Jan. 8, 1969. Voting for governor: Ogilvie 2,307,295. Samuel H. Shapiro, 2,179,501.

Governor Richard B. Ogilvie, res. Cook Co. Rep. b. Chicago, Feb. 22, 1923. Tank officer World War II, purple heart. A.B. Yale, 1948, LL.B. Chicago-Kent College of Law, admitted Ill. bar, 1950. Sheriff Cook Co., 1962–66. Pres. Cook Co. Board of Supervisors, 1966 to Nov. 1968. Mem. Society of Trial Lawyers, Amvets, American Legion, American Bar Association.

Lieutenant Governor Paul Simon, res. Madison Co. Dem. b. Eugene, Oreg., Nov. 29, 1928. Attended Oregon and Dana. Publisher at Troy; author. Counter Intelligence Corps U.S.A., 1948–50. Ill. H.R., 1955–62; Ill. Sen., 1963–68. Received five awards for outstanding services from Independent Voters of Illinois.

Secretary of State Paul Powell[38].

Auditor Michael J. Howlett[37].

Treasurer Adlai E. Stevenson III[38].

Superintendent of Public Instruction Ray Page[37].

Attorney General William J. Scott[37].

United States Senators Everett M. Dirksen[30]; Charles H. Percy[38].

United States Congressmen Leslie C. Arends[30]; William L. Dawson[32]; Charles M. Price[33]; John C. Kluczynski[34]; William L. Springer[34]; Sidney R. Yates[34]; Kenneth J. Gray[35]; Harold R. Collier[36]; Edward J. Derwinski[36]; Robert H. Michel[36]; William T. Murphy[36]; Roman C. Pucinski[36]; Daniel Rostenkowski[36]; George E. Shipley[36]; John B. Anderson[37]; Paul Findley[37]; Robert McClory[37]; Charlotte T. Reid[37]; Donald Rumsfeld[37]; Frank Annunzio[38]; John M. Erlenborn[38]; Daniel J. Ronan[38]; Thomas F. Railsback[38].

Abner J. Mikva, res. Cook Co. Dem. U.S.H.R. from Jan. 3, 1969. b. Milwaukee, Wis., Jan. 21, 1926. U.S.A.F. pvt., 1944; 2nd lieut., 1945. J.D. Chicago Law, admitted Ill. bar, 1951. Licensed to pract. Ill. Supreme Court, 1957, U.S. Supreme Court, 1960. Ill. H.R., 1956–66. Chm. House Judiciary Commission, 1966.

Justices Illinois Supreme Court Roy J. Solfisberg[36], C.J.; Walter V. Schaefer[34]; Ray I. Klingbiel[35]; Byron O. House[36]; Robert C. Underwood[37]; Thomas E. Kluczynski[38]; Daniel P. Ward[38].

No complicated machinery was needed for the government of Illinois in 1818. The constitutional convention in August of that year was setting up administrative, judicial, and legislative departments to govern a rural area populated by fewer than 50,000 persons and containing only three incorporated places: Shawneetown, Kaskaskia, and Cairo. Malefactors were few and could be cared for in the scattered jails of the fourteen counties that had been organized. The poor were not so poor that they would fail to grub out a living from the soil or the forests. The crippled were cared for by their kinfolk, and lone indigents would always find some place to hang their coonskin caps.

Delegates to the convention were united in desiring a constitution that would contain adequate checks and balances among the three divisions of state government, for the erection of which the federal constitution provided a guide.

Purely personal considerations, however, brought about a tighter control of the executive than was the case in many other states. Whereas in most states members of the immediate official family of the governor were appointed by him with the consent of state senates, in Illinois only the secretary of state was so chosen. The auditor of public accounts, the treasurer, and the attorney general were elected by joint vote of the two houses of the General Assembly. This situation arose because of the desire of most delegates to the constitutional convention, many of whom would become legislators, to have Elijah C. Berry, the territorial auditor, continue in office. It was also certain that Shadrach Bond, who in August of 1818 had the inside track for the post of governor, would not appoint him.

Since it would not do to make only one executive officer beholden to the General Assembly, the convention decided that there should be three, leaving with the governor power to appoint his closest associate. The relationship of the governor and the secretary of the territory, whose assignments the secretary of state would take over, was indicated by the fact that one of the territorial secretary's duties was procurement of firewood for the governor.

It is not surprising, then, that the mixture of political acumen and political expediency which motivated the framers of the first organic law of Illinois, together with the primitive character of the new state, should combine to dictate a document which would soon be inadequate.

9

Executive Department: Administrative Structure

Agitation for constitutional changes became insistent in the third decade of Illinois statehood, and resulted in a convention call in 1847 and a new constitution effective in 1848. This document made all principal offices of the executive department elective but, by a strange lack of coordination, neglected to provide for an attorney general and left the governor without a needed legal arm. Thus in 1848 the executive office embraced five elective offices and four institutions—a school for the deaf, two hospitals for the insane, and a penitentiary at Alton.

The next twenty-two years which culminated in the adoption of the constitution of 1870 saw the addition to the executive department of two elective offices—attorney general and superintendent of public instruction—eight institutions, a state university, two teachers' colleges or normal schools, seven executive boards and offices, and eight independent organizations. Some of the independent organizations, like the Illinois Agricultural Association, were private in character but, as recipients of state support, were under the supervisory attention of the executive.

No provisions were made in the constitution of 1870 for a businesslike organization of the executive department, and for the next forty years or more it continued to grow haphazardly as a need or an apparent need arose. By 1910 there were more than 100 quasi-independent agencies overlapping in duties and authority, loosely banded together by the fact that their appropriations were a part of the executive department budget and their heads reported to the governor.

In 1912 the Republican party of Illinois, which had dominated state politics since 1856, divided over the Progressive issue and was badly defeated by the Democrats. Four years were spent in patching up intraparty troubles, and in 1916 Republican Frank Orren Lowden, candidate for governor, went to the electorate on the issue of reorganization of the executive department. Lowden had given the problem several years of study, he had a workable plan, and most important, he carried into office with him a sizable majority in the General Assembly. In his message to the assembly on assuming office he detailed the measures he needed to make good his campaign pledges, and in less than two months Illinois had a new administrative code which became the pattern for reform in many parts of the nation.

The act establishing a civil administrative code for Illinois was passed by the Fiftieth General Assembly on March 7, 1917, and became effective July 1, 1917. The new law provided for nine departments in addition to the elective offices, applied civil service regulations to most of the positions throughout the executive department, and provided machinery for a workable division of labor and an effective nonofficial advisory arm to oversee administration of the code.

Under the act of March 7, 1917, each department had several divisions (from two to twelve) for effective distribution of work and coordination with advisers. There were a director, an assistant director, and specialists heading up divisions, plus sufficient civil service personnel to staff departments and divisions. The original nine code departments and their divisional administrative officers and boards were:

Department of Finance: Director, assistant director, administrative auditor, superintendent of the budget, superintendent of department reports, and tax commissioner.

Department of Agriculture: Director, assistant director, general manager of the Illinois State Fair, superintendent of foods and dairies, superintendent of animal industry, superintendent of plant industry, chief veterinarian, chief game and fish warden, food standards commission, board of agricultural advisers, and board of State Fair advisers.

Department of Labor: Director, assistant director, chief factory inspector, superin-

tendent of employment offices, industrial commission, board of Illinois free employment advisers, local boards for each of five local free employment offices.

Department of Mines and Minerals: Director, assistant director, mining board, miners' examining board.

Department of Public Works and Buildings: Director, assistant director, superintendent of highways, chief highway engineer, supervising architect, supervising engineer, superintendent of waterways, superintendent of printing, superintendent of purchasing and supplies, superintendent of purchases, board of art advisers, board of water resource advisers, board of highway advisers, board of parks and buildings.

Department of Public Welfare: Director, assistant director, alienist, criminologist, fiscal supervisor, supervisor of charities, superintendent of prisons, superintendent of pardons and paroles, board of public welfare commissioners.

Department of Public Health: Director, assistant director, superintendent of lodging house inspection, board of public health advisers.

Department of Trade and Commerce: Director, assistant director, superintendent of insurance, fire marshal, superintendent of standards, chief grain inspector, public utilities commission.

Department of Registration and Education: Director, assistant director, superintendent of registration, normal school board, board of natural resources and conservation advisers, board of state museum advisers, immigrants' commission.

In addition to the nine code departments, there were twenty-one boards, commissions, and departments not under the civil administrative code. Three of these were appointed by the governor: the Adjutant General (Illinois National Guard and Naval Militia); the Commission for Uniformity of Legislation in the United States; and the Penitentiary Commission. Four were appointed by the governor with the advice and consent of the Senate: the Civil Service Commission; the Court of Claims; the Historical Library; and the Lincoln Park and West Chicago Park Commissioners. Six were ex-officio: Board for Vocational Education; Board of Commissioners of the State Library; Joint Legislative Reference Bureau; Primary Canvassing Board; State Canvassing Board; and the Tax Levy Board. Three were partly ex-officio and partly appointed by the governor: Board of Trustees of the Illinois State Teachers Pension and Retirement Fund; Board of Voting Machine Commissioners; and the Centennial Building Commissioners. The Board of Trustees of the University of Illinois was in part elected by the people and in part ex-officio. The Library Extension Committee was partly ex-officio and partly appointed by an ex-officio board. The Farmers' Institute was partly ex-officio and partly appointed from among officers and members of interested groups. The Teachers' Examining Board was partly ex-officio and partly appointed by the superintendent of public instruction. The Board of Examiners in Accounting was appointed by the University of Illinois.

Following the passage of the act, Governor Lowden let it be known that he was still not entirely satisfied with the provisions when considered from the standpoint of future needs. He felt that there should be changes in the organic law of the state to make possible the creation of boards, commissions, and offices as they became needed. Through Bulletin Number 9 of the Legislative Reference Bureau, composed of himself as chairman, two state senators, and two state representatives, which was preparing recommendations for a constitutional convention, he criticized overlapping of functions and lack of coordination in matters of finance administration, in the educational agencies, in the control of corporations, and in the voting machinery and the supervision of elections. The report, after discussing these matters, stated: "The functions of state government are constantly changing and increasing and it is necessary to have broad constitutional provisions for the exercise of these functions."

Such provisions were contained in a draft constitution submitted to the people of Illinois in 1922, which failed of acceptance. However, since that time legislation has provided for new departments, boards, commissions, and offices as they became needed, with strict attention to prevention of overlapping and wasteful functions.

Despite defeat of a new constitution, ten new departments under the Administrative Code were organized by legislation between 1917 and 1967; one, the Department of Trade and Commerce, was dropped and its functions taken over by other departments; and the name of one was changed, the Department of Public Welfare becoming the Department of Mental Health. This brings to eighteen the number of departments functioning under the Lowden Code. Legislation also has provided for many

permanent boards and commissions and for temporary commissions as required.

Governor

As chief executive of the state, the governor is elected for a four-year term, but without limitation on the number of terms he can serve. He must be at least thirty years of age when he takes office, and is required to have resided in Illinois for at least five years. The functions of his office are spelled out in the constitution of 1870 as amended since that date, and by legislation.

As noted above, the governor appoints, with the advice and consent of the Senate, the heads of the eighteen code departments and the heads of many boards and commissions, in addition to serving as a member or an ex-officio member on a multitude of boards.

The governor issues certificates of election and commissions to members of Congress from Illinois, judges and clerks of courts, members of the General Assembly, and certain other elective officers. He has the power of appointment to vacancies in the elective offices that are part of the executive department, and, until the ensuing Congressional election, to vacancies in the United States Senate. If less than a year of tenure remains, he can fill judicial vacancies by appointment.

Every odd-numbered year during his administration, the governor delivers a message on the condition of the state and recommends legislation which he deems necessary to the orderly conduct of state government. Early in each legislative term he submits a budget estimating the amount of money that will be required to finance the state's business during the ensuing two years.

When bills passed by the legislature reach the governor's desk he may sign them, veto them, or allow them to become law by holding them for a period of ten working days without acting. He may veto any portion of an appropriation bill and still sign the remainder of it. If he vetoes a bill, it may be overridden by vote of two-thirds of the elected members of both houses.

If he deems a condition of emergency to exist that requires legislative action, he may call the legislature back into session, stating the purposes for which it is convened. In this event only the specific matters mentioned in the proclamation may be acted upon.

The constitution gives the governor specific powers to grant pardons and reprieves to convicted persons and to reduce their sentences. Parole, however, rests with the Parole and Pardon Board of the Department of Public Safety. The governor may issue warrants to petition governors of other states for the return of fugitives to Illinois. He may offer rewards for the apprehension of criminals and may restore the citizenship rights of convicted felons.

As commander-in-chief of the state's military and naval forces, the governor may call up the state's armed forces to execute laws, suppress riots and insurrection, or repel invasion. He appoints and commissions the officers of the militia.

The governor may approve construction contracts in excess of $1,000 for state buildings, approve permits and leases for extraction of petroleum from state lands and state park concessions. He may also, through the attorney general, institute proceedings in eminent domain to acquire sites for housing developments and certain other purposes.

While the governor does not exercise direct control over other elective offices of the executive department, he has the power to require information relating to management or expenses of those offices at any time.

In 1967 the governor had a staff of eight administrative assistants to help him in the multitude of duties his office entails.

Lieutenant Governor

The lieutenant governor of Illinois is the presiding officer of the state Senate. He votes on legislative matters, however, only in the event of a tie. He represents the governor at many public functions and, if the governor is incapacitated or out of the state, he serves as acting governor. In the event of resignation or death of the governor he becomes the chief executive. The lieutenant governor is the only elective officer of the governor's official family who is not required to reside in Springfield during his term of office.

Secretary of State

A century and a half ago the secretary of state of Illinois functioned principally as a confidential aide to the governor. He was the only officer appointed by the chief executive. He was the governor's clerk as well as his principal adviser. Today the secretary of state operates an office with almost as many ramifications as that of the chief executive. Under his direction are more than twenty major divisions and technical service units.

To help the secretary of state there are an assistant secretary of state and two administrative assistants in Springfield, a third administrative assistant in Chicago, a supervisor of personnel, an internal auditor, a general office supervisor and comptroller, a supervisor and chief clerk for grounds and buildings, a plant engineer, and a chief clerk for the telephone exchange.

The secretary of state has responsibility for administration of the motor vehicle laws of Illinois. He has jurisdiction over corporations registered in Illinois and maintains records of the securities they issue.

The personnel division has the responsibility for screening and updating the classification of the 2,400 employees of the secretary of state, adjusts payrolls, and maintains records of job requirements.

Three divisions concern themselves with automobiles and drivers. They are the Automobile Registration Division, the Title Division, and the Drivers' License Division. The Motor Vehicle divisions and the Drivers' License Division have responsibility for administering the motor vehicle laws of Illinois. The Auto Investigating Branch of the Automobile Registration Division maintains liaison with new and used car dealers and helps them keep purchase and sales records clear for title data. Investigators and Drivers' License examiners serve the public on matters concerning registrations, titles, and drivers' licenses. Investigators are charged with enforcement of revocation of registration and of driver licenses. In the interest of public safety, investigators serve as highway enforcement officers during holidays.

The Motor Vehicle divisions maintain offices in Chicago, Springfield, and several other points in the state. They concern themselves with investigation of doubtful cars as well as providing the license plates required by the motoring public. The Title Division, as well as issuing certificates of title for automobiles, provides watchdog service that keeps auto theft at a low rate in Illinois. The Drivers' License Division conducts tests of all drivers seeking a first license in Illinois and maintains constant watch over aging drivers by tests which must be repeated every three years after age sixty-nine.

The Division of Research and Development concerns itself principally with problems relating to motor vehicles. It is the chief arm of the secretary of state for promotion of driver safety. It provides research reports for legislators when new motor vehicle laws are being considered and maintains liaison with other agencies such as the University of Illinois Highway Traffic Safety Center and the driver training programs of the larger high schools of the state.

Activities of all divisions are brought to the attention of the public through the Public Information Division, which serves all departments of the secretary of state's office.

The foremost task of the Index Division relates to elections. All nominating petitions and certificates of nomination and election are filed in the division and later reviewed by the state electoral board. Returns from primary and general elections are received, compiled, and presented to the state electoral board to be canvassed. Certificates of nomination and election are issued by the division immediately after the official canvass. Another duty of the division is compilation of session laws and Senate and House journals, containing a complete record of all bills introduced in both houses, the action taken, and the final disposition. Certified copies of laws are issued in pamphlet form. The division issues certificates of incorporation to municipalities that have adopted a village or city code, and maintains a record of incorporation proceedings from 1818 to present. Legislators may file with the Index Division bills for introduction at an ensuing session of the General Assembly, in order that they may be printed prior to the opening of the session. Registration of lobbyists as required by state law is also a function of the Index Division.

The secretary of state is state librarian and state archivist, and in these capacities directs and supervises library services, library extension activities, and the keeping of state and local records. A guide service maintained by the secretary of state explains to visitors the functions of all state offices and buildings.

Auditor of Public Accounts

The auditor of public accounts is the chief fiscal officer of the state. He keeps records of the state's financial transactions and writes warrants, which are equivalent to checks on state funds, to pay all state obligations. Warrants issued in the course of a year number more than 5,000,000 and call for a total of more than $2,000,000,000 to be paid from the state treasury. Paid warrants are cancelled by the office of the state treasurer, after which they are returned to the auditor, microfilmed, and become permanent records available for public inspection.

Municipal audits, prepared under the supervision of the auditor of public accounts, are summarized for ready comparison of municipal financial transactions. The same is true of audits for counties of 10,000 to 500,000 population. Members of the Municipal and County Audit Advisory boards are appointed by the auditor. They consist of three municipal officers, three accountants, and three persons representing the public on municipal boards. The county board has an additional representative of the public.

Under the Funeral or Burial Funds Law the auditor licenses trustees of funeral and burial trust funds and sees that they are properly bonded. The auditor also supervises 933 licensed cemeteries in Illinois with trust fund assets totaling $37,000,000. This function was transferred from the Department of Financial Institutions in 1963.

Treasurer

The treasurer of Illinois is charged by law with responsibility for the receipt and investment of the state's funds. The term of office was changed in 1958 from two to four years, and the treasurer is prohibited from succeeding himself. Election of the treasurer takes place at the time of non-Presidential national elections.

In keeping with his fiscal responsibilities, the treasurer receives all money paid into the state treasury, countersigns all warrants prepared by the state auditor, and pays warrants when they have been properly presented. Funds that are not required for the state's daily needs are invested in United States government securities and in deposits in banks and savings and loan associations throughout the state. The duration and interest rates of such deposits are negotiated by the treasurer, within the framework of a competitive bidding statute, and a record of all investments is available for public inspection. As collateral for all bank deposits, United States government securities are pledged to the treasurer. As of 1966 approximately $2,000,000,000 in securities owned by other state agencies are held in a modern vault, equipped with time locks and protected by a twenty-four-hour security guard patrol.

The treasurer shares responsibility with the attorney general for the administration of the Illinois inheritance tax law. This involves the inspection of all safety deposit boxes owned by Cook County decedents, and the collection from county treasurers of the inheritance tax levy.

The treasurer's present staff includes a special administrative assistant, a chief financial officer, an assistant financial officer, an administrator of the Unemployment Compensation Division, administrators in Chicago and Springfield for the Inheritance Tax Division, and a chief of the Warrant Processing Division in Springfield.

Attorney General

The attorney general of Illinois is the chief law officer of the state. Since 1867 his has been an elective office, elections being held at the time of national Presidential elections. The term is four years.

The attorney general is the official legal adviser to, and attorney for, the governor and other executive officers, all code departments and officers, boards, commissions, and agencies of the state government. Additionally the attorney general consults with the 102 state's attorneys of Illinois on matters pertaining to their offices and furnishes legal opinions on problems they face as prosecutors and legal advisers to county governments. Three divisions organized in the last five years brought to seventeen the total of divisions in which the office is organized.

The attorney general's staff, in addition to secretaries, clerks, and other civil service employees, includes first assistant attorney general, administrative assistants, and chiefs of the divisions of Civil Rights, Consumer Fraud, Charitable Trusts and Charitable Solicitations, and Inheritance Tax in both Springfield and Chicago. The Springfield office has, in addition, chiefs of eight divisions: Litigation, Opinions, Public Assistance Claims Enforcement, Revenue, Criminal Law, Financial Institutions, Air Pollution Control, and Stream Control. In Chicago there are chiefs of five additional divisions: Antitrust, Appeals, Investigation, Revenue Litigation, and Unemployment Compensation.

Still another function of the attorney general's office has to do with the dissolution, voluntary or involuntary, and the reinstatement of corporations.

The attorney general defends custodial officers in cases filed against them in federal courts under the Habeas Corpus or Civil Rights acts. He represents the Illinois Commerce Commission, Toll Highway Commission, and Racing Board. He defends state offices and departments in claims filed against them with the Industrial Commission, prosecutes violations of the insurance code, prosecutes wage claims of individuals against employers, represents the Medical Center Association and other state departments in condemnation proceedings, and represents the Department of Public Aid in recovering sums from the estates of recipients, or sums in overpayment of aid due.

Superintendent of Public Instruction

Joseph Duncan, Kentucky-born hero of the War of 1812 and fifth governor of Illinois, during the first year of his term in the Illinois Senate, drafted and introduced a bill for free schools. The future governor, a man with a flair for sonorous and inspiring language, wrote in the preamble: "To enjoy our rights and liberties, we must understand them. Their security and protection ought to be the first object of a free people, and it is a well-established fact that no nation has ever continued long in the enjoyment of civil and political freedom which was not both virtuous and enlightened ... It is therefore considered the peculiar duty of a free government, like ours, to encourage and extend the improvement and cultivation of the intellectual energies of the whole: Therefore, Section 1, be it enacted by the people of the State of Illinois represented in General Assembly, that there shall be established a common school or common schools in each of the counties of the state."

The bill was placed before the legislature in December 1824 and was passed by both houses and signed by Governor Edward Coles January 15, 1825. It provided for the formation of school districts by county commissioners' courts, the election of trustees, methods of taxation, and apportionment of the rents from the school lands given the people of Illinois by the federal government. It also specified that the tax could be paid in good merchandisable products and that such products might be transferred to any teacher who might be employed.

There was no doubt about the need for schools on what was then the western frontier. Theron Baldwin, traveler and writer who became a trustee of Illinois College at Jacksonville in 1832, described the extensive illiteracy in Illinois, reporting a village of fifty-two families in which twenty-seven had no member who could read, write, or cipher. Of the schools in Illinois and Missouri, Baldwin reported, one third were public nuisances due to the immorality and incompetence of the teachers, one third did as much harm as good, and one third were of some public usefulness.

There was little improvement in conditions during the first two decades of school organization under the act of 1825. No supervision was exercised by the state government, and most county officers and trustees lacked the experience necessary to organize good schools or hire good teachers. Accommodations and furniture in the county schools were of the crudest sort. They generally were one-room log cabins with oiled paper for windows. Desks and benches were rough-hewn puncheons—split logs round side down with legs driven into augur holes. Heat in winter was supplied by open fireplaces which did little good except for students placed close to the fire. Flies and mosquitoes abounded during warm weather, with no screens available to keep them out. Discipline was maintained by frequent and vigorous application of the hand of authority to the seat of understanding.

After two decades of this kind of county school, the state legislature recognized the inadequacy of the act of 1825 and passed a new school act in 1845 which gave to the state supervision of the common schools. The secretary of state was charged with responsibility for administration. The first three to undertake the assignment, Thompson Campbell (1845–46), Horace S. Cooley (1847–50), and David L. Gregg (1850–53), had no experience in education or school administration and did little to improve the situation. In the face of this second failure, the legislature again acted and in 1854 created the office of superintendent of public instruction, authorized the governor to appoint the first incumbent, and instructed candidates to file for election to the post in November 1856, to take office on January 12, 1857.

Joel Aldrich Matteson, governor of Illi-

nois from 1853 to 1857, found an able man to organize the new department of the executive branch, Ninian Wirt Edwards, son of Illinois' territorial governor and third state governor, brother-in-law of Mary Lincoln, and friend of the man soon to be President. Edwards took office March 24, 1854, and tackled the problem at the roots. Massachusetts had had excellent results from a normal school (from the French *école normale*) for teacher training. Edwards recommended such a school for Illinois and progressed so rapidly in implementing his program that in 1857 the first elected superintendent of public instruction, William H. Powell, Peoria schoolman, presided at laying the cornerstone of Illinois' first state-supported university, Illinois State at Normal.

Since that day many notable men have held the post. In 1879 James P. Slade, a life-long administrator of public schools in Belleville and East St. Louis, established a model grade school at Normal to give student teachers practical training in their chosen profession. He called to the office of principal a young man from Evanston High School, Edmund Janes James, who later was to become a well-loved president of Northwestern University and of the University of Illinois.

Peoria was the first city of the state to establish a public high school (1853). Two years later the legislature authorized establishment of such schools throughout the state. Under the act of 1855 Galesburg organized a high school in 1861 and Decatur in 1862. Springfield graduated its first high school class in 1867. The first township high school was established at Princeton in that year.

The constitution of 1870 charged the General Assembly with providing "a thorough and efficient system of free schools whereby the children of this state may receive a good common school education." From this admonition came the General Township High School Law of 1872, resulting in establishment of Lake View and Jefferson Township high schools in Cook County in 1874, Tolono Township High School in Champaign County that same year, Streator in 1875, Ottawa in 1879, and Evanston and Nauvoo in 1883. In 1905 the legislature provided that any school district could establish a high school. Under this legislation and a supplementary act of 1911,

193 high schools were provided in Illinois prior to 1917. In that year a special tax was authorized to pay tuition of eighth-grade graduates of nonhigh school districts in the nearest high school. On July 1, 1952, the School Code of Illinois provided that all nonhigh school territory should be eliminated and the said territory annexed to or included in a high school district.

On July 1, 1962, Black Hawk Junior College District, which includes Rock Island, East Moline, and Moline, became the first junior college district in the state. Early normal schools were junior colleges for teacher training, since teachers' certificates were issued after two years. Following the first school near Bloomington, normal schools were established in 1869 at Carbondale (now Southern Illinois University), in 1895 at Charleston and DeKalb (now Eastern Illinois and Northern Illinois universities) and in 1899 at Macomb (now Western Illinois University).

In 1910 the scope of these schools was widened and, from that year, four-year courses leading to degrees other than pedagogic were granted. Southern Illinois University now has two campuses, at Carbondale and Edwardsville.

Illinois' largest public institution of higher learning resulted from a plan first proposed in the 1850's by the United States Congress to use lands of the public domain to finance education at the college level. When the former Indian lands were surveyed early in the nineteenth century, one township in almost every western state was reserved for a "seminary," and one section in each township for a school.

Jonathan Baldwin Turner, Illinois educator and agronomist, frequently is credited with being the first to suggest the plan and was certainly the man who revived it after a veto by President Buchanan in 1859. Turner's espousal of the plan, Lincoln's predilection to it, and Senator Ben Wade's (of Ohio) sponsorship of the bill in the United States Senate brought success. Turner's dream of agricultural and industrial colleges was realized in Illinois, after much political maneuvering as to the site, with the establishment of Illinois Industrial University, now the University of Illinois, in Urbana. With John Milton Gregory as first president, the school was opened in 1867. Students were required to be at least fifteen years of age. On the campus the young men wore uniforms of cadet gray much like those of the military at West Point. Two hours daily of manual labor were obligatory, as were three hours weekly of military drill. Shop practices and the science of agriculture were important in the curriculum. The first graduating class in 1869 had six members. Today the University of Illinois has campuses for undergraduate and graduate students in Champaign-Urbana and in Chicago; also, schools of medicine, dentistry, nursing, and pharmacy in Chicago. In the school year of 1965–66, the University of Illinois enrollments were as follows:

Champaign-Urbana Campus:		
Undergraduate and professional	20,863	
Graduate	7,078	27,941
Chicago Circle Campus		
Undergraduate	8,530	
Graduate School, Social Work	99	8,629
Medical Center- Chicago Campus:		
Undergraduate and professional	1,832	
Post graduate and graduate	551	2,383
Total		38,953

The constitution states that the superintendent of public instruction shall be the chief professional educational leader of the state and sets forth his duties. The Illinois statutes require him to supervise the public schools and see that the schools are organized and conducted according to the School Code of Illinois. The office had few prescribed statutory duties during the early years, the responsibilities of the superintendent were relatively simple, and his staff was small. Gradually the population grew. Farming became more complex and scientific. Industrial and business activities increasingly supplemented agriculture as a way of life. With these changes came migration from rural areas into ever-larger urban centers. These developments brought to the citizens of Illinois many different and more difficult problems with which they could only deal effectively by achieving new understandings and competencies. All this has meant providing additional and improved educational opportunities.

The chart shown on page 167 outlines the present organization of the office of the superintendent of public instruction.

Other boards and commissions which give advice and counsel to the superintendent of public instruction include the University

ORGANIZATIONAL CHART

SUPERINTENDENT OF PUBLIC INSTRUCTION

Deputy Superintendent

Associate Superintendent   Associate Superintendent   Associate Superintendent

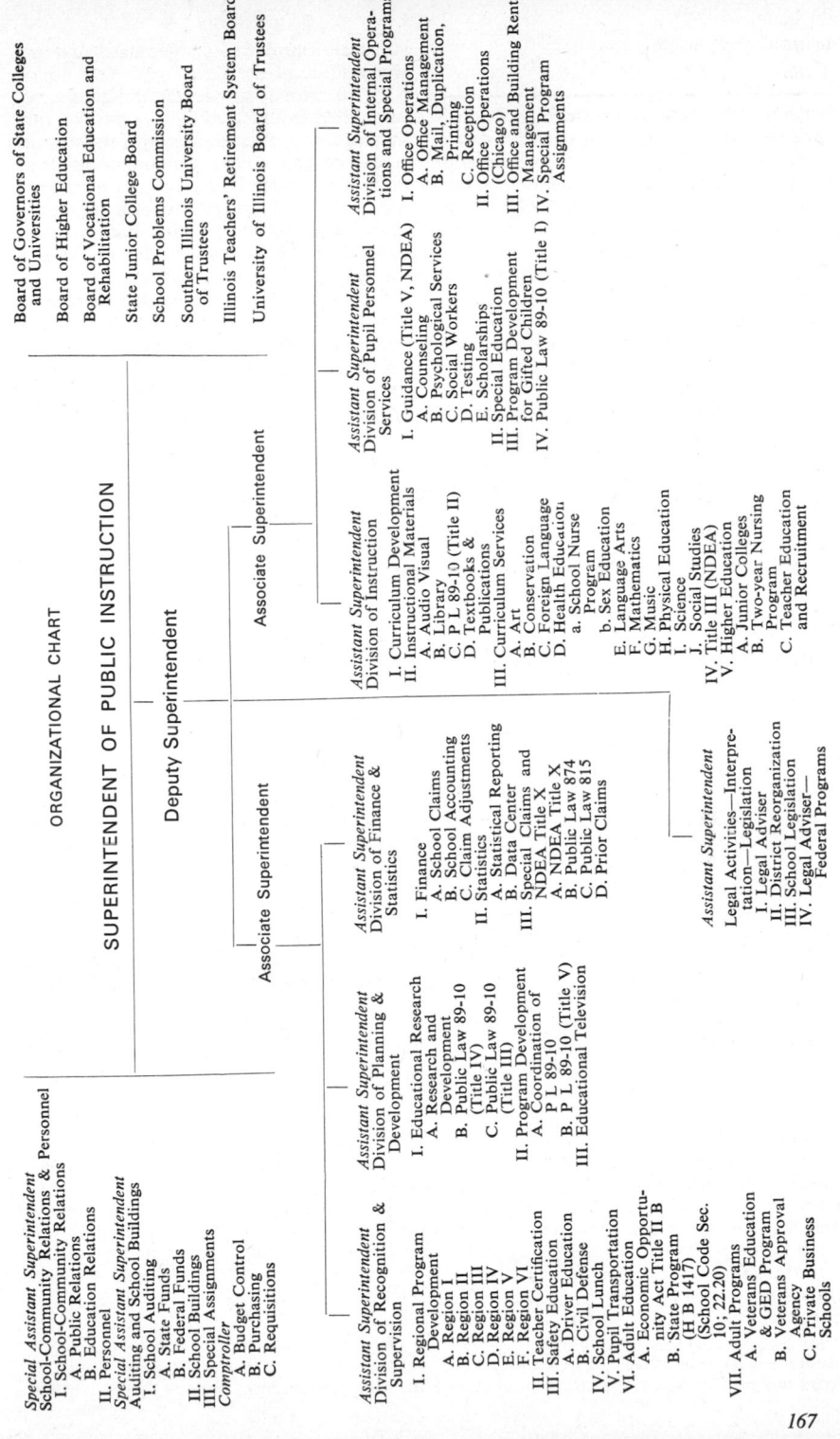

Boards:
- Board of Governors of State Colleges and Universities
- Board of Higher Education
- Board of Vocational Education and Rehabilitation
- State Junior College Board
- School Problems Commission
- Southern Illinois University Board of Trustees
- Illinois Teachers' Retirement System Board
- University of Illinois Board of Trustees

Special Assistant Superintendent
School-Community Relations & Personnel
I. School-Community Relations
  A. Public Relations
  B. Education Relations
II. Personnel
Special Assistant Superintendent
Auditing and School Buildings
I. School Auditing
  A. State Funds
  B. Federal Funds
II. School Buildings
III. Special Assignments
Comptroller
  A. Budget Control
  B. Purchasing
  C. Requisitions

Assistant Superintendent
Division of Internal Operations and Special Programs
I. Office Operations
  A. Office Management
  B. Mail, Duplication, Printing
  C. Reception
II. Office Operations (Chicago)
III. Office and Building Rental Management
IV. Special Program Assignments

Assistant Superintendent
Division of Pupil Personnel Services
I. Guidance (Title V, NDEA)
  A. Counseling
  B. Psychological Services
  C. Social Workers
  D. Testing
  E. Scholarships
II. Special Education
III. Program Development for Gifted Children
IV. Public Law 89-10 (Title I)

Assistant Superintendent
Division of Instruction
I. Curriculum Development
II. Instructional Materials
  A. Audio Visual
  B. Library
  C. P L 89-10 (Title II)
  D. Textbooks & Publications
III. Curriculum Services
  A. Art
  B. Conservation
  C. Foreign Language
  D. Health Education
    a. School Nurse Program
    b. Sex Education
  E. Language Arts
  F. Mathematics
  G. Music
  H. Physical Education
  I. Science
  J. Social Studies
IV. Title III (NDEA)
V. Higher Education
  A. Junior Colleges
  B. Two-year Nursing Program
  C. Teacher Education and Recruitment

Assistant Superintendent
Division of Finance & Statistics
I. Finance
  A. School Claims
  B. School Accounting
  C. Claim Adjustments
II. Statistics
  A. Statistical Reporting
  B. Data Center
III. Special Claims and NDEA Title X
  A. NDEA Title X
  B. Public Law 874
  C. Public Law 815
  D. Prior Claims

Assistant Superintendent
Legal Activities—Interpretation—Legislation
I. Legal Adviser
II. District Reorganization
III. School Legislation
IV. Legal Adviser—Federal Programs

Assistant Superintendent
Division of Planning & Development
I. Educational Research
  A. Research and Development
  B. Public Law 89-10 (Title IV)
  C. Public Law 89-10 (Title III)
II. Program Development
  A. Coordination of NDEA 89-10
  B. P L 89-10 (Title V)
III. Educational Television

Assistant Superintendent
Division of Recognition & Supervision
I. Regional Program Development
  A. Region I
  B. Region II
  C. Region III
  D. Region IV
  E. Region V
  F. Region VI
II. Teacher Certification
III. Safety Education
  A. Driver Education
  B. Civil Defense
IV. School Lunch
V. Pupil Transportation
VI. Adult Education
  A. Economic Opportunity Act Title II B
  B. State Program (H B 1417) (School Code Sec. 10; 22.20)
VII. Adult Programs
  A. Veterans Education & GED Program
  B. Veterans Approval Agency
  C. Private Business Schools

Civil Service Merit Board, with public and professional members; the State Universities Retirement System, of which the superintendent of public instruction is president; the Joint Council on Higher Education, composed of the presidents of the state universities; and the Illinois Junior College Board, composed of the superintendent of public instruction and eight public members, one of whom serves as chairman.

While the office of the superintendent of public instruction has no direct control over private colleges and secondary schools in Illinois, it does have responsibility for see-

ing that the laws of the state are not violated.

For almost forty years after Illinois became a state small colleges controlled and financed by religious denominations provided the only college training available in Illinois and much of the training at the high school level via preparatory departments. McKendree College, an institution under control of the Methodist Church; Illinois College, a Presbyterian effort; and Alton College, under Baptist sponsorship, were chartered by the same act of the General Assembly in 1835. Alton became Shurtleff College in 1836, and about 120 years later became a part of Southern Illinois University.

Universities, colleges, and junior colleges with an enrollment of 100 or more

Universities and colleges

Institution	Site	Control and date founded		Principal officer	Fall 1966 Students	Fall 1966 Faculty
Aero-Space Institute	Chicago	Pr	1959	Alfred F. Stott	100	13
American Academy of Art	Chicago	P	1923	Frank H. Young	700	15
American Conservatory of Music	Chicago	P	1886	John R. Hattstaedt	1,557	115
Art Institute, Schools of the	Chicago	P	1866	William M. Blair	2,887	117
Augustana	Rock Island	D	1860	C. W. Sorensen	1,688	114
Aurora	Aurora	D	1893	James E. Crimi	1,450	94
Barat (W)	Lake Forest	D	1918	Mother Margaret Burke	444	48
Blackburn	Carlinville	P	1857	Glenn R. McConagha	488	36
Bradley University	Peoria	P	1897	Abram L. Sachar	2,200	320
*Carthage	Carthage	D	1847	Harold F. Lentz	1,747	85
Chicago Academy of Fine Arts	Chicago	P	1902	Nickolas J. Matkovic	370	22
*Chicago College of Osteopathy	Chicago	P	1913	R. N. McBain	246	75
Chicago Conservatory College	Chicago	P	1857	Francois D'Albert	200	64
*Chicago Kent College of Law	Chicago	P	1887	E. Douglas Swantes	490	21
*Chicago- Medical School	Chicago	P	1912	Walter S. Wiggins, M.D.	282	755
Chicago State College	Chicago	S	1869	Milton B. Bird	5,753†	273†
*Chicago Theological Seminary	Chicago	D	1855	Howard Schomer	137	14
Chicago, University of	Chicago	P	1890	George W. Beadle	7,780	923
Columbia College	Chicago	Pr	1890	Mirron Alexandroff	370	na
Concordia Teachers	River Forest	D	1864	Martin L. Koehneke	1,223	120
Concordia Theological Seminary (M)	Springfield	D	1846	J. A. O. Preus	371	28
De Lourdes College (W)	Des Plaines	D	1927	Sister M. Canisia	108	15
De Paul University	Chicago	D	1898	V. Rev. John R. Cortelyou	8,416	527
Eastern Illinois University	Charleston	S	1895	Quincy Doudna	6,638	374
Elmhurst	Elmhurst	D	1871	Robert C. Stanger	2,314	131
Eureka	Eureka	D	1855	Ira W. Langston	380	29
*Garrett Theological Seminary	Evanston	D	1853	Orville H. McKay	337	30
George Williams	Downers Grove	P	1890	Richard E. Hamlin	616	45
Greenville	Greenville	D	1892	Glenn A. Richardson	759	51
Illinois	Jacksonville	D	1835	L. Vernon Caine	688	45
*Illinois College of Optometry	Chicago	P	1872	Eugene W. Strawn	250	28
Illinois Institute of Technology	Chicago	P	1892	John T. Rettaliata	7,454	593

Institution	Site	Control and date founded	Principal officer	Fall 1966 Students	Fall 1966 Faculty
Illinois State University	Normal	S 1857	Robert G. Bone	8,301	660
Illinois, University of	Champaign, Chicago	S 1867	David Dodds Henry	37,164	6,749
Illinois Wesleyan University	Bloomington	D 1850	Lloyd M. Berthoff	1,407	97
Jewish Studies, College of	Chicago	D 1924	David Weinstein	352	20
*John Marshall Law School	Chicago	P 1899	Noble W. Lee, dean	1,053	81
Knox	Galesburg	P 1837	Sharvy G. Umbeck	1,240	104
Lake Forest	Lake Forest	D 1857	William G. Cole	1,124	88
Lewis	Lockport	D 1930	Brother L. Paul	1,003	52
Lincoln Christian	Lincoln	D 1944	Earl C. Hargrove	593	30
Loyola University	Chicago	D 1870	V. Rev. James F. Maguire	11,714	1,247
*Lutheran School of Theology	Chicago	D 1860	Stewart W. Herman	420	31
*McCormick Theological Seminary	Chicago	D 1830	Rev. Arthur R. McKay	199	32
McKendree	Lebanon	D 1835	Edwin E. Voigt	497	25
MacMurray	Jacksonville	D 1846	Gordon E. Michaelson	1,068	70
Maryknoll Seminary (M)	Glen Ellyn	D 1949	V. Rev. Charles H. Cappel	355	38
Millikin University	Decatur	D 1901	Paul L. McKay	1,791	100
Monmouth	Monmouth	D 1853	G. Duncan Wimpress	898	79
Mundelein (W)	Chicago	D 1929	Sister Mary Ann Ida	1,419	101
National College of Education	Evanston	P 1886	K. Richard Johnson	850	60
North Central	Naperville	D 1861	Arlo L. Schilling	1,040	89
North Park College and Theological Seminary	Chicago	D 1891	Karl A. Olsson	1,309	89
Northeastern Illinois University	Chicago	S 1961	Jerome M. Sachs	6,043†	238†
Northern Illinois University	DeKalb	S 1895	Leslie A. Holmes	13,896	830
Northwestern University	Evanston	P 1851	J. Roscoe Miller	19,722	2,245
Olivet Nazarene	Kankakee	D 1908	Harold W. Reed	1,545	85
Parks (aeronautical technology branch of St. Louis University)	East St. Louis	D 1927	Leon Z. Seltzer, dean	650	47
Pestalozzi Froebel Teachers	Chicago	P 1896	Herman H. Hegner	479	32
Principia	Elsah	P 1898	David K. Andrews	618	55
Quincy	Quincy	D 1859	Rev. Gabriel Brinkman	1,460	103
Rockford	Rockford	P 1847	John A. Howard	1,217	80
Roosevelt University	Chicago	P 1945	Rolf A. Weil	6,177	292
Rosary (W)	River Forest	D 1848	Sister Mary Candida	1,123*	93
*St. Francis, College of (W)	Joliet	D 1925	Sister Anita Marie	695	65
St. Mary of the Lake Seminary (M)	Mundelein	D 1844	Rt. Rev. M. P. Foley	389	24
St. Procopius (M)	Lisle	D 1887	Rev. D. W. Kucera	815	69
St. Xavier (W)	Chicago	D 1847	Sister Mary Olivia	1,030	106
Sherwood Music School	Chicago	Pr 1911	Walter A. Erley	100	40
Shimer	Mt. Carroll	P 1858	F. Joseph Mullin	471	44
Southern Illinois University	Carbondale, Edwardsville	S 1869	Delyte W. Morris	23,865	1,855
Trinity	Deerfield	D 1897	Harry L. Evans	403	24
Vandercook College of Music	Chicago	Pr 1909	John H. Beckerman	140	18
Western Illinois University	Macomb	S 1899	Arthur L. Knoblauch	5,521	398
Wheaton	Wheaton	P 1860	Hudson T. Armerding	1,876	146

Junior colleges (2-year certificates)

Institution	Site	Control and date founded	Principal officer	Fall 1966 Students	Fall 1966 Faculty
Belleville	Belleville	Di 1946	H. J. Haberaecker	3,100	185
Black Hawk	Moline	Di 1946	Marvin W. Schiese	1,797	128
Bloom Community	Chicago Heights	Di 1958	Albert Martin	1,350	43
Canton Community	Canton	Di 1959	Phillip S. Osborn, dean	850	44
Central YMCA	Chicago	P 1960	Donald A. Canar	3,511	134
Chicago City (9 campuses)	Chicago	Mu 1934	C. G. Erickson	27,466	705
Chicago Technical College	Chicago	P 1904	Leslie G. Morey	1,106	35
Danville	Danville	Mu 1946	Mary Miller, dean	1,200	75

Table—continued

Institution	Site	Control and date founded	Principal officer	Fall 1966 Students	Fall 1966 Faculty
DeVry Technical Institute	Chicago	Pr 1931	Theo J. Laefert	3,150	160
Elgin Community	Elgin	Di 1949	Gilbert I. Renner, dean	1,682	136
Freeport Community	Freeport	Mu 1962	Burton B. Brackney	609	78
Illinois Valley Community	LaSalle	Mu 1924	Francis H. Dolan	1,589	79
Immaculata (W)	Bartlett	D 1955	Sister Mary Fidelia	113	15
Joliet	Joliet	Mu 1901	William C. French	2,079	146
Kaskaskia (formerly Centralia)	Centralia	Di 1940	Virgil Bolerjack	847	44
Kendall	Evanston	D 1934	Wesley M. Westerberg	685	51
Lincoln	Lincoln	P 1865	Raymond N. Dooley	589	50
Lyons Township	LaGrange	Mu 1929	Donald D. Reber	1,370	65
MacCormac	Chicago	P 1904	Gordon C. Borchardt	290	14
Monticello (W)	Godfrey	P 1835	John R. Haines	375	40
*Moody Bible Institute	Chicago	D 1886	William Culbertson	1,850	75
Morton	Cicero	Mu 1924	Walter L. Cooper	1,927	125
Mt. Vernon Community	Mt. Vernon	Di 1956	Howard E. Rawlinson, dean	569	35*
Olney Community	Olney	Di 1963	Gail L. Lathrop, dean	455	18
Robert Morris	Carthage	P 1965	Lawrence W. Sherman, Jr.	437	32
Rock Valley	Rockford	Di 1965	Forest D. Etheredge, dean	2,434	74
Sauk Valley	Dixon	Di 1965	Edward J. Sabol	651	37
Southeastern Illinois	Harrisburg	Di 1960	John R. Murphy, dean	500	27
Springfield	Springfield	D 1929	Mother Mary Celeste	792	48
Thornton	Harvey	Mu 1927	James D. Logsdon, supt.	2,516	184
Trinity Christian	Palos Heights	D 1959	Robert E. VanderVennen, dean	206	15
Triton	Northlake	Di 1964	Herbert Zeitlin	2,524	184
Wabash Valley	Mt. Carmel	Di 1960	C. Edwin Pearson, dean	250	45
Winston Churchill	Pontiac	P 1965	Dr. Andreas A. Paloumpis	185	14

Note: Unless otherwise stated, college or junior
college is part of name.
   M—Men   W—Women
* College not approved for teacher certification or
junior college not approved under Postsecondary
Education Act.
† Fall 1967 figures.
na—Data not available.

Control indicated as follows:
   D—Religious denomination
   Di—School District
   Mu—Municipal
   P—Private, by endowment or otherwise
   Pr—Proprietary
   S—State

Administrative Code Departments

Aeronautics

This department was organized under authority of the Aeronautics Act of 1945. Under the original legislation, the department was authorized to promulgate and enforce rules and regulations, and to implement procedures which would augment and serve as an adjunct to the Civil Air Regulations, so as to produce an effective degree of control and direction over aeronautical activity within the state. Since 1945 constructive amendments and additional legislation have greatly strengthened the basic law. Among these was legislation authorizing the state itself, the counties, municipalities, park districts, and a special type of municipal corporation called an airport authority to engage in the development and operation of airports. Development of adequate zoning laws has been a major accomplishment of the department. Under authority of the basic act, the Airport Au-

thority Act, and amendments, the department is authorized to adopt and enforce adequate zoning regulations in respect to approaches to publicly owned and publicly used airports. In line with this legislation the department has issued zoning guides to all interested public corporations and agencies.

As a practical service to pilots, the department air-marked more than 600 communities in its first two decades, published an air map of Illinois to replace seven overlapping federal charts, and an airport directory with photographs and pertinent data which are constantly revised to keep them up to date.

Education in soil conservation as an assist to local soil conservation districts is another important function of the department. Airlifts to fly farmers over nearby areas in order that they may observe proper soil conservation methods have been popular and helpful in furthering the statewide program of conservation.

Funds have been made available for a program of education for the air age, a program which gives the children in Illinois schools a knowledge of aviation and its many uses as a method of transportation for business and industry.

The department has assisted communities in coordinating their local efforts with the statewide program of civil defense. The department cooperates with the Department of Public Safety and the state police in obtaining better air traffic control and flight discipline. It also promotes a "safety through education" program to familiarize pilots with safe flying habits and practices. Included in this program is an energetic campaign to convince all pilots that they must have good instrument flight skills before taking off in questionable weather. Thanks to this program the loss ratio experienced by major underwriters in Illinois is less than half the national average.

Administrative personnel of the Department of Aeronautics include the director, an assistant director, an administrative aide, a chief engineer, a chief of safety, a chief of registration, and a board of aeronautical advisers of nine regular members and two ex-officio experts in aviation.

Agriculture

This was one of the original departments organized in 1917 under the Lowden Administrative Code. Since that time, it has been largely extended and its basic organization revised to meet changing needs of agriculture. The general office in the new Junior Livestock Building at the state fairgrounds supervises the work of ten divisions. Administrative personnel include the director, assistant director, general auditor, executive secretary, administrative secretary, four administrative assistants, and the following division superintendents: Agricultural Statistics; Apiary Inspection; County Fairs; Feeds, Fertilizers and Standards; Grain Inspection; Livestock and Poultry Industry; Markets; Meat and Poultry Inspection; Plant Industry; and Soil and Water Conservation.

There are also a board of fifteen agricultural advisers, a board of six official and ten nonofficial livestock commissioners, and seven members of the State Soil and Water Districts Advisory Board.

The Division of Agricultural Statistics is a joint undertaking of the Illinois Department of Agriculture and the United States Department of Agriculture. Statistics on crops, livestock numbers, and other needed facts are collected and forwarded to the department by nearly 40,000 farmers and businessmen connected with agriculture. Out of this information 200 reports are prepared annually and 1,000,000 copies distributed.

The Division of Apiary Inspection is concerned with maintaining a balanced bee population, not only for production of honey but for cross-pollination of food and farm crops. This is accomplished by continuing inspection to prevent and eradicate diseases which otherwise might destroy the bees of the state.

The Division of County Fairs is in charge of state aid moneys to agricultural and industrial fairs throughout the state of Illinois. It is in charge of supervision of these fairs and 4-H shows and home economics shows.

The Division of Feeds, Fertilizers and Standards was created in 1961 to enforce laws, rules, and regulations pertinent to commercial feeds, fertilizers, economic poisons, anhydrous ammonia, and weights and measures. The division supervises enforcement of full measure from all metered dispensers, including gasoline pumps and the large meters used on pipelines and at airports. Inspection is on an annual basis, and pumps and scales are sealed against tampering after each inspection.

The Division of Grain Inspection might well be called international, because in addition to two major check points in Illinois —Chicago and East St. Louis—it extends its services to all parts of the United States and many foreign countries. Division duties include preventing marketing of adulterated grain, examination of vessels in foreign commerce, and certification for cleanliness, dryness, and freedom from insect infestation; coordination with the Commodity Credit Corporation on shipments of grain under loan in order to expedite grain movements; provision of laboratories with special equipment for making quality determinations required by millers who purchase grain through Illinois markets.

The Division of Livestock and Poultry Industry, perhaps better known as the office of the state veterinarian, is charged with research and eradication of livestock and poultry diseases. The duties include licensing of livestock dealers, pet-shop dealers, etc.

The Division of Markets provides market information to buyer and seller, shipping point inspection of fruits and vegetables, grading of processed and shell eggs, poultry and poultry products, and terminal inspection of perishable products. It also has regulatory and enforcement functions, including administration of laws relative to agricultural products. Activities are at the wholesale level, but are designed to benefit the ultimate consumer as well.

The Division of Meat and Poultry Inspection is charged with ante-mortem and post-mortem inspection of all food animals produced in Illinois. The division approves labels, spices, additives, and binders used in meat processing and enforces all sanitary regulations of the state as far as the meat and poultry industries are concerned.

The Division of Plant Industry is charged with protecting the state's farms from poor seed, plant diseases, insect pests, weeds, and chemical misuse. The agency is responsible for enforcement of the Illinois Seed Law, the Insect Pest and Plant Disease Act, the Illinois Weed Law, and the 2-4D and Related Herbicides Act. In addition to law enforcement, the division is active in eradicating pests and noxious weeds which threaten Illinois crops.

Ninety-eight districts for soil and water conservation in Illinois include all of the agricultural land of the state. These districts, governed by elected local boards, look to the Division of Soil and Water Conservation for guidance and assistance in the important task of protecting Illinois farms from soil erosion and flood damage. The division recommends the type of man who should be elected to local boards, provides instructions and conducts administrative training programs, assists with program development, provides technical help, information, and advice on watershed development projects, disperses the state funds appropriated for the conservation program, provides supplemental surveys in areas where work is to be done and, in cooperation with the Soil Conservation authorities of the United States Department of Agriculture, provides for the employment of engineers in the preparation of watershed plans and development projects.

Business and Economic Development

In July of 1965 the Board of Economic Development was elevated to departmental status and renamed the Department of Business and Economic Development.

The primary functions of the department are reflected in its eight divisions: Export Expansion, Industrial and Community Development, Information and Publications, State and Local Planning, Research and Economic Analysis, Technical Services, Tourism, and Water and Natural Resources. The department has also been designated as the official state planning agency in Illinois.

The department's activities are under the supervision of the director, an assistant director, an administrative assistant, and eight division chiefs. With headquarters in Springfield, the department maintains three regional offices located at Chicago, Herrin, and Washington, D.C. The latter office serves as liaison between the state, Illinois' Congressional delegation, and the several federal agencies.

The Division of Export Expansion promotes the foreign sale of Illinois products through meetings, consultations, direct mailings, and research data. Aids to prospective exporters as well as existing exporters include foreign economic data, information on export pricing, marketing techniques, and transportation procedures. Overseas promotion is handled through mailings, trade missions, and participation in trade fairs. The division's program offers "in-plant" consultation services when desired and feasible. Many services are coordinated with the Illinois Department of Agriculture for the sale abroad of agricultural products. An Export Advisory Committee assists the division in these efforts.

The Division of Industrial and Community Development offers programs specially planned to promote industrial, commercial, and community growth in specific areas. It also cooperates with private development programs of Illinois business groups and communities. The division's Industrial Development Section uses personal contact, direct mail, and displays to interest prospects in locating or expanding in Illinois. It also provides industrial prospects with statewide and area data as they request. Representatives of the division arrange itineraries for prospects and accompany them on personal visits. The Community Development Section assists communities to prepare themselves for industrial expansion through educational and technical assistance programs. The Business Services Section assists local businesses and industry by providing personal consultation on business problems, furnishing a wide range of data to assist local decision-making relative to business expansion, and providing aids to Illinois businessmen in federal procurement.

An essential element of Illinois' successful economic expansion program is the effective use of all available means of promotion and communication to inform business and community leaders of the advantages of doing business in the state. This function is carried out by the Division of Information and Publications. The department's information program tells the story of the state's economic growth and the development of a healthy business climate through news releases, newsletters, pamphlets, brochures, and radio and television interviews. Economic facts are supplied to newspapers, trade magazines, radio and television stations, special supplements, and national magazines.

The Division of State and Local Planning provides encouragement and technical assistance to communities in initiating and developing comprehensive planning programs. In this effort, it administers the federal Urban Planning Assistance Program which provides financial aid to communities for planning purposes. The division develops guides suggesting sound procedures which can be profitably used in preparing a comprehensive planning program. It also encourages cooperation between local, county, and regional planning programs.

The Division of Research and Economic Analysis provides research and information services to the department's other divisions. It undertakes special studies needed in the implementation of governmental programs, and responds to informational requests from other state agencies, from public and private organizations, and from individuals. The division also carries out the program of statewide planning coordination and research assigned to the department as the official state planning agency.

To implement the State Technical Services Act of 1965, the Division of Technical Services was established as part of the Department of Business and Economic Development. The purpose of the act is to "place the findings of science usefully in the hands of American enterprise." The division administers funds made available under the act. It also serves as a liaison between industry and universities in conducting industrial workshops, seminars, training programs, extension courses, and other technical services. Headquartered in Springfield, the division is assisted by a planning committee composed of representatives from

universities, industry, consulting organizations, and government.

The Division of Tourism is responsible for promoting increased tourist traffic and travel business. Publicity, public relations, advertising, and other promotional tools are used to stimulate interest in Illinois as a destination or stopover for the traveling public. This promotion often results in more than a thousand requests a day for information. The traveling public is interested in information on routes and planned highway tours, places to camp, overnight accommodations, boating facilities, festivals, and other matters of interest to visitors. Schools, businesses, and a variety of other organizations seek information on meeting sites for their groups. The Division of Tourism provides special attention to these inquiries. This information function is a dual service. It assists the tourism industry by protecting existing jobs and creating new ones. It also creates a demand for new and expanded facilities for out-of-state visitors and Illinois citizens alike. A Tourism Advisory Committee of four legislative and five public members advises the division on its many programs and activities.

The Division of Water and Natural Resources serves as a coordinating unit for water resources planning and development activities in Illinois. In this capacity, the division undertakes water resources planning studies, coordinates the state's evaluation of federal water projects, reviews new state and federal legislation, represents the state in federal comprehensive planning studies, and serves as staff to the department's Technical Advisory Committee on Water Resources. The division, in cooperation with eight other state agencies, has recently completed a state water resources plan.

Children and Family Services

This department was created by legislation in 1963. It is organized into three program divisions—Child Welfare, Children's Schools, and Rehabilitation Services—and three supportive divisions—Administrative Services; Personnel Administration; and Planning, Research and Statistics. The department is administered by a director, a deputy director, and a chief for each division.

The act creating the department defines child welfare services as public social services that supplement or substitute for parental care and supervision for the purpose of (1) preventing, remedying, or assisting in the solution of problems that arise from neglect, abuse, or exploitation of children; (2) protecting and caring for homeless, neglected, or dependent children; (3) promoting the welfare of children, including the strengthening of their own families and giving counsel to family members; (4) providing adequate care for children away from their homes, where needed, in foster family, day care, or other care facilities; (5) providing counseling for mentally retarded, physically handicapped, or socially deprived children and their parents when such service is not otherwise available.

The department operates eight regional and twenty-six district offices throughout the state for administration of field service programs. These offices also serve as referral centers for persons interested in services provided by department institutions.

Schools operated by the department provide educational opportunities for physically handicapped or dependent children whose home communities lack specialized resources or who cannot progress satisfactorily in local schools. Schools include the Illinois School for the Deaf at Jacksonville, oldest charitable institution in the state (dating from 1839); the Illinois Braille and Sight Saving School, Jacksonville, which has one of the eight programs in the United States for deaf-blind children; the Illinois Children's Hospital-School in Chicago for children with severe orthopedic handicaps; the Illinois Soldiers' and Sailors' Children's School at Normal, established soon after the Civil War to care for dependent children of war veterans; and the Southern Illinois Children's Service Center at Hurst, also for dependent and neglected children.

The Rehabilitation Services Division is chiefly concerned with adults who are handicapped, have serious medical problems, or are homeless. The three institutions in this division include the Illinois Visually Handicapped Institute, Chicago, a rehabilitation center for the blind; the Illinois Eye and Ear Infirmary, Chicago, a hospital-clinic serving persons suffering from diseases or injuries of the eye, ear, nose, or throat; and the Illinois Soldiers' and Sailors' Home, Quincy, a residential facility providing care and medical treatment for war veterans, their wives, or widows. Through a corps of counseling home teachers, the division also provides instruction and guidance for some 3,000 blind persons each year in their own homes.

Conservation

This department, created under the Civil Administrative Code in 1925, is concerned with outdoor recreation facilities and opportunities in Illinois. It is responsible for management of game, fish, and forest resources to insure continuing crops of these renewable resources, the acquisition and maintenance of state parks, administration of the boating act, and the reclamation of mined lands.

The department is administered by a director, assistant director, administrative assistants, and nine division superintendents or chiefs. An advisory board of nine conservation experts who are not state employees counsel the department on programs.

The primary responsibility of the Division of Law Enforcement is to implement the game, fish, and boating codes. Conservation officers cooperate with personnel in other divisions in game propagation, wildlife cover restoration, and fisheries management. They discuss conservation programs and goals with civic organizations, sportsmen's clubs, and schools.

The Division of Education explains conservation programs to the public through newspapers, radio and television, and the speakers bureau. About five hundred films are maintained in a library for loan to interested groups. A staff of instructors trains adults and youths in hunter safety.

The Division of Parks and Memorials is charged with the management and operation of state parks, memorials, and conservation areas, which were visited by over 20,000,000 people in 1966; almost 600,000 of these were campers. (See chapter "State Parks, Memorials, Recreation and Conservation Areas" for description of facilities.)

The primary responsibility of the Game Division is the management of waterfowl, small game, and deer populations through improvements of the environment and research. Cover restoration on private farmlands helps to provide the environment required by quail, pheasants, rabbits, and Hungarian partridge. Waterfowl refuges along the main flyways and in Southern Illinois provide sanctuary and undisturbed resting and feeding places for migrating ducks and geese. The Game Division manages public small game and waterfowl hunting areas throughout the state and cooperates with the United States Corps of Engineers and the Bureau of Sport Fisheries and Wildlife in the maintenance of refuge lands and public hunting areas on federal lands along the Mississippi and lower Illinois rivers. The division cooperates with the United States Forest Service in the improvement of game environment in the Shawnee National Forest of Southern Illinois.

The Engineering Division consolidates the planning, engineering, construction, and land acquisition projects of other divisions. Included are parks and recreation development and access to public waterways, lake development, and improvement of public hunting and fishing facilities. The study of future lake sites and planning for projects to be constructed with federal aid are important aspects of the division's responsibilities.

The Division of Fisheries is responsible for the establishment and maintenance of sport fishing on public waters. The division investigates water pollution and reports its findings to the Sanitary Water Board. The division cooperates with landowners who wish to maintain good fishing in their ponds or lakes. Two state hatcheries provide fish for stocking public lakes and also private waters where the owner has shown an interest in fisheries management and public fishing. The division cooperates with the Illinois Natural History Survey in basic fisheries research.

In 1961 the General Assembly passed a law requiring strip mine operators to reclaim lands they mined. The Department of Conservation was entrusted with the supervision of this program and the Division of Open Cut Mining Land Reclamation was established. The division provides technical assistance to mine owners and inspects reclaimed lands. Mine owners may plant trees, grasses, or row crops on renovated spoil banks, or they may develop wildlife areas, public fishing waters, camping or picnic grounds, or other recreational facilities. Cooperation between major mine owners and the Department of Conservation has been good and thousands of acres of spoil banks have been converted to productive land.

The Division of Forestry is responsible for fire control, native timber management, and reforestation in Illinois. Two state tree nurseries grow and sell from six million to ten million trees and shrubs to rural landowners for Christmas tree production, timber management, wildlife cover, and soil erosion control. Farm foresters are ready

and willing to advise landowners interested in harvesting and selling tree products, tree planting, forest disease control, fire control, or other management problems. Foresters and forest fire wardens watch for and fight fires on private and public timberlands in Southern Illinois. The division maintains 11,000 acres of state forest lands for demonstration purposes and recreation, and it cooperates with other state and federal agencies.

Finance

Shortly after adoption of the Civil Administrative Code on March 7, 1917, a legislative committee investigating the haphazard financial operations in state offices recommended creation of a Department of Finance. Recommendation was quickly followed by legislation, and the department was organized with three divisions. The department's officers presently include the director, assistant director, superintendent of budgets, superintendent of accounting, superintendent of administrative services, and superintendent of management information. Working under the direction of these officers are a state purchasing agent, a supervisor of printing, a supervisor of voucher control, a supervisor of research, a supervisor of property control, a supervisor of the Illinois information service, and a supervisor of federal surplus property utilization.

The governor's adviser on fiscal affairs is the director of the department. After basic plans and policies have been laid down, he prepares estimates of expected revenue, summarizes requests by the various state agencies for appropriations, the revenue requirements under proposed new legislation, and prepares the biennial budget for approval of the governor. Organization, classification, and summarization of the mass of detail entailed by this document is accomplished through procedures expertly designed, resulting from fifty years of operation. In its final form the budget is a blueprint of the requirements to keep the machinery of government operating and to provide for needed expansion of the state services.

The Management Information Division of the department was created by legislation enacted in 1965. The division is responsible for providing the governor with timely, comprehensive, and meaningful information pertinent to the formulation and execution of fiscal policy. In performing this responsibility the division has the power and duty to control procurement, installation, and operation of electronic data processing equipment used by state agencies subject to the governor; to establish standards of statistical reporting; to improve the utilization of such equipment by arranging for use of available machine-time by agencies in need of this service, and to obtain reimbursement for the cost of such services; to install and operate a modern information system to meet the needs of the state government.

Management of the state office building in Chicago, occupied by some 2,500 state employees, is a function of the director's office.

Pursuant to 1957 legislation, the Accounting Division of the department has established uniform accounting standards for all agencies in the state's executive branch, including the elective offices. Following long-established practices, expenditures are classified and monthly statements prepared. These statements cover all areas of government except the legislature and the courts. Cash receipts are reported by all executive agencies. The Accounting Division reconciles monthly expenditure data with the records of the auditor of public accounts, and confirms the reported cash receipts by reference to records of the state treasurer. The division also allocates monthly motor fuel tax income to the 102 counties, 1,200 cities and villages, and 1,600 townships which participate in this source of revenue. At the present time the annual total is in excess of $100,000,000.

The Department of Finance is the state's purchasing agent. This function is exercised by the purchases and supplies section of the Administrative Services Division. Purchase of materials through this section is obligatory for the eighteen code departments subject to the Administrative Code. Agencies not obliged to utilize the procurement facilities of the section are required to submit their purchasing rules and regulations to the Department of Finance for approval.

Printing and paper required by state agencies are purchased by the printing section of the Administrative Services Division, which also operates a multigraphing division and a paper warehouse.

Control of state property became a function of the Department of Finance in 1957. Records of all tangible property, including real estate, are kept. The director of finance is administrator of the Property Control Act and receives an accounting from the responsible officer in each state agency.

Effective January 1, 1959, the Department of Finance assumed responsibility for distribution of federal surplus property to eligible educational institutions, hospitals, and accredited civil defense organizations. This section for property utilization is entirely supported by a small service charge to recipients of federal surplus property.

Financial Institutions

In 1957 the legislature transferred from the auditor of public accounts to a new Department of Financial Institutions supervision of savings and loan associations, credit unions, currency exchanges, cemetery care trust funds, foreign exchange departments, trust departments, remittance agents, financial planning and management services, and title guarantee companies. This new department also received from the Department of Insurance supervision of consumer finance companies.

The department has chartering, investigative, and supervisory responsibility for several thousand financial institutions. It maintains an office in Chicago with 100 examiners for Cook County and the northern part of the state, and one in Springfield for the central and southern Illinois areas. The department is divided into eight separate operating divisions. It is staffed by a director, assistant director, two technical advisers, general office supervisor, supervisor of banks, and supervisors for the divisions of Abandoned Property, Consumer Finance and Installment Loan, Credit Unions, Currency Exchanges, Sales Finance Agencies, Foreign Exchange, and Title Insurance.

Each division is charged with supervisory, investigative, and enforcement responsibilities in its field. More than 5,000 institutions with revealed assets of more than $13,000,000,000 are regulated by the department.

Department officers are assisted in their responsibilities by a credit union advisory board of five members and a currency exchange advisory board of five members.

Insurance

The Department of Insurance, which regulates the activities of the insurance companies located in or operating in Illinois, originally was a division in the Department of Trade and Commerce, one of the departments organized under the Civil Administrative Code in 1917. In 1933 the legislature, cognizant of the needs of this fast-growing industry, made the division a department responsible directly to the governor.

In 1937 the legislature, with the assistance of the director of insurance, codified insurance laws.

The responsibilities of the Department of Insurance are carried out by a director, an assistant director who heads the Chicago office of the department, technical advisers in Springfield and Chicago, a chief deputy, a chief actuary, supervisors of the fourteen divisions, and five counseling deputies, three in Springfield and two in Chicago. There are also a chief examiner and an assistant chief examiner in the Chicago office.

The Life Division supervises the several hundred life and accident and health companies licensed to do business in Illinois. This includes all types of legal reserve companies, assessment companies, mutual benefit associations, and burial insurance societies. Names of the other divisions describe their duties. They are the Fraternal Division, the Fire and Casualty Division, the Policy Examination Division, the Claims Division, the Tax, Audit and Securities Division, the Rating Division, the License Division, the Company Examination Division, the Bail Bond Division, the Liquidation Division, the Public Employees Pension Fund Division, the Legal Division, and the Administrative Division. An advisory committee of five members assists in administration.

Labor

The Department of Labor was organized in 1917, one of the original nine administrative code departments. It is administered by a director, an assistant director, and division heads for each of the eight divisions that share the work load of the department.

The statutes of Illinois contain fifty-four laws which relate to the state's workers. Of these, the Department of Labor is charged with administering and enforcing twenty-two, of which five are the concern of the Division of Safety Inspection and Education. These include the Health and Safety Act and specific safety rules enforced by the department; the Structural Work Law, the Compressed Air Act, the Washrooms in Certain Employments Act, and the Sanitary Standards for Butterine and Ice Cream Factories Act. The functions of the division are organized into four units—factory in-

spection, construction inspection, industrial hygiene, and safety education.

The Division of Women's and Children's Employment has responsibility and authority for enforcement of four Illinois labor laws which limit the hours, days, and conditions of employment of women and children. These are the Six Day Week Law, the Eight Hour Day for Women Law, the Child Labor Law, and the Industrial Home Work Law.

A special division regulates the activities of private employment agencies. A Statistics and Research Division provides to all divisions statistics that relate to labor and industry. A Wage Claims Section represents workers in claims for money due from employers. A Conciliation and Mediation Service referees labor-management disputes and assists them to reach agreement. It also enforces the Prevailing Wage Act. There is a Bureau of Employment Security that has overall responsibility for two divisions— Unemployment Compensation and the Illinois State Employment Service, which maintains a network of local offices and matches available jobs and labor. The first of these divisions collects contributions from employers and pays benefits to persons who are temporarily unemployed, administers the Illinois temporary emergency benefit program, and administers federal benefit programs within the state. The Board of Review is the final reviewing agency with respect to all appeals on claims for benefits filed under the Unemployment Compensation Act, except those arising from unemployment because of labor disputes. Its decisions are subject to judicial review.

Services of state employment offices are available not only to unemployed persons who have previously been gainfully employed, but also to those entering the labor market for the first time. It maintains a counseling service for young people seeking their first jobs, for discharged servicemen, and for persons whose job skills are no longer required. It also provides labor market information and job opportunity data for employers and workers. Aptitude and proficiency tests used by the division insure utilization of the right man in the right job and make for greater labor stability.

The Illinois Office of Economic Opportunity was established in October of 1964 to bring to the state the benefits of the Federal Economic Opportunity Act. It became a part of the Department of Labor in 1967. This office provides a wide range of programs to combat the causes of poverty. These programs include education and training, loans, grants, and the establishment of service agencies with both professional and volunteer staffs. The numerous programs and projects include: Head Start, Community Action, Neighborhood Youth Corps, Adult Basic Education, Work Experience Projects, Rural Loans, Small Business Loans, Job Corps Centers, College Work Study, Volunteers in Service to America (VISTA), and related programs. The Illinois Office of Economic Opportunity has established offices in Springfield, Carbondale, and Chicago to coordinate the efforts across the state.

Mental Health

Mental health in Illinois originally was the responsibility of a Department of Public Welfare created under the Civil Administrative Code in 1917. In 1962 that department's functions were divided between two new departments—Mental Health and Children and Family Services. Transfer of nonmental health functions of the department became effective January 1, 1964. The work of the department is almost exclusively concerned with operation of the thirteen state hospitals, including the Illinois Security Hospital for dangerously disturbed persons and the Chicago Mental Health Center; five institutions for the mentally retarded; and statewide diagnostic centers. The administrative personnel includes a director, an assistant to the director, an administrative assistant, an administrator of public information, and three deputy directors heading as many services. Two advisory boards are appointed by the governor, and an out-of-state board is available for special consultations. There are also several advisory committees.

In order to bring services of the department as close as possible to those persons who require help, the state is divided into eight zones: Rockford, Chicago North, Chicago South, Peoria, Springfield, Decatur-Champaign, East St. Louis, and Carbondale. In these zones, since 1962 when federal funds became available for community health centers to be constructed over a three-year period, have been built seven diagnostic centers, each named for a pioneer in mental care in Illinois: H. Douglas Singer Zone Center at Rockford; Charles F. Read

Zone Center, Chicago North; John J. Madden Zone Center, Chicago South; George A. Zeller Zone Center, Peoria; Andrew McFarland Zone Center, Springfield; Adolph Meyer Zone Center, Decatur; and Herman M. Adler Zone Center in Champaign. In-patient and out-patient services are available.

To provide more facilities for the care of the mentally retarded the Warren G. Murray Children's Center in Centralia and the A. L. Bowen Children's Center in Harrisburg have been built, opening in 1964 and 1965 respectively. Of the total cost of approximately $300,000,000 for these nine beautifully designed and landscaped one-story establishments, the state of Illinois supplied $150,000,000 and the federal government a like amount.

Illinois established the first institute for juvenile research in the country in 1909 under direction of Dr. William Healy. It has been under the supervision of the department since it was created as a division of the Department of Public Welfare in 1917. In addition to the research institute, the Department of Mental Health also supervises the Illinois State Psychiatric Institute and the Illinois State Pediatric Institute, which was founded in 1962 for the study of mental retardation. The department also provides community services, licenses private facilities, and operates facilities for the cure of alcoholism and drug addiction.

Mines and Minerals

The Illinois Department of Mines and Minerals is one of the original nine code departments organized in 1917. It has responsibility for inspection of mines, analysis of coal quality, certification of miners, oversight of mine safety provisions, operation of mine rescue stations, and control of oil and gas production. Administration is the function of a director, an assistant director, and three boards—the Mining Board, the Miners' Examining Board, and the Oil and Gas Advisory Board. There is also a Division of Oil and Gas administered by a petroleum engineer and a field supervisor.

The Mining Board consists of two coal miners, two coal mine operators, and the director of the Department of Mines and Minerals, who acts as executive officer. The board operates sixteen inspection districts, an analytical laboratory, a safety division, four mine rescue stations at Springfield, Du Quoin, Benton, and Eldorado, and four mobile rescue units at the same cities.

The Miners' Examining Board consists of four members, appointed by the director and approved by the governor. This board certifies all personnel working at the face of the coal.

Fluorspar is an important mineral product of Southern Illinois, the deposits representing the nation's most important supply of the material. Fluorspar has been mined in Illinois since 1842. Mining costs relative to that of imported spar keep down production, but at any time of need output could be greatly raised.

The Division of Oil and Gas was first authorized and staffed in 1941. It is charged by law with enforcement of legislation relative to prevention of waste and dissipation of our natural resources. By strict application of the spacing law, the division prevents drilling of an excessive number of wells in any area. The division acts as arbiter in disputes among operators, landowners, and royalty owners. The Oil and Gas Advisory Board is appointed by the governor. Four members are drawn from the industry. The fifth is the director of the Department of Mines and Minerals, who acts as chairman.

Personnel

The state of Illinois has more than 46,000 employees, exclusive of the staffs of the state universities. The Department of Personnel, which was authorized under the Personnel Code of 1955, is charged with selecting, training, and classifying state employees. While retaining merit principles embodied in the Civil Service Act of 1905, the Personnel Code recognizes added factors as vital to sound personnel management. These include equal pay for equal work and equal opportunity for all, regardless of race, religion, or politics.

Administrative personnel of the department include a director, an assistant director, an executive assistant to the director, a technical adviser, and chiefs of the Employee Relations Office, the Training Office, Classification and Pay division, Recruitment and Selection division, Administrative and Services division, and the Transactions and General Services sections.

The department is established in three jurisdictions; classification and pay, merit and fitness, and conditions of employment. A nine-member board appointed by the governor advises the personnel director, the Civil Service Commission, and the governor on personnel policies.

Public Aid

The Department of Public Aid, which administers the state's public assistance programs, has its headquarters in Springfield. Responsibility for the overall administration of the public aid programs is delegated by the governor to the director of the Department of Public Aid.

The federally aided assistance programs— Old Age Assistance, Blind Assistance, Disability Assistance, Aid to Dependent Children, and Medical Assistance—are administered through 102 county departments. The Cook County Department of Public Aid has district offices in locations accessible to residents of each district.

The department director is assisted in discharging administrative and supervisory responsibilities by a state-level staff of eight divisions: Accounting and Data Processing, Administrative Services, Community Services, Downstate Operations, Medical Services, Program Development, Special Investigations, and Special Services.

Other duties of the department include: allocation of state funds to qualifying township and county units to finance general assistance programs, and the administration of the food commodity distribution and food stamp programs, in cooperation with the United States Department of Agriculture.

In addition to providing material help to needy persons of the state, the department offers education, vocational training, and employment placement programs designed to return recipients to self-support. A comprehensive range of social services is available to help recipients overcome problems which limit their capacities to enjoy a normal, productive role in community life.

Public Health

The Department of Public Health is one of the original nine code departments organized in 1917. The director is the chief executive officer of the department, and there are two assistants to the director, administrative and medical. Functions of the department are organized into ten divisions, with the chiefs of the divisions forming a cabinet to assist the director in the establishment of policies and programs pertinent to the obligations of the department.

The divisions are General Administration, Preventive Medicine, Hospitals and Chronic

Illness, Laboratories, Sanitary Engineering, Tuberculosis Control, Local Health Services, Dental Health, Foods and Dairies, and Milk Control. Specific state statutes and services which have been found essential are administered through these divisions.

Basically the department provides services which the individual cannot provide for himself, develops understanding in people on what they need to do for themselves and what can be accomplished cooperatively in their communities, and gives the public assurance that its efforts will be backed by the department. The department seeks to keep the people abreast of health conditions through timely information and advice through news media, exhibits, brochures, films, and a monthly publication.

Certain segments of the population, such as low income groups, dependent age groups (the "over sixty-five" and the "under fifteen"), and mothers and infants, receive special attention from the department. A measure of its effectiveness has been the reduction in infant deaths from about 70 per 1,000 live births in 1925 to the present rate of about 25 per 1,000.

Preventive medical services of the department have greatly expanded in the last decade, due in part to advances in medical knowledge as well as collaboration with other agencies in health-related programs. Clinical studies have pointed the way to dietary control of phenylketonuria, a hereditary disorder often causing mental retardation. The introduction of an oral polio vaccine marked a spectacular decline in this highly contagious disease. Measles, another disease often causing serious complications, also showed a dramatic decrease after a vaccine was made available for widespread use. Many of the diseases which were still present in excessive numbers a quarter of a century ago, such as diphtheria, typhoid, tetanus, and smallpox, are no longer a menace thanks to educational programs, quality control of drinking water, and distribution of preventive vaccines.

An immediate problem for department attention is the spread of infectious syphilis and gonorrhea among teenagers and young adults. Cooperation of the United States Public Health Service with the Illinois Department of Public Health is making possible a visitation program to all physicians in the state to stress the importance of reporting *all* cases encountered, so that contacts may be traced to halt the spread of the disease. Public educational programs have also been activated.

Deaths among children from accidental poisoning have been in constant decline since the Uniform Hazardous Substances Labeling Act gave the department a needed tool for control of poisons commercially available in many common household products.

In the schools, an expanding health program is achieving excellent results. Vision and hearing conservation coordinators on the public health staff began programing statewide efforts in these fields in 1963 and 1964, respectively. In addition, school nurses and classroom teachers throughout the state are now being offered in-service training programs on dental health.

The veterinary health program was reinstated in 1963, with emphasis on the study of transmission of disease from animals to man. Current studies under way include leptospirosis and problems of occupational infections among plant workers. Statutes relating to rabies are being revised in accordance with current knowledge of the disease.

Laboratory services have greatly increased due to innovations in diagnostic procedures. There are department laboratories available to all sections of the state. They are located in Chicago, Springfield, Champaign, Carbondale, East St. Louis, and Rock Island.

Major activities of the department are embodied in programs designed to abate and control pollution of water, streams, and air, due to natural as well as man-made hazards in the environment. These hazards include the increasing use of radiological and nuclear fission materials. The department administers extensive surveillance, inspectional and licensing programs in areas that concern people's health.

All eligible facilities which participate in the medicare program in the state must be approved by the department and it actively encourages the establishment of more and better facilities and services in areas where they are needed.

The department administers grant-in-aid funds to thirty-two counties and nine cities or districts where full-time public health programs are in operation. Expansion of local services is a worthwile goal of the department. Six boards and commissions aid in program planning.

Public Safety

The Department of Public Safety, created by legislation in 1941, basically is charged with the overall safety of citizens of Illinois. To accomplish its mission it has responsibilities in law enforcement, prevention of crime, control and rehabilitation of offenders, granting of paroles, supervision of parolees, safety on the highways, safety from fire and explosion, and control of traffic in narcotics and dangerous drugs.

The department is administered by a director, who is provided with an assistant director, a legal adviser, an administrative assistant, a statistical consultant, and sufficient personnel to man the several divisions, bureaus, and boards that share the work load. These include Prisons, State Highway Police, State Police Merit Board which screens and approves candidates for the 1,200-man force, the Parole and Pardon Board, Bureau of Criminal Identification and Investigation, and the divisions of the Criminologist, Supervision of Parolees, Fire Prevention, Boiler Inspection, and Narcotic Control.

The department carries on a continuous campaign for the reduction of highway accidents and extends complete cooperation to all law enforcement agencies in the state on all levels—city, township, county—in matters involving law enforcement. In fact, approximately 80 per cent of the work of one bureau, that of Criminal Identification and Investigation, is at the service of city and county law enforcement units in need of expert technological assistance.

The general offices of the department are in the State Armory in Springfield. Offices also are maintained in the State of Illinois Building, Chicago.

Centralized accounting, personnel and payroll, budgeting and related records are maintained in the Springfield offices. All procedures involving funds, expenditures, revenues, and other essential items are supervised in Springfield. Procedures are under constant review as are budgeted items, all of which are subject to regular audit.

As rehabilitation of the 8,900 inmates is the major objective of the penitentiary system, academic education, training in trades and crafts, and materials production for use of other tax-supported agencies in Illinois receive considerable attention of departmental personnel.

Stateville prison near Joliet is a $120,000,000 plant with a 2,200-acre farm on which inmates produce much of the food they consume. At Stateville are factories producing mattresses, textiles, clothing, shoes, soap, sheet metal products of various kinds,

concrete products, and others. At the same time, inmates may receive instruction in a variety of trades and crafts to fit them for the eventual return to a free society. Approximately fifty trades or crafts are taught, and educational facilities are available through the third year of college. Stateville's population is just under 4,200.

Menard Branch penitentiary, at Chester, about sixty-five miles south of East St. Louis, is another maximum security prison. A diagnostic depot is maintained at Menard and a modern psychiatric treatment facility also is in operation. Menard provides instruction in many crafts and trades and education of its inmates from early grade school level through two years of college. The large farm there provides agricultural training and therapeutic assistance for the inmates and supplies the institution with much of its food and dairy products. At Menard many of the inmates are training in the use of heavy machinery used in clearing land, building drainage ditches, and restoring formerly unusable land to useful purposes by proper drainage and in other ways. Approximately 2,200 inmates are housed at Menard.

Improvable-type offenders are usually housed in the branch of the penitentiary system at Pontiac, where approximately 1,200 youthful offenders are receiving training in most of the crafts and trades available at the other two penitentiary branches, Stateville and Menard. Schooling also is an important aspect of rehabilitation at Pontiac. A large sign shop there produces many of the road and other signs which appear on Illinois highways.

The Illinois State Farm near Vandalia is for short-term misdemeanants whose sentences usually are from sixty days to twelve months. Inmates are assigned to services in and about the institution as well as in the farming and dairying operations. The state farm has one of the finest herds of dairy cattle in the state, both private and institutional.

At Vienna, a new concept in minimal security is being tried where the inmates are prepared for reintegration into free society. At Vienna the inmates work an eight-hour day so they can become accustomed to do as they will on the outside, and are thereby prepared to fulfill their obligations when released. Vienna is built without the usual signs of a prison as it has no walls, gun turrets, or other prison appurtenances.

The sixth major correctional institution is the State Reformatory for Women near Dwight, the only Illinois institution for adult female offenders. The reformatory has an average population of approximately 120 who are trained in home economics and commercial studies and prepared for their return to either business and commercial activities or to their own homes.

Many professional men and women, as well as others less skilled but trained for specific tasks, are used in the penal institutions in the quest for rehabilitation of the individual and his restoration to society.

At the beginning of incarceration, the individual is examined by sociologists, clinical psychologists, and psychiatrists who are assigned to the state criminologist's staff. This staff is engaged in separating inmates into groups with similar training needs; the evaluation of inmates' progress prior to release, and the professional assistance of inmates with mental health and behavior problems. An internship program for university graduates and statistical research and reporting are other functions of the Criminologist Division.

Inmates ready to seek release come before the Illinois Parole and Pardon Board, comprising seven members appointed by the governor. The board has the responsibility for approving or denying paroles and for recommendation of pardons to the governor. Hundreds of appeals are heard by the board annually.

Following parole, supervision is maintained by the Division of Supervision of Parolees, and help is accorded the paroled inmate to assist him in reestablishing himself in the community. The parole officer often finds homes and employment for those about to be paroled.

The division of the department which most closely relates to the public is the 1,200-man state police, started about forty years ago with 100 men. The division maintains a large fleet of modern automobiles, all radio equipped; four planes, two mobile communications centers, and other equipment. All maintain close liaison with the fifteen districts and six subdistricts from which they operate, as well as with the central office. The police enforce the state's motor vehicle laws, work with law enforcement agencies throughout the state,

maintain a special crime section, and, because of its special needs, maintain police training academies.

To insure professionalism in the selection of men for the state police, a State Police Merit Board has been established, whose three members are appointed by the governor. These men are the sole judges of the fitness of a candidate for the state police, and the board also conducts hearings into complaints filed against the police.

The Bureau of Criminal Identification and Investigation is an agency which cooperatively works with city, township, and county law enforcement agencies in criminal matters. The bureau maintains records of crimes and criminals, and provides a modern laboratory for use of all law enforcement officials throughout the state. The staff in this office is always available on request of law enforcement officials anywhere in the state.

Three other important safety functions are directed by the Department of Public Safety: fire prevention, narcotic control, and boiler inspection.

The Division of Fire Prevention is engaged in highly technical work in the field of fire prevention, the detection of arson, and in providing information for fire departments in the field of fire prevention. One of the major functions of the division is that of cooperation with the offices of the various state departments on all fire prevention matters, particularly in maintaining all possible safety measures in schools—private, parochial, and public.

The Division of Narcotic Control has become an increasingly busy agency in the department, and is concerned with the control of the illegal sale and use of drugs and narcotics. The division also is charged with enforcement of the Illinois Uniform Dangerous Drug, Device and Cosmetic Act. The division also cooperates very closely with the federal agencies involved in the control of narcotics and illicit use of drugs. The narcotic control division has become an important protective force for the public.

The Division of Boiler Inspection is charged with inspection and approval of boilers used in public and large private structures, and its major objective is the safety of those occupying the buildings. This bureau establishes rules and regulations governing the use of boilers and enforces all state statutes on the use of boilers and on boiler inspections in apartments and in commercial and business structures.

The Department of Public Works and Buildings was the center of an expanding program for hard roads when the administrative Code Act became law in 1917. In the half century since that time, it has achieved the programs outlined by a long line of governors and authorized by legislatures that have been awake to the needs of highway communications in a great agricultural state.

Today the department is principally concerned with completion of more than 1,600 miles of multiple lane limited access highways, part of the national network of more than 41,000 miles of interstate through routes. It is estimated that in another few years the interstate system will carry about a fifth of all motor vehicle traffic in the state.

In the early 1920's Illinois began a heroic effort to get out of the mud. Prior to the authorization of the interstate system in 1956, 13,000 miles of rural and another 2,000 miles of urban hard-surfaced roads had been built. These will continue to be maintained, improved, reconstructed, and augmented to accommodate the 80 per cent of traffic not using the interstate highways.

The department is staffed by a director, an assistant director, and chief engineers of three divisions. While roads represent by far the largest volume of construction and the Division of Highways requires the largest staff, the Division of Waterways and the Division of Architecture and Engineering are major enterprises in their own right. The Division of Waterways traces its lineage to the Illinois and Michigan Canal commissioners appointed by the legislature February 14, 1823, to plan and construct a canal from the Chicago River to the Illinois River and complete an all-water route from New York City to central Illinois and St. Louis. A constitutional amendment approved by the people in 1908 authorized the General Assembly to implement a proposal for a deep waterway along the route of the then obsolete Illinois and Michigan Canal. In 1911 a Rivers and Lakes Commission was formed and in 1914 the General Assembly established the Illinois Waterways Commission to build the new deep waterway. These two commissions were superseded by the Division of Waterways of the Department of Public Works and Buildings in 1917. Construction of the deep waterway was placed in the hands of a specially created Department of Purchases and Construction in 1925, a body that was

abolished in 1933 on completion of the project, and the Divison of Waterways reestablished in the Department of Public Works and Buildings.

Architectural and engineering functions for construction of state buildings of every sort are the responsibility of the Division of Architecture and Engineering, which recommends awards of construction contracts that are the responsibility of the governor, supervises construction, and performs frequent on-site inspections for the various state agencies for which the work is being done. All technical work in preparation for contracting the construction work is handled by the division, including bonding, insurance, advertising for bids, and, upon award, checking claims for payment. An office of the division is maintained in Chicago in addition to the principal one at Springfield.

Registration and Education

This department, which supervises a wide variety of state services, was among the nine original departments authorized in 1917. It is organized in six divisions, with a director, an assistant director, an administrative assistant, a superintendent of registration, and chiefs of the State Geological Survey, the Natural History Survey, the Water Survey, and the State Museum.

The General Office Division handles the administration of the department, determines policies, supervises publications, exercises fiscal control, and directs the department's legislative programs. Its offices are in Springfield, as is the state museum.

The Geological, Natural History, and Water Survey divisions are located on the campus of the University of Illinois in Urbana.

The Division of Registration, with offices in Springfield, licenses, inspects, and regulates twenty-eight occupations, trades, and professions. Its functions are exercised by examining committees, over the findings of which the director has power of veto. Licensing information is available at the Springfield headquarters of the department and at an office in the State of Illinois Building in Chicago. Approximately 300,000 licenses are issued each year.

The State Geological Survey is the agency of state government responsible for a continuing research program on the geology of Illinois. Its program and personnel policies are directed by a Board of Natural Resources and Conservation. Results of division activities are published in technical reports and maps, and basic data cataloged and made easily available to the public. A major program is the development of new uses for Illinois coal, and it has resulted in greatly increased use of this product for metallurgical coke. The survey furnishes information relative to suitable natural storage places for gas, and to new deposits of fluorspar, silica, clay products, and zinc-lead ores. The survey pioneered in the application of geological data to engineering problems. It also is the agency, in cooperation with the United States Geological Survey, for topographic mapping of the state. The educational extension program translates data developed by research into usable information for teachers, students, and the general public.

The Natural History Survey, existing for more than a century, has responsibility for control of insect pests and diseases of trees, plants, and flowers. It furnishes data on the relation of fish population to pollution in streams, maintains a continuing study of pheasant, waterfowl, and small game populations, and of disease and other factors which affect the availability of game.

The State Water Survey has the responsibility for the continuing study of the water resources of Illinois. It develops methods of water use, measurement and conservation, and, when need arises, studies ways to extend water resources in areas where the supply is becoming critical. The water survey was established in 1895 and became a division of the Department of Registration and Education in 1917. Organized to study methods of typhoid prevention, its program now encompasses available ground and surface water, water usage, development of water supplies, situation of reservoirs, quality and treatment of water, and meteorological factors affecting water resources.

Fluctuation of groundwater levels is studied through a network of 220 observation wells in 42 counties, representative of all regions of the state, with special studies at East St. Louis, Peoria, and Chicago. Studies of groundwater recharge at a few locations indicates the possibility of obtaining substantial increases in groundwater supplies. Surface water studies, hydraulic research, studies of water quality, chemistry

services, and meteorological research complete a well-rounded program of the water survey.

The Illinois State Museum in 1963 moved into a new building which is part of the complex of state facilities on the capitol grounds. This handsome structure houses what is recognized as one of the finest state-operated museums in the country. The first floor is given over to exhibits which display the natural resources of Illinois, and include extensive showings of animal life in situations that closely resemble its natural habitat. The second floor is occupied by exhibits relating to the subject of man interpreted through anthropology, particularly in Illinois. Dioramas trace the development of paleolithic man from the last ice age to the historic tribes and the early settlers of Illinois.

The museum furnishes audio-visual materials to students, and a museumobile serves 500 students daily in its continuing tours of the state. It is administered under the general direction of a board of museum advisers.

Revenue

The Department of Revenue came into existence July 1, 1943, when it assumed the tax administration functions of the Department of Finance and all duties of the State Tax Commission. It is administered by a director, an assistant director, executive officers in Springfield and Chicago, superintendent of the Property Tax Division, and chiefs of departments of Field Operations, Rules and Regulations, Miscellaneous Return Processing (liquor and cigarette taxes, motor vehicle use tax, public utility tax, hotel operators' occupation tax, and coin-operated amusement tax), Retailers' Occupation Tax Return Processing, Retailers' Occupation Tax Accounting, Assessment Section, and Audit Section.

The retailers' occupation tax, generally called the sales tax, was authorized in Illinois in 1933. It provides most of the state revenue. The use tax was established in 1955, and the 1961 session of the legislature broadened the retailers' occupation tax to overcome inequities by enacting the service occupation tax and the service use tax. The same session enacted the hotel operators' occupation tax.

The task of enforcing tax payment occupies much of the time of the department auditors, who are charged with the responsibility of determining the correct liability and of assisting taxpayers to understand their obligations to the state.

The Board of Tax Appeals acts independently of the director to provide a procedure for property tax relief.

Noncode Departments, Boards, and Commissions

Close liaison with an alert and interested citizenry and with the legislative branch of the state government is maintained by the executive branch through a number of boards and commissions having public, legislative, and executive membership. Others have only public, only executive, only legislative members, or combination of any two. There are also several executive departments and commissions outside the Civil Administrative Code which perform important functions within the executive branch of the state government. Chief among these are the Office of the Auditor General, the Illinois Civil Defense Agency, the Illinois Commerce Commission, the Court of Claims, the Illinois Board of Higher Education, the Historical Library, the Military and Naval Department, the Illinois Selective Service System, the Board of Vocational Education and Rehabilitation, and the Youth Commission.

The Department of Audits was established by the General Assembly in 1957. To this department were given all the post-audit functions formerly assigned to the auditor of public accounts. The office is administered by an auditor general, an assistant auditor general, and an advisory board of citizens familiar with public-accounting practices. The auditor general is appointed by the governor for a term of six years. He must be a certified public accountant licensed to practice in Illinois with at least seven years experience in the practice of public, industrial, or governmental accounting. It is the duty of the auditor general to audit the transactions of all departments of the state government at least biennially, and oftener if the auditor general feels it is needed. Copies of the audits are furnished to the governor, the Budgetary Commission, and the Illinois Legislative Audit Commission.

Administration of the Military and Naval Department of Illinois is a function of the adjutant general, who serves as chief of staff. He is aided by an assistant adjutant general, a United States property and fiscal officer, and a state maintenance officer. The governor is commander-in-chief of the

National Guard and the Illinois Naval Militia.

The Army National Guard consists of one infantry division and two infantry battalions attached for administration, supply, and training; one air defense Nike-Hercules battalion, one ordnance battalion, and state headquarters and headquarters detachment. The Air National Guard consists of a headquarters, one air refueling wing, two tactical groups, one ground electronics engineering installation, one communications squadron, and the air force band. The Naval Militia has a brigade staff, two battalion staffs, and seven divisions.

The 1st Missile Battalion of the 202nd Artillery (air defense) of the National Guard mans five Nike-Hercules sites in the Chicago-Gary air defense area, and is an integral part of the air defense system of the continental United States.

The Illinois Civil Defense Agency is administered by a director, a chief of administration and personnel, a deputy chief, chiefs of plans and training, field services, shelter services, communications, and public affairs, a resources control officer, a state police liaison officer, a surplus property officer, and a liaison officer. The adjutant general, directors of twelve of the state's eighteen administration departments, and fifteen public members act as a committee to assist the director in plans and administration. All counties and all cities of more than 1,000 population have been required to prepare plans which enable local government to handle the problems associated with an air attack. State emergency services are available, under the direction of the governor, to assist local efforts where possible and to channel federal assistance to areas most in need of such help. The counties of the state are grouped in ten mutual aid areas where the greatest benefits can be enjoyed. A training program is in effect which embraces all code departments that have any connection with civil defense.

The Illinois Selective Service System, an arm of the federal government in Illinois, is administered by a director appointed by the President of the United States on recommendation of the governor. Illinois state headquarters supervises 217 local boards and 3 appeal boards. Members of these boards serve without pay. During the decade of the fifties, Illinois furnished about 7 per cent of all draftees in the United

States, in addition to many enlistments. The decade of the sixties sees the ratio maintained. The Selective Service, in addition to its classification and call-up duties, monitors the standby reserve of the army, navy, and air force.

The Commission of Banks and Trust Companies was authorized by legislation in 1965 and approved by referendum at the general election of November 8, 1966, to assume all powers of the Division of Banks in the Department of Financial Institutions on January 1, 1967. The commission is staffed by a commissioner, a deputy commissioner in Chicago, a deputy commissioner in Springfield, and more than 100 supervisory and clerical personnel who formerly made up the staff of the Division of Banks.

The commission is advised by a Board of Banks and Trust Companies, of which the commissioner is chairman. The board is composed of six bankers and four non-professional members appointed by the governor. The commissioner has power to move rapidly to curb bank law violators. He may also issue new banking regulations, subject to the approval of the board.

The Illinois Commerce Commission regulates several thousand utility companies selling their services in Illinois. They include telephone, electric, gas, water, heating, railroad, street railway, gas pipeline, water pipeline, express and sleeping car companies, motor carriers, public grain elevators, public warehouses, wharf service facilities, airline and sewage companies. Municipally owned utilities are not under the jurisdiction of the commission. The commission is advised by a committee of five members. The primary duty of the commission is to see that every citizen of Illinois using utilities receives continually safe, efficient, and uninterrupted services at reasonable prices. The commission watches the financial soundness of the companies in order to assure continuity of service.

The Board of Higher Education was established by an act of the General Assembly, approved by the governor August 22, 1961. The board is composed of eight members appointed by the governor by and with the consent of the Illinois Senate, the chairmen of the boards of trustees of the University of Illinois and Southern Illinois University, the boards of governors of state universities, the Junior

College Board, and the superintendent of public instruction. The act gave the board three specific powers:

1. To analyze all university budget requests and to report, by February 1 of each legislative year, its recommendations concerning them to the governor, the General Assembly, and their respective budget agencies. This power is advisory.

2. To approve or disapprove all new programs of instruction, research, or service before any university may initiate them. This is a substantive power. No governing board or state university may institute a new branch, department, degree, or any other major program except by approval of the Board of Higher Education.

3. To develop a master plan for higher education in Illinois for the next dozen years.

Assisting the board in its studies and recommendations are three advisory committees, one of distinguished citizens, one of faculty members elected by their peers in all types of institutions, and one of sixteen college and university presidents, public and private.

The Board of Vocational Education and Rehabilitation includes six public members appointed by the governor by and with the consent of the Illinois Senate, the superintendent of public instruction, and directors of five code departments, Agriculture, Labor, Mental Health, Public Health, and Registration and Education. Divisions, each with a chief and one or more supervisors, include Agricultural Education, Business and Distributive Education, Technical Education, Trade and Industrial Education, Home Economics Education, Vocational Guidance, Manpower Training and Area Development, Research, and Statistics. The Division of Vocational Rehabilitation has responsibility for administering a program initiated by the Congress, which is financed by matching state and federal funds. This division is staffed by a director, assistant director, administrative assistant, and five deputy directors, each assigned to special areas of service. There is a staff of 42 professional persons, 8 regional supervisors, 165 counselors, and 246 clerical personnel. A special section relating to social security payments and the "disability freeze" designed by Congress to protect benefit rights of persons in employment covered by Old Age and Survivors Insurance is entirely financed by federal funds. This section is staffed by 7 persons in supervisory positions, 48 disability claims examiners, 15 medical consultants, and 53 clerical personnel.

In 1961 the Illinois legislature enacted the Fair Employment Practices Law, which established the right to equality of employment opportunity in Illinois and created a commission to help bring about fulfillment of this right. The commission has responsibility for enforcement of the act and punishment of violators. It consists of a chairman, four commissioners, an executive director, a Springfield office director, a director of field activities and sufficient investigative and clerical personnel to assure that every complaint of discrimination because of race, color, religion, national origin, or ancestry be properly studied.

The Illinois Toll Highway Commission of three members, with the governor, director of public works, and attorney general serving ex-officio, administers the operation of 187 miles of toll road which skirt Chicago from the Indiana line to the Wisconsin border, with branches to Aurora and the Wisconsin line near Beloit. Operation of the toll highway is entirely self-supporting. State police who patrol the lanes are paid out of highway income and the commission furnishes the patrol cars and microwave communications systems required.

The Illinois Veterans Commission was established in 1945 to assist veterans, their dependents and survivors in securing those benefits due them as the result of military service. The commission has four administrative members, a chairman, an administrator, an assistant administrator, and an administrative assistant. Members of the commission are appointed by the governor by and with the consent of the Illinois Senate.

The Illinois State Historical Library makes available to the public historical material, much of it not to be found elsewhere in the state. The library was chartered by the General Assembly in 1889 "to procure all books, pamphlets, manuscripts, monographs, writings, and other material of historic interest and useful to the historian, bearing upon political, physical, religious, or social history of Illinois from the earliest known period of time."

The library now has more than 100,000 bound volumes, 1,500,000 manuscripts, and the finest collection of newspapers in the state. The library has a complete set of laws relating to the state from Henning's *Statutes at Large of Virginia* (of which Illinois was briefly a county) to texts of all

laws passed by the General Assembly in its session of 1967. Precious volumes in the field of Lincolniana, the Civil War, the Black Hawk War, the Mormon troubles in Nauvoo, and many biographical records not obtainable elsewhere are on its shelves. The manuscript collection contains the papers of twelve governors. Many manuscripts in other libraries, including Robert Todd Lincoln's collections of his father's papers, have been microfilmed. More than 28,000 reels of microfilm hold the library's collection of Illinois newspapers.

When the General Assembly, in 1953, authorized the creation of a Youth Commission, it took one more step of the many that have kept Illinois a leader in the treatment and care of straying children. Illinois had the first juvenile court in the world, the first institute for juvenile research, and, in 1954, established the first commission which would take from the courts the final decision as to where and how every juvenile offender should be treated. From that time courts have discontinued committing boys under the age of seventeen and girls under the age of eighteen to specific institutions. All commitments are made to the commission and the youngsters at odds with the law are studied at the reception and diagnostic centers at Joliet (boys) and Geneva (girls), where they may be paroled to their parents, placed in foster homes, or committed to one of the forestry camps of the commission, to the Illinois Training School for Boys at St. Charles, the Illinois Training School for Girls at Geneva, or the State Industrial School for Boys at Sheridan.

The commission is administered by a chairman and four commissioners, two division superintendents, and two advisory boards with legislative and public members, one board assisting the Division of Community Services, and the other, the Division of Correctional Services. In addition to the schools the commission operates twelve forestry camps, two of them organized to receive and serve younger boys.

The Division of Community Services is concerned with delinquency prevention, concentrating its efforts largely in deprived or problem neighborhoods. As many as 5,000 adults have served annually in neighborhood programs for delinquency prevention. Children who find themselves at cross-purposes with the law frequently are referred to neighborhood organizations for help that in many cases makes their committal to the Youth Commission unnecessary.

Not only the children who have taken a first step toward delinquency are a concern of the state of Illinois. The crippled, the mentally retarded, the brilliant-minded child born into deprived surroundings, the average healthy youngster are the concern of the Illinois Commission on Children. Membership of this body includes clergymen, educators, physicians, psychologists, sociologists, legislators, businessmen, representative members of many communities, directors of five code departments, the superintendent of public instruction, the chairman of the Youth Commission, the director of the Illinois services for crippled children, and the director of vocational rehabilitation. The work of this commission is administered by an executive committee of the chairman and three members, and by an executive director.

The constitution of 1870 provides in Section 26 of Article IV that the state of Illinois shall never be made defendant in any court of law or equity. Because of this provision, it early became evident that some agency should be created to consider just claims against the state of Illinois and, in 1877, a commission on claims was authorized by the General Assembly with one justice of the Illinois Supreme Court as president of the commission and two judges of the circuit courts as associates, the judges to be assigned by the chief justice of the Illinois Supreme Court. In 1881 Alfred M. Craig, chief justice, refused to appoint members to the commission on the grounds that the commission was not a part of the judicial system of Illinois and that it would be improper for members of the court to serve as members of the commission.

The commission was inactive until 1889, when the legislature empowered the governor by and with the consent of the Senate to appoint a Commission of Claims of three members "learned in the law and experienced in its practice" not more than two of whom could be members of the same political party. In 1903 the legislature replaced the commission with a Court of Claims, appointed in the same manner as the commission. In 1917, with the advent of the Lowden Administrative Code, the old court was abolished and a new one set up appointed as before, consisting of a chief justice and two judges. The act, approved June 25, 1917, defined the duties of the justices, described the claims that might be brought before them and named the secretary of state as secretary of the court. New legislation passed by the General Assembly and filed without approval of the governor on July 17, 1945, made important changes in the procedures and prerogatives of the court, such as limiting awards for damages in a case sounding in tort (negligence) and bringing awards for personal injuries in line with the compensation section of the Workmen's Occupational Diseases Act. In 1951 the term of office for judges of the Court of Claims was fixed at six years.

Other boards and commissions of the state with public and/or professional members only, with advisory duties and in many cases administrative and enforcement functions, include the Illinois Armory Board, the Illinois Arts Council, the State Athletic Commission, the Beekeepers' Commission, the Illinois Building Authority, the Chicago Transit Authority, the Civil Service Commission, the State Housing Board, the Human Relations Commission, the Industrial Commission, the Illinois Liquor Control Commission, the Medical Center Commission, the Illinois Nature Preserves Commission, the Illinois Racing Board, the Savings and Loan Commission, the Illinois State Scholarship Commission, the Spanish-American War Veterans Commission, and the Commission on Uniformity of Legislation in the United States.

Boards and commissions composed of members of the executive department, public and/or professional members include the Illinois Air Pollution Control Board, composed of the director of the Department of Public Health and public members; Metropolitan Fair and Exposition Authority, with the governor, the mayor of Chicago, and public members; the Illinois Municipal Retirement Fund, with the state treasurer and public members; the School Building Commission, with the superintendent of public instruction, the director of finance, and public members; the State Employees Retirement System, with public members; the Sanitary Water Board, with public members; and the Teachers' Retirement System, with the superintendent of public instruction and public members.

Boards and commissions having members of the legislative department, public and/or professional members include the American Heritage Commission, the Cities and Villages

Municipal Problems Commission, the County Problems Commission, the Crime Investigating Commission, the Election Laws Commission, the Executive Mansion Commission, the Higher Education Assisttance Corporation, the Judicial Advisory Council, the Legislative Staff Internship Sponsoring Committee, the Pension Laws Commission, the School Problems Commission, the Waterways, Drainage and Flood Control Commission, and the Chicago World's Fair of 1976 Commission.

Boards and commissions of mixed membership include the General Assembly Retirement System Trustees, with a public chairman, the state treasurer, and members of the legislature; the Intergovernmental Cooperation Committee with the governor, the chief justice of the Supreme Court, the secretary of state, and the director of finance as ex-officio members, the lieutenant governor and the speaker of the house as honorary members, and members of the General Assembly; the Judges' Retirement System Trustees, with the chief justice of the Supreme Court, the state treasurer, and three circuit judges; the Legislative Reference Bureau, with the governor, two senators, and two representatives; the Mental Health Commission, with the lieutenant governor, the director of mental health, legislative and public members; the Narcotics Advisory Council, chaired by the director of the Department of Mental Health, with legislative, private, and professional membership. The directors of the departments of Public Aid, Public Health, Public Safety, the Division of Vocational Rehabilitation, and the superintendent of police of the city of Chicago are members ex-officio. There is also the Illinois Sesquicentennial Commission, with a public chairman, the director of business and economic development, the director of the state museum, the state historian, and legislative and public members.

Boards and commissions composed entirely of legislators include the Illinois Budgetary Commission, the Legislative Audit Commission, the Illinois Legislative Council, the Motor Vehicle Laws Commission, the Senate Chambers Maintenance Commission, and the Commission to Visit and Examine State Institutions.

Those boards and commissions with only executive department membership include the Building Bond Board, the State Electrical Commission, the State Employees Housing Commission, the State Records Commission, the State Employees Group Insurance Commission, the Kaskaskia Common School Fund Trustees, and the State Tax Levy Board.

There are two Metropolitan Area Planning commissions, one for the area around Chicago and the other for the middle Mississippi Valley, which includes East St. Louis, Belleville, Alton, Edwardsville, Collinsville, and Granite City. Both are composed entirely of public members.

Eight Regional Port District boards, composed entirely of public members, administer affairs of Illinois river and lake ports: Chicago, Joliet, Little Egypt, Seneca, Shawneetown, Southwest, Tri-City, and Waukegan.

Two commissions with Illinois and Iowa membership administer toll bridges across the Mississippi at Canton and Muscatine.

Interstate agencies include the Bi-State Development Agency (Missouri and Illinois), the Ohio River Valley Water Sanitation Commission, and the Wabash Valley Interstate Commission.

Boards and commissions working directly with one code department only are described in the paragraphs devoted to that department.

10

Legislative Department

By the time Illinois was admitted to the Union as the twenty-first state a preference for bicameral legislatures was well established. In a frontier community, however, it was difficult to find a measure of differentiation for the so-called upper house. In theory it would be composed of men with superior education and cultural advantages. In a brawling backwoods community, aside from a few college-bred attorneys and a few adventurous spirits with university backgrounds, such men were hard to find. In the first dozen or more General Assemblies community leaders of equal ability might serve either in the Senate or the House of Representatives, and occasionally over a period of years a man who began with election to the Senate might well conclude his career in the legislature as a member of the House.

The first constitutional convention steered clear of any social or educational requirements in establishing criteria for the two chambers. Duties, prerogatives, and tenure of service were included, but the convention specified, on manner of choice, only that the Senate would number no more than half nor less than a third as many members as the House, which was to include no fewer than twenty-seven and no more than thirty-six members until the state attained a population of 100,000, and that a senator must be at least twenty-five years old, whereas a member of the House could sit when he had reached his twenty-first birthday. The tenure of a senator was to be four years, that of a representative two years. In order that half the Senate might be elected every two years, the constitutional convention provided for

choice by lot of half the Senate to continue in office four years and half for only two, all being eligible for reelection.

Laws could be introduced into either house of the General Assembly. Before a bill could become law it was required to obtain a majority of votes in both houses, and be signed by the governor. It could also be viewed by a council of revision composed of the governor and the four members of the Illinois Supreme Court. Should the Council of Revision rule against the provisions of a law it could be returned to the General Assembly, where it could be adopted by a simple majority of those eligible to vote in each house.

During the first thirty years of statehood the General Assembly had considerable appointive power, as well as authority to charter banks, corporations, and communities, to establish roads, and to approve toll highways, ferries, and bridges by private law.

The first General Assembly, which met at Kaskaskia October 5, 1818, consisted of fourteen senators and twenty-eight representatives. Fourteen of the fifteen counties then organized had representation in the Senate. Only Franklin County had none. In the House four counties—Gallatin, Madison, St. Clair, and White—had three seats each. Five counties—Crawford, Edwards, Pope, Randolph, and Union—held two seats each. One member from each of the other counties—Bond, Franklin, Jackson, Johnson, Monroe, and Washington—brought the total to twenty-eight. Between the first and second session, which convened January 18, 1819, John Marshall of Gallatin County resigned his seat, and John G. Daimwood was elected in his place.

When the General Assembly convened December 6, 1830, in Vandalia, there were eighteen senators and thirty-six representatives from twenty-six counties. Only two counties, neither of them yet formed when the first assembly sat, were entitled to three members in the House. They were Clark, organized in 1819, and busy Sangamon, chartered in 1821 and already thinking about getting the capital moved to Springfield.

By 1837 the "Long Nine" of which Abraham Lincoln was a moving force, had brought the capital to Springfield. Thirty-nine senators and ninety-one representatives from sixty-five counties met there November 23, 1840. Among them were a future President of the United States, Abraham Lincoln; a man who already had been governor for a short term and a United States senator, W. E. D. Ewing; one man who would be governor, William H. Bissell; and two who would be United States senators, William A. Richardson and Lyman Trumbull. Nor was this unusual, except for the office of President, for many congressmen and senators from Illinois served their political apprenticeships in the statehouse at Springfield.

Illinois' second constitution, written in convention in 1847 and ratified by the people in 1848, sharply reduced the number of legislators. It provided for a Senate of twenty-five members elected in twenty-five districts, and "a House of Representatives numbering seventy-four, until the population should amount to one million souls, when five members may be added to the House for every 500,000, until the whole numbers shall amount to 100, after which the number shall be neither increased nor diminished, to be apportioned among the several counties in proportion to the number of white inhabitants."

This was the third apportionment to be adopted in Illinois after organization of the first General Assembly. In 1836, a ratio of one Senate seat for each 7,000 white inhabitants and one seat in the House of Representatives for each 3,000 white inhabitants had resulted in election of 40 senators and 91 representatives. In 1841, so rapidly was the state growing that a ratio of a senator for every 12,000 whites and a representative for every 4,000 whites found 41 senators and 121 representatives seated.

The new constitution tried to reduce the work load of the legislature by severely restricting private legislation. How badly the provision worked is attested by the 3,351 pages of private laws compiled by the last General Assembly to meet under the constitution of 1848, whereas the second under the constitution of 1870 required only 142 pages to record all its acts.

The General Assembly that established the record for enacting private laws also was the largest in point of membership under the first two constitutions. An amendment to the constitution of 1848 permitted two senators from each of the twenty-five senatorial districts and increased the number of representatives to 179 from ninety-seven districts. Three of these, in Cook County, elected 22 members to the assembly in 1870.

The constitution of 1870 solved the problem of private legislation by making private laws illegal. It established a basic law for

incorporation of towns, cities, and villages under jurisdiction of the secretary of state, set up local boards to govern the location and construction of roads and bridges, and put corporations under the secretary of state. It also established fifty-one electoral districts for the General Assembly, with one senator and three representatives elected from each. In order to assure a representative minority in the lower house, a plan for cumulative voting was devised whereby electors could cast one vote for each of three candidates, one and a half for each of two, or three votes for any one candidate. The system generally resulted in election of not more than two representatives from one party in a district. The plan endures today after almost a century.

After the original apportionment under the constitution of 1870, there was reapportionment on the basis of the United States census in 1883, 1893, and 1901. Cook County, in 1872, had seven election districts, of which five were wholly within the city of Chicago. In 1882 seven of ten districts were wholly within the city and one entirely outside city limits. In 1893 Cook County had fifteen districts, thirteen of which were within the city of Chicago, one contained city and county areas, and one was wholly outside the city limits.

The apportionment of 1901 in Cook County, based on the census of 1900, was made to include an average district population of 94,500. The Sixth District included the city of Evanston with that part of Chicago north of the Chicago River between Racine and Western Avenue. The Thirteenth District contained the area between the Indiana line and Western Avenue from 138th Street north to 104th Street, thence east to State, north to 71st, east to Cottage Grove, north to 63rd Street, and east to the lake. The Nineteenth included the towns of Cicero, Berwyn, and Riverside with Chicago's far west side between Kinzie Street and what is now Pershing Road. The Twenty-third included the village of Oak Park with that part of Chicago between North Avenue and Chicago Avenue west of Ashland Avenue. Only the Seventh District was entirely outside the city limits of Chicago.

The apportionment of 1901 remained in force for half a century. By 1950 it had become glaringly inequitable. Parts of the state had lost population in that fifty years, while the metropolitan areas along Lake Michigan and in the vicinity of Peoria, Alton, and East St. Louis had gained heavily. District 7 in Cook County elected one senator and three representatives from a population of more than 600,000. District 41, Will and Du Page counties, with a senator and three representatives, had nearly 300,000. Lake, Boone, and McHenry counties of District 8 had about 250,000. St. Clair County, which constituted District 49, had more than 200,000. On the other hand, there were four districts with less than 80,000 population, two with 80,000 to 90,000, and two between 90,000 and 100,000. Or, to put it another way, more than 5,000,000 persons in the Chicago metropolitan area elected twenty-one senators and sixty-three representatives, while less than 3,000,000 persons in the rest of the state elected thirty senators and ninety representatives.

To correct these inequities the General Assembly, in 1953, offered a constitutional amendment increasing senatorial districts to fifty-eight, representative districts to fifty-nine, giving Cook County twenty-four senatorial and thirty representative districts, and calling for new apportionment after the 1960 census. The amendment was accepted by the people of the state at the general election in November 1954, and new districts were agreed to by the members of the General Assembly.

The designation of districts after the census of 1960 was made only after a protracted debate which was not resolved until after the 1964 election. (In that year the Senate was elected on the basis of the 1955 apportionment, and representatives were chosen at large from a statewide slate.)

The present apportionment, finally agreed upon in 1965, was made on a basis of 173,985 average population for senatorial districts and 56,956 population per seat in the House of Representatives. Under it the largest senatorial district is the fortieth, Grundy and Will counties, with a population of 213,967 and the smallest the forty-fourth, Coles, Edgar, and Vermilion counties, with a population of 161,586. Average for Cook County outside of Chicago (nine districts) is 175,480, and for the city of Chicago (twenty-one districts) is 169,067. The average for the entire county is 170,990.

Political complexion of the first General Assembly under the new apportionment,

which convened in Springfield, January 9, 1967, was: Senate, thirty-eight Republicans and twenty Democrats; House ninety-nine Republicans and seventy-eight Democrats. All senators elected in 1966 were to serve full four-year terms, and the assembly was charged with developing a plan whereby a return could be made to hold biennial elections of half the Senate no later than 1974, by which time a new apportionment hopefully will have been completed.

The legislative pattern in Illinois is similar to that of Congress. The constitution provides that every bill shall be read at large three different days in each house, that the bill and all amendments shall be printed before vote is taken, and that every bill, having passed both houses, shall be signed by the speakers thereof. Bills become law on July 1 at the end of the fiscal year in which passed, except when an emergency is deemed to exist, when by two-thirds majority in both houses a bill may become law at once. The governor may veto a bill or portions of a bill sent to him. It is then returned to the house in which it originated. The veto then may be overridden by two-thirds of members elected. A bill may also become law if the governor fails to return it within ten days (Sundays excepted) after it has been presented to him, unless the General Assembly, by adjournment, prevents its return. In such case, the bill must be filed within ten days in the office of the secretary of state with the governor's objections, or become a law.

There are twenty-five standing committees in the Senate and twenty-four in the House which consider legislation in their fields of special interest. They may or may not make recommendations on bills that have been introduced.

The standing committees of the House and Senate do not originate legislation. This is done by individual members who, since 1913, have had the assistance of the Legislative Reference Bureau, and occasionally by commissions composed of senators and representatives, with a sufficient staff. A typical body of this kind is the Motor Vehicle Laws Commission, created in 1951. The Illinois Motor Vehicle Code, adopted by the legislature in 1957, resulted from six years of research and study by this group.

The Legislative Reference Bureau furnishes aid to members of the General Assembly in the preparation of bills, amendments, and resolutions. It is composed of the governor as chairman, and the chairmen of committees on appropriations and judiciary from each house. There also is a staff, all attorneys, who give advice to members of the assembly, in a relationship which is identical with that of lawyer and client.

The Legislative Reference Bureau is not a policy-making body, nor does it suggest ideas for legislation. It is concerned with the form of bills, with their language, and with their compliance with the constitution of Illinois. It also is charged with responsibility for recommending revision, simplification, and rearrangement of existing laws. It proposes elimination of obsolete, duplicated, and unconstitutional statutes, but does not recommend substantive changes. The staff drafts proposed measures in compliance with the wishes of the legislator concerned.

Each week when the General Assembly is in session the bureau publishes a digest and legislative synopsis which is furnished to all legislators. This cumulative booklet contains in summary form each legislative proposal to the date of publication of the issue and shows its progress in committee or on various readings. After the General Assembly adjourns and the governor has acted on all bills passed, the bureau publishes a digest of laws enacted, which contains summaries of all bills that became law, and a final issue of the legislative synopsis.

In the comprehensive library of the Legislative Reference Bureau will be found Illinois session laws from territorial times, annotated statutes, Illinois digests of cases, opinions of the Illinois Supreme Court and appellate courts, the journals of the House and Senate, and from territorial times until 1923, when publication was discontinued, texts of legislative debates and the discussions of the constitutional conventions.

There is a continuing need in the General Assembly for compilation of facts and of alternative remedies in preparation for legislative action. This is met by a Legislative Council, established in 1937, and by its research organization, which consists of a director, an assistant director, an administrative assistant, a research coordinator, research assistants, and a secretary of the legislative service unit. Membership in the council includes ten senators and ten representatives, with the lieutenant governor and speaker of the House who appoint the members serving ex-officio. Formal research proposals are approved by the council in quarterly meetings. Spot research is available to legislators, and during the sessions of the General Assembly this

activity requires most of the time of the research staff. Research findings are published in official reports and in personalized memoranda.

The Legislative Budgetary Commission of fourteen members, seven each from the House and the Senate, has the responsibility of advising the governor during his preparation of the biennial budget. Public hearings on budget requests of all state agencies are held by the commission each even-numbered year, generally beginning in September and continuing until the budget is presented, most often in April of the following year. Members are conversant with the principal features of the budget and are qualified to lead discussions during the preparation of appropriation bills. The commission is empowered by law to make cost studies and management analysis of all operations of the state government. All audits made by or for the auditor general are received by the commission to be kept on file for public inspection. The commission has a duty to check license tax fees to determine that they are sufficient to cover services rendered by the state. The commission, when conducting its investigations,

Representation of counties in the Illinois General Assembly under the several apportionments, 1832–1965

	Senators		Representatives	
Year	Cook County	Other counties	Cook County	Other counties
1832	1	25	0	55
1842	2	44	3	118
1848	1	24	2	73
1854	1	24	4	71
1861	2*	23	7	78
1869	4	46	22	155
1872	7	44	21	132
1882	10	41	30	123
1893	15	36	45	108
1901	19	32	57	96
1955	24	34	90	87
1965	30	28	90	87

* In this reapportionment, Bloom, Thornton, and Worth townships were part of the Twenty-third District, which included Boone, Lake, McHenry, and Winnebago counties. The Twenty-fourth District included a small part of Lake County. The Twenty-fifth District was entirely in Cook County.

Political complexion of the Illinois General Assembly, 1880–1968 (count as of opening session)

Election year	Gov. and lt. gov.	Senate Rep.	Senate Dem.	Senate Other	House Rep.	House Dem.	House Other
1880	Rep.	32	18	1 (Soc.)	82	71	
1882	Rep.	31	20		77	75	1 (Ind.)
1884	Rep.	26	25		76	76	1 (Ind.)
1886	Rep.	32	18	1 (Labor)	79	64	9 (Labor), 1 (Proh.)
1888	Rep.	35	15	1 (Labor)	82	70	1 (Ind.)
1890	Rep.	27	24		73	77	3 (Farmers' Alliance)
1892	Dem.	22	29		75	78	
1894	Dem.	33	18		92	61	
1896	Rep.	39	11	1 (Peoples)	89	62	2 (Peoples)
1898	Rep.	34	16	1 (Peoples)	81	71	1 (Proh.)
1900	Rep.	32	19		81	72	
1902	Rep.	36	15		88	62	2 (Pub. Ownership), 1 (Proh.)
1904	Rep.	41	10		91	57	3 (Proh.), 2 (Soc.)
1906	Rep.	44	7		90	60	3 (Proh.)
1908	Rep.	38	13		88	65	
1910	Rep.	34	17		82	68	1 (Proh.), 2 (Ind.)
1912	Dem.	25	24	2 (Prog.)	52	71	27 (Prog.), 3 (Soc.)
1914	Dem.	25	25	1 (Prog.)	79	70	1 (Ind.), 1 (Prog.), 2 (Soc.)
1916	Rep.	33	18		85	67	1 (Ind.)
1918	Rep.	34	17		90	63	
1920	Rep.	43	8		95	58	
1922	Rep.	42	9		89	63	1 (Ind.)
1924	Rep.	38	13		94	59	
1926	Rep.	41	10		93	60	
1928	Rep.	40	11		91	62	
1930	Rep.	33	18		81	72	
1932	Dem.	18	33		73	80	
1934	Dem.	16	35		69	84	
1936	Dem.	17	34		67	86	
1938	Dem.	20	31		80	73	
1940	Rep.	28	23		79	74	
1942	Rep.	28	23		84	69	
1944	Rep.	34	17		78	75	
1946	Rep.	37	14		87	66	
1948	Dem.	33	18		74	79	
1950	Dem.	31	20		84	69	
1952	Rep.	38	13		84	69	
1954	Rep.	32	19		79	74	
1956*	Rep.	38	20		94	83	
1958	Rep.	34	24		85	92	
1960	Dem.	31	27		89	88	
1962	Dem.	35	23		90	87	
1964†	Dem.	33	25		59	118	
1966	Dem.	38	20		99	78	
1968	Rep. (gov.) Dem. (lt. gov.)	38	20		94	83	

* Senatorial districts increased to 58, representative to 59.

† Reapportionment failing, representatives were elected from the state at large.

has the right to compel attendance and examine under oath any person connected directly or indirectly with the fiscal transactions of any state agency.

The Legislative Audit Commission of five senators and five representatives checks the propriety and legality of expenditures made from state funds. The commission is charged with responsibility to ascertain facts, review reports, and make recommendations to the General Assembly concerning the use of money appropriated by the

legislature, and to audit annually the office of the auditor general. The staff of the commission, under an executive director, makes an independent analysis of each audit performed by or for the auditor general. This report is submitted to the commission, and the commission in return makes an annual report to the General Assembly relating to its findings and recommendations.

Legislative accomplishments, 1907–68

Session dates	Bills introduced			Enacted into law	Vetoed	Vetoed in part	Filed without approval
	Senate	House	Total				
Jan. 9 to May 16, 1907 ; Oct. 8, 1907, to May 23, 1908 (one session)	627	966	1,593	272	25	6	9
Jan. 6 to June 4, 1909	528	740	1,268	220	40	0	8
1Dec. 14, 1909, to March 3, 1910	58	47	105	19	4	0	0
Jan. 4 to June 1, 1911	500	677	1,177	255	22	0	0
1June 14 to Nov. 14, 1911	11	2	13	3	0	0	0
2March 26 to June 5, 1912	29	31	60	12	0	0	1
3April 24 to June 5, 1912	9	3	12	5	0	0	0
Jan. 8 to June 30, 1913	695	922	1,617	218	24	0	3
Jan. 6 to June 30, 1915	554	994	1,548	293	22	0	7
1Nov. 22, 1915, to May 10, 1916	51	52	103	35	2	0	0
2Jan. 11 to Feb. 14, 1916	34	29	63	16	0	0	0
Jan. 3 to June 29, 1917	612	1,041	1,653	338	69	0	70
Jan. 8 to June 30, 1919	580	763	1,343	429	39	0	23
Jan. 5 to June 30, 1921	535	868	1,403	318	43	0	17
Jan. 3 to June 30, 1923	556	848	1,404	317	41	0	14
Jan. 7 to June 30, 1925	532	683	1,215	278	24	0	23
Jan. 5 to June 30, 1927	614	758	1,372	446	32	0	6
1Jan. 10 to Feb. 16, 1928	40	41	81	30	0	0	0
2May 15 to June 6, 1928	20	15	35	8	0	0	0
3June 18 to June 22, 1928	12	10	22	6	0	0	0
Jan. 9 to June 20, 1929	547	819	1,366	417	33	0	2
1May 12 to June 25, 1930	40	43	83	39	0	0	11
Jan. 27 to June 30, 1931	769	1,262	2,031	440	52	0	5
1Nov. 5, 1931, to May 3, 1932	187	334	521	60	0	0	2
2Jan. 19 to May 3, 1932	1	20	21	3	0	0	0
3Feb. 1 to May 3, 1932	45	67	112	16	0	0	0
4Sept. 7 to Dec. 21, 1932	50	53	103	19	1	0	1
Jan. 4 to July 1, 1933	791	1,098	1,889	493	51	0	29
1Nov. 3 to Nov. 9, 1933	32	51	83	26	2	0	1
2Nov. 22, 1933, to May 10, 1934	41	40	81	9	2	0	1
3Feb. 13 to May 11, 1934	92	177	269	70	1	0	5
4Nov. 19 to Nov. 23, 1934	4	4	8	4	0	0	0

Session dates	Bills introduced			Enacted into law	Vetoed	Vetoed in part	Filed without approval
	Senate	House	Total				
Jan. 8 to June 29, 1935	670	1,168	1,838	563	47	0	55
[1]Oct. 28, 1935, to March 6, 1936	67	130	197	79	4	2	5
[2]Jan. 8 to Dec. 10, 1936	51	100	151	46	2	0	2
[3]Feb. 5 to March 6, 1936	18	26	44	15	0	0	2
[4]May 19 to June 19, 1936	41	52	93	24	0	0	3
Jan. 1 to June 30, 1937	535	1,079	1,614	341	62	7	45
[1]May 20 to July 1, 1938	67	95	162	43	2	0	3
[2]June 23 to July 1, 1938	3	6	9	7	0	0	0
Jan. 4 to June 30, 1939	631	1,128	1,759	421	53	6	95
[1]April 30 to June 5, 1940	20	41	61	33	0	0	0
Jan. 8 to June 30, 1941	720	987	1,707	563	88	0	43
[1]Dec. 18, 1941, to Jan. 15, 1942	14	26	40	11	0	0	0
Jan. 6 to June 29, 1943	610	891	1,501	615	40	1	14
[1]Jan. 7 to 13, 1944	6	6	12	5	0	0	0
Jan. 3 to June 30, 1945	672	835	1,507	691	51	3	9
[1]May 24 to June 14, 1946	5	9	14	5	0	0	0
[2]July 23 to Aug. 1, 1946	8	11	19	0	0	0	0
Jan. 8 to June 30, 1947	675	1,000	1,675	701	37	0	9
Jan. 5 to June 30, 1949	692	1,133	1,825	833	66	5	16
[1]June 19 to 30 ,1950	14	18	32	6	0	0	0
Jan. 3 to June 30, 1951	786	1,258	2,044	1,040	134	7	0
Jan. 7 to June 27, 1953	661	1,004	1,665	941	136	7	0
Jan. 5 to June 30, 1955	879	1,279	2,158	1,162	182	7	0
Jan. 9 to June 29, 1957	899	1,415	2,314	1,313	124	6	0
[1]June 16 to June 20, 1958	1	4	5	5	0	0	0
Jan. 7 to June 30, 1959	1,047	1,652	2,699	1,362	215	5	0
[1]May 3 to 25, 1960	7	16	23	11	3	0	0
[2]May 11 to 23, 1960	5	2	7	4	1	1	0
Jan. 4 to June 30, 1961	908	1,772	2,680	1,464	258	9	0
[1]Oct. 10 to Nov. 22, 1961	34	26	60	19	0	0	0
[2]Nov. 12 to 16, 1962	7	8	15	5	3	0	0
Jan. 9 to June 29, 1963	1,238	1,678	2,916	1,383	232	8	0
[1]Jan. 6 to 28, 1964	15	18	33	8	0	0	0
Jan. 6 to June 30, 1965	1,321	2,269	3,590	2,211	267	13	0
Jan. 5, 1967 to Jan. 8, 1969	2,177	2,894	5,071	3,060	458	0	0

[1] First special session.
[2] Second special session.
[3] Third special session.
[4] Fourth special session.

This roster of the Illinois General Assembly has been completely revised and the many errors of earlier listings corrected. For the years prior to 1848 the manuscript journals of the House of Representatives and the Senate, manuscript reports of elections, copies of warrants paid to members, and original documents containing the signatures of members were helpful. Theodore Calvin Pease's *Illinois Election Returns from 1818 to 1848* published by the Illinois State Historical Library in 1923 generally was considered correct. For the years from 1848 to 1880 manuscript journals, payroll records, and many other manuscript sources were compared. After 1880 the signed oaths of all members, held in the files of the Illinois State Archives, were available. In the four cases in which signatures were illegible the spelling used by the justice of the Illinois Supreme Court who administered the oaths prevailed.

In cases where elections were contested and members unseated after they had taken office the outcome is reported in the footnotes, as are death dates of members who died in office, when those dates are available.

Composition of the General Assembly by party, kept after 1880, has been checked with the records of secretaries of the Senate and clerks of the House as well as with the tally sheets in the manuscript journals. Members are listed alphabetically prior to 1848, and by districts after that date, when districts were designated by numbers for the first time. In earlier years, when a member is shown as representing more than one county, the last named is his county of residence.

First General Assembly, 1818–20

First session convened at Kaskaskia, Oct. 5, 1818; adjourned Oct. 13, 1818. Second session convened Jan. 18, 1819; adjourned March 31, 1819.

Senate

President	Pierre Menard
Secretary	William C. Greenup

Member	County
Lewis Barker	Pope
George Cadwell	Madison
Thomas Cox	Union
Willis Hargrave	White
Alexander Jameson	Monroe
Martin Jones	Bond
Michael Jones	Gallatin
William Kinney	St. Clair
Joseph Kitchell	Crawford

11

Members of the General Assembly 1818-1969

Member	County
John McFerron[1]	Randolph
Zachariah Maddux	Washington
Thomas Roberts	Johnson
Guy W. Smith	Edwards
Conrad Will	Jackson

[1] Resigned July 1, 1819.

House of Representatives

Speaker	John Messinger
Speaker pro tempore	Risdon Moore
Clerk	Thomas Reynolds

Member	County
William Alexander	Monroe
Levi Compton	Edwards
John G. Daimwood[1]	Gallatin
Jesse Echols	Union
Elijah Ewing	Franklin
Green B. Field	Pope
Jesse Griggs	Jackson
Robert Hamilton	Pope
John Howard	Madison
Adolphus F. Hubbard	Gallatin
Edward Humphreys	Randolph
Francis Kirkpatrick	Bond
Samuel McClintock	Gallatin
William McHenry	White
John Marshall[2]	Gallatin
John Messinger	St. Clair
Risdon Moore	St. Clair
William Nash	White
Alexander Philips	White
David Porter	Crawford
Abraham Prickett	Madison
Scott Riggs	Crawford
Daniel Swearengen	Washington
James D. Thomas	St. Clair

Member	County
Henry Utter	Edwards
Samuel Walker	Randolph
Samuel Whiteacre	Union
Samuel Whiteside	Madison
Isaac D. Wilcox	Johnson

[1] Vice Marshall.
[2] Resigned.

Second General Assembly, 1820–22

Convened at Vandalia, Dec. 4, 1820; adjourned Feb. 15, 1821.

Senate

President	Pierre Menard
Secretary	James Turney

Member	County
Lewis Barker	Pope
William Boone	Jackson
George Cadwell	Madison
Samuel Crozier	Randolph
Robert Frazier	Edwards
Alexander Jameson	Monroe
Edmond B. W. Jones	Union
Martin Jones	Bond
Michael Jones	Gallatin
Joseph Kitchell	Crawford
Milton Ladd	Johnson
James Lemen	St. Clair
Zachariah Maddux	Washington
Leonard White	White

House of Representatives

Speaker	John McLean
Clerk	Thomas Reynolds

Member	County
Samuel Alexander[1]	Pope
William M. Alexander	Union
David Blackwell	St. Clair
Joseph Borough	Madison
Nathaniel Buckmaster	Madison
Abraham Cairns	Crawford
Alexander Campbell	Edwards
William M. Crisp	Bond
Thomas M. Dorriss	Franklin
Henry Eddy	Gallatin
Wyckliffe Kitchell	Crawford
George R. Logan	White
Samuel McClintock	Gallatin
William McFatridge	Johnson
John McLean	Gallatin
William B. McLean	White
Charles R. Matheny	St. Clair

Member	County
Thomas Mather	Randolph
Moses Michaels	Edwards
Enoch Moore	Monroe
Risdon Moore	St. Clair
Samuel Omelveny[2]	Union
William Otwell	Madison
Alexander Philips	White
Edward Robertson	Pope
Charles Slade	Washington
Raphael Widen	Randolph
Conrad Will	Jackson
Richard M. Young	Union

[1] Seat contested.
[2] Vice Samuel Alexander deprived of seat.

Third General Assembly, 1822–24

Convened at Vandalia, Dec. 2, 1822; adjourned Feb. 18, 1823.

Senate

President	Adolphus F. Hubbard
Secretary	Thomas Lippincott

Member	County
Andrew Bankson	Washington
Lewis Barker	Pope
Joseph Beaird	Monroe
William Boone	Jackson
George Cadwell	Greene & Pike
Samuel Crozier	Randolph
Robert Frazier	Edwards
John Grammar	Alexander & Union
Martin Jones	Fayette, Montgomery, & Bond
Michael Jones	Gallatin
William Kinkade	Wayne & Lawrence
William Kinney	St. Clair
Milton Ladd	Franklin & Johnson
Daniel Parker	Clark & Crawford
Archibald Roberts	Wayne
Thomas Sloo, Jr.	Hamilton
Theophilus W. Smith	Madison
Stephen Stillman	Sangamon
Leonard White	White

House of Representatives

Speaker	William M. Alexander
Clerk	Charles Dunn

Member	County
Samuel Alexander	Pope
William Alexander	Monroe
William M. Alexander	Alexander
William Berry	Montgomery & Fayette
Curtis Blakeman	Madison
Abraham Cairns	Lawrence
Alexander Campbell	Wayne

Member	County
Zadok Casey	
Hamilton, Marion, & Jefferson	
George Churchill	Madison
John G. Daimwood	Gallatin
Marmaduke S. Davenport	Gallatin
Thomas M. Dorriss	Franklin
John Emmett	White
Alexander P. Field	Union
Robert C. Ford	Crawford
Nicholas Hansen[1]	Pike
George R. Logan	White
William Lowery	Clark
William McFatridge	Johnson
John McFerron	Randolph
David McGahey	Crawford
John McIntosh	Union
Thomas Mather	Randolph
Risdon Moore	St. Clair
Jacob Ogle	St. Clair
Gilbert T. Pell	Edwards
Alexander Philips	White
Jonathan H. Pugh	Bond
Thomas Rattan	Greene
John Shaw[2]	Pike
James Simms	Sangamon
Joseph Trotier	St. Clair
James Turney[3]	Washington
Emanuel J. West	Madison
James A. Whiteside	Pope
Raphael Widen	Randolph
Conrad Will	Jackson

[1] Seat contested.
[2] Vice Hansen deprived of seat.
[3] Resigned Feb. 18, 1823.

Fourth General Assembly, 1824–26

First session convened at Vandalia, Nov. 15, 1824; adjourned Jan. 18, 1825. Second session convened Jan. 2, 1826; adjourned Jan. 18, 1826.

Senate

President, first session
Adolphus P. Hubbard
President, second session   Raphael Widen
Secretary   Emanuel J. West

Member	County
Andrew Bankson	Washington
Lewis Barker	Pope
Joseph A. Beaird	Monroe
James Bird	Lawrence & Wayne
Stephen Bliss	Edwards
Thomas Carlin[1]	
Fulton, Morgan, Pike, & Greene	
Joseph Conway[2]	Madison

Member	County
Joseph Duncan	Jackson
John Ewing	Franklin & Johnson
John Grammar	Alexander & Union
Daniel Hay	White
Michael Jones	Gallatin
Francis Kirkpatrick	
Fayette, Montgomery, & Bond	
James Lemen	St. Clair
Daniel Parker	Clark, Edgar, & Crawford
Thomas Sloo, Jr.	
Jefferson, Marion, & Hamilton	
Theophilus W. Smith[3]	Madison
Stephen Stillman	Sangamon
Raphael Widen	Randolph

[1] Contested; seat declared vacant, Carlin elected at special election Dec. 13, 1824.
[2] Second session, vice Smith.
[3] Resigned.

House of Representatives

Speaker, first session   Thomas Mather
Speaker, second session   David Blackwell
Clerk   Charles Dunn

Member	County
William B. Archer	Clark
Curtis Blakeman	Madison
David Blackwell	St. Clair
Philo Beers	Washington
John Bridges	Johnson
Zadok Casey	
Hamilton, Marion, & Jefferson	
George Churchill	Madison
Thomas M. Dorriss	Franklin
Abraham Eyman	St. Clair
George Forquer[1]	Monroe
Timothy Guard	Gallatin
John S. Hacker	Union
William S. Hamilton	Sangamon
Nicholas Hansen[1]	Pike & Fulton
Thomas James[2]	Monroe
Archibald Job	Greene & Morgan
Gabriel Jones[3]	Randolph
Richard T. Jones	Gallatin
Elias Kent Kane	Randolph
George R. Logan	White
David McGahey	Crawford
William McHenry	White
Thomas Mather[1]	Randolph
Risdon Moore	St. Clair
Asa Norton	Lawrence
William Otwell	Madison
Alexander Philips	White
Levi Roberts[4]	Fulton & Pike

Member	County
John Russell	Bond
John Shaw[5]	Fulton & Pike
William Sims	Pope
Rigdon B. Slocumb	Wayne
Samuel Smith[6]	Randolph
David Stewart	Crawford
Henry Utter	Edwards
John A. Wakefield	Montgomery & Fayette
Samuel Walker	Randolph
Henry L. Webb	Alexander
John Whitaker	Union
James A. Whiteside	Pope
Conrad Will	Jackson

[1] Resigned.
[2] Vice Forquer, appointed sec. state Jan. 15, 1825.
[3] Second session, vice Kane, elected U.S. Sen.
[4] Vice Hansen. House refused to seat Roberts.
[5] Vice Roberts in special election.
[6] Vice Mather.

Fifth General Assembly, 1826–28

Convened at Vandalia, Dec. 4, 1826; adjourned Feb. 19, 1827.

Senate

President	William Kinney
Secretary	Emanuel J. West

Member	County
Samuel Alexander	Pope
William B. Archer	Clark
Joseph A. Beaird[1]	Clinton, Wabash, & Monroe
James Bird	Lawrence & Wayne
Stephen Bliss	Wabash & Edwards
Thomas Carlin	Greene
Zadok Casey	Hamilton, Marion, Clay, & Jefferson
Joseph Conway	Madison
Joseph Duncan[2]	Jackson
John Ewing	Franklin & Johnson
Timothy Guard	Gallatin
Daniel Hay	White
George Hunsacker	Johnson, Alexander, & Union
Elijah Iles	Sangamon
Archibald Job	Morgan
Francis Kirkpatrick	Bond, Fayette, & Montgomery
James Lemen	St. Clair
Raphael Widen	Randolph

[1] Died.
[2] Resigned Feb. 19, 1827, to take seat in Congress.

House of Representatives

Speaker	John McLean
Clerk	William Lee D. Ewing

Member	County
John Alexander	Edgar, Vermilion, & Clark
John C. Alexander	Crawford
John Allen	Calhoun & Greene
William Berry	Bond, Montgomery, & Fayette
David Blackwell	St. Clair
Benjamin W. Brooks	Alexander, Johnson, & Union
Alfred W. Cavarly	Calhoun & Greene
George Churchill	Madison
Samuel H. Clubb	Lawrence
William B. Davis	Wayne
Thomas M. Dorriss	Franklin
Alexander P. Field	Alexander, Johnson, & Union
Job Fletcher	Sangamon
James Hall	Hamilton
Charles Ives	Edgar, Vermilion, & Clark
Thomas James	Monroe
John Lacy	Randolph
Daniel Leib	Morgan
John Leiper	Morgan
William McHenry	White
Robert K. McLaughlin	Bond, Montgomery, & Fayette
John McLean	Gallatin
Henry I. Mills	Edwards
Mordecai Mobley	Sangamon
David Prickett	Madison
Francis Prince	Gallatin
Jonathan H. Pugh	Sangamon
John Reynolds	St. Clair
Thomas Reynolds	Randolph
John Ridgeway	White
Henry J. Ross	Pike
William Sims	Pope
Charles Slade	Clinton & Washington
Henry Utter	Wabash
Conrad Will	Jackson
Nicholas Wren	Clay, Marion, & Jefferson

Sixth General Assembly, 1828–30

Convened at Vandalia, Dec. 1, 1828; adjourned Jan. 23, 1829.

Senate

President	William Kinney
Secretary	Emanuel J. West

Member	County
Samuel Alexander	Pope
William B. Archer	
	Edgar, Vermilion, & Clark
Enoch Beach	
	Edwards, Wabash, & Wayne
Thomas Carlin	
	Calhoun, part of Macoupin, & Greene
Zadok Casey	
	Clay, Hamilton, Marion, & Jefferson
Joseph Conway	Madison
Samuel Crawford	
	Part of Perry & Randolph
Timothy Guard	Gallatin
George Hunsacker	
	Alexander, Johnson, & Union
Elijah Iles	Sangamon
Archibald Job	Morgan
Wyckliffe Kitchell	Lawrence & Crawford
William McHenry	White
Robert K. McLaughlin	Bond,
	Montgomery, Tazewell, & Fayette
Samuel McRoberts[1]	
	Monroe, Washington, & Clinton
Risdon Moore[2]	St. Clair
Henry J. Ross	Adams, Fulton,
	JoDaviess, Peoria, Schuyler, & Pike
Conrad Will	
	Franklin, part of Perry, & Jackson

[1] Vice Beaird, died.
[2] Died after session was over.

House of Representatives

Speaker	John McLean
Clerk	William Lee D. Ewing

Member	County
John C. Alexander	Crawford
John Allen	Calhoun & Greene
James Black	Bond, Montgomery
	Shelby, Tazewell, & Fayette,
William G. Brown	St. Clair
John S. Carrigan	Washington & Clinton
Peter Cartwright	Sangamon
George Churchill	Madison
John Dement	Franklin
William F. Elkin	Sangamon
William Eubanks	White
Alexander P. Field	
	Alexander, Johnson, & Union
Henry M. Gilham	Lawrence
Willie B. Green	Morgan
James Hall	Hamilton
Charles Ives	Edgar, Vermilion, & Clark
Israel Jennings	
	Clay, Jefferson, & Marion
Singleton H. Kimmel	Perry & Jackson
Moses Lemen	Monroe
John McLean	Gallatin

Member	County
Thomas Mather	Randolph
William L. May	Morgan
Hypolite Menard	Randolph
Samuel Mundy	Wabash
Gilbert T. Pell	Edwards
Charles Prentice	Bond, Montgomery,
	Shelby, Tazewell, & Fayette
Francis Prince	Gallatin
Jonathan H. Pugh	Sangamon
Thomas Rattan	Calhoun & Greene
John Reynolds	St. Clair
Stephen B. Shellody	
	Edgar, Vermilion, & Clark
Rigdon B. Slocumb	Wayne
Josiah Stewart	White
John Turney	
	Fulton, Peoria, Schuyler, & Pike
John Whitaker	
	Alexander, Johnson, & Union
James A. Whiteside	Pope

Seventh General Assembly, 1830–32

Convened at Vandalia, Dec. 6, 1830; adjourned Feb. 16, 1831.

Senate

President	Zadok Casey
Secretary	Jesse B. Thomas, Jr.

Member	County
Samuel Alexander[1]	Pope
William B. Archer	
	Edgar, Vermilion, & Clark
Enoch Beach	Edwards, Wabash, & Wayne
Thomas Carlin	Greene
Joseph Conway	Madison
Samuel Crawford	Randolph
James Evans	Morgan
John Grammar	
	Alexander, Johnson, & Union
Timothy Guard[1]	Gallatin
Elijah Iles	Sangamon
Wyckliffe Kitchell	Crawford
Jonathan Lynch	
	Clinton, Monroe, & Washington
William McHenry	White
Robert K. McLaughlin	
	Bond, Montgomery, Tazewell, & Fayette
Enos Maulding	
	Clay, Jefferson, Marion, & Hamilton
Henry J. Ross	Adams, Henry,
	JoDaviess, Peoria, Schuyler, & Pike

Member — **County**
Adam W. Snyder — St. Clair
Conrad Will
Franklin, part of Perry, & Jackson

¹Resigned.

House of Representatives

Speaker — William Lee D. Ewing
Clerk — David Prickett

Member — **County**
John C. Alexander — Crawford
John Atkins — Part of Perry & Randolph
Daniel Beckwith — Edgar, Vermilion, & Clark
William G. Brown — St. Clair
John B. E. Canal¹
Attached part of Macoupin & Madison
John S. Carrigan — Wabash & Clinton
George Churchill
Attached part of Macoupin & Madison
Alexander Clark — Wayne
Newton Cloud — Morgan
John Davenport — Hamilton
John Dawson — Sangamon
John Dement — Franklin
William Eubanks — White
William Lee D. Ewing — Bond, Macon,
Montgomery, Shelby, Tazewell, & Fayette
Joseph M. Fairfield — Morgan
William J. Gatewood — Gallatin
Charles Gregory
Calhoun, part of Macoupin, & Greene
Alexander M. Jenkins
Part of Perry & Jackson
James Jordan — Edwards
James M. McLean — Lawrence
William Marshall
Clay, Marion, & Jefferson
Samuel Mundy — Wabash
Jacob Ogle — St. Clair
Thomas J. Owen — Randolph
Benjamin Parker²
Clark, Edgar, & Vermilion
Samuel C. Pierce — Attached part of
Macoupin, Calhoun, & Greene
John F. Posey — Bond, Macon,
Montgomery, Shelby, Tazewell, & Fayette
Joseph L. Priestly — Union
Jonathan H. Pugh — Sangamon
John Y. Sawyer³ — Madison
Stephen B. Shellody⁴
Edgar, Macon, & Clark
Josiah Stewart — White
Edward D. Taylor — Sangamon

Member — **County**
Joseph E. Watkins — Gallatin
John Whitaker — Union
James A. Whiteside — Pope
John D. Whiteside — Monroe
Joel Wright
Fulton, JoDaviess, Peoria, & Pike

¹ Resigned.
² Contested by Shellody.
³ Vice Canal.
⁴ Vice Parker, unseated.

Eighth General Assembly, 1832–34

Convened at Vandalia, Dec. 3, 1832; adjourned March 2, 1833.

Senate

President — Zadok Casey¹
President pro tempore
William Lee D. Ewing
Secretary — Jesse B. Thomas, Jr.

Member — **County**
William B. Archer — Coles, Edgar &, Clark
James Bird — Tazewell
Joseph Conway — Madison
Larkin Craig
Macoupin, Montgomery, & Bond
William H. Davidson — White
James Evans — Morgan
William Lee D. Ewing
Clay, Marion, & Fayette
George Forquer — Sangamon
John Grammar — Alexander & Union
Elijah Iles — Sangamon
Waller Jones — Morgan
Jonathan Lynch — Clinton & Monroe
William McCreery — Schuyler
David McGahey — Lawrence & Crawford
Thomas Mather — Perry & Randolph
Enos Maulding — Jefferson & Hamilton
Henry I. Mills
Wabash, Wayne, & Edwards
Thomas Rattan — Greene
John Raum² — Johnson & Pope
Adam W. Snyder — St. Clair
James M. Strode — JoDaviess, La Salle,
Peoria, Putnam, & Cook
John W. Vance — Vermilion
Joseph B. Watkins³ — Gallatin
Conrad Will
Franklin, Washington, & Jackson
Archibald Williams
Pike, Hancock, & Adams
William Williamson — Shelby & Macon

¹ Lt. gov. from Dec. 9, 1830, to March 1, 1833; resigned to take seat in Congress.
² Vice Samuel Alexander, resigned.
³ Vice Timothy Guard, resigned.

Speaker   Alexander M. Jenkins
Clerk   David Prickett

Member	County
Wilson Able	Alexander
Stinson H. Anderson	Jefferson
William G. Anderson	Wabash
David Baldridge	Perry & Randolph
George Barnett	Vermilion
George H. Beeler	Macon & Shelby
Robert Blackwell	Fayette
Christian B. Blockburger	Montgomery
Joseph Borough	Macoupin
George P. Bowyer	
	Washington & Franklin
Benjamin Briggs	Tazewell & McLean
John Carrico	Coles
John S. Carrigan	Clinton
Peter Cartwright	Sangamon
Alexander Clark	Wayne
John Dougherty	Union
William Edmonston	Calhoun,
	Mercer, Warren, & McDonough
Cyrus Edwards	Madison
Benjamin S. Enloe	Johnson
Jesse Essery	Clark
William G. Flood	
	Adams, Pike, & Hancock
William Goode	Greene
John C. Goudy	White
Abner Greer	Lawrence
Samuel Hackleton	
	Henry, Knox, & Fulton
James Hall	Hamilton
John Henry	Morgan
William Highsmith	Crawford
Gurdon S. Hubbard	Vermilion
Thomas Hunt	Edwards
William Hunter	Bond
Alexander M. Jenkins	Jackson
Michael Jones	Gallatin
Lewis W. Link	Greene
Samuel McClintock	Gallatin
Murray McConnell	Morgan
John McGown	White
William Marshall	Clay & Marion
Philip W. Martin	
	Adams, Pike, & Hancock
Samuel T. Mathews	Morgan
John Middlecoff	St. Clair
Benjamin Mills	Cook, La Salle, Peoria,
	Putman, & JoDaviess
William A. Minshall	Schuyler
Achilles Morris	Sangamon
Richard G. Murphy	Perry & Randolph
Lunsford R. Noel	Edgar
Samuel C. Pierce	Greene
James Semple	Madison
John Todd Stuart	Sangamon

Member	County
John Stuntz	St. Clair
Edward D. Taylor	Sangamon
James A. Whiteside	Pope
John D. Whiteside	Monroe
Johnson Wren	Washington & Franklin
John Wyatt	Morgan

Ninth General Assembly, 1834–36

First session convened at Vandalia, Dec. 1, 1834; adjourned Feb. 13, 1835. Second session convened Dec. 7, 1835; adjourned Jan. 18, 1836.

Senate

President   Alexander M. Jenkins
Secretary   Leonard White

Member	County
Benjamin Bond	Clinton & Monroe
Larkin Craig	
	Macoupin, Montgomery, & Bond
William H. Davidson	White
Cyrus Edwards	Madison
William Lee D. Ewing[1]	Fayette
Job Fletcher[2]	Sangamon
George Forquer[1]	Sangamon
William J. Gatewood	Gallatin
John S. Hacker	Union & Alexander
Archer G. Herndon[3]	Sangamon
Waller Jones[4]	Morgan
Levin Lane	Jefferson & Hamilton
David McGahey[1]	Lawrence & Crawford
Thomas Mather[1]	Perry & Randolph
George W. P. Maxwell	Calhoun,
	Fulton, Knox, McDonough, Warren, & Schuyler
Henry I. Mills	
	Wabash, Wayne, & Edwards
Benjamin Mitchell	McLean & Tazewell
Lunsford R. Noel	Clark, Coles, & Edgar
Braxton Parrish[5]	
	Franklin, Washington, & Jackson
Thomas Rattan	Greene
Richard B. Servant[6]	Perry & Randolph
Adam W. Snyder	St. Clair
James W. Stephenson[1]	Cook, La Salle,
	Peoria, Putnam, Rock Island, & JoDaviess
James M. Strode[7]	JoDaviess, La Salle,
	Peoria, Putnam, Rock Island, & Cook
Edward D. Taylor[1]	Sangamon
William Thomas	Morgan
John W. Vance	
	Champaign, Iroquois, & Vermilion

Member	County
William Weatherford[8]	Morgan
James A. Whiteside	Johnson & Pope
Conrad Will[9]	Jackson
Archibald Williams	
	Pike, Hancock, & Adams
William Williamson	Shelby & Macon

[1] Resigned.
[2] Vice Taylor.
[3] Vice Forquer.
[4] Died.
[5] Vice Will.
[6] Vice Mather.
[7] Vice Stephenson.
[8] Vice Jones.
[9] Died June 11, 1835.

House of Representatives

Speaker	James Semple
Clerk	David Prickett

Member	County
Wilson Able	Alexander
Stinson H. Anderson[1]	Jefferson
Nathaniel Blackford[3]	White
Robert Blackwell	Effingham & Fayette
Christian B. Blockburger	Montgomery
George P. Bowyer	Washington & Franklin
William Brown	Tazewell & McLean
Nathaniel Buckmaster[4]	Madison
Peter Butler	Calhoun, McDonough, Mercer, & Warren
Milton Carpenter	Hamilton
William Carpenter	Sangamon
Benjamin A. Clark[2]	Wayne
Newton Cloud	Morgan
Basil Craig[5]	Union
James T. Cunningham	Coles
John Dawson	Sangamon
John Dougherty[1]	Union
Jesse K. Dubois	Lawrence
Charles Dunn	Pope
Asa Elliott	
	Champaign, Edgar, & Vermilion
Orlando B. Ficklin[1]	Wabash
William Fithian	
	Champaign, Edgar, & Vermilion
Elijah S. Frazer	Marion
William Gordon	Morgan
Charles Gregory	Greene
Samuel Hackelton	
	Henry, Knox, & Fulton
John Hamlin[1]	Cook, JoDaviess, La Salle, Putnam, Rock Island, & Peoria
James Hampton	Gallatin
James Harreld	Jackson
John Harris	Macoupin

Member	County
John Henry	Morgan
John D. Hughes	St. Clair
Thomas Hunt	Edwards
William Hunter	Bond
Abraham Lincoln	Sangamon
Lewis W. Link[1]	Greene
James D. McGahey[2]	Crawford
William McHenry[2]	White
Uri Manly	Clark
William Moore	St. Clair
Richard G. Murphy	Randolph & Perry
Nelson W. Nunnally	Edgar
John Oliver	Johnson
James Outhouse	Clinton
Thomas H. Owen	Hancock, Pike, & Adams
Harvey T. Pace[6]	Jefferson
David Porter[7]	Crawford
William Ross	Hancock, Pike, & Adams
Stephen R. Rowan[1]	Gallatin
James Semple	Madison
Edward Smith[8]	Wabash
John Todd Stuart	Sangamon
Jesse B. Thomas, Jr.[1]	Madison
John Thompson[2]	Randolph & Perry
Thomas B. Trower	Shelby & Macon
Calvin Tunnel	Greene
James Turney[9]	Greene
Jacob Vandeventer	Schuyler
Edwin B. Webb	White
John D. Whiteside	Monroe
Daniel Wood[10]	Gallatin
Johnson Wren	Franklin & Washington
John Wyatt	Morgan

[1] Resigned.
[2] Died.
[3] Vice McHenry, died Feb. 3, 1835.
[4] Vice Thomas, resigned Feb. 12, 1835.
[5] Vice Dougherty.
[6] Vice Anderson.
[7] Vice McGahey.
[8] Vice Ficklin, resigned to become state's att., Coles Co.
[9] Vice Link.
[10] Vice Rowan.

Tenth General Assembly, 1836–38

First session convened at Vandalia, Dec. 5, 1836; adjourned March 6, 1837. Second session convened July 10, 1837; adjourned July 22, 1837.

Senate

President	William H. Davidson
Secretary	Jesse B. Thomas, Jr.

Member	County
James Allen	Macon & McLean
John Allen[3]	Greene & Calhoun

Member	County
Benjamin Bond	Clinton & Marion
Joseph Borough	Macoupin
Orville H. Browning	Adams
Peter Butler	Knox, Warren, & Henry
Larkin Craig	Montgomery & Bond
William H. Davidson	White
Cyrus Edwards	Madison
Job Fletcher	Sangamon
William J. Gatewood	Gallatin
John S. Hacker	Alexander & Union
Samuel Hackleton	Fulton
John Hamlin	Peoria & Putnam
Archer G. Herndon	Sangamon
Levin Lane	Jefferson & Hamilton
Robert K. McLaughlin	
	Clay, Effingham & Fayette
George W. P. Maxwell	Schuyler
Henry I. Mills	
	Wabash, Wayne, & Edwards
Benjamin Mitchell	Tazewell
James B. Moore[2]	
	Monroe, St. Clair, & Madison
John Murray	St. Clair
Lunsford R. Noel	Edgar
William O'Rear	Morgan
Thomas H. Owen	Hancock & McDonough
Nathaniel Parker[3]	Coles & Clark
Braxton Parrish	Franklin & Jackson
Peter Pruyne	Will & Cook
John C. Reilly	
	Crawford, Jasper, & Lawrence
William Ross[3]	Pike
Richard B. Servant	Randolph
William Stadden[3]	
	Iroquois, Kane, & La Salle
William Thomas	Morgan
James Turney	Greene
John W. Vance	Champaign & Vermilion
Peter Warren	Shelby
William Weatherford	Morgan
James A. Whiteside	Johnson & Pope
John D. Whiteside[1]	
	Madison, St. Clair, & Monroe
A. G. S. Wight	
	JoDaviess, Rock Island, & Mercer
John D. Wood[3]	Washington & Perry

[1] Resigned March 6, 1837.
[2] Vice Whiteside.
[3] Elected to two-year term.

House of Representatives

Speaker	James Semple
Clerk	David Prickett

Member	County
Wilson Able	Alexander
Mark Aldrich	Hancock
Thomas Atwater	Putnam

GENERAL ASSEMBLY

205

Member	County
Edward D. Baker[3]	Sangamon
Asel F. Ball	Fulton
George Barnett	Vermilion
S. M. Bartlett[4]	Boone, Mercer, Ogle,
	Rock Island, Stephenson, Winnebago,
	& JoDaviess
Richard Bentley	Bond
Milton Carpenter	Hamilton
Elijah Charles[1]	
	Mercer, Rock Island, & JoDaviess
Newton Cloud	Morgan
Samuel Connelly[5]	Edgar
James Copeland[6]	Johnson
Isaac Courtright	Iroquois
James Craig	Boone, Mercer, Ogle,
	Rock Island, Stephenson, Winnebago, &
	JoDaviess
John Crain	Washington
Richard N. Cullom	Tazewell
James T. Cunningham[7]	Coles
William Davidson	Marion
Cyrus A. Davis	Greene
John Dawson	Sangamon
John Dement[1]	Fayette & Effingham
Jonathan Diarman	Pope
Achilles D. Dollins	Franklin
John Dougherty	Union
Stephen A. Douglas[1]	Morgan
Jesse K. Dubois	Lawrence
Alexander P. Dunbar	Coles
Tarlton Dunn[8]	Gallatin
William Edmonston	McDonough
Ninian W. Edwards	Sangamon
William F. Elkin	Sangamon
Revill W. English	Greene
Benjamin S. Enloe[1]	Johnson
William Lee D. Ewing	
	Effingham & Fayette
Augustus C. French[1]	Edgar
George Galbreath[2]	Adams
Resolve Graham[2]	Gallatin
John Green[10]	Calhoun & Greene
Joseph Green	St. Clair
Peter Green	Clay
William J. Hankins[9]	Effingham & Fayette
William W. Happy	Morgan
John J. Hardin	Morgan
John Harris	Macoupin
George Henshaw	McLean
John Hogan	Madison
Joseph Huey	Clinton
Thomas Hunt	Edwards
Wilson Lagow	Jasper & Crawford
William Lane[1]	Calhoun & Greene
Albert C. Leary	Cook
Abraham Lincoln	Sangamon

Member	County
Usher F. Linder[1]	Coles
John Logan	Jackson
James H. Lyons	Champaign
John A. McClernand[1]	Gallatin
Andrew McCormick	Sangamon
John McGown	White
William McMurtry	Henry, Warren, & Knox
Henry Madden	La Salle
William B. Marrs	Clark
Gideon Minor	Edgar
William A. Minshall	Schuyler
John Moore	McLean
William Moore	St. Clair
Joseph Morton	Morgan
John H. Murphy	Vermilion
Richard G. Murphy	Perry
Joseph Naper	Cook
David Nowlin[2]	Monroe
Dempsey Odam	Franklin
Edward J. O'Neille	Lawrence
Harvey T. Pace	Jefferson
Parvin Paullen	Pike
James H. Ralston	Adams
James Rawalt	Fulton
William G. Reddick	Macon
William A. Richardson	Schuyler
George Scarborough	Vermilion
James Semple	Madison
James Shields	Randolph
Edward Smith	Wabash
Robert Smith	Madison
John A. Somerville[11]	Monroe
Dan Stone[1]	Sangamon
Robert Stuart	Tazewell
John Stuntz	St. Clair
Samuel G. Thompson	Randolph
John S. Turley	Shelby
Daniel Turney	Wayne
Francis Voris	Peoria
James Walker	Cook
Richard S. Walker	Morgan
Joseph E. Watkins[12]	Gallatin
Edwin B. Webb	White
Alpheus Wheeler	Pike
Easton Whitten	Montgomery
Archibald Williams[13]	Adams
Robert L. Wilson	Sangamon
Franklin Witt	Greene
Daniel Wood	Gallatin
John Wyatt[14]	Morgan

[1] Resigned.
[2] Died.
[3] Vice Stone.
[4] Vice Charles.
[5] Vice French.
[6] Vice Enloe.
[7] Vice Linder.
[8] Vice McClernand.
[9] Vice Dement.
[10] Vice Lane.
[11] Vice Nowlin, died Jan. 31, 1836.
[12] Vice Graham, died Dec. 27, 1836.
[13] Vice Galbreath.
[14] Vice Douglas, resigned March 5, 1837.

Eleventh General Assembly, 1838–40

First session convened at Vandalia, Dec. 3, 1838; adjourned March 4, 1839. Second session convened at Springfield, Dec. 9, 1839; adjourned Feb. 3, 1840.

Senate

President	Stinson H. Anderson
Secretary	Benjamin Bond

Member	County
James Allen	Macon & McLean
Robert Blackwell	Fayette, Effingham, & Clay
Joseph Borough	Macoupin
Manoah Bostwick[2]	Jersey & Greene
Orville H. Browning	Adams
Peter Butler	Henry, Knox, & Warren
George Churchill	Madison
William H. Davidson	White
William Fithian	Champaign & Vermilion
Job Fletcher	Sangamon
William Gaston	Marion & Clinton
William J. Gatewood	Gallatin
Worthington J. Gibbs	Johnson & Pope
Abner Greer	Crawford, Jasper, & Lawrence
John S. Hacker	Alexander & Union
Samuel Hackelton[1]	Fulton
John Hamlin	Peoria & Putnam
George W. Harrison	Boone, Mercer, Ogle, Rock Island, Stephenson, Winnebago, & JoDaviess
Archer G. Herndon	Sangamon
William Hunter	Montgomery & Bond
Noah Johnson	Hamilton & Jefferson
Sidney H. Little	Hancock & McDonough
David Markley[3]	Morgan, Cass, Scott, & Fulton
Henry I. Mills	Wabash, Wayne, & Edwards
Benjamin Mitchell	Tazewell
Byrd Monroe	Clark & Coles
James B. Moore	Monroe, St. Clair, & Madison
John Murray	St. Clair
Nelson W. Nunnally	Edgar
William O'Rear	Morgan
Braxton Parrish	Franklin & Jackson

Member	County
Ebenezer Peck[1]	Du Page, Lake, McHenry, Will, & Cook
William A. Richardson	Schuyler
William Ross	Pike
William L. Sargeant[4]	Cass, Scott, & Morgan
Richard B. Servant	Randolph
William Stadden	De Kalb, Iroquois, Kane, & La Salle
William Thomas[1]	Cass, Scott, & Morgan
James Turney[1]	Greene
Peter Warren	Shelby
William Weatherford	Morgan
Franklin Witt	Calhoun & Greene
John D. Wood	Washington & Perry
James H. Woodworth[5]	Du Page, Lake, McHenry, Will, & Cook

[1] Resigned.
[2] Vice Turney.
[3] Vice Hackelton.
[4] Vice Thomas.
[5] Vice Peck.

House of Representatives

Speaker	William Lee D. Ewing
Clerk	David Prickett, resigned
Clerk	John Calhoun, succeeded Prickett

Member	County
Wilson Able[1]	Alexander
Mark Aldrich	Hancock
Harmon Alexander	Jasper & Crawford
John Allen	Greene
Willis Allen	Franklin
William B. Archer	Clark
Allen Bainbridge	Franklin
Edward D. Baker	Sangamon
Joseph B. Bowman[2]	Wabash
John Brown	Schuyler
John Calhoun[9]	Sangamon
Milton Carpenter	Hamilton
Joseph W. Churchill	De Kalb, Kane, & La Salle
Newton Cloud	Morgan
William Campher[9]	Peoria
James Copeland	Johnson
James Craig	Mercer, Ogle, Rock Island, Stephenson, Winnebago, & JoDaviess
John Crain	Washington
James T. Cunningham	Coles
Edward M. Daley	Greene
John Dawson	Sangamon
Jesse K. Dubois	Lawrence
Tarlton Dunn	Gallatin
William Edmonston	McDonough
Ninian W. Edwards[9]	Sangamon
William F. Elkin	Sangamon
Asa Elliott	Vermilion
Allan Emmerson	Edwards

Member	County
Revill W. English	Greene
William Lee D. Ewing	Effingham & Fayette
Orlando B. Ficklin	Coles
Josiah Fisk	Montgomery
William G. Flood[9]	Adams
Hardy Foster	Marion
Augustus C. French[9]	Edgar
William Gilham	Morgan
Jesse Wilson Gouge[3]	Macon
John Green	Calhoun & Greene
Peter Green	Clay
William J. Hankins	Effingham & Fayette
William W. Happy[12]	Morgan
John J. Hardin	Morgan
Moses Harlin[13]	Peoria
John Harris	Macoupin
William H. Henderson	Putnam & Bureau
John Henry	Morgan
William Holmes	Cass
John Houston	Jasper & Cass
Joseph Huey	Clinton
Alden Hull	Tazewell
Vital Jarrott	St. Clair
Benjamin Johnson	Bond
Gabriel Jones	Randolph
Germanicus Kent	Mercer, Ogle, Rock Island, Stephenson, Winnebago, & JoDaviess
Gholson Kercheval	McHenry, Will, & Cook
Richard Kerr[10]	Pike
Abraham Lincoln	Sangamon
Oscar Love[10]	Pike
John Logan	Jackson
James H. Lyons	Champaign
Andrew McCormick	Sangamon
Jesse M. McCutcheon	Schuyler
Robert McMillan	Edgar
James McWilliams	Pike
Samuel D. Marshall	Gallatin
William S. Maus	Tazewell
Edmund Menard	Randolph
John Moore	McLean
Edward T. Morgan	Monroe
John H. Murphy	Vermilion
Richard Murphy	McHenry, Will, & Cook
Thomas J. Nance[4]	Sangamon
Joseph Naper	McHenry, Will, & Cook
William Otwell	Madison
Harvey T. Pace	Jefferson
Alexander Philips	White
Jonas Rawalt	Fulton
John W. Read	Pope

Member	County
William G. Reddick[8]	Macon
Louis Roberts	Iroquois
Jeffrey Robinson[9]	Wayne
William W. Rowan	St. Clair
Hall Simms[6]	Edgar
Edward Smith[8]	Wabash
George Smith	Madison
Robert Smith	Madison
Wyatt B. Stapp	Henry, Knox, & Warren
Richard W. Starr[5]	Adams
Cheney Thomas	McLean
John Thomas	St. Clair
William F. Thornton[9]	Shelby
Daniel Turney[11]	Wayne
Isaac P. Walker	Vermilion
Newton Walker	Fulton
Edwin B. Webb	White
Henry L. Webb[9]	Alexander
Archibald Williams	Adams
William Williamson[7]	Shelby
Daniel Wood	Gallatin
Jacob Zimmerman	Union

[1] Vice Webb.
[2] Vice Edward Smith.
[3] Vice Reddick, died Nov. 16, 1838.
[4] Vice Edwards.
[5] Vice Flood.
[6] Vice French.
[7] Vice Thornton.
[8] Died.
[9] Resigned.
[10] Seat contested by Oscar Love on grounds Kerr left state. Love won special election, but House ruled Kerr entitled to sit.
[11] Vice Robinson.
[12] Seat contested by John T. Cassell; special election Oct. 19, 1838, returned Happy, who was seated Dec. 3, 1838.
[13] Vice Campher.

Twelfth General Assembly, 1840–42

First session convened at Springfield, Nov. 23, 1840; adjourned Dec. 5, 1840. Second session convened Dec. 7, 1840; adjourned March 1, 1841.

Senate

President	Stinson H. Anderson
Secretary	Merrit L. Covell

Member	County
John Allen[1]	Greene
Edward D. Baker	Christian, Logan, Menard, & Sangamon
George Churchill	Madison
Richard N. Cullom	Tazewell
William H. Davidson	White

Member	County
Aiken Evans	Clay, Effingham, & Fayette
Jacob Feaman	Randolph
William Fithian	Champaign & Vermilion
William Gaston	Marion & Clinton
William J. Gatewood	Gallatin
Worthington J. Gibbs	Johnson & Pope
John S. Hacker	Alexander & Union
John Hamlin	Bureau, Marshall, Putnam, Stark, & Peoria
John Harris	Macoupin
George W. Harrison	Boone, Carroll, Lee, Mercer, Ogle, Rock Island, Stephenson, Whiteside, Winnebago, & JoDaviess
John Henry	Morgan
Archer G. Herndon	Sangamon
John Houston	Jasper, Lawrence, & Crawford
William Hunter	Bond
James A. James	Madison, St. Clair, & Monroe
Noah Johnson	Hamilton & Jefferson
Thomas M. Killpatrick	Morgan & Scott
Sidney H. Little	Hancock & McDonough
David Markley	Fulton
Byrd Monroe	Coles & Clark
John Moore[2]	De Witt, Livingston, Macon, & McLean
Nelson W. Nunnally	Edgar
Braxton Parrish	Franklin, Williamson, & Jackson
John Pearson	Du Page, Lake, McHenry, Will, & Cook
James H. Ralston	Adams
William A. Richardson	Brown & Schuyler
William Ross	Pike
William L. Sargeant	Cass, Scott, & Morgan
Rigdon B. Slocumb	Edwards, Wabash, & Wayne
Adam W. Snyder	St. Clair
William Stadden	De Kalb, Iroquois, Kane, & La Salle
Wyatt B. Stapp	Knox, Henry, & Warren
Peter Warren	Shelby
Franklin Witt	Calhoun, Jersey, & Green
John D. Wood	Washington & Perry

[1] Died June 29, 1841.
[2] Resigned, elected lt. gov.

House of Representatives

Speaker	William Lee D. Ewing
Clerk	John Calhoun

Member	County
Wilson Able	Alexander
William B. Archer	Clark
William W. Bailey	McDonough
Daniel Baldwin	St. Clair
Robert F. Barnett	Macon & De Witt
James Beall	Wabash
John Bennett	Menard
Richard Bentley	Bond
William H. Bissell	Monroe
David J. Blackman	Gallatin
James M. Bradford	Sangamon
James N. Brown	Sangamon
John J. Brown	Vermilion
Mathew W. Busey	Champaign
John Canady	Vermilion
Milton Carpenter[1]	Hamilton
Aldred W. Cavarly	Greene & Jersey
John F. Charles	Hancock
Isaac Courtright	Iroquois
Jeremiah Cox	Morgan
John Crain	Washington
James T. Cunningham	Coles
John Darneille	Sangamon
John Denny	Henry, Warren, & Knox
Abram R. Dodge	La Salle
Achilles D. Dollins	Williamson & Franklin
John Dougherty	Union
Thomas Drummond	Boone, Carroll, Lee, Mercer, Ogle, Rock Island, Stephenson, Whiteside, Winnebago, & JoDaviess
Samuel Dunlap	Lawrence
Cyrus Edwards	Madison
Allan Emmerson	Edwards
Revill W. English	Greene & Jersey
William Lee D. Ewing	Effingham & Fayette
Josiah Francis	Sangamon
Isaac Froman	Vermilion
Isaac Funk	McLean
Joseph Gillespie	Madison
Peter Green	Clay
Asahel Gridley	McLean
William J. Hankins	Effingham & Fayette
John J. Hardin	Morgan
William H. Henderson	Marshall, Stark, Putnam, & Bureau
Stephen G. Hicks	Jefferson
Alden Hull	Tazewell
John G. Humphrey	Adams
John M. Kelly	Edgar
Wyckliffe Kitchell	Crawford
William Laughlin	Adams
Albert G. Leary	McHenry, Will, & Cook
Harvey Lester	Brown
Abraham Lincoln	Sangamon
John Logan	Jackson
John A. McClernand	Gallatin

Member	County
James McClurken	Randolph
John McDonald	Calhoun, Jersey, & Greene
John P. McGinnis	Randolph
James M. McLean	Lawrence
James Marshall	Marion
Pierre Menard	Tazewell
William A. Minshall	Schuyler
Daniel T. Moore	St. Clair
Leander Munsell	Edgar
Richard Murphy	McHenry, Will, & Cook
Richard G. Murphy	Perry
Dempsey Odam	Williamson & Franklin
Francis A. Olds	Macoupin
John Oliver	Johnson
Joseph W. Ormsbee	Scott
James Parkinson	Morgan
Solomon Parsons	Pike
Ebenezer Peck	McHenry, Will, & Cook
William J. Phelps	Peoria
Alexander Philips	White
Owen Prentice	Shelby
James Reynolds	Madison
Lewis W. Ross	Fulton
John Scott	Clinton
Oliver Shepley	Fulton
Hiram W. Thornton	Boone, Carroll, Lee, Mercer, Ogle, Rock Island, Stephenson, Whiteside, Winnebago, & JoDaviess
Thomas Threlkeld	Coles
Daniel Troy	Morgan
Lyman Trumbull	St. Clair
Daniel Turney	Wayne
George T. Waters	Pope
Edwin B. Webb	White
Amos S. West	Cass
Alpheus Wheeler	Pike
Martin White	Christian & Logan
William Wilson	Jasper & Crawford
Daniel Wood	Gallatin
David M. Woodson	Jersey & Greene

[1] Resigned March 6, 1841, to become treas.

Thirteenth General Assembly, 1842–44

Convened Dec. 5, 1842; adjourned March 6, 1843.

Senate

President	John Moore
Secretary	Isaac A. Berry

Member	County
Edward D. Baker	Christian, Logan, Menard, & Sangamon

Member	County
Robert F. Barnett	De Witt, part of

Greene, Livingston, Macon, Piatt,
part of Woodford, & McLean

John Buford	
Henry, Lee, Whiteside, & Rock Island	
Seth Catlin	St. Clair
Alfred W. Cavarly[2]	Jersey & Greene
John Crain	Perry
Richard N. Cullom	Tazewell
William H. Davidson	White
Jacob C. Davis	Hancock
John Dougherty	Alexander & Union
Revill W. English[2]	Calhoun & Greene
Aiken Evans	Effingham & Fayette
Jacob Feaman	Randolph
William Fithian	Champaign & Vermilion
James Gilham	Cass & Scott
John Harris	Macoupin
George W. Harrison	
Carroll, Stephenson, & JoDaviess	
Reuben Harrison[3]	Sangamon
John Henry	Morgan
Samuel Hoard	Lake & Cook
John Houston	
Jasper, Lawrence, & Crawford	
James A. James	
Madison, St. Clair, & Monroe	
Benjamin Johnson	
Christian, Montgomery, & Bond	
Thomas M. Killpatrick	Morgan & Scott
George Leviston	Gallatin
William McMurtry	Mercer & Knox
David Markley	Fulton
Joel A. Matteson[4]	
Du Page, Iroquois, & Will	
Ira Minard	
Boone, De Kalb, McHenry, & Kane	
Nelson W. Nunnally	Edgar
Nathaniel Parker	Coles & Clark
Braxton Parrish	
Franklin, Williamson, & Jackson	
John Pearson[1]	
Du Page, Lake, McHenry, Will, & Cook	
James H. Ralston	Adams
Spooner Ruggles	Winnebago & Ogle
Michael Ryan	La Salle
Rigdon B. Slocumb	
Edwards, Wabash, & Wayne	
George Smith	Madison
Wyatt B. Stapp	Henry, Knox, & Warren
William W. Thompson	
Bureau, Stark, & Peoria	
Jacob Vandeventer	Schuyler & Brown
Peter Warren	Shelby
George W. Waters	
Hardin, Johnson, & Pope	

Member	County
Robert A. D. Willbanks	
Hamilton, Marion, & Jefferson	
Thomas Worthington	Pike
Lewis B. Wynne	
Logan, Mason, & Menard	

[1] Resigned.
[2] Seat contested, English seated but resigned Dec. 22, 1842, after redistricting.
[3] Right to sit challenged, as Baker represented Sangamon County. Harrison evidently unseated, but no positive evidence found.
[4] Matteson's right to sit after redistricting questioned. Matteson reelected Jan. 2, 1843, seated Jan. 7, 1843.

House of Representatives

Speaker	Samuel Hackelton
Clerk	William Lee D. Ewing

Member	County
Darius Adams	Winnebago
Robert Aldrich	Madison
Alfred E. Ames	Boone
William G. Anderson	Lawrence
Leonard Andrus	Ogle
Isaac N. Arnold	Cook
John Bailhache	Madison
Robert F. Bell	Putnam & Marshall
Elisha Bibbens	La Salle
Mahlon Bishop	McLean
William Blair	Pike
Curtis Blakeman	Madison
Elisha Bone	Menard
Richard A. Bradley	Jackson
William Brinkley	
Jefferson, Marion, & Hamilton	
Benjamin D. Brown	Pike
James N. Brown	Sangamon
Orville H. Browning	Adams
John H. Bryant	Peoria, Stark, & Bureau
John D. Burklow	Perry
Mathew W. Busey	Champaign
William Caldwell	Sangamon
John Canady	Vermilion
Newton Cloud	Morgan
John Cochran	Alexander & Union
Addison Collins	
Iroquois, Will, & Du Page	
John Compton	Wabash
Isaac Courtright	
Du Page, Will, & Iroquois	
William H. W. Cushman	La Salle
Jacob J. Danner	Randolph & Monroe
James M. Davis	Bond
John T. Davis	Williamson
Elias S. Dennis	Washington & Clinton
Andrew J. Dickinson	
Randolph & Monroe	
Achilles D. Dollins	Franklin
Willis Dougherty	Clark

Member	County
John Douglass	Hamilton
Jesse K. Dubois	Lawrence
Lorenzo Edwards	Scott
David Epler	Morgan
Hugh Ervin	McDonough
Charles F. Ewing	Macon & Logan
Orlando B. Ficklin[1]	Coles
Abner Flanders	Gallatin
Joseph Fowler	Coles
Peter B. Garrett	Adams
Robert W. Glass	Macoupin
Sargeant Gobble	Macoupin
Hubbard Graves	Stephenson & Carroll
John Green[2]	Greene
Peter Green	Clay
David L. Gregg	Iroquois, Will, & Du Page
Samuel Hackelton	Peoria & Fulton
Maximilian Haley	Warren
Stephen D. Hambaugh	Brown
Levi A. Hannaford	Peoria
George M. Hanson	Coles
Joshua Harper	Henry & Rock Island
Jeduthan Hatch	Iroquois, Will, & Du Page
Thomas S. Hick	Gallatin
William Hickman	Sangamon
Stephen G. Hicks	Jefferson
Alfred Hinton	Greene
Samuel Horney	Schuyler
Jonathan B. Howard	Shelby
James J. Hunsacker	Alexander & Union
Aaron C. Jackson	Whiteside & Lee
William M. Jackson	Boone, De Kalb, McHenry, & Kane
Abraham Jonas	Adams
Samuel T. Kendall	Jersey
Gustave Philipp Koerner	St. Clair
Andrew J. Kuykendall	Johnson
Cyrus Langworthy	Bureau & Stark
John S. Lawler	White
James Lockhard	Clark
Stephen T. Logan	Sangamon
Thomas M. Loy	Effingham & Fayette
William McBride	Randolph & Monroe
John A. McClernand	Gallatin
John McDonald	Calhoun & Greene
John McDonald	JoDaviess
Andrew McMillan	Livingston & McLean
Henry Madden	Boone, De Kalb, Kane, & McHenry
Julius Manning	Knox
James Marshall	Marion
Pierre Menard	Tazewell
Harry L. Miller	Fulton
Edward Mitchell	Scott
Richard Murphy	Lake
Samuel G. Nesbit	Piatt & Macon
James Norris	Vermilion

Member	County
Thomas H. Owen	Hancock
Philip Penn	St. Clair
William Pickering	Edwards
John W. Pratt	Cass
James K. Scott	De Witt
Joseph L. Sharp	Fulton
John Shirley	Effingham & Fayette
Hall Simms	Edgar
Guy W. Smith	Crawford & Jasper
William Smith	Hancock
Reuben H. Spicer	Knox & Mercer
Alexander Starne	Pike
Richard W. Starr	Adams
Hart L. Stewart	Cook
William S. Stockton	Henderson & Warren
Middleton Tackerberry	Tazeweil
Amos Thompson	St. Clarl
Horace Turner	Fulton
P. C. Vance	Brown & Schuyler
Horatio M. Vandeveer	Christian
Phillip Vineyard	Hardin & Pope
William Weatherford	Morgan
Almeron Wheat	Adams
Lot Whitcomb	Cook
John White	Washington & Clinton
Easton Whitten	Montgomery
William Wilson	Jasper & Crawford
Edward Wirt	Wayne
James H. Woodworth	Cook
Richard Yates	Morgan

[1] Resigned, elected to U.S.H.R.
[2] Died Feb. 3, 1843.

Fourteenth General Assembly, 1844–46

Convened Dec. 2, 1844; adjourned March 3, 1845.

Senate

President — John Moore
Secretary — Merrit L. Covell

Member	County
Willis Allen	Jackson, Williamson, & Franklin
Robert Boal	Putnam, Tazewell, part of Woodford, & Marshall
John Buford	Henry, Lee, Whiteside, & Rock Island
Seth Catlin	St. Clair
Alfred W. Cavarly	Calhoun & Greene
Charles H. Constable	Edwards, Wayne, & Wabash
John Crain	Clinton, Washington, & Perry

Member	County
Jacob C. Davis	Hancock
John Dougherty	Alexander & Union
Samuel Dunlap	Crawford, Jasper, part of Richland, & Lawrence
Ninian W. Edwards	Sangamon
William Fithian	Vermilion
Ferris Forman	Clay, Effingham, part of Richland, & Fayette
John Harris	Jersey & Macoupin
George W. Harrison	Carroll, Stephenson, & JoDaviess
John Henry	Morgan
Benjamin Johnson	Christian, Montgomery, & Bond
Norman B. Judd	Lake & Cook
Thomas M. Killpatrick	Cass & Scott
George Leviston	Gallatin
William McMillan	McDonough & Warren
William McMurtry	Mercer & Knox
David Markley	Fulton
Joel A. Matteson	Du Page, Iroquois, & Will
Ira Minard	Boone, De Kalb, McHenry, & Kane
Joseph Morrison	Monroe & Randolph
Nelson W. Nunnally	Edgar
Nathaniel Parker	Coles & Clark
George W. Powers	De Witt, Livingston, Macon, Piatt, & McLean
Spooner Ruggles	Winnebago & Ogle
Michael Ryan	La Salle
George Smith	Madison
Jacob Smith	Adams
William W. Thompson	Bureau, Starke, & Peoria
Jacob Vandeventer	Schuyler & Brown
Peter Warren	Moultrie & Shelby
Edwin B. Webb	White
George W. Waters	Hardin, Johnson, & Pope
Robert A. D. Willbanks	Hamilton, Marion, & Jefferson
Thomas Worthington	Pike
Lewis B. Wynne	Logan, Mason, & Menard

House of Representatives

Speaker	William A. Richardson
Clerk	Newton Cloud

Member	County
Elijah Adams	Randolph & Monroe
Cyrus Aldrich	JoDaviess
Washington Alexander	Edgar
Samuel Anderson	St. Clair
William G. Anderson	Lawrence

Member	County
Francis Arenz	Morgan
George W. Armstrong	Grundy, Kendall, & La Salle
Isaac N. Arnold	Cook
Almon W. Babbitt	Hancock
Jacob R. Backenstos	Hancock
George Barnsback	Madison
Kirby Benedict	Macon & Piatt
Isaac S. Berry	Effingham & Fayette
William Blair	Pike
Henderson P. Boyakin	Marion
Richard A. Bradley	Jackson
William Brinkley	Hamilton
John Brown	Schuyler
John M. Burnett	Gallatin
Horace Butler	Lake
Joseph Campbell	Wayne
George Churchill	Madison
John Cochran	Alexander & Union
Addison Collins	Iroquois, Will, & Du Page
David Cox	Champaign
William H. W. Cushman	Grundy, Kendall, & La Salle
David Davis	McLean
John T. Davis	Williamson
William A. Denning	Franklin, Pulaski, & Alexander
John Deskins	Mason & Logan
Alexander P. Dunbar	Coles
Reuben R. Emerson[1]	White
Job Fletcher	Sangamon
Presley Funkhouser	Fayette & Effingham
David L. Gregg	Iroquois, Will, & Du Page
Maximilian Haley	Henderson & Warren
Levi A. Hannaford	Peoria
George M. Hanson	Coles
Hiram Hardie	Mercer & Knox
Joshua Harper	Henry & Rock Island
James Harriott	Jersey
William D. Henderson	Henderson & Warren
William Hendry	Adams
William D. Herndon	Sangamon
Thomas S. Hick	Gallatin
Stephen G. Hicks	Jefferson
Samuel M. Hitt	Ogle
Samuel Huffman	Vermilion
Barnabas M. Jackson	Bureau, Stark, & Peoria
William M. Jackson	Boone, De Kalb, McHenry, & Kane
Eldredge S. Janney	Jasper & Crawford
Eli G. Jewel	Boone, De Kalb, McHenry, & Kane
John Kirkpatrick	Montgomery
Andrew J. Kuykendall	Massac & Johnson

Member	County
James Leighton	Scott
James Lockhard	Clark
Stephen T. Logan	Sangamon
James L. Loop	
Boone, De Kalb, McHenry, & Kane	
Peter Lott	Adams
John McDonald	Calhoun & Greene
Julius Manning	Knox
Samuel T. Mathews	Morgan
Benjamin B. Metz	Pike
Anson S. Miller	Winnebago
Harry L. Miller	Fulton
Warren Miller	Adams
William J. Moore	Vermilion
Jacob C. Morrille	Putnam & Marshall
Richard G. Morris	Jasper & Crawford
James L. D. Morrison	St. Clair
Elias B. Myers	Livingston & McLean
Iram Nye	Brown
Ambrose O'Connor	
Grundy, Kendall, & La Salle	
John M. Oglesby	
Jefferson, Marion, & Hamilton	
Braxton Parrish	Franklin
William Pickering	Edwards
Franklin R. Pitner	Clay
John W. Pratt	Cass
Samuel Prevo	Clark
William H. Randolph	McDonough
Isaac D. Rawlings	Morgan
J. H. Reed	Lawrence & Richland
William A. Richardson	
Brown & Schuyler	
William S. Ricks	Christian
Ezekiel W. Robbins	Randolph & Monroe
Lewis W. Ross	Fulton
James K. Scott	De Witt
John Scott	Macoupin
Orval Sexton	Gallatin
Joseph L. Sharp	Fulton
Francis C. Sherman	Cook
Benjamin L. Smith	Stark & Bureau
Henry Smith	Stephenson & Carroll
Joseph Smith	Sangamon
Elisha H. Starkweather	Cumberland
Alexander Starne	Pike
John Steele	Perry
Hart L. Stewart	Cook
Newton D. Strong	Madison
Amos Thompson	St. Clair
Calvin Tunnel	Greene
John S. Turley	Shelby
F. P. Vedder	Greene
Phillip Vineyard	Hardin & Pope
Jacob Wagner	Iroquois, Will, & Du Page
J. M. Warren	Iroquois, Will, & Du Page
James White	Menard
John White	Washington & Clinton
John White	Scott

Member	County
John D. Whiteside	Randolph & Monroe
Charles C. Wilcox	Woodford & Tazewell
Winfield S. Wilkinson	Lee & Whiteside
Isaac Williams	Woodford & Tazewell
John T. Wood	Macoupin
William Woodburn	Washington & Clinton
James B. Woolard	Bond
Richard Yates	Morgan
John F. Youngkin	Wabash
John S. Zeiber	Fulton & Peoria

[1] Election voided, new election ordered Nov. 5, 1844, which Emerson won.

Fifteenth General Assembly, 1846–48

Convened Dec. 7, 1846; adjourned March 1, 1847.

Senate

President	Joseph B. Wells
Secretary	Henry W. Moore

Member	County
Willis Allen	
Jackson, Williamson, & Franklin	
John T. Allison	Edgar
Robert Boal	Putnam, Tazewell, part of
Woodford, & Marshall	
John Brown	Brown & Schuyler
Seth Catlin	St. Clair
Alfred W. Cavarly	Calhoun & Greene
Oliver Coudy	Bond
Charles H. Constable	
Edwards, Wayne, & Wabash	
Jacob C. Davis	Hancock
Thomas G. C. Davis	
Hardin, Johnson, & Pope	
Elias S. Dennis	
Perry, Washington, & Clinton	
John Denny	Mercer & Knox
John Dougherty	
Alexander, Pulaski, & Union	
Samuel Dunlap	Crawford, Jasper, part
of Richland, & Lawrence	
Ninian W. Edwards	Sangamon
Joseph Gillespie	Madison
George M. Hanson	
Clark, Cumberland, & Coles	
John Harris	Jersey & Macoupin
John Henry	Morgan
Samuel Houston[1]	
Clay, part of Richland, & Fayette	
Norman B. Judd	Lake & Cook
Thomas M. Killpatrick	Cass & Scott

Member	County
George Leviston	Gallatin
William McMillan	
Henderson, McDonough, & Warren	
Josiah McRoberts	Champaign & Vermilion
David Markley	Fulton
Joel A. Matteson	
	Du Page, Iroquois, & Will
Anson S. Miller	Ogle & Winnebago
Joseph Morrison	Monroe & Randolph
Silas R. J. Noble	
	Henry, Rock Island, Whiteside, & Lee
George W. Powers	De Witt, Livingston,
	Macon, Piatt, & McLean
William Reddick	Grundy & La Salle
Lorenzo P. Sanger	
	Carroll, Stephenson, & JoDaviess
Jacob Smith	Adams
William J. Stevenson	
	Jefferson, Marion, & Hamilton
Hugh L. Sutphin	Pike
Peter Sweat	Bureau, Stark, & Peoria
Peter Warren	Moultrie & Shelby
Edwin B. Webb	White
Elijah Wilcox	
	Boone, De Kalb, McHenry, & Kane

[1] Elected Dec. 30, 1846. No senator sat for first part of session.

House of Representatives

Speaker	Newton Cloud
Clerk	John McDonald

Member	County
Walter Aiken[3]	Franklin
William B. Archer	Clark
Henry S. Austin[5]	Peoria & Fulton
Even Baly	Fulton
John S. Bailey	Schuyler & Brown
William Bailey	Henry & Rock Island
William Barber	
	Grundy, Kendall, & La Salle
Curtis Blakeman	Madison
Henderson P. Boyakin	Marion
Marmontel Boyle	Jasper & Crawford
Henry Bragg	Greene
James N. Brown	Sangamon
Edward H. Buckley	Marquette[6]
John B. Campbell	Scott
William Cantrell	Piatt & Macon
Lewis F. Casey	Jefferson
Josiah Caswell	Greene
Wyllys H. Chapman	Marquette[6]
Resin H. Constant	Sangamon
Berryman Creel	Clinton
Robert J. Cross	Winnebago

Member	County
Thomas Cummings	Jersey
John W. Cunningham	Williamson
John Curts	Henderson & Warren
Joseph Dairman[4]	Hardin & Pope
William G. Dana	Ogle
William P. Davis	Vermilion
John Dawson	Brown
William A. Denning[1]	
	Franklin, Pulaski, & Alexander
William F. DeWolf	Madison
Abner Eads	JoDaviess
Henry Eddy	Gallatin
George Ela	Lake
Enoch Enloe	Massac & Johnson
Thomas Epperson	Bureau, Peoria, & Stark
Lewis D. Erwin	Schuyler
Jesse J. Everett	Cook
John D. Fry	Calhoun & Greene
Presley Funkhouser	Fayette & Effingham
Ephraim Gilmore	Mercer & Knox
Samuel P. Glenn	De Witt
Joseph O. Glover	
	Grundy, Kendall, & La Salle
John M. Griffith	Clay
Alfred Grubb	Pike
Charles Hansford	Knox
William P. Harpole	Pike
James Harrington	
	Boone, De Kalb, McHenry, & Kane
Thomas Hart	Macoupin
Samuel S. Hayes	White
William Hendry[7]	Adams
Thomas S. Hick	Gallatin
James M. Higgins	Pike
John Hodges	Pulaski & Alexander
Samuel Huffman	Vermilion
Eldredge S. Janney	Jasper & Crawford
Noah Johnson	
	Hamilton, Marion, & Jefferson
Captain E. Kinney	
	Du Page, Iroquois, & Will
George W. Kretzinger	
	Boone, De Kalb, McHenry, & Kane
Usher F. Linder	Coles
Thomas J. Little	Fulton
William E. Little	Du Page, Iroquois, & Will
John Logan	Jackson
Stephen T. Logan	Sangamon
William H. Long	Morgan
Samuel S. Lukins	Wabash
Robert McConnell	Carroll & Stephenson
Reuben R. McDowell	Fulton
Richard C. McLean	Richland & Lawrence
Robert Mann	Monroe & Randolph
Samuel S. Marshall[1]	Hamilton
William Martin	Madison
John Miller	Du Page, Iroquois, & Will
Edward G. Miner	Scott
Isaac N. Morris	Adams

Member	County
John Morrison	Monroe & Randolph
Thomas Morrison	Hancock
Joseph Morton	Morgan
Ambrose O'Connor	Grundy, Kendall, & La Salle
Edward Omelveny	Monroe & Randolph
Hawkins S. Osburn	Perry
William Pickering	Edwards
James T. Pierson	Boone, De Kalb, McHenry, & Kane
Samuel Prevo	Clark
William H. Randolph	McDonough
Frederick Remann	Effingham & Fayette
John Reynolds	St. Clair
William Rhodes[2]	Hardin & Pope
Mathew Robb	McLean
James Robeson	Livingston, Woodford, & McLean
James M. Robinson	Menard
John M. Ruddle[3]	Adams
James M. Rutledge	Montgomery
James M. Seehorn	Marquette[6] & Adams
Francis C. Sherman	Cook
Dorice D. Shumway	Christian
Hall Simms	Edgar
Mark Skinner	Cook
Rigdon B. Slocumb	Wayne
William S. Smith	Bond
Micajah J. Stanley	Du Page, Iroquois, & Will
James Stark	Hancock
Elisha H. Starkweather	Cumberland
William H. Stickney	Gallatin
Mathew Stokes	Union
Samuel Stuckey	St. Clair
Michael W. Swing	Mason & Logan
Harman V. A. Tappan	Macoupin
Samuel Thomas	Stark & Brown
William Thomas	Morgan
James Tucker	Henderson & Warren
Edward W. Turner	Cass
William H. Underwood	St. Clair
Hugh Wallace	Lee & Whiteside
Andrew Wardlaw	Putnam & Marshall
William D. Watson	Coles
Benjamin West	Sangamon
John White	Washington
Charles C. Wilcox	Woodford & Tazewell
Isaac Williams	Woodford & Tazewell
William Williamson	Shelby
James S. Wright	Champaign
Josiah R. Wynne	Richland & Lawrence

[1] Resigned.
[2] Died Jan. 3, 1847.
[3] Vice Denning.
[4] Vice Rhodes.
[5] Elected Dec. 21, 1846. No reason given for special election.
[6] Marquette County formed 1843 from eastern part of Adams County. Renamed Highland County in 1847. Returned to Adams County in 1848.

[7] Died Dec. 30, 1846.
[8] Vice Hendry special election Jan. 16, 1847.

Original districting under constitution of 1848; twenty-five Senate and fifty-four House districts

Senate district — *Counties*

1 Alexander, Hardin, Johnson, Massac, Pope, Pulaski, Union
2 Franklin, Gallatin, Saline, White, Williamson
3 Hamilton, Jefferson, Marion, Wayne
4 Jackson, Perry, Randolph, Washington
5 Monroe, St. Clair
6 Clinton, Madison
7 Bond, Christian, Fayette, Montgomery, Shelby
8 Clay, Edwards, Effingham, Jasper, Lawrence, Richland, Wabash
9 Clark, Crawford, Edgar
10 Champaign, Coles, Cumberland, Moultrie, Piatt, Vermilion
11 De Witt, Logan, McLean, Macon, Tazewell
12 Mason, Menard, Sangamon
13 Calhoun, Greene, Jersey, Macoupin
14 Cass, Morgan, Scott
15 Adams, Pike
16 Brown, Highland*, McDonough, Schuyler
17 Hancock, Henderson
18 Fulton, Peoria
19 Henry, Knox, Mercer, Rock Island, Stark, Warren
20 Bureau, Grundy, La Salle, Livingston, Marshall, Putnam, Woodford
21 Du Page, Iroquois, Kendall, Will
22 De Kalb, Kane, Lee, Ogle
23 Carroll, JoDaviess, Stephenson, Whiteside
24 Boone, McHenry, Winnebago
25 Cook, Lake

House district	*Counties*	*Number of representatives*
1	Alexander, Pulaski, Union	1
2	Hardin, Massac, Pope	1
3	Gallatin, Saline	1
4	Johnson, Williamson	1
5	Franklin, Jackson	1
6	Hamilton, Jefferson, Marion, Wayne	3
7	White	1
8	Edwards, Wabash	1
9	Lawrence, Richland	1
10	Crawford, Jasper	1
11	Coles	1
12	Clark	1
13	Clay, Cumberland, Effingham	1
14	Fayette	1
15	Bond, Clinton, Montgomery	2
16	Perry, Washington	2
17	Randolph	1
18	Monroe	1
19	St. Clair	2
20	Madison	2

House district	Counties	Number of representatives
21	Macoupin	1
22	Greene, Jersey	2
23	Scott	1
24	Morgan	2
25	Cass, Menard	1
26	Sangamon	2
27	Logan, Mason	1
28	Tazewell	1
29	De Witt, McLean	1
30	Vermilion	1
31	Edgar	1
32	Champaign, Macon, Moultrie, Piatt	1
33	Christian, Shelby	1
34	Calhoun, Pike	2
35	Adams, Brown, Highland*	3
36	Schuyler	1
37	Hancock	2
38	McDonough	1
39	Fulton	2
40	Peoria	1
41	Knox	1
42	Henderson, Mercer, Warren	2
43	Henry, Rock Island, Stark	1
44	Lee, Whiteside	1
45	Carroll, Ogle	1
46	JoDaviess, Stephenson	2
47	Winnebago	1
48	Marshall, Putnam, Woodford	1
49	Bureau, Grundy, La Salle, Livingston	2
50	Du Page, Iroquois, Kendall, Will	3
51	De Kalb, Kane	2
52	Boone, McHenry	2
53	Lake	1
54	Cook	2

* This county, originally named Marquette, was organized in 1843, from the eastern part of Adams County. In 1847 it was somewhat enlarged and renamed Highland. In 1848 it was abolished and the land returned to Adams County.

Sixteenth General Assembly, 1849–50

First session convened Jan. 1, 1849; adjourned Feb. 12, 1849. Second session convened Oct. 22, 1849; adjourned Nov. 7, 1849.

Senate

President	William McMurtry
Secretary	William Smith

District	Member	County
1	William Y. Davis	Johnson
2	Dempsey Odam	Williamson
3	Jeduthan P. Hardy	Hamilton
4	Hawkins S. Osburn	Perry
5	James L. D. Morrison	St. Clair
6	Joseph Gillespie	Madison
7	Hiram Rountree	Montgomery
8	Alfred H. Grass	Lawrence

District	Member	County
9	William Tichenor	Edgar
	Uri Manly[1]	Clark
10	Josiah McRoberts	Vermilion
11	Edward O. Smith	Macon
12	John Todd Stuart	Sangamon
13	Franklin Witt	Greene
14	Newton Cloud	Morgan
15	Hugh L. Sutphin	Pike
16	John P. Richmond	Schuyler
17	Azro Patterson	Henderson
18	David Markley	Fulton
19	John Denny	Knox
20	William Reddick	La Salle
21	Joel A. Matteson	Will
22	William B. Plato	Kane
23	Hezekiah H. Gear	JoDaviess
24	Alfred E. Ames	Winnebago
25	Norman B. Judd	Cook

[1] Vice Tichenor, absent from state.

House of Representatives

Speaker	Zadok Casey
Clerk	Nathaniel Niles

District	Member	County
1	John Cochran	Union
2	Wesley Sloan	Pope
3	David J. Blackman	Saline
4	David Y. Bridges	Johnson
5	Richard A. Bradley	Jackson
6	James J. Richardson	Marion
	John A. Campbell	Wayne
	Zadok Casey	Jefferson
7	Samuel S. Hayes	White
8	William Pickering	Edwards
9	Ebenezer Z. Ryan	Lawrence
10	Richard G. Morris	Crawford
11	Usher F. Linder	Coles
12	Joshua P. Cooper	Clark
13	Elisha H. Starkweather	Cumberland
14	John McDonald	Fayette
15	Edward Y. Rice	Montgomery
	Richard S. Bond	Clinton
16	Zenas H. Vernon	Washington
17	Samuel S. Guthrie	Randolph
18	Xerxes F. Trail	Monroe
19	Samuel Stuckey[1]	St. Clair
	Samuel B. Chandler[2]	St. Clair
	Edward Abend	St. Clair
20	Edward Keating	Madison
	Curtis Blakeman	Madison
21	Francis A. Olds	Macoupin
22	Isaac Darniel[1]	Jersey
	Joel Corey[3]	Jersey
	John D. Fry[4]	Greene
	Thomas Carlin[5]	Greene
23	Charles F. Keener	Scott
24	George B. Waller	Morgan
	Richard Yates	Morgan
25	Richard S. Thomas	Cass
26	Ninian W. Edwards	Sangamon
	John W. Smith	Sangamon
27	John Lucas	Logan
28	Middleton Tackerberry	Tazewell
29	James B. Price	McLean
30	John J. Sconce	Vermilion

District	Member	County
31	George W. Rives	Edgar
32	Reuben B. Ewing	Moultrie
33	Edward Evey	Shelby
34	Tyre Jennings	Pike
	George Pattison	Calhoun
35	Onias C. Skinner	Adams
	Jonathan Dearborn	Brown
	John Marrett	Adams
36	Jesse Darnell	Schuyler
37	George Walker	Hancock
	Stephen H. Tyler	Hancock
38	Josiah Harrison	McDonough
39	William Kellogg	Fulton
	Edward Sayre	Fulton
40	Ezra G. Singer	Peoria
41	Henry J. Runkle	Knox
42	Gilbert Turnbull	Henderson
	Abner C. Harding	Warren
43	John W. Henderson	Stark
44	Joseph Crawford	Lee
45	Dauphin Brown	Ogle
46	Abner Aeds	JoDaviess
	Cyrenius B. Denio	JoDaviess
47	Wilson H. Crandell	Winnebago
48	John Page	Woodford
49	George W. Wilson	La Salle
	Melancthon E. Lasher	Bureau
50	William E. Little	Will
	Warren L. Wheaton	Du Page
	Lorenzo D. Brady[4]	Kendall
	Orlando H. Haven[6]	Kendall
51	H. W. Fay	De Kalb
	E. W. Austin	Kane
52	John F. Gray	McHenry
	Selby Leach	Boone
53	Life Wilson	Lake
54	Philip Maxwell	Cook
	Francis C. Sherman	Cook

[1] Died.
[2] Vice Stuckey.
[3] Vice Darniel.
[4] Resigned.
[5] Vice Fry.
[6] Vice Brady.

Seventeenth General Assembly, 1851–52

First session convened Jan. 6, 1851; adjourned Feb. 17, 1851. Second session convened June 7, 1852; adjourned June 23, 1852.

Senate

President	William McMurtry
Secretary	William Smith

District	Member	County
1	Andrew J. Kuykendall	Johnson
2	Dempsey Odam	Williamson
3	Jeduthan P. Hardy	Jefferson
	Hugh Gregg[1]	Hamilton
4	Hawkins S. Osburn	Perry
5	James L. D. Morrison	St. Clair
6	Joseph Gillespie	Madison
7	Hiram Rountree	Montgomery
	Jacob D. Lansing[2]	[unknown]

District	Member	County
8	Alfred H. Grass	Lawrence
9	Josiah R. Wynne	Crawford
10	Nathaniel Parker	Colès
11	Asahel Gridley	McLean
12	John Todd Stuart	Sangamon
13	Franklin Witt	Greene
	John M. Palmer[3]	Macoupin
14	Newton Cloud	Morgan
15	John Wood	Adams
16	John P. Richmond	Schuyler
17	Jacob C. Davis	Hancock
18	Peter Sweat	Peoria
19	John Denny	Knox
	Samuel Webster[4]	Rock Island
20	William Reddick	La Salle
21	Joel A. Matteson	Will
22	William B. Plato	Kane
23	Hugh Wallace	Whiteside
24	Thomas B. Talcott	Winnebago
25	Norman B. Judd	Cook

[1] Vice Hardy, resigned.
[2] Vice Rountree, resigned.
[3] Vice Witt, died.
[4] Vice Denny, resigned.

House of Representatives

Speaker	Sidney Breese
Clerk	Isaac R. Diller

District	Member	County
1	Cyrus G. Simonds	Union
2	Wesley Sloan	Pope
3	Albert G. Caldwell	Gallatin
	Orval Sexton[1]	Gallatin
4	Wilfred Ferrell	Williamson
5	Thomas M. Sams	Franklin
6	Zadok Casey	Jefferson
	Isham N. Haynie	Marion
	William L. Gash	Wayne
7	Samuel H. Martin	White
8	William Pickering	Edwards
9	Aaron Shaw	Lawrence
10	James C. Allen	Crawford
11	Usher F. Linder	Coles
12	T. C. Moore	Clark
13	William H. Blakely	Effingham
14	Aiken Evans	Fayette
15	Sidney Breese	Clinton
	William Brewer	Montgomery
16	Richard G. Murphy	Perry
17	John E. Detrich	Randolph
18	Thomas Quick	Monroe
19	William H. Snyder	St. Clair
	Harbert Patterson	St. Clair
	Philip B. Fouke[2]	St. Clair
20	Andrew Miller	Madison
	Nelson G. Edwards	Madison
	Samuel A. Buckmaster[3]	Madison
21	Beatty T. Burke	Macoupin
22	Charles D. Hodges	Greene
	J. C. Winters	Jersey

District	Member	County
23	Nathan M. Knapp	Scott
24	William Thomas	Morgan
	Benjamin F. Bristow	Morgan
25	William T. Beekman	Menard
26	Ninian W. Edwards	Sangamon
	Preston Breckenridge	Sangamon
	James C. Conkling⁴	Sangamon
27	John Pemberton	Mason
28	Robert W. Briggs	Tazewell
29	Robert F. Barnett	De Witt
30	Oliver L. Davis	Vermilion
31	Ozias Bailey	Edgar
32	Charles Emmerson	Macon
33	Anthony Thornton	Shelby
34	William D. Hamilton	Calhoun
	Ozias M. Hatch	Pike
35	James W. Singleton	Brown
	J. R. Hobbs	Adams
	James M. Pitman	Adams
36	Allen Persinger	Schuyler
37	Joseph Sibley	Hancock
	John Carlin	Hancock
38	John Houston	McDonough
39	Thomas J. Little	Fulton
	Isaac Linley	Fulton
40	David Sanborn	Peoria
41	Henry Arms	Knox
42	Azro Patterson	Henderson
	Thomas Willits	Mercer
43	James M. Allen	Henry
44	Van J. Adams	Whiteside
45	William T. Miller	Carroll
46	Daniel Wilson	Stephenson
	Bushrod B. Howard	JoDaviess
47	Horace Miller	Winnebago
48	Eli B. Ames	Putnam
49	Abraham L. Phillips	Bureau
	John Hise	La Salle
50	Sylvester W. Randall	Kendall
	Jesse O. Norton	Will
	W. F. Jones	Du Page
	Julius M. Warren⁵	Du Page
51	Augustus Adams	Kane
	Benjamin F. Hall	De Kalb
52	Alexander H. Nixon	McHenry
	George Gage	McHenry
53	Hurlbut Swan	Lake
54	Philip Maxwell	Cook
	Thomas Dyer	Cook

¹ Vice Caldwell, died.
² Vice Patterson, resigned.
³ Vice Nelson G. Edwards, resigned.
⁴ Vice Ninian W. Edwards, resigned.
⁵ Vice Jones, left state.

Eighteenth General Assembly, 1853–54

First session convened Jan. 3, 1853; adjourned Feb. 14, 1853. Second session convened Feb. 9, 1854; adjourned March 4, 1854.

Senate

President	Gustave Philipp Koerner
Secretary	Roswell Eaton Goodell

District	Member	County
1	Andrew J. Kuykendall	Johnson
2	Anderson P. Corder	Williamson
3	Silas L. Bryan	Marion
4	John E. Detrich	Randolph
5	Edward Omelveny	Monroe
6	Joseph Gillespie	Madison
7	Gabriel R. Jernigan	Christian
8	Mortimer O'Kean	Jasper
9	Josiah R. Wynne	Crawford
10	Nathaniel Parker	Coles
11	Asahel Gridley	McLean
12	James M. Ruggles	Mason
13	John M. Palmer	Macoupin
14	Joseph Morton	Morgan
15	John Wood¹	Adams
16	James M. Campbell	McDonough
17	Jacob C. Davis	Hancock
18	Peter Sweat²	Peoria
19	Benjamin Graham	Henry
20	Burton C. Cooke	La Salle
21	Uri Osgood	Will
22	William B. Plato	Kane
23	Hugh Wallace³	Whiteside
24	Thomas B. Talcott	Winnebago
25	Norman B. Judd	Cook

¹ Resigned; succeeded by Solomon Parsons, Pike Co.
² Resigned; succeeded by Washington Cockle, Peoria Co.
³ Resigned; succeeded by Bushrod B. Howard, JoDaviess Co.

House of Representatives

Speaker	John Reynolds
Clerk	Isaac R. Diller, resigned
Clerk	John Calhoun, vice Diller

District	Member	County
1	John Cochran	Union
2	Wesley Sloan	Pope
3	David B. Russell	Saline
4	David Y. Bridges	Johnson
5	John A. Logan	Jackson
6	John Wilbanks	Jefferson
	Alexander Campbell	Wayne
	John A. Wilson	Hamilton
7	Daniel L. Jones	White
8	Victor B. Bell	Wabash
9	William H. Christy	Lawrence
10	William H. Sterrett	Crawford
11	William D. Watson	Coles
12	Uri Manly	Clark
13	Presley Funkhouser	Effingham
14	A. J. Gallagher	Fayette
	N. M. McCurdy¹	Fayette
15	William H. Maddux	Clinton
	William Young	Montgomery
16	William M. Phillips	Washington
17	Joseph Williamson	Randolph
18	Thomas Winstanley	Monroe
19	John Reynolds	St. Clair
	William H. Snyder	St. Clair

District	Member	County
20	Samuel A. Buckmaster	Madison
	Thomas Judy	Madison
21	Lewis Solomon	Macoupin
22	Giles H. Turner	Jersey
	Charles D. Hodges	Greene
23	Royal Mooers	Scott
24	William Brown	Morgan
	Edward Lusk	Morgan
25	Cyrus Wright	Cass
26	Pascal P. Enos	Sangamon
	James N. Brown	Sangamon
27	Colby Knapp	Logan
28	Richard N. Cullom	Tazewell
29	John E. McClun	McLean
30	Thomas Heywood	Vermilion
31	William Shields	Edgar
32	Henry Prather	Macon
33	Samuel W. Moulton	Shelby
34	Henry B. Buchanan	Calhoun
	Hugh L. Sutphin	Pike
35	James M. Pitman	Adams
	John C. Moses	Brown
	David Wolf	Adams
	James W. Singleton[2]	Brown
	Hiram Boyle[3]	Adams
36	Francis E. Bryant	Schuyler
37	David Gochenour	Hancock
	Joseph Sibley	Hancock
38	James M. Randolph	McDonough
39	W. K. Johnson	Fulton
	L. H. Bradbury	Fulton
40	Charles P. King	Peoria
41	Thomas McKee	Knox
42	Samuel Darnell	Henderson
	E. A. Paine	Warren
43	William Marshall	Rock Island
44	Joseph Crawford	Lee
45	Elias S. Potter	Ogle
46	Cyrenius B. Denio	JoDaviess
	W. P. Narramore	Stephenson
47	A. J. Enoch	Winnebago
48	Silas Ramsey	Marshall
49	C. R. Potter	La Salle
	C. L. Starbuck	Grundy
50	Joseph Thomas	Iroquois
	R. N. Matthews	Kendall
	Joseph Naper	Du Page
51	John Ransted	Kane
	William Shepherdson	De Kalb
52	Hiram C. Miller	Boone
	Alexander H. Nixon	McHenry
53	Henry W. Blodgett	Lake
54	William B. Egan	Cook
	Homer Wilmarth	Cook

[1] Vice Gallagher, resigned.
[2] Vice Moses, resigned.
[3] Vice Pitman.

Redistricting of 1854 authorized by act of Feb. 27, 1854; twenty-five Senate and fifty-eight House districts

*Senate
district*   *Counties*
1 Cook
2 Lake, McHenry

*Senate
districts*   *Counties*
3 Boone, Carroll, Ogle, Winnebago
4 JoDaviess, Stephenson
5 De Kalb, Kane, Lee, Whiteside
6 Du Page, Iroquois, Kankakee, Kendall, Will
7 Bureau, Grundy, La Salle, Livingston
8 Marshall, Peoria, Putnam, Woodford
9 Henry, Knox, Mercer, Rock Island, Stark, Warren
10 Fulton, McDonough
11 Hancock, Henderson, Schuyler
12 Adams, Brown
13 Calhoun, Pike, Scott
14 Greene, Jersey, Macoupin
15 Morgan, Sangamon
16 Champaign, Christian, De Witt, McLean, Macon, Moultrie, Piatt. Shelby
17 Cass, Logan, Mason, Menard, Tazewell
18 Coles, Cumberland, Edgar, Vermilion
19 Clark, Crawford, Effingham, Fayette, Jasper, Lawrence
20 Clay, Edwards, Jefferson, Marion, Richland, Wabash, Wayne
21 Bond, Madison, Montgomery
22 Monroe, St. Clair
23 Franklin, Hamilton, Saline, White, Williamson
24 Clinton, Jackson, Perry, Randolph, Washington
25 Alexander, Gallatin, Hardin, Johnson, Massac, Pope, Pulaski, Union

*House
district*   *Counties*
1 Alexander, Pulaski, Union
2 Hardin, Massac, Pope
3 Johnson, Williamson
4 Gallatin, Saline
5 Franklin, Jackson
6 Randolph
7 Perry, Washington
8 Hamilton, Jefferson, Marion
9 Wabash, White
10 Edwards, Wayne
11 Monroe
12 St. Clair
13 Bond, Clinton
14 Madison
15 Effingham, Fayette
16 Clay, Jasper, Richland
17 Crawford, Lawrence
18 Clark
19 Cumberland, Shelby
20 Christian, Montgomery
21 Macoupin
22 Calhoun, Jersey
23 Greene
24 Edgar
25 Coles, Moultrie
26 Sangamon
27 Morgan, Scott
28 Brown, Pike
29 Adams

House district	Counties
30 Schuyler	
31 Hancock	
32 McDonough	
33 Fulton	
34 Cass, Menard	
35 Logan, Mason	
36 Champaign, De Witt, Macon, Piatt	
37 Vermilion	
38 McLean	
39 Tazewell	
40 Henderson, Warren	
41 Peoria, Stark	
42 Marshall, Putnam, Woodford	
43 Grundy, La Salle, Livingston	
44 Kendall	
45 Du Page, Iroquois, Kankakee, Will	
46 De Kalb, Kane	
47 Bureau	
48 Henry, Mercer, Rock Island	
49 Lee, Whiteside	
50 Ogle	
51 Carroll, JoDaviess	
52 Stephenson	
53 Winnebago	
54 Boone, McHenry	
55 Lake	
56 Cook	
57 Cook	
58 Knox	

Nineteenth General Assembly, 1855–56

Convened Jan. 1, 1855; adjourned Feb. 15, 1855.

Senate

President	Gustave Philipp Koerner
Secretary	George T. Brown

District	Member	County
1	Norman B. Judd	Cook
2	George Gage	McHenry
3	Wait Talcott	Winnebago
4	John H. Addams	Stephenson
5	Augustus Adams	Kane
6	Uri Osgood	Will
7	Burton C. Cooke	La Salle
8	J. D. Arnold	Peoria
9	Benjamin Graham	Henry
10	James M. Campbell	McDonough
11	Jacob C. Davis[1]	Hancock
12	William H. Carlin	Adams
13	Hugh L. Sutphin	Pike
14	John M. Palmer[1]	Macoupin
15	Joseph Morton	Morgan
16	Gabriel R. Jernigan	Christian
17	James M. Ruggles	Mason
18	William D. Watson	Coles
19	Mortimer O'Kean	Jasper
20	Silas L. Bryan	Marion

District	Member	County
21	Joseph Gillespie	Madison
22	James L. D. Morrison	St. Clair
23	Anderson P. Corder	Williamson
24	John E. Detrich	Randolph
25	Andrew J. Kuykendall	Johnson

[1] Resigned.

House of Representatives

Speaker	Thomas J. Turner
Clerk	Edwin T. Bridges

District	Member	County
1	F. M. Rawlings	Alexander
2	George W. Gray	Massac
3	William J. Allen	Williamson
4	Benjamin P. Hinch	Gallatin
5	Thomas M. Sams	Franklin
6	James C. Holbrook	Randolph
7	Ptolemy E. Hosmer	Washington
8	Tazewell B. Tanner	Jefferson
	Hugh Gregg	Marion
9	Samuel H. Martin	White
10	C. C. Hopkins	Edwards
11	William R. Morrison	Monroe
12	Albert H. Trapp	St. Clair
	William C. Kinney	St. Clair
13	J. Bradford	Bond
14	George T. Allen	Madison
	Henry S. Baker	Madison
15	Presley Funkhouser	Effingham
16	Finney D. Preston	Richland
17	Randolph Heath	Crawford
18	Thomas R. McClure	Clark
19	Samuel W. Moulton	Shelby
20	Henry Richmond	Montgomery
21	George H. Holiday	Macoupin
22	Lafayette McCrillis	Jersey
23	James M. Pursley	Greene
24	Dudley McClain	Edgar
25	Albert G. Jones	Coles
26	Stephen T. Logan	Sangamon
	Jonathan McDaniel[1]	Sangamon
27	Isaac R. Bennett	Scott
	Horace A. Brown	Morgan
28	Chauncey L. Higbee	Pike
	Jonathan Dearborn	Brown
29	Eli Seehorn	Adams
	Henry Sullivan	Adams
30	John P. Richmond	Schuyler
31	George Walker	Hancock
32	Louis H. Waters	McDonough
33	William M. Cline	Fulton
	Amos C. Babcock	Fulton
34	S. D. Masters	Cass
35	Samuel C. Parks	Logan
36	Harry C. Johns	Macon
37	James Courtney	Vermilion
38	John E. McClun	Mclean
39	Henry Riblett	Tazewell
40	William C. Rice	Henderson
41	Henry A. Grove	Peoria
	Thomas J. Henderson	Stark
42	Robert Boal	Marshall
43	David Strawn	La Salle
	Frederick S. Day	Grundy

District	Member	County
44	Alanson K. Wheeler	Kendall
45	G. D. A. Park	Will
	John Strunk	Kankakee
	Erastus O. Hall	Du Page
46	Benjamin Hackney	Kane
	William Patten	De Kalb
47	Owen Lovejoy	Bureau
48	William L. Lee	Rock Island
49	Miles S. Henry	Whiteside
50	Daniel J. Pinckney	Ogle
51	Porter Sargent	Carroll
	Wallace A. Little	JoDaviess
52	Thomas J. Turner	Stephenson
53	William Lyman	Winnebago
54	Luther W Lawrence	Boone
	Wesley Higgins	McHenry
55	Hurlbut Swan	Lake
56	Robert H. Foss	Cook
	Thomas Richmond	Cook
57	L. M. Dunlap	Cook
	George F. Foster	Cook
58	Samuel W. Brown	Knox

¹Vice Abraham Lincoln, resigned before beginning of session.

Twentieth General Assembly, 1857–58

Convened Jan. 5, 1857; adjourned Feb. 19, 1857.

Senate

President	John Wood
Secretary	Benjamin Bond

District	Member	County
1	Norman B. Judd	Cook
2	George Gage	McHenry
3	Wait Talcott	Winnebago
4	John H. Addams	Stephenson
5	Augustus Adams	Kane
6	G. D. A. Park	Will
7	Burton C. Cooke	La Salle
8	J. D. Arnold	Peoria
9	Thomas J. Henderson	Stark
10	William C. Goudy	Fulton
11	Hiram Rose	Henderson
12	William H. Carlin	Adams
13	Hugh L. Sutphin	Pike
14	Linus E. Worcester¹	Greene
15	Cyrus W. Vanderen	Sangamon
16	Joel S. Post	Macon
17	Samuel W. Fuller	Tazewell
18	William D. Watson	Coles
19	Mortimer O'Kean	Jasper
20	Silas L. Bryan	Marion
21	Joseph Gillespie	Madison
22	William H. Underwood	St. Clair
23	Samuel H. Martin	White
24	Elzey C. Coffey	Washington
25	Andrew J. Kuykendall	Johnson

¹ Vice Palmer, resigned.

House of Representatives

Speaker	Samuel Holmes
Clerk	Charles Leib

District	Member	County
1	John Dougherty	Union
2	Wesley Sloan	Pope
3	Thomas Jones	Johnson
4	Ebon C. Ingersoll	Gallatin
5	John A. Logan	Jackson
6	James H. Watt	Randolph
7	Hawkins S. Osburn	Perry
8	John A. Wilson	Hamilton
	William B. Anderson	Jefferson
9	John E. Whiting	White
10	Charles P. Burns	Wayne
11	William R. Morrison	Monroe
12	Vital Jarrott	St. Clair
	William W. Roman	St. Clair
13	William A. J. Sparks	Clinton
14	Lewis Ricks	Madison
	Aaron P. Mason	Madison
15	Daniel Gregory	Fayette
16	Finney D. Preston	Richland
17	Isaac Wilkins	Crawford
18	Nathan Willard	Clark
19	Samuel W. Moulton	Shelby
20	Calvin Goudy	Christian
21	Beatty T. Burke	Macoupin
22	Wright Casey	Jersey
23	John W. Huitt	Greene
24	Samuel Connelly	Edgar
25	James E. Wuche	Coles
26	James J. Megredy	Sangamon
	Shelby M. Cullom	Sangamon
27	Cyrus Epler	Morgan
	Elisha B. Hitt	Scott
28	John L. Grimes	Pike
	King Kerley	Brown
29	Samuel Holmes	Adams
	Moses M. Bane	Adams
30	Lewis D. Erwin	Schuyler
31	William Tyner	Hancock
32	George Hire	McDonough
33	Joseph Dyckes	Fulton
	James H. Stipp	Fulton
34	Samuel Christy	Cass
35	Alexander W. Morgan	Logan
36	Jerome R. Gorin	Macon
37	Oliver L. Davis	Vermilion
38	John H. Wickizer	McLean
39	Daniel Trail	Tazewell
40	A. T. V. Gilbert	Warren
41	Martin Shallenberger	Stark
	John T. Lindsay	Peoria
42	Robert Boal	Marshall
43	Elmer Baldwin	La Salle
	James M. Reading	Grundy
44	John M. Crothers	Kendall
45	Truman W. Smith	Will
	Franklin Blades	Iroquois
	William A. Chatfield	Kankakee
46	David M. Kelsey	De Kalb

District	Member	County
	William R. Parker	Kane
47	George W. Radcliffe	Bureau
48	Henry G. Little	Henry
49	John V. Eustace	Lee
50	Daniel J. Pinckney	Ogle
51	Cyrenius B. Denio	JoDaviess
	Rollin Wheeler	Carroll
52	John A. Davis	Stephenson
53	William Lathrop	Winnebago
54	Lawrence S. Church	McHenry
	Luther W. Lawrence	Boone
55	William M. Burbank	Lake
56	John H. Dunham	Cook
	George W. Morris	Cook
57	Isaac N. Arnold	Cook
	A. F. C. Mueller	Cook
58	David H. Frisbie	Knox

Twenty-first General Assembly, 1859–60

Convened Jan. 3, 1859; adjourned Feb. 24, 1859.

Senate

President	John Wood
Secretary	Finney D. Preston

District	Member	County
1	Norman B. Judd	Cook
2	Henry W. Blodgett	Lake
3	Zenos Applington	Ogle
4	John H. Addams	Stephenson
5	Richard F. Adams	Lee
6	G. D. A. Park	Will
7	Burton C. Cooke	La Salle
8	George C. Bestor	Peoria
9	Thomas J. Henderson	Stark
10	William C. Goudy	Fulton
11	John P. Richmond	Schuyler
12	Austin Brooks	Adams
13	Chauncey L. Higbee	Pike
14	Antony L. Knapp	Jersey
15	Cyrus W. Vanderen	Sangamon
16	Joel S. Post	Macon
17	Samuel W. Fuller	Tazewell
18	Thomas A. Marshall	Coles
19	Mortimer O'Kean	Jasper
20	Silas L. Bryan	Marion
21	Samuel A. Buckmaster	Madison
22	William H. Underwood	St. Clair
23	Samuel H. Martin	White
24	Elzey C. Coffey	Washington
25	Andrew J. Kuykendall	Johnson

House of Representatives

Speaker	William R. Morrison
Clerk	David E. Head

District	Member	County
1	William A. Hacker	Union
2	William H. Green	Massac
3	James D. Pulley	Johnson
4	Thomas S. Hick	Gallatin
5	James Hampton	Franklin
6	John E. Detrich	Randolph
7	John D. Wood	Washington
8	John McIlvane	Hamilton
	William B. Anderson	Jefferson
9	John G. Powell	White
10	Robert T. Forth	Wayne
11	William R. Morrison	Monroe
12	John Scheel	St. Clair
	Vital Jarrott	St. Clair
13	Charles D. Hoiles	Bond
14	Z. B. Job	Madison
	Joseph H. Sloss	Madison
15	Stephen Hardin	Effingham
16	William J. Stephenson	Clay
17	Henry C. McCleave	Crawford
18	Joseph Updegraff	Clark
19	Thomas Brewer	Cumberland
20	James M. Davis	Montgomery
21	William C. Shirley	Macoupin
22	Francis P. Rush	Calhoun
23	Alexander King, Jr.	Greene
24	Robert Mosely	Edgar
25	William W. Craddock	Coles
26	James W. Barrett	Sangamon
	Daniel Short	Sangamon
27	Cyrus Epler	Morgan
	Elisha B. Hitt	Scott
28	Gilbert J. Shaw	Pike
	King Kerley	Brown
29	Moses M. Bane	Adams
	Western Metcalf	Adams
30	Lewis D. Erwin	Schuyler
31	William H. Rolloson	Hancock
32	William Berry	McDonough
33	John G. Graham	Fulton
	Samuel P. Cummings	Fulton
34	William Engle	Menard
35	George H. Campbell	Logan
36	Daniel Stickel	De Witt
37	Oscar F. Harmon	Vermilion
38	Leonard Swett	McLean
39	R. B. M. Wilson	Tazewell
40	William C. Rice	Henderson
41	Thomas C. Moore	Peoria
	Myrtle G. Brace	Stark
42	John A. McCall	Marshall
43	Alexander Campbell	La Salle
	Richardson S. Hick	Livingston
44	Valentine Vermilyea	Kendall
45	Hiram Norton	Will
	Alonzo W. Mack	Kankakee
	J. M. Hood	Iroquois
46	William Patten	De Kalb
	William B. Plato	Kane
47	John H. Bryant	Bureau
48	Ephraim Gilmore, Jr.	Rock Island
49	William Prothrow	Whiteside
50	Joshua White	Ogle
51	James DeWolf	Carroll
	Halstead S. Townsend	JoDaviess
52	John A. Davis	Stephenson
53	Elijah W. Blaisdell, Jr.	Winnebago

District	Member	County
54	Lawrence S. Church	McHenry
	Stephen A. Hurlbut	Boone
55	Elijah M. Haines	Lake
56	Van H. Higgins	Cook
	Samuel L. Baker	Cook
57	Ebenezer Peck	Cook
	Casper Butz	Cook
58	Rufus W. Miles	Knox

Twenty-second General Assembly,
1861–62

First session convened Jan. 7, 1861; adjourned Feb. 22, 1861. Second session convened April 23, 1861; adjourned May 3, 1861.

Senate

President	Francis A. Hoffman
President pro tempore	
	Thomas A. Marshall
Secretary	Campbell W. Waite

District	Member	County
1	William B. Ogden	Cook
2	Henry W. Blodgett	Lake
3	Zenos Applington	Ogle
4	John H. Addams	Stephenson
5	Richard F. Adams	Lee
6	Alonzo W. Mack	Kankakee
7	Washington Bushnell	La Salle
8	George C. Bestor	Peoria
9	Thomas J. Pickett	Rock Island
10	William Berry	McDonough
11	John P. Richmond	Schuyler
12	Austin Brooks[1]	Adams
13	Chauncey L. Higbee	Pike
14	Anthony L. Knapp	Jersey
15	William Jayne	Sangamon
16	Richard J. Oglesby	Macon
17	Henry E. Dummer	Cass
18	Thomas A. Marshall	Coles
19	Presley Funkhouser	Effingham
20	Zadok Casey[2]	Jefferson
21	Samuel A. Buckmaster	Madison
22	William H. Underwood	St. Clair
23	Hugh Gregg	Williamson
24	James M. Rodgers	Clinton
25	Andrew J. Kuykendall	Johnson

[1] Resigned Jan. 18, 1861; reelected Jan. 29, 1861.
[2] Died Sept. 4, 1862.

House of Representatives

Speaker	Shelby M. Cullom
Clerk	Harley Wayne

District	Member	County
1	William A. Hacker	Union
2	William H. Green	Massac
3	James D. Pulley	Johnson
4	William Elder	Saline
5	Peter Keifer	Jackson
6	Edmund Faherty ·	Randolph
7	Orson Kellogg	Perry
8	Cloyd Crouch	Hamilton
	Cyrus W. Webster	Marion
9	James M. Sharp	White
10	Nathan Crews	Wayne
11	Henry C. Talbott	Monroe
12	Vital Jarrott	St. Clair
	Samuel Stuckey	St. Clair
13	Joshua P. Knapp	Clinton
14	Cyrus Edwards	Madison
	Garrett Crownover	Madison
15	F. H. Stoddard	Fayette
16	Isaac H. Walker	Clay
17	Aaron Shaw	Crawford
18	John Scholfield	Clark
19	Thomas W. Harris	Shelby
20	Horatio M. Vandeveer	Christian
21	James T. Pennington	Macoupin
22	John N. English	Jersey
23	Benjamin Baldwin	Greene
24	Napoleon B. Stage	Edgar
25	Smith Nichols	Coles
26	Shelby M. Cullom	Sangamon
	Norman M. Broadwell	Sangamon
27	Isaiah Turner	Morgan
	Albert G. Burr	Scott
28	William R. Archer	Pike
	Benjamin F. DeWitt	Brown
29	James W. Singleton	Adams
	William C. Harrington	Adams
30	Lewis D. Erwin	Schuyler
31	William H. Rolloson	Hancock
32	Samuel H. McCandless	McDonough
33	John G. Graham	Fulton
	Samuel P. Cummings	Fulton
34	Frederick Rearick	Menard
35	Robert B. Latham	Logan
36	Lawrence Weldon	De Witt
37	Samuel G. Craig	Vermilion
38	Harvey Hogg	McLean
39	David Kyes	Tazewell
40	William C. Maley	Warren
41	Elbridge G. Johnson	Peoria
	Theodore F. Hurd	Stark
42	Henry D. Cook	Woodford
43	Andrew J. Cropsey	La Salle
	John W. Newport	Grundy
44	Valentine Vermilyea	Kendall
45	Franklin Blades	Iroquois
	Samuel Stover	Will
	Frederick H. Mather	Du Page
46	Edward R. Allen	Kane
	Thomas S. Terry	De Kalb
47	Joseph W. Harris	Bureau
48	Robert W. Smith	Rock Island
49	George Ryan	Lee
50	Francis A. McNeil	Ogle
51	Benjamin L. Patch	Carroll
	J. Russell Jones	JoDaviess
	Robert H. McClellan[1]	JoDaviess
52	John F. Ankeny	Stephenson

District	Member	County
53 Alfred A. Hale		Winnebago
54 Stephen A. Hurlbut		Boone
Lawrence S. Church		McHenry
55 Elijah M. Haines		Lake
56 J. Young Scammon		Cook
William E. Brown		Cook
57 Solomon M. Willson		Cook
Homer Wilmarth		Cook
58 Arthur A. Smith		Knox

¹ Vice Jones, resigned.

Redistricting of 1861 authorized by act of Jan. 31, 1861 ; twenty-five Senate and sixty-one House districts

Senate
district   *Counties*
1 Alexander, Gallatin, Hardin, Johnson, Massac, Pope, Pulaski, Saline, Union
2 Clay, Edwards, Hamilton, Lawrence, Richland, Wabash, Wayne, White
3 Franklin, Jackson, Jefferson, Monroe, Randolph, Williamson
4 Bond, Clinton, Fayette, Marion, Perry, Washington
5 Madison, St. Clair
6 Calhoun, Greene, Jersey, Pike, Scott
7 Christian, Macoupin, Montgomery, Shelby
8 Clark, Crawford, Cumberland, Edgar, Effingham, Jasper
9 Champaign, Coles, Douglas, Ford, Iroquois, Vermilion
10 De Witt, McLean, Macon, Moultrie, Piatt
11 Logan, Sangamon, Tazewell
12 Brown, Cass, Menard, Morgan, Schuyler
13 Adams, Hancock
14 Henderson, McDonough, Mercer, Warren
15 Fulton, Knox, Mason
16 Marshall, Peoria, Putnam, Stark
17 La Salle, Livingston, Woodford
18 Grundy, Kankakee, Kendall, Will
19 De Kalb, Du Page, Kane
20 Lee, Ogle, Whiteside
21 Bureau, Henry, Rock Island
22 Carroll, JoDaviess, Stephenson
23 Boone, Lake, McHenry, Winnebago
24 Cook
25 Cook

House
district   *Counties*
1 Alexander, Pulaski, Union
2 Johnson, Massac, Pope
3 Gallatin, Hardin, Saline
4 Lawrence, Wabash
5 Franklin, Jefferson
6 Jackson, Williamson
7 Clinton, Washington
8 Monroe, Perry, Randolph
9 Marion
10 Hamilton, Wayne
11 Crawford, Jasper

House
district   *Counties*
12 Clay, Richland
13 Effingham, Fayette
14 Edwards, White
15 St. Clair
16 Bond, Madison
17 Clark, Cumberland
18 Shelby
19 Christian, Montgomery
20 Logan, Sangamon
21 Macoupin
22 Calhoun, Jersey
23 Greene
24 Pike, Scott
25 Brown, Cass
26 Mason, Menard
27 Morgan
28 Adams
29 McDonough
30 Schuyler
31 Hancock
32 Henderson, Mercer
33 Warren
34 Knox
35 Fulton
36 Peoria, Stark
37 Tazewell
38 De Witt, McLean
39 Coles, Douglas, Edgar, Vermilion
40 Champaign, Macon, Moultrie, Piatt
41 Kankakee
42 Ford, Iroquois
43 Grundy, Will
44 La Salle, Livingston
45 Bureau, Marshall, Putnam, Woodford
46 Henry
47 Rock Island
48 Whiteside
49 Lee
50 Ogle
51 Boone, De Kalb
52 Kane, Kendall
53 Lake
54 McHenry
55 Winnebago
56 Stephenson
57 Carroll, JoDaviess
58 Du Page
59 Cook
60 Cook
61 Cook

Twenty-third General Assembly, 1863–64

Convened Jan. 5, 1863; adjourned Feb. 14, 1863, until June 2, 1863; prorogued by the governor, June 10, 1863, until Dec. 31, 1864; convened and adjourned Dec. 31, 1864.

Senate
President   Francis A. Hoffman
Secretary   Manning Mayfield

District	Member	County
1	William H. Green	Massac
2	Hugh Gregg	Hamilton
3	Israel Blanchard	Jackson
4	James M. Rodgers	Clinton
	William A. J. Sparks¹	Clinton
5	William H. Underwood	St. Clair
6	Linus E. Worcester	Greene
7	Horatio M. Vandeveer	Christian
8	Samuel Moffat	Effingham
9	Joseph Peters	Vermilion
10	Isaac Funk	McLean
11	Colby Knapp	Logan
12	Henry E. Dummer	Cass
13	Bryant T. Schofield	Hancock
14	William Berry	McDonough
15	Albert C. Mason	Knox
16	John T. Lindsay	Peoria
17	Washington Bushnell	La Salle
18	Alonzo W. Mack	Kankakee
19	Edward R. Allen	Kane
20	Daniel Richards	Whiteside
21	Thomas J. Pickett	Rock Island
22	John H. Addams	Stephenson
23	Cornelius Lansing	McHenry
24	William B. Ogden	Cook
25	Joseph D. Ward	Cook

¹ Vice Rodgers, died Feb. 12, 1863.

House of Representatives

Speaker	Samuel A. Buckmaster
Clerk	John Q. Harman

District	Member	County
1	James H. Smith	Union
2	Theodore B. Hick	Massac
3	James B. Turner	Gallatin
4	James M. Sharp	Wabash
5	Henry M. Williams	Jefferson
6	James M. Washburn	Williamson
7	Jesse R. Ford	Clinton
8	Stephen W. Miles	Monroe
	Edmund Menard	Randolph
9	John W. Merritt	Marion
10	James M. Heard	Wayne
11	David W. Odell	Crawford
12	John W. Wescott	Clay
13	Robert H. McCann	Fayette
14	Chauncey S. Conger	White
15	Joseph B. Underwood	St. Clair
	John Thomas	St. Clair
16	Samuel A. Buckmaster	Madison
	William Watkins	Bond
17	Philander Daugherty	Clark
18	Reuben Roessler	Shelby
19	Gustavus F. Coffeen	Montgomery
20	Ambrose M. Miller	Logan
	Charles A. Keyes	Sangamon
21	Charles A. Walker	Macoupin
22	John N. English	Jersey
23	William B. Pitt	Greene
24	Scott Wike	Pike
	Albert G. Burr	Scott

District	Member	County
25	James M. Epler	Cass
26	Lyman Lacy	Menard
27	John T. Springer	Morgan
28	Alexander E. Wheat	Adams
	William J. Brown	Adams
29	Lewis J. Reid	McDonough
30	Joseph Sharon	Schuyler
31	Milton M. Morrill	Hancock
32	Thomas B. Cabeen	Mercer
33	Henry R. Peffer	Warren
34	Joseph M. Holyoke	Knox
35	John G. Graham	Fulton
	Simeon P. Shope	Fulton
36	James Holgate	Stark
	William W. O'Brien	Peoria
37	Elias Wenger	Tazewell
38	Harrison Noble	McLean
	Boynton Tenny	De Witt
39	John TenBrook	Coles
	John Gerrard	Edgar
	John Monroe	Vermilion
40	James Elder	Macon
	William N. Coler	Champaign
	John S. Busey¹	Champaign
41	Chauncey A. Lake	Kankakee
42	Addison Goodell	Iroquois
43	John W. Newport	Grundy
	Charles E. Boyer	Will
	Perry A. Armstrong²	Grundy
44	Theodore C. Gibson	La Salle
	Marcy B. Patty	Livingston
	John O. Dent	La Salle
45	George Dent	Putnam
	Jefferson A. Davis	Woodford
	Daniel R. Howe	Bureau
46	Nelson Lay	Henry
47	John Kistler	Rock Island
48	Leander Smith	Whiteside
49	Demas L. Harris	Lee
50	James V. Gale	Ogle
51	Westel W. Sedgwick	De Kalb
	Luther W. Lawrence	Boone
52	Sylvester S. Mann	Kane
	Jacob P. Black	Kendall
53	Elijah M. Naines	Lake
54	Thaddeus B. Wakeman	McHenry
55	Seldon M. Church	Winnebago
56	Horatio C. Burchard	Stephenson
57	Henry Green	JoDaviess
	John F. Chapman	Carroll
58	Algernon S. Barnard	Du Page
59	Ansel B. Cook	Cook
	Amos G. Throop	Cook
60	Melville W. Fuller	Cook
	George W. Gage	Cook
	Michael Brand³	Cook
61	Francis A. Eastman	Cook
	Lorenzo Brentano	Cook

¹ Successfully contested election of William N. Coler.
² Vice John W. Newport, died.
³ Successfully contested election of George W. Gage.

Twenty-fourth General Assembly,
1865–66

Convened Jan. 2, 1865; adjourned Feb. 16,
1865.

Senate

President   William Bross
Secretary   John F. Nash

District	Member	County
1	William H. Green	Alexander
2	John W. Wescott	Clay
3	Daniel Reily	Randolph
4	David K. Green	Marion
5	Andrew W. Metcalf	Madison
6	Linus E. Worcester	Greene
7	Horatio M. Vandeveer	Christian
8	Andrew J. Hunter	Edgar
9	Joseph Peters	Vermilion
10	Isaac Funk[1]	McLean
11	John B. Cohrs	Tazewell
12	Murray McConnell	Morgan
13	Bryant T. Schofield	Hancock
14	James Strain	Warren
15	Albert C. Mason	Knox
16	John T. Lindsay	Peoria
17	Washington Bushnell	La Salle
18	Alonzo W. Mack	Kankakee
19	Edward R. Allen	Kane
20	Daniel Richards	Whiteside
21	Alfred Webster	Rock Island
22	John H. Addams	Stephenson
23	Cornelius Lansing	McHenry
24	Francis A. Eastman	Cook
25	Joseph D. Ward	Cook

[1] Died Jan. 9, 1865.

House of Representatives

Speaker   Allen C. Fuller
Clerk   Walter S. Frazier

District	Member	County
1	Henry Watson Webb	Alexander
2	William A. Looney	Johnson
3	Charles Burnett	Hardin
4	Daniel H. Morgan	Lawrence
5	John Ward	Franklin
6	William H. Logan	Jackson
7	Isaac Miller	Washington
8	William K. Murphy	Perry
	Austin James	Monroe
9	Samuel E. Stephenson	Marion
10	Valentine S. Benson	Hamilton
11	Thomas Cooper	Jasper
12	Lewis W. Miller	Richland
13	George H. Deickman	Fayette
14	Jonathan Shelby	Edwards
15	Nathaniel Niles	St. Clair
	John Thomas	St. Clair
16	Julius A. Barnsback	Madison

District	Member	County
	Hiram Dresser	Madison
17	Hiram B. Decius	Clark
18	William Middlesworth	Shelby
19	Elisha E. Barrett	Montgomery
20	Ambrose M. Miller	Logan
	James W. Patton	Sangamon
21	Sargeant Gobble	Macoupin
22	John McDonald	Calhoun
23	Nathaniel M. Perry	Greene
24	James F. Curtis	Scott
	Scott Wike	Pike
25	King Kerley	Brown
26	John Hill	Menard
27	John T. Springer	Morgan
28	Thomas Redmond	Adams
	William T. Yeargain	Adams
29	William H. Neece	McDonough
30	Joseph Sharon	Schuyler
31	Milton M. Morrill	Hancock
32	Jonathan Simpson	Henderson
33	James H. Martin	Warren
34	Joseph M. Holyoke	Knox
35	Lawrence W. James	Fulton
	Timothy M. Morse	Fulton
36	Richard C. Dunn	Stark
	Alexander McCoy	Peoria
37	Samuel R. Saltonstall	Tazewell
38	Harrison Noble	McLean
	John Warner	De Witt
39	Malden Jones	Douglas
	John L. Tincher	Vermilion
	Solomon L. Spink	Edgar
40	Isaac C. Pugh	Macon
	Lewis J. Bond	Piatt
41	Chauncey A. Lake	Kankakee
42	Charles H. Wood	Iroquois
43	Archibald J. McIntyre	Will
	William T. Hopkins	Grundy
44	Franklin Corwin	La Salle
	John Miller	La Salle
	Jason W. Strevelle	Livingston
45	Henry D. Cook	Woodford
	George D. Henderson	Putnam
	William C. Stacy	Bureau
46	Milton M. Ford	Henry
47	Joseph W. Lloyd	Rock Island
48	Leander Smith	Whiteside
49	Obed W. Bryant	Lee
50	Daniel J. Pinckney	Ogle
51	Allen C. Fuller	Boone
	Ira V. Randall	De Kalb
52	Oliver C. Johnson	Kendall
	Sylvester S. Mann	Kane
53	Eugene B. Payne	Lake
54	Merritt L. Joslyn	McHenry
55	William Brown	Winnebago
56	Horatio C. Burchard	Stephenson
57	John D. Platt	JoDaviess
	Daniel W. Dame	Carroll
58	Henry C. Childs	Du Page
59	Nathan W. Huntley	Cook
	Ansel B. Cook	Cook
	William Jackson	Cook
60	Edward S. Isham	Cook
	Andrew M. Dolton	Cook
61	Alexander F. Stevenson	Cook
	George Strong	Cook

First session convened Jan. 7, 1867; adjourned Feb. 28, 1867. Second session convened June 11, 1867; adjourned June 13, 1867. Third session convened June 14, 1867; adjourned June 28, 1867.

Senate

President   William Bross
Secretary   Charles E. Lippincott, resigned
Secretary
        Chauncey Elwood, vice Lippincott

District	Member	County
1	Daniel W. Munn	Alexander
2	John W. Wescott	Clay
3	Daniel Reily	Randolph
4	David K. Green	Marion
5	Andrew W. Metcalf	Madison
6	William Shepherd	Jersey
7	John M. Woodson	Macoupin
8	Andrew J. Hunter	Edgar
9	John L. Tincher	Vermilion
10	William H. Cheney	McLean
11	John B. Cohrs	Tazewell
12	Murray McConnell	Morgan
13	Samuel R. Chittenden	Adams
14	James Strain	Warren
15	Thomas A. Boyd	Fulton
16	Greenbury L. Fort	Marshall
17	Washington Bushnell	La Salle
18	Alonzo W. Mack	Kankakee
19	William S. Patten	De Kalb
20	Daniel J. Pinckney	Ogle
21	Alfred Webster	Rock Island
22	John H. Addams	Stephenson
23	Allen C. Fuller	Boone
24	Francis A. Eastman	Cook
25	Joseph D. Ward	Cook

House of Representatives

Speaker   Franklin Corwin
Clerk   Stephen G. Paddock

District	Member	County
1	Newton R. Casey	Pulaski
2	Philip G. Clemins	Pope
3	James Macklin	Saline
4	James M. Sharp	Wabash
5	Noah Johnson	Jefferson
6	Hugh Gregg	Williamson
7	Daniel Hay	Washington
8	William K. Murphy	Perry
	John Campbell	Randolph
9	Erastus N. Bates	Marion
10	Robert P. Hanna	Wayne
11	David W. Odell	Crawford
12	Ely Bowyer	Richland
13	George W. Cornwell	Effingham
14	Patrick Dolan	White
15	Abraham B. Pope	St. Clair
	Amos Thompson	St. Clair
16	John H. Yager	Madison

District	Member	County
	Jediah F. Alexander	Bond
17	Edwin Harlan	Clark
18	Charles Voris	Shelby
19	John B. Ricks	Christian
20	James C. Conkling	Sangamon
	William McGalliard	Logan
21	William C. Shirley	Macoupin
22	Robert M. Knapp	Jersey
23	Henry C. Withers	Greene
24	James H. Dennis	Pike
	Thomas Hollowbush	Scott
25	James M. Epler	Cass
26	John M. Beeseley	Mason
27	Felix G. Farrell	Morgan
28	Henry L. Warren	Adams
	Philip G. Corkins	Adams
29	Amaziah Hanson	McDonough
30	George W. Metz	Schuyler
31	John G. Fonda	Hancock
32	Daniel W. Sedwick	Mercer
33	Francis M. Bruner	Warren
34	John Gray	Knox
35	Caleb B. Cox	Fulton
	George W. Fox	Fulton
36	Thomas C. Moore	Peoria
	Sylvester F. Otman	Stark
37	William W. Sellers	Tazewell
38	William M. Smith	McLean
	Henry S. Green	De Witt
39	James M. True	Coles
	Malden Jones	Douglas
	Napoleon B. Stage	Edgar
40	Clark R. Griggs	Champaign
	Abraham B. Bunn	Macon
41	Daniel S. Parker	Kankakee
42	George E. King	Iroquois
43	Philip Collins	Grundy
	Robert Clow	Will
44	William Strawn	Livingston
	Elmer Baldwin	La Salle
	Franklin Corwin	La Salle
45	William C. Stacy	Bureau
	Robert T. Cassell	Woodford
	Alanson P. Webber	Marshall
46	Augustus Allen	Henry
47	Albert S. Coe	Rock Island
48	James Dinsmoor	Whiteside
49	George Ryan	Lee
50	Thomas J. Hewitt	Ogle
51	Stephen A. Hurlbut	Boone
	Robert Hampton	De Kalb
52	James W. Eddy	Kane
	William P. Pierce	Kendall
53	Eugene B. Payne	Lake
54	Thaddeus B. Wakeman	McHenry
55	Abraham I. Enoch	Winnebago
56	Joseph M. Bailey	Stephenson
57	Elijah Funk	Carroll
	Henry Green	JoDaviess
58	Henry C. Childs	Du Page
59	Lester L. Bond	Cook
	Joseph S. Reynolds	Cook
	Horace M. Singer	Cook

District	Member	County
60	Moses W. Leavitt	Cook
	Henry M. Shepard	Cook
61	Alexander F. Stevenson	Cook
	Edward S. Taylor	Cook

Twenty-sixth General Assembly, 1869–70

Convened Jan. 4, 1869; adjourned April 20, 1869.

Senate

President   John Dougherty
Secretary   Chauncey Elwood

District	Member	County
1	Daniel W. Munn	Alexander
2	J. J. R. Turney	Wayne
3	Samuel K. Casey	Jefferson
4	John P. VanDorston	Fayette
5	Willard C. Flagg	Madison
6	William Shepherd	Jersey
7	John M. Woodson	Macoupin
8	Edwin Harlan	Clark
9	John L. Tincher	Vermilion
10	John McNulta	McLean
11	Aaron B. Nicholson	Logan
12	James M. Epler	Cass
13	Samuel R. Chittenden	Adams
14	Isaac McManus	Mercer
15	Thomas A. Boyd	Fulton
16	Greenbury L. Fort	Marshall
17	Jason W. Strevelle	Livingston
18	Henry Snapp	Will
19	William S. Patten	De Kalb
20	Daniel J. Pinckney	Ogle
21	Andrew Crawford	Henry
22	John H. Addams	Stephenson
23	Allen C. Fuller	Boone
24	John C. Dore	Cook
25	Joseph D. Ward	Cook

House of Representatives

Speaker   Franklin Corwin
Clerk   James P. Root

District	Member	County
1	Newton R. Casey	Pulaski
2	Jonathan C. Willis	Massac
3	Charles Burnett	Gallatin
4	Daniel H. Morgan	Lawrence
5	C. C. M. V. B. Payne	Franklin
6	Edward L. Dennison	Williamson
7	George Gundlach	Clinton
8	John M. McCutcheon	Randolph
	Thomas H. Burgess	Perry
9	Thomas E. Merritt	Marion
10	John Halley	Hamilton
11	Joseph Cooper	Jasper

District	Member	County
12	Alexander W. Bothwell	Clay
13	Leonard Rush	Fayette
14	John Landrigan	Edwards
15	James R. Miller	St. Clair
	Alexander Ross	St. Clair
16	Daniel Kerr	Madison
	Samuel H. Challis	Bond
17	Lewis Brookhart	Cumberland
18	Charles Voris	Shelby
19	Ephraim M. Gilmore	Montgomery
20	John Cook	Sangamon
	Silas Beason	Logan
21	Beatty T. Burke	Macoupin
22	Thomas B. Fuller	Calhoun
23	David M. Woodson	Greene
24	Abraham Mittower	Pike
	Henry Dresser	Scott
25	James G. Phillips	Brown
26	Edward Lanning	Menard
27	Smith M. Palmer	Morgan
28	Thomas Jasper	Adams
	James E. Downing	Adams
29	Humphrey Horrabin	McDonough
30	John Ewing	Schuyler
31	Andrew J. Bradshaw	Hancock
32	David M. Findley	Henderson
33	John Porter	Warren
34	William Seldon Gale	Knox
35	Timothy M. Morse	Fulton
	John W. Ross	Fulton
36	William E. Phelps,	Peoria
	Bradford F. Thompson	Stark
37	Jonathan Merriam	Tazewell
	Samuel R. Saltonstall[1]	Tazewell
38	William M. Smith	McLean
	Jacob Swigart	De Witt
39	George W. Parker	Coles
	James E. Callaway	Douglas
	Silas H. Elliot	Edgar
40	Wilson M. Stanley	Moultrie
	John W. Scroggs	Champaign
41	James M. Perry	Kankakee
42	Calvin H. Frew	Ford
43	George Gaylord	Will
	Philip Collins	Grundy
44	William Strawn	Livingston
	Franklin Corwin	La Salle
	Samuel Wiley	La Salle
45	Lorenzo D. Whiting	Bureau
	Charles G. Reed	Bureau
	Joel W. Hopkins	Putnam
46	Philip K. Hanna	Henry
47	Hiram F. Sickles	Rock Island
48	James Dinsmoor	Whiteside
49	Alonzo Kinyon	Lee
50	Ogden B. Young	Ogle
51	Charles W. Marsh	De Kalb
	Elisha H. Talbott	Boone
52	Irus Coy	Kendall
	Needham N. Ravlin	Kane
53	Ansel B. Cook	Lake
54	Peter W. Deitz	McHenry
55	Ephraim Sumner	Winnebago
56	Joseph M. Bailey	Stephenson
57	Adam Nase	Carroll
	Henry Green	JoDaviess
58	Henry C. Childs	Du Page

District	Member	County
59	Henry B. Miller	Cook
	Lester L. Bond	Cook
	Joseph S. Reynolds	Cook
60	Francis Munson	Cook
	Joshua C. Knickerbocker	Cook
61	Iver Lawson	Cook
	Edward S. Taylor	Cook

¹ Successfully contested election of Merriam.

Redistricting of 1869 made by governor and secretary of state as ordered by the constitutional convention; twenty-five Senate districts (unchanged), each with two senators, and ninety-seven House districts with one to ten representatives

House district and counties

1	Alexander	50	Champaign
2	Massac, Pulaski	51	Piatt
3	Pope	52	De Witt
4	Johnson	53	Logan
5	Union	54	Cass, Menard
6	Jackson	55	Brown
7	Williamson	56	Schuyler
8	Saline	57	Adams
9	Gallatin, Hardin	58	Hancock
10	White	59	McDonough
11	Hamilton	60	Fulton
12	Franklin	61	Mason
13	Perry	62	Tazewell
14	Randolph	63	McLean
15	Monroe	64	Iroquois
16	St. Clair	65	Livingston
17	Washington	66	Woodford
18	Jefferson	67	Peoria
19	Wayne	68	Knox
20	Edwards, Wabash	69	Warren
21	Lawrence	70	Henderson
22	Richland	71	Mercer
23	Clay	72	Rock Island
24	Marion	73	Henry
25	Clinton	74	Stark
26	Madison	75	Marshall, Putnam
27	Bond	76	Bureau
28	Fayette	77	La Salle
29	Effingham	78	Grundy
30	Jasper	79	Ford, Kankakee
31	Crawford	80	Will
32	Clark	81	Kendall
33	Cumberland	82	Du Page
34	Shelby	83	Kane
35	Christian	84	De Kalb
36	Montgomery	85	Lee,
37	Macoupin	86	Ogle
38	Calhoun, Jersey	87	Whiteside
39	Greene	88	Carroll
40	Pike	89	JoDaviess
41	Scott	90	Stephenson
42	Morgan	91	Winnebago
43	Sangamon	92	Boone
44	Macon	93	McHenry
45	Moultrie	94	Lake
46	Coles	95	Cook
47	Edgar	96	Cook
48	Douglas	97	Cook
49	Vermilion		

Twenty-seventh General Assembly, 1871–72

First session convened Jan. 4, 1871; adjourned April 17, 1871, until Nov. 15, 1871. First special session convened May 24, 1871; adjourned June 22, 1871. Second special session convened Oct. 13, 1871; adjourned Oct. 21, 1871. Convened in regular adjourned session Nov. 15, 1871; adjourned *sine die* April 9, 1872.

Senate

President	John Dougherty
Secretary	E. H. Griggs

District	Member	County
1	Simeon K. Gibson¹	Gallatin
	Thomas A. E. Holcomb	Union
	William C. Bowman³	Alexander
2	John Jackson	Lawrence
	John Landrigan	Edwards
3	Samuel K. Casey¹	Jefferson
	James M. Washburn⁴	Williamson
	William B. Anderson	Jefferson
4	John P. VanDorston	Fayette
	Jediah F. Alexander	Bond
5	Willard C. Flagg	Madison
	William H. Underwood	St. Clair
6	William Shepherd²	Jersey
	Joseph M. Bush	Pike
	William H. Allen⁵	Jersey
7	Lewis Solomon	Macoupin
	Charles Voris	Shelby
8	Edwin Harlan	Clark
	Robert N. Bishop	Edgar
9	John L. Tincher	Vermilion
	James W. Langley	Champaign
10	John McNulta	McLean
	Michael Donahue	De Witt
11	Aaron B. Nicholson	Logan
	Alexander Starne	Sangamon
12	James M. Epler	Cass
	Edward Lanning	Menard
13	James H. Richardson	Adams
	Jesse C. Williams	Hancock
14	Benjamin R. Hampton	McDonough
	Harvey S. Senter	Mercer
15	Thomas A. Boyd	Fulton
	Henry J. Vaughn	Knox
16	Mark Bangs	Marshall
	Lucien H. Kerr	Peoria
17	Jason W. Strevelle	Livingston
	William Reddick	La Salle
18	Henry Snapp²	Will
	William P. Pierce	Grundy
	John F. Daggett⁶	Will
19	Charles W. Marsh	De Kalb
	James W. Eddy	Kane
20	James K. Edsall	Lee
	Winfield S. Wilkinson	Whiteside

District	Member	County
21	Andrew Crawford	Henry
	Lorenzo D. Whiting	Bureau
22	Wallace A. Little[1]	JoDaviess
	James M. Hunter	Carroll
23	Allen C. Fuller	Boone
	John Early	Winnebago
24	John C. Dore	Cook
	John N. Jewett	Cook
25	Willard Woodard	Cook
	John L. Beveridge[2]	Cook
	Artemas Carter[7]	Cook

[1] Died.
[2] Resigned.
[3] Vice Gibson.
[4] Vice Casey.
[5] Vice Shepherd.
[6] Vice Snapp.
[7] Vice Beveridge.

House of Representatives

Speaker	William M. Smith
Clerk	Daniel Shepard

District	Member	County
1	Henry Watson Webb	Alexander
2	William R. Brown	Massac
3	George W. Waters	Pope
4	James B. Morray	Johnson
5	William C. Rich	Union
6	William Schwartz[1]	Jackson
	William A. Lemma[3]	Jackson
7	Addison Reese, Jr.	Williamson
8	William Elder	Saline
9	William N. Ayers	Hardin
10	Frank E. Hay	White
11	Calvin Allen	Hamilton
12	William W. Barr	Franklin
13	William R. Gass	Perry
14	James M. Ralls	Randolph
	Daniel R. McMaster	Randolph
15	William R. Morrison	Monroe
16	James R. Miller	St. Clair
	Gustave Philipp Koerner	St. Clair
	John Hinchcliffe	St. Clair
17	A. S. Rowley	Washington
18	Thomas S. Casey	Jefferson
19	Ashley T. Galbraith	Wayne
20	Walter L. Mayo	Edwards
21	John D. Sage	Lawrence
22	Israel A. Powell	Richland
23	Osman Pixley	Clay
24	Thomas E. Merritt	Marion
	Samuel L. Dwight	Marion
25	Samuel Burnside	Clinton
26	Daniel D. Gillham	Madison
	Andrew F. Rodgers	Madison
	Theodore Miller	Madison
27	William Brown	Bond
28	Jacob Fouke	Fayette
29	David Leith[1]	Effingham
	B. F. Kagey[4]	Effingham

District	Member	County
30	William McElwee	Jasper
31	William C. Jones	Crawford
32	William T. Briscoe	Clark
33	Edward Barrett	Cumberland
34	John Casey	Shelby
	Edward Roessler	Shelby
35	William B. Hundley	Christian
	Thomas Finley[1]	Christian
	Benjamin Dornblaser[5]	Christian
36	James M. Berry	Montgomery
	James N. McElvain	Montgomery
37	John L. McMillan	Macoupin
	George A. W. Cloud	Macoupin
38	George W. Herdman	Jersey
	Robert A. King	Jersey
39	Thomas H. Boyd	Greene
40	Charles Kenney	Pike
	Albert Landrum	Pike
41	James M. Riggs	Scott
42	Newton Cloud	Morgan
	William H. Barnes	Morgan
43	Charles H. Rice	Sangamon
	William M. Springer	Sangamon
	Ninian R. Taylor	Sangamon
44	William E. Nelson	Macon
	William T. Moffett	Macon
45	Jonathan Meeker	Moultrie
46	James R. Cunningham	Coles
	Azariah Jefferies	Coles
47	James Gaines	Edgar
	George W. Rives	Edgar
48	John Cofer	Douglas
49	John C. Short	Vermilion
	William P. Chandler	Vermilion
50	Randolph C. Wright	Champaign
	Jarius C. Sheldon	Champaign
51	Andrew L. Rodgers	Piatt
52	William R. Carle	De Witt
53	Peter J. Hawes	Logan
	Augustus Reise	Logan
54	William W. Easley	Cass
	Samuel S. Knoles	Menard
55	James G. Phillips	Brown
56	Samuel S. Benson	Schuyler
57	Arthur H. Trimble	Adams
	Maurice Kelly	Adams
	Joseph H. Stewart	Adams
	George J. Richardson	Adams
58	Lemuel Mussetter	Hancock
	Milton M. Morrill	Hancock
59	William H. Neece	McDonough
	James Manley	McDonough
60	John W. Ross	Fulton
	Samuel P. Cummings	Fulton
	Timothy M. Morse	Fulton
61	Matthew Langston	Mason
62	Caesar A. Roberts	Tazewell
	Ira B. Hall	Tazewell
63	William M. Smith	McLean
	Edward R. Roe[2]	McLean
	Warren C. Watkins	McLean
	George W. Funk	McLean
	Leonidas H. Kerrick[6]	McLean
64	Addison Goodell	Iroquois
	Thomas Vennum	Iroquois
65	John Stillwell	Livingston
	James G. Strong	Livingston

District	Member	County
66	Allison M. Cavan	Woodford
67	James M. Rice	Peoria
	Samuel Caldwell	Peoria
	John S. Lee	Peoria
68	Oscar F. Price	Knox
	Joseph F. Latimer	Knox
	Patrick H. Sanford	Knox
69	Samuel T. Shelton	Warren
	John T. Morgan	Warren
70	William A. M. Crouch	Henderson
71	Stephen F. Fleharty	Mercer
72	John Morris	Rock Island
	Edwin H. Johnston	Rock Island
73	Levi North	Henry
	Jonas W. Olson	Henry
74	Miles A. Fuller	Stark
75	Joseph H. Jones	Marshall
	Joseph Reinhardt	Putnam
76	Robert Hunter	Bureau
	Perry F. Remsburg	Bureau
77	George W. Armstrong	La Salle
	Benjamin Edgcomb	La Salle
	James Clark	La Salle
	H. M. Gallagher	La Salle
78	Philip Collins	Grundy
79	Warren R. Hickox	Kankakee
	Calvin H. Frew	Ford
80	John H. Daniels	Will
	William S. Brooks	Will
	Robert Clow	Will
81	Henry Sherrill	Kendall
82	William M. Whitney	Du Page
83	Anson L. Clark	Kane
	Julius A. Carpenter	Kane
	William H. Miller	Kane
84	Reuben M. Prichard	De Kalb
	Lewis M. McEwen	De Kalb
85	Norman H. Ryan	Lee
	Miles J. Braiden	Lee
86	Mortimer W. Smith	Ogle
	Jeremiah Davis	Ogle
87	Nathan Williams	Whiteside
	Dean S. Efner	Whiteside
88	James Shaw	Carroll
89	William Carey	JoDaviess
	Halstead S. Townsend	JoDaviess
90	Thomas J. Turner	Stephenson
	William Massenberg	Stephenson
91	James M. Wight	Winnebago
	D. Emmons Adams	Winnebago
92	Jesse S. Hildrup	Boone
93	William A. McConnell	McHenry
	Ira R. Curtiss	McHenry
94	William B. Dodge	Lake
	Elijah M. Haines	Lake
95	Henry W. Austin	Cook
	Robert H. Foss	Cook
	James L. Campbell	Cook
	Carlile Mason	Cook
	Wiley M. Egan	Cook
	Richard P. Deriekson	Cook
	John D. Easter	Cook
	John Humphrey	Cook
	Alexander L. Morrison	Cook
	John W. Heafield	Cook
96	Andrew J. Galloway	Cook
	Hardin B. Brayton	Cook

District	Member	County
	Simon D. Phelps	Cook
	James P. Root	Cook
	William H. King	Cook
	Arthur Dixon	Cook
97	Horace F. Waite	Cook
	Rollin S. Williamson	Cook
	Augustus H. Burley	Cook
	William Vocke	Cook
	W. K. Sullivan	Cook
	Henry C. Senne	Cook

¹ Died.
² Resigned.
³ Vice Schwartz.
⁴ Vice Leith.
⁵ Vice Finley.
⁶ Vice Roe.

Redistricting of 1872 authorized by act of March 1, 1872; fifty-one districts, each electing one senator and three representatives

District	Counties
1 to 7	Cook
8	Lake, McHenry
9	Boone, Winnebago
10	JoDaviess, Stephenson
11	Carroll, Whiteside
12	Lee, Ogle
13	De Kalb, Grundy, Kendall
14	Du Page, Kane
15	Will
16	Iroquois, Kankakee
17	La Salle
18	Ford, Livingston
19	Bureau, Stark
20	Marshall, Putnam, Woodford
21	Henry, Rock Island
22	Knox, Mercer
23	McDonough, Warren
24	Hancock, Henderson
25	Fulton, Schuyler
26	Peoria
27	Logan, Tazewell
28	McLean
29	De Witt, Macon
30	Champaign, Piatt
31	Edgar, Vermilion
32	Coles, Douglas, Moultrie
33	Cumberland, Effingham, Shelby
34	Christian, Montgomery
35	Sangamon
36	Brown, Cass, Mason, Menard
37	Adams
38	Calhoun, Pike, Scott
39	Greene, Morgan
40	Jersey, Macoupin
41	Madison
42	Bond, Clinton, Washington
43	Fayette, Marion
44	Clay, Edwards, Richland, Wabash, Wayne

District	Counties
45	Clark, Crawford, Jasper, Lawrence
46	Hamilton, Jefferson, White
47	Franklin, Gallatin, Saline, Williamson
48	Monroe, Perry, Randolph
49	St. Clair
50	Alexander, Jackson, Union
51	Hardin, Johnson, Massac, Pope, Pulaski

Twenty-eighth General Assembly, 1873–74

First session convened Jan. 8, 1873; adjourned May 6, 1873, until Jan. 6, 1874. Convened Jan. 6, 1874; adjourned *sine die* March 31, 1874.

Senate

President	John L. Beveridge[1]
President	John Early[2]
Secretary	Daniel A. Ray

District	Member	County
1	Joseph S. Reynolds	Cook
2	Richard S. Thompson	Cook
3	Miles Kehoe	Cook
4	Samuel K. Dow	Cook
5	James J. McGrath	Cook
6	Horace F. Waite	Cook
7	Rollin S. Williamson	Cook
8	Clark W. Upton	Lake
9	John Early	Winnebago
10	Henry Green	JoDaviess
11	Joseph M. Patterson	Whiteside
12	George P. Jacobs	Ogle
13	Miles B. Castle	De Kalb
14	Eugene B. Canfield	Kane
15	William S. Brooks	Will
16	Almon S. Palmer	Iroquois
17	Elmer Baldwin	La Salle
18	James G. Strong	Livingston
19	Lorenzo D. Whiting	Bureau
20	Edward A. Wilcox	Woodford
21	William H. Shepard	Henry
22	Patrick H. Sanford	Knox
23	Benjamin R. Hampton	McDonough
24	Benjamin Warren	Hancock
25	Samuel P. Cummings	Fulton
26	John S. Lee	Peoria
27	Aaron B. Nicholson	Logan
28	John Cusey	McLean
29	Michael Donahue	De Witt
30	Jarius C. Sheldon	Champaign
31	John C. Short	Vermilion
32	Charles B. Steele	Coles
33	Charles Voris	Shelby
34	William B. Hundley	Christian
35	Alexander Starne	Sangamon
36	Archibald A. Glenn	Brown
37	George W. Burns[3]	Adams
	Maurice Kelly[4]	Adams

District	Member	County
38	William R. Archer	Pike
39	William Brown	Morgan
40	Beatty T. Burke	Macoupin
41	John H. Yager	Madison
42	George Gundlach	Clinton
43	John Cunningham	Marion
44	George W. Henry	Clay
45	William J. Crews	Lawrence
46	Thomas S. Casey	Jefferson
47	Francis M. Youngblood	Franklin
48	William K. Murphy	Perry
49	John Hinchcliffe	St. Clair
50	Jesse Ware	Union
51	Charles M. Ferrell	Hardin

[1] Became gov.
[2] Vice Beveridge.
[3] Resigned.
[4] Vice Burns.

House of Representatives

Speaker	Shelby M. Cullom
Clerk	Daniel Shepard

District	Member	County
1	James B. Brudwell	Cook
	John A. Lomax	Cook
	William Wayman	Cook
2	Solomon P. Hopkins	Cook
	Francis T. Sherman	Cook
	Charles G. Wicker	Cook
3	E. F. Cullerton	Cook
	Constantine Kann	Cook
	Thomas M. Halpin	Cook
4	John F. Scanlan	Cook
	Thomas E. Ferrier	Cook
	William H. Condon	Cook
5	William A. Herting	Cook
	Ingwell Oleson	Cook
	Hugh McLaughlin	Cook
6	Otto Peltzer	Cook
	John M. Rountree	Cook
	George E. Washburn	Cook
7	Daniel Booth	Cook
	Charles H. Dolton	Cook
	Henry C. Senne	Cook
8	Richard Bishop	McHenry
	Flavel K. Granger	McHenry
	Elisha Gridley	Lake
9	Robert J. Cross[1]	Winnebago
	Jesse S. Hildrup	Boone
	Duncan J. Stewart	Winnebago
	Richard F. Crawford[3]	Winnebago
10	Edward L. Cronkrite	Stephenson
	Alfred M. Jones	JoDaviess
	James S. Taggart	Stephenson
11	James Shaw	Carroll
	James E. McPherran	Whiteside
	Dean S. Efner	Whiteside
12	Isaac Rice	Ogle
	Henry D. Dement	Lee
	Frederick H. Marsh	Ogle
13	Lyman B. Ray	Grundy
	George M. Hollenback	Kendall
	Perry A. Armstrong	Grundy

District	Member	County
14	Sylvester S. Mann	Kane
	Julius A. Carpenter	Kane
	James Herrington	Kane
15	Amos Savage	Will
	John S. Jessup	Will
	Jabez Harvey	Will
16	Milliard J. Sheridan	Kankakee
	Erasmus B. Collins	Kankakee
	Thomas S. Sawyer	Iroquois
17	Lewis Soule	La Salle
	Joseph Hart	La Salle
	George W. Armstrong	La Salle
18	John P. Middlecoff	Ford
	Lucian Bullard	Livingston
	John Pollock	Ford
19	Joab R. Mulvane	Bureau
	Cyrus Bocock	Stark
	Martin R. Dewey	Bureau
20	J. Dwight Weber	Woodford
	Nathaniel Moore	Marshall
	John G. Freeman	Putnam
21	Wilder W. Warner	Henry
	Edwin H. Johnston	Rock Island
	Charles Dunham	Henry
22	Alson J. Streeter	Mercer
	George P. Graham	Mercer
	Jacob S. Chambers	Knox
23	William A. Grant	Warren
	John E. Jackson	McDonough
	E. K. Westfall	McDonough
24	William Scott	Hancock
	David Rankin	Henderson
	Edward E. Lane	Hancock
25	Stephen Y. Thornton	Fulton
	John A. Gray	Fulton
	John M. Darnell	Schuyler
26	Julius S. Starr	Peoria
	Michael C. Quinn	Peoria
	Ezra G. Webster	Peoria
27	Laban M. Stroud	Logan
	Peter J. Hawes	Logan
	Herman W. Snow	Tazewell
28	Archibald E. Stewart	McLean
	Thomas P. Rogers	McLean
	John Cassedy	McLean
29	Job A. Race	Macon
	Tillman Lane	De Witt
	William T. Moffet	Macon
30	John Penfield	Champaign
	Chester P. Davis	Piatt
	Francis E. Bryant	Piatt
31	Willis O. Pinnell	Edgar
	Henri B. Bishop	Edgar
	Jacob H. Oakwood	Vermilion
32	William T. Sylvester[4]	Douglas
	John A. Freeland	Moultrie
	James A. Connolly	Coles
	Joseph H. Ewing[5]	Douglas
33	William H. McDonald	Cumberland
	William H. Blakely	Effingham
	Benson Wood	Effingham
34	James M. Truitt	Montgomery
	Hiram P. Shumway	Christian
	Elias J. C. Alexander	Montgomery
35	Alfred Orendorff	Sangamon
	Milton Hay	Sangamon
	Shelby M. Cullom	Sangamon

District	Member	County
36	Henry H. Moose	Mason
	William W. Easley	Cass
	Nathaniel W. Branson	Menard
37	Charles Ballou	Adams
	Nehemia Bushnell[6]	Adams
	Ira M. Moore	Adams
	John Tillson[7]	Adams
	Albert J. Griffith[8]	Adams
38	Melville D. Massie	Scott
	Stephen G. Lewis	Calhoun
	Henry Dresser	Scott
39	Jerome B. Nulton	Greene
	John W. Meacham	Morgan
	John Gordon	Morgan
40	William McAdams	Jersey
	Jonathan Plowman	Macoupin
	Archibald L. Virden	Macoupin
41	Henry Weinheimer	Madison
	Benjamin R. Hite	Madison
	Thomas T. Ramey	Madison
42	Fred A. Lietze	Clinton
	Charles D. Hoiles	Bond
	Andrew G. Henry	Bond
43	Napoleon B. Morrison	Marion
	Charles G. Smith	Fayette
	Ziba S. Swan[2]	Fayette
	Alfred P. Crosby[9]	Fayette
44	Isaac N. Jaquess	Wabash
	Robert T. Forth	Wayne
	David W. Barkley	Wayne
45	John L. Flanders	Clark
	Thomas J. Golden	Clark
	Harmon Alexander	Crawford
46	Leonidas Walker	Hamilton
	Robert S. Anderson	Hamilton
	Patrick Dolan	White
47	John G. Newton	Williamson
	James R. Loomis	Gallatin
	Samuel M. Mitchell	Williamson
48	John W. Pyatt	Perry
	William Neville	Randolph
	Austin James	Monroe
49	Bernhard Wick[2]	St. Clair
	Luke H. Hite	St. Clair
	John Thomas	St. Clair
	Spencer M. Kase[10]	St. Clair
50	William A. Lemma	Jackson
	Matthew J. Inscore	Union
	John H. Oberly	Alexander
51	James L. Wymore	Johnson
	Francis M. McGee	Johnson
	Newton R. Casey	Pulaski

[1] Died Feb. 17, 1873.
[2] Resigned.
[3] Vice Cross.
[4] Moved from district.
[5] Vice Sylvester.
[6] Died Jan. 31, 1873.
[7] Vice Bushnell.
[8] Vice Tillson.
[9] Vice Swan.
[10] Vice Wick.

Twenty-ninth General Assembly,
1875–76

Convened Jan. 6, 1875; adjourned April 15,
1875.

Senate

President   Archibald A. Glenn
Secretary   R. R. Townes

District	Member	County
1	John C. Haines	Cook
2	Richard S. Thompson	Cook
3	Miles Kehoe	Cook
4	Samuel K. Dow	Cook
5	John Buehler	Cook
6	Horace F. Waite	Cook
7	Michael W. Robinson	Cook
8	Clark W. Upton	Lake
9	John Early	Winnebago
10	Henry Green	JoDaviess
11	Henry A. Mills	Carroll
12	George P. Jacobs	Ogle
13	Miles B. Castle	De Kalb
14	Eugene B. Canfield	Kane
15	Albert O. Marshall	Will
16	Almon S. Palmer	Iroquois
17	Fawcett Plumb	La Salle
18	James G. Strong	Livingston
19	Lorenzo D. Whiting	Bureau
20	Edward A. Wilcox	Woodford
21	Erastus C. Moderwell	Henry
22	Patrick H. Sanford	Knox
23	John T. Morgan	Warren
24	Benjamin Warren	Hancock
25	Robert Broun	Schuyler
26	John S. Lee	Peoria
27	James W. Robison	Tazewell
28	John Cusey	McLean
29	Jesse F. Harrold	De Witt
30	Jarius C. Sheldon	Champaign
31	George Hunt	Edgar
32	Charles B. Steele	Coles
33	Thomas Brewer	Cumberland
34	William B. Hundley	Christian
35	William E. Shutt	Sangamon
36	Archibald A. Glenn	Brown
37	Bernard Arntzen	Adams
38	William R. Archer	Pike
39	Charles D. Hodges	Greene
40	Beatty T. Burke	Macoupin
41	William H. Krome	Madison
42	George Gundlach	Clinton
43	John Thompson	Fayette
44	George W. Henry	Clay
45	O. V. Smith	Lawrence
46	Thomas S. Casey	Jefferson
47	William H. Parish	Saline
48	William K. Murphy	Perry
49	Jefferson Rainey	St. Clair
50	Jesse Ware	Union
51	Samuel M. Glassford	Johnson

House of Representatives

Speaker   Elijah M. Haines
Clerk   Jeremiah J. Crowley

District	Member	County
1	James B. Brudwell	Cook
	Lincoln Dubois	Cook
	Moses J. Wentworth	Cook
2	John Hise	Cook
	George M. Bogue	Cook
	Solomon P. Hopkins	Cook
3	William Honan	Cook
	Conrad L. Neihoff	Cook
	Thomas M. Halpin	Cook
4	Orrin L. Mann	Cook
	William H. Condon	Cook
	Michael M. Miller	Cook
5	Michael J. Dunne	Cook
	John M. Arwedson	Cook
	Carl L. Linderborg	Cook
6	Robert Thiem	Cook
	John C. Barker	Cook
	William H. Stickney	Cook
7	William H. Skelly, Jr.	Cook
	George Dunlap	Cook
	William Freise	Cook
8	William A. James	Lake
	Elijah M. Haines	Lake
	Flavel K. Granger	McHenry
9	Andrew Ashton	Winnebago
	Richard F. Crawford	Winnebago
	Myron K. Avery	Boone
10	Forest Turner	JoDaviess
	Edward L. Cronkrite	Stephenson
	Alfred M. Jones	JoDaviess
11	Albert R. McCoy	Whiteside
	Norman D. French	Carroll
	Tyler McWhorter	Whiteside
12	Henry D. Dement	Lee
	Isaac Rice	Ogle
	Frederick H. Marsh	Ogle
13	Philip Collins	Grundy
	Joshua S. McGrath	Kendall
	D. B. Bailey	Grundy
14	Victor Fredenhagen	Du Page
	James F. Claflin	Du Page
	James Herrington	Kane
15	William Mooney	Will
	Henry H. Stassen, Jr.	Will
	Luke H. Goodrich	Will
16	George W. Parker	Iroquois
	George C. Wilson	Iroquois
	Reuben Richardson	Kankakee
17	Charles L. Hoffmann	La Salle
	George W. Armstrong	La Salle
	Elijah H. Spicer	La Salle
18	Albert M. Haling	Ford
	Joseph I. Robinson	Ford
	David McIntosh	Livingston
19	A. G. Hammond	Stark
	J. H. Moore	Bureau
	James J. Herron	Bureau
20	Henry J. Frantz	Woodford
	James T. Thornton	Putnam
	Nathaniel Moore	Marshall
21	Rufus M. Grennell	Rock Island
	John T. Browning	Rock Island

District	Member	County
	John P. Fox	Henry
22	John H. Lewis	Knox
	John T. McGinnis	Mercer
	C. K. Harvey	Knox
23	Isaac L. Christie	Warren
	C. W. Boydston	Warren
	A. W. King	McDonough
24	David Rankin	Henderson
	Wellington Jenney	Hancock
	Paul D. Salter	Henderson
25	James DeWitt	Schuyler
	Samuel P. Cummings	Fulton
	Stephen Y. Thornton	Fulton
26	William Rowcliff	Peoria
	Julius S. Starr	Peoria
	Patrick W. Dunne	Peoria
27	Richard Holmes	Tazewell
	Robert A. Talbot	Logan
	Thomas Windle	Logan
28	Thomas P. Rogers	McLean
	John F. Winter	McLean
	Archibald E. Stewart	McLean
29	Shaw Pease	Macon
	John H. Tyler	De Witt
	Samuel S. Jack	Macon
30	William M. Phillips	Champaign
	George H. Benson	Champaign
	William C. Hubbart	Piatt
31	William S. O'Hair	Edgar
	John Sidell	Vermilion
	Andrew Gundy	Vermilion
32	James A. Connolly	Coles
	E. W. Vanse	Coles
	R. A. Wilson	Moultrie
33	William Gillmore	Effingham
	William Middlesworth	Shelby
	William Chew	Shelby
34	Levi Scott	Christian
	John C. Hagler	Christian
	William F. Mulkey	Montgomery
35	Joseph L. Wilcox	Sangamon
	Frederick Gehring	Sangamon
	Shelby M. Cullom	Sangamon
36	Nathaniel W. Branson	Menard
	A. G. Nance	Menard
	John W. Pugh	Menard
37	Thomas J. Bates	Adams
	Ira M. Moore	Adams
	Rezon H. Dowling	Adams
38	James Callans	Scott
	John Moses	Scott
	Joseph S. Harvey	Calhoun
39	Andrew J. Thompson	Morgan
	Samuel Wood	Morgan
	John Gordon	Morgan
40	Samuel S. Gilbert	Macoupin
	Oliver P. Powell	Jersey
	Henry F. Martin	Macoupin
41	Franklin S. Pike	Madison
	George A. Smith	Madison
	George H. Weigler	Madison
42	J. K. McMasters	Washington
	Andrew G. Henry	Bond
	W. Henry Moore	Washington
43	William R. Hubbard	Marion
	Thomas E. Merritt	Marion
	John B. Johnson	Marion

District	Member	County
44	Samuel R. Hall	Edwards
	Byron J. Rotan	Clay
	John Landrigan	Edwards
45	Ethelbert Callahan	Crawford
	John H. Halley	Jasper
	John W. Briscoe	Clark
46	Hiram W. Hall	Hamilton
	Amos B. Barrett	Jefferson
	Boone Kershaw	White
47	John N. Wasson	Gallatin
	Alexander C. Neilson	Williamson
	Isaac Smith	Gallatin
48	Joseph W. Rickert	Monroe
	Samuel McKee	Randolph
	Jonathan Chesnutwood	Randolph
49	William G. Kase	St. Clair
	John Thomas	St. Clair
	James Rankin	St. Clair
50	Fontaine E. Albright	Jackson
	Matthew J. Inscore	Union
	Claiborne Winston	Alexander
51	Benjamin O. Jones	Massac
	James R. Steagall	Pope
	Lewis F. Platen	Hardin

Thirtieth General Assembly, 1877–78

Convened Jan. 3, 1877; adjourned May 24, 1877.

Senate

President	Andrew Shuman
Secretary	James H. Paddock

District	Member	County
1	John C. Haines	Cook
2	Daniel N. Bash	Cook
3	Miles Kehoe	Cook
4	Francis A. Riddle	Cook
5	John Buehler	Cook
6	Martin A. Delaney	Cook
7	Michael W. Robinson	Cook
8	Merritt L. Joslyn	McHenry
9	John Early	Winnebago
10	Robert H. McClellan	JoDaviess
11	Henry A. Mills	Carroll
12	Henry D. Dement	Lee
13	Miles B. Castle	De Kalb
14	Joseph H. Mayborne	Kane
15	Albert O. Marshall	Will
16	Thomas P. Bonfield	Kankakee
17	Fawcett Plumb	La Salle
18	Samuel T. Fosdick	Livingston
19	Lorenzo D. Whiting	Bureau
20	Henry J. Frantz	Woodford
21	Erastus C. Moderwell	Henry
22	Benjamin C. Taliaferro	Mercer
23	John T. Morgan	Warren
24	William Scott	Hancock
25	Robert Broun	Schuyler
26	John S. Lee	Peoria

District	Member	County
27	James W. Robison	Tazewell
28	John M. Hamilton	McLean
29	Jesse F. Harrold	De Witt
30	Chester P. Davis	Piatt
31	George Hunt	Edgar
32	Malden Jones	Douglas
33	Thomas Brewer	Cumberland
34	Elizur Southworth	Montgomery
35	William E. Shutt	Sangamon
36	Luther Dearborn	Mason
37	Bernard Arntzen	Adams
38	William R. Archer	Pike
39	Charles D. Hodges	Greene
40	George W. Herdman	Jersey
41	William H. Krome	Madison
42	Frederick E. W. Brink	Washington
43	John Thompson	Fayette
44	Robert P. Hanna	Wayne
45	O. V. Smith	Lawrence
46	Charles E. McDowell	White
47	William H. Parish	Saline
48	Ambrose Hoener	Monroe
49	Jefferson Rainey	St. Clair
50	Jesse Ware	Union
51	Samuel M. Glassford	Johnson

House of Representatives

Speaker		James Shaw
Clerk		E. F. Dutton

District	Member	County
1	William H. Thompson	Cook
	Charles L. Easton	Cook
	Moses J. Wentworth	Cook
2	Solomon P. Hopkins	Cook
	John W. E. Thomas	Cook
	Joseph E. Smith	Cook
3	John B. Taylor	Cook
	Henry F. Sheridan	Cook
	P. J. Hickey	Cook
4	Elijah B. Sherman	Cook
	George W. Reed	Cook
	Joseph J. Kearney	Cook
5	John A. Roche	Cook
	Peter Kiolbassa	Cook
	Michael J. Dunne	Cook
6	Eugene A. Sittig	Cook
	Arno Voss	Cook
	Austin O. Sexton	Cook
7	John S. Bielefeldt	Cook
	John H. Kedzie	Cook
	George C. Klehm	Cook
8	Flavel K. Granger	McHenry
	William A. James	Lake
	Edward M. Dennis	Lake
9	George H. Hollister	Winnebago
	John Budlong	Winnebago
	Andrew Ashton	Winnebago
10	James S. Taggart	Stephenson
	Hiram Tyrrell	JoDaviess
	Edward L. Cronkrite	Stephenson
11	James Shaw	Carroll

District	Member	County
	Edward H. Nevitt	Whiteside
	John M. Stowell	Carroll
12	Abijah Powers	Lee
	Frank N. Tice	Ogle
	Bernard H. Trusdell	Lee
13	Peter S. Lott	Kendall
	William M. Byers	De Kalb
	Amos D. Clover	Grundy
14	Henry H. Evans	Kane
	James G. Wrigh	Du Page
	James Herrington	Kane
15	Frederick Kouka	Will
	Luke H. Goodrich	Will
	Daniel H. Pinney	Will
16	Conrad Secrest	Iroquois
	John A. Koplin	Iroquois
	Daniel C. Taylor	Kankakee
17	Lucien B. Crooker	La Salle
	Samuel M. Heslet	La Salle
	George W. Armstrong	La Salle
18	George B. Gray	Livingston
	John H. Collier	Ford
	Eben C. Allen	Livingston
19	Charles Baldwin	Bureau
	Daniel J. Hurd	Stark
	James J. Herron	Bureau
20	Joel A. Ranney	Woodford
	Charles Fosbender	Marshall
	Eli V. Raley	Putnam
21	John T. Browning	Rock Island
	John P. Fox	Henry
	Rufus M. Grennell	Rock Island
22	Alfred S. Curtis	Knox
	Joseph F. Latimer	Knox
	Abraham M. Brown	Knox
23	C. W. Boydston	Warren
	E. K. Westfall	McDonough
	Charles H. Whitaker	McDonough
24	Charles F. Gill	Hancock
	George P. Walker	Hancock
	John J. Reaburn	Hancock
25	John A. Leeper	Fulton
	Charles F. Robison	Fulton
	William T. McCreery	Schuyler
26	Latham A. Wood	Peoria
	Nelson D. Jay	Peoria
	Robert S. Bibb	Peoria
27	Joseph C. Ross	Logan
	Dieterich C. Smith	Tazewell
	William A. Moore	Tazewell
28	Thomas F. Mitchell	McLean
	John F. Winter'	McLean
	Thomas P. Rogers	McLean
29	Thomas J. Abel	Macon
	Samuel S. Jack	Macon
	William L. Chambers	De Witt
30	Robert J. Bower	Champaign
	Emory C. Bartholow	Champaign
	Simeon H. Busey	Champaign
31	Jacob H. Oakwood	Vermilion
	Alvan Gilbert	Vermilion
	Robert L. McKinlay	Edgar
32	Henry A. Neal	Coles
	Rodolphus Heffernan	Coles
	Stephen Cannon	Moultrie
33	Gesham Monohon	Cumberland
	Nathaniel P. Robinson	Effingham

District	Member	County
	Thomas J. Fritts	Shelby
34	David H. Zepp	Montgomery
	William E. Morrison	Christian
	Burrel Phillips	Montgomery
35	John Foutch	Sangamon
	John Mayo Palmer	Sangamon
	Dewitt W. Smith	Sangamon
36	Jacob Wheeler	Mason
	William L. Vandeventer	Brown
	Cornelius Rourke	Menard
37	Thomas G. Black	Adams
	Hope S. Davis	Adams
	James H. Hendrickson	Adams
38	Asa C. Mathews	Pike
	Starkey B. Powell	Scott
	B. J. Hall	Calhoun
39	Isaac L. Morrison	Morgan
	William P. Callon	Morgan
	Lucian King	Greene
40	Richard Rowett	Macoupin
	Hampton W. Wall	Macoupin
	John N. English	Jersey
41	John S. Dewey	Madison
	Samuel A. Buckmaster	Madison
	Francis M. Pearce	Madison
42	Richard Tierney	Washington
	William M. Evans	Bond
	George F. Berry	Bond
43	Frederick Remann	Fayette
	Andrew J. Hogge	Fayette
	Thomas E. Merritt	Marion
44	Hiram H. Chesley	Clay
	William R. Wilkinson	Wabash
	George D. Ramsey	Clay
45	William Lindsey	Clark
	John H. Halley[1]	Jasper
	Andrew J. Reavill	Crawford
46	Ross Graham	White
	Thomas Connelly	Hamilton
	Thomas J. Williams	Jefferson
47	Peter Phillips	Franklin
	James M. Washburn	Williamson
	Thomas M. Mooneyham	Franklin
48	Theophilus T. Fountain	Perry
	John Boyd	Perry
	Septimus P. Mace	Randolph
49	John W. Wells	St. Clair
	Alonzo S. Wilderman	St. Clair
	James M. Whitaker	St. Clair
50	William H. Woodward	Jackson
	Alexander H. Irwin	Alexander
	Fontaine E. Albright	Jackson
51	William S. Morris	Hardin
	Alonzo D. Pierce	Pope
	Ephraim B. Watkins	Pulaski

[1] Resigned.

Thirty-first General Assembly,
1879–80

Convened Jan. 8, 1879; adjourned May 31, 1879.

Senate

President	Andrew Shuman
Secretary	James H. Paddock

District	Member	County
1	George E. White	Cook
2	Daniel N. Bash	Cook
3	Sylvester Artley	Cook
4	Francis A. Riddle	Cook
5	William T. Johnson	Cook
6	Martin A. Delaney	Cook
7	William J. Campbell	Cook
8	Merritt L. Joslyn	McHenry
9	Charles E. Fuller	Boone
10	Robert H. McClellan	JoDaviess
11	Charles Bent	Whiteside
12	Henry D. Dement	Lee
13	John R. Marshall	Kendall
14	Joseph H. Mayborne	Kane
15	Sylvester W. Munn	Will
16	Thomas P. Bonfield	Kankakee
17	Samuel R. Lewis	La Salle
18	Samuel T. Fosdick	Livingston
19	Lorenzo D. Whiting	Bureau
20	Henry J. Frantz	Woodford
21	Milton M. Ford	Henry
22	Benjamin C. Taliaferro	Mercer
23	William H. Neece	McDonough
24	William Scott	Hancock
25	Meredith Walker	Fulton
26	John S. Lee	Peoria
27	Abram Mayfield	Logan
28	John M. Hamilton	McLean
29	William T. Moffett	Macon
30	Chester P. Davis	Piatt
31	George Hunt	Edgar
32	Malden Jones	Douglas
33	Erastus N. Rinehart	Effingham
34	Elizur Southworth	Montgomery
35	William E. Shutt	Sangamon
36	Luther Dearborn	Mason
37	Maurice Kelly	Adams
38	William R. Archer	Pike
39	William P. Callon	Morgan
40	George W. Herdman	Jersey
41	Alfred J. Parkinson	Madison
42	Frederick E. W. Brink	Washington
43	Thomas E. Merritt	Marion
44	Robert P. Hanna	Wayne
45	William C. Wilson	Crawford
46	Charles E. McDowell	White
47	Samuel L. Cheaney	Saline
48	Ambrose Hoener	Monroe
49	John Thomas	St. Clair
50	Jesse Ware	Union
51	Andrew J. Kuykendall	Johnson

House of Representatives

Speaker	William A. James
Clerk	W. B. Taylor

District	Member	County
1	William H. Thompson	Cook
	Moses J. Wentworth	Cook
	David W. Clark, Jr.	Cook
2	Benjamin M. Wilson	Cook
	Solomon P. Hopkins	Cook

District	Member	County
	Patrick T. Barry	Cook
3	Leo Meilbeck	Cook
	Thomas J. Walsh	Cook
	John B. Taylor	Cook
4	Lewis H. Bisbee	Cook
	Elijah B. Sherman	Cook
	James Emmett Murray	Cook
5	William E. Mason	Cook
	Charles Erhardt	Cook
	Thomas F. O'Malley	Cook
6	Christian Meier	Cook
	Austin O. Sexton	Cook
	Horace H. Thomas	Cook
7	Lorin C. Collins, Jr.	Cook
	George G. Struckmann	Cook
	Bernard F. Weber	Cook
8	Flavel K. Granger	McHenry
	William A. James	Lake
	William Price	Lake
9	Omar H. Wright	Boone
	Thomas Butterworth	Winnebago
	Horace W. Taylor	Winnebago
10	James I. Neff	Stephenson
	Andrew Hinds	Stephenson
	Charles S. Burt	JoDaviess
11	James Shaw	Carroll
	William H. Allen	Whiteside
	James M. Pratt	Whiteside
12	Frank N. Tice	Ogle
	Bernard H. Trusdell	Lee
	Alexander P. Dysart	Lee
13	William M. Byers	De Kalb
	Robert M. Brigham	De Kalb
	Alonzo B. Smith	Kendall
14	Edward C. Lovell	Kane
	James G. Wright	Du Page
	James Herrington	Kane
15	Jerry Keniston	Will
	Frederick Kouka	Will
	William P. Thomson	Will
16	Conrad Secrest	Iroquois
	Matthew H. Peters	Iroquois
	Azariah Buck	Kankakee
17	Lucien B. Crooker	La Salle
	Francis Bowen	La Salle
	David Richey	La Salle
18	George B. Gray	Livingston
	Norman E. Stevens	Ford
	Calvin H. Frew	Ford
19	Albert G. Scott	Bureau
	Sylvester F. Otman	Stark
	Simon Elliot	Bureau
20	Joel A. Ranney	Woodford
	George F. Wightman	Marshall
	Charles Fosbender	Marshall
21	Anthony R. Mock	Henry
	John W. Foy	Henry
	James W. Simonson	Rock Island
22	Rufus W. Miles	Knox
	Joseph F. Latimer	Knox
	John Sloan	Knox
23	Henry M. Lewis	Warren
	Henry Black	McDonough

District	Member	County
	Edwin W. Allen	Warren
24	Thomas B. Brumback	Hancock
	John J. Reaburn	Hancock
	Brooks R. Hamilton	Hancock
25	Hosea Davis	Schuyler
	Charles F. Robison	Fulton
	William T. McCreery	Schuyler
26	Horace R. Chase	Peoria
	Bernard Cremer	Peoria
	Washington Cockle[1]	Peoria
27	David H. Harts	Logan
	Green P. Orendorff	Tazewell
	William R. Hall	Tazewell
28	Thomas F. Mitchell	McLean
	Henry A. Ewing	McLean
	Thomas P. Rogers	McLean
29	John H. Tyler	De Witt
	George K. Ingham	De Witt
	Bradford K. Durfee	Macon
30	George Scroggs[1]	Champaign
	James Core	Champaign
	William A. Day	Champaign
31	John G. Holden	Vermilion
	Lyford Marston	Vermilion
	Robert L. McKinlay	Edgar
32	Orlando B. Ficklin	Coles
	Arnold Thomason	Moultrie
	Henry A. Neal	Coles
33	William A. Abraham	Effingham
	James L. Ryan	Cumberland
	Bartley Scarlette	Shelby
34	John B. Jones	Christian
	William Y. Crosthwait	Christian
	George L. Zink	Montgomery
35	William L. Gross	Sangamon
	John C. Snigg	Sangamon
	Carter Tracy	Sangamon
36	John F. Snyder	Cass
	John W. Savage	Cass
	Jacob Wheeler[1]	Mason
37	Samuel Mileham	Adams
	Absalom M. Samuel	Adams
	Joseph N. Carter	Adams
38	Asa C. Mathews	Pike
	Starkey B. Powell	Scott
	James H. Pleasants	Calhoun
39	Isaac L. Morrison	Morgan
	Richardson Vasey	Morgan
	Frank M. Bridges	Greene
40	Hampton W. Wall	Macoupin
	John N. English	Jersey
	George E. Warren	Jersey
41	William R. Prickett	Madison
	John M. Pearson	Madison
	John S. Dewey	Madison
42	T. Duane Hinckley	Washington
	Samuel W. Jones	Washington
	John L. Nichols	Clinton
43	John E. W. Hammond	Marion
	Francis M. Bolt	Fayette
	James S. Jackson	Marion
44	Jacob Zimmerman	Wabash
	William Bower	Richland
	Charles Churchill	Edwards
45	Jesse R. Johnson	Jasper
	James W. Graham	Clark
	Andrew J. Reavill	Crawford

District	Member	County
46	Alfred M. Green	Jefferson
	John R. Moss	Jefferson
	Charles M. Lyon	Hamilton
47	John M. Gregg	Saline
	Samuel C. Hall	Gallatin
	Wesley Trammell	Williamson
48	John T. McBride	Randolph
	John R. McFie	Randolph
	Philip C. C. Provart	Perry
49	Thomas C. Jennings	St. Clair
	Joseph Veile	St. Clair
	Henry Seiter	St. Clair
50	Charles H. Layman	Jackson
	Thomas T. Robinson	Jackson
	Thomas W. Halliday	Alexander
51	James H. Carter	Johnson
	Henry H. Spencer	Pulaski
	Thomas G. Farris[2]	Johnson
	William V. Eldredge[3]	Pope

[1] Resigned.
[2] Died Dec. 10, 1878.
[3] Vice Farris, elected Jan. 4, 1879.

Thirty-second General Assembly
1881–82

Convened Jan. 5, 1881; adjourned May 30, 1881. Second session convened March 23, 1881; adjourned May 6, 1882.

Senate

President   John M. Hamilton
President pro tempore
     William. J. Campbell
Secretary   James H. Paddock

District	Member	County
1	George E. White, Rep.	Cook
2	Leander D. Condee, Rep.	Cook
3	Sylvester Artley, Soc.	Cook
4	Christopher Mamer, Rep.	Cook
5	William T. Johnson, Rep.	Cook
	Frederick C. DeLang,[1] Rep.	Cook
6	George E. Adams, Rep.	Cook
7	William J. Campbell, Rep.	Cook
8	George Kirk, Rep.	Lake
9	Charles E. Fuller, Rep.	Boone
10	David H. Sunderland, Rep.	Stephenson
11	Charles Bent, Rep.	Whiteside
12	Isaac Rice, Rep.	Ogle
13	John R. Marshall, Rep.	Kendall
14	Henry H. Evans, Rep.	Kane
15	Sylvester W. Munn, Rep.	Will
16	Conrad Secrest, Rep.	Iroquois
17	Samuel R. Lewis, Rep.	La Salle
18	George Torrance, Rep.	Livingston
19	Lorenzo D. Whiting, Rep.	Bureau
20	Thomas M. Shaw, Dem.	Marshall
21	Milton M. Ford, Rep.	Henry
22	August W. Berggren, Rep.	Knox
23	William H. Neece, Dem.	McDonough
24	John Fletcher, Rep.	Hancock
25	Meredith Walker, Dem.	Fulton
26	Andrew J. Bell, Dem.	Peoria
27	Abram Mayfield, Dem.	Logan

District	Member	County
28	Joseph W. Fifer, Rep.	McLean
29	William T. Moffett, Rep.	Macon
30	James S. Wright, Rep.	Champaign
31	George Hunt, Rep.	Edgar
32	Horace S. Clark, Rep.	Coles
33	Erastus N. Rinehart, Dem.	Effingham
34	William T. Vandeveer, Dem.	Christian
35	William E. Shutt, Dem.	Sangamon
36	Edward Lanning, Dem.	Menard
37	Maurice Kelly, Dem.	Adams
38	William R. Archer, Dem.	Pike
39	William P. Callon, Dem.	Morgan
40	Charles A. Walker, Dem.	Macoupin
41	Alfred J. Parkinson, Rep.	Madison
42	Thomas B. Needles, Rep.	Washington
43	Thomas E. Merritt, Dem.	Marion
44	John R. Tanner, Rep.	Clay
45	William C. Wilson, Dem.	Crawford
46	John C. Edwards, Dem.	Hamilton
47	Samuel L. Cheaney, Dem.	Saline
48	Louis Ihorn, Rep.	Monroe
49	John Thomas, Rep.	St. Clair
50	William A. Lemma, Dem.	Jackson
51	Andrew J. Kuykendall, Rep.	Johnson

[1] Vice Johnson, resigned.

House of Representatives

Speaker   Horace H. Thomas
Clerk   W. B. Taylor

District	Member	County
1	David Sullivan, Dem.	Cook
	Aldis L. Rockwell, Rep.	Cook
	Madison R. Harris, Rep.	Cook
2	John R. Cook, Dem.	Cook
	Randall H. Wite, Rep.	Cook
	Orrin S. Cook, Rep.	Cook
3	Thomas Cloonan, Dem.	Cook
	George W. Kroll, Rep.	Cook
	Joseph R. Gorman, Dem.	Cook
4	Patrick J. McMahon, Dem.	Cook
	John L. Parish, Rep.	Cook
	Robert N. Pearson, Rep.	Cook
5	William A. Phelps, Rep.	Cook
	Thomas H. McKone, Dem.	Cook
	S. D. Mieroslawski, Dem.	Cook
6	Austin O. Sexton, Dem.	Cook
	Horace H. Thomas, Rep.	Cook
	Nathan M. Plotke, Rep.	Cook
7	George G. Struckmann, Rep.	Cook
	Lorin C. Collins, Jr., Rep.	Cook
	Bernard F. Weber, Dem.	Cook
8	Orson C. Diggins, Rep.	McHenry
	James Thompson, Dem.	McHenry
	James Pollock, Rep.	Lake
9	Edward B. Sumner, Rep.	Winnebago
	Omar H. Wright, Rep.	Boone
	Laurence McDonald, Dem.	Winnebago
10	William Cox, Rep.	Stephenson
	Edward L. Cronkrite, Dem.	Stephenson
	Joseph Moore,[1] Rep.	Stephenson
	James Bayne,[2] Rep.	JoDaviess

District	Member	County
11	William H. Allen, Rep.	Whiteside
	Emanuel Stover, Rep.	Carroll
	Henry Bitner, Dem.	Carroll
12	John H. White,[1] Dem.	Ogle
	Frank N. Tice,[3] Rep.	Ogle
	Alexander P. Dysart, Rep.	Lee
	Albert F. Brown, Rep.	Ogle
13	Henry Wood, Rep.	De Kalb
	Hiram Louck, Rep.	De Kalb
	John Clark, Dem.	De Kalb
14	Oliver P. Chisholm, Rep.	Kane
	James Herrington, Dem.	Kane
	James G. Wright, Rep.	Du Page
15	E. B. Shumway, Dem.	Will
	Michael Collins, Rep.	Will
	Harvey Stratton, Rep.	Will
16	George B. Winter, Dem.	Iroquois
	James Chatfield, Rep.	Kankakee
	Edward Rumley, Rep.	Iroquois
17	Alexander Vaughey, Dem.	La Salle
	Isaac Ames, Rep.	La Salle
	Francis M. Robinson, Rep.	La Salle
18	John H. Collier, Rep.	Ford
	Albert G. Goodspeed, Rep.	Livingston
	Leander L. Green, Dem.	Livingston
19	John H. Welsh, Dem.	Bureau
	Sylvester F. Otman, Rep.	Stark
	Charles Baldwin, Rep.	Bureau
20	Euclid Martin, Dem.	Woodford
	Calvin Stowell, Rep.	Marshall
	James T. Thornton, Rep.	Putnam
21	Anthony R. Mock, Rep.	Henry
	James W. Simonson, Rep.	Rock Island
	Patrick O'Mara, Dem.	Rock Island
22	Martin A. Boyd, Dem.	Mercer
	Alexander P. Petrie, Rep.	Mercer
	Hannibal P. Wood, Rep.	Knox
23	William C. McLeod, Dem.	McDonough
	Simeon B. Davis, Rep.	McDonough
	Daniel A. Perry, Rep.	Warren
24	Robert A. McKinley, Dem.	Henderson
	Henry M. Whiteman, Rep.	Henderson
	James Peterson, Rep.	Henderson
25	Joseph L. McCune, Rep.	Fulton
	William C. Reno, Dem.	Schuyler
	Inmon Blackaby, Dem.	Fulton
26	Joseph Gallup, Dem.	Peoria
	David Herver, Rep.	Peoria
	John M. Niehaus, Dem.	Peoria
27	John H. Crandall, Dem.	Tazewell
	Wesley B. Harvey, Rep.	Tazewell
	Allen Lucas, Dem.	Logan
28	William Hill, Dem.	McLean
	George B. Okeson, Rep.	McLean
	Thomas F. Mitchell, Rep.	McLean
29	Lewis Ludington, Rep.	De Witt
	Jasoɔ Rogers, Rep.	Macon
	Bradford K. Durfee, Dem.	Macon
30	Charles F. Tenney, Dem.	Piatt
	Ashbel H. Bailey, Rep.	Champaign
	Herbert D. Peters, Rep.	Piatt
31	Joseph B. Mann, Dem.	Vermilion
	Bradley Butterfield, Rep.	Vermilion
	John G. Holden, Rep.	Vermilion
32	Thomas E. Bundy, Dem.	Douglas
	John W. R. Morgan, Dem.	Moultrie
	Eugene B. Buck, Rep.	Coles
33	George D. Chafee, Rep.	Shelby
	Alfred C. Campbell, Dem.	Shelby
	Francis M. Richardson, Dem.	Cumberland
34	Robert McWilliams, Rep.	Montgomery
	George R. Sharp, Dem.	Christian
	George W. Paisley, Dem.	Montgomery
35	A. N. J. Crook, Dem.	Sangamon
	Dewitt W. Smith, Dem.	Sangamon
	James M. Garland, Rep.	Sangamon
36	Linus C. Chandler, Rep.	Cass
	William M. Duffy, Dem.	Mason
	J. Henry Shaw, Dem.	Cass
37	Joseph N. Carter, Rep.	Adams
	John McAdams, Dem.	Adams
	William A. Richardson, Dem.	Adams
38	John L. Underwood, Rep.	Pike
	William Mortland, Dem.	Pike
	Starkey B. Powell, Dem.	Scott
39	Ornan Pierson, Rep.	Greene
	Oliver Coultas, Dem.	Morgan
	Joseph S. Carr, Dem.	Greene
40	Balfour Cowen, Rep.	Macoupin
	John N. English, Dem.	Jersey
	Archelaus N. Yancey, Dem.	Macoupin
41	Henry O. Billings, Dem.	Madison
	John M. Pearson, Rep.	Madison
	Jones Tontz, Rep.	Madison
42	Frederick Becker, Dem.	Clinton
	John L. Nichols, Rep.	Clinton
	Ervin H. Simmons, Rep.	Bond
43	Iverson M. Little, Rep.	Fayette
	Tillman Raser,[1] Dem.	Marion
	Dwight W. Andrews,[4] Dem.	Marion
44	Mancil A. Harris, Dem·	Fayette
	Nathan Crews, Rep.	Wayne
	James Keen, Dem.	Wayne
45	Ezra B. Keen, Rep.	Wabash
	Jacob C. Olwin, Rep.	Crawford
	James C. Bryan, Dem.	Clark
46	William H. H. Mieure, Dem.	Lawrence
	Charles T. Strattan, Rep.	Jefferson
	Samuel H. Martin, Dem.	White
47	Robert A. D. Willbanks, Dem.	Jefferson
	Milo Erwin, Rep.	Williamson
	Francis M. Youngblood, Dem.	Franklin
48	John M. Gregg, Dem.	Saline
	Isaac M. Kelley, Rep.	Perry
	William K. Murphy, Dem.	Perry
49	Austin James, Dem.	Monroe
	John N. Perrin, Dem.	St. Clair
	Philip H. Postel, Rep.	St. Clair
50	Joseph Veile, Rep.	St. Clair
	Harmon H. Black, Rep.	Alexander
	David T. Linegar, Dem.	Alexander
51	Holly R. Buckingham, Dem.	Union
	William A. Spann, Dem.	Johnson
	William S. Morris, Rep.	Hardin
	John D. Young, Rep.	Massac

[1] Died.
[2] Vice Moore March 21, 1882.
[3] Vice White March 21, 1882.
[4] Vice Raser March 21, 1882.

Redistricting of 1882 authorized by act of
May 6, 1882 ; fifty-one districts, each electing one senator and three representatives

GENERAL ASSEMBLY

241

District	Counties
1 to 7	Cook
8	Boone, Lake, McHenry
9	Cook
10	Ogle, Winnebago
11	Cook
12	Carroll, JoDaviess, Stephenson
13	Cook
14	Du Page, Kane
15	Will
16	Iroquois, Kankakee
17	De Kalb, Grundy, Kendall
18	Ford, Livingston
19	Lee, Whiteside
20	Marshall, Tazewell, Woodford
21	Henry, Rock Island
22	Fulton, Knox
23	La Salle
24	Hancock, Henderson, Mercer
25	Bureau, Putnam, Stark
26	Peoria
27	McDonough, Warren
28	McLean
29	Logan, Macon
30	Champaign, De Witt, Piatt
31	Edgar, Vermilion
32	Coles, Cumberland, Douglas
33	Effingham, Moultrie, Shelby
34	Cass, Mason, Menard, Schuyler
35	Adams
36	Brown, Calhoun, Pike
37	Greene, Jersey, Scott
38	Macoupin, Morgan
39	Sangamon
40	Christian, Montgomery
41	Madison
42	Bond, Clinton, Washington
43	Fayette, Jefferson, Marion
44	Clay, Edwards, Richland, Wayne
45	Clark, Crawford, Jasper
46	Hamilton, Lawrence, Wabash, White
47	St. Clair
48	Monroe, Perry, Randolph
49	Gallatin, Hardin, Massac, Pope, Saline
50	Alexander, Jackson, Union
51	Franklin, Johnson, Pulaski, Williamson

Thirty-third General Assembly, 1883–84

Convened Jan. 3, 1883; adjourned June 18, 1883.

Senate

President	John M. Hamilton
President pro tempore	
	William J. Campbell
Secretary	Lorenzo F. Watson

District	Member	County
1	George E. White, Rep.	Cook
2	Leander D. Condee, Rep.	Cook

District	Member	County
3	John H. Clough, Rep.	Cook
4	Christopher Mamer, Rep.	Cook
5	William H. Ruger, Rep.	Cook
6	George E. Adams,[1] Rep.	Cook
	Henry Van Seller,[2] Rep.	Cook
7	William J. Campbell, Rep.	Cook
8	George Kirk, Rep.	Lake
9	William E. Mason, Rep.	Cook
10	Isaac Rice, Rep.	Ogle
11	Thomas Cloonan, Dem.	Cook
12	David H. Sunderland, Rep.	Stephenson
13	Millard B. Hereley, Dem.	Cook
14	Henry H. Evans, Rep.	Kane
15	E. B. Shumway, Dem.	Will
16	Conrad Secrest. Rep.	Iroquois
17	Lyman B. Ray, Rep.	Grundy
18	George Torrance, Rep.	Livingston
19	William C. Snyder, Rep.	Whiteside
20	Thomas M. Shaw, Dem.	Marshall
21	Henry A. Ainsworth, Rep.	Rock Island
22	August W. Berggren, Rep.	Knox
23	James W. Duncan, Dem.	La Salle
24	John Fletcher, Rep.	Hancock
25	Lorenzo D. Whiting, Rep.	Bureau
26	Andrew J. Bell, Dem.	Peoria
27	Henry Tubbs, Rep.	Warren
28	Joseph W. Fifer, Rep.	McLean
29	Jason Rogers, Rep.	Macon
30	James S. Wright, Rep.	Champaign
31	George Hunt,[1] Rep.	Edgar
32	Horace S. Clark, Rep.	Coles
33	Erastus N. Rinehart, Dem.	Effingham
34	Edward Lanning, Dem.	Menard
35	Maurice Kelly, Dem.	Adams
36	William R. Archer, Dem.	Pike
37	Frank M. Bridges, Dem.	Greene
38	Charles A. Walker, Dem.	Macoupin
39	Lloyd F. Hamilton, Dem.	Sangamon
40	William T. Vandeveer, Dem.	Christian
41	Daniel B. Gillham, Dem.	Madison
42	Thomas B. Needles, Rep.	Washington
43	Thomas E. Merritt, Dem.	Marion
44	John R. Tanner, Rep.	Clay
45	William H. McNary, Dem.	Clark
46	John C. Edwards, Dem.	Hamilton
47	Henry Seiter, Dem.	St. Clair
48	Louis Thorn, Rep.	Monroe
49	William S. Morris, Rep.	Pope
50	William A. Lemma, Dem.	Jackson
51	Daniel Hogan, Rep.	Pulaski

[1] Resigned.
[2] Vice Adams.

House of Representatives

Speaker	Lorin C. Collins, Jr.
Clerk	John A. Reeve

District	Member	County
1	John Fairbanks, Rep.	Cook
	Robert B. Kennedy, Rep.	Cook
	David Sullivan, Dem.	Cook
2	William H. Harper, Rep.	Cook

District	Member	County
	Hilon A. Parker, Rep.	Cook
	Eugene J. Fellows, Dem.	Cook
3	John W. E. Thomas, Rep.	Cook
	Thomas J. McNally, Dem.	Cook
	Isaac Abrahams, Dem.	Cook
4	John L. Parish, Rep.	Cook
	Joseph F. Lawrence, Rep.	Cook
	Redmond F. Sheridan, Dem.	Cook
5	David W. Walsh, Dem.	Cook
	James A. Taylor, Dem.	Cook
	Erwin E. Wood, Rep.	Cook
6	Edward Dean Cooke, Rep.	Cook
	Theodore Stimming, Rep.	Cook
	Austin O. Sexton, Dem.	Cook
7	Lorin C. Collins, Jr., Rep.	Cook
	George G. Struckmann, Rep.	Cook
	Clayton E. Crafts, Dem.	Cook
8	Charles E. Fuller, Rep.	Boone
	Charles H. Tryon, Rep.	McHenry
	Elijah M. Haines, Ind.	Lake
9	Julius Pedersen, Rep.	Cook
	A. Wendell, Rep.	Cook
	Mark J. Clinton, Dem.	Cook
10	Albert F. Brown, Rep.	Ogle
	Edward B. Sumner, Rep.	Winnebago
	John C. Seyster, Dem.	Ogle
11	Jesse J. Rook, Rep.	Cook
	John O'Shea, Dem.	Cook
	August Mette, Dem.	Cook
12	George L. Hoffman, Rep.	Carroll
	Julius A. Hammond, Rep.	JoDaviess
	Edward L. Cronkrite, Dem.	Stephenson
13	Peter A. Sundelius, Rep.	Cook
	Gregory A. Klupp, Dem.	Cook
	John F. Dugan, Dem.	Cook
14	Luther L. Hiatt, Rep.	Du Page
	Henry F. Walker, Rep.	Du Page
	James Herrington, Dem.	Kane
15	George Bez, Dem.	Will
	John O'Connell, Dem.	Will
	James L. Owen, Rep.	Will
16	John H. Jones, Rep.	Iroquois
	William S. Hawker, Rep.	Kankakee
	Daniel C. Taylor, Dem.	Kankakee
17	Henry Wood, Rep.	De Kalb
	Henry M. Boardman, Rep.	De Kalb
	Andrew Welch, Dem.	Kendall
18	John H. Collier, Rep.	Ford
	Albert G. Goodspeed, Rep.	Livingston
	Michael H. Cleary, Dem.	Livingston
19	Solomon H. Bethea, Rep.	Lee
	John G. Manahan, Rep.	Whiteside
	John B. Felker, Dem.	Lee
20	Revilo Newton, Dem.	Woodford
	John H. Crandall, Dem.	Tazewell
	Robert S. Hester, Rep.	Marshall
21	Thomas Nowers, Jr., Rep.	Henry
	Henry C. Cleaveland, Rep.	Rock Island
	Patrick O'Mara, Dem.	Rock Island
22	William H. Emerson, Rep.	Fulton
	Alfred S. Curtis, Rep.	Knox
	Frederick A. Willoughby, Dem.	Knox
23	Wright Adams, Rep.	La Salle
	Alexander Vaughey, Dem.	La Salle
	Samuel C. Wiley, Dem.	La Salle
24	David Rankin, Rep.	Henderson
	J. M. Ansley, Rep.	Mercer
	John D. Stevens, Dem.	Hancock
25	James T. Thornton, Rep.	Putnam
	John Lackie, Rep.	Stark
	John H. Welsh, Dem.	Bureau
26	Samuel H. Thompson, Rep.	Peoria
	Joseph Gallup, Dem.	Peoria
	Michael C. Quinn, Dem.	Peoria
27	Isaac N. Pearson, Rep.	McDonough
	Calvin M. Rogers, Rep.	Warren
	Isaac L. Pratt, Dem.	Warren
28	Thomas F. Mitchell, Rep.	McLean
	Lafayette Funk, Rep.	McLean
	Simeon H. West, Dem.	McLean
29	John H. Crocker, Rep.	Macon
	John T. Foster, Rep.	Logan
	Richard H. Templeman, Dem.	Logan
30	William F. Calhoun , Rep.	De Witt
	James A. Hawks, Rep.	Piatt
	William A. Day, Dem.	Champaign
31	William J. Calhoun. Rep.	Vermilion
	Robert B. Ray, Rep.	Vermilion
	Erneis R. E. Kimbrough, Dem.	Vermilion
32	Joseph H. Ewing, Rep.	Douglas
	William H. DeBord, Rep.	Cumberland
	Francis M. Richardson, Dem.	Cumberland
33	Charles L. Roane, Rep.	Moultrie
	Thomas N. Henry, Dem.	Shelby
	John H. Baker, Dem.	Moultrie
34	Trevanion L. Mathews, Rep.	Cass
	William M. Duffy, Dem.	Mason
	H. C. Thompson, Dem.	Cass
35	Thomas G. Black, Rep.	Adams
	James E. Purnell, Dem.	Adams
	James E. Downing, Dem.	Adams
36	Thomas Worthington, Jr., Rep.	Pike
	John W. Moore, Dem.	Brown
	Francis M. Greathouse,' Dem.	Calhoun
37	John H. Coats, Rep.	Scott
	Walter E. Carlin, Dem.	Jersey
	George W. Murray, Dem.	Scott
38	Isaac L. Morrison, Rep.	Morgan
	Archelaus N. Yancey, Dem.	Macoupin
	Edward M. Kinman, Dem.	Morgan
39	David T. Littler, Rep.	Sangamon
	Ben F. Caldwell, Dem.	Sangamon
	George W. Murray, Dem.	Sangamon
40	Edward F. Cowperthwaite, Rep.	Christian
	George M. Stevens, Dem.	Montgomery
	John B. Ricks, Dem.	Christian
41	John M. Pearson, Rep.	Madison
	Henry O. Billings, Dem.	Madison
	Robert D. Utiger, Dem.	Madison
42	John L. Nichols, Rep.	Clinton
	Frederick E. W. Brink, Dem.	Washington
	James M. Rountree, Dem.	Washington
43	Seth F. Crews, Rep.	Jefferson
	George H. Varnell, Dem.	Jefferson
	Jesse D. Jennings, Dem.	Fayette
44	Henry Studer, Rep.	Richland
	John S. Symonds, Rep.	Clay
	Elbert Rowland, Dem.	Richland

District	Member	County
45	J. M. Honey, Rep.	Jasper
	Grandison Clark, Dem.	Jasper
	William Updyke, Dem.	Crawford
46	William H. Johnson, Rep.	White
	Lowry Hay, Dem.	White
	Flemin Willet Cox, Dem.	Lawrence
47	Joseph B. Messick, Rep.	St. Clair
	Louis C. Starkel, Dem.	St. Clair
	Michael A. Sullivan, Dem.	St. Clair
48	John R. McFie, Rep.	Randolph
	James F. Canniff,[2] Dem.	Monroe
	John J. Higgins, Dem.	Perry
49	Robert W. McCartney, Rep.	Massac
	William H. Boyer, Rep.	Saline
	John M. Gregg, Dem.	Saline
50	James M. Scurlock, Rep.	Jackson
	Sidney Grear, Dem.	Union
	David T. Linegar, Dem.	Alexander
51	William W. Hoskinson, Rep.	Franklin
	Milo Erwin, Rep.	Williamson
	Augustus N. Lodge,[3] Dem.	Williamson
	William A. Spann,[4] Dem.	Williamson

[1] Resigned.
[2] Died April 22, 1883.
[3] Unseated.
[4] Successfully contested election of Lodge.

Thirty-fourth General Assembly, 1885-86

Convened Jan. 7, 1885; adjourned June 26, 1885.

Senate

President	John C. Smith
President pro tempore	William J. Campbell
Secretary	Lorenzo F. Watson

District	Member	County
1	George E. White, Rep.	Cook
2	Charles H. Crawford, Rep.	Cook
3	John H. Clough, Rep.	Cook
4	Thomas A. Cantwell, Dem.	Cook
5	William H. Ruger, Rep.	Cook
6	Henry W. Laman, Rep.	Cook
7	William J. Campbell, Rep.	Cook
8	Ira R. Curtiss, Rep.	McHenry
9	William E. Mason, Rep.	Cook
10	Edward B. Sumner, Rep.	Winnebago
11	Thomas Cloonan, Dem.	Cook
12	James S. Cochran, Rep.	Stephenson
13	Millard B. Hereley, Dem.	Cook
14	Henry H. Evans, Rep.	Kane
15	E. B. Shumway, Dem.	Will
16	Hamilton K. Wheeler, Rep.	Kankakee
17	Lyman B. Ray, Rep.	Grundy
18	George Torrance, Rep.	Livingston
19	William C. Snyder, Rep.	Whiteside
20	Green P. Orendorff, Dem.	Tazewell
21	Henry A. Ainsworth, Rep.	Rock Island
22	August W. Berggren, Rep.	Knox
23	James W. Duncan, Dem.	La Salle
24	Alson J. Streeter, Dem.	Mercer

District	Member	County
25	Lorenzo D. Whiting, Rep.	Bureau
26	Andrew J. Bell, Dem.	Peoria
27	Henry Tubbs, Rep.	Warren
28	Lafayette Funk, Rep.	McLean
29	Jason Rogers, Rep.	Macon
30	Martin B. Thompson, Rep.	Champaign
31	Henry Van Sellar, Rep.	Edgar
32	William B. Galbreath,[1] Dem.	Coles
	Thomas L. McGrath,[2] Rep.	Coles
33	Erastus N. Rinehart, Rep.	Effingham
34	John M. Darnell, Dem.	Schuyler
35	Maurice Kelly,[3] Dem.	Adams
36	James W. Johnson, Dem.	Pike
37	Frank M. Bridges,[4] Dem.	Greene
	Robert H. Davis,[5] Dem.	Greene
38	David Gore, Dem.	Macoupin
39	Lloyd F. Hamilton, Dem.	Sangamon
40	Elizur Southworth, Dem.	Montgomery
41	Daniel B. Gillham, Dem.	Madison
42	William S. Forman. Dem.	Washington
43	Thomas E. Merritt, Dem.	Marion
44	Robley D. Adams, Rep.	Wayne
45	William H. McNary, Dem.	Clark
46	Richard L. Organ, Dem.	White
47	Henry Seiter, Dem.	St. Clair
48	John J. Higgins, Dem.	Perry
49	William S. Morris, Rep.	Pope
50	George W. Hill, Dem.	Jackson
51	Daniel Hogan, Rep.	Pulaski

[1] Died during recess.
[2] Vice Galbreath.
[3] Resigned.
[4] Died March 19, 1885.
[5] Vice Bridges.

House of Representatives

Speaker	Elijah M. Haines
Clerk	Robert A. D. Willbanks

District	Member	County
1	Robert B. Kennedy, Rep.	Cook
	Francis W. Parker, Rep.	Cook
	James McHale, Dem.	Cook
2	William H. Harper, Rep.	Cook
	Hilon A. Parker, Rep.	Cook
	Ernst Hummel, Dem.	Cook
3	Abner Taylor, Rep.	Cook
	John W. E. Thomas, Rep.	Cook
	Thomas J. McNally, Dem.	Cook
4	Thomas C. MacMillan, Rep.	Cook
	Matthew Murphy, Dem.	Cook
	James F. Quinn, Dem.	Cook
5	William S. Powell, Rep.	Cook
	Joseph P. Mahoney, Dem.	Cook
	William A. Dorman, Dem.	Cook
6	Henry S. Boutell, Rep.	Cook
	Eugene A. Sittig, Rep.	Cook
	Stephen F. Sullivan, Dem.	Cook
7	John Humphrey, Rep.	Cook
	George G. Struckmann, Rep.	Cook
	Clayton E. Crafts, Dem.	Cook
8	James Pollock, Rep.	Lake

District	Member	County
	Charles E. Fuller, Rep.	Boone
	Elijah M. Haines, Ind.	Lake
9	Frederick S. Baird, Rep.	Cook
	Charles E. Scharlau, Rep.	Cook
	Dennis Considine, Dem.	Cook
10	Albert F. Brown, Rep.	Ogle
	David Hunter, Rep.	Winnebago
	Edwin M. Winslow, Dem.	Winnebago
11	Adam C. Oldenberg, Rep.	Cook
	John O'Shea, Dem.	Cook
	J. J. Schlessinger, Dem.	Cook
12	Daniel A. Sheffield, Rep.	JoDaviess
	Simon Greenleaf, Rep.	Carroll
	Edward L. Cronkrite, Dem.	Stephenson
13	Peter A. Sundelius, Rep.	Cook
	Barney Brachtendorf, Dem.	Cook
	Thomas, F. Mulheran, Dem.	Cook
14	Luther L. Hiatt, Rep.	Du Page
	John Stewart, Rep.	Kane
	Thomas O'Donnell, Dem.	Kane
15	Henry H. Stassen, Rep	Will
	James C. Morgan, Dem.	Will
	George Bez, Dem.	Will
16	Matthew F. Campbell, Rep.	Kankakee
	John L. Hamilton, Rep.	Iroquois
	Freeman P. Morris, Dem.	Iroquois
17	Henry C. Whittemore, Rep.	De Kalb
	William M. Hanna, Rep.	Kendall
	Andrew Welch, Dem.	Kendall
18	Albert G. Goodspeed, Rep.	Livingston
	Charles Bogardus, Rep.	Ford
	Michael H. Cleary, Dem.	Livingston
19	Charles H. Ingalls, Rep.	Whiteside
	Robert E. Logan,[1] Rep.	Whiteside
	Caleb C. Johnson, Dem.	Whiteside
	Dwight S. Spafford,[2] Rep.	Whiteside
20	Julius Watercott, Dem.	Marshall
	Samuel Patrick, Dem.	Woodford
	Ernest F. Unland, Rep.	Tazewell
21	Henry C. Cleaveland, Rep.	Rock Island
	Thomas Nowers, Jr., Rep.	Henry
	James H. Paddelford, Dem.	Henry
22	Orrin P. Cooley, Rep.	Knox
	William J. Orendorf, Rep.	Fulton
	Samuel P. Marshall, Dem.	Fulton
23	Samuel C. Wiley, Dem.	La Salle
	Charles L. Hoffmann, Dem.	La Salle
	Frank P. Snyder, Rep.	La Salle
24	Abner W. Graham, Rep.	Henderson
	Clarence R. Gittings, Rep.	Hancock
	Alfred N. Cherry, Dem.	Henderson
25	Albert W. Boyden, Rep.	Bureau
	James H. Miller, Rep.	Stark
	Eli V. Raley, Dem.	Putnam
26	Mark M. Bassett, Rep.	Peoria
	John Downs, Dem.	Peoria
	William McLean, Dem.	Peoria
27	Calvin M. Rogers, Rep.	Warren
	William H. McCord, Rep.	McDonough
	William H. Wear, Dem.	McDonough
28	Samuel B. Kinsey, Rep.	McLean
	Ivory H. Pike, Rep.	McLean
	Simeon H. West, Dem.	McLean

District	Member	County
29	Charles S. Lawrence, Rep.	Logan
	Richard H. Templeman, Dem.	Logan
	James M. Graham, Dem.	Macon
30	William F. Calhoun, Rep.	De Witt
	Virgil S. Ruby, Rep.	Piatt
	William B. Webber, Dem.	Champaign
31	Elliott E. Boudinot, Rep.	Vermilion
	Charles A. Allen, Rep.	Vermilion
	Erneis R. E. Kimbrough, Dem.	Vermilion
32	Stroder M. Long, Rep.	Douglas
	Henry Sheplor, Dem.	Cumberland
	James Park McGee, Dem.	Douglas
33	Thomas N. Henry, Dem.	Shelby
	John H. Baker, Dem.	Moultrie
	Walter C. Headen, Rep.	Shelby
34	Perry Logsdon, Rep.	Schuyler
	J. Henry Shaw,[3] Dem.	Cass
	George W. Langford, Dem.	Mason
	William H. Weaver,[4] Rep.	Menard
35	Fred P. Taylor, Dem.	Adams
	Samuel Mileham, Dem.	Adams
	William H. Collins, Rep.	Adams
36	William H. Brackenridge, Rep.	Brown
	John W. Moore, Dem.	Brown
	Peter C. Barry, Dem.	Calhoun
37	Henry C. Massey, Dem.	Jersey
	Bryon McEvers, Dem.	Scott
	Theodore S. Chapman, Rep.	Jersey
38	Edward L. McDonald, Dem.	Morgan
	Frank R. McAliney, Dem.	Macoupin
	George J. Castle, Rep.	Macoupin
39	Ben F. Caldwell, Dem.	Sangamon
	Charles A. Keyes, Dem.	Sangamon
	Charles Kerr, Rep.	Sangamon
40	Robert A. Gray, Dem.	Christian
	George M. Stevens, Dem.	Montgomery
	Humphrey H. Hood, Rep.	Montgomery
41	William R. Prickett, Dem.	Madison
	William W. Pearce, Dem.	Madison
	Jones Tontz, Dem.	Madison
42	Matthew A. Morgan, Rep.	Washington
	Milton M. Sharp, Dem.	Bond
	Charles C. Moore, Dem.	Clinton
43	George H. Varnell, Dem.	Jefferson
	George H. Dieckmann, Dem.	Fayette
	Henry C. Goodnow, Rep.	Marion
44	William T. Prunty, Rep.	Richland
	Alfred Brown, Rep.	Edwards
	Edward McClung, Dem.	Wayne
45	John M. Highsmith, Dem.	Crawford
	Isaac M. Shup, Dem.	Jasper
	David Trexler, Rep.	Jasper
46	James R. Campbell, Dem.	Hamilton
	James M. Sharp, Dem.	Wabash
	William T. Buchanan, Rep.	Lawrence
47	James M. Dill, Dem.	St. Clair
	Ferdinand Heim, Dem.	St. Clair
	Joseph B. Messick, Rep.	St. Clair
48	Thomas James, Dem.	Randolph
	Peter Bickelhaupt, Dem.	Monroe
	Henry Clay, Rep.	Perry
49	John Yost, Rep.	Gallatin
	Simon S. Barger, Rep.	Pope
	W. V. Choisser, Dem.	Saline
50	David T. Linegar, Dem.	Alexander
	Philip V. N. Davis, Dem.	Union
	William S. Rogers, Rep.	Jackson

District	Member	County
51	James M. Fowler, Rep.	Williamson
	William C. Allen, Rep.	Johnson
	Quincy E. Browning, Dem.	Franklin

¹ Died Feb. 25, 1885.
² Vice Logan.
³ Died April 12, 1885.
⁴ Vice Shaw.

Thirty-fifth General Assembly,
1887–88

Convened Jan. 5, 1887; adjourned June 15, 1887.

Senate
President   John C. Smith
President pro tempore
                          August W. Berggren
Secretary   Lorenzo F. Watson

District	Member	County
1	Bernard A. Eckhart, Rep.	Cook
2	Charles H. Crawford, Rep.	Cook
3	George A. Gibbs, Rep.	Cook
4	Thomas A. Cantwell, Dem.	Cook
5	James Monahan, Rep.	Cook
6	Henry W. Laman, Rep.	Cook
7	John Humphrey, Rep.	Cook
8	Ira R. Curtiss, Rep.	McHenry
9	Philip Knopf, Rep.	Cook
10	Edward B. Sumner, Rep.	Winnebago
11	Richard M. Burke, Labor	Cook
12	James S. Cochran, Rep.	Stephenson
13	Michael F. Garrity, Rep.	Cook
14	Henry H. Evans, Rep.	Kane
15	Charles H. Bacon, Rep.	Will
16	Hamilton K. Wheeler, Rep.	Kankakee
17	Charles F. Greenwood, Rep.	De Kalb
18	George Torrance, Rep.	Livingston
19	John D. Crabtree,¹ Rep.	Lee
20	Green P. Orendorff, Dem.	Tazewell
21	John H. Pierce, Rep.	Henry
22	August W. Berggren, Rep.	Knox
23	Joseph Reinhardt, Rep.	La Salle
24	Alson J. Streeter, Dem.	Mercer
25	Edward A. Washburn, Rep.	Bureau
26	Andrew J. Bell, Dem.	Peoria
27	Isaac N. Pearson,² Rep.	McDonough
28	Lafayette Funk, Rep.	McLean
29	William C. Johns, Rep.	Macon
30	Martin B. Thompson, Rep.	Champaign
31	George E. Bacon, Rep.	Edgar
32	Thomas L. McGrath, Rep.	Coles
33	Lloyd B. Stephenson, Dem.	Shelby
34	John M. Darnell, Dem.	Schuyler
35	George W. Dean, Dem.	Adams
36	James W. Johnson, Dem.	Pike
37	Theodore S. Chapman, Rep.	Jersey
38	David Gore, Dem.	Macoupin
39	William E. Shutt, Dem.	Sangamon
40	Elizur Southworth, Dem.	Montgomery
41	William F. L. Hadley, Rep.	Madison
42	William S. Forman, Dem.	Washington
43	Augustus M. Strattan, Dem.	Jefferson

District	Member	County
44	Robley D. Adams, Rep.	Wayne
45	Andrew J. Reavill, Dem.	Crawford
46	Richard L. Organ, Dem.	White
47	Henry Seiter, Dem.	St. Clair
48	John J. Higgins, Dem.	Perry
49	John Yost, Rep.	Gallatin
50	George W. Hill, Dem.	Jackson
51	Daniel Hogan, Rep.	Pulaski

¹ Resigned May 29, 1888.
² Resigned, elected sec. of state.

House of Representatives
Speaker   William F. Calhoun
Clerk   John A. Reeve

District	Member	County
1	David W. Clark, Rep.	Cook
	John S. Ford, Rep.	Cook
	James O'Connor, Labor	Cook
2	Durfee C. Chase, Rep.	Cook
	John W. Farley, Dem.	Cook
	William P. Wright, Labor	Cook
3	Francis A. Brokoski, Rep.	Cook
	George F. Ecton, Rep.	Cook
	Thomas J. Moran, Dem.	Cook
4	James F. Gleason, Dem.	Cook
	Thomas C. MacMillan, Rep.	Cook
	John Meyer, Rep.	Cook
5	Kirk N. Eastman, Rep.	Cook
	Joseph P. Mahoney, Dem.	Cook
	Leo P. Dwyer, Labor	Cook
6	James H. Farrell, Labor	Cook
	Michael J. Dwyer, Labor	Cook
	Charles G. Neeley, Rep.	Cook
7	Clayton E. Crafts, Dem.	Cook
	Orrigen W. Herrick, Rep.	Cook
	Stephen A. Reynolds, Rep.	Cook
8	Charles E. Fuller, Rep.	Boone
	Charles A. Partridge, Rep.	Lake
	George Wait, Dem.	Lake
9	Charles E. Scharlau, Rep.	Cook
	Henry Decker, Rep.	Cook
	Charles D. Nixon, Labor	Cook
10	David Hunter, Rep.	Winnebago
	James P. Wilson, Dem.	Ogle
	James Lamont, Proh.	Winnebago
11	George F. Rohrback, Labor	Cook
	Thomas G. McElligott, Dem.	Cook
	Bryan Conway, Dem.	Cook
12	Emanuel Stover, Rep.	Carroll
	George W. Pepoon, Rep.	JoDaviess
	James Carr, Dem.	JoDaviess
13	Frank E. Schoenewald, Rep.	Cook
	Victor Karlowski, Labor	Cook
	John J. Furlong, Dem.	Cook
14	Charles Curtiss, Rep.	Du Page
	James Herrington, Dem.	Kane
	John Stewart, Rep.	Kane
15	Dwight Haven, Rep.	Will
	Daniel McLaughlin, Rep.	Will
	Thomas H. Riley, Dem.	Will

District	Member	County
16	Hiram M. Keyser, Rep.	Kankakee
	John L. Hamilton, Rep.	Iroquois
	Truman Huling, Dem.	Kankakee
17	Daniel D. Hunt, Rep.	De Kalb
	Edgar W. Faxon, Rep.	Kendall
	Hiram Holcomb, Dem.	De Kalb
18	O. W. Pollard, Rep.	Livingston
	Charles Bogardus, Rep.	Ford
	Michael H. Cleary, Dem.	Livingston
19	Benjamin H. Bradshaw, Rep.	Lee
	John W. White, Rep.	Whiteside
	Caleb C. Johnson, Dem.	Whiteside
20	Aaron H. Brubaker, Rep.	Woodford
	William H. Kister, Rep.	Marshall
	Samuel Patrick,[1] Dem.	Woodford
	Samuel Miller,[2] Dem.	Woodford
21	Hendrick V. Fisher, Rep.	Henry
	William F. Crawford, Rep.	Rock Island
	John T. Piatt, Dem.	Henry
22	Orrin P. Cooley, Rep.	Knox
	Thomas Hamer, Rep.	Fulton
	Samuel P. Marshall, Dem.	Fulton
23	James P. Trench, Dem.	La Salle
	Edgar S. Browne, Rep.	La Salle
	Lewis M. Sawyer, Rep.	La Salle
24	Wesley C. Williams, Dem.	Hancock
	Clarence R. Gittings, Rep.	Henderson
	William C. Galloway, Rep.	Mercer
25	James H. Miller, Rep.	Stark
	Sterling Pomeroy, Rep	Bureau
	Anthony Morrasy, Dem.	Bureau
26	Nelson D. Jay, Dem.	Peoria
	James Kenny, Dem.	Peoria
	John M. Hart, Rep.	Peoria
27	James P. Firoved, Dem.	Warren
	Henry W. Allen, Rep.	Warren
	Richard G. Breeden, Rep.	McDonough
28	Frank Y. Hamilton, Rep.	McLean
	Samuel B. Kinsey, Rep.	McLean
	John Eddy, Dem.	McLean
29	Hiram L. Pierce, Dem.	Logan
	William H. Kretzinger,, Rep.	Logan
	William Grason, Rep.	Macon
30	Francis M. Peel, Dem.	Piatt
	William F. Calhoun, Rep.	De Witt
	Virgil S. Ruby, Rep.	Piatt
31	Hiram P. Blackburn, Rep.	Vermilion
	Charles A. Allen, Rep.	Vermilion
	Robert L. McKinlay, Dem.	Edgar
32	Samuel F. Wilson, Rep.	Cumberland
	Eugene Rice, Rep.	Douglas
	Francis M. Richardson, Dem.	
		Cumberland
33	John H. Baker, Dem.	Moultrie
	John J. Schneider, Dem.	Effingham
	Joseph P. Condo, Rep.	Effingham
34	Michael D. Halpin, Dem.	Cass
	Fred Wilkinson, Dem.	Menard
	James M. Ruggles, Dem.	Mason
35	Albert W. Wells, Dem.	Adams
	Ira Tyler, Dem.	Adams
	William H. Collins, Rep.	Adams
36	William R. Archer, Dem.	Pike

District	Member	County
	John McNabb, Dem.	Calhoun
	Alexander K. Lowry, Rep.	Brown
37	William M. Ward, Rep.	Greene
	Joseph D. Sawyers, Dem.	Scott
	Robert H. Davis, Dem.	Greene
38	George W. Smith, Dem.	Morgan
	James B. Wilson, Dem.	Macoupin
	John E. Wright, Rep.	Morgan
39	Albert J. Converse, Dem.	Sangamon
	Wiley E. Jones, Dem.	Sangamon
	David T. Littler,[3] Rep.	Sangamon
40	Robert A. Gray, Dem.	Christian
	Colman C. George, Rep.	Christian
	Burrel Phillips, Dem.	Montgomery
41	John W. Coppinger, Dem.	Madison
	Isaac Cox, Rep.	Madison
	John Wedig, Rep.	Madison
42	Matthew A. Morgan, Rep.	Washington
	H. H. Heiman,[4] Dem.	Clinton
	William G. Kaune,[5] Dem.	Clinton
	C. H. Seawell, Dem.	Bond
43	Thomas E. Merritt, Dem.	Marion
	Granville V. E. Fletcher, Dem.	Fayette
	John J. Brown, Rep.	Fayette
44	John S. Symonds, Dem.	Clay
	Thomas A. Wilson, Rep.	Clay
	Alfred Brown,[6] Rep.	Edwards
	Albert Rude,[7] Rep.	Edwards
45	Charles A. Purdunn, Dem.	Clark
	James Larrabee, Dem.	Jasper
	Alfred H. Jones, Rep.	Crawford
46	James R. Campbell, Dem.	Hamilton
	George F. French, Dem.	Lawrence
	Edward B. Green, Rep.	Wabash
47	Joseph B. Messick, Rep.	St. Clair
	Joseph Veile, Rep.	St. Clair
	George S. Bailey, Labor	St. Clair
48	Everett J. Murphy, Rep.	Randolph
	Charles B. Cole, Dem.	Randolph
	Peter Bickelhaupt, Dem.	Monroe
49	William G. Sloan, Rep.	Saline
	Simon S. Barger, Rep.	Pope
	Jonathan F. Taylor, Dem.	Hardin
50	Reuben S. Yocum, Dem.	Alexander
	William Scott Day, Dem.	Union
	Charles S. Nellis, Rep.	Alexander
51	William H. Bundy, Dem.	Williamson
	William W. Hoskinson,[8] Rep.	Franklin
	William L. Crim,[9] Rep.	Franklin
	Alonzo K. Vickers, Rep.	Johnson

[1] Died Dec. 19, 1886.
[2] Vice Patrick Jan. 18, 1887.
[3] Resigned.
[4] Died Jan. 17, 1887.
[5] Vice Heiman Feb. 15, 1887.
[6] Died Feb. 21, 1887.
[7] Vice Brown.
[8] Died Feb. 25, 1887.
[9] Vice Hoskinson.

Thirty-sixth General Assembly,
1889–90

Convened Jan. 9, 1889; adjourned May 22, 1889. Second session convened July 23, 1890; adjourned August 1, 1890.

President   Lyman B. Ray

President pro tempore

Theodore S. Chapman	Speaker	William G. Cochran[3]
Secretary Lorenzo F. Watson	Clerk	John A. Reeve

District	Member	County
1	Bernard A. Eckhart, Rep.	Cook
2	Charles H. Crawford, Rep.	Cook
3	George A. Gibbs, Rep.	Cook
4	Thomas C. MacMillan, Rep.	Cook
5	James Monahan, Rep.	Cook
6	Horace H. Thomas, Rep.	Cook
7	John Humphrey, Rep.	Cook
8	Charles E. Fuller, Rep.	Boone
9	Philip Knopf, Rep.	Cook
10	Benjamin F. Sheets, Rep.	Ogle
11	Richard M. Burke, Labor	Cook
12	Robert H. Wiles, Rep.	Stephenson
13	Michael F. Garrity, Rep.	Cook
14	Henry H. Evans, Rep.	Kane
15	Charles H. Bacon, Rep.	Will
16	Conrad Secrest, Rep.	Iroquois
17	Charles F. Greenwood, Rep.	De Kalb
18	Charles Bogardus, Rep.	Ford
19	Charles A. Griswold,[1] Rep.	Whiteside
20	Martin L. Newell, Dem.	Woodford
21	John H. Pierce, Rep.	Henry
22	Thomas Hamer, Rep.	Fulton
23	Joseph Reinhardt, Rep.	La Salle
24	Orville F. Berry, Rep.	Hancock
25	Edward A. Washburn, Rep.	Bureau
26	Mark M. Bassett, Rep.	Peoria
27	William J. Frisbee,[2] Rep.	McDonough
28	Thomas C. Kerrick, Rep.	McLean
29	William C. Johns, Rep.	Macon
30	Milton W. Mathews, Rep.	Champaign
31	George E. Bacon, Rep.	Edgar
32	Lewis L. Lehman,[3] Rep.	Coles
33	Lloyd B. Stephenson, Dem.	Shelby
34	Arthur A. Leeper, Dem.	Cass
35	George W. Dean, Dem.	Adams
36	Harry Higbee, Dem.	Pike
37	Theodore S. Chapman, Rep.	Jersey
38	Edward L. McDonald, Dem.	Morgan
39	William E. Shutt, Dem.	Sangamon
40	Hiram P. Shumway, Dem.	Christian
41	William F. L. Hadley, Rep.	Madison
42	Frederick E. W. Brink, Dem.	Washington
43	Augustus M. Strattan, Dem.	Jefferson
44	Dios C. Hagle, Rep.	Clay
45	Andrew J. Reavill, Dem.	Crawford
46	James R. Campbell, Dem.	Hamilton
47	Henry Seiter, Dem.	St. Clair
48	Joseph W. Rickert, Dem.	Monroe
49	John Yost, Rep.	Gallatin
50	David W. Karraker, Dem.	Union
51	Daniel Hogan,[4] Rep.	Pulaski

[1] Vice Crabtree, resigned.
[2] Vice Pearson, resigned.
[3] Vice McGrath, died Dec. 1888.
[4] Resigned July 23, 1890.

House of Representatives

Speaker   Asa C. Matthews[1]
Speaker   James H. Miller[2]

Clerk   George Buckingham[3]

[1] Resigned to be first comptroller of the treasury, May 10.
[2] Succeeded Matthews, died before second session.
[3] Second session.

District	Member	County
1	John S. Ford, Rep.	Cook
	Jethro M. Getman, Rep.	Cook
	James Walsh, Dem.	Cook
2	Bushrod E. Hoppin, Rep.	Cook
	James N. Buchanan, Rep.	Cook
	James J. O'Toole, Dem.	Cook
3	Francis A. Brokoski, Rep.	Cook
	George F. Ecton, Rep.	Cook
	William Buckley, Dem.	Cook
4	John Meyer, Rep.	Cook
	Quida J. Chott, Rep.	Cook
	James F. Quinn, Dem.	Cook
5	James L. Monaghan, Rep.	Cook
	Joseph P. Mahoney, Dem.	Cook
	Frank J. Wisner, Dem.	Cook
6	Jacob Miller, Rep.	Cook
	George S. Baker, Rep.	Cook
	James H. Farrell, Dem.	Cook
7	Stephen A. Reynolds, Rep.	Cook
	Edward J. Whitehead, Rep.	Cook
	Clayton E. Crafts, Dem.	Cook
8	Charles A. Partridge, Rep.	Lake
	G. S. Southworth, Rep.	McHenry
	Elijah M. Haines,[1] Ind.	Lake
	Robert J. Beck,[2] Rep.	McHenry
9	Samuel C. Hayes, Rep.	Cook
	William F. Wilk, Rep.	Cook
	Joseph A. O'Donnell, Dem.	Cook
10	David Hunter, Rep.	Winnebago
	William H. Cox, Rep.	Ogle
	Robert Simpson, Dem.	Winnebago
11	William E. Kent, Rep.	Cook
	Thomas G. McElligott, Dem.	Cook
	Henry P. Carmody, Dem.	Cook
12	George W. Pepoon, Rep.	JoDaviess
	Levi T. Bray, Rep.	Carroll
	Michael Stoskopf, Dem.	Stephenson
13	Peter A. Sundelius, Rep.	Cook
	Stanley H. Kunz, Dem.	Cook
	William H. Lyman, Dem.	Cook
14	Edgar C. Hawley, Rep.	Kane
	Robert M. Ireland, Rep.	Kane
	Nicholas R. Graham, Dem.	Du Page
15	Daniel McLaughlin, Rep.	Will
	Fred Wilke, Rep.	Will
	William Mooney, Dem.	Will
16	William L. R. Johnson, Rep.	Iroquois
	Daniel H. Paddock, Rep.	Kankakee
	Freeman P. Morris, Dem.	Iroquois
17	Daniel D. Hunt, Rep.	De Kalb
	Reuben W. Willett, Rep.	Kendall
	Dwight Crossett, Dem.	De Kalb
18	O. W. Pollard, Rep.	Livingston

District	Member	County
	Nelson J. Myer, Rep.	Livingston
	James A. Smith, Dem.	Livingston
19	Benjamin H. Bradshaw, Rep.	Lee
	John W. White, Rep.	Whiteside
	Sherwood Dixon, Dem.	Lee
20	Peter A. Coen, Rep.	Woodford
	Jonas T. Ball, Dem.	Marshall
	John W. White, Dem.	Tazewell
21	William F. Crawford, Rep.	Rock Island
	Hendrick V. Fisher, Rep.	Henry
	Elmore W. Hurst, Dem.	Rock Island
22	Orrin P. Cooley, Rep.	Knox
	George W. Prince, Rep.	Knox
	James W. Hunter, Dem.	Knox
23	David Ross, Rep.	La Salle
	Edgar S. Browne, Dem.	La Salle
	James P. Trench, Dem.	La Salle
24	James O. Anderson, Rep.	Henderson
	John P. McClanahan, Rep.	Mercer
	Tom A. Marshall, Dem.	Mercer
25	James H. Miller,[3] Rep.	Stark
	Peter McCall, Rep.	Bureau
	Anthony Morrasy, Dem.	Bureau
	Samuel White,[4] Rep.	Stark
26	John M. Hart, Rep.	Peoria
	James Kenny, Dem.	Peoria
	David B. Stookey, Dem.	Peoria
27	Henry W. Allen, Rep.	Warren
	Richard G. Breeden, Rep.	McDonough
	Horatio R. Bartleson, Dem.	McDonough
28	Ivory H. Pike, Rep.	McLean
	Henry L. Terpening, Rep.	McLean
	John Eddy, Dem.	McLean
29	William H. Kretzinger, Rep.	Logan
	David P. Keller, Rep.	Macon
	Robert H. Hill, Dem.	Macon
30	Julius A. Brown, Rep.	Piatt
	William H. Oglevee, Rep.	De Witt
	Joseph C. Myers, Dem.	De Witt
31	Charles A. Allen, Rep.	Vermilion
	Milton Lee, Rep.	Vermilion
	George R. Tilton, Dem.	Vermilion
32	Eugene Rice, Rep.	Douglas
	James Park McGee, Dem.	Douglas
	Isaac B. Craig, Dem.	Coles
33	William G. Cochran, Rep.	Moultrie
	John J. Schneider, Dem.	Effingham
	Frank Spitler, Dem.	Moultrie
34	Perry Logsdon, Rep.	Schuyler
	John W. Pugh, Dem.	Mason
	William T. McCreery, Dem.	Schuyler
35	Andrew S. McDowell,[5] Rep.	Adams
	Albert W. Wells, Dem.	Adams
	Ira Tyler, Dem.	Adams
	Mitchell Dazey,[6] Dem.	Adams
36	Asa C. Mathews,[5] Rep.	Pike
	John J. Teefey,[7] Dem.	Brown
	George B. Childs,[5] Rep.	Calhoun
	George M. Black,[8] Dem.	Brown
	John McDonald, Dem.	Calhoun
37	Edwin A. Doolittle, Rep.	Greene
	Robert H. Davis, Dem.	Greene
	Sylvester Allen, Dem.	Scott

District	Member	County
38	Watson Towse, Rep.	Macoupin
	David C. Enslow, Dem.	Macoupin
	Eugene K. Blair, Dem.	Morgan
39	Andrew J. Lester, Rep.	Sangamon
	Wiley E. Jones, Dem.	Sangamon
	Albert J. Converse, Dem.	Sangamon
40	John Carstens, Rep.	Montgomery
	Pierson B. Updike, Dem.	Montgomery
	Josiah A. Hill, Dem.	Christian
41	David R. Sparks, Rep.	Madison
	Thomas T. Ramey, Rep.	Madison
	Henry H. Padon, Dem.	Madison
42	Joseph A. Combs, Rep.	Bond
	Rufus N. Ramsay, Dem.	Clinton
	Edward L. Willeford, Dem.	Bond
43	Matthew Telford, Rep.	Jefferson
	Thomas E. Merritt, Dem.	Marion
	William M. Farmer, Dem.	Fayette
44	Edson Gould, Rep.	Edwards
	Joseph B. Scudamore, Rep.	Wayne
	John S. Cochennour, Dem.	Richland
45	Walter Cole, Rep.	Clark
	William G. Williams, Dem.	Jasper
	William G. Delashmutt, Dem.	Clark
46	Charles M. Lyon,, Rep.	Hamilton
	J. Edwin Black,[9] Dem.	Lawrence
	William H. H. Mieure, Dem.	Lawrence
	Samuel H. Martin, Dem.	White
47	Samuel C. Smiley, Rep.	St. Clair
	Frederick B. Phillips, Dem.	St. Clair
	William H. Bowler, Dem.	St. Clair
48	James R. Walker, Rep.	Monroe
	William M. Schuwerk, Dem.	Randolph
	Thomas J. Rice, Dem.	Perry
49	William G. Sloan, Rep.	Saline
	Royal R. Lacey, Rep.	Hardin
	Hugh C. Gregg, Dem.	Gallatin
50	Robert B. Stinson, Rep.	Union
	Reed Green, Dem.	Alexander
	Joseph B. Gill, Dem.	Jackson
51	Thomas Sullivan, Jr., Rep.	Franklin
	James M. Fowler, Dem.	Williamson
	Isaac A. J. Parker, Dem.	Johnson

[1] Died April 24, 1889.
[2] Vice Haines.
[3] Died.
[4] Vice Miller.
[5] Resigned.
[6] Vice McDowell.
[7] Vice Matthews.
[8] Vice Childs.
[9] Vice Lyon.

Thirty-seventh General Assembly, 1891–92

Convened Jan. 7, 1891; adjourned June 12, 1891.

Senate

President	Lyman B. Ray
President pro tempore	Milton W. Matthews
Secretary	Lorenzo F. Watson

District	Member	County
1	Edward T. Noonan, Dem.	Cook
2	Charles H. Crawford, Rep.	Cook
3	George Bass, Rep.	Cook
4	Thomas C. MacMillan, Rep.	Cook
5	Joseph P. Mahoney, Dem.	Cook
6	Horace H. Thomas, Rep.	Cook
7	John Humphrey, Rep.	Cook
8	Charles E. Fuller, Rep.	Boone
9	Philip Knopf, Rep.	Cook
10	Benjamin F. Sheets, Rep.	Ogle
11	Emil Thiele, Dem.	Cook
12	Robert H. Wiles, Rep.	Stephenson
13	John F. O'Malley, Dem.	Cook
14	Henry H. Evans, Rep.	Kane
15	John W. Arnold, Dem.	Will
16	Conrad Secrest, Rep.	Iroquois
17	Daniel D. Hunt, Rep.	De Kalb
18	Charles Bogardus, Rep.	Ford
19	Virgil S. Ferguson, Rep.	Whiteside
20	Martin L. Newell, Dem.	Woodford
21	William F. Crawford, Rep.	Rock Island
22	Thomas Hamer, Rep.	Fulton
23	Andrew J. O'Conor, Dem.	La Salle
24	Orville F. Berry, Rep.	Hancock
25	Louis Zearing, Rep.	Bureau
26	Mark M. Bassett, Rep.	Peoria
27	Perry Anderson, Rep.	Warren
28	Thomas C. Kerrick, Rep.	McLean
29	Harmon Manecke, Dem.	Macon
30	Milton W. Mathews, Rep.	Champaign
31	George E. Bacon, Rep.	Edgar
32	Lewis L. Lehman, Rep.	Coles
33	Samuel W. Wright, Jr., Dem.	Moultrie
34	Arthur A. Leeper, Dem.	Cass
35	Albert W. Wells, Dem.	Adams
36	Harry Higbee, Dem.	Pike
37	Sylvester Allen, Dem.	Scott
38	Edward L. McDonald, Dem.	Morgan
39	Ben F. Caldwell, Dem.	Sangamon
40	Hiram P. Shumway, Dem.	Christian
41	John W. Coppinger, Dem.	Madison
42	Frederick E. W. Brink, Dem.	Washington
43	William M. Farmer, Rep.	Fayette
44	Dios C. Hagle, Rep.	Clay
45	Andrew J. Reavill, Dem.	Crawford
46	James R. Campbell, Dem.	Hamilton
47	Peter Seibert, Dem.	St. Clair
48	Joseph W. Rickert, Dem.	Monroe
49	Thomas H. Sheridan, Rep.	Pope
50	David W. Karraker, Dem.	Union
51	Pleasant T. Chapman, Rep.	Johnson

House of Representatives

Speaker	Clayton E. Crafts
Clerk	William H. Hinrichsen

District	Member	County
1	William Burke, Dem.	Cook
	James J. Townsend, Dem.	Cook
	W. A. Hutchings, Rep.	Cook
2	Michael McInerney, Dem.	Cook
	William J. Kenney, Dem.	Cook
	H. Dorsey Patton, Rep.	Cook
3	Solomon Van Praag, Dem.	Cook

District	Member	County
	Stephen D. May, Dem.	Cook
	Edward H. Morris, Rep.	Cook
4	James F. Quinn, Dem.	Cook
	Quida J. Chott, Rep.	Cook
	Wilson Brooks, Rep.	Cook
5	Jacob J. Kern, Dem.	Cook
	William E. Burns, Dem.	Cook
	Augustus W. Nohe, Rep.	Cook
6	James H. Farrell, Dem.	Cook
	Edward H. Griggs, Rep.	Cook
	Jacob Miller, Rep.	Cook
7	Clayton E. Crafts, Dem.	Cook
	Edward J. Whitehead, Rep.	Cook
	William Thiemann, Rep.	Cook
8	John C. Donnelly, Dem.	McHenry
	Charles A. Partridge, Rep.	Lake
	George Reed, Rep.	Boone
9	Joseph A. O'Donnell, Dem.	Cook
	Samuel C. Hayes, Rep.	Cook
	William F. Wilk, Rep.	Cook
10	James P. Wilson, Dem.	Ogle
	David Hunter, Rep.	Winnebago
	Prescott H. Talbot, Rep.	Ogle
11	Henry P. Carmody, Dem.	Cook
	Bryan Conway, Dem.	Cook
	Julius A. Lense, Rep.	Cook
12	George W. Curtiss, Dem.	JoDaviess
	Daniel S. Berry, Rep.	Carroll
	Henry N. Frentress, Rep.	JoDaviess
13	William H. Lyman, Dem.	Cook
	John A. Kwasigroch, Dem.	Cook
	Samuel E. Erickson, Rep.	Cook
14	Luther M. Dearborn, Dem.	Kane
	Edgar C. Hawley, Rep.	Kane
	Charles P. Bryan, Rep.	Du Page
15	David Forsythe, Dem.	Will
	Fred Wilke, Rep.	Will
	John Corlett, Rep.	Will
16	J. W. Allison, Dem.	Kankakee
	Daniel H. Paddock, Rep.	Kankakee
	John L. Hamilton, Rep.	Iroquois
17	William G. Dawkins, Dem.	Grundy
	William Scaife, Rep.	Grundy
	Charles T. Cherry, Rep.	Kendall
18	James A. Smith, Dem.	Livingston
	Nelson J. Myer, Rep.	Livingston
	Rufus C. Straight, Rep.	Livingston
19	Sherwood Dixon, Dem.	Lee
	John W. White, Rep.	Whiteside
	Luther W. Mitchell, Rep.	Lee
20	John W. White, Dem.	Tazewell
	James O. Garrett, Dem.	Marshall
	John H. Anthony, Rep.	Tazewell
21	George W. Vinton, Dem.	Rock Island
	Reuben F. Beals, Rep.	Henry
	William C. Collins,[1] Rep.	Rock Island
	William Payne,[2] Rep.	Rock Island
22	James W. Hunter, Dem.	Knox
	George W. Prince, Rep.	Knox
	Oscar J. Boyer, Rep.	Fulton
23	Louis Rohrer, Dem.	La Salle
	Michael O'Loughlin, Dem.	La Salle
	Urbin S. Ellsworth, Rep.	La Salle

District	Member	County
24	Amos Edmunds, Dem.	Hancock
	William H. Myers, Dem.	Henderson
	James O. Anderson, Rep.	Henderson
25	Michael Barton, Dem.	Bureau
	Samuel White, Rep.	Stark
	Archibald W. Hopkins, Rep.	Putnam
26	John Johnston, Dem.	Peoria
	John L. Geher, Dem.	Peoria
	Thomas J. Edwards, Rep.	Peoria
27	Eli Dixson, Dem.	Warren
	Charles V. Chandler, Rep.	McDonough
	Dominick C. Graham, Rep.	Warren
28	John Eddy, Dem.	McLean
	Henry L. Terpening, Rep.	McLean
	Edmund O'Connell, Rep.	McLean
29	Lawrence B. Stringer, Dem.	Logan
	Washington S. Smith, Dem.	Macon
	David P. Keller, Rep.	Macon
30	Thomas B. Carson, Dem.	Champaign
	Julius A. Brown, Rep.	Piatt
	Jacob Zeigler, Rep.	De Witt
31	John F. Rowand, Dem.	Vermilion
	Charles A. Allen, Rep.	Vermilion
	Thomas L. Spellman, Rep.	Vermilion
32	Isaac B. Craig, Dem.	Coles
	Henry J. Jansen, Dem.	Cumberland
	George A. Neal, Rep.	Cumberland
33	James Laughlin, Dem.	Shelby
	Philip Wiwi, Dem.	Effingham
	Walter C. Headen, Rep.	Shelby
34	Fred Wilkinson, Dem.	Menard
	Bernard P. Preston, Dem.	Schuyler
	Homer J. Tice, Rep.	Menard
35	Ira Tyler, Dem.	Adams
	Jonathan Parkhurst, Dem.	Adams
	George C. McCrone, Rep.	Adams
36	Ernst Meyer, Dem.	Calhoun
	Joseph M. Hambaugh, Dem.	Brown
	H. D. L. Grisby, Rep.	Pike
37	Thomas F. Ferns, Dem.	Jersey
	Frederick M. Fishback, Dem.	Greene
	Henry Miner, Rep.	Scott
38	David C. Enslow, Dem.	Macoupin
	John W. Springer, Dem.	Morgan
	Edward P. Kirby, Rep.	Morgan
39	Edward L. Merritt, Dem.	Sangamon
	Frank H. Jones, Dem.	Sangamon
	John S. Lyman, Rep.	Sangamon
40	Elijah H. Donaldson, Dem.	Montgomery
	Joseph Adams, Dem.	Christian
	William W. Weedon, Rep.	Christian
41	Henry C. Picker, Dem.	Madison
	William H. Faires, Dem.	Madison
	William McKittrick, Rep.	Madison
42	Rufus N. Ramsay, Dem.	Clinton
	William H. Dawdy, Dem.	Bond
	William D. Jacobs, Rep.	Washington
43	James H. Watson, Dem.	Jefferson
	Eugene L. Stoker, Rep.	Marion
	James Cockrell, Farm. Alli.	Marion
44	Elijah S. Shirley, Dem.	Clay
	Gideon D. Slanker, Rep.	Richland

District	Member	County
	Hosea H. Moore, Farm. Alli.	Wayne
45	Lawrence Kelly, Dem.	Clark
	Ethelbert Callahan, Rep.	Crawford
	Herman E. Taubeneck, Farm. Alli.	Clark
46	John T. Norsworthy, Dem.	White
	Albert B. Denham, Dem.	Wabash
	Thomas G. Parker, Rep.	White
47	Daniel G. Ramsey, Dem.	St. Clair
	Nicholas Boul, Dem.	St. Clair
	Louis Perrottet, Rep.	St. Clair
48	John T. Pollock, Dem.	Randolph
	John A. Bowlin, Dem.	Perry
	Albert H. Evans, Rep.	Perry
49	George B. Parsons, Dem.	Gallatin
	Fowler A. Armstrong, Rep.	Massac
	Thomas R. Reid, Rep.	Gallatin
50	Reed Green, Dem.	Alexander
	Joseph B. Gill, Dem.	Jackson
	Walter Warder, Rep.	Alexander
51	M. N. Webb, Dem.	Franklin
	W. J. N. Moyers, Rep.	Franklin
	John H. Duncan, Rep.	Williamson

¹ Resigned.
² Vice Collins.

Thirty-eighth General Assembly, 1893–94

Convened Jan. 4, 1893; adjourned June 16, 1893.

Senate

President   Joseph B. Gill

President pro tempore

       John W. Coppinger

Secretary   Finis E. Downing

District	Member	County
1	Edward T. Noonan, Dem.	Cook
2	C. Porter Johnson, Dem.	Cook
3	George Bass, Rep.	Cook
4	Moses Salomon, Dem.	Cook
5	Joseph P. Mahoney, Dem.	Cook
6	Henry C. Bartling, Dem.	Cook
7	John Humphrey, Rep.	Cook
8	Reuben W. Coon, Rep.	Lake
9	Philip Knopf, Rep.	Cook
10	David Hunter, Rep.	Winnebago
11	Emil Thiele, Dem.	Cook
12	Homer F. Aspinwall, Rep.	Stephenson
13	John F. O'Malley, Dem.	Cook
14	Henry H. Evans, Rep.	Kane
15	John W. Arnold, Dem.	Will
16	George R. Letourneau, Rep.	Kankakee
17	Daniel D. Hunt, Rep.	De Kalb
18	Charles Bogardus, Rep.	Ford
19	Virgil S. Ferguson, Rep.	Whiteside
20	Charles N. Barnes, Dem.	Marshall
21	William F. Crawford, Rep.	Rock Island
22	Thomas Hamer, Rep.	Fulton
23	Andrew J. O'Conor, Dem.	La Salle
24	Orville F. Berry, Rep.	Hancock
25	Louis Zearing, Rep.	Bureau

District	Member	County
26	John M. Niehaus, Dem.	Peoria
27	Perry Anderson, Rep.	Warren
28	Vinton E. Howell, Rep.	McLean
29	Harmon Manecke, Dem.	Macon
30	Henry M. Dunlap, Rep.	Champaign
31	George E. Bacon, Rep.	Edgar
32	Isaac B. Craig, Dem.	Coles
33	Samuel W. Wright, Jr., Dem.	Moultrie
34	Arthur A. Leeper, Dem.	Cass
35	Albert W. Wells, Dem.	Adams
36	Harry Higbee, Dem.	Pike
37	Sylvester Allen, Dem.	Scott
38	Hampton W. Wall, Dem.	Macoupin
39	Ben F. Caldwell, Dem.	Sangamon
40	George W. Paisley, Dem.	Montgomery
41	John W. Coppinger, Dem.	Madison
42	Thomas E. Ford, Dem.	Clinton
43	William M. Farmer, Dem.	Fayette
44	William A. Mussett, Rep.	Edwards
45	Andrew J. Reavill, Dem.	Crawford
46	James R. Campbell, Dem.	Hamilton
47	Peter Seibert, Dem.	St. Clair
48	Albert L. Brands, Dem.	Randolph
49	Thomas H. Sheridan, Rep.	Pope
50	Reed Green, Dem.	Alexander
51	Pleasant T. Chapman, Rep.	Johnson

House of Representatives

Speaker   Clayton E. Crafts
Clerk   Robert W. Ross

District	Member	County
1	James O'Connor, Dem.	Cook
	William Burke, Dem.	Cook
	William W. Wheelock, Rep.	Cook
2	Michael McInerney, Dem.	Cook
	Charles S. Deneen, Rep.	Cook
	Robert McMurdy, Rep.	Cook
3	Stephen D. May, Dem.	Cook
	James E. Bish, Rep.	Cook
	William H. King, Rep.	Cook
4	James E. McGinley, Dem.	Cook
	James F. Gleason, Dem.	Cook
	John Meyer, Rep.	Cook
5	Edward J. Novak, Dem.	Cook
	Edward J. Hayes, Dem.	Cook
	Augustus W. Nohe, Rep.	Cook
6	James H. Farrell, Dem.	Cook
	Edward H. Griggs, Rep.	Cook
	Godfrey Laughenry, Rep.	Cook
7	Clayton E. Crafts, Dem.	Cook
	Robert H. Muir, Rep.	Cook
	William Thiemann, Rep.	Cook
8	John C. Donnelly, Dem.	McHenry
	Robert J. Beck, Rep.	McHenry
	George Reed, Rep.	Boone
9	Benjamin M. Mitchell, Dem.	Cook
	Joseph A. O'Donnell, Dem.	Cook
	Daniel A. Campbell, Rep.	Cook
10	James P. Wilson, Dem.	Ogle
	Prescott H. Talbot, Rep.	Ogle
	Lars M. Noling, Rep.	Winnebago
11	Bryan Conway, Dem.	Cook
	Henry P. Carmody, Dem.	Cook
	William E. Kent, Rep.	Cook
12	John N. Brandt, Dem.	Carroll
	John C. McKenzie, Rep.	JoDaviess
	Daniel S. Berry, Rep.	Carroll
13	William H. Lyman, Dem.	Cook
	John A. Kwasigroch, Dem.	Cook
	Samuel E. Erickson, Rep.	Cook
14	Luther M. Dearborn, Dem.	Kane
	Edgar C. Hawley, Rep.	Kane
	Charles P. Bryan, Rep.	Du Page
15	Conrad Wilkening, Dem.	Will
	David Forsythe, Dem.	Will
	Fred Wilke, Rep.	Will
16	Freeman P. Morris, Dem.	Iroquois
	Daniel H. Paddock, Rep.	Kankakee
	Alba M. Jones, Rep.	Iroquois
17	Edgar L. Henning, Dem.	Kendall
	Charles F. Meyer, Rep.	De Kalb
	Charles T. Cherry, Rep.	Kendall
18	James A. Smith, Dem.	Livingston
	Rufus C. Straight, Rep.	Livingston
	Bailey A. Gower, Rep.	Livingston
19	Caleb C. Johnson, Dem.	Whiteside
	Washington I. Guffin, Rep.	Lee
	John Dyer, Rep.	Whiteside
20	William A. Moore, Dem.	Tazewell
	Samuel H. McClure, Dem.	Woodford
	Oscar Painter, Rep.	Woodford
21	Joseph H. Mulligan, Dem.	Henry
	William Payne, Rep.	Rock Island
	Reuben F. Beals, Rep.	Henry
22	D. E. Carlin, Dem.	Fulton
	Jay L. Hastings, Rep.	Knox
	Frank Murdoch, Rep.	Knox
23	Michael O'Loughlin, Dem.	La Salle
	Louis Rohrer, Dem.	La Salle
	Urbin S. Ellsworth, Rep.	La Salle
24	William H. Myers, Dem.	Henderson
	Noah H. Guthrie, Rep.	Mercer
	James O. Anderson, Rep.	Henderson
25	Michael Barton, Dem.	Bureau
	Archibald W. Hopkins, Rep.	Putnam
	George Murray, Rep.	Stark
26	Peter Cahill, Dem.	Peoria
	John Holmes, Dem.	Peoria
	William O. Clark, Rep.	Peoria
27	Thomas J. Sparks, Dem.	McDonough
	Louis Kaiser, Rep.	McDonough
	D. Caswell Hanna, Rep.	Warren
28	Bernard J. Claggett, Dem.	McLean
	Edmund O'Connell, Rep.	McLean
	Edward Stubblefield, Rep.	McLean
29	Lawrence B. Stringer, Dem.	Logan
	Washington S. Smith, Dem.	Macon
	Thomas N. Leavitt, Rep.	Macon
30	Thomas B. Carson, Dem.	Champaign
	John Cusey, Rep.	De Witt
	James A. Hawks, Rep.	Piatt
31	Robert L. McKinlay, Dem.	Edgar
	Thomas L. Spellman, Rep.	Vermilion
	James P. Fletcher, Rep.	Vermilion
32	James Park McGee, Dem.	Douglas
	Charles Hanker, Rep.	Cumberland

District	Member	County
	William H. Wallace, Rep.	Coles
33	Philip Wiwi, Dem.	Effingham
	Leverett S. Baldwin, Dem.	Shelby
	Albert Campbell, Rep.	Effingham
34	Bernard P. Preston, Dem.	Schuyler
	Robert S. Carter, Dem.	Menard
	Homer J. Tice, Rep.	Menard
35	Mitchell Dazey, Dem.	Adams
	Joel W. Bonney, Dem.	Adams
	George C. McCrone, Rep.	Adams
36	Ernst Meyer,[1] Dem.	Calhoun
	William Mortland,[2] Dem.	Calhoun
	Frederick W. Rottger, Dem.	Brown
	Augustow Dow, Rep.	Pike
37	Thomas F. Ferns, Dem.	Jersey
	Norman L. Jones, Dem.	Greene
	Orville A. Snedeker, Rep.	Jersey
38	William L. Mounts, Dem.	Macoupin
	James T. McMillan, Dem.	Morgan
	Sargeant McKnight, Rep.	Macoupin
39	Edward L. Merritt, Dem.	Sangamon
	Langley Whitley, Dem.	Sangamon
	H. Clay Wilson, Rep.	Sangamon
40	Walter S. Parrott, Dem.	Montgomery
	Alexander B. Herdman, Dem.	Christian
	Charles A. Ramsey, Rep.	Montgomery
41	Michael J. Gill, Dem.	Madison
	Conrad A. Ambrosius, Dem.	Madison
	Thomas T. Ramey, Rep.	Madison
42	James J. Anderson, Dem.	Washington
	Charles W. Seawell, Dem.	Bond
	George S. Caughlan, Rep.	Clinton
43	James H. Watson, Dem.	Jefferson
	Daniel W. Holstlaw, Dem.	Marion
	Richard T. Higgins, Rep.	Fayette
44	Captain T. Taggart, Dem.	Wayne
	Thomas H. Creighton, Rep.	Wayne
	John D. Edmiston, Rep.	Richland
45	Lawrence Kelly, Dem.	Clark
	James D. Warren, Dem.	Jasper
	Ethelbert Callahan, Rep.	Crawford
46	J. Edwin Black, Dem.	Lawrence
	Jacob Zimmerman, Dem.	Wabash
	John S. Martin, Rep.	Lawrence
47	William H. Snyder, Jr., Dem.	St. Clair
	Joseph E. Miller, Dem.	St. Clair
	Frederick S. Weckler, Rep.	St. Clair
48	Joseph W. Drury, Dem.	Monroe
	Joseph L. Murphy, Dem.	Perry
	John J. Douglas, Rep.	Randolph
49	H. Robert Fowler, Dem.	Hardin
	Fowler A. Armstrong, Rep.	Massac
	Albert W. Lewis, Rep.	Saline
50	Philip H. Kroh, Dem.	Union
	William C. Dean, Dem.	Jackson
	Walter Warder, Rep.	Alexander
51	Samuel H. Goodall, Dem.	Williamson
	John H. Duncan, Rep.	Williamson
	Richard M. Johnson, Rep.	Pulaski

[1] Died May 11, 1893.
[2] Vice Meyer, June 19, 1893.

Redistricting of 1893 authorized by act of June 15, 1893; fifty-one districts, each electing one senator and three representatives

District	Counties
1 to 7	Cook
8	Boone, Lake, McHenry
9	Cook
10	Ogle, Winnebago
11	Cook
12	Carroll, JoDaviess, Stephenson
13	Cook
14	Du Page, Kane
15	Cook
16	Iroquois, Kankakee
17	Cook
18	Ford, Vermilion
19	Cook
20	Livingston, Marshall, Woodford
21	Cook
22	McLean
23	Cook
24	Peoria
25	Will
26	Fulton, Tazewell
27	La Salle
28	Hancock, McDonough, Schuyler
29	De Kalb, Grundy, Kendall, Lee
30	Champaign, De Witt, Piatt
31	Bureau, Putnam, Stark, Whiteside
32	Cass, Logan, Mason, Menard
33	Henry, Rock Island
34	Morgan, Pike, Scott
35	Henderson, Knox, Mercer, Warren
36	Greene, Macoupin
37	Adams, Brown
38	Bond, Fayette, Montgomery
39	Sangamon
40	Coles, Douglas, Shelby
41	Christian, Macon, Moultrie
42	Clay, Clinton, Marion, Washington
43	Clark, Cumberland, Edgar, Effingham
44	Edwards, Gallatin, Hardin, Wabash, White
45	Crawford, Jasper, Lawrence, Richland
46	Franklin, Hamilton, Jefferson, Wayne
47	Calhoun, Jersey, Madison
48	Jackson, Monroe, Perry, Randolph
49	St. Clair
50	Alexander, Union, Williamson
51	Johnson, Massac, Pope, Pulaski, Saline

Thirty-ninth General Assembly, 1895–96

Convened Jan. 9, 1895; adjourned June 11, 1895. Second session convened June 25, 1895; adjourned Aug. 2, 1895.

Senate

President	Joseph B. Gill
President pro tempore	Charles Bogardus
Secretary	James H. Paddock

District	Member	County
1	Patrick V. Fitzpatrick, Rep.	Cook
2	Moses Salomon, Dem.	Cook
3	Sidney McCloud, Rep.	Cook
4	C. Porter Johnson, Dem.	Cook
5	Charles H. Crawford, Rep.	Cook
6	Henry C. Bartling, Dem.	Cook
7	John Humphrey, Rep.	Cook
8	Reuben W. Coon, Rep.	Lake
9	William J. O'Brien, Dem.	Cook
10	David Hunter, Rep.	Winnebago
11	Frederick Lundin, Rep.	Cook
12	Homer F. Aspinwall, Rep.	Stephenson
13	Joseph P. Mahoney, Dem.	Cook
14	Henry H. Evans, Rep.	Kane
15	John J. Morrison, Rep.	Cook
16	George R. Letourneau, Rep.	Kankakee
17	Edward J. Dwyer, Rep.	Cook
18	Charles Bogardus, Rep.	Ford
19	Daniel A. Campbell, Rep.	Cook
20	Charles N. Barnes, Dem.	Marshall
21	Charles M. Netterstrom, Rep.	Cook
22	Vinton E. Howell, Rep.	McLean
23	George D. Anthony, Rep.	Cook
24	John M. Niehaus, Dem.	Peoria
25	George H. Munroe, Rep.	Will
26	Thomas Hamer, Rep.	Fulton
27	Lewis M. Sawyer, Rep.	La Salle
28	Orville F. Berry, Rep.	Hancock
29	Daniel D. Hunt, Rep.	De Kalb
30	Henry M. Dunlap, Rep.	Champaign
31	James W. Templeton, Rep.	Bureau
32	Arthur A. Leeper, Dem.	Cass
33	Hendrick V. Fisher, Rep.	Henry
34	Harry Higbee, Dem.	Pike
35	Fred E. Harding, Rep.	Warren
36	Hampton W. Wall, Dem.	Macoupin
37	Albert W. Wells, Dem.	Adams
38	George W. Paisley, Dem.	Montgomery
39	David T. Littler, Rep.	Sangamon
40	Isaac B. Craig, Dem.	Coles
41	M. F. Kanan, Rep.	Macon
42	Thomas E. Ford, Dem.	Clinton
43	Robert L. McKinlay, Dem.	Edgar
44	William A. Mussett, Rep.	Edwards
45	Hiram H. Kingsbury, Rep.	Richland
46	James R. Campbell, Dem.	Hamilton
47	Charles A. Herb, Rep.	Madison
48	Albert L. Brands, Dem.	Randolph
49	James Amos Willoughby, Rep.	St. Clair
50	Reed Green, Dem.	Alexander
51	Pleasant T. Chapman, Rep.	Johnson

House of Representatives

Speaker	John Meyer'
Speaker	William G. Cochran
Clerk	John A. Reeve

District	Member	County
1	John C. Sterchie, Dem.	Cook
	Stephen D. May, Dem.	Cook
	William E. Kent, Rep.	Cook
2	Rudolph Mulac, Rep.	Cook
	Oscar L. Dudley, Rep.	Cook
	Sherman P. Cody, Dem.	Cook
3	Alexander J. Jones, Dem.	Cook
	George W. Miller, Rep.	Cook

District	Member	County
	Solomon L. Lowenthal, Rep.	Cook
4	William C. Eakins, Rep.	Cook
	Timothy Hogan, Rep.	Cook
	Daniel F. Curley, Dem.	Cook
5	Milroy H. Gibson, Rep.	Cook
	John C. Buckner, Rep.	Cook
	Angelo S. Cella, Dem.	Cook
6	George M. Boyd, Rep.	Cook
	Bernard J. Mahony, Dem.	Cook
	Isadore Plotke, Rep.	Cook
7	Robert H. Muir, Rep.	Cook
	Clayton E. Crafts, Dem.	Cook
	William Thiemann, Rep.	Cook
8	George Reed, Rep.	Boone
	Robert J. Beck, Rep.	McHenry
	Patrick H. DeLany, Dem.	Lake
9	Christian R. Walleck, Dem.	Cook
	Philip Steiner, Dem.	Cook
	David E. Shanahan, Rep.	Cook
10	Lars M. Noling, Rep.	Winnebago
	C. Harry Woolsey, Dem.	Winnebago
	Victor H. Bovey, Rep.	Ogle
11	Joseph S. Schwab, Dem.	Cook
	Ernest Schubert, Rep.	Cook
	M. G. Mauritzon, Rep.	Cook
12	Daniel S. Berry, Rep.	Carroll
	Michael Stoskopf, Dem.	Stephenson
	John C. McKenzie, Rep.	JoDaviess
13	James P. Cavanagh, Rep.	Cook
	Simon Shaffer, Dem.	Cook
	Edward J. Novak, Rep.	Cook
14	Charles P. Bryan, Rep.	Du Page
	Edgar C. Hawley, Rep.	Kane
	Luther M. Dearborn, Dem.	Kane
15	John Meyer, Rep.	Cook
	John T. Fleming. Dem.	Cook
	William F. McCarthy, Rep.	Cook
16	Edward C. Curtis, Rep.	Kankakee
	Freeman P. Morris, Dem.	Iroquois
	Alba M. Jones, Rep.	Iroquois
17	William Burke, Dem.	Cook
	Frank Brignadello, Dem.	Cook
	Albert Glade, Rep.	Cook
18	James P. Fletcher, Rep.	Vermilion
	Martin B. Bailey, Rep.	Vermilion
	William M. Bines, Dem.	Vermilion
19	James Fitzsimmons, Dem.	Cook
	Sewell B. Weston, Rep.	Cook
	Charles G. Johnson, Rep.	Cook
20	Isaac B. Hammers, Rep.	Woodford
	John L. McGuire, Dem.	Woodford
	Bailey A. Gower, Rep.	Livingston
21	James H. Farrell, Dem.	Cook
	David Revell, Rep.	Cook
	Fred A. Busse, Rep.	Cook
22	Edward Stubblefield, Rep.	McLean
	James F. O'Donnell, Dem.	McLean
	John L. White, Rep.	McLean
23	William H. Lyman, Dem.	Cook
	Albert J. Olson, Rep.	Cook
	Lawrence Kilcourse, Rep.	Cook
24	Aquilla J. Daugherty, Rep.	Peoria
	Alva Merrill, Rep.	Peoria

District	Member	County
	Peter Cahill, Dem.	Peoria
25	John M. Thompson, Dem.	Will
	Addison B. Hallock, Rep.	Will
	William H. Stein, Rep.	Will
26	Lute C. Breeden, Dem.	Fulton
	Jonathan Merriam, Rep.	Tazewell
	John W. Johnson, Rep.	Fulton
27	John Wylie, Rep.	La Salle
	Urbin S. Ellsworth, Rep.	La Salle
	John McLauchlan, Dem.	La Salle
28	Ulysses A. Wilson, Rep.	Schuyler
	Louis Kaiser, Rep.	McDonough
	James A. Teel, Dem.	Schuyler
29	Washington I. Guffin, Rep.	Lee
	John K. Ely, Rep.	Grundy
	James Branen, Dem.	De Kalb
30	William H. Taylor, Rep.	De Witt
	William C. Hubbart, Rep.	Piatt
	James Ownby, Dem.	Piatt
31	John W. White, Rep.	Whiteside
	William M. Pilgrim, Dem.	Stark
	George Murray, Rep.	Stark
32	William S. Dunham, Rep.	Logan
	George Wendell, Dem.	Logan
	Emeziah J. Mell, Dem.	Mason
33	Joseph H. Mulligan, Dem.	Henry
	William C. Stickney, Rep.	Henry
	William Payne, Rep.	Rock Island
34	John D. Huffman, Dem.	Scott
	Wilfred I. Klein, Rep.	Pike
	Edward McConnell, Dem.	Morgan
35	Frank Murdoch, Rep.	Knox
	Noah H. Guthrie, Rep.	Mercer
	LaVergne B. DeForest, Dem.	Mercer
36	William L. Mounts, Dem.	Macoupin
	James W. Kitzmiller, Rep.	Macoupin
	Norman L. Jones, Dem.	Greene
37	Elmer A. Perry, Dem.	Brown
	George W. Dean, Dem.	Adams
	Charles F. Kincheloe, Rep.	Adams
38	John R. Challacombe, Rep.	Montgomery
	Emmet P. Poindexter, Dem.	Bond
	James G. Miller, Rep.	Fayette
39	Charles E. Selby, Rep.	Sangamon
	Edward L. Merritt, Dem.	Sangamon
	William J. Butler, Rep.	Sangamon
40	Alexander H. McTaggart, Rep.	Shelby
	Joseph P. Barricklow, Dem.	Douglas
	William H. Wallace, Rep.	Coles
41	Murray McDonald, Dem.	Moultrie
	James E. Sharrock, Rep.	Christian
	William G. Cochran, Rep.	Moultrie
42	Thomas B. Needles, Rep.	Washington
	Morrison J. O'Harnett, Rep.	Clinton
	John A. Barnes, Dem.	Clay
43	Joseph P. Condo, Rep.	Effingham
	Polk B. Briscoe, Dem.	Clark
	George M. LeCrone, Dem.	Effingham
44	Samuel M. Smyth, Rep.	Gallatin
	Melville W. Spencer, Dem.	White
	Ross Graham, Rep.	White
45	Ethelbert Callahan, Rep.	Crawford
	J. Edwin Black, Dem.	Lawrence

District	Member	County
	Thomas Tippitt, Dem.	Richland
46	William H. Green, Dem.	Jefferson
	Samuel H. Watson, Rep.	Jefferson
	Charles A. Aiken, Rep.	Franklin
47	Thomas F. Ferns, Dem.	Jersey
	Orville A. Snedeker, Rep.	Jersey
	Thomas P. McFee, Rep.	Madison
48	Ezekiel J. Ingersoll, Rep.	Jackson
	John J. Douglas, Rep.	Randolph
	Harmon P. Burroughs, Dem.	Jackson
49	William H. Snyder, Dem.	St. Clair
	Michael Kelly, Rep.	St. Clair
	Louis Perrottet, Rep.	St. Clair
50	Martin M. McDonald, Rep.	Williamson
	Andrew J. Pickrell, Rep.	Union
	William T. Davis, Dem.	Williamson
51	Fowler A. Armstrong, Rep.	Massac
	Richard M. Johnson, Rep.	Pulaski
	C. A. F. Rondeau, Dem.	Pope

' Died during session.

Fortieth General Assembly, 1897–98

Convened Jan. 6, 1897; adjourned June 4, 1897. Special session convened Dec. 7, 1897; adjourned Feb. 24, 1898.

Senate

President	William A. Northcott
President pro tempore	
	Hendrick V. Fisher
Secretary	James H. Paddock

District	Member	County
1	Patrick V. Fitzpatrick, Rep.	Cook
2	Selon H. Chase, Rep.	Cook
3	Sidney McCloud, Rep.	Cook
4	Daniel F. Curley, Dem.	Cook
5	Charles H. Crawford, Rep.	Cook
6	William Sullivan, Rep.	Cook
7	John Humphrey, Rep.	Cook
8	Flavel K. Granger, Rep.	McHenry
9	William J. O'Brien, Dem.	Cook
10	Delos W. Baxter, Rep.	Ogle
11	Frederick Lundin, Rep.	Cook
12	Homer F. Aspinwall, Rep.	Stephenson
13	Joseph P. Mahoney, Dem.	Cook
14	Henry H. Evans, Rep.	Kane
15	John J. Morrison, Dem.	Cook
16	Isaac M. Hamilton, Rep.	Iroquois
17	Edward J. Dwyer, Rep.	Cook
18	Charles Bogardus, Rep.	Ford
19	Daniel A. Campbell, Rep.	Cook
20	Robert B. Fort, Rep.	Marshall
21	Charles M. Netterstrom, Rep.	Cook
22	George W. Stubblefield, Rep.	McLean
23	George D. Anthony, Rep.	Cook
24	James D. Putnam, Rep.	Peoria
25	George H. Munroe, Rep.	Will
26	W. Scott Edwards, Rep.	Fulton
27	Lewis M. Sawyer, Rep.	La Salle

District	Member	County
28	William E. Manifold,[1] Dem.	Hancock
	Orville F. Berry,[2] Rep.	Hancock
29	Daniel D. Hunt, Rep.	De Kalb
30	Henry M. Dunlap, Rep.	Champaign
31	James W. Templeton, Rep.	Bureau
32	Arthur A. Leeper, Dem.	Cass
33	Hendrick V. Fisher, Rep.	Henry
34	Edward McConnell, Dem.	Morgan
35	Fred E. Harding, Rep.	Warren
36	William L. Mounts, Dem.	Macoupin
37	Albert W. Wells,[3] Dem.	Adams
	John McAdams,[4] Dem.	Adams
38	Nathaniel S. Dressor, Peo.	Bond
39	David T. Littler, Rep.	Sangamon
40	Stanton C. Pemberton, Rep.	Coles
41	M. F. Kanan, Rep.	Macon
42	Charles E. Hull, Dem.	Marion
43	Robert L. McKinlay, Dem.	Edgar
44	John Landrigan, Dem.	Edwards
45	Hiram H. Kingsbury, Rep.	Richland
46	Joseph T. Payne, Rep.	Jefferson
47	David R. Sparks,[5] Rep.	Madison
48	Albert C. Bollinger, Rep.	Monroe
49	James Amos Willoughby, Rep.	St. Clair
50	Walter Warder, Rep.	Alexander
51	Pleasant T. Chapman, Rep.	Johnson

[1] Unseated March 18, 1897.
[2] Vice Manifold, seated March 18, 1897.
[3] Died March 5, 1897.
[4] Vice Wells, elected June 7, 1897.
[5] Vice Charles A. Herb, died 1896.

House of Representatives

Speaker	Edward C. Curtis
Clerk	John A. Reeve

District	Member	County
1	William G. Laub, Rep.	Cook
	Charles A. Wathier, Rep.	Cook
	John C. Sterchie, Dem.	Cook
2	Peter A. Rowe, Rep.	Cook
	Augustus W. Nohe, Rep.	Cook
	Peter J. McGinnis, Dem.	Cook
3	George W. Miller, Rep.	Cook
	Charles W. Nothnagel, Rep.	Cook
	John P. McGoorty, Dem.	Cook
4	Charles F. Wiedmaier, Rep.	Cook
	Michael J. Butler, Dem.	Cook
	John Staudacher, Dem.	Cook
5	John C. Buckner, Rep.	Cook
	William O. LaMonte, Rep.	Cook
	Joseph Powell, Ind. Rep.	Cook
6	George M. Boyd, Rep.	Cook
	Charles M. Eldredge, Rep.	Cook
	Henry C. Bartling, Dem.	Cook
7	William Thiemann, Rep.	Cook
	Clark J. Tisdel, Rep.	Cook
	Ross C. Hall, Dem.	Cook
8	DuFay A. Fuller, Rep.	Boone
	George R. Lyon, Rep.	Lake
	Jacob S. Edelstein, Dem.	Boone
9	David E. Shanahan, Rep.	Cook
	John O'Shea, Dem.	Cook
	Christian R. Walleck, Dem.	Cook

District	Member	County
10	Lars M. Noling, Rep.	Winnebago
	Victor H. Bovey, Rep.	Ogle
	Henry Andrus, Rep.	Winnebago
11	Ernest Schubert, Rep.	Cook
	Walter Sayler, Rep.	Cook
	Joseph S. Schwab, Dem.	Cook
12	James R. Berryman, Rep.	JoDaviess
	David C. Busell, Rep.	Carroll
	Michael Stoskopf, Dem.	Stephenson
13	James P. Cavanagh, Rep.	Cook
	William Carmody, Dem.	Cook
	Edward J. Novak, Dem.	Cook
14	Charles P. Bryan, Rep.	Du Page
	William F. Hunter, Rep.	Kane
	Samuel Alschuler, Dem.	Kane
15	Patrick J. Meaney, Rep.	Cook
	Henry D. Nicholls, Rep.	Cook
	Peter F. Galligan, Dem.	Cook
16	Edward C. Curtis, Rep.	Kankakee
	Almet Powell, Rep.	Iroquois
	Freeman P. Morris, Dem.	Iroquois
17	Albert Glade, Rep.	Cook
	Daniel V. McDonough, Dem.	Cook
	Frank Brignadello, Dem.	Cook
18	Charles A. Allen, Rep.	Vermilion
	Martin B. Bailey, Rep.	Vermilion
	G. W. Salmans, Dem.	Vermilion
19	Robert C. Busse, Rep.	Cook
	John F. Quanstrom, Rep.	Cook
	Benjamin M. Mitchell, Dem.	Cook
20	Oscar F. Avery, Rep.	Livingston
	Isaac B. Hammers, Rep.	Woodford
	John L. McGuire, Dem.	Woodford
21	Fred A. Busse, Rep.	Cook
	David Revell, Rep.	Cook
	James H. Farrell, Dem.	Cook
22	Duncan M. Funk, Rep.	McLean
	Arthur J. Scrogin, Rep.	McLean
	James F. O'Donnell, Dem.	McLean
23	Lawrence Kilcourse, Rep.	Cook
	Albert J. Olson, Rep.	Cook
	Denis E. Sullivan, Dem.	Cook
24	Aquilla J. Daugherty, Rep.	Peoria
	Alva Merrill, Rep.	Peoria
	Almon H. Bristol, Dem.	Peoria
25	John Kolstedt, Rep.	Will
	William H. Stein, Rep.	Will
	Joseph Kain, Dem.	Will
26	Jonathan Merriam, Rep.	Tazewell
	John W. Johnson, Rep.	Fulton
	Simon B. Beer, Dem.	Fulton
27	John Wylie, Rep.	La Salle
	Irving H. Trowbridge, Rep.	La Salle
	John McLauchlan, Dem.	La Salle
28	Lawrence Y. Sherman, Rep.	McDonough
	Ulysses A. Wilson, Rep.	Schuyler
	William A. Compton, Dem.	McDonough
29	Washington I. Guffin, Rep.	Lee
	John K. Ely, Rep.	Grundy
	James Branen, Dem.	De Kalb
30	Samuel B. Garver, Rep.	De Witt
	Seymour Marquiss, Rep.	Piatt
	Henry C. Suttle, Dem.	De Witt

Convened Jan. 4, 1899; adjourned April 14, 1899.

District	Member	County
31	George Murray, Rep.	Stark
	Jerry W. Dinneen, Rep.	Whiteside
	Caleb C. Johnson, Dem.	Whiteside
32	David C. White, Rep.	Mason
	Joseph A. Horn, Dem.	Logan
	James M. Large, Dem.	Menard
33	William Payne, Rep.	Rock Island
	Edwin W. Houghton, Rep.	Henry
	William McEwing, Dem.	Rock Island
34	John B. Joy, Rep.	Morgan
	John D. Huffman, Dem.	Scott
	Frank L. Hall, Dem.	Pike
35	Frank Murdoch, Rep.	Knox
	James O. Anderson, Rep.	Henderson
	James R. Barnett, Dem.	Warren
36	George B. Metcalf, Rep.	Greene
	William T. Conlee, Dem.	Macoupin
	William V. Rhodes, Dem.	Greene
37	Charles F. Kincheloe, Rep.	Adams
	Elmer A. Perry, Dem.	Brown
	George W. Montgomery, Dem.	Adams
38	Thomas P. Morey, Rep.	Bond
	Obed E. Lovett, Dem.	Fayette
	Joseph P. Price, Dem.	Montgomery
39	Charles E. Selby, Rep.	Sangamon
	Abner G. Murray, Dem.	Sangamon
	George L. Harnsberger, Dem.	Sangamon
40	Caleb R. Torrence, Rep.	Shelby
	Isaac B. Craig, Dem.	Coles
	Joseph P. Barricklow, Dem.	Douglas
41	James E. Sharrock, Rep.	Christian
	William G. Cochran, Rep.	Moultrie
	Oliver T. Achison, Dem.	Moultrie
42	Thomas B. Needles, Rep.	Washington
	John A. Barnes, Dem.	Clay
	Hugh V. Murray, Dem.	Clinton
43	Fenton W. Booth, Rep.	Clark
	Bernard L. Hussman, Dem.	Effingham
	Eb Stewart, Dem.	Cumberland
44	Samuel A. Williams, Rep.	Wabash
	Benjamin S. Origin, Dem.	Wabash
	Nathan D. Bryant, Peo.	Gallatin
45	William H. Lathrop, Rep.	Jasper
	Duane Gaines, Dem.	Jasper
	William Hart, Dem.	Crawford
46	Wallace B. Flannigan, Rep.	Hamilton
	Daniel R. Webb, Dem.	Franklin
	F. G. Blood, Peo.	Jefferson
47	Charles L. Wood, Rep.	Calhoun
	John A. Shephard, Dem.	Jersey
	Robert B. English, Rep.	Jersey
48	Harry B. Ward, Rep.	Perry
	Robert C. Brown, Rep.	Randolph
	Robert H. Allen, Dem.	Randolph
49	John E. Thomas, Rep.	St. Clair
	Louis Perrottet, Rep.	St. Clair
	Jule C. Jarvis, Dem.	St. Clair
50	Elbert H. Dickson, Rep.	Union
	William D. Dewoody, Rep.	Williamson
	William Q. McGee, Dem.	Alexander
51	Joseph W. King, Rep.	Pope
	William H. Parish, Rep.	Saline
	Fletcher A. Trousdale, Dem.	Massac

Senate

President	William A. Northcott
President pro tempore	Walter Warder
Secretary	James H. Paddock

District	Member	County
1	Daniel J. May, Rep.	Cook
2	Selon H. Chase, Rep.	Cook
3	Sidney McCloud, Rep.	Cook
4	Daniel F. Curley, Dem.	Cook
5	Thomas E. Milchrist, Rep.	Cook
6	William Sullivan, Rep.	Cook
7	John Humphrey, Rep.	Cook
8	Flavel K. Granger, Rep.	McHenry
9	Bernard J. Maguire, Dem.	Cook
10	Delos W. Baxter, Rep.	Ogle
11	Niels Juul, Rep.	Cook
12	Homer F. Aspinwall, Rep.	Stephenson
13	Joseph P. Mahoney, Dem.	Cook
14	Henry H. Evans, Rep.	Kane
15	Peter F. Galligan, Dem.	Cook
16	Isaac M. Hamilton, Rep.	Iroquois
17	John Broderick, Dem.	Cook
18	Charles Bogardus, Rep.	Ford
19	Daniel A. Campbell, Rep.	Cook
20	Robert B. Fort, Rep.	Marshall
21	Fred A. Busse, Rep.	Cook
22	George W. Stubblefield, Rep.	McLean
23	Harry G. Hall, Rep.	Cook
24	James D. Putnam, Rep.	Peoria
25	William M. Odell, Rep.	Will
26	W. Scott Edwards, Rep.	Fulton
27	Corbus P. Gardner, Rep.	La Salle
28	Orville F. Berry, Rep.	Hancock
29	Daniel D. Hunt, Rep.	De Kalb
30	Henry M. Dunlap, Rep.	Champaign
31	James W. Templeton, Rep.	Bureau
32	Arthur A. Leeper, Dem.	Cass
33	William Payne, Rep.	Rock Island
34	Edward McConnell, Dem.	Morgan
35	Leon A. Townsend, Rep.	Knox
36	William L. Mounts, Dem.	Macoupin
37	John McAdams, Dem.	Adams
38	Nathaniel S. Dressor, Peo.	Bond
39	George W. Funderburk, Dem.	Sangamon
40	Stanton C. Pemberton, Rep.	Coles
41	John N. C. Shumway, Dem.	Christian
42	Charles E. Hull, Dem.	Marion
43	Bernard L. Hussman, Dem.	Effingham
44	John Landrigan, Dem.	Edwards
45	Charles A. Davidson, Dem.	Jasper
46	Joseph T. Payne, Rep.	Jefferson
47	John J. Brenholt, Rep.	Madison
48	Albert C. Bollinger, Rep.	Monroe
49	Henry C. Begole, Rep.	St. Clair
50	Walter Warder, Rep.	Alexander
51	Pleasant T. Chapman, Rep.	Johnson

House of Representatives

Speaker	Lawrence Y. Sherman
Clerk	John A. Reeve

District	Member	County
1	Albert J. Kettering, Rep.	Cook
	Denis J. Leahy, Dem.	Cook
	James Hackett, Dem.	Cook
2	John S. Varley, Rep.	Cook
	John R. Newcomer, Rep.	Cook
	Francis J. Sullivan, Dem.	Cook
3	Charles N. Goodnow, Rep.	Cook
	William Mayhew, Rep.	Cook
	John P. McGoorty, Dem.	Cook
4	Patrick E. Callaghan, Rep.	Cook
	Michael J. Butler, Dem.	Cook
	Joseph Friechel, Dem.	Cook
5	Linn H. Young, Rep.	Cook
	William L. Martin, Rep.	Cook
	Robert Redfield, Dem.	Cook
6	George M. Boyd, Rep.	Cook
	Edward J. Brundage, Rep.	Cook
	John M. Nowicki, Dem.	Cook
7	Edward H. Alling, Rep.	Cook
	William Thiemann, Rep.	Cook
	Walter A. Lantz, Dem.	Cook
8	George R. Lyon, Rep.	Lake
	DuFay A. Fuller, Rep.	Boone
	John C. Donnelly, Dem.	McHenry
9	David E. Shanahan, Rep.	Cook
	John J. Morley, Dem.	Cook
	C. J. Belinski, Dem.	Cook
10	Henry Andrus, Rep.	Winnebago
	James A. Countryman, Rep.	Ogle
	Frank S. Regan, Proh.	Winnebago
11	Peter B. Olsen, Rep.	Cook
	William Barclay, Rep.	Cook
	George H. Harris, Dem.	Cook
12	David C. Busell, Rep.	Carroll
	James R. Berryman, Rep.	JoDaviess
	Michael H. Cleary, Dem.	JoDaviess
13	James P. Cavanagh, Rep.	Cook
	John Churan, Dem.	Cook
	William Carmody, Dem.	Cook
14	Guy L. Bush, Rep.	Du Page
	John Stewart, Rep.	Kane
	Samuel Alschuler, Dem.	Kane
15	Patrick J. Meaney, Rep.	Cook
	Edward H. Rorig, Dem.	Cook
	John Dockery, Dem.	Cook
16	John L. Hamilton, Rep.	Iroquois
	Edward C. Curtis, Rep.	Kankakee
	James J. Kirby, Dem.	Kankakee
17	Albert Glade, Rep.	Cook
	Daniel V. McDonough, Dem.	Cook
	Stephen A. Malato, Dem.	Cook
18	Charles A. Allen, Rep,	Vermilion
	William G. Herron, Rep.	Vermilion
	John E. P. Butz, Dem.	Vermilion
19	Charles G. Johnson, Rep.	Cook
	John Meier, Rep.	Cook
	Daniel V. Harkin, Dem.	Cook
20	Melancthon C. Eignus, Rep.	Livingston
	Josiah Kerrick, Rep.	Woodford
	Michael Cleary, Dem.	Livingston
21	Henry C. Beitler, Rep.	Cook
	Carl Mueller, Rep.	Cook
	James H. Farrell, Dem.	Cook
22	Arthur J. Scrogin, Rep.	McLean
	Duncan M. Funk, Rep.	McLean
	Miles Brooks, Dem.	McLean
23	Samuel E. Erickson, Rep.	Cook

District	Member	County
	John F. O'Malley, Dem.	Cook
	Denis E. Sullivan, Dem.	Cook
24	Alva Merrill, Rep.	Peoria
	Edward D. McCulloch, Rep.	Peoria
	Peter Cahill, Dem.	Peoria
25	John Kolstedt, Rep.	Will
	Samuel J. Drew, Rep.	Will
	Michael F. Hennebry, Dem.	Will
26	John W. Johnson, Rep.	Fulton
	Ubbo J. Albertsen, Rep.	Tazewell
	Jesse Black, Jr., Dem	Tazewell
27	Irving H. Trowbridge, Rep.	La Salle
	Joseph J. Pool, Rep.	La Salle
	John McLauchlan, Dem.	La Salle
28	Lawrence Y. Sherman, Rep.	McDonough
	James A. Anderson, Dem.	Hancock
	George M. Black, Dem.	Schuyler
29	Washington I. Guffin, Rep.	Lee
	Charles T. Cherry, Rep.	Kendall
	James Branen, Dem.	De Kalb
30	Samuel B. Garver, Rep.	De Witt
	Oscar Mansfield, Rep.	Piatt
	Hugh J. Robinson, Dem.	Champaign
31	Alfred N. Abbott, Rep.	Whiteside
	Archibald W. Hopkins, Rep.	Putnam
	Michael Kennedy, Dem.	Bureau
32	David C. White, Rep.	Mason
	John C. Young, Dem.	Mason
	Nicholas P. Casaway, Dem.	Logan
33	George W. Johnson, Rep.	Rock Island
	William W. Cole, Rep.	Henry
	Elmore W. Hurst, Dem.	Rock Island
34	John A. McKeene, Rep.	Scott
	Thomas A. Retallic, Dem.	Pike
	Thomas Meehan, Dem.	Scott
35	George C. Rankin, Rep.	Warren
	Charles A. Samuelson, Rep.	Mercer
	Charles C. Craig, Dem.	Knox
36	James B. Searcy, Rep.	Macoupin
	William V. Rhodes, Dem.	Greene
	William T. Conlee, Dem.	Macoupin
37	William Schlagenhauf, Rep.	Adams
	Jacob Groves, Dem.	Adams
	Elmer A. Perry, Dem.	Brown
38	Thomas Zinn, Rep.	Fayette
	Garrett Carstens, Rep.	Montgomery
	Robert W. Ross, Dem.	Fayette
39	Harry A. Kumler, Rep.	Sangamon
	John A. Vincent, Dem.	Sangamon
	S. P. V. Arnold, Dem.	Sangamon
40	Carl S. Burgett, Rep.	Douglas
	George R. Graybill, Dem.	Shelby
	Charles L. Lee, Dem.	Coles
41	Thomas L. McDaniel, Rep.	Moultrie
	James M. Gray, Dem.	Macon
	Rufus Huff, Dem.	Moultrie
42	Thomas S. Williams, Rep.	Clay
	Charles E. Phillips, Dem.	Clay
	George Louden, Dem.	Clinton
43	John W. Lewis, Rep.	Clark
	Isaac T. Hackley, Dem.	Cumberland
	Charles A. Purdunn, Dem.	Clark
44	Jasper Partridge, Rep.	White

District	Member	County
	James B. Bryant, Dem.	Gallatin
	Joseph L. Howell, Dem.	Gallatin
45	James H. Wood, Rep.	Crawford
	Thomas Tippit, Dem.	Richland
	Carl Busse, Dem.	Lawrence
46	Norman H. Moss, Rep.	Jefferson
	Samuel H. Rea, Dem.	Wayne
	Pinkney L. McNabb, Dem.	Hamilton
47	Jesse K. Cadwallader, Rep.	Jersey
	William McKittrick, Rep.	Madison
	John A. Shephard, Dem.	Jersey
48	Robert C. Brown, Rep.	Randolph
	Arthur M. Lee, Rep.	Jackson
	Joseph W. Drury, Dem.	Monroe
49	William E. Trautmann, Rep.	St. Clair
	Herman R. Heimberger, Rep.	St. Clair
	John Green, Dem.	St. Clair
50	James E. N. Edwards, Rep.	Union
	J. Henry Hilboldt, Dem.	Union
	William H. Warder, Dem.	Williamson
51	Oliver J. Page, Rep.	Massac
	George E. Martin, Rep.	Pulaski
	Albert G. Abney, Dem.	Saline

District	Member	County
25	William M. Odell, Rep.	Will
26	Ubbo J. Albertsen, Rep.	Tazewell
27	Corbus P. Gardner, Rep.	La Salle
28	William F. Harris, Dem.	Hancock
29	Daniel D. Hunt, Rep.	De Kalb
30	Henry M. Dunlap, Rep.	Champaign
31	James W. Templeton, Rep.	Bureau
32	Lawrence B. Stringer, Dem.	Logan
33	William Payne, Rep.	Rock Island
34	Thomas Meehan, Dem.	Scott
35	Leon A. Townsend, Rep.	Knox
36	James K. P. Farrelly, Dem.	Greene
37	John McAdams, Dem.	Adams
38	C. F. Coleman, Dem.	Fayette
39	George W. Funderburk, Dem.	Sangamon
40	Stanton C. Pemberton, Rep.	Coles
41	John N. C. Shumway, Dem.	Christian
42	John O. Koch, Rep.	Clinton
43	Bernard L. Hussman, Dem.	Effingham
44	H. Robert Fowler, Dem.	Hardin
45	Charles A. Davidson, Dem.	Jasper
46	James H. Watson, Dem.	Jefferson
47	John J. Brenholt, Rep.	Madison
48	Roy Alden, Dem.	Perry
49	Henry C. Begole, Rep.	St. Clair
50	Otis H. Burnett, Rep.	Williamson
51	Pleasant T. Chapman, Rep.	Johnson

Forty-second General Assembly, 1901–2

Convened Jan. 9, 1901; adjourned May 4, 1901.

Senate

President William A. Northcott
President pro tempore John J. Bernholt
Secretary James H. Paddock

District	Member	County
1	Daniel J. May, Rep.	Cook
2	William U. Riley, Rep.	Cook
3	Sidney McCloud, Rep.	Cook
4	Michael J. Butler, Dem.	Cook
5	Thomas E. Milchrist, Rep.	Cook
6	Thomas J. Dawson, Dem.	Cook
7	John Humphrey, Rep.	Cook
8	DuFay A. Fuller, Rep.	Boone
9	Bernard J. Maguire, Dem.	Cook
10	Henry Andrus, Rep.	Winnebago
11	Niels Juul, Rep.	Cook
12	John C. McKenzie, Rep.	JoDaviess
13	Joseph P. Mahoney, Dem.	Cook
14	Henry H. Evans, Rep.	Kane
15	Peter F. Galligan, Dem.	Cook
16	Len Small, Rep.	Kankakee
17	John Broderick, Dem.	Cook
18	Martin B. Bailey, Rep.	Vermilion
19	Daniel A. Campbell, Rep.	Cook
20	Robert B. Fort, Rep.	Marshall
21	Fred A. Busse, Rep.	Cook
22	George W. Stubblefield, Rep.	McLean
23	Harry G. Hall, Rep.	Cook
24	James D. Putnam, Rep.	Peoria

House of Representatives

Speaker Lawrence Y. Sherman
Clerk John A. Reeve

District	Member	County
1	Albert J. Kettering, Rep.	Cook
	Patrick J. Wall, Dem.	Cook
	Samuel W. Arrand, Dem.	Cook
2	Frank C. Farnum, Rep.	Cook
	Augustus W. Nohe, Rep.	Cook
	Francis J. Sullivan, Dem.	Cook
3	Chester W. Church, Rep.	Cook
	Kitt Gould, Rep.	Cook
	Michael E. Hunt, Dem.	Cook
4	Frank E. Christian, Rep.	Cook
	Edward M. Cummings, Dem.	Cook
	John E. Doyle, Dem.	Cook
5	John G. Jones, Rep.	Cook
	Hamlin M. Spiegel, Rep.	Cook
	George E. Lapsley, Dem.	Cook
6	William Sullivan, Rep.	Cook
	William Kreicker, Dem.	Cook
	John M. Nowicki, Dem.	Cook
7	George Struckman, Rep.	Cook
	Stacy W. Osgood, Rep.	Cook
	Clayton E. Crafts, Dem.	Cook
8	Edward D. Shurtleff, Rep.	McHenry
	George R. Lyon, Rep.	Lake
	Cornelius V. O'Connor, Dem.	Boone
9	David E. Shanahan, Rep.	Cook
	John J. Morley, Dem.	Cook
	James D. O'Meara, Dem.	Cook
10	James A. Countryman, Rep.	Ogle
	David Hunter, Rep.	Winnebago
	James P. Wilson, Dem.	Ogle
11	Robert E. Pendarvis, Rep.	Cook
	Peter B. Olsen, Rep.	Cook
	Henry L. Drevs, Dem.	Cook

District	Member	County
12	Charles W. Middlekauff, Rep.	Carroll
	James E. Taggart, Rep.	Stephenson
	Bertrand F. Lichtenberger, Dem.	Carroll
13	James P. Cavanagh, Rep.	Cook
	Cyril R. Jandus, Dem.	Cook
	William Carmody, Dem.	Cook
14	Guy L. Bush, Rep.	Du Page
	Charles H. Backus, Rep.	Kane
	John A. Logan, Dem.	Kane
15	Charles W. Kopf, Rep.	Cook
	William J. Moran, Dem.	Cook
	Francis E. Donoghue, Dem.	Cook
16	Edward C. Curtis, Rep.	Kankakee
	William A. Rankin, Rep.	Iroquois
	Frank M. Crangle, Dem.	Iroquois
17	Albert Glade, Rep.	Cook
	Daniel V. McDonough, Dem.	Cook
	Richard F. Shay, Dem.	Cook
18	John A. Montelius, Rep.	Ford
	Charles A. Allen, Rep.	Vermilion
	Coulson V. McClenathan, Dem.	Vermilion
19	Morton G. Smith, Rep.	Cook
	Benjamin M. Mitchell, Dem.	Cook
	Joseph F. Helminiak, Dem.	Cook
20	Josiah Kerrick, Rep.	Woodford
	Melancthon C. Eignus, Rep.	Livingston
	Christian Haase, Dem.	Woodford
21	Henry C. Beitler, Rep.	Cook
	Carl Mueller, Rep.	Cook
	James H. Farrell, Dem.	Cook
22	Arthur J. Scrogin, Rep.	McLean
	Duncan M. Funk, Rep.	McLean
	John F. Heffernan, Dem.	McLean
23	Samuel E. Erickson, Rep.	Cook
	Michael J. Kelly, Dem.	Cook
	Denis E. Sullivan, Dem.	Cook
24	Alva Merrill, Rep.	Peoria
	Edward D. McCulloch, Rep.	Peoria
	John F. Buckley, Dem.	Peoria
25	Samuel J. Drew, Rep.	Will
	Thomas J. Neese, Rep.	Will
	William A. Bowles, Dem.	Will
26	John W. Johnson, Rep.	Fulton
	Jasper S. Onion, Rep.	Fulton
	John Hughes, Dem.	Fulton
27	William D. Isermann, Rep.	La Salle
	Joseph J. Pool, Rep.	La Salle
	Lee O'Neil Browne, Dem.	La Salle
28	Lawrence Y. Sherman, Rep.	McDonough
	S. J. Grigsby, Jr., Dem.	McDonough
	J. E. Wyand, Dem.	Schuyler
29	Charles H. Hughes, Rep.	Lee
	Charles T. Cherry, Rep.	Kendall
	O. Prescott Bennett, Dem.	Grundy
30	Thomas Lamb, Jr., Rep.	Piatt
	Carl Swigart, Rep.	De Witt
	Hugh J. Robinson, Dem.	Champaign
31	Alfred N. Abbott, Rep.	Whiteside
	Allen P. Miller, Rep.	Stark
	Edward Devine, Dem.	Whiteside
32	James C. Taylor, Rep.	Logan
	John C. Young, Dem.	Mason
	John A. Petrie, Dem.	Menard
33	William W. Cole, Rep.	Henry
	George W. Johnson, Rep.	Rock Island
	James H. Andrews, Dem.	Henry

District	Member	County
34	Albert G. Crawford, Rep.	Pike
	Edwin Johnston, Dem.	Pike
	Edward McConnell, Dem.	Morgan
35	Charles A. Samuelson, Rep.	Mercer
	George C. Rankin, Rep.	Warren
	Charles C. Craig, Dem.	Knox
36	Thomas Rinaker, Rep.	Macoupin
	William T. Conlee, Dem.	Macoupin
	George W. Witt, Dem.	Greene
37	William Schlagenhauf, Rep.	Adams
	John M. Murphy, Dem.	Brown
	Jacob Groves, Dem.	Adams
38	Frank R. Milnor, Rep.	Montgomery
	Edward A. Rice, Dem.	Montgomery
	Samuel Vaughn, Dem.	Bond
39	Samuel H. Jones, Rep.	Sangamon
	John A. Wheeler, Rep.	Sangamon
	Redick M. Ridgely, Dem.	Sangamon
40	W. H. Beem, Rep.	Shelby
	Carl S. Burgett, Rep.	Douglas
	Robert G. Hammond, Dem.	Coles
41	John H. Uppendahl, Rep.	Moultrie
	James C. Hunter, Rep.	Christian
	James M. Gray, Dem.	Macon
42	William F. Bundy, Rep.	Clinton
	Charles L. Farris, Dem.	Clay
	George Louden, Dem.	Clinton
43	Charles M. Connor, Rep.	Cumberland
	Ferdinand W. Loy, Dem.	Effingham
	Charles A. Purdunn, Dem.	Clark
44	Jasper Partridge, Rep.	White
	Joseph L. Howell, Dem.	Gallatin
	James B. Bryant, Dem.	Gallatin
45	Philip W. Barnes, Rep.	Lawrence
	Thomas Tippit, Dem.	Richland
	Carl Busse, Dem.	Lawrence
46	John H. Miller, Rep.	Hamilton
	William H. Smith, Dem.	Franklin
	Robert P. Hanna, Dem.	Wayne
47	George L. Aderton, Rep.	Calhoun
	Louis E. Walter, Rep.	Madison
	John A. Shephard, Dem.	Jersey
48	Robert C. Brown, Rep.	Randolph
	Alfred D. Riess, Dem.	Randolph
	David Huggins, Dem.	Jackson
49	John M. Chamberlain, Jr., Rep.	St. Clair
	William E. Trautmann, Rep.	St. Clair
	George F. Wombacher, Dem.	St. Clair
50	Sidney B. Miller, Rep.	Alexander
	James E. N. Edwards, Rep.	Union
	William H. Warder, Dem.	Williamson
51	Charles P. Skaggs, Rep.	Saline
	S. Bartlett Kerr, Rep.	Massac
	Lewis H. Frizzell, Dem.	Johnson

Redistricting of 1901 authorized by act of May 10, 1901; fifty-one districts, each electing one senator and three representatives

District	Counties
1 to 7	Cook
8	Boone, Lake, McHenry

District	Counties
9	Cook
10	Ogle, Winnebago
11	Cook
12	Carroll, JoDaviess, Stephenson
13	Cook
14	Kane, Kendall
15	Cook
16	Livingston, Marshall, Putnam, Woodford
17	Cook
18	Peoria
19	Cook
20	Grundy, Iroquois, Kankakee
21	Cook
22	Edgar, Vermilion
23	Cook
24	Champaign, Moultrie, Piatt
25	Cook
26	Ford, McLean
27	Cook
28	De Witt, Logan, Macon
29	Cook
30	Brown, Cass, Mason, Menard, Schuyler, Tazewell
31	Cook
32	Hancock McDonough, Warren
33	Henderson, Mercer, Rock Island
34	Clark, Coles, Douglas
35	De Kalb, Lee, Whiteside
36	Adams, Calhoun, Pike, Scott
37	Bureau, Henry, Stark
38	Greene, Jersey, Macoupin, Montgomery
39	La Salle
40	Christian, Cumberland, Fayette, Shelby
41	Du Page, Will
42	Clay, Clinton, Effingham, Marion
43	Fulton, Knox
44	Jackson, Monroe, Perry, Randolph, Washington
45	Morgan, Sangamon
46	Jasper, Jefferson, Richland, Wayne
47	Bond, Madison
48	Crawford, Edwards, Gallatin, Hardin, Lawrence, Wabash, White
49	St. Clair
50	Alexander, Franklin, Pulaski, Union, Williamson
51	Hamilton, Johnson, Massac, Pope, Saline

Forty-third General Assembly,
1903–4

Convened Jan. 7, 1903; adjourned May 7, 1903.

Senate

President   William A. Northcott
President pro tempore   John C. McKenzie
Secretary   James H. Paddock

District	Member	County
1	George William Dixon, Rep.	Cook
2	William U. Riley, Rep.	Cook
3	Michael E. Maher, Dem.	Cook
4	Michael J. Butler, Dem.	Cook
5	Francis W. Parker, Rep.	Cook
6	Thomas J. Dawson, Dem.	Cook
7	John Humphrey, Rep.	Cook
8	DuFay A. Fuller, Rep.	Boone
9	Edward J. Rainey, Dem.	Cook
10	Henry Andrus, Rep.	Winnebago
11	Carl Lundberg, Rep.	Cook
12	John C. McKenzie, Rep.	JoDaviess
13	Albert C. Clark, Rep.	Cook
14	Henry H. Evans, Rep.	Kane
15	Cyril R. Jandus, Dem.	Cook
16	Robert B. Fort, Rep.	Marshall
17	John Powers, Dem.	Cook
18	James D. Putnam, Rep.	Peoria
19	Frank C. Farnum, Rep.	Cook
20	Len Small, Rep.	Kankakee
21	Daniel A. Campbell, Rep.	Cook
22	Martin B. Bailey, Rep.	Vermilion
23	Niels Juul, Rep.	Cook
24	Henry M. Dunlap, Rep.	Champaign
25	Joseph F. Haas, Rep.	Cook
26	George W. Stubblefield, Rep.	McLean
27	Stanley H. Kunz, Dem.	Cook
28	Lawrence B. Stringer, Dem.	Logan
29	Harry G. Hall, Rep.	Cook
30	Ubbo J. Albertsen, Rep.	Tazewell
31	Carl Mueller, Rep.	Cook
32	Orville F. Berry, Rep.	Hancock
33	Levi S. McCabe, Rep.	Rock Island
34	Stanton C. Pemberton, Rep.	Coles
35	Charles H. Hughes, Rep.	Lee
36	Thomas Meehan, Dem.	Scott
37	James W. Templeton, Rep.	Bureau
38	James K. P. Farrelly, Dem.	Greene
39	Corbus P. Gardner, Rep.	La Salle
40	C. F. Coleman, Dem.	Fayette
41	Richard J. Barr, Rep.	Will
42	John O. Koch, Rep.	Clinton
43	Leon A. Townsend, Rep.	Knox
44	Roy Alden, Dem.	Perry
45	Thomas Rees, Dem.	Sangamon
46	James H. Watson, Dem.	Jefferson
47	Louis E. Walter, Rep.	Madison
48	H. Robert Fowler, Dem.	Hardin
49	Robert S. Hamilton, Rep.	St. Clair
50	Otis H. Burnett, Rep.	Williamson
51	Douglas W. Helm, Rep.	Massac

House of Representatives

Speaker   John H. Miller
Clerk   John A. Reeve

District	Member	County
1	Jacob Boll, Rep.	Cook
	Edward H. Morris, Rep.	Cook
	Samuel W. Arrand, Dem.	Cook
2	Charles W. Kopf, Rep.	Cook
	Benjamin F. Greenebaum, Rep.	Cook
	Francis E. Donoghue, Dem.	Cook
3	Sigmund S. Jonas, Rep.	Cook
	Frederick L. Davies, Rep.	Cook
	Richard E. Corigan, Dem.	Cook
4	Frank E. Christian, Rep.	Cook
	Isaac Miller, Dem.	Cook
	Edward M. Cummings, Dem.	Cook

District	Member	County
5	Aaron Norden, Rep.	Cook
	Michael E. Hunt, Dem.	Cook
	Oliver W. Stewart, Proh.	Cook
6	Harry Oldam, Rep.	Cook
	Edward J. Brundage, Rep.	Cook
	M. L. McKinley, Dem.	Cook
7	George Struckman, Rep.	Cook
	James W. Turner, Rep.	Cook
	John W. Farley, Dem.	Cook
8	Edward D. Shurtleff, Rep.	McHenry
	George R. Lyon, Rep.	Lake
	William Desmond, Dem.	McHenry
9	David E. Shanahan, Rep.	Cook
	Anton J. Cermak, Dem.	Cook
	Thomas J. Deady, Dem.	Cook
10	Frederick Haines, Rep.	Winnebago
	Johnson Lawrence, Rep.	Ogle
	James P. Wilson, Dem.	Ogle
11	Chester W. Church, Rep.	Cook
	Nicholas J. Nagel, Rep.	Cook
	John E. Doyle, Dem.	Cook
12	James E. Taggart, Rep.	Stephenson
	William W. Gillespie, Rep.	Carroll
	Douglas Pattison, Dem.	Stephenson
13	Benton F. Kleeman, Rep.	Cook
	James H. Wilkerson, Rep.	Cook
	Henry V. Meeteren, Dem.	Cook
14	Charles H. Backus, Rep.	Kane
	Charles T. Cherry, Rep.	Kendall
	John W. Linden, Dem.	Kane
15	James P. Cavanagh, Rep.	Cook
	Peter Knolla, Dem.	Cook
	Ladislas J. Fligel, Dem.	Cook
16	Ira M. Lish, Rep.	Livingston
	Josiah Kerrick, Rep.	Woodford
	John P. Moran, Dem.	Livingston
17	Edward J. Smejkal, Rep.	Cook
	John Noonan, Dem.	Cook
	Clarence S. Darrow, P. O.¹	Cook
18	William G. McRoberts, Rep.	Peoria
	Charles F. Black, Rep.	Peoria
	Jefferson R. Boulware, Dem.	Peoria
19	Augustus W. Nohe, Rep.	Cook
	William W. Weare, Rep.	Cook
	Richard E. Burke, Dem.	Cook
20	Edward C. Curtis, Rep.	Kankakee
	Horace Russell, Rep.	Iroquois
	W. W. Parish, Jr., Dem.	Kankakee
21	Frederick E. Erickson, Rep.	Cook
	Benjamin M. Mitchell, Dem.	Cook
	John J. McManaman, P. O.¹	Cook
22	Charles A. Allen, Rep.	Vermilion
	George H. Gordon, Rep.	Edgar
	Coulson V. McClenathan, Dem.	Vermilion
23	Henry W. Austin, Rep.	Cook
	Abel Davis, Rep.	Cook
	John S. Clark, Dem.	Cook
24	Julius N. Rodman, Rep.	Piatt
	John H. Uppendahl, Rep.	Moultrie
	Evan Stevenson, Dem.	Piatt
25	Robert E. Pendarvis, Rep.	Cook
	Herman H. Breidt, Rep.	Cook
	Frank H. Landmesser, Dem.	Cook
26	Wesley M. Owen, Rep.	McLean
	John A. Montelius, Rep.	Ford
	John F. Heffernan, Dem.	McLean

District	Member	County
27	Albert Glade, Rep.	Cook
	Joseph S. Geshkewich, Dem.	Cook
	Daniel V. McDonough, Dem.	Cook
28	Carl Swigart, Rep.	De Witt
	Arthur J. Gallagher, Rep.	Macon
	James M. Gray, Dem.	Macon
29	Samuel E. Erickson, Rep.	Cook
	Bernard F. Clettenberg, Rep.	Cook
	M. B. McNulty, Dem.	Cook
30	Homer J. Tice, Rep.	Menard
	John A. Petrie, Dem.	Menard
	Henry H. Elliot, Dem.	Mason
31	Henry C. Beitler, Rep.	Cook
	Joseph M. Patterson, Rep.	Cook
	John C. Werdell, Dem.	Cook
32	Lawrence Y. Sherman, Rep.	McDonough
	Everitt C. Hardin, Rep.	Warren
	William McKinley, Dem.	Warren
33	Lawrence M. Magill, Rep.	Rock Island
	Charles A. Samuelson, Rep.	Mercer
	George A. Cooke, Dem.	Mercer
34	D. B. Miller, Rep.	Clark
	Carl S. Burgett, Rep.	Douglas
	J. T. Hinds, Dem.	Douglas
35	John B. Castle, Rep.	De Kalb
	Charles A. Wetherbee, Rep.	Whiteside
	Caleb C. Johnson, Dem.	Whiteside
36	William Schlagenhauf, Rep.	Adams
	Jacob Groves, Dem.	Adams
	Irvin D. Webster, Dem.	Pike
37	Nathaniel W. Tibbetts, Rep.	Henry
	James E. Noyes, Rep.	Stark
	James K. Blish, Dem.	Henry
38	Thomas Rinaker, Rep.	Macoupin
	Frank W. Burton, Dem.	Macoupin
	Edward A. Rice, Dem.	Montgomery
39	William D. Isermann, Rep.	La Salle
	Enoch H. Pedersen, Rep.	La Salle
	Lee O'Neil Browne, Dem.	La Salle
40	George T. Turner, Rep.	Fayette
	Henry O. Minnis, Dem.	Christian
	William O. Wallace, Dem.	Shelby
41	Samuel J. Drew, Rep.	Will
	Guy L. Bush, Rep.	Du Page
	William A. Bowles, Dem.	Will
42	William F. Bundy, Rep.	Clinton
	Charles L. Farris, Dem.	Clay
	Fred Pullen, Dem.	Marion
43	Wilfred Arnold, Rep.	Knox
	Burnett M. Chiperfield, Rep.	Fulton
	John Hughes, Dem.	Fulton
44	Robert J. McElvain, Rep.	Jackson
	Sylvester W. McGuire, Rep.	Randolph
	Charles S. Luke, Dem.	Washington
45	John A. Wheeler, Rep.	Sangamon
	Abner G. Murray, Rep.	Sangamon
	William S. Lurton, Dem.	Morgan
46	Lowry E. Sunderland, Rep.	Wayne
	Thomas Tippit, Dem.	Richland
	John M. Rapp, Dem.	Wayne
47	Cicero J. Lindly, Rep.	Bond
	William Montgomery, Rep.	Madison
	Charles Carrillon, Dem.	Bond

District	Member	County
48	John W. Leaverton, Rep.	Crawford
	Mahlon H. Mundy, Dem.	Wabash
	Carl Busse, Dem.	Lawrence
49	William E. Trautmann, Rep.	St. Clair
	Martin Schnipper, Rep.	St. Clair
	James O. Miller, Dem.	St. Clair
50	James E. N. Edwards, Rep.	Union
	Charles M. Gaunt, Rep.	Pulaski
	William L. Eskew, Dem.	Franklin
51	A. W. Walker, Rep.	Pope
	John H. Miller, Rep.	Hamilton
	David J. Underwood, Dem.	Hamilton

[1] P.O.—Public Ownership.

Forty-fourth General Assembly, 1905–6

Convened Jan. 4, 1905; adjourned May 6, 1905.

Senate

President	Lawrence Y. Sherman
President pro tempore	
	Leon A. Townsend[1]
Secretary	James H. Paddock

District	Member	County
1	George William Dixon, Rep.	Cook
2	Homer K. Galpin, Rep.	Cook
3	Michael E. Maher, Dem.	Cook
4	Patrick J. McShane, Rep.	Cook
5	Francis W. Parker, Rep.	Cook
6	William M. Brown, Rep.	Cook
7	John Humphrey, Rep.	Cook
8	Albert N. Tiffany, Rep.	Lake
9	Edward J. Rainey, Dem.	Cook
10	Andrew J. Anderson, Rep.	Winnebago
11	Carl Lundberg, Rep.	Cook
12	John C. McKenzie, Rep.	JoDaviess
13	Albert C. Clark, Rep.	Cook
14	Henry H. Evans, Rep.	Kane
15	Cyril R. Jandus, Dem.	Cook
16	Ira M. Lish, Rep.	Livingston
17	John Powers, Dem.	Cook
18	George B. Sucher,[2] Dem.	Peoria
	James D. Putnam,[3] Rep.	Peoria
19	Frank C. Farnum, Rep.	Cook
20	Edward C. Curtis, Rep.	Kankakee
21	Daniel A. Campbell, Rep.	Cook
22	William M. Acton, Rep.	Vermilion
23	Niels Juul, Rep.	Cook
24	Henry M. Dunlap, Rep.	Champaign
25	Joseph F. Haas, Rep.	Cook
26	George W. Stubblefield, Rep.	McLean
27	Stanley H. Kunz, Dem.	Cook
28	James A. Henson, Rep.	Macon
29	Harry G. Hall, Rep.	Cook
30	George W. Cunningham, Dem.	Tazewell
31	Carl Mueller, Rep.	Cook

District	Member	County
32	Orville F. Berry, Rep.	Hancock
33	Levi S. McCabe, Rep.	Rock Island
34	Stanton C. Pemberton, Rep.	Coles
35	Charles H. Hughes, Rep.	Lee
36	Thomas D. Bare, Rep.	Calhoun
37	James W. Templeton, Rep.	Bureau
38	Frank W. Burton, Dem.	Macoupin
39	Corbus P. Gardner, Rep.	La Salle
40	George D. Chafee, Rep.	Shelby
41	Richard J. Barr, Rep.	Will
42	Charles E. Hull, Dem.	Marion
43	Leon A. Townsend, Rep.	Knox
44	Robert J. McElvain, Rep.	Jackson
45	Thomas Rees, Dem.	Sangamon
46	John L. Houser, Rep.	Richland
47	Louis E. Walter, Rep.	Madison
48	Jesse E. Bartly, Rep.	Gallatin
49	Robert S. Hamilton, Rep.	St. Clair
50	Otis H. Burnett, Rep.	Williamson
51	Douglas W. Helm, Rep.	Massac

[1] Resigned May 6, 1905. Orville F. Berry elected to replace him.
[2] Unseated May 5, 1905, contested.
[3] Seated vice Sucher May 5, 1905.

House of Representatives

Speaker	Edward D. Shurtleff
Clerk	John A. Reeve

District	Member	County
1	Francis P. Brady, Rep.	Cook
	Edward D. Green, Rep.	Cook
	Samuel W. Arrand, Dem.	Cook
2	Paul I. Zaabel, Rep.	Cook
	Frank J. McNichols, Rep.	Cook
	Frank D. Comerford,[1] Dem.	Cook
3	Daniel Buettner, Rep.	Cook
	Walter E. Beebe, Rep.	Cook
	John P. Walsh, Dem.	Cook
4	Emil O. Kowalski, Rep.	Cook
	John C. Russell, Dem.	Cook
	Joseph A. Ambroz, Soc.	Cook
5	Aaron Norden,[2] Rep.	Cook
	William H. McSurely, Rep.	Cook
	John P. McGoorty, Dem.	Cook
6	John W. Hill, Rep.	Cook
	John C. Williams, Rep.	Cook
	M. L. McKinley, Dem.	Cook
7	George Struckman, Rep.	Cook
	Louis J. Pierson, Rep.	Cook
	John W. Farley, Dem.	Cook
8	Frank R. Covey, Rep.	Boone
	Edward D. Shurtleff, Rep.	McHenry
	Dennis E. Gibbons, Dem.	Lake
9	David E. Shanahan, Rep.	Cook
	Anton J. Cermak, Dem.	Cook
	Andrew Olson, Soc.	Cook
10	Wilbur B. McHenry, Rep.	Ogle
	Frederick Haines, Rep.	Winnebago
	Charles E. Martin, Dem.	Winnebago
11	Chester W. Church, Rep.	Cook
	Nicholas J. Nagel, Rep.	Cook
	John R. Reilly, Dem.	Cook
12	James E. Taggart, Rep.	Stephenson
	William W. Gillespie, Rep.	Carroll

District	Member	County
	Douglas Pattison, Dem.	Stephenson
13	Benton F. Kleeman, Rep.	Cook
	William T. Monroe, Rep.	Cook
	John J. Poulton, Dem.	Cook
14	Charles T. Cherry, Rep.	Kendall
	Charles H. Backus, Rep.	Kane
	John W. Linden, Dem.	Kane
15	James P. Cavanagh, Rep.	Cook
	William J. Laskowski, Dem.	Cook
	Dennis J. Egan, Dem.	Cook
16	Josiah Kerrick, Rep.	Woodford
	Harrison T. Ireland, Rep.	Woodford
	John P. Moran, Dem.	Livingston
17	Edward J. Smejkal, Rep.	Cook
	Edward J. Glackin, Dem.	Cook
	Edward W. Gillespie, Dem.	Cook
18	John Dailey, Rep.	Peoria
	Otis S. Mills, Rep.	Peoria
	Daniel R. Sheen, Proh.	Peoria
19	Charles A. Schumacher, Rep.	Cook
	James M. Kittleman, Rep.	Cook
	Richard E. Burke, Dem.	Cook
20	Horace Russell, Rep.	Iroquois
	Israel Dudgeon, Rep.	Grundy
	Frank M. Crangle, Dem.	Iroquois
21	William H. Troyer, Rep.	Cook
	Frederick E. Erickson, Rep.	Cook
	Benjamin M. Mitchell, Dem.	Cook
22	Charles A. Allen, Rep.	Vermilion
	J. Russ Grace, Rep.	Edgar
	Clay F. Gaumer, Proh.	Vermilion
23	Henry W. Austin, Rep.	Cook
	Christopher Beck, Rep.	Cook
	Joseph Grein, Dem.	Cook
24	Julius N. Rodman, Rep.	Piatt
	John R. Pogue, Rep.	Moultrie
	Peter P. Schaefer, Dem.	Champaign
25	Herman H. Breidt, Rep.	Cook
	Robert E. Pendarvis, Rep.	Cook
	Frank J. Wilson, Dem.	Cook
26	Cassius M. Coyle, Rep.	McLean
	A. L. Phillips, Rep.	Ford
	Paul Finnan, Dem.	McLean
27	Albert Glade, Rep.	Cook
	Daniel V. McDonough, Dem.	Cook
	Joseph S. Geshkewich, Dem.	Cook
28	John G. Oglesby, Rep.	Logan
	John R. Robinson, Rep.	De Witt
	James M. Gray, Dem.	Macon
29	Bernard F. Clettenberg, Rep.	Cook
	Samuel E. Erickson, Rep.	Cook
	Patrick J. Sullivan, Dem.	Cook
30	Louis Zinger, Rep.	Tazewell
	Walter I. Manny, Dem.	Brown
	J. Joseph Cook, Dem.	Cass
31	Charles E. Erby, Rep.	Cook
	Lewis Rinaker, Rep.	Cook
	John C. Werdell, Dem.	Cook
32	Everitt C. Hardin, Rep.	Warren
	J. Edward Harris, Rep.	McDonough
	William McKinley, Dem.	Warren
33	Lawrence M. Magill, Rep.	Rock Island
	Monroe G. Reynolds, Rep.	Mercer
	George W. McCaskrin,[3] Ind.	Rock Island
	George A. Cooke,[4] Dem.	Mercer
34	D. B. Miller, Rep.	Clark
	Carl S. Burgett, Rep.	Douglas

District	Member	County
	Isaac B. Craig, Dem.	Coles
35	John B. Castle, Rep.	De Kalb
	Harvey L. Sheldon, Rep.	Whiteside
	James Branen, Dem.	De Kalb
36	Randall B. Echols, Rep.	Adams
	Campbell S. Hearn, Dem.	Adams
	Irvin D. Webster, Dem.	Pike
37	James E. Noyes, Rep.	Stark
	Nathaniel W. Tibbetts, Rep.	Henry
	James E. Dabler, Rep.	Bureau
38	William J. Donahue, Rep.	Macoupin
	Stephen D. Canaday, Dem.	Montgomery
	George W. Witt, Dem.	Greene
39	Enoch H. Pedersen, Rep.	La Salle
	William D. Isermann, Rep.	La Salle
	John J. McClusky,[3] Dem.	La Salle
	Lee O'Neil Browne,[5] Dem.	La Salle
40	Walter M. Provine, Rep.	Christian
	C. F. Coleman, Dem.	Fayette
	Henry O. Minnis, Dem.	Christian
41	Guy L. Bush, Rep.	Du Page
	Samuel J. Drew, Rep.	Will
	William A. Bowles,[3] Dem.	Will
	Alonzo E. Wilson,[6] Proh.	Du Page
42	Harvey W. Shriner, Rep.	Clay
	James H. Loy, Rep.	Effingham
	Charles L. Farris, Dem.	Clay
43	Wilfred Arnold, Rep.	Knox
	William H. Emerson, Rep.	Fulton
	Michael J. Daugherty, Dem.	Knox
44	Sample G. Parks,[7] Rep.	Perry
	Sylvester W. McGuire, Rep.	Randolph
	Charles S. Luke, Dem.	Washington
45	Frank J. Heinl, Rep.	Morgan
	Charles Fetzer, Rep.	Sangamon
	William S. Lurton, Dem.	Morgan
46	Robert E. Mabry, Rep.	Wayne
	Thomas Tippit, Dem.	Richland
	John M. Rapp, Dem.	Wayne
47	Cicero J. Lindly, Rep.	Bond
	William Montgomery, Rep.	Madison
	Amos E. Benbow, Dem.	Madison
48	Daniel E. Rose, Rep.	White
	Mahlon H. Mundy, Dem.	Wabash
	Bruce A. Campbell, Dem.	Edwards
49	William E. Trautmann, Rep.	St. Clair
	Fred Keck, Rep.	St. Clair
	Charles A. Karch, Dem.	St. Clair
50	Charles M. Gaunt, Rep.	Pulaski
	R. D. Kirkpatrick, Rep.	Franklin
	Walter W. Williams, Dem.	Williamson
51	John S. Organ, Rep.	Hamilton
	Kenneth C. Ronalds, Rep.	Saline
	John W. Shaw, Dem.	Saline

[1] Expelled Feb. 8, 1905; reelected as Independent April 4, 1905; seated April 21, 1905.
[2] Died July 5, 1905.
[3] Unseated.
[4] Vice McCaskrin.
[5] Vice McCluskey.
[6] Vice Bowles.
[7] Died Feb. 12, 1905.

Forty-fifth General Assembly,
1907–8

Beginning with this General Assembly, session dates are included in the table of legislative accomplishments, 1907–68, at the end of the previous chapter, "Legislative Department."

Senate

President   Lawrence Y. Sherman
President pro tempore
                     Stanton C. Pemberton
Secretary   James H. Paddock

District	Member	County
1	Charles L. Billings, Rep.	Cook
2	Homer K. Galpin, Rep.	Cook
3	Samuel A. Ettleson, Rep.	Cook
4	Patrick J. McShane, Rep.	Cook
5	Walter Clyde Jones, Rep.	Cook
6	William M. Brown, Rep.	Cook
7	John Humphrey, Rep.	Cook
8	Albert N. Tiffany, Rep.	Lake
9	Edward J. Rainey, Dem.	Cook
10	Andrew J. Anderson, Rep.	Winnebago
11	Carl Lundberg, Rep.	Cook
12	John C. McKenzie, Rep.	JoDaviess
13	Albert C. Clark, Rep.	Cook
14	Henry H. Evans, Rep.	Kane
15	Cyril R. Jandus, Dem.	Cook
16	Ira M. Lish, Rep.	Livingston
17	Edward J. Glackin, Dem.	Cook
18	James D. Putnam, Rep.	Peoria
19	Charles E. Cruikshank, Rep.	Cook
20	Edward C. Curtis, Rep.	Kankakee
21	Daniel A. Campbell,[1] Rep.	Cook
22	William M. Acton, Rep.	Vermilion
23	Niels Juul, Rep.	Cook
24	Henry M. Dunlap, Rep.	Champaign
25	Herman H. Breidt, Rep.	Cook
26	George W. Stubblefield, Rep.	McLean
27	John Broderick, Dem.	Cook
28	James A. Henson, Rep.	Macon
29	Harry G. Hall, Rep.	Cook
30	George W. Cunningham, Dem.	Tazewell
31	Frank G. Schmitt, Rep.	Cook
32	Orville F. Berry, Rep.	Hancock
33	Frank A. Landee, Rep.	Rock Island
34	Stanton C. Pemberton, Rep.	Coles
35	Charles H. Hughes,[2] Rep.	Lee
36	Thomas D. Bare, Rep.	Calhoun
37	B. Frank Baker, Rep.	Henry
38	Frank W. Burton, Dem.	Macoupin
39	Corbus P. Gardner, Rep.	La Salle
40	George D. Chafee, Rep.	Shelby
41	Richard J. Barr, Rep.	Will
42	Charles E. Hull, Dem.	Marion
43	Charles F. Hurburgh, Rep.	Knox
44	Robert J. McElvain, Rep.	Jackson
45	Logan Hay, Rep.	Sangamon
46	John L. Houser, Rep.	Richland
47	George M. McCormick, Rep.	Madison
48	Jesse E. Bartly, Rep.	Gallatin
49	Robert S. Hamilton, Rep.	St. Clair
50	W. O. Potter, Rep.	Williamson
51	Douglas W. Helm, Rep.	Massac

[1] Resigned April 15, 1907.
[2] Died May 15, 1907.

House of Representatives

Speaker   Edward D. Shurtleff
Clerk   John A. Reeve

District	Member	County
1	Francis P. Brady, Rep.	Cook
	Alexander Lane, Rep.	Cook
	Thomas J. McNally, Jr., Dem.	Cook
2	Frank J. McNichols, Rep.	Cook
	Paul I. Zaabel, Rep.	Cook
	Francis E. Donoghue, Dem.	Cook
3	Daniel Buettner,[1] Rep.	Cook
	William M. Ostrom,[2] Rep.	Cook
	Oliver Sollitt, Rep.	Cook
	John P. Walsh, Dem.	Cook
4	Emil O. Kowalski, Rep.	Cook
	George C. Hilton, Dem.	Cook
	John C. Russell, Dem.	Cook
5	William Tudor ApMadoc, Rep.	Cook
	Morton D. Hull, Rep.	Cook
	John P. McGoorty, Dem.	Cook
6	John W. Hill, Rep.	Cook
	William C. Levere, Rep.	Cook
	Robert E. Wilson, Dem.	Cook
7	Louis J. Pierson, Rep.	Cook
	Frederick B. Roos, Rep.	Cook
	Walter A. Lantz, Dem.	Cook
8	Frank R. Covey, Rep.	Boone
	Edward D. Shurtleff, Rep.	McHenry
	Dennis E. Gibbons, Dem.	Lake
9	David E. Shanahan, Rep.	Cook
	Anton J. Cermak, Dem.	Cook
	Eugene J. Danaher, Dem.	Cook
10	Earl D. Reynolds, Rep.	Winnebago
	Johnson Lawrence, Rep.	Ogle
	James H. Corcoran, Dem.	Winnebago
11	Chester W. Church, Rep.	Cook
	Henry D. Fulton, Rep.	Cook
	Robert W. McKinlay, Dem.	Cook
12	William W. Gillespie, Rep.	Carroll
	William W. Krape, Rep.	Stephenson
	Douglas Pattison, Dem.	Stephenson
13	Cornelius J. Ton, Rep.	Cook
	Edward C. Fitch, Rep.	Cook
	John J. Poulton, Dem.	Cook
14	Charles H. Backus, Rep.	Kane
	Charles C. Hoge, Rep.	Kendall
	Nicholas L. Johnson, Proh.	Kane
15	Thomas Curran, Rep.	Cook
	Dennis J. Egan, Dem.	Cook
	John O. Hruby, Jr., Dem.	Cook
16	Harrison T. Ireland, Rep.	Marshall
	Josiah Kerrick, Rep.	Woodford
	Christian Haase, Dem.	Marshall
17	Edward J. Smejkal, Rep.	Cook
	William Navigato, Dem.	Cook
	Emanuel M. Abrahams, Dem.	Cook

District	Member	County
18	William G. McRoberts, Rep.	Peoria
	Charles F. Black, Rep.	Peoria
	Jefferson R. Boulware, Dem.	Peoria
19	Charles A. Schumacher, Rep.	Cook
	James M. Kittleman, Rep.	Cook
	John J. McLaughlin, Dem.	Cook
20	Israel Dudgeon, Rep.	Grundy
	George H. Hamilton, Rep.	Iroquois
	J. W. Allison, Dem.	Kankakee
21	Frederick E. Erickson, Rep.	Cook
	William H. Troyer, Rep.	Cook
	Thomas J. O'Brien, Dem.	Cook
22	Walter V. Dysert, Rep.	Vermilion
	Charles A. Allen, Rep.	Vermilion
	Clay F. Gaumer, Proh.	Vermilion
23	Henry W. Austin, Rep.	Cook
	Christopher Beck, Rep.	Cook
	Patrick F. Murray, Dem.	Cook
24	Charles Adkins, Rep.	Piatt
	John R. Pogue, Rep.	Moultrie
	Peter P. Schaefer, Dem.	Champaign
25	Albert F. Keeney, Rep.	Cook
	Charles L. Fieldstack, Rep.	Cook
	Frank H. Landmesser, Dem.	Cook
26	Cassius M. Coyle, Rep.	McLean
	Paul Finnan, Dem.	McLean
	John R. Golden, Proh.	Ford
27	Albert Glade, Rep.	Cook
	Daniel V. McDonough, Dem.	Cook
	Joseph S. Geshkewich, Dem.	Cook
28	John G. Oglesby, Rep.	Logan
	John R. Robinson, Rep.	De Witt
	Byron F. Staymates, Dem.	De Witt
29	Charles A. Nelson, Rep.	Cook
	Edward Hope, Rep.	Cook
	Patrick J. Sullivan, Dem.	Cook
30	Louis Zinger, Rep.	Tazewell
	Alrick Mann Foster, Dem.	Schuyler
	Walter I. Manny, Dem.	Brown
31	Matthew Mills, Rep.	Cook
	Charles E. Erby, Rep.	Cook
	John C. Werdell, Dem.	Cook
32	J. Edward Harris, Rep.	McDonough
	Henry L. Jewell, Rep.	Warren
	John A. Califf, Dem.	Hancock
33	Thomas Campbell, Rep.	Rock Island
	Frank E. Abbey, Rep.	Henderson
	Everett L. Werts, Dem.	Henderson
34	William T. Hollenbeck, Rep.	Clark
	John F. Martin, Rep.	Douglas
	Seymour Hurst, Dem.	Clark
35	Harvey L. Sheldon, Rep.	Whiteside
	George M. Tindall, Rep.	De Kalb
	Henry F. Gehant, Dem.	Lee
36	Chauncey H. Castle, Rep.	Adams
	Campbell S. Hearn, Dem.	Adams
	Charles E. Bolin, Dem.	Pike
37	Francis J. Liggett, Rep.	Stark
	Clayton C. Pervier, Rep.	Bureau
	William J. McGuire, Dem.	Henry
38	William H. Behrens, Rep.	Macoupin
	Stephen D. Canaday, Dem.	Montgomery
	George W. Witt, Dem.	Greene
39	William R. Lewis, Rep.	La Salle
	Al A. Clapsaddle, Rep.	La Salle
	Lee O'Neil Browne, Dem.	La Salle
40	Walter M. Provine, Rep.	Christian

District	Member	County
	Joseph S. Clark, Dem.	Fayette
	John C. Richardson, Dem.	Christian
41	Guy L. Bush, Rep.	Du Page
	Frank L. Parker, Rep.	Will
	Thomas H. Riley, Dem.	Will
42	Charles L. McMackin, Rep.	Marion
	John A. Read, Dem.	Effingham
	H. J. C. Beckemeyer, Dem.	Clinton
43	Burnett M. Chiperfield, Rep.	Fulton
	Edward J. King, Rep.	Knox
	Michael J. Daugherty, Dem.	Knox
44	William Stevenson, Rep.	Randolph
	Porter Baird, Rep.	Perry
	Charles S. Luke, Dem.	Washington
45	Frank J. Heinl, Rep.	Morgan
	Charles McBride, Dem.	Sangamon
	Charles Schermerhorn, Dem.	Sangamon
46	Lester Leamon, Rep.	Jasper
	William C. Blair, Dem.	Jefferson
	J. W. Templeman, Dem.	Wayne
47	William Montgomery,[3] Rep.	Madison
	Cicero J. Lindly, Rep.	Bond
	Michael S. Link, Dem.	Madison
48	Charles H. Musgrave, Rep.	Crawford
	Daniel E. Rose, Rep.	White
	E. M. Young, Dem.	White
49	Fred Keck, Rep.	St. Clair
	John L. Flannigen, Rep.	St. Clair
	George F. Smith, Rep.	St. Clair
50	Charles M. Gaunt, Rep.	Pulaski
	R. D. Kirkpatrick, Rep.	Franklin
	Richard E. Powers, Dem.	Alexander
51	Lewis E. York, Rep.	Saline
	Charles Durfee, Rep.	Pope
	George W. English, Dem.	Johnson

[1] Died Jan. 16, 1907.
[2] Elected April 2, 1907. vice Buettner.
[3] Died during recess.

Forty-sixth General Assembly, 1909–10

Senate

President	John G. Oglesby
Secretary	James H. Paddock

District	Member	County
1	Charles L. Billings, Rep.	Cook
2	Lewis C. Ball, Rep.	Cook
3	Samuel A. Ettelson, Rep.	Cook
4	Al F. Gorman, Dem.	Cook
5	Walter Clyde Jones, Rep.	Cook
6	William M. Brown, Rep.	Cook
7	John Humphrey, Rep.	Cook
8	Albert J. Olson, Rep.	McHenry
9	Edward J. Rainey, Dem.	Cook
10	Henry Andrus, Rep.	Winnebago
11	Carl Lundberg, Rep.	Cook
12	John C. McKenzie, Rep.	JoDaviess
13	Albert C. Clark, Rep.	Cook

District	Member	County
14	Thomas B. Stewart, Rep.	Kane
15	Cyril R. Jandus, Dem.	Cook
16	Ira M. Lish, Rep.	Livingston
17	Edward J. Glackin, Dem.	Cook
18	John Dailey, Rep.	Peoria
19	Charles E. Cruikshank, Rep.	Cook
20	Edward C. Curtis, Rep.	Kankakee
21	William H. Dellenback, Rep.	Cook
22	Martin B. Bailey, Rep.	Vermilion
23	Niels Juul, Rep.	Cook
24	Henry M. Dunlap, Rep.	Champaign
25	Herman H. Breidt, Rep.	Cook
26	Frank H. Funk, Rep.	McLean
27	John Broderick, Dem.	Cook
28	James A. Henson, Rep.	Macon
29	Harry G. Hall, Rep.	Cook
30	Walter I. Manny, Dem.	Brown
31	Frank G. Schmitt, Rep.	Cook
32	James F. Gibson, Dem.	Hancock
33	Frank A. Landee, Rep.	Rock Island
34	Stanton C. Pemberton, Rep.	Coles
35	B. F. Downing, Rep.	Lee
36	Campbell S. Hearn, Dem.	Adams
37	B. Frank Baker, Rep.	Henry
38	Frank W. Burton, Dem.	Macoupin
39	Corbus P. Gardner, Rep.	La Salle
40	F. Jeff Tossey, Dem.	Cumberland
41	Richard J. Barr, Rep.	Will
42	Daniel W. Holstlaw, Dem.	Marion
43	Charles F. Hurburgh, Rep.	Knox
44	Robert J. McElvain, Rep.	Jackson
45	Logan Hay, Rep.	Sangamon
46	Albert E. Isley, Dem.	Jasper
47	George M. McCormick, Rep.	Madison
48	James A. Womack, Dem.	Hardin
49	Robert S. Hamilton, Rep.	St. Clair
50	W. O. Potter, Rep.	Williamson
51	Douglas W. Helm, Rep.	Massac

House of Representatives

Speaker Edward D. Shurtleff
Clerk   Bert H. McCann

District	Member	County
1	Alexander Lane, Rep.	Cook
	Francis P. Brady, Rep.	Cook
	John J. Griffin, Dem.	Cook
2	Paul I. Zaabel,[1] Rep.	Cook
	Roger J. Marcy,[2] Rep.	Cook
	Frank J. McNichols, Rep.	Cook
	George L. McConnell, Dem.	Cook
3	Oliver Sollitt, Rep.	Cook
	Charles Lederer, Rep.	Cook
	John P. Walsh, Dem.	Cook
4	Emil O. Kowalski, Rep.	Cook
	William Murphy, Dem.	Cook
	George C. Hilton, Dem.	Cook
5	Morton D. Hull, Rep.	Cook
	William Tudor ApMadoc, Rep.	Cook
	Charles Naylor, Dem.	Cook
6	William F. Zipf, Rep.	Cook

District	Member	County
	Richard P. Hagan, Rep.	Cook
	Robert E. Wilson, Dem.	Cook
7	William H. Maclean, Rep.	Cook
	Louis J. Pierson, Rep.	Cook
	Walter A. Lantz, Dem.	Cook
8	A. K. Stearns, Rep.	Lake
	Edward D. Shurtleff, Rep.	McHenry
	Thomas F. Burns, Dem.	Boone
9	David E. Shanahan, Rep.	Cook
	Edward J. Murphy, Dem.	Cook
	Anton J. Cermak, Dem.	Cook
10	Johnson Lawrence, Rep.	Ogle
	Earl D. Reynolds, Rep.	Winnebago
	James H. Corcoran, Dem.	Winnebago
11	Henry D. Fulton, Dem.	Cook
	Chester W. Church, Rep.	Cook
	James J. O'Toole, Dem.	Cook
12	Stephen Rigney, Rep.	Stephenson
	William W. Gillespie, Rep.	Carroll
	Martin J. Dillon, Dem.	JoDaviess
13	Benton F. Kleeman, Rep.	Cook
	Cornelius J. Ton, Rep.	Cook
	John J. Poulton, Dem.	Cook
14	Arwin E. Price, Rep.	Kane
	Frank W. Shepherd, Rep.	Kane
	George W. Alschuler, Dem.	Kane
15	Thomas Curran, Rep.	Cook
	John O. Hruby, Jr., Dem.	Cook
	Edward J. Forst, Dem.	Cook
16	Josiah Kerrick, Rep.	Woodford
	Harrison T. Ireland, Rep.	Marshall
	Michael Fahy, Dem.	Marshall
17	Edward J. Smejkal, Rep.	Cook
	Emanuel M. Abrahams, Dem.	Cook
	Peter F. Galligan, Dem.	Cook
18	Charles F. Black, Rep.	Peoria
	Lucas I. Butts, Rep.	Peoria
	Thomas N. Gorman, Dem.	Peoria
19	James M. Kittleman, Rep.	Cook
	Charles A. Schumacher, Rep.	Cook
	John J. McLaughlin, Dem.	Cook
20	Israel Dudgeon, Rep.	Grundy
	George H. Hamilton, Rep.	Iroquois
	J. W. Allison, Dem.	Kankakee
21	William H. Troyer, Rep.	Cook
	Frederick E. Erickson, Rep.	Cook
	Thomas J. O'Brien, Dem.	Cook
22	William P. Holaday, Rep.	Vermilion
	J. Russ Grace, Rep.	Edgar
	George W. Myers, Dem.	Edgar
23	Christopher Beck, Rep.	Cook
	Charles Richter, Rep.	Cook
	Patrick F. Murray, Dem.	Cook
24	Charles Adkins, Rep.	Piatt
	Joseph Carter, Rep.	Champaign
	Homer E. Shaw, Rep.	Piatt
25	Lewis Hutzler, Rep.	Cook
	Charles L. Fieldstack, Rep.	Cook
	Frank J. Wilson, Dem.	Cook
26	John A. Montelius, Rep.	Ford
	William H. Wright, Rep.	McLean
	Daniel D. Donahue, Dem.	McLean
27	Albert Glade, Rep.	Cook
	John O'Neil, Dem.	Cook
	Joseph S. Geshkewich, Dem.	Cook
28	Edwin C. Perkins, Rep.	Logan
	John R. Robinson, Rep.	De Witt

District	Member	County
	Byron F. Staymates, Dem.	De Witt
29	Edward Hope, Rep.	Cook
	Charles A. Nelson, Rep.	Cook
	Patrick J. Sullivan, Dem.	Cook
30	Louis Zinger, Rep.	Tazewell
	Alrick Mann Foster, Dem.	Schuyler
	William M. Groves, Dem.	Menard
31	Matthew Mills, Rep.	Cook
	Charles E. Erby, Rep.	Cook
	John C. Werdell, Dem.	Cook
32	Henry Terrill, Rep.	McDonough
	Henry L. Jewell, Rep.	Warren
	John Huston, Dem.	McDonough
33	Thomas Campbell, Rep.	Rock Island
	Frank E. Abbey, Rep.	Henderson
	Henry L. Wheelan, Dem.	Rock Island
34	Carl S. Burgett, Rep.	Douglas
	William T. Hollenbeck, Rep.	Clark
	Polk B. Briscoe, Dem.	Clark
35	John H. Gray, Rep.	Whiteside
	Adam C. Cliffe, Rep.	De Kalb
	William A. Kannally, Dem.	Whiteside
36	George H. Wilson, Rep.	Adams
	Charles E. Bolin, Dem.	Pike
	Jacob Groves, Dem.	Adams
37	Francis J. Liggett, Rep.	Stark
	Clayton C. Pervier, Rep.	Bureau
	William J. McGuire, Dem.	Henry
38	William H. Behrens, Rep.	Macoupin
	Henry A. Shephard, Dem.	Jersey
	Louis P. Daley, Dem.	Macoupin
39	William M. Scanlan, Rep.	La Salle
	William R. Lewis, Rep.	La Salle
	Lee O'Neil Browne, Dem.	La Salle
40	Dell D. Brownback, Rep.	Shelby
	John C. Richardson, Dem.	Christian
	Joseph S. Clark, Dem.	Fayette
41	Guy L. Bush, Rep.	Du Page
	Frank L. Parker, Rep.	Will
	Thomas H. Riley, Dem.	Will
42	Charles L. McMackin, Rep.	Marion
	H. J. C. Beckemeyer, Dem.	Clinton
	Harvey D. McCollum, Dem.	Clay
43	Burnett M. Chiperfield, Rep.	Fulton
	Edward J. King, Rep.	Knox
	J. H. DeWolf, Dem.	Fulton
44	William Stevenson, Rep.	Randolph
	James M. Etherton, Dem.	Jackson
	Charles S. Luke, Dem.	Washington
45	Thomas E. Lyon, Rep.	Sangamon
	Harry W. Wilson, Rep.	Sangamon
	James F. Morris, Dem.	Sangamon
46	George B. Welborn, Rep.	Jefferson
	William C. Blair, Dem.	Jefferson
	Thomas Tippit, Dem.	Richland
47	J. G. Bardill, Rep.	Madison
	Norman G. Flagg, Rep.	Madison
	Michael S. Link, Dem.	Madison
48	John A. Logan, Rep.	Gallatin
	William E. Finley, Dem.	Lawrence
	Charles L. Scott, Dem.	Edwards
49	Fred Keck, Rep.	St. Clair
	John L. Flannigen, Rep.	St. Clair
	Charles A. White, Dem.	St. Clair
50	R. D. Kirkpatrick, Rep.	Franklin
	James W. Crawford, Rep.	Franklin
	Sidney B. Espy, Dem.	Franklin

District	Member	County
51	Lewis E. York, Rep.	Saline
	Charles Durfee, Rep.	Pope
	George W. English, Dem.	Johnson

[1] Died Jan. 13, 1909.
[2] Vice Zaabel.

Forty-seventh General Assembly, 1911–12

Senate

President	John G. Oglesby
President pro tempore	Henry M. Dunlap
Secretary	James H. Paddock

District	Member	County
1	Francis P. Brady, Rep.	Cook
2	Lewis C. Ball, Rep.	Cook
3	Samuel A. Ettleson, Rep.	Cook
4	Al F. Gorman, Dem.	Cook
5	Walter Clyde Jones, Rep.	Cook
6	William M. Brown, Rep.	Cook
7	William H. Maclean, Rep.	Cook
8	Albert J. Olson, Rep.	McHenry
9	Patrick J. Carroll, Dem.	Cook
10	Henry Andrus, Rep.	Winnebago
11	Carl Lundberg, Rep.	Cook
12	John C. McKenzie,[1] Rep.	JoDaviess
13	Albert C. Clark, Rep.	Cook
14	Thomas B. Stewart, Rep.	Kane
15	Edward J. Forst, Dem.	Cook
16	Ira M. Lish, Rep.	Livingston
17	Edward J. Glackin, Dem.	Cook
18	John Dailey, Rep.	Peoria
19	John T. Denvir, Dem.	Cook
20	Edward C. Curtis, Rep.	Kankakee
21	John E. Madigan, Dem.	Cook
22	Martin B. Bailey, Rep.	Vermilion
23	Niels Juul, Rep.	Cook
24	Henry M. Dunlap, Rep.	Champaign
25	John Waage, Dem.	Cook
26	Frank H. Funk, Rep.	McLean
27	John Broderick, Dem.	Cook
28	James A. Henson, Rep.	Macon
29	John M. O'Connor, Dem.	Cook
30	Walter I. Manny, Dem.	Brown
31	Willett H. Cornwell, Rep.	Cook
32	James F. Gibson, Dem.	Hancock
33	Frank A. Landee, Rep.	Rock Island
34	Stanton C. Pemberton, Rep.	Coles
35	John H. Gray, Rep.	Whiteside
36	Campbell S. Hearn, Dem.	Adams
37	H. S. Magill, Jr., Rep.	Bureau
38	Frank W. Burton, Dem.	Macoupin
39	Henry W. Johnson, Rep.	La Salle
40	F. Jeff Tossey, Dem.	Cumberland
41	Richard J. Barr, Rep.	Will
42	Daniel W. Holtslaw,[2] Dem.	Marion
	Erastus D. Telford,[3] Rep.	Marion
43	Charles F. Hurburgh, Rep.	Knox
44	Robert J. McElvain, Rep.	Jackson

District	Member	County
45	Logan Hay, Rep.	Sangamon
46	Albert E. Isley, Dem.	Jasper
47	Edmond Beall, Rep.	Madison
48	James A. Womack, Dem.	Gallatin
49	John M. Chamberlain, Jr., Rep.	St. Clair
50	W. O. Potter, Rep.	Williamson
51	Douglas W. Helm, Rep.	Massac

[1] Resigned May 11, 1911.
[2] Resigned Jan. 4, 1911.
[3] Elected April 4, 1911, vice Holtslaw.

House of Representatives

Speaker	Charles Adkins
Clerk	Bert H. McCann

District	Member	County
1	Noble B. Judah, Jr., Rep.	Cook
	Edward D. Green, Rep.	Cook
	John J. Griffin, Dem.	Cook
2	Roger J. Marcy, Rep.	Cook
	Frank J. McNichols, Rep.	Cook
	George L. McConnell, Dem.	Cook
3	William M. Ostrom, Rep.	Cook
	John P. Walsh, Dem.	Cook
	Patrick J. Wall, Dem.	Cook
4	John Hrubee, Rep.	Cook
	George C. Hilton, Dem.	Cook
	Hubert Kilens, Dem.	Cook
5	Morton D. Hull, Rep.	Cook
	William Tudor ApMadoc, Rep.	Cook
	Hiram T. Gilbert, Dem.	Cook
6	Richard P. Hagan, Rep.	Cook
	William E. Anderson, Rep.	Cook
	Robert E. Wilson, Dem.	Cook
7	Louis J. Pierson, Rep.	Cook
	Frederick B. Roos, Rep.	Cook
	J. J. O'Rourke, Dem.	Cook
8	Edward D. Shurtleff, Rep.	McHenry
	James H. Vickers, Rep.	McHenry
	Joseph E. Anderson, Proh.	Lake
9	David E. Shanahan, Rep.	Cook
	Edward J. Murphy, Dem.	Cook
	Rudolph Stocklasa, Dem.	Cook
10	John A. Atwood, Rep.	Ogle
	Alexander Collier, Rep.	Winnebago
	John Coleman, Dem.	Ogle
11	Chester W. Church, Rep.	Cook
	James J. O'Toole, Dem.	Cook
	Frank J. Ryan, Dem.	Cook
12	W. T. Rawleigh, Rep.	Stephenson
	Martin J. Dillon, Dem.	JoDaviess
	R. R. Thompson, Dem.	Stephenson
13	Benton F. Kleeman, Rep.	Cook
	John A. Swanson, Rep.	Cook
	Timothy Dunne, Dem.	Cook
14	Frank W. Shepherd, Rep.	Kane
	Frank R. Reid, Rep.	Kane
	George W. Alschuler, Dem.	Kane
15	Thomas Curran, Rep.	Cook
	John O. Hruby, Jr., Dem.	Cook
	Peter F. Smith, Dem.	Cook

District	Member	County
16	Josiah Kerrick, Rep.	Woodford
	Harrison T. Ireland, Rep.	Woodford
	Michael Fahy, Dem.	Marshall
17	Edward J. Smejkal, Rep.	Cook
	Tony Trimarco, Dem.	Cook
	Peter F. Galligan, Dem.	Cook
18	Lucas I. Butts, Rep.	Peoria
	Ira J. Covey, Rep.	Peoria
	Thomas N. Gorman, Dem.	Peoria
19	Joseph C. Blaha, Rep.	Cook
	John J. McLaughlin, Dem.	Cook
	Frank G. Smith, Ind.	Cook
20	Israel Dudgeon, Rep.	Grundy
	George H. Hamilton, Rep.	Iroquois
	Frank M. Crangle, Dem.	Iroquois
21	Frederick E. Erickson, Rep.	Cook
	Charles J. Burke, Rep.	Cook
	Benjamin M. Mitchell, Dem.	Cook
22	William P. Holaday, Rep.	Vermilion
	Isaac N. Cooley, Rep.	Edgar
	Andrew B. Dennis, Dem.	Vermilion
23	George A. Miller, Rep.	Cook
	Joseph P. Kinsella, Rep.	Cook
	Joseph Strauss, Dem.	Cook
24	Charles Adkins, Rep.	Piatt
	Joseph Carter, Rep.	Champaign
	W. E. Stedman, Dem.	Moultrie
25	Lewis Hutzler, Rep.	Cook
	Charles McParland, Dem.	Cook
	Frank C. Burke,[1] Dem.	Cook
	Thomas H. Donoghue,[2] Dem.	Cook
26	William H. Wright, Rep.	McLean
	John A. Montelius, Rep.	Ford
	Daniel D. Donahue, Dem.	McLean
27	Robert J. Collins, Dem.	Cook
	Daniel J. Sullivan, Dem.	Cook
	Joseph Pitlock, Dem.	Cook
28	Edwin C. Perkins, Rep.	Logan
	Thomas N. Leavitt, Rep.	Macon
	Cyrus J. Tucker, Dem.	Macon
29	James F. Burns, Rep.	Cook
	Bernard J. Conlon, Dem.	Cook
	Patrick J. Sullivan, Dem.	Cook
30	Homer J. Tice, Rep.	Menard
	Alrick Mann Foster, Dem.	Schuyler
	William M. Groves, Dem.	Menard
31	Harry L. Shaver, Rep.	Cook
	Franklin S. Catlin, Rep.	Cook
	John C. Werdell, Dem.	Cook
32	Henry Terrill, Rep.	McDonough
	Isaac M. Martin, Rep.	Hancock
	John Huston, Dem.	McDonough
33	Thomas Campbell, Rep.	Rock Isladn
	Frank E. Abbey, Rep.	Henderson
	Henry L. Wheelan, Dem.	Rock Island
34	D. B. Miller, Rep.	Clark
	William T. Hollenbeck, Rep.	Clark
	Edward F. Poorman, Dem.	Coles
35	Albert T. Tourtillott, Rep.	Lee
	Alfred N. Abbott, Rep.	Whiteside
	Burr S. Smiley, Ind.	De Kalb
36	George H. Wilson, Rep.	Adams
	William H. Hoffman, Dem.	Adams
	Charles E. Bolin, Dem.	Pike
37	Clayton C. Pervier, Rep.	Bureau
	John Robert Moore, Rep.	Henry
	William J. McGuire, Dem.	Henry

District	Member	County
38	S. Elmer Simpson, Rep.	Greene
	Louis P. Daley, Dem.	Macoupin
	Stephen D. Canaday, Dem.	Montgomery
39	William R. Lewis, Rep.	La Salle
	William M. Scanlan, Rep.	La Salle
	Lee O'Neil Browne, Dem.	La Salle
40	Walter M. Provine, Rep.	Christian
	John C. Richardson, Dem.	Christian
	William H. Harp, Dem.	Christian
41	James H. Alexander, Rep.	Will
	Richard Prendergast, Rep.	Du Page
	Bernard L. Keyll, Dem.	Will
42	Robert S. Jones, Rep.	Clay
	Fred J. Koch, Dem.	Clinton
	Walter E. Rinehart, Dem.	Effingham
43	Burnett M. Chiperfield, Rep.	Fulton
	Edward J. King, Rep.	Knox
	M. P. Rice, Dem.	Fulton
44	Dempsey Winthrop, Rep.	Perry
	William Stevenson, Rep.	Randolph
	James M. Etherton, Dem.	Jackson
45	Thomas E. Lyon, Rep.	Sangamon
	James F. Morris, Dem.	Sangamon
	James M. Bell, Dem.	Sangamon
46	George B. Welborn, Rep.	Jefferson
	John M. Rapp, Dem.	Wayne
	W. Duff Piercy, Dem.	Jefferson
47	Norman G. Flagg, Rep.	Madison
	J. G. Bardill, Rep.	Madison
	William Dickman, Dem.	Madison
48	James A. Watson, Rep.	Hardin
	Charles L. Scott, Dem.	Edwards
	William E. Finley, Dem.	Lawrence
49	John L. Flannigen, Rep.	St. Clair
	Alonzo A. Miller, Rep.	St. Clair
	Charles A. Karch, Rep.	St. Clair
50	Hall Whiteaker, Rep.	Pulaski
	R. D. Kirkpatrick, Rep.	Franklin
	Robert P. Hill, Dem.	Williamson
51	Elwood Barker, Rep.	Hamilton
	John P. Mathis, Rep.	Johnson
	George W. English, Dem.	Johnson

[1] Died Feb. 8, 1911.
[2] Elected April 15, 1911, vice Burke.

Forty-eighth General Assembly, 1913–14

Senate

President	Barratt O'Hara
President pro tempore	Walter J. Manny
Secretary	James H. Paddock

District	Member	County
1	Francis P. Brady, Rep.	Cook
2	Francis A. Hurley, Dem.	Cook
3	Samuel A. Ettelson, Rep.	Cook
4	Al F. Gorman, Dem.	Cook
5	Walter Clyde Jones, Prog.	Cook
6	George W. Harris, Prog.	Cook
7	William H. Maclean, Rep.	Cook
8	Albert J. Olson, Rep.	McHenry
9	Patrick J. Carroll, Dem.	Cook
10	Henry Andrus, Rep.	Winnebago
11	Carl Lundberg, Rep.	Cook

District	Member	County
12	Michael H. Cleary, Dem.	JoDaviess
13	Albert C. Clark, Rep.	Cook
14	Thomas B. Stewart, Rep.	Kane
15	Edward J. Forst, Dem.	Cook
16	Christian Haase, Dem.	Woodford
17	Edward J. Glackin, Dem.	Cook
18	John Dailey, Rep.	Peoria
19	John T. Denvir, Dem.	Cook
20	Edward C. Curtis, Rep.	Kanakakee
21	John E. Madigan, Dem.	Cook
22	Martin B. Bailey, Rep.	Vermilion
23	Niels Juul, Rep.	Cook
24	Raymond D. Meeker, Dem.	Moultrie
25	John Waage, Dem.	Cook
26	Noah Elmo Franklin, Rep.	McLean
27	John Broderick, Dem.	Cook
28	Willis R. Shaw, Dem.	Macon
29	John M. O'Connor, Dem.	Cook
30	Walter I. Manny, Dem.	Brown
31	Willett H. Cornwell, Rep.	Cook
32	William A. Compton, Dem.	McDonough
33	Frank A. Landee, Rep.	Rock Island
34	John R. Hamilton, Rep.	Coles
35	John H. Gray, Rep.	Whiteside
36	Campbell S. Hearn, Dem.	Adams
37	H. S. Magill, Jr., Rep.	Bureau
38	Stephen D. Canaday, Dem.	Montgomery
39	Henry W. Johnson, Rep.	La Salle
40	F. Jeff Tossey, Dem.	Cumberland
41	Richard J. Barr, Rep.	Will
42	F. C. Campbell, Dem.	Clay
43	Charles F. Hurburgh, Rep.	Knox
44	Kent E. Keller, Dem.	Jackson
45	Logan Hay, Rep.	Sangamon
46	W. Duff Piercy, Dem.	Jefferson
47	Edmond Beall, Rep.	Madison
48	James A. Womack, Dem.	Gallatin
49	John M. Chamberlain, Jr., Rep.	St. Clair
50	D. T. Woodard, Dem.	Franklin
51	Douglas W. Helm, Rep.	Massac

House of Representatives

Speaker	William McKinley
Clerk	Bert H. McCann

District	Member	County
1	Maurice J. Clarke, Rep.	Cook
	John J. Griffin, Dem.	Cook
	John H. Taylor, Prog.	Cook
2	Frank J. McNichols, Rep.	Cook
	John F. McCarty, Dem.	Cook
	Frank J. Snite, Prog.	Cook
3	John P. Walsh, Dem.	Cook
	Henry M. Ashton,[1] Dem.	Cook
	Robert R. Jackson,[2] Rep.	Cook
	F. E. Lloyd, Prog.	Cook
4	Thomas A. Boyer, Rep.	Cook
	George C. Hilton, Dem.	Cook
	Hubert Kilens, Dem.	Cook
5	Isaac S. Rothschild, Rep.	Cook
	Morton D. Hull, Rep.	Cook
	Michael L. Igoe, Dem.	Cook

District	Member	County
6	Robert E. Wilson, Dem.	Cook
	Joseph A. Weber, Dem.	Cook
	Charles S. Graves, Prog.	Cook
7	Frederick B. Roos, Rep.	Cook
	J. J. O'Rourke, Dem.	Cook
	John M. Curran, Prog.	Cook
8	Edward D. Shurtleff, Rep.	McHenry
	Thomas E. Graham, Dem.	Lake
	Fayette S. Munro, Prog.	Lake
9	David E. Shanahan, Rep.	Cook
	Rudolph Stocklasa, Dem.	Cook
	Robert J. Mulcahy, Dem.	Cook
10	John A. Atwood, Rep.	Ogle
	Andrew J. Lovejoy, Rep.	Winnebago
	John Coleman, Dem.	Ogle
11	Frank J. Ryan, Dem.	Cook
	Henry F. Schuberth, Dem.	Cook
	Robson Barron, Prog.	Cook
12	Martin J. Dillon, Dem.	JoDaviess
	R. R. Thompson, Dem.	Stephenson
	Thomas H. Hollister, Prog.	Stephenson
13	Benton F. Kleeman, Rep.	Cook
	Seymour Stedman, Soc.	Cook
	Elmer J. Snackenberg, Prog.	Cook
14	Frank W. Shepherd, Rep.	Kane
	Charles F. Clyne, Dem.	Kane
	Henry B. Fargo, Prog.	Kane
15	Thomas Curran, Rep.	Cook
	Peter F. Smith, Dem.	Cook
	Joseph O. Hruby, Dem.	Cook
16	Michael Fahy, Dem.	Marshall
	Henry A. Foster, Dem.	Livingston
	Charles H. Carmon, Prog.	Livingston
17	Edward J. Smejkal, Rep.	Cook
	Tony Trimarco, Dem.	Cook
	John S. Burns, Dem.	Cook
18	Lucas I. Butts, Rep.	Peoria
	Thomas N. Gorman, Dem.	Peoria
	George Fitch, Prog.	Peoria
19	Joseph C. Blaha, Rep.	Cook
	John J. McLaughlin, Dem.	Cook
	Richard E. Sherman, Prog.	Cook
20	Israel Dudgeon, Rep.	Grundy
	Daniel O'Connell, Dem.	Grundy
	William H. Dunn, Dem.	Kankakee
21	Benjamin M. Mitchell, Dem.	Cook
	H. W. Harris,[3] Soc.	Cook
	Edwin T. Farrar,[4] Rep.	Cook
	John Grunau, Prog.	Cook
22	William P. Holaday, Rep.	Vermilion
	George W. Myers, Dem.	Edgar
	Charles W. Fleming, Prog.	Vermilion
23	George A. Miller, Rep.	Cook
	Christian M. Madsen, Soc.	Cook
	Emil N. Zolla, Prog.	Cook
24	William F. Burres, Rep.	Champaign
	Francis E. Williamson, Dem.	Champaign
	Joseph Carter, Prog.	Champaign
25	Charles G. Hutchinson, Rep.	Cook
	Edward J. Costello, Dem.	Cook
	Joseph M. Mason, Soc.	Cook
26	William Rowe, Rep.	McLean
	Frank Gillespie, Prog.	McLean

District	Member	County
	Abraham C. Thompson, Prog.	Ford
27	Albert Rostenkowski, Rep.	Cook
	Joseph Pitlock, Dem.	Cook
	James M. Donlan, Dem.	Cook
28	William McGinley, Rep.	Macon
	Cyrus J. Tucker, Dem.	Macon
	William W. McCormick, Dem.	Logan
29	Patrick J. Sullivan, Dem.	Cook
	James H. Farrell, Dem.	Cook
	Medill McCormick, Prog.	Cook
30	Homer J. Tice, Rep.	Menard
	Alrick Mann Foster, Dem.	Schuyler
	William M. Groves, Dem.	Menard
31	Franklin S. Catlin, Rep.	Cook
	Harry L. Shaver, Rep.	Cook
	William McKinley, Dem.	Cook
32	John Huston, Dem.	McDonough
	Robert A. Elliott, Dem.	Warren
	J. H. Jayne, Prog.	Warren
33	Thomas Campbell, Rep.	Rock Island
	Everett L. Werts, Dem.	Henderson
	William Hartquist, Prog.	Henderson
34	William T. Hollenbeck, Rep.	Clark
	Polk B. Briscoe, Dem.	Clark
	Edward F. Poorman, Dem.	Coles
35	Alfred N. Abbott, Rep.	Whiteside
	John P. Devine, Dem.	Lee
	Roy D. Hunt, Prog.	De Kalb
36	George H. Wilson, Rep.	Adams
	William H. Hoffman, Dem.	Adams
	Edwin T. Strubinger, Dem.	Pike
37	Randolph Boyd, Rep.	Henry
	Clayton C. Pervier, Rep.	Bureau
	Frank W. Morrasy, Dem.	Bureau
38	S. Elmer Simpson, Rep.	Greene
	William A. Hubbard, Dem.	Greene
	Henry A. Shephard, Dem.	Jersey
39	Ole E. Benson, Rep.	La Salle
	William M. Scanlan, Rep.	La Salle
	Lee O'Neil Browne, Dem.	La Salle
40	Walter M. Provine, Rep.	Christian
	Arthur Roe, Dem.	Fayette
	John C. Richardson, Dem.	Christian
41	James H. Alexander,[5] Rep.	Will
	Michael F. Hennebry,[6] Dem.	Will
	George B. Boardman,[7] Prog.	Will
	William R. McCabe, Rep.	Will
	Ezra E. Miller, Prog.	Du Page
42	Robert S. Jones, Rep.	Clay
	Walter E. Rinehart, Dem.	Effingham
	Fred J. Koch, Dem.	Clinton
43	Edward J. King, Rep.	Knox
	E. W. Duvall, Dem.	Fulton
	William B. Elliott, Prog.	Knox
44	Judson E. Harris, Rep.	Perry
	James M. Etherton, Dem.	Jackson
	A. H. Cohlmeyer, Dem.	Washington
45	Thomas E. Lyon, Rep.	Sangamon
	James F. Morris, Dem.	Sangamon
	James M. Bell, Dem.	Sangamon
46	Charles L. Wood, Rep.	Wayne
	John M. Rapp, Dem.	Wayne
	John Kasserman, Dem.	Jasper
47	Norman G. Flagg, Rep.	Madison
	Ferdinand A. Garesche, Dem.	Madison
	William Dickman, Dem.	Madison
48	James A. Watson, Rep.	Hardin

District	Member	County
	Charles L. Scott, Dem.	Edwards
	William E. Finley, Dem.	Lawrence
49	Fred Keck, Rep.	St. Clair
	Charles A. Karch, Dem.	St. Clair
	Lewis S. McWilliams, Dem.	St Clair
50	Charles Curren, Rep.	Pulaski
	R. D. Kirkpatrick, Rep.	Franklin
	George W. Crawford, Dem.	Union
51	George B. Baker, Rep.	Pope
	Elwood Barker, Rep.	Hamilton
	W. C. Kane, Dem.	Saline

¹ Seat contested.
² Seated vice Ashton.
³ Seat contested.
⁴ Seated vice Harris.
⁵ Died Dec. 13, 1912.
⁶ Elected to fill vacancy; seat contested.
⁷ Seated vice Hennebry.

District	Member	County
36	Charles R. McNay, Dem.	Adams
37	Clayton C. Pervier, Rep.	Bureau
38	Stephen D. Canaday, Dem.	Montgomery
39	Peter E. Coleman, Dem.	La Salle
40	F. Jeff Tossey, Dem.	Cumberland
41	Richard J. Barr, Rep.	Will
42	F. C. Campbell, Dem.	Clay
43	William S. Jewell, Rep.	Fulton
44	Kent E. Keller, Dem.	Jackson
45	Elbert S. Smith, Rep.	Sangamon
46	W. Duff Piercy, Dem.	Jefferson
47	J. G. Bardill, Rep.	Madison
48	James A. Womack, Dem.	Gallatin
49	Paul W. Abt, Rep.	St. Clair
50	D. T. Woodard, Dem.	Franklin
51	Sam W. Latham, Rep.	Saline

Forty-ninth General Assembly, 1915-16

Senate

President Barratt O'Hara
President pro tempore
    Stephen D. Canaday
Secretary A. A. Eden

District	Member	County
1	George F. Harding, Jr., Rep.	Cook
2	Francis A. Hurley, Dem.	Cook
3	Samuel A. Ettelson, Rep.	Cook
4	Al F. Gorman, Dem.	Cook
5	Morton D. Hull, Rep.	Cook
6	George W. Harris, Prog.	Cook
7	Frederick B. Roos, Rep.	Cook
8	Albert J. Olson, Rep.	McHenry
9	Patrick J. Carroll, Dem.	Cook
10	Henry Andrus, Rep.	Winnebago
11	Percival G. Baldwin, Rep.	Cook
12	Michael H. Cleary, Dem.	JoDaviess
13	John A. Swanson, Rep.	Cook
14	Thomas B. Stewart, Rep.	Kane
15	John J. Boehm, Dem.	Cook
16	Christian Haase, Dem.	Woodford
17	Edward J. Glackin, Dem.	Cook
18	John Dailey, Rep.	Peoria
19	John T. Denvir, Dem.	Cook
20	Edward C. Curtis, Rep.	Kankakee
21	Edward J. Hughes, Dem.	Cook
22	Martin B. Bailey, Rep.	Vermilion
23	Henry W. Austin, Rep.	Cook
24	Raymond D. Meeker, Dem.	Moultrie
25	Daniel Herlihy, Dem.	Cook
26	Noah Elmo Franklin, Rep.	McLean
27	John Broderick, Dem.	Cook
28	Willis R. Shaw, Dem.	Macon
29	Patrick J. Sullivan, Dem.	Cook
30	Walter I. Manny, Dem.	Brown
31	Willett H. Cornwell, Rep.	Cook
32	William A. Compton, Dem.	McDonough
33	Frank A. Landee, Rep.	Rock Island
34	John R. Hamilton, Rep.	Coles
35	Adam C. Cliffe, Rep.	De Kalb

House of Representatives

Speaker David E. Shanahan
Clerk Bert H. McCann

District	Member	County
1	John J. Griffin, Dem.	Cook
	William M. Brinkman, Rep.	Cook
	Shadrick B. Turner, Rep.	Cook
2	George U. Lipshulch, Dem.	Cook
	Frank Ryan, Dem.	Cook
	John J. Gardner, Rep.	Cook
3	John P. Walsh, Dem.	Cook
	Edward M. Santry, Dem.	Cook
	Robert R. Jackson, Rep.	Cook
4	George C. Hilton, Dem.	Cook
	Hubert Kilens, Dem.	Cook
	Thomas A. Boyer, Rep.	Cook
5	Michael L. Igoe, Dem.	Cook
	Isaac S. Rothschild, Rep.	Cook
	John H. Helwig, Rep.	Cook
6	Joseph A. Weber, Dem.	Cook
	Robert E. Wilson, Dem.	Cook
	William M. Brown, Rep.	Cook
7	Louis J. Pierson, Rep.	Cook
	Frederic R. DeYoung, Rep.	Cook
	J. J. O'Rourke, Dem.	Cook
8	Thomas E. Graham, Dem.	Lake
	Edward D. Shurtleff, Rep.	McHenry
	James H. Vickers, Rep.	McHenry
9	Robert J. Mulcahy, Dem.	Cook
	Joseph Placek, Dem.	Cook
	David E. Shanahan, Rep.	Cook
10	Herbert S. Hicks, Ind.	Winnebago
	John A. Atwood, Rep.	Ogle
	Emil A. Festerling, Rep.	Winnebago
11	Frank J. Ryan, Dem.	Cook
	Henry F. Schuberth, Dem.	Cook
	John H. Lyle, Rep.	Cook
12	Charles D. Franz, Dem.	Stephenson
	R. R. Thompson, Dem.	Stephenson
	John D. Turnbaugh, Rep.	Carroll
13	James W. Ryan, Dem.	Cook
	Gotthard A. Dahlberg, Rep.	Cook
	C. A. Young, Rep.	Cook

District	Member	County
14	Frank R. Dalton, Dem.	Kane
	DeGoy B. Ellis, Rep.	Kane
	Harold C. Kessinger, Rep.	Kane
15	Joseph O. Hruby, Dem.	Cook
	Peter F. Smith, Dem.	Cook
	Thomas Curran. Rep.	Cook
16	Michael Fahy, Dem.	Marshall
	Simon E. Lantz, Rep.	Woodford
	William H. Bentley, Rep.	Livingston
17	John S. Burns, Dem.	Cook
	Jacob W. Epstein, Dem.	Cook
	Edward J. Smejkal, Rep.	Cook
18	Thomas N. Gorman, Dem.	Peoria
	Robert Scholes Rep.	Peoria
	John F. Lynch, Rep.	Peoria
19	James T. Prendergast, Dem.	Cook
	James C. McGloon, Dem.	Cook
	Solomon P. Roderick, Rep.	Cook
20	Daniel O'Connell, Dem.	Grundy
	Richard R. Meents, Rep.	Iroquois
	Israel Dudgeon, Rep.	Grundy
21	Benjamin M. Mitchell, Dem.	Cook
	Frederick J. Bippus, Rep.	Cook
	Thomas P. Devereux, Rep.	Cook
22	G. A. Ray, Dem.	Vermilion
	William P. Holaday, Rep.	Vermilion
	Abraham L. Stanfield, Rep.	Edgar
23	George R. Bruce, Dem.	Cook
	William G. Thon, Rep.	Cook
	Christian M. Madsen, Soc.	Cook
24	Francis E. Williamson, Dem.	Champaign
	William F. Burres, Rep.	Champaign
	Charles A. Gregory, Rep.	Moultrie
25	John G. Jacobson, Dem.	Cook
	Charles L. Fieldstack, Rep.	Cook
	Joseph M. Mason, Soc.	Cook
26	Daniel D. Donahue, Dem.	McLean
	William Rowe, Rep.	McLean
	James C. Harvey, Rep.	McLean
27	Joseph A. Trandel, Dem.	Cook
	James M. Donlan, Dem.	Cook
	Albert Rostenkowski, Rep.	Cook
28	Clifford Quisenberry, Dem.	Logan
	Edwin C. Perkins, Rep.	Logan
	T. C. Buxton, Rep.	Macon
29	James H. Farrell, Dem.	Cook
	Bernard J. Conlon, Dem.	Cook
	Medill McCormick, Prog.	Cook
30	Alrick Mann Foster, Dem.	Schuyler
	William M. Groves, Dem.	Menard
	Homer J. Tice, Rep.	Menard
31	Frank J. Seif, Jr., Dem.	Cook
	Harry F. Hamlin, Rep.	Cook
	E. I. Frankhauser, Rep.	Cook
32	John Huston, Dem.	McDonough
	Robert A. Elliott, Dem.	Warren
	James M. Pace, Rep.	McDonough
33	William C. Maucker, Dem.	Rock Island
	Thomas Campbell, Rep.	Rock Island
	William J. Graham, Rep.	Mercer
34	C. A. Purdunn, Dem.	Clark
	Harry W. Drake, Rep.	Clark
	E. Walter Green, Rep.	Douglas

District	Member	County
35	John P. Devine, Dem.	Lee
	William L. Leech, Rep.	Lee
	Frederick A. Brewer, Rep.	Whiteside
36	William H. Hoffman, Dem.	Adams
	Edwin T. Strubinger, Dem.	Pike
	George H. Wilson, Rep.	Adams
37	Frank W. Morrasy, Dem.	Bureau
	Randolph Boyd, Rep.	Henry
	John Robert Moore, Rep.	Henry
38	William A. Hubbard, Dem.	Greene
	Henry A. Shephard, Dem.	Jersey
	Otto C. Sonnemann, Rep.	Macoupin
39	Lee O'Neil Browne, Dem.	La Salle
	Ole E. Benson, Rep.	La Salle
	William M. Scanlan, Rep.	La Salle
40	Arthur Roe, Dem.	Fayette
	John C. Richardson, Dem.	Christian
	Walter M. Provine, Rep.	Christian
41	Michael F. Hennebry, Dem.	Will
	William R. McCabe, Rep.	Will
	Squire F. Tompkins, Rep.	Will
42	Walter E. Rinehart, Dem.	Effingham
	John W. Thomason, Dem.	Clay
	Charles W. Vursell, Rep.	Marion
43	William H. Basel, Dem.	Fulton
	Owen B. West, Rep.	Knox
	James E. Davis, Rep.	Knox
44	W. T. Morris, Dem.	Perry
	Harry Wilson, Rep.	Perry
	Hawkins O. Murphy, Rep.	Perry
45	Edward L. Merritt, Dem.	Sangamon
	William J. Butler, Rep.	Sangamon
	Thomas E. Lyon, Rep.	Sangamon
46	John Kasserman, Dem.	Jasper
	John L. Cooper, Dem.	Wayne
	Charles L. Wood, Rep.	Wayne
47	Ferdinand A. Garesche, Dem.	Madison
	Norman G. Flagg, Rep.	Madison
	Chris Rethmeier, Rep.	Madison
48	Carl Green, Dem.	Crawford
	Richard F. Taylor, Dem.	Hardin
	James A. Watson, Rep.	Hardin
49	John T. Desmond, Dem.	St. Clair
	Stephen T. LePage, Rep.	St. Clair
	James W. Rentchler, Rep.	St. Clair
50	James H. Felts, Dem.	Williamson
	Charles Curren, Rep.	Pulaski
	C. A. Stewart, Rep.	Franklin
51	W. C. Kane, Dem.	Saline
	Elwood Barker, Rep.	Hamilton
	Oral P. Tuttle, Rep.	Saline

Fiftieth General Assembly, 1917–18

Senate

President	John G. Oglesby
President pro tempore	Adam C. Cliffe
Secretary	James H. Paddock

District	Member	County
1	George F. Harding, Jr., Rep.	Cook
2	John M. Powell, Rep.	Cook
3	Samuel A. Ettelson, Rep.	Cook
4	Al F. Gorman, Dem.	Cook
5	Morton D. Hull, Rep.	Cook
6	James J. Barbour, Rep.	Cook

District	Member	County
7	Frederick B. Roos. Rep.	Cook
8	Rodney B. Swift, Rep.	Lake
9	Patrick J. Carroll. Dem.	Cook
10	John A. Atwood, Rep.	Ogle
11	Percival G. Baldwin, Rep.	Cook
12	John D. Turnbaugh, Rep.	Carroll
13	John A. Swanson,[1] Rep.	Cook
	Albert C. Clark,[2] Rep.	Cook
14	Harold C. Kessinger, Rep.	Kane
15	John J. Boehm, Dem.	Cook
16	Simon E. Lantz, Rep.	Woodford
17	Edward J. Glackin, Dem.	Cook
18	John Dailey, Rep.	Peoria
19	John T. Denvir, Dem.	Cook
20	Edward C. Curtis, Rep.	Kankakee
21	Edward J. Hughes, Dem.	Cook
22	Martin B. Bailey, Rep.	Vermilion
23	Henry W. Austin, Rep.	Cook
24	Henry M. Dunlap, Rep.	Champaign
25	Daniel Herlihy, Dem.	Cook
26	William H. Wright, Rep.	McLean
27	John Broderick, Dem.	Cook
28	William G. McCullough, Dem.	Macon
29	Patrick J. Sullivan, Dem.	Cook
30	Walter I. Manny, Dem.	Brown
31	Willett H. Cornwell, Rep.	Cook
32	Clarence F. Buck, Rep.	Warren
33	Frank A. Landee,[3] Rep.	Rock Island
34	John R. Hamilton, Rep.	Coles
35	Adam C. Cliffe, Rep.	De Kalb
36	Charles R. McNay, Dem.	Adams
37	Clayton C. Pervier, Rep.	Bureau
38	Stephen D. Canaday, Dem.	Montgomery
39	Peter E. Coleman, Dem.	La Salle
40	Frank B. Wendling, Dem.	Shelby
41	Richard J. Barr, Rep.	Will
42	F. C. Campbell, Dem.	Clay
43	William S. Jewell, Rep.	Fulton
44	Frank M. Hewitt, Rep.	Randolph
45	Elbert S. Smith,[4] Rep.	Sangamon
46	Charles L. Wood, Rep.	Wayne
47	J. G. Bardill, Rep.	Madison
48	Raleigh M. Shaw, Dem.	Lawrence
49	Paul W. Abt, Rep.	St. Clair
50	Sidney B. Miller, Rep.	Alexander
51	Sam W. Latham, Rep.	Saline

[1] Resigned.
[2] Vice Swanson April 10, 1917.
[3] Died March 23, 1917.
[4] Resigned to accept judgeship.

House of Representatives

Speaker   David E. Shanahan
Clerk   Bert H. McCann

District	Member	County
1	John J. Griffin, Dem.	Cook
	William M. Brinkman, Rep.	Cook
	Benjamin H. Lucas, Rep.	Cook
2	Randall E. Marshall, Dem.	Cook
	Roger J. Marcy, Rep.	Cook
	Frank Ryan, Dem.	Cook
3	John P. Walsh, Dem.	Cook
	Robert R. Jackson, Rep.	Cook
	Herman E. Schultz, Rep.	Cook
4	Timothy D. Murphy, Dem.	Cook

District	Member	County
	Hubert Kilens, Dem.	Cook
	Thomas A. Boyer, Rep.	Cook
5	Michael L. Igoe, Dem.	Cook
	Guy Guernsey, Rep.	Cook
	Sidney Lyon, Rep.	Cook
6	Joseph A. Weber, Dem.	Cook
	Allan J. Carter, Rep.	Cook
	Ralph E. Church, Rep.	Cook
7	John W. McCarthy, Dem.	Cook
	Frederic R. DeYoung, Rep.	Cook
	Albert F. Volz, Rep.	Cook
8	Thomas E. Graham, Dem.	Lake
	James H. Vickers, Rep.	McHenry
	Edward D. Shurtleff, Rep.	McHenry
9	Robert J. Mulcahy, Dem.	Cook
	Joseph Placek, Dem.	Cook
	David E. Shanahan, Rep.	Cook
10	Charles W. Baker, Rep.	Ogle
	Emil A. Festerling, Rep.	Winnebago
	Herbert S. Hicks, Ind.	Winnebago
11	Henry F. Schuberth, Dem.	Cook
	John H. Lyle, Rep.	Cook
	Alfred Van Dusen, Rep.	Cook
12	Charles D. Franz, Dem.	Stephenson
	Robert Irwin, Rep.	Carroll
	Joseph L. Meyers, Rep.	Stephenson
13	James W. Ryan, Dem.	Cook
	Gotthard A. Dahlberg, Rep.	Cook
	C. A. Young, Rep.	Cook
14	R. A. Milroy, Dem.	Kane
	William J. Tyers, Rep.	Kane
	DeGoy B. Ellis, Rep.	Kane
15	Peter F. Smith, Dem.	Cook
	Joseph O. Hruby, Dem.	Cook
	Thomas Curran, Rep.	Cook
16	Michael Fahy, Dem.	Marshall
	Charles H. Carmon, Rep.	Livingston
	Charles M. Turner, Rep.	Marshall
17	Jacob W. Epstein, Dem.	Cook
	John S. Burns, Dem.	Cook
	Edward J. Smejkal, Rep.	Cook
18	Thomas N. Gorman, Dem.	Peoria
	John F. Lynch, Rep.	Peoria
	James D. Putnam,[1] Rep.	Peoria
	Shelton P. McGrath,[2] Rep.	Peoria
19	James T. Prendergast, Dem.	Cook
	James C. McGloon, Dem.	Cook
	Solomon P. Roderick, Rep.	Cook
20	Daniel O'Connell, Dem.	Grundy
	Israel Dudgeon, Rep.	Grundy
	Richard R. Meents, Rep.	Iroquois
21	Michael F. Maher, Dem.	Cook
	Thomas P. Devereux, Rep.	Cook
	Frederick J. Bippus, Rep.	Cook
22	P. J. Breen, Dem.	Edgar
	Abraham L. Stanfield, Rep.	Edgar
	William P. Holaday, Rep.	Vermilion
23	George R. Bruce, Rep.	Cook
	William G. Thon, Rep.	Cook
	Edward M. Overland, Rep.	Cook
24	Fred H. Cole, Dem.	Piatt
	William H. H. Miller, Rep.	Champaign
	Charles A. Gregory, Rep.	Moultrie

District	Member	County
25	John G. Jacobson, Dem.	Cook
	Frank P. Caviezel, Rep.	Cook
	Charles L. Fieldstack, Rep.	Cook
26	Daniel D. Donahue, Dem.	McLean
	William Rowe, Rep.	McLean
	W. A. Cameron, Rep.	Ford
27	Joseph A. Trandel, Dem.	Cook
	Joseph Petlak, Dem.	Cook
	Edward Walz, Rep.	Cook
28	Horace W. McDavid, Dem.	Macon
	Peter Murphy, Dem.	Logan
	Edwin C. Perkins, Rep.	Logan
29	Bernard J. Conlon, Dem.	Cook
	Lawrence C. O'Brien, Dem.	Cook
	Bernard F. Clettenberg, Rep.	Cook
30	William H. Dieterich, Dem.	Cass
	James H. Kirby, Dem.	Menard
	Elmer O. Neef, Rep.	Tazewell
31	Frank J. Seif, Jr., Dem.	Cook
	Carl Mueller, Rep.	Cook
	Harry F. Hamlin, Rep.	Cook
32	Ernest O. Reaugh, Dem.	Hancock
	James M. Pace, Rep.	McDonough
	Rollo R. Robbins, Rep.	Hancock
33	William C. Maucker, Dem.	Rock Island
	Frank E. Abbey, Rep.	Henderson
	James A. Wells, Rep.	Mercer
34	Robert Howard, Dem.	Coles
	E. Walter Green, Rep.	Douglas
	Harry W. Drake, Rep.	Clark
35	John P. Devine, Dem.	Lee
	Frederick A. Brewer, Rep.	Whiteside
	George L. Carpenter, Rep.	Lee
36	Edwin T. Strubinger, Dem.	Pike
	Rolland M. Wagner, Dem.	Adams
	Samuel H. Thompson, Rep.	Adams
37	Frank W. Morrasy, Dem.	Bureau
	Randolph Boyd, Rep.	Henry
	John W. Walters, Rep.	Stark
38	Henry A. Shephard, Dem.	Jersey
	Truman A. Snell, Dem.	Macoupin
	Otto C. Sonnemann, Rep.	Macoupin
39	Lee O'Neil Browne, Dem.	La Salle
	Ole E. Benson, Rep.	La Salle
	William M. Scanlan, Rep.	La Salle
40	Arthur Roe, Dem.	Fayette
	John J. Bullington, Dem.	Christian
	Lincoln Bancroft, Rep.	Cumberland
41	Michael F. Hennebry, Dem.	Will
	James R. Bentley, Rep.	Will
	William R. McCabe, Rep.	Will
42	John W. Thomason, Dem.	Clay
	Alois B. Lager, Dem.	Clinton
	Charles L. McMackin, Rep.	Marion
43	Patrick W. Gallagher, Dem.	Fulton
	Owen B. West, Rep.	Knox
	James E. Davis, Rep.	Knox
44	James M. Etherton, Dem.	Jackson
	William C. Fridrichs, Rep.	Monroe
	Harry Wilson, Rep.	Perry
45	Clarence A. Jones, Dem.	Sangamon
	Jacob Frisch, Rep.	Sangamon
	Thomas E. Lyon, Rep.	Sangamon

District	Member	County
46	John Kasserman, Dem.	Jasper
	John L. Cooper, Dem.	Wayne
	Frank Vice, Jr., Rep.	Richland
47	Ferdinand A. Garesche, Dem.	Madison
	Norman G. Flagg, Rep.	Madison
	Chris Rethmeier, Rep.	Madison
48	Carl Green, Dem.	Crawford
	Rene Havill, Dem.	Wabash
	James A. Watson, Rep.	Hardin
49	John T. Desmond, Dem.	St. Clair
	Frank Holten, Dem.	St. Clair
	James W. Rentchler, Rep.	St. Clair
50	James H. Felts, Dem.	Williamson
	Charles Curren, Rep.	Pulaski
	Ernest J. Odum, Rep.	Franklin
51	Austin Hill, Dem.	Hamilton
	Oral P. Tuttle, Rep.	Saline
	Claude F. Lacey, Rep.	Massac

[1] Died Feb. 13, 1917.
[2] Vice Putnam May 11, 1917.

Fifty-first General Assembly, 1919–20

Senate

President	John G. Oglesby
President pro tempore	Adam C. Cliffe
Secretary	James H. Paddock

District	Member	County
1	Francis P. Brady, Rep.	Cook
2	John M. Powell, Dem.	Cook
3	Samuel A. Ettelson, Rep.	Cook
4	Al F. Gorman, Dem.	Cook
5	Morton D. Hull, Rep.	Cook
6	James J. Barbour, Rep.	Cook
7	Frederick B. Roos, Rep.	Cook
8	Rodney B. Swift, Rep.	Lake
9	Patrick J. Carroll, Dem.	Cook
10	John A. Atwood, Rep.	Ogle
11	Frank P. Sadler, Rep.	Cook
12	John D. Turnbaugh, Rep.	Carroll
13	Albert C. Clark, Rep.	Cook
14	Harold C. Kessinger, Rep.	Kane
15	John J. Boehm, Dem.	Cook
16	Simon E. Lantz, Rep.	Woodford
17	Edward J. Glackin, Dem.	Cook
18	John Dailey, Rep.	Peoria
19	John T. Denvir, Dem.	Cook
20	Edward C. Curtis, Rep.	Kankakee
21	Edward J. Hughes, Dem.	Cook
22	Martin B. Bailey, Rep.	Vermilion
23	Henry W. Austin, Rep.	Cook
24	Henry M. Dunlap, Rep.	Champaign
25	Daniel Herlihy, Dem.	Cook
26	William H. Wright, Rep.	McLean
27	John Broderick, Dem.	Cook
28	William G. McCullough, Dem.	Macon
29	Patrick J. Sullivan, Dem.	Cook
30	Walter I. Manny, Dem.	Brown
31	Willett H. Cornwell, Rep.	Cook
32	Clarence F. Buck, Rep.	Warren
33	Martin R. Carlson. Rep.	Rock Island
34	John R. Hamilton, Rep.	Coles

District	Member	County
35	Adam C. Cliffe, Rep.	De Kalb
36	Charles R. McNay, Dem.	Adams
37	Clayton C. Pervier, Rep.	Bureau
38	Stephen D. Canaday, Dem.	Montgomery
39	Thurlow G. Essington, Rep.	La Salle
40	Frank B. Wendling, Dem.	Shelby
41	Richard J. Barr, Rep.	Will
42	F. C. Campbell, Dem.	Clay
43	William S. Jewell, Rep.	Fulton
44	Frank M. Hewitt, Rep.	Jackson
45	John A. Wheeler, Rep.	Sangamon
46	Charles L. Wood, Rep.	Wayne
47	J. G. Bardill, Rep.	Madison
48	Raleigh M. Shaw, Dem.	Lawrence
49	R. E. Duvall, Rep.	St. Clair
50	Sidney B. Miller,[1] Rep.	Alexander
51	W. A. Spence, Rep.	Massac

[1] Died Feb. 16, 1919.

House of Representatives

Speaker   David E. Shanahan
Clerk   Bert H. McCann

District	Member	County
1	William M. Brinkman, Rep.	Cook
	Shadrick B. Turner, Rep.	Cook
	John J. Griffin, Dem.	Cook
2	Roger J. Marcy, Rep.	Cook
	Frank Ryan, Dem.	Cook
	Samuel E. Weinshenker, Dem.	Cook
3	Warren B. Douglas, Rep.	Cook
	Adelbert H. Roberts, Rep.	Cook
	George Gary Noonan, Dem	Cook
4	Emil O. Kowalski, Rep.	Cook
	James P. Boyle, Dem.	Cook
	Frank J. McDermott, Dem.	Cook
5	Theodore K. Long, Rep.	Cook
	Sidney Lyon, Rep.	Cook
	Michael L. Igoe, Dem.	Cook
6	Ralph E. Church, Rep.	Cook
	Emil A. W. Johnson, Rep.	Cook
	Robert E. Wilson, Dem.	Cook
7	Albert F. Volz, Rep.	Cook
	Howard P. Castle, Rep.	Cook
	John W. McCarthy, Dem.	Cook
8	Edward D. Shurtleff, Rep.	McHenry
	James H. Vickers, Rep.	McHenry
	Thomas E. Graham, Dem.	Lake
9	David E. Shanahan, Rep.	Cook
	Thomas A. Doyle, Dem.	Cook
	Joseph Placek, Dem.	Cook
10	Charles W. Baker, Rep.	Ogle
	Herbert S. Hicks, Rep.	Winnebago
	Guy W. Ginders, Rep.	Winnebago
11	William H. Cruden, Rep.	Cook
	Edward B. Lucius, Rep.	Cook
	Frank J. Ryan, Dem.	Cook
12	Robert Irwin, Rep.	Carroll
	Joseph L. Meyers, Rep.	Stephenson
	Charles D. Franz, Dem.	Stephenson
13	Gotthard A. Dahlberg, Rep.	Cook
	C. A. Young, Rep.	Cook
	James W. Ryan, Dem.	Cook
14	DeGoy B. Ellis, Rep.	Kane
	Frank A. McCarthy, Rep.	Kane

District	Member	County
	Fred B. Shearer, Rep.	Kane
15	Thomas Curran, Rep.	Cook
	Joseph Perina, Dem.	Cook
	Peter F. Smith, Dem.	Cook
16	William H. Bentley, Rep.	Livingston
	Charles M. Turner, Rep.	Marshall
	Michael Fahy, Dem.	Marshall
17	Edward J. Smejkal, Rep.	Cook
	Charles Coia, Dem.	Cook
	Jacob W. Epstein, Dem.	Cook
18	Charles W. LaPorte, Rep.	Peoria
	Charles S. Stubbles. Rep.	Peoria
	Thomas N. Gorman, Dem.	Peoria
19	Solomon P. Roderick, Rep.	Cook
	James P. O'Brien,[1] Dem·	Cook
	James T. Prendergast, Dem.	Cook
20	Israel Dudgeon, Rep.	Grundy
	Richard R. Meents, Rep.	Iroquois
	Ben W. Alpiner, Dem.	Kankakee
21	Frederick J. Bippus, Rep.	Cook
	Michael F. Maher, Dem.	Cook
	Benjamin M. Mitchell, Dem.	Cook
22	William P. Holaday, Rep.	Vermilion
	Abraham L. Stanfield, Rep.	Edgar
	Archie N. Vance, Dem.	Edgar
23	Edward M. Overland, Rep.	Cook
	William G. Thon, Rep.	Cook
	Thomas P. Keane, Dem.	Cook
24	Charles A. Gregory, Rep.	Moultrie
	William H. H. Miller, Rep.	Champaign
	Jacob R. Drake, Dem.	Moultrie
25	Charles L. Fieldstack, Rep.	Cook
	Theodore R. Steinert, Rep.	Cook
	John G. Jacobson, Dem.	Cook
26	William Noble, Rep.	Ford
	William Rowe, Rep.	McLean
	George E. Dooley, Dem.	McLean
27	Edward Walz, Rep.	Cook
	James M. Donlan, Dem.	Cook
	Joseph Petlak, Dem.	Cook
28	Edwin C. Perkins, Rep.	Logan
	Orpheus W. Smith, Rep.	Macon
	Horace W. McDavid, Dem.	Macon
29	Bernard F. Clettenberg,[2] Rep.	Cook
	Bernard J. Conlon, Dem.	Cook
	Lawrence C. O'Brien, Dem.	Cook
30	Homer J. Tice, Rep.	Menard
	William H. Dieterich, Dem.	Cass
	Ben L. Smith, Dem.	Tazewell
31	Carl Mueller, Rep.	Cook
	James A. Steven, Rep.	Cook
	Frank J. Seif, Jr., Dem.	Cook
32	James M. Pace, Rep.	McDonough
	Rollo R. Robbins, Rep.	Hancock
	Ernest O. Reaugh, Dem.	Hancock
33	Frank E. Abbey, Rep.	Henderson
	James A. Wells, Rep.	Mercer
	Everett L. Werts, Dem.	Henderson
34	E. Walter Green, Rep.	Douglas
	A. L. Ruffner, Rep.	Clark
	Robert Howard, Dem.	Coles
35	Frederick A. Brewer, Rep.	Whiteside
	Albert T. Tourtillott, Rep.	Lee

District	Member	County
	John P. Devine, Dem.	Lee
36	A. Otis Arnold, Rep.	Adams
	Henry Bowers, Dem.	Pike
	Rolland M. Wagner, Dem.	Adams
37	Randolph Boyd, Rep.	Henry
	John W. Walters, Rep.	Stark
	Frank W. Morrasy, Dem.	Bureau
38	Otto C. Sonnemann, Rep.	Macoupin
	Henry A. Shephard, Dem.	Jersey
	Truman A. Snell, Dem.	Macoupin
39	William M. Scanlan, Rep.	La Salle
	R. G. Soderstrom, Rep.	La Salle
	Lee O'Neil Browne, Dem.	La Salle
40	Lincoln Bancroft, Rep.	Cumberland
	John C. Richardson, Dem.	Christian
	Arthur Roe, Dem.	Fayette
41	James R. Bentley, Rep.	Will
	William R. McCabe, Rep.	Will
	Michael F. Hennebry, Dem.	Will
42	Charles L. McMackin, Rep.	Marion
	Alois B. Lager, Dem.	Clinton
	John W. Thomason, Dem.	Clay
43	A. O. Lindstrum, Rep.	Knox
	Owen B. West, Rep.	Knox
	M. P. Rice, Dem.	Fulton
44	W. George Beever, Rep.	Randolph
	Harry Wilson, Rep.	Perry
	James M. Etherton, Dem.	Jackson
45	Jacob Frisch, Rep.	Sangamon
	Fred W. Wanless, Rep.	Sangamon
	Clarence A. Jones, Dem.	Sangamon
46	W. B. Phillips, Rep.	Jefferson
	Frank Vice, Jr., Rep.	Richland
	John Kasserman, Dem.	Jasper
47	Norman G. Flagg, Rep.	Madison
	Chris Rethmeier, Rep.	Madison
	Ferdinand A. Garesche, Dem.	Madison
48	Samuel R. Thomas, Rep.	Crawford
	James A. Watson, Rep.	Hardin
	Rene Havill, Dem.	Wabash
49	James W. Rentchler, Rep.	St. Clair
	Charles F. Short, Rep.	St. Clair
	Frank Holten, Dem.	St. Clair
50	Charles Curren, Rep.	Pulaski
	James P. Mooneyham, Rep.	Franklin
	J. L. Hammond, Dem.	Union
51	Claude F. Lacey, Rep.	Massac
	Kenneth C. Ronalds, Rep.	Saline
	John J. Parish, Dem.	Saline

[1] Died April 12, 1919.
[2] Died May 28, 1919.

Fifty-second General Assembly,
1921–22

Senate

President	Fred E. Sterling
President pro tempore	William S. Jewell
Secretary	Theresa Gorman[1]
Secretary	A. G. Murray

District	Member	County
1	Adolph Marks,[2] Rep.	Cook
2	George Van Lent, Rep.	Cook
3	Samuel A. Ettelson, Rep.	Cook
4	Robert W. Schulze, Rep.	Cook
5	James E. MacMurray,[3] Rep.	Cook
6	James J. Barbour, Rep.	Cook
7	Frederick B. Roos, Rep.	Cook
8	Rodney B. Swift, Rep.	Lake
9	Patrick J. Carroll, Dem.	Cook
10	Herbert S. Hicks, Rep.	Winnebago
11	Frank P. Sadler, Rep.	Cook
12	John D. Turnbaugh, Rep.	Carroll
13	Albert C. Clark, Rep.	Cook
14	Harold C. Kessinger, Rep.	Kane
15	John J. Boehm, Dem.	Cook
16	Simon E. Lantz, Rep.	Woodford
17	Edward J. Glackin, Dem.	Cook
18	John Dailey, Rep.	Peoria
19	John T. Denvir, Dem.	Cook
20	Richard R. Meents, Rep.	Iroquois
21	Edward J. Hughes, Dem.	Cook
22	Martin B. Bailey, Rep.	Vermilion
23	Henry W. Austin, Rep.	Cook
24	Henry M. Dunlap, Rep.	Champaign
25	Daniel Herlihy, Dem.	Cook
26	Frank O. Hanson, Rep.	McLean
27	John Broderick, Dem.	Cook
28	Orpheus W. Smith, Rep.	Macon
29	Patrick J. Sullivan, Dem.	Cook
30	Epler C. Mills, Rep.	Cass
31	Willett H. Cornwell, Rep.	Cook
32	Clarence F. Buck, Rep.	Warren
33	Martin R. Carlson, Rep.	Rock Island
34	John R. Hamilton, Rep.	Coles
35	Harry G. Wright,[4] Rep.	De Kalb
36	William S. Gray, Rep.	Adams
37	Clayton C. Pervier, Rep.	Bureau
38	Andrew S. Cuthbertson, Rep.	Macoupin
39	Thurlow G. Essington, Rep.	La Salle
40	James H. Forrester, Rep.	Christian
41	Richard J. Barr, Rep.	Will
42	Erastus D. Telford, Rep.	Marion
43	William S. Jewell, Rep.	Fulton
44	Otis F. Glenn, Rep.	Jackson
45	John A. Wheeler, Rep.	Sangamon
46	Charles L. Wood, Rep.	Wayne
47	J. G. Bardill, Rep.	Madison
48	Nathan E. Smith, Rep.	Edwards
49	R. E. Duvall, Rep.	St. Clair
50	William J. Sneed, Rep.	Williamson
51	W. A. Spence, Rep.	Massac

[1] Resigned.
[2] Vice Francis P. Brady, resigned.
[3] Vice Morton D. Hull, resigned.
[4] Vice Adam C. Cliffe, resigned.

House of Representatives

Speaker	Gotthard A. Dahlberg
Clerk	Bert H. McCann

District	Member	County
1	William M. Brinkman, Rep.	Cook
	Shadrick B. Turner, Rep.	Cook
	John J. Griffin, Dem.	Cook
2	Peter S. Krump, Rep.	Cook
	Frank Ryan, Dem.	Cook

District	Member	County
	Samuel E. Weinshenker, Dem.	Cook
3	Adelbert H. Roberts, Rep.	Cook
	Warren B. Douglas, Rep.	Cook
	George Gary Noonan, Dem.	Cook
4	Arthur J. Rutshaw, Rep.	Cook
	Thomas J. O'Grady, Dem.	Cook
	James P. Boyle, Dem.	Cook
5	Sidney Lyon, Rep.	Cook
	Charles W. Baldwin, Rep.	Cook
	John F. Healy, Dem.	Cook
6	Ralph E. Church, Rep.	Cook
	Emil A. W. Johnson, Rep.	Cook
	Robert E. Wilson, Dem.	Cook
7	Albert F. Volz, Rep.	Cook
	Howard P. Castle, Rep.	Cook
	John W. McCarthy, Dem.	Cook
8	William F. Weiss, Rep.	Lake
	William L. Pierce, Rep.	Boone
	Charles H. Francis, Rep.	McHenry
9	David E. Shanahan, Rep.	Cook
	Joseph Placek, Dem.	Cook
	Thomas A. Doyle, Dem.	Cook
10	Charles W. Baker, Rep.	Ogle
	Harlan B. Kauffman, Rep.	Ogle
	Guy W. Ginders, Rep.	Winnebago
11	William H. Cruden, Rep.	Cook
	Philip M. Giesler, Rep.	Cook
	Frank J. Ryan, Dem.	Cook
12	Robert Irwin, Rep.	Carroll
	Joseph L. Meyers, Rep.	Stephenson
	Charles D. Franz, Dem.	Stephenson
13	C. A. Young, Rep.	Cook
	Gotthard A. Dahlberg, Rep.	Cook
	James W. Ryan, Dem.	Cook
14	Frank W. Hopp, Rep.	Kane
	John P. Hart, Rep.	Kane
	Fred B. Shearer, Rep.	Kane
15	Thomas Curran, Rep.	Cook
	Joseph Perina, Dem.	Cook
	Peter F. Smith, Dem.	Cook
16	Charles M. Turner, Rep.	Marshall
	D. S. Myers, Jr., Rep.	Livingston
	Michael Fahy, Dem.	Marshall
17	Edward J. Smejkal, Rep.	Cook
	Charles Coia, Dem.	Cook
	Jacob W. Epstein, Dem.	Cook
18	Charles W. LaPorte, Rep.	Peoria
	Charles S. Stubbles, Rep.	Peoria
	David H. McClugage, Dem.	Peoria
19	Solomon P. Roderick, Rep.	Cook
	Charles E. Marinier, Rep.	Cook
	John F. Berry, Dem.	Cook
20	C. B. Sawyer, Rep.	Kankakee
	J. H. Francis, Rep.	Grundy
	Ben W. Alpiner, Dem.	Kankakee
21	Frederick J. Bippus, Rep.	Cook
	Charles S. Rasmussen, Rep.	Cook
	Michael F. Maher, Dem.	Cook
22	Abraham L. Stanfield, Rep.	Edgar
	William P. Holaday, Rep.	Vermilion
	P. J. Breen, Dem.	Edgar
23	William G. Thon, Rep.	Cook
	Edward M. Overland, Rep.	Cook
	Thomas P. Keane, Dem.	Cook
24	Roger F. Little, Rep.	Champaign
	Charles A. Gregory, Rep.	Moultrie
	Thomas M. Lyman, Dem.	Champaign

District	Member	County
25	John P. Remus, Rep.	Cook
	Theodore R. Steinert, Rep.	Cook
	John Paul, Rep.	Cook
26	William Rowe, Rep.	McLean
	G. J. Johnson, Rep.	Ford
	Martin A. Brennan, Dem.	McLean
27	Edward Walz, Rep.	Cook
	Joseph Petlak, Dem.	Cook
	Joseph A. Trandel, Dem.	Cook
28	E. B. Bentley, Rep.	De Witt
	John Clark, Rep.	Macon
	Albert A. Hill, Dem.	Macon
29	John T. Joyce, Rep.	Cook
	Bernard J. Conlon, Dem.	Cook
	Lawrence C. O'Brien, Dem.	Cook
30	Homer J. Tice, Rep.	Menard
	Ben L. Smith, Dem.	Tazewell
	George B. Steele, Dem.	Schuyler
31	Carl Mueller, Rep.	Cook
	George A. Williston, Rep.	Cook
	Frank J. Seif, Jr., Dem.	Cook
32	James M. Pace, Rep.	McDonough
	Rollo R. Robbins, Rep.	Hancock
	Charles E. Flack, Dem.	McDonough
33	Harry M. McCaskrin, Rep.	Rock Island
	Frank E. Abbey, Rep.	Henderson
	William C. Maucker, Dem.	Rock Island
34	E. Walter Green, Rep.	Douglas
	Charles E. Moore, Rep.	Douglas
	Seymour Hurst, Dem.	Clark
35	John H. Byers, Rep.	Lee
	Albert T. Tourtillott, Rep.	Lee
	John P. Devine, Dem.	Lee
36	A. Otis Arnold, Rep.	Adams
	Henry Bowers, Dem.	Pike
	J. H. Paxton, Dem.	Adams
37	Randolph Boyd, Rep.	Henry
	John W. Walters, Rep.	Stark
	Frank W. Morrasy, Dem.	Bureau
38	Otto C. Sonnemann, Rep.	Macoupin
	David Davis, Rep.	Montgomery
	Truman A. Snell, Dem.	Macoupin
39	William M. Scanlan, Rep.	La Salle
	John Wylie, Rep.	La Salle
	Lee O'Neil Browne, Dem.	La Salle
40	Lincoln Bancroft, Rep.	Cumberland
	Arthur Roe, Dem.	Fayette
	John C. Richardson, Dem.	Christian
41	John L. Walker, Rep.	Will
	William R. McCabe, Rep.	Will
	Michael F. Hennebry, Dem.	Will
42	Charles L. McMackin, Rep.	Marion
	Alois B. Lager, Dem.	Clinton
	Ben Phillips, Dem.	Marion
43	Owen B. West, Rep.	Knox
	A. O. Lindstrum. Rep.	Knox
	M. P. Rice, Dem.	Fulton
44	A. H. Fridrichs, Rep.	Monroe
	Harry Wilson, Rep.	Perry
	James M. Etherton, Dem.	Jackson
45	Jacob Frisch, Rep.	Sangamon
	Earl B. Searcy, Rep.	Sangamon
	B. L. Barber, Dem.	Sangamon

District	Member	County
46	W. B. Phillips, Rep.	Jefferson
	Frank Vice, Jr., Rep.	Richland
	John A. MacNeil, Dem.	Richland
47	Norman G. Flagg, Rep.	Madison
	Chris Rethmeier, Rep.	Madison
	Ferdinand A. Garesche, Dem.	Madison
48	James A. Watson, Rep.	Hardin
	Samuel R. Thomas, Rep.	Crawford
	Lyman W. Emmons, Dem.	Lawrence
49	Charles F. Short, Rep.	St. Clair
	James W. Rentchler, Rep.	St. Clair
	Frank Holten, Dem.	St. Clair
50	James P. Mooneyham, Rep.	Franklin
	Charles Curren, Rep.	Pulaski
	J. L. Hammond, Dem.	Union
51	Claude F. Lacey, Rep.	Massac
	Claude L. Rew, Rep.	Saline
	John J. Parrish, Dem.	Saline

Fifty-third General Assembly, 1923–24

Senate

President	Fred E. Sterling
President pro tempore	Richard J. Barr
Secretary	James H. Paddock

District	Member	County
1	Adolph Marks, Rep.	Cook
2	George Van Lent, Rep.	Cook
3	Samuel A. Ettelson, Rep.	Cook
4	Robert W. Schulze, Rep.	Cook
5	James E. MacMurray, Rep.	Cook
6	James J. Barbour, Rep.	Cook
7	Frederick B. Roos, Rep.	Cook
8	Rodney B. Swift, Rep.	Lake
9	Patrick J. Carroll, Dem.	Cook
10	Herbert S. Hicks, Rep.	Winnebago
11	Frank J. Ryan, Dem.	Cook
12	John D. Turnbaugh, Rep.	Carroll
13	Albert C. Clark, Rep.	Cook
14	Harold C. Kessinger, Rep.	Kane
15	John J. Boehm, Dem.	Cook
16	Simon E. Lantz, Rep.	Woodford
17	Edward J. Glackin, Dem.	Cook
18	John Dailey, Rep.	Peoria
19	John T. Denvir, Dem.	Cook
20	Richard R. Meents, Rep.	Iroquois
21	Edward J. Hughes, Dem.	Cook
22	Martin B. Bailey, Rep.	Vermilion
23	Lowell B. Mason, Rep.	Cook
24	Henry M. Dunlap, Rep.	Champaign
25	Daniel Webster, Rep.	Cook
26	Frank O. Hanson, Rep.	McLean
27	John A. Piotrowski, Dem.	Cook
28	Orpheus W. Smith, Rep.	Macon
29	John T. Joyce, Rep.	Cook
30	Epler C. Mills, Rep.	Cass
31	Herman J. Haenisch, Rep.	Cook
32	Clarence F. Buck, Rep.	Warren
33	Martin R. Carlson, Rep.	Rock Island
34	John R. Hamilton, Rep.	Coles
35	Harry G. Wright, Rep.	De Kalb
36	William S. Gray, Rep.	Adams
37	Randolph Boyd, Rep.	Henry
38	Andrew S. Cuthbertson, Rep.	Macoupin
39	Thurlow G. Essington, Rep.	La Salle
40	James H. Forrester, Rep.	Christian
41	Richard J. Barr, Rep.	Will
42	Erastus D. Telford, Rep.	Marion
43	William S. Jewell, Rep.	Fulton
44	Otis F. Glenn, Rep.	Jackson
45	Earl B. Searcy, Rep.	Sangamon
46	Charles L. Wood, Rep.	Wayne
47	Herbert G. Giberson, Dem.	Madison
48	Nathan E. Smith, Rep.	Edwards
49	R. E. Duvall, Rep.	St. Clair
50	William J. Sneed, Rep.	Williamson
51	John W. Shaw, Dem.	Saline

House of Representatives

Speaker	David E. Shanahan
Clerk	Bert H. McCann

District	Member	County
1	William M. Brinkman, Rep.	Cook
	Shadrick B. Turner, Rep.	Cook
	John J. Griffin, Dem.	Cook
2	Peter S. Krump, Rep.	Cook
	Harry C. Van Norman, Dem.	Cook
	Frank Ryan, Dem.	Cook
3	George T. Kersey, Rep.	Cook
	Adelbert H. Roberts, Rep.	Cook
	George Gary Noonan, Dem.	Cook
4	Arthur J. Rutshaw, Rep.	Cook
	James P. Boyle, Dem.	Cook
	Thomas J. O'Grady, Dem.	Cook
5	Sidney Lyon, Rep.	Cook
	Thomas J. Hair, Rep.	Cook
	Michael L. Igoe, Dem.	Cook
6	Ralph E. Church, Rep.	Cook
	John W. Gibson, Rep.	Cook
	Charles H. Weber, Dem.	Cook
7	Howard P. Castle, Rep.	Cook
	Lewis B. Springer, Rep.	Cook
	John W. McCarthy, Dem.	Cook
8	William L. Pierce, Rep.	Boone
	William F. Weiss, Rep.	Lake
	Charles H. Francis, Rep.	McHenry
9	David E. Shanahan, Rep.	Cook
	Joseph Placek, Dem.	Cook
	Thomas A. Doyle, Dem.	Cook
10	Leroy M. Green, Rep.	Winnebago
	David Hunter, Jr., Rep.	Winnebago
	Charles W. Baker, Rep.	Ogle
11	David I. Swanson, Rep.	Cook
	John M. Lee, Dem.	Cook
	George A. Fitzgerald, Dem.	Cook
12	Robert Irwin, Rep.	Carroll
	Joseph L. Meyers, Rep.	Stephenson
	Charles D. Franz, Dem.	Stephenson
13	Gotthard A. Dahlberg, Rep.	Cook
	Elmer J. Schnackenberg, Rep.	Cook
	William W. Powers, Dem.	Cook
14	Frank A. McCarthy, Rep.	Kane
	John P. Hart, Rep.	Kane
	Ralph H. Hoar, Rep.	Kane

District	Member	County
15	Thomas Curran, Rep.	Cook
	Joseph Perina, Dem.	Cook
	Peter F. Smith, Dem.	Cook
16	Calistus A. Bruer, Rep.	Livingston
	Charles M. Turner, Rep.	Marshall
	Michael Fahy, Dem.	Marshall
17	Edward J. Smejkal, Rep.	Cook
	Jacob W. Epstein, Dem.	Cook
	Thomas F. Frole, Dem.	Cook
18	Robert Scholes, Rep.	Peoria
	Charles S. Stubbles,[1] Rep.	Peoria
	David H. McClugage, Dem.	Peoria
19	Charles E. Marinier, Rep.	Cook
	John F. Berry, Dem.	Cook
	Walter Francis Gallas, Dem.	Cook
20	C. B. Sawyer, Rep.	Kankakee
	L. S. Holderman, Rep.	Grundy
	J. W. Rausch, Dem.	Grundy
21	William F. Daley, Rep.	Cook
	Michael F. Maher, Rep.	Cook
	Benjamin M. Mitchell, Dem.	Cook
22	Abraham L. Stanfield, Rep.	Edgar
	Hugh M. Luckey, Rep.	Vermilion
	P. J. Breen, Dem.	Edgar
23	Edward M. Overland, Rep.	Cook
	William G. Thon, Rep.	Cook
	Thomas P. Keane, Dem.	Cook
24	Roger F. Little, Rep.	Champaign
	James A. Reeves, Rep.	Champaign
	Francis E. Williamson, Dem.	Champaign
25	Theodore R. Steinert, Rep.	Cook
	John Paul, Rep.	Cook
	John G. Jacobson, Dem.	Cook
26	H. N. Boshell, Rep.	Ford
	G. J. Johnson, Rep.	Ford
	Martin A. Brennan, Dem.	McLean
27	Albert Rostenkowski, Rep.	Cook
	Joseph A. Trandel, Dem.	Cook
	William Lipka, Dem.	Cook
28	E. B. Bentley, Rep.	De Witt
	John Clark, Rep.	Macon
	Albert A. Hill, Dem.	Macon
29	Michael R. Durso, Rep.	Cook
	Ernest W. Turner, Rep.	Cook
	Lawrence C. O'Brien, Dem.	Cook
30	Homer J. Tice, Rep.	Menard
	Ben L. Smith, Dem.	Tazewell
	Martin B. Lohmann, Dem.	Tazewell
31	George A. Williston, Rep.	Cook
	Carl Mueller, Rep.	Cook
	James J. O'Toole, Dem.	Cook
32	Rollo R. Robbins, Rep.	Hancock
	James H. Foster, Rep.	McDonough
	Charles E. Flack, Rep.	McDonough
33	Harry M. McCaskrin, Rep.	Rock Island
	Frank E. Abbey, Rep.	Henderson
	William C. Maucker, Dem.	Rock Island
34	Charles E. Moore, Rep.	Douglas
	Robert Howard, Dem.	Coles
	Seymour Hurst, Dem.	Clark
35	Henry C. Allen, Rep.	Whiteside
	John H. Byers, Rep.	Lee
	John P. Devine, Dem.	Lee
36	A. Otis Arnold, Rep.	Adams
	Samuel S. Hyatt, Dem.	Adams
	Henry Bowers, Dem.	Pike
37	Frederick W. Rennick, Rep.	Bureau

District	Member	County
	John Robert Moore, Rep.	Henry
	Frank W. Morrasy, Dem.	Bureau
38	Otto C. Sonnemann, Rep.	Macoupin
	Henry A. Shephard, Dem.	Jersey
	Harry S. Hargrave, Dem.	Montgomery
39	R. G. Soderstrom, Rep.	La Salle
	Lee O'Neil Browne, Dem.	La Salle
	Ole E. Benson, Ind.	La Salle
40	Lincoln Bancroft, Rep.	Cumberland
	Arthur Roe, Dem.	Fayette
	John C. Richardson, Dem.	Christian
41	John L. Walker, Rep.	Will
	William R. McCabe,[2] Rep.	Will
	Michael F. Hennebry,[3] Dem.	Will
	Lottie Holman O'Neill, Rep.	Du Page
42	Charles L. McMackin, Rep.	Marion
	Alois B. Lager, Rep.	Clinton
	J. E. McMackin, Dem.	Marion
43	Owen B. West, Rep.	Knox
	Reed F. Cutler, Rep.	Fulton
	M. P. Rice, Dem.	Fulton
44	A. H. Fridrichs, Rep.	Monroe
	Harry Wilson, Rep.	Perry
	Charles J. Kribs, Dem.	Randolph
45	Samuel E. Moore, Rep.	Sangamon
	Euclid B. Rogers, Rep.	Sangamon
	B. L. Barber, Dem.	Sangamon
46	W. B. Phillips, Rep.	Jefferson
	Laurence F. Arnold, Dem.	Jasper
	H. S. Burgess, Dem.	Wayne
47	Norman G. Flagg, Rep.	Madison
	Chris Rethmeier, Rep.	Madison
	Ferdinand A. Garesche, Dem.	Madison
48	Ed Ryan, Rep.	Lawrence
	Lyman W. Emmons, Dem.	Lawrence
	James L. Guard, Dem.	Gallatin
49	James W. Rentchler, Rep.	St. Clair
	Thomas L. Fekete, Jr., Rep.	St. Clair
	Frank Holten, Dem.	St. Clair
50	Wallace A. Bandy, Rep.	Williamson
	Carl Choisser, Rep.	Franklin
	Thomas J. Myers, Dem.	Franklin
51	Kenneth C. Ronalds, Rep.	Saline
	John P. Mathis, Rep.	Johnson
	John McElvain, Dem.	Hamilton

[1] Died February 13, 1923.
[2] Seat contested, unseated June 6, 1923.
[3] Seated June 6, 1923, vice McCabe.

Fifty-fourth General Assembly, 1925–26

Senate

President	Fred E. Sterling
President pro tempore	Richard J. Barr
Secretary	James H. Paddock

District	Member	County
1	Adolph Marks, Rep.	Cook
2	George Van Lent, Rep.	Cook

District	Member	County
3	Adelbert H. Roberts,[1] Rep.	Cook
4	Frank J. McDermott, Dem.	Cook
5	James E. MacMurray, Rep.	Cook
6	James J. Barbour, Rep.	Cook
7	Frederick B. Roos, Rep.	Cook
8	Rodney B. Swift, Rep.	Lake
9	Patrick J. Carroll, Dem.	Cook
10	Herbert S. Hicks, Rep.	Winnebago
11	Frank J. Ryan, Dem.	Cook
12	Joseph L. Meyers, Rep.	Stephenson
13	Albert C. Clark, Rep.	Cook
14	Harold C. Kessinger, Rep.	Kane
15	John J. Boehm, Dem.	Cook
16	Simon E. Lantz, Rep.	Woodford
17	Edward J. Glackin, Dem.	Cook
18	John Dailey, Rep.	Peoria
19	John T. Denvir, Dem.	Cook
20	Richard R. Meents, Rep.	Iroquois
21	Edward J. Hughes, Dem.	Cook
22	Martin B. Bailey, Rep.	Vermilion
23	Lowell B. Mason, Rep.	Cook
24	Henry M. Dunlap, Rep.	Champaign
25	Daniel Webster, Rep.	Cook
26	Florence Fifer Bohrer, Rep.	McLean
27	John A. Piotrowski, Dem.	Cook
28	Jesse E. Deck, Rep.	Macon
29	John T. Joyce, Rep.	Cook
30	Ben L. Smith, Dem.	Tazewell
31	Herman J. Haenisch, Rep.	Cook
32	John S. Brown, Rep.	Warren
33	Martin R. Carlson, Rep.	Rock Island
34	John R. Hamilton, Rep.	Coles
35	Harry G. Wright, Rep.	De Kalb
36	Charles R. McNay, Dem.	Adams
37	Randolph Boyd, Rep.	Henry
38	Andrew S. Cuthbertson, Rep.	Macoupin
39	Thurlow G. Essington, Rep.	La Salle
40	James H. Forrester, Rep.	Christian
41	Richard J. Barr, Rep.	Will
42	Erastus D. Telford, Rep.	Marion
43	William S. Jewell, Rep.	Fulton
44	Harry Wilson, Rep.	Perry
45	Earl B. Searcy, Rep.	Sangamon
46	H. S. Burgess, Dem.	Wayne
47	Herbert G. Giberson, Rep.	Madison
48	Lyman W. Emmons, Dem.	Lawrence
49	R. E. Duvall, Rep.	St. Clair
50	William J. Sneed, Rep.	Williamson
51	John W. Shaw, Dem.	Saline

[1] Vice Samuel A. Ettelson, resigned.

House of Representatives

Speaker		Robert Scholes
Clerk		Bert H. McCann

District	Member	County
1	Shadrick B. Turner, Rep.	Cook
	Charles A. Griffin, Rep.	Cook
	John J. Griffin, Dem.	Cook
2	Peter S. Krump, Rep.	Cook
	Harry C. Van Norman, Dem.	Cook

District	Member	County
	Frank Ryan, Dem.	Cook
3	Warren B. Douglas, Rep.	Cook
	William E. King, Rep.	Cook
	George Gary Noonan, Dem.	Cook
4	Arthur J. Rutshaw, Rep.	Cook
	James P. Boyle, Dem.	Cook
	Thomas J. O'Grady, Dem.	Cook
5	Katherine Hancock Goode, Rep.	Cook
	Sidney Lyon, Rep.	Cook
	Thomas F. Reilly, Dem.	Cook
6	Ralph E. Church, Rep.	Cook
	John W. Gibson, Rep.	Cook
	Charles H. Weber, Dem.	Cook
7	Lewis B. Springer, Rep.	Cook
	Howard P. Castle, Rep.	Cook
	Martin H. Finneran, Dem.	Cook
8	William F. Weiss, Rep.	Lake
	Charles H. Francis, Rep.	McHenry
	Noyes L. Jackson, Rep.	Boone
9	David E. Shanahan, Rep.	Cook
	William J. Gormley, Dem.	Cook
	Joseph Placek, Dem.	Cook
10	David Hunter, Jr., Rep.	Winnebago
	Leroy M. Green, Rep.	Winnebago
	Emmet F. Wilson, Rep.	Winnebago
11	David I. Swanson, Rep.	Cook
	Walter R. Miller, Rep.	Cook
	John M. Lee, Dem.	Cook
12	Alfred S. Babb, Rep.	Carroll
	John Acker, Rep.	Carroll
	Charles D. Franz, Dem.	Stephenson
13	Elmer J. Schnackenberg, Rep.	Cook
	Theo D. Smith, Rep.	Cook
	William W. Powers, Dem.	Cook
14	Frank A. McCarthy, Rep.	Kane
	John M. Peffers, Rep.	Kane
	Ralph H. Hoar, Rep.	Kane
15	Thomas Curran, Rep.	Cook
	Joseph Perina, Dem.	Cook
	Matt Franz, Dem.	Cook
16	Charles M. Turner, Rep.	Marshall
	Calistus A. Bruer, Rep.	Livingston
	Michael Fahy, Dem.	Marshall
17	William V. Pacelli, Rep.	Cook
	Charles Coia, Dem.	Cook
	Jacob W. Epstein, Dem.	Cook
18	Robert Scholes, Rep.	Peoria
	Charles W. LaPorte, Rep.	Peoria
	David H. McClugage, Dem.	Peoria
19	Charles E. Marinier, Rep.	Cook
	Harry I. Weisbrod, Rep.	Cook
	John R. McSweeney, Dem.	Cook
20	C. B. Sawyer, Rep.	Kankakee
	John Trotter, Rep.	Grundy
	Claude N. Saum, Dem.	Iroquois
21	Frederick J. Bippus, Rep.	Cook
	Michael F. Maher, Dem.	Cook
	Benjamin M. Mitchell, Dem.	Cook
22	Hugh M. Luckey, Rep.	Vermilion
	Abraham L. Stanfield, Rep.	Edgar
	Edgar B. Brown, Dem.	Edgar
23	William G. Thon, Rep.	Cook
	Edward M. Overland, Rep.	Cook
	Fred W. Hrdlicka, Dem.	Cook
24	Roger F. Little, Rep.	Champaign
	James A. Reeves, Rep.	Champaign
	Thompson J. Anderson, Dem.	Piatt

District	Member	County
25	Theodore R. Steinert, Rep.	Cook
	Rena Elrod, Rep.	Cook
	John G. Jacobson, Dem.	Cook
26	G. J. Johnson, Rep.	Ford
	A. L. Hutson, Rep.	McLean
	Jacob Martens, Dem.	McLean
27	Albert Rostenkowski, Rep.	Cook
	A. L. Auth, Dem.	Cook
	William Lipka, Dem.	Cook
28	W. C. Chynoweth, Rep.	Macon
	John Clark, Rep.	Macon
	Grover C. Hoff, Dem.	De Witt
29	Ernest W. Turner, Rep.	Cook
	Michael R. Durso, Rep.	Cook
	Lawrence C. O'Brien, Dem.	Cook
30	Homer J. Tice, Rep.	Menard
	Herschel V. Teel, Dem.	Schuyler
	Martin B. Lohmann, Dem.	Tazewell
31	Carl Mueller,[1] Rep.	Cook
	George A. Williston, Rep.	Cook
	James J. O'Toole, Dem.	Cook
32	Rollo R. Robbins, Rep.	Hancock
	James H. Foster, Rep.	McDonough
	William Adcock, Dem.	Warren
33	Harry M. McCaskrin, Rep.	Rock Island
	Frank E. Abbey, Rep.	Henderson
	Thomas P. Sinnett, Dem.	Rock Island
34	Walter E. Cork, Rep.	Clark
	Harry Baxter, Rep.	Douglas
	Norman Bennett, Dem.	Clark
35	Albert T. Tourtillott, Rep.	Lee
	Henry C. Allen, Rep.	Whiteside
	John P. Devine, Dem.	Lee
36	A. Otis Arnold, Rep.	Adams
	Samuel S. Hyatt,[2] Dem.	Adams
	Carroll Bush, Dem.	Pike
37	Frederick W. Rennick, Rep.	Bureau
	John Robert Moore, Rep.	Henry
	Milton T. Booth, Rep.	Henry
38	Otto C. Sonnemann, Rep.	Macoupin
	Robert Whiteley, Rep.	Macoupin
	Truman A. Snell, Dem.	Macoupin
39	R. G. Soderstrom, Rep.	La Salle
	John Wylie, Rep.	La Salle
	Lee O'Neil Browne, Dem.	La Salle
40	Henry D. Sparks, Rep.	Shelby
	Lincoln Bancroft, Rep.	Cumberland
	Arthur Roe, Dem.	Fayette
41	Lottie Holman O'Neill, Rep.	Du Page
	John L. Walker, Rep.	Will
	Michael F. Hennebry, Dem.	Will
42	R. J. Branson, Rep.	Marion
	J. E. McMackin, Dem.	Marion
	Alois B. Lager, Dem.	Clinton
43	Owen B. West, Rep.	Knox
	Reed F. Cutler, Rep.	Fulton
	M. P. Rice, Dem.	Fulton
44	Elbert Waller, Rep.	Perry
	Henry Eisenbart, Rep.	Monroe
	Charles J. Kribs, Dem.	Randolph
45	James H. Ashby, Rep.	Sangamon
	Euclid B. Rogers, Dem.	Sangamon
	Marion U. Woodruff, Dem.	Sangamon
46	W. B. Phillips, Rep.	Jefferson
	Laurence F. Arnold, Dem.	Jasper
	H. W. Faulkner, Dem.	Jefferson
47	Norman G. Flagg, Rep.	Madison

District	Member	County
	Earl Herrin, Rep.	Madison
	Charles F. Malloy, Dem.	Bond
48	Ed Ryan, Rep.	Lawrence
	F. W. Lewis, Dem.	Crawford
	Jerome L. Harrell, Dem.	White
49	Ed P. Petri, Rep.	St. Clair
	Thomas L. Fekete, Jr., Rep.	St. Clair
	Frank Holten, Dem.	St. Clair
50	Wallace A. Bandy, Rep.	Williamson
	Carl Choisser, Rep.	Franklin
	Thomas J. Meyers, Dem.	Franklin
51	W. V. Rush, Rep.	Massac
	Claude L. Rew, Rep.	Saline
	John McElvain, Dem.	Hamilton

[1] Died July 12, 1925.
[2] Died April 3, 1925.

Fifty-fifth General Assembly, 1927–28

Senate

President	Fred E. Sterling
Secretary	James H. Paddock

District	Member	County
1	Adolph Marks, Rep.	Cook
2	George Van Lent, Rep.	Cook
3	Adelbert H. Roberts, Rep.	Cook
4	Frank J. McDermott, Dem.	Cook
5	Roy C. Woods, Rep.	Cook
6	James J. Barbour, Rep.	Cook
7	Arthur A. Huebsch, Rep.	Cook
8	Rodney B. Swift, Rep.	Lake
9	Patrick J. Carroll, Dem.	Cook
10	Herbert S. Hicks, Rep.	Winnebago
11	Thomas J. Courtney, Dem.	Cook
12	Joseph L. Meyers, Rep.	Stephenson
13	Harry W. Starr, Rep.	Cook
14	Harold C. Kessinger, Rep.	Kane
15	John J. Boehm, Dem.	Cook
16	Simon E. Lantz, Rep.	Woodford
17	James B. Leonardo, Rep.	Cook
18	John Dailey, Rep.	Peoria
19	John T. Denvir, Rep.	Cook
20	Richard R. Meents, Rep.	Iroquois
21	Edward J. Hughes, Dem.	Cook
22	Martin B. Bailey, Rep.	Vermilion
23	Lowell B. Mason, Rep.	Cook
24	Henry M. Dunlap, Rep.	Champaign
25	Theodore R. Steinert, Rep.	Cook
26	Florence Fifer Bohrer, Rep.	McLean
27	John Broderick, Dem.	Cook
28	Jesse E. Deck, Rep.	Macon
29	John T. Joyce, Rep.	Cook
30	Ben L. Smith, Rep.	Tazewell
31	Herman J. Haenisch, Rep.	Cook
32	John S. Brown, Rep.	Warren
33	Martin R. Carlson, Rep.	Rock Island
34	John R. Hamilton, Rep.	Coles
35	Harry G. Wright, Rep.	De Kalb

District	Member	County
36	Charles R. McNay, Dem.	Adams
37	Randolph Boyd, Rep.	Henry
38	Andrew S. Cuthbertson, Rep.	Macoupin
39	George M. Reynolds, Rep.	La Salle
40	James H. Forrester, Rep.	Christian
41	Richard J. Barr, Rep.	Will
42	Erastus D. Telford, Rep.	Marion
43	William S. Jewell, Rep.	Fulton
44	Harry Wilson, Rep.	Perry
45	Earl B. Searcy, Rep.	Sangamon
46	H. S. Burgess, Dem.	Wayne
47	Norman G. Flagg, Rep.	Madison
48	Lyman W. Emmons, Dem.	Lawrence
49	E. J. Abt, Rep.	St. Clair
50	William J. Sneed, Rep.	Williamson
51	Charles H. Thompson, Rep.	Saline

House of Representatives

Speaker	Robert Scholes
Clerk	Bert H. McCann

District	Member	County
1	Shadrick B. Turner,[1] Rep.	Cook
	Charles A. Griffin, Rep.	Cook
	John J. Griffin, Dem.	Cook
2	Peter S. Krump, Rep.	Cook
	Frank Ryan, Dem.	Cook
	Harry C. Van Norman, Dem.	Cook
3	George T. Kersey, Rep.	Cook
	Warren B. Douglas, Rep.	Cook
	George Gary Noonan, Dem.	Cook
4	Elmer N. Holmgren, Rep.	Cook
	James P. Boyle, Dem.	Cook
	Thomas J. O'Grady, Dem.	Cook
5	Katherine Hancock Goode,[2] Rep.	Cook
	Sidney Lyon, Rep.	Cook
	Michael L. Igoe, Dem.	Cook
6	Emil A. W. Johnson, Rep.	Cook
	Ralph E. Church, Rep.	Cook
	Charles H. Weber, Dem.	Cook
7	William F. Propper, Rep.	Cook
	Howard P. Castle, Rep.	Cook
	Martin H. Finneran, Dem.	Cook
8	William F. Weiss, Rep.	Lake
	Roy J. Stewart, Rep.	McHenry
	Noyes L. Jackson, Rep.	Boone
9	David E. Shanahan, Rep.	Cook
	Joseph Placek, Dem.	Cook
	William J. Gormley, Dem.	Cook
10	Charles W. Baker, Rep.	Ogle
	Leroy M. Green, Rep.	Winnebago
	David Hunter, Jr., Rep.	Winnebago
11	David I. Swanson, Rep.	Cook
	Calvin T. Weeks, Rep.	Cook
	John M. Lee, Dem.	Cook
12	John Acker, Rep.	Carroll
	Alfred S. Babb, Rep.	Carroll
	Charles D. Franz, Dem.	Stephenson
13	Elmer J. Schnackenberg, Rep.	Cook
	John C. Garriott, Jr., Rep.	Cook
	William W. Powers, Dem.	Cook
14	Frank A. McCarthy, Rep.	Kane

District	Member	County
	John M. Peffers, Rep.	Kane
	Ralph H. Hoar, Rep.	Kane
15	Thomas Curran, Rep.	Cook
	Matt Franz, Dem.	Cook
	Joseph Perina, Dem.	Cook
16	Charles M. Turner, Rep.	Marshall
	Calistus A. Bruer, Rep.	Livingston
	Michael Fahy, Dem.	Marshall
17	William V. Pacelli, Rep.	Cook
	Charles Coia, Dem.	Cook
	Henry Minsky, Dem.	Cook
18	Robert Scholes, Rep.	Peoria
	Sherman W. Eckley, Rep.	Peoria
	David H. McClugage, Dem.	Peoria
19	Charles E. Marinier, Rep.	Cook
	John R. McSweeney, Dem.	Cook
	Walter Francis Gallas, Dem.	Cook
20	John Trotter,[3] Rep.	Iroquois
	J. Bert Miller, Rep.	Kankakee
	Louis E. Beckman, Rep.	Kankakee
21	Frederick J. Bippus, Rep.	Cook
	Benjamin M. Mitchell,[4] Dem.	Cook
	Joseph L. Rategan, Dem.	Cook
22	Hugh M. Luckey, Rep.	Vermilion
	Abraham L. Stanfield,[5] Rep.	Edgar
	P. J. Breen, Dem.	Edgar
23	Charles A. Mugler, Rep.	Cook
	Edward M. Overland, Rep.	Cook
	Fred W. Hrdlicka, Dem.	Cook
24	Roger F. Little, Rep.	Champaign
	James A. Reeves, Rep.	Champaign
	H. H. Hawkins, Dem.	Moultrie
25	Rena Elrod, Rep.	Cook
	Frank T. Baird, Rep.	Cook
	John G. Jacobson, Dem.	Cook
26	G. J. Johnson, Rep.	Ford
	A. L. Hutson, Rep.	McLean
	Jacob Martens, Dem.	McLean
27	Joseph F. Murray, Rep.	Cook
	William Lipka, Dem.	Cook
	Joseph A. Trandel, Dem.	Cook
28	W. C. Chynoweth, Rep.	Macon
	John Clark, Rep.	Macon
	Grover C. Hoff, Dem.	Macon
29	Ernest W. Turner, Rep.	Cook
	Michael R. Durso, Rep.	Cook
	Lawrence C. O'Brien, Dem.	Cook
30	Homer J. Tice, Rep.	Menard
	Martin B. Lohmann, Dem.	Tazewell
	Herschel V. Teel, Dem.	Schuyler
31	Roy Juul, Rep.	Cook
	James A. Steven, Rep.	Cook
	Joseph L. Gill, Dem.	Cook
32	Rollo R. Robbins, Rep.	Hancock
	James H. Foster, Rep.	McDonough
	Sarah Bond Hanley, Dem.	Warren
33	Harry M. McCaskrin, Rep.	Rock Island
	Clinton Searle, Rep.	Rock Island
	Thomas P. Sinnett, Dem.	Rock Island
34	Harry Baxter, Rep.	Douglas
	Walter E. Cork, Rep.	Clark
	Harvey Z. O'Hair, Dem.	Coles
35	Henry C. Allen, Rep.	Whiteside
	Alvin Warren, Rep.	De Kalb
	John P. Devine, Dem.	Lee
36	A. Otis Arnold, Rep.	Adams
	Carroll Bush, Dem.	Pike

District	Member	County
	Mary Cowan McAdams, Dem.	Adams
37	John Robert Moore, Rep.	Henry
	Frederick W. Rennick, Rep.	Bureau
	Frank W. Morrasy,[6] Dem.	Bureau
38	Robert Whiteley, Rep.	Macoupin
	Truman A. Snell, Dem.	Macoupin
	M. E. Bray, Dem.	Montgomery
39	John Wylie, Rep.	La Salle
	R. G. Soderstrom, Rep.	La Salle
	Lee O'Neil Browne,[7] Dem.	La Salle
40	Henry D. Sparks, Rep.	Shelby
	Roy A. Corzine, Rep.	Christian
	Arthur Roe, Dem.	Fayette
41	Lottie Holman O'Neill, Rep.	Du Page
	John M. Jenco, Rep.	Will
	Michael F. Hennebry, Dem.	Will
42	R. J. Branson, Rep.	Marion
	Alois B. Lager, Dem.	Marion
	George J. Bauer, Dem.	Effingham
43	Clinton L. Ewing, Rep.	Knox
	Reed F. Cutler, Rep.	Fulton
	M. P. Rice, Dem.	Fulton
44	Elbert Waller, Rep.	Perry
	Henry Eisenhart, Rep.	Monroe
	Joseph H. Davis, Dem.	Jackson
45	Carl E. Robinson, Rep.	Morgan
	Henry H. Mester, Rep.	Sangamon
	T. J. Sullivan, Dem.	Sangamon
46	Charles L. Wood, Rep.	Wayne
	W. B. Phillips, Rep.	Jefferson
	John Kasserman, Dem.	Jasper
47	Schuyler B. Vaughan, Rep.	Bond
	William H. Martin, Rep.	Madison
	Charles F. Malloy, Dem.	Bond
48	Ed Ryan, Rep.	Lawrence
	Jerome L. Harrell, Dem.	White
	Ivan Wright, Dem.	Lawrence
49	Ed P. Petri, Rep.	St. Clair
	Thomas L. Fekete, Jr., Rep.	St. Clair
	Frank Holten, Dem.	St. Clair
50	Wallace A. Bandy, Rep.	Williamson
	Carl Choisser, Rep.	Franklin
	Alexander Wilson, Dem.	Alexander
51	Claude L. Rew, Rep.	Saline
	W. V. Rush, Rep.	Massac
	Frank Porter, Dem.	Hamilton

[1] Died Sept. 30, 1927.
[2] Died Jan. 12, 1928.
[3] Died during session, did not sit.
[4] Died March 11, 1927.
[5] Died Aug. 7, 1927.
[6] Died Dec. 8, 1926.
[7] Died Feb. 15, 1928.

District	Member	County
3	Adelbert H. Roberts, Rep.	Cook
4	Frank J. McDermott, Dem.	Cook
5	Roy C. Woods, Rep.	Cook
6	James J. Barbour, Rep.	Cook
7	Arthur A. Huebsch, Rep.	Cook
8	Ray Paddock, Rep.	Lake
9	Patrick J. Carroll, Dem.	Cook
10	Charles W. Baker, Rep.	Ogle
11	Thomas J. Courtney, Dem.	Cook
12	Joseph L. Meyers, Rep.	Stephenson
13	Harry W. Starr, Rep.	Cook
14	Harold C. Kessinger, Rep.	Kane
15	John J. Boehm, Dem.	Cook
16	Simon E. Lantz, Rep.	Woodford
17	James B. Leonardo, Rep.	Cook
18	Victor P. Michel, Rep.	Peoria
19	John T. Denvir, Dem.	Cook
20	Richard R. Meents, Rep.	Iroquois
21	Edward J. Hughes, Dem.	Cook
22	Martin B. Bailey, Rep.	Vermilion
23	Lowell B. Mason, Rep.	Cook
24	Henry M. Dunlap, Rep.	Champaign
25	Theodore R. Steinert, Rep.	Cook
26	Florence Fifer Bohrer, Rep.	McLean
27	John Broderick, Dem.	Cook
28	Charles E. Lee, Rep.	Macon
29	John T. Joyce, Rep.	Cook
30	Epler C. Mills, Rep.	Cass
31	Herman J. Haenisch, Rep.	Cook
32	Louis H. Hanna, Rep.	Warren
33	Martin R. Carlson, Rep.	Rock Island
34	John R. Hamilton, Rep.	Coles
35	Harry G. Wright, Rep.	De Kalb
36	J. Leroy Adair, Dem.	Adams
37	Randolph Boyd, Rep.	Henry
38	Andrew S. Cuthbertson, Rep.	Macoupin
39	George M. Reynolds, Rep.	La Salle
40	Guy L. Smith, Rep.	Christian
41	Richard J. Barr, Rep.	Will
42	Walter L. Finn, Dem.	Marion
43	William S. Jewell, Rep.	Fulton
44	Harry Wilson, Rep.	Perry
45	Earl B. Searcy, Rep.	Sangamon
46	William R. McCauley, Rep.	Richland
47	Norman G. Flagg, Rep.	Madison
48	Arthur A. Miles, Rep.	Hardin
49	E. J. Abt, Rep.	St. Clair
50	James H. Felts, Dem.	Williamson
51	Charles H. Thompson, Rep.	Saline

Fifty-sixth General Assembly, 1929–30

Senate

President	Fred E. Sterling
President pro tempore	Martin R. Carlson
Secretary	James H. Paddock

District	Member	County
1	Adolph Marks, Rep.	Cook
2	Joseph Mendel, Dem.	Cook

House of Representatives

Speaker	David E. Shanahan
Clerk	George C. Blaeuer

District	Member	County
1	George W. Blackwell, Rep.	Cook
	Harris B. Gaines, Rep.	Cook
	John J. Griffin, Dem.	Cook
2	Albert J. Mancin, Rep.	Cook
	Thomas J. Clancy, Dem.	Cook
	Frank Ryan, Dem.	Cook

District	Member	County
3	George T. Kersey, Rep.	Cook
	William E. King, Rep.	Cook
	George Gary Noonan, Dem.	Cook
4	Michael A. Ruddy, Rep.	Cook
	James P. Boyle, Dem.	Cook
	Thomas J. O'Grady, Dem.	Cook
5	Flora S. Cheney,[1] Rep.	Cook
	William J. Warfield, Rep.	Cook
	Michael L. Igoe, Dem.	Cook
6	Ralph E. Church, Rep.	Cook
	Emil A. W. Johnson, Rep.	Cook
	Charles H. Weber, Dem.	Cook
7	Anna Wilmarth Ickes, Rep.	Cook
	William F. Propper, Rep.	Cook
	Emmett McGrath, Dem.	Cook
8	Lee McDonough, Rep.	Lake
	Noyes L. Jackson, Rep.	Boone
	Richard J. Lyons, Rep.	Lake
9	David E. Shanahan, Rep.	Cook
	Henry Sonnenschein, Dem.	Cook
	William J. Gormley, Dem.	Cook
10	Leroy M. Green, Rep.	Winnebago
	David Hunter, Jr., Rep.	Winnebago
	Emmet F. Wilson,[2] Rep.	Winnebago
11	David I. Swanson, Rep.	Cook
	Calvin T. Weeks, Rep.	Cook
	John M. Lee, Dem.	Cook
12	John A. Bingham, Rep.	JoDaviess
	John Acker, Rep.	Carroll
	Charles D. Franz, Dem.	Stephenson
13	John C. Garriott, Jr., Rep.	Cook
	Elmer J. Schnackenberg, Rep.	Cook
	William W. Powers, Dem.	Cook
14	Frank A. McCarthy, Rep.	Kane
	John M. Peffers, Rep.	Kane
	John F. Petit, Dem.	Kane
15	Thomas Curran,[3] Rep.	Cook
	Matt Franz, Dem.	Cook
	Edward Skarda, Dem.	Cook
16	Calistus A. Bruer, Rep.	Livingston
	Charles M. Turner, Rep.	Marshall
	Michael Fahy, Dem.	Marshall
17	William V. Pacelli, Rep.	Cook
	Charles Coia, Dem.	Cook
	Henry Minsky, Dem.	Cook
18	Robert Scholes,[4] Rep.	Peoria
	Leo D. Crowley, Rep.	Peoria
	David H. McClugage, Dem.	Peoria
19	Charles E. Marinier, Rep.	Cook
	Richey V. Graham, Dem.	Cook
	John R. McSweeney, Dem.	Cook
20	Louis E. Beckman, Rep.	Kankakee
	Elmer C. Wilson, Rep.	Kankakee
	James T. Burns, Dem.	Kankakee
21	J. W. Harris, Rep.	Cook
	Joseph L. Rategan, Dem.	Cook
	Thomas J. O'Brien, Dem.	Cook
22	Hugh M. Luckey, Rep.	Vermilion
	Karl R. O'Hair, Rep.	Edgar
	P. J. Breen, Dem.	Edgar
23	William G. Thon, Rep.	Cook
	Edward M. Overland, Rep.	Cook
	Thomas P. Keane, Dem.	Cook
24	Roger F. Little, Rep.	Champaign
	William Z. Black, Rep.	Champaign
	William E. Gilmore, Dem.	Champaign
25	Edwin B. Bederman, Rep.	Cook
	Rena Elrod, Rep.	Cook
	John G. Jacobson,[5] Dem.	Cook
26	G. J. Johnson, Rep.	Ford
	Gordon W. Childers, Rep.	McLean
	Charles P. Kane, Dem.	McLean
27	A. O. Galvin, Rep.	Cook
	A. L. Auth, Dem.	Cook
	Joseph A. Trandel, Dem.	Cook
28	W. C. Chynoweth, Rep.	Macon
	John Clark, Rep.	Macon
	Grover C. Hoff, Dem.	Macon
29	Ernest W. Turner, Rep.	Cook
	Michael R. Durso, Rep.	Cook
	Lawrence C. O'Brien, Dem.	Cook
30	Homer J. Tice, Rep.	Menard
	Martin B. Lohmann, Dem.	Tazewell
	Herschel V. Teel, Dem.	Schuyler
31	Roy Juul, Rep.	Cook
	James J. McVicker, Rep.	Cook
	Joseph L. Gill, Dem.	Cook
32	James H. Foster, Rep.	McDonough
	Rollo R. Robbins, Rep.	Hancock
	Sarah Bond Hanley, Dem.	Warren
33	Clinton Searle, Rep.	Rock Island
	Harry M. McCaskrin, Rep.	Rock Island
	Thomas P. Sinnett, Dem.	Rock Island
34	John W. Lewis, Rep.	Clark
	Harry Baxter, Rep.	Douglas
	Harvey Z. O'Hair, Dem.	Coles
35	George C. Dixon, Rep.	Lee
	Henry C. Allen, Rep.	Whiteside
	John P. Devine, Dem.	Lee
36	Henry F. Scarborough, Rep.	Adams
	Carroll Bush, Dem.	Pike
	Mary Cowan McAdams, Dem.	Adams
37	Frederick W. Rennick, Rep.	Bureau
	William H. Jackson, Rep.	Stark
	Robert J. Wilson, Dem.	Henry
38	Robert Whiteley, Rep.	Macoupin
	Henry W. Smith, Rep.	Greene
	M. E. Bray, Dem.	Montgomery
39	R. G. Soderstrom, Rep.	La Salle
	Ole E. Benson, Rep.	La Salle
	Edmond P. Conerton, Dem.	La Salle
40	Henry D. Sparks, Rep.	Shelby
	Roy A. Corzine, Rep.	Christian
	Arthur Roe, Dem.	Fayette
41	Lottie Holman O'Neill, Rep.	Du Page
	John L. Walker, Rep.	Will
	Michael F. Hennebry, Dem.	Will
42	R. J. Branson, Rep.	Marion
	George J. Bauer, Dem.	Effingham
	J. E. McMackin, Dem.	Marion
43	Clinton L. Ewing, Rep.	Knox
	Reed F. Cutler, Rep.	Fulton
	M. P. Rice, Dem.	Fulton
44	Charles Johnson, Rep.	Jackson
	Elbert Waller, Rep.	Perry
	Charles J. Kribs, Dem.	Randolph
45	Carl E. Robinson, Rep.	Morgan
	Henry H. Mester, Rep.	Sangamon
	T. J. Sullivan, Dem.	Sangamon
46	W. B. Phillips,[6] Rep.	Jefferson

District	Member	County
Charles L. Wood, Rep.	Wayne
Sidney Parker, Dem.	Jefferson
47	William H. Martin, Rep.	Madison
Schuyler B. Vaughan, Rep.	Bond
Charles F. Malloy, Dem.	Bond
48	Ed Ryan, Rep.	Lawrence
John R. Thompson, Rep.	Lawrence
F. W. Lewis, Dem.	Crawford
49	Ed P. Petri, Rep.	St. Clair
Frank Holten, Dem.	St. Clair
Grover C. Borders, Dem.	St. Clair
50	Wallace A. Bandy, Rep.	Williamson
Alexander Wilson, Dem.	Alexander
Earl C. Kimbro, Dem.	Union
51	Claude L. Rew, Rep.	Saline
W. V. Rush, Rep.	Massac
Frank Porter, Dem.	Hamilton

[1] Died April 8, 1929.
[2] Died Nov. 12, 1928.
[3] Died Nov. 12, 1928.
[4] Died Oct. 23, 1929.
[5] Died May 24, 1929.
[6] Died April 21, 1929.

District	Member	County
33	Martin R. Carlson, Rep.	Rock Island
34	John R. Hamilton, Rep.	Coles
35	Harry G. Wright, Rep.	De Kalb
36	J. Leroy Adair, Dem.	Adams
37	Thomas P. Gunning, Rep.	Bureau
38	Andrew S. Cuthbertson, Rep.	Macoupin
39	N. M. Mason, Rep.	La Salle
40	Guy L. Smith, Rep.	Christian
41	Richard J. Barr, Rep.	Will
42	Walter L. Finn, Dem.	Marion
43	Clinton L. Ewing, Rep.	Knox
44	Harry Wilson, Rep.	Perry
45	Earl B. Searcy, Rep.	Sangamon
46	William R. McCauley, Rep.	Richland
47	James O. Monroe, Dem.	Madison
48	Arthur A. Miles, Rep.	Hardin
49	E. P. Kline, Dem.	St. Clair
50	James H. Felts,[1] Dem.	Williamson
51	Charles H. Thompson, Rep.	Saline

[1] Died Jan. 13, 1932.

Fifty-seventh General Assembly, 1931–32

Senate

President	Fred E. Sterling
President pro tempore	Richard J. Barr
Secretary	James H. Paddock

District	Member	County
1	Daniel A. Serritella, Rep.	Cook
2	Joseph Mendel, Dem.	Cook
3	Adelbert H. Roberts, Rep.	Cook
4	Frank J. McDermott, Dem.	Cook
5	Roy C. Woods, Rep.	Cook
6	James J. Barbour, Rep.	Cook
7	Arthur A. Huebsch, Rep.	Cook
8	Ray Paddock, Rep.	Lake
9	Patrick J. Carroll, Dem.	Cook
10	Charles W. Baker, Rep.	Ogle
11	Thomas J. Courtney, Dem.	Cook
12	Joseph L. Meyers, Rep.	Stephenson
13	Francis J. Loughran, Dem.	Cook
14	Harold C. Kessinger, Rep.	Kane
15	Peter P. Kielminski, Dem.	Cook
16	Simon E. Lantz, Rep.	Woodford
17	James B. Leonardo, Rep.	Cook
18	Victor P. Michel, Rep.	Peoria
19	Richey V. Graham, Dem.	Cook
20	Richard R. Meents, Rep.	Iroquois
21	George M. Maypole, Dem.	Cook
22	Martin B. Bailey, Rep.	Vermilion
23	William F. Gillmeister, Dem.	Cook
24	Henry M. Dunlap, Rep.	Champaign
25	Frank J. Huckin, Jr., Dem.	Cook
26	Florence Fifer Bohrer, Rep.	McLean
27	John Broderick, Dem.	Cook
28	Charles E. Lee, Rep.	Macon
29	Edward P. O'Grady, Dem.	Cook
30	Epler C. Mills, Rep.	Cass
31	Harold G. Ward, Dem.	Cook
32	Louis H. Hanna, Rep.	Warren

House of Representatives

Speaker	David E. Shanahan
Clerk	George C. Blaeuer

District	Member	County
1	George W. Blackwell, Rep.	Cook
Harris B. Gaines, Rep.	Cook
John J. Griffin,[1] Dem.	Cook
2	Albert J. Mancin, Rep.	Cook
John M. Bolton, Dem.	Cook
Frank Ryan, Dem.	Cook
3	William E. King, Rep.	Cook
Charles J. Jenkins, Rep.	Cook
George Gary Noonan, Dem.	Cook
4	Michael A. Ruddy, Rep.	Cook
Thomas J. O'Grady, Dem.	Cook
James P. Boyle, Dem.	Cook
5	William J. Warfield, Rep.	Cook
Josephine Perry, Rep.	Cook
Michael L. Igoe, Dem.	Cook
6	Ralph E. Church, Rep.	Cook
Arthur E. Fischer, Dem.	Cook
Joseph H. Donahue, Dem.	Cook
7	Anna Wilmarth Ickes, Rep.	Cook
Frank E. Foster, Rep.	Cook
Emmett McGrath, Dem.	Cook
8	Richard J. Lyons, Rep.	Lake
William M. Carroll, Rep.	McHenry
Thomas A. Bolger, Dem.	McHenry
9	David E. Shanahan, Rep.	Cook
Henry Sonnenschein, Dem.	Cook
William J. Gormley, Dem.	Cook
10	Leroy M. Green, Rep.	Winnebago
Carl O. Nyman, Rep.	Winnebago
David Hunter, Jr., Rep.	Winnebago
11	David I. Swanson, Rep.	Cook
John M. Lee, Dem.	Cook
George A. Fitzgerald, Dem.	Cook
12	Alfred S. Babb, Rep.	Carroll
John Acker, Rep.	Carroll
Charles D. Franz, Dem.	Stephenson

District	Member	County
13	Elmer J. Schnackenberg, Rep.	Cook
	John C. Garriott, Jr., Rep.	Cook
	William W. Powers, Dem.	Cook
14	Frank A. McCarthy, Rep.	Kane
	John M. Peffers, Rep.	Kane
	John F. Petit, Dem.	Kane
15	James Curran, Rep.	Cook
	Joseph Perina, Dem.	Cook
	Edward Skarda, Dem.	Cook
16	Charles M. Turner, Rep.	Marshall
	Fred Bestold, Rep.	Marshall
	Michael Fahy, Dem.	Marshall
17	Roland V. Libonati, Rep.	Cook
	Charles Coia, Dem.	Cook
	Anthony Pintozzi, Dem.	Cook
18	Carl J. Jobst, Rep.	Peoria
	Leo D. Crowley, Rep.	Peoria
	David H. McClugage, Dem.	Peoria
19	Solomon P. Roderick, Rep.	Cook
	John O. Hruby, Dem.	Cook
	John R. McSweeney, Dem.	Cook
20	Elmer C. Wilson, Rep.	Kankakee
	Luther B. Bratton, Rep.	Kankakee
	James T. Burns, Dem.	Kankakee
21	J. W. Harris, Rep.	Cook
	Thomas J. O'Brien, Dem.	Cook
	Joseph L. Rategan, Dem.	Cook
22	Hugh M. Luckey, Rep.	Vermilion
	P. J. Breen, Dem.	Vermilion
	W. O. Edwards, Dem.	Vermilion
23	William G. Thon, Rep.	Cook
	Edward M. Overland,[2] Rep.	Cook
	Thomas P. Keane, Dem.	Cook
24	Roger F. Little, Rep.	Champaign
	William Z. Black, Rep.	Champaign
	William E. Gilmore, Dem.	Champaign
25	Edwin B. Bederman, Rep.	Cook
	Benjamin S. Adamowski, Dem.	Cook
	Raymond W. O'Keefe, Dem.	Cook
26	G. J. Johnson, Rep.	Ford
	Gordon W. Childers, Rep.	McLean
	Charles P. Kane, Dem.	McLean
27	A. O. Galvin, Rep.	Cook
	A. L. Auth, Dem.	Cook
	Joseph P. Rostenkowski, Dem.	Cook
28	W. C. Chynoweth, Rep.	Macon
	Evan Worth, Rep.	Logan
	Howard L. Doyle, Dem.	Macon
29	Robert M. Woodward, Rep.	Cook
	Michael R. Durso, Rep.	Cook
	Lawrence C. O'Brien, Dem.	Cook
30	Homer J. Tice, Rep.	Menard
	Herschel V. Teel, Dem.	Schuyler
	Martin B. Lohmann, Dem.	Tazewell
31	James J. McVicker, Rep.	Cook
	Mason S. Sullivan, Dem.	Cook
	Pierce L. Shannon, Dem.	Cook
32	Roy R. Barnes, Rep.	McDonough
	Rollo R. Robbins, Rep.	Hancock
	Mary Davidson, Dem.	Hancock
33	Harry M. McCaskrin, Rep.	Rock Island
	Clinton Searle, Rep.	Rock Island
	Thomas P. Sinnett, Dem.	Rock Island

District	Member	County
34	John W. Lewis, Rep.	Clark
	Sol Handy, Dem.	Clark
	John F. Brewster, Dem.	Coles
35	Henry C. Allen, Rep.	Whiteside
	Dennis J. Collins, Rep.	De Kalb
	John P. Devine, Dem.	Lee
36	Henry F. Scarborough, Rep.	Adams
	Henry D. Sullivan, Jr., Dem.	Adams
	Carroll Bush, Dem.	Pike
37	Frederick W. Rennick, Rep.	Bureau
	William H. Jackson, Rep.	Stark
	Robert J. Wilson, Dem.	Henry
38	Robert Whiteley, Rep.	Macoupin
	Truman A. Snell, Dem.	Macoupin
	M. E. Bray, Dem.	Montgomery
39	R. G. Soderstrom, Rep.	La Salle
	Ole E. Benson, Rep.	La Salle
	Edmond P. Conerton, Dem.	La Salle
40	Roy A. Corzine, Rep.	Christian
	Henry D. Sparks, Rep.	Shelby
	Arthur Roe, Dem.	Fayette
41	John L. Walker, Rep.	Will
	Otto A. Buck, Rep.	Du Page
	Michael F. Hennebry, Dem.	Will
42	R. J. Branson, Rep.	Marion
	Alois B. Lager, Dem.	Clinton
	J. E. McMackin, Dem.	Marion
43	E. W. Mureen, Rep.	Knox
	Henry G. Hawkinson, Rep.	Knox
	Frank W. McClure, Dem.	Knox
44	Elbert Waller, Rep.	Perry
	Joseph H. Davis, Dem.	Jackson
	Charles J. Kribs, Dem.	Randolph
45	D. Logan Giffin, Rep.	Sangamon
	William J. Lawler, Rep.	Sangamon
	T. J. Sullivan, Dem.	Sangamon
46	Frank G. Thompson, Rep.	Jefferson
	Sidney Parker, Dem.	Jefferson
	F. W. Kuechler, Dem.	Jasper
47	Schuyler B. Vaughan, Rep.	Bond
	Schaefer O'Neill, Dem.	Madison
	Charles F. Malloy, Dem.	Bond
48	John R. Thompson, Rep.	Lawrence
	Ed Ryan,[3] Rep.	Lawrence
	F. W. Lewis, Dem.	Crawford
49	R. H. Huschle, Rep.	St. Clair
	Frank Holten, Dem.	St. Clair
	Grover C. Borders, Dem.	St. Clair
50	M. F. Browner, Rep.	Pulaski
	Earl C. Kimbro, Dem.	Union
	Alexander Wilson, Dem.	Alexander
51	W. V. Rush, Rep.	Massac
	Claude L. Rew, Dem.	Saline
	Frank Porter, Dem.	Hamilton

[1] Died July 6, 1931.
[2] Died Dec. 14, 1931.
[3] Died Feb. 17, 1932.

Fifty-eighth General Assembly, 1933–34

Senate

President   Thomas F. Donovan
President pro tempore   Richey V. Graham
Secretary   Alfred E. Eden

District	Member	County
1	Daniel A. Serritella, Rep.	Cook
2	Joseph Mendel, Dem.	Cook
3	Adelbert H. Roberts, Rep.	Cook
4	Frank J. McDermott, Dem.	Cook
5	Roy C. Woods, Rep.	Cook
6	James J. Barbour, Rep.	Cook
7	Arthur A. Huebsch, Rep.	Cook
8	Ray Paddock, Rep.	Lake
9	Patrick J. Carroll, Dem.	Cook
10	Charles W. Baker, Rep.	Ogle
11	Thomas J. Courtney,[1] Dem.	Cook
12	Harry C. Boeke, Dem.	Stephenson
13	Francis J. Loughran, Dem.	Cook
14	Arnold P. Benson, Rep.	Kane
15	Peter P. Kielminski, Dem.	Cook
16	Simon E. Lantz, Rep.	Woodford
17	James B. Leonardo, Rep.	Cook
18	Carl Behrman, Dem.	Peoria
19	Richey V. Graham, Dem.	Cook
20	Jerome O'Connell, Dem.	Grundy
21	George M. Maypole, Dem.	Cook
22	Wilber D. Hickman, Dem.	Edgar
23	William F. Gillmeister, Dem.	Cook
24	W. E. C. Clifford, Dem.	Champaign
25	Frank J. Huckin, Jr., Dem.	Cook
26	L. C. Sieberns, Dem.	McLean
27	John Broderick, Dem.	Cook
28	Louis O. Williams, Dem.	De Witt
29	Edward P. O'Grady, Dem.	Cook
30	Martin B. Lohmann, Dem.	Tazewell
31	Harold G. Ward, Dem.	Cook
32	James C. Mayor, Dem.	Hancock
33	Martin R. Carlson, Rep.	Rock Island
34	J. S. Mundy, Dem.	Clark
35	Harry G. Wright, Rep.	De Kalb
36	Mark A. Penick, Dem.	Adams
37	Thomas P. Gunning, Rep.	Bureau
38	Harry C. Stuttle, Dem.	Montgomery
39	N. M. Mason, Rep.	La Salle
40	Clifford J. Vogelsang,[2] Dem.	Christian
41	Richard J. Barr, Rep.	Will
42	Walter L. Finn, Dem.	Marion
43	Clinton L. Ewing, Rep.	Knox
44	Charles J. Kribs, Dem.	Randolph
45	Earl B. Searcy, Rep.	Sangamon
46	H. S. Burgess, Dem.	Wayne
47	James O. Monroe, Dem.	Madison
48	Raleigh M. Shaw, Dem.	Lawrence
49	E. P. Kline, Dem.	St. Clair
50	R. Wallace Karraker, Dem.	Union
51	Charles H. Thompson, Rep.	Saline

[1] Died Dec. 2, 1932.
[2] Died May 8, 1933.

House of Representatives

Speaker	Arthur Roe
Clerk	Charles P. Casey

District	Member	County
1	Harris B. Gaines, Rep.	Cook
	Arthur T. Broche, Rep.	Cook
	Harry L. Williams, Dem.	Cook
2	Albert J. Mancin, Rep.	Cook
	John M. Bolton, Dem.	Cook
	Frank Ryan, Dem.	Cook

District	Member	County
3	William E. King, Rep.	Cook
	Charles J. Jenkins, Rep.	Cook
	George Gary Noonan, Dem.	Cook
4	Michael A. Ruddy, Rep.	Cook
	John C. Kluczynski, Dem.	Cook
	James P. Boyle, Dem.	Cook
5	William J. Warfield, Rep.	Cook
	Josephine Perry, Rep.	Cook
	Bernard J. Kewin, Dem.	Cook
6	Arthur E. Fischer, Rep.	Cook
	Drennan J. Slater, Rep.	Cook
	Joseph H. Donahue, Dem.	Cook
7	Anna Wilmarth Ickes, Rep.	Cook
	Frank E. Foster, Rep.	Cook
	Emmett McGrath, Dem.	Cook
8	Richard J. Lyons, Rep.	Lake
	William M. Carroll, Rep.	McHenry
	Thomas A. Bolger, Dem.	McHenry
9	David E. Shanahan, Rep.	Cook
	Peter P. Jezierny, Dem.	Cook
	William J. Gormley, Dem.	Cook
10	Leroy M. Green, Rep.	Winnebago
	David Hunter, Jr., Rep.	Winnebago
	Frank B. Wilson, Dem.	Winnebago
11	David I. Swanson, Rep.	Cook
	George A. Fitzgerald, Dem.	Cook
	Michael E. Hannigan, Dem.	Cook
12	John Acker,[1] Rep.	Carroll
	John A. Bingham, Rep.	JoDaviess
	Charles D. Franz, Dem.	Stephenson
13	Elmer J. Schnackenberg, Rep.	Cook
	William W. Powers, Dem.	Cook
	John G. Ryan, Dem.	Cook
14	Frank A. McCarthy, Rep.	Kane
	John M. Peffers, Rep.	Kane
	John F. Petit, Dem.	Kane
15	James L. Kostka, Rep.	Cook
	Matt Franz, Dem.	Cook
	Edward Skarda, Dem.	Cook
16	Calistus A. Bruer, Rep.	Livingston
	Charles M. Turner, Rep.	Marshall
	Michael Fahy, Dem.	Marshall
17	Roland V. Libonati, Rep.	Cook
	Charles Coia, Dem.	Cook
	Anthony Pintozzi,[2] Dem.	Cook
18	Clarence P. Scott, Rep.	Peoria
	Thomas J. Stack, Rep.	Peoria
	David H. McClugage, Dem.	Peoria
19	Solomon P. Roderick, Rep.	Cook
	John R. McSweeney, Dem.	Cook
	John O. Hruby, Dem.	Cook
20	Luther B. Bratton, Rep.	Kankakee
	Elmer C. Wilson, Rep.	Kankakee
	James T. Burns, Dem.	Kankakee
21	Robert Petrone, Rep.	Cook
	Joseph L. Rategan, Dem.	Cook
	Edward J. Upton, Dem.	Cook
22	Walter J. Bookwalter, Rep.	Vermilion
	P. J. Breen, Dem.	Vermilion
	W. O. Edwards, Dem.	Vermilion
23	William G. Thon, Rep.	Cook
	Arthur M. Kaindl, Dem.	Cook
	N. A. Waterloo, Dem.	Cook

District	Member	County
24	Roger F. Little, Rep.	Champaign
	William Z. Black, Rep.	Champaign
	Thompson J. Anderson, Dem.	Piatt
25	Edwin B. Bederman, Rep.	Cook
	Benjamin S. Adamowski, Dem.	Cook
	Raymond V. O'Keefe, Dem.	Cook
26	Maurice O. Kalahar, Rep.	McLean
	G. J. Johnson, Rep.	Ford
	Joseph W. Russell, Dem.	Ford
27	A. O. Galvin, Rep.	Cook
	Edward J. Petlak, Dem.	Cook
	A. L. Auth, Dem.	Cook
28	W. C. Chynoweth, Rep.	Macon
	Howard L. Doyle, Dem.	Macon
	William D. Gayle, Dem.	Logan
29	Robert M. Woodward, Rep.	Cook
	Joseph E. Farina, Rep.	Cook
	William J. Connors, Dem.	Cook
30	Jesse Hall, Rep.	Tazewell
	Herschel V. Teel, Dem.	Schuyler
	Glen Petefish, Dem.	Cass
31	James J. McVicker, Rep.	Cook
	Pierce L. Shannon, Dem.	Cook
	Mason S. Sullivan, Dem.	Cook
32	Claude R. Thomas, Rep.	Hancock
	Rodmon E. Grigsby, Dem.	McDonough
	Mary Davidson, Dem.	Hancock
33	Harry M. McCaskrin, Rep.	Rock Island
	Clinton Searle, Rep.	Rock Island
	Thomas P. Sinnett, Dem.	Rock Island
34	Charles G. Strohm, Rep.	Clark
	Sol Handy, Dem.	Clark
	Harvey Z. O'Hair, Dem.	Coles
35	Dennis J. Collins, Rep.	De Kalb
	Henry C. Allen, Rep.	Whiteside
	John P. Devine, Dem.	Lee
36	Henry F. Scarborough, Rep.	Adams
	Joseph E. Heckenkamp, Dem.	Adams
	Thomas J. Lenane, Dem.	Adams
37	William H. Jackson, Rep.	Stark
	Frederick W. Rennick, Rep.	Bureau
	Robert J. Wilson, Dem.	Henry
38	Hugh W. Cross, Rep.	Jersey
	M. E. Bray, Dem.	Montgomery
	Frank A. Stewart, Dem.	Macoupin
39	R. G. Soderstrom, Rep.	La Salle
	Ole E. Benson, Rep.	La Salle
	Edmond P. Conerton, Dem.	La Salle
40	Henry D. Sparks, Rep.	Shelby
	Arthur Roe, Dem.	Fayette
	Sam S. Lorton, Dem.	Shelby
41	John L. Walker, Rep.	Will
	Lottie Holman O'Neill, Rep.	Du Page
	Michael F. Hennebry, Dem.	Will
42	R. J. Branson, Rep.	Marion
	Alois B. Lager, Dem.	Clinton
	George J. Bauer, Dem.	Effingham
43	Henry G. Hawkinson,[3] Rep.	Knox
	E. W. Mureen, Rep.	Knox
	Frank W. McClure, Dem.	Knox
44	R. G. Crisenberry, Rep.	Jackson
	Joseph H. Davis, Dem.	Jackson
	A. A. Brands, Dem.	Randolph

District	Member	County
45	William J. Lawler, Rep.	Sangamon
	Hugh Green, Rep.	Morgan
	David Evans, Dem.	Sangamon
46	Glenn H. Sunderland, Rep.	Jasper
	Laurence F. Arnold, Dem.	Jasper
	Sidney Parker, Dem.	Jefferson
47	I. H. Streeper III, Rep.	Madison
	Schaefer O'Neill, Dem.	Madison
	C. W. Burton, Dem.	Madison
48	John R. Thompson, Rep.	Lawrence
	F. W. Lewis, Dem.	Crawford
	D. T. Woodard, Dem.	White
49	R. H. Huschle, Rep.	St. Clair
	Frank Holten, Dem.	St. Clair
	Grover C. Borders, Dem.	St. Clair
50	M. F. Browner, Rep.	Pulaski
	Louie E. Lewis, Dem.	Franklin
	Ray C. Carroll, Dem.	Williamson
51	W. V. Rush, Rep.	Massac
	John D. Upchurch, Dem.	Saline
	Frank Porter, Dem.	Hamilton

[1] Died Aug. 6, 1933.
[2] Died April 2, 1933.
[3] Died Oct. 11, 1933.

Fifty-ninth General Assembly, 1935–36

Senate

President   Thomas F. Donovan
President pro tempore   Richie V. Graham
Secretary   Alfred E. Eden

District	Member	County
1	Daniel A. Serritella, Rep.	Cook
2	Joseph Mendel, Dem.	Cook
3	William E. King, Rep.	Cook
4	Frank J. McDermott, Dem.	Cook
5	Thomas V. Smith, Dem.	Cook
6	James J. Barbour, Rep.	Cook
7	Arthur J. Bidwill,[1] Rep.	Cook
	Charles F. Baumrucker,[2] Dem.	Cook
8	Ray Paddock, Rep.	Lake
9	Patrick J. Carroll, Dem.	Cook
10	Charles W. Baker, Rep.	Ogle
11	John M. Lee, Dem.	Cook
12	Harry C. Boeke, Dem.	Stephenson
13	Francis J. Loughran, Dem.	Cook
14	Arnold P. Benson, Rep.	Kane
15	Peter P. Kielminski, Dem.	Cook
16	Simon E. Lantz, Rep.	Woodford
17	James B. Leonardo, Rep.	Cook
18	Carl Behrman, Dem.	Peoria
19	Richey V. Graham, Dem.	Cook
20	Jerome O'Connell, Dem.	Grundy
21	George M. Maypole, Dem.	Cook
22	Wilber D. Hickman, Dem.	Edgar
23	Thomas E. Keane, Dem.	Cook
24	W. E. C. Clifford, Dem.	Champaign
25	Frank J. Huckin, Jr., Dem.	Cook
26	L. C. Sieberns, Dem.	McLean
27	John Broderick, Dem.	Cook
28	Louis O. Williams, Dem.	De Witt
29	William J. Connors, Dem.	Cook
30	Martin B. Lohmann, Dem.	Tazewell
31	Harold G. Ward, Dem.	Cook
32	James C. Mayor, Dem.	Hancock

District	Member	County
33	Robert M. Harper, Dem.	Rock Island
34	J. S. Mundy, Dem.	Clark
35	George C. Dixon, Rep.	Lee
36	Mark A. Penick, Dem.	Adams
37	Thomas P. Gunning, Rep.	Bureau
38	Harry C. Stuttle, Dem.	Montgomery
39	N. M. Mason, Rep.	La Salle
40	John W. Fribley, Dem.	Christian
41	Richard J. Barr, Rep.	Will
42	Walter L. Finn, Dem.	Marion
43	Clinton L. Ewing, Rep.	Knox
44	Charles J. Kribs, Dem.	Randolph
45	Earl B. Searcy, Rep.	Sangamon
46	H. S. Burgess, Dem.	Wayne
47	James O. Monroe, Dem.	Madison
48	Raleigh M. Shaw, Dem.	Lawrence
49	Louis J. Menges, Dem.	St. Clair
50	R. Wallace Karraker, Dem.	Union
51	Oral P. Tuttle, Rep.	Saline

¹ Election contested.
² Seated May 21, 1935, vice Bidwill.

House of Representatives

Speaker	John P. Devine
Clerk	Harold J. Taylor

District	Member	County
1	Harry L. Williams, Dem.	Cook
	Arthur T. Broche, Rep.	Cook
	Harris B. Gaines, Rep.	Cook
2	John M. Bolton, Dem.	Cook
	Frank Ryan, Dem.	Cook
	James J. Adduci, Rep.	Cook
3	George Gary Noonan, Dem.	Cook
	Charles J. Jenkins, Rep.	Cook
	Warren B. Douglas,¹ Rep.	Cook
4	John C. Kluczynski, Dem.	Cook
	James P. Boyle, Dem.	Cook
	Michael A. Ruddy, Rep.	Cook
5	Louis G. Berman, Dem.	Cook
	Bernard J. Kewin, Dem.	Cook
	William J. Warfield, Rep.	Cook
6	Joseph H. Donahue, Dem.	Cook
	Charles H. Weber, Dem.	Cook
	Drennan J. Slater, Rep.	Cook
7	Frank G. Ring, Dem.	Cook
	Frank E. Foster, Rep.	Cook
	Bernice T. Van Der Vries, Rep.	Cook
8	Thomas A. Bolger, Dem.	McHenry
	Richard J. Lyons, Rep.	Lake
	William M. Carroll, Rep.	McHenry
9	Peter P. Jezierny, Dem.	Cook
	William J. Gormley, Rep.	Cook
	David E. Shanahan, Rep.	Cook
10	Frank B. Wilson, Dem.	Ogle
	Leroy M. Green, Rep.	Winnebago
	David Hunter, Jr., Rep.	Winnebago
11	George A. Fitzgerald, Dem.	Cook
	Michael E. Hannigan, Dem.	Cook
	David I. Swanson, Rep.	Cook
12	Charles D. Franz, Dem.	Stephenson
	John A. Bingham, Rep.	JoDaviess
	Edward E. Laughlin, Rep.	Stephenson
13	William W. Powers, Dem.	Cook
	John G. Ryan, Dem.	Cook
	Elmer J. Schnackenberg, Rep.	Cook

District	Member	County
14	John F. Petit, Dem.	Kane
	John M. Peffers, Rep.	Kane
	Frank A. McCarthy, Rep.	Kane
15	Edward Skarda, Dem.	Cook
	Matt Franz, Dem.	Cook
	James L. Kostka, Rep.	Cook
16	William Vicars, Dem.	Livingston
	Calistus A. Bruer, Rep.	Livingston
	Charles M. Turner, Rep.	Marshall
17	A. J. Prignano, Dem.	Cook
	Charles Coia, Dem.	Cook
	Peter C. Granata, Rep.	Cook
18	Howard J. Gorman, Dem.	Peoria
	Clarence P. Scott, Rep.	Peoria
	Leo D. Crowley, Rep.	Peoria
19	John O. Hruby, Dem.	Cook
	John R. McSweeney, Dem.	Cook
	Solomon P. Roderick, Rep.	Cook
20	James T. Burns, Dem.	Kankakee
	Ben W. Alpiner, Dem.	Kankakee
	Harry L. Topping, Rep.	Kankakee
21	Joseph L. Rategan, Dem.	Cook
	Edward J. Upton, Dem.	Cook
	Robert Petrone, Rep.	Cook
22	P. J. Breen, Dem.	Edgar
	W. O. Edwards, Dem.	Vermilion
	Hugh M. Luckey, Rep.	Vermilion
23	Arthur M. Kaindl, Dem.	Cook
	Stanley A. Halick, Dem.	Cook
	Daniel A. Roberts, Rep.	Cook
24	Hugh M. Rigney, Dem.	Moultrie
	E. E. Sturdyvin, Dem.	Champaign
	Everett R. Peters, Rep.	Champaign
25	Benjamin S. Adamowski, Dem.	Cook
	Raymond V. O'Keefe, Dem.	Cook
	Elroy C. Sandquist, Rep.	Cook
26	Joseph W. Russell, Dem.	Ford
	Maurice O. Kalahar, Rep.	McLean
	G. J. Johnson, Rep.	Ford
27	A. L. Auth, Dem.	Cook
	Edward J. Petlak, Dem.	Cook
	Joseph N. DeGrazio, Rep.	Cook
28	Verne R. Johnson, Dem.	Logan
	Nicholas L. Hubbard, Dem.	Logan
	Dan Dinneen, Rep.	Macon
29	Arthur J. Quinn, Dem.	Cook
	Edward P. O'Grady, Dem.	Cook
	Joseph E. Farina, Rep.	Cook
30	Herschel V. Teel, Dem.	Schuyler
	Glen Petefish, Dem.	Cass
	Robert H. Allison, Rep.	Tazewell
31	Pierce L. Shannon, Dem.	Cook
	Mason S. Sullivan, Dem.	Cook
	Edward P. Saltiel, Rep.	Cook
32	Lawrence H. Stice, Dem.	Warren
	Claude R. Thomas, Rep.	Hancock
	T. Mac Downing, Rep.	McDonough
33	Thomas P. Sinnett, Dem.	Rock Island
	Clinton Searle, Dem.	Rock Island
	Harry M. McCaskrin, Rep.	Rock Island
34	Victor H. McDonald, Dem.	Douglas
	J. M. Turner, Dem.	Clark
	Charles G. Strohm, Rep.	Clark

District	Member	County
35	John P. Devine, Dem.	Lee
	Dennis J. Collins, Rep.	De Kalb
	Henry C. Allen, Rep.	Whiteside
36	Joseph E. Heckenkamp, Dem.	Adams
	Thomas J. Lenane, Dem.	Adams
	Henry F. Scarborough, Rep.	Adams
37	Henry Knauf, Dem.	Bureau
	Frederick W. Rennick, Rep.	Bureau
	James A. Nowlan, Rep.	Stark
38	Frank W. Fries, Dem.	Macoupin
	Frank A. Stewart, Dem.	Macoupin
	Hugh W. Cross, Rep.	Jersey
39	Edward G. Hayne, Dem.	La Salle
	Ole E. Benson, Rep.	La Salle
	R. G. Soderstrom, Rep.	La Salle
40	Sam S. Lorton, Dem.	Shelby
	C. F. Easterday, Dem.	Fayette
	Henry D. Sparks, Rep.	Shelby
41	Michael F. Hennebry, Dem.	Will
	Lottie Holman O'Neill, Rep.	Du Page
	Warren L. Wood, Rep.	Will
42	George J. Bauer, Dem.	Effingham
	Alois B. Lager, Dem.	Clinton
	R. J. Branson, Rep.	Marion
43	Frank W. McClure, Dem.	Knox
	Ray Simkins, Dem.	Knox
	Reed F. Cutler, Rep.	Fulton
44	Joseph H. Davis, Dem.	Jackson
	A. A. Brands, Dem.	Randolph
	R. G. Crisenberry, Rep.	Jackson
45	Warren E. Brockhouse, Dem.	Morgan
	Hugh Green, Rep.	Morgan
	William J. Lawler, Rep.	Sangamon
46	Laurence F. Arnold, Dem.	Jasper
	Hardy M. Swift, Dem.	Jefferson
	Glenn H. Sunderland, Rep.	Jasper
47	Schaefer O'Neill, Dem.	Madison
	Lloyd Harris, Dem.	Madison
	I. H. Streeper III, Rep.	Madison
48	F. W. Lewis, Dem.	Crawford
	Thomas W. Hall, Dem.	White
	Fred A. Reavill, Rep.	Crawford
49	Frank Holten, Dem.	St. Clair
	A. H. Smith, Dem.	St. Clair
	Calvin D. Johnson, Rep.	St. Clair
50	Louie E. Lewis, Dem.	Franklin
	Charles A. Koehler, Dem.	Alexander
	M. F. Browner, Rep.	Pulaski
51	Paul Powell, Dem.	Johnson
	Abner Field, Rep.	Pope
	R. R. Randolph, Rep.	Saline

[1] Died Dec. 3, 1934.

Sixtieth General Assembly, 1937–38

Senate

President　　　　　　　　　　John Stelle
President pro tempore
　　　　　　　　　　George M. Maypole
Secretary　　　　　　　　　　Alfred E. Eden

District	Member	County
1	Daniel A. Serritella, Rep.	Cook
2	Joseph Mendel, Dem.	Cook
3	William E. King, Rep.	Cook
4	Frank J. McDermott, Dem.	Cook
5	Thomas V. Smith, Dem.	Cook
6	John J. Myers, Dem.	Cook
7	Charles F. Baumrucker, Dem.	Cook
8	Ray Paddock, Rep.	Lake
9	Patrick J. Carroll,[1] Dem.	Cook
10	Charles W. Baker, Rep.	Ogle
11	John M. Lee, Dem.	Cook
12	Edward E. Laughlin, Rep.	Stephenson
13	Francis J. Loughran, Dem.	Cook
14	Arnold P. Benson, Rep.	Kane
15	Peter P. Kielminski, Dem.	Cook
16	Simon E. Lantz, Rep.	Woodford
17	James B. Leonardo, Dem.	Cook
18	Thomas E. Madden, Dem.	Peoria
19	Richey V. Graham, Dem.	Cook
20	Louis E. Beckman, Rep.	Kankakee
21	George M. Maypole, Dem.	Cook
22	Wilber D. Hickman, Dem.	Edgar
23	Thomas E. Keane, Dem.	Cook
24	W. E. C. Clifford, Dem.	Champaign
25	Frank J. Huckin, Jr., Dem.	Cook
26	L. C. Sieberns, Dem.	McLean
27	John Broderick, Dem.	Cook
28	Louis O. Williams, Dem.	De Witt
29	William J. Connors, Dem.	Cook
30	Martin B. Lohmann, Dem.	Tazewell
31	Harold G. Ward, Dem.	Cook
32	T. Mac Downing, Rep.	McDonough
33	Robert M. Harper, Dem.	Rock Island
34	Melvin Thomas, Dem.	Coles
35	George C. Dixon, Rep.	Lee
36	Joseph E. Heckenkamp, Dem.	Adams
37	Thomas P. Gunning, Rep.	Bureau
38	Harry C. Stuttle, Dem.	Montgomery
39	N. M. Mason, Rep.	La Salle
40	John W. Fribley, Dem.	Christian
41	Richard J. Barr, Rep.	Will
42	Walter L. Finn,[2] Dem.	Marion
43	Clinton L. Ewing, Rep.	Knox
44	R. G. Crisenberry, Rep.	Jackson
45	Earl B. Searcy, Rep.	Sangamon
46	H. S. Burgess, Dem.	Wayne
47	James O. Monroe, Dem.	Madison
48	D. T. Woodard, Dem.	White
49	Louis J. Menges, Dem.	St. Clair
50	R. Wallace Karraker, Dem.	Union
51	Oral P. Tuttle, Rep.	Saline

[1] Died Jan. 15, 1938.
[2] Died Nov. 7, 1936.

House of Representatives

Speaker　　　　　　　　　　Louie E. Lewis
Clerk　　　　　　　　　　Harold J. Taylor

District	Member	County
1	Harry L. Williams,[1] Dem.	Cook
	Ernest A. Greene, Rep.	Cook
	Arthur T. Broche, Rep.	Cook
2	Frank Ryan, Dem.	Cook
	James J. Ryan, Dem.	Cook

District	Member	County
	James J. Adduci, Rep.	Cook
3	George Gary Noonan, Dem.	Cook
	Charles J. Jenkins, Rep.	Cook
	Richard A. Harewood, Rep.	Cook
4	John C. Kluczynski, Dem.	Cook
	James P. Boyle, Dem.	Cook
	Michael A. Ruddy, Rep.	Cook
5	Louis G. Berman, Dem.	Cook
	Bernard A. Kewin, Dem.	Cook
	William J. Warfield, Rep.	Cook
6	Charles H. Weber, Dem.	Cook
	George H. Smith, Dem.	Cook
	Drennan J. Slater, Rep.	Cook
7	Emmett McGrath, Dem.	Cook
	Bernice T. Van Der Vries, Rep.	Cook
	Frank E. Foster, Rep.	Cook
8	Thomas A. Bolger, Dem.	McHenry
	Richard J. Lyons, Rep.	Lake
	Nick Keller, Rep.	Lake
9	Peter P. Jezierny, Dem.	Cook
	William J. Gormley, Dem.	Cook
	Richard J. Daley, Dem.	Cook
10	Edward C. Hunter, Dem.	Winnebago
	Frank B. Wilson, Dem.	Ogle
	David Hunter, Jr., Rep.	Winnebago
11	Michael E. Hannigan, Dem.	Cook
	George A. Fitzgerald, Dem.	Cook
	Calvin T. Weeks, Rep.	Cook
12	Charles D. Franz, Dem.	Stephenson
	John A. Bingham, Rep.	JoDaviess
	Franklin U. Stransky, Rep.	Carroll
13	William W. Powers,[2] Dem.	Cook
	John G. Ryan, Dem.	Cook
	Elmer J. Schnackenberg, Rep.	Cook
14	John F. Petit, Dem.	Kane
	John M. Peffers,[3] Rep.	Kane
	John C. Friedland, Rep.	Kane
15	Edward Skarda, Dem.	Cook
	Matt Franz, Dem.	Cook
	John A. Pelka, Rep.	Cook
16	William Vicars, Dem.	Livingston
	Charles M. Turner, Rep.	Marshall
	Calistus A. Bruer, Rep.	Livingston
17	Carmen Vacco, Dem.	Cook
	Nicholas J. Mastro, Dem.	Cook
	Peter C. Granata, Rep.	Cook
18	Howard J. Gorman, Dem.	Peoria
	Leo D. Crowley, Rep.	Peoria
	Clarence P. Scott, Rep.	Peoria
19	John O. Hruby, Dem.	Cook
	John R. McSweeney, Dem.	Cook
	Solomon P. Roderick, Rep.	Cook
20	Ben W. Alpiner, Dem.	Kankakee
	Harry L. Topping, Rep.	Kankakee
	George B. Allen, Rep.	Grundy
21	Edward J. McCabe, Dem.	Cook
	Joseph L. Rategan, Dem.	Cook
	Robert Petrone, Rep.	Cook
22	P. J. Breen, Dem.	Edgar
	Oda M. Sizemore, Dem.	Edgar
	John W. Speakman, Rep.	Vermilion
23	Arthur M. Kaindl, Dem.	Cook
	Stanley A. Halick, Dem.	Cook
	William G. Thon, Rep.	Cook
24	Tom M. Garman, Dem.	Champaign
	F. E. Sturdyvin, Dem.	Champaign
	Everett R. Peters, Rep.	Champaign

District	Member	County
25	Benjamin S. Adamowski, Dem.	Cook
	Raymond V. O'Keefe, Dem.	Cook
	Elroy C. Sandquist, Rep.	Cook
26	Joseph W. Russell, Dem.	Ford
	Maurice O. Kalahar, Rep.	McLean
	Homer Caton, Rep.	McLean
27	Edward J. Petlak, Dem.	Cook
	A. L. Auth, Dem.	Cook
	Joseph N. DeGrazio, Rep.	Cook
28	Nicholas L. Hubbard, Dem.	Logan
	Dean S. McGaughey, Dem.	Macon
	Dan Dinneen, Rep.	Macon
29	Edward P. O'Grady, Dem.	Cook
	Arthur J. Quinn, Dem.	Cook
	Robert M. Woodward, Rep.	Cook
30	Major T. Flowerree, Dem.	Mason
	Herschel V. Teel,[4] Dem.	Schuyler
	Robert H. Allison, Rep.	Tazewell
31	Pierce L. Shannon, Dem.	Cook
	Mason S. Sullivan, Dem.	Cook
	Edward P. Saltiel, Rep.	Cook
32	Ross E. Noper, Dem.	McDonough
	Claude R. Thomas, Rep.	Hancock
	Matt J. Gross, Rep.	Warren
33	Thomas A. Brennan, Dem.	Rock Island
	Ora Smith, Dem.	Henderson
	Harry M. McCaskrin, Rep.	Rock Island
34	J. M. Turner, Dem.	Clark
	Victor H. McDonald, Dem.	Douglas
	Andrew Knapp, Rep.	Douglas
35	Henry J. White, Dem.	De Kalb
	Dennis J. Collins, Rep.	De Kalb
	Henry C. Allen,[5] Rep.	Whiteside
36	Thomas J. Lenane, Dem.	Adams
	William F. Gibbs, Dem.	Adams
	Henry F. Scarborough, Rep.	Adams
37	Henry Knauf, Dem.	Bureau
	Frederick W. Rennick, Rep.	Bureau
	James A. Nowlan, Rep.	Stark
38	Howard Manning, Dem.	Jersey
	Frank A. Stewart, Dem.	Macoupin
	Hugh W. Cross, Rep.	Jersey
39	Jeremiah F. Walsh, Dem.	La Salle
	Edward G. Hayne, Dem.	La Salle
	Ole E. Benson, Rep.	La Salle
40	Sam S. Lorton, Dem.	Shelby
	C. F. Easterday, Dem.	Fayette
	Henry D. Sparks, Rep.	Shelby
41	Joseph Sam Perry, Dem.	Du Page
	Lottie Holman O'Neill, Rep.	Du Page
	Warren L. Wood, Rep.	Will
42	Alois B. Lager, Dem.	Clinton
	George J. Bauer, Dem.	Effingham
	R. J. Branson, Rep.	Marion
43	Ray Simkins, Dem.	Knox
	James E. Davis, Rep.	Knox
	Reed F. Cutler, Rep.	Fulton
44	Joseph H. Davis, Dem.	Jackson
	A. A. Brands, Dem.	Randolph
	Thomas J. Thornton, Rep.	Randolph
45	Andrew P. O'Neill, Dem.	Sangamon
	Hugh Green, Rep.	Morgan
	William J. Lawler, Rep.	Sangamon

District	Member	County
46	Hardy M. Swift, Dem.	Jefferson
	Sidney Parker, Dem.	Jefferson
	S. O. Dale, Rep.	Wayne
47	Schaefer O'Neill, Dem.	Madison
	Lloyd Harris, Dem.	Madison
	I. H. Streeper III, Rep.	Madison
48	Thomas W. Hall,[6] Dem.	White
	F. W. Lewis, Dem.	Crawford
	Fred A. Reavill, Rep.	Crawford
49	Ben Emge, Dem.	St. Clair
	Frank Holten, Dem.	St. Clair
	Calvin D. Johnson, Rep.	St. Clair
50	Louie E. Lewis, Dem.	Franklin
	Baker McAlpin Dem.	Franklin
	I. A. Palmer, Rep.	Franklin
51	Paul Powell, Dem.	Johnson
	R. R. Randolph, Rep.	Saline
	Abner Field, Rep.	Pope

[1] Died Jan. 4, 1938.
[2] Died July 14, 1938.
[3] Died Nov. 29, 1936.
[4] Died May 27, 1938.
[5] Died Dec. 15, 1937.
[6] Died Feb. 12, 1937.

District	Member	County
25	Frank J. Huckin, Jr., Dem.	Cook
26	L. C. Sieberns, Dem.	McLean
27	John Broderick,[1] Dem.	Cook
28	Nicholas L. Hubbard, Dem.	Logan
29	William J. Connors, Dem.	Cook
30	Martin B. Lohmann, Dem.	Tazewell
31	Harold G. Ward, Dem.	Cook
32	T. Mac Downing, Rep.	McDonough
33	Charles F. Carpentier, Rep.	Rock Island
34	Melvin Thomas, Dem.	Coles
35	George C. Dixon, Rep.	Lee
36	Joseph E. Heckenkamp, Dem.	Adams
37	Thomas P. Gunning, Rep.	Bureau
38	Harry C. Stuttle, Dem.	Montgomery
39	Ole E. Benson, Rep.	La Salle
40	John W. Fribley, Dem.	Christian
41	Richard J. Barr, Rep.	Will
42	John J. Parish, Dem.	Marion
43	Clinton L. Ewing, Rep.	Knox
44	R. G. Crisenberry, Rep.	Jackson
45	Earl B. Searcy, Rep.	Sangamon
46	H. S. Burgess, Dem.	Wayne
47	Norman G. Flagg, Rep.	Madison
48	D. T. Woodard, Dem.	White
49	Louis J. Menges, Dem.	St. Clair
50	R. Wallace Karraker, Dem.	Union
51	Charles H. Thompson, Rep.	Saline

[1] Died Aug. 9, 1939.

Sixty-first General Assembly 1939–40

Senate

President John Stelle
President pro tempore
          George M. Maypole
Secretary Alfred E. Eden

District	Member	County
1	Daniel A. Serritella, Rep.	Cook
2	Joseph Mendel, Dem.	Cook
3	William A. Wallace, Dem.	Cook
4	Frank J. McDermott, Dem.	Cook
5	John B. Geary, Dem.	Cook
6	John J. Myers, Dem.	Cook
7	Arthur J. Bidwill, Rep.	Cook
8	Ray Paddock, Rep.	Lake
9	Richard J. Daley, Dem.	Cook
10	Charles W. Baker, Rep.	Ogle
11	John M. Lee, Dem.	Cook
12	Edward E. Laughlin, Rep.	Stephenson
13	Francis J. Loughran, Dem.	Cook
14	Arnold P. Benson, Rep.	Kane
15	Peter P. Kielminski, Dem.	Cook
16	Simon E. Lantz, Rep.	Woodford
17	James B. Leonardo, Rep.	Cook
18	Thomas E. Madden, Dem.	Peoria
19	Abraham L. Marovitz, Dem.	Cook
20	Louis E. Beckman, Rep.	Kankakee
21	George M. Maypole, Dem.	Cook
22	Wilber D. Hickman, Dem.	Edgar
23	Thomas E. Keane, Dem.	Cook
24	W. E. C. Clifford, Dem.	Champaign

House of Representatives

Speaker Hugh W. Cross
Clerk R. R. Randolph

District	Member	County
1	Daniel M. Flanigan, Dem.	Cook
	Arthur T. Broche, Rep.	Cook
	Ernest A. Greene, Rep.	Cook
2	Frank Ryan, Dem.	Cook
	James J. Ryan, Dem.	Cook
	James J. Adduci, Rep.	Cook
3	George Gary Noonan, Dem.	Cook
	Charles J. Jenkins, Rep.	Cook
	A. Andrew Torrence,[1] Rep.	Cook
4	John C. Kluczynski, Dem.	Cook
	James P. Boyle,[2] Dem.	Cook
	Michael A. Ruddy, Rep.	Cook
5	James Weber Linn,[3] Dem.	Cook
	Louis G. Berman, Dem.	Cook
	William J. Warfield, Rep.	Cook
6	Charles H. Weber, Dem.	Cook
	George H. Smith, Dem.	Cook
	Drennan J. Slater, Rep.	Cook
7	Emmett McGrath, Dem.	Cook
	Bernice T. Van Der Vries, Rep.	Cook
	Arthur W. Sprague, Rep.	Cook
8	Thomas A. Bolger, Dem.	McHenry
	Nick Keller, Dem.	Lake
	Harold D. Kelsey, Rep.	Lake
9	Peter P. Jezierny, Dem.	Cook
	William J. Gormley, Dem.	Cook
	William S. Finucane, Rep.	Cook
10	John Baumgarten, Dem.	Winnebago
	David Hunter, Jr., Rep.	Winnebago

District	Member	County
	Leroy M. Green, Rep.	Winnebago
11	Michael E. Hannigan, Dem.	Cook
	George A. Fitzgerald, Dem.	Cook
	David I. Swanson, Rep.	Cook
12	Charles D. Franz, Dem.	Stephenson
	John A. Bingham, Rep.	JoDaviess
	Franklin U. Stransky, Rep.	Carroll
13	John G. Ryan, Dem.	Cook
	Adam S. Mioduski, Dem.	Cook
	Elmer J. Schnackenberg, Rep.	Cook
14	Leon M. Schuler, Dem.	Kane
	John C. Friedland, Rep.	Kane
	Maud N. Peffers, Rep.	Kane
15	Edward Skarda, Dem.	Cook
	Matt Franz, Dem.	Cook
	John A. Pelka, Rep.	Cook
16	William Vicars, Dem.	Livingston
	Calistus A. Bruer, Rep.	Livingston
	Rollie C. Carpenter, Rep.	Livingston
17	Carmen Vacco, Rep.	Cook
	Nicholas J. Mastro, Dem.	Cook
	Peter C. Granata, Rep.	Cook
18	Howard J. Gorman, Dem.	Peoria
	August C. Grebe, Rep.	Peoria
	Leo D. Crowley, Rep.	Peoria
19	John O. Hruby, Dem.	Cook
	John J. Gorman, Dem.	Cook
	Arnold L. Lund, Rep.	Cook
20	Ben W. Alpiner, Dem.	Kankakee
	Harry L. Topping, Rep.	Kankakee
	George B. Allen, Rep.	Grundy
21	Edward J. McCabe, Dem.	Cook
	Joseph L. Rategan, Dem.	Cook
	Robert Petrone, Rep.	Cook
22	W. O. Edwards, Dem.	Vermilion
	John W. Speakman, Rep.	Vermilion
	Augustus F. DeGafferelly, Rep.	Vermilion
23	Arthur M. Kaindl, Dem.	Cook
	Stanley A. Halick, Dem.	Cook
	William G. Thon, Rep.	Cook
24	Tom M. Garman, Dem.	Champaign
	Everett R. Peters, Rep.	Champaign
	Charles W. Clabaugh, Rep.	Champaign
25	Benjamin S. Adamowski, Dem.	Cook
	Raymond V. O'Keefe, Dem.	Cook
	Elroy C. Sandquist, Rep.	Cook
26	Joseph W. Russell, Dem.	Ford
	Ben S. Rhodes, Rep.	McLean
	Homer Caton, Rep.	McLean
27	Edward J. Petlak, Dem.	Cook
	John C. Kuklinski, Dem.	Cook
	Stanley E. Martynowski, Rep.	Cook
28	Dean S. McGaughey, Dem.	Macon
	Dan Dinneen, Rep.	Macon
	Ray A. Dillinger, Rep.	Macon
29	Edward P. O'Grady, Dem.	Cook
	Arthur J. Quinn, Dem.	Cook
	Robert M. Woodward, Rep.	Cook
30	Ed Teefey, Dem.	Brown
	Major T. Flowerree, Dem.	Mason
	Robert H. Allison, Rep.	Tazewell
31	Pierce L. Shannon, Dem.	Cook
	William B. Greene, Dem.	Cook
	Edward P. Saltiel, Rep.	Cook
32	Ross E. Noper, Dem.	McDonough
	Claude R. Thomas, Rep.	Hancock
	Sam Schaumleffel, Rep.	Warren

District	Member	County
33	Ora Smith, Dem.,	Henderson
	Clinton Searle, Rep.	Rock Island
	Harry M. McCaskrin, Rep.	Rock Island
34	J. M. Turner, Dem.	Clark
	Lew Wallace, Rep.	Coles
	Raymond C. Gillogly, Rep.	Douglas
35	Henry J. White, Dem.	De Kalb
	Dennis J. Collins, Rep.	De Kalb
	George S. Brydia, Rep.	Whiteside
36	Thomas J. Lenane, Dem.	Adams
	William F. Gibbs, Dem.	Adams
	Henry F. Scarborough, Rep.	Adams
37	Henry Knauf, Dem.	Bureau
	Frederick W. Rennick, Rep.	Bureau
	James A. Nowlan, Rep.	Stark
38	Frank A. Stewart, Dem.	Macoupin
	Raymond S. Richmond, Dem.	Montgomery
	Hugh W. Cross, Rep.	Jersey
39	Edward G. Hayne, Dem.	La Salle
	J. Ward Smith, Rep.	La Salle
	Elmer P. Hitter, Rep.	La Salle
40	Sam S. Lorton, Dem.	Shelby
	Ed Marvel, Dem.	Christian
	Henry D. Sparks, Rep.	Shelby
41	Joseph Sam Perry, Dem.	Du Page
	Warren L. Wood, Rep.	Will
	Lottie Holman O'Neill, Rep.	Du Page
42	George J. Bauer, Dem.	Effingham
	Alois B. Lager, Dem.	Clinton
	R. J. Branson, Rep.	Marion
43	Jesse J. Fidler, Dem.	Fulton
	Reed F. Cutler, Rep.	Fulton
	James E. Davis, Rep.	Knox
44	W. H. Owen, Dem.	Perry
	Elbert Waller, Rep.	Perry
	Thomas J. Thornton, Rep.	Randolph
45	Andrew P. O'Neill, Dem.	Sangamon
	Hugh Green, Rep.	Morgan
	William J. Lawler, Rep.	Sangamon
46	Clyde Lee, Dem.	Jefferson
	Sidney Parker, Dem.	Jefferson
	S. O. Dale, Rep.	Wayne
47	Schaefer O'Neill, Dem.	Madison
	I. H. Streeper III, Rep.	Madison
	Schuyler B. Vaughan, Rep.	Bond
48	Lizzie Barnes, Dem.	White
	Fred A. Reavill,[4] Rep.	Crawford
	John R. Thompson, Rep.	Lawrence
49	Frank Holten, Dem.	St. Clair
	J. L. Wellinghoff, Dem.	St. Clair
	Calvin D. Johnson, Rep.	St. Clair
50	J. Will Howell, Dem.	Franklin
	I. A. Palmer, Rep.	Franklin
	M. F. Browner, Rep.	Pulaski
51	Paul Powell, Dem.	Johnson
	Oral P. Tuttle, Rep.	Saline
	Abner Field, Rep.	Pope

[1] Died April 8, 1940.
[2] Died Sept. 24, 1939.
[3] Died July 16, 1939.
[4] Died April 27, 1939.

Sixty-second General Assembly, 1941–42

Senate

President Hugh W. Cross
President pro tempore Arnold P. Benson
Secretary Edward H. Alexander

District	Member	County
1	Daniel A. Serritella, Rep.	Cook
2	Frank Ryan, Dem.	Cook
3	William A. Wallace, Dem.	Cook
4	Frank J. McDermott, Dem.	Cook
5	John B. Geary, Dem.	Cook
6	William G. Knox, Rep.	Cook
7	Arthur J. Bidwill, Rep.	Cook
8	Ray Paddock, Rep.	Lake
9	Richard J. Daley, Dem.	Cook
10	Charles W. Baker, Rep.	Ogle
11	John M. Lee, Dem.	Cook
12	Edward E. Laughlin, Rep.	Stephenson
13	Francis J. Loughran, Dem.	Cook
14	Arnold P. Benson, Rep.	Kane
15	Peter P. Kielminski, Dem.	Cook
16	Simon E. Lantz, Rep.	Woodford
17	James B. Leonardo, Rep.	Cook
18	Thomas E. Madden, Dem.	Peoria
19	Abraham L. Marovitz, Dem.	Cook
20	Louis E. Beckman, Rep.	Kankakee
21	George M. Maypole, Dem.	Cook
22	John W. Speakman, Rep.	Vermilion
23	Thomas E. Keane, Dem.	Cook
24	Everett R. Peters, Rep.	Champaign
25	Frank J. Huckin, Jr., Dem.	Cook
26	Wilbur J. Cash, Rep.	McLean
27	Stanley J. Mondala, Dem.	Cook
28	Nicholas L. Hubbard, Dem.	Logan
29	William J. Connors, Dem.	Cook
30	Martin B. Lohmann, Dem.	Tazewell
31	Harold G. Ward, Dem.	Cook
32	T. Mac Downing, Rep.	McDonough
33	Charles F. Carpentier, Rep.	Rock Island
34	Robert W. Lyons, Rep.	Coles
35	George C. Dixon, Rep.	Lee
36	A. Otis Arnold,[1] Rep.	Adams
37	Thomas P. Gunning, Rep.	Bureau
38	Elmer H. Droste, Rep.	Macoupin
39	Ole E. Benson, Rep.	La Salle
40	John W. Fribley, Dem.	Christian
41	Richard J. Barr, Rep.	Will
42	John J. Parish, Dem.	Marion
43	Clinton L. Ewing, Rep.	Knox
44	R. G. Crisenberry, Rep.	Jackson
45	Earl B. Searcy, Rep.	Sangamon
46	Clyde Lee, Dem.	Jefferson
47	Norman G. Flagg, Rep.	Madison
48	George C. Armstrong, Rep.	Lawrence
49	Louis J. Menges, Rep.	St. Clair
50	J. Will Howell, Dem.	Franklin
51	Charles H. Thompson, Rep.	Saline

[1] Died Sept. 11, 1941.

House of Representatives

Speaker Elmer J. Schnackenberg
Clerk R. R. Randolph

District	Member	County
1	Daniel M. Flanigan, Dem.	Cook
	Ernest A. Greene, Rep.	Cook
	Arthur T. Broche, Rep.	Cook
2	James J. Ryan, Dem.	Cook
	Vito Marzullo, Dem.	Cook
	James J. Adduci, Rep.	Cook
3	George Gary Noonan, Dem.	Cook
	Charles H. Jenkins, Rep.	Cook
	Dudley S. Martin, Rep.	Cook
4	John C. Kluczynski, Dem.	Cook
	John F. Boyle, Dem.	Cook
	Michael A. Ruddy, Rep.	Cook
5	Louis G. Berman, Dem.	Cook
	William J. Warfield, Rep.	Cook
	Noble W. Lee, Rep.	Cook
6	Charles H. Weber, Dem.	Cook
	Alan E. Ashcraft, Jr., Rep.	Cook
	James J. Barbour, Rep.	Cook
7	Emmett McGrath, Dem.	Cook
	Bernice T. Van Der Vries, Rep.	Cook
	Arthur W. Sprague, Rep.	Cook
8	Thomas A. Bolger, Dem.	McHenry
	Nick Keller, Rep.	Lake
	Harold D. Kelsey, Rep.	Lake
9	William J. Gormley, Dem.	Cook
	Peter P. Jezierny, Dem.	Cook
	William S. Finucane, Rep.	Cook
10	Edward C. Hunter, Dem.	Winnebago
	David Hunter, Jr., Rep.	Winnebago
	Leroy M. Green,[1] Rep.	Winnebago
11	Michael E. Hannigan, Dem.	Cook
	George A. Fitzgerald, Dem.	Cook
	David I. Swanson, Rep.	Cook
12	Charles D. Franz, Dem.	Stephenson
	John A. Bingham, Rep.	JoDaviess
	Franklin U. Stransky, Rep.	Carroll
13	John G. Ryan, Dem.	Cook
	Adam S. Mioduski, Dem.	Cook
	Elmer J. Schnackenberg, Rep.	Cook
14	Leon M. Schuler, Dem.	Kane
	Maud N. Peffers, Rep.	Kane
	John C. Friedland, Rep.	Kane
15	Edward Skarda, Dem.	Cook
	Matt Franz, Dem.	Cook
	Joseph Zientek, Rep.	Cook
16	William Vicars, Dem.	Livingston
	Rollie C. Carpenter, Rep.	Livingston
	Calistus A. Bruer, Rep.	Livingston
17	Carmen Vacco,[2] Dem.	Cook
	Roland V. Libonati, Dem.	Cook
	Peter C. Granata, Rep.	Cook
18	Howard J. Gorman, Dem.	Peoria
	August C. Grebe, Rep.	Peoria
	Leo D. Crowley, Rep.	Peoria
19	John J. Gorman, Dem.	Cook
	John O. Hruby, Dem.	Cook
	Frank Houcek, Rep.	Cook
20	Ben W. Alpiner, Dem.	Kankakee
	Harry L. Topping, Rep.	Kankakee
	H. Victor McBroom, Rep.	Kankakee
21	Joseph L. Rategan, Dem.	Cook
	Edward J. McCabe, Dem.	Cook

District	Member	County
	Robert Petrone. Rep.	Cook
22	W. O. Edwards, Dem.	Vermilion
	Hugh M. Luckey, Rep.	Vermilion
	Augustus F. DeGafferelly, Rep.	Vermilion
23	Arthur M. Kaindl, Dem.	Cook
	Stanley A. Halick, Dem.	Cook
	William G. Thon, Rep.	Cook
24	Tom M. Garman, Dem.	Champaign
	Charles W. Clabaugh, Rep.	Champaign
	Ora D. Dillavou, Rep.	Champaign
25	Raymond V. O'Keefe, Dem.	Cook
	Stanley R. Kosinski, Dem.	Cook
	Elroy C. Sandquist, Rep.	Cook
26	Joseph W. Russell, Dem.	Ford
	Homer Caton, Rep.	McLean
	Ben S. Rhodes, Rep.	McLean
27	John C. Kuklinski, Dem.	Cook
	A. L. Auth, Dem.	Cook
	Eugene P. Dukes, Rep.	Cook
28	Dean S. McGaughey, Dem.	Macon
	Dan Dinneen, Rep.	Macon
	William Querfeld, Rep.	De Witt
29	Edward P. O'Grady, Dem.	Cook
	Arthur J. Quinn, Dem.	Cook
	Robert M. Woodward, Rep.	Cook
30	Major T. Flowerree, Dem.	Mason
	Ed Teefey, Dem.	Brown
	Robert H. Allison, Rep.	Tazewell
31	Pierce L. Shannon, Dem.	Cook
	Edward P. Saltiel, Rep.	Cook
	George A. Williston, Rep.	Cook
32	Albert Salisbury, Dem.	Hancock
	Sam Schaumleffel, Rep.	Warren
	Rollo R. Robbins, Rep.	Hancock
33	Ora Smith, Dem.	Henderson
	Francis J. Coyle, Dem.	Rock Island
	Clinton Searle, Rep.	Rock Island
34	J. S. Mundy, Dem.	Clark
	Raymond C. Gillogly, Rep.	Douglas
	John W. Lewis, Jr., Rep.	Clark
35	Henry J. White, Dem.	De Kalb
	Dennis J. Collins, Rep.	De Kalb
	George S. Brydia, Rep.	Whiteside
36	W. Roy Donohoo, Dem.	Pike
	William F. Gibbs, Dem.	Adams
	Henry F. Scarborough, Rep.	Adams
37	Henry J. Knauf, Dem.	Bureau
	Frederick W. Rennick, Rep.	Bureau
	James A. Nowlan, Rep.	Stark
38	Frank A. Stewart, Dem.	Macoupin
	Timothy C. Donnelly, Dem.	Macoupin
	William Robison, Rep.	Macoupin
39	Edward G. Hayne, Dem.	La Salle
	Elmer P. Hitter, Rep.	La Salle
	J. Ward Smith, Rep.	La Salle
40	Ed Marvel, Dem.	Christian
	Sam S. Lorton, Dem.	Shelby
	Will P. Welker, Rep.	Fayette
41	Joseph Sam Perry, Dem.	Du Page
	Warren L. Wood, Rep.	Will
	Lottie Holman O'Neill, Rep.	Du Page
42	George J. Bauer, Dem.	Effingham
	Miles E. Mills, Dem.	Effingham
	R. J. Branson, Rep.	Marion
43	A. W. Ray, Dem.	Fulton
	James E. Davis, Rep.	Knox
	Reed F. Cutler, Rep.	Fulton

District	Member	County
44	A. A. Brands, Dem.	Randolph
	Thomas J. Thornton, Rep.	Randolph
	W. J. McDonald, Rep.	Jackson
45	T. J. Sullivan, Dem.	Sangamon
	Hugh Green, Rep.	Morgan
	William J. Lawler, Rep.	Sangamon
46	H. S. Burgess, Dem.	Wayne
	Homer Kasserman, Dem.	Jasper
	S. O. Dale, Rep.	Wayne
47	Anthony W. Daly, Dem.	Madison
	Lloyd Harris, Dem.	Madison
	Milton M. Mueller, Rep.	Madison
48	Jesse Higgins, Dem.	Crawford
	John R. Thompson, Rep.	Lawrence
	John R. Funkhouser, Rep.	Edwards
49	Frank Holten, Dem.	St. Clair
	J. L. Wellinghoff, Dem.	St. Clair
	Max L. Bowler, Rep.	St. Clair
50	E. N. Bowen, Dem.	Williamson
	Herbert L. Upchurch, Dem.	Franklin
	M. F. Browner,[3] Rep.	Pulaski
51	Paul Powell, Dem.	Johnson
	Arthur Van Hooser, Rep.	Massac
	Oral P. Tuttle, Rep.	Saline

[1] Died March 8, 1941.
[2] Died Nov. 7, 1940.
[3] Died Oct. 14, 1941.

Sixty-third General Assembly, 1943–44

Senate

President	Hugh W. Cross
President pro tempore	Arnold P. Benson
Secretary	Edward H. Alexander

District	Member	County
1	Lawrence E. Dowd, Dem.	Cook
2	Frank Ryan, Dem.	Cook
3	Christopher C. Wimbish, Dem.	Cook
4	Frank J. McDermott, Dem.	Cook
5	George D. Mills, Rep.	Cook
6	William G. Knox, Rep.	Cook
7	Arthur J. Bidwill, Rep.	Cook
8	Ray Paddock, Rep.	Lake
9	Richard J. Daley, Dem.	Cook
10	Charles W. Baker, Rep.	Winnebago
11	John M. Lee, Dem.	Cook
12	Edward E. Laughlin, Rep.	Stephenson
13	Walker Butler, Rep.	Cook
14	Arnold P. Benson, Rep.	Kane
15	Peter P. Kielminski, Dem.	Cook
16	Simon E. Lantz, Rep.	Woodford
17	Roland V. Libonati, Dem.	Cook
18	Thomas E. Madden, Dem.	Peoria
19	Abraham L. Marovitz, Dem.	Cook
20	Louis E. Beckman, Rep.	Kankakee
21	Norman C. Barry, Dem.	Cook
22	Hugh M. Luckey, Rep.	Vermilion
23	Thomas E. Keane, Dem.	Cook

District	Member	County
24	Everett R. Peters, Rep.	Champaign
25	Frank J. Huckin, Jr., Dem.	Cook
26	Wilbur J. Cash, Rep.	McLean
27	Stanley J. Mondala, Dem.	Cook
28	Nicholas L. Hubbard, Dem.	Logan
29	William J. Connors, Dem.	Cook
30	Martin B. Lohmann, Dem.	Tazewell
31	Milton D. Smith,[1] Dem.	Cook
32	T. Mac Downing, Rep.	McDonough
33	Charles F. Carpentier, Rep.	Rock Island
34	Robert W. Lyons, Rep.	Coles
35	Dennis J. Collins, Rep.	De Kalb
36	Frank J. Dick, Rep.	Adams
37	Thomas P. Gunning,[2] Rep.	Bureau
38	Rice W. Miller, Rep.	Montgomery
39	Ole E. Benson, Rep.	La Salle
40	John W. Fribley, Dem.	Christian
41	Richard J. Barr, Rep.	Will
42	John J. Parish, Dem.	Marion
43	Wallace Thompson, Rep.	Knox
44	R. G. Crisenberry, Rep.	Jackson
45	Earl B. Searcy, Rep.	Sangamon
46	Clyde Lee, Dem.	Jefferson
47	Norman G. Flagg, Rep.	Madison
48	George C. Armstrong, Rep.	Lawrence
49	Louis J. Menges,[3] Dem.	St. Clair
	John T. Thomas, Rep.	St. Clair
50	J. Will Howell, Dem.	Franklin
51	Arthur Van Hooser, Rep.	Massac

[1] Died Nov. 9, 1943.
[2] Died Nov. 8, 1943.
[3] Resigned.

House of Representatives

Speaker	Elmer J. Schnackenberg
Clerk	R. R. Randolph

District	Member	County
1	Corneal A. Davis, Rep.	Cook
	Daniel M. Flanigan, Dem.	Cook
	Ernest A. Greene, Rep.	Cook
2	James J. Adduci, Rep.	Cook
	Vito Marzullo, Dem.	Cook
	James J. Ryan, Dem.	Cook
3	Charles J. Jenkins, Rep.	Cook
	George Gary Noonan, Dem.	Cook
	Fred J. Smith, Dem.	Cook
4	John F. Boyle, Dem.	Cook
	John C. Kluczynski, Dem.	Cook
	Michael A. Ruddy, Rep.	Cook
5	Lewis G. Berman, Dem.	Cook
	Noble W. Lee, Rep.	Cook
	William J. Warfield, Rep.	Cook
6	Stanley C. Armstrong, Rep.	Cook
	Alan E. Ashcraft, Jr., Rep.	Cook
	Charles H. Weber, Dem.	Cook
7	Emmett McGrath, Dem.	Cook
	Bernice T. Van Der Vries, Rep.	Cook
	Frederick A. Virkus, Rep.	Cook
8	Thomas A. Bolger, Dem.	McHenry
	Nick Keller, Rep.	Lake

District	Member	County
	Harold D. Kelsey, Rep.	Lake
9	William S. Finucane, Rep.	Cook
	William J. Gormley, Dem.	Cook
	Peter P. Jezierny, Dem.	Cook
10	James M. White, Rep.	Ogle
	David Hunter, Jr., Rep.	Winnebago
	Edward C. Hunter, Dem.	Winnebago
11	Michael E. Hannigan, Dem.	Cook
	Walter McAvoy, Rep.	Cook
	David I. Swanson, Rep.	Cook
12	John A. Bingham, Rep.	JoDaviess
	Charles D. Franz, Dem.	Stephenson
	Franklin U. Stransky, Rep.	Carroll
13	Ragner G. Nelson, Rep.	Cook
	John G. Ryan, Dem.	Cook
	Elmer J. Schnackenberg, Rep.	Cook
14	John C. Friedland, Rep.	Kane
	Maud N. Peffers, Rep.	Kane
	Leon M. Schuler, Dem.	Kane
15	Matt Franz, Dem.	Cook
	Edward Skarda, Dem.	Cook
	Joseph Zientek, Rep.	Cook
16	Calistus A. Bruer, Rep.	Livingston
	Rollie C. Carpenter, Rep.	Livingston
	William Vicars, Dem.	Livingston
17	Alfred J. Cillela, Dem.	Cook
	Andrew A. Euzzino, Dem.	Cook
	Frank Novelli, Rep.	Cook
18	Leo D. Crowley, Dem.	Peoria
	Howard J. Gorman, Dem.	Peoria
	August C. Grebe, Rep.	Peoria
19	John J. Gorman, Dem.	Cook
	Frank Houcek, Rep.	Cook
	John O. Hruby, Dem.	Cook
20	Ben W. Alpiner, Dem.	Kankakee
	H. Victor McBroom, Rep.	Kankakee
	Harry L. Topping, Rep.	Kankakee
21	Edward J. McCabe, Dem.	Cook
	Robert Petrone, Rep.	Cook
	Joseph L. Rategan, Dem.	Cook
22	W. O. Edwards, Dem.	Vermilion
	John S. Lavezzi, Rep.	Vermilion
	M. R. Walker, Rep.	Vermilion
23	Stanley A. Halick, Dem.	Cook
	Arthur M. Kaindl, Dem.	Cook
	William G. Thon, Rep.	Cook
24	Charles W. Clabaugh, Rep.	Champaign
	Ora D. Dillavou, Rep.	Champaign
	Tom M. Garman, Dem.	Champaign
25	Stanley R. Kosinski, Dem.	Cook
	Jacob A. Mueller, Dem.	Cook
	Elroy C. Sandquist, Rep.	Cook
26	Homer Caton, Rep.	McLean
	Ben S. Rhodes, Rep.	McLean
	Joseph W. Russell Dem.	Ford
27	A. L. Auth, Dem.	Cook
	John C. Kuklinski, Dem.	Cook
	Anthony C. Prusinski, Dem.	Cook
28	Dan Dinneen, Rep.	Macon
	Homer B. Harris, Rep.	Logan
	Felix E. Wilson, Dem.	De Witt
29	Edward P. O'Grady, Dem.	Cook
	Arthur J. Quinn, Dem.	Cook
	Robert M. Woodward, Rep.	Cook
30	Robert H. Allison, Rep.	Tazewell
	William G. Burnsmier, Rep.	Mason
	Major T. Flowerree, Dem.	Mason

District	Member	County
31	Edward P. Saltiel, Rep.	Cook
	Pierce L. Shannon, Dem.	Cook
	George A. Williston, Rep.	Cook
32	Rollo R. Robbins, Rep.	Hancock
	Albert Salisbury, Dem.	Hancock
	Sam Schaumleffel, Rep.	Warren
33	Bertrand C. Schuemann, Rep.	Rock Island
	Clinton Searle, Rep.	Rock Island
	Ora Smith, Dem.	Henderson
34	John W. Lewis, Jr., Rep.	Clark
	J. S. Mundy, Dem.	Clark
	Charles G. Strohm,[1] Rep.	Clark
35	George S. Brydia, Rep.	Whiteside
	Lyle M. Prescott, Rep.	Lee
	Henry J. White, Dem.	De Kalb
36	W. Roy Donohoo, Dem.	Pike
	William F. Gibbs, Dem.	Adams
	Henry F. Scarborough, Rep.	Adams
37	Henry J. Knauf, Dem.	Bureau
	John T. Nowlan, Rep.	Henry
	Frederick W. Rennick, Rep.	Bureau
38	Timothy C. Donnelly, Dem.	Macoupin
	Ed Fellis, Rep.	Montgomery
	William Robison, Rep.	Macoupin
39	Fred J. Hart, Rep.	La Salle
	Edward G. Hayne, Dem.	La Salle
	J. Ward Smith, Rep.	La Salle
40	Sam S. Lorton, Dem.	Shelby
	Henry D. Sparks, Rep.	Shelby
	Will P. Welker, Rep.	Fayette
41	John J. Maloney,[2] Dem.	Will
	Lottie Holman O'Neill, Rep.	Du Page
	Warren L. Wood, Rep.	Will
42	R. J. Branson, Rep.	Marion
	J. E. McMackin, Dem.	Marion
	Paul Taylor, Dem.	Effingham
43	Reed F. Cutler, Rep.	Fulton
	James E. Davis, Rep.	Knox
	A. W. Ray, Dem.	Fulton
44	A. A. Brands, Dem.	Randolph
	W. J. McDonald, Rep.	Jackson
	Thomas J. Thornton, Rep.	Randolph
45	Hugh Green, Rep.	Morgan
	William J. Lawler, Rep.	Sangamon
	T. J. Sullivan, Dem.	Sangamon
46	Paul W. Broyles, Rep.	Jefferson
	Charles W. Creighton, Dem.	Wayne
	Leonard F. Samford, Rep.	Wayne
47	Lloyd Harris, Dem.	Madison
	Milton M. Mueller, Rep.	Madison
	Schaefer O'Neill, Dem.	Madison
48	Jesse Higgins, Dem.	Crawford
	S. R. Stanley, Rep.	White
	John R. Thompson, Rep.	Lawrence
49	Frank Holten, Dem.	St. Clair
	Otis L. Miller, Sr., Rep.	St. Clair
	J. L. Wellinghoff, Dem.	St. Clair
50	Homer Butler, Rep.	Williamson
	Roy A. Gulley, Rep.	Franklin
	Herbert L. Upchurch, Dem.	Franklin
51	Abner Field, Rep.	Pope
	Paul Powell, Dem.	Johnson
	W. B. Westbrook, Rep.	Saline

[1] Died June 9, 1943.
[2] Died Dec. 17, 1943.

Sixty-fourth General Assembly, 1945-46

Senate

President	Hugh Cross
President pro tempore	Edward E. Laughlin
Secretary	Edward H. Alexander

District	Member	County
1	Lawrence E. Dowd, Dem.	Cook
2	Frank Ryan, Dem.	Cook
3	Christopher C. Wimbish, Dem.	Cook
4	Frank J. McDermott, Dem.	Cook
5	George D. Mills, Rep.	Cook
6	William G. Knox, Rep.	Cook
7	Arthur J. Bidwill, Rep.	Cook
8	Ray Paddock, Rep.	Lake
9	Richard J. Daley, Dem.	Cook
10	Charles W. Baker, Rep.	Winnebago
11	John M. Lee, Dem.	Cook
12	Edward E. Laughlin, Rep.	Stephenson
13	Walker Butler, Rep.	Cook
14	Merritt J. Little, Rep.	Kane
15	Peter P. Kielminski, Dem.	Cook
16	Simon E. Lantz, Rep.	Woodford
17	Roland V. Libonati, Dem.	Cook
18	Clyde C. Trager, Rep.	Peoria
19	Abraham L. Marovitz, Dem.	Cook
20	Louis E. Beckman,[1] Rep.	Kankakee
21	Norman C. Barry, Dem.	Cook
22	Hugh M. Luckey, Rep.	Vermilion
23	Thomas E. Keane, Dem.	Cook
24	Everett R. Peters, Rep.	Champaign
25	Frank J. Huckin, Jr., Dem.	Cook
26	Wilbur J. Cash, Rep.	McLean
27	Stanley J. Mondala, Dem.	Cook
28	Lawrence Rotz, Rep.	Macon
29	William J. Connors, Dem.	Cook
30	Martin B. Lohmann, Dem.	Tazewell
31	Albert L. Schwartz, Dem.	Cook
32	T. Mac Downing, Rep.	McDonough
33	Charles F. Carpentier, Rep.	Rock Island
34	Robert W. Lyons, Rep.	Coles
35	Dennis J. Collins, Rep.	De Kalb
36	Frank J. Dick, Rep.	Adams
37	Frederick W. Rennick, Rep.	Bureau
38	Rice W. Miller, Rep.	Montgomery
39	Ole E. Benson, Rep.	La Salle
40	John W. Fribley, Dem.	Christian
41	Richard J. Barr, Rep.	Will
42	Ora A. Oldfield, Rep.	Marion
43	Wallace Thompson, Rep.	Knox
44	R. G. Crisenberry, Rep.	Jackson
45	D. Logan Giffin, Rep.	Sangamon
46	Paul W. Broyles, Rep.	Jefferson
47	Norman G. Flagg, Rep.	Madison
48	George C. Armstrong, Rep.	Lawrence
49	John T. Thomas, Rep.	St. Clair
50	Homer Butler, Rep.	Williamson
51	Arthur Van Hooser, Rep.	Massac

[1] Died Jan. 7, 1946.

House of Representatives

Speaker	Hugh Green
Clerk	Fred W. Ruegg

District	Member	County
1	Corneal A. Davis, Dem.	Cook
	Daniel M. Flanigan, Dem.	Cook
	Edward A. Welters, Rep.	Cook
2	James J. Adduci, Rep.	Cook
	Vito Marzullo, Dem.	Cook
	James J. Ryan, Dem.	Cook
3	Charles J. Jenkins, Rep.	Cook
	George Gary Noonan, Dem.	Cook
	Fred J. Smith, Dem.	Cook
4	John F. Boyle, Dem.	Cook
	John C. Kluczynski, Dem.	Cook
	Michael A. Ruddy, Rep.	Cook
5	Louis G. Berman, Dem.	Cook
	Noble W. Lee, Rep.	Cook
	Charles M. Skyles, Dem.	Cook
6	Stanley C. Armstrong, Rep.	Cook
	W. Russell Arrington, Rep.	Cook
	Charles H. Weber, Dem.	Cook
7	Emmett McGrath, Dem.	Cook
	Bernice T. Van Der Vries, Rep.	Cook
	Frederick A. Virkus, Rep.	Cook
8	Thomas A. Bolger, Dem.	McHenry
	Nick Keller, Rep.	Lake
	Harold D. Kelsey, Rep.	Lake
9	William S. Finucane, Rep.	Cook
	William J. Gormley, Dem.	Cook
	Peter P. Jezierny, Dem.	Cook
10	Delbert J. Hilvers, Dem.	Winnebago
	David Hunter, Jr., Rep.	Winnebago
	Carl A. Lagerstrom, Rep.	Winnebago
11	George A. Fitzgerald, Dem.	Cook
	Michael E. Hannigan, Dem.	Cook
	Walter McAvoy, Rep.	Cook
12	Marvin F. Burt, Rep.	Stephenson
	Charles D. Franz, Dem.	Stephenson
	Franklin U. Stransky, Rep.	Carroll
13	Adam S. Mioduski, Dem.	Cook
	Ragner G. Nelson, Rep.	Cook
	John G. Ryan, Dem.	Cook
14	J. Lisle Laufer, Rep.	Kane
	Maud N. Peffers, Rep.	Kane
	Leon M. Schuler, Dem.	Kane
15	Matt Franz, Dem.	Cook
	Edward J. Zeman, Dem.	Cook
	Joseph Zientek, Rep.	Cook
16	Calistus A. Bruer, Rep.	Livingston
	Rollie C. Carpenter, Rep.	Livingston
	James P. Lannon, Dem.	Livingston
17	John D'Arco, Dem.	Cook
	Andrew A. Euzzino, Dem.	Cook
	Peter C. Granata, Rep.	Cook
18	Leo D. Crowley, Rep.	Peoria
	Howard J. Gorman, Dem.	Peoria
	August C. Grebe, Rep.	Peoria
19	John J. Gorman, Dem.	Cook
	Frank Houcek, Rep.	Cook
	John O. Hruby, Dem.	Cook
20	Ben W. Alpiner,[1] Dem.	Kankakee
	H. Victor McBroom, Rep.	Kankakee
	Harry L. Topping, Rep.	Kankakee
21	Edward J. McCabe, Dem.	Cook
	Robert Petrone, Rep.	Cook
	Joseph L. Rategan, Dem.	Cook
22	W. O. Edwards, Dem.	Vermilion
	John S. Lavezzi, Rep.	Vermilion
	M. R. Walker, Rep.	Vermilion
23	Stanley A. Halick, Dem.	Cook
	Arthur M. Kaindl, Dem.	Cook
	William G. Thon, Rep.	Cook
24	Charles W. Clabaugh, Rep.	Champaign
	Ora D. Dillavou, Rep.	Champaign
	Tom M. Garman, Dem.	Champaign
25	Stanley R. Kosinski, Dem.	Cook
	Jacob A. Mueller, Dem.	Cook
	Elroy C. Sandquist, Rep.	Cook
26	Homer Caton, Rep.	McLean
	Edward T. Kane, Dem.	McLean
	Ben S. Rhodes, Rep.	McLean
27	A. L. Auth, Dem.	Cook
	John C. Kuklinski, Dem.	Cook
	Anthony C. Prusinski, Dem.	Cook
28	Dan Dinneen, Rep.	Macon
	Homer B. Harris, Rep.	Logan
	Felix E. Wilson, Dem.	De Witt
29	Edward P. O'Grady, Dem.	Cook
	Arthur J. Quinn,[2] Dem.	Cook
	Paul J. Randolph, Rep.	Cook
30	Robert H. Allison, Rep.	Tazewell
	William G. Burnsmier, Rep.	Mason
	Major T. Flowerree, Dem.	Mason
31	William J. Mullaley, Dem.	Cook
	Pierce L. Shannon, Dem.	Cook
	George A. Williston, Rep.	Cook
32	Rollo R. Robbins, Rep.	Hancock
	Albert Salisbury, Dem.	Hancock
	Sam Schaumleffel, Rep.	Warren
33	Clinton Searle, Rep.	Rock Island
	Ora Smith, Dem.	Henderson
	Donald C. Teigland, Dem.	Rock Island
34	G. O. Frazier, Dem.	Clark
	George A. Jones,[3] Rep.	Douglas
	John W. Lewis, Jr., Rep.	Clark
35	George S. Brydia, Rep.	Whiteside
	George B. Shaw, Rep.	Lee
	Henry J. White, Dem.	De Kalb
36	W. Roy Donohoo, Dem.	Pike
	William F. Gibbs, Dem.	Adams
	Henry F. Scarborough, Rep.	Adams
37	Orville G. Chapman, Rep.	Stark
	Henry J. Knauf, Dem.	Bureau
	John T. Nowlan, Dem.	Henry
38	Timothy C. Donnelly, Dem.	Macoupin
	Ed Fellis, Rep.	Montgomery
	William Robison, Rep.	Macoupin
39	Fred J. Hart, Rep.	La Salle
	Edward G. Hayne,[4] Dem.	La Salle
	J. Ward Smith, Rep.	La Salle
40	Clifford C. Hunter, Rep.	Christian
	Carl H. Preihs, Dem.	Christian
	Will P. Welker, Rep.	Fayette
41	J. Harold Downey, Dem.	Will
	Morton H. Hollingsworth, Rep.	Will
	Lottie Holman O'Neill, Rep.	Du Page
42	R. J. Branson, Rep.	Marion
	Raymond O. Horn, Dem.	Marion

District	Member	County
	Paul Taylor, Dem.	Effingham
43	Reed F. Cutler, Rep.	Fulton
	Kenneth J. Peel, Rep.	Knox
	A. W. Ray, Dem.	Fulton
44	A. A. Brands, Dem.	Randolph
	W. J. McDonald, Rep.	Jackson
	Thomas J. Thornton, Rep.	Randolph
45	Hugh Green, Rep.	Morgan
	William J. Lawler, Rep.	Sangamon
	T. J. Sullivan, Dem.	Sangamon
46	Samuel Tilden Coffman, Dem.	Jefferson
	Leonard F. Samford, Rep.	Wayne
	Claude D. Travers, Rep.	Richland
47	Lloyd Harris, Dem.	Madison
	James O. Monroe, Dem.	Madison
	Milton M. Mueller, Rep.	Madison
48	Jesse Higgins, Dem.	Crawford
	S. R. Stanley, Rep.	White
	John R. Thompson, Rep.	Lawrence
49	Frank Holten, Dem.	St. Clair
	Otis L. Miller, Sr., Rep.	St. Clair
	J. L. Wellinghoff, Dem.	St. Clair
50	Roy A. Gulley,[5] Rep.	Franklin
	John E. Miller, Rep.	Alexander
	Herbert L. Upchurch, Dem.	Franklin
51	Abner Field,[6] Rep.	Pope
	Paul Powell, Dem.	Johnson
	W. B. Westbrook, Rep.	Saline

[1] Died July 15, 1946.
[2] Died May. 3, 1945.
[3] Died Dec. 13, 1945.
[4] Died Sept. 30, 1945.
[5] Died Jan. 8, 1945.
[6] Died April 26, 1946.

District	Member	County
20	H. Victor McBroom, Rep.	Kankakee
21	Norman C. Barry, Dem.	Cook
22	Hugh M. Luckey,[2] Dem.	Vermilion
23	William J. Walsh, Rep.	Cook
24	Everett R. Peters, Rep.	Champaign
25	Peter J. Miller, Rep.	Cook
26	Wilbur J. Cash, Rep.	McLean
27	Stanley J. Mondala, Dem.	Cook
28	Lawrence Rotz, Rep.	Macon
29	William J. Connors, Dem.	Cook
30	Martin B. Lohmann, Dem.	Tazewell
31	Edward P. Saltiel, Rep.	Cook
32	T. Mac Downing, Rep.	McDonough
33	Charles F. Carpentier, Rep.	Rock Island
34	Robert W. Lyons, Rep.	Coles
35	Dennis J. Collins, Rep.	De Kalb
36	Frank J. Dick, Rep.	Adams
37	Frederick W. Rennick, Rep.	Bureau
38	Rice W. Miller, Rep.	Montgomery
39	Ole E. Benson, Rep.	La Salle
40	John W. Fribley, Dem.	Christian
41	Richard J. Barr, Rep.	Will
42	Ora A. Oldfield, Rep.	Marion
43	Wallace Thompson, Rep.	Knox
44	R. G. Crisenberry, Rep.	Jackson
45	D. Logan Giffin, Rep.	Sangamon
46	Paul W. Broyles, Rep.	Jefferson
47	Milton M. Mueller, Rep.	Madison
48	George C. Armstrong, Rep.	Lawrence
49	John T. Thomas, Rep.	St. Clair
50	Homer Butler, Rep.	Williamson
51	Arthur Van Hooser, Rep.	Massac

[1] Died March 13, 1947.
[2] Died Dec. 29, 1946.

Sixty-fifth General Assembly, 1947–48

Senate

President   Hugh Cross
President pro tempore   Edward E. Laughlin
Secretary   Edward H. Alexander

District	Member	County
1	Lawrence E. Dowd, Dem.	Cook
2	Frank Ryan, Dem.	Cook
3	Christopher C. Wimbish, Dem.	Cook
4	Frank J. McDermott,[1] Dem.	Cook
5	George D. Mills, Rep.	Cook
6	William G. Knox, Rep.	Cook
7	Arthur J. Bidwill, Rep.	Cook
8	Ray Paddock, Rep.	Lake
9	Thaddeus V. Adesko, Dem.	Cook
10	Charles W. Baker, Rep.	Ogle
11	Arthur E. Larson, Rep.	Cook
12	Edward E. Laughlin, Rep.	Stephenson
13	Walker Butler, Rep.	Cook
14	Merritt J. Little, Rep.	Kane
15	Edward J. Zeman, Dem.	Cook
16	Simon E. Lantz, Rep.	Woodford
17	Roland V. Libonati, Dem.	Cook
18	Clyde C. Trager, Rep.	Peoria
19	Abraham L. Marovitz, Dem.	Cook

House of Representatives

Speaker   Hugh Green
Clerk   Fred W. Ruegg

District	Member	County
1	Corneal A. Davis, Dem.	Cook
	Daniel M. Flanigan,[1] Dem.	Cook
	Edward A. Welters, Rep.	Cook
2	Vito Marzullo, Dem.	Cook
	James J. Ryan, Dem.	Cook
	James J. Adduci, Rep.	Cook
3	Charles J. Jenkins, Rep.	Cook
	George Gary Noonan, Dem.	Cook
	Fred J. Smith, Dem.	Cook
4	John F. Boyle, Dem.	Cook
	John C. Kluczynski, Dem.	Cook
	Michael A. Ruddy, Rep.	Cook
5	Louis G. Berman, Dem.	Cook
	Noble W. Lee, Rep.	Cook
	Charles M. Skyles, Dem.	Cook
6	Stanley C. Armstrong, Rep.	Cook
	W. Russell Arrington, Rep.	Cook
	Charles H. Weber, Dem.	Cook
7	Emmett McGrath, Dem.	Cook
	Vernon W. Reich, Rep.	Cook

District	Member	County
	Bernice T. Van Der Vries, Rep.	Cook
8	Thomas A. Bolger, Dem.	McHenry
	Nick Keller, Rep.	Lake
	Harold D. Kelsey,[2] Rep.	Lake
9	William S. Finucane, Rep.	Cook
	William J. Gormley, Dem.	Cook
	Peter P. Jezierny, Dem.	Cook
10	David Hunter, Jr., Rep.	Winnebago
	Edward C. Hunter, Dem.	Winnebago
	James M. White, Rep.	Ogle
11	Michael E. Hannigan, Dem.	Cook
	Walter McAvoy, Rep.	Cook
	David I. Swanson, Rep.	Cook
12	Marvin F. Burt, Rep.	Stephenson
	John K. Morris, Dem.	Carroll
	Franklin U. Stransky, Rep.	Carroll
13	Ragner G. Nelson, Rep.	Cook
	John G. Ryan, Dem.	Cook
	Edward Schneider, Rep.	Cook
14	J. Lisle Laufer, Rep.	Kane
	Maud N. Peffers, Rep.	Kane
	Leon M. Schuler, Dem.	Kane
15	Matt Franz, Dem.	Cook
	Frank J. Krasniewski, Dem.	Cook
	Joseph Zientek, Rep.	Cook
16	Calistus A. Bruer, Rep.	Livingston
	Rollie C. Carpenter, Rep.	Livingston
	James P. Lannon, Dem.	Livingston
17	John D'Arco, Dem.	Cook
	Andrew A. Euzzino, Dem.	Cook
	Peter C. Granata, Rep.	Cook
18	James D. Carrigan, Dem.	Peoria
	Leo D. Crowley, Rep.	Peoria
	August C. Grebe, Rep.	Peoria
19	John J. Gorman, Dem.	Cook
	Frank Houcek, Rep.	Cook
	John O. Hruby, Dem.	Cook
20	Siets D. Kamp, Rep.	Iroquois
	Samuel H. Shapiro, Dem.	Kankakee
	Harry L. Topping, Rep.	Kankakee
21	Edward J. McCabe, Dem.	Cook
	Robert Petrone, Rep.	Cook
	Joseph L. Rategan, Rep.	Cook
22	W. O. Edwards, Dem.	Vermilion
	M. R. Walker, Rep.	Vermilion
	William E. Wayland, Rep.	Vermilion
23	Arthur M. Kaindl, Dem.	Cook
	Thomas A. Patton, Rep.	Cook
	William G. Thon, Rep.	Cook
24	Charles W. Clabaugh, Rep.	Champaign
	Ora D. Dillavou, Rep.	Champaign
	Charles Simpson, Dem.	Champaign
25	Harold R. Blomstrand, Rep.	Cook
	Stanley R. Kosinski, Dem.	Cook
	Elroy C. Sandquist, Rep.	Cook
26	Homer Caton, Rep.	McLean
	Edward T. Kane, Dem.	McLean
	Ben S. Rhodes, Rep.	McLean
27	A. L. Auth, Dem.	Cook
	John C. Kuklinski, Dem.	Cook
	Anthony C. Prusinski, Dem.	Cook
28	Dan Dinneen, Rep.	Macon
	Paul H. Ferguson, Dem.	Macon

District	Member	County
	Homer B. Harris, Rep.	Logan
29	Joseph L. De La Cour, Dem.	Cook
	Edward P. O'Grady, Dem.	Cook
	Paul J. Randolph, Rep.	Cook
30	Robert H. Allison, Rep.	Tazewell
	William G. Burnsmier, Rep.	Mason
	C. R. Ratcliffe, Dem.	Cass
31	Alan Best, Rep.	Cook
	Pierce L. Shannon, Dem.	Cook
	George A. Williston, Rep.	Cook
32	Rollo R. Robbins, Rep.	Hancock
	Albert Salisbury, Dem.	Hancock
	Sam Schaumleffel, Rep.	Warren
33	Hazel A. McCaskrin, Rep.	Rock Island
	Clinton Searle, Rep.	Rock Island
	Ora Smith, Dem.	Henderson
34	G. O. Frazier, Dem.	Clark
	John W. Lewis, Jr., Rep.	Clark
	Myron E. Lollar, Rep.	Douglas
35	George S. Brydia, Rep.	Whiteside
	Hubert D. Considine, Dem.	Lee
	Lyle M. Prescott, Rep.	Lee
36	William F. Gibbs, Dem.	Adams
	H. B. Ihnen, Rep.	Adams
	Henry F. Scarborough, Rep.	Adams
37	Orville G. Chapman, Rep.	Stark
	Henry J. Knauf, Dem.	Bureau
	John T. Nowlan, Rep.	Henry
38	Ed Fellis, Rep.	Montgomery
	William Robison, Rep.	Macoupin
	Charles Ed Schaefer, Dem.	Montgomery
39	Vincent J. Dimond, Dem.	La Salle
	Fred J. Hart, Rep.	La Salle
	J. Ward Smith, Rep.	La Salle
40	Clifford C. Hunter, Rep.	Christian
	Carl H. Preihs, Dem.	Christian
	Will P. Welker, Dem.	Fayette
41	J. Harold Downey, Dem.	Will
	Lottie Holman O'Neill, Rep.	Du Page
	Warren L. Wood, Rep.	Will
42	R. J. Branson, Rep.	Marion
	Joseph B. Siemer, Rep.	Effingham
	Paul Taylor, Dem.	Effingham
43	Reed F. Cutler, Rep.	Fulton
	Kenneth J. Peel, Rep.	Knox
	A. W. Ray, Dem.	Fulton
44	A. A. Brands, Dem.	Randolph
	W. J. McDonald, Rep.	Jackson
	Thomas J. Thornton, Rep.	Randolph
45	Hugh Green, Rep.	Morgan
	G. William Horsley, Rep.	Sangamon
	T. J. Sullivan, Dem.	Sangamon
46	Clyde Lee, Dem.	Jefferson
	Leonard F. Samford, Rep.	Wayne
	Claude D. Travers, Rep.	Richland
47	Lloyd Harris, Dem.	Madison
	Orville E. Hodge, Rep.	Madison
	Leland J. Kennedy, Dem.	Madison
48	Herschel S. Green, Rep.	Crawford
	James W. Karber, Dem.	Gallatin
	S. R. Stanley, Rep.	White
49	Frank, Holten, Dem.	St. Clair
	James W. McRoberts, Rep.	St. Clair
	Otis L. Miller, Sr., Rep.	St. Clair
50	Clyde L. Choate, Dem.	Union
	Harry W. McClintock, Rep.	Franklin
	John E. Miller, Rep.	Alexander

District	Member	County
51	Paul Powell, Dem.	Johnson
	W. O. Verhines, Rep.	Johnson
	W. B. Westbrook, Rep.	Saline

Died Nov. 26, 1946.
Died Feb. 26, 1948.

District	Member	County
49	John T. Thomas, Rep.	St. Clair
50	Robert J. Young, Jr., Dem.	Williamson
51	Arthur Van Hooser, Rep.	Massac

¹ Resigned, elected U.S.H.R.
² Died Aug. 21, 1948.

Sixty-sixth General Assembly, 1949–50

Senate

President	Sherwood Dixon
President pro tempore	Wallace Thompson
Secretary	Edward H. Alexander

District	Member	County
1	Lawrence E. Dowd, Dem.	Cook
2	Frank Ryan, Dem.	Cook
3	Christopher C. Wimbish, Dem.	Cook
4	John C. Kluczynski,¹ Dem.	Cook
5	George D. Mills,² Rep.	Cook
6	William G. Knox, Rep.	Cook
7	Arthur J. Bidwill, Rep.	Cook
8	Ray Paddock, Rep.	Lake
9	Thaddeus V. Adesko, Dem.	Cook
10	Charles W. Baker, Rep.	Ogle
11	Arthur E. Larson, Rep.	Cook
12	Edward E. Laughlin, Rep.	Stephenson
13	Walker Butler, Rep.	Cook
14	Merritt J. Little, Rep.	Kane
15	Edward J. Zeman, Dem.	Cook
16	Simon E. Lantz, Rep.	Woodford
17	Roland V. Libonati, Dem.	Cook
18	Clyde C. Trager, Rep.	Peoria
19	Abraham L. Marovitz, Dem.	Cook
20	H. Victor McBroom, Rep.	Kankakee
21	Norman C. Barry, Dem.	Cook
22	William E. Wayland, Rep.	Vermilion
23	William J. Walsh, Rep.	Cook
24	Everett R. Peters, Rep.	Champaign
25	Peter J. Miller, Rep.	Cook
26	Wilbur J. Cash, Rep.	McLean
27	Stanley J. Mondala, Dem.	Cook
28	Elbert S. Smith, Rep.	Macon
29	William J. Connors, Dem.	Cook
30	Martin B. Lohmann, Dem.	Tazewell
31	Edward P. Saltiel, Rep.	Cook
32	T. Mac Downing, Rep.	McDonough
33	Charles F. Carpentier, Rep.	Rock Island
34	Robert W. Lyons, Rep.	Coles
35	Dennis J. Collins, Rep.	De Kalb
36	Russell A. Waters, Dem.	Adams
37	Frederick W. Rennick, Rep.	Bureau
38	Timothy C. Donnelly, Dem.	Macoupin
39	Ole E. Benson, Rep.	La Salle
40	John W. Fribley, Dem.	Christian
41	Richard J. Barr, Rep.	Will
42	John J. Parish, Dem.	Marion
43	Wallace Thompson, Rep.	Knox
44	R. G. Crisenberry, Rep.	Jackson
45	D. Logan Giffin, Rep.	Sangamon
46	Paul W. Broyles, Rep.	Jefferson
47	Milton M. Mueller, Rep.	Madison
48	Kent Lewis, Dem.	Crawford

House of Representatives

Speaker	Paul Powell
Clerk	Charles F. Kervin

District	Member	County
1	Joseph Clark, Dem.	Cook
	Corneal A. Davis, Dem.	Cook
	James Rinella, Rep.	Cook
2	Vito Marzullo, Dem.	Cook
	James J. Ryan, Dem.	Cook
	James J. Adduci, Rep.	Cook
3	Charles J. Jenkins, Rep.	Cook
	George Gary Noonan, Dem.	Cook
	Fred J. Smith, Dem.	Cook
4	John F. Boyle, Dem.	Cook
	Michael A. Ruddy, Rep.	Cook
	Theodore A. Swinarski, Dem.	Cook
5	Louis G. Berman, Dem.	Cook
	Noble W. Lee, Rep.	Cook
	Charles M. Skyles, Dem.	Cook
6	Stanley C. Armstrong, Rep.	Cook
	W. Russell Arrington, Rep.	Cook
	Charles H. Weber, Dem.	Cook
7	Emmett McGrath, Dem.	Cook
	Vernon W. Reich, Rep.	Cook
	Bernice T. Van Der Vries, Rep.	Cook
8	Thomas A. Bolger, Dem.	McHenry
	Nick Keller, Rep.	Lake
	Harvey Pearson, Rep.	Lake
9	William S. Finucane, Rep.	Cook
	William J. Gormley, Dem.	Cook
	Peter P. Jezierny,¹ Dem.	Cook
10	Mabel E. Green, Rep.	Winnebago
	David Hunter, Jr., Rep.	Winnebago
	Edward C. Hunter, Dem.	Winnebago
11	A. L. Cronin, Rep.	Cook
	Michael E. Hannigan, Dem.	Cook
	David I. Swanson,² Rep.	Cook
12	Marvin F. Burt, Rep.	Stephenson
	John K. Morris, Dem.	Carroll
	Franklin U. Stransky, Rep.	Carroll
13	Adam S. Mioduski, Dem.	Cook
	John G. Ryan, Dem.	Cook
	Edward Schneider, Rep.	Cook
14	J. Lisle Laufer, Rep.	Kane
	Maud N. Peffers, Rep.	Kane
	Leon M. Schuler, Dem.	Kane
15	Joseph G. Kohout, Dem.	Cook
	Frank J. Krasniewski, Dem.	Cook
	Joseph Zientek, Rep.	Cook
16	Calistus A. Bruer,³ Rep.	Livingston
	Rollie C. Carpenter, Rep.	Livingston
	James P. Lannon, Dem.	Livingston
17	John D'Arco, Dem.	Cook
	Andrew A. Euzzino, Dem.	Cook
	Peter C. Granata, Rep.	Cook

District	Member	County
18	Robert L. Burhans, Rep.	Peoria
	James D. Carrigan, Dem.	Peoria
	August C. Grebe, Rep.	Peoria
19	John J. Gorman, Dem.	Cook
	John O. Hruby, Dem.	Cook
	Frank A. Marek, Rep.	Cook
20	Siets D. Kamp, Rep.	Iroquois
	Samuel H. Shapiro, Dem.	Kankakee
	Harry L. Topping, Rep.	Kankakee
21	Edward J. McCabe, Dem.	Cook
	Robert Petrone, Rep.	Cook
	Daniel J. Ronan, Dem.	Cook
22	W. O. Edwards, Dem.	Vermilion
	John P. Meyer, Rep.	Vermilion
	M. R. Walker, Rep.	Vermilion
23	Stanley A. Halick, Dem.	Cook
	Arthur M. Kaindl, Dem.	Cook
	William G. Thon, Rep.	Cook
24	Charles W. Clabaugh, Rep.	Champaign
	Ora D. Dillavou, Rep.	Champaign
	Charles Simpson, Dem.	Champaign
25	Stanley R. Kosinski, Dem.	Cook
	Charles O. Miller, Rep.	Cook
	Jacob A. Mueller, Dem.	Cook
26	Homer Caton, Rep.	McLean
	Edward T. Kane, Dem.	McLean
	Ben S. Rhodes, Rep.	McLean
27	John C. Kuklinski, Dem.	Cook
	Anthony C. Prusinski,[4] Dem.	Cook
	John P. Touhy, Dem.	Cook
28	Paul H. Ferguson, Dem.	Macon
	Barrett F. Rogers, Rep.	Logan
	Felix E. Wilson, Dem.	De Witt
29	Joseph L. De La Cour, Dem.	Cook
	Edward P. O'Grady, Dem.	Cook
	Paul J. Randolph, Rep.	Cook
30	Robert H. Allison, Rep.	Tazewell
	Major T. Flowerree, Dem.	Mason
	C. R. Ratcliffe, Dem.	Cass
31	Alan Best, Rep.	Cook
	Irving J. Melites, Dem.	Cook
	Pierce L. Shannon, Dem.	Cook
32	John B. Monroe, Dem.	McDonough
	Rollo R. Robbins, Rep.	Hancock
	Sam Schaumleffel, Rep.	Warren
33	Virgil Bozeman, Dem.	Rock Island
	Clinton Searle, Rep.	Henderson
	Richard Stengel, Dem.	Rock Island
34	John W. Lewis, Jr., Rep.	Clark
	W. Henry Waltrip, Rep.	Douglas
	Frank C. Welsh, Dem.	Clark
35	George S. Brydia, Rep.	Whiteside
	Hubert D. Considine, Dem.	Lee
	Charles K. Willett, Rep.	Lee
36	W. Roy Donohoo, Dem.	Pike
	William F. Gibbs, Dem.	Adams
	William J. Thornton, Rep.	Pike
37	Orville G. Chapman, Rep.	Stark
	Frank P. Johnson, Rep.	Henry
	Henry J. Knauf,[5] Dem.	Bureau
38	William Robison, Rep.	Macoupin
	Delbert O. Shade, Dem.	Greene
	Charles Ed Schaefer, Dem.	Montgomery

District	Member	County
39	Fred J. Hart, Rep.	La Salle
	J. Ward Smith, Rep.	La Salle
	Joseph P. Stremlau, Dem.	La Salle
40	Clifford C. Hunter, Rep.	Christian
	Sam S. Lorton, Dem.	Shelby
	Clyde A. Roberts, Dem.	Fayette
41	J. Harold Downey, Dem.	Will
	Lottie Holman O'Neill, Rep.	Du Page
	Warren L. Wood, Rep.	Will
42	R. J. Branson, Rep.	Marion
	Edwin R. Haag, Dem.	Clinton
	Paul Taylor, Dem.	Effingham
43	Reed F. Cutler, Rep.	Fulton
	Kenneth J. Peel, Rep.	Knox
	A. W. Ray, Dem.	Fulton
44	A. A. Brands, Dem.	Randolph
	W. J. McDonald, Rep.	Jackson
	Thomas J. Thornton, Rep.	Randolph
45	Hugh Green, Rep.	Morgan
	G. William Horsley, Rep.	Sangamon
	T. J. Sullivan, Dem.	Sangamon
46	Warren D. Crippen, Dem.	Wayne
	Clyde Lee, Dem.	Jefferson
	Claude D. Travers, Rep.	Richland
47	Lloyd Harris, Dem.	Madison
	Orville E. Hodge, Rep.	Madison
	Leland J. Kennedy, Dem.	Madison
48	James P. Alexander, Jr., Dem.	Lawrence
	Herschel S. Green, Rep.	Crawford
	James W. Karber, Dem.	Gallatin
49	Frank Holten, Dem.	St. Clair
	James W. McRoberts, Rep.	St. Clair
	Otis L. Miller, Sr., Rep.	St. Clair
50	Clyde L. Choate, Dem.	Union
	Harry W. McClintock, Rep.	Franklin
	Ora Collard, Dem.	Williamson
51	Paul Powell, Dem.	Johnson
	W. O. Verhines, Rep.	Johnson
	W. B. Westbrook, Rep.	Saline

[1] Died Jan. 1, 1949.
[2] Died April 11, 1950.
[3] Died Oct. 1, 1949.
[4] Died Jan. 2, 1950.
[5] Died April 16, 1950.

Sixty-seventh General Assembly, 1951–52

Senate

President   Sherwood Dixon

President pro tempore

       Wallace Thompson

Secretary   Edward H. Alexander

District	Member	County
1	Fred B. Roti, Dem.	Cook
2	Frank Ryan, Dem.	Cook
3	Christopher C. Wimbish, Dem.	Cook
4	Donald J. O'Brien, Dem.	Cook
5	Marshall Korshak, Dem.	Cook
6	William G. Knox, Rep.	Cook
7	Arthur J. Bidwill, Rep.	Cook
8	Ray Paddock, Rep.	Lake
9	William J. Lynch, Dem.	Cook

District	Member	County
10	Charles W. Baker, Rep.	Ogle
11	Arthur E. Larson, Rep.	Cook
12	Edward E. Laughlin, Rep.	Stephenson
13	Walker Butler, Rep.	Cook
14	Merritt J. Little, Rep.	Kane
15	Frank J. Kocarek, Dem.	Cook
16	Simon E. Lantz,[1] Rep.	Woodford
17	Roland V. Libonati, Dem.	Cook
18	Clyde C. Trager, Rep.	Peoria
19	John J. Gorman, Dem.	Cook
20	H. Victor McBroom, Rep.	Kankakee
21	Norman C. Barry, Dem.	Cook
22	William E. Wayland, Rep.	Vermilion
23	William J. Walsh, Rep.	Cook
24	Everett R. Peters, Rep.	Champaign
25	Peter J. Miller, Rep.	Cook
26	Wilbur J. Cash, Rep.	McLean
27	Stanley J. Mondala, Dem.	Cook
28	Elbert S. Smith, Rep.	Macon
29	William J. Connors, Dem.	Cook
30	Martin B. Lohmann, Dem.	Tazewell
31	Edward P. Saltiel, Rep.	Cook
32	T. Mac Downing, Rep.	McDonough
33	Charles F. Carpentier, Rep.	Rock Island
34	Robert W. Lyons, Rep.	Coles
35	Dennis J. Collins, Rep.	De Kalb
36	Russell A. Waters, Dem.	Adams
37	Frank P. Johnson, Rep.	Henry
38	Timothy C. Donnelly, Dem.	Macoupin
39	Fred J. Hart, Rep.	La Salle
40	John W. Fribley, Dem.	Christian
41	Lottie Holman O'Neill, Rep.	Du Page
42	John J. Parish, Dem.	Marion
43	Wallace Thompson,[2] Rep.	Knox
44	R. G. Crisenberry, Rep.	Jackson
45	George E. Drach, Rep.	Sangamon
46	Paul W. Broyles, Rep.	Jefferson
47	Milton M. Mueller, Rep.	Madison
48	Kent Lewis, Dem.	Crawford
49	James W. Gray, Dem.	St. Clair
50	Robert J. Young, Jr., Dem.	Williamson
51	Arthur Van Hooser, Rep.	Massac

[1] Died Dec. 27, 1952.
[2] Died Jan. 22, 1952.

House of Representatives

Speaker		Warren L. Wood
Clerk		Fred W. Ruegg

District	Member	County
1	Corneal A. Davis, Dem.	Cook
	James Rinella, Rep.	Cook
	Robert E. Romano, Dem.	Cook
2	Vito Marzullo, Dem.	Cook
	James J. Ryan, Dem.	Cook
	James J. Adduci, Rep.	Cook
3	Charles J. Jenkins, Rep.	Cook
	George Gary Noonan, Dem.	Cook
	Fred J. Smith, Dem.	Cook
4	John F. Boyle, Dem.	Cook
	Michael A. Ruddy, Rep.	Cook
	Theodore A. Swinarski, Dem.	Cook
5	Louis G. Berman, Dem.	Cook

District	Member	County
	Noble W. Lee, Rep.	Cook
	Charles M. Skyles, Dem.	Cook
6	W. Russell Arrington, Rep.	Cook
	William E. Pollack, Rep.	Cook
	Charles H. Weber, Dem.	Cook
7	Emmett McGrath,[1] Dem.	Cook
	Arthur W. Sprague, Rep.	Cook
	Bernice T. Van Der Vries, Rep.	Cook
8	Thomas A. Bolger, Dem.	McHenry
	Robert McClory, Rep.	Lake
	Harvey Pearson, Rep.	Lake
9	William S. Finucane,[2] Rep.	Cook
	William J. Gormley, Dem.	Cook
	Lillian Piotrowski, Dem.	Cook
10	Mabel E. Green, Rep.	Winnebago
	David Hunter, Jr., Rep.	Winnebago
	William Pierce, Dem.	Winnebago
11	A. L. Cronin, Dem.	Cook
	Walter McAvoy, Rep.	Cook
	William J. Morgensen, Rep.	Cook
12	Marvin F. Burt, Rep.	Stephenson
	John K. Morris, Dem.	Carroll
	Franklin U. Stransky, Rep.	Carroll
13	John G. Ryan, Dem.	Cook
	Edward Schneider, Rep.	Cook
	Marie H. Suthers, Rep.	Cook
14	J. Lisle Laufer, Rep.	Kane
	Maud N, Peffers, Rep.	Kane
	Leon M. Schuler, Dem.	Kane
15	Clem Graver, Rep.	Cook
	Joseph G. Kohout, Dem.	Cook
	Frank J. Krasniewski, Dem.	Cook
16	Dean McCully, Rep.	Woodford
	Rollie C. Carpenter, Rep.	Livingston
	James P. Lannon, Dem.	Livingston
17	Anthony J. De Tolve, Dem.	Cook
	Andrew A. Euzzino, Dem.	Cook
	Peter C. Granata, Rep.	Cook
18	Robert L. Burhans, Rep.	Peoria
	James D. Carrigan, Dem.	Peoria
	August C. Grebe, Rep.	Peoria
19	Samuel S. Epstein,[3] Dem.	Cook
	John O. Hruby, Dem.	Cook
	Frank A. Marek, Rep.	Cook
20	Louis E. Beckman, Rep.	Kankakee
	Samuel H. Shapiro, Dem.	Kankakee
	Harry L. Topping, Rep.	Kankakee
21	Edward J. McCabe, Dem.	Cook
	Robert Petrone, Rep.	Cook
	Daniel J. Ronan, Dem.	Cook
22	W. O. Edwards, Dem.	Vermilion
	John P. Meyer, Rep.	Vermilion
	M. R. Walker, Rep.	Vermilion
23	Stanley A. Halick, Dem.	Cook
	Thomas A. Patton, Rep.	Cook
	William G. Thon, Rep.	Cook
24	Charles W. Clabaugh, Rep.	Champaign
	Ora D. Dillavou, Rep.	Champaign
	Paul Stone, Dem.	Moultrie
25	Stanley R. Kosinski, Dem.	Cook
	Charles O. Miller, Rep.	Cook
	Elroy C. Sandquist, Rep.	Cook
26	Homer Caton, Rep.	McLean

District	Member	County
	Edward T. Kane, Dem.	McLean
	Ben S. Rhodes, Rep.	McLean
27	John C. Kuklinski, Dem.	Cook
	Bernard C. Prusinski, Dem.	Cook
	John P. Touhy, Dem.	Cook
28	James L. Atkins, Rep.	Macon
	Paul H. Ferguson, Dem.	Macon
	Barrett F. Rogers, Rep.	Logan
29	Joseph L. De La Cour, Dem.	Cook
	Edward P. O'Grady, Dem.	Cook
	Paul J. Randolph, Rep.	Cook
30	Robert H. Allison, Rep.	Tazewell
	William D. Burnsmier, Rep.	Mason
	Major T. Flowerree, Dem.	Mason
31	Alan Best, Rep.	Cook
	Thomas Patrick Henehan, Dem.	Cook
	Samuel Kart, Rep.	Cook
32	John B. Monroe, Dem.	McDonough
	Rollo R. Robbins, Rep.	Hancock
	Sam Schaumleffel, Rep.	Warren
33	Hazel A. McCaskrin, Rep.	Rock Island
	Clinton Searle, Rep.	Henderson
	Richard Stengel, Dem.	Rock Island
34	John W. Lewis, Jr., Rep.	Clark
	Lee Lynch,[4] Dem.	Coles
	W. Henry Waltrip, Rep.	Douglas
35	George S. Brydia, Rep.	Whiteside
	Hubert D. Considine, Dem.	Lee
	Charles K. Willett, Rep.	Lee
36	W. Roy Donohoo, Dem.	Pike
	H. B. Ihnen, Rep.	Adams
	William J. Thornton,[5] Rep.	Pike
37	Tobias Barry, Sr., Dem.	Bureau
	Milo L. Craig, Rep.	Henry
	Joseph R. Peterson, Rep.	Bureau
38	William Lyons, Dem.	Macoupin
	William Robison, Rep.	Macoupin
	Charles Ed Schaefer, Dem.	Montgomery
39	J. Ward Smith, Rep.	La Salle
	Carl W. Soderstrom, Rep.	La Salle
	Joseph P. Stremlau, Dem.	La Salle
40	Carl H. Preihs, Dem.	Christian
	Clyde A. Roberts, Dem.	Fayette
	Will P. Welker, Rep.	Fayette
41	J. Harold Downey, Dem.	Will
	John M. King, Rep.	Du Page
	Warren L. Wood, Rep.	Will
42	R. J. Branson, Rep.	Marion
	Edwin R. Haag, Dem.	Clinton
	Paul Taylor, Dem.	Effingham
43	Reed F. Cutler, Rep.	Fulton
	Kenneth J. Peel, Rep.	Knox
	A. W. Ray, Dem.	Fulton
44	Dean R. Hammack, Dem.	Perry
	W. J. McDonald, Rep.	Jackson
	Thomas J. Thornton, Rep.	Randolph
45	Hugh Green, Rep.	Morgan
	G. William Horsley, Rep.	Sangamon
	T. J. Sullivan, Dem.	Sangamon
46	Clyde Lee, Dem.	Jefferson
	Claude D. Travers, Rep.	Richland
	Frank H. Walker, Rep.	Jefferson

District	Member	County
47	Lloyd Harris, Dem.	Madison
	Orville E. Hodge, Rep.	Madison
	Leland J. Kennedy, Dem.	Madison
48	W. V. Brown, Rep.	Wabash
	Herschel S. Green, Rep.	Crawford
	Paul A. Ziegler, Dem.	White
49	Alan J. Dixon, Dem.	St. Clair
	Frank Holten, Dem.	St. Clair
	Otis L. Miller, Sr., Rep.	St. Clair
50	Homer Butler, Rep.	Williamson
	Clyde L. Choate, Dem.	Union
	Harry W. McClintock, Rep.	Franklin
51	Gordon E. Kerr, Rep.	Massac
	Paul Powell, Dem.	Johnson
	W. B. Westbrook, Rep.	Saline

[1] Died Nov. 24, 1951.
[2] Died Oct. 26, 1951.
[4] Died April 21, 1951.
[3] Died Feb. 1951.
[5] Died May 7, 1951.

Sixty-eighth General Assembly,
1953–54

Senate

President   John W. Chapman
President pro tempore   Walker Butler
Secretary   Edward H. Alexander

District	Member	County
1	Fred B. Roti, Dem.	Cook
2	Frank Ryan, Dem.	Cook
3	Christopher C. Wimbish, Dem.	Cook
4	Donald J. O'Brien, Dem.	Cook
5	Marshall Korshak, Dem.	Cook
6	William G. Knox,[1] Rep.	Cook
7	Arthur J. Bidwill, Rep.	Cook
8	Robert McClory, Rep.	Lake
9	William J. Lynch, Dem.	Cook
10	Charles W. Baker, Rep.	Ogle
11	Arthur E. Larson, Rep.	Cook
12	Marvin F. Burt, Rep.	Stephenson
13	Walker Butler, Rep.	Cook
14	Merritt J. Little, Rep.	Kane
15	Frank J. Kocarek, Dem.	Cook
16	Simon E. Lantz,[2] Rep.	Woodford
	Rollie C. Carpenter,[3] Rep.	Livingston
17	Roland V. Libonati, Dem.	Cook
18	Clyde C. Trager, Rep.	Peoria
19	John J. Gorman, Dem.	Cook
20	H. Victor McBroom, Rep.	Kankakee
21	Norman C. Barry, Dem.	Cook
22	John P. Meyer, Rep.	Vermilion
23	William J. Walsh, Rep.	Cook
24	Everett R. Peters, Rep.	Champaign
25	Peter J. Miller, Rep.	Cook
26	David Davis, Rep.	McLean
27	Stanley J. Mondala, Dem.	Cook
28	Elbert S. Smith, Rep.	Macon
29	William J. Connors, Dem.	Cook
30	Egbert B. Groen, Rep.	Tazewell
31	Edward P. Saltiel, Rep.	Cook
32	T. Mac Downing, Rep.	McDonough

GENERAL ASSEMBLY

305

District	Member	County
33	Charles F. Carpentier,[4] Rep.	Rock Island
34	Robert W. Lyons, Rep.	Coles
35	Dennis J. Collins, Rep.	De Kalb
36	Lillian E. Schlagenhauf, Rep.	Adams
37	Frank P. Johnson, Rep.	Henry
38	W. P. Cuthbertson, Rep.	Macoupin
39	Fred J. Hart, Rep.	La Salle
40	Lloyd E. Davis, Rep.	Christian
41	Lottie Holman O'Neill, Rep.	Du Page
42	Dwight P. Friedrich, Rep.	Marion
43	Albert Scott, Rep.	Fulton
44	R. G. Crisenberry, Rep.	Jackson
45	George E. Drach, Rep.	Sangamon
46	Paul W. Broyles, Rep.	Jefferson
47	Milton M. Mueller, Rep.	Madison
48	William F. Hensley, Rep.	Lawrence
49	James W. Gray, Dem.	St. Clair
50	Homer Butler, Rep.	Williamson
51	Arthur Van Hooser, Rep.	Massac

[1] Died Nov. 20, 1953.
[2] Died Dec. 27, 1952.
[3] Vice Lantz.
[4] Resigned, elected sec. state.

House of Representatives

Speaker   Warren L. Wood
Clerk   Fred W. Ruegg

District	Member	County
1	Corneal A. Davis, Dem.	Cook
	James Rinella, Rep.	Cook
	Robert E. Romano, Dem.	Cook
2	Vito Marzullo, Dem.	Cook
	James J. Ryan, Dem.	Cook
	James J. Yacullo, Rep.	Cook
3	Charles J. Jenkins, Rep.	Cook
	George Gary Noonan, Dem.	Cook
	Fred J. Smith, Dem.	Cook
4	Michael A. Ruddy, Rep.	Cook
	Frank J. Smith, Dem.	Cook
	Theodore A. Swinarski, Dem.	Cook
5	Louis G. Berman,[1] Dem.	Cook
	Noble W. Lee, Rep.	Cook
	Charles M. Skyles, Dem.	Cook
6	W. Russell Arrington, Rep.	Cook
	William E. Pollack, Rep.	Cook
	Charles H. Weber, Dem.	Cook
7	Joseph L. Lelivelt, Dem.	Cook
	Arthur W. Sprague, Rep.	Cook
	Bernice T. Van Der Vries, Rep.	Cook
8	Jack Bairstow, Dem.	Lake
	A. B. McConnell, Rep.	McHenry
	Harvey Pearson, Rep.	Lake
9	Hector A. Brouillet, Rep.	Cook
	William J. Gormley, Dem.	Cook
	Lillian Piotrowski, Dem.	Cook
10	Mabel E. Green, Rep.	Winnebago
	David Hunter, Jr., Rep.	Winnebago
	William Pierce, Dem.	Winnebago
11	Michael E. Hannigan, Dem.	Cook
	Walter McAvoy, Rep.	Cook
	William J. Morgensen, Rep.	Cook
12	Harold W. Widmer, Rep.	Stephenson
	John K. Morris, Dem.	Carroll

District	Member	County
	Franklin U. Stransky, Rep.	Carroll
13	Henry M. Lenard, Dem.	Cook
	John G. Ryan, Dem.	Cook
	Edward Schneider, Rep.	Cook
14	J. Lisle Laufer, Rep.	Kane
	Maud N. Peffers, Rep.	Kane
	Leon M. Schuler, Dem.	Kane
15	Charles S. Bonk, Dem.	Cook
	Clem Graver, Rep.	Cook
	Joseph G. Kohout, Dem.	Cook
16	Dean McCully, Rep.	Woodford
	Rollie C. Carpenter, Rep.	Livingston
	James P. Lannon, Dem.	Livingston
17	Anthony J. De Tolve, Dem.	Cook
	Andrew A. Euzzino, Dem.	Cook
	Peter C. Granata, Rep.	Cook
18	Robert L. Burhans, Rep.	Peoria
	James D. Carrigan, Dem.	Peoria
	August C. Grebe, Rep.	Peoria
19	Frank A. Marek, Rep.	Cook
	Benjamin Nelson, Dem.	Cook
	Frank C. Wolf, Dem.	Cook
20	Louis E. Beckman, Rep.	Kankakee
	Samuel H. Shapiro, Dem.	Kankakee
	Harry L. Topping, Rep.	Kankakee
21	Nicholas E. Caruso, Dem.	Cook
	Peter K. Vuono, Rep.	Cook
	William G. Clark, Dem.	Cook
22	W. O. Edwards, Dem.	Vermilion
	Clarence G. Hall, Rep.	Vermilion
	M. R. Walker, Rep.	Vermilion
23	Stanley A. Halick, Dem.	Cook
	Walter J. Reum, Rep.	Cook
	William G. Thon,[2] Rep.	Cook
24	Charles W. Clabaugh, Rep.	Champaign
	Ora D. Dillavou, Rep.	Champaign
	Leo Pfeffer, Dem.	Champaign
25	Stanley R. Kosinski, Dem.	Cook
	Charles O. Miller, Dem.	Cook
	Elroy C. Sandquist, Rep.	Cook
26	Homer Caton, Rep.	McLean
	Edward T. Kane, Dem.	McLean
	Ben S. Rhodes, Rep.	McLean
27	Bernard C. Prusinski, Dem.	Cook
	Daniel D. Rostenkowski, Dem.	Cook
	John P. Touhy, Dem.	Cook
28	James L. Atkins, Rep.	Macon
	Paul H. Ferguson, Dem.	Macon
	Barrett F. Rogers, Rep.	Logan
29	Joseph L. De La Cour, Dem.	Cook
	Edward P. O'Grady,[3] Dem.	Cook
	Paul J. Randolph, Rep.	Cook
30	Robert H. Allison, Rep.	Tazewell
	William D. Burnsmier, Rep.	Mason
	C. R. Ratcliffe, Dem.	Cass
31	Alan Best,[4] Rep.	Cook
	Albert W. Hachmeister, Rep.	Cook
	Kenneth R. Wendt, Dem.	Cook
32	Robert T. McLoskey, Rep.	Warren
	John B. Monroe, Dem.	McDonough
	Rollo R. Robbins, Rep.	Hancock
33	Hazel A. McCaskrin, Rep.	Rock Island

District	Member	County
	Richard Stengel, Dem.	Rock Island
	Ralph Stephenson, Rep.	Rock Island
34	Myron E. Lollar, Rep.	Douglas
	William K. Kidwell, Dem.	Coles
	John W. Lewis, Jr., Rep.	Clark
35	George S. Brydia, Rep.	Whiteside
	Hubert D. Considine, Dem.	Lee
	Charles K. Willett, Rep.	Lee
36	Fred L. Goodwin, Dem.	Adams
	H. B. Ihnen, Rep.	Adams
	George W. Wilson, Rep.	Pike
37	Tobias Barry, Sr., Dem.	Bureau
	Orville G. Chapman, Rep.	Stark
	Joseph R. Peterson, Rep.	Bureau
38	William Lyons, Dem.	Macoupin
	William Robison, Dem.	Macoupin
	Pauline B. Rinaker, Rep.	Macoupin
39	J. Ward Smith,[5] Rep.	La Salle
	Carl W. Soderstrom, Rep.	La Salle
	Joseph P. Stremlau, Dem.	La Salle
40	Carl H. Preihs, Dem.	Christian
	Clarence E. Sprinkle, Rep.	Christian
	Will P. Welker, Rep.	Fayette
41	J. Harold Downey, Dem.	Will
	John M. King, Rep.	Du Page
	Warren L. Wood, Rep.	Will
42	R. J. Branson, Rep.	Marion
	Joseph B. Siemer, Rep.	Effingham
	Paul Taylor, Dem.	Effingham
43	Reed F. Cutler, Rep.	Fulton
	Richard R. Larson, Rep.	Knox
	A. W. Ray, Dem.	Fulton
44	Dean R. Hammack, Dem.	Perry
	W. J. McDonald, Rep.	Jackson
	Thomas J. Thornton, Rep.	Randolph
45	Hugh Green, Rep.	Morgan
	G. William Horsley, Rep.	Sangamon
	T. J. Sullivan, Dem.	Sangamon
46	S. O. Dale, Rep.	Hamilton
	Clyde Lee, Dem. /	Jefferson
	Claude D. Travers, Rep.	Richland
47	Edward D. Groshong, Rep.	Madison
	Lloyd Harris, Dem.	Madison
	Leland J. Kennedy, Dem.	Madison
48	W. V. Brown, Rep.	Wabash
	Herschel S. Green, Rep.	Crawford
	Paul A. Ziegler, Dem.	White
49	Alan J. Dixon, Rep.	St. Clair
	Frank Holten, Dem.	St. Clair
	Otis L. Miller, Sr., Rep.	St. Clair
50	Clyde L. Choate, Dem.	Union
	Harry W. McClintock, Rep.	Franklin
	John E. Miller, Rep.	Alexander
51	Gordon E. Kerr, Rep.	Massac
	Paul Powell, Dem.	Johnson
	W. O. Verhines, Rep.	Johnson

[1] Died July 21, 1954.
[2] Died May 23, 1953.
[3] Died Dec. 25, 1952.
[4] Died April 23, 1953.
[5] Died Sept. 27, 1953.

Senate

President	John W. Chapman
President pro tempore	Arthur J. Bidwill
Secretary	Edward H. Alexander

District	Member	County
1	Fred B. Roti, Dem.	Cook
2	Frank Ryan, Dem.	Cook
3	Fred J. Smith, Dem.	Cook
4	Donald J. O'Brien, Dem.	Cook
5	Marshall Korshak, Dem.	Cook
6	W. Russell Arrington, Rep.	Cook
7	Arthur J. Bidwill, Rep.	Cook
8	Robert McClory, Rep.	Lake
9	William J. Lynch, Dem.	Cook
10	Charles W. Baker, Rep.	Ogle
11	A. L. Cronin, Dem.	Cook
12	Marvin F. Burt, Rep.	Stephenson
13	Daniel Dougherty, Dem.	Cook
14	Merritt J. Little, Rep.	Kane
15	Frank J. Kocarek, Dem.	Cook
16	Rollie C. Carpenter, Rep.	Livingston
17	Roland V. Libonati, Dem.	Cook
18	Clyde C. Trager, Rep.	Peoria
19	John J. Gorman, Dem.	Cook
20	H. Victor McBroom, Rep.	Kankakee
21	William G. Clark, Dem.	Cook
22	John P. Meyer, Rep.	Vermilion
23	Benedict Garmisa, Dem.	Cook
24	Everett R. Peters, Rep.	Champaign
25	Robert J. Graham, Dem.	Cook
26	David Davis, Rep.	McLean
27	Daniel D. Rostenkowski, Dem.	Cook
28	Elbert S. Smith, Rep.	Macon
29	William J. Connors, Dem.	Cook
30	Egbert B. Groen, Rep.	Tazewell
31	Robert E. Cherry, Dem.	Cook
32	T. Mac Downing, Rep.	McDonough
33	Morris E. Muhleman, Rep.	Rock Island
34	Robert W. Lyons, Rep.	Coles
35	Dennis J. Collins, Rep.	De Kalb
36	Lillian E. Schlagenhauf, Rep.	Adams
37	Frank P. Johnson,[1] Rep.	Henry
	Joseph R. Peterson,[2] Rep.	Bureau
38	W. P. Cuthbertson, Rep.	Macoupin
39	Fred J. Hart, Rep.	La Salle
40	Lloyd E. Davis, Rep.	Christian
41	Lottie Holman O'Neill, Rep.	Du Page
42	Dwight P. Friedrich, Rep.	Marion
43	Albert Scott, Rep.	Fulton
44	R. G. Crisenberry, Rep.	Jackson
45	George E. Drach, Rep.	Sangamon
46	Paul W. Broyles, Rep.	Jefferson
47	James O. Monroe, Dem.	Madison
48	William F. Hensley, Rep.	Lawrence
49	James W. Gray, Dem.	St. Clair
50	Homer Butler, Rep.	Williamson
51	Glen O. Jones, Rep.	Saline

[1] Died March 19, 1955.
[2] Vice Johnson.

Speaker   Warren L. Wood
Clerk   Fred W. Ruegg

District	Member	County
1	Corneal A. Davis, Dem.	Cook
	Ernest A. Greene, Rep.	Cook
	Robert E. Romano, Dem.	Cook
2	James J. Adduci, Rep.	Cook
	Sam Romano, Dem.	Cook
	James J. Ryan, Dem.	Cook
3	James Y. Carter, Dem.	Cook
	William H. Robinson, Rep.	Cook
	George Gary Noonan, Dem.	Cook
4	Michael A. Ruddy, Rep.	Cook
	Frank J. Smith, Dem.	Cook
	Theodore A. Swinarski, Dem.	Cook
5	Noble W. Lee, Rep.	Cook
	Charles M. Skyles, Dem.	Cook
	Kenneth E. Wilson, Dem.	Cook
6	Irwin L. Marty, Rep.	Cook
	William E. Pollack, Rep.	Cook
	Charles H. Weber, Dem.	Cook
7	Joseph L. Lelivelt, Dem.	Cook
	Arthur W. Sprague, Rep.	Cook
	Bernice T. Van Der Vries, Rep.	Cook
8	Jack Bairstow, Dem.	Lake
	A. B. McConnell, Rep.	McHenry
	W. J. Murphy, Rep.	Lake
9	Hector A. Brouillet, Rep.	Cook
	John G. Fary, Dem.	Cook
	Lillian Piotrowski, Dem.	Cook
10	Mabel E. Green, Rep.	Winnebago
	David Hunter, Jr., Rep.	Winnebago
	William Pierce, Dem.	Winnebago
11	Michael E. Hannigan, Dem.	Cook
	Walter McAvoy, Rep.	Cook
	Michael H. McDermott, Dem.	Cook
12	Harold M. Widmer, Rep.	Stephenson
	John K. Morris, Dem.	Carroll
	Franklin U. Stransky, Rep.	Carroll
13	Henry M. Lenard, Dem.	Cook
	John G. Ryan, Dem.	Cook
	Edward Schneider, Rep.	Cook
14	J. Lisle Laufer, Rep.	Kane
	Maud N. Peffers, Rep.	Kane
	Leon M. Schuler, Dem.	Kane
15	Thomas J. Curran, Rep.	Cook
	Joseph G. Kohout,[1] Dem.	Cook
	Mitchell Ropa, Dem.	Cook
16	William C. Harris, Rep.	Livingston
	James P. Lannon, Dem.	Livingston
	Dean McCully, Rep.	Woodford
17	Anthony J. De Tolve, Dem.	Cook
	Andrew A. Euzzino, Dem.	Cook
	Peter C. Granata, Rep.	Cook
18	Robert L. Burhans, Rep.	Peoria
	James D. Carrigan, Dem.	Peoria
	August C. Grebe, Rep.	Peoria
19	Frank A. Marek, Rep.	Cook
	Benjamin Nelson, Dem.	Cook
	Frank C. Wolf, Dem.	Cook
20	Louis E. Beckman, Rep.	Kankakee
	Samuel L. Martin, Rep.	Iroquois
	Samuel H. Shapiro, Dem.	Kankakee
21	Louis F. Capuzi, Rep.	Cook
	Nicholas E. Caruso, Dem.	Cook
	Robert Cutro, Dem.	Cook
22	Robert Craig, Dem.	Vermilion
	Clarence G. Hall, Rep.	Vermilion
	M. R. Walker, Rep.	Vermilion
23	Stanley A. Halick, Dem.	Cook
	Richard A. Napolitano, Dem.	Cook
	Walter J. Reum, Rep.	Cook
24	Charles W. Clabaugh, Rep.	Champaign
	Ora D. Dillavou, Rep.	Champaign
	Leo Pfeffer, Dem.	Champaign
25	Stanley R. Kosinski, Dem.	Cook
	Robert L. Massey, Dem.	Cook
	Elroy C. Sandquist, Rep.	Cook
26	Homer Caton, Rep.	McLean
	Ben S. Rhodes, Rep.	McLean
	Joe W. Russell, Dem.	Ford
27	Louis Janczak, Rep.	Cook
	Edward J. Shaw, Dem.	Cook
	John P. Touhy, Dem.	Cook
28	Robert W. McCarthy, Dem.	Logan
	David M. Peters,[2] Dem.	Macon
	Barrett F. Rogers, Rep.	Logan
29	Joseph L. De La Cour, Dem.	Cook
	George W. Dunne, Dem.	Cook
	Paul J. Randolph, Rep.	Cook
30	C. R. Ratcliffe, Dem.	Cass
	J. Norman Shade, Rep.	Tazewell
	George L. Saal, Dem.	Tazewell
31	Albert W. Hachmeister, Rep.	Cook
	Harry D. Lavery, Rep.	Cook
	Kenneth R. Wendt, Dem.	Cook
32	Everett L. Falder, Dem.	McDonough
	Robert T. McLoskey, Rep.	Warren
	Rollo R. Robbins, Rep.	Hancock
33	Hazel A. McCaskrin,[3] Rep.	Rock Island
	Richard Stengel, Dem.	Rock Island
	Ralph Stephenson, Rep.	Rock Island
34	Myron E. Lollar,[4] Rep.	Douglas
	John W. Lewis, Jr., Rep.	Clark
	William K. Kidwell, Dem.	Coles
35	George S. Brydia, Rep.	Whiteside
	Hubert D. Considine, Dem.	Lee
	Charles K. Willett, Rep.	Lee
36	H. B. Ihnen, Rep.	Adams
	George W. Wilson, Rep.	Pike
	Carl H. Wittmond, Dem.	Calhoun
37	Tobias Barry, Sr., Dem.	Bureau
	Orville G. Chapman, Rep.	Stark
	Joseph R. Peterson, Rep.	Bureau
38	William Lyons, Dem.	Macoupin
	Pauline B. Rinaker, Rep.	Macoupin
	Charles Ed Schaefer, Dem.	Montgomery
39	Clayton C. Harbeck, Rep.	La Salle
	Carl W. Soderstrom, Rep.	La Salle
	Joseph P. Stremlau, Dem.	La Salle
40	Edward C. Eberspacher, Dem.	Shelby
	Carl H. Preihs, Dem.	Christian
	Clarence E. Sprinkle, Rep.	Christian
41	John M. King, Rep.	Du Page
	Francis J. Loughran, Dem.	Will
	Warren L. Wood, Rep.	Will

District	Member	County
42	Warren O. Billhartz, Rep.	Clinton
	Edwin R. Haag, Dem.	Clinton
	Joseph B. Siemer, Rep.	Effingham
43	Richard R. Larson, Rep.	Knox
	Martin P. Sutor, Dem.	Knox
	Paul C. Zempel, Rep.	Fulton
44	G. R. Beckmeyer, Rep.	Washington
	Dean R. Hammack, Dem.	Perry
	Thomas J. Thornton, Rep.	Randolph
45	Hugh Green, Rep.	Morgan
	G. William Horsley, Rep.	Sangamon
	Alan T. Lucas, Dem.	Sangamon
46	S. O. Dale, Rep.	Hamilton
	Clyde Lee, Dem.	Jefferson
	Claude D. Travers, Rep.	Richland
47	Lloyd Harris, Dem.	Madison
	Paul Simon, Dem.	Madison
	Ralph T. Smith, Rep.	Madison
48	Garrel Burgoon, Rep.	Lawrence
	Herschel S. Green, Rep.	Crawford
	Paul A. Ziegler, Dem.	White
49	Alan J. Dixon, Dem.	St. Clair
	Frank Holten, Dem.	St. Clair
	Otis L. Miller, Sr., Rep.	St. Clair
50	Bert Baker, Jr., Dem.	Franklin
	Clyde L. Choate, Dem.	Union
	John E. Miller, Rep.	Alexander
51	Gordon E. Kerr, Rep.	Massac
	Paul Powell, Dem.	Johnson
	W. O. Verhines, Rep.	Johnson

[1] Died Nov. 10, 1955.
[2] Died Jan. 14, 1956.
[3] Died Dec. 2, 1954.
[4] Died April 4, 1956.

Redistricting of 1955 authorized by act of July 29, 1955; fifty-eight Senate districts, each electing one senator; fifty-nine House districts, each electing three representatives

Senate

district	Counties
1 to 15	Cook (6 outside of Chicago)
16	Livingston, Woodford
17	Cook
18	Marshall, Peoria, Stark
19	Cook
20	Iroquois, Kankakee
21	Cook
22	Edgar, Vermilion
23	Cook
24	Champaign, Moultrie, Piatt
25	Cook
26	Ford, McLean
27	Cook
28	De Witt, Logan, Macon
29	Cook
30	Mason, Menard, Tazewell
31	Cook
32	Hancock, McDonough
33	Cook
34	Clark, Coles, Cumberland, Douglas

Senate

district	Counties
35	De Kalb, Lee, Whiteside
36	Adams, Calhoun, Pike, Scott
37	Bureau, Henry
38	Bond, Macoupin, Montgomery
39	La Salle, Putnam
40	Christian, Fayette, Shelby
41	Du Page, Will
42	Clay, Clinton, Effingham, Marion
43	Brown, Fulton, Schuyler
44	Jackson, Monroe, Randolph
45	Cass, Morgan, Sangamon
46	Edwards, Jefferson, Wabash, Wayne
47	Greene, Jersey, Madison
48	Crawford, Jasper, Lawrence, Richland
49	Perry, St. Clair, Washington
50	Alexander, Pulaski, Union, Williamson
51	Franklin, Hardin, Johnson, Massac, Pope, Saline
52	Boone, Lake, McHenry
53	Henderson, Mercer, Rock Island
54	Ogle, Winnebago
55	Gallatin, Hamilton, White
56	Carroll, JoDaviess, Stephenson
57	Knox, Warren
58	Grundy, Kane, Kendall

House

district	Counties
1 to 30	Cook
31	Lake
32	Boone, De Kalb, McHenry, Ogle
33	Winnebago
34	Carroll, JoDaviess, Stephenson, Whiteside
35	Kane
36	Du Page
37	Will
38	Grundy, Kendall, La Salle
39	Mercer, Rock Island
40	Bureau, Henry, Lee, Stark
41	Ford, Kankakee, Livingston
42	De Witt, McLean, Marshall, Putnam, Woodford
43	Peoria
44	Champaign, Moultrie, Piatt
45	Iroquois, Vermilion
46	Cass, Fulton, Mason, Tazewell
47	Logan, Macon, Menard
48	Sangamon
49	Adams, Calhoun, Greene, Morgan, Pike, Scott
50	Brown, Hancock, Henderson, Knox, McDonough, Schuyler, Warren
51	Clark, Coles, Crawford, Cumberland, Douglas, Edgar
52	Christian, Jersey, Macoupin, Montgomery, Shelby
53	Madison
54	St. Clair
55	Bond, Clinton, Effingham, Fayette, Marion
56	Clay, Edwards, Jasper, Lawrence, Richland, Wabash, Wayne, White
57	Franklin, Jefferson, Perry, Washington
58	Alexander, Jackson, Monroe, Pulaski, Randolph, Union
59	Gallatin, Hamilton, Hardin, Johnson, Massac, Pope, Saline, Williamson

Senate

President	John W. Chapman	
President pro tempore	Arthur J. Bidwill	
Secretary	Edward E. Fernandes	

District	Member	County
1	Arthur J. Bidwill, Rep.	Cook
2	Arthur W. Sprague, Rep.	Cook
3	Jackson L. Boughner, Rep.	Cook
4	W. Russell Arrington, Rep.	Cook
5	Marshall Korshak, Dem.	Cook
6	Frank M. Ozinga, Rep.	Cook
7	Roland V. Libonati,[1] Dem.	Cook
8	Hayes Robertson, Rep.	Cook
9	William J. Lynch,[1] Dem.	Cook
10	Albert E. Bennett, Rep.	Cook
11	Fred J. Smith, Dem.	Cook
12	Edmund G. Sweeney, Dem.	Cook
13	Daniel D. Dougherty, Dem.	Cook
14	Donald J. O'Brien, Dem.	Cook
15	A. L. Cronin, Dem.	Cook
16	Rollie C. Carpenter, Rep.	Livingston
17	John J. Donovan, Rep.	Cook
18	Hubert W. Woodruff, Rep.	Peoria
19	Herbert M. Johnson, Rep.	Cook
20	H. Victor McBroom, Rep.	Kankakee
21	William G. Clark,[1] Dem.	Cook
22	John P. Meyer, Rep.	Vermilion
23	Frank J. Kocarek, Dem.	Cook
24	Everett R. Peters, Rep.	Champaign
25	William J. Connors, Dem.	Cook
26	David Davis, Rep.	McLean
27	Robert E. Cherry, Dem.	Cook
28	George P. Johns, Rep.	Macon
29	Robert J. Graham, Dem.	Cook
30	Egbert B. Groen, Rep.	Tazewell
31	John J. Gorman,[2] Dem.	Cook
32	T. Mac Downing, Rep.	McDonough
33	Daniel D. Rostenkowski, Dem.	Cook
34	Robert W. Lyons,[3] Rep.	Coles
35	Dennis J. Collins, Rep.	De Kalb
36	Lillian E. Schlagenhauf, Rep.	Adams
37	Joseph R. Peterson, Rep.	Bureau
38	William Lyons, Dem.	Macoupin
39	Fred J. Hart, Rep.	La Salle
40	Clarence E. Sprinkle, Rep.	Christian
41	Lottie Holman O'Neill, Rep.	Du Page
42	Dwight P. Friedrich, Rep.	Marion
43	Albert Scott, Rep.	Fulton
44	R. G. Crisenberry, Rep.	Jackson
45	George E. Drach, Rep.	Sangamon
46	Paul W. Broyles, Rep.	Jefferson
47	James O. Monroe, Dem.	Madison
48	Herschel S. Green, Rep.	Crawford
49	James W. Gray, Dem.	St. Clair
50	William L. Grindle, Dem.	Williamson
51	Glen O. Jones,[4] Rep.	Saline
52	Robert McClory, Rep.	Lake
53	Morris E. Muhleman, Rep.	Rock Island
54	Robert R. Canfield, Rep.	Winnebago
55	Paul A. Ziegler, Dem.	White
56	Marvin F. Burt, Rep.	Stephenson

District	Member	County
57	Richard R. Larson, Rep.	Knox
58	Merritt J. Little, Rep.	Kane

[1] Resigned.
[2] Died March 23, 1957.
[3] Died Sept. 27, 1957.
[4] Died Nov. 2, 1957.

House of Representatives

Speaker	Warren L. Wood
Clerk	Fred W. Ruegg

District	Member	County
1	Jack E. Walker, Rep.	Cook
	Maurino R. Richton, Rep.	Cook
	Anthony Scariano, Dem.	Cook
2	Terrel E. Clarke, Rep.	Cook
	Harold A. Hoover, Rep.	Cook
	Frank X. Downey, Dem.	Cook
3	Frank A. Marek, Rep.	Cook
	George E. Dolezal, Rep.	Cook
	Paul G. Ceaser, Dem.	Cook
4	Walter J. Reum, Rep.	Cook
	Claude A. Walker, Rep.	Cook
	Raymond J. Welsh, Jr., Dem.	Cook
5	Elmer W. Conti, Rep.	Cook
	Joseph L. Lelivelt, Dem.	Cook
	Harry J. Smith, Rep.	Cook
6	John W. Carroll, Rep.	Cook
	Thomas J. Halpin, Dem.	Cook
	Arthur E. Simmons, Rep.	Cook
7	Marion E. Burks, Rep.	Cook
	Frances L. Dawson, Rep.	Cook
	Jeanne C. Hurley, Dem.	Cook
8	Paul F. Elward, Dem.	Cook
	Esther Saperstein, Dem.	·Cook
	Michael F. Zlatnik, Rep.	Cook
9	Joseph F. Fanta, Dem.	Cook
	Kenneth E. Moberley, Rep.	Cook
	William E. Pollack, Rep.	Cook
10	Albert W. Hachmeister, Rep.	Cook
	Carl W. Stolteben, Dem.	Cook
	Kenneth R. Wendt, Dem.	Cook
11	Joseph L. De La Cour, Dem.	Cook
	George W. Dunne, Dem.	Cook
	Paul J. Randolph, Rep.	Cook
12	Kenneth W. Course, Dem.	Cook
	Charles H. Kordowski, Dem.	Cook
	Charles O. Miller, Rep.	Cook
13	Nathan J. Kaplan, Dem.	Cook
	James P. Loukas, Dem.	Cook
	Elroy C. Sandquist, Rep.	Cook
14	Horace H. Brock, Rep.	Cook
	Oscar Hansen, Rep.	Cook
	Harry H. Semerow, Dem.	Cook
15	Peter J. Miller, Rep.	Cook
	Al Sakowicz, Rep.	Cook
	Chester R. Wiktorski, Dem.	Cook
16	William G. Clark, Dem.	Cook
	Bernard McDevitt, Rep.	Cook
	Bernard S. Neistein, Dem.	Cook

District	Member	County
17	Andrew A. Euzzino, Dem.	Cook
	Peter C. Granata, Rep.	Cook
	Sam Romano, Dem.	Cook
18	Louis F. Capuzi, Rep.	Cook
	Nicholas E. Caruso, Dem.	Cook
	John P. Touhy, Dem.	Cook
19	Louis Janczak, Rep.	Cook
	Richard A. Napolitano, Dem.	Cook
	Edward J. Shaw, Dem.	Cook
20	Corneal A. Davis, Dem.	Cook
	Richard A. Harewood, Dem.	Cook
	William H. Robinson, Rep.	Cook
21	James Y. Carter, Dem.	Cook
	J. Horace Gardner, Rep.	Cook
	Kenneth E. Wilson, Dem.	Cook
22	Charles F. Armstrong, Dem.	Cook
	Elwood Graham, Rep.	Cook
	Cecil A. Partee, Dem.	Cook
23	Nathan J. Kinnally, Dem.	Cook
	Noble W. Lee, Rep.	Cook
	Abner J. Mikva, Dem.	Cook
24	Edward J. Derwinski, Rep.	Cook
	Henry M. Lenard, Dem.	Cook
	Nick Svalina, Dem.	Cook
25	John G. Ryan, Dem.	Cook
	Edward Schneider, Rep.	Cook
	Peter J. Whalen, Dem.	Cook
26	John P. Downes, Dem.	Cook
	William J. Morgensen,[1] Rep.	Cook
	George F. Stastny, Rep.	Cook
27	Michael E. Hannigan, Dem.	Cook
	Walter McAvoy, Rep.	Cook
	Michael H. McDermott, Dem.	Cook
28	John G. Fary, Dem.	Cook
	Michael A. Ruddy, Rep.	Cook
	Frank J. Smith, Dem.	Cook
29	Thomas J. Curran, Rep.	Cook
	George Gary Noonan, Dem.	Cook
	Matt Ropa, Dem.	Cook
30	Hector A. Brouillet, Rep.	Cook
	Lillian Piotrowski, Dem.	Cook
	Frank C. Wolf, Dem.	Cook
31	Jack Bairstow, Dem.	Lake
	Robert Coulson, Rep.	Lake
	W. J. Murphy, Rep.	Lake
32	John P. Manning, Rep.	Ogle
	A. B. McConnell, Rep.	McHenry
	Ferne Carter Pierce, Dem.	De Kalb
33	Mabel E. Green, Rep.	Winnebago
	David Hunter, Rep..	Winnebago
	Wiiliam Pierce, Dem.	Winnebago
34	George S. Brydia, Rep.	Whiteside
	John K. Morris, Dem.	Carroll
	Harold W. Widmer, Rep.	Stephenson
35	Robert F. Casey, Rep.	Kane
	J. Lisle Laufer, Rep.	Kane
	Leon M. Schuler, Dem.	Kane
36	Fred W. Anderson, Dem.	Du Page
	Lee E. Daniels, Rep.	Du Page
	John N. Erlenborn, Rep.	Du Page
37	Louis F. Bottino, Rep.	Will
	Francis J. Loughran, Dem.	Will
	Warren L. Wood, Rep.	Will
38	Clayton C. Harbeck, Rep.	La Salle

District	Member	County
	Carl W. Soderstrom, Rep.	La Salle
	Joseph P. Stremlau, Dem.	La Salle
39	Robert Austin, Rep.	Rock Island
	Paul E. Rink, Dem.	Rock Island
	Ralph Stephenson, Rep.	Rock Island
40	Tobias Barry, Sr.,[2] Dem.	Bureau
	W. K. Davidson, Rep.	Henry
	Charles K. Willett, Rep.	Lee
41	Louis E. Beckman, Rep.	Kankakee
	William C. Harris, Rep.	Livingston
	Samuel H. Shapiro, Dem.	Kankakee
42	Dean McCully, Rep.	Woodford
	Ben S. Rhodes, Rep.	McLean
	J. W. Scott, Dem.	McLean
43	Robert L. Burhans, Rep.	Peoria
	James D. Carrigan, Dem.	Peoria
	August C. Grebe, Rep.	Peoria
44	Charles W. Clabaugh, Rep.	Champaign
	Ora D. Dillavou, Rep.	Champaign
	Leo Pfeffer, Dem.	Champaign
45	Robert Craig, Dem.	Vermilion
	Clarence G. Hall, Rep.	Vermilion
	Samuel L. Martin, Rep.	Iroquois
46	C. R. Ratcliffe, Dem.	Cass
	George L. Saal, Dem.	Tazewell
	J. Norman Shade, Rep.	Tazewell
47	George M. Grandfield, Rep.	Macon
	Robert W. McCarthy, Dem.	Logan
	Barrett F. Rogers, Rep.	Logan
48	George P. Coutrakon, Rep.	Sangamon
	G. William Horsley, Rep.	Sangamon
	Alan T. Lucas, Dem.	Sangamon
49	Hugh Green, Rep.	Morgan
	H. B. Ihnen, Rep.	Adams
	Carl H. Wittmond, Dem.	Calhoun
50	Robert T. McLoskey, Rep.	Warren
	Rollo R. Robbins, Rep.	Hancock
	Guy D. Seckman, Dem.	Brown
51	Dave Glenn, Dem.	Cumberland
	John W. Lewis, Jr., Rep.	Clark
	A. Lincoln Stanfield, Rep.	Edgar
52	Edward C. Eberspacher, Dem.	Shelby
	Orval Hittmeier, Rep.	Montgomery
	Charles Ed Schaefer, Dem.	Montgomery
53	Lloyd Harris, Dem.	Madison
	Paul Simon, Dem.	Madison
	Ralph T. Smith, Rep.	Madison
54	Alan J. Dixon, Dem.	St. Clair
	Frank Holten, Dem.	St. Clair
	Otis L. Miller, Sr., Rep.	St. Clair
55	Warren O. Billhartz, Rep.	Clinton
	Edwin R. Haag, Dem.	Clinton
	Joseph B. Siemer, Rep.	Effingham
56	Garrel Burgoon, Rep.	Lawrence
	S. O. Dale, Rep.	Wayne
	Ray Koehler, Dem.	White
57	Bert Baker, Jr., Dem.	Franklin
	Wayne Fitzgerrell, Rep.	Franklin
	Clyde Lee, Dem.	Jefferson
58	Clyde L. Choate, Dem.	Union
	W. J. McDonald, Rep.	Jackson
	John E. Miller, Rep.	Alexander
59	Gordon E. Kerr, Rep.	Massac
	C. L. McCormick, Rep.	Johnson
	Paul Powell, Dem.	Johnson

[1] Died May 20, 1958.
[2] Died June 17, 1958.

Senate

President   John W. Chapman
President pro tempore   Arthur J. Bidwill
Secretary   Edward E. Fernandes

House of Representatives

Speaker   Paul Powell
Clerk   Clarence Boyle

District	Member	County
1	Arthur J. Bidwill, Rep.	Cook
2	Arthur W. Sprague, Rep.	Cook
3	John A. Graham, Rep.	Cook
4	W. Russell Arrington, Rep.	Cook
5	Marshall Korshak, Dem.	Cook
6	Frank M. Ozinga, Rep.	Cook
7	Anthony J. De Tolve, Dem.	Cook
8	Hayes Robertson, Rep.	Cook
9	Morgan M. Finley, Dem.	Cook
10	Albert E. Bennett, Rep.	Cook
11	Fred J. Smith, Dem.	Cook
12	Edmund G. Sweeney, Dem.	Cook
13	Daniel D. Dougherty, Dem.	Cook
14	Donald J. O'Brien, Dem.	Cook
15	A. L. Cronin, Dem.	Cook
16	Rollie C. Carpenter, Rep.	Livingston
17	Robert B. Maher, Dem.	Cook
18	Hubert W. Woodruff, Rep.	Peoria
19	Phillip J. Carey, Dem.	Cook
20	H. Victor McBroom,[1] Rep.	Kankakee
21	Thomas A. McGloon, Dem.	Cook
22	John P. Meyer, Rep.	Vermilion
23	Frank J. Kocarek, Dem.	Cook
24	Everett R. Peters, Rep.	Champaign
25	William J. Connors, Dem.	Cook
26	David Davis, Rep.	McLean
27	Robert E. Cherry, Dem.	Cook
28	George P. Johns, Rep.	Macon
29	James E. Strunk, Dem.	Cook
30	Egbert B. Groen, Rep.	Tazewell
31	Bernard S. Neistein, Dem.	Cook
32	T. Mac Downing, Rep.	McDonough
33	Thad L. Kusibab, Dem.	Cook
34	John W. Lewis, Jr., Rep.	Clark
35	Dennis J. Collins, Rep.	De Kalb
36	Lillian E. Schlagenhauf, Rep.	Adams
37	Joseph R. Peterson, Rep.	Bureau
38	William Lyons, Dem.	Macoupin
39	Fred J. Hart, Rep.	La Salle
40	Clarence E. Sprinkle, Rep.	Christian
41	Lottie Holman O'Neill, Rep.	Du Page
42	Dwight P. Friedrich, Rep.	Marion
43	Robert A. Welch, Dem.	Fulton
44	R. G. Crisenberry, Rep.	Jackson
45	George E. Drach, Rep.	Sangamon
46	Paul W. Broyles, Rep.	Jefferson
47	James O. Monroe, Dem.	Madison
48	Herschel S. Green, Rep.	Crawford
49	James W. Gray, Dem.	St. Clair
50	William L. Grindle, Dem.	Williamson
51	Gordon E. Kerr, Rep.	Massac
52	Robert McClory, Rep.	Lake
53	Ora Smith, Dem.	Henderson
54	Robert R. Canfield, Rep.	Winnebago
55	Paul A. Ziegler, Dem.	White
56	Marvin F. Burt, Rep.	Stephenson
57	Richard R. Larson, Rep.	Knox
58	Merritt J. Little, Rep.	Kane

[1] Died Feb. 21, 1959.

District	Member	County
1	Jack E. Walker, Rep.	Cook
	Maurino R. Richton, Rep.	Cook
	Anthony Scariano, Dem.	Cook
2	Terrel E. Clarke, Rep.	Cook
	Harold A. Hoover, Rep.	Cook
	Frank X. Downey, Dem.	Cook
3	Frank A. Marek, Rep.	Cook
	George E. Dolezal, Rep.	Cook
	Paul G. Ceaser, Dem.	Cook
4	Walter J. Reum, Rep.	Cook
	Claude A. Walker, Rep.	Cook
	Raymond J. Welsh, Jr., Dem.	Cook
5	Elmer W. Conti, Rep.	Cook
	Joseph L. Lelivelt, Dem.	Cook
	Joseph P. Sandro, Dem.	Cook
6	John W. Carroll, Rep.	Cook
	Bernard M. Peskin, Dem.	Cook
	Arthur E. Simmons, Rep.	Cook
7	Marion E. Burks, Rep.	Cook
	Frances L. Dawson, Rep.	Cook
	Jeanne C. Hurley, Dem.	Cook
8	Paul F. Elward, Dem.	Cook
	Esther Saperstein, Dem.	Cook
	Michael F. Zlatnik, Rep.	Cook
9	Joseph F. Fanta, Dem.	Cook
	William E. Pollack, Rep.	Cook
	Nicholas Zagone, Dem.	Cook
10	Albert W. Hachmeister, Rep.	Cook
	Frank Lyman, Dem.	Cook
	Kenneth R. Wendt, Dem.	Cook
11	Joseph L. De La Cour, Dem.	Cook
	George W. Dunne, Dem.	Cook
	Paul J. Randolph, Rep.	Cook
12	Kenneth W. Course, Dem.	Cook
	Charles H. Kordowski, Dem.	Cook
	Charles O. Miller, Rep.	Cook
13	Nathan J. Kaplan, Dem.	Cook
	James P. Loukas, Dem.	Cook
	Elroy C. Sandquist, Rep.	Cook
14	Bernard J. Fio Rito, Dem.	Cook
	Oscar Hansen, Rep.	Cook
	Harry H. Semerow, Dem.	Cook
15	Peter J. Miller, Rep.	Cook
	John F. Leon, Dem.	Cook
	Chester R. Wiktorski, Dem.	Cook
16	William G. Clark, Dem.	Cook
	Peter M. Callan, Dem.	Cook
	Bernard McDevitt, Rep.	Cook
17	Andrew A. Euzzino, Dem.	Cook
	Peter C. Granata, Rep.	Cook
	Sam Romano, Dem.	Cook
18	Louis F. Capuzi, Rep.	Cook
	Nicholas E. Caruso, Dem.	Cook
	John P. Touhy, Dem.	Cook
19	Louis Janczak, Rep.	Cook
	Richard A. Napolitano, Dem.	Cook
	Edward J. Shaw, Dem.	Cook
20	James Y. Carter, Dem.	Cook
	Corneal A. Davis, Dem.	Cook

District	Member	County
	William H. Robinson, Rep.	Cook
21	J. Horace Gardner, Rep.	Cook
	Cecil A. Partee, Dem.	Cook
	Kenneth E. Wilson, Dem.	Cook
22	Charles F. Armstrong, Dem.	Cook
	Floy Clements, Dem.	Cook
	Elwood Graham, Rep.	Cook
23	Nathan J. Kinnally, Dem.	Cook
	Noble W. Lee, Rep.	Cook
	Abner J. Mikva, Dem.	Cook
24	Henry M. Lenard, Dem.	Cook
	August J. Ruf, Rep.	Cook
	Nick Svalina, Dem.	Cook
25	John G. Ryan, Dem.	Cook
	Edward Schneider, Rep.	Cook
	Peter J. Whalen, Dem.	Cook
26	John M. Daley, Dem.	Cook
	John P. Downes, Dem.	Cook
	George F. Stastny, Rep.	Cook
27	Michael E. Hannigan, Dem.	Cook
	Walter McAvoy, Rep.	Cook
	Michael H. McDermott, Dem.	Cook
28	John G. Fary, Dem.	Cook
	Michael A. Ruddy, Rep.	Cook
	Frank J. Smith, Dem.	Cook
29	Thomas J. Curran, Rep.	Cook
	George Gary Noonan, Dem.	Cook
	Matt Ropa, Dem.	Cook
30	Hector A. Brouillet, Rep.	Cook
	Lillian Piotrowski, Dem.	Cook
	Frank C. Wolf, Dem.	Cook
31	Jack Bairstow, Dem.	Lake
	Robert Coulson, Rep.	Lake
	W. J. Murphy, Rep.	Lake
32	John P. Manning, Rep.	Ogle
	A. B. McConnell, Rep.	McHenry
	Ferne Carter Pierce, Dem.	De Kalb
33	Mabel E. Green, Rep.	Winnebago
	David Hunter, Rep.	Winnebago
	William Pierce, Dem.	Winnebago
34	George S. Brydia, Rep.	Whiteside
	John K. Morris, Dem.	Carroll
	Harold W. Widmer, Rep.	Stephenson
35	Robert F. Casey, Rep.	Kane
	J. Lisle Laufer, Dem.	Kane
	John Jerome Hill, Dem.	Kane
36	Lee E. Daniels, Rep.	Du Page
	John N. Erlenborn, Rep.	Du Page
	William A. Redmond, Dem.	Du Page
37	Louis F. Bottino, Rep.	Will
	Francis J. Loughran, Dem.	Will
	Warren L. Wood, Rep.	Will
38	Clayton C. Harbeck, Rep.	La Salle
	Carl W. Soderstrom, Rep.	La Salle
	Joseph P. Stremlau, Dem.	La Salle
39	Robert Austin, Rep.	Rock Island
	Paul E. Rink, Dem.	Rock Island
	Ralph Stephenson, Rep.	Rock Island
40	W. K. Davidson, Rep.	Henry
	William C. Hollerich, Dem.	Bureau
	Charles K. Willett, Rep.	Lee
41	William C. Harris, Rep.	Livingston
	George E. Luehrs, Rep.	Kankakee
	Samuel H. Shapiro, Dem.	Kankakee

District	Member	County
42	Dean McCully, Rep.	Woodford
	Ben S. Rhodes, Rep.	McLean
	J. W. Scott, Dem.	McLean
43	Robert L. Burhans, Rep.	Peoria
	James D. Carrigan, Dem.	Peoria
	John C. Parkhurst, Rep.	Peoria
44	Charles W. Clabaugh, Rep.	Champaign
	Edwin E. Dale, Rep.	Champaign
	Leo Pfeffer, Dem.	Champaign
45	Robert Craig, Dem.	Vermilion
	Clarence G. Hall, Rep.	Vermilion
	Samuel L. Martin, Rep.	Iroquois
46	Walter E. Hill, Rep.	Fulton
	C. R. Ratcliffe, Dem.	Cass
	Willis L. Stamm, Dem.	Tazewell
47	John W. Alsup, Dem.	Macon
	Robert W. McCarthy, Dem.	Logan
	Barrett F. Rogers, Rep.	Logan
48	George P. Coutrakon, Rep.	Sangamon
	G. William Horsley, Rep.	Sangamon
	Alan T. Lucas, Dem.	Sangamon
49	Hugh Green, Rep.	Morgan
	H. B. Ihnen, Rep.	Adams
	Carl H. Wittmond, Dem.	Calhoun
50	Robert T. McLoskey, Rep.	Warren
	Rollo R. Robbins, Rep.	Hancock
	Martin P. Sutor, Dem.	Knox
51	Dave Glenn, Dem.	Cumberland
	Paul Graham, Rep.	Coles
	A. Lincoln Stanfield, Rep.	Edgar
52	Edward C. Eberspacher, Dem.	Shelby
	Orval Hittmeier, Rep.	Montgomery
	Charles Ed Schaefer, Dem.	Montgomery
53	Lloyd Harris, Dem.	Madison
	Paul Simon, Dem.	Madison
	Ralph T. Smith, Rep.	Madison
54	Alan J. Dixon, Dem.	St. Clair
	Frank Holten, Dem.	St. Clair
	Otis L. Miller, Sr.,' Rep.	St. Clair
55	Warren O. Billhartz, Rep.	Clinton
	Edwin R. Haag, Dem.	Clinton
	Miles E. Mills, Dem.	Effingham
56	S. O. Dale, Rep.	Wayne
	Ray Koehler, Dem.	White
	William A. Moore, Dem.	Richland
57	Bert Baker, Jr., Dem.	Franklin
	Wayne Fitzgerrell, Rep.	Franklin
	Clyde Lee, Dem.	Jefferson
58	Clyde L. Choate, Dem.	Union
	James D. Holloway, Dem.	Randolph
	W. J. McDonald, Rep.	Jackson
59	Homer Butler, Rep.	Williamson
	C. L. McCormick, Rep.	Johnson
	Paul Powell, Dem.	Johnson

' Died July 26, 1959.

Seventy-second General Assembly, 1961-62

Senate

President	Samuel H. Shapiro
President pro tempore	Arthur J. Bidwill
Secretary	Edward E. Fernandes

District	Member	County
1	Arthur J. Bidwill, Rep.	Cook
2	Arthur W. Sprague, Rep.	Cook

District	Member	County
3	John A. Graham, Rep.	Cook
4	W. Russell Arrington, Rep.	Cook
5	Marshall Korshak, Dem.	Cook
6	Frank M. Ozinga, Rep.	Cook
7	Anthony J. De Tolve, Dem.	Cook
8	Arthur R. Gottschalk, Rep.	Cook
9	Morgan M. Finley, Dem.	Cook
10	Seymour Fox, Dem.	Cook
11	Fred J. Smith, Dem.	Cook
12	Edmund G. Sweeney, Dem.	Cook
13	Daniel D. Dougherty, Dem.	Cook
14	Donald J. O'Brien, Dem.	Cook
15	A. L. Cronin, Dem.	Cook
16	William C. Harris, Rep.	Livingston
17	Robert B. Maher, Dem.	Cook
18	Hudson R. Sours, Rep.	Peoria
19	Phillip J. Carey, Dem.	Cook
20	Samuel L. Martin, Rep.	Iroquois
21	Thomas A. McGloon, Dem.	Cook
22	John P. Meyer, Rep.	Vermilion
23	Frank J. Kocarek, Dem.	Cook
24	Everett R. Peters, Rep.	Champaign
25	William J. Connors,[1] Dem.	Cook
26	David Davis, Rep.	McLean
27	Robert E. Cherry, Dem.	Cook
28	Robert W. McCarthy, Dem.	Logan
29	James E. Strunk, Dem.	Cook
30	Egbert B. Groen, Rep.	Tazewell
31	Bernard S. Neistein, Dem.	Cook
32	T. Mac Downing, Rep.	McDonough
33	Thad L. Kusibab, Dem.	Cook
34	Paul Graham, Rep.	Coles
35	Dennis J. Collins, Rep.	De Kalb
36	Lillian E. Schlagenhauf, Rep.	Adams
37	Joseph R. Peterson, Rep.	Bureau
38	William Lyons, Dem.	Macoupin
39	Fred J. Hart, Rep.	La Salle
40	Edward C. Eberspacher, Dem.	Shelby
41	Lottie Holman O'Neill, Rep.	Du Page
42	Dwight P. Friedrich, Rep.	Marion
43	Robert A. Welch, Dem.	Fulton
44	John G. Gilbert, Rep.	Jackson
45	George E. Drach, Rep.	Sangamon
46	Paul W. Broyles, Rep.	Jefferson
47	James O. Monroe, Dem.	Madison
48	Herschel S. Green, Rep.	Crawford
49	James W. Gray, Dem.	St. Clair
50	William L. Grindle, Dem.	Williamson
51	Gordon E. Kerr, Rep.	Massac
52	Robert McClory,[2] Rep.	Lake
53	Ora Smith, Dem.	Henderson
54	Robert R. Canfield, Rep.	Winnebago
55	Paul A. Ziegler, Dem.	White
56	Everett E. Laughlin, Rep.	Stephenson
57	Richard R. Larson, Rep.	Knox
58	Merritt J. Little, Rep.	Kane

[1] Died June 24, 1961.
[2] Resigned, candidate for U.S.H.R.

House of Representatives

Speaker   Paul Powell
Clerk   Charles F. Kervin

District	Member	County
1	Jack E. Walker, Rep.	Cook
	Edwin A. McGowan, Rep.	Cook

District	Member	County
	Anthony Scariano, Dem.	Cook
2	Terrel E. Clarke, Rep.	Cook
	Harold A. Hoover, Rep.	Cook
	Frank X. Downey, Dem.	Cook
3	Frank A. Marek, Rep.	Cook
	George E. Dolezal, Rep.	Cook
	Paul G. Ceaser, Dem.	Cook
4	Walter J. Reum, Rep.	Cook
	Claude A. Walker, Rep.	Cook
	Raymond J. Welsh, Dem.	Cook
5	Elmer W. Conti, Rep.	Cook
	Joseph L. Lelivelt, Dem.	Cook
	William D. Walsh, Rep.	Cook
6	John W. Carroll, Rep.	Cook
	Bernard M. Peskin, Dem.	Cook
	Arthur E. Simmons, Rep.	Cook
7	Marion E. Burks, Rep.	Cook
	Frances L. Dawson, Rep.	Cook
	Robert Marks, Dem.	Cook
8	Paul F. Elward, Dem.	Cook
	Esther Saperstein, Dem.	Cook
	Michael F. Zlatnik, Rep.	Cook
9	Joseph F. Fanta, Dem.	Cook
	Kenneth E. Moberley, Rep.	Cook
	William E. Pollack, Rep.	Cook
10	Albert W. Hachmeister, Rep.	Cook
	Frank Lyman, Dem.	Cook
	Kenneth R. Wendt, Dem.	Cook
11	Joseph L. De La Cour, Dem.	Cook
	George W. Dunne, Dem.	Cook
	Paul J. Randolph, Rep.	Cook
12	Kenneth W. Course, Dem.	Cook
	LaSalle J. DeMichaels, Dem.	Cook
	Charles O. Miller, Rep.	Cook
13	Nathan J. Kaplan, Dem.	Cook
	James P. Loukas, Dem.	Cook
	Elroy C. Sandquist, Rep.	Cook
14	Oscar Hansen, Rep.	Cook
	Walter P. Hoffelder, Rep.	Cook
	Harry H. Semerow,[3] Dem.	Cook
15	John F. Leon, Dem.	Cook
	Peter J. Miller, Rep.	Cook
	Chester R. Wiktorski, Dem.	Cook
16	Peter M. Callan, Dem.	Cook
	Bernard McDevitt, Rep.	Cook
	Robert F. McPartlin, Dem.	Cook
17	Andrew A. Euzzino, Dem.	Cook
	Peter C. Granata, Rep.	Cook
	Sam Romano, Dem.	Cook
18	Louis F. Capuzi, Rep.	Cook
	Nicholas E. Caruso, Dem.	Cook
	John P. Touhy, Dem.	Cook
19	Louis Janczak, Rep.	Cook
	Richard A. Napolitano, Dem.	Cook
	Edward J. Shaw, Dem.	Cook
20	James Y. Carter, Dem.	Cook
	Corneal A. Davis, Dem.	Cook
	William H. Robinson, Dem.	Cook
21	J. Horace Gardner, Rep.	Cook
	Cecil A. Partee, Dem.	Cook
	Kenneth E. Wilson, Dem.	Cook
22	Charles F. Armstrong, Dem.	Cook
	Lycurgus J. Conner, Dem.	Cook
	Elwood Graham, Rep.	Cook

District	Member	County
23	Nathan J. Kinnally, Dem.	Cook
	Noble W. Lee, Rep.	Cook
	Abner J. Mikva, Dem.	Cook
24	Henry M. Lenard, Dem.	Cook
	August J. Ruf, Rep.	Cook
	Nick Svalina, Dem.	Cook
25	John G. Ryan, Dem.	Cook
	Edward Schneider, Rep.	Cook
	Peter J. Whalen, Dem.	Cook
26	John M. Daley, Dem.	Cook
	John P. Downes, Dem.	Cook
	George F. Stastny, Rep.	Cook
27	Michael E. Hannigan, Dem.	Cook
	Walter McAvoy, Rep.	Cook
	Michael H. McDermott, Dem.	Cook
28	John G. Fary, Dem.	Cook
	Michael A. Ruddy, Rep.	Cook
	Frank J. Smith, Dem.	Cook
29	Thomas J. Curran, Rep.	Cook
	Matt Ropa, Dem.	Cook
	John M. Vitek, Dem.	Cook
30	Hector A. Brouillet, Rep.	Cook
	Lillian Piotrowski, Dem.	Cook
	Frank C. Wolf, Dem.	Cook
31	Jack Bairstow, Dem.	Lake
	Robert Coulson, Rep.	Lake
	W. J. Murphy, Rep.	Lake
32	John P. Manning, Rep.	Ogle
	A. B. McConnell, Rep.	McHenry
	Ferne Carter Pierce, Dem.	De Kalb
33	Mabel E. Green, Rep.	Winnebago
	William Pierce, Dem.	Winnebago
	Bertil T. Rosander, Rep.	Winnebago
34	George S. Brydia, Rep.	Whiteside
	John K. Morris, Dem.	Carroll
	Harold W. Widmer, Rep.	Stephenson
35	Robert F. Casey, Rep.	Kane
	J. Lisle Laufer, Rep.	Kane
	John Jerome Hill, Dem.	Kane
36	Lee E. Daniels, Rep.	Du Page
	John N. Erlenborn, Rep.	Du Page
	William A. Redmond, Dem.	Du Page
37	Meade Baltz, Rep.	Will
	Francis J. Loughran, Dem.	Will
	Warren L. Wood, Rep.	Will
38	Clayton C. Harbeck, Rep.	La Salle
	Carl W. Soderstrom, Rep.	La Salle
	Joseph P. Stremlau, Dem.	La Salle
39	Paul E. Rink, Dem.	Rock Island
	Leonard W. Ross, Dem.	Rock Island
	Ralph Stephenson, Rep.	Rock Island
40	Tobias Barry, Jr., Dem.	Bureau
	W. K. Davidson, Rep.	Henry
	Charles K. Willett, Rep.	Lee
41	Arthur R. Falter, Rep.	Livingston
	Carl T. Hunsicker, Rep.	Livingston
	Joe W. Russell, Dem.	Ford
42	Dean McCully, Rep.	Woodford
	Ben S. Rhodes, Rep.	McLean
	J. W. Scott, Dem.	McLean
43	Robert L. Burhans, Rep.	Peoria
	James D. Carrigan, Dem.	Peoria
	John C. Parkhurst, Rep.	Peoria
44	Charles W. Clabaugh, Rep.	Champaign

District	Member	County
	Edwin E. Dale, Rep.	Champaign
	Leo Pfeffer, Dem.	Champaign
45	Robert Craig, Dem.	Vermilion
	Clarence G. Hall, Rep.	Vermilion
	Melvin A. Weyand, Rep.	Vermilion
46	Walter E. Hill, Rep.	Fulton
	C. R. Ratcliffe, Dem.	Cass
	Ray C. Heiple II,[1] Rep.	Tazewell
	Willis L. Stamm,[2] Dem.	Tazewell
47	John W. Alsup, Dem.	Macon
	Herman L. Dammerman, Dem.	Logan
	Hilmer C. Landholt, Rep.	Macon
48	George P. Coutrakon, Rep.	Sangamon
	G. William Horsley, Rep.	Sangamon
	Alan T. Lucas, Dem.	Sangamon
49	H. B. Ihnen, Rep.	Adams
	Harris Rowe, Rep.	Morgan
	Carl H. Wittmond, Dem.	Calhoun
50	Robert T. McLoskey, Rep.	Warren
	Rollo R. Robbins, Rep.	Hancock
	Dan Teefey, Dem.	Brown
51	Edward M. Finfgeld, Rep.	Douglas
	Dave Glenn, Dem.	Cumberland
	A. Lincoln Stanfield, Rep.	Edgar
52	Orval Hittmeier, Rep.	Montgomery
	Charles Ed Schaefer, Dem.	Montgomery
	Stuart J. Traynor, Dem.	Christian
53	Lloyd Harris, Dem.	Madison
	Paul Simon, Dem.	Madison
	Ralph T. Smith, Rep.	Madison
54	Alan J. Dixon, Dem.	St. Clair
	Frank Holten, Dem.	St. Clair
	Otis L. Miller, Jr., Rep.	St. Clair
55	Fred Branson, Rep.	Marion
	James H. Donnewald, Dem.	Clinton
	Miles E. Mills, Dem.	Effingham
56	Garrel Burgoon, Rep.	Lawrence
	Norman L. Benefiel, Dem.	Jasper
	S. O. Dale, Rep.	Wayne
57	Bert Baker, Jr., Rep.	Franklin
	Wayne Fitzgerrell, Rep.	Franklin
	Clyde Lee, Dem.	Jefferson
58	Clyde L. Choate, Dem.	Union
	James D. Holloway, Dem.	Randolph
	Gale Williams, Rep.	Jackson
59	Homer Butler, Rep.	Williamson
	C. L. McCormick, Rep.	Johnson
	Paul Powell, Dem.	Johnson

[1] Willis L. Stamm contested election, Heiple unseated.
[2] Vice Heiple.
[3] Resigned.

Seventy-third General Assembly, 1963–64

Senate

President	Samuel H. Shapiro
President pro tempore	Arthur J. Bidwill
Secretary	Edward E. Fernandes

District	Member	County
1	Arthur J. Bidwill, Rep.	Cook
2	Arthur W. Sprague, Rep.	Cook
3	John A. Graham, Rep.	Cook
4	W. Russell Arrington, Rep.	Cook

District	Member	County
5	Nathan J. Kinnally, Dem.	Cook
6	Frank M. Ozinga, Rep.	Cook
7	Anthony J. De Tolve, Dem.	Cook
8	Arthur R. Gottschalk, Rep.	Cook
9	Morgan M. Finley, Dem.	Cook
10	Seymour Fox, Dem.	Cook
11	Fred J. Smith, Dem.	Cook
12	Edmund G. Sweeney, Dem.	Cook
13	Daniel D. Dougherty, Dem.	Cook
14	Donald J. O'Brien, Dem.	Cook
15	A. L. Cronin, Dem.	Cook
16	William C. Harris, Rep.	Livingston
17	Arthur R. Swanson, Rep.	Cook
18	Hudson R. Sours, Rep.	Peoria
19	Robert F. Hatch, Rep.	Cook
20	Samuel L. Martin, Rep.	Iroquois
21	Thomas A. McGloon, Dem.	Cook
22	John P. Meyer, Rep.	Vermilion
23	Frank J. Kocarek, Dem.	Cook
24	Everett R. Peters, Rep.	Champaign
25	Joseph L. De La Cour, Dem.	Cook
26	David Davis, Rep.	McLean
27	Robert E. Cherry, Dem.	Cook
28	Robert W. McCarthy, Dem.	Logan
29	Walter P. Hoffelder, Rep.	Cook
30	Egbert B. Groen, Rep.	Tazewell
31	Bernard S. Neistein, Dem.	Cook
32	T. Mac Downing, Rep.	McDonough
33	Thad L. Kusibab, Dem.	Cook
34	Paul Graham, Rep.	Coles
35	Dennis J. Collins, Rep.	De Kalb
36	Lillian E. Schlagenhauf, Rep.	Adams
37	Joseph R. Peterson, Rep.	Bureau
38	William Lyons, Dem.	Macoupin
39	Fred J. Hart, Rep.	La Salle
40	Edward C. Eberspacher, Dem.	Shelby
41	Harris W. Fawell, Rep.	Du Page
42	Dwight P. Friedrich, Rep.	Marion
43	Robert A. Welch, Dem.	Fulton
44	John G. Gilbert, Rep.	Jackson
45	George E. Drach, Rep.	Sangamon
46	Paul W. Broyles, Rep.	Jefferson
47	Paul Simon, Dem.	Madison
48	Madge Miller Green, Rep.	Crawford
49	Alan J. Dixon, Dem.	St. Clair
50	William L. Grindle, Dem.	Williamson
51	Gordon E. Kerr, Rep.	Massac
52	Robert Coulson,[1] Rep.	Lake
53	Donald D. Carpentier, Rep.	Rock Island
54	Robert R. Canfield, Rep.	Winnebago
55	Paul A. Ziegler, Dem.	White
56	Everett E. Laughlin, Rep.	Stephenson
57	Richard R. Larson, Rep.	Knox
58	Merritt J. Little, Rep.	Kane

[1] Vice McClory, elected U.S.H.R. Nov. 6, 1962.

House of Representatives

Speaker	John W. Lewis, Jr.
Clerk	Frederic B. Selcke

District	Member	County
1	Edwin A. McGowan, Rep.	Cook
	Anthony Scariano, Dem.	Cook
	Jack E. Walker, Rep.	Cook
2	Terrel E. Clarke, Rep.	Cook
	Frank X. Downey, Dem.	Cook

District	Member	County
	Don A. Moore, Rep.	Cook
3	Paul G. Ceaser, Dem.	Cook
	George E. Dolezal, Rep.	Cook
	Frank A. Marek, Rep.	Cook
4	Claude A. Walker, Rep.	Cook
	Richard A. Walsh, Rep.	Cook
	Raymond J. Welsh, Jr., Dem.	Cook
5	Leo J. Bartoline,[1] Dem.	Cook
	Richard L. LoDestro, Rep.	Cook
	William D. Walsh, Rep.	Cook
6	John W. Carroll, Rep.	Cook
	Bernard M. Peskin, Dem.	Cook
	Arthur E. Simmons, Rep.	Cook
7	Frances L. Dawson, Rep.	Cook
	Alan R. Johnston, Rep.	Cook
	Robert Marks, Dem.	Cook
8	Paul F. Elward, Dem.	Cook
	Esther Saperstein, Dem.	Cook
	Michael F. Zlatnik, Rep.	Cook
9	Kenneth E. Moberley, Rep.	Cook
	William E. Pollack, Rep.	Cook
	Nicholas Zagone, Dem.	Cook
10	Albert W. Hachmeister, Rep.	Cook
	Frank Lyman, Dem.	Cook
	John Merlo, Dem.	Cook
11	Harry P. Bauler,[2] Dem.	Cook
	Paul J. Randolph, Rep.	Cook
	Edward W. Wolbank, Dem.	Cook
12	Kenneth W. Course, Dem.	Cook
	LaSalle J. DeMichaels, Dem.	Cook
	Charles O. Miller, Rep.	Cook
13	Nathan J. Kaplan,[3] Dem.	Cook
	James P. Loukas, Dem.	Cook
	Elroy C. Sandquist, Rep.	Cook
14	Oscar Hansen, Rep.	Cook
	Chester P. Majewski, Dem.	Cook
	Helmut W. Stolle, Rep.	Cook
15	John F. Leon, Dem.	Cook
	Peter J. Miller, Rep.	Cook
	Chester R. Wiktorski, Dem.	Cook
16	Peter M. Callan, Dem.	Cook
	Bernard McDevitt, Rep.	Cook
	Robert F. McPartlin, Dem.	Cook
17	Andrew A. Euzzino, Dem.	Cook
	Peter C. Granata, Rep.	Cook
	Sam Romano, Dem.	Cook
18	Louis F. Capuzi, Rep.	Cook
	Lawrence DiPrima, Dem.	Cook
	John P. Touhy, Dem.	Cook
19	Louis Janczak, Dem.	Cook
	Richard A. Napolitano, Dem.	Cook
	Edward J. Shaw, Dem.	Cook
20	James Y. Carter, Dem.	Cook
	Corneal A. Davis, Dem.	Cook
	William H. Robinson, Rep.	Cook
21	J. Horace Gardner, Rep.	Cook
	Cecil A. Partee, Dem.	Cook
	Kenneth E. Wilson, Dem.	Cook
22	Charles F. Armstrong, Dem.	Cook
	Lycurgus Conner,[4] Dem.	Cook
	Elwood Graham, Rep.	Cook
23	Noble W. Lee, Rep.	Cook
	Robert E. Mann, Dem.	Cook
	Abner J. Mikva, Dem.	Cook

District	Member	County
24	John J. Donovan, Rep.	Cook
	Henry M. Lenard, Dem.	Cook
	Nick Svalina, Dem.	Cook
25	John G. Ryan,[5] Dem.	Cook
	Edward Schneider, Rep.	Cook
	Peter J. Whalen, Dem.	Cook
26	John P. Downes, Dem.	Cook
	Raymond J. Kahoun, Rep.	Cook
	George F. Stastny, Rep.	Cook
27	Michael E. Hannigan, Dem.	Cook
	Walter McAvoy, Rep.	Cook
	Michael H. McDermott, Dem.	Cook
28	John G. Fary, Dem.	Cook
	Michael A. Ruddy, Rep.	Cook
	Frank J. Smith, Dem.	Cook
29	Matt Ropa, Dem.	Cook
	John M. Vitek, Dem.	Cook
	John F. Wall, Rep.	Cook
30	Hector A. Brouillet, Rep.	Cook
	Lillian Piotrowski, Dem.	Cook
	Frank C. Wolf, Dem.	Cook
31	Jack Bairstow,[6] Dem.	Lake
	John H. Conolly, Rep.	Lake
	W. J. Murphy, Rep.	Lake
32	Paul F. Jones, Rep.	Ogle
	A. B. McConnell, Rep.	McHenry
	Albert H. Pearson,[7] Dem.	McHenry
33	Merle K. Anderson, Rep.	Winnebago
	William Pierce, Dem.	Winnebago
	Bertil T. Rosander, Rep.	Winnebago
34	George S. Brydia, Rep.	Whiteside
	Kenneth W. Miller, Rep.	Whiteside
	John K. Morris, Dem.	Carroll
35	John Jerome Hill, Dem.	Kane
	J. Lisle Laufer, Rep.	Kane
	Allen L. Schoeberlein, Rep.	Kane
36	John N. Erlenborn, Rep.	Du Page
	Lewis V. Morgan, Jr., Rep.	Du Page
	William A. Redmond, Dem.	Du Page
37	Meade Baltz, Rep.	Will
	Francis J. Loughran, Dem.	Will
	Warren L. Wood, Rep.	Will
38	Carl W. Soderstrom, Rep.	La Salle
	Joseph P. Stremlau, Dem.	La Salle
	Harlan D. Warren, Rep.	La Salle
39	Robert Austin, Rep.	Rock Island
	Thomas F. Railsback, Rep.	Rock Island
	Paul E. Rink, Dem.	Rock Island
40	Tobias Barry, Jr., Dem.	Bureau
	W. K. Davidson, Rep.	Henry
	Charles K. Willett, Rep.	Lee
41	Carl T. Hunsicker, Rep.	Livingston
	Edward McBroom, Rep.	Kankakee
	Joe W. Russell, Dem.	Ford
42	Dean McCully, Rep.	Woodford
	Ben S. Rhodes, Rep.	McLean
	J. W. Scott, Dem.	McLean
43	Robert L. Burhans, Rep.	Peoria
	James D. Carrigan, Dem.	Peoria
	John C. Parkhurst, Rep.	Peoria
44	Edwin E. Dale, Rep.	Champaign
	Charles W. Clabaugh, Rep.	Champaign
	Leo Pfeffer, Dem.	Champaign

District	Member	County
45	Charles M. Campbell, Rep.	Vermilion
	Robert Craig, Dem.	Vermilion
	Clarence G. Hall, Rep.	Vermilion
46	Ray C. Heiple II, Rep.	Tazewell
	C. R. Ratcliffe, Dem.	Cass
	George L. Saal, Dem.	Tazewell
47	John W. Alsup, Dem.	Macon
	Herman L. Dammerman, Dem.	Logan
	George P. Johns, Rep.	Macon
48	George P. Coutrakon, Rep.	Sangamon
	G. William Horsley, Rep.	Sangamon
	Alan T. Lucas, Dem.	Sangamon
49	H. B. Ihnen, Rep.	Adams
	Harris Rowe, Rep.	Morgan
	Carl H. Wittmond, Dem.	Calhoun
50	Raymond E. Anderson, Rep.	Knox
	Clarence E. Neff, Rep.	Henderson
	Dan Teefey, Dem.	Brown
51	Edward M. Finfgeld, Rep.	Douglas
	Dave Glenn,[8] Dem.	Cumberland
	John W. Lewis, Jr., Rep.	Clark
52	Orval Hittmeier, Rep.	Montgomery
	Charles Ed Schaefer, Dem.	Montgomery
	Stuart J. Traynor, Dem.	Christian
53	Lloyd Harris, Dem.	Madison
	Leland J. Kennedy, Dem.	Madison
	Ralph T. Smith, Rep.	Madison
54	Daniel E. Costello, Dem.	St. Clair
	Frank Holten, Dem.	St. Clair
	Edward Lehman, Rep.	St. Clair
55	Fred Branson, Rep.	Marion
	James H. Donnewald, Dem.	Clinton
	Miles E. Mills, Dem.	Effingham
56	Ben C. Blades, Rep.	Wayne
	Garrel Burgoon, Rep.	Lawrence
	Robert V. Walsh, Dem.	White
57	Bert Baker, Jr., Dem.	Franklin
	Wayne Fitzgerrell, Rep.	Franklin
	Clyde Lee, Dem.	Jefferson
58	Clyde L. Choate, Dem.	Union
	James D. Holloway, Dem.	Randolph
	Gale Williams, Rep.	Jackson
59	Joseph R. Hale, Rep.	Gallatin
	C. L. McCormick, Rep.	Johnson
	Paul Powell, Dem.	Johnson

[1] Died June 10, 1963.
[2] Died Dec. 6, 1962.
[3] Resigned.
[4] Died May 28, 1963.
[5] Died Dec. 17, 1963.
[6] Died Oct. 28, 1963.
[7] Died Nov. 16, 1963.
[8] Died April 1, 1964.

Seventy-fourth General Assembly, 1965–66

Senate

President   Samuel H. Shapiro
President pro tempore
            W. Russell Arrington
Secretary   Edward E. Fernandes

District	Member	County
1	Arthur J. Bidwill, Rep.	Cook
2	Arthur W. Sprague, Rep.	Cook

Member	County
3 John A. Graham, Rep.	Cook
4 W. Russell Arrington, Rep.	Cook
5 Nathan J. Kinnally, Dem.	Cook
6 Frank M. Ozinga, Rep.	Cook
7 Anthony J. De Tolve, Dem.	Cook
8 Arthur R. Gottschalk, Rep.	Cook
9 Morgan M. Finley, Dem.	Cook
10 Thomas G. Lyons, Dem.	Cook
11 Fred J. Smith, Dem.	Cook
12 John J. Lanigan, Rep.	Cook
13 Daniel D. Dougherty, Dem.	Cook
14 Theodore A. Swinarski, Dem.	Cook
15 A. L. Cronin, Dem.	Cook
16 William C. Harris, Rep.	Livingston
17 Arthur R. Swanson, Rep.	Cook
18 Hudson R. Sours, Rep.	Peoria
19 Robert F. Hatch, Rep.	Cook
20 Samuel L. Martin, Rep.	Iroquois
21 Thomas A. McGloon, Dem.	Cook
22 Tom Merritt, Rep.	Vermilion
23 Frank J. Kocarek, Dem.	Cook
24 Everett R. Peters, Rep.	Champaign
25 Joseph L. De La Cour, Dem.	Cook
26 David Davis, Rep.	McLean
27 Robert E. Cherry, Dem.	Cook
28 Robert W. McCarthy, Dem.	Logan
29 Walter P. Hoffelder, Rep.	Cook
30 Egbert B. Groen, Rep.	Tazewell
31 Bernard S. Neistein, Dem.	Cook
32 Clifford B. Latherow, Rep.	Hancock
33 Thad L. Kusibab, Dem.	Cook
34 Paul Graham,[1] Rep.	Coles
35 Dennis J. Collins, Rep.	De Kalb
36 Thomas J. Awerkamp, Dem.	Adams
37 Joseph R. Peterson, Rep.	Bureau
38 William Lyons, Dem.	Macoupin
39 Fred J. Hart, Rep.	La Salle
40 Stuart J. Traynor, Dem.	Christian
41 Harris W. Fawell, Rep.	Du Page
42 James H. Donnewald, Dem.	Clinton
43 Robert A. Welch, Dem.	Fulton
44 John G. Gilbert, Rep.	Jackson
45 George E. Drach, Rep.	Sangamon
46 Paul W. Broyles, Rep.	Jefferson
47 Paul Simon, Dem.	Madison
48 Phillip B. Benefiel, Dem.	Lawrence
49 Alan J. Dixon, Dem.	St. Clair
50 William L. Grindle, Dem.	Williamson
51 Gordon E. Kerr, Rep.	Massac
52 Robert Coulson, Rep.	Lake
53 Donald D. Carpentier, Rep.	Rock Island
54 Bertil T. Rosander, Rep.	Winnebago
55 Paul A. Ziegler, Dem.	White
56 Everett E. Laughlin, Rep.	Stephenson
57 Richard R. Larson, Rep.	Knox
58 Robert W. Mitchler, Rep.	Kendall

[1] Died June 18, 1965.

House of Representatives

Speaker	John P. Touhy
Clerk	Charles F. Kervin

(Members elected at large)

Member	County
John W. Alsup, Dem.	Macon
Charles F. Armstrong,[1] Dem.	Cook

Member	County
Bert Baker, Jr., Dem.	Franklin
Tobias Barry, Jr , Dem.	Bureau
Francis J. Berry, Rep.	Lake
W. Robert Blair, Rep.	Will
William L. Blaser, Rep.	Cook
Paul P. Boswell, Rep.	Cook
Jack E. Bowers, Rep.	Du Page
Frank J. Broucek, Dem.	Cook
George M. Burditt, Rep.	Cook
Joseph Callahan, Dem.	Iroquois
Peter M. Callan,[2] Dem.	Cook
Robert R. Canfield, Rep.	Winnebago
James D. Carrigan, Dem.	Peoria
John W. Carroll, Rep.	Cook
James Y. Carter, Dem.	Cook
John E. Cassidy, Jr., Dem.	Peoria
Eugenia S. Chapman, Dem.	Cook
Clyde L. Choate, Dem.	Union
Charles W. Clabaugh, Rep.	Champaign
Terrel E. Clarke, Rep.	Cook
Otis G. Collins, Dem.	Cook
Joseph T. Connelly, Dem.	Coles
John H. Conolly, Rep.	Lake
Daniel E. Costello, Dem.	St. Clair
Kenneth W. Course, Dem.	Cook
Robert Craig, Dem.	Vermilion
William J. Cunningham, Rep.	Perry
Edwin E. Dale, Rep.	Champaign
John M. Daley, Dem.	Cook
Corneal A. Davis, Dem.	Cook
Frances L. Dawson, Rep.	Cook
LaSalle J. DeMichaels, Dem.	Cook
Lawrence DiPrima, Dem.	Cook
John P. Downes, Dem.	Cook
Frank X. Downey, Dem.	Cook
Earl D. Eisenhower, Rep.	Cook
Paul F. Elward, Dem.	Cook
Andrew A. Euzzino, Dem.	Cook
Joseph F. Fanta, Dem.	Cook
John G. Fary, Dem.	Cook
Joseph Fennessey, Dem.	La Salle
Wayne Fitzgerrell,[3] Rep.	Franklin
William J. Frey, Rep.	Sangamon
Benedict Garmisa, Dem.	Cook
Herbert F. Geisler, Rep.	Cook
William A. Giblin, Dem.	McHenry
E. J. Giorgi, Dem.	Winnebago
Philip C. Goldstick, Dem.	Cook
Dorah Grow, Dem.	Adams
Albert W. Hachmeister, Rep.	Cook
Thomas J. Hanahan, Jr., Dem.	McHenry
Michael E. Hannigan, Dem.	Cook
Lloyd Harris, Dem.	Madison
William E. Hartnett, Dem.	Lake
John Jerome Hill, Dem.	Kane
James D. Holloway, Dem.	Randolph
G. William Horsley, Rep.	Sangamon
John J. Houlihan, Dem.	Will
Ronald A. Hurst, Rep.	Peoria
Oral Jacobs, Dem.	Rock Island
Edward H. Jenison, Rep.	Edgar
Alan R. Johnston, Rep.	Cook
J. David Jones, Rep.	Sangamon

Member	County
Leslie N. Jones, Rep.	Clay
Harold A. Katz, Dem.	Cook
John A. Kennedy, Dem.	Cook
Leland J. Kennedy, Dem.	Madison
James C. Kirie, Dem.	Cook
Carl L. Klein, Rep.	Cook
John H. Kleine, Rep.	Lake
Jack T. Knuepfer, Rep.	Du Page
Clyde Lee, Dem.	Jefferson
Noble W. Lee, Rep.	Cook
Edward Lehman, Rep.	St. Clair
Henry M. Lenard, Dem.	Cook
John F. Leon, Dem.	Cook
John W. Lewis, Jr., Rep.	Clark
Marvin S. Lieberman, Dem.	Macon
Francis J. Loughran, Dem.	Will
James P. Loukas, Dem.	Cook
Alan T. Lucas, Dem.	Sangamon
Frank Lyman, Dem.	Cook
Elmo McClain, Dem.	Adams
C. L. McCormick, Rep.	Johnson
Hope McCormick, Rep.	Cook
Dean McCully, Rep.	Woodford
Michael H. McDermott, Dem.	Cook
Bernard McDevitt, Rep.	Cook
James A. McLendon, Dem.	Cook
Melvin McNairy, Dem.	Cook
John J. McNichols, Dem.	Cook
Robert F. McPartlin, Dem.	Cook
Francis X. Mahoney, Dem.	Stephenson
Chester P. Majewski, Dem.	Cook
Robert E. Mann, Dem.	Cook
Mary K. Meany, Rep.	Cook
John Merlo, Dem.	Cook
Abner J. Mikva, Dem.	Cook
Miles E. Mills, Dem.	Effingham
Don A. Moore, Rep.	Cook
William A. Moore, Dem.	Richland
James B. Moran, Dem.	Cook
Lewis V. Morgan, Jr., Rep.	Du Page
John K. Morris, Dem.	Carroll
Clarence E. Neff, Rep.	Henderson
Leo B. Obernuefemann, Dem.	St. Clair
Leo F. O'Brien, Dem.	Knox
Daniel O'Neill, Dem.	Madison
James H. Oughton, Jr., Rep.	Livingston
Stanley A. Papierz, Rep.	Cook
John C. Parkhurst, Rep.	Peoria
Cecil A. Partee, Dem.	Cook
Marjorie Pebworth, Rep.	Cook
Bernard M. Peskin, Dem.	Cook
Leo Pfeffer, Dem.	Champaign
Daniel M. Pierce, Dem.	Lake
William Pierce, Dem.	Winnebago
William E. Pollack, Rep.	Cook
Lawrence X. Pusateri, Rep.	Cook
Thomas F. Railsback, Rep.	Rock Island
Paul J. Randolph, Rep.	Cook
C. R. Ratcliffe, Dem.	Cass
Leland H. Rayson, Dem.	Cook
William A. Redmond, Dem.	Du Page
Ben S. Rhodes, Rep.	McLean
Paul E. Rink, Dem.	Rock Island

Member	County
Sam Romano, Dem.	Cook
Matt Ropa, Dem.	Cook
Harris Rowe, Rep.	Morgan
Michael A. Ruddy, Rep.	Cook
Joe W. Russell, Dem.	Ford
Omer Sanders, Dem.	Williamson
Esther Saperstein, Dem.	Cook
Anthony Scariano, Dem.	Cook
Charles Ed Schaefer, Dem.	Montgomery
Eugene F. Schlickman, Rep.	Cook
William V. Schoeninger, Dem.	Cook
Fred J. Schraeder, Dem.	Peoria
J. W. Scott, Dem.	McLean
Edward F. Sensor, Dem.	Kane
Edward J. Shaw, Dem.	Cook
Arthur E. Simmons, Rep.	Cook
George F. Sisler, Rep.	Cook
Howard R. Slater, Dem.	Lake
Roy C. Small, Dem.	Saline
Calvin L. Smith, Dem.	Cook
Frank J. Smith, Dem.	Cook
Ralph T. Smith, Rep.	Madison
Carl W. Soderstrom, Rep.	La Salle
Harold D. Stedelin, Dem.	Marion
Adlai E. Stevenson III, Dem.	Cook
Joseph P. Stremlau, Dem.	La Salle
Nick Svalina, Dem.	Cook
H. B. Tanner, Dem.	Saline
Dan Teefey, Dem.	Brown
George Thiem, Rep.	Cook
John P. Touhy, Dem.	Cook
Joseph Tumpach, Dem.	Du Page
James Van Boeckman, Dem.	Tazewell
John M. Vitek, Dem.	Cook
Richard A. Walsh, Rep.	Cook
Robert V. Walsh, Dem.	White
William D. Walsh, Rep.	Cook
Edward A. Warman, Dem.	Cook
Harold Washington, Dem.	Cook
Raymond J. Welsh, Jr., Dem.	Cook
Peter J. Whalen, Dem.	Cook
Chester R. Wiktorski, Dem.	Cook
Carl H. Wittmond, Dem.	Calhoun
Edward W. Wolbank, Dem.	Cook
Bernard B. Wolfe, Dem.	Cook
Frank C. Wolf, Dem.	Cook
Robert M. Woodward, Rep.	Cook
John Clinton Youle, Rep.	Kane
Nicholas Zagone, Dem.	Cook

[1] Died March 8, 1965.
[2] Died Jan. 9, 1965.
[3] Died May 12, 1965.

Redistricting of 1965 authorized by act of Dec. 1, 1965; fifty-eight Senate districts, each electing one senator; fifty-nine House districts, each electing three representatives

Senate
district — Counties
1 to 30 Cook (nine outside of Chicago)
31 Lake (eastern part)
32 Lake (western part), McHenry (eastern part)
33 Boone, De Kalb, Kane (western part), Kendall (western part), McHenry (western part)

Senate
district   *Counties*

34 Winnebago (southern part)
35 Carroll, JoDaviess, Ogle, Stephenson, Whiteside, Winnebago (northern part)
36 Bureau, Henry, La Salle (northern part), Lee
37 La Salle (southern part), Livingston, McLean
38 Kane (eastern part), Kendall (eastern part)
39 Du Page (northern part)
40 Du Page (southern part)
41 Grundy, Will
42 Cass, Fulton, Knox, Mason, Menard, Peoria (western part), Warren
43 Henderson, Mercer, Rock Island
44 Coles, Edgar, Vermilion
45 Peoria (eastern part), Stark
46 Champaign (northern part), Ford, Iroquois, Kanakakee
47 Champaign (southern part), De Witt, Douglas, Moultrie, Piatt
48 Logan, Marshall, Putnam, Tazewell, Woodford
49 Morgan, Sangamon
50 Christian, Macon, Shelby
51 Bond, Clinton, Cumberland, Effingham, Fayette, Jasper, Marion, Montgomery
52 Calhoun, Jersey, Macoupin, Madison (eastern part), St. Clair (northern part)
53 Madison (western part)
54 St. Clair (East St. Louis and environs)
55 Clark, Clay, Crawford, Edwards, Hamilton, Jefferson, Lawrence, Richland, Wabash, Wayne
56 Alexander, Jackson, Monroe, Perry, Randolph, St. Clair (southern part), Union, Washington
57 Franklin, Gallatin, Hardin, Johnson, Massac, Pope, Pulaski, Saline, White, Williamson
58 Adams, Brown, Greene, Hancock, Mc-Donough, Pike, Schuyler, Scott

House
district   *Counties*

1 to 30 Cook (nine outside of Chicago)
31 Lake (eastern part)
32 Lake (western part), McHenry (eastern part)
33 Boone, De Kalb, Kane (western part), Kendall, McHenry (western part)
34 Winnebago (southern part)
35 JoDaviess, Lee, Ogle, Stephenson, Winnebago (northern part)
36 Kane (eastern part)
37 Du Page (northern part)
38 Du Page (southern part)
39 Bureau, Carroll, Henry, Stark, Whiteside
40 La Salle, Livingston, Marshall, Putnam
41 Will (except southwest corner)
42 Ford, Grundy, Iroquois, Kankakee, Will (southwest corner)
43 Peoria (northern part)
44 Mercer, Rock Island
45 Brown, Cass, Hancock, Henderson, Knox, McDonough, Schuyler, Warren
46 Fulton, Peoria (southern part), Tazewell

House
district   *Counties*

47 De Witt, Logan, McLean, Piatt, Woodford
48 Champaign, Douglas, Moultrie
49 Coles, Edgar, Vermilion
50 Adams, Calhoun, Greene, Jersey, Morgan, Pike, Scott
51 Mason, Menard, Sangamon
52 Christian, Macon, Shelby
53 Bond, Clinton, Macoupin, Madison Montgomery
54 Clark, Clay, Crawford, Cumberland, Edwards, Effingham, Fayette, Jasper, Lawrence, Richland, Wabash
55 Madison (metropolitan area)
56 St. Clair (East St. Louis and environs)
57 Monroe, Perry, Randolph, rest of St. Clair, Washington
58 Franklin, Hamilton, Jefferson, Marion, Saline, Wayne, White
59 Alexander, Gallatin, Hardin, Jackson, Johnson, Massac, Pope, Pulaski, Union, Williamson

Seventy-fifth General Assembly, 1967–68

Senate

President   Samuel H. Shapiro
President pro tempore
     W. Russell Arrington
Secretary   Edward J. Fernandes

District	Member	County
1	W. Russell Arrington, Rep.	Cook
2	Arthur J. Bidwill, Rep.	Cook
3	John A. Graham, Rep.	Cook
4	John W. Carroll, Rep.	Cook
5	Howard R. Mohr, Rep.	Cook
6	Frank M. Ozinga, Rep.	Cook
7	James C. Soper, Rep.	Cook
8	Arthur R. Gottschalk, Rep.	Cook
9	Terrel E. Clarke, Rep.	Cook
10	Esther Saperstein, Dem.	Cook
11	Robert E. Cherry, Dem.	Cook
12	Joseph L. De La Cour,¹ Dem.	Cook
13	James P. Loukas, Dem.	Cook
14	Albert E. Bennett, Rep.	Cook
15	Walter Duda, Rep.	Cook
16	Walter P. Hoffelder, Rep.	Cook
17	Thad L. Kusibab, Dem.	Cook
18	Thomas A. McGloon, Dem.	Cook
19	Zygmunt A. Sokolniki, Dem.	Cook
20	Sam Romano, Dem.	Cook
21	Bernard S. Neistein, Dem.	Cook
22	Fred J. Smith, Dem.	Cook
23	Edward A. Nihill, Dem.	Cook
24	Richard H. Newhouse, Dem.	Cook
25	Joseph L. Krasowski, Rep.	Cook
26	Cecil A. Partee, Dem.	Cook
27	John T. Lanigan, Rep.	Cook

District	Member	County
28	Arthur R. Swanson, Rep.	Cook
29	Charles Chew, Jr., Dem.	Cook
30	Daniel D. Dougherty, Dem.	Cook
31	Robert Coulson, Rep.	Lake
32	Karl Berning, Rep.	Lake
33	Dennis J. Collins, Rep.	De Kalb
34	Bertil T. Rosander, Rep.	Winnebago
35	Everett E. Laughlin, Rep.	Stephenson
36	Joseph R. Peterson,[2] Rep.	Bureau
37	William C. Harris, Rep.	Livingston
38	Robert W. Mitchler, Rep.	Kendall
39	Jack T. Knuepfer, Rep.	Du Page
40	Harris W. Fawell, Rep.	Du Page
41	Meade Baltz, Rep.	Will
42	Richard R. Larson, Rep.	Knox
43	Donald D. Carpentier, Rep.	Rock Island
44	Tom Merritt, Rep.	Vermilion
45	Hudson R. Sours, Rep.	Peoria
46	Edward McBroom, Rep.	Kankakee
47	Everett R. Peters, Rep.	Champaign
48	Egbert B. Groen, Rep.	Tazewell
49	G. William Horsley, Rep.	Sangamon
50	Robert W. McCarthy, Dem.	Macon
51	James H. Donnewald, Dem.	Clinton
52	William Lyons, Dem.	Macoupin
53	Paul Simon, Dem.	Madison
54	Alan J. Dixon, Dem.	St. Clair
55	Paul W. Broyles, Rep.	Jefferson
56	John G. Gilbert, Rep.	Jackson
57	Delmer R. Mitchell, Rep.	Williamson
58	Clifford B. Latherow, Rep.	Hancock

[1] Died Feb. 11, 1967.
[2] Died Aug. 26, 1967.

House of Representatives

Speaker — Ralph T. Smith
Clerk — Frederic Selcke

District	Member	County
1	Frances L. Dawson, Rep.	Cook
	Alan R. Johnston, Rep.	Cook
	Harold A. Katz, Dem.	Cook
2	Edward E. Bluthardt, Rep.	Cook
	James C. Kirie, Dem.	Cook
	Richard A. Walsh, Rep.	Cook
3	Eugenia S. Chapman, Dem.	Cook
	David J. Regner, Rep.	Cook
	Eugene F. Schlickman, Rep.	Cook
4	Robert S. Juckett, Sr., Rep.	Cook
	Arthur E. Simmons, Rep.	Cook
	Edward A. Warman, Dem.	Cook
5	Joseph P. McGah, Dem.	Cook
	Lawrence X. Pusateri, Rep.	Cook
	William D. Walsh, Rep.	Cook
6	Ralph A. Beezhold, Rep.	Cook
	Marjorie Pebworth, Rep.	Cook
	Harry Yourell, Dem.	Cook
7	Henry J. Klosak, Rep.	Cook
	Joseph G. Sevcik, Rep.	Cook
	Gerald W. Shea, Dem.	Cook
8	Anthony Scariano, Dem.	Cook

District	Member	County
	John W. Thompson, Rep.	Cook
	Jack E. Walker, Rep.	Cook
9	George M. Burditt, Rep.	Cook
	Don A. Moore, Rep.	Cook
	Leland H. Rayson, Dem.	Cook
10	Edward J. Copeland, Rep.	Cook
	Paul F. Elward, Dem.	Cook
	Michael F. Zlatnik, Rep.	Cook
11	Frank Lyman, Dem.	Cook
	John Merlo, Dem.	Cook
	Arthur A. Telcser, Rep.	Cook
12	Paul J. Randolph, Rep.	Cook
	William V. Schoeninger, Dem.	Cook
	Edward W. Wolbank, Dem.	Cook
13	LaSalle J. DeMichaels, Dem.	Cook
	William E. Pollack,[1] Rep.	Cook
	Elroy C. Sandquist, Rep.	Cook
14	Kenneth W. Course, Dem.	Cook
	Herbert F. Geisler, Rep.	Cook
	Jacob John Wolf, Rep.	Cook
15	Peter J. Miller, Rep.	Cook
	Chester R. Wiktorski, Dem.	Cook
	Bernard B. Wolfe, Dem.	Cook
16	Henry J. Hyde, Rep.	Cook
	Helmut W. Stolle, Rep.	Cook
	William M. Zachacki, Sr., Dem.	Cook
17	Benedict Garmisa, Dem.	Cook
	Louis Janczak, Rep.	Cook
	Edward J. Shaw, Dem.	Cook
18	Lawrence DiPrima Dem.	Cook
	Bernard McDevitt, Rep.	Cook
	Robert F. McPartlin, Dem.	Cook
19	Louis F. Capuzi, Rep.	Cook
	Isaac Sims, Dem.	Cook
	John P. Touhy, Dem.	Cook
20	Victor A. Arrigo, Dem.	Cook
	Peter C. Granata, Rep.	Cook
	Matt Ropa, Dem.	Cook
21	Lawrence J. Bartels, Rep.	Cook
	Otis G. Collins, Dem.	Cook
	Frank C. Wolf, Dem.	Cook
22	James Y. Carter, Dem.	Cook
	Corneal A. Davis, Dem.	Cook
	Genoa S. Washington, Rep.	Cook
23	John G. Fary, Dem.	Cook
	Frank J. Smith, Dem.	Cook
	John F. Wall, Rep.	Cook
24	Noble W. Lee, Rep.	Cook
	Robert E. Mann, Dem.	Cook
	Calvin L. Smith, Dem.	Cook
25	Michael E. Hannigan, Dem.	Cook
	Raymond J. Kahoun, Rep.	Cook
	Michael H. McDermott, Dem.	Cook
26	Horace J. Gardner, Rep.	Cook
	Owen D. Pelt,[2] Dem.	Cook
	Harold Washington, Dem.	Cook
27	Carl L. Klein, Rep.	Cook
	Walter McAvoy, Rep.	Cook
	Frank D. Savickas, Dem.	Cook
28	John P. Downes, Dem.	Cook
	Mary K. Meany, Rep.	Cook
	J. Theodore Meyer, Rep.	Cook
29	Lewis A. H. Caldwell, Dem.	Cook
	Raymond W. Ewell, Dem.	Cook
	Elwood Graham, Rep.	Cook
30	Phillip W. Collins, Rep.	Cook
	Henry M. Lenard, Dem.	Cook

District	Member	County
	Nick Svalina, Dem.	Cook
31	John H. Conolly, Rep.	Lake
	John S. Matijevich, Dem.	Lake
	W. J. Murphy, Rep.	Lake
32	John H. Kleine, Rep.	Lake
	George W. Lindberg, Rep.	McHenry
	Daniel M. Pierce, Dem.	Lake
33	Lester Cunningham, Rep.	Boone
	Thomas J. Hanahan, Jr., Dem.	McHenry
	John B. Hill, Rep.	Kane
34	E. J. Giorgi, Dem.	Winnebago
	David W. Johnson, Rep.	Winnebago
	Frank P. North, Rep.	Winnebago
35	Merle K. Anderson, Rep.	Winnebago
	Robert E. Brinkmeier, Dem.	Ogle
	Robert D. Law, Rep.	Stephenson
36	John Jerome Hill, Dem.	Kane
	Charles L. Hughes, Rep.	Kane
	Allen L. Schoeberlein, Rep.	Kane
37	Gene L. Hoffman, Rep.	Du Page
	James Philip, Rep.	Du Page
	William A. Redmond, Dem.	Du Page
38	Jack E. Bowers, Rep.	Du Page
	Lewis V. Morgan, Jr., Rep.	Du Page
	Joseph Tumpach,[1] Dem.	Du Page
39	Tobias Barry, Dem.	Bureau
	W. K. Davidson, Rep.	Henry
	Kenneth W. Miller, Rep.	Whiteside
40	Joseph Fennessey, Dem.	La Salle
	Carl T. Hunsicker, Rep.	Livingston
	Carl W. Soderstrom, Rep.	La Salle
41	William G. Barr, Rep.	Will
	W. Robert Blair, Rep.	Will
	John J. Houlihan, Dem.	Will
42	Thomas R. Houde, Rep.	Kankakee
	Joe W. Russell, Dem.	Ford
	James R. Washburn, Rep.	Grundy
43	John E. Cassidy, Jr., Dem.	Peoria
	Robert G. Day, Rep.	Peoria
	John C. Parkhurst, Rep.	Peoria
44	Donald A. Henss, Rep.	Rock Island
	Pete Pappas, Rep.	Rock Island
	Paul E. Rink, Dem.	Rock Island
45	Raymond E. Anderson, Rep.	Knox
	Clarence E. Neff, Rep.	Henderson
	Leo F. O'Brien, Dem.	Knox
46	Wilbur H. Lauterbach, Rep.	Peoria
	George L. Saal, Dem.	Tazewell
	J. Norman Shade, Rep.	Tazewell
47	Harber H. Hall, Rep.	McLean
	Edward Madigan, Rep.	Logan
	J. W. Scott,[4] Dem.	McLean
48	Charles W. Clabaugh, Rep.	Champaign
	Edwin E. Dale, Rep.	Champaign
	Paul Stone, Dem.	Moultrie
49	Charles M. Campbell, Rep.	Vermilion
	William D. Cox, Rep.	Coles
	Robert Craig, Dem.	Vermilion
50	H. B. Ihnen, Rep.	Adams
	Elmo McClain, Dem.	Adams
	Thomas C. Rose, Rep.	Morgan
51	William K. Cavanagh, Rep.	Sangamon
	J. David Jones, Rep.	Sangamon
	Alan T. Lucas, Dem.	Sangamon
52	John W. Alsup, Dem.	Macon
	George P. Johns, Rep.	Macon
	Rolland F. Tipsword, Dem.	Christian

District	Member	County
53	Ben C. Harpstrite, Rep.	Clinton
	Charles Ed Schaefer, Dem.	Montgomery
	Sam M. Vadalabene, Dem.	Madison
54	Garrel Burgoon, Rep.	Lawrence
	John W. Lewis, Jr., Rep.	Clark
	Miles E. Mills, Dem.	Effingham
55	Lloyd Harris, Dem.	Madison
	Leland J. Kennedy, Dem.	Madison
	Ralph T. Smith, Rep.	Madison
56	Kenneth Hall, Dem.	St. Clair
	James G. Krause, Dem.	St. Clair
	Edward Lehman, Rep.	St. Clair
57	William J. Cunningham, Rep.	Perry
	James D. Holloway, Dem.	Randolph
	Norbert G. Springer, Rep.	Randolph
58	Ben C. Blades, Rep.	Wayne
	James E. Eatherly, Rep.	Saline
	Harold D. Stedelin, Dem.	Marion
59	Clyde L. Choate, Dem.	Union
	C. L. McCormick, Rep.	Johnson
	Gale Williams, Rep.	Jackson

[1] Died March 18, 1968.
[2] Died Sept. 18, 1968.
[3] Died Oct. 20, 1968.
[4] Died Oct. 7, 1967.

Seventy-sixth General Assembly, 1969–70

Senate

President	Paul Simon
President pro tempore	W. Russell Arrington
Secretary	Edward J. Fernandes

District	Member	County
1	W. Russell Arrington, Rep.	Cook
2	Arthur J. Bidwill, Rep.	Cook
3	John A. Graham, Rep.	Cook
4	John W. Carroll, Rep.	Cook
5	Howard R. Mohr, Rep.	Cook
6	Frank M. Ozinga, Rep.	Cook
7	James C. Soper, Rep.	Cook
8	Arthur R. Gottschalk, Rep.	Cook
9	Terrel E. Clarke, Rep.	Cook
10	Esther Saperstein, Dem.	Cook
11	Robert E. Cherry, Dem.	Cook
12	William V. Schoeninger, Dem.	Cook
13	James P. Loukas, Dem.	Cook
14	Albert E. Bennett, Rep.	Cook
15	Walter Duda, Rep.	Cook
16	Walter P. Hoffelder, Rep.	Cook
17	Thad L. Kusibab, Dem.	Cook
18	Thomas A. McGloon, Dem.	Cook
19	Zygmunt A. Sokolniki, Dem.	Cook
20	Sam Romano, Dem.	Cook
21	Bernard S. Neistein, Dem.	Cook
22	Fred J. Smith, Dem.	Cook
23	Edward A. Nihill, Dem.	Cook
24	Richard H. Newhouse, Dem.	Cook

District	Member	County
25	Joseph L. Krasowski, Rep.	Cook
26	Cecil A. Partee, Dem.	Cook
27	John J. Lanigan, Rep.	Cook
28	Arthur R. Swanson, Rep.	Cook
29	Charles Chew, Jr., Dem.	Cook
30	Daniel D. Dougherty, Dem.	Cook
31	Robert Coulson, Rep.	Lake
32	Karl Berning, Rep.	Lake
33	Dennis J. Collins, Rep.	De Kalb
34	Bertil T. Rosander, Rep.	Winnebago
35	Everett E. Laughlin, Rep.	Stephenson
36	W. K. Davidson, Rep.	Henry
37	William C. Harris, Rep.	Livingston
38	Robert W. Mitchler, Rep.	Kendall
39	Jack T. Knuepfer, Rep.	Du Page
40	Harris W. Fawell, Rep.	Du Page
41	Meade Baltz, Rep.	Will
42	Richard R. Larson, Rep.	Knox
43	Donald D. Carpentier, Rep.	Rock Island
44	Tom Merritt, Rep.	Vermilion
45	Hudson R. Sours, Rep.	Peoria
46	Edward McBroom, Rep.	Kankakee
47	Everett R. Peters, Rep.	Champaign
48	Egbert B. Groen, Rep.	Tazewell
49	G. William Horsley, Rep.	Sangamon
50	Robert W. McCarthy, Dem.	Macon
51	James H. Donnewald, Dem.	Clinton
52	William Lyons, Dem.	Macoupin
53	Paul Simon,[1] Dem.	Madison
54	Alan J. Dixon, Dem.	St. Clair
55	Paul W. Broyles, Rep.	Jefferson
56	John G. Gilbert, Rep.	Jackson
57	Delmer R. Mitchell, Rep.	Williamson
58	Clifford B. Latherow, Rep.	Hancock

[1] Elected lt. gov., Nov. 5, 1968.

House of Representatives

Speaker	Ralph T. Smith
Clerk	Frederic B. Selcke

District	Member	County
1	Frances L. Dawson, Rep.	Cook
	Alan R. Johnston, Rep.	Cook
	Harold A. Katz, Dem.	Cook
2	Edward E. Bluthardt, Rep.	Cook
	Richard A. Walsh, Dem.	Cook
	James C. Kirie, Dem.	Cook
3	Eugenia S. Chapman, Dem.	Cook
	David J. Regner, Rep.	Cook
	Eugene F. Schlickman, Rep.	Cook
4	Robert S. Juckett, Sr., Rep.	Cook
	Arthur E. Simmons, Rep.	Cook
	Edward A. Warman, Dem.	Cook
5	Joseph P. McGah, Dem.	Cook
	William D. Walsh, Rep.	Cook
	Ronald K. Hoffman, Rep.	Cook
6	Harry Yourell, Dem.	Cook
	Romie J. Palmer, Rep.	Cook
	Edward L. Kipley, Rep.	Cook
7	Henry J. Klosak, Rep.	Cook
	Joseph G. Sevcik, Rep.	Cook

District	Member	County
	Gerald W. Shea, Dem.	Cook
8	Anthony Scariano, Dem.	Cook
	John W. Thompson, Rep.	Cook
	Jack E. Walker, Rep.	Cook
9	George M. Burditt, Rep.	Cook
	Don A. Moore, Rep.	Cook
	Leland H. Rayson, Dem.	Cook
10	Paul F. Elward, Dem.	Cook
	Edward J. Copeland, Rep.	Cook
	Arthur L. Berman, Dem.	Cook
11	Arthur A. Telcser, Rep.	Cook
	Frank Lyman, Dem.	Cook
	John Merlo, Dem.	Cook
12	Paul J. Randolph, Rep.	Cook
	Edward W. Wolbank, Dem.	Cook
	Robert L. Thompson, Dem.	Cook
13	Elroy C. Sandquist, Rep.	Cook
	Richard J. Elrod, Dem.	Cook
	John B. Brandt, Dem.	Cook
14	Kenneth W. Course, Dem.	Cook
	Herbert F. Geisler, Rep.	Cook
	Jacob John Wolf, Rep.	Cook
15	Peter J. Miller, Rep.	Cook
	Bernard B. Wolfe, Dem.	Cook
	Thaddeus S. Lechowicz, Dem.	Cook
16	Henry J. Hyde, Rep.	Cook
	Helmut W. Stolle, Rep.	Cook
	William M. Zachacki, Sr., Dem.	Cook
17	Benedict Garmisa, Dem.	Cook
	Louis Janczak, Rep.	Cook
	Edward J. Shaw, Dem.	Cook
18	Lawrence DiPrima, Dem.	Cook
	Bernard McDevitt, Rep.	Cook
	Robert F. McPartlin, Dem.	Cook
19	Louis F. Capuzi, Rep.	Cook
	Isaac Sims, Dem.	Cook
	John P. Touhy, Dem.	Cook
20	Victor A. Arrigo, Dem.	Cook
	Peter C. Granata, Rep.	Cook
	Matt Ropa, Dem.	Cook
21	Otis G. Collins, Dem.	Cook
	Frank C. Wolf, Dem.	Cook
	Lillian Karmazyn, Dem.	Cook
22	James Y. Carter, Dem.	Cook
	Corneal A. Davis, Dem.	Cook
	Genoa S. Washington, Rep.	Cook
23	John G. Fary, Dem.	Cook
	Frank J. Smith, Dem.	Cook
	John F. Wall, Rep.	Cook
24	Robert E. Mann, Dem.	Cook
	Bernard E. Epton, Rep.	Cook
	James A. McLendon, Dem.	Cook
25	Raymond J. Kahoun, Rep.	Cook
	Michael H. McDermott, Dem.	Cook
	Bernard J. O'Hallaren, Dem.	Cook
26	J. Horace Gardner, Rep.	Cook
	Harold Washington, Dem.	Cook
	James C. Taylor, Dem.	Cook
27	Carl L. Klein, Rep.	Cook
	Walter McAvoy, Rep.	Cook
	Frank D. Savickas, Dem.	Cook
28	John P. Downes, Dem.	Cook
	J. Theodore Meyer, Rep.	Cook
	James E. Peterson, Rep.	Cook
29	Lewis A. H. Caldwell, Dem.	Cook
	Raymond W. Ewell, Dem.	Cook
	Elwood Graham, Rep.	Cook

District	Member	County
30	Phillip W. Collins, Rep.	Cook
	Henry M. Lenard, Dem.	Cook
	Samuel C. Maragos, Dem.	Cook
31	John H. Conolly, Rep.	Lake
	John S. Matijevich, Dem.	Lake
	W. J. Murphy, Rep.	Lake
32	John H. Kleine, Rep.	Lake
	George W. Lindberg, Rep.	Lake
	Daniel M. Pierce, Dem.	Lake
33	Lester Cunningham, Rep.	Boone
	Thomas J. Hanahan, Dem.	McHenry
	John B. Hill,¹ Rep.	Kane
34	E. J. Giorgi, Dem.	Winnebago
	David W. Johnson, Rep.	Winnebago
	Frank P. North, Rep.	Winnebago
35	Merle K. Anderson, Rep.	Winnebago
	Robert E. Brinkmeier, Dem.	Ogle
	David C. Shapiro, Rep.	Stephenson
36	John Jerome Hill, Dem.	Kane
	Allen L. Schoeberlein, Rep.	Kane
	John E. Friedland, Rep.	Kane
37	Gene L. Hoffman, Rep.	Du Page
	James Philip, Rep.	Du Page
	William A. Redmond, Dem.	Du Page
38	Lewis V. Morgan, Jr., Rep.	Du Page
	Goudyloch Dyer, Rep.	Du Page
	James Wright, Dem.	Du Page
39	Tobias Barry, Dem.	Bureau
	Kenneth W. Miller, Rep.	Whiteside
	James D. Nowlan, Rep.	Stark
40	Joseph Fennessey, Dem.	La Salle
	Carl T. Hunsicker, Rep.	Livingston
	Carl W. Soderstrom, Rep.	La Salle
41	William G. Barr, Rep.	Will
	W. Robert Blair, Rep.	Will
	John J. Houlihan, Dem.	Will
42	Thomas R. Houde, Rep.	Kankakee
	James R. Washburn, Rep.	Grundy
	C. R. Hamilton, Dem.	Kankakee
43	Robert G. Day, Rep.	Peoria
	Fred J. Tuerk, Rep.	Peoria
	James D. Carrigan, Dem.	Peoria
44	Donald A. Henss, Rep.	Rock Island
	Pete Pappas, Rep.	Rock Island
	Oral Jacobs, Dem.	Rock Island
45	Raymond E. Anderson, Rep.	Knox
	Clarence E. Neff, Rep.	Henderson
	Louis A. Markert, Dem.	Brown

District	Member	County
46	Wilbur H. Lauterbach, Rep.	Peoria
	J. Norman Shade, Rep.	Tazewell
	Gale Schisler, Dem.	Fulton
47	Harber H. Hall, Rep.	McLean
	Edward Madigan, Rep.	Logan
	Gerald A. Bradley, Dem.	McLean
48	Charles W. Clabaugh, Rep.	Champaign
	Paul Stone, Dem.	Moultrie
	Stanley B. Weaver, Rep.	Champaign
49	Charles M. Campbell, Rep.	Vermilion
	William D. Cox, Rep.	Coles
	Robert Craig, Dem.	Vermilion
50	Jerry Corbett, Dem.	Calhoun
	Thomas C. Rose, Rep.	Morgan
	Elmo McClain, Dem.	Adams
51	J. David Jones, Rep.	Sangamon
	Christian H. Homeier, Rep.	Sangamon
	James T. Londrigan, Dem.	Sangamon
52	John W. Alsup, Rep.	Macon
	Rolland F. Tipsword, Dem.	Christian
	Webber Borchers, Rep.	Macon
53	Ben C. Harpstrite, Rep.	Clinton
	Sam M. Vadalabene, Dem.	Madison
	Don Barry, Dem.	Montgomery
54	Garrel Burgoon, Rep.	Lawrence
	Leslie N. Jones, Rep.	Clay
	Charles F. Keller, Dem.	Effingham
55	Leland J. Kennedy, Dem.	Madison
	Ralph T. Smith, Rep.	Madison
	Horace L. Calvo, Dem.	Madison
56	Kenneth Hall, Dem.	St. Clair
	James G. Krause, Rep.	St. Clair
	Edward Lehman, Rep.	St. Clair
57	William J. Cunningham, Rep.	Perry
	James D. Holloway, Dem.	Randolph
	Norbert G. Springer, Rep.	Randolph
58	Ben C. Blades, Rep.	Wayne
	Harold D. Stedelin, Dem.	Marion
	Richard O. Hart, Dem.	Franklin
59	Clyde L. Choate, Dem.	Union
	C. L. McCormick, Rep.	Johnson
	Gale Williams, Rep.	Jackson

¹ Died Nov. 23, 1968.

12

Courts in Illinois

The constitution of Illinois, adopted in 1818, established a basic plan for the administration of justice, from which there has been no significant deviation. It is expressed in these words: "The judicial power of the state shall be vested in one supreme court and such inferior courts as the General Assembly shall from time to time ordain and establish."

The final responsibility of a supreme court and of the right of the legislature to establish courts as they are needed has not been altered. Methods of choosing judges, tenure of office, and general organization of the courts have been varied at the will of the legislature as dictated by the needs of the time, but the basic chain of responsibility from lowest to highest courts remains.

Municipal courts at various levels, recorders' courts, and appellate courts have been established to lighten the load of the Supreme Court, circuit and county courts, and at long last the entire structure of Illinois courts has been streamlined, but final responsibility has remained with the highest court of the state.

The first Supreme Court consisted of four justices chosen by joint ballot of the two houses of the General Assembly, and the constitution required that for the first eight years these four judges should also serve as judges of circuit courts in the four judicial districts into which the state had been divided, all of them south of the Illinois River. Commissions, signed by Governor Shadrach Bond, ran to 1825, and thereafter tenure was to continue during good behavior. The court had appellate jurisdiction only, save in cases relating to revenue, in cases of mandamus, and in such cases of impeachment as might be required to be tried before it.

Joseph Phillips was elected chief justice and Thomas C. Browne, John Reynolds, and William P. Foster were elected associate justices October 9, 1818, effective December 3. Phillips resigned his post in 1822 to run for governor as an advocate of a constitutional convention to legalize slavery in Illinois. Judge Browne also ran for governor as a proslavery man, but he was more cautious and did not resign his judgeship. Beaten by Edward Coles, onetime Virginia slaveholder become abolitionist, Phillips returned to his birthplace in Tennessee, and Illinois heard of him no more. Judge Browne remained on the Supreme Court bench until 1848. John Reynolds resigned from the court in 1825 to practice law and serve as a member of the General Assembly, later as governor and as a representative in Congress for six terms. Foster, completely unqualified as lawyer or jurist, never held court or sat on the supreme bench, collected his salary of $1,000, and disappeared, where no one knew or cared.

Foster was replaced by William Wilson, Virginia-born, who became chief justice a few years later and held that position until the reorganization of the court under the constitution of 1848. Succeeding Phillips and John Reynolds were Thomas Reynolds as chief justice and Samuel D. Lockwood. Lockwood had been attorney general under Governor Shadrach Bond. Thomas Reynolds resigned after brief service, moved to Missouri, and died a suicide February 9, 1844, during his third year as governor of that state. Replacing Reynolds was Theophilus Washington Smith, who was impeached in 1832 but not convicted.

The first circuit court in Illinois was held at Covington, Washington County, during the spring of 1819 by John Reynolds. Court was opened by the sheriff, seated astride a puncheon bench, with these words, according to Thomas Ford, seventh governor of Illinois: "Boys, come in. Our John is going to hold court." A week or so later circuit court for Montgomery County was held in the bedroom of a two-room house. Reynolds, again presiding, seated himself on the bed in lieu of a bench, and the jury, after hearing evidence, retired to the warm, dappleshadowed woods to deliberate.

Below the four circuit courts in 1819 were justices of the peace, who handled minor misdemeanors and civil causes in which little money was involved, and county commissioners' courts.

The General Assembly made several changes in the organization of the courts between 1826 and 1847, when a constitutional convention was called. On January 8, 1829, a circuit north of the Illinois River was added to the four southern circuits. On January 7, 1835, an act was approved which established a uniform mode for holding circuit courts, and ten days later division of the state into six judicial circuits was enacted. On February 4, 1837, a seventh circuit was added and on February 23, 1839, an eighth, and new rules were enacted with reference to terms of the various courts.

In December 1840 a long-smoldering dissatisfaction in the Democratic party flared up as the result of two decisions, both of which were good law but bad politics. From 1826 the court had consisted of three Whigs and one Democrat. Gradually Whig power in the state had decreased while the Democratic party had gained larger and larger control of the state political machinery.

Under the terms of their tenure, established by the organic law of the state, the sitting justices could only be turned out of office by impeachment, which required a two-thirds vote of the Illinois Senate. This the Democrats had found in 1832 to be unattainable. But the General Assembly could change the structure of the court, and did. On February 10, 1841, after nearly two months of acrimonious debate, led on the Democratic side by John A. McClernand and Stephen A. Douglas, "an act reorganizing the judiciary of Illinois" was passed. It placed on the supreme bench five eminent individuals, all men of unquestioned probity and also of unquestioned party loyalty, and all Democrats. They were Samuel Hubbel Treat, who by the end of his life would have devoted forty-eight years to service on state and federal courts; Thomas Ford, soon to become governor of Illinois; Sidney Breese, whose decisions while chief justice gained international attention; Walter B. Scates, respected Chicago lawyer and jurist; and Douglas. When Justice Smith resigned the following year he was replaced by another Democrat, Richard M. Young. Ford resigned August 1, 1842, to run successfully for governor, and was succeeded by John D. Caton, who served twenty-two years on the supreme bench.

The act of February 10, 1841, placed the administration of justice entirely in the hands of these men by specifying that each

of them sit as a circuit court judge, and increasing to nine the judicial circuits into which the state was divided. With the Supreme Court justices holding original responsibility as judges of circuit court and appellate authority in the Supreme Court over their decisions on the circuit and over the inferior courts as well, a hammerlock was achieved.

Other problems of judicial administration were becoming pressing. Of these, those encountered in Chicago were an example. The crowded docket, which later became a continuing cause of complaint, was already in evidence. A small measure of relief was available in the first city charter, which authorized the mayor to establish a court of his own and gave him the same rights, responsibilities, and recompense as a justice of the peace. In 1849 Mayor James H Woodworth briefly held such a court to help lighten the case load. The city charter also provided for a municipal court to have jurisdiction concurrent with the circuit court in civil and criminal cases arising within the city limits.

Chicago's first courts had been set up in 1825, when John Kinzie, Alexander Wolcott, and Jean Beaubien were appointed justices of the peace by the commissioners of Peoria County, of which Chicago was then a precinct. At the same time Archibald Clyborn was named constable. There is no record of a trial by any of these.

Orrin N. Carter, a justice of the Illinois Supreme Court from 1906 to 1924, in an address before the Illinois State Historical Society on May 8, 1914, stated his belief that Russell E. Heacock, appointed September 10, 1831, was the first justice of the peace in Chicago before whom trials were held. Justice Carter also described the organization and authority of county commissioners' courts in the early days of Illinois justice. These bodies, long since become purely administrative in the seventeen counties in southern Illinois where a commission form of county government exists, originally had judicial jurisdiction in disputes over public roads, turnpikes, canals, toll bridges, and all things concerning public revenues, county taxes and licenses, but no original or appellate jurisdiction in civil or criminal actions, except where the public concerns of a county were involved. There was a commissioners' court in Cook County in 1831, and one in Alton as late as 1845, with which

John Jones, first Negro officeholder in Illinois, deposited his freedom papers, documents which a Negro under the "black laws" then in force had to display on entering Illinois.

John D. Caton, in his reminiscences, said, and Judge Carter agreed, that the first term of the circuit court in Chicago was held in May 1834 and that a case which Judge Caton tried as a lawyer was the first on the docket. Judge Carter reported that the judge at this term of court was Richard M. Young. Sessions were held in Fort Dearborn, "in the brick house, and in the lower room of said house." The following May sessions were held in the still-incomplete wooden structure that was to become the first Tremont House. Judge Sidney Breese presided, and in September he shared the bench with Judge Stephen T. Logan of Springfield. Other famous jurists to sit at a term of the circuit court in Chicago included Governor Thomas Ford and the much-maligned Whig, Associate Justice Theophilus Washington Smith.

Meanwhile, in Illinois, as in other parts of the nation where justices were appointed by majority vote in legislatures, a considerable body of opinion was coming to favor choice by ballot. There was also dissatisfaction with the variety of practices in municipal courts of the state. The fact that the Supreme Court had power to revise all laws passed by the legislature became increasingly a cause for complaint.

Dissatisfaction with other provisions of the constitution of 1818 (or a lack of needed restraints) added to the pressure for constitutional reform. The result was a convention call initiated during the second session of the General Assembly in Ford's administration, approved by the people and activated in 1847. The constitution then framed, ratified by the electors at a special election and made effective as of April 1, 1848, overhauled the entire judicial system of the state. It again vested the judicial power in one supreme court, in circuit courts and county courts. Justices of the peace became mandatory instead of optional at the pleasure of the General Assembly, and inferior local courts might be established by the General Assembly in the cities of the state, but such courts should have a uniform organization and jurisdiction.

The new Supreme Court was to consist of three justices, two of whom would

constitute a quorum. Three grand divisions were delineated, in each of which one justice would be elected. In the first election one judge would be chosen for three years, one for six, and one for nine. Thereafter there would be elections in one of the three divisions every three years. The senior judge in point of commission date would serve as chief justice. Tenure after 1854 would be nine years.

Nine judicial circuits were retained, each circuit electing a judge of the circuit court for six years. Provision was made to increase the number of circuits as needed. Except where a vacancy had less than a year to run, all vacancies would be filled by election. Salaries were $1,200 a year for justices of the Supreme Court and $1,000 for judges of the circuit courts. There were residential requirements of five years in the state and two years in division or district. Age qualifications were thirty-five years for the Supreme Court and thirty years for circuit courts.

"Circuit rider" was a term as applicable to judges, attorneys, and other officers of the court as it was to the ministers and missionaries for whom it was first used. Until the 1850's men traveled mostly by horseback or buggy. The entourage moved from county to county, and since accommodations were meager, judges, lawyers, and clerks doubled up in the few tavern rooms available. Most popular lawyers in Chicago, Peoria, and Springfield had partners in the county seats who accepted commitments and prepared cases to be tried by their traveling associates.

Below the circuit courts were county courts restricted to cases where punishment by fine in criminal actions was limited to $100 and to civil actions in which not more than $1,000 was involved.

This multiplication of courts was not sufficient, however, to keep pace with the growth of the state and particularly of Cook County. By 1868 the case load of the Supreme Court had become too great a burden for three men, and a crowded docket was the rule in almost every district, county, and incorporated city of the state. This was one of the many considerations that led to a constitutional convention in 1869 and the adoption of the constitution of 1870, which, with a few amendments, is still the organic law of the state.

The judicial structure set up in this document continued in force until January 1, 1964. It increased the number of Supreme Court justices to seven, with the office of chief justice rotating annually June to June and passing to the senior member who had not served within six years. Tenure continued to be nine years. Seven Supreme Court districts were created. the voters in each district electing one member of the court as a vacancy occurred or tenure ended. Four judges made a quorum.

The constitution of 1870 further ordained that a new group of courts of uniform organization and jurisdiction should be created beginning in 1874, to be known as appellate courts. For these the state was divided into four districts, of which Cook County was the first. Each district would have three judges, except the first which would have three divisions (later to be increased to four) each with three judges. The appellate courts of Illinois were staffed by justices of the circuit courts in addition to their other duties, an honor much sought despite the added work. The appellate courts cannot entertain cases that lie to the Supreme Court as a matter of right under the constitution, such as criminal cases, or those in which a franchise, a freehold, or the validity of a law is involved. Except in three classes of cases the decision of the appellate court is final. These exceptions include those mentioned above, those where a majority of the judges desire review of an important matter, or those cases which the Supreme Court grants leave to appeal.

Salaries were fixed at $3,000 for Supreme Court justices and $2,500 for judges of the circuit and appellate courts. Provision was made for future changes in remuneration. Age qualifications were reduced to thirty years for the Supreme Court. Two or more terms each year of the Supreme Court and two or more terms of circuit courts in every county were required by the constitution, which fixed at thirty the number of circuit court districts, but made provision for future increase.

Under the new constitution the Superior Court of Chicago, established shortly after 1848, became the Superior Court of Cook County, and the Recorder's Court of Chicago became the Criminal Court of Cook County. Probate courts were provided for every county with more than 50,000 inhabitants to handle matters of estates, wills, and inheritances. In smaller counties, county courts retained probate jurisdiction. The constitution, while requiring a county court in every county, made an exception for smaller counties, granting them the privilege of uniting with a contiguous county

in a court that served both counties and had the same jurisdiction as a county court.

In 1904 the General Assembly gave the city of Chicago the right to replace justices of the peace and police magistrates with the Municipal Court of Chicago, composed of five districts (reduced to two in 1907). This change created courts of limited jurisdiction but of wider area than the ones they replaced. In civil cases the municipal court was limited to causes involving not more than damages of $1,000 (in 1951 raised to $5,000 and in 1957 to $10,000) and in criminal cases to those where punishment was less than confinement in the penitentiary. The Municipal Court of Chicago, unlike justices' and magistrates' courts, was a court of record and its actions were subject to review by the appellate courts of Illinois.

Important in the structure of Chicago courts was the creation of special facilities for handling juveniles. In 1892 a special police court for young offenders was established, and in 1899 the first juvenile court in the world came into being in Cook County. Called the Family Court since 1949, this agency works in close harmony with the Illinois Youth Commission, to which it can remand juveniles for correction, rehabilitation, or supervision.

In the beginning the court structure of 1870 proved as satisfactory as any in the country, but in a fast-growing area fifty years can bring a multitude of changes. By 1920, despite judicial improvements, it became apparent that inequities existed in court structure and practice that could be corrected only by constitutional amendment. One judicial district—Cook County—by that time contained about half the population of the state, but elected only one Supreme Court judge while the rest of the state chose six. Cook County, with well over half of the cases on appeal, had much less than half of the judicial personnel, including appellate court judges, available to care for that load.

Courts where fees provided for the remuneration of the judges, particularly those that adjudicated traffic violations, were under constant bombardment. Several constitutional amendments to remedy these ills were offered, but all failed until the general election of 1962, when an amendment incorporating long-sought changes, and completely streamlining the structure of the Illinois courts, was approved by the voters by a margin of more than four to one, to become effective January 1, 1964.

This amendment left the number of justices of the Supreme Court at seven, but provided five judicial districts, the first being Cook County which would elect three justices to one by each of the other districts. Tenure of Supreme Court justices is ten years. The chief justice is chosen by the court for a term of three years.

The Supreme Court may exercise original jurisdiction in cases relating to the revenue, mandamus, prohibition of specific acts, and habeas corpus, and such original jurisdiction as may be necessary to complete determination of any cause on review (such powers also apply to the appellate courts). In all other cases only appellate jurisdiction is held.

Appeals from final judgments in the circuit courts lie directly to the Supreme Court as a matter of right only in cases involving revenue, in cases involving a question arising under the Constitution of the United States or of the state of Illinois, in cases of habeas corpus, and, by the defendant, from sentence in capital cases. Subject to laws hereafter to be enacted, the Supreme Court has authority to provide by rule for appeal in other cases from the circuit courts directly to the Supreme Court.

The Supreme Court has broad advisory powers over all courts and convenes judicial conferences annually to consider the business of the several courts and suggest improvements in the administration of justice. A report in writing of the accomplishments of such conferences must be made to the General Assembly not later than January 31 of each uneven-numbered year.

Appellate courts are organized in the same five judicial districts as the Supreme Court. District One, at present, has four divisions and twelve judges. All others have one division and three judges, a total of twenty-four in the five districts. Judges no longer are appointed to appellate courts, nor are justices of the circuit courts called to sit in review on the work of the circuit courts. The Supreme Court, as need arises, may create new divisions in any of the districts, with three judges in each. A majority of a division constitutes a quorum, and concurrence of a majority is necessary for a decision. Times and places of sittings are prescribed by the Supreme Court.

In all cases other than those applicable to the Supreme Court, appeals from judgments of a circuit court lie as a matter of right to the appellate court in the district in which the circuit court is located. There is no appeal from acquittal in a criminal case.

The state has been divided into twenty-one judicial circuits of one or more counties. Cook County is one circuit, which is unnumbered. Each circuit has one chief judge, two or more judges, and as many associate judges and magistrates as are needed to conduct the business of the courts. Provision has been made for increasing the number of circuits as required.

Circuit courts are the only trial courts in Illinois. Judges of the Superior Court of Cook County, the county courts, and the chief justice of the municipal court were named judges of circuit court on January 1, 1964. On the same date judges of downstate county and probate courts, of municipal, village, and incorporated-town courts, and the judges of the Municipal Court of Chicago became associate judges, and justices of the peace and police magistrates became magistrates of the circuit court.

Masters in chancery and referees in office on January 1, 1964, continued in office until the expiration of their terms, and thereafter by order of the court, wherever justice requires, were empowered to conclude matters in which testimony had been received.

The chief judge of a circuit, chosen by his fellow judges, has general administrative authority in his area. Judges and associate judges may hear any kind of case assigned by the chief judge. Magistrates may be assigned civil cases when the amount at litigation does not exceed $10,000 and criminal cases when the maximum penalty does not exceed a fine of $1,000 or one year in jail.

The circuit court has unlimited original jurisdiction in all justiciable matters and such powers of review of administrative action as may be provided by law.

At the general elections of 1964 the first judges were elected under the new amendment. Procedure is nomination by party convention or primary if a vacancy exists. In this event, two or more candidates may be submitted on the judicial ballot (or one if the parties are in agreement on the man). However, if a sitting judge wishes to succeed himself, and if he has notified the secretary of state in writing six months prior to election day, he may run unopposed on the sole question as to whether he should be retained in office. His name is submitted to the voters on a special judicial ballot without party designation and, if he receives a majority of affirmative votes cast on the judicial ballot, he remains in office.

Judges are required to devote full time to their elected task, and they are prohibited from holding office in any political party. The General Assembly may provide by law for retirement of judges at a prescribed age. Subject to rules of procedure to be established by the Supreme Court, and after notice and hearing, any judge may be retired for disability, suspended without pay, or removed for cause by a commission composed of one judge of the Supreme Court selected by that court, two judges of the appellate courts selected by those courts, and two circuit judges selected by the Supreme Court. Such commission shall be convened by the chief justice upon order of the Supreme Court or request of the Senate of the state of Illinois.

Judicial districts for the Supreme Court and appellate courts of Illinois by counties (as defined in the *Illinois Blue Book, 1965–1966*)

First District

Cook (Voters resident in Cook County elect three justices resident in the county to the Supreme Court and twelve to the appellate courts.)

Second District

Boone	Kane	McHenry
Carroll	Kendall	Ogle
De Kalb	Lake	Stephenson
Du Page	Lee	Winnebago
JoDaviess		

Third District

Bureau	Kankakee	Putnam
Grundy	Knox	Rock Island
Fulton	La Salle	Stark
Hancock	McDonough	Tazewell
Henderson	Marshall	Warren
Henry	Mercer	Whiteside
Iroquois	Peoria	Will

Fourth District

Adams	Edgar	Menard
Brown	Ford	Morgan
Calhoun	Greene	Moultrie
Cass	Jersey	Piatt
Champaign	Livingston	Pike
Clark	Logan	Sangamon
Coles	McLean	Schuyler
Cumberland	Macon	Scott
De Witt	Macoupin	Vermilion
Douglas	Mason	Woodford

Fifth District

Alexander	Jackson	Pulaski
Bond	Jasper	Randolph
Christian	Jefferson	Richland
Clay	Johnson	St. Clair
Clinton	Lawrence	Saline
Crawford	Madison	Shelby
Edwards	Marion	Union
Effingham	Massac	Wabash
Fayette	Monroe	Washington
Franklin	Montgomery	Wayne
Gallatin	Perry	White
Hamilton	Pope	Williamson
Hardin		

Judicial circuits by counties (number of judges in each circuit as recorded in the Index Division of the Office of the Secretary of State, January 1968)

Unnumbered

Cook
Seventy-six circuit judges, sixty-one associate judges.

First Judicial Circuit

Alexander	Massac	Saline
Jackson	Pope	Union
Johnson	Pulaski	Williamson

Three judges, fifteen associate judges

Second Judicial Circuit

Crawford	Hamilton	Richland
Edwards	Hardin	Wabash
Franklin	Jefferson	Wayne
Gallatin	Lawrence	White

Three judges, fourteen associate judges

Third Judicial Circuit

Bond	Madison

Three judges, five associate judges

Fourth Judicial Circuit

Christian	Effingham	Marion
Clay	Fayette	Montgomery
Clinton	Jasper	Shelby

Three judges, eleven associate judges

Fifth Judicial Circuit

Clark	Cumberland	Vermilion
Coles	Edgar	

Three judges, seven associate judges

Sixth Judicial Circuit

Champaign	Douglas	Moultrie
De Witt	Macon	Piatt

Four judges, eight associate judges

Seventh Judicial Circuit

Greene   Macoupin   Sangamon
Jersey   Morgan   Scott

Four judges, seven associate judges

Eighth Judicial Circuit

Adams   Cass   Pike
Brown   Mason   Schuyler
Calhoun   Menard

Three judges, eight associate judges

Ninth Judicial Circuit

Fulton   Henderson   McDonough
Hancock   Knox   Warren

Three judges, seven associate judges

Tenth Judicial Circuit

Marshall   Putnam   Tazewell
Peoria   Stark

Four judges, six associate judges

Eleventh Judicial Circuit

Ford   Logan   Woodford
Livingston   McLean

Three judges, six associate judges

Twelfth Judicial Circuit

Iroquois   Kankakee   Will

Four judges, five associate judges

Thirteenth Judicial Circuit

Bureau   Grundy   La Salle

Three judges, five associate judges

Fourteenth Judicial Circuit

Henry   Rock Island   Whiteside
Mercer

Three judges, eight associate judges

Fifteenth Judicial Circuit

Carroll   Lee   Stephenson
JoDaviess   Ogle

Three judges, five associate judges

Sixteenth Judicial Circuit

De Kalb   Kane   Kendall

Three judges, seven associate judges

Seventeenth Judicial Circuit

Boone   Winnebago

Three judges, three associate judges

Eighteenth Judicial Circuit

Du Page

Four judges, two associate judges

Nineteenth Judicial Circuit

Lake   McHenry

Four judges, five associate judges

Twentieth Judicial Circuit

Monroe   Randolph   Washington
Perry   St. Clair

Four judges, eight associate judges

The state of Illinois cannot be sued or made party to any suit, but claims against the state may be heard. For the purpose of adjudicating them a Court of Claims was established in October 1903, consisting of a chief justice and two judges. The secretary of state of Illinois is ex-officio clerk of the court.

In the federal judicial system, Illinois is in the seventh circuit and is divided into three districts. The Northern District has two divisions, with twelve judges. It holds terms on the first Monday of each calendar month of the year in Chicago and on the third Mondays of April and October in Freeport.

There are two judges in the Eastern District, who sit the first Mondays of March and September in Danville, the first Mondays of April and October in Cairo, the first Mondays of May and November in East St. Louis, and the first Mondays of June and December in Benton.

The Southern District, with two judges, holds terms of court the third Mondays in April and October in Peoria, the first Mondays of January and June in Springfield, and the first Mondays of March and September in Quincy.

The United States Court of Appeals, consisting of nine judges, sits in Chicago.

Canals

From the late summer of 1673, when Louis Jolliet and Father Marquette reached the Chicago portage on their return from the lower Mississippi, a canal connecting the headwaters of the Illinois River with Lake Michigan was seen as a solution of the travel problems of the Illinois country. Every explorer, trader, and trapper to visit what was to become the twenty-first state of the Union experienced the rigors of a transit of Mud Lake, the bog stretching from the south branch of the Chicago and the Des Plaines and draining into both. Gurdon Saltonstall Hubbard, then a youth of sixteen on his first assignment with the American Fur Company, tells of a crossing in September 1818, which required three days from stream to stream—and that was during the dry season. As he and other voyageurs fought their way across the morasses, they doubtless dreamed of an open, navigable passage uncluttered by marsh, mud, or mosquito.

First to propose the canal to the Congress of the United States was Peter B. Porter of New York in 1810. The federal government was favorably impressed with the idea, and Ninian Edwards, territorial governor of Illinois and agent for Indian affairs, was instructed in 1816 to obtain cession by Indian claimants of a tract 20 miles wide and 100 miles long where a future canal would be located. The canal strip, given up by the United Tribes of the Chippewa, Ottawa, and Potawatami at St. Louis, stretched from the 36 square-mile area at the mouth of the Chicago River ceded by the Indians in the Treaty of Greenville (1795), southwest a distance of 100 miles to the main stream of the Illinois, and included the lower reaches of the Kankakee, Des Plaines, Du Page, and Fox rivers.

In 1817 Major Stephen Long, an engineer officer of the United States Army, surveyed the proposed canal route and reported to the War Department. In 1819 John C. Calhoun, then the secretary of war in President Monroe's cabinet, urged Congress to authorize construction as a military measure. No action was taken until a resolution of the Illinois General Assembly in 1821 asked for authority to build the canal. An act passed in Congress March 30, 1822, authorized Illinois to build the canal, and granted a right of way, plus an additional ninety feet on each side of the waterway to be used as the state saw fit. The Illinois legislature appointed commissioners under this authority to lay out the route and

estimate the cost. After the survey engineers named a figure of $639,000 to $713,000 for the construction of ditch, locks, and towpaths. Governor Edward Coles, in his message of November 26, 1824, to the General Assembly, urged establishment of a fund in the latter amount, but the legislature could not find the money. A proposal to charter a private company with a capitalization of $1,000,000 to build and hold the canal for its profit for fifty years or until construction costs plus interest at 6 per cent per year had been recovered was accepted, and the charter granted to a company headed by the first and second governors of Illinois, Shadrach Bond and Edward Coles. Under the charter the company was to "receive all lands the Congress might grant and all donations private persons and the various states might make in aid of the undertaking." Opposition from both Whig and Democrat leaders, and particularly Daniel Pope Cook, Illinois' sole representative in the lower house of Congress, to the private construction of the canal led the company to give up its charter January 12, 1826.

Cook then requested additional land grants by Congress to aid in building the canal, and in March 1827 half of the lands lying along the canal strip to a depth of five miles was granted to Illinois. Governor Ninian Edwards then proposed that the canal be constructed on a loan secured by the canal lands. Commissioners were appointed under the authority of an act of the General Assembly of January 29, 1829, the towns of Chicago and Ottawa were platted at the ends of the proposed canal, and the town lots offered for sale. A disappointing $18,000 was all that was realized at the first auction.

Several years of political wrangling, debate pro and con canals or railroads, and opposition to pledging the credit of the state followed. Southern counties could see little advantage to them of a canal across Mud Lake, or in the platting of a town on Lake Michigan. There also was debate as to whether the canal should be on a shallow-cut plan with feeder canals from the Calumet, Kankakee, Des Plaines, Du Page, and Fox rivers, or a deep cut which would reverse the flow of the Chicago River and eliminate locks between Lake Michigan and Lockport. It was said that cost of the deep cut would be substantially double that of the shallow cut. The deep cut won, construction was authorized, bonds approved, and a new auction of town lots in Chicago and Ottawa brought the sum of $1,355,755 at Chicago and $21,358 at Ottawa, mostly in promises to pay in the future. New York and London bankers were persuaded to underwrite a bond issue backed only by the canal lands and appurtenances. Contracts were let June 6, 1836, for the first part of the work between Bridgeport on the south branch of the Chicago River and Summit, the crest of the very shallow divide marking the area beyond which waters flowed into rivers that eventually reached the Mississippi and the gulf.

On the morning of July 4, 1836, a gaily decorated boat left the vicinity of Wolf's Point with the notables of the young city of Chicago aboard. As the boat neared what now is Roosevelt Road it passed a brickyard, where it was greeted by a shower of missiles from would-be hitchhikers. The notables went ashore, surrounded and captured their assailants, handled them none too gently, and carried them aboard the boat, where they were secured below deck. The ceremonies of the day were only slightly delayed.

First official shovelful of earth was turned by several notables at Bridgeport after long orations on Chicago's future during which mischievous youngsters filled the official wheelbarrow with unofficial earth. An unknown man who predicted a population of 50,000 for Chicago was thought to be drunk, and he received a dunking in the river to cool him off.

The work began. Ample money seemed to be on hand. The ditch, sixty feet wide at the water surface, thirty-six feet wide at the bottom, and six feet deep, progressed according to plan. Then panic struck—the panic of 1837. The State Bank suspended specie payments. Special legislation and heroic efforts were required to safeguard canal funds and permit the work to continue. The canal commissioners arranged to provide supplies unavailable to their contractors. Despite hard times, Lockport, headquarters for the canal project from early 1838, was a boom town. Canal script bearing no interest was accepted as money by merchants throughout the canal region. Contractors took canal bonds in payment for their work and discounted these bonds in London for as little as eighty-three cents on the dollar. It was not until 1842 that this frantic financing caught up with the canal. The debt had reached a total of $4,436,408. Work ceased.

However, that amount of money could not be permitted to go down the drain. In the face of strong opposition the General Assembly accepted a plan for completion of the canal on the shallow-cut plan at an estimated cost of $1,600,000, sterling bond-holders (London) agreed to lend $600,000 of that amount, dollar bondholders (New York) took up the balance, and the state guaranteed the bonds and appropriated one mill per dollar of assessed valuation from the state's share of tax receipts to service the new loan. Work was resumed under direction of three trustees, two selected by the bondholders and one appointed by the governor. It was provided that the trust would continue in force and the trustees in authority until the bonds were retired.

Finally, in 1848, the canal was completed. (For detailed summary of the canal financing, see *Illinois Improvements 1818 to 1848* by John H. Krenkel, published by The Torch Press, Cedar Rapids, Iowa, 1958, pp. 195–96.) The cost was $6,468,854.25. The indebtedness to be funded, which included discounts on the lands sold and interest claims, amounted to $8,042,622. The funds by which the canal debt was liquidated over a period of years were derived from sale of canal lands ($4,706,482.68), tolls and collections ($4,405,658.27), and smaller amounts from leases of lands in the ninety-foot strips, from the Illinois Central Railroad fund, from the sale of water power, used machinery, wood, timber, and stone. The last bond was retired April 30, 1871, and the trust dissolved May 1, 1871, with a cash balance of $95,742.41, which was paid to the canal commissioners who took over operation. Illinois had its canal, free and paid for and transporting more than 500,000 tons of freight yearly. Operation of the canal, however, was not without its headaches. During periods of heavy rainfall, floodwaters found their way into the system and out into Lake Michigan, polluting the city's drinking water. In 1865 the General Assembly authorized reconstruction of the canal on the deep-cut plan which would permanently reverse the flow of the Chicago River. This solved a problem for Chicago and created one for Joliet and other towns on the canal—the problem of midsummer odors. By 1889 the situation had become so bad that heroic measures were necessary. The General Assembly authorized a Chicago Sanitary District which would take steps to control and deodorize sewage that reached the country towns by way of the canal. The trustees of the Sanitary District proposed and the General Assembly accepted a program for a new canal, much deeper and wider, paralleling the old, the establishment of sewage treatment plants where solids would be removed, and the diversion of considerably more water from Lake Michigan than had been authorized to service the new canal. Work was begun on the Chicago Sanitary and Ship Canal in 1890 and, after prolonged litigation over water diversion from the lake which delayed the completion by several years, the water was turned into the canal from Lake Michigan January 2, 1900. The section of the Illinois and Michigan Canal from the lake to Lockport became obsolete.

The capacity of the new canal, built wisely with a far look into the future, changed the entire aspect of canal operation in Illinois. The federal government had done much to improve the channel of the Illinois River below La Salle, and would do more in the future. The canal commissioners and others began talking about a new concept for the waterways of Illinois—a deep, well-controlled channel with locks and dams at required intervals, to provide not just a water route, but a deep waterway from New York to New Orleans by way of the Great Lakes, the Illinois River, and the Mississippi—a sort of River Rhine on a grander scale than existed in Germany. In 1908 the people of Illinois approved by referendum a bond issue of $20,000,000 to carry on the work between the terminal of the Chicago Sanitary and Ship Canal at Lockport and Utica on the Illinois River. Six years later the Illinois Waterways Commission was created to replace the

canal commissioners, and in 1917, with the adoption of the Lowden code, it became the Division of Waterways, Department of Public Works.

A war intervened and was won. In 1919 the General Assembly passed the Illinois Deep Waterways Act and put the waterway under authority of a Department of Construction and Purchases. Litigation delayed work. Finally, in 1930, after the courts had cleared away all legal difficulties, the federal government appropriated $7,500,000 to offset increased costs, and the Deep Waterway entered its final stage. In 1933 the waterway was opened, and the Illinois and Michigan Canal, which had been completely revamped from Lockport to La Salle in 1918 and 1919, was no longer required for commerce. Illinois' first canal, come of age, was the most important segment of the lakes-to-gulf waterway.

Illinois' second canal, the Hennepin, from the Illinois River near Hennepin to the Mississippi at Rock Island, was a war baby. Construction was recommended in 1862 as a military measure, but no action resulted. A favorable report finally was made by army engineers to the War Department in 1871. In 1886 Congress authorized construction of the canal, plus a feeder canal from Lake Sinissippi near Sterling to the Hennepin at about midpoint of its length. Construction got under way in 1892 and three years later the lower part of the canal from the Mississippi around the falls of the Rock River was opened. In 1907 the canal was nagivable throughout. It carried important cargos of iron and steel from the Chicago area to the arsenal at Rock Island during World War I and World War II, but never paid its way commercially. In 1951 it was declared obsolete and closed.

Still another canal, the Calumet-Sag channel from the Calumet River near its mouth to the Sanitary and Ship Canal southwest of the Argonne Forest at route U.S. 83, was authorized in 1904 and, after years of litigation with other states in federal courts, was opened in 1922. This canal has been widened to 225 feet, deepened to 9 feet, and the control works removed from Blue Island to the Little Calumet River south of Lake Calumet. An alternate mouth for the canal is being provided at Indiana Harbor, Indiana, by way of the Grand Calumet and the Indiana Harbor Canal, to be ready in the early 1970's.

Other canal proposals in Illinois have received little support. However, waterborne commerce carried by what once was the Illinois and Michigan Canal has reached monumental proportions, inconceivable to the men who proposed the original canal and those who carried it through to completion.

DATES FOR REFERENCE

1810   Peter B. Porter of New York memorialized Congress on need for a canal connecting Lake Michigan with the Illinois River.

Aug. 24, 1816   Treaty of St. Louis between the United States and the United Tribes of the Chippewa, Ottawa, and Potawatami ceded strip of land 20 miles wide running southwest from the 36 square-mile holding of the federal government at the mouth of the Chicago River ceded to the United States by Indian confederates in the Treaty of Greenville (1795). The 100-mile-long strip included the lower reaches of the Kankakee, Des Plaines, Du Page, and Fox rivers.

1817   Major Stephen Long, Corps of Engineers, United States Army, surveyed route of canal and reported construction feasible.

1819   Secretary of War John C. Calhoun recommended immediate construction of a canal from Lake Michigan to the Illinois River. General Assembly of Illinois received and tabled a canal bill.

1821   The Illinois General Assembly asked Congress to cede lands in the canal strip to the state of Illinois and to authorize the state to begin construction of the canal.

Mar. 30, 1822   Congress authorized construction of the canal and granted a 40-foot right-of-way plus 90 feet on each side of the canal bed, a total of 220 feet, to the state of Illinois from Bridgeport on the south branch of the Chicago River to the present site of Ottawa.

Feb. 24, 1823   General Assembly appointed canal commissioners to lay out and survey a route and to estimate costs.

Mar. 2, 1827   Congress granted alternate sections of public lands in the canal strip, to a depth of five miles on each side, to the state of Illinois. The state was authorized to sell or lease these lands or to pledge them to meet construction costs of a canal.

Jan. 29, 1829   The Illinois General Assembly appointed canal commissioners to lay out a canal forty feet wide at the surface, twenty-eight feet wide at the bottom, and four feet deep. The commissioners were instructed to plat the towns of Chicago and Ottawa, and to sell the town lots at auction.

Apr. 19, 1830   Town lots at canal terminals offered at public sale in Springfield found few purchasers.

Sept. 27, 1830 Auction at Chicago also was disappointing. Total realized from both sales about $18,000.

1832–34   Prolonged debate over use of state credit for the canal and the cost of a shallow ditch in which canal boats would be lifted to the summit by locks versus cost of a deep-cut ditch reversing the flow of the Chicago River finally resulted in an act by the General Assembly approving the deep-cut plan and authorizing canal lands, locks, and dams, but not the credit of the state of Illinois, to be pledged for funds to accomplish the project. Canal dimensions were to be sixty feet wide at the surface, thirty-six feet wide at the bottom, and six feet deep.

June 6, 1836   Contracts were let for parts of the first section of the Illinois and Michigan Canal, from Chicago to Lockport.

June 20, 1836   Auction of lots on canal lands in the Chicago region brought more than $1,300,000, mostly in promises to pay at a future date.

July 4, 1836   First official shovel of earth turned by William B. Ogden and others at Bridgeport on the south branch of the Chicago River.

1837–42   State Bank suspended specie payments. Special legislation passed to protect canal funds on deposit in state banks. Canal scrip issued to pay for construction work. Contractors accepted canal bonds in payment and discounted them when necessary to meet payrolls. Short-term loans made. Bonds held by contractors sold on the London market as low as eighty-three cents on the dollar.

1842 Canal debt reached $4,436,408. Work was discontinued.

1844 The General Assembly approved completion of the canal on the shallow-cut plan with feeders from the Calumet, Kankakee, Des Plaines, Fox, and Du Page rivers. The assembly authorized a loan of $1,600,000, to be paid by a tax of one mill per dollar assessed valuation, out of the state's share of tax receipts. The act provided for three trustees to supervise the work, two to be selected by the bondholders and one appointed by the governor. European bondholders provided $600,000 of the new money; New York raised $1,000,000.

June 24, 1845 Trustees appointed William Gooding as chief engineer and ordered work to be resumed.

Apr. 10, 1848 The canal boat *General Fry* traversed the Illinois and Michigan Canal from Lockport to Chicago.

Apr. 21, 1848 The canal opened from Ottawa to Chicago.

1862 A canal from the Illinois River near Hennepin to the Mississippi River at or near Rock Island was proposed in Congress as a military measure.

1865 Because of pollution of Chicago's water supply (Lake Michigan) by floodwaters, the General Assembly authorized reconstruction of the Chicago-Lockport section of the Illinois and Michigan Canal on the deep-cut plan, permanently reversing the flow of the Chicago River.

1871 Report by United States Army engineers to secretary of war estimated a ratio of benefits to costs of the canal from the Illinois to the Mississippi (later called the Hennepin Canal) as 1 to 1.15, and recommended construction of the canal at an estimated cost of $12,479,000.

Apr. 30, 1871 Last Illinois and Michigan Canal bond was retired.

May 1, 1871 Canal trust was dissolved and a board of canal commissioners

assumed operating control of the Illinois and Michigan Canal.

1886 Congress authorized construction of the Hennepin Canal and a feeder canal from Lake Sinissippi near Sterling, Illinois.

1889 Because of continuing pollution problems in Cook County, the General Assembly authorized, among others, organization of the Chicago Sanitary District charged with designing and constructing a sanitary and ship canal paralleling the Illinois and Michigan Canal from Bridgeport to Lockport, treating sewage of the metropolitan area at suitable plants and discharging it into the new canal through which the effluent would eventually reach the Mississippi River.

1890 After litigation to test constitutionality of Sanitary District Act, work began on the ship canal.

1892 Route of Hennepin Canal determined to be from a point one mile east of Bureau, Illinois, to a point on the Mississippi just below Rock Island. Construction by Army Corps of Engineers began.

Apr. 17, 1895 Hennepin Canal opened to traffic from Mississippi River to a point above the falls on the Rock River.

Jan. 2, 1900 Water turned into the new Sanitary and Ship Canal near Bridgeport, increasing the diversion of Lake Michigan waters to the Illinois River, and providing the beginning of a deep waterway from Lake Michigan to the Gulf of Mexico.

May 1904 Sanitary District trustees, on advice of their engineering staff, approved construction of the Calumet-Sag channel, which would bring about an additional diversion of water from Lake Michigan.

Oct. 24, 1907 Hennepin Canal filled with water and opened for its entire length.

1908 A bond issue of $20,000,000 authorized by referendum for completion of a deep waterway from the terminus of the Chicago Sanitary and Ship Canal at Lockport to the Illinois River at Utica.

Oct. 13, 1913 United States attorney general filed suit against Sanitary District to prevent excessive diversion of lake waters. (For complete details see report of Chief of Engineers, United States Army, 1916, p. 1831.)

1914 Control and operation of the Illinois and Michigan Canal passed from the Board of Canal Commissioners to the Illinois Waterways Commission.

1917 Authority over the canal passed to the newly organized Department of Public Works, of which the Illinois Waterways Commission became the Division of Waterways.

1918–19 The Illinois and Michigan Canal completely rehabilitated from Lockport to Utica.

June 17, 1919 The Illinois General Assembly passed the Illinois Deep Waterways Act, which provided for dams and locks from Lockport to Utica, where the canal would join the deep channel maintained in the Illinois and Mississippi rivers by the federal government.

1922 After years of litigation and delay, involving the federal government and several states, the Calumet-Sag channel was opened.

1925 Authority to construct the Deep Waterway from Lockport to Utica passed from the Department of Public Works to a new Department of Construction and Purchases.

1930 The federal government appropriated $7,500,000 to aid the state of Illinois to complete the Deep Waterway.

1933 Major facilities completed, the Deep Waterway was opened and the Illinois and Michigan Canal was closed to navigation. The right of way was opened in places for recreational uses.

1947 Congress passed act enabling the state of Illinois to use lands occupied by the Illinois and Michigan Canal for highway, park, and recreational purposes.

1951 After various proposals for redesign of locks and modernization the

Hennepin Canal was declared obsolete and closed to navigation as of June 30.

1954 Constitutional amendment authorizing sale or lease of the Illinois and Michigan Canal or other waterways owned by the state of Illinois was approved by voters.

Illinois and Michigan Canal, 1848–1930, generally at five-year intervals (pleasure boats excluded)

Year	Expense	Tolls	Boats operating	Tons transported
1848	$43,197	$87,890	na	na
1853	44,870	118,375	na	na
1858	58,088	197,171	na	na
1860	82,583	138,554	201	367,437
1865	124,869	300,810	228	616,140
1870	108,695	149,635	179	585,970
1875	74,511	107,081	142	676,025
1880[1]	125,601	92,296	133	751,360
1882[2]	105,412	85,947	132	1,011,287
1885	86,393	66,800	135	827,355
1890	75,125	55,112	104	742,392
1895	71,142	39,106	88	591,507
1900	88,317	13,867	60	121,759
1905	50,890	4,950	124	38,820
1910[3]	57,938	3,754	357	374,500
1914[4]	49,995	3,292	407	487,328
1920	32,119	442	114	na
1925	40,634	112	64	178
1930	23,229	127	36	na

na—Data not available.
[1] Tolls reduced in 1877.
[2] Peak year for freight under commissioners.
[3] Tolls drastically reduced in 1908.
[4] Illinois Waterways Commission assumed control.

Hennepin Canal between the Illinois and Mississippi rivers, at five-year intervals, 1905–50

(As of June 30, 1916, the canal with additions and improvements cost $8,911,511. Pleasure boats excluded.)

Year	Number of boats	Tons transported	Number of passengers	Cost of operation
1905	1,261	10,555	2,310	$13,602
1910	505	22,388	4,827	28,863
1915	1,790	32,276	24,354	90,769
1920	224	7,428	17,909	107,177
1925	na	14,929	17,316	143,974
1930	393	19,142	15,376	190,331
1935	na	11,578	13,138	102,687
1940	733	14,542	1,817	176,272
1945	285	14,146	839	71,396
1950	39	1,198	0	187,160

na—Data not available.

Illinois River—Traffic at Grafton and the Kampsville Lock, 1890–1930

(The United States Army Corps of Engineers began keeping records relative to the Illinois River in 1890. Those for traffic between La Salle and Grafton, 1890–1930, and at the Kampsville Lock, 1905–30, are given below. Beginning with 1935 the statistics cover the entire Illinois Deep Waterway from Grafton to Chicago. Pleasure boats excluded.)

| Year | Between La Salle and Grafton | | | | Kampsville Lock | | |
	Tons transported	Value of tonnage	Number of passengers	Number of boats	Tons transported	Number of passengers
1890	26,300	na	na			
1895	37,640	na	na			
1900	25,925	na	na			
1905	14,950	na	na	587	114,366	16,600
1910	106,320	$2,841,520	75,200	750	139,481	6,655
1915	234,677	3,702,832	74,172	780	186,884	18,393
1920	187,007	7,567,135	81,930	1,057	30,325	6,365
1925	96,080	4,828,588	17,315	511	13,170	4,808
1930	74,786	2,121,595	23,872	394	5,277	5,611

| Year | Illinois Deep Waterway Grafton to Chicago | | | | Chicago Sanitary and Ship Canal Chicago to Lockport (included in Deep Waterway) | | |
	Number of boats	Tons transported	Value of tonnage*	Number of passengers	Number of boats	Tons transported	Value of tonnage*
1925					na	688,295	$1,543,705
1930					589	92,228	2,501,468
1935	4,623	1,584,428	$48,710,394	288,373	1,715	1,004,829	na
1940	14,462	5,729,356		135,684	13,516	4,668,712	
1945	16,382	6,590,639		na	12,285	5,106,678	
1950	23,274	16,420,619		na	14,798	12,045,910	
1955	30,000†	21,362,852		30,409	12,000†	16,386,596	
1960	32,000†	26,929,167		9,158	13,142	19,966,596	
1965	40,000†	30,812,773		10,820	19,010	20,109,654	

na—Data not available.
* The Corps of Engineers discontinued publication of cargo values 1936.
† Estimated.

1964 Southwest Expressway (later renamed for Adlai E. Stevenson) occupying much of the right of way of the Illinois and Michigan Canal between Bridgeport and Lockport was opened from the Cook County line to the Dan Ryan Expressway.

1966 The Illinois and Michigan Canal office closed the year with a substantial cash balance derived from leases of the ninety-foot parcels along the canal right-of-way.

Railroads

From the earliest exploration of Illinois, routes of transportation and travel were recognized by forward-looking men as the key to progress. Water routes generally were followed by newcomers into the southern counties. Settlement of the northern areas of the state was greatly advanced by the completion of the Erie Canal, which provided an all-water route from New York to the Chicago portage and thence by way of the Illinois River to St. Louis and New Orleans.

During his administration Governor Edward Coles (1822–26) suggested a canal along the eastern border of the state from Lake Michigan to the Wabash River, with the Wabash furnishing a water route to the eastern and southern counties. A great central highway was proposed from Cairo to the Illinois River near Ottawa, before there was an Ottawa.

A railroad, the Chicago & Vincennes, was chartered in 1834, but no work was done on the line for many years. Meanwhile, A. M.

Jenkins, lieutenant governor of Illinois from 1834 to 1836, brought a proposal before the General Assembly for a railroad from Cairo to Galena by way of the southwest terminus of the Illinois and Michigan Canal. On January 18, 1836, the assembly chartered a company to build the Illinois Central Railroad. Among the directors were Governor John Reynolds (1830–34) and Jenkins. Financing of construction was a major project, and no work would be done for more than a decade.

In that same year, Illinois got its first railroad, a line six miles long from the coal mines on the Mississippi bluffs to Illinois-town, now East St. Louis. It was not much of a railroad, for it had wooden rails and mules for motive power, but it hauled considerable coal from the mines to the river before the first locomotive was brought to Illinois. Governor Reynolds was one of the incorporators of the line, which became known as John Reynolds' railroad and was officially called the Coal Mine Bluffs Railroad. In 1841 it was chartered as the St. Clair Railroad, renamed the Pittsburgh Railway & Coal Company in 1859, and finally renamed the Illinois & St. Louis Railroad. Meanwhile it had been extended to Belleville and powered with steam locomotives. Still another mule-power road four miles long from the Illinois River at Naples into the prairie was built in 1837. It was known as Charles Collins' railroad. Neither of these roads was a common carrier, neither had a schedule or hauled passengers or freight, but they were the first railways to haul commodities of any kind in Illinois.

On February 27, 1837, an internal improvement act was passed by the General Assembly which was to put Illinois into the railroad business in a large way and almost bankrupt the state. The new law established a $10,000,000 project that called for more than 1,300 miles of railroad, together with roads, canals, and improved waterways. Backbone of the proposed undertaking was to be the central line, which had not yet been privately financed under its charter of 1836. To it would be added a branch from Hillsboro to the Indiana line; the Southern Cross Railway from Alton to Mount Carmel; the Northern Cross from Quincy to the Indiana line via Springfield; a line from Peoria to Warsaw, one from Alton east to intercept the Central, one from Belleville to intercept the Southern Cross, and one from Bloomington to Mackinaw with a branch to Pekin and Peoria.

The Central might have been the first railroad on which construction would begin had it not been for the panic of 1837. Bonds were difficult—almost impossible—to sell. There was little cash in the treasury. Governor Joseph Duncan and his director of public works determined to begin a line they thought they might finish, and a section of the Northern Cross was selected. Henry Brown reports in his *History of Illinois* (1844) that first surveys were undertaken at Meredosia on the Illinois River on May 11, 1837, and were completed to Jacksonville late that year. The first rail was laid May 9, 1838, and on November 8, 1838, the first locomotive to reach Illinois was unloaded from a barge at Meredosia and placed on the rails. As was the early custom, the locomotive had a name—the "Rogers."

The road was completed to Jacksonville on January 1, 1840, with appropriate New Year's ceremonies. By February 15, 1842, it was close to Springfield, and a second locomotive, the "Illinois," had been purchased and received at Meredosia. On March 18, 1842, regular service was established from Jacksonville to Springfield, thirty-three and a half miles in two hours, eight minutes elapsed time. On May 13 the entire stretch of railroad from Meredosia to Springfield was in operation at a cost of $1,000,000. It never made any money, and finally was sold by the state, but it was secure in its title of the first railroad with steam motive power and the first common carrier to be built in the West. Several years later it became a part of the Wabash, St. Louis & Pacific. Needless to say, it never reached the Pacific.

The first railway into or out of Chicago had a difficult time getting under way. It was the Galena & Chicago Union Railroad, chartered in 1836. Work was begun on the line that year, but soon came to a stop because of the money shortage created by the panic of 1837. Early in 1845 the charter was bought by Elisha Townsend of New York and Thomas Mather of Springfield, who turned it over to a group of residents of the area through which it would pass, receiving a promise of stock in payment. On November 28, 1845, 319 delegates from along the right-of-way, meeting in Rockford under leadership of William B. Ogden, J. Young Scammon, Walter L. Newberry, and others of Chicago, and Thomas Drummond of Galena, determined that the entire capital stock in the enterprise except some shares for the owners of the charter and some for construction financing be offered at public subscription. On February 17, 1846, Ogden was elected first president of the railroad and construction got under way. Rails of the steel-strap type, to be nailed to wooden stringers, were purchased from the Michigan Central, which, after building a few miles of road, had converted to iron rails. A franchise to use public streets in Chicago was granted and the first rails laid. Soon the need for a locomotive became pressing, yet money was scarce. Ogden solved this difficulty by offering the Michigan Central forty shares of stock for the wood-burning locomotive "Alert." The offer was accepted and the Galena & Chicago Union was in the railroad business. Trains were running to the Des Plaines River at Maywood in the fall of 1848; to Turner Junction (West Chicago) in the spring of 1849; to Elgin January 22, 1850; to Belvidere December 3, 1851; to Rockford August 22, 1852, and to Freeport September 1, 1853. That became the end of the line when an agreement was reached with the Illinois Central, already building its branch from La Salle to Galena and Dunleith (East Duluth), to use the Central's rails from Freeport into Dunleith. The Central completed its branch June 12, 1855. After nine years of operation over the width of the state the Galena & Chicago Union was merged with other lines of Illinois and Wisconsin into the Chicago & North Western Railway.

Meanwhile another little railway with a big future, the Aurora Branch Railroad, twelve miles long, had been constructed from Aurora to connect with the Galena & Chicago Union at Turner Junction, linking Aurora with Chicago. The schedule called for morning and evening trains daily. Sometime later the Aurora Branch was extended to Mendota. Finally it was merged with the Central Military Tract Railroad and the Peoria & Oquawka Railroad to become the Chicago, Burlington & Quincy. Thus, in 1850, Chicago had a railway as far as Aurora and Elgin, a plank road from Chicago to Naperville (later to become Ogden Avenue), a plank road to what is now Wheeling (Milwaukee Avenue), and a canal from Lake Michigan to the Illinois River near Ottawa.

While this activity was going on around Springfield and Chicago, the Central Railroad was showing signs of life. In 1850 Senator Stephen A. Douglas secured agreement of Congress to subsidize railroads with public lands in Illinois, Alabama, and Mississippi. Later these roads would be joined in a lakes-to-gulf line. The grant in Illinois, 2,595,000 acres, was turned over to a newly organized private Illinois Central corporation, since the state was out of the railroad business under provisions of the constitution of 1848. Construction was begun, and by 1855 rails had been laid from Cairo to Galena and Dunleith by way of Centralia and La Salle, and a branch was being built from Centralia to Chicago. Within the city of Chicago trains of the Michigan Central were running from Calumet to the Illinois Central depot at Twelfth Street and Michigan Avenue on Illinois Central tracks. At the time of completion of the branch line, September 27, 1856, the Illinois Central was the longest railroad in the world. The land, almost 10 per cent of Illinois' total acreage and some of its richest soil, had built a railroad.

The first railways into Chicago from the east, the Southern Michigan & Northern Indiana from Toledo and Monroe, Michigan, (completed in 1852) and the Michigan Central, which reached Chicago from Michigan City on May 20, 1852, were bitter rivals. The Michigan Central, refused a charter across Indiana, obtained access through the subterfuge of an agreement in perpetuity with the Monon (building from New Albany to Michigan City) which constructed trackage from Michigan City to the Illinois line and leased it to the Michigan Central. The Pittsburgh, Fort Wayne & Chicago brought the Pennsylvania system into Chicago in 1857.

Other railways built in the fifties developed into giant carriers before a new century began, and helped make Chicago the undisputed leader of the Western Hemisphere as a railroad center. Among these were the Rock Island & Chicago, now the Chicago, Rock Island & Pacific, which did reach the western ocean via Southern Pacific tracks from Tucumcari, New Mexico; the St. Louis, Alton & Chicago, which became the Chicago & Alton, and in recent years was merged with the Gulf, Mobile & Ohio; the Dixon Airline, which became a part of the North Western system; the Terre Haute & Alton, which now is part of the New York Central lines; the Ohio & Mississippi, now part of the Baltimore & Ohio; the Great Western of Illinois, which was absorbed by the Wabash, and in recent years with the Nickle Plate, became a part of the Norfolk & Western Railroad; and the Chicago & Milwaukee Railroad, which developed into the Chicago, Milwaukee, St. Paul & Pacific. By 1860 Illinois had 2,790 miles of railroad, second only to Ohio. In 1871 total trackage was 4,648 miles, in 1901 it was 8,577, and in 1935 it reached a peak of 24,993 miles.

One of the great Illinois railroads, the Atchison, Topeka & Santa Fe, was built in the 1880's. As a latecomer it fathered many legends, developed the system of railway-sponsored eating places and inns along the route, and set up an out-of-work miner, called Death Valley Scotty, to help obtain railway mail contracts by dramatizing the first run ever made from Los Angeles to Chicago in less than forty hours. Scott— whose only mine was an almost worthless

hole called the Golden Ophir, in what is now the Joshua Tree National Monument in California's desert—was established as the owner of a fabulously wealthy mine in Death Valley more than 150 miles away. The publicity resulting from his spectacular dash as the sole passenger from Los Angeles to Chicago gave the Santa Fe a lever for mail contracts that could not be disregarded, and from 1906 until mid-October 1967 Santa Fe mail trains made daily Chicago-Los Angeles runs in just over thirty-nine hours.

Statistics on total revenue miles of Illinois railways begin in 1871, when seven railroads submitted figures. By 1881 the number had increased to twelve, and the reports included totals of passenger and freight revenues. Since 1915 statistics have been fairly complete. Appended are tables showing mileage, freight and passenger miles, and earnings for the twenty principal long-line railroads and the six principal switching railroads of Illinois.

Recapitulation, 1871–1965, generally at ten-year intervals

Year	Miles of track	Freight train miles	Passenger train miles	Long-haul carriers Tonnage revenue freight	Freight revenue	Passenger revenue
1871	4,648	12,459,695	6,236,673	$6,089,810	$20,533,894	$7,961,521
1881	5,156	ns	ns	17,373,398	25,652,781	7,549,568
1891	6,516	15,689,939	12,004,900	31,228,564	32,178,707	12,110,604
1901	8,577	37,234,176	26,412,947	51,979,449	56,564,692	18,464,446
1905	9,480	34,972,591	31,769,734	72,706,429	69,035,754	27,253,352
1915	18,488	31,027,298	34,224,293	124,120,725	103,797,494	34,105,179
1925	21,245	37,061,405	36,417,142	205,867,938	264,063,677	59,365,743
1935	24,993	29,759,170	29,462,524	155,092,941	177,538,335	23,708,028
1945	23,755	40,158,015	33,483,118	320,757,345	413,370,310	97,378,918
1955	23,643	27,834,115	23,501,362	283,187,847	547,692,447	61,612,481
1965	22,125	25,316,054	15,947,939	309,128,936	582,998,976	65,756,582

Switching carriers

Year	Miles of track	Number of cars	Tonnage	Revenue
1871	na	na	na	na
1881	81	ns	14,843	$144,130
1891	41	ns	3,545,443	1,164,924
1901	61	ns	2,986,020	1,196,854
1905	111	ns	3,034,073	2,922,154
1915	940	1,911,543	ns	8,310,481
1925	1,131	1,796,776	ns	19,507,722
1935	1,441	1,704,639	ns	14,616,947
1945	1,377	1,971,023	ns	26,786,577
1955	1,327	3,669,452	ns	47,031,342
1965	1,273	749,729	ns	46,470,374

na—Data not available.
ns—Data not stated.

Record of earnings—twenty selected long-haul railroads, 1871–1965, generally at ten-year intervals

Railroad[1]	Miles of track	Freight train miles	Passenger train miles	Tonnage revenue freight	Freight revenue	Passenger revenue
			1871			
A T & S F						
B & O						
C B & Q	893	1,825,792	1,298,157	ns	ns	ns
C & E I						
C G W						
C & I M						
C M St. P & P						
C & N W	1,416	3,852,750	1,882,380	2,289,915	$7,556,022	$3,289,906
C R I & P	707	2,312,516	953,903	1,011,019	3,942,974	1,602,298
G M & O	582	1,937,710	727,348	1,190,776	3,646,261	1,233,725
I T						
I C	798	2,145,792	1,078,501	1,598,100	4,672,570	1,578,002
L & N						
M P						
N Y C						
N & W						
Penn.						
Sou.						
St. L. SW						
T P & W	252	385,135	296,384	ns	716,067	257,590
Total	4,648	12,459,695	6,236,673	6,089,810	$20,533,894	$7,961,521
			1881			
A T & S F						
B & O	17	ns	ns	223,589	$37,464	$12,252
C B & Q	1,132	ns	ns	4,525,691	7,592,578	1,927,416
C & E I	177	ns	ns	948,278	1,041,042	173,070
C G W						
C & I M						
C M St. P & P	296	ns	ns	720,331	1,453,575	503,870
C & N W	636	ns	ns	2,344,999	2,396,600	801,303
C R I & P	398	ns	ns	2,490,129	2,674,459	857,562
G M & O	754	ns	ns	3,029,110	4,373,832	1,302,271
I T						
I C	1,108	ns	ns	2,349,285	4,747,248	1,424,546
L & N	207	ns	ns	456,636	477,101	215,021
M P						
N Y C	96	ns	ns	154,585	347,876	166,736
N & W						
Penn.	53	ns	ns	130,765	244,377	80,726
Sou.						
St. L SW						
T P & W (3 months)	282	ns	ns	ns	266,629	84,795
Total	5,156			17,373,398	$25,652,781	$7,549,568
			1891			
A T & S F	295	1,380,162	872,800	1,674,452	$2,382,347	$467,706
B & O	14	62,316	56,643	1,241,673	91,544	34,029
C B & Q	1,229	ns	ns	2,819,375	4,123,900	1,678,393
C & E I	203	744,885	393,465	2,052,372	1,598,121	444,994
C G W						
C & I M						
C M St. P & P	339	747,817	442,585	578,075	1,089,597	351,573
C & N W	593		2,675,301	1,883,144	2,777,408	951,582
C R I & P	236		1,232,028	3,123,391	2,738,962	1,250,186
G M & O	586	2,357,484	1,454,544	3,061,163	3,621,564	1,702,801
I T						

Railroad[1]	Miles of track	Freight train miles	Passenger train miles	Tonnage revenue freight	Freight revenue	Passenger revenue
I C	1,285	4,691,428	2,685,788	5,656,066	6,348,959	2,219,917
L & N	180	394,610	275,423	755,097	581,653	276,510
M P						
N Y C	532	2,020,530	1,468,856	4,243,898	2,841,358	1,276,570
N & W	750	2,566,835	1,200,000[3]	3,200,570	3,152,850	1,103,829
Penn.	27	145,438	110,415	356,963	262,265	109,962
Sou.						
St. L SW						
T P & W	247	578,434	319,710	582,325	568,181	242,552
Total	6,516	15,689,939	13,187,558	31,228,564	$32,178,707	$12,110,604

1901

Railroad[1]	Miles of track	Freight train miles	Passenger train miles	Tonnage revenue freight	Freight revenue	Passenger revenue
A T & S F	291	861,039	464,631	1,118,625	$1,513,287	$443,166
B & O	401	1,398,690	1,141,038	4,911,838	4,435,031	1,129,481
C B & Q	1,447	5,444,807	3,653,804	ns	6,174,618	2,133,643
C & E I	485	1,505,308	1,077,504	4,613,227	3,526,429	787,478
C G W	178	953,753	543,670	790,316	1,058,020	251,647
C & I M						
C M St. P & P	377	2,883,782	1,508,268	2,505,286	5,052,432	1,078,779
C & N W	594	6,117,565	3,167,277	2,737,528	3,436,083	1,045,750
C R I & P	237	1,361,821	1,604,388	4,258,052	4,308,604	1,503,590
G M & O	655	2,044,425	2,121,259	4,439,149	4,866,847	2,068,160
I T	14	ns	ns	164,367	48,293	9,786
I C	1,982	8,407,507	5,996,184	12,923,753	12,634,495	4,044,167
L & N	179	554,636	365,767	1,370,836	831,492	321,864
M P						
N Y C	540	1,963,703	1,594,610	5,323,742	3,406,235	1,453,706
N & W	762	2,711,633	2,513,677	3,895,619	3,776,980	1,701,079
Penn.	31	209,081	139,180	1,251,038	414,510	106,573
Sou.	156	220,160	137,280	754,592	363,278	85,216
St. L SW						
T P & W	248	596,266	384,410	921,482	718,058	300,381
Total	8,577	37,234,176	26,412,947	51,979,449	$56,564,692	$18,464,446

1905

Railroad[1]	Miles of track	Freight train miles	Passenger train miles	Tonnage revenue freight	Freight revenue	Passenger revenue
A T & S F	291	1,281,743	996,309	1,836,203	$3,103,728	$1,059,983
B & O	400	702,185	1,053,549	5,692,400	2,888,245	1,356,556
C B & Q	1,580	4,186,375	3,518,297	3,733,119	7,932,392	2,871,044
C & E I	683	2,565,081	1,796,985	7,609,134	5,502,182	1,080,896
C G W ·	177	726,079	495,434	2,005,015	1,762,788	292,758
C & I M						
C M St. P & P	472	3,094,721	1,757,909	3,155,349	6,171,478	1,460,362
C & N W	707	3,590,454	4,331,762	2,878,518	3,633,356	1,233,506
C R I & P	364	1,497,895	2,208,604	5,585,174	5,108,353	2,050,620
G M & O	651	2,211,311	2,414,480	5,586,223	5,520,791	3,345,795
I T	19	22,320	30,840	402,219	85,702	9,813
I C	2,043	8,560,383	6,581,225	16,875,288	15,700,082	6,086,302
L & N	182	544,455	485,791	1,589,076	1,170,017	734,495
M P						
N Y C	574	1,975,698	1,976,137	6,763,391	3,501,539	1,962,612
N & W	763	2,582,165	2,985,824	4,164,761	4,095,238	2,688,745
Penn.	31	256,722	205,670	1,436,100	526,990	143,195
Sou.	163	437,937	365,173	1,899,061	960,980	392,718
St. L SW	132	102,786	169,751	540,738	577,207	140,871
T P & W	248	634,281	395,994	954,660	794,686	343,081
Total	9,480	34,972,591	31,769,734	72,706,429	$69,035,754	$27,253,352

Railroad[1]	Miles of track	Freight train miles	Passenger train miles	Tonnage revenue freight	Freight revenue	Passenger revenue
			1915			
A T & S F	715	1,196,021	1,419,438	3,386,838	$5,256,685	$1,454,910
B & O	586	769,263	1,300,541	5,994,031	3,732,269	1,230,729
C B & Q	3,163	5,117,551	4,420,652	18,065,243	19,739,381	4,811,973
C & E I	1,402	2,369,135	1,980,424	9,295,216	7,516,013	1,786,079
C G W	352	543,937	437,639	2,919,938	2,506,289	309,266
C & I M	33	38,215	36,657	1,202,923	188,425	43,068
C M St. P & P	1,150	2,124,774	2,107,022	13,621,017	7,408,359	1,881,982
C & N W	2,042	3,057,456	5,499,233	18,544,019	11,110,781	5,694,560
C R I & P	958	1,618,869	2,754,852	8,760,540	7,440,604	3,126,116
G M & O	1,376	2,197,538	2,507,509	7,500,244	6,821,449	2,929,877
I T	37	ns	ns	ns	281,354	39
I C	3,609	7,583,148	6,881,182	22,162,383	19,944,129	6,755,727
L & N	237	647,587	458,105	1,648,344	1,111,746	581,060
M P						
N Y C[2]	325	284,419[3]	666,695[3]	863,607[3]	1,133,463	277,351
N & W	1,437	2,423,208	2,390,686	4,819,187	6,190,506	2,105,836
Penn.	156	212,115	233,234	1,379,505	688,488	229,283
Sou.	259	383,100	425,671	2,043,216	1,103,862	325,221
St. L SW	355	182,284	187,919	1,014,530	967,014	121,836
T P & W	295	278,678	516,834	899,944	656,677	440,266
Total	18,487	31,027,298	34,224,293	124,120,725	$103,797,494	$34,105,179
			1925			
A T & S F	764	1,256,904	1,510,210	5,857,604	$12,557,504	$3,346,179
B & O	589	1,031,846	1,172,928	8,180,013	14,903,993	2,061,444
C B & Q	3,703	5,515,588	4,715,916	25,174,192	40,652,466	6,960,931
C & E I	1,380	2,120,294	1,861,138	7,909,239	15,094,733	2,841,571
C G W	357	678,685	405,824	3,443,796	4,416,931	370,971
C & I M	48	69,195	38,226	3,009,362	952,622	23,471
C M St. P & P	1,446	2,563,314	2,314,033	20,556,432	17,685,641	2,411,833
C & N W	2,094	3,428,295	4,819,427	26,908,790	24,303,011	8,908,722
C R I & P	958	1,750,554	2,354,659	11,758,024	14,926,882	5,175,466
G M & O	1,464	2,496,246	2,799,085	12,239,754	16,722,321	5,141,155
I T	52	53,929		2,344,348	1,440,997	
I C	4,122	8,964,329	8,813,752	35,980,169	50,854,191	13,756,000
L & N	245	935,442	493,389	2,804,518	3,535,336	859,874
M P	517	803,773	171,133	10,151,249	9,501,452	82,346
N Y C	350	633,646	568,886	2,024,271	4,370,099	1,761,025
N & W	1,404	2,441,356	2,026,585	13,170,930	17,771,844	2,734,936
Penn.	932	1,309,165	1,627,638	8,239,917[3]	7,976,179	2,202,176
Sou.	257	525,060	289,250	2,862,143	2,349,962	312,040
St. L SW	265	191,534	94,338	2,041,059	2,851,070	128,764
T P & W	299	292,250	340,725	1,211,328	1,196,443	286,839
Total	21,246	37,061,405	36,417,142	205,867,938	$264,063,677	$59,365,743
			1935			
A T & S F	800	950,993	1,150,757	4,610,579	$7,556,014	$1,183,365
B & O	757	788,938	878,915	4,929,595	9,970,355	802,883
C B & Q	3,558	3,749,114	3,715,161	13,513,069	20,372,348	2,639,730
C & E I	1,347	1,312,568	1,344,990	6,082,215	7,406,677	739,930
C G W	342	524,945	235,035	2,476,385	3,063,329	43,698
C & I M	211	315,634	97,351	5,168,087	3,138,750	12,985
C M St. P & P	1,704	1,976,838	1,617,460	14,308,116	12,339,234	957,850
C & N W	2,329	2,178,888	3,373,493	15,160,692	16,357,341	3,949,641
C R I & P	1,043	1,084,760	2,089,986	7,078,180	8,170,460	2,069,694
G M & O	1,374	1,634,956	1,550,040	6,268,567	8,017,259	1,586,487
I T	709	694,313	2,695,379	4,620,972	4,094,974	734,669
I C	4,408	7,049,792	5,749,037	24,576,904	37,832,085	5,399,667

343

Railroad[1]	Miles of track	Freight train miles	Passenger train miles	Tonnage revenue freight	Freight revenue	Passenger revenue
L & N	256	378,453	393,381	1,105,267	1,605,894	210,345
M P	625	733,247	142,691	6,813,461	6,444,640	12,258
N Y C	1,809	2,116,741	1,911,671	4,712,159	9,862,701	1,422,515
N & W	1,875	2,607,032	1,231,942	11,386,317[3]	12,160,617	998,320
Penn.	1,026	683,141	967,579	17,342,113	4,613,653	869,785
Sou.	252	418,369	222,850	1,762,152	1,794,708	64,468
St. L SW	269	275,598	94,768	1,641,623	923,699	9,563
T P & W	300	284,850	38	1,536,488	1,813,597	175
Total	24,994	29,759,170	29,462,524	155,092,941	$177,538,335	$23,708,028

1945

Railroad[1]	Miles of track	Freight train miles	Passenger train miles	Tonnage revenue freight	Freight revenue	Passenger revenue
A T & S F	805	2,162,749	2,002,529	12,274,402	$21,482,356	$8,165,231
B & O	728	1,334,052	919,054	16,582,082	25,123,266	4,127,275
C B & Q	3,350	4,726,220	4,399,333	33,591,779	50,250,382	10,491,229
C & E I	1,207	2,152,840	1,516,259	11,039,572	14,828,698	3,589,283
C G W	327	797,812	320,160	5,036,223	5,564,661	608,341
C & I M	215	551,239	56,544	10,005,860	6,306,954	8,460
C M St. P & P	1,673	2,228,774	1,966,831	27,409,876	28,266,941	4,948,453
C & N W	2,095	2,852,203	4,340,320	30,438,584	32,461,118	12,836,724
C R I & P	1,018	1,361,066	2,473,728	14,896,068	17,267,855	7,108,839
G M & O	1,580	2,364,438	2,060,627	13,646,222	19,258,797	7,747,467
I T	650	65,652	229,158	458,990	481,028	164,354
I C	4,164	7,538,817	6,566,834	48,686,660	80,449,084	19,966,453
L & N	238	730,862	427,730	3,824,329	5,631,941	1,511,083
M P	621	1,322,429	138,537	20,461,431	17,048,925	50,694
N Y C	1,770	3,097,316	2,281,757	11,102,367	22,397,435	5,083,325
N & W	1,784	4,186,725	1,533,277	27,311,894	36,721,173	4,193,111
Penn.	1,031	1,619,406	1,996,783	23,825,937	17,818,514	5,967,977
Sou.	234	657,159	137,823	3,281,138	4,237,075	446,630
St. L SW	267	408,256	115,834	6,883,931	7,774,107	363,989
T P & W[4]						
Total	23,757	40,158,015	33,483,118	320,757,345	$413,370,310	$97,378,918

1955

Railroad[1]	Miles of track	Freight train miles	Passenger train miles	Tonnage revenue freight	Freight revenue	Passenger revenue
A T & S F	806	1,528,412	1,824,804	10,474,986	$28,613,979	$4,120,082
B & O	717	921,118	487,929	12,357,681	31,253,972	914,166
C B & Q	3,303	3,534,827	3,757,167	29,070,667	58,086,685	8,125,417
C & E I	1,155	1,064,008	732,904	13,143,691	19,491,018	1,389,531
C G W	290	269,883	128,240	3,955,561	7,046,994	24,919
C & I M	234	245,456	1,344	8,359,572	7,487,847	5,027
C M St. P & P	1,612	1,328,339	1,584,013	22,505,300	25,189,114	3,521,704
C & N W	2,070	1,742,441	3,323,684	29,598,104	48,515,218	11,429,261
C R I & P	1,070	1,005,646	1,878,806	12,658,786	20,487,478	5,129,091
G M & O	1,534	999,680	542,871	8,276,917	27,120,955	3,489,394
I T	532	549,859	648,566	6,780,737	10,301,942	479,318
I C	4,161	6,199,582	5,026,117	46,603,966	117,455,810	16,073,308
L & N	234	272,599	165,439	2,268,482	5,169,242	272,628
M P	629	807,564		13,583,689	17,761,495	
N Y C	1,717	2,244,764	1,270,161	11,510,784	28,542,200	2,400,824
N & W	1,776	2,899,795	1,180,803	22,944,959	52,749,610	2,490,540
Penn.	1,022	1,107,091	857,108	17,137,445	20,612,609	1,683,749
Sou.	221	321,501	882	3,292,649	6,176,094	4,761
St. L SW	263	364,174	90,524	5,053,861	8,692,397	58,761
T P & W	298	427,376		3,610,010	6,937,788	
Total	23,644	27,834,115	23,501,362	283,187,847	$547,692,447	$61,612,481

Railroad[1]	Miles of track	Freight train miles	Passenger train miles	Tonnage revenue freight	Freight revenue	Passenger revenue
			1965			
A T & S F	827	1,559,317	1,261,750	12,329,518	$29,018,080	$3,771,282
B & O	697	815,278	264,800	13,916,519	31,722,086	723,055
C B & Q	3,118	3,197,903	2,463,134	32,372,291	62,219,262	9,936,944
C & E I	1,056	1,215,661	246,502	13,764,380	24,856,269	781,417
C G W	285	266,675		3,944,952	6,196,625	
C & I M	178	175,737		6,942,823	7,738,862	
C M St. P & P	1,574	1,101,103	1,502,905	21,434,238	22,258,744	5,765,421
C & N W	2,091	1,904,274	2,599,618	32,843,448	57,017,847	15,859,057
C R I & P	1,070	1,340,984	1,353,236	14,072,565	25,189,315	5,497,628
G M & O	1,418	1,001,545	701,535	15,411,320	30,404,433	2,325,674
I T	511	251,505		6,218,733	8,057,759	
I C	3,983	4,575,492	3,715,126	45,948,404	106,903,587	17,194,101
L & N	232	405,625	100,322	4,712,217	8,818,787	184,943
M P	589	760,938		16,462,493	19,910,329	
N Y C	914	1,470,655	418,291	10,564,810	33,742,373	1,224,869
N & W	1,793	2,850,777	700,970	25,981,904	56,718,189	1,300,574
Penn.	985	1,112,126	619,750	20,887,510	23,383,368	1,191,587
Sou.	218	315,411		4,583,935	8,747,798	30
St. L SW	265	577,248		2,330,114	12,445,586	
T P & W	321	417,800		4,406,762	7,649,677	
Total	22,125	25,316,054	15,947,939	309,128,936	$582,998,976	$65,756,582

ns—Data not stated.
[1] A T & S F—Atchison, Topeka and Santa Fe; B & O—Baltimore & Ohio; C B & Q—Chicago, Burlington & Quincy; C & E I—Chicago & Eastern Illinois; CGW—Chicago Great Western; C & I M—Chicago & Illinois Midland; C M St. P & P—Chicago, Milwaukee, St. Paul & Pacific; C & N W—Chicago & North Western; C R I & P—Chicago, Rock Island & Pacific; G M & O—Gulf, Mobile & Ohio (includes Chicago & Alton); I T—Illinois Terminal; I C—Illinois Central; L & N—Louisville &

Nashville; M P—Missouri Pacific; N Y C—New York Central (includes Cleveland, Cincinnati, Chicago & St. Louis and Michigan Central); N & W—Norfolk & Western (includes Nickle Plate and Wabash); Penn.—Pennsylvania; Sou.—Southern Railway; St. L SW—St. Louis Southwestern; T P & W—Toledo, Peoria & Western.
[2] Report incomplete.
[3] Estimated figure.
[4] Under federal control.

Record of earnings—six switching railroads, 1881–1965, generally at ten-year intervals

	Miles of track	Number of cars	Tonnage	Revenue
		1881		
Belt Railway of Chicago Chicago & Western Indiana East St. Louis Junction Indiana Harbor Belt	48	ns	ns	$72,759
Peoria & Pekin Union Term. RR Ass'n of St. Louis	33	ns	14,843	71,371
Total	81		14,843	$144,130
		1891		
Belt Railway of Chicago Chicago & Western Indiana East St. Louis Junction Indiana Harbor Belt	21	ns	ns	$675,668
Peoria & Pekin Union	18	ns	184,471	50,507
Term. RR Ass'n of St. Louis.	2	ns	3,360,972	438,549
Total	41		3,545,443	$1,164,724

Table—continued

	Miles of track	Number of cars	Tonnage	Revenue
1901				
Belt Railway of Chicago	21	ns	ns	$814,116
Chicago & Western Indiana	20	ns	ns	ns
East St. Louis Junction				
Indiana Harbor Belt				
Peoria & Pekin Union	18	ns	223,624	382,738
Term. RR Ass'n of St. Louis	2	ns	2,762,396	
Total	61		2,986,020	$1,196,854
1905				
Belt Railway of Chicago	47	ns	ns	$1,671,887
Chicago & Western Indiana	27	ns	ns	ns
East St. Louis Junction				
Indiana Harbor Belt				
Peoria & Pekin Union	18	ns	269,578	484,696
Term. RR Ass'n of St. Louis	19	ns	2,764,495	765,571
Total	111		3,034,073	$2,922,154
1915				
Belt Railway of Chicago	349.96	666,370	ns	$3,142,057
Chicago & Western Indiana	150.11	17,815	ns	88,281
East St. Louis Junction				
Indiana Harbor Belt	204.01	572,612	ns	3,170,371
Peoria & Pekin Union	148.46	53,671	ns	721,758
Term. RR Ass'n of St. Louis	87.49	601,075	ns	1,188,014
Total	940.03	1,911,543		$8,310,481
1925				
Belt Railway of Chicago	354.07	784,864	ns	$6,933,767
Chicago & Western Indiana	167.92	16,514	ns	213,158
East St. Louis Junction	41.86	178,867	ns	645,650
Indiana Harbor Belt	314.52	566,546	ns	8,083,325
Peoria & Pekin Union	163.67	54,223	ns	1,391,835
Term. RR Ass'n of St. Louis	89.54	195,762	ns	2,239,987
Total	1,131.58	1,796,776		$19,507,722
1935				
Belt Railway of Chicago	460.35	470,782	ns	$4,630,661
Chicago & Western Indiana	179.19	4,480	ns	67,013
East St. Louis Junction	38.88	80,366	ns	290,326
Indiana Harbor Belt	377.55	431,114*	ns	4,942,040
Peoria & Pekin Union	159.88	206,117	ns	961,269
Term. RR Ass'n of St. Louis	225.55	511,780*	ns	3,725,638
Total	1,441.40	1,704,639		$14,616,947
1945				
Belt Railway of Chicago	440.51	734,911	ns	$7,250,335
Chicago & Western Indiana	167.70	5,871	ns	85,360
East St. Louis Junction	37.33	80,012	ns	369,667
Indiana Harbor Belt	364.43	788,215	ns	9,201,239
Peoria & Pekin Union	156.54	362,014	ns	1,713,952
Term. RR Ass'n of St. Louis	210.35	ns	ns	8,166,024
Total	1,376.86	1,971,023		$26,786,577

	Miles of track	Number of cars	Tonnage	Revenue
1955				
Belt Railway of Chicago	438.77	684,332	ns	$14,128,430
Chicago & Western Indiana	158.54	6,012	ns	152,051
East St. Louis Junction	22.89	42,386	ns	426,614
Indiana Harbor Belt	384.71	1,346,707	ns	17,944,487
Peoria & Pekin Union	119.82	301,561	ns	2,813,493
Term. RR Ass'n of St. Louis	201.90	1,288,454	ns	11,566,267
Total	1,326.63	3,669,452		$47,031,342
1965				
Belt Railway of Chicago	440.91	532,040	ns	$13,946,133
Chicago & Western Indiana	146.10	2,827	ns	125,214
East St. Louis Junction	20.91	10,720	ns	300,507
Indiana Harbor Belt	358.50	ns	ns	16,137,268
Peoria & Pekin Union	117.83	204,142	ns	2,685,488
Term. RR Ass'n of St. Louis	188.46	ns	ns	13,275,764
Total	1,272.71	749,729		$46,470,374

ns—Data not stated.   * Report incomplete.

Roads and Bridges

In territorial Illinois, with its few thousand inhabitants scattered over several million acres of rich, black soil, hardwood forest, and mucky bottomlands, passable roads existed only in the late summer and early fall, or when an unusually hard winter froze the quagmires solid enough to bear the weight of a team of oxen or horses. Places like Purgatory Swamp, across the Wabash from Vincennes, where George Rogers Clark's men waded to their armpits in the campaign of February 1779 to capture the British garrison, were passable at any time only by the most arduous toil. Actually, in all of Illinois, except the area from Kaskaskia to Cahokia settled almost a century earlier, was there anything but cart tracks that followed old Indian trails and buffalo traces.

In Kaskaskia, after Illinois became a territory in its own right, considerable interest in a road from Shawneetown was evident, but Washington was a long way from the Mississippi. There was much talk but little action. It was not until 1814, when a land office was opened in Shawneetown and the trickle of pioneers crossing the Ohio became a stream, that postal routes were laid out and bids were asked for carrying mail. There were seven designated circuits, stretching from Shawneetown to Kaskaskia and Ste. Genevieve, from Kaskaskia by way of Cahokia to St. Louis and St. Charles in the newly formed territory of Missouri, and between other settlements in Illinois Territory, which at the time had fewer than 20,000 inhabitants.

An act of Congress April 27, 1816, provided government assistance for building roads in the territories, and on July 13 of that year Illinois residents petitioned for a road from Kaskaskia to Shawneetown. The petition was granted, a survey of the route ordered, and the survey lost somewhere between Kaskaskia and Washington. Finally, on June 23, 1818, when Illinois was about to become a state, the treasurer of the United States authorized Agent John Caldwell at Shawneetown to advance funds for construction, and dragging of the "highway" began.

First legislation by the General Assembly of Illinois relating to roads was approved by Governor Shadrach Bond on March 24, 1819. It provided for commissioners to "view and mark" a road from Golconda to Kaskaskia by way of Brownsville. Three days later an act was approved by Governor Bond authorizing county commissioners to license toll bridges and turnpikes. The General Assembly approved construction of a toll road 100 feet wide from a point on the Mississippi opposite St. Louis to the bluffs about six miles across the bottomlands toward Belleville. Licensee was one Samuel Wiggins.

Basic legislation relating to roads and bridges was contained in an act approved by Governor Bond March 29, 1819. It was entitled An Act for Opening, Repairing, Improving and Regulating Roads and Highways, and it established principles of county responsibility that in essence were unchanged until the creation of a highway commission in 1905. In fact county responsibility over many roads of the state continues today.

The legislature declared that roads designated by the territorial legislature were in fact public roads of the state of Illinois. It placed jurisdiction for roads in the commissioners' courts of the several counties and ordered these courts to appoint a sufficient number of freeholders as supervisors. It authorized these supervisors to call all able-bodied men eighteen to fifty-five years of age to work on the roads not less than one nor more than five days a year. County commissioners' courts also were authorized to receive petitions from a designated number of freeholders for opening roads in their jurisdictions and to lay out such roads. Highways that would pass through more than one county required action by the General Assembly, and the first three legislatures authorized construction of many through roads or declared existing roads to be public highways.

On June 15, 1825, an act of the General Assembly, approved by Governor Edward Coles, revised the basic highway law. This act instructed county commissioners to divide their counties into road districts, authorized a road tax not to exceed one half of 1 per cent of assessed valuation of taxable property, and provided that this tax could be paid by road work, with additional credit for implements and animals used on the highways.

First mention of state roads as such occurred in acts of the General Assembly during 1832 and 1833, which ordered survey and construction of seventy-seven roads, chiefly in the Military Tract and in the northern counties newly opened to settlement by Indian cessions. Among these was a road from Chicago to Galena, one from Chicago to Peoria, and one from Peoria to Galena. In 1835 the General Assembly declared the Old Vincennes Trace to Chicago by way of Vermilion and Iroquois counties a state road. The street by which it entered the village of Chicago became State Street. This assembly also spelled out the powers and duties of county commissioners in greater detail, and ordered roads to be laid

out not more than fifty nor less than thirty feet wide, a provision later changed to sixty and forty feet.

The Tenth General Assembly, which convened in December 1836, gave long and earnest consideration to transportation problems and finally laid out a program of public roads, toll roads, railroads, and canals, to be financed by a bond issue. The assembly created a Board of Commissioners of Public Works to lay out and initiate the program, and a Board of Fund Commissioners to market the bonds and administer the financial details of the program. Among the proposals was a Great Western Mail Route from Vincennes to St. Louis, completion of the National Road from Vandalia to St. Louis by way of Greenville, without taking into account the many sections of the road from Terre Haute to Vandalia that were more often than not impassable, and construction of a Chicago-Fox River turnpike following the first section of the old army trail blazed to Galena during the Black Hawk War. This turnpike was to terminate at Elgin. Unfortunately, the panic of 1837 dried up the money well, the bonds could not be sold, and the program collapsed. However, even during the panic period, some state roads were laid out and work done on them when the counties had sufficient manpower or money muscle.

For several decades highways laid out by the legislature carried a provision that they should follow the most direct route. By 1840 the highway maps of Illinois showed roads radiating like the spokes of a wheel from a number of centers which were the hubs. Shawneetown, Golconda, Metropolis, Jonesboro, Vienna, Kaskaskia, Benton, Carmi, Lawrenceville, Effingham, Belleville, Vandalia, Edwardsville, Alton, Jacksonville, Springfield, Decatur, Livingston, Danville, Urbana, Bloomington, Peoria, Macomb, Monmouth, Ottawa, Juliet (now Joliet), Chicago, Elgin, Belvidere, Middletown (now Rockford), Dixon, Freeport, and Galena were the centers from which nearly 500 designated state highways radiated to serve the country around them and more distant parts of the state.

County roads, on the other hand, followed township lines, interlacing the state routes. The procedure for laying out a new road in a county was for a number of freeholders to sign a petition asking for the road. Whereupon the road commissioners, after ascertaining that funds were available under a road tax limited to anywhere from $0.20 to $1.00 per $100 of assessed valuation, could order the work to proceed. Meanwhile some of the roads into Illinois from other states were in trouble. In 1833 federal maintenance and toll gathering ceased on the National Road, originally mapped from Washington to St. Louis and constructed from Washington to Richmond, Indiana. The road reverted to the states, most of the toll gates were removed, and by 1840 what had been a good stone or macadam highway from Cumberland, Maryland, to Richmond had deteriorated. Across Indiana and Illinois, the road, while authorized, had not been completely laid out. Macadam in Ohio gave way to mud in Indiana and Illinois. The National Road became a trace at times not even marked, at others filled with chuckholes and studded with stumps. An Indiana rhymster, quoted by Phillip Dillon Jordan in *The National Road*, described the highway thus: "The roads are impassable, / Hardly jackassable. / I think those that travel 'em / Should get out and gravel 'em."

The principal highway from the East into northern Illinois and Wisconsin stretched across Ohio and northern Indiana from Port Lawrence (Toledo) to Michigan City, where it was joined by a much-used route from Madison, Indiana, on the Ohio, by way of Indianapolis. From Michigan City the road pretty much followed the beach north of the sand dunes to avoid the bogs, and the Calumet River was negotiated by way of a sandbar at its mouth. Later a somewhat flexible and frightening but sturdy bridge, built entirely of poles and supported on cribs of poles and brush, spanned the river near its mouth. Durability of the structure was proved early in its life when a runaway team driven by a frightened girl negotiated the span at full gallop without damaging a sapling.

Travel on a north-south line followed the Vincennes Trace along the valley of the Vermilion of the Wabash and across the watershed toward the Iroquois to the point where that river turned eastward to its confluence with the Kankakee. From that place the route was more or less direct to Chicago. In the 1820's the road was followed so much by youthful Gurdon Saltonstall Hubbard from his trading post on the Iroquois that it became known as Hubbard's Trace. This energetic pioneer, later to be counted as a builder of Chicago, lived and traded with the Indians at the confluence of the Iroquois and Sugar Creek. When he was away his store was kept by his Indian wife, Watseka, for whom the

county seat of Iroquois County was named.

Much of Hubbard's travel was on horseback or by canoe along the trails first made by the Weas of central Indiana, the Potawatami, and the Kickapoo. The trace, which was to be designated a state highway only a few years later, was no way for wagons. In fact, whether the roads entered Illinois at Golconda, Shawneetown, or Mount Carmel, near Lawrenceville, Marshall, or Danville, or along the Lake Michigan shore, the problem of quagmire and bog, of mud and muck, would be most vexing for a century after Illinois became a state. The Fifteenth General Assembly gave official recognition to this fact in 1846 by authorizing organization of road associations to keep highways open in difficult river-bottom areas.

In the late 1840's a Canadian development, the plank road, reached Illinois. Soon these tollways, built of three-inch planks laid on stringers in the mud, eight feet wide and with frequent gravel turnouts, had become the recognized way of easy travel and easy money up and down the state. The volume of private legislation grew as the legislature freely gave authority to build and authorized county commissioners to fix tolls. Dividends of 30 to 40 per cent frequently were paid, without regard for a sinking fund to maintain the roadways. One of the longest plank tollways was from Milwaukee Road at Graceland in Lakeview (now part of Chicago) to Geneva by way of Elgin. Connection with Chicago was via the Northwest Plank Road from Lake Street to Dutchman's Point (Niles). There was another route along Ogden Avenue to the east branch of the Du Page River in Downers Grove township, and a southbound road from Lake Street to Blue Island. The first few miles of the Chicago-Vincennes state highway were planked from a point near present Fifty-fifth Street to the end of State Street.

The plank-road era lasted little more than a decade, with many men getting rich for a few years. Toward the end of the decade the legislature became almost as busy authorizing the sale or dismantling of plank roads as it had been authorizing their construction. By the time of the Civil War they were almost out of existence, although a few well-maintained and well-managed turnpikes were still in use at the beginning of the twentieth century.

In 1865 Illinois got its first macadamized roads built with public money. On February 16 of that year voters of the top tier of townships in Madison County elected to build free hard-surfaced roads. Two years later, February 25, 1867, the General Assembly authorized county and township governing bodies to form public corporations for construction of hard-surfaced toll highways and to sell bonds to meet the cost. This and the succeeding assembly were the last to authorize roads by private legislation, which was forbidden by the constitution of 1870. Whereas the General Assembly needed 3,351 pages for so-called private laws and about 500 for public acts, the assembly sitting in 1871, although required to rewrite many Illinois statutes to conform with constitutional provisions, managed with less than 500 pages and the succeeding assembly needed only 142 pages to record all its acts.

The basic highway legislation passed by the General Assembly sitting in 1871, and liberally amended by two succeeding assemblies, was sufficient to the needs of Illinois until the end of the nineteenth century, at which time a new factor entered the road picture throughout the country. Illinois never succumbed to the mania for legislation restricting and harassing the automobile, but the necessity for regulating self-propelled vehicles was recognized by the state's legislators. No laws such as the one passed in many states requiring a flagman with a red warning flag to walk ahead of automobiles on public highways found their way into the statutes of Illinois, but in 1903 a speed law restricted the rate of travel to fifteen miles an hour, while authorizing higher or lower speeds by order of local laws.

In addition to passing the first speed laws in the history of the state, the General Assembly in 1903 authorized the governor to appoint a "Good Roads" commission which was to inquire into materials and methods for constructing all-weather roads. Under this act twenty-five townships petitioned during the first two years to be permitted to lay out experimental roads. Most influential on future construction was the Bates Experimental Road near Springfield, where many of the state's decisions as to materials and methods were arrived at, and which continued to be used for tests well into the twenties.

A decision of lasting importance was made by the General Assembly in 1905, when it established an Illinois State Highway Commission as an arm of the executive department, and gave it broad powers over the highways of the state. This act was approved by Governor Charles S. Deneen on May 18. The initial report of the commission, late in 1906, contained the first authoritative record of highways in the state and the aggregate cost of new construction and maintenance for the year 1905. The people of Illinois learned that the state had more than 94,000 miles of public roads, that more than 7,000 miles were hard-surfaced, and that more than $4,000,000 in cash and almost $500,000 in labor were spent by counties and the state in building and repairing highways.

The first commission also reported that it found road administration inefficient, work poorly done, specifications for bridges inadequate, and money wastefully expended. Local road districts were too many and too small, the average supervisor or commissioner of highways at that level having less than twenty miles of road under his jurisdiction. Work performed under provisions of the labor tax was badly organized and expensively completed.

Out of the first two years of study by the commission came recommendations for a motor vehicle act, one of the first in the nation. This act, approved May 28, 1907, defined motor vehicles, required their registration with the office of the secretary of state, display of license numbers on vehicles, use of lamps from sunset to an hour before sunrise, and provided that lamps should carry license numbers and state identification. Speeds were limited to six miles an hour on turns, ten miles an hour in congested areas, fifteen miles an hour in other built-up areas, and twenty miles an hour on open highways. Motor vehicles were required to stop when it became apparent that horses were being frightened.

The commission also asked for and received authorization to appoint county superintendents of highways with final authority over roads in their jurisdiction. Intensive study of existing legislation and highway needs brought a recommendation at the end of 1910 for codification of existing laws, and passage of a number of additional statutes. In meeting these needs, the General Assembly established an important precedent for financing improved roads with an act approved June 10, 1911.

which directed that license fees be paid into a road fund and used only for construction and repair of roads and bridges outside cities, villages, and towns. The assembly also codified highway legislation and created a State Highway Department consisting of members of the State Highway Commission, the chief engineer of the Highway Commission, and his principal assistant. The legislation established the method of appointing county superintendents of highways and authorized state aid to county highways. County superintendents were instructed to recommend roads to be built or improved under the measure, with the state furnishing half of the necessary funds. Implementation of the act was celebrated April 15, 1914, with ground-breaking ceremonies at several points in the state.

The cry for good roads, heard throughout the country, was the result of the increased range, reliability, and usefulness of the automobile. Cross-country tours became almost a mania with many car owners. Road associations as well as city, county, and state officers were engaged in locating and marking through routes. By 1914 two transcontinental routes were on the road maps of Illinois. One, the Lincoln Highway which became U.S. 30, was completely marked. The other, the Ocean-to-Ocean Highway, which entered Illinois not far from Terre Haute, Indiana, and left the state at Quincy, was in process of being laid out. Within Illinois fifty-one roads and trails were designated, among them the Egyptian Trail from Chicago to Cairo, the Diagonal Trail from Danville to Moline, and the Lincoln Trail from Vincennes to St. Louis. The act of designating and marking, however, did not make them easily passable. Help from the federal government was needed, and it was on the way. In 1912 the postmaster general persuaded President William Howard Taft to cause a study to be made of the efficiency of the rural mail carrier in an area served by hard roads, compared with his efficiency in a rural community served only by earth roads. President Taft asked for a commission of five senators and five representatives to direct and evaluate the study, and the Congress gave it to him, together with $500,000 to finance hard roads in selected areas in cooperation with state highway departments. The survey required four years. The findings were conclusive.

On July 11, 1916, President Woodrow Wilson signed an act authorizing the secretary of agriculture to cooperate with the

states through their respective highway departments in construction of rural post roads. A post road was so defined that almost any public highway in Illinois qualified for the state's share of a federal appropriation of $75,000,000 to be spent over a period of five years. The statute required formal acceptance by state legislatures, an agreement to maintain the roads constructed or improved by aid of federal funds, and obliged the states to obtain approval of the secretary of agriculture for plans, specifications, and surveys. The federal cost was to be 50 per cent. Later a limit cost per mile was established and frequently amended as requirements for qualifying roads became stiffer and overall costs of highway work increased.

With this considerable sum of money just over the horizon—Illinois' share for the five-year period would be several million—and with income from license fees increasing, the General Assembly, acting on recommendations of Governor Frank O. Lowden, approved an act that was to accomplish much in getting Illinois out of the mud. The legislation asked for a referendum at the next general election to approve a bond issue of $60,000,000 to be used over a period of several years for constructing hard roads, and designated forty-six state highways to be built with the bond money, the unappropriated portions of license income, and whatever portion of federal funds was applicable to the system. The bonds were approved by a large margin and Illinois highways 1 to 46 were laid out.

Two succeeding General Assemblies codified laws regulating motor vehicle traffic, limited weights and dimensions of trucks and buses using state highways, authorized policing of highways by state officers, and accepted federal aid in building the primary highway system, directing that such aid be paid into the general road fund. The Division of Highways, Department of Public Works and Buildings, was given supervision of all roads constructed in whole or in part with state or federal funds. During the next ten years the federal appropriation for Illinois highway costs would be $19,082,899.14.

In 1923 the General Assembly, subject to referendum, authorized issue of $100,000,000 in road bonds to aid in construction of an additional 138 state highways. Speed limit for motor cars in open country was raised to thirty-five miles an hour, and speed limits for trucks were graduated by weight, with a high speed in open country of twenty-five miles an hour for trucks weighing 5,000 pounds or less. The next piece of important legislation in the field of roads and bridges was an act approved June 29, 1927, establishing a tax of two cents a gallon on motor fuel used on the highways. During the same session of the assembly all roads constructed with state or federal aid were consolidated into the state highway system. In 1929 the legislature added a cent to the motor fuel tax, directed that it be paid into a fund used only for roads, and provided that two-thirds of the fund would be expended by the Department of Public Works and Buildings and one-third by county road authorities, in proportion to the amount of tax collected in each county. Automobile speed limits were increased to forty-five miles an hour in open country, to fifteen, twenty, and twenty-five miles an hour in urban areas. At a third special session of the General Assembly in 1932 counties were authorized to use proceeds of the motor fuel tax to pay interest on or redeem bonds issued under an emergency relief act. In 1933 the legislature divided the motor fuel tax income into thirds, one-third to the Department of Public Works and Buildings for highway use, one-third to counties, and one-third to municipalities, with cities authorized to spend the income for streets directly connecting with or related to state highways.

Counties and cities also benefited from federal funds, which from 1934 to 1940 totaled $2,368,250,000, of which Illinois received $82,451,025.90. Much of this money was included in pump-priming operations of the federal government for emergency aid.

On July 9, 1935, a new act codifying traffic regulations was approved by Governor Henry Horner. Among other things this act authorized "a reasonable and proper" speed, a provision that was to remain on the books for sixteen years, and for the first time imposed a mileage weight tax on trucks and buses. This tax measure, with several minor modifications and additions, has remained in force for more than thirty years, as has a school bus act designed to protect children boarding or alighting from school buses.

Laws regulating operation of motor trucks and buses were completely revised by the legislature in 1939 to require permit, registration, bonding, insurance, safety certification, and tests and inspection of all commercial carriers. In 1943 the General Assembly, after studying highway requirements of a wartime economy, took a careful look at the future, recognized the need for greater capacity for arterial roads, and in an act not approved by Governor Dwight H. Green but filed July 29, 1943, authorized construction of a system of freeways. In a further act, approved by the governor July 9, the assembly created the Illinois State Superhighway Commission, a board of five members appointed by the governor from the state at large. This commission was instructed to study, plan, and construct a system of limited-access highways and / or toll roads throughout Illinois. The General Assembly also revised the basic legislation relating to roads and bridges to remove obsolete language.

The new laws were most timely and enabled Illinois to be ready when Congress passed the Highway Act of 1944, approved by President Roosevelt on December 20 of that year, which appropriated $1,500,000,000 for highway construction during the first three years after war's end, and directed the states to begin planning for postwar highway needs.

Under the act of July 29, 1943, the highway authorities of Chicago and Cook County proceeded with their plans for limited-access highways into and within the city. Chicago already had one limited-access expressway for passenger vehicles along the Outer Drive, built during the twenties in accordance with the Burnham Plan. Purchase of right-of-way for an expressway along Congress Street from the Outer Drive to the western city limits, under discussion in 1906 and authorized by an appropriation act of the city council in 1940, was begun in 1943. An offer of state aid for the expressway and extension to U.S. 45 was accepted by the aldermen in 1945. Purchase of right-of-way within the city was completed in 1949 and demolition begun. The freeway was opened in sections, beginning in 1952, and was finally completed October 12, 1960. Edens Expressway was authorized by the Board of Cook County Commissioners in 1944, so far as territory beyond Chicago was concerned, and by the city council that same year for territory within the city limits. The Northwest expressway was provided for in 1945.

During the years from the end of World War II to the middle fifties road and bridge legislation was passed chiefly by amendment to basic laws. In 1949 the General Assembly provided a new act, approved by Governor Adlai E. Stevenson August 12, 1949, which classified public roads as primary, secondary, municipal, and local, in line with new federal designations, and assigned responsibility for each class. The primary division was to be a complete and integrated system of trunk highways to serve interstate travel, connect counties, municipalities, and various regional areas. In general it would consist of the public highways having the largest volume of travel. In unincorporated areas the system would contain not less than 9,000 miles nor more than 11,000 miles of highway, plus right-of-way within incorporated places. The secondary system would form countywide networks of farm-to-market, mine-to-market, and feeder roads. During the same session of the legislature the motor fuel tax was increased to five cents a gallon.

On June 21, 1951, Governor Stevenson approved an act creating a Motor Vehicle Laws Commission consisting of five members from the House of Representatives, appointed by the speaker, and five from the Senate, appointed by the president pro tempore, to study existing laws and their administration, the construction and condition of the highways, the effect on such highways of vehicles of different sizes and weights, and to present to each succeeding assembly a comprehensive program which would permit maximum efficiency in transporting persons in times of war as well as in times of peace, while conserving and protecting the highways of Illinois.

During the next several years the commission made recommendations for amendments to existing laws, particularly the motor vehicle acts of June 30, 1919, and July 9, 1935, and, when the Seventieth General Assembly convened in January 1957, the commission presented a draft for complete revision of these two acts which was finally approved July 11, 1957, as the Illinois Motor Vehicle Law, the provisions of which are stated in another section of this chapter.

Meanwhile the General Assembly had produced several pieces of legislation of much importance to the Illinois highway program. An act approved July 13, 1953, provided for a system of toll highways within and through the state and created an Illinois State Toll Highway Commission

composed of the governor, the director of public works and buildings, and three members appointed by the governor from the state at large. The commission was empowered to issue bonds for the construction of toll highways, to bear interest of not more than 5 per cent, which would be liquidated by toll charges. When the bonds should be retired the roads would become part of the system of state highways and freeways, tolls no longer would be charged, and the roads would be maintained by the Division of Highways of the Department of Public Works and Buildings.

By 1955 a study of routes and probable revenues had indicated a system of toll roads in northern Illinois would be feasible. An issue of $415,000,000 in bonds was approved, of which $60,000,000 later was withdrawn, and after a year's delay because of litigation the sale of the bonds was completed January 23, 1956, and construction was begun July 1 of that year. Additional bonds were sold for added mileage, amounting to $94,000,000 on April 28, 1958, and in August the first section, from River Road west of Chicago to South Beloit was opened. By December the entire system was in use. It consisted of the first section opened, plus an eighty-three-mile toll road from a junction with the Calumet and Kingery expressways to the Wisconsin border, and a twenty-eight-mile branch from Roosevelt Road west of U.S. 45 to Illinois highway 47, west of Aurora. Total mileage of the system is 187 miles, and it provided a high-speed bypass of Chicago which had been under discussion for many years.

Another piece of legislation, approved July 7, 1953, was the Illinois Motor Carrier of Property Act, which provided a basic law placing motor carriers under control of the Illinois Commerce Commission, classifying them as common carriers or contract carriers and establishing regulations governing licensing, bonding, and operation of such carriers in Illinois.

An amendment to the motor fuel tax statute made provision for distribution of proceeds of the tax, after administrative costs, as follows: to the Department of Public Works and Buildings, 35 per cent; to municipalities of the state, in proportion to their contribution to the tax fund, 32 per cent; to counties having a population of 500,000 or more (a euphemism for Cook County) 11 per cent; to counties having less than 500,000 population (the other 101 counties) 12 per cent; and for townships 10 per cent.

In 1954 Chicago authorities were faced with the necessity of providing access to downtown Chicago from the Indiana Toll Road soon to be opened. Its western terminus was at 106th Street and Indianapolis Boulevard at the eastern city limits of Chicago. To provide entry into Chicago a Skyway toll highway was authorized, with egress to the Outer Drive by way of Stony Island Avenue, to the Loop by way of Indiana Avenue and eventually to the Dan Ryan Expressway at Sixty-third Street. This seven-mile road on stilts, with a bridge over the Calumet River high above the masts of ocean-going steamships, was completed at a cost of more than $100,000,000, derived from a Skyway bond issue. It was opened April 16, 1958.

When the General Assembly convened in January 1957, it met with an emergency and an opportunity that required immediate action. During the previous year Congress had passed legislation providing for a system of interstate and defense highways at a cost in excess of $25,000,000,000. The federal government was to pay 90 per cent of the cost, the states 10 per cent, and the states were to obligate themselves to maintain the highways in perpetuity. An act was introduced into the General Assembly accepting the plan so far as it concerned Illinois and appropriating $70,000,000 for immediate needs. On approval of the bill March 29, 1957, by Governor Wliliam G. Stratton, Illinois became a participant in the interstate highway system. The following highways were approved for Illinois.

Interstate 24 from a point near Paducah, Kentucky, to the junction of I-57 and Ill. 148 near Pulley's Mill in Williamson County. This highway originates at Nashville, Tennessee.

Interstate 55 from Chicago via Springfield and St. Louis to Cape Girardeau, Missouri; Memphis, Tennessee; Jackson, Mississippi; and New Orleans, Louisiana.

Interstate 57 from Chicago via Kankakee, Champaign, Effingham, Mount Vernon, and Cairo to a junction with I-55 at Sikeston, Missouri.

Interstate 64 from the Wabash near Grayville to St. Louis. This route originates at Norfolk, Virginia, and proceeds by way of Richmond, Virginia; Charleston, West Virginia; and Louisville, Kentucky, to a junction with I-70 at St. Louis.

Interstate 70 from Terre Haute, Indiana, to St. Louis. This highway, the old National Road, originates at Baltimore, Maryland, and crosses the greater portion of the United States via Cumberland, Maryland; Washington, Pennsylvania; Wheeling, West Virginia; Columbus and Dayton, Ohio; Indianapolis, Indiana, into Illinois, thence via Kansas City, Missouri, and Denver, Colorado, to join the north-south Interstate 15 at Salina, Utah, for travel to Las Vegas, Nevada, and Los Angeles, California.

Interstate 74 from Danville to Moline. This highway originates at Cincinnati, Ohio, and will join I-80 near Moline.

Interstate 80 from the Indiana line on the Kingery Expressway to Moline by way of Joliet and La Salle. The highway originates in New York City, proceeds across central Pennsylvania to Youngstown, Ohio, thence via the Ohio and Indiana toll roads and the Tri-State highway into Illinois. From Moline the road passes through Iowa City and Des Moines, Iowa; Omaha, Nebraska; Cheyenne, Wyoming; Salt Lake City, Utah; and Reno, Nevada, to San Francisco, California. This is the second longest continuous highway of the interstate and national defense system.

Interstate 90, longest of the interstates, enters Illinois via the Skyway, proceeds by way of the Dan Ryan and Eisenhower expressways to the Northwest toll road near Elk Grove Village and thence to the Wisconsin line at South Beloit. The highway originates in Boston, Massachusetts, enters the New York toll road at Albany and proceeds via the New York, Ohio, and Indiana toll roads to Illinois. From the Wisconsin line the road is routed across the state to Madison and La Crosse, thence across the Mississippi River, through Minnesota to Sioux Falls, South Dakota; Sheridan, Wyoming; Billings and Missoula, Montana; Coeur d'Alène, Idaho, to Spokane and Seattle, Washington.

Interstate 94, which originates at Port Huron, Michigan, reaches Illinois via Detroit, Battle Creek, and St. Joseph, Michigan; and the Tri-State highway to the Kingery Expressway. It follows the Calumet and Dan Ryan expressways, the Kennedy and Edens expressways to the Cook County line, thence to toll highway I-294, which then becomes I-94. The road continues to Milwaukee, Madison, and Eau Claire, Wisconsin: St. Paul, Minnesota; Fargo and Bismarck, North Dakota; and Glendive and Billings, Montana, where it joins I-90.

Because of provisions of the federal legislation which required that work be carried on across the entire system simultaneously, I-94, I-270, and I-294 were the only interstates finished within Illinois at the end of 1967.

While the interstate system was taking shape, Illinois legislators were busying themselves with the revision and codification of highway and motor vehicle legislation. On July 11, 1957, Governor Stratton approved a bill entitled the Illinois Motor

Vehicle Law, which completely revised and brought up-to-date the motor vehicle act of July 9, 1935, as amended. This legislation resulted from studies of the Motor Vehicle Laws Commission, initiated in 1951. The succeeding General Assembly occupied itself with codification of laws relating to roads and bridges into an Illinois Highway Code approved by the governor June 8, 1959, which brought highway laws into line with the vigorous program for interstates, primary highways, and secondary farm-to-market and mine-to-market roads. This legislation again accepted the aid of the federal government for interstate and defense highways, restated provisions for laying out, constructing, widening, altering, and vacating public highways and bridges; methods of financing, sale and retirement of bonds, and all other matters relating to the administration of state, county, and township roads.

Illinois, in prior legislation, had already made safety belts and some other safety devices mandatory, and amendments to the act of 1935 already approved were included in the new Highway Code. This legislation paved the way for Illinois' participation in a compact with other states relating to motor vehicle safety equipment. When a joint resolution in Congress approved by President Johnson August 28, 1965, ordered all states receiving highway federal aid to prepare safety programs to be approved by the secretary of commerce, Illinois already was nearing completion of a more-than-adequate program. Within days after the secretary of commerce issued his directive the Illinois plan was ready. Before the end of the year it had been approved. In January 1966 contracts were let for eliminating hazards for 50 of the 235 specific locations on the primary system and 159 on the secondary system and more than $14,000,000 authorized for expenditure in 1966. The authorization for 1967 was more than $18,000,000. When the first stages of the program are completed in 1969, all designated hazards will have been remedied at a cost of $87,000,000, divided between the state and federal governments.

Meanwhile construction of superhighways not eligible for the 90 per cent bracket of federal aid had proceeded, especially in the Chicago metropolitan area. The Congress Street expressway is completed as far as the north limits of Elmhurst. It will be continued to the Northwest Tollway. This expressway was named for President Eisenhower on January 10, 1964, when the

northwest one was named for President Kennedy and the south one for Dan Ryan, former president of the Board of Cook County Commissioners. The southwest expressway, named for Governor Adlai E. Stevenson in 1965, was completed to the Dan Ryan in 1964 and to the Outer Drive in the fall of 1966.

Studies for a west side expressway were sufficiently matured in 1966 for the highway program for 1967 to carry a $1,000,000 appropriation for acquisition of right-of-way. This new expressway, to be called I-494, will follow Cicero Avenue from a point near the junction of the John F. Kennedy and Edens expressways to Forty-seventh Street. Thence it will continue, probably in a direct line, to a junction with the Dan Ryan at Sixty-third Street. At some future time it may be extended along Cicero Avenue to the Tri-State Tollway and eventually to I-57.

In the East St. Louis area construction is well under way on both I-55 and I-70. Interstate 55 has been completed from the end of the Stevenson expressway southwest of Chicago to a junction with U.S. 66, south of Joliet, and in the vicinity of Bloomington and Springfield. At the end of 1967, I-70 had been completed between Montrose and Vandalia.

During 1967 a total of $268,500,000 was scheduled to be spent on primary highways in Illinois. Of this amount $195,941,000 is in federal aid, $57,895,000 in state funds, and $14,664,000 in funds of other agencies, chiefly Cook County. Roads to benefit were selected from projects to the amount of $203,000,000 approved by the Federal Bureau of Roads for interstate highways, and $88,934,000 for other highways. Most of the money (anywhere from a third to a half) was scheduled to go toward completion of I-57, which in addition benefited from Cook County funds expended during the year on the west leg of the Dan Ryan south from 103rd Street. Next largest amount of federal and state funds was earmarked for I-70, on which more than $39,000,000 of projects have been approved. For I-64 more than $19,000,000 had obtained federal approval by the end of 1966 for consideration during 1967. A small but significant portion of the 1967 money was programmed for beautification of highways. Of a total of $4,300,000 more than half had been earmarked for rest areas.

Non urban road mileage and maintenance cost for 1905

County	Public roads			Highway bridges	Cash expenditures		Money value of labor tax	Total cost in money and labor for roads and bridges
	Total mileage	Miles of gravel and macadam	Per-centage gravel and macadam		Road construction and repairs	Roads and bridges		
Adams	1,543	161	10.4%	$20,275	$27,867	$48,142	$1,551	$49,693
Alexander	427	20	4.7	500	11,823	12,323	1,281	13,604
Bond	674	1	0.0	7,962	13,419	21,381	606	21,987
Boone	510	227	44.5	8,954	18,030	26,984	5,300	32,284
Brown	462			2,734	9,650	12,384	2,539	14,923
Bureau	1,583	477	28.2	42,344	49,784	92,128	7,503	99,631
Calhoun	288	2	0.1	2,654	6,129	8,783	2,779	11,562
Carroll	807	42	5.2	24,813	51,329	76,142	3,540	79,682
Cass	523			3,411	17,091	20,502	679	21,181
Champaign	1,830	5	0.3	33,155	56,959	90,114	6,007	96,121
Christian	1,351	14	1.0	24,126	22,812	46,938	14,265	61,203
Clark	1,063	43	4.0	9,835	25,622	35,457	10,494	45,951
Clay	922			8,820	7,755	16,575	3,230	19,805
Clinton	704			13,575	14,103	27,678	3,860	31,538
Coles	897	23	2.6	12,879	20,690	33,569	3,300	36,869
Cook	1,450	734	50.6	47,828	20,821	68,649		68,649
Crawford	715	10	1.4	8,447	16,600	25,047	4,374	29,421
Cumberland	687	5	0.7	6,655	11,865	18,520	8,120	26,640
De Kalb	1,096	392	35.8	32,560	37,199	69,759	4,589	74,348
De Witt	737			5,015	27,901	32,916	200	33,116
Douglas	709			12,065	11,231	29,296	3,665	32,961
Du Page	629	392	62.3	13,124	39,914	53,038	1,650	54,688
Edgar	1,187	212	17.9	13,820	53,565	67,385	4,972	72,357
Edwards	460			4,009	5,694	9,703	1,772	11,475
Effingham	930	2	0.2	14,466	8,610	23,076	4,685	27,761
Fayette	1,163	4	0.3	17,226	19,610	36,836	5,112	41,948
Ford	785	85	10.8	25,091	31,028	56,119	9,686	65,805
Franklin	740	2	0.3	6,611	8,072	14,683	2,372	17,055
Fulton	1,698	1	0.0	22,989	24,493	47,482	8,459	55,941
Gallatin	491			4,813	7,392	12,205	2,160	14,365
Greene	805		0.0	14,184	16,589	30,773	4,150	34,923

Grundy	41,691	600	41,091	20,962	20,129	9.5	71	748
Hamilton	12,201	2,662	9,539	6,628	2,911			744
Hancock	86,663	7,765	78,898	22,719	56,179	1.9	22	1,178
Hardin	5,638	1,353	4,285	3,803	482			245
Henderson	19,494	664	18,830	9,780	9,050	0.0	3	607
Henry	61,630	3,505	58,125	30,225	27,900	3.0	58	1,430
Iroquois	100,351	12,917	87,434	42,493	44,941	0.5	4	1,919
Jackson	34,331	4,133	30,198	17,016	13,182			871
Jasper	17,756	6,551	11,205	6,120	5,085			844
Jefferson	31,861	9,606	22,255	13,438	8,817	0.3	2	1,174
Jersey	18,772	1,405	17,367	7,699	9,668	4.5	47	598
JoDaviess	41,160	8,128	33,032	15,193	17,839			1,034
Johnson	11,255	2,480	8,775	3,675	5,100			605
Kane	54,275	6,300	47,975	30,705	17,270	74.6	724	971
Kankakee	67,978	6,877	61,101	33,086	28,015	12.2	138	1,127
Kendall	37,193	3,500	33,693	20,075	13,618	45.7	242	530
Knox	39,465	1,920	37,545	16,764	20,781	0.4	3	743
Lake	53,582	8,434	45,148	30,209	14,939	34.1	285	835
La Salle	181,013	5,860	175,153	105,099	70,054	24.0	461	1,919
Lawrence	21,309	2,092	19,217	10,348	8,869	3.9	25	636
Lee	74,286	5,688	68,598	37,135	31,463	11.4	135	1,189
Livingston	110,981	21,839	89,142	48,278	40,864	3.9	68	1,734
Logan	92,214	2,500	80,714	43,196	46,518	0.5	5	1,014
McDonough	50,621	3,558	47,063	24,413	22,650			1,196
McHenry	54,483	1,500	52,983	35,907	17,076	54.6	619	1,134
McLean	104,033	5,381	98,652	45,133	53,519	5.1	106	2,069
Macon	50,506	1,110	49,396	32,748	16,648	6.0	61	1,025
Macoupin	57,844	8,544	49,300	25,751	23,549			1,369
Madison	92,938	6,344	86,594	43,693	42,901	1.7	26	1,509
Marion	23,066	7,763	15,303	7,371	7,932	0.2	2	1,145
Marshall	33,171	1,850	31,321	20,215	11,106	7.3	46	634
Mason	34,450	950	33,500	14,401	19,099			771
Massac	12,786	2,000	10,786	9,606	1,180	11.1	45	403
Menard	15,246	1,607	13,639	4,301	9,338			411
Mercer	56,823	4,320	52,503	20,691	31,812	2.7	19	904
Monroe	17,567	3,824	13,743	10,131	3,612	0.2	3	703
Montgomery	45,358	5,284	40,074	15,638	24,236			1,220
Morgan	32,444	555	31,889	18,419	13,470			832
Moultrie	36,641	10,550	26,091	5,357	20,734			551
Ogle	93,929	4,179	89,750	37,905	51,845	14.1	172	1,222

County	Public roads			Cash expenditures			Money value of labor tax	Total cost in money and labor for roads and bridges
	Total mileage	Miles of gravel and macadam	Per-centage gravel and macadam	Highway bridges	Road construction and repairs	Roads and bridges		
Peoria	983	222	22.6	45,205	28,069	73,274	4,275	77,549
Perry	668			5,035	10,745	15,780	3,945	19,725
Piatt	621	51	3.8	21,952	15,950	37,902	1,396	39,298
Pike	1,347	7	1.5	17,078	12,760	29,838	2,807	32,645
Pope	465	4	0.1	204	9,133	9,337	5,477	14,814
Pulaski	346	34	11.8	4,438	6,139	10,577	3,074	13,651
Putnam	287	10	1.0	4,800	6,740	11,540	700	12,240
Randolph	974			9,548	13,805	23,353	6,532	29,885
Richland	770			5,450	4,407	9,857	3,135	12,992
Rock Island	784	30	3.8	15,893	20,658	36,551	10,852	47,403
St. Clair	1,139	26	2.3	31,987	34,905	66,892	1,733	68,625
Saline	354			3,461	7,682	11,143	5,708	16,851
Sangamon	1,220	1	0.0	16,571	37,419	53,990	7,908	61,898
Schuyler	736	4	0.5	13,604	13,406	27,010	10,570	37,580
Scott	440			4,584	8,513	13,097	605	13,702
Shelby	1,575	1	0.0	29,400	26,808	56,208	14,750	70,958
Stark	443	2	0.5	11,365	11,208	22,573	1,085	23,658
Stephenson	959	93	9.7	23,147	15,724	38,871	12,724	51,595
Tazewell	998	50	5.0	26,253	23,138	49,391	821	50,212
Union	626	23	3.7	1,889	12,110	13,999	3,115	17,114
Vermilion	1,598	188	11.8	53,865	66,625	120,490	6,900	127,390
Wabash	401			6,585	4,819	11,404	2,231	13,635
Warren	1,045	6	0.6	22,564	22,100	44,664	1,625	46,289
Washington	772			6,338	10,980	17,318	2,205	19,523
Wayne	1,263			11,184	9,500	20,684	7,144	27,828
White	600			8,645	11,904	20,549	6,430	26,979
Whiteside	1,120	179	16.0	38,954	34,425	73,379	9,057	82,436
Will	1,534	343	22.4	42,992	46,327	89,319	8,392	97,711
Williamson	587			4,283	13,221	17,504	4,768	22,272
Winnebago	931	367	39.4	31,485	48,398	79,883	3,200	83,083
Woodford	896	7	0.1	20,644	12,287	32,931	8,401	41,332
Total	94,141	7,864	8.3%	$1,888,724	$2,240,078	$4,125,802	$490,563	$4,625,365

During 1968 the Illinois section of I-80 was opened, completing a limited-access route from the east coast almost to the Missouri River north of Council Bluffs, Iowa. New sections of I-57 were readied and progress was made on I-64, I-70 and I-74. An extension of the Illinois tollway westward from Aurora was in the planning stage. Planning for the future of the primary highways of Illinois, beyond the interstate system, is now in the hands of a commission created by the General Assembly in 1963, which includes five senators, five

representatives, and seven public members. The commission was ordered to study public roads and streets in Illinois, to classify them into systems according to their functional characteristics, and to analyze existing practices and future needs. Special emphasis is to be given to requirements of urban areas. The commission made an interim report to the General Assembly in 1965.

Pavement mileage constructed by the state and by the counties, cities, and townships under state supervision, 1914–67

Year	State construction			County construction	City work	Total state, county, and city work[3]	Township work[3]
	Federal-aid interstate[1]	Primary	Secondary[2]				
1914				53.58		53.58	
1915				100.27		100.27	
1916				135.41		135.41	
1917				184.38		184.38	
1918		6.77		93.36		100.13	
1919		152.54		102.06		254.60	
1920		270.60		94.92		365.52	
1921		285.62		128.32		413.94	
1922		546.95		194.15		741.10	
1923		858.31		226.71		1,085.02	
1924		1,018.21		211.27		1,229.48	
1925		786.86		119.54		906.40	
1926		361.79		101.95		463.74	
1927		522.98		145.46		668.44	
1928		1,075.27		229.48		1,304.75	
1929		629.51		126.11		755.62	
1930		790.22		291.17		1,081.39	
1931		759.87		663.67		1,423.54	
1932		726.86		818.57		1,545.43	
1933		730.55	10.97	513.10		1,254.62	
1934		287.91	275.10	397.53	90.55	1,051.09	
1935		287.35	176.75	399.00	136.94	1,000.04	
1936		154.69	230.01	752.69	228.53	1,365.92	
1937		284.63	131.26	649.00	299.69	1,364.58	
1938		392.91	228.03	780.92	263.42	1,665.28	
1939		309.96	163.68	726.43	293.20	1,493.27	
1940		268.55	131.31	677.74	276.13	1,353.73	
1941		295.04	102.12	740.50	251.36	1,389.02	
1942		300.31	131.35[4]	443.53	147.26	1,022.45	
1943		315.67	127.70[4]	320.34	87.31	851.02	
1944		380.38	175.85[4]	257.41	98.62	912.26	
1945		224.62	56.02[4]	204.74	71.12	556.50	
1946		250.37	87.46	222.10	100.33	660.26	8,176.94[6]
1947		311.32[5]	159.51	293.88	133.96	898.67	8,504.41[6]
1948		324.14[5]	487.38	270.40	136.77	1,218.69	6,419.33[6]
1949		434.13[5]	298.41	353.79	181.58	1,267.91	7,047.57[6]
1950		295.70[5]	164.73	354.40	160.48	975.31	
1951		756.97[5]	150.92	343.94	166.70	1,418.53	
1952		1,441.27[5]	460.47	438.28	200.31	2,540.33	642.70[6]
1953		872.12[5]	562.19	323.34	230.61	1,988.26	1,666.29[6]

Table—continued

Year	State construction			County construction	City work	Total state, county, and city work[3]	Township work[3]
	Federal-aid interstate[1]	Primary	Secondary[2]				
1954		741.82[5]	343.49	267.73	204.23	1,557.27	1,809.58[6]
1955		371.86[5]	535.69	331.65	301.34	1,540.54	2,018.60[6]
1956		560.61[5]	491.05	334.19	258.78	1,644.63	1,646.61[6]
1957		510.96[5]	524.93	273.17	213.67	1,522.73	1,753.53[6]
1958	37.37	1,035.49[5]	588.33	238.95	244.26	2,144.40	1,612.23[6]
1959	40.77	648.20[5]	672.36	346.09	208.17	1,915.59	1,563.98[6]
1960	95.19	611.55[5]	545.15	291.76	224.96	1,768.61	1,451.23[6]
1961	45.94	571.20[5]	457.84	255.12	196.84	1,526.94	1,301.17[6]
1962	73.71	639.83[5]	484.14	271.46	226.49	1,695.63	1,106.77[6]
1963	86.34	616.65[5]	428.64	212.43	258.97	1,603.03	963.06[6]
1964	89.84	399.89[5]	352.55	193.68	272.00	1,307.96	1,003.63[6]
1965	69.98	364.10[5]	255.84	188.98	136.93	1,015.83	722.99[6]
1966	62.08	222.95[5]	218.47	229.60	204.17	936.27	852.76[6]
1967	64.19	233.92[5]	117.11	181.83	177.70	774.75	675.62[6]
Total	665.41	25,239.98	10,326.81	17,100.08	6,683.38	60,014.66	50,939.00

[1] Previous to 1958, interstate work was included in the column showing primary mileage.
[2] Includes surfacing constructed with state and federal funds on state-aid or federal-aid secondary routes, access roads not on the state system, and mileage built in state parks, state institutions, etc.
[3] Oiled earth, and grading not included.
[4] Includes access roads not on the state system.
[5] Includes full-width portland cement concrete base course and widening of existing portland cement concrete pavement prior to surfacing with bituminous concrete. Mileage of base course and widening (most of which has been surfaced with bituminous concrete) was as follows: 1947—5.77 miles; 1948—6.86 miles; 1949—40.35 miles; 1950—73.29 miles; 1951—284.24 miles; 1952—551.15 miles; 1953—294.97 miles; 1954—252.05 miles; 1955—81.51 miles; 1956—117.84 miles; 1957—105.35 miles; 1958—174.40 miles; 1959—94.78 miles; 1960—81.04 miles; 1961—60.03 miles; 1962—70.69 miles; 1963—47.07 miles; 1964—28.30 miles; 1965—19.32 miles; 1966—19.12 miles; 1967—7.20 miles.
[6] The figures for 1946 through 1952 are the mileages approved for construction and those for 1953 through 1967 are the mileages actually constructed.

Status of work on federal-aid interstate routes in Illinois at December 31, 1967

FAI route	Miles opened to traffic		Miles under construction	Status of remaining mileage			Total miles
	Open	Toll		Right-of-way being acquired	Plans being prepared	Location under way	
24				37.46	0.47		37.93
55	234.27		0.31	3.36	15.08	17.97	270.99
57	138.57		129.21	84.73	0.20		352.71
64			1.57	86.35	35.12		123.04
70	93.95		27.26	39.04			160.25
74	114.38	0.74	33.19	65.85			214.16
80	129.26	4.83	29.44				163.53
90	19.98	73.41	0.55	9.07	2.85		105.86
94	46.31	28.58					74.89
180			12.36	0.79			13.15
255	2.31			7.80	9.24		19.35
270	14.97						14.97
280	2.81		4.42	0.55	0.35		8.13
294		48.10					48.10
474				14.54			14.54
494						20.87	20.87
Total	796.81	155.66	238.31	349.54	63.31	38.84	1,642.47

Motor vehicles registered in Illinois, 1911–67, by number of vehicles

Year	Passenger cars	Trucks and buses	Motor-cycles	Trailers	Dealers' licenses	Chauffeur registrations
1911	39,269		4,346			
1912	68,012		9,238		874	8,162
1913	94,646		12,183		1,041	13,153
1914	131,140		14,852		1,198	17,827
1915	180,832		15,710		1,458	22,995
1916	248,429		14,931		2,671	33,022
1917	340,292		13,740		3,745	43,679
1918	389,701		10,834		3,548	45,096
1919	478,438		10,920		4,960	53 123
1920	503,762	65,307	10,597		6,282	69,365
1921	583,441	80,031	8,935		7,041	69,226
1922	682,250	99,876	7,871		4,214	56,789
1923	847,005	122,282	7,612		4,516	92,871
1924	981,859	141,706	6,873	2,044	4,488	96,924
1925	1,101,943	161,234	6,603	3,777	4,557	99,372
1926	1,195,014	175,489	6,156	3,350	4,688	102,849
1927	1,254,421	184,564	6,135	3,489	4,594	100,398
1928	1,314,003	190,356	5,826	3,742	4,548	94,169
1929	1,410,913	204,175	6,055	5,068	4,605	106,551
1930	1,429,146	209,114	6,245	7,341	4,368	108,538
1931	1,411,261	201,509	5,811	9,283	3,883	93,056
1932	1,311,783	181,715	5,274	8,950	3,266	70,788
1933	1,276,864	186,186	4,959	9,228	2,922	66,559
1934	1,285,434	178,496	4,766	10,792	3,449	70,584
1935	1,342,904	190,843	5,291	14,636	3,896	78,931
1936	1,459,195	208,926	5,924	18,408	3,963	90,228
1937	1,556,702	220,639	6,490	23,475	4,329	97,573
1938	1,567,775	222,582	6,848	23,396	4,199	88,974
1939	1,626,689	232,888	7,227	25,296	4,363	123,313
1940	1,707,512	228,889	7,742	29,349	4,679	135,299
1941	1,825,142	234,703	7,672	32,236	4,862	141,199
1942	1,747,253	233,386	9,242	30,429	3,742	141,680
1943	1,592,837	221,634	8,247	26,014	3,282	125,576
1944	1,518,629	216,930	8,381	26 371	3 904	125,182
1945	1,508,222	224,929	8,834	31,776	4,595	142,714
1946	1,614,490	254,059	16,016	45,998	6,332	193,854
1947	1,753,109	291,773	22,506	51,810	7,028	214,618
1948	1,904,991	317,048	30,369	56,365	7,603	232,637
1949	2,078,704	336,044	28,627	56,943	7,349	242,192
1950	2,286,572	362,975	26,682	60,776	7,347	252,993
1951	2,407,130	382,335	24,782	64,971	7,560	262,366
1952	2,458,462	382,873	24,020	68,222	7,783	267,150
1953	2,580,668	377,073	23,637	72,699	7,941	270,046
1954	2,694,253	393,045	22,880	80,545	7,680	267,115
1955	2,858,869	409,217	23,263	90,249	7,868	270,500
1956	2,984,584	423,910	24,004	104,549	8,321	300,146
1957	3,076,362	436,382	24,755	116,493	8,502	298,746
1958	3,127,657	441,880	33,436	131,524	9,174	301,185
1959	3,221,902	457,633	27,904	146,319	9,015	297,064
1960	3,312,800	464,447	26,123	158,316	8,850	299,497
1961	3,389,608	469,910	25,617	167,968	8,828	297,390
1962	3,496,232	481,897	27,091	179,684	8,562	305,764
1963	3,607,545	496,261	30,131	200,160	8,596	307,116
1964	3,744,086	514,156	37,043	218,030	8,760	314,173
1965	3,902,342	538,740	56,753	238,741	8,811	321,632
1966	4,025,773	565,667	81,688	268,636	7,116	332,124
1967	4,206,628	592,300	93,867	289,471	6,927	340,121

Year	Motor license and operators' license fees	Federal aid	Miscellaneous	Motor fuel tax[1]	Total
1911	$74,552.59				$74,552.59
1912	364,708.03				364,708.03
1913	499,802.45				499,802.45
1914	700,233.00				700,233.00
1915	903,284.09				903,284.09
1916	1,238,483.92				1,238,483.92
1917	1,629,445.26				1,629,445.26
1918	2,770,084.60		$85.00		2,770,169.60
1919	3,236,448.71	$527,709.65	1,443.50		3,765,601.86
1920	5,856,044.48	5,197,089.40	58,861.68		11,111,995.56
1921	6,862,125.83	3,802,430.46	221,645.55		10,886,201.84
1922	7,904,219.71	1,733,334.86	132,495.77		9,770,050.34
1923	9,689,702.77	4,257,276.06	135,485.61		14,082,464.44
1924	11,557,838.94	3,565,058.69	300,045.58		15,422,943.21
1925	13,050,977.39	2,717,923.43	514,260.69		16,283,161.51
1926	13,937,579.64	2,036,921.95	214,330.36		16,188,831.95
1927	15,589,365.19	2,997,912.78	216,671.59	$3,953,047.72	22,756,997.28
1928	15,069,830.33	4,054,652.00	425,556.10	2,439,728.14	21,989,766.57
1929	17,035,596.03	3,482,065.67	454,193.15		20,971,854.85
1930	18,353,865.44	4,089,891.72	347,066.64	14,813.95	22,805,637.75
1931	19,201,521.14	10,063,542.21	293,793.69	36,530.40	29,595,387.44
1932	16,812,097.50	4,888,086.14	195,232.94	502,762.35	22,398,178.93
1933	15,544,501.29	7,271,723.92	272,550.28		23,088,775.49
1934	18,189,190.93	13,663,956.76	178,430.17		32,031,577.86
1935	19,988,807.85	8,880,882.56	197,548.18		29,067,238.59
1936	18,685,682.83	18,449,527.07	180,772.26		37,315,982.16
1937	21,283,188.44	15,648,505.31	299,437.77		37,231,131.52
1938	21,754,616.24	9,194,477.62	231,517.19		31,180,611.05
1939	24,678,040.42	7,283,227.14	604,474.51		32,565,742.07
1940	24,037,765.01	9,330,449.44	637,548.51		34,005,762.96
1941	25,852,799.98	5,586,877.20	591,285.65		32,030,962.83
1942	23,771,384.62	3,970,309.57	527,099.93		28,268,794.12
1943	24,037,431.29	7,182,876.22	159,735.91		31,380,043.42
1944	22,942,106.55	2,717,935.17	140,916.12[3]		25,800,957.84
1945	23,396,891.33	1,405,921.39	496,090.29[4]		25,298,903.01
1946	27,917,192.83	2,754,479.49	295,731.69		30,967,404.01
1947	30,492,814.24	6,227,802.26	993,400.15		37,714,016.65
1948	32,892,386.26	14,827,994.23	2,645,795.30		50,366,175.79
1949	41,986,130.32	15,526,936.34	2,693,251.72	9,809,067.97	70,015,386.35
1950	40,437,007.68	14,553,825.13	1,762,456.26	19,632,478.32	76,385,767.39
1951	44,607,331.92	18,413,925.26	907,511.57	20,018,519.39	83,947,288.14
1952	52,327,170.57	26,908,982.94	2,546,878.69	27,448,212.23	109,231,244.43
1953	69,647,775.00	25,800,389.22	6,700,031.16	38,636,458.54	140,784,653.92
1954	71,942,193.55	26,955,333.75	5,014,534.97	38,518,698.60	142,430,760.87
1955	74,929,696.50	35,140,812.81	6,730,105.38	43,289,613.36	160,090,228.05
1956	86,103,830.45	32,445,599.00	7,088,621.34	43,701,119.35	169,339,170.14
1957	89,472,754.46	32,899,818.43	8,221,293.43	45,611,615.12	176,205,481.44
1958	95,583,744.21	107,089,299.33	7,477,916.44	46,864,864.08	257,015,824.06
1959	94,745,386.67	183,086,159.17	9,451,191.46	48,518,034.89	335,800,772.19
1960	98,704,381.89	186,893,487.35	8,704,826.48	49,608,695.65	343,911,391.37
1961	100,729,647.65	133,343,534.61	9,130,007.87	50,882,962.17	294,086,152.30
1962	110,755,846.75	162,916,652.73	12,223,553.41	52,452,213.22	338,348,266.11
1963	110,081,741.53	163,360,224.89	10,138,266.55	54,162,002.78	337,742,235.75
1964	113,807,987.13	248,027,456.42	11,815,655.94	56,609,269.60	430,260,369.07
1965	132,742,182.43	137,477,854.09	11,327,426.49	60,486,545.03	342,034,008.04
1966	134,140,443.66	151,856,052.04	15,635,944.25	63,519,841.36	365,152,281.31
Total	$2,120,547,859.52	$1,890,507,183.88	$149,532,975.17	$776,717,094.20	$4,937,305,122.77

[1] Revenue received prior to 1933 consists of 1927 gas tax receipts, subsequent to 1933 consists of 1929 motor fuel tax collections deposited in road fund.

[2] The $21,526,300.00 shown consists of $17,624,000.00 from the $60M issue and $3,902,300.00 from the $100M issue. All bond fund receipts before 1924 are from the $60M issue and after 1924 from the $100M issue.

[3] Does not agree with figure published in 1944 annual report because of auditing adjustments.

for highway purposes, 1911–66

Bond funds $60M and $100M issues	Motor fuel tax fund	Grade crossing protection fund	Trust fund	General revenue fund allocations for highway purposes	Total
					$74,552.59
					364,708.03
				$48,747.07	548,549.52
				100,938.11	801,171.11
				140,903.07	1,044,187.16
				236,651.02	1,475,134.94
				69,529.12	1,698,974.38
					2,770,169.60
					3,765,601.86
					11,111,995.56
$4,709,477.78					15,595,679.62
12,023,966.76					21,794,017.10
24,100,867.70					38,183,332.14
21,526,300.00[2]					36,949,243.21
19,630,300.00					35,913,461.51
4,953,100.00				4,863.73	21,146,795.68
12,157,100.00				34,559.44	34,948,656.72
35,048,600.00				296,531.80	57,334,898.37
19,566,600.00	$1,616,185.06			374,021.42	42,520,661.33
	34,175,312.05			167,425.43	57,148,375.23
	30,222,440.40			223,585.88	60,041,413.72
1,983,500.00	29,060,264.01			27,801.78	53,469,744.72
	30,920,366.65			23,918.20	54,033,060.34
	31,006,380.09				63,037,957.95
	31,771,511.28				60,838,749.87
	35,433,014.14				72,748,996.30
	38,950,820.29				76,181,951.81
	39,536,348.09				70,716,959.14
	42,327,572.43				74,893,314.50
	45,286,015.72				79,291,778.68
	48,648,263.73				80,679,226.56
	44,584,819.98				72,853,614.10
	34,015,607.91			221,026.40	65,616,677.73
	35,166,506.80			853,119.84	61,820,583.48
	37,486,710.53			287,265.11	63,072,878.65
	48,711,836.17			13,420,060.59	93,099,300.77
	53,801,933.48			2,187,074.84	93,703,024.97
	58,889,358.50			13,189,757.18	122,445,291.47
	52,599,525.21			2,817,380.87	125,432,292.43
	48,530,845.50		$1,347,061.42	343,391.77	126,607,066.08
	57,836,644.17		2,471,795.73	354,071.26	144,609,799.30
	69,707,721.74		1,343,596.23	333,296.04	180,615,858.44
	87,314,714.65		376,553.62	327,836.95	228,803,759.14
	92,846,072.45		130,718.46	287,931.54	235,695,483.32
	94,336,154.26	$125,000.00		284,371.77	254,835,754.08
	98,837,789.35	300,000.00		288,821.22	268,765,780.71
	100,530,159.38	300,000.00		155,513.08	277,191,153.90
	102,479,709.73	300,000.00			359,795,533.79
	107,367,787.08	475,000.00			443,643,559.27
	108,656,774.66	600,555.49			453,168,721.52
	109,935,185.24	600,200.83			404,621,538.37
	114,017,606.59	600,074.76			452,965,947.46
	116,844,317.74[5]	600,000.00			455,186,553.49
	121,045,528.60[6]	600,000.00			551,905,897.67
	128,044,708.34[6]	903,442.21			470,982,158.59
	131,591,168.15[6]	1,200,000.00			497,943,449.46
$155,699,812.24	$2,494,133,679.15	$6,604,273.29	$5,669,725.46	$37,100,394.53	$7,636,512,997.44

[4] Includes $250,000.00 transferred from the state garage revolving fund as a reimbursement of funds advanced in 1943.

[5] Includes $210,000.00 transferred to the State Boating Act fund for the use of the Department of Conservation.

[6] Includes $504,000.00 transferred to the State Boating Act fund for the use of the Department of Conservation in 1964, 1965, and 1966 and $750,000.00 payment of judgments against the Kaneland Community Unit School District by the auditor of public accounts in 1964 only.

Levy and payment schedule for Cook County expressway bond issue

Year	Levy schedule Principal	Levy schedule Interest	Payment schedule Principal due each year	Payment schedule Interest due each year	Payment schedule Total bond service each year
1955	$2,000,000.00	$2,047,500.00			
1956	2,000,000.00	945,000.00	$2,000,000.00	$1,050,000.00	$3,050,000.00
1957	2,500,000.00	1,280,000.00	2,000,000.00	997,500.00	2,997,500.00
1958	8,250,000.00	3,664,479.17	2,500,000.00	1,332,500.00	3,832,500.00
1959	10,750,000.00	3,991,783.33	7,000,000.00	3,021,041.67	10,021,041.67
1960	14,250,000.00	5,178,450.00	9,500,000.00	3,663,958.33	13,163,958.33
1961	14,500,000.00	5,604,700.00	13,000,000.00	5,350,625.00	18,350,625.00
1962	16,000,000.00	6,109,700.00	14,000,000.00	5,356,875.00	19,356,875.00
1963	16,500,000.00	5,772,825.00	15,000,000.00	5,954,375.00	20,954,375.00
1964	16,500,000.00	4,931,575.00	16,500,000.00	5,700,000.00	22,200,000.00
1965	17,500,000.00	4,390,325.00	16,500,000.00	5,158,750.00	21,658,750.00
1966	19,500,000.00	3,799,075.00	17,500,000.00	4,617,500.00	22,117,500.00
1967	18,250,000.00	3,161,575.00	18,500,000.00	4,043,750.00	22,543,750.00
1968	15,750,000.00	2,566,250.00	19,500,000.00	3,420,625.00	22,920,625.00
1969	13,250,000.00	2,063,125.00	17,000,000.00	2,783,125.00	19,783,125.00
1970	12,000,000.00	1,653,750.00	14,500,000.00	2,230,000.00	16,730,000.00
1971	12,000,000.00	1,288,125.00	12,000,000.00	1,820,625.00	13,820,625.00
1972	12,000,000.00	922,500.00	12,000,000.00	1,455,000.00	13,455,000.00
1973	8,500,000.00	607,500.00	12,000,000.00	1,089,375.00	13,089,375.00
1974	8,500,000.00	343,125.00	8,500,000.00	723,750.00	9,223,750.00
1975	4,000,000.00	131,250.00	8,500,000.00	459,375.00	8,959,375.00
1976	500,000.00	19,375.00	4,500,000.00	195,000.00	4,695,000.00
1977			2,500,000.00	48,125.00	2,548,125.00
Total	$245,000,000.00	$60,471,987.50	$245,000,000.00	$60,471,875.00	$305,471,875.00

Percentage of total motor vehicle license fees paid by residents of each county in 1967

County	All counties	Counties other than Cook*
Adams	.816%	1.421%
Alexander	.128	.222
Bond	.200	.348
Boone	.261	.455
Brown	.094	.164
Bureau	.497	.866
Calhoun	.079	.137
Carroll	.236	.411
Cass	.219	.381
Champaign	1.318	2.296
Christian	.482	.839
Clark	.222	.386
Clay	.225	.392
Clinton	.345	.602
Coles	.690	1.203
Cook	42.592	
Crawford	.315	.548
Cumerland	.116	.203
De Kalb	.703	1.225
De Witt	.243	.423
Douglas	.279	.486
Du Page	3.231	5.627
Edgar	.303	.528
Edwards	.122	.212
Effingham	.264	.460
Fayette	.260	.453
Ford	.275	.478
Franklin	.388	.677
Fulton	.520	.906
Gallatin	.109	.189
Greene	.221	.386
Grundy	.296	.516
Hamilton	.121	.210
Hancock	.354	.617
Hardin	.061	.106
Henderson	.112	.195
Henry	.653	1.137
Iroquois	.503	.876
Jackson	.460	.801
Jasper	.151	.263
Jefferson	.383	.667
Jersey	.191	.333
JoDaviess	.211	.368
Johnson	.091	.159
Kane	2.317	4.035
Kankakee	1.043	1.818
Kendall	.262	.457
Knox	.716	1.247
Lake	2.749	4.789
La Salle	1.468	2.558
Lawrence	.221	.384
Lee	.431	.750

County	All counties	Counties other than Cook*	County	All counties	Counties other than Cook*
Livingston	.600	1.046	Union	.200	.348
Logan	.451	.785	Vermilion	1.062	1.850
McDonough	.364	.633	Wabash	.181	.316
McHenry	1.128	1.965	Warren	.272	.474
McLean	1.041	1.813	Washington	.187	.326
Macon	1.289	2.246	Wayne	.303	.528
Macoupin	.569	.991	White	.288	.501
Madison	2.222	3.870	Whiteside	.713	1.243
Marion	.476	.829	Will	2.072	3.609
Marshall	.190	.331	Williamson	.493	.859
Mason	.243	.423	Winnebago	2.287	3.983
Massac	.189	.330	Woodford	.384	.668
Menard	.149	.260			
Mercer	.219	.382	Total	100.000%	100.000%
Monroe	.194	.338			
Montgomery	.422	.736			
Morgan	.435	.759			
Moultrie	.185	.323			
Ogle	.519	.903			
Peoria	1.991	3.469			
Perry	.246	.428			
Piatt	.223	.388			
Pike	.275	.478			
Pope	.040	.070			
Pulaski	.072	.126			
Putnam	.081	.142			
Randolph	.361	.629			
Richland	.245	.426			
Rock Island	1.905	3.319			
St. Clair	2.331	4.060			
Saline	.313	.546			
Sangamon	1.575	2.744			
Schuyler	.119	.208			
Scott	.117	.203			
Shelby	.319	.555			
Stark	.125	.218			
Stephenson	.494	.860			
Tazewell	1.294	2.253			

* The 12 per cent of motor fuel tax which is allotted counties is allocated to each county on the basis of the state license fees collected in that county in comparison with those collected in all counties during the previous year. The percentages indicate the approximate share of allotments for each county in 1968.

Cook County expressway bond issue to be retired out of share of motor fuel tax

Series	Amount	Date of issue	Interest rate
A	$40,000,000	Oct. 1, 1955	$2\frac{5}{8}$%
B	10,000,000	Oct. 1, 1957	$3\frac{1}{8}$
C	25,000,000	June 1, 1958	$2\frac{3}{4}$
D	25,000,000	Dec. 1, 1958	$3\frac{3}{8}$
E	25,000,000	Nov. 1, 1959	4
F	25,000,000	May 1, 1960	$3\frac{1}{2}$
G	25,000,000	Dec. 1, 1960	$3\frac{1}{4}$
H	25,000,000	Oct. 1, 1961	$3\frac{1}{2}$
I	25,000,000	May 1, 1962	$2\frac{7}{8}$
J	20,000,000	Dec. 1, 1963	3
Total	$245,000,000		

Record of bridge work 1906–30 and annually, 1931–67

Year	Plans and specifications prepared	Contracts let on state plans	Contract price	Foreign plans approved*
1906–30	8,319	6,137	$34,692,985.27	16,987
1931	673	437	3,997,361.24	6,221
1932	683	603	3,988,988.46	7,546
1933	482	390	2,815,976.05	4,410
1934	419	299	4,547,005.88	5,020
1935	342	300	4,394,287.12	2,441
1936	319	258	7,742,110.07	3,060
1937	288	254	4,506,279.14	1,952
1938	304	236	3,921,100.75	1,050
1939	272	217	2,817,481.72	1,044
1940	266	194	2,838,897.03	832
1941	138	130	3,067,158.02	666
1942	220	106	1,104,427.66	279

Year	Plans and specifications prepared	Contracts let on state plans	Contract price	Foreign plans approved*
1943	122	62	418,753.64	198
1944	149	74	817,973.77	223
1945	110	90	1,682,640.00	226
1946	128	141	3,545,550.62	450
1947	137	135	4,767,188.35	189
1948	122	93	6,779,175.89	196
1949	90	86	4,952,839.41	132
1950	164	99	2,750,017.08	122
1951	108	130	6,566,189.53	98
1952	133	120	10,785,576.92	185
1953	109	132	9,287,045.05	218
1954	171	155	13,354,854.18	324
1955	146	146	13,850,013.76	349
1956	137	166	15,167,468.10	429
1957	139	216	38,769,316.32	350
1958	171	229	36,037,644.77	427
1959	185	197	38,445,040.49	543
1960	170	258	39,001,753.11	351
1961	172	188	34,813,839.70	372
1962	158	325	48,528,443.12	274
1963	140	232	43,727,449.23	283
1964	166	259	47,057,369.07	207
1965	200	214	37,153,437.00	209
1966	132	217	42,858,040.22	162
1967	127	231	64,143,588.20	184
Total	16,311	13,756	$645,695,265.94	58,209

Note: Included are all bridges for state and county highways whether built as independent contracts or included in the general road contracts.

* Plans prepared by county superintendents of highways and others outside of the Division of Highways.

Comparison of average weights of loaded and empty commercial vehicles for selected years, 1936–66

Vehicle type and year weighed	All vehicles		Loaded vehicles		Empty vehicles	
	Percentage distribution by type	Average weight (in pounds)	Percentage of total weighed	Average weight (in pounds)	Percentage of total weighed	Average weight (in pounds)
Single-unit trucks						
Year 1936	79.67%	7,690	63.52%	8,975	36.48%	5,452
Year 1942	71.00	9,233	54.74	11,633	45.26	6,330
Year 1959	43.53	9,299	59.41	11,518	40.59	6,034
Year 1966	38.51	8,531	38.59	11,782	61.41	6,490
Tractor-truck semitrailers						
Year 1936	18.42	22,212	79.78	24,868	20.22	11,736
Year 1942	27.56	26,000	68.48	30,676	31.52	16,144
Year 1959	55.90	38,808	72.70	45,169	27.30	21,964
Year 1966	59.87	45,527	72.22	53,162	27.78	25,672
Trailer combinations*						
Year 1936	1.91	24,588	59.26	31,881	40.74	13,982
Year 1942	1.44	25,807	59.26	32,613	40.74	15,909
Year 1959	0.57	38,872	71.19	40,561	28.81	26,588
Year 1966	1.62	46,613	82.97	50,909	17.03	25,667

* Includes combinations consisting of tractor-truck semitrailers with trailers as well as combinations consisting of trucks with trailers.

Revenue and expenditures for highway purposes, 1911–67 (in thousands)

Revenue from		
Road fund	$2,271,044	
Federal aid	2,063,181	
Portion of motor fuel tax	851,577	
Miscellaneous	162,152	
Total		$5,347,954
Revenue from		
Highway bonds to 1932	$155,700	
Motor fuel tax	2,636,243	
Grade crossing trust fund	7,804	
Trust fund	5,670	
General revenue	37,100	
Total		2,842,517
Total revenue		$8,190,471
Expenditures, Division of Highways		
Construction	$3,632,564	
Maintenance	794,328	
Highway debt service	290,582	
Buildings, overhead, policing, etc.	550,565	
Total		$5,268,039

Expenditures, counties, townships, municipalities		
Refunds	$41,541	
Motor fuel tax to counties	730,405	
Motor fuel tax to townships and road districts	207,195	
Motor fuel tax to municipalities	887,328	
State share of secondary roads	29,617	
Advances	40,266	
Flood damage funds	790	
Total		$1,937,142
Other state departments for administration, etc.		705,364
Diversions for school funds, service of relief bonds, and emergency relief— Kaneland Community Unit School District judgment and development of Lake Taylorville		93,427
Total expenditures		$8,048,972
Balance on hand		141,499
		$8,190,471

Approved interstate projects from which selection would be made for 1968 action

Interstate route	Funds	Construction	Right of way	Total
24	Federal and state	$3,400,000	$100,000	$3,500,000
55	Federal and state	7,447,000	865,000	8,312,000
57	Cook County	13,882,000		13,882,000
	Federal and state	63,506,000	1,585,000	65,091,000
64	Federal and state	9,007,000	2,415,000	11,422,000
70	Federal and state	38,715,000	623,000	39,338,000
74	Federal and state	27,568,000	3,295,000	30,863,000
80	Federal and state	7,328,000	25,000	7,353,000
90	Federal and state	20,200,000	7,100,000	27,300,000
94	Federal and state	4,417,000		4,417,000
180	Federal and state	5,025,000		5,025,000
255	Federal and state	242,000	2,397,000	2,639,000
280	Federal and state	1,314,000	100,000	1,414,000
474	Federal and state		536,000	536,000
494	Federal and state	200,000	8,800,000	9,000,000
Total		$202,251,000	$27,841,000	$230,092,000

Funds available for the 1968 interstate and primary highway improvement program

	Interstate	Other primary	Total
Federal	$186,900,000	$28,800,000	$215,700,000
State	19,400,000	60,300,000	79,700,000
Other agencies	1,400,000	22,000,000	23,400,000
Total	$207,700,000	$111,100,000	$318,800,000

Summary of primary highway contracts (including federal-aid

Year	Rigid-type pavement[1]		Bituminous surface on flexible base[2]		Gravel or crushed stone[3]	
	Miles	Cost	Miles	Cost	Miles	Cost
1918–29	6,398.75	$180,977,894.27				
1930	943.18	24,361,360.36				
1931	851.65	20,674,468.63				
1932	966.31	21,653,238.74				
1933	318.35	10,668,618.73			2.33	$73,444.82
1934	327.29	12,109,016.10	1.11	$11,581.43	.92	43,618.84
1935	188.30	9,422,414.96	5.32	116,810.01		
1936	195.78	10,904,152.33	0.81	19,965.66	42.75	456,181.85
1937	159.82	7,618,065.49			93.08	891,571.60
1938	194.08	9,879,465.49	71.92	460,027.13	67.67	750,076.65
1939	169.37	9,722,071.99	81.84	788,941.72	24.18	381,336.47
1940	178.14	7,531,631.24	24.16	271,963.03	63.05	1,046,002.97
1941	112.84	7,287,661.71	17.15	246,833.30	13.47	365,087.91
1942	278.75	15,546,937.21		88,313.18	11.57	73,817.33
1943	149.05	9,684,627.25	18.23	262,924.28	10.71	114,926.07
1944	215.00	9,003,166.62	1.65	294,142.53	1.91	47,334.88
1945	207.83	9,494,309.89		301,986.07	0.90	44,924.17
1946	180.28	8,937,963.46	42.01	428,314.96	6.35	296,468.77
1947	332.65	16,991,253.50	28.51	619,200.80	1.50	57,478.53
1948	130.21	10,690,263.73	10.52	223,422.04	10.14	445,049.46
1949	269.81	20,484,006.43	54.79	864,297.81	0.50	41,942.75
1950	166.99	10,541,566.55	14.05	97,720.06	0.38	22,499.87
1951	578.53	32,589,431.82	12.56	237,494.65		
1952	1,081.51	61,872,623.68	105.22	2,109,239.09		
1953	446.05	30,654,204.85	28.89	795,926.99		
1954	717.64	43,156,715.64	17.34	243,793.04		
1955	416.70	43,493,537.82	61.87	1,081,026.33		
1956	540.39	44,785,993.93	49.37	2,602,538.85		
1957	677.52	36,640,700.15	26.49	1,584,938.55		
1958	1,603.70	80,439,657.12	18.69	1,375,810.77	78.03	4,054,615.68
1959	433.82	93,604,201.65	90.21	1,973,203.14	0.39	64,149.87
1960	804.62	88,796,450.00	34.69	1,993,251.07		
1961	533.12	73,972,728.04	13.63	1,162,105.91	2.89	352,965.08
1962	884.38	98,255,280.71	20.15	1,881,997.14	8.39	1,198,683.64
1963	655.75	110,555,657.14	4.98	1,050,148.31	7.65	1,273,353.13
1964	518.75	94,287,564.88	9.24	1,636,755.06		
1965	550.06	80,507,570.26	7.92	909,648.38	7.93	1,022,891.23
1966	376.72	81,310,447.18	10.48	2,438,019.50	5.21	966,959.72
1967	488.96	147,168,248.59	8.88	3,331,394.83	4.43	861,511.47
Total	24,242.64	$1,686,275,167.14	892.68	$31,503,735.62	466.33	$14,946,892.76

Note Contracts awarded by Cook County and the city of Chicago are not included in this table.
[1] Includes concrete pavement, concrete base course, and bituminous concrete surfacing; but mileage does not include seal coats, concrete base repair, patching, or concrete pavement widening, but cost includes all these items. [2] Cost includes seal coats bituminous surface treatment, and repair of base and surface courses, but mileage is excluded.

	Grading[4]		Structures[5]	Miscellaneous items[6]	Total cost
Miles	Cost	Number	Cost	Cost	
1,768.06	$19,765,795.01	1,487	$21,239,693.95		$221,983,383.23
152.05	2,162,973.57	136	2,692,560.27		29,216,894.20
169.04	1,932,957.25	138	3,243,492.85		25,850,918.73
190.02	1,895,751.32	169	3,525,399.65		27,074,389.71
42.47	643,000.10	73	1,979,479.13		13,364,542.78
105.63	1,597,610.65	129	4,717,863.41		18,479,690.43
117.80	2,342,939.73	86	3,494,429.76	$31,169.49	15,407,763.95
130.82	2,618,921.15	128	7,113,311.90	151,081.16	21,263,614.05
146.13	2,146,642.80	97	3,331,017.45	53,576.00	14,040,873.34
74.27	1,316,976.05	70	3,907,178.43	13,770.90	16,327,494.65
68.37	1,468,430.66	67	3,185,949.08	241,461.83	15,788,191.75
88.02	1,801,582.16	38	2,088,929.55	508,172.66	13,248,281.61
12.67	249,932.21	36	3,143,428.81	360,247.61	11,653,191.55
12.26	725,263.53	20	713,813.53	5,000.00	17,153,144.78
1.15	134,035.24	5	309,888.59	28,052.56	10,534,453.99
1.75	320,495.87	14	429,325.66	72,906.34	10,167,371.90
	527,017.84	22	1,329,042.96	255,316.65	11,952,597.58
	274,695.67	29	2,788,282.15	550,635.67	13,276,360.68
11.83	1,448,207.65	42	3,791,027.50	540,322.22	23,447,490.20
43.77	3,694,321.53	28	4,392,732.87	1,362,298.50	20,808,088.13
2.82	409,674.12	33	4,392,104.94	480,183.15	26,672,209.20
0.76	211,710.37	17	2,122,684.34	726,653.34	13,722,834.53
9.60	524,194.94	66	5,720,996.03	1,367,559.66	40,439,677.10
4.32	1,187,178.24	79	9,938,257.23	2,411,641.09	77,518,939.33
3.43	923,073.23	110	13,108,725.63	982,243.33	46,464,174.03
2.11	1,151,936.22	138	15,689,551.99	2,735,265.12	62,977,261.01
0.68	788,734.45	85	15,865,443.70	3,070,766.42	64,299,508.72
32.09	3,067,486.38	108	16,011,210.53	4,036,223.76	70,503,453.45
27.90	4,506,176.73	167	36,580,830.49	9,660,341.00	88,972,986.92
34.09	2,794,857.57	166	40,077,166.08	6,984,517.41	135,726,624.63
41.78	2,519,432.54	177	32,553,234.90	9,202,115.13	139,916,337.23
32.35	7,329,982.66	240	35,287,332.57	15,250,361.11	148,657,377.41
43.55	2,569,834.98	132	23,334,504.40	14,330,544.66	115,722,683.07
36.20	3,404,944.75	260	38,115,180.28	13,667,119.09	156,523,205.61
20.56	15,001,562.13	218	40,845,652.28	16,651,548.03	185,377,921.02
50.70	7,772,734.42	189	41,327,890.36	17,921,484.76	162,946,429.48
80.14	3,148,648.91	129	33,079,525.01	14,896,431.42	133,564,715.21
34.10	8,652,345.83	186	36,676,934.25	18,754,769.20	148,799,475.68
22.77	9,106,416.72	207	58,116,791.63	39,254,857.52	257,839,220.76
3,616.06	$122,138,475.18	5,521	$576,260,864.14	$196,558,636.79	$2,627,683,771.63

[3] Includes base and surface courses, granular embankment-special, soil cement, waterbound macadam, and bituminous stabilized base courses.

[4] Includes roadway and roadbed construction grading separate from other work; only cost includes other items of earth moving.

[5] Includes only bridges, railroad and highway grade separation structures, elevated highway structures, major culverts, and special structures.

[6] Includes items such as railroad grade crossing improvements, highway lighting, traffic control signals, highway signing, and landscaping.

Summary of secondary road contracts awarded

Year	Rigid-type pavement[1]		Bituminous surface on flexible base[2]		Gravel or crushed stone[3]	
	Miles	Cost	Miles	Cost	Miles	Cost
1933–42	129.70	$5,805,660.07	437.65	$2,198,482.33	890.22	$8,892,813.96
1943	19.38	747,741.33	16.26	168,227.47	22.22	325,247.73
1944	22.81	805,464.67	22.94	292,709.39	21.51	291.343,64
1945	16.55	578,905.81		170,536.87	14.09	232,012.25
1946	15.71	495,613.35	14.87	221,237.37	17.95	412,884.21
1947	57.78	2,411,603.43	161.67	2,813,024.80	153.68	3,222,092.24
1948	8.45	852,921.76	145.05	3,596,940.14	175.44	4,081,884.47
1949	17.93	710,587.67	86.54	1,511,091.90	29.07	710,902.70
1950	6.30	286,456.04	97.83	1,561,673.09	94.17	1,369,801.02
1951	19.69	951,849.88	81.35	1,597,737.83	51.06	1,058,978.27
1952	38.30	1,834,170.46	220,83	4,488,003.27	87.25	1,983,171.76
1953	56.07	2,601,049.28	285.77	7,326,834.26	142.37	3,241,836.72
1954	9.35	497,045.51	215.02	4,342,166.56	91.15	1,731,106.45
1955	64.59	2,753,059.21	344.70	6,927,467.78	146.23	2,479,224.75
1956	56.75	2,763,053.01	306.54	7,526,801.50	148.85	3,462,362.01
1957	52.30	2,352,939.44	329.84	8,384,424.32	141.34	3,288,658.94
1958	87.42	5,698,177.40	552.06	14,314,033.80	190.50	4,735,658.17
1959	41.90	3,373,734.63	274.92	7,625,752.42	103.58	3,323,693.75
1960	64.82	7,388,775.70	234.59	8,930,220.24	127.87	3,670,709.36
1961	145.77	8,795,478.15	191.20	7,068,363.37	108.10	2,697,724.29
1962	93.35	7,649,696.99	233.47	9,805,704.13	110.32	3,396,462.45
1963	92.34	10,865,163.75	136.21	7,835,407.54	117.09	2,936,057.68
1964	73.27	6,004,963.03	115.74	6,718,084.89	87.34	2,976,052.26
1965	108.58	7,109,122.96	93.49	5,670,141.47	73.14	2,911,432.80
1966	85.39	6,544,386.37	26.28	1,972,523.11	44.02	1,471,765.58
1967	35.27	5 657,756.46	53.08	4,959,389.17	35.72	1,270,327.79
Total	1,419.77	$95,535,376.36	4,650.90	$128,026,979.02	3,224.28	$66,174,205.25

Note: This table includes improvements contracted by the state on federal-aid secondary roads, secondary roads established prior to the federal-aid secondary road system, state-aid roads, secondary forest highways, defense access roads, roads serving state parks and institutions, and county highways added to the state's secondary road system.
[1] Includes concrete pavement, full width concrete base course, and bituminous concrete surfacing; mileage does not include seal coat on bituminous surfaces, repair and preparation of rigid base course, or patching and widening of rigid pavements, but cost includes all of these items.
[2] Mileage does not include seal coats on flexible bituminous surfaced pavements, bituminous surface treatment for gravel or crushed stone base.

Grading[4]		Structures[5]		Miscellaneous items[6]	Total cost
Miles	Cost	Number	Cost	Cost	
465.89	$4,179,015.84	261	$6,140,326.41	$371,330.99	$27,587,629.60
0.56	20,836.65	5	201,148.68	13,494.80	1,476,696.66
0.78	18,937.50		7,603.00	8,550.00	1,424,608.20
	36,618.98			9,432.26	1,027,506.17
3.71	154,579.46	10	415,441.03	27,730.58	1,727,486.00
27.50	435,855.38	17	715,187.68	35,446.00	9,633,209.53
22.84	594,337.16	22	2,105,393.44	59,371.76	11,290,848.73
12.63	192,778.93	12	537,534.52	122,158.64	3,785,054.36
11.62	176,226.21	11	577,441.31	158,483.10	4,130,080.77
10.62	564,539.68	13	689,815.02	69,642.63	4,932,563.31
18.83	285,781.22	20	1,204,636.23	263,382.21	10,059,145.15
20.08	360,152.21	31	1,422,198.32	230,426.68	15,182,497.47
11.90	137,890.39	22	979,771.87	315,658.98	8,003,639.76
26.96	456,048.21	59	3,149,576.80	461,646.91	16,227,023.66
7.34	216,814.92	32	2,013,524.71	430,080.05	16,412,636.20
24.08	460,246.55	51	2,794,080.08	627,107.77	17,907,457.10
28.68	754,010.91	87	5,460,774.10	219,512.51	31,182,166.89
		45	3,254,797.91	719,300.46	18,297,279.17
11.84	286,251.45	35	2,742,173.76	1,938,910.72	24,957,041.23
9.16	267,387.83	51	3,561,705.20	842,104.10	23,232,762.94
7.70	1,198,367.19	57	2,343,932.93	2,320,451.98	26,714,615.67
6.85	147,208.60	34	2,550,848.06	1,164,246.18	25,498,931.81
14.87	317,809.87	29	1,631,840.89	801,553.18	18,450,304.12
3.00	58,136.71	37	2,724,634.30	1,100,743.50	19,574,211.74
9.46	371,290.00	33	2,545,847.88	540,176.08	13,445,989.02
1.31	83,869.76	27	3,741,667.58	1,431,591.81	17,144,602.57
758.21	$11,774,991.61	1,001	$53,511,901.71	$14,282,533.88	$369,305,987.83

and the repair of flexible base and surface courses, but cost includes all of these items.

[3] Includes base and surface courses, granular embankment-special, and soil cement, waterbound macadam, and bituminous stabilized base courses.

[4] Includes roadway and roadbed construction grading separate from other work; only cost includes additional items of earth grading.

[5] Includes only the awarded cost of bridges, railroad and highway grade separation structures, elevated highway structures, major culverts, and special structures.

[6] Includes items such as railroad grade crossing improvements highway lighting, traffic control signals, highway signing, and landscaping.

371

Comparison of annual maintenance and highway operation costs, 1930–67

Year	Mileage	Maintenance cost		Operation cost		Total maintenance and operation cost	
		Total	Per mile	Total	Per mile	Total	Per mile
1930	8,519	$1,749,647.18	$205.38	$1,337,611.34	$157.02	$3,087,258.52	$362.40
1931	9,530	1,958,134.12	205.47	1,328,918.40	139.45	3,287,052.52	344.92
1932	10,459	2,332,253.28	222.99	1,558,649.90	149.02	3,890,903.18	372.01
1933	11,234	1,819,343.39	161.95	1,162,922.67	103.52	2,982,266.06	265.47
1934	11,886	2,267,471.80	109.77	1,444,799.78	121.55	3,712,271.58	312.32
1935	12,223	2,391,909.55	195.69	1,574,893.43	128.85	3,966,802.96	324.54
1936	12,515	2,271,627.77	181.51	2,388,325.20	190.84	4,659,952.97	372.35
1937	12,742	2,935,431.25	230.38	2,365,445.29	185.64	5,300,876.54	416.02
1938	13,067	2,730,534.68	208.96	2,669,708.79	204.31	5,400,243.47	413.27
1939	13,319	3,041,150.70	228.33	2,619,706.72	196.69	5,660,857.42	425.02
1940	13,558	3,079,790.06	227.16	3,253,101.04	239.94	6,332,891.10	467.10
1941	13,853	3,562,474.79	257.16	2,873,841.57	207.46	6,436,316.36	464.62
1942	13,941	3,618,649.34	259.57	3,321,607.68	238.26	6,940,257.02	497.83
1943	14,052	3,090,481.85	219.92	3,311,451.68	235.65	6,401,933.53	455.57
1944	14,093	3,485,901.75	247.36	3,536,330.40	250.94	7,022,232.15	498.30
1945	14,109	3,720,034.95	263.66	4,403,280.19	312.08	8,123,315.14	575.74
1946	14,113	4,061,284.79	287.78	4,650,465.67	329.52	8,711,750.46	617.30
1947	14,125	4,942,038.49	349.87	5,766,839.11	408.26	10,708,877.60	758.13
1948	14,134	6,129,120.23	433.65	6,339,784.75	448.55	12,468,904.98	882.20
1949	14,168	6,973,572.39	492.21	6,455,231.18	455.62	13,428,803.57	947.83
1950	14,224	9,355,382.15	657.70	7,201,589.64	506.29	16,556,971.79	1,163.99
1951	14,248	10,292,240.95	722.39	8,647,635.99	606.95	18,939,876.94	1,329.34
1952	14,256	11,250,460.33	789.20	9,244,739.81	648.50	20,495,200.14	1,437.70
1953	14,233	11,026,356.90	774.71	8,511,335.77	598.00	19,537,692.67*	1,372.71
1954	14,297	11,994,706.34	840.71	10,968,394.01	768.77	22,963,100.35*	1,609.48
1955	14,297	11,578,217.78	809.85	11,285,006.47	789.34	22,863,224.25*	1,599.19
1956	14,344	11,929,219.50	831.65	12,328,119.61	859.46	24,257,339.11*	1,691.11
1957	14,414	11,984,745.70	831.45	12,702,170.46	881.22	24,686,916.16*	1,712.67
1958	14,400	13,352,896.89	927.30	13,637,589.64	947.07	26,990,486.53*	1,874.37

1959	14,434	12,087,221.86	837.41	16,016,040.96	1,109.59	28,103,262.82*	1,947.00
1960	14,553	13,497,741.50	927.50	18,976,670.78	1,303.98	32,474,412.28*	2,231.48
1961	14,645	13,742,780.14	938.36	18,466,948.19	1,260.93	32,209,728.33*	2,199.29
1962	14,711	16,927,645.10	1,150.70	20,951,989.47	1,424.26	37,879,634.57**	2,574.96
1963	14,757	15,789,078.72	1,069.94	24,153,293.47	1,636.73	39,942,372.19*	2,706.67
1964	14,869	17,015,581.32	1,144.37	26,417,991.21	1,776.72	43,433,572.53*	2,921.08
1965	14,957	19,589,676.39	1,309.73	28,323,228.24	1,893.64	47,912,904.63*	3,203.37
1966	15,073†	20,614,034.19	1,367.61	27,224,479.65	1,806.18	47,838,513.84**	3,173.79
1967	16,023**	52,744,683.49	3,291.81	na	na	na	na

Note: Before 1941 the mileages did not include
detours, unpaved and temporary routes.
* Does not include costs for maintenance or traffic
operation of expressways.

† Includes 732.82 miles of interstate highways and
14,340.26 miles of other state-maintained roads.
** Includes 809.57 miles of municipal streets.
na—Data not available (included in maintenance
costs after 1966).

Comparison of annual snow removal and ice control costs, 1931–67

Year	Entire state			Northern zone only		
	Miles reported	Total cost	Cost per mile	Miles reported	Total cost	Cost per mile
1931	5,944.40	$289,915.67	$48.77	4,362.06	$240,903.51	$55.23
1932	8,499.36	279,710.14	32.91	6,565.95	206,045.27	37.02
1933	7,255.60	230,684.53	31.93	4,918.07	194,962.85	39.64
1934	9,159.49	270,675.51	29.55	5,312.61	172,411.55	52.45
1935	9,516.82	419,872.34	44.12	5,750.52	321,588.88	55.92
1936	12,693.90	1,098,427.54	87.01	6,930.00	806,784.24	116.42
1937	12,831.64	674,985.18	52.60	7,031.49	429,241.04	61.05
1938	13,175.75	593,173.22	45.02	7,186.40	458,994.91	63.87
1939	13,378.67	625,905.25	46.78	7,251.10	434,373.90	59.90
1940	13,615.49	1,109,962.53	81.52	7,351.29	719,854.25	97.92
1941	13,852.98	710,839.77	51.31	7,444.68	545,360.40	73.26
1942	13,940.95	847,779.92	60.81	7,475.51	587,462.68	78.58
1943	14,052.40	889,063.48	63.27	7,510.40	695,844.49	92.65
1944	14,092.54	849,457.98	60.28	7,524.38	568,333.34	75.53
1945	14,109.26	1,321,678.97	93.67	7,533.07	899,401.49	119.39
1946	14,112.63	1,106,379.30	78.40	7,528.65	742,121.84	98.57
1947	14,125.36	1,591,399.16	112.66	7,539.85	1,225,436.24	162.53
1948	14,133.95	1,747,642.76	123.65	7,543.44	1,236,310.15	163.89
1949	14,167.90	2,080,265.35	146.83	7,543.39	1,566,023.89	207.60
1950	14,224.37	2,281,113.17	160.37	7,549.64	1,621,433.03	214.77
1951	14,247.54	3,108,455.28	218.17	7,555.10	2,216,405.30	293.37
1952	14,255.57	3,166,286.93	222.11	7,558.39	2,254,554.09	298.28
1953	14,232.91	2,130,092.51	149.66	7,527.05	1,464,028.79	194.50
1954	14,267.41	2,408,941.59	168.84	7,539.21	1,758,156.08	233.20
1955	14,296.73	3,238,918.88	226.55	7,534.88	2,205,043.94	292.64
1956	14,344.06	3,141,550.47	219.01	7,550.62	2,006,771.16	265.78
1957	14,414.25	3,607,152.08	250.25	7,577.97	2,344,306.69	309.36
1958	14,399.75	3,682,249.99	255.72	7,551.42	2,560,757.60	339.11
1959	14,434.12	4,848,497.71	335.91	7,546.71	3,409,560.55	451.79
1960	14,552.86	6,501,513.74	446.75	7,580.21	4,556,140.51	601.06
1961	14,645.49	4,641,459.79	316.92	7,596.24	2,701,978.65	355.70
1962	14,710.79	7,731,480.26	525.57	7,591.37	5,528,379.93	728.25
1963	14,757.20	7,338,857.41	497.31	7,601.05	4,950,347.37	651.27
1964	14,869.39	7,417,795.67	498.86	7,633.54	4,810,267.29	630.15
1965	14,957.39	8,923,493.86	596.59	7,657.86	5,931,750.77	774.60
1966	15,073.08*	6,050,220.95	401.39	7,723.63†	4,391,510.28	568.58
1967	15,107.01	7,544,870.94	499.43	7,745.95	5,843,920.21	754.45

Note: Costs subsequent to 1952 do not include cost of removing snow and ice from expressways.
* Included in the costs are 774.19 miles of interstate highways and 14,332.82 miles of other state-maintained highways.
† Included in the costs are 372.69 miles of interstate highways and 7,373.26 miles of other state-maintained highways.

Motor vehicle fatalities, injuries, miles of travel, and death rate in Illinois, 1920–67

Year	Number of fatalities	Number of injuries	Number of vehicle miles (in millions)	Death rate per 100 million vehicle miles
1920	728	na	3,462	21.0
1925	1,533	na	7,749	19.8
1930	2,285	na	12,737	17.9
1935	2,334	na	13,359	17.5
1940	2,328	na	17,908	13.0
1945	1,587	19,265	13,800	11.5
1950	1,973	70,654	25,964	7.6
1955	2,195	82,051	32,659	6.7
1960	1,725	104,832	36,508	4.7
1961	1,822	110,193	37,646	4.8
1962	1,890	112,310	38,735	4.9
1963	2,028	119,894	40,090	5.1
1964	2,207	134,163	42,519	5.2
1965	2,256	145,544	44,180	5.1
1966	2,522	149,137	48,359	5.2
1967	2,493	149,512	58,574	4.3

na—Data not available.

The state of Illinois had barely come of age when, in 1840, the first flying machine was built within its borders. It was an ornithopter (wing flapper). The inventor was Hugh Newell—Crazy Hugh—a farmer living in the village of Newton, six miles west of Danville. He had the backing of well-to-do Jesse Liggate and the help of a blacksmith. When Newell thought his "Flying Carr" was ready, he and friends carried it to the top of a haystack. Newell entered the craft and started turning the crank that caused the wings to flap. The friends shoved. But instead of rising the ornithopter plunged to the barnyard below. Newell, it was reported, was not badly hurt.

Newell, his "Flying Carr" and the village of Newton are gone, but curiosity about flight, kept alive by the many pioneers who followed him, finally was rewarded—and man flew in a craft that was heavier than air. One of the great contributors to this triumph was a Chicago resident, Paris-born Octave Chanute, brought to New York by his parents at age six in 1838. Chanute, after obtaining an engineering degree, came to Chicago as chief engineer for the Chicago & Alton Railroad. He built railroads, bridged the Missouri at Kansas City, and returned to Chicago in 1873 to open a consulting office. In 1883 he began his study of airfoils, to which he devoted the rest of his life.

While Chanute was working on the theory of flight and problems of stability in the air another Illinois pioneer was engaged in aerial activities that were far from stable. Thomas Scott Baldwin was born in Quincy, Illinois, on June 30, 1860, five years after the first balloon ascension in Illinois was made from Peoria and Randolph streets in Chicago by Silas M. Brooks. Baldwin trained himself as an acrobat and made a youthful living with carnivals, performing on the high wire and trapeze. Before he was twenty he took his trapeze into the air and gave the stagnating profession of carnival aeronaut a big boost by his daring antics high above the crowds. In 1886, while working as acrobat and balloonist at the Cliff House in San Francisco, he began developing an aerial safeguard, the parachute. He literally "tried it on the dog." It worked. On January 30, 1887, after having set a fee of a dollar a foot with the carnival manager, Baldwin made the first parachute jump in history from a point 1,000 feet above the beach, and landed safely on the barrens that were soon to become a part of Golden Gate Park. Having established a fee of $1,000 a

performance, Baldwin took his act to Chicago, St. Louis, and other cities. Soon bookings were so heavy his brother doubled in filling them, while Tom Baldwin went to England and France to make first jumps in those countries. By the age of thirty he was a wealthy young man. He spent some of that wealth in building a glider and successfully flew it in 1892.

Meanwhile, in Chicago, Chanute experimented with multiwinged kites and gliders, determined airfoil shapes, and looked into stability devices. He presided over the Third International Conference on Aerial Navigation (the first to be held in the United States) at the World's Columbian Exposition in the summer of 1893, where he was a featured speaker and seminar leader. His work at the fair and his later writings came to the attention of two young men in Dayton, Ohio, Orville and Wilbur Wright, who determined to visit him for consultation relative to the final form of their first experimental craft. These conferences occurred in Chicago in 1901, and contributed largely to the decision to build a biplane, and also pointed the way to the use of fins for lateral stability, the rudder well out in front of the lifting planes for easy control of longitudinal stability, the warping wing for maneuverability, and other details so carefully worked out before the triumph of Kitty Hawk in December 1903, when man first flew.

Tom Baldwin, in the meantime, was progressing toward navigable flight in a lighter-than-air machine. In 1898 the Brazilian Alberto Santos-Dumont, at Paris, France, had achieved controlled flight in a dirigible. Baldwin, inspired by Santos-Dumont's example, and needing a new carnival attraction to replace the dwindling income from the parachute descents that no longer interested blasé picnickers, devoted his entire time to duplicating Santos-Dumont's success. He had his gasbag and catwalk long before he had an engine. Finally he encountered a motorcycle with a lightweight motor made by a young man named Glenn Curtiss. He sent Curtiss an order for an engine to his specifications. It was accepted and filled. On August 3, 1904, Baldwin flew for more than two hours at Oakland, California, and landed within a few feet of his takeoff point. Baldwin, not Curtiss, got the first Curtiss engine into the air. From that time until the end of 1905

Baldwin, who weighed 200 pounds, and two youngsters who weighed about that much together, Roy Knabenshue and Lincoln Beachey, made more than 170 flights with a fleet of five machines. Two of the big gasbags were lost in accidents, and the other three were destroyed in San Francisco, together with shop, tools, and equipment, by the fire that followed the earthquake of April 18, 1906. Baldwin flew no more carnival dirigibles, but he celebrated his fiftieth birthday by piloting a Red Devil biplane of his own construction. By that year he and Lincoln Beachey, together with two army officers, Frank Kennedy of Aurora, Illinois, and Frank Lahm of Mansfield, Ohio, were triple-rated pilots, accredited for balloons, dirigibles, and airplanes.

The first decade of the twentieth century saw increasing activity in aviation in Illinois. Even before the Wrights were in the air a Chicagoan, Charles S. Bates, advertised airplanes built to order and manufactured his first aero engine. He did not get off the ground, however, until 1908, when he made several short hops from Washington Park. In the fall of 1909 Glenn Curtiss, fresh from his speed triumphs at Rheims, France, gave an exhibition of flight at Hawthorn racetrack. On September 27, 1910, Walter Brookins of the Wright Brothers exhibition team, won $10,000 for cross-country flight from Chicago to Springfield, Illinois. In August 1911 airmen from France, England, Canada, and the United States, competed for $100,000 in prizes in a nine-day aviation meet on Chicago's lakefront which cost two lives. When the meet was repeated the following year a Mississippi lass, Katherine (Kitty) Stinson, recently graduated from Max Lillie's aviation school in Chicago, became the first woman to enter a major meet. Illinois' first aviatrix, Julia Clark, Chicago stenographer and graduate of the Curtiss school at San Diego, California, had been killed at Springfield, Illinois, a few weeks before the second Chicago meet, which she was scheduled to enter as one of William Pickens' team, the International Flying Circus.

In 1911 and 1912 fliers in Illinois participated in several experiments relating to delivery of mail by aircraft. Airmail was carried from Minneapolis to Rock Island in the fall of 1911, when a proposed flight to New Orleans terminated for lack of incentive money. On May 25, 1912, Farnum Fish of the Wright exhibition team, who a bit later was to fly briefly for Pancho Villa, carried letters, four bolts of cloth, and 7,500 circulars from Chicago to Milwaukee. He dropped the circulars, delivered the mail to the post office, and the cloth to a Milwaukee department store. Flight time was two hours six minutes. Later the same year mail was carried from Hawthorn racetrack to Elmhurst, Wheaton, and Aurora; from Springfield fairgrounds to Williamsville; and from McLeansboro fairgrounds to the post office in the town. Participants were Max Lillie and Horace F. Kearney, both flying Wright biplanes.

Illinois quickly came of age in the air when preparedness became a national watchword in 1916. The Signal Corps, which was the army agency responsible for aviation at that time, established a school for reserve military aviators at Ashburn Field in the Chicago area at Cicero Avenue from Seventy-ninth to Eighty-seventh Street. This program began at Ashburn June 29, 1916, moved to Memphis, Tennessee, for the winter, and returned to Ashburn in the early spring. Meanwhile, at Rantoul, Chanute Field was being readied to train pilots, observers, gunners, mechanics, riggers, and other specialists while at the nearby University of Illinois aviation cadets were receiving an eight-week ground course. In July the Signal Corps school moved from Ashburn to Chanute in the first mass flight in the nation's history. Only one of the twenty-three Curtiss "Jenny" trainers failed to complete the flight the first day.

Flight training began at Chanute July 17, 1917, and by the first of October three squadrons had been trained, equipped, and shipped out—two to Issoudun, France, to prepare the huge complex of eight fields for advance pursuit training, and one to Waco, Texas, to man a primary training school. Meanwhile training, which, on the non-flying side was concerned with air communications, began at Scott Field, Belleville. By 1919, when the massive training program ended, Chanute had sent ten squadrons into combat and Scott had supplied another four, Illinois thus furnishing more than 30 per cent of the squadrons that saw combat duty. In addition, two Chanute-trained squadrons remained at Issoudun for school assignment and four more from Scott were used for other than combat duty. Many pilot graduates from Chanute and Scott, for whom there was no immediate squadron assignment, were shipped as casuals to

England, where they were brigaded with the British for advance training and combat. America's first two aces, Reed G. Landis of Chicago and Howard C. Knotts of Springfield, were among them.

In the area of navy training Illinois contributed both in pilot training and in the education of specialists. The navy flight school for both lighter and heavier than air at Newport News, Virginia, engaged Tom Baldwin, most experienced dirigible pilot in America, as chief instructor. Among the men who trained the first navy pilots was Eddie Stinson. It was at Newport News that Stinson, in 1916, logically explained the cause of spinning in flight, which was killing so many army and navy flight cadets, and advanced a method for correcting the spin. He pointed out that spinning only occurred when the aircraft lost flying speed. The plane spun in a nose-down position, and a student's normal reaction would be to haul back on the stick and rudder against the spin. This, believed Stinson, only made the spin tighter and faster. Having thought through his theory, Stinson deliberately gambled his life on it by taking a trainer to 6,000 feet, putting it in a spin, and clearing the spin by placing the rudder control in neutral and the elevator control a bit forward of neutral. Stinson lived through this experiment and hundreds of pilots lived after him because of his courage and acumen.

It is a pity to destroy the legend that Stinson, caught in a spin, decided to make a potential crash spectacular and shoved the elevator all the way forward. However, his deliberate action reflects more credit on his memory than any romantic tale of a glorious end could do. After the war Stinson became a resident of Chicago and a successful designer and manufacturer of aircraft. In both army and navy the watchword of the pilot in training in 1916 was "keep your nose clean." After Stinson's successful test it became "get your nose down."

At Great Lakes Naval Training Center near Waukegan emphasis in 1917 and 1918 was on training mechanics, riggers, communications specialists, and other skilled personnel needed to keep the pilots in the air. Philip K. Wrigley, first as chief machinist's mate and later as lieutenant, was in charge of the School of Aviation Mechanics, first to be set up in the country. There was also preliminary training for pilots of flying boats. Officers and cadets, completing their courses at Great Lakes, took their advanced training at Pensacola. But despite the fact

that flight skills were a side issue at Great Lakes, the training center was a major instrument in the creation of the splendid Navy combat and reconnaissance squadrons of World War I.

After the war, except for the airmail operated by the Post Office Department and a curtailed military program, aviation in the United States remained with the barnstormers. A notable exception was Tom Baldwin. When the navy no longer required him he was employed by Goodyear Tire and Rubber Company as head of their dirigible division, and participated in many experiments and developments right up to the time of his death in Buffalo on May 17, 1923.

When the post office went into the airmail business seriously in 1919, Chicago, because of its geographical location, became the most important center of airmail development for the same reason it had become the rail center of the nation sixty years earlier. The backbone of the airmail operation was the New York-Chicago-San Francisco axis, and Chicago was the logical point at which the populous areas of the nation west of the Alleghenies could feed into and out of the transcontinental route.

The development of coast-to-coast airmail began in 1918, two months before the armistice of November 11. Max Miller, a civilian pilot employed by the Post Office Department, carried mail from Mineola, Long Island, to Grant Park in Chicago in less than ten hours on September 5, 1918. The return flight on September 10 resulted in a crash landing near Hicksville, Long Island, but this did not prevent delivery of the mail in New York that evening.

After this pair of trial flights the Post Office Department announced that airmail service between New York and Chicago would begin December 18, 1918. However, no flight got through because of the bad weather, and it was not until May 15, 1919, that a scheduled airmail operation was inaugurated, with service between Cleveland and Chicago, one flight in each direction daily. On July 1 scheduled service between New York and Chicago got under way. It cut sixteen hours from the delivery time of mail between the nation's two largest cities.

The following year the service was extended from Chicago to Omaha (May 20), two feeder routes were opened—Minneapolis to Chicago (August 10) and St.

Louis to Chicago (August 16)—and on September 10, 1920, airmail service was extended from Omaha to San Francisco. DeHaviland bombers powered with Liberty engines were used on the early airmail flights. No passengers were carried. An economy wave in 1921 terminated both feeder routes and the Chicago landing field was moved to Checkerboard Field at First Avenue and Roosevelt Road in suburban Maywood, and a few weeks later to government-owned land near Hines Hospital, which continued to receive the airmail for several years. When the Post Office Department turned the mail over entirely to private contractors June 30, 1927, the flying postmen had carried 298,517,610,000 pieces of mail on scheduled operations that involved more than 13,500,000 miles of flight. A lighted airway had been established from New York to San Francisco, and radio beacons were being installed to aid airmail flights in bad weather.

There were no scheduled passenger-carrying airlines available in the United States such as those established in 1919 between Paris and London, Paris and Brussels, and Paris and Geneva, and extended to Berlin, Vienna, The Hague, Amsterdam, Rome, and Madrid a year or so later. Passenger flying in this country was confined to charter flights in revamped World War I aircraft, of which most major cities in Illinois boasted at least one. Courier aircraft occasionally took passengers when they were flying to deliver photographs of important events to the newspapers in larger cities.

In February 1925, however, a firm base for transport flying was created when President Calvin Coolidge signed a bill introduced into Congress by Representative Melville Clyde Kelly of Pennsylvania authorizing the Post Office Department to employ contract carriers for the airmail. The Post Office Department continued to operate the New York-Chicago-San Francisco service. The two discontinued feeder routes were reauthorized together with ten others that brought feeder mileage to 5,500. The contracts were let by the postmaster general, who had sole responsibility under the act.

The first company to get under way, Robertson Aircraft Company of St. Louis, with the St. Louis-Chicago route, had as its chief pilot a young Minnesotan named Charles Augustus Lindbergh. No passengers were carried. In 1928 Robertson would become a division of Universal Airways, Inc., which would be absorbed by American Airways. A feeder route was established by Ford Motor Company from Dearborn, Michigan, to Chicago in single-engine all-metal aircraft in 1925, and two years later passengers were carried in three-engined Ford transports. Stinson began manufacture of cabin aircraft, seating the pilot and three passengers, that same year. The year also marked the genesis of Northwest Airways, Inc., which took over the Minneapolis-Chicago feeder airline and equipped DeHaviland bombers with small cabins for passengers, as had been done in London seven years earlier. Lindbergh's flight to Paris May 20–21, 1927, gave the public increased confidence in flight safety, and soon all contract airmail carriers had passenger service.

On July 1, 1927, Boeing Air Transport took over the New York-Chicago-San Francisco airmail route and the government was out of the airmail business except for a brief period in 1934. Boeing immediately advertised for passengers, two and later four per scheduled flight. In 1929 they went from single-engine biplanes to three-motor transports of their own make, carrying nine. As better engines became available both Boeing and a newcomer in the field, Douglas Aircraft Company of Santa Monica, California, which had built the biplanes Captain Lowell Smith led around the world in 1925, developed sleek twin-engine all-metal monoplane transports. The Douglas craft, the famous DC3, carried twenty-one passengers. Boeing's 247 had accommodations for twelve. A year later the Lockheed Electra, which Amelia Erhardt would fly from Los Angeles to Honolulu and from United States to Europe, entered the field. It also carried twelve passengers.

While the first models of the Douglas and Boeing aircraft were still in Chicago awaiting the reopening of the Century of Progress Exposition in 1934, Postmaster General James A. Farley canceled all airmail contracts, charging that they had been obtained by collusion during the Hoover administration, and the President ordered the Army Air Force to carry the mail. Mr. Farley's action threw the air transport industry into a flat spin. The airmail contracts provided the thin cushion of financial safety required by the airlines. The result was financial distress and a series of mergers from which the transport giants of the present emerged, and a sorry situation on the airmail routes. However, despite a record of sixty-six accidents, twelve deaths, and an increase of four times in the cost of carrying the mail, the experiment was not without its long-range benefits. From it the Air Force gained experience that led to the revamping of the entire training program. From it the airlines, with new contracts awarded in April and May of 1934, emerged stronger and with more solid financial foundation.

These were the companies operating into and out of Illinois at that time:

American Airlines, formerly American Airways, Inc., with eight contracts including Chicago-New York, Chicago-Washington, and Chicago-Fort Worth.

Braniff, with the Chicago-Dallas-Houston contract.

Chicago & Southern, with a contract to serve Memphis, Jackson, and other cities to the south.

Eastern Airlines, headed by America's ace of aces, Eddie Rickenbacker, flying the mail to Louisville, Atlanta, and Florida cities.

Northwest Airlines, with the Chicago-Minneapolis-Seattle route and a service from Chicago to Winnipeg.

Trans World Airlines, successor to Transcontinental and Western Air Express, Chicago-Los Angeles.

United Air Lines, successor, with several other merged lines, to Boeing Air Transport, holding the New York-Chicago-San Francsico airmail contract. (Boeing was devoting all its energies to production of the B-17 bomber.)

Pacific Air Transport received the Chicago-New Orleans contract, but discontinued operations out of Chicago before the year was over, and Chicago & Southern succeeded to the contract.

Progress in air technology, which resulted in faster aircraft that required longer and longer takeoff and landing runs, inspired continuing development of airfields. In the Chicago area Grant Park soon was abandoned. Checkerboard Field in Maywood, where many Illinoisans learned to fly, and where E. M. Laird and Yackey Aircraft rebuilt war-weary planes for private flying, became inadequate. In 1925 the city of Chicago leased a small parcel at Cicero Avenue and Sixty-third Street from the Board of Education, and on May 8, 1926, opened Chicago Municipal Airport. By the end of 1927, when all the contract mail

carriers were operating out of Municipal, the field extended along Cicero Avenue from Sixty-third Street to the Chicago Belt Line tracks, then located on Fifty-ninth Street, and west to Laramie Avenue. There were two miles of cinder runways, the longest 3,600 feet, ample for the Curtiss Condors and Ford Tri-Motors which were the largest aircraft then carrying passengers in America.

Advent of the DC3 in 1934 made further development necessary, and Chicago received a $6,000,000 grant for airport improvement under the Works Progress Administration. The program involved acquiring by lease and purchase all of the section of land extending from Fifty-fifth to Sixty-third Street, and from Cicero to Central Avenue. The Belt Line tracks were to be relocated north of Fifty-fifth Street. When the work was completed in 1940 the field had six runways, two of them more than a mile in length, storm sewers, well-equipped passenger terminals, and hangars for the eight airlines using the field (Pennsylvania Airlines had reached Chicago in 1938), for many private enterprises, and for the Army Air Force and the Illinois Air National Guard.

In 1940 more than 700,000 passengers arrived at or departed from Chicago Municipal Airport. This figure was far in excess of any other airport in the world that year. An aircraft took off or landed on an average of every six minutes, day and night, throughout the year. By the same token, small fields began disappearing from the scene. Checkerboard Field had become a part of the Cook County Forest Preserve. Ashburn Field was no longer useful. The most important remaining landing areas were Orchard Place Airport on Mannheim Road north of Lawrence Avenue, Sky Harbor in Northbrook, Palwaukee at Palatine and Milwaukee roads, and Rubicam near Harvey.

Other sections of Illinois had usable airports, but not many were served by the airlines. First airport in the Rock Island area was a farmer's field where gasoline storage was installed and the field rented to barnstormers in 1919. It lay close to Prospect Park. In 1922 activity moved to the Weaver Farm on Colona Avenue in the outskirts of Moline. This thirty-acre tract was purchased by the city of Moline in 1935 and developed into a good landing place with shops. The field, enlarged several times, is now the Quad Cities Airport, accommodating jets on daily schedule, and outside the Chicago area, one of the busiest airports in Illinois.

Springfield, Aurora, Peoria, and Rockford all have fields dating back to 1927 and continuously operated since that time. Bloomington, Danville, Joliet, Lansing, and a number of other Illinois cities had airfields with shops and hangar space for permanently based and visiting aircraft before 1930. Airport development was one of the areas of improvement authorized under WPA grants, and used to advantage in many parts of the state as well as at Chicago Municipal Airport.

Not only was the decade of the thirties one of progress in transport flying, but military aviation was again to the fore. Illinois did not share in the large development contracts for army and navy, but it remained important in the training program. Chanute Field at Rantoul, which had been the air technical training center of the Army from 1921, had more and more trainees in its shops and hangars. Scott Field, inland base for army lighter-than-air operations from 1920 until the program was abandoned in May 1937, was selected as general headquarters of the Army Air Force in 1938. The same year navy air training operations returned to the Chicago area, when Glenview Naval Air Station was activated on the site of Curtiss-Reynolds Field. By the end of World War II Chanute had graduated more than 200,000 air technicians, including many of the crews that made up the personnel of the Eighth Air Force, flying out of England, and the Twentieth Air Force, bombing Japan from Guam, Saipan, and Tinian. Most of the flying radio operators and ground radio technicians received their training at Scott.

With the outbreak of war with Japan, Orchard Place Airport became of great importance to the military. The government took over the field, enlarged it, provided it with four runways 150 feet wide and from 5,500 to 5,700 feet long, and the world's largest wooden structure, and turned it over to Douglas Aircraft Company of Santa Monica as an assembly and fly-away point for the large C54 four-engine transports. Ground was broken June 30, 1942, and the field and plant completed August 31, 1943. From then until October 1945, 655 of the big troop and cargo carriers were built and

delivered to army and navy. In addition the field accommodated some military traffic.

Illinois also had a Civil Air wing of nine groups, created by executive order in December 1941. The civilian aircraft manned by volunteer pilots towed targets for gunnery training, checked blackout security, performed search and rescue missions and scores of military chores that released Air Force planes for other duties. The nine groups, in numerical order, were stationed at Sky Harbor, Northbrook; McChesney Airport, Rockford; Rubicam Airport, Harvey; Municipal Airport, Moline; Municipal Airport, Peoria; Municipal Airport, Bloomington; Southwest Airport, Springfield; Parks Air College, East St. Louis; and Salem Airport, Salem.

During the war members of the Illinois wing received 825 air medals and 25 War Department citations for exceptional service. In 1968 the wing had 1,300 adults and 1,900 teenage cadets. The men participate in state and regional civilian defense airlift exercises, search and rescue operations, and other requested tasks. The cadets receive orientation flights and sound basic education for the space age. Twenty-four of the youngsters were rewarded for specially meritorious effort by participating in a glider-training program at Eastern Illinois University in 1966. Approximately 400 attend summer camps at Chanute Field or Scott Air Force Base each year. Adults maintain liaison with the Illinois Aerospace Education Committee, assist in school training programs, and maintain an aerospace research center at wing headquarters. Members serve without pay and provide their own aircraft, maintenance, and uniforms.

One of the largest flying clubs in the world came into being during the last year of World War II, when the Chicago magazine *Prairie Farmer* invited 50 aircraft-owning farmers of Vermilion County, Indiana, to fly into Chicago for a performance of the WLS Barn Dance. The club, from this modest beginning, attracted 670 farmer-flown planes from Illinois, Indiana, Michigan, and Wisconsin to its first field day at Purdue University, Lafayette, Indiana, July 30, 1946, and has had from that many to 1,000 participants in this annual event, which alternates between Purdue and the University of Illinois.

This kind of activity was an indication of the tremendous surge of interest in flying evident all over Illinois as service pilots returned home. It also pointed up the necessity for tighter control and better discipline in the air. During the pioneering era of aviation in Illinois much was attempted but little accomplished to legislate safety into air activities. However, aircraft do not forgive mistakes, and the facts of life and death in the air did a pretty fair job of policing the airspace. Between the end of World War I and the year 1926 twenty-four bills to regulate flying were introduced into Congress, the first by Senator Lawrence Y. Sherman of Springfield, Illinois, in 1919. None passed. Finally, in 1926, a Federal Air Commerce Act was approved and signed into law by President Coolidge. Legislation by the Illinois General Assembly followed. An act was passed in the second special session of the Fifty-fifth General Assembly in 1928 which stipulated the licensing and registration clauses of the Federal Air Commerce Act were to apply to all airmen engaged in commercial flight in Illinois. Amendments to this act, accepted by the legislature early in 1929, covered matters such as types of licenses to be held by airmen engaged in various kinds of flying and established minimum altitudes for flights over inhabited places. However, no appropriations or provisions for enforcement of the act were forthcoming, and it could not be made effective.

These inherent shortcomings were apparent almost at once, and toward the end of the same session an Aerial Navigation Commission was authorized and instructed to investigate legislative requirements and report to the next session of the assembly. This commission, headed by Major Reed G. Landis (now a retired colonel) recommended a permanent aerial navigation commission which would have regulatory and enforcing authority in the interest of public safety. Members were to be appointed by the governor for four-year terms.

The Aerial Navigation Act of 1931 was the first workable legislation relating to aircraft in Illinois. It established rules for flight, created a permanent commission, members of which would serve without pay, and gave the commission authority and some money to enforce the new air laws. Even though handicapped by lack of funds during the depression years, the commission accomplished much to further the development of aviation. The secretary, World War I ace Howard C. Knotts of Springfield, was also air adviser to the Illinois Commerce Commission, and in his dual capacity was able to coordinate the efforts of the two bodies until his death in Springfield, November 23, 1942.

By the end of the decade it was apparent that further legislation was needed, and the Illinois Aviation Conference of the Illinois Chamber of Commerce, the members of the Aerial Navigation Commission, volunteers working for the commission, and other interested persons set about getting it. In 1941 nine amendments to the Illinois Aeronautics Act were introduced in the General Assembly by Senator Earl B. Searcy of Springfield, passed by both houses, and signed by Governor Dwight H. Green. Most important of the changes, all designed to strengthen the Aerial Navigation Commission, was one making the commission, except for municipal corporations of more than 500,000 population, the sole state agency eligible to receive federal aid for airports and for the development of aeronautics in Illinois.

Further overhauling of air legislation was in abeyance from 1941 until nearly the end of World War II. Early in 1945 a number of agencies and individuals became active in work for new air laws to meet postwar needs. All were agreed that a stronger air authority was advisable and immediately after victory in Europe legislation was passed creating a Department of Aeronautics under the administrative code originally enacted in 1917. By means of an Illinois Aeronautics Act, a County Airports Act, a Municipal Airport Authority Act, and an Airport Zoning Act, postwar aviation was placed on a sound footing, with ample provision for the future.

The new organization was given authority to carry out multiple duties affecting every aspect of aviation in Illinois. The Aeronautics Act directed the new code department to cooperate with the federal government and with municipalities in regulation, promotion, and development of aviation and to render financial assistance to communities in the planning, construction, and improvement of airports and navigational facilities. It was authorized to receive federal funds (of which it was expected Illinois would share to the extent of about $40,000,000) on behalf of the state, municipalities, and political subdivisions and to enter into contracts for construction and development of aviation facilities. Regulatory duties included registration of federal aircraft certificates, pilot certificates, and flight instructor certificates, classification of and approval of airports and their operations, and the preparation of zoning plans for publicly owned airports.

The Municipal Airport Authority Act authorized creation of an airport authority to construct, develop, and maintain an airport in any territory of not less than 5,000 persons and containing one or more municipalities, subject to a referendum in the area affected, and approval by a majority of voters.

Emphasis on aviation has given Illinois a high place among the states in air activity. In aircraft population the state is third, surpassed only by California and Texas. In number of landing fields, airports, and heliports per square mile or per capita Illinois' rank has been first for a number of years. Thanks to an energetic safety program and an unsurpassed educational endeavor, the state is the national leader. This has been accomplished without making large increases in personnel. In fact the Department of Aeronautics today has fewer employees than it had shortly after organization in 1945.

The Department of Aeronautics has had four directors in its twenty-two years of service. First was Robert E. Dewey, appointed by Governor Green on his release from active duty as a military pilot in 1945. Joseph K. McLaughlin, also a service pilot, was appointed by Governor Stevenson in 1949. Mr. McLaughlin had served as a legal adviser to the Civil Aeronautics Administration. He was succeeded by Arthur E. Abney, an attorney with military background who had served as Mr. McLaughlin's assistant. J. E. "Jack" Wenzel, attorney and naval aviator, was appointed director by Governor Kerner in 1961 and served through 1968.

Meanwhile, city planners in Chicago were much concerned with the future of commercial aviation. The world's busiest airport was getting busier. During 1944, takeoffs and landings at Chicago Municipal Airport had reached a total of 120,783. More than a million inbound and outbound passengers were carried. This traffic was not maximum for the facilities of Chicago Municipal Airport, but the rate of increase began to be alarming. It indicated that by 1955 air traffic would be close to the danger point.

Nine airlines were providing scheduled service into and out of Chicago Municipal Airport. Three of these, American Airlines, Pan American Airways, and Trans World

Airlines, held certificates to provide service to cities around the world. This busiest of all airports was also one of the smallest, with less than 640 acres overcrowded as to hangars and shops and with approaches over solidly built-up areas. An army B24 had removed the most obvious hazard to traffic, a large gasholder a mile or so south of the field at a cost of ten lives early in the war, but there were other conditions that invited costly accidents, and proper zoning regulations in the vicinity of the field could not be established except at great expense.

The answer obviously was a new airport, and Orchard Place Airport, a government-owned tract more than twice the size of Chicago Municipal Airport, with open fields to north, west, and south where man-made hazards could be prevented by adequate zoning laws, and where land could be had at reasonable cost, was the obvious answer. On March 26, 1946, the city of Chicago received from the federal government as surplus property 1,080.61 acres of the total 1,371 acres, together with one small hangar. The military retained about 300 acres, including the huge assembly plant, the hangars, tower, and other buildings for reserve and Air National Guard use. By the middle of 1948 two air transport reserve wings had been created and one was ready for active service, as were several National Guard units.

Immediate relief for Chicago Municipal Airport, so far as nonscheduled operations were concerned, was provided at another area. A federal act setting up grants for airport construction and improvement was passed in 1946. Development of a landing strip on Northerly Island along the lakeshore south of Fourteenth Street had been determined upon and a lease signed between the city and the Chicago Park District, which held title to the land. When federal funds became available Chicago was the first city in the nation to benefit. Construction work began early in 1947 and the lakefront airport was ready to receive traffic December 10, 1948, just about the time Orchard Place Airport was completing its first year of operation under authority of the city of Chicago.

On June 30, 1949, the Chicago City Council passed a resolution renaming the three city-owned airports. Chicago Municipal became Chicago Midway Airport. Northerly Island was named Merrill C. Meigs Field in honor of a descendant of a pioneer family who had become one of Chicago's leading journalists and publishers. Orchard Place Airport became Chicago-O'Hare International Airport in memory of Lieutenant Commander Edward H. "Butch" O'Hare who received the Congressional Medal of Honor posthumously for flying alone into an enemy formation and shooting down six of nine attacking enemy land-based bombers bent on destroying the carrier on which he served. This action, resulting in O'Hare's death, occurred February 20, 1942, off Tarawa in the Gilberts during a reconnaissance raid.

Acquisition of land at O'Hare continued. Railroads west of the field were relocated along York Road. On October 30, 1955, American Airlines, Delta, Northwest, Trans World, and United transferred a portion of their scheduled operations to O'Hare. Six months later British Overseas Airways Company moved all its flights to O'Hare.

During 1955, almost 381,000 aircraft with more than 9,000,000 passengers operated into or out of Midway Airport. Flights were landing or taking off on an average of every minute and a half, day and night. Allowing for instrument flying conditions during the winter months, actually spacing probably was closer to one minute.

The next three years saw much progress at O'Hare. By 1958, 7,200 acres of land had been acquired and an issue of $120,000,000 revenue bonds approved under agreement with the airlines to provide the interest and retirement costs. In 1959 American Airlines instituted the first jet flights from runways more than two miles long, and O'Hare accommodated more than 200,000 aircraft, many of them exceeding a fifty-passenger capacity, and more than 2,000,000 passengers.

From that year scheduled airline operations were phased out at Midway and by 1962 all had been transferred to O'Hare. On December 15, 1962, the Federal Aeronautics Authority approved simultaneous approaches under instrument conditions, with ceilings as low as 900 feet. O'Hare thus became, and still is, the only airport in the world with simultaneous bad weather approaches, thanks to parallel northwest-southeast runways more than a mile apart. Takeoffs and landings averaged 47.7 per hour for the year 1962. During the preceding ten years passengers landing and taking off from the three Chicago fields had

more than doubled—from 6,162,097 in 1952 to 14,466,208 in 1962. Of these, 13,525,955 were accommodated at O'Hare.

In 1964 it was apparent that O'Hare was approaching the saturation point, and it was determined to reactivate Midway as a port for scheduled airlines. By the end of 1966 passengers flying into and out of Chicago's oldest commercial field had passed the number accommodated there in 1944, when traffic first passed the 1,000,000 mark, while at O'Hare 23,589,683 persons arrived or departed. An aircraft was landing or taking off on an average of fifty-eight seconds.

As traffic continued to increase in early 1967, it was obvious that a new facility with large capacity must be provided. Plans, under consideration for several years, were announced for a full-scale commercial field to be built on made land in the lake, close to the downtown area of Chicago or at another suitable place in the metropolitan area. Chicago and all of Illinois were well into the jet age.

Number of aircraft and passengers arriving at and departing from Chicago Midway Airport 1927–46

Year	Aircraft	Passengers
1927	800	0
1928	41,660	14,498
1929	93,613	44,452
1930	58,688	62,456
1931	71,083	97,070
1932	60,947	100,847
1933	63,252	133,247
1934	80,492	175,538
1935	60,727*	191,738
1936	73,345	260,863
1937	79,919	315,283
1938	69,604	352,563
1939	79,350	501,164
1940	88,201	704,846
1941	87,837	804,461
1942	88,349	720,746
1943	118,477	802,490
1944	120,783	1,089,553
1945	153,007	1,496,634
1946	190,338	2,598,418
Total	1,681,742	10,468,867

* DC3 aircraft, carrying twenty-one passengers, in service.

Amount and source of funds for public airport construction to December 31, 1966

Airport	Date of certificate or opening	Federal funds	State funds	Local funds	Longest runway (in feet)
Aledo	June 15, 1954	$0.00	$15,000.00	$8,000.00	2,100[2]
Alexander County, Cairo[1]	April 3, 1947	292,218.03	375,733.50	218,539.16	3,600
Aurora	Jan. 13, 1964	612,941.00	355,220.45	379,280.00	3,000
Benton	April 30, 1946	76,938.57	64,666.19	33,092.97	2,800
Bi-State Municipal, East St. Louis	July 19, 1944	1,006,400.39	205,478.99	61,143.96	4,000
Bloomington-Normal[1]	May 5, 1964	274,259.58	277,910.45	252,199.94	3,720[3]
Carmi	May 24, 1955	0.00	85,116.29	7,000.00	2,700
Casey	Nov. 8, 1946	47,890.81	54,677.14	3,577.23	2,200
Centralia	March 6, 1947	229,966.46	235,783.32	218,143.08	4,100
Champaign-Willard	Feb. 25, 1946	2,159,458.84	677,203.42	721,550.00	5,300
Civic Memorial, Alton[1]	July 3, 1946	1,079,722.87	697,379.85	994,092.34	5,100[3]
Coles County, Charleston-Mattoon[1]	May 28, 1946	857,512.69	492,357.74	383,075.90	4,400[3]
Decatur	Jan. 21, 1947	1,715,990.53	240,987.51	666,174.87	5,300
De Kalb	April 26, 1949	0.00	64,934.40	125,000.00	3,020
Dixon	Aug. 8, 1944	74,452.98	194,698.94	215,371.15	3,160
Effingham	Jan. 17, 1947	88,974.83	147,698.80	122,150.16	3,400
Fairfield	April 19, 1954	45,500.00	55,607.82	51,000.00	2,000
Flora[1]	July 1, 1957	84,574.40	196,143.01	79,500.00	3,500
Freeport	Oct. 30, 1946	76,759.77	276,975.34	258,929.43	3,600
Galesburg (old site)		103,570.00	50,000.00	65,000.00	closed
Galesburg (new site)	March 18, 1957	786,409.13	472,822.11	523,704.01	5,800
Greater Peoria[1]	June 15, 1950	1,839,533.82	1,130,303.60	2,230,978.63	7,150
Greater Rockford[1]	May 6, 1946	1,530,367.29	1,277,412.75	2,612,058.18[4]	6,000
Greenville, Bond County[1]	May 27, 1963	186,616.02	138,753.75		4,000
Harrisburg-Raleigh[1]	July 7, 1947	274,705.64	255,029.28	212,516.15	3,500
Havana	Oct. 11, 1952	0.00	20,000.00	27,000.00	2,000[2]
Jacksonville[1]	March 22, 1946	178,467.97	285,974.44	287,065.13	4,000
Joliet	1933	406,679.07	57,151.70	368,468.03	2,980
Kankakee Valley[1]	May 3, 1957	770,070.86	600,624.44	287,588.57[4]	4,300[3]
Kewanee[1]	July 3, 1964	77,898.89	75,788.03		3,200[3]
Lacon	Nov. 25, 1949	31,519.71	94,490.53	57,000.00	2,200
Lawrenceville	Sept. 30, 1948	50,063.92	75,524.26	100,500.00	5,200

Airport	Date				Runway
Lincoln	Jan. 1, 1950	136,305.20	136,400.00	190,455.37	2,700
Litchfield[1]	March 3, 1947	136,992.93	123,207.76	65,778.87	3,300
McLeansboro	April 22, 1955	0.00[5]	87,000.00	11,000.00	1,800
Macomb[1]	Jan. 8, 1965				
Metropolis	June 2, 1948	0.00	107,999.24	50,000.00	2,500
Morris	May 16, 1947	0.00	77,000.00	89,000.00	2,900
Mount Carmel	July 3, 1947	50,720.00	42,219.91	0.00	4,500
Mount Vernon[1]	May 7, 1956	575,635.57	600,605.95	458,418.94	4,000
Olney-Noble[1]	Sept. 28, 1956	223,061.04	179,258.44	224,999.22	3,600
Pekin	May 1, 1964	104,309.26	101,463.22	0.00	3,000
Quincy	Jan. 2, 1948	1,635,454.35	238,060.50	432,002.62	5,400
Robinson Community[1]	March 7, 1960	136,463.17	139,353.43	0.00[4]	3,400[3]
Rochelle	March 4, 1947	73,488.53	40,000.00	0.00	2,500
Rock Island County Metropolitan[1]	Nov. 28, 1947	2,393,351.78	1,559,815.70	2,906,134.19	6,505[3]
Salem[1]	Dec. 24, 1942	167,194.32	166,536.99	245,582.50	3,500
Savanna	Aug. 20, 1947	0.00	50,000.00	36,000.00	2,500
Shelbyville	Nov. 17, 1947	77,702.93	139,484.81	72,000.00	2,500
Southern Illinois, Carbondale-Murphysboro[1]	Nov. 13, 1946	481,610.38	403,125.18	349,630.15	4,400
Sparta Community[1]	Aug. 1, 1957	156,655.29	87,221.18	82,831.82	3,300
Springfield[1]	Nov. 9, 1945	2,372,091.71	881,006.91	1,592,857.84	7,000
Sterling-Rock Falls	April 22, 1947	148,826.93	312,257.34	201,500.00	5,600
Taylorville	June 7, 1946	0.00	147,803.07	63,000.00	2,240
Vandalia	Oct. 16, 1943	227,412.76	35,084.20	52,000.00	3,900
Vermilion County, Danville[1]	Feb. 5, 1946	302,469.11	768,318.24	757,632.14	5,400
Waukegan	Sept. 30, 1946	536,004.17	358,435.93	379,472.46	4,500
West Chicago	July 2, 1943	1,109,675.75	400,770.81	849,579.09	4,000
Williamson County, Marion-Herrin[1]	June 5, 1947	812,499.78	500,686.28	714,831.74	5,100
Chicago Municipal Airports					
Midway	May 8, 1926	7,086,935.57[6]	1,636,836.96	3,355,129.00	6,520
Merrill C. Meigs	Jan. 6, 1947	1,285,555.67	504,365.96	972,910.00	3,950
O'Hare	Jan. 1, 1947	14,817,623.07	10,061,245.55	16,092,799.34[7]	11,660
Total		$50,507,503.34	$29,133,011.61	$41,815,244.18	

1 Incorporated Airport Authority.
2 Sod runway
3 Runway being lengthened, end of 1966.
4 Under construction, end of 1966.
5 Construction not begun, end of 1966.
6 Includes WPA grant of $6,000,000 in 1935.
7 Plus $149,000,000 in bonds being retired by the airlines using the field.

Number of aircraft and passengers arriving at and departing from Chicago municipal airports 1927–46 and annually, 1947–66

Year	Midway		Meigs		O'Hare		Total	
	Aircraft	Passengers	Aircraft	Passengers	Aircraft	Passengers	Aircraft	Passengers
1927–46	1,681,742	10,468,867						
1947	206,140	2,645,674			108,704	217,412	314,844	2,863,086
1948	221,552	2,564,103	958	1,908	121,416	238,314	343,926	2,804,325
1949	223,493	3,246,963	23,589	43,355	124,519	259,408	371,601	3,549,726
1950	234,331	3,820,165[1]	25,812	50,788	94,682[2]	176,902	354,825	4,047,855
1951	263,737	4,953,160	26,394	55,460	80,519	146,278	370,650	5,154,898
1952	295,456	5,945,436	32,438	88,865	70,958	127,796	398,852	6,162,097
1953	331,297	7,151,474	37,611	103,893	90,940	201,968	459,848	7,457,335
1954	348,909	7,935,879	46,573	127,341	117,461	311,530	512,943	8,374,750
1955	380,996	9,134,483	56,178	169,266	142,912	471,170	580,086	9,774,919
1956	368,580	9,174,930	65,254	209,630	156,043	723,296[3]	589,877	10,107,856
1957	408,128	9,709,633	80,066	268,658	207,498	1,030,346	695,692	11,008,637
1958	420,193	9,667,696	93,585	309,268	231,412	1,263,147	745,190	11,240,111
1959	431,400	10,040,353	97,656	332,225	231,636	2,156,755[4]	760,692	12,529,333
1960	376,168	6,981,667	109,570	421,611	252,799	5,691,446	738,537	13,094,724
1961	249,852	3,565,561	97,598	356,231	322,054	9,615,480	669,504	13,537,272
1962	107,768	659,549	74,235	280,704	416,991	13,525,955	598,994	14,466,208
1963	126,959	417,544	75,860	286,911	426,098	16,163,464	628,917	16,867,919
1964	217,057	823,676[5]	71,942	201,586	458,460	18,394,126	747,459	19,419,388
1965	216,043	882,349	65,320	165,227	509,621	20,998,325	790,984	22,045,901
1966	258,491	1,094,878	72,906	192,194	543,500	23,589,683	874,897	24,876,755
Total	7,466,939	110,884,040	1,153,545	3,665,121	4,708,223	115,302,801	13,328,707	230,321,561

[1] Aircraft carrying fifty passengers in service.
[2] Two reserve wings from O'Hare go on active duty in Korean War.
[3] Thirty per cent of airline flights transferred to O'Hare.
[4] First jets in service from O'Hare.
[5] Limited passenger service restored at Midway.

**Comparison of number of airports in Illinois and in the forty-eight
contiguous states of the United States, 1928–65, by five-year intervals,
with number of Illinois aircraft and pilots by ten-year intervals**

Year	Number of Illinois airports			Number of airports in U.S.*	Per-centage in Illinois	Number in Illinois	
	Com-mercial	Private	Total			Aircraft	Registered pilots
1928	na	na	58	1,036	5.6%		
1930	na	na	69	1,550	4.5		
1935	48	11	59	2,207	2.6		
1940	44	12	56	2,280	2.5		
1945	60	11	71	3,427	2.1		
1946						3,245	8,483
1950	166	382	548	6,484	8.4		
1955	130	495	625	6,839	9.1		
1956						3,566	10,891
1960	122	480	602	6,881	8.7		
1965	129	459	588	6,910	8.5		
1966						3,705	12,869

na—Data not available.
* Statistical base changed in 1946 to include small
landing strips.

14

Farms, Mines, and Factories

During the second decade of the eighteenth century a Scotsman named John Law brought to Paris a modest fortune and an idea for replenishing the almost empty treasury of France. He persuaded Louis XV to sanction the consolidation of three French trading companies in a new venture. The Company of the West, concerned with the Mississippi Valley and particularly with Illinois, the older French East India Company, and the Company of Africa became the worldwide Company of the Indies.

Law was a brilliant pamphleteer. In modern times he probably would have been head of his own vast advertising agency. He promised gold and silver, jewels and furs, plantations and trading posts. He created paper money, the French *billets d'état*, persuaded the people to accept them in payment of claims against the state, and offered shares in the new trading company in exchange for the paper, thereby touching off the wildest speculative spree in the history of Europe until that time.

As English, Swiss, Italians, and citizens of the German states joined the French in a wild scramble, the shares doubled, tripled, and doubled again in value, a great shining bubble, a Mississippi bubble. But there were no gold or jewels and very little silver. Most of the furs were finding their way to Albany instead of to Montreal or Mobile. There was no trade with the colonies of Spain. The bubble burst. Hundreds all over Europe, once wealthy, were penniless. Law returned to London with only small change in his pockets—to die in poverty.

Law was a man born long before his time. His extravagant promises of wealth and luxury that failed so spectacularly of realization actually were far short of the mark. From the soil of Illinois and from the depths of the earth beneath this soil have come tens of billions of dollars in corn and wheat, hogs and cattle, in coal and petroleum, in cut stone and crushed stone, bright sands and rich clays, lead, fluorspar, and even a little silver. Corn alone has yielded more than $20,000,000,000 in the last hundred years. Coal, the presence of which was reported in Jesuit journals of the late seventeenth century, has brought more than $8,000,000,000 at the mines. It promises future production ten times as great (1965 values) from strip mines alone. Petroleum, natural gasoline, and gas have provided between six billion and seven billion dollars. The point in time when Illinois coal, mined at the present rate, may be exhausted is fantastically remote. The 140,000,000,000 tons within the state, mined at a rate of 50,000,000 tons a year, would not be entirely exhausted until the year 4300.

From Fields and Orchards

The story of farming in Illinois in the twentieth century may be summed up thus: 54.6 per cent fewer people, tilling 8.2 per cent fewer acres, are producing almost three times as much of Illinois' major crops today as in 1899. Farm population has decreased from a high of 1,215,000 in 1900 (one-fourth of the total population) to 551,000 in 1966 (one-twentieth of the people who live in Illinois). Land farmed has decreased from 91.5 per cent of total Illinois acreage to 85.6 per cent.

Corn, the number one crop, has shown a spectacular advance from an average of 30.9 bushels per acre in the first decade of record, January 1, 1871–December 31, 1880, to an average of 83.2 bushels per acre for the five years ending December 31, 1965. In this period, with less than 10 per cent more acres planted, the average annual crop showed an increase of nearly 300 per cent.

Soybeans, second in importance of Illinois' major crops, were introduced into the state at the time of World War I. For the decade ending in 1930 the average production was 15 bushels per acre. For the five years ending in 1965 that average had risen to 28.1 bushels per acre. Acreage planted in 1929 was 226,000 acres. In 1965 it was 6,021,000 acres.

In third place in 1965—second place prior to 1940—both in tonnage and value is hay. The average crop for the ten-year period ending December 31, 1880, was 1.38 tons per acre. From 1960 to 1965 the average was 2.16 tons per acre. With acreage down 352,000 acres in the five years ending in 1965 relative to the 1870's, the average yield was 1,000,000 tons greater.

Wheat gains since 1880 are even more dramatic. Average yield for the seventies was 12.7 bushels per acre. The five-year period ending in 1965 provided an average of 36.3 bushels per acre. During the five years ending December 31, 1965, Illinois produced an average crop 60 per cent greater than that of the 1870's on slightly more than half as many acres.

Oats, up to the time of the automobile Illinois' second largest crop, now is in fourth position. Acreage was down nearly 500,000 acres in 1965 from that of 1880. Not so production, where there is a gain of 16,500,000 bushels accruing from a production of 54.4 bushels per acre in the five years ending 1965, compared with an average of 31.0 bushels per acre in the seventies.

These increases came about because of better machinery, better farming methods, better seeds, and, in the last quarter of a century, far better fertilizer applied with more knowledge and care. Large farms, where machinery and equipment are instantly available for the operations that have brought about much of the increase, are a major factor. Despite the fact that many farms of five to twenty acres worked by part-time farmers on the fringes of cities and manufacturing areas are included, average farm size was at an all-time high of 218 acres in 1966, compared with a low point of 124 acres in 1880 and again in 1900. If we excluded the acreage farmed by industrial and clerical workers, retired persons, and others to whom farming is of secondary importance, the average probably would have been more than half a section (320 acres).

Much of the tonnage of field crops, particularly of corn and hay, is converted at the farm into pork, beef, and lamb; milk, butter, and cheese; eggs and poultry. Cash sales usually represent less than 10 per cent of the value of hay, 25 per cent of the value of oats, 40 per cent of the value of corn, 80 per cent of the value of wheat, and 90 per cent of the value of soybeans, which is largely a cash crop. A measure of actual farm income is found by combining cash income from all sales and value of products consumed in the home, plus government payments for acreage left fallow. This is presented in the table showing total farm income.

As production of the land increased by better farming, the number of meat animals increased. From 1870 to 1900 hogs on the farm averaged about 4,500,000, beef cattle and calves about 1,000,000. For the five years from 1961 to 1965 hogs averaged 7,500,000 and beef cattle 3,000,000. Numbers of sheep and lambs for slaughter have shown a somewhat smaller increase.

Appended are tables which show farm size and population, farm production and value, cash and gross income, value of products consumed in farm households, and amounts of other farm income by decades as far back as statistics are available. These tables, based on statistics published by the Illinois Cooperative Crop Reporting Service, reflect the growth of agriculture in Illinois from 1866 through 1965 (crops) and from 1924 through 1965 (livestock and products). Reporting periods are decades except 1866 through 1870 and 1961 through 1965 (crops); 1924 through 1930 and 1961 through 1965 (livestock). All figures are annual averages. Acres are cultivated acres, and, except in the first table, omit barnyards, work areas, woodlots, pasturage, and land left fallow.

Total farm income for selected periods, 1924–65 (annual average totals in thousands)

Period	Receipts for livestock and products	Receipts for crops	Government payments	Value of home consumption	Gross farm income
1924–30	$355,964	$218,908		$63,733	$638,605
1931–40	269,645	146,291	$18,261	43,086	477,283
1941–50	850,950	518,506	27,843	72,536	1,469,834
1951–60	1,147,114	811,772	18,172	50,583	2,027,641
1961–65	1,171,386	1,069,774	118,110	31,106	2,390,376

Annual average production and value of livestock and products for selected periods, 1924–65 (in thousands)

Period	Marketed (pounds)	Cash receipts	Value of home consumption	Gross income	Inshipments	Gross income less inshipments
			Hogs			
1924–30	1,291,874	$128,464	$13,033	$141,497	$651	$140,846
1931–40	1,362,255	86,105	8,173	94,278	1,034	93,244
1941–50	1,919,535	334,937	16,866	351,803	1,232	350,571
1951–60	2,482,504	430,472	10,032	440,504	2,330	438,174
1961–65	2,834,824	470,105	5,021	475,126	3,740	471,386

Period	Meat	Wool	Cash receipts	Value of home consumption	Gross income	Inshipments	Gross income less inshipments
			Sheep, lambs, and wool				
1924–30	50,514	1,355	7,712	25	7,737	2,601	5,136
1931–40	72,475	1,171	6,187	28	6,215	2,131	4,084
1941–50	70,375	2,029	12,785	34	12,819	4,824	7,995
1951–60	64,653	2,182	15,198	23	15,221	5,409	9,812
1961–65	63,793	2,077	12,687	38	12,725	3,873	8,852

Period	Marketed (pounds)	Cash receipts	Value of home consumption	Gross income	Inshipments	Gross income less inshipments
			Cattle			
1924–30	896,923	78,078	571	78,649	27,042	51,607
1931–40	1,018,116	71,700	857	72,557	27,225	45,332
1941–50	1,428,568	243,740	3,701	247,441	102,985	144,456
1951–60	2,000,753	434,603	8,189	442,792	176,809	265,983
1961–65	2,270,182	475,123	9,955	485,078	195,479	289,599

Period	Number (includes commercial broilers)	Cash receipts	Value of home consumption	Gross income
			Chickens	
1924–30	37,443	24,165	8,392	32,557
1931–40	35,479	15,165	5,547	20,712
1941–50	40,611	35,334	7,037	42,371
1951–60	26,041	17,672	3,268	20,940
1961–65	9,468	5,062	708	5,770

Period	Production (number)	Cash receipts	Value of home consumption	Gross income
			Eggs	
1924–30	2,001,000	35,699	6,870	42,569
1931–40	1,885,000	20,542	4,970	25,512
1941–50	2,672,000	65,624	8,795	74,419
1951–60	2,824,000	72,073	5,693	77,766
1961–65	2,040,000	45,969	2,345	48,314

Period	Marketed (pounds)	Cash receipts	Value of home consumption	Gross income
			Milk and dairy products	
1924–30	3,498,000	80,599	17,874	98,473
1931–40	4,085,000	65,571	11,844	77,415
1941–50	4,755,000	148,162	17,005	165,167
1951–60	4,482,000	164,108	12,188	176,296
1961–65	3,990,000	149,886	4,650	154,536

Period	Gross income
	All other animal products
1924–30	1,247
1931–40	4,375
1941–50	10,368
1951–60	12,988
1961–65	12,554

Annual average production and value of selected field crops which have represented more than 90 per cent of all crop values in Illinois since accurate reporting began in 1866

Period	Acreage (in thousands)	Bushels (in thousands)	Price per bushel	Yield, bushels per acre	Value per acre	Total value (in thousands)
			Corn			
1866–70	5,540	171,772	$0.46	31.0	$14.26	$78,987
1871–80	7,875	243,741	0.32	30.9	9.93	78;192
1881–90	8,836	297,024	0.31	33.6	10.47	92,490
1891–1900	9,974	333,220	0.29	34.1	9.86	96,356
1901–10	10,412	389,564	0.44	37.4	16.48	171,549
1911–20	9,592	327,334	0.93	34.1	31.85	305,537
1921–30	8,891	312,092	0.72	35.1	25.35	225,404
1931–40	8,687	326,910	0.51	37.6	19.23	167,039
1941–50	8,726	476,062	1.18	54.6	64.54	563,135
1951–60	9,093	544,562	1.32	59.9	78.83	716,835
1961–65	8,836	745,382	1.10	83.2	91.47	808,201
			Soybeans			
1921–30	154	2,310	1.56	15.0	23.36	33,604
1931–40	1,136	22,504	0.77	19.8	15.29	17,373
1941–50	3,383	74,342	2.22	22.0	48.74	164,878
1951–60	4,416	110,543	2.33	25.0	58.36	257,742
1961–65	5,685	159,654	2.15	28.1	60.29	342,756
			Wheat			
1866–70	2,480	27,037	1.31	10.9	14.30	35,463
1871–80	3,049	38,591	0.99	12.7	12.61	38,129
1881–90	2,730	35,946	0.81	13.2	10.66	29,112
1891–1900	2,013	28,025	0.65	13.9	9.04	18,198
1901–10	2,269	37,134	0.83	16.4	13.52	30,681
1911–20	2,572	43,140	1.52	16.8	25.52	65,632
1921–30	2,448	40,766	1.12	16.7	18.65	45,658
1931–40	2,126	37,358	0.74	17.6	13.03	27,711
1941–50	1,391	27,306	1.72	19.6	33.79	46,999
1951–60	1,718	47,460	1.91	27.6	52.76	90,642
1961–65	1,687	61,216	1.66	36.3	60.37	101,847
			Oats			
1866–70	1,222	38,050	0.37	31.1	11.56	14,122
1871–80	1,759	54,722	0.26	31.1	7.99	14,056
1881–90	3,209	105,491	0.27	32.9	8.93	28,670
1891–1900	4,111	134,154	0.23	32.6	7.56	31,092
1901–10	4,362	136,807	0.34	31.4	10.77	46,972
1911–20	4,379	159,360	0.50	36.4	18.27	80,025
1921–30	4,361	139,086	0.38	31.9	12.17	53,083
1931–40	3,656	117,310	0.26	32.1	8.33	30,465
1941–50	3,566	141,681	0.69	39.7	27.55	98,240
1951–60	2,833	124,575	0.67	44.0	29.28	82,939
1961–65	1,311	71,291	0.63	54.4	34.32	44,989

Period	Acreage (in thousands)	Tons	Per ton	Tons per acre	Value per acre	Total value (in thousands)
			Hay			
1866–70	1,680	2,414	9.78	1.44	14.05	23,602
1871–80	2,286	3,149	8.14	1.38	11.22	25,643
1881–90	2,922	3,949	7.79	1.35	10.53	30,772
1891–1900	2,989	3,541	7.27	1.18	8.61	25,738
1901–10	3,012	3,662	9.72	1.22	11.82	35,592

Table—continued

Period	Acreage (in thousands)	Tons (in thousands)	Price per ton	Yield, tons per acre	Value per acre	Total value (in thousands)
1911–20	2,960	3,215	16.25	1.09	17.65	52,243
1921–30	3,022	3,430	12.77	1.14	14.49	43,793
1931–40	2,785	3,467	8.27	1.24	10.30	28,680
1941–50	2,719	3,983	18.65	1.46	27.33	74,298
1951–60	2,525	4,786	20.54	1.90	38.93	98,296
1961–65	1,934	4,174	22.31	2.16	48.14	93,112

Annual average production and value of all crops, 1866–1965 (in thousands)

Period	Acreage Selected field crops	Total value	Acreage All other crops	Total value	Acreage All crops	Total value
1866–70	10,922	$152,174	364	$10,218	11,286	$162,392
1871–80	14,969	156,020	516	12,746	15,485	168,766
1881–90	17,697	181,044	462	8,903	18,159	189,947
1891–1900	18,887	171,384	308	7,742	19,195	179,126
1901–10	20,055	284,794	299	9,339	20,354	294,133
1911–20	19,503	503,437	446	28,211	19,949	531,648
1921–30	18,876	371,542	880	38,115	19,756	409,657
1931–40	18,390	271,268	702	21,969	19,092	293,237
1941–50	19,785	947,550	366	29,418	20,151	976,968
1951–60	20,585	1,246,454	267	21,471	20,852	1,267,925
1961–65	19,453	1,390,905	450	85,319	19,903	1,476,224

Percentage of Illinois population on farms and size of farms, selected years, 1870–1966

Year	Population Number (in thousands) Total	Farm	Percentage on farms	Farms Number (in thousands)	Acres (in thousands)	Average acreage
1870	2,540	1,165*	45.8%	203	25,883	128
1880	3,078	1,210*	39.3	256	31,674	124
1890	3,826	1,195*	31.2	241	30,498	127
1900	4,822	1,215*	25.2	264	32,795	124
1910	5,639	1,158	20.6	253	32,523	129
1920	6,574	1,107	16.8	240	31,975	133
1930	7,630	1,002	13.1	230	30,695	133
1940	7,897	979	12.4	221	31,033	140
1950	8,712	763	8.8	203	31,700	156
1960	10,081	621	6.2	159	30,700	193
1966	10,800†	551†	5.1	138	30,100	218‡

* Farm population before 1910 not available from the United States Census; estimated from various studies by the Illinois Cooperative Crop Reporting Service and universities.
† Population estimates for 1966 by Illinois Cooperative Crop Reporting Service, compiled from inter-mediate special censuses, metropolitan planning commission estimates, and Illinois Department of Public Health estimates.
‡ Average size of farms is misleading, since totals include many holdings of part-time farmers near cities and industrial areas.

Mines and Minerals

Father Louis Hennepin, in his narrative printed at Paris in 1698, reported that he had first seen stone coal on the North American continent near what is now Ottawa, Illinois, in 1668. However, his-torians are inclined to discount this state-ment, pointing out that Hennepin's first journey into the Illinois country was with Robert Cavelier, Sieur de la Salle, and Henri de Tonti more than ten years later. If this is so, the first white men, other than an occasional *courrier des bois*, to see coal outcroppings near the mouth of the Fox River were Father Jacques Marquette and Louis Jolliet in 1673.

Zinc and lead were mined by the Indians, French, British, and Americans in the Fever River area long before the year 1800. It is probable that coal was grubbed out of the ground by early settlers, but it had little use outside the blacksmith shop. Wood was plentiful, easier to obtain, and simpler to ignite. It is possible that farmers used coal to heat the stones for the hog-scalding vats or to maintain at a boil the huge open-air kettles used in butchering.

By 1831 it was recognized that coal was plentiful in almost every part of the state. At first found only in outcroppings along the Mississippi, the Illinois, and the lower reaches of the Rock, it appeared far from these streams when water wells began to be dug in the interior of Illinois.

The coal fields of Illinois form a major part of the Eastern Interior Basin which covers most of the state and extends into Indiana and Kentucky. The coal lies in beds that slope gently from the perimeter toward the center of the basin. Forty or fifty beds are distributed under 25,000,000 of the state's 35,000,000 acres. The coal-bearing strata are a part of the Pennsylvania system, and the beds, one upon another, vary in thickness from a few feet to a maximum of 2,600 feet in Jasper County, where a majority of the forty or fifty beds of the basin has been identified. For purposes of identification the beds are numbered. Many of the coal seams are mineable throughout, varying in thickness from twenty-eight inches to fourteen feet. Others develop mineable thickness only in widely separated areas.

First record of coal mining in 1810 tells of operations on the banks of the Big Muddy River in Jackson County. In 1833, when production reports were first gathered in Illinois, a total of 6,000 tons was mined. This figure rose to 10,000 in 1836, when commercial mining began on the Mississippi bluffs south of Illinoistown, now East St. Louis. In 1840, according to the United States census, 16,967 tons were mined in nineteen counties by 152 men.

For forty years after 1840, increasing railroad mileage was a principal factor leading to increased coal production, with a generous assist from new industries such as agricultural machinery in the late fifties. Coal replaced wood as fuel for railroad engines, and rails transported coal from the

mines to cities at low cost. A comparison of tons of coal mined and miles of railway in operation emphasizes this relationship.

Year	Tons of coal mined in Illinois	Miles of railroad in Illinois
1840	16,967	6
1850	300,000	111
1860	728,400	2,790
1870	2,624,123	4,823
1880	6,115,377	7,851

When the constitution of 1848 was adopted, there was little need for special legislation covering the coal mining industry. Even in 1870 it was felt that county supervision would be sufficient for policing mining practices, and the new fundamental law of Illinois adopted that year so stated. By 1880, however, it was becoming apparent that special laws were needed and, in 1883, the General Assembly created a Bureau of Mines and Minerals and defined the authority and responsibility of that office. From that time, mine operators made reports of industry operations, mine accidents, and other pertinent statistics yearly, based on a fiscal year running from July 1 to June 30 of the following year. This was changed to a calendar year in 1925, with production figures and other statistics covering the eighteen months prior to December 31, 1925.

The basic act of 1883 tightened the discipline within the mining industry. As a result, the accident rate (fatal) per million tons of coal mined showed a decline every decade but one from a high of 5.3 during the eight years ending June 30, 1890, to a low of 0.25 for the five years ending December 31, 1965. During the same eighty-three and a half years, production rate increased from 397 tons per man average to 5,805 tons per man average.

When the Bureau of Mines and Minerals became one of the first nine code departments created under the Lowden Code of 1917, the basic legislation required that the department be staffed with men experienced in mining. Regulations governing all phases of underground operation were made more stringent. Ventilating requirements have been increased from year to year, permissible methane at any face reduced, and a greater number of emergency exits made mandatory. Today any man employed as a face boss must hold a certificate of competency as a mine examiner, and a list of certificates in force is published at stated intervals.

Mechanization of Illinois mines began to show important economies shortly before World War I. In the last four years of the first decade of the twentieth century an average of 107 shipping mines were using undercutting machines below ground and 91 employed electric trains for underground haulage, while strip mining was converting from horse-drawn scrapers to self-propelled shovels.

At the time of World War II automation both underground and above made its bow in the coal industry. Continuous mining, using conveyor belts, effected important economies in production costs. By 1966 one mine of the many automated had more than thirty miles of three- and four-foot conveyor belts, while in the strip mines self-propelled wheel excavators weighing 3,600 tons and taking twenty-two yards at every turn were in use.

The changeover from men to machines reduced the labor force by almost 90 per cent from the twenties to the present decade. In the peak year of employment, July 1, 1922, to June 30, 1923, 103,566 men mined 75,514,095 tons of coal. Of this total, 412 men in strip shipping mines produced 895,608 tons, an average of 2,174 tons per man; 4,485 men in local underground mines and local strip mines produced 3,318,900 tons, an average of 740 tons per man. (Local mines supply only their immediate area.) In 1965, year of lowest employment until that time per ton of coal mined, 8,790 men produced 58,232,480 tons. Of this total, 2,780,350 was produced in local mines by 655 men, an average of 4,245 tons per man. Twenty-four underground shipping mines with 5,082 men employed produced 24,737,416 tons, an average per man of 4,867 tons, and in thirty-nine strip mines, 3,053 men mined 30,714,714 tons, an average of 10,060 tons per man employed.

Much more coal could be mined in Illinois if the market existed. The state has the largest reserves in the nation, except for the lignite beds of Wyoming and Montana. The Department of Mines and Minerals, with the support of the State Geological Survey, the University of Illinois, and Southern Illinois University, is cooperating with the principal coal producers in the development of new uses for coal. Chief among these are the production of pipeline gas at the mines and the conversion of coal to liquid fuels, also at the mines. Progress in both these areas was reported on a national basis at the annual meeting of Bituminous Coal Research, Inc., and the National Coal Association Conference in Pittsburgh, Pennsylvania, September 14 and 15, 1966. A summary of progress to date in conversion of coal to pipeline gas and to liquid fuel indicated that commercial production in Illinois might be expected in the early 1970's. An annual consumption of more than 50,000,000 tons, almost as much as that mined and shipped in Illinois during the sixties, was foreshadowed.

Another important effort by the Department of Mines and Minerals in cooperation with the principal producers of coal from strip mines is the use of exhausted strip-mining areas for recreation facilities, for pasture, and for reforestation. Good conservation practices are making many of the strip-mined areas more useful today than they were before they were touched by the power shovels of the miners.

Petroleum was discovered in Illinois during the late eighties and has been produced continuously since that time. New fields proved up in Hamilton, Wayne, and White counties during the thirties made Illinois one of the major six states producing oil and gas. During 1940 Illinois output was 146,788,000 barrels of crude oil, worth $160,000,000 plus 21,432,000 gallons of natural gasoline worth another million. This represented 10.8 per cent of all United States production. Since that time production has declined to an annual average of a bit more than 70,000,000 barrels in the period from 1961 to 1965. New reserves found in recent years show a backlog of 371,000,000 barrels. Waterflood operations since 1944 have resulted in production of more than 40,000,000 barrels of oil annually during the last ten years. Twenty-one wildcat wells and 581 development wells were brought into production during 1965. Production of natural gas adds considerable amounts each year to the cash receipts for petroleum products.

In addition to coal and petroleum, Illinois produces much of the fluorspar mined in the United States, about a fourth of the glass sand, and much of the tripoli, a special silica sand used for glazes, enamels, and similar products. Illinois also produces a modest tonnage of lead, considerably more zinc, and quantities of special clays. Stone, particularly limestone, which is abundant in many parts of the state, is high on the list of Illinois minerals. In 1965 stone accounted for 16.6 per cent of the state's mineral production. In all the years that records have been kept, starting in 1821, Illinois has produced 171,751 troy ounces of silver, worth $131,284, and no gold at all.

Appended are tables which show annual averages by decades or shorter periods as indicated at mines, wells, or quarries, of coal, petroleum products, and other minerals, together with statistics on strip mining, mine mechanization, and percentages of annual production contributed by each group.

Annual average production and value of coal at all Illinois mines and number of miners for stated periods, 1882–1965

Period	Tons mined	Value	Number of	Tons per	Value per
	(in thousands)		miners	miner	ton
8 yrs., 7/1/1882–6/30/1890	10,570	$10,436	26,605	397	$0.99
10 yrs. ending 6/30/1900	19,537	16,810	36,121	541	0.86
10 yrs. ending 6/30/1910	39,914	44,118	60,117	664	1.11
10 yrs. ending 6/30/1920*	66,890	111,264	66,024	1,013	1.66
10½ yrs. ending 12/31/1930†	65,004	109,253	77,818	835	1.68
10 yrs. ending 12/31/1940	45,015	67,523	46,924	959	1.50
10 yrs. ending 12/31/1950	64,845	178,928	33,020	1,964	2.76
10 yrs. ending 12/31/1960	46,354	183,361	16,092	2,881	3.96
5 years ending 12/31/65	51,639	196,554	8,896	5,805	3,81

* 1919–20 values estimated. year. 1921–30 values estimated.
† Reporting period changed from fiscal to calendar

Annual average comparison of production, men employed, and tons per man output for underground shipping mines and strip shipping mines for stated periods, 1920–65

Period	Number of mines	Tons mined (in thousands)	Number of of miners	Tons per man
Underground shipping mines				
10½ yrs. ending 12/31/1930	268	63,241	75,370	839
10 yrs. ending 12/31/1940	138	32,946	36,558	901
10 yrs. ending 12/31/1950	117	45,628	26,086	1,749
10 yrs. ending 12/31/1960	64	26,643	11,576	2,302
5 yrs. ending 12/31/1965	28	21,310	5,035	4,232
Strip shipping mines				
10½ yrs. ending 12/31/1930	12	2,781	897	3,100
10 yrs. ending 12/31/1940	24	8,333	2,417	3,448
10 yrs. ending 12/31/1950	36	15,630	3,129	4,995
10 yrs. ending 12/31/1960	30	17,833	3,129	5,699
5 yrs. ending 12/31/65	38	25,451	3,066	8,301
All shipping mines				
10½ yrs. ending 12/31/1930	280	66,022	76,267	866
10 yrs. ending 12/31/1940	162	41,279	38,975	1,059
10 yrs. ending 12/31/1950	153	61,258	29,215	2,097
10 yrs. ending 12/31/1960	94	44,476	14,705	3,025
5 yrs. ending 12/31/1965	66	46,761	8,101	5,772

Annual average mechanization in underground shipping mines for stated periods, 1906–65

Period	Number of mines using	Number of machines	Tons undercut (in thousands)	Percentage of mines using	Percentage of production
Machine cutting					
4 yrs. ending 6/30/1910	107	1,187	16,072	26.8%	33.8%
10 yrs. ending 6/30/1920	154	1,846	36,688	44.5	54.3
10½ yrs. ending 12/31/1930	177	2,455	45,446	63.2	69.9
10 yrs. ending 12/31/1940	104	1,019	30,378	64.2	73.6
10 yrs. ending 12/31/1950	99	636	44,239	64.7	72.2
10 yrs. ending 12/31/1960*	52	224	26,593	55.4	59.8
5 yrs. ending 12/31/1965	22	66	23,309	33.4	49.8

Period	Number of trains	Tons hauled (in thousands)			
Motor trains					
4 yrs. ending 6/30/1910	91	188	20,141	22.8	42.4
10 yrs. ending 6/30/1920	200	709	53,932	57.5	79.7
10½ yrs. ending 12/31/1930	206	1,344	57,099	73.5	86.5
10 yrs. ending 12/31/1940	119	1,178	32,591	73.5	79.0
10 yrs. ending 12/31/1950	100	1,209	44,269	65.3	72.3
10 yrs. ending 12/31/1960*	49	521	21,673	52.1	48.7
5 yrs. ending 12/31/1965	22	66	11,324	33.3	24.2

* Conveyor belts in increasing use this decade.

Annual average value of clay products, amount and value of sand and gravel, glass sand, and tripoli for stated periods, 1894–1965

Period	Clay products* Value (in thousands)	Sand and gravel Tons (in thousands)	Sand and gravel Value (in thousands)
6 yrs. ending 6/30/1900	$6,909		
10 yrs. ending 6/30/1910	12,079	3,443	$898
10 yrs. ending 6/30/1920	16,368	7,745	3,055
10½ yrs. ending 12/31/1930	23,650	14,119	5,756
10 yrs. ending 12/31/1940	9,382	9,509	4,728
10 yrs. ending 12/31/1950	28,271	13,145	7,653
10 yrs. ending 12/31/1960	53,518	20,921	17,376
5 yrs. ending 12/31/1965	54,126	30,363	17,969

	Glass sand† Tons	Glass sand† Value	Tripoli‡ Tons	Tripoli‡ Value
1913–20	570,834	$727,807	15,242	$139,406
1921–30	548,029	525,851	12,262	143,165
1931–40	575,941	541,592	9,835	126,537
1941–50	961,420	1,592,230	12,827	222,212
1951–60	1,238,192	2,942,753		
1961–65	1,534,519	3,457,726		

* No tonnage figures available.
† Figures for glass sand concealed for 1938, 1951, and 1954 because of limited number of producers; production included in sand and gravel. Figures for glass sand available from 1914–65.
‡ Figures for tripoli available from 1913–47.

Annual average number of accidents and rate per tons of coal mined for stated periods, 1882–1965

Period	Number of miners		Rate per million tons	
	Killed	Injured	Killed	Injured*
8 yrs., 7/1/1882–6/30/1890	55.8	183.3	5.3	17.3
10 yrs. ending 6/30/1900	73.2	510.2	3.7	26.2
10 yrs. ending 6/30/1910	183.2	585.1	4.6	14.7
10 yrs. ending 6/30/1920	187.1	1,591.8	2.8	23.8
10½ yrs. ending 12/31/1930	146.7	2,982.3	2.3	45.9
10 yrs. ending 12/31/1940	86.6	1,062.0	1.9	23.6
10 yrs. ending 12/31/1950	86.1	965.5	1.3	14.9
10 yrs. ending 12/31/1960	32.4	304.8	0.7	6.6
5 yrs. ending 12/31/1965	13.0	194.9	0.25	3.8

* Cases involving thirty days or more loss of work.

Annual average amount and value of fluorspar, lead, and zinc for stated periods, 1882–1965

Period	Fluorspar		Lead*		Zinc†	
	Tons	Value (in thousands)	Tons	Value (in thousands)	Tons	Value (in thousands)
8 yrs. ending 6/30/1890	5,844	$30				
10 yrs. ending 6/30/1900	6,488	46				
10 yrs. ending 6/30/1910	25,453	151			1,690	$198
10 yrs. ending 6/30/1920	84,539	1,200	1,924‡	$26	2,786	563
10½ yrs. ending 12/31/1930	52,823	1,021	748	102	1,448	187
10 yrs. ending 12/31/1940	52,716	1,041	342	30	515	61
10 yrs. ending 12/31/1950	158,723	5,331	2,818	650	11,700	2,800
10 yrs. ending 12/31/1960	157,737	7,924	3,257	933	21,880	5,141
5 yrs. ending 12/31/1965	133,678	6,642	3,025	701	21,272	5,249

* Negligible production, 1850–1919.   ‡ Average of 1919 and 1920 only.
† No production prior to 1906.

Annual average value of stone products and amount and value of lime and cement for stated periods, 1890–1965

Period	Stone* Value (in thousands)	Lime		Portland cement	
		Tons	Value (in thousands)	Barrels	Value (in thousands)
10 yrs. ending 6/30/1900	$2,321†	na	na	312	$301
10 yrs. ending 6/30/1910	3,353	109	$480	1,802	2,193
10 yrs. ending 6/30/1920	3,502	86	413	4,694	5,488
10½ yrs. ending 12/31/1930	23,522	26	228	6,644	10,637
10 yrs. ending 12/31/1940	3,907	38	286	4,746	5,761
10 yrs. ending 12/31/1950	16,015	296	2,664	5,951	11,711
10 yrs ending 12/31/1960	35,189	655	8,905	9,247	26,183
5 yrs. ending 12/31/1965	70,234	na	na	9,751	32,004

na—Data not available.   † Average of seven years, 1894–1900.
* No tonnage figures available.

Annual average amount and value of crude oil, natural gasoline, and natural gas for stated periods, 1889–1965

Period	Crude oil Barrels	Value	Natural gasoline Gallons	Value	Natural gas Cubic feet (in millions)	Value (in thousands)
	(in thousands)		(in thousands)			
2 yrs., 1889, 1890	2	$8			na	$17
10 yrs. ending 6/30/1900	4	17			na	74
10 yrs. ending 6/30/1910	12,713	81,935			4,348*	389
10 yrs. ending 6/30/1920	19,436	28,025	383†	$660		
10½ yrs. ending 12/31/1930	7,366	13,718	7,830	776	3,313	475
10 yrs. ending 12/31/1940	29,990	30,388	5,256	231	2,303	123
10 yrs. ending 12/31/1950	80,870	143,400	53,470	3,650	14,138	1,066
10 yrs. ending 12/31/1960	72,122	212,900	3,888	296	10,061	1,506
5 yrs. ending 12/31/1965	72,981	216,497	14,832‡	1,110	9,059	1,156

na—Data not available.
* Average for five years, 1906–10.
† Average for seven years, 1914–20.
‡ Production ceased 1964.

Annual average of mineral production and commodity groups as a percentage of total production for stated periods, 1883–1965. (Because of restrictions in publishing figures for individual commodities, this table is at variance with some of the individual tables and reflects greater accuracy.)

Value in thousands and percentage of total production

Period	Total production value	Coal	Oil and products	Stone products	Clay products	Sand and gravel	Fluorspar and metals
7 yrs. ending 6/30/1890	$ 12,159	$ 12,104 99.6%	$ 25 0.2%	na	na	na	$ 30 0.2%
10 yrs. ending 6/30/1900	24,105	16,810 69.7%	91 0.4%	$ 2,321 9.6%	$ 4,837 20.1%	na	46 0.2%
10 yrs. ending 6/30/1910	69,033	44,118 63.9%	8,388 12.2%	3,353 4.8%	12,019 17.4%	$ 905 1.3%	250 0.4%
10 yrs. ending 6/30/1920	165,240	111,264 67.3%	29,013 17.6%	3,501 2.1%	16.368 9.9%	3,326 2.0%	1,768 1.1%
10½ yrs. ending 12/31/1930	208,357	116,715 56.0%	27,545 13.2%	26,026 12.5%	30,082 14.4%	6,613 3.2%	1,376 0.7%
10 yrs. ending 12/31/1940	123,585	67,523 54.6%	33,451 27.1%	6,437 5.2%	9,882 7.9%	5,160 4.2%	1,132 1.0%
10 yrs. ending 12/31/1950	412,414	178,929 43.4%	152,553 37.0%	30,616 7.4%	28,271 6.9%	13,264 3.2%	8,781 2.1%
10 yrs. ending 12/31/1960	581,512	183,361 31.5%	238,277 41.0%	64,934 11.2%	53,518 9.2%	27,422 4.7%	14,000 2.4%
5 yrs. ending 12/31/1965	614,813	196,554 32.0%	219,700 35.8%	102,238 16.6%	54,126 8.8%	29,603 4.8%	12,592 2.0%

na—Data not available

Manufacturing in Illinois during the first two decades of statehood was confined largely to blacksmith shops, water-powered mills for grinding, extracting, and sawing, and to stills and vats for making whiskey and beer. First reliable statistics regarding numbers employed in manufacturing, kinds and value of products, and money invested were contained in the federal census of 1840. They revealed the following facts:

There were 13,185 persons in forty-nine counties employed in factories, mills, and distilleries. In each of the other counties, fewer than 100 men were similarly occupied. Seven hundred eighty-two persons were engaged in mining of whom 617 worked in the lead mines of JoDaviess County. Commerce provided a living for 2,506 persons. The rest of the state was concerned almost entirely with agriculture. The professions supported comparatively few.

Of the 13,185 factory hands, 2,304 were employed in mills of various kinds—flour and grist mills, oil presses, and sawmills. They produced goods worth $2,417,826. Investment totaled $2,147,618. There were four iron furnaces in the state, with seventy-four men on the payrolls. Investment in the four was $40,300. Metalworking kept thirty-five men busy, and the goods they produced were worth $33,500. Thirty-four persons were employed in the manufacture of woolens, valued at $9,540. Investment was $26,205. One hundred and fifty distilleries and eleven breweries in thirty-nine counties produced 1,551,684 gallons of spirits and 90,300 gallons of beer on an investment of $138,155. Bourbon whiskey was an export commodity.

Manufacture of soap, tallow, and whale-oil candles employed twenty-five men in thirteen counties and produced 520,000 pounds of soap, 118,000 pounds of tallow and 42 pounds of candles on an investment of $17,345. Farms, almost without exception, made their own soap and candles.

Manufacture of carriages and wagons kept 307 men busy in twenty-one counties. Product was valued at $144,362. Capital was $59,263. Seventy-one men were employed in making and repairing machinery with an output worth $37,720. Furniture was made in nineteen counties and provided a living for 176 men, who produced goods valued at $80,905 on an investment of $26,555.

Other census figures for 1840 are of interest. There were five colleges with a total enrollment of 311. Children in school numbered 38,857, less than 10 per cent of the total population. On the other hand, the literacy ratio was more than 85 per cent, with only 27,502 illiterate adults recorded.

The decade ending December 31, 1849, saw a considerable advance in manufacturing. In the year 1850 there were 3,162 manufacturing establishments with a capital of $6,218,000 and a net product value (selling price less manufacturing costs) of $7,575,000. This figure or something very much like it was later to be defined as value added in manufacture, and in the tables relating to employment, earnings, and value of manufactured goods from 1850 through 1963 that terminology has been used. It is slightly inaccurate during the early decades, but serves as a good basis of comparison.

Total value of production in 1850 was $17,236,073, a sevenfold increase over 1840, and this output was accomplished by about two thousand fewer workers. One and four-tenths per cent of the population was employed in the manufacture of durable and nondurable goods.

Additional information beyond that contained in the decennial census covering the early years of industry in Illinois is to be found in a thesis by Mary Oona Marquardt, who took her bachelor's and master's degrees at the University of Illinois in her early twenties, and her doctorate at the same university after she had passed the half-century mark. Her doctoral dissertation, entitled "Sources of Capital of Early Illinois Manufacturers, 1840 to 1880," was presented in 1960, and may be read at the library of the University of Illinois or that of the Chicago Historical Society. The splendid biographical material concerning the industrial pioneers is too voluminous to be included here, but from her admirable research we learn that so far as the number of establishments was concerned JoDaviess County led the state in 1850 with 279 plants or workshops. Cook County was second. In volume of production, however, Cook County had attained the position of leadership it never relinquished. Miss Marquardt's employment totals vary slightly from those of the federal census. She shows a total of 11,632 men and 433 women earning wages of $3,286,249 that year, while the federal census records 11,559.

In the statistics for 1860 coal is included as a manufactured product, with seventy-three miners and a product value of $1,285,501. Cook County continued to lead the state in value of product with a total of $13,555,671 of the state's $57,580,887. (Net, or value added in manufacture, was $22,022,000.) A large part of Cook County's total came from the manufacture of agricultural machinery.

Two great needs spurred the inventive genius of pioneer blacksmiths of the forties and fifties—a machine to replace the scythe, sickle, and cradle in the grainfields, and a plow that would clean itself and turn a good furrow in the rich, black, recalcitrant soil of the Illinois prairies. As has been the case since man first made fire with a stick and a deer thong, the need led to the solutions and in so doing created great wealth for the state of Illinois, and several huge fortunes among the state's industrialists. Two names are outstanding—John Deere of Vermont and Cyrus Hall McCormick of Virginia. McCormick, with his father, patented a reaping machine in 1834 and erected a factory in Chicago in 1847. John Deere, journeyman blacksmith, who arrived in Grand Detour at the age of twenty-two in 1836, made the first successful steel plow in 1837. Deere moved from what started as a home workshop into a new factory in Moline the same year McCormick located in Chicago. Out of these beginnings Illinois became the dominant state of the Union by 1860 so far as manufacture of agricultural machinery was concerned.

Nor was the inventive genius and adaptive talent in Illinois confined to reapers and plows. Many labor-saving devices, some of them applicable to production methods in factories, appeared, and the business of manufacturing showed steady gains in the efficiency of the men it employed. Average value added in manufacture, reduced to the output of one man, increased more than twentyfold, from $656 in 1850 to about $16,000 in 1964. Much of the benefit accruing from more efficient production was passed along to the workers in the form of higher wages paid, as indicated by the almost static curve for value added per dollar of wages. This figure was $2.36 for 1850, and had increased only by one-third to $3.145 in 1963.

Other statistics highlight industrial progress in the last century. Annual value added in manufacture rose from $7,575,000 in 1850 to an estimated $16,129,000,000 in 1964. Capital invested increased from $6,218,000 in 1850 to $3,366,453,000 in 1919, after which the statistic was not published. Total persons employed in manufacturing increased from 11,559 or 1.4 per cent of population in 1850 to an estimated 1,252,000 or 11.9 per cent of population in 1964. Annual average wage rose from $277 in 1850 to $5,439 for wage earners and $8,178 for salaried employees in 1963.

In the statistics appended, the first table reflects the progress of industrial activity with reasonable accuracy. Figures withheld from publication in selected categories to avoid revealing records of individual companies (generally when there were fewer than three producers), have in the main been included in the overall totals. While there have been many changes in methods of reporting factory production over the years, every effort has been made to reconcile the figures and bring production in different categories into relationship with the reporting method used since 1954, when major changes were made by the Department of Commerce in the base for the census of manufactures. Selection of years for reports is not capricious. The year 1933 is included because it represented the lowest point, since World War I, of industrial activity. No biennial census of manufacturers was published during the years of World War II. Otherwise we have tried to conform to a publication at ten-year intervals until 1900 and at five-year intervals thereafter.

The table showing employment and value added by kinds of products contains many inaccuracies, and cannot be used except as an approximate indication of growth of individual categories, for reasons stated above. Used with reasonable caution, however, the table may be of some value to students of industrial progress.

Illinois Exports

In 1961 the Department of Commerce of the United States instituted a study of the origin of exports by states and geographical regions, based on estimated export totals for the year 1960. Only the standard categories of the census of manufactures were used. Manufacturers employing more than 100 men were given questionnaires with reference to export products at plant value, cost of transportation to shipping port, warehousing, and wholesale margin costs from plant to port. Export of agricultural products, in which Illinois was frequently the leader for many years, was not included in the study. Had it been, the report would have shown Illinois to be in first place.

Reports were received from plants producing about two-thirds of export products. They included exports to Puerto Rico and bunkered fuel sold to foreign vessels in United States ports. The totals, released early in 1962, were well documented, and the survey so well received by American manufacturers that a second study was made in 1964 of exports in 1963. On this occasion exports to Puerto Rico and fuel sold for shipboard use were omitted.

This second census of origins of foreign commerce revealed that Illinois, second to California in 1960 and just above New York and Ohio, with an increase of 17 per cent in 1963 over 1960, had slipped to third by $6,500,000. New York had gained 18 per cent in the three year period. California, with a gain of 11 per cent, still led all the states, but the margin between first and second places, $138,400,000 in 1960, had narrowed to $83,200,000 in 1963.

A third census of exports, covering 1966, was published in the fall of 1967 by the United States Bureau of the Census in *Current Industrial Reports*, Series MA-161 (66)-1. Controls were approximately the same as for the 1963 census. This report showed a spread of $105,700,000 among the three leaders, with Illinois overtaking and passing New York, and California dropping to third position. Illinois also retained leadership in exports of agricultural products—and total exports.

Position of the three leaders was:

		Value at the plant
1960	California	$1,373,000,000
	Illinois	1,234,600,000
	New York	1,228,400,000
1963	California	1,530,200,000
	New York	1,447,000,000
	Illinois	1,440,500,000
1966	Illinois	1,883,700,000
	New York	1,807,700,000
	California	1,778,000,000

The Illinois total for 1966 was larger than that of five geographical divisions—New England with six states, the West North Central division with seven states, the East South Central division with four states, the West South Central division with four states, and the Mountain division of eight states. The East North Central division, which includes Illinois, Indiana, Michigan, Ohio, and Wisconsin, for the third time, had the largest total of any geographical division.

Illinois held first place in the manufacturing classification only in one category, machinery except electrical, which furnished slightly more than half of the Illinois export total of manufactured products. Illinois was second in food and related products, and printing and publishing; third in rubber and plastics, fabricated metal products, and unclassified products; and fourth in apparel and related products, and instruments and related products.

Illinois furnished 8.9 per cent of the national industrial exports. Important in Illinois' position of leadership in recent years has been the achievement of two trade missions, to Europe in 1963 and to Asia in 1965; the work of the Department of Business and Economic Development, for which it received a Presidential "E" certificate, and the enthusiastic cooperation of organizations like the Chicago Association of Commerce and Industry.

Illinois shipments of pig iron, 1940–65

Year	Tons	Value
1940	4,093,623	$73,882,065
1941	5,461,459	113,558,606
1942	5,871,858	125,662,134
1943	5,920,894	126,910,295
1944	5,686,397	118,953,078
1945	5,061,368	116,303,897
1946	4,359,719	109,717,853
1947	5,607,680	173,679,369
1948	5,503,437	196,586,808
1949	4,904,281	204,467,609
1950	6,038,572	258,242,109
1951	6,592,721	306,764,003
1952	5,461,716	263,873,529
1953	6,531,839	325,582,535
1954	4,534,969	227,159,687
1955	6,466,534	331,126,618
1956	6,537,451	356,432,770
1957	6,195,023	359,569,000
1958	4,217,898	258,661,000
1959	5,327,000	320,243,000
1960	5,247,000	316,382,000
1961	4,775,000	288,469,000
1962	4,775,000	282,210,000
1963	4,541,000	261,186,000
1964	5,579,000	322,098,000
1965	6,407,000	361,819,000

Employment and value added by kinds of products* for selected years, 1929–63

	1929		1933		1939		1947	
	Wage earners	Value added (in thousands)	Wage earners	Value added (in thousands)	Wage earners	Value added (in thousands)	Wage earners	Value added (in thousands)
Durable goods								
Primary metals	65,151	$406,906	24,448	$53,934	57,129	$158,515	101,334	$556,338
Forest products	11,953	36,342	7,325	16,289	11,699	28,478	na	na
Furniture and fixtures	35,851	121,184	12,100	19,618	22,364	51,253	29,193	141,142
Stone, clay, and glass products	20,707	73,862	7,067	21,225	10,418	26,758	30,705	175,996
Fabricated metal products	49,200	185,293	27,644	68,387	64,838	200,826	115,129	616,579
Machinery, except electrical	53,625	214,627	40,466	92,561	62,807	227,587	218,096	1,097,751
Electrical equipment and supplies	61,931	288,469	na	na	13,871	56,612	129,841	675,767
Transportation equipment	22,871	74,087	24,849	56,105	17,510	47,496	46,227	253,413
Instruments and related products including watches	12,848	43,655	na	na	20,834	65,202	31,163	145,195
Not otherwise classified	14,944	58,697	11,548	25,669	13,958	34,044	na	na
Nondurable goods								
Food and kindred products	55,854	323,371	63,384	187,641	79,589	307,268	na	na
Textile mill products	9,998	24,807	7,714	13,892	6,425	12,230	11,733	58,980
Apparel	46,511	133,191	44,509	66,984	47,315	239,846	60,390	252,257
Paper and allied products	11,306	48,268	8,966	29,176	16,077	56,335	28,129	158,113
Printing and publishing	50,808	332,063	34,008	157,623	47,856	239,846	91,421	541,841
Chemicals, paints, soaps, and allied products	16,040	134,179	11,835	72,728	15,880	115,425	47,537	438,305
Rubber and rubber goods	1,496	5,087	1,343	2,562	4,486	10,667	5,279	na
Leather and leather products	6,297	21,648	19,540	31,875	25,264	49,472	28,847	115,201
Petroleum and coal products	na	na	4,571	25,839	9,217	64,300	14,140	208,297
Not otherwise classified	31,038	133,808	ra	na	6,107	16,994	na	na

	1954		1958		1963	
	Wage earners	Value added (in thousands)	Wage earners	Value added (in thousands)	Wage earners	Value added (in thousands)
Durable goods						
Primary metals	96,200	$840,000	89,432	$906,854	97,851	$1,176,747
Forest products	12,495	69,020	11,836	77,460	11,088	88,819
Furniture and fixtures	27,363	179,575	24,705	188,082	23,500	208,986
Stone, clay and glass products	na	na	37,724	418,759	37,603	488,113
Fabricated metal products	130,150	1,005,400	127,744	1,201,866	121,879	1,366,458
Machinery, except electrical	na	na	164,447	1,723,164	178,573	2,264,672

Electrical equipment and supplies	na	na	162,255	1,455,423	167,834	1,806,838
Transportation equipment	50,986	475,528	44,673	535,606	40,819	601,088
Instruments and related products including watches	31,879	234,404	30,962	302,905	36,592	474,806
Not otherwise classified	37,903	262,292	31,229	264,738	31,827	309,286
Nondurable goods						
Food and kindred products	140,151	1,337,334	128,982	1,653,037	116,063	2,059,037
Textile mill products	10,080	61,885	8,126	60,082	6,728	54,192
Apparel	50,817	232,526	44,345	246,407	40,467	266,218
Paper and allied products	30,760	229,403	31,922	386,977	35,506	375,438
Printing and publishing	93,944	756,506	94,445	918,520	95,476	1,197,739
Chemicals, paints, soaps, and allied products	50,403	663,699	46,189	847,870	47,468	1,218,465
Rubber and rubber goods	6,054	30,030	22,143	185,240	28,489	308,077
Leather and leather products	21,871	116,627	na	na	16,242	117,229
Petroleum and coal products	16,618	214,596	14,140	208,297	11,346	250,378
Not otherwise classified	na	na	na	na	na	na

na—Data not available.
* Figures on products withheld when competitive information would be revealed, or for other reasons. Therefore totals will not correspond with those of preceding tables.

Record of employment in factories for selected years, 1850–1964

Year	Number of establishments	Capitalization[2] (in thousands)	Employees[1]			
			Number of salaried	Number of wage earners	Total	Percentage of population
1850	3,162	$6,218	na	na	11,559	1.4%
1860	4,268	27,549	na	na	22,968	1.3
1870	12,597	94,368	na	na	82,979	3.3
1880	14,549	140,652	na	na	144,727	4.7
1890	20,482	502,005	31,980	280,218	312,198	7.3
1899[3]	38,360	776,830	85,533	395,110	480,643	10.2
1899[4]	14,374	732,830	40,964	332,871	373,835	7.1
1904	14,921	975,845	68,511	379,436	447,947	9.0
1909	18,026	1,548,171	85,280	465,764	551,044	10.1
1914	18,388	1,733,327	110,984	506,943	617,927	10.4
1919	18,539	3,366,453	151,691	653,114	804,805	12.4
1925	14,117		na	622,368	na	na
1929	15,333		144,792	691,555	836,347	11.0
1933	10,740		na	420,334	na	na
1939	11,983		151,733	590,995	742,728	9.6
1947	15,988		230,405	954,415	1,184,820	14.0
1954	17,628		274,076	902,967	1,177,043	12.7
1958	18,100		304,179	835,233	1,139,412	11.6
1963	18,592		354,980	855,820	1,210,800	11.6
1964	na		na	na	1,252,000[5]	11.9

na—Data not available.
[1] Includes proprietors who drew a salary.
[2] Not published after 1919.
[3] Includes home industry establishments, carried in earlier years but dropped with the census of manufacturing in 1904.
[4] Excludes home industry establishments for comparison with later figures.
[5] Estimated from preliminary data.

Salaries, wages, and value added by manufacture for selected years, 1850–1964

Year	Salaries		Wages		Value added		
	Paid (in thousands)	Average annual	Paid[1] (in thousands)	Average annual	By manufacture (in thousands)	Average per wage earner	Average per thousand dollars wages paid
1850	na	na	$3,204	$277	$7,575	$655	$2,364
1860	na	na	7,633	333	22,022	959	2,885
1870	na	na	31,100	375	78,021	940	2,509
1880	na	na	57,429	397	125,021	864	2,177
1890	$28,650	$896	142,873	510	379,621	1,355	2,657
1899[2]	43,337	507	191,511	485	519,976	1,316	2,715
1899[3]	40,549	990	159,104	478	439,418	1,320	2,762
1904	60,560	884	208,405	549	570,285	1,503	2,736
1909	91,449	1,072	273,318	587	758,350	1,628	2,774
1914	128,478	1,158	340,910	672	907,139	1,789	2,661
1919	274,616	1,810	801,087	1,227	1,936,974	2,966	2,418
1925	na	na	897,970	1,443	2,395,774	3,849	2,668
1929	368,722	2,547	1,024,870	1,482	2,930,038	4,237	2,859
1933	na	na	403,682	960	1,200,784	2,857	2,975
1939	365,174	2,407	742,451	1,256	2,187,240	3,701	2,946
1947	957,775	4,157	2,627,318	2,753	6,680,137	6,999	2,543
1954	1,616,315	5,897	3,518,602	3,897	9,663,848	10,702	2,747
1958	2,031,124	6,677	3,833,476	4,245	11,664,070	13,966	3,042
1963	2,902,922	8,178	4,655,057	5,439	14,640,121	17,107	3,145
1964	na	na	na	na	16,129,000[4]	na	na

na—Data not available.
[1] Includes salaried employees through 1880.
[2] Includes home industry establishments, carried in earlier years but dropped with the census of manufacturing in 1904.
[3] Excludes home industry establishments for comparison with later figures.
[4] Estimated from preliminary data.

Illinois exports, rank, and percentage of national total in reporting categories for 1966, and change from 1960

Product	Illinois exports at the plant 1966 (in millions)	Index of export change (1963 = 100) 1966	Index of export change (1963 = 100) 1960	Rank in 1966	National exports at the plant 1966 (in millions)	Illinois percentage of national total
Total exports manufactured	$1,883.7	129	86	1	$21,299.2	8.8%
Food and kindred	205.8	107	81	2	1,908.1	10.7
Tobacco products	0.5	2,479	84	12	578.3	0.1
Textile mill	4.3	173	98	14	335.3	1.3
Apparel and related	12.0	120	91	4	198.9	6.1
Lumber and wood	5.3	146	75	18	284.3	1.8
Furniture and fixtures	2.2	130	114	5	36.1	6.1
Paper and allied	10.5	171	68	17	599.7	3.7
Printing and publishing	36.0	175	61	2	258.9	13.9
Chemicals and allied	86.5	138	80	13	2,438.6	3.6
Petroleum and coal	11.2	171	92	6	400.9	2.8
Rubber and plastics	22.1	161	81	3	337.2	6.5
Leather	2.3	104	98	10*	60.4	3.8
Stone, clay and glass	17.2	145	73	7	283.3	6.1
Primary metals	44.0	154	122	7	1,080.7	4.1
Fabricated metals	89.3	151	87	3	948.0	9.4
Machinery except electrical	917.9	128	83	1	4,722.3	19.4
Electrical machinery	151.6	161	81	5	1,605.4	9.6
Transportation equipment	139.2	158	143	7	3,452.4	4.0
Instruments and related	59.8	148	87	4	791.9	7.6
Miscellaneous	66.0	117	64	3	978.5	6.1

* Tied with Tennessee.

15

Libraries, Museums, and Historical Societies

In what Illinois community was the first library established? There are two possible places—Albion and Edwardsville. To some extent the answer depends on the identity of the benefactor who gave the town of Edwardsville the 133 volumes cataloged under 79 titles in November 1819. The catalog gives no founding date. No formal association was chartered. There is no record of the date in the files of the *Edwardsville Spectator*. An examination of the listed titles, which include twelve volumes of American state papers, Gibbon's *Rome* (the four-volume edition), Shakespeare's works, Burns' poems, Scott's works, ten bound volumes of the *London Spectator*, titles by both Addison and Steele, and a translation of *Gil Blas*, indicate that the books were presented by a person of education and considerable property.

Examination of the census of 1820, which lists heads of families by communities, shows the presence of one man who fits this description. He was Edward Coles, soon to be the second governor of Illinois. Coles, son and heir of a wealthy Virginia planter, private secretary to James Madison and his special envoy to Russia, on his father's death sold the plantation and brought his chattels, animate and inanimate, to Edwardsville. The slaves, who had already been freed on the voyage down the Ohio River, he established in the vicinity as farmers, purchasing 160 acres of land for each head of a family or single man twenty-four or more years of age. His goods he had placed in a commodious home.

But if it was Coles who benefited Edwardsville with a gift of books, and if they were the first received by the Edwardsville library, then the Albion library can claim priority, for Coles only arrived in Edwardsville as a resident during the summer of 1819. He had made a brief visit there a couple of years earlier on a journey to select a place of residence in the Illinois country.

On the other hand, the *Edwardsville Spectator*, in its edition of December 26, 1820, stated that a library had been established at Albion in the year 1818. Existence of the library is attested in a letter written by Richard Flower from Albion August 8, 1819. Flower, on a visit to his son, the founder of the English settlement of Albion, mentions a library in the village church containing several volumes of sermons and a few volumes of Shaw's *General Zoology or Systematic Natural History*, publication of which had begun in 1800 and the work, in fourteen volumes, completed in 1826.

Evidence favoring either town is inconclusive, but seems to point to Albion. In any event, both towns had the beginnings of libraries before the Social Library Association at Kaskaskia was chartered (1826). In Chicago a few books were available in Mark Beaubien's cabin for children of the Sunday School in 1832. In 1834, the year after Chicago was chartered as a village, the Chicago Lyceum, a reading room supplied with 300 volumes, a lecture platform, and chairs for about one hundred members, was opened. A library with reading room and lecture hall was established at Belleville July 17, 1836, by German scholars who had fled their fatherland in the early 1830's after the Frankfurt rebellion and settled on farms near Belleville. To the local residents these newcomers were known as the Latin farmers, since their knowledge of the dead languages exceeded that of agronomy. Their St. Clair Library Association was chartered by the General Assembly February 22, 1837.

In Chicago a Young Men's Association was organized in 1841. Two dates are given, January 16 and January 30; take your choice. The association maintained a reading room and lecture hall and was charged with obtaining "literary and scientific" lecturers. This group had as its first president Walter Loomis Newberry, a merchant who had settled in Chicago in 1833. This estimable gentleman, several times president of the Chicago Board of Education, was later to give half his fortune to establish one of the world's great reference libraries in Chicago.

Other private reading rooms and libraries existed in Illinois during the early years of statehood. One of record was established at Alton in 1852. Schools and colleges had collections open to students and in some cases to others. Public libraries supported by municipalities did not exist until 1872, when the first library enabling act was passed by the General Assembly. Impetus for the legislation, according to some commentators, was engendered by the Chicago fire of October 1871. This is not strictly in accord with the facts.

At the time of the fire there were several worthy collections of books and manuscripts in the city. In 1868 the Young Men's Association became the Chicago Library Association, with pleasant quarters at Randolph and La Salle streets. The Chicago Historical Society, organized in 1856, already had a significant collection of manuscripts, periodicals, and books, a total of 16,000 volumes of which about half related to the history of Chicago and the state of Illinois. They included the original draft of the Emancipation Proclamation, a documentary history of Chicago, 1,738 files of newspapers, the Gould manuscripts on crustaceans of the world, and the Kinzie collection of portraits of noted men. The Academy of Sciences, established in 1857, had a small, well-chosen library relating to plants, animals, and geological formations of the Chicago region. They were housed in the society's "fireproof" building at Wabash and Van Buren streets, together with numerous private collections sent to the academy for safekeeping. The Academy of Design had a small, highly specialized library consisting of books, prints, and drawings relating to the arts.

The year before the fire citizens of Peoria, which already had a library association and a collection of books, wished to give those volumes to the city of Peoria for a public library. They found that there was no legal way for the city to maintain such an institution with public funds. At their urging Samuel Caldwell, representative from Peoria County, on March 23, 1871, introduced a bill to provide for public support of libraries. Required readings were had that year in House and Senate, but because of pressure of other business the act did not reach a vote, and passed over to the special session of the legislature scheduled to convene in November.

At this juncture, a fire started in Patrick O'Leary's cow barn on DeKoven Street, and Chicago was in flames. The fire that raged from the evening of October 9, 1871, to the morning of the eleventh devoured businesses, homes, and all the downtown collections of books, art objects, and museum treasures.

In London, Thomas Hughes, whom men over sixty will remember as the author of that classic of schoolboy life, Tom Brown's Schooldays, read the cables. Scarcely two years before, Hughes had been in Chicago, had visited and probably lectured at the library association, and had been amazed to find in the hinterlands of America a collection of 30,000 volumes available to readers at a modest fee. Hughes had been a favorite pupil of Dr. Thomas Arnold, headmaster at Rugby and the father of the poet Matthew Arnold. He acted quickly, and with the help of the poet and others plus the backing of an existing Anglo-American association, began to collect books for Chicago. Before the end of the year 7,000 volumes were dispatched, and during 1872 another 5,000 were added. Among the donors were Queen Victoria, who autographed The Early Years of the Prince Consort, Disraeli, Gladstone, Matthew Arnold, Herbert Spencer, Charles Kingsley, the Duke of Wellington, John Stuart Mill, and many other famous men and women. Hughes procured a special bookplate for the collection which read: "Presented to the City of Chicago Toward the Formation of a Public Library after the Fire of 1871 as a Token of English Sympathy." Upon receipt, the books were housed in a water tank owned by the city at Adams and La Salle streets. The Chicago Library Board was organized January 8, 1872, and sent a representative to Springfield to urge passage of the library bill. This was accomplished March 7, 1872.

While Chicago was the first to establish a library board, it was not the first with a public library. That honor went to Elgin, which organized its library immediately after passage of the bill, and to Rockford, which organized after Elgin, but opened its doors a few days earlier.

Chicago, a devastated area being transformed into a new metropolis, needed a bit more time to prepare fitting premises. First the tank was lined with brick set five inches away from the steel walls. Next shelving was erected sufficient for 17,000 volumes. A reading room, attached to the stack room by an outside staircase, was built beneath the tank. The library was opened with fitting ceremonies on New Year's Day, 1873, and was followed the same year by public libraries at Earlville, East St. Louis, Moline, Oregon, Rock Island, and Warsaw. By 1879 there were 26 public libraries in Illinois, and in 1900 there were 129.

First librarian of the Chicago Public Library was W. B. Wickersham, who filled an interim appointment in 1873 until the arrival in Chicago of William Frederick Poole, the man selected by the library board from among a number of trained applicants for permanent tenure. He remained with the library until 1887, when he resigned to organize the newly endowed Newberry Library.

In 1904 a library census revealed that 112 of the 146 libraries in Illinois were supported by public funds. Fourteen libraries reported more than 20,000 volumes on their shelves. Chicago led the list with 298,743. The others were Peoria, Springfield, Rockford, Evanston, Galesburg, Quincy, Bloomington, Elgin, Decatur, East St. Louis, Champaign, Danville, and Belleville. Some Illinois libraries already were receiving help from Andrew Carnegie.

It was only a year after the Chicago Public Library opened its doors that a tank, even one fifty-eight feet in diameter and twenty-one feet high, became too small to house its books. Quarters were rented at Madison Street and Wabash Avenue and occupied in March 1874. In May 1875 the library moved again, into less expensive and roomier quarters in the Dickey Building at Lake and Dearborn, where it remained eleven years. On May 24, 1886, the library once again removed to the fourth floor of the new City Hall.

In 1893 funds were made available for a public library building which would occupy Dearborn Park, city property which formerly was part of the Fort Dearborn military reservation. On this block bounded by Washington Street, Michigan Avenue, Randolph Street, and Garland Court was constructed an elegant building of stone and steel, four vaulted stories high, with several acres of reading rooms and stacks sufficient for 2,000,000 volumes. The structure, with its marble wainscoating, its domes of Tiffany stained glass, its many mottos, intricate mosaics, and its sturdy chairs and tables of native oak, was opened to an admiring public in 1897.

Before 1911 there were no branch libraries in Chicago. Books were provided for schoolchildren and others at distribution centers to which the books were brought by "circulating libraries"—horse-drawn book carts that went from center to center on regular schedules and stated days to deliver and pick up books. Four of these traveling branches (of which there were 25 in 1911 serving 110 stations) are still in use and long since motorized. Every weekday and Saturday they take up their stations—different for every day—and remain for six hours. There are now 24 designated locations. In 1912 two branch libraries were opened. By 1967 the number had grown to sixty-one, with a total of 3,366,605 books on the shelves of the main library and branches.

First library supported by public funds in Illinois was one established by the General Assembly in 1839 to serve the Illinois Supreme Court and the legislature. Appropriation for the first biennium was $5,000. In 1843 the Supreme Court became custodian, and the library became exclusively a law library. It was quartered in the capitol until 1906, when it occupied appropriate quarters in the new Supreme Court building. At that time the library had 40,000 volumes. In 1967 the library had grown to 70,000, including legislation, trial records, and opinions from all fifty states, the federal courts and the Supreme Court of the United States and the courts and legislative bodies of Canada, Great Britain, Australia, and South Africa. It is open to the general public for study, as well as to lawyers, judges, legislators, and students.

The Illinois State Library at Springfield was established by an act of the General Assembly in 1842 separating it from the library of the Supreme Court as of January 1, 1843. The secretary of state was designated librarian. During the first three decades of its life it offered restricted service to state officials and employees. Since that time it has become increasingly important to libraries and individuals, including rural residents with no local library service, who borrow from its shelves by mail. Most rapid growth has occurred since passage by Congress of the Library Services Act of 1957, which among other things provides matching funds for state activities in the library field.

In 1962, by aid from a Library Services Act grant, an examination of public libraries in Illinois revealed that despite increased services at the local level more persons were without library service than when a similar survey was made in 1947— 2,109,554 compared with 1,275,277. The investigation resulted in an act by the Illinois legislature creating a network of library systems which would receive monetary support from the state and would be eligible to borrow specialized collections from the Illinois State Library. The act is applicable to areas where libraries are tax-supported by a tax of at least six-tenths of a mill of the full, fair cash value of all taxable property. Should this not equal $1.50 per capita the state would be authorized to make an equalization grant.

Organization grants to library systems serving participating libraries were authorized in areas with populations of at least 150,000 or containing 4,000 or more square miles. The establishment grant was fixed at $25,000 for the first county or part of county in the system and $15,000 for each additional county or part of county. Continued support of the system was made subject to annual review, and was contingent on appropriations for the first biennium and each succeeding biennium by the state legislature. The annual assistance for the first biennium was fixed at $0.40 per capita, plus $5 per square mile if the system were within a single county or $15 per square mile if the system included areas in two or more counties. All systems within the network are autonomous and serve as a pool for all libraries within the systems. For the equalization grants the legislature appropriated $510,000. The appropriation for establishing grants was $770,000. For continuing support of the systems $3,063,082 was appropriated for the first biennium.

The act also designated the University of Illinois library, the Chicago Public Library, the Southern Illinois University library, and the Illinois State Library as research centers. The grant for support of research was fixed at $400,000 for the first year. The four libraries had almost 10,000,000 volumes on their shelves on January 1, 1967, of which more than 4,000,000 were at the University of Illinois, 3,366,605 at the Chicago Public Library, more than 1,400,000 at the Illinois State Library, and more than 1,150,000 at Southern Illinois University.

In 1963 the Illinois State Library was designated a regional depository for United States government documents. As of January 1, 1967, more than 500,000 federal and state documents were on its shelves. In 1964 the library reorganized its services,

creating a library development service section which offers broader services to libraries which are members of library systems. Services include loan of audio-visual material, of which the audio-visual unit has close to 100,000 films, film strips, recordings, art reproductions, and related materials available. Lists of local library facilities may be had on written application. The entire record-keeping system of the Illinois State Library has been computerized, using the machines of the driver-license division of the office of the secretary of state. A catalog of the four designated research libraries is in preparation.

In 1851 the Illinois legislature passed an act which directed that "specimens of the recently formed Illinois State Geological Survey shall be properly arranged in a cabinet available to the public and deposited in some apartment in or convenient to the Capitol." This was the origin of the Illinois State Museum. However, specimens already collected by the Geological Survey remained in New Harmony, Indiana, for several years, and none reached Springfield, where they were treated with scant respect, until the end of the Civil War.

In 1877 the Illinois legislature established the Illinois State Museum as an entity apart from the Geological Survey. However, it still did not come to life. The physical possessions of the museum were shunted from room to room in the Illinois Arsenal, then to the capitol, where they were stacked in unmarked boxes in the cellar. Finally, in 1906, the collection was ordered exhumed from the dust of the capitol and, after being cataloged and labeled, it was established again in the arsenal where an orderly display came into being.

In 1923, when the Centennial Building was finished, the museum was assigned permanent quarters on the fifth floor. Its departments were specified as covering the fields of economic geology, mineralogy, petrography, zoology, entomology, ichthyology, and conchology. To this successive directors added historical displays covering implements and wagons, tools, weapons, and other things of interest in an expanding economy.

The museum soon overflowed its quarters and further room was found at the state fairgrounds, where many of the larger exhibits were exposed to a much larger audience than they would have had in downtown Springfield. At the same time the museum directors and staff began taking an active part in the study of prehistoric Illinois. Thorne Deuel, a West Pointer who became an anthropologist, brought the museum into harmony with the universities of Chicago and Illinois in excavating at the Modoc Rock Shelter, where earliest evidences of a communal life were unearthed, at the Dickson Mounds, Cahokia, and other places in the state where evidence of development of paleolithic and prehistoric man existed. He also got the museum down to ground level in the state's educational program, furnishing traveling displays of ingenuity and interest for the schoolchildren of the state.

Right after World War II planning began for a building that would be entirely devoted to the museum, unifying displays and providing much needed working space for the staff. Ground was broken for the building January 5, 1961, and the $2,200,000 structure was dedicated and opened to the public February 4, 1963.

The Illinois State Historical Library, established in 1889 by an act of the General Assembly, has 106,000 bound volumes and 1,600,000 manuscripts relating to the history of Illinois. The collection of Lincolniana is second largest in the nation, the largest being the collection of the federal government housed in the Library of Congress and the National Archives in Washington. The library has a complete set of laws which concern Illinois, beginning with Hening's *Statutes at Large: Being a Collection of All the Laws of Virginia.*

The shelves contain histories of the state, of all 102 counties, and of many cities, towns, and villages of Illinois. The Illinois State Historical Library has more Illinois newspapers than any other institution, including a copy of the first issue of the first newspaper published in Illinois, the *Illinois Herald*, which was printed at Kaskaskia December 14, 1814. There are three copies of the only issue of the *Nauvoo Expositor*, anti-Mormon newspaper, and all issues but one of Elijah Lovejoy's abolitionist newspaper, the *Alton Observer*.

The manuscript files contain papers of twelve Illinois governors, 1,250 Lincoln manuscripts, including one of the five known copies of the Gettysburg Address in Lincoln's handwriting, and the original manuscript of Edward Everett's dedicatory address at the battlefield. The Lincoln display in the Horner-Lincoln room is changed at intervals, but it always includes fifty or more letters and documents, plus many pictures and mementos of the sixteenth president. Exclusive of the Lincoln collection there are 10,000 volumes of the Alfred Whital Stern collection of Civil War material.

The Illinois State Historical Society is the collecting arm of the Historical Library, and has provided a great deal of material both for the library and the State Museum. The members, all volunteers, are enthusiastic historians of their local scene, as well as the state of Illinois at large. The library publishes four journals of the Historical Society each year, containing new material relating to Illinois persons, places, or organizations. The Historical Society encourages schoolchildren to participate in the program, setting topics and publishing the best papers at quarterly intervals. The library operates the David Davis mansion in Bloomington and the Robert Rutherford McCormick Historymobile, a traveling historical display which tours Illinois schools.

Another important library supported by public funds, not only of Illinois but also of several other states and two Canadian provinces is the Center for Research Libraries, established in 1949 by thirteen universities; it now includes thirty members from coast to coast and across the border to the north. They are the universities of British Columbia, California, Chicago, Cornell, Harvard, Illinois, Illinois Institute of Technology, Indiana, Iowa, Iowa State, Kansas, Kentucky, Loyola of Chicago, Marquette, Michigan State, Minnesota, Missouri, Nebraska, Northwestern, Notre Dame, Ohio State, Princeton, Purdue, St. Louis, Southern Illinois, Toronto, Wayne State, Wisconsin, the Wisconsin State Historical Society, and the John Crerar Library.

The library exists for the joint use of its membership, and eventually will have on its shelves 2,000,000 volumes, mostly research material which ordinarily would not be available at the average university library. The library building at 5700 Cottage Grove Avenue, Chicago, was dedicated October 29, 1950.

The state universities of Illinois have a number of fine museums and art galleries, all of them designed to aid university students and graduate students in their studies. In fact, the collections might well be said to constitute working museums, and this classification fits another important activity of the state educational system, for loan collections of many kinds, many in the fine arts, are sent to schools throughout the state and to smaller public galleries. These collections travel to the people who cannot travel to the collections.

The Natural History Museum of the University of Illinois was a natural outgrowth of the "specimen case" featured in the laboratory of the College of Natural Science when the school was known as Illinois Industrial University. By the middle seventies the name had become the University of Illinois, and the specimen case had become a museum with 4,500 square feet of display space. Until recent years the museum was part of the Department of Natural History. It is now an independent department, as is the case at Harvard, Iowa, Michigan, Oregon, and Yale. Photographs and descriptive materials are available for research students.

The museum has accumulated many specimens from field expeditions in Illinois and as far away as Tibet. Work of university professors and students in excavating the Modoc Rock Shelter, Dickson Mounds, and the Cahokia Mounds has been very rewarding. Major contributions have been made in the study of early man in the Mississippi Valley and in many parts of Illinois. Presence of man in Southern Illinois 10,000 years ago has been confirmed by carbon-dating of uncovered objects, and his presence in Illinois prior to the fourth ice age is inferred from recovery of projectile points at an area covered by ice as late as 15,000 years ago. Much of this research has been a cooperative effort of the state of Illinois, the University of Chicago, the University of Illinois, and Southern Illinois University.

As of September 1, 1967, the museum contained 90,000 specimens of reptiles and amphibians, 38,000 specimens of mammals, 5,000 specimens of fish, 3,000 specimens of fossil plants (mostly from Illinois), large collections of objects from Indian sites, skeletal material of birds, 10,000 species of birds, and more than 200,000 specimens of mollusks. The museum is located in the Natural History building at Green and Mathews streets, near the Student Union, and is open to the public weekdays from 8 A.M. to 5 P.M.

The Classical and European Culture Museum on the fourth floor of Lincoln Hall, south of the Union, was established in 1912 to provide resources for graduate students in archeology and for the general use of the student body. The museum collection includes replicas of the masterpieces of sculpture from ancient Greece and Rome and many thousands of original coins, inscribed clay tablets, Sumerian figurines, and other materials that offer a panorama of 100,000 years of human history. The collections form a teaching museum of great value for research in depth, and a reservoir of teaching materials for Illinois schools. The exhibits are open to the public from 2 P.M. to 5 P.M. on Fridays and Sundays, and 9 A.M. to noon on Saturdays.

The Krannert Art Museum, an adjunct of the College of Fine and Applied Arts, was opened in 1961. Its construction was made possible by a large gift from Mr. and Mrs. Herman C. Krannert of Indianapolis, Indiana. Mr. Krannert was a graduate of the University of Illinois in 1912. Many smaller contributions were included in the available funds, through the University of Illinois Foundation.

The museum and galleries are the outgrowth of earlier galleries, the first of which was founded in 1876. In 1938 the university received a collection of forty old masters from Mr. and Mrs. Merle J. Trees of Chicago. Other works have been purchased out of collections exhibited by the University of Illinois Festival of Contemporary Art, held annually from 1948 to 1953, and biennially from 1954. New works are acquired frequently with money from the Elenora D. Krannert acquisition fund. Obtained through the fund during 1966–67 were a Rubens, an Ingres, and a granite sculpture from the Nineteenth Egyptian Dynasty. There were thirty-six other works from twelve donors and fifty-seven art objects acquired by purchase that same year. Sixteen exhibitions of loan collections were displayed, which included 1,182 objects from 163 lenders.

The museum lent special collections during 1967 to the Chicago Circle campus, the University of Illinois College of Medicine in Chicago, the Ben and Abby Grey Foundation, and the University of Chicago. Special loans were made for exhibit in California, Kentucky, Michigan, New York, Ohio, Rhode Island, and Brazil. Museum attendance in 1966–67 was 112,798, an increase of 20,413 over the previous year. Eighteen traveling exhibits were shown 142 times in 47 areas and viewed by 193,328 persons. Most of the exhibits were in Illinois, but locations in Indiana, Michigan, Missouri, New York, Ohio, and Oregon were included. A major addition to gallery space was authorized and a contract signed February 9, 1967. The museum is open to the public from 9 A.M. to 5 P.M. Monday through Saturday, and from 2 P.M. to 5 P.M. on Sundays.

Amid the university buildings on the Circle campus of the University of Illinois in Chicago stands Hull House, restored to its original form. The building is a memorial to Jane Addams and her colleagues, to Charles J. Hull, who was an early benefactor of homeless boys, and to his cousin, Helen Culver, who wisely distributed the Hull fortune which was left in her care to further the ideals and purposes of one of Chicago's early philanthropists. A principal feature of the house will be a research library specializing in material relating to Jane Addams and the many people who worked with her, to the Hull family, and to the work of the first large settlement house in America. Accumulation of books, papers, manuscripts, microfilms, and other materials that will preserve the Hull House story is in progress.

The house, stripped of the many accretions of the busy settlement project, such as the coffee house, theater, nursery, gymnasium, and boys' club, has only the restored residents' dining hall as a companion. The two buildings contain furnishings, paintings, silver, pewter, and brass treasured by Miss Addams. In the Octagon Room is a pedestaled bust of Miss Addams by Lawrence Taylor. The restored Hull House on June 14, 1967, was declared by the federal government to be a national historic landmark. Hull House is open Monday through Friday from 9 A.M. to 5 P.M., on Saturday from 10 A.M. to 3 P.M., and on Sunday from noon to 4 P.M.

The University Museum, on the Carbondale campus of Southern Illinois University, was inaugurated in 1875. A collection of archeological specimens donated by Cyrus Thomas, an amateur archeologist and traveler in the Mississippi Valley, served as the nucleus of the exhibit program. Originally housed in the main building of the university, the museum's operation was temporarily disturbed when the building was destroyed by fire in 1883. The museum was again in operation by 1886 and has functioned regularly since that date. With the advent of a professional staff, the University Museum, particularly in the past twenty years, has grown to be a multidiscipline adjunct to the overall educational program of the university.

The museum, destroyed by fire in June 1969, stressed an interpretative exhibits program; a rapidly growing educational program intended for both the university and for the surrounding communities in Southern Illinois; a dynamic program of research in the fields of Meso-American, Mayan, and North American archeology, and in geology; and is responsible for virtually all salvage archeology carried out in Southern Illinois.

The primary objective of the University Museum will continue to be education and interpretation through the acquisition, preservation, exhibition, and circulation of historical scientific, artistic, anthropological, and archeological objects and specimens. New exhibit halls will feature special traveling exhibits in addition to the exhibits on Earth Sciences, Life Sciences, Behavioral Sciences, Social Sciences, and Communications. The museum, when restored, will be open to the public from 8.30 A.M. to 4.30 P.M. Monday through Friday, and from 2.30 P.M. to 4.30 P.M. on Sunday.

The art department of Eastern Illinois University, Charleston, has a representative art gallery which is open to the public from 2 P.M. to 5 P.M. Monday through Thursday and from 12.30 P.M. to 4 P.M. on Sundays. The Merritt Art Gallery at Northern Illinois University, De Kalb, is open to the public Monday through Friday from 8 A.M. to 9 P.M., and on Saturdays from 9 A.M. to noon. At Western Illinois University, Macomb, an art gallery with exhibits designed for educational purposes is open to the public from 8 A.M. to 5 P.M. Monday through Friday during the school year. Traveling exhibits are changed frequently.

A museum of prehistory and pioneer days at Illinois State University in Normal presents a fine collection of Indian artifacts, weapon points, and other relics from the distant past, and pioneer mementos of value and interest. The museum is open to the public from 10 A.M. to 5 P.M. Monday through Friday, 10 A.M. to 4 P.M. on Saturday, and 2 P.M. to 5 P.M. on Sunday, during the school year.

Privately endowed libraries and museums are among the institutions that make Illinois important in many fields of research, as well as offering unusual advantages to the schoolchildren of the state. Among the more important, in the order of their founding, are the Chicago Historical Society Museum and Library (1856); the Chicago Academy of Sciences Museum (1857); the Chicago Law Institute Library (1857); the Art Institute of Chicago Gallery (1879) with the Ryerson Library of Art (1901) and the Daniel Burnham Library of Architecture (1912); the Walter Loomis Newberry Research Library (1887); the Field Museum of Natural History (1893); the John Crerar Library (1894—opened 1897); the Evanston Historical Society (1898); the American Medical Association Library (1903); the Museum and Library of the Oriental Institute of the University of Chicago (1919); the Morton Arboretum (1921); the John G. Shedd Aquarium (1926 —opened 1929); the Adler Planetarium (1929); the Rosenwald Museum of Science and Industry (1929—opened 1933); the Library of International Relations (1932); the Stephenson County Historical Society (1944); the Hinsdale Health Museum (1958); the Cantigny War Memorial Museum (1960); and the Julius Sterling Morton Memorial Library (1961).

The announced purpose of the Chicago Historical Society in its application for a charter in 1856 was the collection and dissemination of information concerning Chicago, the state of Illinois, and the Old Northwest. The reference library which was to be a major part of the society's program began with collections made by the first librarian, William Barry, on journeys downstate and efforts in Chicago. On the occasion of the first annual meeting of the society June 9, 1857, Mr. Barry reported that the shelves contained 3,577 bound volumes, the yearly files of newspapers, 4,966 public documents, reports of institutions and similar pamphlets and broadsides, 101 charts in bound volumes and single sheets, and 9,000 manuscripts. That library, considerably expanded by 1871, became a total loss in the great fire, and nothing was done to restore it or the building that housed it until several years had passed, when a small and admittedly temporary building was constructed at Dearborn and Ontario streets and opened in January 1878.

Through the rest of the seventies and the eighties the society pursued its aims with zeal and decorum. A plaque marking the site of Fort Dearborn was unveiled in the presence and with the vocal participation of Isaac N. Arnold, Gurdon S. Hubbard, John Wentworth, and Thomas Hoyne

among others. Robert Lincoln was announcing to the society that there was nothing in his father's papers worthy of preservation by a historical society, and Levi Z. Leiter, soon to shake the dust of Chicago from his feet for the earth of England, was financing the publication of George Flower's *History of the English Settlement in Edwards County, Illinois*. To enliven a meeting of the society in 1891 Major Joseph Kirkland read a paper setting forth his recollections of the death of John Lalime, purchaser of Du Sable's trading post, during a personal encounter with John Kinzie, who bought the post from Lalime. After establishing the identity of the relics as those of the deceased he presented the society with Lalime's bones.

Now money became available for a new building, thanks to settlement of the will of Henry D. Gilpin of Philadelphia, who had left a considerable legacy to the society, plus a gift from John Crerar and other donations. Construction of the building, which still stands at Dearborn and Ontario, began in November 1892 under direction of the architect Henry Ives Cobb, who had designed the Newberry Library a few blocks farther north. The building was opened December 15, 1896. Its street address was 142 Dearborn Avenue. The Gilpin Library on the first and second floors already was a most important tool of historical research.

In the late twenties the society had entirely outgrown the building it then occupied. Almost priceless treasures accumulated over the years could not be placed on display because there was no room. One collection, acquired in 1920, the Gunther Collection of books, art treasures, prints, manuscripts, and historic objects, could be shown only in part for lack of space. In spite of depression and hard times the million dollars needed for the new building was raised, the park commissioners allocated a site, and in 1932 the building was opened.

The emphasis Mr. Barry placed on pamphlets and other source material continues to the present. The clipping file is maintained on a day-to-day basis, items being cataloged within twenty-four hours of their printing. A card catalog gives birth and death dates of a substantial percentage of historically important people of Illinois. Among the thousands of volumes relating to Illinois are the journals of the Senate and House from 1819, county histories, publications of the Illinois State Historical Society including the name by name censuses of 1810, 1818, and 1820, the *Jesuit Relations* in the original French with English translations on facing pages, the proceedings of the Chicago Bar Association, accounts of travel in early Illinois, early school books, Civil War records and relics, and a mass of manuscript material which will afford subject matter for study for many years. The society possesses an unusually fine collection of material on sports. It also has the Civil War library of the Loyal Legion, the papers of the Aero Club of Illinois, and the Agnes Nestor papers relating to women in the labor force.

In the chart room is a road map in color dated 1838 and showing a network of "highways" almost as numerous as those on the average map of today. The principal difference is that there are no indications of what roads were passable and at what seasons. In showrooms and storage areas (the displays are changed frequently) are furniture, guns, swords, carriages, uniforms, dresses, many of George Peter Alexander Healy's portraits of early Chicago leaders, Mrs. Lincoln's White House piano and the bed on which Lincoln died, a cabin like the one in which he was born, a dramatic series of dioramas showing principal incidents from his life, and a fine collection of Lincoln portraits. There is a quantity of commercial catalogs, sheet music, opera and theater programs, and all the ephemera and memorabilia of the social and political history of Illinois. The society is currently raising funds for an addition planned for the immediate future.

Less than half a mile from the Historical Society, at 2001 Clark Street, stands the museum of the Chicago Academy of Sciences. Organized in 1857, its first curator was Illinoisan Robert Kennicott, who was more often absent on collecting tours than present at the academy, and who brought to the academy and the Smithsonian Institution in Washington some of their most interesting exhibits. Kennicott was a money raiser as well as a scientist, and under his leadership a fund of $60,000 was raised in 1864 for exhibits. The society occupied rented space until it completed its own building at Wabash and Van Buren streets in 1868. This building was described as so nearly fireproof no insurance needed to be carried. Unfortunately this was not the case.

Building and contents were destroyed by the great fire of 1871.

Rented quarters were occupied (and a rent-free space in an exhibition hall where the Art Institute now stands) from the fire until 1894, when Matthew Laflin gave $75,000 and the city through the Lincoln Park commissioners $25,000 to build the present building. Others provided funds for equipping and endowing the academy.

The museum activities are largely restricted to the ecology of the Chicago region and to the plant and animal life of the Chicago metropolitan area from the last ice age to the present. Dioramas and open displays emphasize the times of the great river that flowed out of Lake Michigan, through the Kankakee and Des Plaines River basins to the present course of the Illinois River, and so by way of the vast Mississippi to the Gulf of Mexico. The recession of the lake and the development of dune areas, where once there was only water, are part of the picture.

In 1912 the Chicago Academy of Sciences had the only celestial globe of record on the North American continent. The viewers, as many as twenty if they are small enough, sit at the center of the globe and look above and around at the heavens which have been accurately cut into the metal of the globe. This device is still in daily use and has given thousands upon thousands of Chicago youngsters their introduction to astronomy. It is mechanically operated and was built by William Atwood, who then was the museum director. One other device of this character is of record—built at Cambridge University in 1758 by the Lowndes professor of astronomy, Roger Long.

There is a busy program of lectures that attract audiences of a hundred or more to Albert Dickinson Memorial Hall, completed in 1957. Field trips within fifty miles of Chicago are frequent and groups as well as individuals are accommodated. Occasional papers and monographs by members of the academy have contributed consistently to the program of public education on the importance of ecological balance to the continued health of woods and fields in Illinois.

The Chicago Law Institute was officially established in 1857, but it had its unofficial beginnings in a communal collection of law books kept in a lawyer's office near the courthouse from 1837. When the Chicago Law Institute was chartered these books and many others that had been added to the working collection were placed on shelves in the Cook County Courthouse, and for more than a hundred years enjoyed the hospitality of the county. As 1966 dawned they had been on the tenth floor of the county building for sixty years.

When the plans for the new Civic Center were drawn by the city and county one of the topmost floors—the twenty-ninth—was reserved for the Chicago Law Institute Library. Shelving was constructed, desks, counters, and all the paraphernalia of a major library were installed and the institute was invited to move into its new and commodious quarters. Some of the members objected. After all, the move would cost the institute an estimated $130,000, and with dues far short of half that amount annually the members could not justify moving the 140,000 volumes (at a cost of $45,000) and repairing old bindings (at a cost of $85,000). They preferred to stay where they were.

The membership voted to support the dissenters. The Cook County authorities said they had other plans for the space in the county building and it would have to be vacated. Being lawyers, the members of the institute went to law. Meanwhile, the county had been quietly building up a fund to support the library. Lawyers were asked to pay a dollar for each case filed. By the spring of 1966 more than $800,000 was in the fund. Since the institute would not move its books, the county did. By the end of August 1966 the transfer had been completed, necessary repairs had been made, and on the day after Labor Day the library was opened. But not as the library of the Chicago Law Institute. It had become the Cook County Law Library. Even the uniforms of the stack attendants carry that name.

There were still two causes running in the dispute in the summer of 1967. One has reached the Supreme Court of the United States, and before these words reach print, probably will have been decided. The other is still in the circuit court in Cook County, and should be there another year or more. Meanwhile the same lawyers who consulted the books before the dispute are making use of the library, and finding the things they need, for this is the third largest private law library in the world, containing almost every useful record of every English-speaking country.

In the 1870's the men of means in Chicago thought in large sums. Fun was poked at them by New York newspapers which said Chicagoans bought their books by the foot, and when plans for an art

institute and gallery were announced five years after the Chicago fire, the New York journals said Chicago probably would buy its art by the yard. Such pleasantries did not bother Chicagoans. They had skinned many a tough New York hide. (The Bulls and the Bears who played games in· the seventies weren't basketball or football teams, but they played for keeps.)

The Art Institute of Chicago was chartered May 24, 1879, as the Chicago Academy of Fine Arts. First president was George Armour. Its purpose was to provide the best possible instruction in the fields of painting, sculpture, and other arts, and to display the world's greatest examples of those arts. In 1882 the name was changed to the Art Institute of Chicago and the organization bought property at Michigan and Van Buren, where a brick building housed school and gallery. In 1885 John W. Root designed a Romanesque four-story stone building to stand at the southwest corner of Michigan and Van Buren. Martin Ryerson and Charles Hutchinson busied themselves with raising the money to build it, and in 1887 the Art Institute moved into its new quarters, which it would occupy for little more than six years.

The first portion of the building on the present site of the Art Institute, Michigan Avenue at the foot of Adams Street, was erected by the trustees and managers of the World's Columbian Exposition. Having appropriated $200,000 for its construction, the exposition people offered to make the central part of the building a permanent structure and deed it to the Art Institute if enough donations could be raised to meet the added cost. The building, on public land, became the property of the city at the close of the exposition, and later was transferred to the South Park commissioners. It cost $648,000, was constructed in the Italian Renaissance manner, and was opened as an art museum after removal of two temporary wings in December 1893. The building at Michigan and Van Buren was sold to the Chicago Club, which still owns and occupies the property.

The Art Institute made its first large purchase of portraits by old masters in 1890, acquiring paintings by Rembrandt, Rubens, Van Dyck, Frans Hals, and Holbein, plus "The Guitar Lesson" by Terburg, "A Family Concert" by Jan Steen, a landscape by Hobbema, and "Jubilee" by Van

Ostade. There were no remarks from New York about "paintings by the yard."

In 1897 a lecture room was built and donated by Charles W. Fullerton as a memorial to his father, Alexander. In 1901 the Ryerson Library, provided for with a gift of $50,000 by Martin A. Ryerson, was assembled. In 1903 Blackstone Hall was given by Mr. and Mrs. Timothy Blackstone. By this time the Art Institute was becoming known worldwide for its examples of the Barbizon School, given by Mrs. Henry Field, including paintings by Millet, Breton, Troyon, Rousseau, Corot, Cazin, Constable, and Daubigny, and for the Albert A. Munger collection, chiefly by French painters of the middle- and late-eighteenth century, and the Nickerson collection of porcelains and Oriental art objects. In 1912 the Art Institute received as the bequest of Daniel Burnham his architectural library, together with the sum of $50,000 to provide a proper accommodation for it. Among other treasures the library contains the Louis Sullivan collection of drawings and the library of Pierre F. L. Fontaine, architect to Napoleon.

In 1931 James O'Donnell Bennett of the *Chicago Tribune* listed six paintings which he described as among the world's greatest art treasures. Leading the list was El Greco's "Assumption of the Virgin," bought by the Art Institute in 1906 at the insistence of Mary Cassatt, the famous Philadelphia painter. The cost of this work had been guaranteed by Martin Ryerson and three other directors of the institute, and later underwritten by Nancy Atwood Sprague. The others were Rembrandt's "Girl at an Open Half-door," John Constable's "Stoke-by-Nayland," Seurat's "Sunday on the Grande Jatte," Manet's "Christ Mocked," and Renoir's "Two Little Circus Girls." To these the Art Institute by gift and purchase has added literally hundreds of canvasses worthy to be called "great," but those six selected by Bennett remain near the top of the list.

Funds for the purchases, which continue ($700,000 for a Picasso and a Correggio in 1966) come from donations, quite a few of which have been in amounts of a million dollars or more. The $6,000,000 building program included a $1,200,000 donation for a new wing, given by the children of Joy Morton and grandchildren of Julius Sterling Morton in memory of the man who originated Arbor Day.

On October 1, 1960, the Art Institute abolished entrance fees, except small amounts for special loan collections which are brought to Chicago at frequent intervals. Meanwhile the schools of the Art Institute, without fanfare, continue to encourage artists of Illinois, and to produce not a few who can take their places in the company of the most capable of our times. The Art Institute collection today is valued at $200,000,000.

A commemorative plaque states that Walter Loomis Newberry died at sea in 1868. But some men never die. Walter Newberry lives in the red English tile that floors the library bearing his name. He lives in the brick, the shelves, the hundreds of thousands of books on those shelves. The library, one of the great research institutions in the field of the humanities, is the living expression of a man who above everything else loved learning.

There was a meeting of the minds in Chicago during the nineties, when the Newberry, the Crerar, and the Chicago Public Library administrators met and divided fields of interest in order that there should be no duplication of effort. To the library of the Chicago Historical Society was left the field of Illinois history and the records of the Old Northwest. To the public library went all wholesomely entertaining and generally instructive books, especially those desired by citizens for home use; also the humdrum things of the library world, the collections of newspapers, patents, government documents, and some of the exotic matters that fascinate the general and instruct the particular—architecture and the decorative arts. To the Crerar went physiology and (somewhat later) medicine, the physical and natural sciences, the useful arts (technology), the fine arts in part, sociology, and economics.

To the Newberry went those things which are so much the blood and bone, the soul and spirit of a community—literature, languages, the vast canvasses of general history, philosophy, religion, theology, the fine arts in part, genealogy, and communications (the printed word). The Newberry Library was established in 1887, almost two decades after the death of the founder. The endowment in that time had accumulated a substantial sum, and the library never has lacked financial sinews. In 1894 it occupied the Spanish Romanesque building designed by Henry Ives Cobb, a New Englander who liked to express himself in Connecticut granite.

The library has on its shelves several hundred thousands of useful books in the fields assigned to it. More important, it has those fabulous treasures which are not for reading but for standing in awe and admiring. Example—the first copy of Homer's poems to be printed. Another—one of the oldest manuscripts of the Christian gospels, dating from the time of the second crusade. Still another—all four folio editions of Shakespeare's plays, printed in 1623, 1632, 1664, and 1685.

Such possessions give the Newberry a special aura, and it has been a policy to acquire them. In 1901 the Newberry bought the library of Prince Louis Lucien Bonaparte, collected in the course of a study of the history of speech, and comprising specimens of every known language with even a rudimentary literature. In 1917 the John M. Wing Foundation gave to the Newberry Library 20,000 volumes collected during a study of the history of printing. Wing was a newspaperman, a bachelor who pursued a rewarding hobby. In 1964, shortly before his death in Rome, Everett Dwight Graf, president of the board of trustees from 1952 to 1964 and president of the Art Institute, gave the Newberry his valuable collection of early Western Americana. That same year the library paid $2,750,000 for the Louis H. Silver collection of rare books, some 800 in all. Then there are those ordinary things, many thousands of volumes, from which the family down the block can trace its ancestry back to Revolutionary times or beyond. If you are curious about your own family background, perhaps you'll find a clue.

When the World's Columbian Exposition drew to a close it seemed that thousands of exhibits might be up for grabs. Marshall Field felt otherwise. "This building," he said referring to the Palace of the Fine Arts along the lakefront at Fifty-seventh Street, "and these treasures," designating the anthropological displays and exhibits in natural history, "must not become a loss." Field, to use a somewhat vulgar expression, put his money where his mouth was— $1,000,000 to be exact, and Chicago got the marvelous Field Museum of Natural History. There were no strings attached to the money, but he suggested that holders of exposition stock donate it to the museum, and he got a lot of it (face value $1,500,000— cash value $193,500), $100,000 from George M. Pullman, and $144,000 from others.

This was enough to assure opening the museum, but there was more to come. H. N. Higinbotham purchased the Tiffany collection of precious stones for $100,000 and tossed it in the pot, while Edward E. Ayer placed his $100,000 anthropological collection at the disposal of the museum director, Dr. Frederick J. V. Skiff, chief of the Department of Mines and Minerals of Illinois and deputy general of the exposition, who was appointed curator. The winter of 1893–94 saw the major part of the collections and exhibits appropriate to the museum packed, crated, transferred to the Palace of Fine Arts, and displayed (an activity to be repeated at the same place forty-one years later from A Century of Progress for the Museum of Science and Industry). The museum opened on June 2, 1894, as the Field Columbian Museum.

A year before Field's death the name was changed to the Field Museum of Natural History. Field's will, probated just after his death on January 16, 1906, bequeathed eight times the amount of his original gift to the institution—$4,000,000 for a new building and $4,000,000 for an endowment fund. It was nine years before the building construction could begin. The site which had been selected by Field was an old pier belonging to the Illinois Central Railroad at the foot of Fourteenth Street, used by the railroad for storing freight cars, the bit of land at pier end, and the water beneath the pier which was to be filled and become land. The railroad contended that the water belonged to the railroad under the doctrine of riparian rights. The state of Illinois also claimed the area, as did the South Park commissioners. Finally the railroad relinquished its rights, the courts, in a friendly suit, decided for the South Park commissioners, and construction began June 26, 1915. It was completed in the summer of 1920, exhausting the treasury while packing chores exhausted the staff, and on April 26, 1920, the move into the not-quite-completed building began. Three hundred and twenty-one freight cars were filled, and there were 354 five-ton loads transported by truck. One stuffed pachyderm didn't quite make it—lost his legs in the unloading process. The museum was opened May 2, 1921, at its present location.

School-extension work by the Field Museum early became important. Originally this was largely supported by money and securities given to the museum by Norman Wait Harris, his children, and grandchildren. The original gift of $250,000 was made in December 1910. Members of the family added $25,000 in 1919 and $100,000 in 1924. In 1938 Albert W. Harris gave an additional $55,000 to offset the shrinkage of securities included in the original bequest. This was backed by an endowment fund of $500,000 established in 1925 by Mrs. James Nelson Raymond as a memorial to her husband. The income was designated for salaries of lecturers from the museum at public schools. When the museum celebrated its first fifty-year mark in 1944, newspapers stated that the museum had received $19,852,752 during that time, and that $13,844,000 of that sum had been given by Marshall Field, Marshall Field III, and Stanley Field, who was president of the board of the museum for more than thirty years.

The museum's building, 350 feet from north to south and 700 feet from east to west, is filled with beautifully arranged displays in the fields of anthropology, botany, ethnology, geology, mineralogy, paleontology, and zoology, gathered from all parts of the world. The museum presents the entire natural history of man and his environment in displays that range from the home life of the Neanderthaler to the cave dweller of the big cities in the twentieth century. Many of the displays are provided with electronic voices which explain their meaning. "Man and His World" might well be an overall title for the museum.

Chicago's noted men of the eighties and nineties appeared in the membership and on the boards of many cultural enterprises. The names of Marshall Field, Levi Z. Leiter, Walter Loomis Newberry, Martin Antoine Ryerson, Charles Hutchinson, Julius Rosenwald, Aaron Montgomery Ward, Potter Palmer, and others are found again and again. In several cases they left one particular monument to their memories. For John Crerar, builder of railroad equipment, benefactor of the Chicago Historical Society, the Young Men's Christian Association, and other Chicago enterprises, the important memorial is a technical library of more than 1,000,000 volumes now housed on the campus of the Illinois Institute of Technology, which is in itself a memorial to Phillip Danforth Armour. John Crerar was born in New York City,

and came to Chicago in 1862 at the age of thirty-five. In addition to managing his own iron and steel enterprises, he was an incorporator and member of the board of the Pullman Company. Crerar's will was in the courts from 1889 to 1893. Among those who defended its bequest to establish the Crerar Library was John H. Mulkey, one-time chief justice of the Illinois Supreme Court. After the will was upheld, June 19, 1893, the Crerar Library was incorporated under a special act of the Illinois legislature to encourage and promote the establishment of free public libraries in cities, villages, and towns of Illinois. The act, passed in 1891, was effective July 1 of that year. Incorporation date of the Crerar Library was October 12, 1894, and the library opened in April 1897 in the Marshall Field & Company building where it remained until 1920. From 1920 to March 1963 the library was in its own building at Randolph and Michigan, and since that date has been in a beautiful modern building on the campus of Illinois Institute of Technology. In 1898 the library had 20,000 volumes on its shelves. Slow but steady acquisition increased this figure to about 350,000 in 1940, and to 1,100,000 volumes in 1963.

In 1904 the Crerar Library obtained a collection of 18,000 volumes and 13,000 pamphlets on the social, political, and legal status of women. In 1906 the medical collection of the Newberry Library, which stemmed from a gift of the American Medical Association in 1897, was purchased. To this were added several gifts of Dr. Nicholas Senn and others, and Dr. Senn's purchases of private medical libraries which he bequeathed to the Crerar Library. A Union Medical Catalog was published in 1935, covering the medical-school libraries of Chicago and the Crerar.

In 1907 the Crerar added a notable collection of botanical volumes, and in 1909, in its first experiment in cooperative buying, it obtained many volumes from the Orient purchased for the Crerar and the Newberry libraries by Dr. Berthold Laufer while he was buying material for the Field Museum. These volumes, in Chinese, Japanese, Manchurian, Mongolian, and Tibetan, were divided among the libraries according to the fields of interest established a decade earlier. In 1911 cooperative buying in Europe added many volumes to the Crerar and the libraries of Harvard University, Northwestern University, and the University of Chicago. In 1962 the Crerar Library was designated a depository for the documents of three agencies of the federal government. It is one of twelve libraries which receive reports of the Atomic Energy Commission, the Department of Defense, and the National Aviation and Space Agency.

The Evanston Historical Society, founded in 1898, in its early years concerned itself with collecting historical documents relating to the town and to Northwestern University. On the death of Charles Gates Dawes in 1951 it acquired the Dawes home. In 1960 the society opened a museum at the Dawes place, containing memorabilia of the former vice president of the United States and Nobel laureate. Among the displays are exhibits relating to all the wars of the United States from the Revolution to the Second World War. There are guided tours of the museum and lectures. The museum is open Monday, Tuesday, Thursday, and Friday from 1 P.M. to 5 P.M. and on Saturday from 9 A.M. to noon.

The American Medical Association at Grand and Dearborn in Chicago has had two libraries. One, gathered during the eighties and nineties, was given to the Newberry Library in 1897 and moved to the John Crerar Library in 1906. In 1903 the association again began accumulating books, and these eventually became an adequate service library for the medical profession. The library publishes a quarterly cumulative *Index Medicus* for members of the association.

The Oriental Institute and Museum of the University of Chicago had its beginnings in 1894 when Mrs. Caroline E. Haskell presented funds to the university for a museum of Oriental antiquities from Far and Near East, which would also house the departments of comparative religions and Semitic languages. When Dr. James Henry Breasted became professor of Egyptology in 1905 emphasis more and more was placed on the Near and Middle East. The Oriental Institute was founded in 1919 with funds provided by John D. Rockefeller, Jr. most of which were to be used for excavations. The actual collection of antiquities was slow in growing. In 1926 the material from the Far East was allocated to the divinity school. The Near Eastern collections remained in custody of the Oriental Institute.

In 1931 the present building of the Oriental Institute at 1155 East Fifty-eighth Street in Chicago was opened and the collections from the Haskell Museum were

transferred to it. There are five exhibition halls designated by the planners as the Egyptian, Assyrian, Babylonian, Persian-Moslem, and Hittite-Syrian-Palestinian. Permanent exhibits include many objects of great antiquity and a number of spectacular materials in stone like the great Assyrian human-headed bull, casts of the Rosetta stone, examples of temple decoration, and other petrographs, reliefs, and carvings.

The museum has a small library, some fine examples of Egyptian papyruses, one of the jars and a fragment of the Dead Sea scrolls, and an Assyrian dictionary on clay tablets, among other treasures. There is a fine collection of ivories from Megiddo in Palestine. Special showings arranged for the sixteenth meeting of the International Assyriological Association in August of 1967 included casts and photographs of tablets from Tel Abu Salabikh which date from about 2300 B.C. Also shown were treasures recovered in the work for the United Nations project for saving the monuments of Nubia, in which the University of Chicago participated with expeditions to Aswan and the Sudan.

Since 1905 the department of Egyptology has been as much an investigative body as an arm of education. The work has greatly accelerated after World War I, and is continuing and expanding despite unsettled conditions today. Between World War I and 1967 the Oriental Institute conducted twenty projects in the Near East. Fourteen of these had been completed by the summer of 1967 and six are still in progress. From all of them, under agreement with the governments concerned, a certain amount of important antiquities have been brought to Chicago. As of 1967, the material for display had outgrown the possibility of finding space to display it. Projects not yet completed are the Iraq-Jarmo project, begun in 1948; the survey of urban development in Southern Mesopotamia, which dates from 1956; the Nippur Expedition, undertaken in 1945; the prehistoric survey of Southwestern Iran started in 1959; the Epigraphic Survey initiated in 1924; and the Nubian Expeditions begun at Aswan and the Sudan in 1960. Additional work in the Euphrates Valley is slated for 1968.

The Morton Arboretum was founded in 1921 by Joy Morton as a memorial to his father, Julius Sterling Morton, a Nebraska pioneer, territorial governor, secretary of agriculture in the cabinet of President Grover Cleveland from 1893 to 1897, and the founder of Arbor Day. In recent years the Arboretum has benefited by very substantial bequests from Joy Morton's daughter, Mrs. Joseph M. Cudahy, and his son, Sterling Morton. The Arboretum, of more than 1,400 acres near Lisle, contains examples of indigenous trees and many from China, Siberia, and the countries of Europe, more than 5,000 in all. In 1961 descendants of Morton established the J. Sterling Morton Memorial Library. It contains many rare volumes on nature, including first editions of the Audubon prints of birds of North America.

Shortly before his death John G. Shedd, president of Marshall Field & Company from 1906 to 1923, established a $3,000,000 fund for building and endowing an aquarium. The beautiful building on the lakefront, just northeast of the Field Museum, was completed and opened in the fall of 1929. The aquarium is the most comprehensive in the Western Hemisphere. It contains about ten thousand specimens of 250 or more species at all times. There are six main galleries and 132 exhibition tanks. Ninety-five reserve tanks hold the stock not on display. Water is maintained at temperatures from arctic to tropical to suit the fish inhabiting the different tanks. There is a special railway car to transport specimens from coastal points, lake and river areas to Chicago. The collection includes sharks, rays, moray eels, piranha, and most varieties of North and South American freshwater and saltwater game fish. Tanks are fitted to simulate the actual conditions in native habitats of the fish. The rainbow reef, for example, is formed of true coral.

The Adler Planetarium, the first optical device for depicting the heavens, was the gift of Max Adler of Chicago. It is located at the edge of Lake Michigan east of the Field Museum. The hemispherical dome with its intricate series of Zeiss projectors and its attendant museum was dedicated by the South Park commissioners on May 10, 1929, and opened its doors to the public two days later.

The interconnected projectors of the system are able to reproduce the positions of stars, planets, and satellites in the heavens at any given time or position in space. The museum houses telescopes, geodetic instruments, and astronomical devices from ancient times to the present, clocks, watches, hour glasses, astrolabs, and kindred materials. Authorities call the Adler Planetarium the world's finest. Lecture topics are announced for six-month periods and group reservations may be made in advance. For large groups this is imperative.

Sometime in the youth of the boy, Julius Rosenwald and his son William visited the huge German museum in Munich. The youngster was entranced and the father much impressed by what he saw there. In the summer of 1926 Rosenwald told the Commercial Club of Chicago that Chicago should have just such a museum, and that he had earmarked $3,000,000 to help equip it, provided the South Park commissioners would restore and rehabilitate the old Palace of the Fine Arts in Jackson Park as its home. Rosenwald pointed out that speedy action would be needed to have the museum ready to receive visitors during the projected Chicago world fair in 1933, and to receive, he hoped, the industrial exhibits contemplated for the fair after it closed.

The South Park commissioners presented a proposal for a $5,000,000 bond issue to voters at the election the following spring, and work of renovating and rebuilding the magnificent old building, uninhabited since 1920, finally got under way in early 1929. A portion of the building was opened in 1933, simultaneously with A Century of Progress exposition. When A Century of Progress was over in the fall of 1934 the entire structure was ready to receive the best industrial and scientific displays of the fair. Major Lennox R. Lohr, general manager of the exposition (a position comparable to that of Deputy General Skiff of the World's Columbian Exposition), helped select the exhibits and in 1941 was named director. The museum, he said when he took office, would emphasize man's progress from cave to industrial city.

The final cost of the new building (very little of the old structure could be saved and used) was $8,000,000. It consisted of three pavilions, 1,145 feet from east to west, with a ground area of 263,000 square feet. The caryatids from the central portico of the Erechtheum at Athens, twenty-four in number and thirty feet tall, again were reproduced in featured and exterior decoration. There was a lecture hall to seat 300, an auditorium that would hold 1,000, and exhibits on three floors (basement, first, and second) with some occupying two stories and one extending from the basement well toward the top of the structure.

Among the things a visitor may see at the Museum of Science and Industry are: a coal mine, an oil well, a German submarine, a streamlined railroad train, a village square, a machine to press bricks, a mechanical milker, a farm, the first locomotive in the United States and many of its successors, a steel mill, and many more. Suspended from the ceiling is a Model B Wright biplane (the one with wheels instead of skids) modified with ailerons instead of wing warping; a Curtis Jenny, a Nieuport monoplane from 1911, and so on and so on, far more than the average youngster can assimilate in a month.

A series of scientific "shows"—animation with music—carry names like Adam to Atom. And not to be forgotten, old 999, the steam locomotive that set the world's record of 112 miles an hour over the New York Central tracks on May 10, 1893, hauling visitors to the World's Columbian Exposition, is among those present in 1968.

Hatching chicks delight the little folk and interest their parents. Old horse-drawn fire engines hold the attention of small boys and their dads. And for the girls there's a half-million-dollar dollhouse. Mr. Rosenwald would be proud of what the people have done with his idea.

On a much smaller scale than the vast projects of the multimillionaire benefactors of Chicago is the Library of International Relations, but it occupies an important place in the cultural picture of Illinois. Founded in 1932, the library received free space in the John Crerar Library for quite a few years. It now occupies quarters of its own at 660 North Wabash Avenue. In addition to an increasing number of books pertinent to its field, the library receives most publications important from an international point of view. These include among many others the publications of the World Health Organization, the International Labor Office, the World Agricultural Organization, the two Courts of International Justice at The Hague, the Council of Europe, the European Steel and Coal Community, and the Organization of American States. The library is a depository for documents of the United Nations, as it was for those of the League of Nations prior to World War II.

The Stephenson County Historical Society was founded in 1944 and opened a museum in Freeport which now displays local industrial products of early days, toys, fans, Indian beadwork and material relating to the Lincoln-Douglas debates, one of which was held in Freeport. There is a Jane Addams room (she was born in Stephenson County). A historic house, the Oscar Taylor home built in 1857, and an arboretum are maintained. The museum is open to the public from 1:30 P.M. to 5 P.M. Friday, Saturday, and Sunday. At other times visits by groups are arranged by appointment.

A museum of importance to parents who wish their children to have the best possible information on physiology and the life functions is the Hinsdale Health Museum at 40 South Clay Street in Hinsdale. The museum is the gift of the Kettering Family Foundation, established by the children and grandchildren of Charles F. Kettering, inventor of the self-starter for automobiles, General Motors executive, and originator of the Kettering Foundation at Yellow Springs, Ohio, which is engaged chiefly in the nationwide program for research in photosynthesis and kindred subjects. The Hinsdale museum has audio-visual animated displays of the human brain, heart, nervous, circulatory, and reproductive systems. The museum was opened to the public in 1958.

A military museum of the first order is the Cantigny War Memorial of the First Division, on the estate of the late Robert Rutherford McCormick at Wheaton. The museum was opened August 20, 1960. It displays information on military equipment and methods, a World War I trench with simulated battle conditions, and a number of push-button displays. There are two dioramas, one of the Battle of Cantigny and the other of the D-Day landing in Normandy.

Museums and historical societies not elsewhere reported

Location	Name	Type of activity	Hours
Albion	Edwards County Historical Society	Museum	By appointment
Aledo	Mercer County Museum and Historical Society	Museum	1 P.M.–5 P.M., Sat., Sun., holidays; by appointment
Aurora	Aurora Historical Museum	Museum and historic house	2:30 P.M.–5 P.M., Mon., Fri., Sun.; by appointment

Table—continued

Location	Name	Type of activity	Hours
Belvidere	Boone County Historical Society	Historical markers	
Bloomington	Bloomington-Normal Art Association	Gallery	10 A.M.–9 P.M., Mon.–Fri.; 10 A.M.–5 P.M., Sat.; 2 P.M.–5 P.M., Sun.
Bloomington	McLean County Historical Society	Museum	9:30 A.M.–Noon, Tues.–Fri.; 1:30 P.M.–4:30 P.M., Sat.
Bloomington	Municipal Zoo	Zoological gardens	Summer, 8 A.M.–8 P.M.; Winter, 8 A.M.–5 P.M.
Cairo	Cairo Historical Association, Inc.	Historic house	8 A.M.–5 P.M., daily
Canton	Moore Museum of Natural History	Museum	9 A.M.–6 P.M., Mon.–Sat.; 10 A.M.–6 P.M., Sun., holidays; evenings in summer
Carmi	White County Historical Society	Museum and historic building	
Carrollton	Greene County Historical Society	Museum	9 A.M.–5 P.M., Mon.–Fri.
Chicago	International College of Surgeons Hall of Fame	Museum	9 A.M.–4 P.M., Mon.–Fri.; 10 A.M.–4 P.M., Sat.
Chicago	Lincoln Park Zoological Gardens	Zoological gardens	Summer, 9 A.M.–6 P.M., Mon.–Fri.; 10 A.M.–6 P.M., Sat., Sun., holidays; Winter, 9 A.M.–5 P.M.
Chicago	Museum of Negro History and Art	Museum and gallery	10 A.M.–5 P.M., Fri.; 1 P.M.–5 P.M., Sat., Sun.
Chicago	Polish Museum of America	Museum	1 P.M.–4 P.M., Tues.–Fri.; 1 P.M.–5 P.M., Sat., Sun.
Chicago	Swedish Pioneer Historical Society	Museum	10 A.M.–4 P.M., Mon.–Sat.
Chicago	University of Chicago Robie House	Historic house	1 P.M.–5 P.M., Sun.; by appointment
Clinton	Fine Arts Center	Gallery and school	10 A.M.–5 P.M., Mon.–Fri.; 10 A.M.–Noon, Sat.; 7 P.M.–10 P.M., Mon., Wed., Thurs.
Decatur	Decatur Arts Center	Gallery	Sept.–May, 1 P.M.–4 P.M., Tues., Thurs., Sat.; 7 P.M.–9 P.M., Wed.; 2 P.M.–5 P.M., Sun.
Edwardsville	Madison County Historical Museum	Museum	9 A.M.–5 P.M., Tues., Thurs.; 1 P.M.–5 P.M., Wed.
Elgin	Audubon Museum	Natural history museum	Sept.–May, Noon–4 P.M., Tues.–Sun.
Elmhurst	DuPage County Historical Society	Museum	2 P.M.–5 P.M., Tues., Thurs.
Freeport	Rawleigh Museum	Gallery	9 A.M.–4 P.M., Mon.–Fri.; by appointment
Galena	Galena Historical Society	Museum	May–Nov., 9 A.M.–5 P.M., daily
Galesburg	Carl Sandburg Birthplace, Inc.	Museum	9 A.M.–Noon, 1 P.M.–5 P.M. Mon.–Sat.; 1 P.M.–5 P.M., Sun.; evenings by appointment
Harrisburg	Saline County Historical Society	Museum	
Hinsdale	Graue Mill	Museum	May–Oct., 1:30 P.M.–8:30 P.M., Mon.–Sat.; 11:30 A.M.–8:30 P.M., Sun.
Jacksonville	David Strawn Art Gallery	Gallery	3:30 P.M.–5:30 P.M., 7 P.M.–9 P.M., Mon.–Fri.; 1 P.M.–5 P.M., Sat., Sun.
Jerseyville	Jersey County Historical Society	Museum	By appointment

Table—continued

Location	Name	Type of activity	Hours
Kankakee	Kankakee County Historical Society	Museum	2 P.M.–5 P.M., Sat., Sun.; by appointment
Knoxville	Knox County Historical Society	Historic places	May–Sept., 2 P.M.– 5 P.M., Sun.
Marion	Williamson County Historical Society	Lectures	
Monticello	Piatt County Historical Society	Lectures	
Morris	Grundy County Historical Society	Historical collection in courthouse	9 A.M.–5 P.M., Mon.–Fri.
Nauvoo	Joseph Smith Homestead	Historic house	May–Oct., 8 A.M.–6 P.M., daily; Nov. – Apr., 8 : 30 A.M.–5 P.M., daily
Nauvoo	Joseph Smith Mansion	Historic house	May–Oct., 8 A.M.–6 P.M., daily; Nov. – Apr., 8 : 30 A.M.–5 P.M., daily
Oglesby	Oglesby Historical Society	Museum (documents)	12 : 30 P.M.–5 P.M., Mon., Wed., Fri., Sat.; 6 : 30 P.M.–8 : 30 P.M., Tues., Thurs., Sat.
Oregon	Ogle County Historical Society	Museum	Apr.–Oct., 2 P.M.–5 P.M., Sun.; by appointment
Peoria	Peoria Historical Society	Historic house	1 P.M.–4 : 30 P.M., Mon.–Sat.; 1 P.M.–5 : 30 P.M., Sun.
Princeton	Bureau County Historical Society	Museum and library	1 P.M.–5 P.M., Thurs., Sat., Sun.; by appointment
Quincy	Historical Society of Quincy and Adams County	Museum and historic house	
Rockford	Burpee Gallery of Art	Gallery and library	9 A.M.–Noon, Tues.–Sat.; 2 P.M.–5 P.M., Sun.
Rockford	Erlander House Museum	Historic house	2 P.M.–5 P.M., Sun.; by appointment
Rockford	Memorial Hall	Military museum and library	9 A.M.–8 P.M., Mon.–Sat.
Rockford	Natural History Museum	Museum	1 P.M.–5 P.M., Tues.–Sat.; 2 P.M.–5 P.M., Sun.
Rock Island	Augustana College Museum	Museum and film library	1 P.M.–4 P.M., Mon.–Fri.
Rock Island	John M. Browning Memorial Museum	Museum (firearms)	11 A.M.–4 P.M., Wed., Sun., holidays
Springfield	Vachel Lindsay Home	Historic house	June–Sept. 9 A.M.– 5 P.M., daily; Oct.–May, by appointment
Steeleville	Randolph County Historical Society	Restoration projects	
Sterling	Sterling-Rock Falls Historical Society	Museum	2 P.M.–4 P.M., Sun., holidays; by appointment
Vandalia	Vandalia Historical Society	Museum	1 P.M.–5 P.M., Tues.–Sat.
Wadsworth	Lake County Museum	Historical museum	10 A.M.–5 P.M., Tues.–Sat.; Noon–5 P.M., Sun.
Wilmette	Wilmette Historical Commission	Museum (costumes)	12 : 30 P.M.–5 P.M., first Sun. each month: by appointment
Winnetka	Winnetka Historical Society	Museum and library	By appointment

16

State Parks, Memorials, Recreation and Conservation Areas

The Department of Conservation of the state of Illinois owns or leases and operates recreational facilities which totaled 187,195 acres in 1967. Of this total 39,656.1 was water acreage devoted to fishing, hunting of waterfowl, boating, swimming, and water sports. Much of the land selected for recreation serves a double purpose, in that it commemorates important events in Illinois history or honors the work of Illinoisans who accomplished great deeds for the state and the nation.

The first of these memorials, at the foot of Thirty-fifth Street in Chicago, was dedicated in 1865 to the memory of Stephen A. Douglas, whose political life was largely devoted to achieving an understanding between slave states and free, and who died in office June 3, 1861, while representing Illinois in the United States Senate. It was not until thirty years later that the first state-established memorial to Abraham Lincoln—the tomb at Oak Ridge Cemetery in Springfield—was formally opened to the public.

A burial ground was dedicated in 1891 on an elevation called Garrison Hill, near the ruins of Fort Kaskaskia. It was provided by the state of Illinois to receive the bodies of pioneers whose graves were threatened with inundation when the Mississippi River cut a new channel after a series of floods during the previous decade. The town of Kaskaskia had been nearly wiped out by flood in 1844, and its destruction was completed in 1910. A park adjacent to the cemetery, which provides 233.83 acres of beautiful camping and picnicking area, was incorporated into the Illinois state park system in 1927. It stands as a memorial to George Rogers Clark, who occupied Kaskaskia July 4, 1778, and to the pioneer French and American settlers who developed Southern Illinois. Nearby is the mansion of Pierre Menard, first lieutenant governor of the state. Across the river, on the site of the vanished village, is a memorial containing the "Liberty Bell of the West," rung when Clark occupied Kaskaskia. It was dedicated in 1961.

Fort Massac State Park, acquired by Illinois in 1903 through the efforts of the Daughters of the American Revolution, was Illinois' first state park. A preliminary restoration of this old French fort shows the location of the moat and the outlines of the palisade and major buildings. In 1843 army officers seeking a site for an arsenal recommended the fort as the best available place, but the arsenal went to Rock Island.

Starved Rock State Park, which embraces the site of La Salle's and Tonti's Fort St. Louis, was opened in 1911. Second on the roster of parks, it offered rooms and fine dining-room service in a beautifully situated lodge, in addition to outdoor camping and picnicking. Of Illinois' fifty-one state parks, five now provide excellent hotel accommodations. They are Giant City, Illinois Beach, Pere Marquette, Starved Rock, and White Pines Forest.

In 1967 fifty-eight Illinois state parks, memorials, and conservation areas had places for tent and / or trailer camping; twenty-nine had electricity available; twenty-three had sanitary facilities for hookup to mobile homes and trailers.

Forty state parks and conservation areas have stocked lakes, and more provide good stream fishing. In addition, most of the navigation pools above the locks and dams of the Mississippi and Illinois rivers have public access areas operated by the Department of Conservation where launching ramps are available. Most have picnicking, but none have camping facilities. Fifteen public campgrounds are available in the Shawnee National Forest. Campgrounds in the Crab Orchard National Wildlife Refuge are located near Carbondale at Crab Orchard, Little Grassy, and Devils Kitchen lakes.

Provision is made for hunting waterfowl along the Illinois and Mississippi rivers, and for hunting pheasant, quail, and upland game in many of the conservation areas, the state forests, and parts of the Shawnee

National Forest which spreads across a large part of Southern Illinois. Family camping can be combined with historical adventure or hunting and fishing in every part of the state. Nowhere in Illinois will a person be more than a couple of hours from one or more state-operated camping places. For groups particularly interested in following the early life, the hardships, the achievements, and the tragic death of Abraham Lincoln, a tour that embraces all the important monuments in Illinois can be arranged by a brief study of the parks and memorials dedicated to his memory. The Lincoln Trail State Park near Marshall is the place through which the Lincoln family passed as they entered Illinois. At the Lincoln Trail Homestead State Park near Decatur Lincoln spent his first winter in Illinois. Lincoln's New Salem State Park near Springfield is where Lincoln passed his young manhood, and Lincoln Log Cabin State Park near Charleston is where Thomas and Sarah Lincoln, father and stepmother of Abraham, spent their last years. Camping facilities are available at all. New Salem State Park is the closest state campground to Springfield. Advance reservations at these four parks and others near the six Lincoln memorials and the three courthouses connected with his law practice are advised.

A tour of Southern Illinois from East St. Louis, where the remains of the world's most extensive pyramid, the Monks' Mound, may be visited, to the southern borders of the state will reveal much early Illinois history. The road leads from St. Clair County into Monroe and Randolph counties, to Fort de Chartres State Park and the Modoc Rock Shelter near Prairie du Rocher (for a glimpse of Illinois' paleolithic history); thence to Ellis Grove for a visit to Fort Kaskaskia State Park and the Pierre Menard home. From Fort Kaskaskia there is a variety of routes, all interesting, and seldom more than an hour from a camping place at a state park or a state conservation area. At Dixon Springs State Park are accommodations for organized youth groups with adult leaders. Facilities are available for as many as forty-two youths and eight adults in modern cabins provided with kitchen, mess hall, utensils, coolers, showers, and flush toilets. These accommodations are not for family groups. There is a swimming pool for families as well as organized youth groups.

The valley of the Illinois River from Peoria to the confluence of the Kankakee

and Des Plaines rivers, is well served with campgrounds and is historically as interesting as any part of the state. Bloody battleground of the Iroquois and Illini Indians, site of Father Marquette's last missionary endeavors and of the colonizing efforts of La Salle and Tonti, the Illinois River is peopled with the shades of the past. From Fort Crevecoeur (Heartbreak) at Peoria to Channahon, where the Illinois and Michigan Canal once crossed the Du Page River, there are things to see, things to do, and places to camp every twenty to fifty miles.

The triangle between the Rock and Mississippi rivers is served by four large scenic and recreational facilities, while another four are available between the Rock River and the northern boundary of the bounty land—the 3,500,000 acres of western Illinois set aside by Congress for rewarding soldiers of the Revolution and the War of 1812 and their heirs.

Within the bounty-land area between the Illinois River west of La Salle and the Mississippi are more than a dozen state-operated parks and conservation areas. The extensive Pere Marquette Conservation Area near Grafton has three camps for organized youth groups with their own adult leaders. Each camp has frame cabins, a large mess hall and kitchen complete with utensils, eight-burner range, and walk-in cooler, staff quarters, recreation buildings, toilets, and showers. Two of the camps, each accommodating 145 persons, have swimming pools. Camp Potawatomie, which has space for 75 persons, has no pool, but campers use one of the pools on a schedule arranged by the ranger. There are churches and a physician at Grafton, six miles from the area, and hospitals at Alton, twenty-five miles distant. Arrangements for camping time from June 1 to September 1 should be made not later than January with the Department of Conservation in Springfield. There is a nominal fee.

Tent-camping youth groups with proper adult leaders are welcome at all state parks and conservation areas where facilities are provided. The office of the Department of Conservation will furnish names of rangers and / or custodians on application. Groups should notify the ranger a few days in advance of their desire to camp at an area under his supervision. Costs are nominal and may be paid by cash or a check drawn in favor of the treasurer of the state of

Illinois. State parks with camping facilities and state conservation areas are open every day of the year when weather permits.

State memorials, which are open every day but Thanksgiving, Christmas, and New Year's, include three to former governors, Shadrach Bond, the first to hold the office, Edward Coles, the second, and Len Small, the twenty-eighth; to the first lieutenant governor, Pierre Menard; to General Ulysses S. Grant, Elijah Parrish Lovejoy, and Wild Bill Hickok; to an early Swedish religious community at Bishop Hill, to Norwegian settlers at Norway, to Jubilee College, an Episcopal institution; to the men who fought an engagement in 1812 partly from canoes at Campbell's Island in the Mississippi at East Moline; to the fort Zachary Taylor, then a lieutenant, built near the present site of Warsaw in 1816; the third Illinois State House (at Vandalia), three courthouses associated with Abraham Lincoln and one commemorating early justice at Cahokia. There is a monument to Lewis and Clark on the Illinois shore of the Mississippi opposite its confluence with the Missouri at the point from which their expedition to explore the northwest set out, and the Kaskaskia Memorial on Kaskaskia

Island housing Illinois' "liberty bell," rung by George Rogers Clark to arouse the inhabitants when he entered the town in 1778. This memorial must be approached from another state—Missouri—since access can be had only from St. Mary's. There is a memorial park of about forty acres at Shawneetown, first city in Illinois to be incorporated (1814), and also the site of the first United States Land Office in Illinois. Finally, there are six monuments memorializing events in the life of Abraham Lincoln. They are the Lincoln Monument at Dixon, showing him as a soldier in the Black Hawk War; the Lincoln Trail Monument, where it is believed the Lincolns crossed the Wabash River into Illinois; Bryant Cottage, where it is said Lincoln and Douglas completed arrangements for the debates of 1858; the Moore Home in Coles County, where Lincoln visited his stepmother for the last time just before his departure for Washington in 1861; the Lincoln Home on South Eighth Street in Springfield, and Lincoln's Tomb at Oak Ridge Cemetery.

While Illinois always has provided good fishing, many new areas are being opened —man-made lakes for control of flood waters, for cooling water at fossil fuel and nuclear power plants, and for impounding runoff. Many of the sites, particularly those

Principal fishing areas, by county, owned and operated by the Illinois Department of Conservation

County	Area	Water acreage
Adams	Siloam Springs Lake	68
	Siloam Springs State Park	
Alexander	Horseshoe Lake	2,400
	Horseshoe Lake Conservation Area	
Clark	Lincoln Trail Lake	146
	Lincoln Trail State Park	
Coles	Fox Ridge Lake	18
	Fox Ridge State Park	
Cook	Wolf Lake	442
	William W. Powers Conservation Area	
De Witt	Weldon Springs Lake	28
	Weldon Springs State Park	
Douglas	Douglas County Lake	59
	Douglas County Conservation Area	
Fayette	Ramsey Lake	49
	Ramsey Lake State Park	
Fulton	Anderson Lake	1,364
	Anderson Lake Conservation Area	
Fulton	Rice Lake	1,384
	Rice Lake Conservation Area	
Hamilton	Dolan Lake	76
	Hamilton County Conservation Area	

County	Area	Water acreage
Henderson	Gladstone Lake	27
	Henderson County Conservation Area	
Henry	Johnson-Sauk Trail Lake	58
	Johnson-Sauk Trail State Park	
Jackson	Murphysboro Lake	145
	Lake Murphysboro State Park	
Jefferson	Mt. Vernon Game Farm Lake	8
	Mt. Vernon Game Farm	
Johnson	Ferne Clyffe Lake	15.8
	Ferne Clyffe State Park	
Lake	Grass Lake	1,360
	Chain O' Lakes Conservation Area	
Lawrence	Red Hills Lake	40
	Red Hills State Park	
McDonough	Argyle Lake	95
	Argyle Lake State Park	
McLean	Dawson Lake	158
	McLean County Conservation Area	
Macoupin	Beaver Dam Lake	56.5
	Beaver Dam State Park	
Marion	Forbes Lake	525
	Stephen A. Forbes State Park	
Marshall	Sparland Public Hunting and Fishing Area	1,280
	Sparland Conservation Area	
Marshall	Marshall County Public Hunting and Fishing Area	2,557
	Marshall County Conservation Area	
Mason	Sanganois Island Area	1,550
	Sanganois Conservation Area	
Massac	Mermet Lake	452
	Mermet Conservation Area	
Randolph	Randolph County Lake	84
	Randolph County Conservation Area	
St. Clair	Frank Holten Lake No. 1	45
	Frank Holten Lake No. 2	40
	Frank Holten Lake No. 3	123
	Frank Holten State Park	
Saline	Jones Lake	105
	Saline County Conservation Area	
Stephenson	Lake Le-Aqua-Na	43
	Le-Aqua-Na State Park	
Tazewell	Spring Lake	1,285
	Spring Lake Conservation Area	
Union	Grassy Lake	310
	Lyrle Lake	260
	Union County Conservation Area	
Vermilion	Kickapoo State Park Lakes	170
	Kickapoo State Park	
Washington	Washington County Lake	248
	Washington County Conservation Area	
Wayne	Dale Lake	194
	Sam Dale Lake Conservation Area	
Whiteside	Coleta Trout Rearing Units	4
Will	Des Plaines Game Farm Pond	7
	Des Plaines Game Farm	
Winnebago	Pierce Lake	162
	Rock Cut State Park	
Woodford	Woodford County Public Fishing Area	2,900
	Woodford County Conservation Area	

Acreage and facilities of properties of the Illinois Department of Conservation as of June 30, 1967 (includes changes resulting from legislation after June 30, 1967)

State Parks

Name of property	Initial acquisition Year	Initial acquisition Acreage	County	Acreage	Water acreage (included in land acreage)	F—Fishing, P—Private boats, R—Rental boats	Hunting	Facilities available C—Camping, P—Picnicking, R—Refreshments, S—Swimming	H—Historical, S—Scenic, T—Trails	Other
Apple River Canyon	1932	157.10	JoDaviess	296.79		F*		C-P-R	H-S-T	
Argyle Lake	1948	1,051.89	McDonough	1,051.89	95.0	F-P-R	Upland Game	C-P-R	S-T	
Beaver Dam	1947	425.00	Macoupin	737.32	56.5	F-P-R		C-P-R	S-T	
Black Hawk	1927	200.00	Rock Island	205.83		F*		C-P-R	H-S-T	
Buffalo Rock	1929	43.00	La Salle	43.00		F*		P-R	H-S-T	
Cahokia Mounds	1925	144.00	Madison-St. Clair	456.19				C-P-R	H-T	
Cave-in-Rock	1929	64.50	Hardin	64.50	45.0	F-P-R		C-P-R	H-S-T	
Chain O'Lakes	1945	840.00	Lake	960.00		F	Pheasant	C-P-R	S	
Channahon Parkway	1963	2.03	Will	2.03				C-P-R		
Delabar	1960	6.00	Henderson	89.13		F*-P		C-P-R-S		
Dixon Springs	1946	391.40	Pope	399.40		F		C-P-R	S-T	
Ferne Clyffe	1949	36.00	Johnson	1,073.19	15.8	F		C-P-R	H	
Fort Chartres	1915	10.27	Randolph	19.60				P	H-S	
Fort Crevecoeur	1920	15.00	Tazewell	86.06				P	H-S-T	
Fort Defiance	1960	19.50	Alexander	38.10		F*		C-P-R	S-T	
Fort Kaskaskia	1891	20.00	Randolph	234.83				C-P-R		
Fort Massac	1903	24.30	Massac	865.50		F*-P		C-P	T	
Fox Ridge	1938	269.81	Coles	751.80	18.0	F by permit		C-P	S-T	
Fox River	1935	86.00	La Salle	64.00		F*			S-T	
Frank Holten	1946	1,125.00	St. Clair	1,125.00	208.0	F-P-R		P	S-T	
Gebhard Woods	1934	29.60	Grundy	29.60		F*-P		C-P-R-S	S-T	
Giant City	1927	1,162.60	Jackson-Union	2,199.26		F*		P	S-T	
Illini	1934	430.00	La Salle	406.00		F*		C-P	H-S-T	
Illinois Beach	1943	1,114.00	Lake	1,701.87		F*-P		C-P-R	S-T	
Johnson-Sauk Trail	1947	16.32	Henry	436.32	58.0	F-P-R		C-P-R	S-T	
Kankakee River	1938	35.60	Will-Kankakee	2,402.64		F*-P		C-P-R	H-S-T	
Kickapoo	1939	1,327.02	Vermilion	1,539.30	170.0	F-P		C-P	S-T	
Lake Le-Aqua-Na	1949	614.58	Stephenson	614.58	43.0	F-P-R		C-P-R	S-T	
Lake Murphysboro	1948	904.00	Jackson	904.00	145.0	F-P-R		C-P-R	H-T	
Lincoln Log Cabin	1929	68.00	Coles	86.00				C-P	H-T	
Lincoln Trail	1936	31.40	Clark	910.82	146.0	F-P-R		C-P-R	S-T	
Lincoln Trail Homestead	1938	62.00	Macon	162.00		F*		C-P	H-T	
Lincoln's New Salem	1919	60.00	Menard	328.89				C-P-R	H-S-T	Rooms
Lowden	1945	207.12	Ogle	207.50				P-R	T	
McHenry Dam	1939	15.00	McHenry	94.50		F*-P		P	S-T	
Matthiessen	1943	174.50	La Salle	174.50		F*-P		P-R	H-T	
Mississippi Palisades	1929	376.96	Carroll	1,560.99		F*		C-P-R	H-S-T	
Nauvoo	1948	143.00	Hancock	147.92		F*-P-R		C-P-R	S-T	
Pere Marquette	1932	1,511.00	Jersey	5,547.40		F*	Upland Game	C-P-R-S	H-S-T	Rooms
Prophetstown	1948	53.50	Whiteside	53.50		F*-P		C-P	S	
Ramsey Lake	1947	815.00	Fayette	815.00	49.0	F-P-R	Upland Game	C-P-R	S-T	
Red Hills	1943	797.00	Lawrence	948.43	40.0	F-P-R	Upland Game	C-P-R	H-S-T	
Rock Cut	1957	13.00	Winnebago	908.84	162.0	F-P-R	Facilities being developed	C-P-R	H-S-T	
Sam Parr	1960	72.09	Jasper	790.09				C-P-R	T	
Siloam Springs	1940	2,665.00	Adams-Brown	3,025.95	68.0	F-P-R		C-P	S-T	
Spitler Woods	1937	172.40	Macon	202.50				C-P	S-T	
Starved Rock	1911	315.00	La Salle	1,451.25		F*-P		P-R	H-T	Rooms
Stephen A. Forbes	1959	20.00	Marion	2,937.00	525.0	F-P-R		C-P-R	S-T	
Weldon Springs	1948	119.96	De Witt	119.96	28.0	F-P-R		C-P-R	H-T	
White Pines Forest	1927	315.00	Ogle	385.00		F*	Upland Game	C-P-R	H-S-T	Rooms
William G. Stratton	1959	3.00	Grundy	6.75		F*-P		P-R	S-T	Rooms
Total acreage				39,662.52	1,872.3					

State Memorials

Name	County	Year	Acreage	State Memorials	Statute	Type	Recreation	Class
Bishop Hill	Henry	1945	4.30	4.30			P	H
Bryant Cottage	Piatt	1947	.47	.47				H
Cahokia Court House	St. Clair	1936	.79	1.50			P	H
Campbell's Island	Rock Island	1929	5.00	5.00	F*			H
Douglas Tomb	Cook	1865	2.20	2.20				H
Fort Edwards Monument	Hancock	1931	.06	.10				H
Governor Bond Monument	Randolph	1946	.46	.46				H
Governor Coles Monument	Madison	1927	.25	.25				H
Governor Small Home	Kankakee	1947	.20	.20				H
Jubilee College	Peoria	1933	96.00	976.00	F*		C-P-R	H-S-T
Kaskaskia	Randolph	1961	.38	.38				H
Lincoln Home	Sangamon	1923	.42	.42				H
Lincoln Monument	Lee	1921	.64	.64				H-S-
Lincoln Tomb	Sangamon	1895	12.40	12.40				H
Lincoln Trail Monument	Lawrence	1936	.64	25.05				H
Lovejoy Monument	Madison	1923	.10	.10				H
Metamora Court House	Woodford	1921	.20	.20				H
Moore Home	Coles	1935	1.50	1.50				H
Mt. Pulaski Court House	Logan	1935	1.30	1.30				H
Norwegian Settlers Monument	La Salle	1934	.10	.10				H
Old Market House	Randolph	1947	.60	.60				H
Pierre Menard Home	Randolph	1959	1.50	1.50			P	H
Shawneetown	Gallatin	1940	40.00	35.05			P-R	H
U. S. Grant Home	JoDaviess	1931	2.00	5.02				H
Vandalia State House	Fayette	1920	2.30	2.30				H
Wild Bill Hickok Monument	La Salle	1929	1.90	1.90				H
Total acreage				**1,078.94**				

Conservation Areas designated by statute

Name	County	Year	Acreage	Area	Statute	Type	Recreation	Class
Anderson Lake	Fulton	1947	911.19	2,067.74	1,364.0 F-P-R		C-P-R	
Barkhousen	Mason	1962	1,163.00	1,163.00	90.0		C-P	S
Beall Woods Nature Preserve and Conservation Area†	Wabash	1965	626.60	626.30				
Burnham Island	Alexander	1952	742.04	779.44		Pheasant		
Des Plaines	Will	1955	273.19	4,252.81	400.0 F	Waterfowl	C-P-R	S-T
Hamilton County†	Hamilton	1960	99.00	720.00	76.0 F-P-R	Upland Game	C-P-R	S
Horseshoe Lake	Alexander	1927	49.56	7,901.30	2,400.0 F-P-R	Upland Game		
Iroquois County	Iroquois	1944	1,920.00	1,920.00		Upland Game		
Lee County	Lee	1940	480.00	2,330.00				
McLean County†	McLean	1959	516.27	759.50	158.0 F-P-R	Waterfowl	C-P-R	S-T
Marshall County	Marshall	1955	2,570.00	2,615.15	2,557.0 F-P	Waterfowl	P	
Mermet Lake	Massac	1949	10.00	2,461.10	452.0 F-P-R	Upland Game	C-P-R	
Randolph County†	Randolph	1958	25.00	1,001.00	84.0 F-P-R	Upland Game	C-P-R	S-T
Rice Lake	Fulton	1945	2,370.00	2,617.51	1,384.0 F-P-R	Upland Game	C-P-R	
Saline County†	Saline	1959	40.00	524.00	105.0 F-P-R	Waterfowl	C-P-R	S-T
Sam Dale Lake†	Wayne	1959	40.00	1,301.00	194.0 F-P	Waterfowl	C-P-R	S
Sanganois	Cass-Mason	1948	3,161.78	6,989.64	1,550.0 F	Waterfowl		
Sparland	Marshall	1925	1,280.60	ns	1,280.0 F			
Spring Branch	Peoria	1953	410.00	410.00	350.0 F-P-R		C-P-R	
Spring Lake†	Tazewell	1950	632.00	1,658.47	1,285.0	Waterfowl		S-T
Union County	Union	1943	42.00	6,201.98	570.0 F-P-R	Waterfowl	C-P	
Washington County†	Washington	1947	160.00	1,377.90	248.0 F-P	Upland Game	P-R	
William W. Powers†	Cook	1947	160.00	580.24	442.0 F-P		C-P-R	S-T
Woodford County	Woodford	1928	60.00	2,896.55	2,900.0 F-P-R	Waterfowl		S
Total acreage			**17,889**	**53,154.93**				

Table—continued

Name of property	Initial acquisition Year	Acreage	County	Acreage	Water acreage (included in land acreage)	F—Fishing P—Private boats R—Rental boats	Hunting	Facilities available C—Camping P—Picnicking R—Refreshments S—Swimming	H—Historical S—Scenic T—Trails	Other
Conservation Areas not designated by statute										
Carlyle Reservoir	1966	39.09	Clinton	39.09						
Castle Rock†	1967	160.00	Ogle	160.00						
Chain O'Lakes	1953	750.00	Lake	3,230.87	1,360.0	F-P-R	Upland Game			
Henderson County	1961	84.02	Henderson	87.52	27.0	F	Upland Game			
Kankakee River†	1966	634.50	Kankakee	604.50						
Pyatt's Strip Mine†	1965	1,600.00	Perry	1,600.00						
Total acreage				5,721.98	1,387.0					
State Forests										
Henderson	1941	1,047.25	Henderson	1,047.25				C P	S-T	
Mason	1939	5,504.06	Mason	5,524.06				P	S-T	
Putnam	1961	40.00	Putnam	80.00						
Shelby	1957	313.92	Shelby	1,025.92						
Union	1932	3,558.00	Union	3,752.74						
Total acreage				11,429.97						
Fish Hatcheries										
Coleta Trout	1948	11.71	Whiteside	11.71	4.0					
Geneseo Fish	1927	13.87	Henry	13.87	7.5	F				
Southern Illinois	1956	98.00	Williamson	110.00	21.6					
Spring Grove	1931	42.50	McHenry	42.00	24.3			P		
Total acreage				177.58	57.4					
Game Farms										
Des Plaines	1960	320.00	Will	320.00	7.0	F				
Mt. Vernon	1931	759.00	Jefferson	719.00	8.0	F				
Yorkville	1934	74.41	Kendall	101.79				P		Wildlife exhibit
Total acreage				1,140.79	15.0					
Forest Towers										
Aden	1938	3.00	Hamilton	3.00						
Cypress	1939	7.05	Johnson	7.05						
Lively Grove	1940	5.00	Washington	5.00						
Pinckneyville	1938	1.00	Perry	1.00						Wildlife exhibit
Total acreage				16.05						
Access Areas										
Piasa Creek	1965	7.10	Jersey	7.10		F*-P-R		P R	H	
Montebello	1958	3.30	Hancock	3.30						
Total acreage				10.40						

Access areas to Shawnee National Forest (Wildlife Management Plan)	Hardin	1962	160.00	<0.00			
	Johnson	1963	40.00	<0.00			
	Pope	1962	107.00	1,347.00			
	Saline	1963	85.00	85.00			
Calhoun County (Red's Landing)	Calhoun	1963	16.35	16.35	F*-P		
Havana Field Headquarters	Mason	1936	3.50	4.71	F*		
Kankakee River Dam	Kankakee	1959	5.57	5.75			
Mason Tree Nursery	Mason	1934	80.00	80.00			
Oquawka Game Refuge	Henderson	1925	200.00	200.00		P	
Owen Lovejoy Home	Bureau	1967	1.20	1.21			H
Postville Court House	Logan	1953	1.14	1.14			
Rock River Dam	Ogle	1959	27.75	27.75	F*		
Sangamon County Game Preserve	Sangamon	1938	126.85	126.85	F*		
Sid Simpson Park	Adams	1960	20.00	20.00	F*-P	P	
Southern Illinois Forestry Headquarters	Franklin	1938	37.27	37.27	.7	F	P
Tazewell County	Tazewell	1947	10.00	10.00	9.3	F	
Wyanet Public Fishing Area	Henry	1926	17.00	18.35	10.0		T
Total acreage				2,461.38			

ns—Total acreage not supplied.
* Fishing in river, stream, or backwater.
† State park operated conservation area.

Acreage and facilities of properties leased and operated by the Illinois Department of Conservation as of June 30, 1967 (includes changes resulting from legislation after June 30, 1967)

Name of nearest municipality	Area	County	Acreage	Water acreage (included in land acreage)	F—Fishing P—Private boats	Hunting	Facilities available C—Camping P—Picnicking R—Refreshments	Other
Carlyle	Clinton County†	Clinton	3,360.00					
Channahon	Channahon Parkway‡	Will	22.03	2.0	F		R	
Channahon	Illinois & Michigan Parkway‡	Will-Grundy	450.00	230.0	F-P		C-P	
Hartford	Lewis & Clark Memorial*	Madison	5.95				P	
Kewanee	Land adjacent to Johnson-Sauk Trail State Park†							
Olney	Richland County†	Richland	3,867.00			Pheasant		
Cowden	Shelby County†	Shelby	3,509.00			Pheasant		
Springfield	State conservation & education area‡	Sangamon	40.00	1.4				Wildlife exhibit

					Facilities available			
Name of nearest municipality	Area	County	Acreage	Water acreage (included in land acreage)‖	F—Fishing P—Private Boats	Hunting	C—Camping P—Picnicking R—Refreshments	Other
			Navigation Pools—Mississippi River*					
East Dubuque	Pool No. 12—Park & recreation	JoDaviess	22.70		F-P		P	
Menominee	Pool No. 12—Park & recreation	JoDaviess	38.00		F-P		P	
Savanna	Pool No. 13—Park & recreation	Carroll	186.00		F-P		P	Boat launching
Fulton	Pool No. 13—Park & recreation	Whiteside	67.00		F-P		P	
Andalusia	Pool No. 16—Public hunting & fishing	Rock Island	4,500.00	2,000.0	F-P	Waterfowl		
Andalusia	Pool No. 16—Wildlife refuge	Rock Island	500.00	200.0				
Andalusia	Pool No. 17—Park & recreation	Rock Island	10.00		F-P		P	Boat launching
New Boston	Pool No. 17—Public hunting fishing, & recreation	Mercer-Rock Island	1,298.00	500.00	F	Waterfowl		Boat launching
Keithsburg	Pool No. 18—Public hunting & fishing	Henderson	2,877.13	1,500.00	F-P	Waterfowl	P	Boat launching
Oquawka	Pool No. 18—Wildlife refuge	Mercer	390.00	190.0	F-P		P	Boat launching
Keithsburg	Pool No. 18—Park & recreation	Henderson	42.00		F-P		P	Boat launching
Gladstone	Pool No. 19—Park & recreation	Henderson	40.00		F-P		P	Boat launching
Hamilton	Pool No. 20—Park & recreation	Hancock	12.00		F-P		P	Boat launching
Meyer	Pool No. 21—Park & recreation	Adams	.53		F-P		P	Boat launching
Quincy	Pool No. 21—Public hunting, fishing, & recreation	Adams	4,214.00	1,700.0	F	Waterfowl		
Quincy & Hull	Pool No. 22—Public hunting, fishing, & recreation	Pike-Adams	3,553.00	1,750.0	F	Waterfowl	P-R	Boat launching
Hannibal	Pool No. 22—Park & recreation	Pike	356.00		F-P		P	
Pleasant Hill	Pool No. 24—Public hunting & fishing	Pike	1,800.00	1,000.0	F-P	Waterfowl	P	Boat launching
Atlas	Pool No. 24—Wildlife refuge	Pike	300.00	225.0	F-P		P	Boat launching
Rockport	Pool No. 24—Park & recreation	Pike	41.00		P		P	
New Canton	Pool No. 24—Park & recreation	Pike	2.62		F-P		P	Boat launching
Hardin	Pool No. 25—Park & recreation	Calhoun	63.76		P		P	Boat launching
Batchtown & Hamburg	Pool No. 25—Public hunting, fishing, & recreation	Calhoun	2,919.00	1,500.0	F-P	Waterfowl	P	Boat launching
Deer Plain	Pool No. 26 Park & recreation	Calhoun	26.00		F-P		P	Boat launching
Deer Plain	Pool No. 26 Park & recreation	Calhoun	78.00		F-P		P	Boat launching
Alton	Pool No. 26—Park & recreation	Jersey	27.10		F-P		P	Boat launching
			Mississippi and Illinois Rivers*					
Grafton	Pool No. 26—Public hunting & fishing	Jersey	8,087.00	3,000.0	F-P	Waterfowl	P-R	Boat launching
Hardin	Pool No. 26—Wildlife refuge	Calhoun	602.00	400.0	F		P	Boat launching
Rosedale	Pool No. 26—Park & recreation	Jersey	25.00		F-P		P	Boat launching
Rosedale	Pool No. 26—Park & recreation	Jersey	31.00		F-P		P	Boat launching
			Federal Reservoirs§					
Carlyle	Park & recreation, game management	Clinton Fayette	3,151.64	15,500.00	F-P		P	Boat launching
Shelbyville	Lake Shelbyville Conservation Area	Shelby-Moultrie	5,121.41	14,198.4‖		Facilities being developed		
Total acreage			67,335.87					
Less state-owned portion	Oquawka-Delabar Wildlife Refuge		289.13					
	Channahon Parkway State Park		2.03					
	Piasa Creek Access Area		7.10					
			298.26					
Net total acreage			67,037.61					

* Federal government property.
‡ Private property.
† State-owned property other than Department of Conservation.

§ Proposed multiple use of recreational development on United States Corps of Engineers land when state funds are made available.
‖ Water acreage does not include river proper.

created to take care of large flocks of waterfowl that winter in central and southern Illinois, are open to hunters. A few of the conservation areas are open for hunting upland game—pheasant, quail, rabbit, squirrel, and the like.

Of the four largest conservation areas, Horseshoe Lake (7,901.3 acres) in Alexander County hosts a famous concentration of wild geese every winter; Sanganois (6,989.6 acres), near Havana in Cass and Mason counties, is a good waterfowl hunting area; Union County (6,201.9 acres) off Illinois Route 3 near Ware is an important Canada Goose refuge; and Des Plaines (4,252.8 acres) in Will County south of Joliet provides "put-and-take" pheasant hunting.

The Department of Conservation operates five state forests where profitable forestry practices are demonstrated. It has four fish hatcheries to provide fish for new ponds and lakes and for renovated waters suitable as fish habitats. There also are three game farms. The *Illinois Surface Water Inventory*, prepared by the Department of Conservation and revised in 1965, gives a total of about 65,000 ponds and lakes in the state with water surface acreage of more than 186,000 acres. This is exclusive of the waters of Lake Michigan under jurisdiction of the state of Illinois, and the pools and backwater areas of the Mississippi River. Of this total, 62,627 are ponds of from 0.1 to 5.9 acres with a total surface acreage of more than 37,900. Lakes from 6 to 500 acres or larger number 2,167, with a total surface acreage of more than 148,500 acres. The *Illinois Surface Water Inventory* also indicates that there are more than 2,700 named streams totaling more than 9,000 miles. Most of the ponds and smaller lakes are in private ownership and not open to the public. Larger bodies of water are under federal, state, county, and municipal ownership.

The Department of Conservation has more than forty sport fishing areas for use by the general public, with a total of over 20,000 acres. County listings in the *Illinois Fishing Guide* show more than 450 lakes and ponds and 200 streams and major rivers open to the public. This publication, described as the source for sport fishing information, has been revised to June 30, 1967, and may be obtained from the Illinois Department of Conservation.

In preparing the list of recreational properties under the jurisdiction of the Department of Conservation we have relied upon

an official document, "Land and Water Acreage—Facilities," revised to June 30, 1967. This document is described by the department as an administrative report. There is some disagreement in the figures presented in this document and those in the *Illinois Fishing Guide*, particularly in water acreage. Statistics and dates furnished by the Department of Conservation vary occasionally from those given on the official state map and in many brochures and pamphlets of an official nature distributed to the public. There may also be differences with locally prepared material. For example, there is a bronze tablet at Fort de Chartres which states that the reservation became the property of the state in 1913. Actually, the deed to this state park was not registered until 1915, which is the official date of acquisition.

Forest Preserve Districts established under the Enabling Act of June 27, 1913

Cook County

The first tentative gropings toward the splendid ensemble of playing fields, picnic grounds, fishing streams and lakes, woodland trails, toboggan slides, waterways, swimming pools, and golf courses, nature centers and wildlife refuges that comprise the Cook County Forest Preserves began in 1899. It was not until 1929 that the last legal battle of the many that plagued the district had been won and the way completely opened to orderly acquisition of access lands as well as forests.

The thirty intervening years were filled with ardent, sometimes hasty, but generally well-oriented efforts to provide outdoor recreation space for the people of Cook County. They were also filled with wrangles between official agencies for control, and with bitter attacks from persons desiring to keep the general population away from their dooryards.

Efforts to create "outer belt" parks and forests began when the Municipal Science Club of Chicago, mindful of a warning that the city had made no provision for popular play space and that land costs were fast going beyond reach, suggested to two qualified members that they study the problem and report their findings to the club. Jens Jensen, Danish-born landscape architect of the West Park Board, was familiar with the thousands of acres of public forests in Paris, Berlin, Vienna, and Copenhagen. He and David H. Perkins, Chicago architect also familiar with European recreation facilities, set about their assignment with an enthusiasm that never waned until their task bore fruit. They pointed out that in and around Paris were more than 400,000 acres of woods and parks; that Berlin enjoyed almost as much open space on its outskirts and a magnificent wood, the Gruenewald, in the heart of the city. They recommended that immediate action be taken and they were specific in suggesting that the natural woods along the Des Plaines River, the forks of the Chicago River's north branch, Salt Creek, Tinley Creek, Thorne Creek, and the Little Calumet be acquired without delay. Their conclusions were published in 1904 and led to the first Forest Preserve Enabling Act, passed by the General Assembly of Illinois in 1905.

Like many bills that attempt to solve long-standing problems with one piece of hasty and ill-considered legislation, this act was faulty. For this reason it met opposition from Jensen, Perkins, and many others who, nonetheless, were keenly anxious for public forests and genuinely concerned that land soon would be unavailable. However, establishment of a Cook County Forest Preserve was attempted by referendum in 1906. The proposition failed because not enough people were sufficiently interested to vote on the referendum, and even unanimous consent of those voting would have fallen short of a majority of ballots cast in the election.

Early in 1909 the Commercial Club of Chicago included the Jensen-Perkins proposals in the plan for Chicago drawn up by Daniel Burnham which stressed creation of a system of boulevards and parks in outlying areas. The Burnham plan led to another enabling act for a forest preserve, which passed almost unopposed in the General Assembly on June 16, 1909.

A referendum under the enabling act, offered to the voters of Chicago and Cicero, led to a bitter controversy between the trustees of the Metropolitan Sanitary District and the Board of Cook County Commissioners as to which body should appoint the officers of the Forest Preserve District. The outgoing board of commissioners, defeated in the same general election that provided for the forest preserves, attempted to name the district officers before the new board took office. Suit and countersuit eventually reached the Illinois Supreme Court, which ruled the referendum void because it had not been offered to all the voters of Cook County, and also declared the enabling legislation unconstitutional.

Proponents of the public forests had better legal advice on the occasion of their next attempt at legislation. A bill was introduced in the General Assembly early in 1913 that attorneys for interested civic organizations believed would stand up in the courts, and it was passed on June 27, 1913. In November of 1914 a referendum for a Cook County Forest Preserve District was offered to the entire county electorate and passed by almost two-thirds majority. The proposition avoided disputes as to authority over the district by designating the county commissioners of Cook County to be commissioners for the forest preserves as well. A friendly suit was brought by Perkins to test the constitutionality of the enabling act and the legality of the referendum. A favorable decision by the courts cleared the way for a bond issue and on September 25, 1916, the Forest Preserve District of Cook County acquired its first land—500 acres of forest in Palatine Township known as Deer Grove.

By the end of 1922 the district had become owner of 21,500 acres of land at an average cost of $433 per acre. Two thousand of those acres were soon to bring further legal dispute. They lay in the Skokie Valley, they were not forest but they represented necessary access to forested land. People who lived in the area and who did not want public woods in their vicinity contended in court that the district could only purchase forest lands. Two suits went to the Illinois Supreme Court before the right of the district to obtain land abutting on forests was confirmed.

Today Jensen's and Perkins' dream of an emerald necklace of parks and forests around the metropolitan area from the Lake Michigan bluffs at the Wisconsin line to the Little Calumet River and the Indiana border is near realization. Cook County, at the end of 1967, had acquired more than 56,000 acres, and was authorized to purchase 19,000 more. Above Cook County's Potawatomi Woods near Wheeling and from there to the Wisconsin line 300 feet of land on each side of the Des Plaines River has been declared forest preserve by Lake County, which has already developed several hundred acres and marked for development several thousand more. The state of Illinois has completed work on more than 1,700 acres of Illinois Beach State Park at Zion.

Within the eleven divisions of the Cook County preserves are now accommodations for more than a quarter million picnickers in areas equipped with dance floors, baseball diamonds, playing fields, and fields for flying model airplanes. There are parking places for about twenty-five thousand automobiles, thousands of fireplaces for cooking over charcoal, nearly a hundred miles of horse trails used also by cyclists and hikers, streams and lakes for fishing, nearly 2,000 acres of lakes and, in designated areas, launching ramps for motorboats and sailboats. Roadside accommodations for family picnic groups abound. No overnight camping is provided except in a few areas designated for scouts and other youth groups which have responsible adult leadership.

Brookfield Zoo. In 1920 the Chicago Zoological Society was formed for the express purpose of promoting a zoological park. The Illinois General Assembly in 1923 provided for the establishment of such an enterprise by amendment to the Forest Preserve Enabling Act. Three hundred acres of land south of Salt Creek near Riverside were donated to the Forest Preserve District by Edith Rockefeller McCormick and, on March 29, 1926, after all legal difficulties had been cleared away and the amendment affirmed by the courts, a contract was signed between the forest preserve commissioners and the Chicago Zoological Society for the establishment, operation, and maintenance of a zoological park on the lands of the Forest Preserve District.

Today the Brookfield Zoo is a famous institution. It contains many innovations and improvements that have been an inspiration to similar enterprises both in the United States and abroad. Cages are practically nonexistent. Animals are housed in areas that closely approximate their native habitats. Rare and exotic creatures are given as good a life as possible in captivity and additions to the population by natural processes and importation maintain the park at a high level of variety and interest.

Chicago Botanic Garden. Early in the present decade the Chicago Horticultural Society was approached by the Chicago Central Area Committee with reference to improvements in Grant Park. Suggestions

for a small botanic garden were well received, but expert opinion was not enthusiastic. Due to the stormy lake winds, and to industrial smog prevailing on the lakefront in the downtown area, the site was deemed unsuitable. The idea of a botanic garden in Grant Park was dropped, but recommendations by qualified persons brought about a plan for a garden of 300 acres on forest preserve land between the northern end of the Skokie Lagoons developed area and the Lake-Cook line.

Toward the end of its 1963 session the Illinois General Assembly passed an amendment to the Forest Preserve Enabling Act similar to the one that provided for the construction, maintenance, and operation of the Brookfield Zoo—with one important difference. No tax money would be asked or granted for construction of the garden. During the succeeding eighteen months individuals, organizations, and foundations subscribed the money necessary to bring the garden into being, and on January 27, 1965, a contract was signed between the Horticultural Society and the commissioners of the Cook County Forest Preserve District for maintenance and operation of the Chicago Botanic Garden.

Ground was broken at the garden on September 25, 1965, and by the summer of 1966 a drainage system had been completed to carry effluent from a sewage-treatment plant in Lake County underground a distance of one mile in a four-foot concrete aqueduct, and to provide clean water for the botanic garden.

On September 21, 1966, a $1,481,773 contract was let for rough grading of the land masses, waterways, islands, and roadways. Final development of the area will be completed in the early 1970's, at which time the Chicago Botanic Garden will provide many acres of flowering plants, shrubs and trees, a chain of lagoons well stocked with fish, and a waterfowl refuge area, together with parking areas to accommodate a large number of cars. As for the garden area, it is the intention of the directors of the Chicago Horticultural Society and the forest preserve commissioners to provide plantings that will rival and, hopefully, surpass the famous gardens of Europe.

Detailed information on the Cook County Forest Preserve system is developed in the tables which follow.

Cook County Forest Preserves

Division	Location	*Total acres*	Water acres	Trails miles	Fishing streams miles
Calumet	S, SE	1,588	63		
Des Plaines	NW	3,971	77	9.0	10
Indian Boundary	W, NW	3,163	27	11.0	9
North Branch	NW	1,692		6.0	
North West	NW	10,103	110	1.0	
Palos Hills	SW	5,760	528	15.0	
Sag Valley	SW	7,787	446	10.0	
Salt Creek	W, SW	3,671	26	7.5	5
Skokie	N	3,406	401	18.0	
Thorn Creek	S	6,288	60	7.0	
Tinley Creek	SW	8,576	37	3.0	
	Total	56,005	1,775	87.5	24

Facilities in the following lists of forest preserve areas are shown by the legend.

A — Parking available (no count)
B — Boating, including canoe and sail
Bb — Baseball diamond with backstop
C — Concession stand
Cp — Camping
D — Dance platform
E — Electricity
F — Flush or Imhof toilets
G — Golf course

H — Horseback riding
L — Lake fishing
M — Motorboats permitted
P — Playfield
R — Launching ramp
S — Shoreline fishing
Sh — Shelter
W — Winter sports area
X — First aid station

All areas have picnic tables, fireplaces, pure drinking water and toilets, unless otherwise noted. Horse trails are used by cyclists and hikers. Foot trails are laid out in most forest preserve areas. Therefore no notation of hiking facilities, common to all, is made.

Area	Location	Family picnic areas	Permit picnic areas	Permit area capacity	Parking capacity	Facilities
Calumet Division						
Beaubien Preserve	Riverdale	1			267	S R
Calumet Woods	Blue Island		2	1,000	105	B Bb D P
Dan Ryan's Woods	87th & Western		4	11,500	1,308	D F P Sh W X[1]
Eggers Woods	112th & Ave. B	1		2,225	397	Bb D F P Sh[2]
Little Calumet Ramp	Blue Island				100	M[3]
Kickapoo Meadows	Dolton			500	168	P[4]
Whistler Woods	Riverdale	1		1,200	264	B D P
Pipe o'Peace Golf Course	Riverdale					A G
Burnham Woods Golf Course	Burnham					A G
Burnham Woods (Powder Horn Lake)	N. of Calumet City				68	B L
Calumet River Ramp	130th W. of Calumet Expressway				100	A B F M P R X

[1] Soccer field.
[2] Horseshoe courts.
[3] Parking for 33 boat trailers.
[4] Model airplane field.

Area	Location	Family picnic areas	Permit picnic areas	Permit area capacity	Parking capacity	Facilities
Des Plaines Division[1]						
Algonquin Woods	Algonquin & Oakton	1				D S
Alleson's Woods	Ill.-21 at Des Plaines River		1	100	57	P Sh
Bartleson Tract (Iroquois Woods)	Touhy at tollway	1			46	S
E. J. Beck Lake	N. end of E. River Rd.					A S
Belleau Woods	Rand & Ballard rds.	1				S
Big Bend Lake	E. River & Golf rds.				196	B L P R S
Camp Ground Road	Des Plaines	1			117	S
Camp Pine Woods	Lake Ave. at Des Plaines River	1			66	S

Areas	Location	Family picnic areas	Permit picnic areas	Permit area capacity	Parking capacity	Facilities
Dam No. 1 Woods	Wheeling		3	1,600		P S Sh
Dam No. 2 Woods	River & Foundry rds.		1	500	200	S
Lake Ave. Woods	Lake Ave. at Des Plaines River		2	1,100	650	P S Sh
Lions Woods	Des Plaines		1	500	100	P S Sh
Northwestern Woods	Des Plaines		1	3,000	100	Bb F P S Sh
Potawatomi Woods	Wheeling		1	500	197	P S Sh

[1] River Trail Nature Center on Milwaukee Ave. just south of Des Plaines River. Horseback riding at all Des Plaines River locations.

Indian Boundary Division[1]

Areas	Location	Family picnic areas	Permit picnic areas	Permit area capacity	Parking capacity	Facilities
Axe Head Lake	Touhy at River Rd.	1			123	S
Che-Ceh-Pin-Qua Woods	Irving Pk. & Cumberland		1	500	70	D H W
Dam No. 4	Devon & River Rd.		2	1,350	228	D H S Sh
Chippewa Woods	River Rd. S. of Touhy	1	1			A H S
Evans Field	River Grove	1	1	500	132	H P S
Fullerton Woods	River Grove		2	1,000	116	Bb H P S Sh
La Framboise Woods	River Grove	(family picnics only)				A S
Thomas Jefferson Woods	River Forest	(family picnics only)				A S
G.A.R. Woods	River Forest	(family picnics only)				A S
Indian Boundary Golf Course	Belmont & Forest Preserve Blvd.					A G
Robinson Woods	Lawrence & E. River Rd.	1			194	H S
Schiller Woods	Cumberland & Montrose		3	5,000	1,827	Bb D F H S[2][3]
Thatcher Woods	Chicago & Thatcher		2	2,775	444	Bb C D F H P S[4]
Maywood Grove	First Ave., Maywood		1	900	65	D P S Sh
Catherine Chevalier Woods	E. River Rd. near Higgins					A H S

[1] Family picnic areas along River Rd. near Lawrence, Irving Park, Belmont, Fifth Ave., and at 1200 First Ave.
[2] Model airplane field.
[3] Playfield, Cumberland and Montrose.
[4] Trailside museum and nature center at Chicago and Thatcher, where there is ice skating.

North Branch Division

Areas	Location	Family picnic areas	Permit picnic areas	Permit area capacity	Parking capacity	Facilities
Billy Caldwell Golf Course	Caldwell NW of Peterson					A G
Bunker Hill	Div. H.Q. Harts near Caldwell	1				A S
Clayton F. Smith Woods	Caldwell near Harts		3	15,650	1,022	Bb D F P Sh[1][2]
Edgebrook Woods and Golf Course	Caldwell & Devon		1	600	115	F G
Forest Glenn	Forest Glenn Ave. at Elston		1	900	148	Bb F
Indian Road Woods	Central at river		1	1,200	190	Bb P Sh
La Bagh Woods	Cicero N. of Foster		1	2,000	550	Bb F P Sh
Linne Woods	Morton Grove		1	800	228	D H P
Miami Woods	Oakton near U.S.-14		2	700	132	H P
St. Paul Woods	End of Lincoln Ave., Morton Grove		1	5,000	229	Bb D H P
Wayside Woods	Morton Grove	1			61	H

[1] Model airplane field at Grove No. 6.
[2] Pool.

North West Division

Areas	Location	Family picnic areas	Permit picnic areas	Permit area capacity	Parking capacity	Facilities
Deer Grove (Grove 5C)	Dundee Rd. & NW. Highway	1			20	P
Deer Grove	Dundee Rd. & NW. Highway		2	1,200	327	P Sh
Busse Forest	Elk Grove Village	1	6	2,200	961	P Sh[1]
Spring Creek Valley	Barrington Hills					none

[1] Model airplane field.

437

Table—*continued*

Area	Location	Family picnic areas	Permit picnic areas	Permit area capacity	Parking capacity	Facilities
Palos Hills Division[1]						
Apple Orchard Woods	107th W. of U.S.-45	1				A H
Belly Deep Slough	Between U.S.-45 & Kean ¼ mile S. of 95th	1			30	H S
Black Partridge Woods	Lemont	1			30	Sh
Buffalo Woods	Willow Springs	1	3	2,750	408	D H
Bullfrog Lake	Wolf Rd. S. of 95th	1			30	S
Columbia Woods[2]	Wolf Rd & Des Plaines River	1	1	400	224	S
Country Lane Woods	95th W. of U.S.-45	1			151	H
Crooked Creek Woods	Between Kean & U.S.-45 near 107th		1	1,500	220	D H
Don McMahon Woods	107th W. of U.S.-45	1				H
Forty Acre Woods	119th E. of U.S.-45		1	250	75	
Henri de Tonti Woods	Archer 2 miles W. of Willow Springs	1			16	H
Hickory Hills Woods	Hickory Hills	1			50	
Hidden Pond Woods	Between U.S.-45 & Kean N. of 95th		2	1,100	164	D H
Maple Lakes Woods	95th & Wolf Rd.	2	2	1,350	402	B D H L
McGinnis Slough	U.S.-45 S. of 135th, Orland Pk.	1	(fishing area)		100	S
Palos Park Woods	Kean Ave. S. of Ill.-13		2	1,000	142	D H P
Pioneer Woods (Tuma Lake)	107th W. of U.S.-45		1	2,500	292	D H P S W
Pulaski Woods	Wolf Rd. S. of Ill.-4A		3	2,600	319	D H Sh
Red Gate Woods	Archer 2½ miles SW. of Willow Springs		1	1,000	95	D H
Sanganashkee Slough	107th W. of Willow Springs	3	(fishing area)		143	H S
Spears Woods	U.S.-45 S. of 87th		1	500	100	D H
White Oaks Woods	U.S.-45 S. of 95th		1	250	44	D H
Willow Springs Woods	Willow Springs	1	1	750	130	D H
Wolf Road Woods	Wolf S. of 95th		1	500	91	D H

[1] Little Red Schoolhouse Nature Center on 104th Ave. one-half mile S. of 95th St. Model airplane field at Palos Hills, US-45 S. of 107th St.

[2] Only entrance to Columbia Woods is from Willow Springs Rd. just N. of Des Plaines River.

Area	Location	Family picnic areas	Permit picnic areas	Permit area capacity	Parking capacity	Facilities
Sag Valley Division						
Cherry Hill Woods	104th Ave. N. of McCarthy	1		200	57	H S
Crab Apple Woods	123rd E. of U.S.-45	1				none
John J. Duffy Preserve (Tampier Slough)	Wolf Rd. from Ford to 135th	(fishing area)				none
McClaughry Springs	Kean Ave. S. of Ill.-83	1			22	H P
Paddock Woods	86th S. of Ill.-83		1	150	20	H P
Papoose Lake	McCarthy Rd. W. of U.S.-45	1	(fishing area)		123	H S
Swallow Cliff Winter Sports Area	Ill.-83 W. of U.S.-45		1	5,000	500	Sh W
Swallow Cliff Woods	U.S.-45 at 119th		1	1,000	95	D F H Sh
Teason's Woods	104th Ave. S. of Ill.-83		1	200	60	H

Area	Location	Family picnic areas	Permit picnic areas	Permit area capacity	Parking capacity	Facilities
Salt Creek Division						
Arie Crown Forest	71st & U.S.-45		3	2,000	539	H P Sh
Bemis Woods	Wolf Rd. & Ogden Ave.		2	2,000	433	H P Sh W
Black Hawk Woods	Ogden at Des Plaines River	1				B
Brezina Woods	U.S.-45 S. of 22nd		1	2,200	262	Bb D Sh
Brookfield Woods	31st at the Zoo	1	1	200	78	P
Cermak Woods	7600 W. Ogden		1	1,800	474	B C D S[1]
Chicago Portage	Harlem S. of 47th	(no picnics, historical site and museum)				

Area	Location	Family picnic areas	Permit picnic areas	Permit area capacity	Parking capacity	Facilities
Hoffman Dam	Lyons	1	(fishing area)			S B
LaGrange Park Woods	U.S.-45 at 31st, La Grange Park		1	300	33	
McCormick Woods	1st Ave. at 31st	1			47	Sh B
Meadow Lark Golf Course	Wolf Rd. & 31st					A G
George A. Miller Meadow	1st Ave., 12th to Cermak, Maywood		1	10,000	870	B P S Sh²
National Woods	26th at Des Plaines River		5	3,100	194	B Bb D P S Sh
Ottawa Trail Woods	Harlem, 39th to 47th		5	2,600	378	B P Sh S
Plank Road Meadow	Ogden at Des Plaines River	1			78	M R S
Possom Hollow Woods	LaGrange Park	1			233	
Schuth's Grove	Des Plaines Ave. at 22nd	1	1	1,500	88	B D S
Stony Ford	U.S.-66 at Des Plaines River	1			59	B S
Twenty-sixth Woods	26th W. of 17th Ave.		2	200	72	P
Westchester Woods	22nd E. of U.S.-45		1	600	241	P
White Eagle Woods	Harlem S. of 39th		3	3,750	327	B Bb D P S Sh
Zoo Woods	31st at 1st Ave.	1				

¹ Pool. ² Model airplane field.

Skokie Division

Area	Location	Family picnic areas	Permit picnic areas	Permit area capacity	Parking capacity	Facilities
Chipilly Woods	Dundee Rd. & Shermer	1				H
Glenview Woods	Harms Rd. between Glenview Rd. & Lake Ave.	1				H
Harms Woods	Harms Rd. between Golf & Glenview rds		4	3,775	259	Bb D H P S Sh
Skokie Lagoons	Forest Ave., Willow Rd. to County Line Rd.		(no picnics, fishing & boating area)			B H L R S
Somme Woods	Dundee Rd. near Ill.-43	1				H
Sunset Ridge Woods	Sunset Ridge Rd. at Middle Fork	1				H
Turnbull Woods	Green Bay Rd. S. of Lake-Cook Rd.		1	200	41	Sh
Willow Road Woods	Willow at Edens	1			71	S Sh
Northwestern Golf Course	Golf Rd. at West Fork					A G

Thorn Creek Division

Area	Location	Family picnic areas	Permit picnic areas	Permit area capacity	Parking capacity	Facilities
Brownell Woods	Thornton		1	250		A D
Clayhole Woods	Torrence N. of 59th		1	1,000	288	
Glenwood Woods	Glenwood		2	1,500	90	P Sh
Green Lake Woods	159th E. of Torrence		1	3,000	680	C D¹
Halsted Woods	Chicago Heights	1				
Indian Hill Woods	Chicago Heights	1	1	street only		Bb W
Joe Orr Woods	Chicago Heights		1	300	105	P
Jurgenson Woods	Glenwood		3	1,450	130	D P Sh²
Lansing Woods	183rd near Torrence		1	400	50	D P
North Creek Meadow	190th & Torrence		1			A P
Sauk Lake Woods	Chicago Heights		2	2,000		A Bb D P S Sh
Sauk Trail Woods	Chicago Heights		1	1,000	85	P Sh
Shubert's Woods	Chicago Heights		1	600	58	Sh
Shabbona Woods	Torrence N. of 159th		1	1,000	85	D³
Steger Woods	Chicago Heights	1				
Sweet Woods	183rd & Cottage Grove, Thornton		2	1,500	215	B D P Sh
Thornton Woods	Thornton	1				
Wampum Lake	Torrence-Lansing Rd.		1	1,500	296	P S Sh
Woodrow Wilson Woods	Chicago Heights	1				Bb P
Zander's Woods	Thornton		(for scouts and church groups only)			

¹ Pool.
² Model airplane field.

³ Sand Ridge Nature Center is located in Shabbona Woods.

Table—continued

Area	Location	Frmily picnic areas	Permit picnic areas	Permit area capacity	Parking capacity	Facilities
Tinley Creek Division						
Bachelor Grove Woods	143rd at Bachelor Grove Rd.	1			74	D
Burr Oak Woods	Harlem S. of 135th		1	1,100	342	P
Carlson Springs	Oak Park Ave. near 143rd		2	600	131	D P
Elizabeth A. Conkey Forest	135th W. of Central		2	1,800	391	P Sh
Rubio Woods	143rd E. of Ridgeland Ave.		1	2,000	321	Bb D P Sh
St. Mihiel Preserve	167th, Central to Cicero					none
Tinley Creek Woods	Harlem N. of 143rd		1	800	89	Sh
Turtle Head Lake	Harlem S. of 135th	1			191	S Sh
Yankee Woods	Central N. of 167th		1	500	191	
Midlothian Meadows	159th, Cicero to Crawford					none

Du Page County

The Du Page County Forest Preserve District, the second in the state to be created under the enabling act of 1913, was authorized by countywide referendum June 7, 1915. The district boundaries are coterminous with those of the county. Administration is by a president, a clerk, and a treasurer appointed by the Forest Preserve Commission of Du Page County. Supervisors of the county constitute the commission. There is an advisory committee in each of the nine townships.

The first land, 78.97 acres known as York Park, lying just west of Illinois route 83 and Roosevelt Road, was purchased by the commission in 1917. Since that time the preserves have grown in number to twenty-four, and in area to 2,727 acres. York, because of road construction, has been reduced to 57 acres. Aware of the fact that acreage for recreational purposes is rapidly disappearing from the market, the Du Page County commissioners are engaged in a program of expansion which will carry well beyond 1970. During 1966 a total of 620 acres was added by purchase or deed of gift. One preserve, Deer Park, was sold, and another, Belleau Woods, was given to the county. Most of the added acreage was in parcels purchased to enlarge existing areas, including 115 acres added to West Du Page Park, and 180 acres added to the Roy C. Blackwell preserve north of Naperville. In the following table, except where indicated, all areas have picnic tables, playfields, good drinking water, and toilets, and most have hiking trails. Areas and their status as of December 31, 1966, include the following:

Area	Location	Access routes	Acreage	Facilities
York Park	S. of Elmhurst at Ill.-83 & Roosevelt Rd.	Alt. U.S.-30, Ill.-83, York Rd.	57	A P
West Du Page Park	West Chicago	Alt. U.S.-30, Ill.-59	427	A L P
Bloomingdale Grove	Bloomingdale	U.S.-20, Ill.-72	40	none (wild flowers)
Maple Grove	Downers Grove	Maple Ave.	80	A
Fullersburg	N. of Hinsdale	York Road, U.S.-34, I-294	130	A P museum
Burlington Park	Naperville	E-W toll road, U.S.-34, Maple Rd.	51	AP S
Belleau Woods	S. of Wheaton	Alt. U.S.-30, Schaffner Rd.	80	under development
Wayne Grove	Near Bartlett	Ill.-59	70	A P
Churchill	Between Lombard & Glen Ellyn	U.S.-64, Ill.-53	136	A P S W
Warrenville	Near Warrenville	Warrenville & River rds.	43	A L P S
Roy C. Blackwell	N. of Warrenville	Ill.-55	325	under development
Herrick Lake	Butterfield & Herrick rds.	Ill.-55	190	A (300) B L P W
Rocky Glenn	SE. corner of Du Page County	I-55, Ill.-83	191	A P (scout camp)
Oak Grove	91st W. of Ill.-83	I-55, Ill.-83	40	under development

Area	Location	Access routes	Acreage	Facilities
Hinterlong Bird Sanctuary	79th & Greene Rd.	75th & Greene Rd.	18	none
Goodrich Woods	SE. edge of Naperville	75th & Hobson Rd.	16	under development
Fischer Woods	S. of Wood Dale on both sides III.-83	III.-19 & 83	10	future site for roadside picnics
Pioneer Park	E. edge of Naperville	Washington St.	19	A S
Wood Dale Grove	Wood Dale	III.-19 & 83	44	A (under development)
McDowell Grove	NW. Naperville	E-W toll road, U.S.-34 & River Rd.	86	A B C P
Salt Creek Park	S. edge of Wood Dale on Addison	U.S.-20, III.-19	80	A C P
Willowbrook	S. of Glen Ellyn on Park Blvd.	III.-55	43	none (wildlife shelter)
Mallard Lake	Off U.S.-20, W. of Bloomingdale	U.S.-20 & Fischer Blvd.	125	A L S
Pratts Wayne Woods	N. of Wayne	Stearns & Army Trail rds.	219	A L (under development)

Winnebago County

Created by popular referendum on November 2, 1922, the Winnebago County Forest Preserve District has grown from 360 acres in 1924 to 2,000 acres at the end of 1966. The fourteen preserves are maintained by a tax rate of $0.0125 per $100 assessed valuation of real property in the county. The township supervisors and assistant supervisors form the Board of Forest Preserve Commissioners. The president appoints a seven-man executive committee to administer the district.

Eight of the fourteen preserves have shelters and / or lodges which are available to county residents on a reservation and permit basis. Some are equipped with electricity and fireplaces. Two areas have been developed for family camping, with pure drinking water, firewood, and sanitary facilities available. All except those designated by deed of gift to remain undeveloped conservation areas have picnic tables and cooking areas. Ample parking space is available.

Two of the preserves, Hononegah and Macktown, honor the memory of the first white settler in Winnebago County, Stephen Mack, and his Indian wife, Hononegah. Four others were donated as memorials to residents of the county.

Preserve	Location	Access routes	Acreage	Facilities
Hononegah	N. bank Rock River between Rockton & Roscoe	U.S.-51	145.0	A Cp E S Sh lodge
Laona Heights	3½ miles NW. of Durand	III.-70 & Anderson Rd.	40.0	A lodge
Kilbuck Bluffs	Baxter Rd. at Kilbuck Creek	U.S.-51 to Baxter Rd.	165.0	A S Sh lodge
Trailsibe	Baxter Rd. at U.S.-51	U.S.-51	9.0	undeveloped area
Sugar River	On the river NW. of Shirland	III.-75 & Forest Preserve Rd.	323.0	A S Sh lodge
Macktown	Near Rockton	III.-2 & 75	214.0	A E G S Sh museum
Kishwaukee River	Near Morristown	U.S.-51 & Blackhawk Rd.	145.0	A E S Sh lodge
Willow Creek	Near Harlem	III.-173 & Harlem Rd.	143.0	A E S lodge
Seward Bluffs	Near Pecatonica	U.S.-20 & a country road	71.0	A S lodge
Hartley Memorial	3 miles S. of Durand	III.-70	40.0	undeveloped conservation area
Fuller Memorial	III.-2 at Meridian Rd.	U.S.-20, III.-2	135.0	bird sanctuary
Hinchcliff Memorial	Confluence of Kishwaukee and Rock rivers	Bypass U.S.-20 & Kishwaukee Rd.	2.0	public fishing area
Four Lakes	7 miles NW. of Rockford on III.-70	III.-70	30.0	A B L W
Atwood Homestead	Old River & Glassman rds.	III.-2	338.2	A B Cp R S

Piatt County

The Piatt County Forest Preserve District was organized by referendum in 1925, and first acquisition was made in 1926. City parks at Monticello, Bement, Mansfield Park, Hammond Park, and Cerro

Gordo Park comprise 41 acres of a total of 573. There is a two-acre park at Atwood. Picnic facilities are available at all of these. Forest properties are Sangamon Park, 60 acres, inaccessible, and Lodge Park, north of Monticello, 470 acres, with a two-acre lake. Minimal camping facilities are provided at Lodge Park. Adequate playing fields are available at most of the locations.

Area	Location	Access routes	Acreage	Facilities
Atwood Park	Atwood	U.S.-36	2	city park Sh
Bement Park	Bement	Ill.-105	10	city park Sh
Cerro Gordo Park	Cerro Gordo	Ill.-105	2	city park
De Land Park	De Land	Ill.-10	5	city park Sh
Hammond Park	Hammond	U.S.-36	1	city park
Lodge Park	N. of Monticello	Ill.-47	470	A Cp P
Mansfield Park	Mansfield	Ill.-150	3	city park Sh
Monticello Park	Monticello	Ill.-47 & 105	20	city park A P Sh

Kane County

The Forest Preserve District of Kane County was organized under the enabling act of 1913 in June 1925. At the end of 1966 the district had eight preserves, six of which were fully developed, one under development, and one purchased during the year. The eight areas encompass 747 acres, of which 595 were developed, 60 acres under development, and 92 acres in the planning stage at the end of 1966.

Johnson's Mound, an area of 98 acres of

gravel hill which geologists call a *kame*, was purchased on April 13, 1927. The Shabbona Tree, an attraction of the area, a gigantic elm, is estimated to be more than 350 years old. It measures thirty-six feet around its base. Picnicking facilities, hiking trails, and coasting in winter make Johnson's Mound a popular spot the year round.

Tent and trailer overnight camping is available at Sugar Grove. All the areas feature hiking and picnicking. Winter sports are available at several.

Preserve	Location	Access routes	Acreage	Facilities
Johnson's Mound	2 miles E. of Ill.-47 on Hughes Rd.	Alt. U.S.-30	98	A P W
Sugar Grove	Bliss Road near Ill.-47	U.S.-30, Ill.-47, E-W toll road	75	A Cp P
Tyler Creek	N. of Elgin	U.S.-31, NW toll road	50	A Bb P
Elburn	Elburn	Ill.-47, Alt. U.S.-30	87	A
Fabyan	Geneva-Batavia	Ill.-31 & 25	245	A Bb P W
Hampshire	Hampshire	U.S.-20, NW toll road	40	A P
Rutland	Big Timber Road near Ill.-47	Ill.-47	60	being developed
Lone Grove	NW. of Sugar Grove	Ill.-47 & Harter Rd.	92	in planning stage

Will County

The Will County Forest Preserve District was authorized by countywide referendum in 1927. The county board of supervisors serves as commissioners of the forest preserves. First land, 146 acres of Messenger Woods on Bruce Road five miles east of Lockport, was purchased January 30, 1930. The tract later was increased to 207 acres. Shortly thereafter the commissioners bought

151 acres at the junction of U.S. route 52 and Illinois highway 59 on the Du Page River. This tract became Hammel Woods. There now are ten forest preserve sites, ranging from the 8.2 acres of Gerdes Woods in Wilton Township, a gift of Mr. and Mrs. Harry Gerdes in the thirties, to the 242 acres of McKinley Woods on the Des Plaines River just north of its confluence with the Kankakee.

Area	Location	Access routes	Acreage	Facilities
McKinley Woods	3 miles SW. of Channahon	U.S.-6 & a country road	242.2	A Cp P
Hammel Woods	Troy, junction of U.S.-52 & Ill.-59	U.S.-52, Ill.-59	151.3	A Bb P
Runyon Woods	On Ill.-4A, NE. of Lockport	U.S.-6, Ill.-4A & 7	20.9	A P W
Messenger Woods	5 miles E. of Joliet	U.S.-6, Bruce Rd., Ill.-4A, Parker Rd.,	207.0	A Cp P
Van Horn Woods	W. of Frankfort on U.S.-30	U.S.-30, Ill.-7 & Wolf Rd.	131.1	A P
Gerdes Woods	Wilton Center	U.S.-52	8.2	A P
Raccoon Woods	1 mile S. of Monee	U.S.-54	57.7	A P Sh
Plum Grove	Junction Ill.-1 & 394	Calumet Expressway, Ill.-394	86.6	A P
Santa Fe Woods	Alt. U.S.-66 1½ miles S. of U.S.-66	Alt. U.S.-66	75.0	A P
Lamb Woods	Lockport, corner Bruce and Farrell	U.S.-6, Ill.-4A	75.0	A P

De Kalb County

The Forest Preserve District of De Kalb County was organized June 13, 1939, under authority of the Forest Preserve Enabling Act of 1913. The countywide referendum made the boundaries coextensive with those of the county. Members of the board of supervisors are the commissioners of the Forest Preserve District. The first land was acquired in 1939. At the end of 1966 the county had three forest preserves totaling 283 acres. They are the Russell Preserve on the South Branch of the Kishwaukee River at Genoa, the Somonauk Preserve on Somonauk Creek at the La Salle County line, and the Shabbona Preserve at the village of Shabbona. Ample parking is available at all three locations. All areas have hiking trails, and two have sliding hills for winter sports.

Preserve	Location	Access routes	Acreage	Facilities
Russell	Genoa	Ill.-72	122	A Bb P S Sh W
Somonauk	Near Sandwich	U.S.-34	73	A P Sh
Shabbona	Shabbona	U.S.-30	88	A Bb P Sh W

Rock Island County

The forest preserves of Rock Island County were authorized by referendum in 1944. First land was acquired on February 8 of that year. Four preserves and the Niabi Zoo, owned by the Forest Preserve District, total 2,261 acres, of which 227 are water acres, a lake in Loud Thunder Forest Preserve.

The Loud Thunder Preserve of 1,600 acres stretches along the Mississippi for several miles from a mile west of Andalusia. There are three launching ramps, three boat docks, a well-marked nature trail, hiking trails, and fifteen miles of bridle paths.

Wood is furnished at picnic areas and the many secluded camping areas. Under construction is a 227-acre lake with a 70 foot dam which will provide a public fishing area. There is an observation tower.

Land was acquired and paid for by two bond issues, one on February 1, 1944, for $115,000.00 and one on October 1, 1946, for $225,000.00. The lake and dam at Loud Thunder are a gift from the Illinois Department of Conservation.

Preserve	Location	Access routes	Acreage	Facilities
Dorrance	Port Byron	Ill.-84	70	A Bb F P W
Iliniwek	Hampton	Ill.-84	180	A B Bb Cp F P R S W
Indian Bluff	½ mile S. of Quad City Airport	Ill.-150 & 67	174	A C F G P
Loud Thunder	Near Andalusia	Ill.-67 & 92	1,600	A B Cp F L P R S water sports
Niabi Zoo	S. of Moline near Coal Valley	U.S.-6 & local road	10	A C P

Champaign County

The Forest Preserve District of Champaign County was organized in 1948 by countywide referendum under authority of the Forest Preserves Enabling Act of June 27, 1913, as amended. First acquisition, about 260 acres northeast of Mahomet, was made the same year. The preserve was named Lake of the Woods. Since that time purchases and gifts have increased the holdings to more than 500 acres. Of this total, 34 are water acres, represented by two lakes, one of 30 acres with extensive bathing facilities and one of 4 acres well stocked with fish. There is also stream fishing from the banks of the Sangamon River, which flows through the preserve. There is ice fishing in winter.

The forest preserve district is administered by the Champaign County Forest Preserve Commission, which operates under authority of the Champaign County Board of Supervisors. It is a municipal taxing body with autonomous taxing powers within the limitations of its charter.

The Isaac Walton League of Champaign County assists the commission in a program of reforestation and development of fishing areas and hiking trails. The league also conducts a summer program of nature study for Unit Four of the Champaign schools. The lectures and classes continue for four weeks during the summer holidays. The league also has built its own building for its headquarters and meeting place.

A large bathhouse and about three acres for sunbathing are provided on the south shore of the larger lake. Paddle boats and rowboats are available on a rental basis, but no power boats are permitted. Three open shelters and two closed pavilions were available as of 1967. There also are two golf courses. A modern museum building was under construction in 1967 to house the William Redhed collection of early American artifacts, agricultural instruments, and devices. It was scheduled to be opened to the public during the Illinois Sesquicentennial. A 100-foot high observation tower, the Hi-Tower, commemorates the work of H. I. Gelvin in developing the area.

Preserve	Location	Access routes	Acreage	Water acreage	Facilities
Lake of the Woods	Mahomet	I-74, Ill.-47	500	34	A B Bb C F G L S X

Lake County

Established November 4, 1958, by countywide referendum, boundaries are coextensive with those of Lake County. The Board of Supervisors is designated by statute as the Board of Forest Preserve Commissioners. First land purchased was 453 acres, the major portion of Van Patten Woods, which lies east of Russell, near I-94 toll road. It was acquired in 1961 and an additional 173 acres of the tract was bought in 1966. The development has been completed, including shelters, baseball diamonds, playing fields, flush toilets, and parking for more than 1,000 cars.

Captain Daniel Wright Woods on Ill.-21

west of Deerfield was completed in 1966. The area contains 413 acres of forest land, with hiking trails, a shelter, a baseball field, toilet facilities, and a two-acre lake. There is parking for 400 cars.

The Spring Bluff Forest Preserve area on Lake Michigan at the Wisconsin line, was completed in 1967. It consists of 300 acres on the wooded bluffs above Lake Michigan. Seven other areas have been designated and a total of 430 acres purchased. Acquisition of 300 feet on each side of the Des Plaines River from the Wisconsin border to the Cook County line is under way. At the end of 1967, 2,002 acres had been acquired.

Area	Location	Access routes	Acreage	Facilities
Gander Mountain	T46N, R9E 3rd PM	Ill.-173	35	under development
Van Patten Woods	Near Russell	I-94, U.S.-41	626	A (1000) Bb F P Sh
Spring Bluff	Winthrop Harbor	Ill.-42	300	A (50) Bb P Sh
Gurnee Woods	N. of Gurnee	none	131	under development
Wilmott Woods	Buckley Rd. at Des Plaines River	Buckley Rd.	100	under development
Captain Daniel Wright Woods	Half Day	I-94 (toll), U.S.-41, Ill.-21	413	A (400) Bb F L S Sh
Edward L. Ryerson Conservation Area	N. of Deerfield Rd. at Des Plaines River	Ill.-21, U.S.-45, U.S.-41, I-94 (toll)	164	under development

Games with stick and ball, with primitive weapons, and with inflated buffalo bladders were played in Illinois in prehistoric times. The "chunkey game" in which young Indian braves gained skill with bow and arrow by propelling a rolling object with repeated arrow shots was a popular pastime in Illinois during the pre-Columbian period. Lacrosse, a sport to which the Algonquin tribes devoted much time, was called by them the "southern game," and since the most southerly of the Algonquin tribes, the Shawnee, were called the men of the south, the game may have originated in southeastern Illinois or northwestern Kentucky.

Early settlers of the Illinois country were pretty well occupied with gaining a living, but certainly the youngsters had a crack at a primitive field hockey they termed shinney. Youths and young adults were adept at wrestling, which in the heat of conflict sometimes degenerated into biting and eye-gouging. Native-bred horses were raced at informal gatherings and at county fairs.

Horse Racing

The sport of trotting to saddle and sulkey, which had begun on Long Island in 1826, reached Chicago in 1845 when the first race meeting in Illinois was held. On successive days, the *Chicago Tribune* records, a bay mare, Lady Jane, won two straight heats of two miles under saddle, trotting, in the feature race of the day (September 1) and a gelding, Byron, defeated a field of five in straight heats under harness (September 2). The names of the owners, W. Graves (Lady Jane) and Harry Jones (Byron) both of Chicago, are known, but the pedigrees of the horses are not. However, it was not long before standard-bred animals from the line of Messenger and the great Hambletonian were seen on the Chicago track.

Messenger was an English thoroughbred imported into Pennsylvania about 1797 and crossed with native stock, much of it with some Arab blood. Hambletonian was his great-grandson, sturdiest and fastest trotter of his times. Some of his descendants, among them Flora Temple and Dexter, appeared in Chicago frequently a century ago guided by the legendary driver Bud Doble.

Harness racing with standard-bred animals imported from New York and Pennsylvania and with native stock gained in popularity after its introduction in Chicago. In 1855 a track and a regular race meeting were established at Carrollton. La Salle, Peoria, and Pittsfield followed in 1857,

17

Sports in Illinois

1858, and 1859. In 1860 meetings were arranged at Dixon, Morrison, and Waukegan; at Brighton, De Kalb, Decatur, and Sandwich in 1863, and at Jacksonville, Ottawa, and Springfield in 1865. By 1869 twenty-eight tracks in Illinois, most of them half-mile ovals, were holding race meetings. Fifty-one were added in the 1870's, forty-six in the 1880's, and fifty in the last decade of the century. Thus, in 1900, eighty county seats and ninety-five other towns and cities were running annual trotting and pacing events. Since that time thirty-three more tracks have been built and the half-mile oval at Du Quoin has been replaced by a mile track and new grandstands.

Meanwhile a man who did much to promote thoroughbred racing in Illinois had arrived as commander of the Department of the Missouri, with headquarters in Chicago. General Phillip Sheridan, Grant's great cavalry leader, was to make his home from that time in Illinois, even when he was stationed in Washington as commander of the armies. Sheridan married a Chicago woman and participated in the social life of the city. In the early eighties he organized and became first president of the Washington Park Jockey Club. Here the American Derby was inaugurated in 1884. Over the years it has attracted the greatest horses of thoroughbred racing.

During the World's Columbian Exposition of 1893 the Washington Park track was the scene of two great races. As an exposition feature the value to the winner of the American Derby had been boosted from less than $20,000 to $49,500, and a ten-heat feature, the Columbian Free for-All

Trot, had been scheduled. The Derby was won by E. J. Cushing's Boundless, and the trot in world record time (first heat) of 2:07$\frac{3}{4}$ by the great Alix, a mare of the Messenger-Hambletonian line seldom beaten when the bets were down.

For almost a century Illinois horses have been leaders in harness racing. Great names in the sport include Colonel E. J. Baker of St. Charles, who owned more "two-minute" trotters and pacers than any other man; the Warren family, who raised many fine standard breds, and the Hayes brothers, Gene and Don, of Du Quoin, who, among many fine horses, raced the second leading money-winning trotter of all time, Pronto Don, who earned $332,363 for them on the nation's tracks.

In the 122 years since the first harness race in Chicago there have been seven miles at better than 1:58 at the fairgrounds in Springfield, more than on any other track in the nation. They were by Greyhound in 1936 (still the world's record trot by a gelding at 1:57$\frac{1}{4}$), Victory Song in 1947, Samson Hanover in 1952, Right Time in 1960, Lang Hanover in 1961, Coffee Break in 1962, and Bret Hanover in 1965. There were two such miles at Du Quoin on the same afternoon in 1952, by Florican and Star's Pride. On September 2, 1964, Ayers tied a record of 1:56$\frac{4}{5}$ for three-year-old colts at Du Quoin. On September 1, 1966, Noble Victory set a world record for the mile trot by a stallion (four-year-old and all-age) at Du Quoin. The time was 1:55$\frac{3}{5}$. In 1960, at Springfield, Bye Bye Byrd set a world record for three heats in an afternoon, with an aggregate time of 5:56$\frac{3}{5}$. A world record for two heats in an afternoon was set at Springfield by Midnight Hardy in 3:56$\frac{4}{5}$. In all there have been 116 miles at two minutes or better on the Springfield track, the first of them by the great Dan Patch in 1906.

Modern racing in Illinois began with the legalization of pari-mutuel betting in 1927. Tracks were placed under supervision of a racing commission in that year and in 1941 the commission became the Illinois Racing Board. In 1946 a harness racing commission was formed. It was merged with the Racing Board in 1965. Until 1944 all racing revenue accruing to the state went into the general revenue fund. In that year the value of uncashed betting tickets was devoted to veterans' rehabilitation, as it has been ever since. In 1946 the tax on the pari-mutuels was increased to provide for interest and amortization of service recognition bonds (the World War II bonus). In that same year mutuel betting was legalized at certain harness tracks.

In 1951 a fund for Illinois colts was established, which received one half of 1 per cent of the total betting at harness tracks where pari-mutuels operated. To this money, which totaled $7,073,023.53 from 1951 through 1967, was added nomination fees and entry charges to provide purses at the Illinois State Fair in Springfield for a series of races to be known as the Illinois State Fair Colt Stakes. More than $200,000 has been made available each year since 1953. Races now include mile trots and paces for two- and three-year-olds (free-for-all), mile trots and paces for fillies, and for four-, five-, and six-year-olds previously nominated for the two- and three-year-old divisions. Money is divided in each race so that there are at least six winners in each of two preliminary heats, and there is a reserve of 10 per cent for the winning horse. The statistical section below includes names of winners and amounts of winning shares from 1952 through 1968.

In 1967 aid to breeders was expanded to make available prize money at county fairs. For 1967 the sum of $80,000 was appropriated for qualified colt associations to distribute. For fiscal 1968 and thereafter the amount was increased to $160,000. Colts entering county races must have been nominated in the Illinois State Fair Colt Stakes. An additional $40,000 annually will be provided for four races at Springfield to be known as the Illinois Colt Association Championship Stakes. It will be divided equally among two- and three-year-old trots and paces, $10,000 for each event.

During the period from 1927 through 1966, out of their share of the mutuels, the various racing associations have provided $259,931,464 in purses for thoroughbred and standard-bred racing. Total mutuel handle increased from $60,078,214 in 1941 to $522,193,681 in 1967. Racing days at tracks where mutuel betting is permitted totaled 222 in 1941. In 1967 there were 664 such days. Races increased from 1,778 to 6,290 in the same period.

Revenue to the state from racing from 1941 through 1967 totaled $421,719,843.44. Of this sum $200,697,419.55 has been used for the Service Recognition Fund,

Distribution of revenue to state funds from racing, 1941–67
(obtained from privilege tax on wagering, admission taxes, application and license fees)

Year	General revenue	Agricultural premium	Fair and Exposition	Service recognition	Veterans' rehabilitation	Illinois colts	Illinois-bred thoroughbred	Total
1941	$895,759.02	$895,759.01						$1,791,518.03
1942	1,222,302.69	1,222,302.69						2,444,605.38
1943	1,404,084.01	1,404,084.01						2,808,168.02
1944	1,941,543.37	1,941,543.37			$34,748.00			3,917,834.74
1945	2,125,729.00	2,125,729.00			88,362.20			4,339,820.20
1946	2,477,507.47	2,634,734.39			93,809.20			5,206,051.06
1947	1,169,008.24	2,398,287.12		$7,701,929.39	115,189.90			11,384,414.65
1948	808,553.35	1,992,184.82		6,659,104.45	87,793.70			9,547,636.32
1949	812,473.40	2,229,819.82		5,554,502.41	76,513.80			8,673,309.43
1950	868,630.20	2,360,065.40		5,797,743.62	58,057.65			9,084,496.87
1951	911,103.60	2,678,946.00	$900,090.77	6,774,123.06	65,963.40	$84,342.67		11,414,566.50
1952	988,638.56	3,389,366.23	1,866,780.68	8,636,015.15	78,559.60	150,018.19		15,109,378.41
1953	995,047.05	3,772,500.75	1,970,071.70	9,067,068.22	99,132.60	177,600.11		16,081,420.43
1954	1,010,133.20	3,907,089.42	1,954,781.32	8,956,387.47	114,726.80	192,515.69		16,135,633.90
1955	1,035,553.60	3,946,643.72	1,914,418.12	9,384,300.97	119,095.00	200,588.40		16,600,599.81
1956	1,027,384.20	4,290,212.67	1,945,766.17	9,929,688.82	111,723.00	231,467.10	$116,995.94	17,536,241.96
1957	995,757.49	4,385,345.95	1,906,714.05	9,784,269.67	117,416.80	244,487.69	253,665.05	17,550,986.59
1958	1,001,204.00	4,425,125.29	1,818,777.44	9,391,781.34	118,773.30	257,597.35	302,287.01	17,266,923.77
1959	981,743.95	4,712,430.90	1,803,883.26	9,336,215.58	112,018.50	287,101.08		17,535,680.28
1960	989,219.20	4,934,158.22	1,840,928.40	9,445,422.81	130,143.30	304,504.79	471,054.62	18,115,431.34
1961	1,170,584.34	5,421,643.37	1,945,211.64	9,916,001.34	114,729.40	342,150.59	654,239.95	19,564,560.63
1962	1,332,944.54	6,795,842.15	2,227,543.29	11,086,468.01	129,926.50	450,696.12	742,679.25	22,766,099.86
1963	1,410,676.05	8,103,926.84	2,386,246.54	11,770,664.49	152,929.60	564,230.21	785,517.63	25,174,191.36
1964	3,465,558.25	9,781,563.30	2,337,679.10	11,319,006.10	165,468.10	734,905.35		27,804,180.20
1965	3,195,734.03	11,220,930.76	2,625,971.40	12,440,653.65	189,186.90	828,952.49		30,501,429.23
1966	3,100,999.33	14,802,582.96	2,904,422.09	13,607,956.13	181,308.00	963,848.11		35,561,116.62
1967	3,308,946.89	16,067,900.27	3,031,330.23	14,138,116.87	199,235.60	1,058,017.59		37,803,547.45
Total	$40,646,819.03	$131,840,718.43	$35,380,616.20	$200,697,419.55	$2,754,806.85	$7,073,023.53	$3,326,439.46	$421,719,843.04

Distribution of money wagered at Illinois tracks, 1941–67

In the column headed "public pool" are included sums donated by the associations to meet race obligations when the "break" to ten cents goes against the track. This money, by law, cannot be taken out of the mutuel handle. Breaks the other way are evenly divided between the state and the associations, and the amount generally is larger than the minus pools. Since minus pools are not separately reported at all tracks (not by thorough-bred tracks before 1948 nor by harness tracks before 1965), the public pool plus association commissions plus state tax will exceed the total mutuel handle by the amount of the minus pools. Over the years this has varied from $1,351.89 for thoroughbred racing in 1950 to $68,216.23 for harness racing in 1966. No record of public pools is available for harness racing prior to 1961, nor any record of minus pools for harness racing prior to 1965, when the Illinois Racing Board assumed the duties of the Illinois Harness Racing Commission. If a figure is not available, this fact is indicated by na.

Year	No. of racing days	Average daily handle	Total handle	Public pool	Association commissions and breakage	State tax and breakage
			Thoroughbred racing			
1941	222	$270,623	$60,078,214.00	na	na	na
1942	227	365,081	82,873,489.00	$73,351,788.90	$7,864,230.32	$1,657,469.78
1943	229	438,445	100,403,826.00	88,932,347.20	9,463,402.28	2,008,076.52
1944	227	656,231	148,964,367.00	131,986,657.50	13,998,422,16	2,979,287.34
1945	222	757,027	168,060,010.00	148,808,302.90	15,890,506.90	3,361,200.20
1946	227	872,436	198,042,882.00	175,399,179.30	18,682,845.06	3,960,857.64
1947	228	728,327	166,058,458.00	142,284,148.10	13,719,793.37	10,054,516.53
1948	168	846,876	142,275,234.00	121,948,740.60	12,304,706.95	8,036.450.77
1949	174	689,516	119,975,759.00	102,871,379.10	10,353,531.92	6,754,260.00
1950	234	537,311	125,730,720.00	107,757,969.60	10,919,051.47	7,055,050.82
1951	234	631,427	147,753,830.00	125,784,950.10	12,820.030.45	9,151,752.13
1952	234	797,770	186,678,068.00	158,070,682.60	16,258,051.57	12,369,576.51
1953	234	842,187	197,007,170.00	166,882,888.00	17,122,179.54	13,007,211.62
1954	298	655,967	195,478,132.00	165,521,645.20	17,092,048.26	12,865,950.11
1955	294	697,248	204,991,019.00	173,654,207.10	18,130,016.92	13,213,137.21
1956	294	727,613	213,918,109.00	180,959,507.50	19,154,999.14	13,821,221.16
1957	295	724,897	213,844,665.00	181,016,475.10	19,121,808.24	13,714,693.71
1958	295	707,802	208,801,666.00	176,864,040.10	18,657,415.73	13,283,001.27
1959	300	689,508	206,852,527.00	175,061,916.70	18,557,388.25	13,246,269.11
1960	301	705,560	212,373,616.00	179,785,761.10	18,990,838.16	13,598,334.23
1961	302	747,598	225,774,520.00	191,180,270.40	20,155,051.94	14,460,664.57
1962	307	822,416	252,481,658,00	213,781,475.16	22,430,558.51	16,284,233.84
1963	307	873,579	268,188,747.00	227,097,978.50	23,781,891.76	17,328,675.20
1964	307	905,807	278,082,705.00	235,518,178.70	24,542,479.50	18,022,046.80
1965	307	940,190	288,638,361.00	243,245,011.80	25,670,001.15	19,723,348.50
1966	307	972,418	298,532,281.00	250,424,510.92	26,341,047.85	21,766,722.23
1967	307	1,011,694	310,590,158.00	260,589,320.30	27,247,154.60	22,753,683.10

Year	No. of racing days	Average daily handle	Total handle	Public pool	Association commisions and breakage	State tax and breakage
			Harness racing			
1946	90	$84,182	$7,576,346.00	na	na	$157,226.92
1947	117	105,265	12,315,947.00	na	na	246,318.94
1948	198	131,929	26,121,889.00	na	na	522,437.78
1949	193	127,448	24,597,495.00	na	na	998,795.63
1950	137	156,785	21,479,570.00	na	na	1,102,758.20
1951	140	168,717	23,620,414.00	na	na	1,285,750.37
1952	156	192,331	30,003,567.00	na	na	1,672,603.74
1953	166	213,976	35,519,937.00	na	na	1,953,596.96
1954	161	239,149	38,503,052.00	na	na	2,117,668.29
1955	163	246,120	40,117,606.00	na	na	2,206,468.70
1956	170	272,314	46,293,322.00	na	na	2,546,133.20
1957	182	268,667	48,897,452.00	na	na	2,126,797.54
1958	167	308,499	51,519,389.00	na	na	2,063,517.27
1959	207	277,392	57,420,110.00	na	na	3,158,106.62
1960	198	307,580	60,900,861.00	na	na	3,349,547.91
1961	211	324,313	68,430,028.00	$57,315,319.50	$7,351,056.48	3,798,444.02
1962	229	393,621	90,139,107.00	75,503,649.70	9,677,505.82	4,993,928.98
1963	235	480,110	112,825,918.00	94,456,113.40	12,164,378.49	6,253,932.51
1964	241	609,880	146,981,026.00	123,128,086.40	15,768,982.55	8,150,217.95
1965	242	702,271	169,949,613.00	142,339,855.70	18,262,528.02	9,347,229.28
1966	321	600,528	192,769,619.00	161,518,781.20	19,120,522.86	11,130,215.14
1967	357	759,856	211,603,523.00	177,256,492.40	21,023,458.95	13,323,571.65

Total mutuel handle (no harness-racing wagering until 1946)

Year	No. of racing days	Total handle	Public pool	Association commisions and breakage	State tax and breakage
1946	317	$205,619,228.00	na	na	$4,118,084.56
1947	345	178,374,405.00	na	na	10,300,835.47
1948	366	168,396,123.00	na	na	8,558,888.55
1949	367	144,573,254.00	na	na	7,753,055.63
1950	371	147,210,290.00	na	na	8,157,809.02
1951	374	171,374,244.00	na	na	10,440,502.50
1952	390	225,681,635.00	na	na	14,242,180.25
1953	400	232,527,107.00	na	na	14,960,808.58
1954	395	233,981,184.00	na	na	14,983,618.40
1955	457	245,108,625.00	na	na	15,419,605.91
1956	464	260,211,431.00	na	na	16,367,354.36
1957	477	262,742,117.00	na	na	15,841,491.25
1958	462	260,321,055.00	na	na	15,346,518.54
1959	507	264,272,637.00	na	na	16,404,375.73
1960	499	273,274,477.00	na	na	16,947,885.14
1961	513	294,204,548.00	$248,495,589.90	$27,506,108.42	18,259,108.59
1962	536	358,327,854.00	302,601,628.20	33,459,397.58	22,322,604.18
1963	542	344,712,055.00	291,149,892.50	32,089,293.47	21,541,124.78
1964	548	386,055,845.00	358,646,265.10	40,311,462.05	26,172,264.75
1965	549	458,587,974.00	385,584,867.50	43,932,529.17	29,070,577.33
1966	628	491,301,900.00	411,943,288.60	45,461,574.03	33,897,037.37
1967	664	522,193,681.00	437,845,812.70	48,270,613.55	36,077,254.75

Thoroughbred racing in Illinois
Days, number of races, purses, and attendance, 1927–67

Year	Days of racing			Number of races	Purses		Attendance	
	Chicago	Southern Illinois	Total		Total	Daily average	Total	Daily average
1927			178	1,254	$1,649,660	$9,268	na	
1928			208	1,477	2,065,087	9,928	na	
1929			206	1,450	2,270,682	11,023	na	
1930			209	1,492	2,370,036	11,340	na	
1931			183	1,335	2,182,700	11,927	na	
1932			203	1,536	1,815,950	8,946	na	
1933	176	37	213	1,638	1,375,115	6,456	na	
1934	158	51	209	1,565	1,249,875	5,980	na	
1935			183	1,410	1,471,575	8,046	na	
1936			157	1,249	1,347,725	8,584	na	
1937			188	1,480	1,531,685	8,147	na	
1938			217	1,716	1,574,615	7,256	na	
1939			200	1,600	1,502,255	7,511	na	
1940			198	1,586	1,659,485	8,381	na	
1941			222	1,778	2,004,320	9,028	1,878,814	8,463
1942	169	58	227	1,828	2;487,150	10,957	2,075,405	9,143
1943	169	60	229	1,859	4,169,062	18,206	1,923,286	8,399
1944	168	59	227	1,844	3,486,139	15,358	2,451,610	10,800
1945	163	59	222	1,807	4,202,055	18,928	2,456,926	11,067
1946	169	58	227	1,827	5,534,390	24,381	2,963,586	13,055
1947	169	59	228	1,847	5,633,775	24,710	2,743,225	12,032
1948	168	*	168	1,364	5,149,625	30,653	2,267,655	13,498
1949	174	*	174	1,410	4,743,625	27,262	2,064,426	11,865
1950	174	60	234	1,935	4,795,420	20,493	2,190,378	9,361
1951	174	60	234†	1,929	5,356,780	23,090	2,413,494	10,403
1952	174	60	234†	1,937	6,537,210	28,672	2,800,125	12,281
1953	174	60	234	1,971	7,417,215	31,655	2,853,326	12,194
1954	168	130	298	2,582	8,238,980	27,648	3,020 920	10,137
1955	174	120	294	2,529	8,528,790	29,009	2,938,772	9,996
1956	174	120	294	2,505	8,547,355	29,072	2,947,558	10,020
1957	175	120	295	2,595	8,742,760	29,636	2,802,222	9,499
1958	175	120	295	2,642	8,877,445	30,093	2,869,512	9,727
1959	180	120	300	2,692	8,965,375	29,885	2,755,740	9,186
1960	181	120	301†	2,682	8,935,115	29,883	2,827,324	9,456
1961	181	121	302	2,702	9,164,905	30,347	3,079,130	10,196
1962	187	120	307	2,766	10,031,460	32,676	3,380,110	11,010
1963	187	120	307	2,762	10,398,919	33,873	3,525,391	11,483
1964	187	120	307	2,756	11,092,720	36,133	3,566,100	11,616
1965	187	120	307	2,768	11,458,120	37,233	3,637,461	11,848
1966	187	120	307†	2,763	11,965,130	38,974	3,606,640	11,748
1967	187	120	307	2,763	12,364,455	40,275	3,636,286	11,845

na—Data not available.
* Harness racing replaced thoroughbred racing at Fairmont Park, Collinsville, in 1948 and 1949.
† While 234 days were allotted in 1951, there were two races only on November 6, none on November 7 and 8; averages are based on 232 days. In 1952, while 234 days were allotted, there was no racing May 5 through May 10; averages are based on 228 days. In 1960, while 301 days were allotted, two days were lost due to a strike of mutuel clerks; averages are based on 299 days. In 1966 two days were lost; averages are based on 305 days.

Harness racing in Illinois
Days, number of races, purses, and attendance at tracks where pari-mutuel betting is permitted, 1946–67

Year	Days of racing			Number of races	Purses		Attendance	
	Chicago	Southern Illinois	Total		Total	Daily average	Total	Daily average
1946	90		90	736	$447,450	$4,972	388,065	4,312
1947	117		117	1,014	507,650	4,339	645,617	5,519
1948	109	89	198	1,736	1,202,450	6,073	1,043,535	5,270
1949	131	62	193	1,734	1,380,242	7,151	1,057,066	5,477
1950	137		137	1,230	868,260	6,338	674,952	4,927
1951	140		140	1,265	1,008,438	7,203	708,399	5,060
1952	156		156	1,409	1,322,761	8,479	676,859	4,339
1953	166		166	1,497	1,377,675	8,299	760,282	4,580
1954	161		161	1,457	1,654,950	10,279	826,363	5,133
1955	163		163	1,480	1,862,308	11,425	828,825	5,085
1956	170		170	1,550	1,862,308	10,955	919,487	5,409
1957	182		182	na	2,199,814	12,087	926,753	5,092
1958	167		167	na	2,126,798	12,735	965,543	5,782
1959	207		207	na	2,460,129	11,885	1,013,566	4,896
1960	198		198	1,972	2,478,320	12,517	1,088,364	5,497
1961	211		211	2,095	2,721,340	12,897	1,193,180	5,655
1962	229		229	2,316	3,775,322	16,486	1,663,909	7,266
1963	235		235	2,350	4,448,614	18,930	2,289,922	9,744
1964	241		241	2,410	5,644,266	23,420	2,633,940	10,929
1965	242		242	2,420	6,599,970	27,273	2,778,439	11,481
1966	242	79	321	3,161	7,299,314	22,739	2,899,739	9,033
1967	247	110	357	3,527	7,530,543	21,094	3,027,306	8,480

Thoroughbred racing, leading money winners on Illinois tracks, 1943–67

	Owners			Horses	
Year	Name	Amount won		Name	Amount won
1943	Marsch, J.	$125,325		Askmenow	$80,650
1944	Calumet Farm	183,515		Free For All	109,575
1945	Main Chance Farm	186,420		Busher	122,925
1946	Calumet Farm	200,450		Education	126,925
1947	Calumet Farm	560,800		Bewitch	193,925
1948	Calumet Farm	348,800		Billings	112,650
1949	Calumet Farm	520,862		Ponder	139,350
1950	Bishop, W. H.	167,745		To Market	115,555
1951	Calumet Farm	180,935		Curandero	142,175
1952	Calumet Farm	349,905		Mark-Ye-Well	229,270
1953	Hasty House Farm	576,344		Hasty Road	208,320
1954	Calumet Farm	180,935		Errard King	173,375
1955	Hasty House Farm	435,785		Swoon's Son	204,470
1956	Drake, E. G.	329,205		Swoon's Son	280,475
1957	Hasty House Farm	245,517		Swoon's Son	204,775
1958	Bishop, W. H.	381,764		Round Table	257,100
1959	Kerr Stable	348,555		Round Table	251,350
1960	Hooper, F. W.	327,124		T. V. Lark	234,100
1961	Jolly, Mrs. M.	329,725		Ridan	279,675
1962	Bishop, W. H.	374,542		Candy Spots	158,312
1963	Bishop, W. H.	231,003		Candy Spots	172,665
1964	Bishop, W. H.	329,944		Umbrella Fella	141,226
1965	Powhatan Stable	309,840		Tom Rolfe	241,600
1966	Peltier, H.	324,109		Diplomat Way	219,525
1967	Van Berg, M. H., Stable	290,810		Dr. Fager	133,360

Three great stake races in Illinois

American Derby—three year olds, distance varied*

Year	Name of horse	Name of owner	Name of trainer	Name of jockey	Weight of jockey	Value to winner
1884	Modesty	Corrigan, E.	Corrigan, E.	Murphy, I.	117	$10,700
1885	Volante	Santa Anita Stable	Cooper, A.	Murphy, I.	123	9,570
1886	Silver Cloud	Santa Anita Stable	Cooper, A.	Murphy, I.	121	8,160
1887	C. H. Todd	McCarthy, H. and J.	Appleby, W.	Hamilton	118	13,690
1888	Emperor of Norfolk	Santa Anita Stable	Cooper, A.	Murphy, I.	123	14,340
1889	Spokane	Armstrong, N.	Rodegap, J.	Kiley, T.	121	15,400
1890	Uncle Bob	Harkins, G. B.	Bryant, S.	Kiley, T.	115½	15,260
1891	Strathmeath	Morris, G. B.	Morris, G. B.	Covington	112	18,610
1892	Carlsbad	Swigert, R. A.	Swigert, R. A.	Williams, R.	122	16,930
1893†	Boundless	Cushing, E. J.	McDaniel, W.	Garrison, E.	122	49,500
1894	Rey el Santa Anita	Santa Anita Stable	McDaniel, H.	Van Kuren, E.	122	19,750
1898	Pink Coat	Woodford and Buckner	Fizer, W. H.	Martin, W.	127	9,225
1900	Sidney Lucas	Thompson Brothers	Thompson R.	Bullman, J.	122	9,425
1901	Robert Waddell	Bradley, Mrs. R.	Bradley, R.	Bullman, J.	119	19,275
1902	Wyeth	Drake, J.	Wishard, E.	Lyne, L.	122	19,875
1903	The Picket	Middleton and Jungbluth	Reid, C. B.	Helgesen	115	27,025
1904	Highball	Sheftel, W. M.	May, J. W.	Fuller, G. C.	122	26,325
1916	Dodge	Weber and Ward	Ward, J. H.	Murphy, F.	126	6,850
1926	Boot to Boot	Bradley, E. R.	Hurley, W.	Johnson, A.	121	89,000
1927	Hydromel	Camden, J. N.	Stewart, D.	McDermott, L.	116	22,750
1928	Toro	McLean, E. B.	Schorr, J. F.	Ambrose, E.	126	21,925
1929	Windy City	Grabiner, F. M.	Lowenstein, J.	McDermott, L.	118	47,550
1930	Reveille Boy	Best, J. A.	Paul, J.	Fronk, W.	118	51,300
1931	Mate	Bostwick, A. C.	Healy, J. W.	Ellis, G.	126	48,675
1932	Gusto	Schwartz, M. L.	Hirsch, M.	Coucci, S.	118	48,200
1933	Mr. Khayyam	Catawba Stable	Brady, M.	Walls, P.	121	23,410
1934	Cavalcade	Brookmeade Stable	Smith, R.	Garner, M.	126	23,310
1935	Black Helen	Bradley, E. R.	Hurley, W.	Meade, D.	118	25,025
1937	Dawn Play	King Ranch	Hirsch, M.	Balaski, L.	116	25,400

452

Year	Winner	Owner/Trainer	Jockey		Wt.	Value
1940	Mioland	Howard, C. S.	Smith, T.	Adams, J.	123	44,900
1941	Whirlaway	Calumet Farm	Jones, B. A.	Robertson, A.	126	44,975
1942	Alsab	Sabath, Mrs. A.	Swenke, A.	Woolf, G.	126	60,850
1943	Askmenow	Headley, H. P.	Osborne, K.	Woolf, G.	115	56,150
1944	By Jimminy	Parker, A.	Smith, J. W.	Woolf, G.	122	61,650
1945	Fighting Step	Murlogg Farm	Norman, C. C.	South, G.	118	68,950
1946	Eternal Reward	Augustus and Nahm	Hall, C. J.	Campbell, R.	118	83,450
1947	Fervent	Calumet Farm	Jones, H. A.	Dodson, D.	118	70,950
1948	Citation	Calumet Farm	Jones, H. A.	Arcaro, E.	126	66,450
1949	Ponder	Calumet Farm	Jones, B. A.	Brooks, S.	126	66,150
1950	Hill Prince	Chenery, C. T.	Hayes, J. H.	Arcaro, E.	126	60,050
1951	Hall of Fame	Greentree Stable	Gaver, G. R.	Atkinson, T.	122	61,200
1952	Mark-Ye-Well	Calumet Farm	Jones, B. A.	Arcaro, E.	120	103,325
1953	Native Dancer	Vanderbilt, A. G.	Winfrey, W. C.	Arcaro, E.	128	66,500
1954	Errard King	Gavegagno, J.	Barry, T. J.	Boulmetis, S.	124	68,900
1955	Swaps	Ellsworth, R. C.	Tenney, M.	Shoemaker, W.	126	89,600
1956	Swoon's Son	Drake, E. G.	Wilson, A. G.	Arcaro, E.	122	102,600
1957	Round Table	Kerr Stable	Jolly, M.	Shoemaker, W.	126	100,350
1958	Nadir	Claiborne Farms	Jolly, M.	Ycaza, M.	120	114,600
1959	Dunce	Claiborne Farms	Jolly, M.	Cook, L. C.	126	93,000
1960	T. V. Lark	C. R. Mac Stable	Miller, P. F.	Sellers, J.	123	70,500
1961	Beau Prince	Calumet Farm	Jones, H. A.	Brooks, S.	112	71,400
1962	Black Sheep	C. R. Mac Stable	Wittingham, C.	Langdon, J.	117	71,250
1963	Candy Spots	Ellsworth, R. C.	Tenney, M.	Shoemaker, W.	126	65,833
1964	Roman Brother	Harbor View Farm	Parker, B.	Alvarez, F.	122	89,300
1965	Tom Rolfe	Powhatan Stable	Whiteley, F. Y., Jr.	Shoemaker, W.	126	83,100
1966	Buckpasser	Phipps, O.	Neloy, E. A.	Baeza, B.	125	84,100
1967	Damascus	Bancroft, Mrs. E.	Whiteley, F. Y., Jr.	Shoemaker, W.	126	75,000
1968	Forward Pass	Calumet Farm	Forrest, H.	Valenzuela, M.	123	70,600

* Race run at old Washington Park 1884–1904, 1½ miles. Hawthorne 1916, 1¼ miles. Variously at Arlington Park and Washington Park from 1927; 1¼ miles 1928–51, 1 1/3 miles, 1952–54, 1 3/16 miles since that date. No racing in Chicago 1895–97, 1899, 1905, and 1906. American Derby was not run 1907–15, 1917–25, 1936, 1938, and 1939.
†Feature of World's Columbian Exposition program.

Arlington Futurity—two year olds, ¾ mile*

Year	Name of horse	Name of owner	Name of trainer	Name of jockey	Weight of jockey	Value to winner
1927	Misstep	LeMar Stock Farm	Knapp. W.	Poole. E.	122	$9,360
1928	Double Heart	Three D Stock Farm	Durnell. C. E.	Geving. L.	115	21,920
1932	Lady's Man	Coe. W. R.	Creech. B.	Jones. R.	117	38,010
1933	Far Star	Dixiana Stable	Van Dusen. C.	Belizzi. D.	116	31,020
1934	Toro Nancy	Church. N. W.	Fitzgerald. E. L.	Jones. R.	112	41,725
1935	Grand Slam	Bomar Stable	Potts. R. E.	Bryson. J.	122	45,135
1936	Case Ace	Milky Way Farm	McGarvey. R.	Robertson. A.	117	36,540
1937	Tiger/Teddy's Comet	Milky Way Farm	McGarvey. R.	Robertson. A.	122	18,000
	(dead heat)	Valdina Farms	Flanigan. J. J.	Smith. G.	117	18,000
1938	Thingumabob	Manhasset Stable	Brennan. W.	Arcaro. E.	117	31,100
1939	Andy K.	Millsdale Stable	Wallace. W.	Oros. J. E.	114	33,735
1940	Swain	Putnam. C.	Durnell. C. E.	Adams. J.	117	34,470
1941	Sun Again	Calumet Farm	Jones. B. A.	Eads. W.	122	34,655
1942	Occupation	Marsch. J.	Parke. B.	Balaski. L.	117	51,500
1943	Jezrahel	Marsch. J.	Parke. B.	Grohs. O.	116	48,650
1944	Free For All	Marsch. J.	Parke. B.	Grohs. O.	122	48,525
1945	Spy Song	Dixiana Stable	Hodgins. J. C.	Brooks. S.	122	58,650
1946	Cosmic Bomb	Helis. W.	Booth. W.	Clark. S.	122	66,875
1947	Piet	Bone and Markey	Potts. R. E.	Jessop. D.	122	66,900
1948	Mr. Busher	Maine Chance Farm	Smith. J. W.	Zufelt. F.	122	62,775
1949	Wisconsin Boy	Peavey. W. M.	Dobson. E. C.	Chestnut. J.	122	60,075
1950	To Market	Mason, S. A., II	Hirsch. W. J.	Rivera. A. D.	122	56,215
1951	Hill Gail	Calumet Farm	Jones. B. A.	Brooks. S.	122	64,140
1952	Mr. Good	Martin and McKinney	Rupelt. A.	Dodson. D.	122	81,575
1953	Hasty Road	Hasty House Farm	Trotsek. H.	Arcaro. E.	122	101,475
1954	Royal Note	Wilton Stable	Gilpin. F.	Arcaro. E.	122	93,345
1955	Swoon's Son	Drake. E. G.	Wilson. A. G.	Erb. D.	122	88,140
1956	Greek Game	Hooper. F. W.	Park. I. H.	Hartack. W.	122	84,410
1957	Leather Button	Dockmoore Farm	Sarner. J. J.. Jr.	Skelly. J.	122	97,575

Year	Winner	Owner	Trainer	Jockey	Wt.	Value
1958	Restless Wind	Llangollen Farm	Wittingham, C.	Shoemaker, W.	122	100,475
1959	T. V. Lark	C. R. Mac Stable	Miller, P. F.	Maese, A.	122	150,312
1960	Pappa's All	King, Mr. and Mrs. G. D.	Leavitt, C. B.	Taniguchi, G.	122	129,086
1961	Ridan	Jolly, Mrs. M.	Jolly, L.	Hartack. W.	122	127,050
1962	Candy Spots	Ellsworth, R. C.	Tenney, M.	Shoemaker, W.	122	142,500
1963	Golden Ruler	Fisher, Mary V.	Hodgins. J.	Hinojosa, E.	122	112,500
1964	Sadair	North 40 Stable	Lear, L.	Shoemaker, W.	122	134,925
1965	Buckpasser	Phipps, O.	Neloy, E. A.	Baeza, B.	122	190,475
1966	Diplomat Way	Pelton, H.	Meaux, J. O.	Shoemaker, W.	122	195,200
1967						
Div. 1	TV Commercial	Bwamazon Farm	Basile, T.	Anderson, P.	122	105,875
Div. 2	Vitriolic	Phipps, O.	Neloy, E. A.	Shoemaker, W.	122	105,875
1968	Strong Strong	Steiner and Resseguet	Resseguet, W.	Gargan, D.	122	212,850

* Run as American National Futurity 1927 and 1928. Not run 1929–31. Run at Washington Park 1943–45. Alhambra finished first 1957, disqualified and placed fourth. Now run as Arlington-Washington Futurity.

Arlington Classic—three year olds, 1 mile*

Year	Winner	Owner	Trainer	Jockey	Wt.	Value
1929	Blue Larkspur	Bradley, E. R.	Hurley, W.	Garner, M.	126	$59,900
1930	Gallant Fox	Belair Stud	Fitzsimmons, J.	Sande, E.	126	64,750
1931	Mate	Bostwick, A. C.	Healy, J. W.	Robertson, A.	126	73,650
1932	Gusto	Schwartz, M. L.	Hirsch, M.	Coucci, S.	126	76,600
1933	Inlander	Brookmeade Stable	Smith, R.	Jones, R.	118	32,777
1934	Cavalcade	Brookmeade Stable	Smith, R.	Garner, M.	126	30,325
1935	Omaha	Belair Stud	Fitzsimmons, J.	Wright, W. P.	126	28,975
1936	Granville	Belair Stud	Fitzsimmons, J	Stout, J.	126	28,400
1937	Flying Scot	Whitney, J. H.	Healy, J. W.	Gilbert, J.	123	27,375
1938	Nedayr	Kilmer, W. S.	Crawford, W. A.	Wright, W. D.	121	27,500
1939	Challedon	Brann, W. L.	Schaefer, L. J.	Richards, H.	126	35,600
1940	Sirocco	Dixiana Stable	Smith, J. W.	Woolf, G.	121	37,935
1941	Attention	Corning, Mrs. P.	Hirsch, M.	Bierman, C.	121	42,450
1942	Shutout	Greentree Stable	Gaver, J. M.	Arcaro, E.	126	69,700
1943	Slide Rule	Boeing, W. E.	Wilhelm, C.	Zufelt, F.	120	53,450
1944	Twilight Tear	Calumet Farm	Jones, B. A.	Haas, L.	114	62,500
1945	Pot O' Luck	Calumet Farm	Jones, B. A.	Dodson, D.	119	67,150

Table—continued

Year	Name of horse	Name of owner	Name of trainer	Name of jockey	Weight of jockey	Value to winner
1946	The Dude	Gaal, Mrs. A.	Gaal, A.	Duhon, M.	119	76,850
1947	But Why Not	King Ranch	Hirsch, M.	Mehrtens, W.	117	71,500
1948	Papa Redbird	Goodwin, J. A.	Goode, J. M.	Baird, R. L.	122	66,600
1949	Ponder	Calumet Farm	Jones, B. A.	Brooks, S.	126	65,450
1950	Greek Song	Brandywine Stable	Raines, V. W.	Scurlock, O.	120	58,950
1951	Hall of Fame	Greentree Stable	Gaver, G. R.	Atkinson, T.	120	62,975
1952	Mark-Ye-Well	Calumet Farm	Jones, B. A.	Arcaro, E.	112	105,375
1953	Native Dancer	Vanderbilt, A. G.	Winfrey, W. C.	Guerin, E.	126	97,725
1954	Errard King	Gavegagno, J.	Barry, T. J.	Boulmetis, S.	120	104,475
1955	Nashua	Belair Stud	Fitzsimmons, J.	Arcaro, E.	126	91,675
1956	Swoon's Son	Drake, E. G.	Wilson, A. G.	Erb, D.	120	102,000
1957	Clem	Rand, Adele L.	Stephens, W. W.	McCreary, C.	117	105,950
1958	A Dragon Killer	Saddaca, Mrs. S. H.	Haymaker, H. L.	Combert, J.	117	101,100
1959	Dunce	Claiborne Farms	Jolly, M.	Cook, L. C.	117	78,700
1960	T. V. Lark	C. R. Mac Stable	Miller, P. F.	Sellers, J.	120	86,500
1961	Globemaster	Sasso, L. P.	Kelly, T. J.	Rotz, J. L.	119	72,900
1962	Ridan	JGW Stable	Jolly, L.	Gomez, A.	123	64,750
1963	Candy Spots	Ellsworth, R. C.	Tenney, M.	Shoemaker, W.	126	86,833
1964	Tosmah	Briardale Farm	Mergier, J. W.	Boulmetis, S.	115	69,000
1965	Tom Rolfe	Powhatan Stable	Whiteley, F. Y., Jr.	Shoemaker, W.	124	62,500
1966	Buckpasser	Phipps, O.	Neloy, E. A.	Baeza, B.	125	63,000
1967	Dr. Fager	Tartan Stable	Nerud, J.	Baeza, B.	120	61,000
1968	Exclusive Native	Harbor View Farm	Parke, I.	Valenzuela, M.	113	63,000

* Run at Washington Park 1943, 1944, and 1945.
Distance 1¼ miles prior to 1952.

456

Leading jockeys and trainers, wins on Illinois tracks, 1943–67

Year	Name of jockey	Number of wins	Name of trainer	Number of wins
1943	Whitney, L.	101	Lewis, G. E.	25
1944	Martin, J. W.	111	Shipp, E. B.	31
1945	Nichols, B.	181	Weil, M.	32
1946	Brooks, S.	125	Bishop, W. H.	42
1947	Brooks, S.	165	Bishop, W. H.	43
1948	Skoronski, A.	130	Bishop, W. H.	41
1949	Brooks, S.	121	Bishop, W. H.	84
1950	Keene, H.	175	Bishop, W. H.	83
1951	Keene, H.	127	Bishop, W. H.	83
1952	Adams, J.	138	Bishop, W. H.	68
1953	Adams, J.	181	Bishop, W. H.	103
1954	Keene, H.	127	Bishop, W. H.	83
1955	Meaux, C.	114	Schmidt, W. J.	53
1956	Hartack, W.	125	Bishop, W. H.	57
1957	Meaux, C.	170	Schmidt, W. J.	48
1958	Landing, R. L.	113	Bishop, W. H.	83
1959	Cook, L. C.	146	Bishop, W. H.	89
1960	Landing, R. L.	137	Bishop, W. H.	69
1961	Hartack, W.	154	Bishop, W. H.	79
1962	Hartack, W.	184	Bishop, W. H.	91
1963	Blum, W.	202	Hammond, E.	72
1964	Blum, W.	153	Hammond, E.	153
1965	Hinojosa, E.	155	Hammond, E.	144
1966	Hinojosa, E.	175	Hammond, E.	92
1967	Hinojosa, E.	205	Hammond, E.	152

Leading trotters, pacers, and drivers on Illinois tracks where pari-mutuel betting is permitted, 1946–67

Year	Name of trotter	Amount won	Name of pacer	Amount won	Name of driver	Number of wins
1946					Leonard, E.	42
1947	Moses	$7,280	Dr. Stanton	$12,175	Stover, D.	46
1948	Pronto Don	8,500	Brucita's Guy	8,362	Burright, H.	108
1949	Billy Carleton	12,067	Highland Ellen	9,670	Burright, H.	59
1950	Moses	12,782	Royal Blackstone	11,250	Burright, H.	85
1951	Clever Sunny	14,548	Grattan Truax	13,239	Burright, H.	82
1952	Johnny Brown	18,142	Choice Hanover	13,375	Stover, D.	33
1953	Royal Vickie	10,923	Irish Hal	5,500	Rouse, W.	65
1954	Jamie	12,325	Billy Wasson	9,515	Bessinger, H.	103
1955	Victor Morris	13,012	B'Haven	26,474	Leonard, E.	54
1956	Sis's Brother	11,934	Hi Hill	17,225	Burright, H.	70
1957	Bold Rodney	9,500	Belle Acton	12,475	Bessinger, H.	76
1958	Annette Sue	10,245	WD Direct	16,687	Insko, D.	117
1959	Senator Frost	35,086	Bye Bye Bird	33,135	Insko, D.	104
1960	Tie Silk	29,986	Adios Butler	29,986	Insko, D.	127
1961	Merrie Duke	34,716	Merrie Gesture	29,998	Burright, H.	156
1962	Duke Rodney	29,372	Harry T. Adios	45,138	Burright, H.	131
1963	Tercel	31,183	Coffee Break	42,154	Boing, C.	72
1964	Nite Shirt	38,230	Pole Adios	44,700	Farrington, R.	266
1965	Argo Kid	51,500	Race Time	54,134	Farrington, R.	300
1966	All A'Flame	57,313	Bret Hanover	78,105	Farrington, R.	251
1967	Carlisle	67,335	Song Cycle	76,682	Farrington, R.	165

Illinois State Fair Colt Stakes: winners of two- and three-year-old free-for-all trots and paces, with owners, positions by heats, and amount won, 1952–68

Trots

Two-year-old trot

Year	Total value all events	Name of horse	Name of owner	Positions by heats	Amount won
1952	$81,075	Steve Tell	Luae, W.	DH-2-1	$11,958.56
1953	224,300	Bagdad	Luae, W.	3-1-1	20,747.75
1954	229,250	Gracie Colleen	Dickey, C. E.	1-1	21,469.24
1955	215,700	Peggy Key	Humphries, O.	5-1-1	13,811.65
1956	251,400	SuMac Lad	SuMac Stable	4-1-1	15,024.75
1957	248,424	Miss Scotbed	Herman Graham Stock Farm	DH-1-1	14,668.50
1958	254,450	Dutchess Ronald	Herman Graham Stock Farm	1-1	21,891.76
1959	261,625	Prince Jamie	Riker and Spencer	1-1	22,586.12
1960	258,125	Volarie	Betty Bee Stable	1-DH-1	14,949.00
1961	252,050	Paul's Best	Flanery, R. C.	1-1	22,207.38
1962	251,695	Windy Skeeter	Davies, J. and Knackmuhs, E.	DH-1-1	14,751.00
1963	245,050	Private Bud	Busse, D. and Welch, E.	DH-DH-1	12,152.00
1964	242,825	Joe Brooke	Redshaw, L.	5-1-1	14,475.57
1965	248,800	Dangerous Storm	Baier, D. and J.	3-1-1	16,067.25
1966	247,600	Rock Springs Jane	Ward, D.	DH-DH-1	14,099.25
1967	333,555	Moon Baby	Bell Shore Farm	10-1-1	11,904.00
1968	337,925	Frosty Radar	Cossey, P.	1-1	16,425.75

Three-year-old trot

Year	Name of horse	Name of owner	Positions by heats	Amount won
1952*				
1953	Still Better	Bredberg, C.	1-1	20,747.74
1954	Bishop's First	Graham, H.	1-1	28,027.50
1955	Marathon Hanover	Grant, H.	3-1-1	14,815.50
1956	An Ka Da	Ward, D. and K.	1-15-1	15,990.86
1957	Cindy Gal	Austin Brothers	3-1-1	11,400.75
1958	Lady Ann Reed	Rhodes, C., Jr.	3-1-1	11,967.75
1959	Greve	Ward, D. and K.	11-1-1	12,901.63
1960	(dead heat)†			9,581.00
1961	Volarie	Betty Bee Stable	DH-1-1	14,157.00
1962	Rona Farcry	Melvin, Mr. and Mrs. O.	DH-DH-1	14,396.25
1963	Windy Skeeter	Davies, J. and Knackmuhs, E.	DH-DH-1	14 247.75

Paces

Two-year-old pace

Year	Name of horse	Name of owner	Positions by heats	Amount won
1952	Gene Jester	Whittaker, G.	DH-1-1	$14,998.87
1953	John Sitzmann	Boner, O. H.	1-3-1	15,701.00
1954	Eclipse Queen	Bredberg, C.	1-1	21,543.24
1955	Double Mc	Shiawassee Stable	1-1	20,511.87
1956	Sunny Byrd	Warren, H. R. and Son	DH-1-1	16,390.92
1957	Bye Bye Byrd	Larkin, Mr. and Mrs. R. C.	DH-DH-1	15,840.00
1958	Roxburgh Leonard	Moody, E.	DH-1-1	12,481.08
1959	Hark Win	Henry, Winters, and Cisna	DH-DH-1	17,175.50
1960	Nibble Byrd	Larkin, Mr. and Mrs. R. C.	1-DH-1	16,755.75
1961	Crystal Byrd	Thiel, O.	DH-1-1	16,062.75
1962	Fly Fly Byrd	Red Sheep Stable	1-1	23,533.00
1963	Don Parker	Riegle, Mr. and Mrs. G.	DH-1-1	15,765.75
1964	Jimmy's Pilot	Ward, D. and K.	1-2-1	13,426.00
1965	King Noble	Peterson, R.	1-DH-1	16,409.25
1966	John L. Purdue	Moffett, R.	DH-1-1	15,708.00
1967	Active Don	Sutton, J. H.	14-1-1	13,266.00
1968		Hanson, V.	1-1-1	13,860.00

Three-year-old pace

Year	Name of horse	Name of owner	Positions by heats	Amount won
1952*				
1953	B'Haven	Austin, S. J.	2-1-1	16,542.12
1954	Peter Van Gundy	Altamont Stable	1-1	21,275.00
1955	Frisco Flyer	Wixom, P.	1-1	19,873.63
1956	Coburn Frost	Castleton Farm	DH-DH-1	18,302.62
1957	Sunny Byrd	Warren, H. R. and Son	DH-1-1	14,388.00
1958	Bye Bye Byrd	Larkin, Mr. and Mrs. R. C.	DH-1-1	14,767.50
1959	Royal Ronald	Herman Graham Stock Farm	2-1-1	13,601.00
1960	Fiddler's Green	Herman Graham Stock Farm	3-DH-1	12,582.00
1961	H. D. Counsel	Pletcher, Mr. and Mrs. L.	2-1-1	13,160.00
1962	Thomas Purdue	Redden, B. N.	5-1-1	14,366.28
1963	Fly Fly Byrd	Red Sheep Stable	DH-DH-1	14,553.00

Year	Name of horse	Name of owner	Positions by heats	Amount won	Name of driver		Placed 1	Amount won
1964	Eyre Royal	Herman Graham Stock Farm				Zweifel, E. T.	Placed 1	12,292.00
1965	Royal Escort	Traub, Mrs. M. and Hankins, Mrs. J.	1–1	20,907.00	Bob Yates‡			
1966	Princess Randolph	Busse, Mrs. G.	2–1–1	11,928.00	Chicago King	Empress Farms	DH–DH–1	14,883.00
1967	Dandy Date	Zweifel, E. T.	1–4–1	10,900.50	Jimmy's Pilot	Peterson, R.	DH–DH–1	15,039.75
			1–1–1	16,112.25	Shore Will	Benson, L.	3–1–1	13,959.00
1968	Empire Squire	Country Squire Stable	1–1–1	15,881.25	Shoestring	Buchen, R. and Davis, E. H.	1–1–1	17,605.50

*Three-year-old trot and pace not run in 1952.
†Volation's Key, owned by Rhodes and Graham. was second in the first heat, first in the second. E. L. Garrison's Petunia's Filly was first in the first heat, second in the second. The third heat was a tie. Times ranged from 2:02 2/5 to 2:05. ‡Bosco Rosco, owned by McCoy, Buchen, and Davis, ran a dead heat with Poplar Aaron (Car-Bon Stable) in the first mile, and a dead heat with Bob Yates in the second mile. Bosco Rosco finished first in the third mile, but fouled. Bob Yates was placed first, Poplar Aaron second, and Bosco Rosco third.

Winners of the Hambletonian,* 1957–68
Three-year-old trot, one mile

Year	Name of horse	Name of owner	Name of driver	Positions by heats	Time of best heat	Amount won
1957	Hickory Smoke	Sheppard, L. B. and Mudge, A. C.	Simpson, J., Sr.	1 1 x x 1	2:00.2	$47,917.62
1958	Emily's Pride	Castleton and Walnut Hall farms	Nipe, F.	1 12 1	1:59.8	62,750.92
1959	Diller Hanover	Hall Stable	Ervin, F.	1 1	2:01.2	73,666.98
1960	Blaze Hanover	S. A. Camp Farms	O Brien, J.	1 7 3 1	1:59.6	85,019.00
1961	Harlan Dean	Keystone Stable	Arthur, J.	1 1	1:58.4	77,364.93
1962	A. C.'s Viking	Peterson, Mr. and Mrs. A. C.	Russell, S.	1 1	1:59.6	62,854.29
1963	Speedy Scott	Castleton Farm	Baldwin, R.	2 1 1	1:58.0	56,619.15
1964	Ayres	Sheppard, C. N.	Simpson, J., Sr.	1 1	1:56.8†	56,487.89
1965	Egyptian Candor	Dancer, Mrs. S.	Cameron, D.	5 1 2 1	2:03.8	59,900.42
1966	Kerry Way	Gainsway Farms	Ervin, F.	1 1	1:58.8	60,044.60
1967	Speedy Streak	Owens, Gaines, and Gaines	Cameron, D.	1 1	2:00.0	60,098.00
1968	Nevele Pride	Nevele Acres Farm	Dancer, S.	1 1	1:59.6	56,933.00

*Established 1926 for top home-breds, nominated in their first year (250 to 650 nominations each year). Run at Syracuse, N.Y.; Lexington, Ky.; Goshen, N.Y., and Yonkers, N.Y., 1926–56; at Du Quoin, Ill., from 1957. No betting.
x—Ran out.
†Record time for the Hambletonian.

$2,754,806.85 for veterans' rehabilitation, various sums for encouragement of agriculture, for fairs and expositions, for development of better standard-bred and thoroughbred colts, and $40,646,819.03 for general revenue.

Baseball

Little is known about baseball in Illinois before the Civil War, although we are aware that the game was played. Documentation concerning the sport, available for New York, is not to be found for Illinois. However, newspaper reports mention baseball as early as 1856. In 1865, when the National Association of Baseball Players convened for the first time since 1861, Illinois was well represented among the 91 clubs in attendance. (There had been 34 in 1861.) Two years later, of the 237 clubs answering roll call, 56 were from Illinois. Ohio was second with 42; Pennsylvania with 27, third; Wisconsin with 25, fourth; and New York, which previously led, had slipped to fifth with 24.

In 1869 the Cincinnati Red Stockings became the first professional baseball club with paid full-time employees on the diamond. Their national tour, during which they won 92 and tied 1 of 93 games before they suffered a defeat, brought them to Chicago and Rockford. In the latter city they faced a wiry youngster named Albert G. Spalding, who gave them a tough battle. Spalding later pitched for Boston, was a great of early baseball with the Chicago White Stockings, and founded a successful sporting goods and sports publishing company.

The success of the Cincinnati club's tour led almost at once to the formation of the first professional baseball league, which appropriated the name National Association of Baseball Players. Two of the nine clubs were from Illinois, a Chicago team later called the White Stockings, which became the Chicago Cubs in 1906, and the Rockford Forest Cities, not to be confused with the Cleveland club of the same name which was briefly a member of the association a few years later.

In 1875 William A. Hulbert of Chicago, newly elected president of the White Stockings, after raiding the Boston team of its four top players, including Spalding, went to the annual meeting of the association armed with proxies and power of attorney from clubs in Cincinnati, Louisville, and St. Louis, which had been crowded out of the league in 1874. After a prolonged battle Hulbert brought about the demise of the National Association and the formation of the National League of Professional Baseball Clubs. (Note the change from "players" to "clubs.") This league, with minor changes in franchises, remains as the senior circuit of organized baseball.

In 1879 the first minor league in Illinois was organized at Rockford as the Northwestern Association. This short-lived venture later blossomed into the Western League with teams in Chicago, Kansas City, Minneapolis, and Milwaukee among others. In 1900, under leadership of President Bancroft Johnson of Chicago, the Western League changed its name and announced itself a major league owing fealty to no other organization, but ready to go along with the National League on a basis of equality. This announcement, together with the signing of several top stars of the National League, led to a baseball war of two years duration, finally resolved by recognition of the American League with clubs in Chicago, St. Louis, Cleveland, Detroit, Washington, Philadelphia, New York, and Boston. This was the fourth of five baseball wars, and except for a brief struggle with a Federal League in 1914 and 1915, it was the last. So far as Illinois was concerned, the principal result of the battle with the Federal League was the moving of the Cubs from their ramshackle west-side park with its separate bleachers in left, center, and right fields, to Wrigley Field, which had been built for the Chicago Federals. William Wrigley, Jr. also acquired control of the Cubs as a result of that conflict.

In amateur baseball Illinois schools and colleges have fielded many fine teams. Little League, Pony League, and Babe Ruth League, for youngsters eight to twelve, thirteen and fourteen, and fifteen to seventeen respectively, have been widely represented in the state, but an Illinois team has yet to win a national championship in any of these groups, or a college or university national championship.

Men of Illinois who have contributed to the thrills and glamour of baseball are legion. Perhaps a fact book should be confined to their deeds as measured in the statistics of the sport. However, as spectator participation in baseball, football, golf, and other games widens through radio and television, a brief backward glance may be excused—a glance at Adrian C. "Cap"

Anson, great batsman and manager who brought five national league pennants to Chicago; at Frank Chance, playing manager of Tinker-to-Evers-to-Chance double-play fame and "peerless leader" of four pennant drives by the Cubs in the first decade of this century; at the "hitless wonders" of 1906, the White Sox who won a pennant and a world championship by superb pitching and fielding, with hardly an extrabase hit in their locker. Nor should one forget Lewis R. "Hack" Wilson whose 56 home runs of 1930 still led the National League in 1967, and whose 190 runs batted in that same year still stood as the major league record as this book went to press.

Among memories of baseball's past in Illinois, most of them pleasant, there is one of another sort. It stemmed from pressure on players by gamblers in an attempt to influence the outcome of games. In the days before there were leagues gambling threatened at one time to destroy the pastime. After baseball became a widespread professional sport, owners and players alike, aware of the peril to their future of any betting scandal, kept the game reasonably honest. A notorious lapse occurred during the world series of 1919 between the Chicago White Sox and the Cincinnati Reds. Glaring pitching inadequacies and fielding errors raised a suspicion that something was rotten. During the fall and winter an investigation brought confessions from eight White Sox players that they had received money for throwing the series. All eight were barred from professional baseball for life, and ended their baseball days in a maverick league on the Mexican border.

The major leagues felt that some firm discipline was needed to prevent another scandal, but they did not act hastily. It was not until 1922 that they arrived at a solution —appointment of a national commissioner with almost unlimited power to control and discipline the sport. First man in the office was Kenesaw Mountain Landis, federal judge for the Northern District of Illinois from 1905, who once fined the Standard Oil Company of Indiana for multiple incidents of rebating, and who resigned his judgeship in 1922 to accept the major league offer. Landis held the post until his death in 1944, when Senator A. B. (Happy) Chandler succeeded him. In 1951 Ford Frick, for many years president of the National League, became commissioner,

Members of Baseball Hall of Fame from Chicago teams and area

Player and position	Club	Year named
Alexander, Grover C. (P)	Phillies and Cubs	1938
Anson, Adrian C. (P, CF)	White Stockings	1939
Appling, Lucius B. (2B)	White Sox	1964
Bresnahan, Roger (M)	Cubs	1945
Brown, Mordecai (P)	Cubs	1949
Chance, Frank L. (1B, M)	Cubs	1946
Clarkson, John G. (P)	White Stockings	1963
Collins, Edward T. (2B)	Athletics and White Sox	1939
Comiskey, Charles A. (M)	White Sox	1939
Cuyler, Hazen (OF)	Cubs	1968
Dean, Jay Hanna (P)	Cardinals and Cubs	1953
Evers, John J. (2B)	Cubs	1946
Faber, Urban C. (P)	White Sox	1964
Griffith, Clark C. (M)	White Sox	1946
Hartnett, Charles L. (C, M)	Cubs	1955
Hornsby, Rogers (IF, M)	Cardinals and Cubs	1942
Landis, Kenesaw M.	(Commissioner)	1943
Lyons, Theodore A. (P)	White Sox	1955
McCarthy, Joseph V. (M)	Cubs and Yankees	1957
Schalk, Raymond W. (C)	White Sox	1955
Spading, Albert G. (P, M)	White Stockings	1939
Tinker, Joseph B. (SS)	Cubs	1946
Walsh, Edward A. (P)	White Sox	1946

Most valuable player awards to members of Chicago teams

Chalmers Award (1911-14)
1911   Schulte, Frank   Cubs

League Award (1924-29)
1929   Hornsby, Rogers   *Cubs*

Baseball Writers Association Award (from 1931)
1935   Harnett, Charles (Gabby) (C)   Cubs
1945   Cavarretta, Phillip (1B)   Cubs
1952   Sauer, Henry (OF)   Cubs
1958   Banks, Ernest (1B)   Cubs
1959   Banks, Ernest (1B)   Cubs
1959   Fox, Nelson (2B)   White Sox

Rookie of the year award to members of Chicago teams

Baseball Writers Association Award (from 1949)
1956   Aparicio, Luis (SS)   White Sox
1961   Williams, William (OF)   Cubs
1962   Hubbs Kenneth (2B)   Cubs
1963   Peters, Gary (P)   White Sox
1966   Agee, Thomas (OF)   White Sox

Pennants won by Chicago teams

Year	Name of manager	Games won	Games lost	Percentage

National League
(White Stockings)

Year	Name of manager	Games won	Games lost	Percentage
1876	Spalding, Albert	52	14	.788
1880	Anson, Adrian C.	67	17	.798
1881	Anson, Adrian C.	56	28	.667
1882	Anson, Adrian C.	55	29	.655
1885	Anson, Adrian C.	87	25	.777
1886	Anson, Adrian C.	90	34	.726

(Cubs)

Year	Name of manager	Games won	Games lost	Percentage
1906	Chance, Frank	116	36	.763
1907	Chance, Frank	107	45	.704*
1908	Chance, Frank	99	55	.643*
1910	Chance, Frank	104	50	.675
1918	Mitchell, Frederick	84	45	.651
1929	McCarthy, Joseph	98	54	.645
1932	Grimm, Charles	90	64	.584
1935	Grimm, Charles	100	54	.649
1938	Hartnett, Charles	89	63	.583
1945	Grimm, Charles	98	56	.636

American League
(White Sox)

Year	Name of manager	Games won	Games lost	Percentage
1901	Griffith, Clark	83	53	.610
1906	Jones, Fielder	93	58	.616*
1917	Rowland, Clarence	100	54	.649*
1919	Gleason, William	88	52	.629
1959	Lopez, Albert	94	60	.610

* Won World Series.

Major league leaders

Individual records: Batting

	White Stockings and Cubs			White Sox		
Department	Year	Player	Record	Year	Player	Record
Average	1879	Anson, Adrian C.	.407	1936	Appling, Lucius B.	.388
Longest hitting streak	1930 1968	Wilson, Lewis R. Beckert, Glenn	27 games	1936	Appling, Lucius B.	27 games
Home runs	1930	Wilson, Lewis R.	56[1]	1950	Zernial, Gustav	29
Hits	1929	Hornsby, Rogers	229	1920	Collins, Edward	222
Runs batted in	1930	Wilson, Lewis R.	190[2]	1936	Bonura, Ezekial	138
Extra-base hits	1930	Wilson, Lewis R.	97	1920	Jackson, Joseph (Shoeless Joe)	74
Two-base hits	1935, 1937	Herman, William	57	1963	Robinson, Floyd	45
Three-base hits	1911 1913	Schulte, Frank Saier, Victor	21	1916	Jackson, Joseph	21
Total bases	1930	Wilson, Lewis R.	423			
Stolen bases	1896	Lang, William	100	1943 1959	Moses, Walter Appling, Lucius B.	56
Bases on balls	1911	Schekard, James	147	1931	Blue, Louis	127
Most strikeouts	1968	Jenkins, Ferguson	160	1963	Nicholson, Donald	175
Fewest strikeouts	1922	Hollocher, Charles	5	1951 1958	Fox, Nelson	11

Batting

	White Stockings and Cubs				White Sox			
Year	Player	Games	Hits	Average	Year	Player	Games	Hits	Average
1876	Barnes, Roscoe C.	66	138	.404	1936	Appling, Lucius B.	138	204	.388
1879	Anson, Adrian C.	49	90	.407	1943	Appling, Lucius B.	155	192	.328
1881	Anson, Adrian C.	84	137	.399					
1887	Anson, Adrian C.	122	224	.421[3]					
1888	Anson, Adrian C.	134	177	.343					
1912	Zimmerman, Henry	145	207	.372					
1945	Cavarretta, Phillip	132	177	.355					

Home runs

Year	Player	Number	Year	Player	Number
1884	Williamson, Edward N.	27	1915	Roth, Robert F.	7
1885	Dalrymple, Abner N.	11			
1910	Schulte, Frank	10[4]			
1911	Schulte, Frank	21			
1912	Zimmerman, Henry	14			
1916	Williams, Frederick	12			
1926	Wilson, Lewis R. (Hack)	21			
1927	Wilson, Lewis R.	30			
1928	Wilson, Lewis R.	31			
1930	Wilson, Lewis R.	56[1]			
1943	Nicholson, William B.	29			
1944	Nicholson, William B.	33			
1952	Sauer, Henry J.	37[4]			
1958	Banks, Ernest	47			
1960	Banks, Ernest	41			

Stolen bases

Year	Player	Number	Year	Player	Number
1896	Lange, William	100	1901	Isbell, Frank	48
1897	Lange, William	83	1908	Dougherty, Patrick	47
1903	Chance, Frank	67	1919	Collins, Edward	33
1928	Cuyler, Hazen (Kiki)	37	1923	Collins, Edward	49
1929	Cuyler, Hazen	43	1924	Collins, Edward	42
1930	Cuyler, Hazen	37	1951	Minoso, Orestes	31
1935	Galan, August	22	1952	Minoso, Orestes	22
1937	Galan, August	23	1953	Minoso, Orestes	25
1938	Hack, Stanley	16	1955	Rivera, James	25
1939	Hack, Stanley	17[4]	1956	Aparicio, Luis	21
			1957	Aparicio, Luis	28
			1958	Aparicio, Luis	29

3,000 or more major league hits

Anson, Adrian C. 3,081   Collins, Edward 3,311

Table—continued

Individual records: Pitching

Department	Year	Pitcher	Record		Year	Pitcher	Record
	White Stockings and Cubs				*White Sox*		
Games won	1885	Clarkson, John W.	52		1908	Walsh, Edward	40
Appearances	1965	Abernathy, Theodore	84[1]		1968	Wood, Wilbur	88[2]
Games started	1920	Alexander, Grover C.	40		1908	Walsh, Edward	49
Complete games	1903	Taylor, John W.	33		1908	Walsh, Edward	42
Bases on balls	1955	Jones, Samuel	185		1936	Kennedy, Vernon	147
Strikeouts	1967	Jenkins, Ferguson	236		1908	Walsh, Edward	269
Shutouts	1906	Brown, Mordecai			1908	Walsh, Edward	12
	1907	Overall, Orval					
	1908	Brown, Mordecai	9				
	1909	Overall, Orval					
	1938	Lee, William					
Most consecutive shutouts	1906	Brown, Mordecai			1904	White, G. Harris (Doc)	5[1]
	1907	Overall, Orval				(Sept. 12, 16, 19, 25, 30)	
	1908	Brown, Mordecai					
	1908	Ruelbach, Edward	4				
	1909	Overall, Orval					
	1920	Alexander, Grover					
	1938	Lee, William					
Innings pitched	1920	Alexander, Grover	363		1908	Walsh, Edward	464
Most appearances lifetime					to 1968	Wilhelm, Hoyt	937[2]

Pitching

	White Stockings and Cubs						*White Sox*			
Year	Pitcher	Won	Lost	Percentage		Year	Pitcher	Won	Lost	Percentage
1876	Spalding, Albert G.	47	14	.770		1901	Griffith, Clark	24	7	.774
1880	Goldsmith, Fred	22	3	.880		1908	Walsh, Edward	40	15	.727
1881	Corcoran, Lawrence J.									
	(Larry)	31	14	.689		1919	Cicotte, Edward	29	7	.806
1882	Corcoran, Lawrence J.	27	13	.675		1954	Consuegra Sandelio	16	3	.842
1885	Clarkson, John	52	16	.765		1957	Donovan, Richard	16	6	.727[4]
1886	Flynn, John	24	6	.800		1959	Shaw, Robert	18	6	.750
1906	Ruelbach, Edward	19	4	.826		1962	Herbert, Ray	20	9	.690
1907	Ruelbach, Edward	17	4	.810						
1908	Ruelbach, Edward	24	7	.774						
1918	Hendrix, C. R.	20	7	.741						
1929	Root, Charles	19	6	.760						
1932	Warneke, Lonnie (Lon)	22	6	.786						
1933	Tinning, Lyle	13	6	.684						
1935	Lee, William	20	6	.769						
1938	Lee, William	22	9	.710						

Earned run average
(record begins in 1912)

Year	Pitcher	Innings pitched	ERA		Year	Pitcher	Innings pitched	ERA
1918	Vaughn, James L.	290	1.74		1917	Cicotte, Edward V.	346	1.53
1919	Alexander, Grover C.	235	1.72		1921	Faber, Urban C.	331	2.48
1920	Alexander, Grover C.	363	1.91		1922	Faber, Urban C.	353	2.81
1932	Warneke, Lonnie	277	2.37		1942	Lyons, Theodore A.	180	2.10
1938	Lee, William	291	2.66		1951	Rogovin, Saul	217	2.78
1945	Borowy, Henry	122	2.14		1955	Pierce, William W.	206	1.97
					1960	Baumann Frank	185	2.68
					1963	Peters, Gary	243	2.33
					1966	Peters, Gary	205	1.98

Winners, 300 major league games

Pitcher	Team	Number of years	Number of games	Won	Lost	Percentage
Alexander, Grover C.	Phillies and Cubs	20	696	373	208	.642
Clarkson, John W.	White Stockings	11	509	328	176	.651

[1] League record.
[2] Major league record.
[3] Only in this year was a base on balls scored as a hit.
[4] Tie with a player from another team.

No-hit games by Chicago teams, 1902-67 *

Year	Pitcher	Teams	Score	
1902	Callahan, James J.	White Sox vs. Detroit	3–0	
1904	Wicker, Robert K.	Cubs vs. New York	1–0	
1905	Smith, Frank E.	White Sox vs. Detroit	15–0	
1908	Smith, Frank E.	White Sox vs. Athletics	1–0	
1911	Walsh, Edward A.	White Sox vs. Boston	0–1	(10 innings) †
1914	Benz, Joseph D.	White Sox vs. Cleveland	6–1	
	Scott, James	White Sox vs. Washington	0–1	(10 innings) †
1915	Lavender, J. S.	Cubs vs. Giants	2–0	
	Hendrix, C. R.	Chicago Federals vs. Pirates	10–0	
1917	Cicotte, Edward V.	White Sox vs. Browns	11–0	
	Vaughn, James L.	Cubs vs. Cincinnati	0–1	(11 innings) †
1922	Robertson, Charles C.	White Sox vs. Detroit	2–0	
1926	Lyons, Theodore	White Sox vs. Boston	6–0	
1935	Kennedy, Vernon	White Sox vs. Cleveland	5–0	
1937	Dietrich, William	White Sox vs. St. Louis	8–0	
1955	Jones, Samuel	Cubs vs. Pittsburgh	4–0	
1957	Keegan, Robert	White Sox vs. Washington	6–0	
1960	Cardwell, Donald	Cubs vs. St. Louis	4–0	
1967	Horlen, Joseph	White Sox vs. Detroit	6–0	

* Larry Corcoran of the White Stockings holds the   † Game lost in extra innings.
record for the most no-hit games (four, 1880-84).

and in 1966 William D. Eckert took over the post.

In 1937 a committee was formed by the major leagues, consisting of Kenesaw Mountain Landis, commissioner of baseball; Ford Frick, president of the National League; William Harridge, president of the American League; and others to select players from the early days of baseball to be honored at a centennial at Cooperstown in 1939. Their selections, made from 1936 to 1938, were augmented by nominations from the baseball writers covering the two leagues. The committee selections included thirteen names, those of the writers thirteen. Since then, centennial players have been added almost every year by a three-fourths vote of the writers.

Football

Intercollegiate Football

There is an old saying—and certainly a true one—that football began with the coaches. The game was played at many Illinois schools, colleges, and universities in the eighties, perhaps even earlier at some, but it was not until 1892 when Amos Alonzo Stagg came to the fledgling University of Chicago, bringing with him football lore gathered from Walter Camp at Yale, that the full potential of the game as an inspiration for school spirit and a financial reservoir for athletic department funds was realized in Illinois.

Stagg coached University of Chicago teams that were among the best in the nation from 1892 to 1933. During his forty-one years he had five undefeated seasons (1899, 1905, 1908, 1913, and 1924). He continued to coach after university retirement rules brought about his resignation at Chicago, and did not quit until his ninety-first year. His most severe disapprobation was expressed by the term "jackass." He applied it singly or doubly. Once he was heard to tell a halfback of considerable merit that he was a triple jackass—an appellation still treasured by that man, who became president of a large Chicago corporation. Stagg had a profound influence on the lives of many of the young men with whom he came in contact.

The Big Ten

Three years after Stagg's arrival at Chicago seven large state universities of the old Northwest Territory and three others formed the first regional football association in the United States—the Western Conference, popularly known as the Big Ten. Participating schools were the University of Illinois, the University of Chicago, and Northwestern University in Illinois, Indiana and Purdue universities in Indiana, Ohio State University, and the universities of Michigan, Wisconsin, Minnesota, and Iowa. The conference played its first schedule in 1896 with Wisconsin the winner, and the repeat winner in 1897.

Robert Zuppke arrived in the Big Ten about fifteen years after Stagg's debut at Chicago. He coached at Illinois for many years. One of his finest teams, that of 1927, was winner of the Knute Rockne trophy, emblematic of the national championship. He was the coach who developed Harold "Red" Grange, the "galloping ghost," one of the all-time greats of college and professional football.

The University of Chicago discontinued football in 1939, and resigned from the Western Conference March 8, 1946. The Big Ten then became the Big Nine until Michigan State was admitted December 12, 1948. Because schedules had been made through 1952, Michigan State did not play its first official Big Ten football game until 1953. However, 1949 was the starting date for all other sports.

Big Ten champions from Illinois

1899	Chicago	1924	Chicago
1905	Chicago	1926	Northwestern[3]
1907	Chicago	1927	Illinois
1908	Chicago	1928	Illinois
1910	Illinois[1]	1930	Northwestern[3]
1913	Chicago	1931	Northwestern[4]
1914	Illinois	1936	Northwestern
1915	Illinois[1]	1946	Illinois
1918	Illinois	1951	Illinois
1919	Illinois	1953	Illinois
1922	Chicago[2]	1963	Illinois[5]
1923	Illinois[3]		

[1] Tied with Minnesota.
[2] Tied with Iowa and Michigan.
[3] Tied with Michigan.
[4] Tied with Purdue and Michigan.
[5] Tied with Michigan State.

The Rose Bowl

The Rose Bowl game, in which the champion of the Pacific Coast meets a team from another part of the country, is an annual feature of Pasadena's Tournament of Roses. The game is played on New Year's Day (the next day if the holiday falls on Sunday). From 1902, when Michigan defeated Stanford in Tournament Park, until 1946 it was an invitational affair. After Michigan's first appearance Big Ten teams were forbidden by conference regulations from participating at Pasadena or in any other post-season game. In 1946 the Big Ten amended its rules to permit signing of a contract with the coast conference that was to continue in force for five years. The agreement has been renewed each time its limiting date was reached. Including the game on January 1, 1968, the Big Ten has won sixteen games, the Pacific Coast Conference six. (When a Big Ten champion repeats, the runner-up goes to the Rose Bowl.) Three-time winners for the Big Ten have been Illinois, Michigan, and Ohio State. Michigan State and Iowa both have won twice, and Northwestern, Minnesota, and Purdue once. Wisconsin suffered three defeats, while Indiana, Michigan State, and Minnesota each lost one game.

Winners from Illinois

1947	Illinois 45, U.C.L.A. 14
1949	Northwestern[1] 20, California 14
1952	Illinois 40, Stanford 7
1964	Illinois 17, Washington 7

[1] Runner-up.

Awards and trophies

All-American selections

From 1889 until his death March 14, 1925, Walter Camp, player and coach, at Yale, coach at Stanford, and football statistician, selected one player for each position on a hypothetical team which he called the All-American. For the first nine years his selections were almost entirely from Yale, Harvard, and Princeton, with an occasional accolade for a Pennsylvania player. First "outlander" to be named an All-American was Clarence B. Herschberger, great fullback of the University of Chicago, in 1898.

Camp's annual selections were a midwinter feature of *Collier's Weekly*. After his death Grantland Rice, Tennessee-born sportswriter and syndicated columnist for the *New York Tribune*, undertook the assignment. He remained with *Collier's* until 1947, when the magazine assembled a panel of coaches. Rice moved on to *Look* magazine with his selections until his death in 1954. *Collier's Weekly* suspended publication in 1957, but the coaches' selections continued as a syndicated feature.

The year of Camp's death the Associated Press, with the aid of its sportswriters in all parts of the country, began publication of its own selections, and has continued to do so. The following year the United Press (now the United Press International) began publication of choices by a panel of coaches across the nation. In 1944 the Football Writers Association added its voice to the confusion.

In 1950 Rice named twenty-two players in recognition of the two-platoon system, which was being employed by many coaches. He continued to select offense and defense until he died. The Associated Press tried the two-platoon system for three years, 1950, 1951, and 1952, and the Football Writers Association picked up the technique in 1954.

Naturally, with so many different groups making selections, there seldom was any unanimity. From Illinois only three were unanimous choices from Camp's death to 1966. They were Harold "Red" Grange of Illinois, halfback, in 1925; Ernest J. "Pug" Rentner of Northwestern, fullback, in 1931; and Jay Berwanger of Chicago, halfback, in 1935.

Early all-American selections were weighted in favor of eastern universities. During his lifetime, Camp chose members of Big Ten teams from Illinois schools only ten times, although these teams were consistently defeating the best the country offered. Rice chose only nine men from Chicago, Illinois, and Northwestern on the twenty teams he nominated. With this in mind, this book records selections of players from Illinois schools from the Walter Camp All-American in 1898 to the choices of the various authorities in 1966.

Helms Foundation Hall, all-time all-Americans

The Helms Athletic Foundation was established at Los Angeles, California, in 1936 by Paul Helms to honor amateur and professional athletes in all fields of sport. The foundation is concerned with past as well as current performances. All awards are made by the board. Three of the eleven men named to an all-time all-American football team were residents of Illinois. They are: William Heffelfinger, Yale 1893, guard,; Walter Eckersall, Chicago 1906, quarterback; and Harold Grange, Illinois 1925, halfback.

Walter Camp's all-American selections
in *Collier's Weekly*

Year	Name	Position	School
1898	Herschberger, Clarence	F	Chicago
1904	Eckersall, Walter	Q	Chicago
1905	Eckersall, Walter	Q	Chicago
1908	Steffen, Walter	Q	Chicago
1913	Des Jardien, Paul	C	Chicago
1920	Carney, Charles	E	Illinois
1921	McGuire, Charles	T	Chicago
1922	Thomas, John	F	Chicago
1923	Grange, Harold	H	Illinois
1924	Grange, Harold	H	Illinois
1925	Grange, Harold	Q	Illinois
1926	Baker, Ralph	H	Northwestern
1931	Rentner, Ernest J.	F	Northwestern
1935	Berwanger, Jay	H	Chicago
1936	Reid, Steven	G	Northwestern
1940	Bauman, Alfred	T	Northwestern
1943	Hein, Herbert	E	Northwestern
1951	Karras, John	OB	Illinois
1953	Caroline, James	OB	Illinois

Other all-American selections
(press associations, writers polls)

Year	Name	Position	School	Chosen by
1925	Grange, Harold	Q, H	Illinois	Consensus
1926	Shively, Bernard	G	Illinois	AP
	Baker, Ralph	H	Northwestern	AP
1930	Woodworth, Wade	G	Northwestern	AP
	Baker, Ralph	H	Northwestern	UP
1931	Rentner, Ernest J.	F	Northwestern	Consensus
	Marvil, Dallas	T	Northwestern	AP
1933	Manske, Edgar	E	Northwestern	UP
1935	Berwanger, Jay	H	Chicago	Consensus
1935	Tangora, Paul	G	Northwestern	AP
1939	Haman, John	C	Northwestern	UP
1940	Bauman, Alfred	T	Northwestern	UP
1942	Agase, Alex	C	Illinois	UP
1943	Graham, Otto	H	Northwestern	AP
1946	Agase, Alex	C	Illinois	AP UP
1948	Murakowski, Arthur	F	Northwestern	AP
1950	Vohaska, William	C	Illinois	AP
	Stonesifer, Donald	OE	Northwestern	AP
1951	Brosky, Albert	DB	Illinois	AP
	Karras, John	H	Illinois	UP
1953	Caroline, James	H	Illinois	UP
1959	Burrell, William	G	Illinois	AP UPI
1963	Butkus, Richard	C	Illinois	AP UPI
1964	Butkus, Richard	C	Illinois	AP UPI
	Grabowski, James	F	Illinois	AP UPI
	Donnelly, George	Saf.	Illinois	AP UPI
1965	Grabowski, James	F	Illinois	AP UPI

The Heisman Memorial Trophy, honoring the memory of John W. Heisman, (Penn '91) has been presented annually since 1936 (for the 1935 season) to the nation's outstanding football player, as determined by a poll of sportswriters and sportscasters. Heisman, coach for thirty-six years (sixteen years at Georgia Tech, where he had a string of thirty-three straight victories), was athletic director of the Downtown Athletic Club of New York from 1927 until his death in 1936. Donor: Downtown Athletic Club.

Rissman and Knute Rockne trophies

The Rissman Trophy, 1924 through 1930, and Knute Rockne Trophy, 1931 through 1940, were emblematic of the national championship. After 1940 the championship was determined by the press polls of writers (AP) and coaches (UPI). When they were not in agreement, the award was shared by the teams selected.

Illinois winner (Heisman Memorial Trophy)

1935 (first award of trophy)   Berwanger, Jay   Chicago

Illinois winner (Rissman Trophy)

		Games			Points	
		Won	Lost	Tied	For	Against
1927	University of Illinois	7	0	1	152	24

Illinois members of College Football Hall of Fame
(at Rutgers University, where the game originated)

Name	School	Position	Last year played
Players			
Agase, Alex	Illinois	C	1946
Berwanger, Jay	Chicago	H	1935
Carney, Charles	Illinois	E	1921
Des Jardien, Paul	Chicago	C	1914
Eckersall, Walter	Chicago	Q	1905
Graham, Otto	Northwestern	H	1943
Grange, Harold	Illinois	H	1925
Wyant, A.	Chicago	G	1895
Coaches			
Stagg, Amos Alonzo	Chicago		
Waldorf, Lynn	Northwestern		
Zuppke, Robert	Illinois		

Chicago Tribune Silver Football

(awarded annually to the most valuable player of the Big Ten)

Year	Name	School
1924	Grange, Harold	Illinois
1925	Lowry, Tim	Northwestern
1927	Rouse, Kenneth	Chicago
1935	Berwanger, Jay	Chicago
1943	Graham, Otto	Northwestern
1946	Agase, Alex	Illinois
1948	Murakowski, Arthur	Northwestern
1959	Burrell, William	Illinois
1963	Butkus, Richard	Illinois
1965	Grabowski, James	Illinois

Professional Football

Professional football was played in Illinois as early as 1895 with little success. Teams in Decatur, Rock Island, and other cities played on Sunday afternoons and passed the hat to pay expenses. It was not until after World War I that the game began to attract widespread attention. Chief figure in its development, not only in Illinois but nationwide, has been George Halas, owner and coach of the Chicago Bears. Halas was an outstanding end in college and professional games. He owns the oldest individual record in the National

Football League—a ninety-eight-yard run to a touchdown after recovery of a fumble by Jim Thorpe, November 4, 1923. When he was no longer active on the field he continued to coach and in this capacity he has served longer than any other man in the professional ranks. His contributions to management and policy have done a great deal toward elevating the sport from a sandlot pastime to its present stature as a favorite spectator sport, and have contributed to financial security for owners, coaches, and players through huge crowds in the stands and multimillion-dollar contracts with the radio and TV networks.

Professional football is a business with a circus angle. The season lasts from early August (preseason exhibition games) until after New Year's Day (championship and bowl games). During the preseason period games are played in cities that get no major league ball during the regular season. In this manner, football offers a lifetime career to a select few—as players for ten or fifteen years, later as coaches, sports announcers, and football management experts.

The success of two great Illinois professional teams, the Bears and the Cardinals (now in St. Louis), is indicated by the records of team and individual achievement. Some examples are: most seasons leading the league in scoring, Bears 9; most seasons leading the league in rushing and passing, Bears 12; best running average for one season, Beattie Feathers of the Bears 9.9 yards per try for 101 tries, 1934; most kickoff returns to touchdown, career, Gale Sayers 6; best total offense, season, Sayers 2,440 yards, 1966. Sayers holds five national league records and is tied for one. He also holds eight team records.

There are two football halls of fame honoring professional athletes. One of these, at Canton, Ohio, was organized in 1962. The other is Helms Hall, one of the several in various fields of sports selected by the Helms Foundation. Twenty-three athletes representing Illinois in the football wars were among fifty-nine selections of Helms Hall to 1968 and the fifty-one elected to the hall at Canton to the same year. John "Paddy" Driscoll, halfback from Northwestern, played with both the Bears and the Cardinals, and remained with the Bears as coach and executive until his death June 30, 1968. James Conzelman played for the Bears and coached the Cardinals. Guy Chamberlain, end from Nebraska, played with Bears and Cardinals. Ernest Nevers, fullback from Stanford, was a member of the Duluth team and the Cardinals; Elroy Hirsch, end from Northwestern, was with the short-lived Rockets before he joined the Los Angeles Rams; Charles Trippi of the Cardinals, selected after the 1967 season by the Canton Hall, was the most recent.

All-time league individual records held by players on Illinois teams

Most seasons as head coach: Halas, George, Bears, 39
Most points, one game: Nevers, Ernest, Cardinals, 40 (6 TDs, 4 PAT)
Most touchdowns, one game: Nevers, Ernest, Cardinals, 6
                             Sayers, Gale, Bears, 6
Most touchdowns, season: Sayers, Gale, Bears, 22
Most touchdowns, kickoff returns, career: Sayers, Gale, Bears, 6
Most yards, total offense, season: Sayers, Gale, Bears, 2,440
Most touchdown passes, one game: Luckman, Sidney, Bears, 7
Best total offense average, one game: Sayers, Gale, Bears, 21 yards (336 yards, 16 tries)
Most points, rookie season: Sayers, Gale, Bears 1965, 132
Most dropkick field goals, career: Driscoll, John, Bears (12), Cardinals (37), 49
Longest field goal, dropkick: Driscoll, John, Cardinals, 50 yards (two times)
Most points after touchdown, game: Harder, Marlin, Cardinals, 9 (tie)
Most consecutive points after touchdown: Blanda, George (school: Kentucky), Bears 1949–56, 156
Most yards gained, career: Matson, Oliver, Cardinals 1951–60, 11,216
Highest average, punt returns, career: McAfee, George, Bears, 12.8 yards (112 returns)
Longest run with recovered fumble: Halas, George, Bears 1923, 98 yards

All-league selections

From 1931 to 1942 an all-league team was selected by the office of the league in consultation with coaches. Thereafter a team was chosen by the Associated Press and another by the United Press (later United Press International), with the press associations agreeing more often than not. Beginning in 1951 eleven players were selected to represent the offense and eleven to represent the defense. George Connor of the Bears, a great tackle equally effective on either assignment, in 1951 and 1952 was selected on offense by the Associated Press and on defense by the United Press. In 1935, 1941, and 1942 five of eleven players were selected from the Bears and Cardinals. In 1943 the two press associations agreed on five out of eleven from the two Illinois teams. Sidney Luckman was named most valuable player in 1943 by the league office. Since 1955 that selection has been made by ballot of all players in the league. The honor carries with it possession of the Jim Thorpe Trophy. The first to be named for that honor, in 1955, was Harlon Hill, great pass-catching end of the Bears.

Year	Player	Team	Position	Selected by	School
1931	McNally, Frank	Cardinals	C	League	St. Mary's (Calif.)
	Grange, Harold	Bears	B	League	Illinois
	Nevers, Ernest	Cardinals	B	League	Stanford
1932	Johnsos, Luke	Bears	E	League	Northwestern
	Carlson, Jules	Bears	G	League	Oregon State
	Kiesling, Walter	Cardinals	T	League	St. Thomas (Minn.)
	Nagurski, Bronko	Bears	B	League	Minnesota
1933	Hewitt, William	Bears	E	League	Michigan
	Kopcha, Joseph	Bears	G	League	Chattanooga
	Nagurski, Bronko	Bears	B	League	Minnesota
1934	Hewitt, William	Bears	E	League	Michigan
	Kopcha, Joseph	Bears	G	League	Chattanooga
	Feathers, Beattie	Bears	B	League	Tennessee
	Nagurski, Bronko	Bears	B	League	Minnesota
1935	Smith, William	Cardinals	E	League	Washington
	Karr, William	Bears	E	League	West Virginia
	Musso, George	Bears	G	League	Milliken
	Kopcha, Joseph	Bears	G	League	Chattanooga
	Mikulak, Michael	Cardinals	B	League	Oregon
1936	None selected from Illinois teams.				
1937	Tinsley, Gaynell	Cardinals	E	League	Louisiana State
	Stydahar, Joseph	Bears	T	League	West Virginia
	Musso, George	Bears	G	League	Milliken
1938	Tinsley, Gaynell	Cardinals	E	League	Louisiana State
	Stydahar, Joseph	Bears	T	League	West Virginia
	Fortmann, Daniel	Bears	G	League	Colgate
1939	Stydahar, Joseph	Bears	T	League	West Virginia
	Fortmann, Daniel	Bears	G	League	Colgate
	Osmanski, William	Bears	B	League	Holy Cross
1940	Stydahar, Joseph	Bears	T	League	West Virginia
	Fortmann, Daniel	Bears	G	League	Colgate
1941	Fortmann, Daniel	Bears	G	League	Colgate
	Kuharich, Joseph	Cardinals	G	League	Notre Dame
	Turner, Clyde	Bears	C	League	Hardin-Simmons
	Luckman, Sidney	Bears	Q	League	Columbia
	McAfee, George	Bears	B	League	Duke
1942	Artoe, Lee	Bears	T	League	Santa Clara
	Fortmann, Daniel	Bears	G	League	Colgate
	Turner, Clyde	Bears	C	League	Hardin-Simmons
	Luckman, Sidney	Bears	Q	League	Columbia
	Famiglietti, Gary	Bears	B	League	Boston Univ.
1943	Rucinski, Edward	Cardinals	E	AP UP	Indiana
	Fortmann, Daniel	Bears	G	AP UP	Colgate
	Turner, Clyde	Bears	C	AP UP	Hardin-Simmons
	Luckman, Sidney	Bears	Q	AP UP	Columbia
	Clark, Harry	Bears	B	AP UP	West Virginia
1944	Turner, Clyde	Bears	C	AP UP	Hardin-Simmons
	Luckman, Sidney	Bears	Q	AP	Columbia
1945	None selected from Illinois teams.				
1946	Kavanaugh, Kenneth	Bears	E	UP	Louisiana State
	Turner, Clyde	Bears	C	AP UP	Hardin-Simmons

Year	Player	Team	Position	Selected by	School
1947	Kavanaugh, Kenneth	Bears	E	UP	Louisiana State
	Kutner, Malcolm	Cardinals	E	UP	Texas
	Turner, Clyde	Bears	C	AP UP	Hardin-Simmons
	Banonis, Vincent	Cardinals	C	UP	Detroit
	Luckman, Sidney	Bears	Q	AP UP	Columbia
	Harder, Marlin	Cardinals	B	UP	Wisconsin
1948	Kutner, Malcom	Cardinals	E	AP UP	Texas
	Bray, Raymond	Bears	G	UP	Western Michigan
	Ramsay, Garrard	Cardinals	G	AP UP	William and Mary
	Turner, Clyde	Bears	C	AP UP	Hardin-Simmons
	Harder, Marlin	Cardinals	B	UP	Wisconsin
	Trippi, Charles	Cardinals	B	AP UP	Georgia
1949	Bray, Raymond	Bears	G	UP	Western Michigan
	Ramsay, Garrard	Cardinals	G	AP UP	William and Mary
	Harder, Marlin	Cardinals	B	UP	Wisconsin
1950	Connor, George	Bears	T	AP UP	Notre Dame
	Barwegan, Richard	Bears	G	AP UP	Notre Dame
	Lujack, John	Bears	Q	AP UP	Notre Dame
1951	Connor, George	Bears	T	(O) AP (D) UP	Notre Dame
	Barwegan, Richard	Bears	G	AP UP	Notre Dame
1952	Connor, George	Bears	T, LB	(O) AP (D) UP	Notre Dame
	Fischer, William	Cardinals	G	UP	Notre Dame
	Matson, Oliver	Cardinals	B	AP UP	San Francisco
1953	Connor, George	Bears	T, LB	(O) AP (D) UP	Notre Dame
1954	Hill, Harlon	Bears	E	UP	Alabama State Teachers
	Matson, Oliver	Cardinals	B	AP UP	San Francisco
1955	Hill, Harlon	Bears	E	UP	Alabama State Teachers
	Wightkin, William	Bears	T	AP	Notre Dame
	Jones, Oliver	Cardinals	B	AP UP	San Francisco
	George, William	Bears	MG	AP	Wake Forest
	Connor, George	Bears	LB	UP	Notre Dame
1956	Hill, Harlon	Bears	E	AP UP	Alabama State Teachers
	Jones, Stanley	Bears	G	AP UP	Maryland
	Strickland, Lawrence	Bears	C	AP	North Texas State
	Matson, Oliver	Cardinals	B	AP UP	San Francisco
	Casares, Ricardo	Bears	B	AP UP	Florida
	George, William	Bears	MG	AP UP	Wake Forest
1957	Strickland, Lawrence	Bears	C	UP	North Texas State
	Matson, Oliver	Cardinals	B	AP UP	San Francisco
	George, William	Bears	LB	AP UP	Wake Forest
1958	George, William	Bears	LB	AP UPI	Wake Forest
1959	Jones, Stanley	Bears	G	AP	Maryland
	George, William	Bears	LB	AP UPI	Wake Forest
1960	Jones, Stanley	Bears	G	UPI	Maryland
	Atkins, Douglas	Bears	DE	UPI	Tennessee
	George, William	Bears	LB	AP UPI	Wake Forest
1961	George, William	Bears	LB	AP	Wake Forest
1962	Ditka, Michael	Bears	E	UPI	Pittsburgh
1963	Ditka, Michael	Bears	E	AP UPI	Pittsburgh
	Atkins, Douglas	Bears	DE	AP UPI	Tennessee
	George, William	Bears	LB	AP UPI	Wake Forest
	Fortunato, Joseph	Bears	LB	AP UPI	Mississippi State
	Petitbon, Richard	Bears	DB	AP UPI	Tulane
	Taylor, Roosevelt	Bears	DB	AP	Grambling
1964	Ditka, Michael	Bears	E	AP UPI	Pittsburgh
	Morris, John	Bears	E	AP UPI	Santa Barbara
	Fortunato, Joseph	Bears	LB	AP	Mississippi State
1965	Sayers, Gale	Bears	B	AP UPI	Kansas
	Butkus, Richard	Bears	LB	AP	Illinois
	Fortunato, Joseph	Bears	LB	AP	Mississippi State
1966	Sayers, Gale	Bears	B	AP UPI	Kansas
	Ditka, Michael	Bears	E	AP UPI	Pittsburgh
1967	Sayers, Gale	Bears	B	AP UPI	Kansas
	Butkus, Richard	Bears	LB	UPI	Illinois

Members of Canton and Helms Halls of Fame from Illinois teams to 1968

Player	Position	Club and years	Hall	School
Benton, William	E	Bears 1943, Cleveland, Canton	Helms	Arkansas
Bray, Raymond	G	Bears 1939–51, Green Bay	Helms	Western Michigan
Chamberlain, Guy	E	Bears 1921, Cardinals 1927–28	Canton	Nebraska
Conzelman, James	B, coach	Bears 1920, Milwaukee, Detroit, coach Cardinals 1946–48	Canton	Washington (St. Louis)
Driscoll, John (Paddy)	B, coach	Cardinals 1921–25, Bears 1926–28, coach Bears 1929–68	both	Northwestern
Fortmann, Dr. Daniel	G	Bears 1946–52	both	Colgate
Grange, Harold (Red)	B	Bears 1925, 1928–34, Yankees	both	Illinois
Halas, George	E, coach	Bears 1920–29, coach Bears 1930–41, 1945–55, 1958–67	both	Illinois
Healy, Edward	T	Bears 1922–27	Canton	Dartmouth
Hewitt, William	E	Bears 1932–36, Eagles	Canton	Michigan
Hirsch, Elroy	G	Rockets 1946–48, Rams	both	Northwestern
Kiesling, Walter	G	Cardinals 1929–33, Bears 1934	both	St. Thomas (Minn.)
Luckman, Sidney	Q, coach	Bears 1939–50, coach Bears from 1951	both	Columbia
Lyman, William Roy	T	Bears 1925–34	both	Nebraska
McAfee, George	B	Bears 1940–50	both	Duke
Musso, George	G	Bears 1933–44	Helms	Milliken
Nagurski, Bronko	B	Bears 1930–37, 1943	both	Minnesota
Nevers, Ernest	B	Cardinals 1929–31	both	Stanford
Sprinkle, Edward	E, G	Bears 1944–55	Helms	Hardin-Simmons
Stydahar, Joseph	T, coach	Bears 1936–42, 1945–46, coach Bears 1963–64	Helms	West Virginia
Trafton, George	C	Bears 1921–32	Both	Notre Dame
Trippi, Charles	B	Cardinals 1947–55	Canton	Georgia
Turner, Clyde (Bulldog)	C	Bears 1940–52	both	Hardin-Simmons

All-time league records held by Illinois teams

Scoring	Bears	9	(1934, 1935, 1939, 1941, 1942, 1943, 1946, 1947, 1956)
Rushes and passes	Bears	12	(1932, 1934, 1935, 1939, 1941, 1942, 1943, 1944, 1947, 1949, 1955, 1956)
Rushes	Bears	9	(1932, 1935, 1939, 1940, 1941, 1942, 1951, 1955, 1956)
Most yards gained punt returns	Bears	781	1948
Most consecutive victories	Bears	18	1933–34, 1941–42
Fewest punts	Bears	32	1941
Most touchdowns on punt returns	Cardinals	5	1959
Most fumbles	Bears	56	1938
Most penalties	Bears	122	1948 (1,066 yards)
Most yards penalized	Bears	1,107	1951
Fewest yards allowed	Cardinals	1,578	1934
Fewest yards allowed rushing	Bears	519	1942
Fewest yards allowed passing	Cardinals	625	1934
Most touchdown passes game	Bears	7	Nov. 14, 1943 (tie)
Most kickoff returns game	Bears	10	Nov. 27, 1955 (tie)
Fewest yards allowed game	Cardinals	53	Oct. 17, 1943

Individual departmental champions

Rushing

Year	Player	Team	Yards gained	Number of attempts	Average gain	School
1934	Feathers, Beattie	Bears	1,004	101	9.9	Tennessee
1935	Russell, Douglas	Cardinals	499	140	3.6	Kansas State
1939	Osmanski, William	Bears	699	121	5.8	Holy Cross
1956	Casares, Ricardo	Bears	1,126	234	4.8	Florida
1966	Sayers, Gale	Bears	1,231	229	5.4	Kansas

Forward passing

Year	Player	Team	Passes attempted	Passes completed	Per-centage	Yards gained	TDs	Inter-ceptions	School
1956	Brown, Edward	Bears	168	96	57.1	1,667	11	12	San Francisco
1965	Bukich, Rudolph	Bears	312	176	56.4	2,641	20	9	Southern California

Pass receiving

Year	Player	Team	Passes caught	Yards gained	TDs	School
1932	Johnsos, Luke	Bears	24	321	2	Northwestern
1964	Morris, John	Bears	93	1,200	10	Santa Barbara

Interceptions

Year	Player	Team	Number of interceptions	Yards	Longest return	School
1942	Turner, Clyde	Bears	8	96	42	Hardin-Simmons
1949	Nussbaumer, Robert	Cardinals	12	157	68	Michigan
1954	Lane, Richard	Cardinals	10	181	64	Scottsbluff, Nebr., J.C.
1963	Taylor, Roosevelt	Bears	9	172	46	Grambling

Field goals

Year	Player	Team	Number of field goals	School
1934	Manders, Jack	Bears	10	Minnesota
1936	Manders, Jack	Bears	7	Minnesota
1937	Manders, Jack	Bears	8	Minnesota

Scoring

Year	Player	Team	TDs	PAT	FG	Total points	School
1934	Manders, Jack	Bears	3	31	10	79	Minnesota
1937	Manders, Jack	Bears	5	15	8	69	Minnesota
1947	Harder, Marlin	Cardinals	7	39	7	102	Wisconsin
1948	Harder, Marlin	Cardinals	6	53	7	110	Wisconsin
1949	Harder, Marlin	Cardinals	8	45	3	102 (tie)	Wisconsin
1965	Sayers, Gale	Bears	22	0	0	132	Kansas

Annual team departmental champions from Illinois, 1932–66

Total yards gained, net
(yards gained by rushing, passing, kick returns, and penalties, less losses)

1932	Bears	2,755
1934	Bears	3,750
1935	Bears	3,454
1939	Bears	3,988
1941	Bears	4,265
1942	Bears	3,900
1943	Bears	4,045
1944	Bears	3,239
1947	Bears	5,053
1948	Cardinals	4,694
1949	Bears	4,873
1955	Bears	4,316
1956	Bears	4,537

Yards gained by rushing

1932	Bears	1,770
1935	Bears	2,096
1939	Bears	2,043
1940	Bears	1,818
1941	Bears	2,156
1942	Bears	1,881
1948	Cardinals	2,560
1951	Bears	2,408
1955	Bears	2,388
1956	Bears	2,468

Yards gained by passing

1932	Bears	1,013
1939	Bears	1,965
1941	Bears	2,002
1943	Bears	2,310
1949	Bears	3,055

| 1954 | Bears | 3,104 |
| 1964 | Bears | 2,841 |

Points scored

1934	Bears (13 games)	286
1935	Bears (12 games)	192
1939	Bears (11 games)	298
1941	Bears (11 games)	396
1942	Bears (11 games)	376
1943	Bears (10 games)	303
1946	Bears (11 games)	289
1947	Bears (12 games)	363
1948	Cardinals (12 games)	395
1956	Bears (12 games)	363

Championships won by Illinois teams

Year	Team	Record[1] Won	Lost	Tied
1921	Bears	10	1	1
1925	Cardinals	11	2	1
1933	Bears	11	2	1
1940	Bears	9	3	0
1941	Bears	11	1	0
1943	Bears	9	1	1
1946	Bears	9	2	1
1947	Cardinals	10	3	0
1963	Bears	12	1	2

[1] Includes playoff games between division champions.

Basketball

Intercollegiate Basketball

Basketball is the favorite spectator sport of Illinois. Estimates indicate that more than 1,500,000 persons attended at least one basketball game in 1967–68. Illinois teams have won one national title designated by the Helms Athletic Foundation (Northwestern in 1931); one National Collegiate Athletic Association title (Loyola in 1963); one so-called small-college championship—the National Association of Intercollegiate Athletics—(Southern Illinois in 1946); five National Invitational tournaments (De Paul in 1945, Bradley in 1957, 1960, and 1964, and Southern Illinois in 1967). Illinois teams have won eleven Big Ten (or Big Nine) championships and shared five since 1907. Eight Amateur Athletic Union championships have come to Illinois since 1900—the Ravenswood Y.M.C.A., Chicago, in 1901; the Armour Playground, Chicago, in 1913 and 1914; the Illinois AC, Chicago, 1917; the Caterpillar Diesels, Peoria, in 1952 and 1953; and the Peoria Cats in 1954 and 1958. George Mikan of De Paul, Harlan Page and John Schommer of Chicago, and Raymond Woods of Illinois have been named to the Helms Basketball

Hall of Fame, as has coach Arthur Lonborg of Northwestern. Scott Steagall of Millikin and Gene Stotlar of Southern Illinois are members of the Helms NAIA Hall of Fame.

Big Ten champions from Illinois

Year	Team	Won	Lost	Percentage
1907	Chicago[1]	6	2	.750
1908	Chicago	8	1	.889
1909	Chicago	12	0	1.000
1910	Chicago	9	3	.750
1915	Illinois	12	0	1.000
1917	Illinois[2]	10	2	.833
1920	Chicago	11	2	.846
1924	Chicago[3]	8	4	.667
1931	Northwestern	11	1	.917
1935	Illinois[4]	9	3	.750
1937	Illinois[2]	10	2	.833
1942	Illinois	13	2	.867
1943	Illinois	12	0	1.000
1949	Illinois	10	2	.833
1951	Illinois	13	1	.929
1952	Illinois	12	2	.857

[1] Tied with Minnesota and Wisconsin.
[2] Tied with Minnesota.
[3] Tied with Wisconsin.
[4] Tied with Wisconsin and Purdue.

National scoring leaders, NCAA

Year	Name	School	Number of games	Total points	Average per game
1945	Mikan, George	De Paul	19	454	23.9
1946	Mikan, George	De Paul	21	485	23.1

National scoring leader, NAIA

Year	Name	School	Number of games	Total points	Average per game
1951	Steagall, Scott	Millikin	31	888	28.6

Scoring leaders, Big Ten

Year	Name	School			
1907	Schommer, John	Chicago	8	95	11.9
1908	Schommer, John	Chicago	9	105	11.7
1909	Schommer, John	Chicago	12	104	8.7
1913	Dahringer, Homer	Illinois	12	125	10.4
1914	Whittle, George	Northwestern	12	109	9.1
1917	Woods, Raymond	Illinois	12	126	10.5
1918	Anderson, Earl	Illinois	12	162	13.5
1919	Gorgas, William	Chicago	12	106	8.8
1920	Carney, Charles	Illinois	12	188	15.7
1922	Carney, Charles	Illinois	12	172	14.3
1931	Reiff, Joseph	Northwestern	12	120	10.0
1933	Reiff, Joseph	Northwestern	12	168	14.0
1935	Haarlow, Arnold W.	Chicago	12	156	13.0
1940	Hapac, William	Illinois	12	164	13.7
1941	Stampf, Joseph	Chicago	12	166	13.8
1943	Phillip, Andrew	Illinois	12	255	21.3
1945	Morris, Max	Northwestern	12	189	15.8
1946	Morris, Max	Northwestern	12	198	16.5
1951	Ragelis, Raymond	Northwestern	14	277	19.8

All-American selections
by Helms Athletic Foundation

(After 1945 forwards and defense only were selected. Centers were listed under defense. In this table we have used the letter C for those players nominally assigned by their coaches for the tip-off when required. In 1967 the foundation, recognizing the difficulties of comparing players from many different leagues, named thirty-six players.)

Year	Name	Position	School
1905	Ozanne, James	F	Chicago
1906	McKeag, James	F	Chicago
	Schommer, John	C	Chicago
1907	Schommer, John	C	Chicago
	Houghton, Albert	G	Chicago
1908	Schommer, John	C	Chicago
	Page, Harlan O.	G	Chicago
1909	Schommer, John	C	Chicago
	Page, Harlan O.	G	Chicago
1910	Page, Harlan O.	G	Chicago
1914	Norgren, Nelson	F	Chicago
1915	Woods, Raymond	G	Illinois
1916	Woods, Raymond	G	Illinois
1917	Alwood, Clyde	C	Illinois
	Woods, Raymond	G	Illinois
1918	Anderson, Earl	F	Illinois
1919	Hinkle, Paul	G	Chicago
1920	Carney, Charles	F	Illinois
	Hinkle, Paul	G	Chicago
1922	Carney, Charles	F	Illinois
1931	Reiff, Joseph	C	Northwestern
1933	Reiff, Joseph	F	Northwestern
1940	Hapac, William	F	Illinois
1942	Phillip, Andrew	G	Illinois
1943	Phillip, Andrew	F	Illinois
	Mikan, George	C	De Paul
1944	Graham, Otto	F	Northwestern
	Mikan, George	C	De Paul
1945	Morris, Max	F	Northwestern
	Mikan, George	C	De Paul
	Kirk, Walton, Jr.	G	Illinois
1946	Morris, Max	F	Northwestern
	Mikan, George	C	De Paul
1947	Humerickhouse, David	G	Bradley
	Smiley, John	G	Illinois
1948	Mikan, Edward	G	De Paul
1949	Erickson, William	G	Illinois
	Unruh, Paul	C	Bradley
1950	Unruh, Paul	G	Bradley
	Melchiorre, Gene	F	Bradley
1951	Melchiorre, Gene	G	Bradley
	Ragelis, Raymond	F	Northwestern
	Sunderlage, Donald	G	Illinois
1952	Fletcher, Rodney	G	Illinois
1953	Bemoras, Irving	G	Illinois
	Carney, Robert	G	Bradley
1954	Carney, Robert	G	Bradley
	Kerr, John	C	Illinois
1955	Ehmann, Frank	F	Northwestern
1956	Sobieszczyk, Ronald	G	De Paul
	Judson, Paul	G	Illinois

Year	Name	Position	School
1957	Mason, Bobby Joe	G	Bradley
	Heise, Richard	F	De Paul
1958	Ohl, Donald	G	Illinois
1959	Mason, Bobby Joe	G	Bradley
1960	Walker, Chester	C	Bradley
1961	Walker, Chester	G	Bradley
1962	Walker, Chester	G	Bradley
1963	Downey, David	F	Illinois
1964	Falk, Richard	G	Northwestern
	Miller, Ronald	G	Loyola
	Tart, Lavern	G	Bradley
1965	Thoren, Duane	F	Illinois
1966	Freeman, Donald	F	Illinois
1967	Allen, Joseph	C	Bradley
	Tillman, James	C	Loyola
	Burns, James	G	Northwestern
	Frazier, Walter	G	Southern Illinois

In 1935 the Helms Athletic Foundation designated twelve Illinois players as members of all-American teams for the years 1905 to 1935. Since that time they have added thirty-five, including those named for 1966–67. One, George Mikan of De Paul, was twice named college player of the year, and is a member of everybody's all-time all-American.

High School Basketball

Basketball training in Illinois, like other states with a sizeable rural and small-town population, begins as soon as a youngster can get two hands on a ball. Against most of the barns in the state are practice baskets, and many small-town and suburban garages have the same equipment. That may be one reason why Chicago, with its large high schools and great records in football, had to wait forty-six years for its first state championship. Play for the state title began in 1908 with an invitational tournament at the Oak Park Y.M.C.A. won by Peoria, with Rock Island the runner-up. In 1909 the first state high school association was formed, and the championship event was the climax of elimination play. Hinsdale was the winner and Washington High the runner-up. For the next nine years the tournaments shuttled from Bloomington to Bradley University to Millikin University to Bradley to Millikin to Springfield High School. In 1919 title play went to the University of Illinois at Champaign, where it has been ever since. In the first fifty years of tournament play Mt. Vernon had four winners, in 1920, 1949, 1950, and 1954. Smallest school to win the title was Hebron of McHenry County, which had an enrollment of fewer than 100 students. Here are the tournament records from 1908.

Year	Champion	Runner-up	Score
1908	Peoria Central	Rock Island	48–29
1909	Hinsdale	Washington	18–13
1910	Bloomington	Rock Island	32–25
1911	Rockford	Mt. Carroll	60–15
1912	Batavia	Galesburg	28–25
1913	Galesburg	Peoria Manual	37–36
1914	Hillsboro	Freeport	42–19
1915	Freeport	Springfield	27–11
1916	Bloomington	Robinson	25–17
1917	Springfield	Belvidere	32–11
1918	Centralia	University High (Normal)	35–29
1919	Rockford	Springfield	39–20

Year	Champion	Runner-up	Score
1920	Mt. Vernon	Canton	18–14
1921	Marion	Rockford	24–23
1922	Centralia	Atwood	24–16
1923	Villa Grove	Rockford	32–29
1924	Elgin	Athens	28–17
1925	Elgin	Champaign	25–17
1926	Freeport	Canton	24–13
1927	Mt. Carmel	Peoria Central	24–18
1928	Canton	West Aurora	18– 9
1929	Johnston City	Champaign	30–21
1930	Peoria Manual	Bloomington	38–25
1931	Decatur	Galesburg	30–26
1932	Morton (Cicero)	Canton	30–16
1933	Thornton (Harvey)	Springfield	14–13
1934	Quincy	Thornton (Harvey)	30–27
1935	Springfield	Thornton (Harvey)	24–19
1936	Decatur	Danville	26–22
1937	Joliet	Decatur	40–20
1938	Dundee	Braidwood	36–29
1939	Rockford	Paris	53–44
1940	Granite City	Herrin	24–22
1941	Morton (Cicero)	Urbana	32–31
1942	Centralia	Paris	35–33
1943	Paris	Moline	46–37
1944	Taylorville	Elgin	56–33
1945	Decatur	Champaign	62–54
1946	Champaign	Centralia	54–48
1947	Paris	Champaign	58–37
1948	Pinckneyville	Rockford East	65–39
1949	Mt. Vernon	Hillsboro	45–39
1950	Mt. Vernon	Danville	85–61
1951	Freeport	Moline	71–51
1952	Hebron	Quincy	64–59
1953	La Grange	Peoria Central	72–60
1954	Mt. Vernon	Du Sable (Chicago)	76–70
1955	Rockford West	Elgin	61–59
1956	Rockford West	Edwardsville	67–65
1957	Herrin	Collinsville	45–42
1958	Marshall (Chicago)	Rock Falls	70–64
1959	Springfield	Aurora West	60–52
1960	Marshall (Chicago)	Bridgeport	79–55
1961	Collinsville	Thornton (Harvey)	84–50
1962	Decatur	Carver (Chicago)	49–48
1963	Carver (Chicago)	Centralia	53–52
1964	Pekin	Cobden	50–45
1965	Collinsville	Quincy	55–52
1966	Thornton (Harvey)	Galesburg	74–60
1967	Pekin	Carbondale	75–59

Most championships: Mt. Vernon 4—1920, 1949, 1950, 1954
              Decatur   4—1931, 1936, 1945, 1962

Most times in finals: Springfield 6—1915, 1917, 1919, 1933,
                                        1935, 1959.

Professional Basketball

Professional basketball has not made much headway in Illinois. Membership in a professional league has been an in-and-out proposition. However, Chicago again is fielding a team, the Bulls, in national professional play. Two fairly successful seasons were enjoyed during 1966–67 and 1967–68, and the backers of the team are looking forward to greater success in the future.

Golf

Historians are agreed that golf was devised by the Scots, perhaps in a very early day. The game received a royal accolade from James IV late in the fifteenth century. He was a capable golfer and taught his grand-daughter, Mary, who lost her head on order of England's first Elizabeth. Mary carried golfing equipment when she went to France to marry the Dauphin. There she taught her French hosts the sport. To carry the clubs Mary had a youngster from the court, a *fils cadet* (pronounced fees caday) from which the term caddy derived. The Royal and Ancient Golf Club of St. Andrews was founded about 1552, during Mary's reign. When England and Scotland were united in the person of Mary's son James (in Scotland the Sixth, in England the First) he introduced the game in England. The Royal Blackheath Club was organized in 1608.

Golf came to fledgling United States when Illinois was still a part of the Northwest Territory—perhaps even earlier. First mention of a golf club is found in an advertisement in a Charleston, South Carolina, newspaper on October 13, 1795, calling members of "the Golf Club" to an anniversary celebration the following Saturday at one o'clock at the clubhouse on Harleston Green. It is not definite that the game got beyond the conversation stage at that time, but why a golf club without golf? Seventy years later there were clubs in Canada and twenty years after that several in the New York area and a couple in Illinois.

The United States Golf Association was organized in the winter of 1895 with four clubs in the vicinity of New York and one, the Chicago Golf Club, at Wheaton. When the U.S.G.A. held its first amateur tournament in 1895 at Newport, Rhode Island, Charles B. McDonald of the Chicago Golf Club beat C. E. Sands, affiliation not recorded, twelve up and eleven to play. McDonald had been runner-up in an unsanctioned tournament the previous year, losing one up to L. B. Stoddard. In 1896 H. G. Whigham of Onwentsia, Lake Forest, beat J. G. Thorpe at the Shinnecock Hills Golf Club, New York, eight and seven in the final match. Whigham repeated in 1897 at the Chicago Golf Club, Wheaton. McDonald won the medal round in 1899 but failed in match play. No more amateur titles came to Illinois until 1916, when Charles (Chick) Evans took both the national amateur and the national open.

Evans was a much-feared competitor for more than twenty years. He was beaten in the finals of the amateur championship in 1912 by Jerome Travers, a four-time winner. He defeated Robert A. Gardner, champion in 1909 and 1915, in the 1916 finals, four up and three to play. Evans' victim in 1920 was Francis Ouimet, first amateur to win the U.S. Open, whom he trounced seven and six at the Engineers Golf Club, Roslyn, New York. Evans was finalist in 1922, losing to Jesse Sweetzer, and in 1927, losing to Bobby Jones. Evans won the Western Open in 1910 and the Western Amateur in 1909, 1912, 1914, 1915, 1920, 1921, 1922, and 1923.

Evans, although not a professional, was elected to the P.G.A. Hall of Fame in recognition of the work he did for the welfare of golfing's indispensable youngsters, the caddies. Evans scholarships made possible college education for many a boy who might otherwise have ended his schooling with graduation from high school.

Except for Evans, Illinois has had only two winners in the Western Amateur— John Lehman of Chicago in 1930 and Jack Westland of Chicago in 1933. No other major tournament has been won by an amateur golfer born in or a resident of Illinois.

Winners of the United States Open among professionals employed by Illinois clubs were Fred Herd, who won with 328 at the Myopia Hunt Club, Hamilton, Massachusetts, in 1898, and Willie Smith, who won at Baltimore, Maryland, in 1899 with 315. Herd represented the Washington Park Golf Club of Chicago and Smith was employed by Midlothian. When the open was played at Chicago Golf Club in 1900, the event was won by the great Harry Vardon of England with a 313. Aside from these early professionals Jock Hutchison of Glenview was most successful in competition. He won the Professional Golfers Association title at Flossmoor in 1920, the Western Open in 1920 and 1923, and the North-South Open in 1921.

In 1957 Illinois ranked third in number of golf courses, with 315. Of this number 156 were private, 106 daily fee, and 53 municipal. Chicago Park District and Cook County Forest Preserve courses were listed among the daily fee layouts.

Bowling

Until the advent of television, bowling was a sport that could in no manner be classified as "spectator." But it was, in Illinois, the sport that drew more participants than any other. More than 1,500,000 men, women, and children bowled in Illinois in 1967. Of the 1,248,423 five-man teams registered with the American Bowling Congress in 1966, more than 100,000 bowled on Illinois lanes.

Bowling was popular in Illinois a hundred years ago. It fell into disrepute through association with saloons and gamblers. The renaissance of bowling began in 1895 with the formation of the American Bowling Congress with 60 teams. When the congress held its first tournament in 1901 in Chicago 41 five-man teams were entered. The fiftieth tournament, also in Chicago, in 1953, drew 8,180 five-man teams. Of those fifty tournaments, six were held in Chicago and four in Peoria.

Illinois bowlers have dominated the

national scene since the first ABC tournament. They had won twenty-seven five-man events, sixteen all-events titles, seventeen doubles championships, and sixteen individual titles in sixty-three tournaments conducted by the ABC from 1901 through 1966. (No competitions were held in 1943, 1944, or 1945.) In addition Illinois women captured twenty-three team titles, eleven all-events, thirteen singles and twelve doubles in the forty-five tournaments conducted by the Woman's International Bowling Congress, organized in 1917, from 1917 through 1966.

Match game championships originated in Chicago. James Blouin of Blue Island won the first and only ABC Open Tournament in 1922 and successfully defended his title for five years. In 1926 he retired because of illness. Frank Kartheiser succeeded to the title and lost it to Charles Daw of Milwaukee in 1927. Adolph Carlson brought the match game championship back to Chicago before 1928 was over, and defended the title until 1929. In 1942 the match game title was turned over to the *Chicago Tribune* for all-star competition. Illinois winners since that date have been Herbert Booth (Buddy) Bomar, Joseph Wilman, Junie McMahon, and William Lillard. Wilman has reached the finals ten times since competition started. Bomar has been nine times in the finals.

Illinois members of Bowling Hall of Fame, established in 1941
Selections by Bowling Writers of America

Bowler	City	Year nominated	Basis of selection
Steers, Harry	Chicago	1941	ABC Doubles 1902, 1918. ABC All-events 1918. ABC average 185 in 52 tournaments.
Carlson, Adolph	Chicago	1941	Six all-events averages of 2,000 or more. ABC average 197 in 32 tournaments.
Howley, Peter	Chicago	1941	Service recognition. Entered all ABC tournaments 1901–40 (later extended to 1948). Average 178.
Wilman, Joseph	Berwyn	1951	All-events 1939, 1946. Team title 1954. Record average 5 successive tournaments (45 games) 214–17.
Blouin, James	Blue Island	1953	All-events 1909. Singles 1911. Match game champion 5 successive years 1922–26.
Norris, Joseph	Chicago	1954	Four all-events averages of 2,000 or more. ABC average 198 in 28 tournaments.
Bomar, Herbert Booth	Chicago	1966	Nine times finalist in match-game competition. Average 201– 167 in 17 years, 1,090 games.
Kawolics, Edward	Chicago	1968	Average for 34 consecutive ABC tournaments, 196. Teacher, exhibition star. Eight consecutive series ABC of 1,800 or better, ending 1948.
Krumske, Paul	Chicago	1968	Chicago's bowler of the half century 1951. National match champion 1944. ABC average 197 in 32 tournaments.

American Bowling Congress

Team champions from Illinois, 1901–66

Year	Team	City	Score
1901	Standards	Chicago	2,720
1903	O'Learys	Chicago	2,819
1904	Ansons	Chicago	2,737
1905	Guenthers	Chicago	2,795
1906	Centurys	Chicago	2,794
1909	Lipmans	Chicago	2,962
1910	Cosmos	Chicago	2,880
1911	Flenners	Chicago	2,924
1915	Barry Kettlers	Chicago	2,907
1916	Commodore Barrys	Chicago	2,905
1917	Birk Brothers	Chicago	3,061
1920	Bruchs No. 1	Chicago	3,096
1926	Castany	Chicago	3,063
1928	O'Henrys	Chicago	3,057
1929	Hub Recreation	Joliet	3,063
1931	S and L Motors	Chicago	3,013
1938	Birk Brothers	Chicago	3,234
1940	Monarchs	Chicago	3,047
1941	Vogel Brothers	Forest Park	3,065
1942	Budweiser	Chicago	3,131
1948	Washington Shirts	Chicago	3,007
1951	O'Malley Olds	Chicago	3,070
1954	TriPar Radio	Chicago	3,226
1956	Falstaff Beer	Chicago	3,092
1957	Peter Hand	Chicago	3,126
1962	Strike 'n Spare	Chicago	3,128
1963	Old Fitzgerald	Chicago	3,180

All-events champions from Illinois, 1901–66

Year	Bowler	City	Score
1901	Brill, Frank	Chicago	1,736
1903	Strong, Frederick	Chicago	1,896
1905	Reilly, Jack G.	Chicago	1,791
1909	Blouin, James	Chicago	1,885
1915	Faetz, Matthew	Chicago	1,876
1916	Thoma, Frank	Chicago	1,919
1918	Steers, Harry	Chicago	1,959
1928	Wolff, Phillip	Chicago	1,937
1930	Morrison, George	Chicago	1,985
1937	Stein, Max	Belleville	2,070
1939	Wilman, Joseph	Berwyn	2,028
1946	Wilman, Joseph	Berwyn	2,054
1947	McMahon, Junie	Chicago	1,965
1949	Small, John	Chicago	1,941
1956	Lillard, William	Chicago	2,018
1964	Zikes, Les	Chicago	2,001

Doubles champions from Illinois, 1901–66

Year	Bowling team	City	Score
1902	Steers, Harry—McLean, James	Chicago	1,237
1905	Stretch, Edward—Rolfe, Robert	Chicago	1,213
1908	Chalmers, James—Kiene, Henry	Chicago	1,254
1916	Thoma, Frank—Marino, Henry	Chicago	1,279

Year	Bowling team	City	Score
1917	Startorious, G.—Holzschuh, William	Peoria	1,346
1918	Steers, Harry—Thoma, Frederick	Chicago	1,331
1920	Erickson, Marvin—Kems, Edward	Chicago	1,301
1924	Thoma, Harry—Thoma, Clarence	Chicago	1,380
1925	Karich, Edward—Schupp, Edward	Chicago	1,318
1928	Hradek, Joseph—Will, Henry	Cicero	1,363
1929	Butler, Peter—Klecz, Walter	Chicago	1,353
1934	Rudolph, George—Ryan, John	Waukegan	1,321
1936	Slanina, Anthony—Straka, Michael	Chicago	1,347
1940	Freitag, Herbert—Sinke, Joseph	Chicago	1,346
1948	Sweeney, William—Towns, James	Chicago	1,361
1956	Lillard, William—Gifford, Stanley	Chicago	1,331
1966	Stephanic, James—Rogoznica	Chicago	1,361

Individual champions from Illinois, 1901–66

Year	Bowler	City	Score
1901	Brill, Frank	Chicago	648
1902	Strong, Frederick	Chicago	649
1908	Wengler, Archie	Chicago	699
1911	Blouin, James	Chicago	681
1920	Shaw, Joseph	Chicago	713
1922	Lundgren, Walter	Chicago	729
1925	Green, Al	Chicago	706
1927	Eggers, William	Chicago	706
1936	Warren, Charles	Springfield	735
1938	Anderson, Knute	Moline	746
1939	Danek, James	Forest Park	730
1941	Ruff, Fred	Belleville	745
1947	McMahon, Junie	Chicago	740
1950	Leins, Everett	Aurora	757
1952	Sharkey, Al	Chicago	758
1964	Stephanic, James	Joliet	726*

* Classic Division.

Match game champions from Illinois

1922–26	Blouin, James (undefeated, retired 1926, illness), Chicago
1926	Kartheiser, Frank Chicago
1928–29	Carlson, Adolph Chicago

In 1942, the match game title was turned over to the *Chicago Tribune*, which instituted a match game championship series. Illinois winners have been:

Year	Bowler	Average*	Peterson point margin†
1944–45	Bomar, Herbert Booth	205–51	8.30
1945–46	Wilman, Joseph	209–61	4.25
1949–50	MaMahon, Junie	214–19	11.20
1951–52	McMahon, Junie	209–53	3.38
1955–56	Lillard, William	207–32	0.08

* Figure that follows whole number is remainder of pins after dividing total by number of games.
† One point for each game won, 1 point for each 50 pins dropped, ½ point for out-totaling opponent while losing majority of games.

Illinois all-star leaders

Bowler	Years	Number of games	Pins dropped	Average per game
Lillard, William	10	900	185,414	206–14
Wilman, Joseph	17	1,297	263,181	202–1,187
Bomar, Herbert Booth	17	1,090	219,257	201–167

All-Americans from Illinois Selected by the editors of the *National Bowlers Journal* beginning in 1940

Year	Bowler	City	Year	Bowler	City
1940	Norris, Joseph	Chicago	1947	Kawolics, Edward	Chicago
	Carlson, Adolph	Chicago		McMahon, Junie	Chicago
1941	Norris, Joseph	Chicago		Norris, Joseph	Chicago
	Carlson, Adolph	Chicago	1948	Krumske, Paul	Chicago
1942	Carlson, Adolph	Chicago		Wilman, Joseph	Berwyn
	Norris, Joseph	Chicago	1949	Bomar, Herbert	Chicago
	Wilman, Joseph	Berwyn	1950	Bomar, Herbert	Chicago
1943	Bomar, Herbert	Chicago		Krumske, Paul	Chicago
	Hargadon, William	Chicago		McMahon, Junie	Chicago
	Krumske, Paul	Chicago	1951	McMahon, Junie	Chicago
	Norris, Joseph	Chicago		Wilman, Joseph	Berwyn
1944	Bomar, Herbert	Chicago	1952	Lillard, William	Chicago
	Krumske, Paul	Chicago		McMahon, Junie	Chicago
	Norris, Joseph	Chicago	1953	Brosius, Edward	Chicago
1945	Bomar, Herbert	Chicago		McMahon, Junie	Chicago
	Krumske, Paul	Chicago	1954	Lillard, William	Chicago
	Norris, Joseph	Chicago		Wilman, Joseph	Berwyn
	Wilman, Joseph	Berwyn	1955	Lillard, William	Chicago
1946	Krumske, Paul	Chicago	1956	Lillard, William	Chicago
	Norris, Joseph	Chicago		Gifford, Stan	Chicago
	Wilman, Joseph	Berwyn	1958	Allison, Glenn	Chicago

Woman's International Bowling Congress

Team champions from Illinois, 1917-66

Year	Team	City	Score
1918	Leffingwell	Chicago	2,479
1921	Grand B and B	Rockford	2,482
1922	Cola Girls	Chicago	2,531
1924	Albert Pick and Co.	Chicago	2,477
1925	Estes Alibis	Chicago	2,518
1926	Taylor Trunks	Chicago	2,525
1927	Boyle Valves	Chicago	2,515
1928	Alberti Jewelers	Chicago	2,682
1930	Finucane Ladies	Chicago	2,784
1933	Alberti Jewelers	Chicago	2,867
1935	Alberti Jewelers	Chicago	2,765
1940	Logan Square Buicks	Chicago	2,689
1941	Rovick Bowling Shoes	Chicago	2,661
1942	Logan Bowling Shoes	Chicago	2,815
1948	Kathryne Cream Pack	Chicago	2,812
1954	Marhofer Wieners	Chicago	2,734
1955	Falstaff of Chicago	Chicago	2,991
1956	Daniel Ryan	Chicago	2,880
1958	Allgauer Restaurant	Chicago	2,972
1964	Allgauer's Villa Moderne	Chicago	2,920
1965	Belmont Bowl Pro Shop	Chicago	2,929
1966	Gossard Girls	Chicago	2,755

All-events champions from Illinois, 1917-66

Year	Bowler	City	Score
1930	Twyford, S.	Aurora	1,727
1932	Warmbler, M.	Chicago	1,807
1933	Twyford, S.	Aurora	1,765
1935	Warmbler, M.	Chicago	1,911
1938	Burmeister, D.	Chicago	1,843
1940	Morris, T.	Chicago	1,777
1941	Twyford, S.	Aurora	1,799
1942	Van Camp, N.	Chicago	1,888
1946	Fellmeth, C.	Chicago	1,835
1949	Winandy, C.	Chicago	1,840
1958	Ploegman, M.	Chicago	1,828

Doubles champions from Illinois, 1917-66

Year	Bowling team	City	Score
1925	Becker, M.—Ebert, M.	Chicago	1,119
1926	Laib, J.—Higgins, A.	Chicago	1,086
1927	Burke, A.—Kerg, E.	Chicago	1,100
1928	Weitler, A.—Estes, E.	Chicago	1,155
1929	Smith, M.—McQuade, D.	Chicago	1,123
1932	Frank, M.—Kerg, E.	Chicago	1,218
1934	Trettin, F.—Miller, D.	Chicago	1,190
1940	Morris, T.—Miller, D.	Chicago	1,181
1949	Elyasovich, A.—Svoboda, E.	Chicago	1,229
1954	Stennett, F.—Gacloch, R.	Chicago	1,244
1957	Vella, N.—Grazelack, J.	Rockford	1,218
1964	Werkmeister, G.—Garms, S.	Chicago	1,248

Individual champions from Illinois, 1917-66

Year	Bowler	City	Score
1925	Reich, E.	Chicago	622
1929	Higgins, A.	Chicago	637
1933	Twyford, S.	Aurora	628
1934	Clemensen, M.	Chicago	712
1938	Warner, B.	Waukegan	622
1940	Twyford, S.	Aurora	636
1948	Wernecke, S.	Chicago	696
1953	Baginski, M.	Chicago	737
1954	Martin, H.	Peoria	668
1955	Vella, N.	Rockford	695
1957	Towles, E.	Peoria	664
1959	Bolt, M.	Chicago	664
1961	Newton, E.	Park Forest	661

Ice Hockey

To excel at hockey a boy needs a sturdy frame, a tendency to mayhem, and a long, hard-frozen winter. The first two ingredients are as often present in Illinois as elsewhere, but before the days of artificial ice the third was problematical. In Canada, on the other hand, the lakes and streams freeze early and thaw late. A hockey stick and puck are as familiar to Canadian youngsters as a ball and bat to those of the United States. Perhaps that is why, in Illinois, hockey is important only as a spectator sport, and most of the great stars are developed in the upper lakes region and across the northern border.

Hockey as a professional sport did not come to Illinois until eight years after

World War I. The Black Hawks of Chicago were franchised in 1926 and for several years, until the stadium was built, played their games at the Coliseum on South Wabash. The Black Hawks have won the Stanley Cup, prize in the "world series" of hockey, three times—1934, 1938, and 1961. The cup was placed in competition throughout Canada in 1893, but until 1968 was the prize in the annual playoff among the top four teams of the National Hockey League. The Hawks have won the league championship only once—in 1966.

In 1964 the Hawks placed five men out of six appointed on the national league all-star team, officially selected by the league executives. They had a sixth on the second team. They had four of the six places on the first team in 1966 and one on the

second. These awards, made since 1930, carry with them $1,000 in prize money for selection on the first team and $500 for selection on the second team. There are also the Hart Trophy, first awarded in 1923 for most valuable player; the Lady Byng Trophy for sportsmanship, awarded annually since 1925; the Vezina Trophy, first granted in 1929, for best goalkeeper record; the Calder Memorial Trophy for rookie of the year, inaugurated in 1937; the Ross Trophy, from 1946, for individual scoring; and the James Norris Memorial Trophy, since 1954, for best defense man. All these trophies have been won three or more times by Black Hawks. A Hawk has won the Ross award ten times out of twenty-three. A Black Hawk, Stanley Mikita, is the only player ever to win hockey's triple crown—the Hart Trophy, the Lady Byng Trophy, and the Ross Trophy. Furthermore, he turned this hat trick twice, in 1967 and 1968.

All-stars from the Black Hawks

Year	On first team	On second team
1931	goal—Gardiner, Charles	
1932	goal—Gardiner, Charles	
1933		goal—Gardiner, Charles
1934	goal—Gardiner, Charles	
1935	goal—Chabot, Lorne	defense—Coulter, Thomas
1936		defense—Seibert, Earl
1937		left wing—Thompson, Paul
		defense—Seibert, Earl
1938	left wing—Thompson, Paul	defense—Seibert, Earl
1939		defense—Seibert, Earl
1940		defense—Seibert, Earl
1941		defense—Seibert, Earl
1942	defense—Seibert, Earl	
1943	defense—Seibert, Earl	
	left wing—Bentley, Douglas	
1944	defense—Seibert, Earl	
	left wing—Bentley, Douglas	
1945		goal—Karakas, Michael
1946	center—Bentley, Max	right wing—Mosienko, William
1947	left wing—Bentley, Douglas	center—Bentley, Max
1948		right wing—Poile, N. R. (Bud)
		left wing—Stewart, Gaye
		center—Bentley, Douglas
1949	left wing—Conacher, Roy	
1953		defense—Gadsby, William
1954		defense—Gadsby, William
1957		center—Litzenberger, Edward
1958	goal—Hall, Glenn	
1960	goal—Hall, Glenn	defense—Pilote, Pierre
	left wing—Hull, Robert	

Year	On first team	On second team
1961		goal—Hall, Glenn
1962	center—Mikita, Stanley left wing—Hull, Robert	goal—Hall, Glenn defense—Pilote, Pierre
1963	goal—Hall, Glenn defense—Pilote, Pierre center—Mikita, Stanley	left wing—Hull, Robert
1964	goal—Hall, Glenn left wing—Hull, Robert center—Mikita, Stanley right wing—Wharram, Kenneth defense—Pilote, Pierre	defense—Vasco, Elmer
1965	defense—Pilote, Pierre left wing—Hull, Robert	center—Mikita, Stanley
1966	goal—Hall, Glenn defense—Pilote, Pierre center—Mikita, Stanley left wing—Hull, Robert	defense—Stapleton, Patrick
1967	center—Mikita, Stanley left wing—Hull, Robert	defense—Pilote, Pierre defense—Wharram, Kenneth
1968	center—Mikita, Stanley left wing—Hull, Robert	

Trophies awarded to Black Hawk players

Hart Trophy (most valuable player)

Year	Player
1946	Bentley, Max
1954	Rollins, Albert
1965	Hull, Robert
1966	Hull, Robert
1967	Mikita, Stanley
1968	Mikita, Stanley

Lady Byng Trophy (sportsmanship)

1936	Romnes, Doc
1943	Bentley, Max
1945	Mosienko, William
1964	Wharram, Kenneth
1965	Hull, Robert
1967	Mikita, Stanley
1968	Mikita, Stanley

Vezina Trophy (best goalkeeper)

1934	Gardiner, Charles
1935	Chabot, Lorne
1963	Hall, Glenn

Calder Memorial Trophy (rookie of the year)

1936	Karakas, Michael
1938	Dahlstrom, Carl
1955	Litzenberger, Edward
1960	Hay, William

Ross Trophy (individual scoring)

Year	Player
1946	Bentley, Max
1947	Bentley, Max
1949	Conacher, Roy
1960	Hull, Robert
1962	Hull, Robert
1964	Mikita, Stanley
1965	Mikita, Stanley
1966	Hull, Robert
1967	Mikita, Stanley
1968	Mikita, Stanley

James Norris Memorial Trophy (best defenseman)

1963	Pilote, Pierre
1964	Pilote, Pierre
1965	Pilote, Pierre

National Hockey League record

Most goals one season:
1965–66   Hull, Robert   54

Players with 200 or more goals lifetime
(includes only goals with NHL)

Bentley, Douglas	219
Bentley, Max	245
Hull, Robert	414
Mikita, Stanley	255
Mosienko, William	258
Conacher, Roy	226

Black Hawks in Hall of Fame

Club presidents
    McLaughlin, Frederick
    Norris, James
 Players
    Bentley, Douglas
    Bentley, Max
    Brinsek, Francis
    Conacher, Charles (also a coach)
    Gardiner, Charles
    Hay, George
    Irvin, James Dickerson (also a coach)
    Lehman, Hugh
    Lorenz, Howard
    Mosienko, William
    Seibert, Earl
    Stewart, John

Academic Degrees

A.B. Bachelor of Arts
A.M. Master of Arts
B.E. Bachelor of Engineering
B.Ed. Bachelor of Education
B.L. Bachelor of Letters
B.Lit. Bachelor of Literature
B.S. Bachelor of Science
B.Sc. Bachelor of Science
B.S. in Ed. Bachelor of Science in Education
D.D. Doctor of Divinity
D.Ed. Doctor of Education
D.Sc. Doctor of Science
Ed.B. Bachelor of Education
Ed.D. Doctor of Education
E.E. Electrical Engineer
J.D. Juris Doctor (Doctor of Laws)
LL.B. Bachelor of Law
LL.D. Doctor of Law
LL.M. Master of Law
M.A. Master of Arts
M.D. Doctor of Medicine
M.Ed. Master of Education
M.S. in Ed. Master of Science in Education
M.S. in Ed. Master of Science in Educational Administration
Adm. Administration
Ph.B. Bachelor of Philosophy
Ph.D. Doctor of Philosophy

General

A.A.F. Army Air Forces
Acad. Academy
Adj. Adjutant
Adm. Administration
Adv. Advocate
A.E.F. American Expeditionary Force
A.F. Air Force
Agr. Agriculture
Ald. Alderman
Amb. Ambassador
App. Appointed
Art. Artillery
Assoc. Associate
Asst. Assistant
Att. Attorney
Aud. Auditor
A.U.S. Army of the United States
B. Born
Biog. Biographical
Brig. Brigadier
Bvt. Brevet or brevetted
C. in C. Commander in Chief
Ca. About

C.J. Chief Justice
Cand. Candidate
Capt. Captain
Cav. Cavalry
Chm. Chairman
Co. County
Col. Colonel
Coll. Collector
Comm. Commissioner
Conf. Conference
Cong. Congress
Const. Constitutional
Conv. Convention
Corp. Corporation
Cpl. Corporal
D. Died
Del. Delegate
Dem. Democrat
Dept. Department
D.F.C. Distinguished Flying Cross
Dir. Director
Dist. District
Div. Division
D.S.C. Distinguished Service Cross
D.S.M. Distinguished Service Medal
Ed. Editor
ETO European Theater of Operations
Exec. Executive
F.A. Field Artillery
FBI Federal Bureau of Investigation
Fed. Federal
G.A.R. Grand Army of the Republic
Gen. General
Gov. Governor
Grad. Graduate or graduated
H.R. House of Representatives
H.S. High School
Indp. Independent (in politics)
Inf. Infantry
Inst. Institute
Instr. Instruction or instructor
Int. Rev. Internal Revenue
J.P. Justice of the Peace
Jud. Judicial
Just. Justice
Leg. Legislature or legislative
Lt. Lieutenant
Maj. Major
M.C. Medical Corps
Med. Medical
Mem. Member
Mfr. Manufacturer
Min. Minister
Mun. Municipal

MTO Mediterranean Theater of Operations
N. Near
Nat. National
N.G. National Guard
O.R.C. Officers' Reserve Corps
O.R.T.C. Officers' Reserve Training Corps
P.M. Postmaster
Pract. Practice or practiced (generally, began practice)
Pres. President or Presidential
Prin. Principal
Prof. Professor
Prog. Progressive
Pros. Prosecuting
PTO Pacific Theater of Operations
Pub. Public
Pvt. Private
Q.M. Quartermaster
Rcvr. Receiver of Public Moneys
Reg. Register
Regt. Regiment
Rep. Republican
Res. Resident
R.R. Railroad
Sec. Secretary
Sem. Seminary
Sen. Senate
Sgt. Sergeant
Spec. Special
Spkr. Speaker
Supt. Superintendent
Tech. Technical
Ter. Territory or territorial
Treas. Treasurer
Twp. Township
U. University
U.S.A. United States Army
U.S.A.F. United States Air Force
U.S.A.R. United States Army Reserve
U.S.M.A. United States Military Academy, West Point
U.S.M.C. United States Marine Corps
U.S.N. United States Navy
U.S.N.A. United States Naval Academy, Annapolis
Vol. Volunteer
V.P. Vice President
Y.M.C.A. Young Men's Christian Association

18

Famous
Illinoisans

This compilation is, of necessity, arbitrary. No living persons have been included. Cross references to the chapter on state officers, senators, and congressmen are to the first office the subject held in Illinois. For instance, Abraham Lincoln is referenced to his term in Congress, 1847–49. Illinois has been omitted after names of places in the state in the following biographies. See page 489 for abbreviations.

Robert Sengstacke Abbott Founder of *Chicago Defender*. b. St. Simon's Island, Ga., Nov. 24, 1870. Attended Claflin and Hampton Inst. LL.B. Chicago-Kent College of Law, 1900; pract. Chicago, and Gary, Ind. Founded *Defender*, May 5, 1905. Mem. Ill. Race Relations Commission; dir. Urban League Chicago; donor Chicago Civic Opera. d. Chicago, Feb. 29, 1940.

Jane Addams Settlement house worker, founder of Hull House. b. Cedarville, Sept. 6, 1860. A.B. Rockford, 1881; studied in Europe. Opened Hull House, 1889. Author *Democracy and Social Ethics* (1902), *Newer Ideals of Peace* (1904), *Twenty Years at Hull House* (1910), and other volumes. Honorary LL.D. Wisconsin, 1904; Smith, 1910; Tufts, 1923; Northwestern, 1929; Chicago, 1930. Honorary A.M. Yale, 1910. Shared Nobel Peace Prize with Nicholas Murray Butler, 1931. d. Chicago, May 21, 1935.

George Ade Author, playwright, fabulist. b. Kentland, Ind., Feb. 9, 1866. B.S. Purdue, 1887. Journalist Lafayette, Ind., 1887–90. Reporter, feature writer *Chicago Morning News* (became *Chicago Record*), 1890–1900. In 1893 Ade and cartoonist John Tinney McCutcheon initiated an un-

signed feature, "Stories of the Streets and the Town" from which Ade developed his first three books: *Artie: A Story of the Streets and the Town* (1896), *Pinky Marsh* (1897), and *Doc Horne* (1899). First "Fable in Slang" appeared in 1897, the year the column was first signed. Collection, *Fables in Slang*, published Dec. 1899, became the Book of the Year, 1900. Ade left *Record* to syndicate "Fables in Slang," 1900, continued column nationally until 1933. Author *The County Chairman, The College Widow, The Sultan of Sulu*, and other memorable books, plays, and operettas. Resided Hazelden Farm, n. Brook, Ind., until his death, May 16, 1944.

Dankmar Adler Architect. b. Langsfeld, Saxe-Weimar, Germany, July 3, 1844. Emigrated as child with parents to Detroit, Mich., 1854. Studied architecture Detroit and Chicago, 1857–62. Served with 1st Ill. Art., 1862–65. Pract. architecture Chicago, 1869; with A. J. Kinney to 1871, Edward Burling, 1871–78, Louis Sullivan, 1880–95. Architect for the Auditorium and McVicker's Theater (with Louis Sullivan), Carnegie Music Hall in New York City, and many churches, synagogues, and office buildings in Chicago, St. Louis, Mo., Buffalo, N.Y., and other cities. d. Chicago, April 15, 1900.

David Adler Architect. b. Chicago, 1882. Mem. Ill. Society of Architects. Designed many large homes and estates in Chicago and North Shore area. d. Libertyville, Sept. 27, 1949.

Peter Akers Clergyman, educator, author. b. Campbell Co., Va., Sept. 1, 1790. Mostly self-educated. Removed to Ky.; read law; admitted Ky. bar, 1817. After four years pract. was converted and became a Methodist min. Removed to Ill., 1832. Pres. McKendree, 1833, 1834, and 1852–57. Presiding elder Jacksonville from 1865. Published scholarly *Biblical Chronology* about 1835. His accounts of life as circuit rider and exhorter in early Ill. were widely read. d. Jacksonville, Feb. 21, 1886.

Robert Allerton Philanthropist. b. Chicago, March 20, 1873 (son of Samuel, founder of Union Stock Yards, Chicago, and owner of 12,000 acres rich Illinois farm land). Ambition to be an artist led to years of study in Munich and Paris and the conviction he had insufficient talent for greatness. On father's death, 1914, returned to Monticello to manage family estate. Made gifts to Art Inst. of Chicago, the last one in 1963, totaling more than $2,000,000. Gave 6,000 acres and the family mansion to U. of Illinois for plant reserve and animal refuge in 1946. Made Lihue, Kauai, Hawaii, his winter home from 1938. Gave $1,000,000 to botanic garden there. d. Lihue, Hawaii, Dec. 22, 1964.

Jean Claude Allouez Jesuit missionary. b. Saint-Didier, Haute-Loire, France, June 6, 1622. Emigrated to Montreal, P.Q., 1658. Founded missions of La Pointe d'Esprit, Ashland, Wis., 1665; St. Francis Xavier, Green Bay, Wis., 1669; Rapides des Pères (Fox River of Wis.), 1671. On Marquette's death, 1675, he was assigned to continue the work at Kaskaskia on the Illinois, but did not reach his post until the spring of 1677. Devoted the rest of his life to the Ill. Indians and to the Miamis. d. Ft. St. Joseph, n. present-day Niles, Mich., Aug. 27, 1689.

John Peter Altgeld Gov. Ill., 1893–97. *See* chapter on state officers.

Adrian Constantine Anson Baseball player, manager Chicago National League club, the White Stockings. b. Marshalltown, Iowa, 1852 (first white child born there). Played amateur ball on Marshalltown team, composed almost entirely of his father and brothers. Joined Rockford Forest Cities professional club, then signed with Chicago. Named manager, 1879; brought five pennants to Chicago between 1880 and 1886; retired 1901. Anson's batting average of .407 in 1879 still tops both Chicago major league clubs. d. Chicago, April 14, 1922.

Phillip Danforth Armour Meat packer, founder Armour & Company. b. Stockbridge, N.Y., May 16, 1832. Common school education. Mined in Calif., 1852–56; commission merchant, Milwaukee, 1856–63. Pres. Armour & Company, 1870. Founder Armour Mission and Armour Inst. of Technology (now Illinois Inst. of Technology). d. Chicago, Jan. 6, 1901.

Isaac Newton Arnold U.S.H.R., 1861–65. *See* chapter on state officers.

Edward Dickinson Baker U.S.H.R., 1845–46, 1849–51. *See* chapter on state officers.

Theron Baldwin Educator, clergyman. b. Goshen, Conn., July 21, 1801. B.A. Yale, 1827. Ordained missionary, 1829; mem. of famous "Yale Band" of home missionaries in Ill. Congregational min. Vandalia, 1830; active in founding Illinois College, Jacksonville; trustee, 1831–70. Prin. Monticello Female Sem., Godfrey, 1838–43. Active as lecturer and preacher in Ill. until late in life. d. Orange, N.J., April 10, 1870.

Oliver Roger Barrett Lawyer, collector of Lincolniana. b. Jacksonville, Oct. 14,

1873. LL.B. Michigan, admitted Ill. bar, 1896; pract. Peoria. Removed to Chicago, 1905. Began search for Lincoln material as young man, achieved most notable collection in private hands. Pres. board of trustees Ill. State Historical Library. His fame as collector overshadowed his considerable reputation as a trial lawyer. d. Kenilworth, March 5, 1950.

Newton Bateman Educator, historian. Supt. pub. instr., 1859–63, 1865–75. *See* chapter on state officers.

Bertha Elizabeth Baur Political and social leader. b. Doppler Mineral Point, Wis., Oct. 22, 1871. Grad. business college; sec. to postmasters Chicago. Married Jacob Baur, pres. Liquid Carbonic. Mem. women's bureau Rep. nat. conv., 1900; precinct capt. Chicago, 1900–1967. Pres. elector, 1924; Rep. nat. committeewoman, 1928–52; hostess Rep. nat. conv., 1952. Trustee Chicago Civic Opera; mem. Mississippi Park Commission; trustee and founder mem. A Century of Progress. d. Chicago, July 10, 1967.

Jean Baptiste Beaubien Fur trader. b. Detroit, Mich., 1780. Moved to Chicago, 1813. J.P. Chicago, 1825. Col. Ill. militia Black Hawk War, 1832, brig. gen., 1850. Claim to seventy-five acres on site of Ft. Dearborn approved by Cong. but disallowed by Supreme Court. Moved to Nashville, Tenn., 1858. d. Nashville, Tenn., Jan. 5, 1863.

Mary Ann Ball Bickerdyke Volunteer army nurse, called by troops "Mother Bickerdyke." b. Knox Co., Ohio, July 19, 1817. Studied at Oberlin; qualified as nurse in Cincinnati, Ohio, hospitals. Married Robert Bickerdyke, 1847; moved to Galesburg, 1856, listed as botanic physician. Established hospital with Grant's forces Cairo; served with Grant and Sherman until March 20, 1865. When Civil War ended, she became pension att. Resettled 300 families of soldiers in Kansas. After missionary work Chicago and New York, N.Y., moved to Bunker Hill, Kans., 1874. d. Bunker Hill, Kans., Nov. 8, 1901.

Frank Billings Physician, surgeon, teacher, administrator. b. Highland, Wis., April 2, 1854. M.D. Northwestern, 1881. Mem. Northwestern Med. faculty, 1882–98. Pres. Chicago Med. Society, 1890. Prof. of med. Rush Med. College, Chicago, 1898; dean of faculty from 1900. Chm. American Red Cross mission to Russia, 1917. Col.

M.C. U.S.A. A.E.F., 1918. Pres. Ill. State Board of Charities and State Charities Commission, 1906–12. d. Chicago, Sept. 20, 1932.

Morris Birkbeck Sec. state Ill., 1824. *See* chapter on state officers.

William Harrison Bissell U.S.H.R., 1849–55; gov. Ill., 1857–60. *See* chapter on state officers.

Greene Vardiman Black Pioneer oral surgeon. b. n. Winchester, Aug. 3, 1836. Studied dentistry, pract. Winchester, 1857. Enlisted 129th Ill. Vols., 1862; discharged for disability, 1863. Lecturer dental pathology, Missouri Dental College, 1870–80; D.D.S., 1877. Prof. dental pathology Chicago Dental School, 1883–89; M.D. Chicago Med., 1884. Prof. dental pathology Iowa, 1890, Northwestern, 1891; dean and prof. operative dentistry, 1897–1915. Many honorary degrees and other honors. d. Chicago, Aug. 31, 1915.

Black Hawk Indian Chief Ma-Ka-Tai-me-she-kia-kiak, leader of Sac and Fox. b. Sac Village (now Rock Island), 1767. Opposed Treaty of St. Louis granting Indian lands to Ind. Ter., 1804. Fought with British under Tecumseh War of 1812. Invaded Ill. from Iowa, 1832, to repossess tribal lands; defeated at Bad Axe, Wis. Deposed by Keokuk, taken to Washington for visit with Pres. Jackson, 1833. d. Sac Village on the Des Moines River, Oct. 3, 1838.

Rufus Blanchard Cartographer, historian. b. Lyndeboro, N.H., 1821. Educated by private tutors. Came to Wheaton as youth; taught in log-cabin schools. Mapped many areas of Northwest. Wrote histories of Ill., Chicago, the Old Northwest, several Indian tribes, and a political history of the U.S. d. Wheaton, 1904.

Shadrach Bond First gov. Ill., 1818–22. *See* chapter on state officers.

Myra Colby Bradwell Lawyer, editor, suffragist. b. Manchester, Vt., Feb. 12, 1831. Removed with parents to Chicago, 1843. Grad. Ladies' Sem., Elgin; taught school. In 1852 married James B. Bradwell; worked and read law with him in Chicago from 1855. Founded *Chicago Legal News*, 1868; edited this weekly publication until her death. In 1869 passed bar examinations but was refused admission Ill. bar on grounds her married status was a disqualifying disability. U.S. Supreme Court upheld decision of Ill. Supreme Court on grounds state had right to prescribe qualifications for practice. In 1882 Mrs. Bradwell procured passage of an act of the Ill. General Assembly guaranteeing to all persons freedom to choose a profession irrespective of sex. Admitted Ill. bar on original application, 1885, and to practice before U.S. Supreme Court, 1892. Mem. of Board of Lady Managers for World's Columbian Exposition, 1893. d. Chicago, Feb. 14, 1894.

James Henry Breasted Archeologist, historian. b. Rockford, Aug. 22, 1865. A.B. North Central; A.M. Yale; Ph.D. U. of Berlin, 1894. Asst. in Egyptology U. of Chicago, 1894–96; asst. dir. Haskell Oriental Museum, 1895–1901; dir., 1901–31. Prof. Egyptology and Oriental history, 1905–33; numerous field expeditions. Dir. Oriental Inst. in Near East, 1915; dir. Oriental Inst., 1919–35. Author many texts on Egyptian history. Honorary degrees from Oxford, Yale, Princeton, and U. of California. d. New York, N.Y., Dec. 2, 1935.

Sidney Breese Just. Ill. Supreme Court, 1841–43, 1857–78. *See* chapter on state officers.

William Bross Lt. gov. Ill., 1865–69. *See* chapter on state officers.

Edward Eagle Brown Banker, lawyer. b. Chicago, June 4, 1885. A.B. Harvard, 1905; LL.B. Harvard, admitted Ill. bar, 1908; pract. Chicago. Gen. counsel First Nat. Bank of Chicago, 1910–23; v.p., 1923–34; pres., 1934–45; Chm. board, 1945–59. Chm. Fed. Advisory Council Fed. Reserve System, 1939–55. d. Chicago, Aug. 24, 1959.

Orville Hickman Browning U.S. Sen., 1861–63. *See* chapter on state officers.

William Jennings Bryan U.S. sec. state. b. Salem, March 18, 1860. LL.B. Union College of Law (now Northwestern), admitted Ill. bar, 1883; pract. Jacksonville, 1883–87, Lincoln, Nebr., 1887–94. U.S.H.R. from Neb., 1891–95. Dem. cand. Pres., 1896, 1900, and 1908. Col. 3rd Nebr. Vols. (which he raised), 1899. App. sec. state by Pres. Wilson, 1913; resigned, June 9, 1915. Helped prosecute John Thomas Scopes for teaching Darwinism in Tenn. schools. d. during trial, Dayton, Tenn., July 26, 1925.

Kate Sturges Buckingham Art patron. b. Zanesville, Ohio, Aug. 3, 1858. Brought to Chicago by parents as infant. Inherited family wealth and art treasures of her brother Clarence, which she gave to the Art Inst. of Chicago. Erected fountain in Grant Park as memorial to her brother. Directed in her will that statue of Alexander statue, be erected in Lincoln Park; after much controversy, statue finally accepted by Chicago and erected near Diversey Parkway in Lincoln Park. Asked for information for the archives of the Chicago Historical Society, she listed her name, address, parents' names, Zanesville as her former home, and wrote in longhand on the data sheet, "If this isn't enough information you may count me *out*! ! !" d. Chicago, Dec. 14, 1937.

Ida B. Wells Burnett Editor. b. Holly Springs, Miss., July 16, 1862. Grad. Fisk. Part owner *Free Speech*, Memphis; driven out by mob, newspaper plant destroyed, 1892. In Chicago joined staff of the *Conservator*, founded by Ferdinand Lee Burnett, whom she married, 1895. Lectured, wrote, campaigned for equal rights for Negroes until her death in Chicago, March 25, 1931.

Daniel Hudson Burnham Architect. b. Henderson, N.Y., Sept. 4, 1846. Moved with parents to Chicago, 1856. Studied architecture at U. of Chicago. Member Burnham & Root, 1873–91; D. H. Burnham & Company, 1891–1912. Designed buildings in Chicago, Cleveland, Ohio, San Francisco, Calif., London. Planned cities of Manila, Bagnio, and portions of Chicago and San Francisco. Architect World's Columbian Exposition, 1893. d. Heidelberg, Germany, June 1, 1912.

Étienne Cabet Philosopher, writer. b. Dijon, France, Jan. 1, 1788. LL.D. Dijon, 1812. Elected deputy, 1831, but exiled for his part in revolution of 1830. Lived in England, where he came under influence of Robert Owen. In *A Voyage en Icaria* (1839; rev. ed., 1840) he proposed a Christian community where an elected government would control business and manufacturing, and, except for the family, would be the only social unit. Migrated to Tex. with followers, 1848. Settlement failed, and in 1849 founded an Icarian community at Nauvoo. Driven out by dissenting members, Cabet died in St. Louis, Mo., Nov. 8, 1856. Fragmentary Icarian communities survived in Iowa until 1898.

Frances Xavier Cabrini Founder Missionary Sisters of the Sacred Heart. b. St. Angelo, Lodigiano, Italy, July 15, 1850. Began work as nun in home parish, 1868; founded missionary order at Codogno, 1880. Came to U.S. to work with Italian immigrants, 1889; in Chicago from 1891. Founded hospitals of same name, Columbus, in New York and Chicago, many schools and orphanages worldwide. Beatification inquiries instituted by Cardinal Mundelein; beatified, Nov. 13, 1938. Canonized (first and only American saint), July 7, 1946; known as Chicago's own saint. d. Chicago, Dec. 22, 1917.

Joseph Gurney Cannon U.S.H.R., 1873–91, 1893–1913, 1915–23. *See* chapter on state officers.

Peter Cartwright Methodist clergyman, circuit rider. b. Amherst Co., Va., Sept. 1, 1775. Moved with parents to Ky., 1801. Converted, received instruction from Bishop William McKendree. Ordained deacon, 1806, elder, 1808. Received $40 a year for preaching in 1824, $60 in 1825, and considered it sufficient. Opposing slavery, asked assignment in Sangamon Co., 1824. Ill. H.R., 1828–30, 1832–34. Defeated by Lincoln for U.S.H.R., 1846. Presiding elder in Ill. forty-five years. d. Pleasant Plains, Sept. 25, 1872.

Mary Hartwell Catherwood Novelist. b. Luray, Ohio, Dec. 16, 1847. Grad. Granville, Ohio, Sem. Taught school, Danville. Married James Catherwood, merchant in Indianapolis, Ind., and later postmaster in Hoopeston. Published many successful romantic novels from 1875 until her death, Chicago, Dec. 26, 1902.

John D. Caton Just. Ill. Supreme Court, 1842–64. *See* chapter on state officers.

Octave Chanute Engineer, aeronaut. b. Paris, France, Feb. 18, 1832. Emigrated to New York with parents, 1838. Educated in private schools. Civil engineer Hudson River R.R., 1853–63. Chief engineer Chicago & Alton R.R., 1863–67. Bridged Missouri River at Kansas City. Consulting engineer, 1873–83. Began study of aerodynamics, 1883. Built and flew successful gliders; published works on aerodynamic theory which helped advance flight. d. Chicago, Nov. 23, 1910.

George Rogers Clark Soldier. b. n, Charlottesville, Va., Nov. 19, 1752, Farmer, surveyor in northeast Ohio, fought Shawnees in 1774. Removed to Ky. 1775. Maj. Ky. militia, 1776; col. and brig. gen., 1778. Led expedition to capture Kaskaskia and the Ill. country, 1778; recaptured Vincennes, Ind., Feb. 1779. After war led militia against Indian marauders in Ind. and Ohio. Settled veterans of his revolutionary command on large tract across Ohio River from Louisville, Ky. d. n. Louisville, Ky., Feb. 18, 1818.

Ralph Clarkson Portraitist. b. Amesbury, Mass., Aug. 3, 1861. Studied at Museum of Fine Arts, Boston, Julian Academy, Paris. Exhibited in Paris and Chicago, 1887. Painted in N.Y. and Europe, 1888–95. Moved to Chicago, 1895. Many times pres. Chicago Society of Artists. Juror Art Section Paris Exposition, 1900; Louisiana Purchase Exposition St. Louis, 1904; Pan-Pacific Exposition San Francisco, 1915. Juror Corcoran Gallery, Art Inst. of Chicago. d. Orlando, Fla., April 3, 1942.

Henry Ives Cobb Architect. b. Brookline, Mass., Aug. 19, 1859. B.S. Harvard, 1880; attended Massachusetts Inst. of Technology; completed architectural training Europe. Moved in 1881 to Chicago as architect for Union Club. Mem. nat. board architects for World's Columbian Exposition. Designed Newberry Library, several buildings of U. of Chicago, and other Chicago buildings now demolished; important work elsewhere, including entire town at South San Francisco, Calif. d. Chicago, March 27, 1931.

Edward Coles Second gov. Ill., 1822–26. See chapter on state officers.

Robert Collyer Clergyman. b. Keighley, Yorkshire, England, Dec. 8, 1823. Worked in linen mill thirteen hours daily from age eight; apprentice blacksmith at age fourteen; self-educated. Began preaching, 1849; emigrated to Philadelphia, 1850; followed blacksmith trade and preached. Became Unitarian, moved to Chicago, 1859, as min.-at-large First Unitarian Church. Later that year invited to become pastor Unity Church. Preached sermon amid ashes of church the Sunday after Chicago fire, 1871. Predicted city would rise and "the glory of the latter house shall be greater than the former." Became pastor Messiah Church, New York, 1879. d. New York, N.Y., Nov. 30, 1912, ripe in years and honors.

Arthur Holly Compton Physicist. b. Wooster, Ohio, Sept. 10, 1892. B.S. Wooster, 1913; A.M. Princeton, 1914; Ph.D. Princeton, 1916. Prof. physics Chicago, 1923–45; Nobel Prize in physics (with Charles T. R. Wilson), 1927. Chm. dept. physics and dean physical sciences, 1940–45. Head physics dept. Washington, St. Louis, 1945–53. Lecturer in many countries, including India, and at many U.S. universities. Regent Smithsonian Inst., 1938–62; trustee John Crerar Library, 1939–45; chm. board Wooster, 1940–53.

Many gold medals and honorary degrees. Mem. advisory board John S. Guggenheim Memorial Foundation, 1938–62. Protestant chm. Nat. Conf. of Christians and Jews, 1938–62. d. Berkeley, Calif., March 15, 1962.

Daniel Pope Cook First att. gen. Ill. See chapter on state officers.

Ira Clifton Copley U.S.H.R., 1911–23. See chapter on state officers.

Frank Crane Minister, journalist, a pioneer syndicated columnist. b. Urbana, May 12, 1861. Ordained min., 1892; Ph.B. Illinois Wesleyan, 1892; D.D. Nebraska Wesleyan, 1894. Pastor Chicago, 1896–1903, Worcester, Mass., 1904–9. Ed. *Current Opinion*; author many books on devotional subjects. Syndicated editorial column in 100 newspapers from 1909 until death, Los Angeles, Calif., Nov. 6, 1928.

Richard Teller Crane Manufacturer. b. Paterson, N.J., May 13, 1832. Laborer; moved to Chicago, 1855. His uncle, Martin Ryerson, helped him start foundry which grew into the huge Crane Company, makers of boilers, elevators, plumbing fixtures. Philanthropist. d. Chicago, Jan. 8, 1912.

John Crerar Financier, philanthropist. b. New York, N.Y., March 8, 1827. Common school education; bookkeeper. Moved to Chicago in 1862; started iron and steel business. By bequest established John Crerar Library specializing in scientific and technical works. Benefactor of Chicago Historical Society. d. Chicago, Oct. 19, 1889.

Edward A. Cudahy Packer, philanthropist. b. Milwaukee, Wis., Feb. 1, 1859 (son of Patrick Cudahy). Moved to Chicago in employ of Armour & Company, 1875. V.P. Cudahy Packing Company, 1887, pres., 1910. Mem. Chicago Historical Society. Built library for Loyola of Chicago as memorial to his wife. d. Chicago, Oct. 18, 1941.

Shelby Moore Cullom U.S.H.R., 1865–71; gov. Ill., 1877–83. See chapter on state officers.

Helen Culver Teacher, philanthropist. b. Cattaraugus Co., N.Y., 1832. Attended acad.; teacher. Came to Chicago to help cousin, Charles J. Hull, when his wife was invalided. Willed the Hull fortune and the family mansion, she leased mansion to Jane Addams at no rent and gave $170,000 to support Miss Addams' work. Continued Hull's social projects. Gave $1,000,000 to U. of Chicago to build Hull Biological Laboratories. Active in aid to homeless boys, other philanthropies until death, Lake Forest, Aug. 19, 1925.

Walter Joseph Cummings Banker. b. on farm n. Springfield, June 24, 1879. Moved to Chicago with parents as young boy. Educated in parochial and pub. schools; LL.B. Loyola of Chicago, 1915. Served in various capacities with Continental Nat. Bank of Chicago from 1915. In 1934 elected chm. board on recommendation of Reconstruction Finance Corp. Retired as chm. bd., 1959, as chm. exec. committee, 1960, and as dir., Jan. 23, 1961. d. Chicago, Aug. 19, 1967.

Clarence Seward Darrow Trial lawyer. b. Kinsman, Ohio, April 18, 1857. Pub. school education. Admitted Ohio bar, 1878; pract. Ashtabula, Ohio. Moved to Chicago, 1888. Defended McNamara brothers, accused of dynamiting *Los Angeles Times*, 1911. Often appeared in defense of labor and leftist individuals and organizations; self-styled "counsel for the damned." Att. for Loeb and Leopold, killers of Bobby Franks in Chicago. Defended John Thomas Scopes, opposing William Jennings Bryan. d. Chicago, March 13, 1938.

Abel Davis Lawyer, soldier. b. Chicago, Dec. 26, 1874. Pvt. Spanish-American War, served in Cuba. LL.B. Northwestern, admitted Ill. bar, 1901; pract. Chicago. Ill. H.R., 1903-4. Recorder Cook Co., 1904-12. Maj. Ill. N.G. on Mexican border, 1915. Col. 132nd Inf., 1917-19; brig. gen. Ill. N.G., 1919-35. V.P. Chicago Title & Trust Company, 1912-31, chm. board, 1931-37. d. Glencoe, Jan. 7, 1937.

David Davis U.S. Sen., 1877-83; just. U.S. Supreme Court, 1862-77. *See* chapter on state officers.

Nathan Smith Davis Known as "father of the American Medical Association." b. Greene, N.Y., Jan. 9, 1817. M.D. College of Physicians and Surgeons, Fairfield, N.Y., 1837. Pract. Vienna, N.Y. Moved to New York City, 1847, to Chicago, 1849. Prof. physiology and pathology Rush Med. College, 1849-59. Leader of movement for pure water and adequate sewers in Chicago which led to establishment of Sanitary Dist. Founder, with others from Rush Med., of Lind Med. College, which became Chicago Med. College and later med. dept. of Northwestern. Dean of faculty and prof. emeritus Northwestern Med. School. A founder of Chicago Historical Society, Chicago Acad. of Sciences, Union College of Law (now Northwestern), Ill. Med. Society, and American Med. Association. Ed. and author, *A Code of Medical Ethics* (1903). d. Chicago, June 16, 1904.

Charles Gates Dawes V.P. U.S. b. Marietta, Ohio, Aug. 27, 1865. A.B. Marietta, 1884; LL.B. Cincinnati Law School, 1886; A.M. Marietta, 1887. Admitted Nebr. bar, 1886; pract. Lincoln, Nebr. to 1894. Moved to Chicago. U.S. comptroller currency, 1897-1901. Pres. Central Trust Company of Ill., 1902-21; chm. board, 1921-25. World War I maj. engineers, June 1917; lt. col., July, col. Jan. 1918, brig. gen. Oct. 1918; gen. purchasing agent A.E.F.; D.S.M. and many allied decorations. Author Dawes Plan for German reparations, which restored German currency and halted financial dissolution. V.P. U.S., 1925-29. Amb. to Great Britain, 1929-32. Nobel Peace Prize (with Sir Austen Chamberlain), 1925. d. Evanston, April 23, 1951.

Rufus Cutler Dawes Utilities executive. b. Marietta, Ohio, July 30, 1867. A.B. Marietta, 1886; A.M. 1889. Adviser to committee preparing plan for German reparations named for his brother, Charles Gates Dawes, 1923. Pres., A Century of Progress exposition Chicago, 1933-34. d. Evanston, Jan. 8, 1940.

John Deere Inventor, manufacturer. b. Rutland, Vt., Feb. 7, 1804. Attended Middlebury. Learned blacksmith trade, moved to Grand Detour, 1836. Made first successful steel plow, 1837. Moved factory to Moline, 1847; sole owner, 1853. Output passed 10,000 plows yearly, 1857; instituted time-payment plan, 1858. First mayor Moline, 1873. Gold Medal Paris Exposition, 1875, for Deere gang plow. In 1883 produced 58 per cent of all plows made in U.S. d. Moline, May 17, 1886.

Charles Samuel Deneen Gov. Ill., 1905-13. *See* chapter on state officers.

Spencer C. Dickerson Physician, surgeon, brig. gen. M.C. U.S.A. b. Austin, Tex., Dec. 1, 1871. Attended Tillotson School, Austin; B.S. Chicago; M.D. Rush Med. College, 1901. Pract. New Bedford, Mass. Moved to Chicago, 1907. Taught at Rush; associated with Provident Hospital forty-one years. From capt. to col. M.C. A.E.F. 1917-19; retired as brig. gen. Specialist eye, ear, nose, throat; internationally recognized in field. d. Chicago, Feb. 25, 1948.

Walter Elias Disney Cartoonist, producer. b. Chicago, Dec. 5, 1901. Red Cross ambulance driver France, 1917 and 1918. Became cartoonist, 1920; created idea of one drawing for each frame in animation. Achieved fame with Mickey Mouse, 1928;

Silly Symphonies followed same year (first animation in color). *Three Little Pigs* (1933), *Snow White and the Seven Dwarfs* (1938). *Fantasia* (1940) was first attempt to couple classical music with animated cartoons. Adventure stories, documentaries, and finally live productions occupied him until his death, Burbank, Calif., Dec. 15, 1966. His fantastic tourist attraction, Disneyland, brings people from around the world to Anaheim, Calif.

Stephen Arnold Douglas Just. Ill. Supreme Court, 1841–43; U.S. Sen., 1847–61. *See* chapter on state officers.

Peter Finley Dunne Satirist. b. Chicago, July 10, 1867. Educated pub. schools, Chicago. Reporter *Chicago Herald* and other Chicago newspapers, 1884–92; ed. *Evening Journal*, 1896. Removed to New York City, 1900; ed. *Morning Telegraph*; part owner *American Magazine*; ed. *Collier's Weekly*. Retired 1911 to write; author of *Mr. Dooley* sketches and satires, of which ten volumes were published between 1898 and 1919, and a collected edition in 1938. d. New York, N.Y., April 14, 1936.

Ninian Edwards U.S. Sen., 1818–24; gov. Ill. Ter., 1809–18. *See* chapter on state officers.

John Evans Founder Evanston, physician. b. Waynesville, Ohio, March 9, 1814. M.D. Lynn Med. College, Cincinnati, 1838. Pract. Attica, Ind., 1838–45. Head Ind. Hospital for the Insane, Indianapolis, Ind., 1845–48. Prof. obstetrics Rush Med. College, 1848–62. Ald., 1853 and 1854. With Orrington Lunt and Nathan Smith Davis, a founder of Northwestern. Made a fortune in Cook Co. real estate. App. ter. gov. Colorado, 1862; served to 1865. Founded Colorado Sem. which became Denver U. Built Denver Pacific (Denver to Cheyenne), South Park, and Denver & New Orleans railroads. Mt. Evans, west of Denver, named for him. d. Denver. Colo., July 3, 1897.

Eugene Field Poet, journalist. b. St. Louis, Mo., Sept. 2, 1850. Early orphaned, raised by relatives in Amherst, Mass. Grad. Missouri, 1872. Reporter, city ed. in Mo. and Colo. Moved to Chicago, 1883; columnist ("Sharps and Flats") *Morning News*, morning edition of *Chicago Daily News*, later renamed *Record*. Wrote poems of childhood of great popular appeal, fiction, and scholarly translations of Horace's *Odes*. d. Chicago, Nov. 4, 1895.

Marshall Field Merchant. b. n. Conway, Mass., Aug. 18, 1834. Boyhood on farm; left school at age eighteen. Clerk Pittsfield, Mass., 1852–56. Moved to Chicago; clerk, manager, Cooley, Wadsworth & Company to 1864; partner, Cooley, Farwell & Company to 1868; partner Milton Palmer and Levi Z. Leiter in 1868. Bought out partners, store became Marshall Field & Company, 1881. Founded Museum of Natural History, now on Chicago lakefront, 1893, with gift of $1,000,000. With nephew, Stanley, and grandson, Marshall Field III, gave $13,844,000 to endow museum and erect present building. d. New York, N.Y., Jan. 16, 1906.

Marshall Field III Publisher, philanthropist. b. Chicago, Sept. 28, 1893. Educated Eton and Cambridge, England. Pres. Field Foundation. Pres. Field Enterprises which publishes *Chicago Daily News, Sun-Times, World Book Encyclopedia*, and *Childcraft*. Trustee Chicago Museum Natural History, Metropolitan Museum of Art, New York. World War I 122nd F.A., promoted through grades pvt. to capt.; two battle stars. Pres. Child Welfare League of America. d. New York, N.Y., Nov. 8, 1956.

Thomas Ford Historian. Gov. Ill., 1842–46. *See* chapter on state officers.

Milton J. Foreman Lawyer, lt. gen. Ill. N.G. b. Chicago, Jan. 26, 1863. Worked from boyhood, studied night school. Admitted Ill. bar, 1899; pract. Chicago. Ald. Chicago, 1899–1911. Capt. 1st Ill. Cav., 1898; col. 1st Cav. Ill. N.G., 1906–17. Col. 122nd F.A. A.E.F., 1917–19; brig. gen. 33rd Div., 1920; maj. gen. commanding 33rd Div., 1921–31. Retired with rank lt. gen. d. Chicago, Oct. 16, 1935.

Henry Blake Fuller Author. b. Chicago, Jan. 9, 1857. Attended h.s. Chicago; studied in Europe. First novel, *The Chevalier of Pensieri-Vani* (1891), ran five editions; best known in Ill. for *The Cliff-Dwellers* (1893). Edited book review section of *Chicago Evening Post*, 1901 and 1902. Editorial writer *Chicago Record-Herald*, 1912 and 1913. Aided Harriet Monroe in publishing *Poetry*. d. Chicago, July 28, 1929.

Melville Weston Fuller C.J. of the United States. b. Augusta, Maine, Feb. 11, 1833. A.B. Bowdoin, 1853; A.M., 1856. Admitted Maine bar; pract. Augusta, Maine, 1855. Moved to Chicago, 1856; pract. Chicago to 1888. Ill. H.R. 1863–64. App. C.J., April 1888; confirmed, July 20; sworn in, Oct. 8. Mem. permanent Court of Arbitration, The Hague, 1900–1910. d. (in office) at summer home, Sorrento, Maine, July 4, 1910.

Lyman Judson Gage Sec. of treasury U.S., banker. b. Deruyter, N.Y., June 28, 1836. Educated Rome, N.Y., Acad. Moved to Chicago, 1855. Bookkeeper, 1858–61, cashier, 1861–68, Merchants Loan & Trust Company. Cashier, 1868–82, v.p., 1882–91, pres., 1891–97, First Nat. Bank of Chicago. Sec. of treasury U.S., 1897–1902. Pres. U.S. Trust Company, New York, N.Y., 1902–6. d. San Diego, Calif., Jan. 26, 1927.

Irene McCoy Gaines Political and social leader. b. Ocala, Fla., ca. 1896. Grad. Fisk, 1917. Three times pres. Nat. Association of Colored Women's Clubs. Pres. Citizens Advisory Committee to Chicago Plan Commission. Honorary degree Doctor of Humanities Wilberforce, 1962. Mem. of exec. board, Illinois Child Labor Committee. d. Chicago, April 8, 1962.

George Washington Gale Clergyman, pioneer in manual arts education. b. Stanford, Dutchess Co. N.Y., Dec. 3, 1789. A.B. Union, 1814; D.D. Princeton, 1816. Licensed to preach. Established Oneida Inst. (manual labor school) at Whitesboro, N.Y., 1827. Removed to Ill., 1835; established Knox Manual Labor College; around it grew city of Galesburg; name changed to Knox College, 1857. With aid of wealthy wife established large endowment. Taught at Knox until his death, Galesburg, Sept. 30, 1861.

Mary Garden Opera star. b. Aberdeen, Scotland, April 13, 1877. Brought to Chicago as child by parents; educated pub. schools. Studied voice with Mme Robinson-Duff, who took her to Paris in 1897; pupil of Fugère and Trabadello; protégée of Sybil Sanderson. Debut Opera Comique as substitute in *Louise* at beginning of second act, 1900. Signed with Hammerstein's Manhattan Opera Company, 1907. Returned to Chicago, 1909, as star of Chicago-Philadelphia Grand Opera Company, later Chicago Grand Opera Company, which she directed, and Chicago Civic Opera Company, with which she remained until its demise, 1932. Greatest roles were Melisande, Thaïs, Fiora in *L'Amore dei Tre Re*, Katusha in *Resurrection* (which she created in Chicago), and Salome, which was barred by Chicago police after third performance, but welcomed in Milwaukee, Wis., and elsewhere. Richard Strauss wrote *Der Rosenkavalier* for her in 1913, but she never performed the role of Octavian, due to outbreak of World War I. Her parents remained in Chicago until late in life.

Mary Garden retired in 1932, except for occasional concert and lecture tours of the U.S. d. Aberdeen, Scotland, Jan. 3, 1967.

Hamlin Garland Author. b. n. Salem, Wis., Sept. 4, 1860. Grad. Cedar Valley Sem., Iowa, 1881. Taught in Ill. rural schools, 1881 and 1882. Moved to Chicago, 1893. Wrote adult and boys' fiction, a biography of U. S. Grant, Indian history. Founder and first pres. The Cliff Dwellers, a Chicago literary and artistic club. d. Los Angeles, Calif., March 4, 1940.

Elbert Henry Gary Lawyer, financier. b. on farm n. Wheaton, Oct. 8, 1846. Attended Wheaton; LL.B. Chicago, admitted Ill. bar, 1867; pract. Chicago and Wheaton. Judge Du Page Co. Court, 1882–90. Pres. Federal Steel Company, 1898. Organized U.S. Steel Corp. with backing of J. P. Morgan & Company, 1900. Chm. and chief exec. officer, 1903–27; Chm. finance committee, 1907–27. d. New York, N.Y., Aug. 15, 1927.

John Warne Gates Promoter, nickname, "Bet-a-Million." b. Turner Junction (now West Chicago), May 8, 1855. Pioneered manufacture of barbed wire, 1878; pres. Ill. Steel Company, 1894. Consolidated wire interests into the American Steel & Wire Company, 1898. Helped form Republic Iron & Steel Company, 1906. Speculator N.Y. Stock Exchange. During last few years of life oil interests in Spindletop took him to Port Arthur, Tex. d. Paris, France, Aug. 9, 1911.

Benjamin Godfrey Sailor, merchant, banker. b. Chatham, Mass., Dec. 4, 1794. Ran away to sea at nine; served U.S.N. War of 1812. Shipwrecked in Gulf of Mexico in 1820's; established a business, liquidated it with profit of $200,000, and lost entire amount to bandits en route from Matamoros to New Orleans; prospered in New Orleans. Moved to Alton, 1832; befriended Elijah Parish Lovejoy, abolitionist ed. With Winthrop S. Gilman, gained control of State Bank at Alton, bankrupted it by loans to themselves to promote river trade at Alton. After bank failed Godfrey pioneered in railroad construction. Founded Monticello Female Sem. d. Godfrey, April 13, 1862.

Ulysses Simpson Grant Pres. U.S., 1869–77. b. Point Pleasant, Ohio, April 27, 1822. Grad. U.S.M.A., 1843. With Taylor in Mexico, 1845–47, with Scott in 1847;

active all battles from Buena Vista to Chapultepec. Bvt. capt., 1848; promoted capt., 1853; resigned commission, 1854. Failed as farmer, 1854–60. Leather merchant Galena, 1860–61. Col. 21st Ill. Vols., June 1861, promoted brig. gen., Aug. 1861. Captured Fts. Donelson and Henry. Promoted maj. gen. vols., 1862. Commanded at Shiloh, 1862; captured Vicksburg, 1863; supreme command U.S.A. in West, defeated Bragg at Chattanooga. Given command of U.S.A. with rank lt. gen., 1864. Defeated Lee after year's campaign, 1865. Promoted gen. (first use of rank since George Washington). Sec. war, 1867. Elected Pres., 1868, reelected, 1872. d. Mount McGregor, N.Y., July 23, 1885.

Benjamin Henry Grierson Maj. gen. U.S.A., cavalry leader. b. Pittsburgh, Pa., July 8, 1826. Taught music Jacksonville, 1850. Grain merchant. Enlisted pvt. Ill. Vols., 1861; commissioned, made aide to Gen. Prentiss, May 1861. Maj. 6th Ill. Cav., Oct. 1861; col., April 8, 1862; brig. gen., 1863; maj. gen. vols., 1865. Led cav. raid from La Grange, Tenn., to Baton Rouge, La., April 1863. Commissioned col. A.U.S., 1866; brig. gen., bvt. maj. gen., 1867. Commanded depts. of Tex. and Ariz. and dist. of N. Mex. Retired to Jacksonville, 1890. d. at summer home, Omena, Mich., Aug. 31, 1911.

Frank Wakeley Gunsaulus Educator, clergyman. b. Chesterville, Ohio, Jan. 1, 1856. Grad. Ohio Wesleyan, 1875. Entered Congregational ministry, 1879. Preached in many states. Came to Chicago, 1887. Left Congregational Church to become pastor of independent Central Church, 1899; preached there until 1919. Pres. Armour Inst. of Technology (now Illinois Inst. of Technology) from founding in 1893 until his death. Noted as lecturer, active in civic affairs; biographer of Martin Luther. d. Chicago, March 19, 1921.

James Hall Author, editor. Treas. Ill., 1827–31. See chapter on state officers.

William Rainey Harper Scholar, educator. b. New Concord, Ohio, July 26, 1856. Grad. Muskingum, 1870; Ph.D. Yale, 1875. Prin. Masonic College, Macon, Tenn., 1875–76. Prof. of Hebrew at Baptist Union Theological Sem., Chicago, 1879–86. Prof. Semitic languages Yale, 1886–91. Head dept. Semitic languages and pres. Chicago until death, Jan. 10, 1906.

Carter Henry Harrison U.S.H.R., 1875–79; mayor Chicago, 1879–87, 1893. See chapter on state officers.

Carter Henry Harrison II Politician (Dem.), writer, mayor of Chicago five times. b. Chicago, April 23, 1860. Grad. St. Ignatius, Chicago, 1881; A.M., LL.B. Yale. Admitted to Ill. bar, 1883; pract. Chicago to 1889. Ed. *Chicago Times*, 1892–95. Mayor, 1897–1905, 1911–15. With American Red Cross in France, 1917 and 1918. Wrote essays, sketches, biographies until death, Chicago, Dec. 25, 1953.

John Milton Hay Diplomat, historian. b. Salem, Ind., Oct. 8, 1838. LL.D. Brown, admitted Ill. bar, 1858; pract. Springfield. Sec. to Pres. Lincoln, 1861–65. Bvt. col. vols. Sec. legation Paris, Madrid, Vienna, chargé d'affaires Vienna, 1865–70. Journalist New York, N.Y., Cleveland, Ohio, and Springfield, 1870–78. Asst. sec. state U.S., 1878–81. Wrote biography of Lincoln, with John G. Nicolay, (ten volumes, 1890). Amb. Great Britain, 1897 and 1898. Sec. state U.S., 1898–1905. Responsible for "open door" policy with China and the Hay-Pauncefote treaties. d. Newberry, N.H., July 1, 1905.

George Peter Alexander Healy Portrait painter. b. Boston, Mass., July 15, 1813. Studied in Paris. Established studio Chicago, 1855, painted many leading citizens; mem. American Acad. of Design. Largest collection of his work in Chicago Historical Society; other work in Art Inst. of Chicago, Metropolitan Museum of Art, New York, and Corcoran Gallery, Washington, D.C. Portrait of C.J. Roger B. Taney in Capitol, Washington, D.C.; self-portrait in Uffizi Gallery, Florence, Italy. After 1866 lived in Europe until 1892, when he returned to Chicago. d. Chicago, June 24, 1894.

Ernest Hemingway Author. b. Oak Park, July 21, 1898. American ambulance driver and with Italian inf. World War I. First success, *The Sun Also Rises*, was written in Paris. Other principal works, *A Farewell to Arms, For Whom the Bell Tolls, Death in the Afternoon, Across the River and into the Trees, The Old Man and the Sea.* Pulitzer Prize, 1953; Nobel Prize, 1954. Suicide, Ketchum. Idaho, July 2, 1961.

James Butler Hickok Known as "Wild Bill," soldier, scout, U.S. marshal border posts. b. Troy Grove, May 27, 1837. Constable in Johnson Co., Kans., 1856. Drove stage, 1857 (killed a bear with a bowie knife); Union scout and spy, 1861–65. Dept. of U.S. marshal Fort Riley, Kans., 1866 and 1867. Marshal, Hays City, Kans., 1869–71, Abilene, Kans., 1871. Toured with

Buffalo Bill Cody, 1872 and 1873. Moved to Deadwood, Dak. Ter. 1873. Murdered, Aug. 2, 1876, by Jack McCall at Deadwood.

James R. Holbert Agronomist, pioneer hybridizer of corn. b. n. Muncie, Ind., July 18, 1890. B.S. (Agr.) Purdue, 1915. Researcher on inbred and hybrid corn at Funk Farms, Bloomington, 1915–18. Dir. U.S. Dept. of Agr. experimental field station on Funk Farms, 1918–37. Developed fungus- and insect-resistant corn hybrids, hardy cold-weather strains, and drought-resistant plants. With R. R. St. John in 1936 produced hybrid U.S. 13, which succeeded during drought years and in arid areas because of low water requirements. As v.p. in charge of research, 1937, he established research program on nation-wide basis and developed hybrids suited to many climatic zones. d. Feb. 8, 1947, at his desk in Bloomington.

Henry Horner Gov. Ill., 1933–40. See chapter on state officers.

Gurdon Saltonstall Hubbard Fur trader, early Chicago packer. b. Windsor, Vt., Aug. 22, 1802. Apprentice American Fur Company, 1818–23, ran station on Iroquois River. Partner, 1827. Bought Ill. interests of American Fur Company, 1828. Ill. H.R. from Vermilion Co., 1832–34. Moved to Chicago, opened packing house, 1834. Suffered heavy losses in Chicago fire, 1871. d. Chicago, Sept. 14, 1886.

Charles J. Hull Social worker, philanthropist. b. n. Manchester, Conn., March 18, 1820. Meager schooling, largely self-educated. Orphan, tended uncle's tavern bar from age twelve to seventeen; teacher, 1837. Removed to Chicago, 1846, became wealthy as owner of hardware store; wiped out by a fire. Entered Rush Med, College, 1849; M.D. Rush, 185Î. Entered Harvard Law School, 1851; LL.B. Harvard, 1853. Bought and sold land, made huge fortune. Founded a home for penitent intemperates; founded Chicago Newsboys' Home; helped poor acquire homes of their own. Built mansion which became Hull House, 1856. When wife became ill, a cousin, Helen Culver, came to his home to help with family. Hull willed his estate to her with broad instructions as to its disposition. d. Chicago, Feb. 12, 1889.

Harvey Bostwick Hurd Father of Chicago Sanitary District. b. Huntington, Conn., Feb. 14, 1828. Attended Jubilee College, Peoria, 1844 and 1845; attended Chicago Law School. Admitted Ill. bar 1848; pract. Chicago. Prof. Chicago (now Chicago-Kent) Law School, 1862–92. Official reviser

of Ill. statutes (seventeen editions). Originated Chicago Drainage Canal system. Author of Torrens Act of Ill. for registration of titles and of first juvenile court act (April 22, 1899) which revolutionized treatment of juvenile dependents and offenders. d. Evanston, Jan. 20, 1906.

Michael Lambert Igoe U.S.H.R., 1935–36. See chapter on state officers.

Robert Green Ingersoll Att. gen. Ill., 1867–69. See chapter on state officers.

Samuel Insull Public utilities executive. b. London, England, Nov. 11, 1859. Attended Oxford. Emigrated to New York, 1881. Pvt. sec. Thomas Edison. Operated Edison Machine Works, Schenectady, N.Y., and after consolidation of Edison enterprises was second v.p. in charge manufacturing. Moved to Chicago, 1892. Pres. Chicago Edison Company and Commonwealth Electric Company, 1892–1907, Commonwealth Edison Company, 1907–30, chm. board, 1930–32. Prin. supporter Chicago Civic Opera. d. Paris, France, July 16, 1938.

Edmund Janes James Educator, author. b. Jacksonville, May 21, 1855. Studied at Harvard; A.M. and Ph.D. from U. of Halle, Germany, 1877; many honorary degrees. Prin. Evanston H.S., 1878 and 1879; prin. of a model h.s. at Normal, 1879–82. Prof. finance Wharton School of Finance, U. of Pennsylvania, 1883–95; prof. political and social science Pennsylvania, 1884–95. Dir. Extension Div. U. of Chicago, 1896–1901. Pres. Northwestern, 1902–4. Pres. Illinois, 1904–19, pres. emeritus, 1920–25. d. Covina, Calif., June 17, 1925.

William Le Baron Jenney Architect, inventor. b. Fairhaven, Mass., Sept. 25, 1832. Grad. Harvard Scientific School and École Centrale des Arts et Manufactures, Paris, 1856. Capt. and maj. on staffs of Grant and Sherman, 1861–66. Moved to Chicago, 1868; pract. architecture. Inventor of skeleton construction for tall buildings, utilizing cast-iron columns and Bessemer steel beams. d. Los Angeles, Calif., June 15, 1907.

Jens Jensen Landscape architect, artist. b. Schleswig, Denmark, Sept. 13, 1860. Emigrated to U.S., 1884, to Chicago, 1886. Supt. Humboldt Park to 1900. Supt. and landscape architect, West Park System from 1900. Creator of Lincoln Memorial Garden at Springfield. Retired to Ellison Bay, Door

Co., Wis., 1935, where he died on Oct. 1, 1951.

Louis Jolliet Explorer. b. n. Beaupré, Quebec, Sept. 21, 1645. Educated in France (hydrographer). Explored for copper on shores of Lake Superior, 1669; pioneered route via Lake St. Clair from Mackinac to Montreal, 1669. As cartographer explored Mississippi and Illinois rivers with Marquette, 1673, Trader and explorer Hudson Bay area, 1694. Royal prof. and hydrographer for Canada. d. while exploring lower St. Lawrence region, May 1700.

John Jones Merchant. b. Greene Co., N.C., Nov. 3, 1816(?). Apprenticed to tailor in Memphis, Tenn. Moved to Alton, 1845, then to Chicago. Opened shop at Clark and Randolph streets; self-educated. Helped obtain repeal of "black laws" just after Civil War. Opposed separate schools for Negro and white children. Donated land for Jones Elementary School at Harrison and Plymouth Court. Cook Co. comm., 1871–75 (first Negro to hold pub. office in Chicago). d. Chicago, May 21, 1879.

J. Wesley Jones Choral leader. b. in Tennessee, Sept. 8, 1884. Postal employee Chicago, 1914–54. First Negro to become supt. of a postal station in Chicago, 1950. A founder of the Nat. Association of Negro Musicians, which granted its first scholarship to Marian Anderson. For twenty-five years leader of one thousand-voice Negro choir at Chicagoland Festival of Music. Dir. music Metropolitan Community Church. Authority on Negro folk music. d. Chicago, Feb. 11, 1961.

Robert Kennicott Naturalist, explorer. b. New Orleans, La., Nov. 13, 1835. Moved with parents as infant to Northfield; educated by father. A founder of Chicago Acad. of Science, 1857, curator, 1863. Organized Museum of Natural History for Northwestern, 1857. Explored northern Canada and collected fauna for Smithsonian Institution, 1859. App. to explore land route to Asia and Europe for Western Union Company, 1865. d. during first stages of task at Ft. Nulato, Alaska, May 13, 1866.

Keokuk Fox Indian leader. b. Sac Village (now Rock Island), 1790. Took over Black Hawk's position, 1812, during latter's absence in Canada. Succeeded Black Hawk as chief Sac and Fox tribes after defeat at Bad Axe, Wis., 1832. d. Sac Indian Agency, Franklin Co., Kans., 1848.

David Kinley Educator. b. Dundee,

Scotland, Aug. 2, 1861. Emigrated to U.S. with father, 1872. A.B. Yale, 1884. Teacher. Postgrad. studies and instructor Johns Hopkins, 1890. Fellow and instructor Wisconsin, 1892 and 1893; Ph.D. Wisconsin, 1893. Asst. prof. economics Illinois, 1893; prof. economics and dean of literature and arts, 1894–1906. Dir. courses in commerce and dean grad. schools, 1906–19. Pres. Illinois, 1920–30; pres. emeritus from 1930. Chm. board First Nat. Bank Champaign, 1932–44. d. Champaign, Dec. 3, 1944.

John Kinzie Fur trader. b. Quebec, P.Q., Dec. 3, 1763. Trader on Maumee River, 1781, on St. Joseph River, 1796. Bought Pointe du Sable's post at mouth Chicago River from Jean Lalime, 1804; enlarged it. Escaped Ft. Dearborn massacre, 1812. Imprisoned Detroit by British; returned to Chicago, 1816. Aided comms. in Indian treaty negotiations, 1821. J.P. Chicago, 1825. d. Chicago, Jan. 6, 1828.

Joseph Kirkland Author. b. Geneva, N.Y., Jan. 7, 1830. Self-taught pioneer in realistic fiction. Moved to Chicago, 1856, employed by Illinois Central R.R. Enlisted U.S.A., 1861; commissioned lt., promoted capt. and maj. on McClellan's staff; discharged, 1863. Admitted Ill. bar at age fifty. Spec. correspondent, reviewer, literary ed., *Chicago Tribune*, 1890. Influenced development of Hamlin Garland. Best-known novel is *Zury: The Meanest Man in Spring County*; wrote a history of Chicago. d. Chicago, April 29, 1894.

Gustave Philipp Koerner Just. Ill. Supreme Court, 1845–48; lt. gov. Ill., 1853–57. *See* chapter on state officers.

Kenesaw Mountain Landis Jurist. b. Millville, Ohio, Nov. 20, 1866. Named for Civil War battle in which father was wounded. LL.B. Union College of Law (now Northwestern). Admitted Ill. bar; pract. Chicago, 1891. App. just. U.S. Dist. Court, Northern Ill. Dist., 1905. Fined Standard Oil Company $20,000 on each of 1,426 counts charging acceptance of rebates from Chicago & Alton R.R. Fine never paid because Supreme Court reversed decision, but Standard Oil was broken up into several smaller corporations. In 1918 Landis tried and sentenced "Big Bill" Haywood and 93 members of Industrial Workers of the World for obstructing war program; Haywood fled to Russia. In 1922 Judge Landis became high comm. baseball; served until his death Chicago, Nov. 25, 1944.

Robert Cavelier, Sieur de la Salle Explorer. b. Rouen, France, Nov. 22, 1643. Trained as Jesuit, left order in 1665.

Established seigniory at Lachine, Canada, 1666. May have discovered upper Ohio River in 1669. Returned to France, received patent of nobility, 1673. Returned to Canada, and undertook exploration of Mississippi and its tributaries. Given fur-trading rights, built Ft. Crevecoeur (now Peoria), 1680. Explored lower Mississippi and claimed all its drainage area for France, 1682. Returned to France, named viceroy of North America, 1683. Killed by own men near Brazos River in what is now Tex., March 19, 1687, while trying to locate mouth of Mississippi.

Albert Davis Lasker Advertising executive. b. of American parents in Germany, 1880. Came to Chicago, 1898. Employed by Lord & Thomas advertising agency the same year and owned the company twelve years later. Pioneered network radio. Asst. sec. agr. U.S., 1917–19. Head of U.S. Shipping Board, 1921. Trustee U. of Chicago, 1937–42. Dir. Jewish Charities Chicago many years. Liquidated advertising agency and retired, 1942. d. New York, N.Y., May 30, 1952.

Julia Clifford Lathrop Social worker. b. Rockford, 1858. A.B. Vassar, 1880. Assoc. of Jane Addams, Hull House, Chicago. Aided in founding world's first juvenile court (Chicago), 1899. Head of U.S. Children's Bureau, 1912–21. Mem. League of Nations Child Welfare Commission, 1925. d. Rockford, April 15, 1932.

Victor Freemont Lawson Editor, publisher *Chicago Daily News*. b. Chicago, Sept. 9, 1850. Attended Phillips-Andover Acad. Bought *News*, 1876, with Melville E. Stone; purchased Stone's interest, 1888. Dir. and pres. Associated Press, 1894–1900. Philanthropist. d. Chicago, Aug. 19, 1925.

James Hamilton Lewis U.S. Sen., 1913–19, 1931–39. *See* chapter on state officers.

Lloyd Downs Lewis Journalist, historian. b. Pendleton, Ind., May 2, 1891. A.B. Swarthmore, 1913. Journalist Philadelphia, Pa., and Chicago, 1913–19; advertising writer, 1920–30. Drama critic, sports ed. *Chicago Daily News*, 1931–43. Lecturer history, U. of Chicago, 1937 and 1938. Managing ed. *Chicago Daily News*, 1943–45. Author *Myths After Lincoln* (1929); *Chicago: The History of Its Reputation*, with Henry Justin Smith, (1929); *Sherman, Fighting Prophet* (1932); *Jayhawker*, with Sinclair Lewis, (1935); *John S. Wright, Prophet of the Prairies* (1941); *It Takes All Kinds* (1947); *Captain Sam Grant* (1949). d. Chicago, April 21, 1949.

Abraham Lincoln U.S.H.R., 1847–49;

Pres. U.S., 1861–65. *See* chapter on state officers.

Robert Todd Lincoln Attorney, sec. war U.S. b. Springfield, Aug. 1, 1843 (son of Abraham Lincoln). A.B. Harvard, 1864. Capt. on Grant's staff, 1864–65. Admitted Ill. bar, 1867; pract. Chicago. Sec. war, 1881–85. U.S. min. to Great Britain, 1889–93. Spec. counsel Pullman Company, 1894–97; pres. Pullman Company, 1897–1911. Moved to Washington, D.C., in 1912 where he died July 26, 1926.

Nicholas Vachel Lindsay Poet. b. Springfield, Nov. 16, 1879. Studied at Hiram, 1897–1900; at Art Inst. of Chicago, 1900–1903; at New York School of Art, 1904 and 1905. Penniless, walked through South, paying way by sale of poems. Best known for his poems "The Congo," "The Eagle That is Forgotten," and "Abraham Lincoln Walks at Midnight." d. by his own hand, Springfield, Dec. 5, 1931.

Henry Demarest Lloyd Journalist, author. b. New York, N.Y., May 1, 1847. A.M. Columbia; admitted N.Y. bar, 1869; pract. New York. Helped defeat Tammany Hall, 1872. Moved to Chicago, joined staff of *Tribune*, 1872. Investigated monopolistic corporations; was called "first of the muckrakers." Left *Tribune*. 1885; traveled and wrote on behalf of labor. d. Winnetka, Sept. 28, 1903.

John Alexander Logan U.S.H.R., 1859–61, 1867–71; U.S. Sen., 1871–77, 1879–86. *See* chapter on state officers.

Stephen Trigg Logan Jurist, a law partner in Springfield of Lincoln. b. Franklin Co., Ky., Feb. 24, 1800. Educated Frankfort pub. schools. Admitted Ky. bar, 1820; pract. Barren Co., Ky., Moved to Sangamon Co., Ill., 1832; farmed. Moved to Springfield, resumed pract. of law. Judge circuit court, 1835–37. Ill. H.R., 1842–48, 1855–56. Lincoln said of him: "The most thorough and accomplished lawyer I have ever known." d. Springfield, July 17, 1880.

Elijah Parish Lovejoy Abolitionist. b. Albion, Kennebec Co., Maine, Nov. 9, 1802. Grad. Waterville (now Colby), 1826. Studied theology at Princeton. Moved to St. Louis, Mo., 1833. Edited *St. Louis Observer*, Presbyterian weekly newspaper, advocated gradual emancipation. Harassed by his enemies, he moved his printing plant to Alton, 1836, and continued to publish his paper. On July 4, 1837, he called a meeting of adherents to establish an Ill.

Auxiliary of the American Antislavery Society. Organization completed Oct. 26, whereupon mob destroyed his press for a third time. On the night of Nov. 7, 1837, while guarding another new press, he was slain by a mob.

Owen Lovejoy Abolitionist. U.S.H.R., 1857–64. *See* chapter on state officers.

Frank Orren Lowden U.S.H.R., 1906–11; gov. Ill., 1917–21. *See* chapter on state officers.

Orrington Lunt Philanthropist. b. Bowdoinham, Maine, Dec. 24, 1815. Partner in father's store. Moved to Chicago, 1842; successful in wheat market. An incorporator of Galena & Chicago R.R. Retired in 1862, devoted rest of life to charities. With John Evans, founder of Northwestern; sec.-treas. for many years. d. Evanston, April 5, 1897.

John Alexander McClernand U.S.H.R., 1843–51, 1859–61. *See* chapter on state officers.

Cyrus Hall McCormick Inventor and manufacturer. b. Rockbridge Co., Va., Feb. 15, 1809. Little schooling. Invented and patented a hillside plow, 1831, and, with father, a reaping machine, 1834. Erected factory Chicago, 1847; developed mower, rake, and other implements. Honored in England, made chevalier and later officer of French Legion of Honor, and mem. French Acad. of Sciences. Pioneer of creative business methods, philanthropist, active Presbyterian layman. d. Chicago, May 13, 1884.

Robert Rutherford McCormick Publisher *Chicago Tribune*. b. Chicago, July 30, 1880. B.A. Yale, 1903; attended Northwestern Law School. Ald. Chicago, 1904–6; pres. Sanitary Dist., 1905–10. Admitted Ill. bar, 1908; pract. Chicago. Maj. 1st Ill. Cav. (border patrol), 1916 and 1917; A.E.F. (Pershing's staff), 1917; maj. 5th F.A., lt. col. 122nd F.A. Ill. N.G.; col. 51st F.A. U.S.A.; D.S.M. Author. Published *Tribune* 1919 to his death, Chicago, April 1, 1955.

Myrtle Reed McCullough (pen name **Myrtle Reed**) Poet, author. b. Norwood Park, Sept. 27, 1874. Grad. West Division H.S. First book, *Love Letters of a Musician* (1899), was a popular success. Best-known work *Lavender and Old Lace* (1902). *The Master's Violin* (1904) was a bestseller. Three works published posthumously included *Threads of Gold and Gray* (1913). d. Chicago, Aug. 17, 1911.

John Tinney McCutcheon Cartoonist, war correspondent. b. n. South Bend, Ind., May 6, 1870. Moved with parents to LaFayette, Ind., 1876; B.S. Purdue, 1889. Cartoonist *Chicago Morning News* (became *Chicago Record*), 1889–1901, *Chicago Record-Herald*, 1901–3, *Chicago Tribune* from 1903. Covered battle of Manila Bay from dispatch boat *McCullough*; with Boers in South Africa, 1900. In Mexico and on border, 1914; with Germans and Belgians, 1914; in France and Balkans, 1915 and 1916. Crossed Gobi Desert, 1925, over Andes and down Amazon same year. Pulitzer Prize (cartoons), 1932. Retired 1946. d. Chicago, June 10, 1949.

James Hubert McVicker Actor, theatrical manager. b. New York, N.Y., Feb. 14, 1822. Moved to St. Louis, Mo., 1837, as printer's apprentice. Moved to New Orleans, La., about 1840, where he joined a repertory company at the St. Charles Theater. Made Chicago debut, 1848; toured U.S. and England for several years. Opened his own theater in Chicago, 1857. Three times remodeled or rebuilt his theater; his last, in 1891, was designed by Louis Sullivan and Dankmar Adler. d. Chicago, March 7, 1896.

Jacques Marquette Jesuit missionary. b. Laon, France, June 1, 1637. Taught in France until 1666. Emigrated to Quebec, then to Three Rivers. Replaced Father Allouez at La Pointe d'Esprit, Ashland, Wis., 1669; founded mission of St. Ignace, Straits of Mackinac, 1671. With Louis Jolliet discovered upper waters of Mississippi, traveling from Green Bay via the Fox and Wisconsin rivers to the Mississippi, canoeing to the mouth of the Arkansas, and returning via the Illinois River, Chicago portage, and Lake Michigan to Green Bay, 1673. Established mission to Ill. Indians at Kaskaskia on the Illinois River, 1675. Died en route from Kaskaskia to Mackinac, near site of Ludington, Mich., on river named for him, May 18, 1675.

Edgar Lee Masters Poet, political essayist, lawyer. b. Garnett, Kans., Aug. 23, 1869. Moved with parents as infant to Petersburg, then to Lewistown. Grad. Knox, 1889. Read law in father's office; admitted Ill. bar, 1891. At one time, partner with Clarence Darrow. First great success, 1915, *Spoon River Anthology*, collection of verse published in *Reedy's Mirror*, St. Louis, Mo. Abandoned flourishing law practice in 1920 to devote entire time to writing. Among noted works a long narrative poem, *Doomsday Book*, and a heroic saga of Robert E. Lee. Among his prose a derogatory book on Abraham Lincoln, the man, was much criticised. d. Philadelphia, Pa., March 5, 1950.

Oscar F. Mayer Meat packer, philanthropist. b. Kasingen, Wurtemberg, Germany, March 29, 1859. Emigrated with parents to U.S., 1871. Moved with brother to Chicago, established meat market which soon became packing house, 1878. Oscar Mayer & Company now has plants in Chicago and Beardstown; Davenport and Perry, Iowa; Philadelphia, Pa., and Los Angeles, Calif. d. Chicago, March 11, 1955.

Joseph Medill Publisher *Chicago Tribune*. b. n. St. John, New Brunswick, April 6, 1823. Moved to Stark Co., Ohio, with parents, 1832. Admitted Ohio bar, 1846; pract. Coshocton, Ohio. Ed. *Coshocton Whig*, which he renamed *Republican*, 1849. Established *Daily Forest City* (Cleveland, Ohio), 1851; merged with *Cleveland Leader*. A founder of the Rep. party. Moved to Chicago, 1854, bought an interest in *Chicago Tribune*; helped elect Lincoln. Became majority stockholder of *Tribune*, 1874. Mayor Chicago, 1871–75. d. San Antonio, Tex., March 16, 1899.

Wesley Merritt Maj. gen. U.S.A. b. New York, N.Y., June 16, 1834. Moved with parents as infant to Belleville, then to Salem. Appointed to West Point, 1855; grad. 1860. Aide to Gen. Philip Cooke, commander cav. Army of Potomac; capt. vols., 1862, brig. gen., 1863; received six successive bvts. for gallantry from Gettysburg to Appomattox. Supt. West Point, 1882–87. Promoted maj. gen. U.S.A., 1897; commanding gen. Manila, 1898, captured city without bombardment. Del. peace conf. Paris. Retired, 1900. d. Natural Bridge, Va., Dec. 3, 1910.

Albert Abraham Michelson Physicist. b. Strelno, Prussia, Dec. 19, 1852. Emigrated to Virginia City, Nev., with parents; attended pub. schools. Removed to San Francisco, Calif., where he led his classes in h.s. Grad. U.S.N.A., 1873; instructor physics Annapolis, 1875–79. Grad. study Berlin, Heidelberg, and Paris. Prof. Case Inst. of Applied Science, 1883–89, Clark, 1889–92. Head physics dept. Chicago, 1892–1931; prof. emeritus, 1931. Nobel Prize in physics, 1907. Pioneer in measuring speed of light. Eleven honorary degrees and gold medals, including grand prize Paris Exposition, 1900. d. Pasadena, Calif., May 9, 1931.

William Henry Milburn Clergyman, author. b. Philadelphia, Pa., Sept. 26, 1823. Almost blinded by glass thrown in eye at age five; largely self-educated. Exhorter

(with Peter Akers) on Illinois circuit. Ordained deacon, Sept. 17, 1845. Chaplain U.S.H.R., 1845; U.S. Cong., 1853; U.S.H.R., 1885 and 1887; U.S. Sen. 1893, 1895, 1897. Traveled, lectured, published accounts of career in early Illinois. d. Santa Barbara, Calif., April 10, 1903.

Robert Andrews Millikan Physicist. b. Morrison, March 22, 1868. A.B. Oberlin, 1891; Ph.D. Columbia, 1895. Asst. in physics Chicago, 1896; assoc., 1897; instructor, 1899; asst. prof. 1902; prof. of physics and dir. Ryerson Physical Laboratory, 1910. Maj., lt. col., Signal Corps, World War I, dir. science research div.; mem. Munitions Board. In 1921 left Chicago to become prof. of physics and dir. of the Norman Bridge Laboratory of Physics at Throop Inst. of Technology, Pasadena, Calif. Received Nobel Prize in physics, 1923, for work on cosmic rays done principally at Chicago. In 1922 Millikan became v.p. board of trustees, and Throop was renamed California Inst. of Technology. As chief exec. officer, Millikan attracted famous men to Pasadena by pointing out proximity of one of the world's great libraries, the Huntington Memorial Library, and the excellent research facilities at the inst. Pres. Medal of Merit World War II, many honors and degrees; mem. Nat. Acad. of Science. Author of advanced and college texts in physics and popular works relating to science. d. Pasadena, Calif., Dec. 19, 1953.

Harriet Monroe Author, poet, b. Chicago, Dec. 23, 1860. Educated Acad. of the Visitation, Georgetown, D.C. Wrote the *Columbian Ode* for opening of World's Columbian Exposition in 1893. Published two volumes of verse, one of prose, between 1893 and 1912. Founded *Poetry: A Magazine of Verse*, Oct. 1912; established large annual prizes. Published work by Sandburg, Vachel Lindsay, and many others. d. Arequipa, Peru, Sept. 26, 1936, on a tour of South America.

Dwight Lyman Moody Lay evangelist. b. Northfield, Mass., Feb. 5, 1837. Education limited, worked on farm until 1854. Clerk Boston, 1854–56. Moved to Chicago, 1856; organized Sunday School class of 1,000 children. Organized an interdenominational church, 1863. Pres. Chicago Y.M.C.A., 1866. Toured world as evangelist 1873–99, returning to Chicago frequently; joined by Ira D. Sankey about

1875. Founded present Moody Bible Institute. Moody was never ordained. d. Northfield, Mass., Dec. 22, 1899.

Ira Nelson Morris Financier, diplomat. b. Chicago, March 8, 1875. Attended Yale. Succeeded father as pres. Nelson Morris & Company. Min. Sweden, 1914-23. Rumanian consul gen. Chicago, 1926-42. Grand officer French Legion of Honor. d. Chicago, Jan. 15, 1942.

James A. Mulligan Soldier. b. Utica, N.Y., June 25, 1830. Removed with parents to Chicago, 1836; Grad. St. Mary's of the Lake, Chicago, 1850; studied law. Col. 23rd Ill. Reg. (Irish Brigade), 1861; refused promotion to stay with regiment. Dashing soldier, severely wounded, returned to action; twice captured; fatally wounded leading charge, Winchester. Died in Confederate hands, July 26, 1864, at Winchester, Va.

George William Mundelein Clergyman. b. New York, N.Y., July 2, 1872. A.B. Manhattan, 1889; studied Rome, ordained 1895. Became monsignor, 1906; auxiliary bishop Brooklyn, 1909. Named archbishop of Chicago, 1915, and a cardinal, 1924. Hosted Eucharistic Congress, 1926. Bitter critic of Hitler. Concerned with poverty, slums, and juvenile delinquency. d. Chicago, Oct. 2, 1939.

Walter Loomis Newberry Philanthropist. b. East Windsor, Conn., Sept. 18, 1804. Moved to Buffalo, 1822, to Detroit, Mich., 1826. Adj. gen. Mich. Ter., 1829-31; ald. Detroit, 1832. Moved to Chicago, 1833. Founder and first pres. Young Men's Library Association, 1841. Made fortune in real estate, bequeathed much of it to found Newberry Library, Chicago. d. at sea, Nov. 6, 1868.

John George Nicolay Biographer of Abraham Lincoln. b. Essingen, Bavaria, Feb. 26, 1832. Brought to Pike Co., by parents, 1837. Reporter *Pittsfield Free Press*; purchased paper, 1854; published it until 1856. Published *Pike Co. Sucker*, 1856-60. Private sec. to Abraham Lincoln 1860-65. With John Hay, published ten-volume biography of Lincoln (1890). d. Washington, D.C., Sept. 26, 1901.

William Butler Ogden First mayor of Chicago. b. Walton, N.Y., June 15, 1805. N.Y.H.R., 1834. Moved to Chicago, 1835. Mayor, 1837, many times an ald. Pres. Galena & Chicago Union R.R., 1846; Chicago, St. Paul & Fond du Lac R.R.,

1857. Guided merger that resulted in Chicago & North Western R.R., 1859; pres. 1859-68. Ill. Sen., 1861-64. First pres. Union Pacific R.R. First pres. Rush Med. College. d. High Bridge, N.Y., Aug. 3, 1877.

Richard James Oglesby Gov. Ill., 1865-69, 1885-89. *See* chapter on state officers.

Alice Elvira Freeman Palmer Educator. b. Broome Co., N.Y., Feb. 21, 1855. A.B. Michigan, 1876. Head history dept. Wellesley, 1879; pres., 1881-87. First dean of women Chicago, 1892. Dir. World's Columbian Exposition, 1893. Resigned Chicago 1895 to be with husband, George Herbert Palmer, prof. philosophy Harvard. Mem. Mass. State Board of Education. d. Paris, France, Dec. 6, 1902.

Bertha Honoré Palmer Social leader. b. Louisville, Ky., *ca.* 1849. Married Potter Palmer, 1871. In 1891 named pres. Board of Lady Managers for the World's Columbian Exposition and toured European countries to persuade governments to participate. Only woman mem. of the Nat. Committee for the Paris Exposition of 1900. French Legion of Honor, the same year. Was undisputed leader Chicago society from nineties until her death in Osprey, Fla., May 5, 1918.

John McAuley Palmer Gov. Ill., 1869-73. *See* chapter on state officers.

Potter Palmer Merchant, capitalist. b. on farm n. Rensselaerville, N.Y., May 20, 1826. Moved to Chicago, 1852, opened dry goods store on Lake Street. Pioneered modern merchandising techniques; retired due to health, 1867. Invested in real estate; built thirty-three buildings, including Palmer House on State Street in 1870 and 1871, making it the business street of Chicago. Wiped out by fire of 1871, rebuilt State Street with help of his bride of a few months, Bertha Honoré. First pres. Chicago Nat. League baseball team, then the White Stockings. Comm. South Park System. d. Chicago, May 4, 1902.

James A. Patten Grain merchant, philanthropist. b. Freeland Corners, May 8, 1852. Attended preparatory dept. Northwestern. Worked for uncle, Gov. John L. Beveridge 1870-74. Clerk, state grain inspection dept. Chicago, 1874-78. Clerk G. P. Comstock Company (Board of Trade), 1878-80. With brother George established cash grain brokerage house, 1880. Mem. Chicago Board of Trade, 1882-1928; dir. 1897; pres., 1918. Founded Chicago Fresh Air Hospital; contributed $500,000 to Chicago Tuberculosis Inst. Left half his multimillion-dollar fortune to Northwestern. d. Chicago, Dec. 8, 1928.

John Mason Peck Clergyman, author. b. Litchfield, Conn., Oct. 31, 1789. Licensed to preach by Baptist Church, 1811; ordained, 1813. With James Welch established western mission in St. Louis, 1818; went as home missionary to Rock Spring (near Alton), 1823. Rode circuit in Ill., Ind., and Mo.; established meeting houses and Bible societies. Helped found Rock Spring Sem., 1827, and, when Benjamin Shurtleff gave $10,000 for its support, renamed it Shurtleff. Edited Baptist publications, travelers' directories (the *Guide for Emigrants* appeared first in 1831). With John Messinger, published a sectional map of Illinois. Wrote biography of Daniel Boone. d. Rock Spring, March 14, 1858.

Jean Baptiste Pointe du Sable Fur trader, Chicago's first settler. b. Haiti, of Negro parents, *ca.* 1740. First Illinois residence, Peoria about 1778. Built fur trading post at mouth of Chicago River, 1779; arrested by British, taken to Detroit, Mich.; returned to his trading post about 1781, where he lived until 1796. Sold the property to Jean Lalime, 1796, who in turn sold to John Kinzie in 1804. Du Sable moved to Peoria, then to St. Charles, Mo. Ter., where he died, August 28, 1818.

John Pope Maj. gen. U.S.A. b. Louisville, Ky., March 16, 1822 (son of Nathaniel Pope, U.S. dist. judge Ill.). App. to U.S.M.A. from Ill., 1838. Bvt. 1st lt. for gallantry at Monterey, bvt. capt. for gallantry Buena Vista. Commanding gen. successful operations at New Madrid, 1862, and at second Battle of Bull Run. Bvt. maj. gen., 1865; promoted to maj. gen. U.S.A., 1882. Dept. and dist. commands to 1886. d. Sandusky, Ohio, Sept. 23, 1892.

Nathaniel Pope Jurist. b. Louisville, Ky., Jan. 5, 1784. Attended Transylvania; admitted Ky. bar, 1808. Moved to Kaskaskia, 1809. Sec. Ill. Ter., 1809–16. Ter. del. U.S.H.R., 1816–18. Framed enabling act which assured lake coastline to Ill. U.S. dist. judge Ill., 1819–50. d. St. Louis, Mo., Jan 22, 1850.

Maud Powell Concert violinist. b. Peru, Aug. 22, 1868. Pub. school education Aurora where father was supt. schools. Studied violin in Chicago, Leipzig, Paris, and Berlin, 1881–85. Debut Berlin age seventeen. Soloist with Damrosch, Thomas, Wood, and other famous orchestras in U.S. and abroad for thirty-five years. d. on tour, Uniontown, Pa., Jan. 8, 1920.

Benjamin Mayberry Prentiss Maj. gen.

vols. b. Belleville, Va., Nov. 23, 1819. Moved with parents to Marion Co., Mo., 1836. Moved to Quincy, 1841. Capt. Ill. Vols. Mexican War. Admitted Ill. bar about 1850; pract. Quincy. Col. militia, 1860; col. 10th Ill. Vols., 1861; promoted brig. gen. Captured at Shiloh after gallant stand; exchanged; promoted maj. gen. vols., 1862. Won victory at Helena, Ark.; resigned, Oct. 1863. Pension agent, 1869–77. Pract. Quincy to 1878. In 1879 moved to Mo. P.M. Bethany, Mo. d. Bethany, Mo., Feb. 8, 1901.

George Mortimer Pullman Inventor, financier. b. Brockton, N.Y., March 3, 1831. Cabinet maker; moved to Chicago, 1858. Contractor, developed methods for raising level of streets and adjacent buildings. Built first sleeping car, the "Pioneer," 1863. Introduced dining cars for railroads. Built the model town of Pullman for his employees. Resisted worker demands in bitter strike, 1894. d. Chicago, Oct. 19, 1897.

Norman Higgins Purple Just. Ill. Supreme Court, 1845–48. *See* chapter on state officers.

John Aaron Rawlins Sec. war U.S. b. Galena, Feb. 13, 1831. Attended Rock River Sem. Admitted Ill. bar; pract. Galena, 1854. Maj. 45th Ill. Vol. Inf., 1861. Aide-de-camp to Grant, Aug. 1861; remained on Grant's staff to 1865. Lt. col. 1862; brig. gen. vols., 1863; chief of staff, U.S.A., bvt. maj. gen. 1865. Sec. war, 1869. d. Washington, D.C., Sept. 9, 1869.

Henry Joseph Reilly Army officer, journalist. b. Ft. Barrancas, Fla., April 29, 1881. Grad. U.S.M.A., 1904. Served in cav. to 1914; resigned. Spec. correspondent *Chicago Tribune* Mexico, 1913; Far East, 1914; Europe, 1914–15 and 1916–17. Joined 42nd (Rainbow) Div. as col. of 149th F.A., 1917; promoted brig. gen. Military writer for *Tribune*, 1919–60. Ed. *Army and Navy Journal*. d. Washington, D.C., Dec. 13, 1963.

John Reynolds Just. Ill. Supreme Court, 1818–25; gov. Ill., 1830–34. *See* chapter on state officers.

George Frederick Root "Song writer to the Union Army." b. Sheffield, Mass., Aug. 30, 1820. Studied music Boston. Singing teacher Abbott's School for Young Ladies, New York, 1844–50. Studied Paris, 1850–53. Established New York Normal Inst., New York City, 1853. Joined brother in publishing firm Chicago, 1859. Composed cantatas, sacred songs, and Civil War songs, including "The Battle Cry of Freedom," "Tramp, Tramp, Tramp, the Boys Are Marching," "Just Before the Battle, Mother," "The Vacant Chair," and many others. d. Chicago, Aug. 6, 1895.

John Wellborn Root Architect. b. Lumpkin, Ga., Jan. 10, 1850. Sent to England in 1864; attended Oxford, 1866. Moved to New York, 1867. B.E. College of City of New York, 1869; headed class. Studied Paris, 1870. Moved to Chicago, 1872; partner with Daniel Burnham. One of several architects who developed floating foundations for tall buildings. Consulting architect World's Columbian Exposition. d. Chicago, Jan. 15, 1891.

Julius Rosenwald Merchant, philanthropist. b. Springfield, Aug. 12, 1862. Moved to New York, N.Y., 1879, to Chicago, 1885. Pres. Rosenwald & Weil, 1885–1906. V.P. and treas. Sears, Roebuck & Company, 1895–1910; pres., 1910–25; chm. board, 1925–32. Gave millions to build modern schools for Negroes in South. Established $30,000,000 Rosenwald Fund "for well-being of mankind." Founded Museum of Science and Industry. Trustee, Rockefeller Foundation, Art Inst. of Chicago, Tuskegee Inst., U. of Chicago, Hull House. Honorary pres. Jewish Charities of Chicago. d. Chicago, Jan. 6, 1932.

Martin Antoine Ryerson Philanthropist, art collector. b. Grand Rapids, Mich., Oct. 26, 1856. Moved to Chicago with parents as infant. Attended preparatory schools Paris, France, and Geneva, Switzerland. LL.B. Harvard, admitted Ill. bar, 1878; pract. Chicago. Headed Chicago office of father's lumber business; owner of Martin Ryerson & Company from 1887. Dir. Northern Trust and Elgin Nat. Watch Company. Governing mem. Art Inst. of Chicago, 1887, trustee, 1890–1932, v.p., 1902–25, pres., 1925 and 1926, honorary pres., 1927–32. d. Chicago, Aug. 11, 1932.

Carl Sandburg Poet, biographer, historian. b. of immigrant parents at Galesburg, Jan. 6, 1878. Worked from age fourteen. Pvt. inf., 1898, served in Puerto Rico. Att. Lombard College, Galesburg, 1902. After variety of jobs, from farmhand to sec. to mayor of Milwaukee, came to Chicago, 1912. Journalist, editorial writer, published first major poem, "Chicago," in Harriet Monroe's *Poetry* magazine, 1914.

Corn Huskers (1918) won American Poetry Society prize. Published first two volumes of monumental Lincoln biography *Abraham Lincoln: The Prairie Years* in 1926, and the final four volumes *Abraham Lincoln: The War Years* in 1939. Three Pulitzer Prizes, one for history, in 1940, and two for poetry, in 1919 and 1951. Condensation of the Lincoln biography from six volumes to one of about 700 pages, an autobiography, *Always the Young Strangers*, a collection of American ballads and folk songs, *The American Song Bag*, the epic novel *Remembrance Rock* were among his thirty successful books. Resided Chicago, 1912–33; Hobart, Mich., 1933–45; Flat Rock, N.C., 1945 until his death, July 22, 1967.

John McAllister Schofield Commanding gen. U.S.A. b. Gerry, N.Y., Sept. 29, 1831. Moved with parents to Bristol, 1843, to Freeport, 1845. Graduated U.S.M.A., 1853. Asst. prof. West Point, 1855–60; acting prof. physics (on leave) St. Louis U., 1860–61. Maj. Mo. Vols., June, brig. gen., Nov. 1861; promotion to maj. gen. vols., Nov. 1862, being unconfirmed for political reasons, Schofield asked for transfer and was given command of the 14th Army Corps in Tenn., March 1863. In May, his promotion finally confirmed, he was made commanding gen. Dept of Mo. In Feb. 1864 he was assigned as commanding gen. 23rd Army Corps and the Dept. of the Ohio. Served Atlanta campaign; captor, with Sherman, of Gen. Joseph E. Johnston, 1865. Sec. war, 1868. Promoted maj. gen. U.S.A., 1869; dept. commands to 1886. Commanding gen. U.S.A., 1886–95. d. St. Augustine, Fla., March 4, 1906.

Walter Dill Scott Educator. b. Cooksville, May 1, 1869. Grad. Illinois State Normal, 1891; A.B. Northwestern, 1895; Ph.D. Leipzig, Germany, 1900; many honorary degrees. Dir. psychological laboratory, Northwestern, 1901–8; prof. psychology, 1908–20. Col. U.S.A., 1918 and 1919; awarded D.S.M. for devising, installing, and supervising army personnel system. Pres. Northwestern, 1920–39; pres. emeritus, 1939–55. Published many books on psychology in business, industry, and advertising. d. Evanston, Sept. 23, 1955.

John L. Scripps Journalist. b. n. Cape Girardeau, Mo., Feb. 18, 1818. Removed with parents as child to Rushville; Grad. McKendree; studied law. In 1847 removed to Chicago and purchased a third interest in *Chicago Tribune*. In 1852 withdrew from *Tribune* and, with William Bross, established the *Daily Democratic Press*, which consolidated with *Tribune*, 1858. Reported Lincoln-Douglas debates. App. by Abraham Lincoln p.m. of Chicago, served 1861-65. Private banker, 1865. d. on visit to Minneapolis, Minn., Sept. 21, 1866.

Nicholas Senn Pioneer in abdominal surgery. b. Buchs, St. Gallen, Switzerland, Oct. 31, 1844. Emigrated with parents to Wisconsin, 1852. M.D. Chicago Med. College, 1868; studied in Europe, received degree Munich, 1877. Joined staff Rush Med. College, 1877. Surg. gen. Ill. N.G., 1893; served as col. Camp Chicamauga and Santiago, Cuba, 1898. d. Chicago, Jan. 2, 1908.

James Shields Aud. Ill., 1841-43; U.S. Sen., 1849-55. *See* chapter on state officers.

Frederick Slater Jurist known as, "Duke." b. Normal, Dec. 9, 1898. Attended h.s. Clinton, Iowa; A.B. Iowa, 1921; LL.B., 1928. All-American tackle, 1921; all-time all-American, 1931 and 1946; professional football Rock Island, 1922-27, Chicago Cardinals, 1928-31. Admitted Ill. bar, 1928; pract. Chicago. Asst. corp. counsel, 1935. Ill. Commerce Commission, 1940-41. Judge municipal court Chicago, 1948-60, Cook Co. Superior Court, 1960-62, circuit court, 1962 until his death Chicago, Aug. 14, 1966.

Giles Alexander Smith Maj. gen. Ill. Vols. b. Jefferson Co., N.Y., Sept. 29, 1829. Merchant Bloomington. Capt. Mo. Vols., 1861; served at Fts. Donelson and Henry, promoted lt. col. and col., 1862; wounded Arkansas Post; promoted brig. gen. for gallantry, 1863. Brigade commander with Sherman Chattanooga, Missionary Ridge, the Atlanta campaign, and march to the sea; maj. gen., 1865. d. Bloomington, Nov. 8, 1876.

Hyrum Smith Brother Joseph, patriarch Mormon Church. b. Tunbridge, Vt., Feb. 9, 1800. Accepted brother's visions, baptized into Mormon Church, 1829. Name affixed to *The Book of Mormon* as one of eight permitted to see golden tablets of the prophet Mormon. One of six organizers of church, named patriarch, 1841. Killed with brother by mob, June 27, 1844, Carthage.

Joseph Smith Religious leader, founder Church of Jesus Christ of the Latter-Day Siants. b. Sharon, Vt., Dec. 23, 1805. Claimed visions and discovery of golden tablets on which were written *The Book of Mormon* which he translated and dictated to associates in 1829; cult grew up around him. Driven out by neighbors, Smith led his people to Ohio, then to Mo. In 1839 Ill. granted him a charter to found a colony at Nauvoo on the Mississippi. There Smith proclaimed a doctrine of plural marriage and took several wives. The settlement prospered. In 1844 Smith announced himself a candidate for Presidency of U.S. Charged with conspiracy he and brother Hyrum were arrested and lodged in jail at Carthage, where they were murdered by a mob on June 27, 1844.

Franklyn Bliss Snyder Educator. b. Middletown, Conn., July 26, 1884. A.B. Beloit, 1905; A.M. Harvard, 1907; Ph.D. Harvard, 1909. Joined faculty of Northwestern in English dept., 1909; instructor, 1909-11; asst. prof., 1911-13; assoc. prof., 1913-18; prof. from 1918. Dean of grad. school, 1934. V.P. and dean of faculty, 1937; pres., 1939; pres. emeritus, 1949. Lectured at many unversities. Published biography of Robert Burns, 1926, and other authoritative works in field of American and English literature. Pres. board of managers Presbyterian Hospital, 1949-56. d. Evanston, May 11, 1958.

Albert Spalding Violinist, composer, author. b. Chicago, Aug. 15, 1888. Studied Chicago and Paris; debut Paris, 1905, New York, 1908. Toured world with Damrosch and the New York Philharmonic, and as concert artist. In World War I, lt., A.A.F.; in World War II, worked behind enemy lines to maintain communications with the Italian underground. Chevalier French Legion of Honor; Cross of the Crown of Italy. Composed two violin concertos, a sonata, and many concert pieces. Author of a successful novel. d. New York, N.Y., May 26, 1953.

Albert Goodwill Spalding Baseball player and manager, merchant. b. Byron, Sept. 2, 1850. Attended Rockford pub. schools and Commercial College. Pitcher Boston, 1871-75, Chicago 1876-91. Established firm of A. G. Spalding & Brothers, 1876. Organized first world tour of baseball with Chicago and an all-American team, 1888 and 1889. d. Point Loma, Calif., Sept. 9, 1915.

Amos Alonzo Stagg Athletic coach and director. b. West Orange, N.J., Aug. 16, 1862. Grad. Phillips-Exeter Acad. End, Yale, '88, the team that rolled up 695 points to 0 for its opponents. Pitched Yale to five championships, striking out 20 Princetonians in one shutout. Grad. Y.M.C.A. Inst. Springfield, Mass., 1890. Coach Springfield, 1890-92; Chicago, 1892-1932; College of Pacific, 1933-47. Asst.

coach (to son) Susquehanna, 1947–53; advisory coach Stockton College, 1953–60. d. Stockton, Calif., March 18, 1965.

Augustus Eugene Staley Manufacturer. b. Julian, N.C., Feb. 25, 1867. Grammar school education; traveled for a tobacco house. Deciding that starch was a demand item, he started packaging starch Baltimore, 1898. In 1909 purchased Wellington Starch Co., Decatur; rebuilt and modernized plant and started making starch there in 1912. Added corn syrup and corn sugars to his line, 1916. Encouraged farmers to grow soybeans and built processing plant in 1919, but bean shortage prevented operation until 1922 when production began by crushing 500 bushels soybeans daily. By 1936 plant crushed 4,000,000 bushels and was important in giving Ill. leadership in soybean production the state has never relinquished. At Staley's death, Dec. 26, 1940, in Miami, Fla., the plant covered 320 acres and was worth $20,000,000.

Ellen Gates Starr Social worker. b. Laona, March 19, 1859. Joined Jane Addams as co-founder Hull House; established first free art school there. Arrested 1914 for interfering with police in arrest of pickets from waitress' union during strike; acquitted. Candidate for ald. on Socialist ticket, 1916. Left Hull House for reasons of health, 1920. Bedridden, died in old peoples' sanatorium Suffern, N.Y., Feb. 10, 1940.

Adlai Ewing Stevenson U.S.H.R., 1875–77; V.P. U.S., 1893–97. See chapter on state officers.

Adlai Ewing Stevenson II Gov. Ill., 1949–53. See chapter on state officers.

Melville Elijah Stone Journalist. b. Hudson, Aug. 22, 1848. Moved with parents to Chicago, 1860. A.M. Yale, 1872. Reporter *Chicago Tribune*, 1864–69. Ran machine shop, 1869–71 (burned out by fire). With Victor Lawson, established *Chicago Daily News*; sold interest in 1888 to Lawson. Gen. manager Associated Press, 1893–1921; counselor, 1921 to his death in New York, N.Y., Feb. 15, 1929.

Julian Monson Sturtevant Educator, member "Yale Band" of home missionaries who participated in establishing the first colleges in Illinois. b. Warren, Conn., July 26, 1805. A.B. Yale, 1826; D.D., 1829; ordained, 1829. First instructor at Illinois College, Jacksonville, 1830. Preached in college chapel, raised funds. Named prof. mathematics, 1833, pres., 1844, a post he held for thirty-two years. Lectured in

England for Union cause during Civil War. His autobiography gives picture of college life in early Ill. Resigned as pres., 1876, but continued to teach until his death, Jacksonville, Feb. 11, 1886.

Louis Henri Sullivan Architect. b. Boston, Mass., Sept. 3, 1856. Studied architecture Massachusetts Inst. of Technology, 1872. Moved to Chicago, 1873, draughtsman with William Le Baron Jenney. Studied École des Beaux Arts Paris, 1874. Returned Chicago, 1875, draughtsman various offices. Joined Dankmar Adler as probationary partner, 1879, became partner, 1880. Remained with Adler fifteen years, designed the Auditorium, McVicker's Theater, the Transportation Building at World's Columbian Exposition, many homes and pub. buildings with Adler, 1880–95, and alone, 1895–1924. His *Autobiography of an Idea* (1924) was called by critics a major contribution to American literature. d. Chicago, Oct. 3, 1924.

Gustavus Franklin Swift Meat packer. b. n. Sandwich, Mass., June 24, 1839. Established packing house Chicago, 1875. First shipper of dressed beef; developed refrigerating system, built own refrigerator cars. Established worldwide distribution network, established plants in many U.S. cities. d. Chicago, March 29, 1903.

David Swing Clergyman. b. Cincinnati, Ohio, Aug. 23, 1930. A.B. Miami of Ohio, 1852; taught school. Studied theology; occasional preacher in Ohio to 1866, when he moved to Chicago to become min. of Westminster Presbyterian Church. In 1874 charged with heresy, acquitted, but when case carried to synod he left the denomination and preached as an independent min. Continued to write and preach at Central Church, organized for him in downtown Chicago, until his death in Chicago, Oct 3, 1894.

Lorado Zodoc Taft Sculptor. b. Elmwood, April 29, 1860. B.L. Illinois, 1879, M.L., 1880; studied at École des Beaux Arts, Paris, 1880–83. Instructor Art Inst. of Chicago, 1886–97; lecturer until 1929. Lecturer, extension div. of U. of Chicago, 1892–1902; professorial lecturer, 1909–36. Among finest works are "Solitude of the Soul," Art Inst. of Chicago; "Black Hawk," n. Oregon; "Columbus Fountain," Washington, D.C. Author, *History of American Sculpture*. d. Chicago, Oct. 30, 1936.

Christian Friederich Theodore Thomas Orchestra leader. b. Esens, Germany, Oct. 11, 1835. Made debut as violinist at age ten; emigrated with parents to New York the same year; toured as a child prodigy.

Organized and conducted Thomas Orchestra New York and on tour, 1867–88; conducted Brooklyn Philharmonic Society, 1862; New York Philharmonic, 1877–91. Moved to Chicago as conductor of the newly organized Chicago Symphony Orchestra, 1891. First concert, Oct. 17, 1891, featured Beethoven's *Fifth Symphony*. Engaged as musical director World's Columbian Exposition, 1893, resigned in controversy over piano Paderewski would use. Interspersed symphonies and lighter works in Chicago concerts. d. Chicago, Jan. 4, 1905.

Thomas Bjerne Thompson Journalist, known as "Barney." b. Nashota, Wis., Jan 20, 1876. B.A. (magna cum laude) Beloit, 1903. Congregational min., Old Stone Church, Rockton; Congregational church, Watertown, Wis.; Plymouth Church, Milwaukee, Wis.; and at First Congregational Church, Rockford. In 1914 left ministry to become ed. *Rockford Daily Republic*. In 1930 became ed. of *Rockford Register-Republic*, publisher and ed., 1945, ed. emeritus, 1953. Wrote column, 1922–67; became radio broadcaster, 1930, made daily newscasts until 1958. His last column, written Aug. 30, 1967, dealt with "death, the ultimate disaster." d. Rockford, Sept. 7, 1967.

Henri de Tonti Explorer, soldier. b. Gaeta, Italy, *ca.* 1650. Lost hand in battle, wore iron substitute. Joined La Salle in Canada, 1678, helped him build forts in Ill., 1679. Saw his allies, the Iliniwek, beaten and almost wiped out by Iroquois. Went with La Salle to mouth of Mississippi, 1682. Built Fort St. Louis (at Starved Rock), 1682, and drove Iroquois from fort in 1684. Remained with Ill. Indians as fur trader, held various posts under the French, brought settlers and supplies to Ft. Crevecoeur (Peoria). d. Mobile, Ala., while on visit to receive orders from French Commandant d'Iberville, 1704.

Melvin Alvah Traylor Banker. b. Breeding, Ky., Oct. 21, 1878. Worked from boyhood; educated in night schools. Moved to Tex., 1898; admitted to Tex. bar; pract. Hillsboro, Tex., 1901. City and co. offices to 1904; became bank employee. Moved to Chicago, 1914; v.p. and pres. Livestock Exchange Nat. Bank and First Union Trust & Savings Bank, 1919–34. V.P. First Nat. Bank of Chicago, 1919–25; pres., 1925–34. Trustee Newberry Library, Northwestern, Berea. d. Chicago, Feb. 14, 1934.

Lambert Tree Jurist, diplomat. b. Washington, D.C., Nov. 29, 1832. LL.B. Virginia; admitted to D.C. bar. Moved to

Chicago, 1855; pract. Chicago. Pres. Chicago Law Inst., 1864–70. Judge Cook Co. Circuit Court, 1870–74. Cand. for U.S. Sen., lost to Logan by one vote, 1885. U.S. min. to Belgium, 1885–88, to Russia, 1888 and 1889. An incorporator of the nat. American Red Cross; pres. Ill. State Historical Library board, 1892–96. d. just after 122nd trans-Atlantic voyage, New York, N.Y., Oct. 9, 1910.

Lyman Trumbull Sec. state Ill., 1841–43; U.S. Sen., 1855–73. *See* chapter on state officers.

Jonathan Baldwin Turner Educator, agronomist. b. Templeton, Mass., Dec. 7, 1805. A.B. Yale, 1833. Instructor, Latin and Greek Illinois College, Jacksonville, 1833 and 1834; prof. of rhetoric and belles lettres, 1834–47. Ed. *Statesman* (antislavery); first pres. Ill. Natural History Society. In 1850 formulated plan for agricultural and industrial universities to be supported by income from fed. lands, which was enacted into law by Cong., and under Turner's persuasion signed by Abraham Lincoln, 1862. Under this act the U. of Illinois was chartered, 1867. Developed Osage orange as a hedge plant; first experimenter with hybrid seed corn; historian. d. Jacksonville, Jan. 19, 1899.

Frank Arthur Vanderlip Banker, author. b. n. Aurora, Nov. 17, 1864. Attended Illinois and Chicago; honorary degrees, A.M. Illinois, 1905; LL.D. Colgate, 1911, Princeton, 1919. Financial ed. *Chicago Tribune*, 1889; ed. *The Economist* Chicago, 1894–97. Asst. sec. of treasury, 1897–1901. V.P. Nat. City Bank of New York, 1901–9, pres. until 1919. Trustee Carnegie Foundation. Decorated by France, Belgium, Montenegro, and Italy, 1919. Retired from banking to write, 1919. d. New York, N.Y., June 29, 1937.

Carl Clinton Van Doren Editor, author, publisher. b. Hope, Sept. 10, 1885. A.B. Illinois, 1907; Ph.D. Columbia, 1911. Lecturer Columbia, 1911–30. Wrote critical analyses, histories, and biographies. Literary ed. *The Nation*, 1919–20; *Century Magazine*, 1922–25; managing ed. the *Cambridge History of American Literature*, 1917–21; ed. Literary Guild, 1926–34. d. Torrington, Conn., July 18, 1950.

Leonard Wells Volk Sculptor. b. Wellstown (now Wells), N.Y., Nov. 7, 1828. Protégé of Stephen A. Douglas, opened studio in Chicago, 1857. Active in founding Chicago Acad. of Design. Made life mask of Abraham Lincoln, cast of his hands, many portrait busts of pioneers, statues of Lincoln and Douglas now standing at Springfield and elsewhere. d. Osceola, Wis., Aug. 19, 1895.

Charles Henry Wacker Brewer, city planner. b. Chicago, Aug. 29, 1856. Attended Lake Forest Acad.; studied in Stuttgart and Baden, Germany, and Geneva, Switzerland. Partner with father in malt business, 1880–84; pres. Wacker & Birk, 1884–1901. Pres. Chicago Heights Land Association, 1902–28; chm. Chicago Planning Commission, 1909–26 (resigned due to illness); first pres. United Charities of Chicago, 1909–12; sec. Chicago Zoning Commission, 1920. d. Chicago, Oct. 31, 1929.

Jesse Walker Methodist missionary, circuit rider. b. Rockingham Co., Va., June 9, 1766. Ordained about 1786. Moved to Tenn. 1802, to Ill. 1806. Held first Ill. camp meeting n. Edwardsville, 1807. Preached Peoria, 1824. Ottawa, 1825, Chicago, 1826. Supt. of mission to Indians of Fox River Valley, Plainfield, until his death Oct. 5, 1835.

Aaron Montgomery Ward Merchant, called father of mail-order business. b. Chatham, N.J., Feb. 17, 1843. Worked from age fourteen; moved to Chicago, 1865. Clerk and traveling salesman, 1866–71. With George Thorne established Montgomery Ward & Company, 1872. Retired to Oconomowoc, Wis., 1901; raised fine stock. Through expensive litigation preserved Chicago's lakefront for the people. d. Highland Park, Dec. 7, 1913. In 1923 and 1926 Ward's widow gave $8,500,000 to establish and equip Northwestern Med. School.

Elihu Benjamin Washburne U.S.H.R., 1853–69. *See* chapter on state officers.

John Wentworth U.S.H.R., 1843–51, 1853–55, 1865–67. *See* chapter on state officers.

Frances Elizabeth Caroline Willard Temperance worker. b. Churchville, N.Y., Sept. 28, 1839. Moved as a child to Ohio, then to Wis. Graduated Northwestern Female College, Evanston, 1859. Taught country schools, 1860–63, Pittsburgh, Pa., 1863 and 1864, Genesee Wesleyan Sem., 1866 and 1867. Traveled in Europe and lectured, 1868–74. Pres. Chicago Woman's Christian Temperance Union, 1874, nat. pres., 1879; and pres. World's Woman's Christian Temperance Union, 1891 to death in New York, N.Y., Feb. 18, 1898. In 1910 named to the Hall of Fame of Great Americans.

Daniel Hale Williams Surgeon, cofounder of Provident Hospital, Chicago. b. Holidaysburg, Pa., Jan. 18, 1856, of Negro, Indian, and German parentage. Moved as child with mother to Rockford. Completed h.s. at Janesville, Wis., while operating own barbershop. While in med. school, helped with employment by widow of John Jones. M.D. Chicago Med. College, 1883; pract. Chicago. Performed world's first open-heart surgery, July 9, 1893, at Provident. Except for four years, 1894–98, as chief surgeon Freedman's Hospital, Washington, D.C., pract. Provident and Cook County hospitals, Chicago. Founding mem. American College of Surgeons. Retired because of illness, 1926. d. Idlewild, Mich., Aug. 4, 1931.

James Harrison Wilson Soldier, traveler, author. b. n. Shawneetown, Sept. 2, 1837. Attended McKendree, grad. U.S.M.A., 1860. Aide to McClellan, 1862; lt. col. vols., 1862, with Army of Tennessee; brig. gen. vols., 1863, maj. gen. vols., 1865. Commissioned lt. col. U.S.A.; bvt. maj. gen., 1866; resigned commission, 1870. Traveled in China, built railways, and wrote. Served as maj. gen. vols. Spanish-American War. d. New York, N.Y., Feb. 23, 1925.

Frank Lloyd Wright Architect. b. Richland Center, Wis., June 8, 1869. Civil engineering degree Wisconsin, 1888. Pract. Chicago, 1893. Recognized as leader of the new school of the Middle West; designed homes, hotels, and pub. buildings worldwide. Many honorary degrees; Royal Gold Medal for architecture England, 1941; Gold Medal American Inst. of Architects, 1948. Published in English and German; among English titles, *The Disappearing City* (1932), *Genius and Mobocracy* (1949). Founder of Taliesin Fellowship, a "cultural experiment" at Spring Green, Wis. (summer) and Paradise Valley, Ariz. (winter). Designed "earthquake-proof" Imperial Hotel, Tokyo, Japan, on a cushion of mud; it withstood destructive quakes, 1923 and 1966. d. Phoenix, Ariz., April 9, 1959.

John Stephen Wright Manufacturer, editor, founder *Prairie Farmer* magazine. b. Sheffield, Mass., July 16, 1815. Removed with father to Chicago, 1832. Built first pub. school building in Chicago at own expense, 1835. Published *Union Agriculturist* for Union Agricultural Society, 1839; combined it with *Western Prairie Farmer*, 1841. Purchased publication, 1843, and changed name to *Prairie Farmer*. Mfr. of reapers and mowers. Helped finance Galena

& Chicago Union R.R. d. Philadelphia, Pa., Sept. 26, 1874.

William Wrigley, Jr. Established and operated chewing gum factory. b. Philadelphia, Pa., Sept. 30, 1861. Educated in pub. schools; business with father, 1882–91. Removed to Chicago; established chewing gum factory. Became principal owner Chicago Cubs, 1918; trustee Field Museum; dir. First Nat. Bank of Chicago; pres. Catalina Island Company. d. Phoenix, Ariz., Jan. 26, 1932.

Richard Yates U.S.H.R., 1851–55; gov. Ill., 1861–65. *See* chapter on state officers.

Richard Yates Gov., Ill., 1901–5; U.S.H.R., 1919–33. *See* chapter on state officers.

Fannie Bloomfield Zeisler Concert pianist. b. Bielitz, Austrian Silesia (now Poland), July 16, 1863. Brought to U.S. by parents, 1866, to Chicago, 1869. Debut Chicago, Feb. 26, 1875, at age eleven, playing Beethoven's *Andante Favori*. Studied in Vienna, 1878–83; popular concert pianist in Europe and America. Founded a musician's relief fund administered by United Charities of Chicago. At golden jubilee, 1925, repeated *Andante Favori* and played two concertos. d. Chicago, Aug. 20, 1927.

Florenz Ziegfeld Theatrical producer. b. Chicago, March 21, 1869. Pub. school education. Brought bands and acts to World's Columbian Exposition, 1893. Manager for Eugene Sandow, professional strong man, 1893–96. Brought Anna Held from Paris to Broadway, 1896. Produced first of a long series of musical revues, later known as the *Ziegfeld Follies*, in 1907, taking name from *Folies Bergères*, Paris. Continued annual production until his death in New York, N.Y., July 22, 1932.

Illinoisans in Hall of Fame for Great Americans

(Established in 1900 by gift of Helen Gould Sheppard. New York University is trustee.)

Name	Year elected
Ulysses Simpson Grant	1900
Abraham Lincoln	1900
Frances Elizabeth Caroline Willard	1910
Jane Addams	1965

Nobel Prize winners, born in or working in Illinois

Year	Winner of award	Illinois connection	Field
1907	Albert Abraham Michelson*	at U. of Chicago	Physics
1923	Robert Andrews Millikan*	at U. of Chicago	Physics
1925	Charles Gates Dawes*	res. Evanston	Peace
1927	Arthur Holly Compton*	at U. of Chicago	Physics
1931	Jane Addams*	at Hull House	Peace
1937	Clinton Joseph Davisson	b. Bloomington at Ill. Bell Tel. Co.	Physics
1943	Edward Adalbert Doisy	b. Hume B.A. U. of Illinois, 1914	Medicine and Physiology
1946	Wendell Meredith Stanley	at U. of Illinois	Chemistry
1952	Edward Mills Purcell	b. Taylorville	Physics
1954	Ernest Hemingway*	b. Oak Park	Literature
1955	Vincent du Vigneaud	b. Chicago B.S. U. of Illinois, 1923	Chemistry
1956	John Bardeen	at U. of Illinois	Physics
1958	George W. Beadle	at U. of Chicago	Medicine and Physiology†
1960	Williard Frank Libby	at U. of Chicago	Chemistry
1962	James Dewey Watson	b. Chicago B.S. U. of Chicago, 1947	Medicine and Physiology
1966	Robert Sanderson Mulliken	at U. of Chicago	Chemistry
	Charles Brenton Huggins	at U. of Chicago	Medicine and Physiology
1968	Roger G. Holly	b. Urbana	Medicine and Physiology

* Detailed biography above.   † Prize awarded for work done elsewhere.

Pulitzer prizes awarded in Illinois

Meritorious Public Service

Year	Winner of award
1950	Chicago Daily News
1957	Chicago Daily News
1963	Chicago Daily News

Local Reporting

1925 James W. Mulroy and Alvin H. Goldstein, *Chicago Daily News*
1943 George Weller, *Chicago Daily News*
1962 George Bliss, *Chicago Tribune*

International Reporting

1929 Paul Scott Mowrer, *Chicago Daily News*
1933 Edgar Ansel Mowrer, *Chicago Daily News*
1936 Wilfred C. Barber, *Chicago Tribune*
1951 Keyes Beech and Fred Sparks, *Chicago Daily News*

Cartooning

1932 John Tinney McCutcheon,* *Chicago Tribune*
1938 Vaughn Shoemaker, *Chicago Daily News*
1941 Jacob Burck, *Chicago Times*
1949 Vaughn Shoemaker, *Chicago Daily News*
1961 Carey Orr, *Chicago Tribune*

Fiction and Literature

1931 Margaret Ayers Barnes, *Years of Grace*
1953 Ernest Hemingway,* *The Old Man and the Sea*

History

1928 Vernon Louis Parrington, *Main Currents in American Thought*
1936 Andrew Cunningham McLaughlin, *A Constitutional History of the United States*
1940 Carl Sandburg,* *Abraham Lincoln: The War Years*
1941 Marcus Lee Hansen, *The Atlantic Migration*

Biography or Autobiography

1922 Hamlin Garland,* *A Daughter of the Middle Border*
1928 Charles Edward Russell,† *The American Orchestra and Theodore Thomas*
1933 Allan Nevins, *Grover Cleveland*
1937 Allan Nevins, *Hamilton Fish: The Inner History of the Great Administration*
1938 Odell Sheppard, *Pedlar's Progress*
1939 Carl Van Doren,* *Benjamin Franklin*
1965 Ernest Samuels, *Henry Adams*

Poetry‡

1919 Carl Sandburg,* *Corn Huskers*
1940 Mark Van Doren, *Collected Poems*
1950 Gwendolyn Brooks, *Annie Allen*
1951 Carl Sandburg,* *Complete Poems*

Music

1946 Leo Sowerby, *The Canticle of the Sun*

---

* Detailed biography above.
† Lived only briefly in Illinois as a journalist.

‡ Prior to 1922 prizes were awarded from gifts made available by the Poetry Society.

INDEX

Map
Section

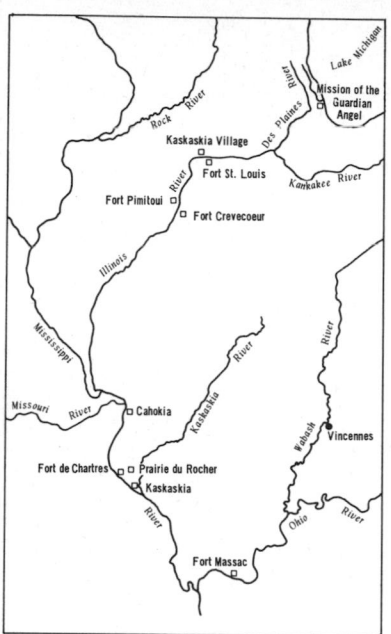

*Illinois under
the French
and English*

*Northwest
Territory*

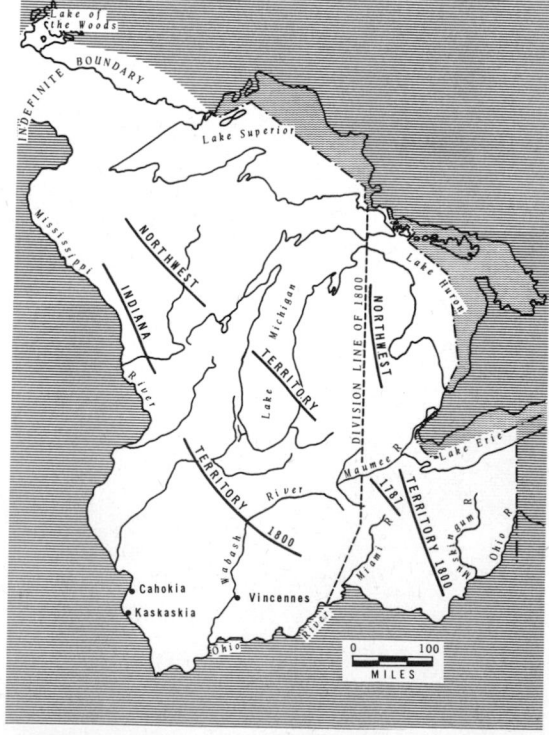

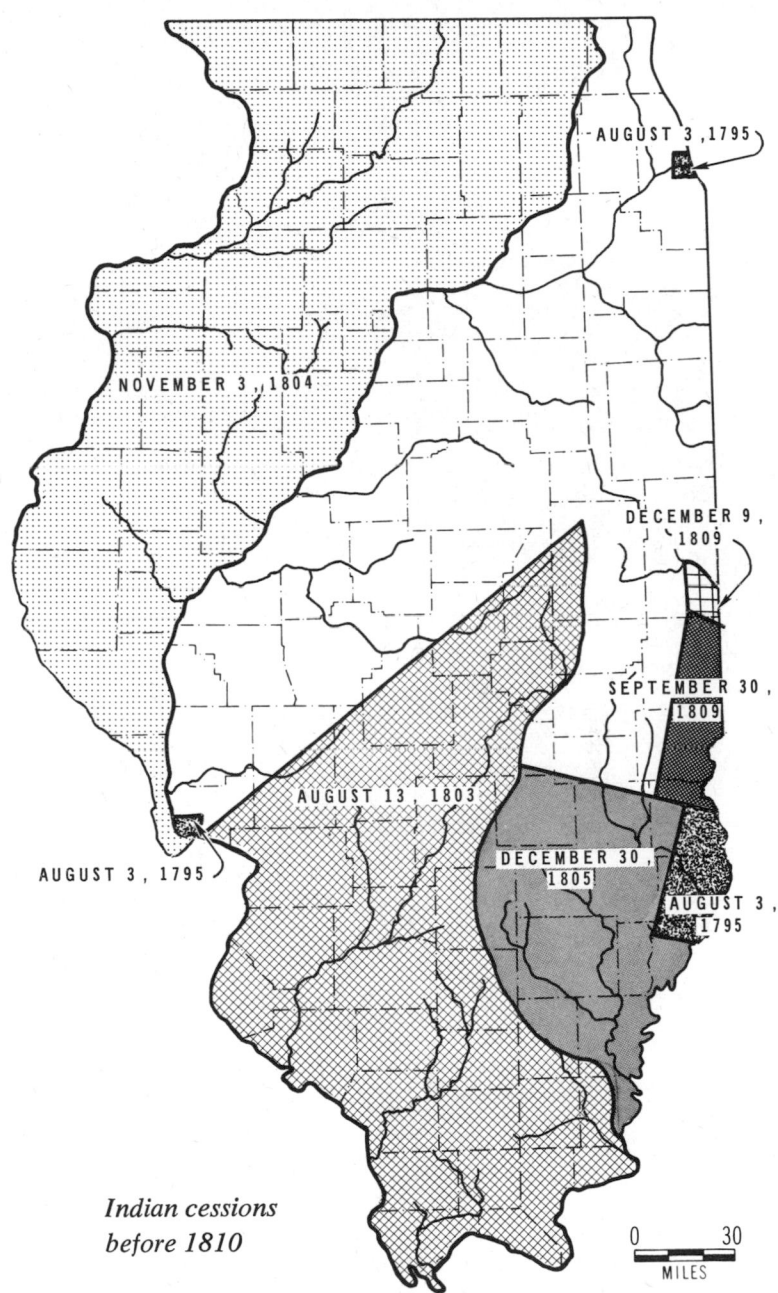

AUGUST 3 ,1795

NOVEMBER 3 ,1804

DECEMBER 9 ,
1809

SEPTEMBER 30 ,
1809

AUGUST 13 , 1803

DECEMBER 30 ,
1805

AUGUST 3 ,
1795

AUGUST 3 , 1795

*Indian cessions
before 1810*

0   30

MILES

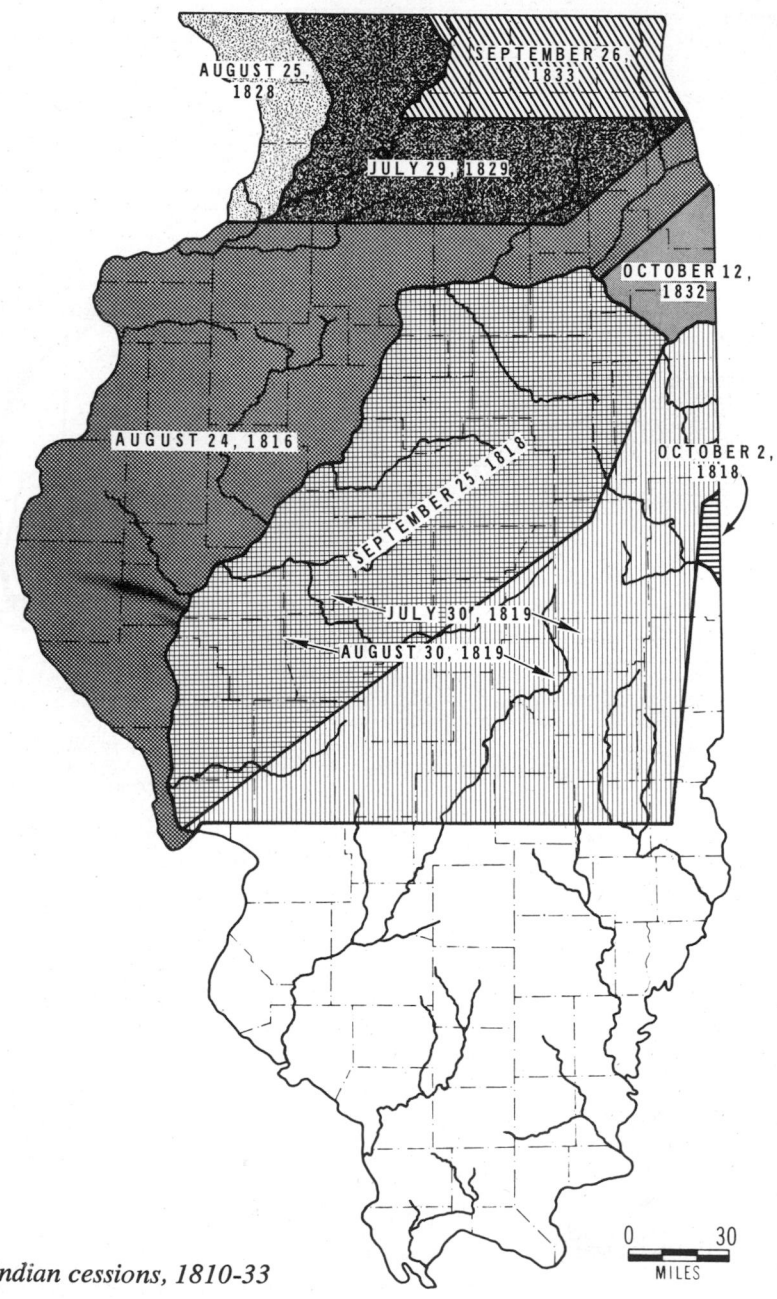

AUGUST 25,
1828

SEPTEMBER 26,
1833

JULY 29, 1829

OCTOBER 12,
1832

AUGUST 24, 1816

SEPTEMBER 25, 1818

OCTOBER 2,
1818

JULY 30, 1819

AUGUST 30, 1819

0   30
MILES

Indian cessions, 1810-33

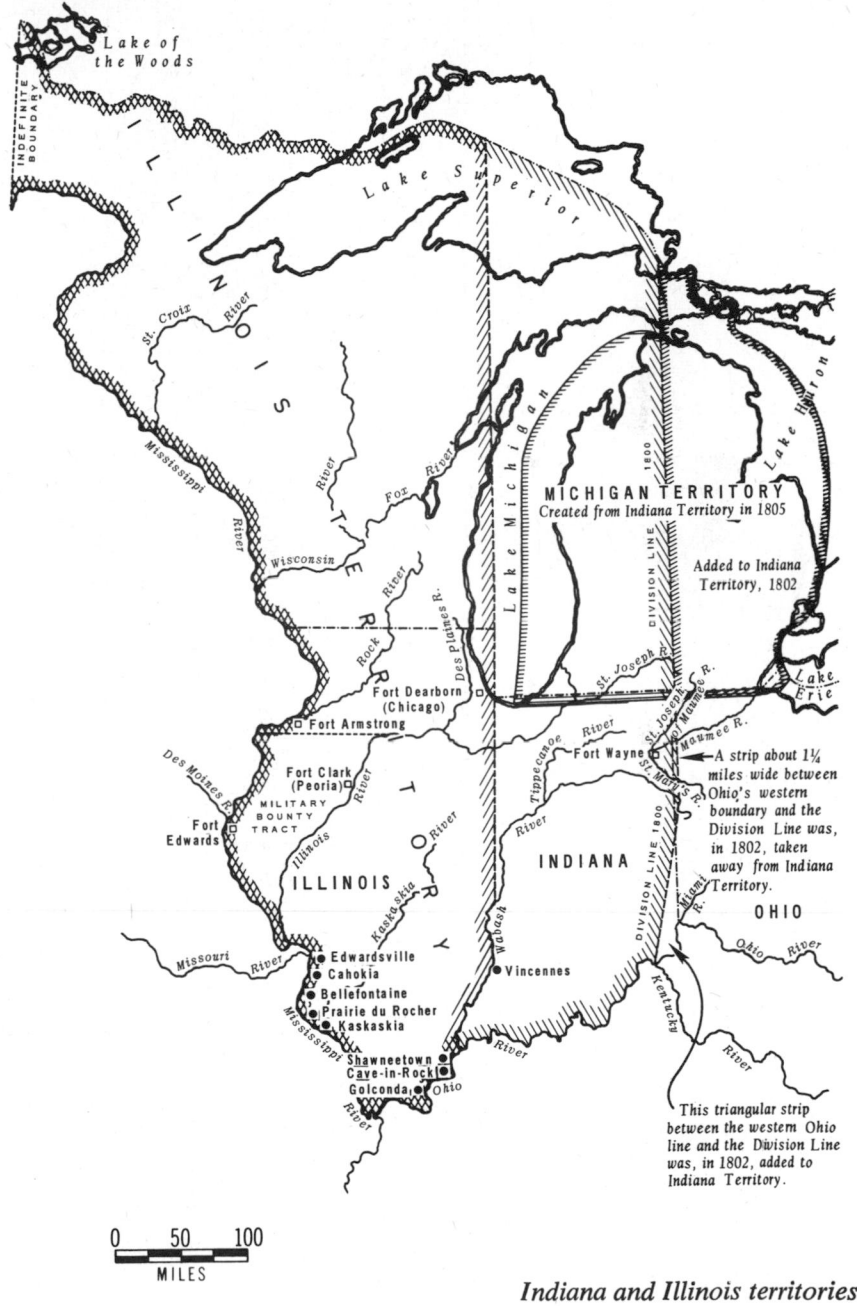

Lake of
the Woods

INDEFINITE
BOUNDARY

I L L I N O I S

Lake Superior

St. Croix River

Mississippi River

Wisconsin River

Fox River

Rock River

Des Plaines R.

Lake Michigan

MICHIGAN TERRITORY
Created from Indiana Territory in 1805

DIVISION LINE 1800

Added to Indiana
Territory, 1802

Lake Huron

T E R R I T O R Y

Fort Dearborn
(Chicago)

☐ Fort Armstrong

Des Moines R.

Fort Clark
(Peoria)

MILITARY
BOUNTY
TRACT

Fort
Edwards

Illinois River

Kaskaskia River

I L L I N O I S

T E R R I T O R Y

St. Joseph R.

St. Joseph R.

Maumee R.

Maumee R.

St. Mary's R.

Fort Wayne

Lake Erie

Tippecanoe River

River

Wabash

I N D I A N A

DIVISION LINE 1800

Miami R.

◄—A strip about 1¼
miles wide between
Ohio's western
boundary and the
Division Line was,
in 1802, taken
away from Indiana
Territory.

O H I O

Missouri River

Mississippi River

● Edwardsville
● Cahokia
● Bellefontaine
● Prairie du Rocher
● Kaskaskia

● Vincennes

Kentucky River

Ohio River

Ohio River

River

Shawneetown ●
Cave-in-Rock ●
Golconda ● ● Ohio

This triangular strip
between the western Ohio
line and the Division Line
was, in 1802, added to
Indiana Territory.

0   50   100
╠══╪══╪══╣
MILES

Indiana and Illinois territories

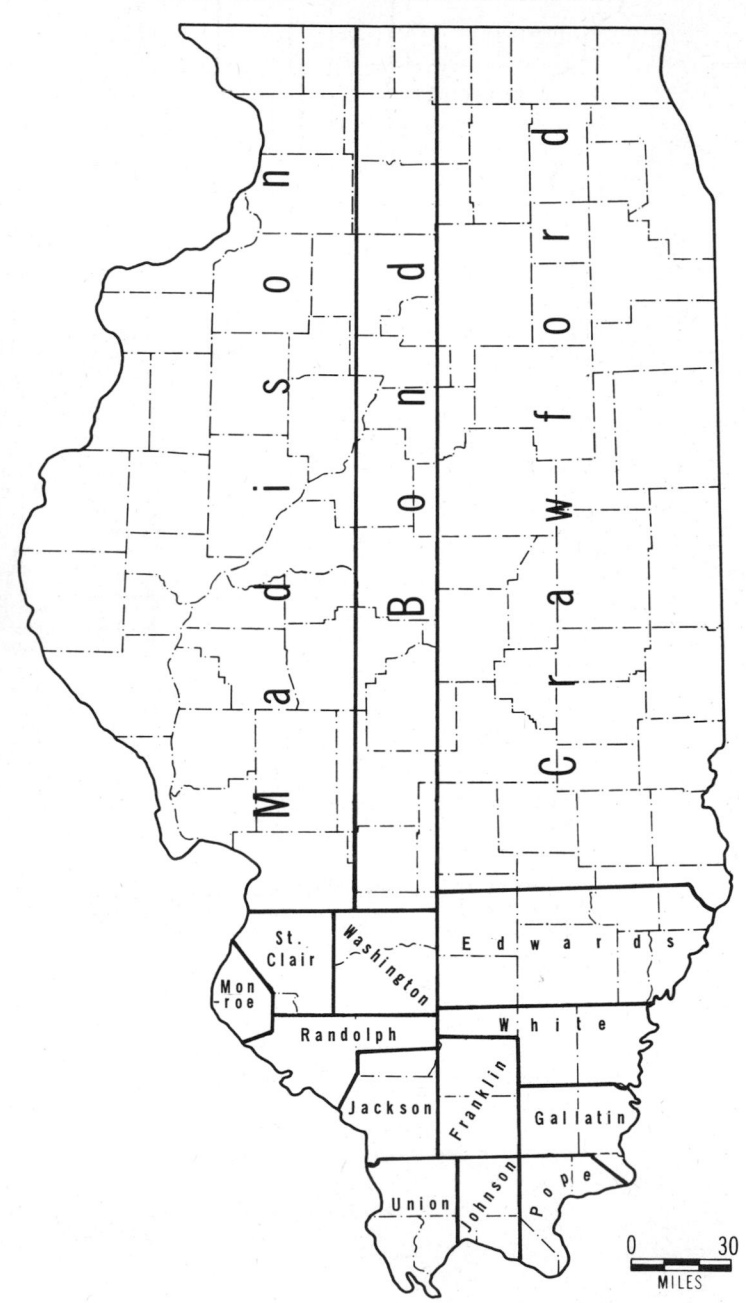

Counties in Illinois, 1818

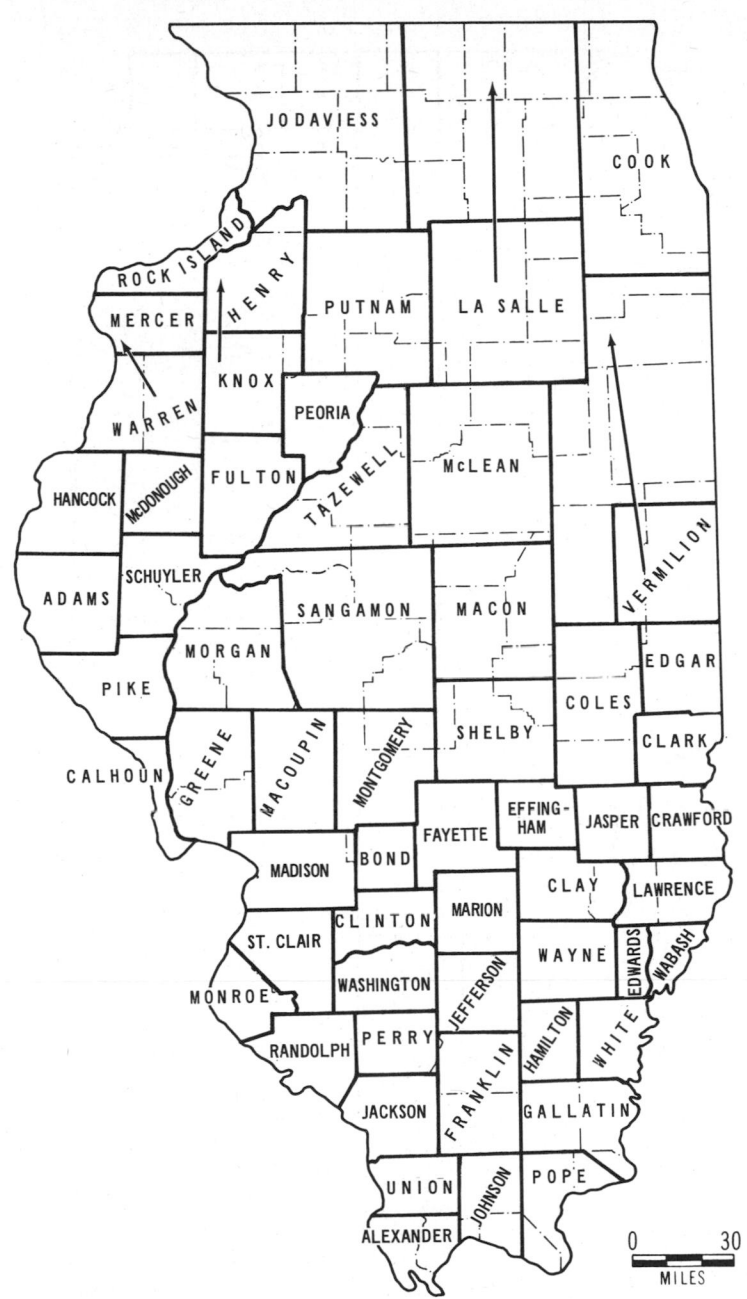

Counties in Illinois, 1831

*Illinois state parks, memorials,
and conservation areas
designated by statute*

P — State Parks

1. Apple River Canyon
2. Lake Le-Aqua-Na
3. Rock Cut
4. McHenry Dam
5. Chain O'Lakes
6. Illinois Beach
7. Mississippi Palisades
8. White Pines Forest
9. Lowden
10. Prophetstown
11. Black Hawk
12. Johnson Sauk Trail
13. Starved Rock
14. Buffalo Rock
15. Matthiessen
16. Fox River
17. Illini
18. Gebhard Woods
19. William G. Stratton
20. Channahon Parkway
21. Kankakee River
22. Delabar
23. Nauvoo
24. Argyle Lake
25. Fort Crevecoeur
26. Siloam Springs
27. Lincoln's New Salem
28. Weldon Springs
29. Kickapoo
30. Lincoln Trail Homestead
31. Spitler Woods
32. Lincoln Log Cabin
33. Fox Ridge
34. Lincoln Trail
35. Beaver Dam
36. Pere Marquette
37. Ramsey Lake
38. Sam Parr
39. Stephen A. Forbes
40. Red Hills
41. Cahokia Mounds
42. Frank Holten
43. Fort Chartres
44. Fort Kaskaskia
45. Lake Murphysboro
46. Giant City
47. Ferne Clyffe
48. Dixon Springs
49. Cave-in-Rock
50. Fort Massac
51. Fort Defiance

M — State Memorials

1. U. S. Grant Home
   Old Market House
2. Douglas Tomb
3. Lincoln Monument
4. Campbell's Island
5. Wild Bill Hickok Monument
6. Norwegian Settlers Monument
7. Bishop Hill
8. Governor Small Home
9. Jubilee College
10. Metamora Court House
11. Fort Edwards Monument
12. Postville Court House
13. Mt. Pulaski Court House
14. Bryant Cottage
15. Lincoln Home
    Lincoln Tomb
16. Moore Home
17. Vandalia State House
18. Lovejoy Monument
19. Lewis and Clark Memorial
20. Governor Coles Monument
21. Cahokia Court House
22. Lincoln Trail Monument
23. Pierre Menard Home
24. Kaskaskia
25. Governor Bond Monument
26. Shawneetown

C — Conservation Areas

1. Lee County
2. William W. Powers
3. Des Plaines
4. Iroquois County
5. Sparland
6. Spring Branch
7. Marshall County
8. Woodford County
9. Rice Lake
10. Spring Lake
11. Barkhousen
12. Anderson Lake
13. Sanganois
14. McLean County
15. Sam Dale Lake
16. Washington County
17. Randolph County
18. Hamilton County
19. Beall Woods
20. Saline County
21. Union County
22. Burnham Island
23. Horseshoe Lake
24. Mermet Lake

Counts of Illinois
since 1859
with county seats
as of 1968

568